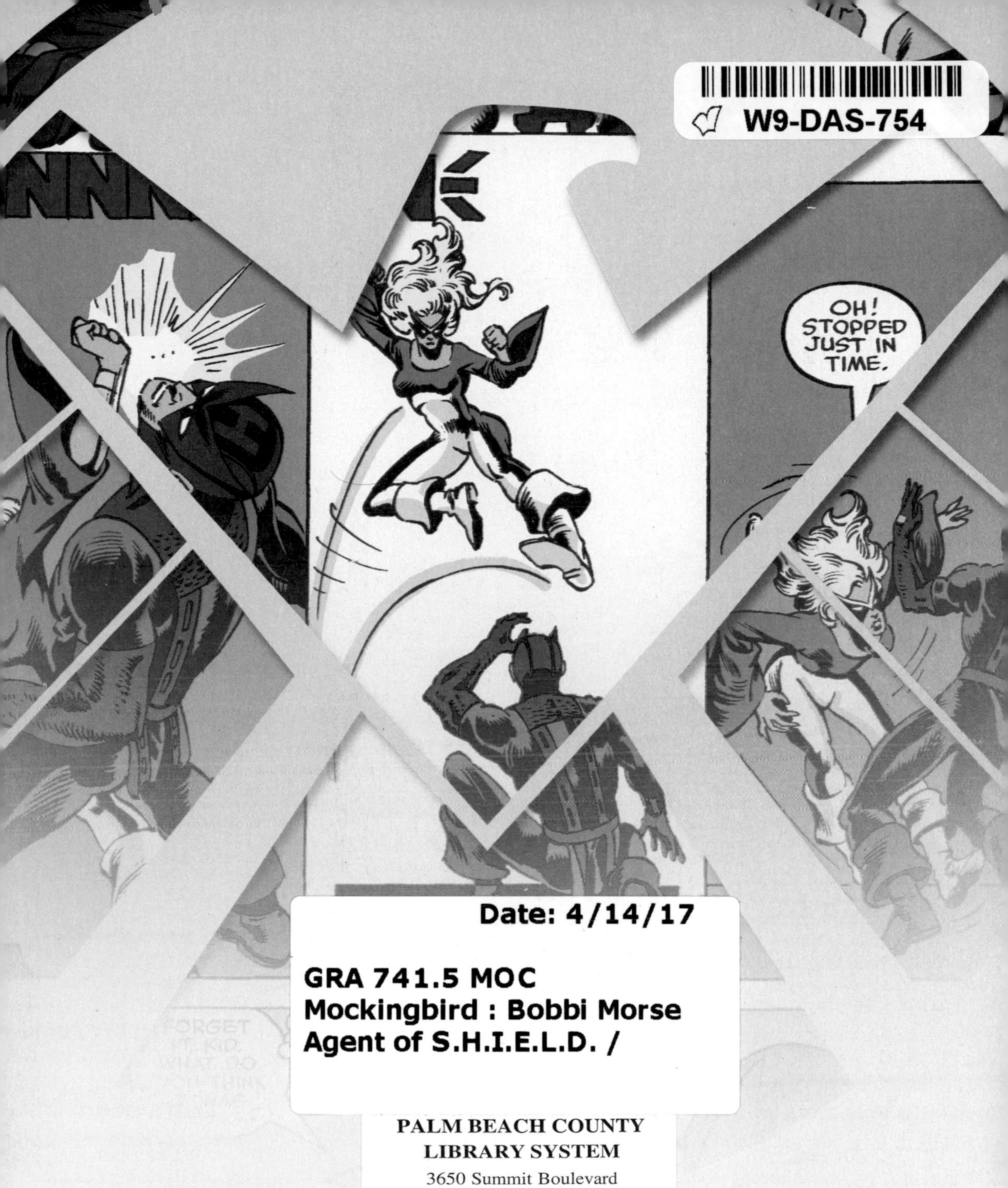
OH! STOPPED JUST IN TIME.

MOCKINGBIRD

BOBBI MORSE AGENT OF S.H.I.E.L.D.

COLLECTION EDITOR **MARK D. BEAZLEY**	VP, PRODUCTION & SPECIAL PROJECTS **JEFF YOUNGQUIST**	SVP PRINT, SALES & MARKETING **DAVID GABRIEL**
ASSOCIATE EDITOR **SARAH BRUNSTAD**	RESEARCH & LAYOUT **JEPH YORK**	EDITOR IN CHIEF **AXEL ALONSO**
ASSOCIATE MANAGER, DIGITAL ASSETS **JOE HOCHSTEIN**	PRODUCTION **COLORTEK & JOE FRONTIRRE**	CHIEF CREATIVE OFFICER **JOE QUESADA**
ASSOCIATE MANAGING EDITOR **ALEX STARBUCK**	MASTERWORKS EDITOR **CORY SEDLMEIER**	PUBLISHER **DAN BUCKLEY**
SENIOR EDITOR, SPECIAL PROJECTS **JENNIFER GRÜNWALD**	BOOK DESIGNER **ADAM DEL RE**	EXECUTIVE PRODUCER **ALAN FINE**

SPECIAL THANKS TO **MIKE HANSEN** & **JESS HARROLD**

MOCKINGBIRD: BOBBI MORSE, AGENT OF S.H.I.E.L.D. Contains material originally published in magazine form as ASTONISHING TALES #10, #12-13 and #15-20; KA-ZAR #3-5; MARVEL TEAM-UP #95; HAWKEYE #1-4; ASTONISHING TALES #8; SAVAGE TALES #8; and MARVEL SUPER ACTION #1. First printing 2016. ISBN# 978-1-302-90086-1. Published by MARVEL WORLDWIDE, INC., a subsidiary of MARVEL ENTERTAINMENT, LLC. OFFICE OF PUBLICATION: 135 West 50th Street, New York, NY 10020. Copyright © 2016 MARVEL No similarity between any of the names, characters, persons, and/or institutions in this magazine with those of any living or dead person or institution is intended, and any such similarity which may exist is purely coincidental. **Printed in the U.S.A.** ALAN FINE, President, Marvel Entertainment; DAN BUCKLEY, President, TV, Publishing & Brand Management; JOE QUESADA, Chief Creative Officer; TOM BREVOORT, SVP of Publishing; DAVID BOGART, SVP of Business Affairs & Operations, Publishing & Partnership; C.B. CEBULSKI, VP of Brand Management & Development, Asia; DAVID GABRIEL, SVP of Sales & Marketing, Publishing; JEFF YOUNGQUIST, VP of Production & Special Projects; DAN CARR, Executive Director of Publishing Technology; ALEX MORALES, Director of Publishing Operations; SUSAN CRESPI, Production Manager; STAN LEE, Chairman Emeritus. For information regarding advertising in Marvel Comics or on Marvel.com, please contact Vit DeBellis, Integrated Sales Manager, at vdebellis@marvel.com. For Marvel subscription inquiries, please call 888-511-5480. **Manufactured between 6/10/2016 and 7/18/2016 by R.R. DONNELLEY, INC., SALEM, VA, USA.**

10 9 8 7 6 5 4 3 2 1

MOCKINGBIRD

BOBBI MORSE AGENT OF S.H.I.E.L.D.

WRITERS

Roy Thomas, Gerry Conway, Mike Friedrich, Steven Grant &
Mark Gruenwald with Gary Friedrich, Len Wein & Co.

PENCILERS

Barry Windsor-Smith, Gil Kane, John Buscema, Rich Buckler, Dan Adkins,
Don Heck, George Evans, Jimmy Janes & Mark Gruenwald with Herb Trimpe,
Neal Adams, Marie Severin, Werner Roth & Eliot R. Brown

INKERS

Tom Sutton, Sal Buscema, Frank Giacoia, Dan Adkins, Chic Stone,
Frank Chiaramonte, Jack Abel, Mike Royer, Mike Esposito, Tony DeZuniga,
Frank Springer, Bruce Patterson, Brett Breeding & Danny Bulanadi with
Bill Everett, Herb Trimpe, Neal Adams, Ian Akin & Brian Garvey

COLORISTS

Stan Goldberg, Dave Hunt, Marie Severin, Linda Lessmann,
George Roussos, Ben Sean, Bob Sharen & Christie Scheele

LETTERERS

Artie Simek, John Costanza, Denise Vladimer, June Braverman,
Tom Orzechowski & Joe Rosen with Sam Rosen

ASSISTANT, ASSOCIATE & CONSULTING EDITORS

John Warner, Marv Wolfman, Mark Gruenwald & Linda Grant with Len Wein & Doug Moench

EDITORS

Stan Lee, Roy Thomas, Gerry Conway, Archie Goodwin & Dennis O'Neil

FRONT COVER ARTIST
Paul Renaud

BACK COVER ARTISTS
Frank Miller & Bob McLeod

The woman who would become known as Mockingbird made her debut in the pages of 1971's *Astonishing Tales #6*. As the jungle man Ka-Zar fought for his life in the Savage Land, a mysterious visitor arrived at his family mansion in England…

Writer: Gerry Conway • Penciler: Barry Windsor-Smith • Inker: Bill Everett • Letterer: Artie Simek • Editor: Stan Lee

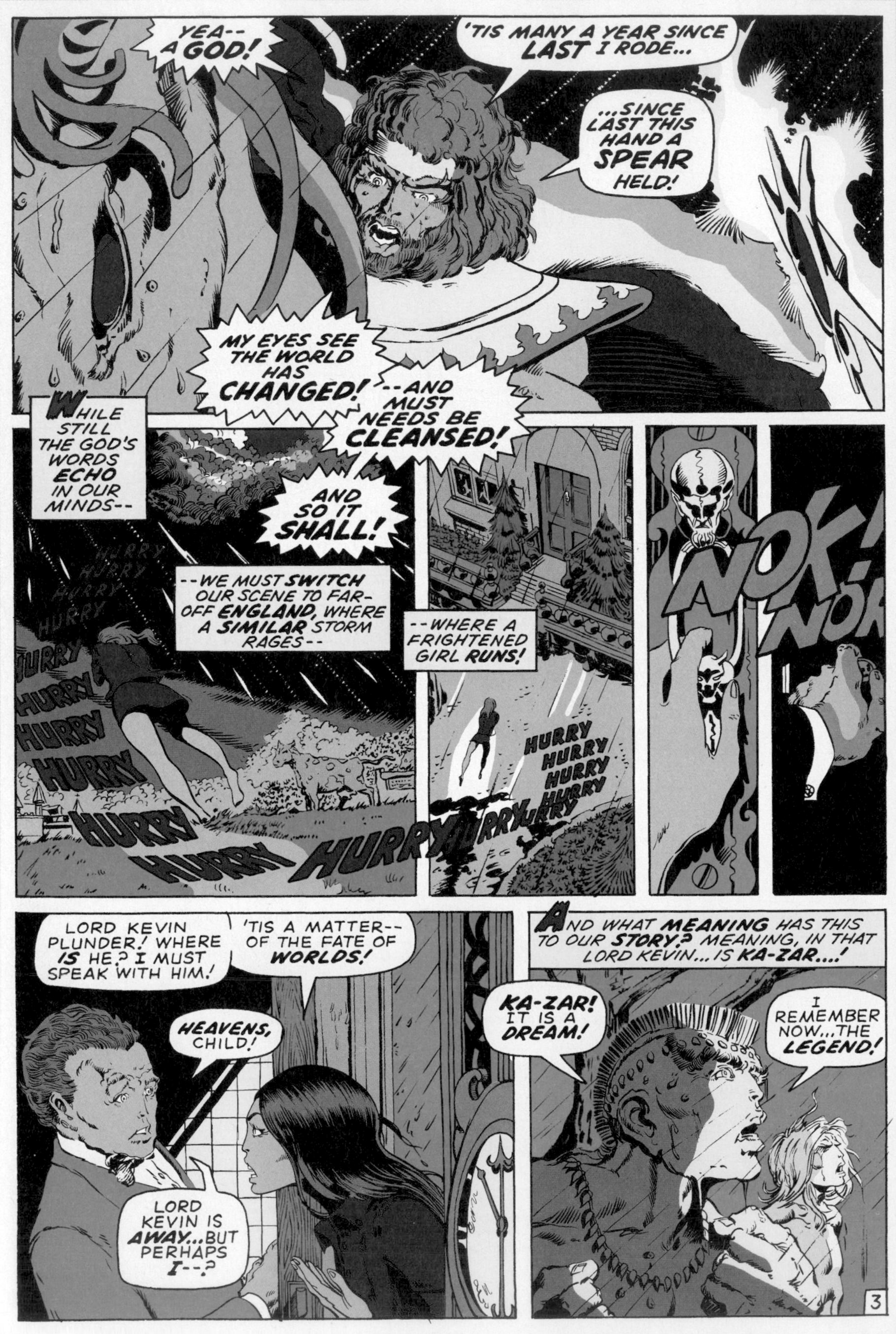
YEA-- A GOD!
'TIS MANY A YEAR SINCE LAST I RODE...
...SINCE LAST THIS HAND A SPEAR HELD!
MY EYES SEE THE WORLD HAS CHANGED!
--AND MUST NEEDS BE CLEANSED!
WHILE STILL THE GOD'S WORDS ECHO IN OUR MINDS--
AND SO IT SHALL!
--WE MUST SWITCH OUR SCENE TO FAR-OFF ENGLAND, WHERE A SIMILAR STORM RAGES--
HURRY HURRY HURRY HURRY
HURRY HURRY HURRY HURRY HURRY HURRY HURRY
--WHERE A FRIGHTENED GIRL RUNS!
HURRY HURRY HURRY HURRY HURRY HURRY
LORD KEVIN PLUNDER! WHERE IS HE? I MUST SPEAK WITH HIM!
'TIS A MATTER-- OF THE FATE OF WORLDS!
HEAVENS, CHILD!
LORD KEVIN IS AWAY... BUT PERHAPS I--?
AND WHAT MEANING HAS THIS TO OUR STORY? MEANING, IN THAT LORD KEVIN... IS KA-ZAR...!
KA-ZAR! IT IS A DREAM!
I REMEMBER NOW... THE LEGEND!
3

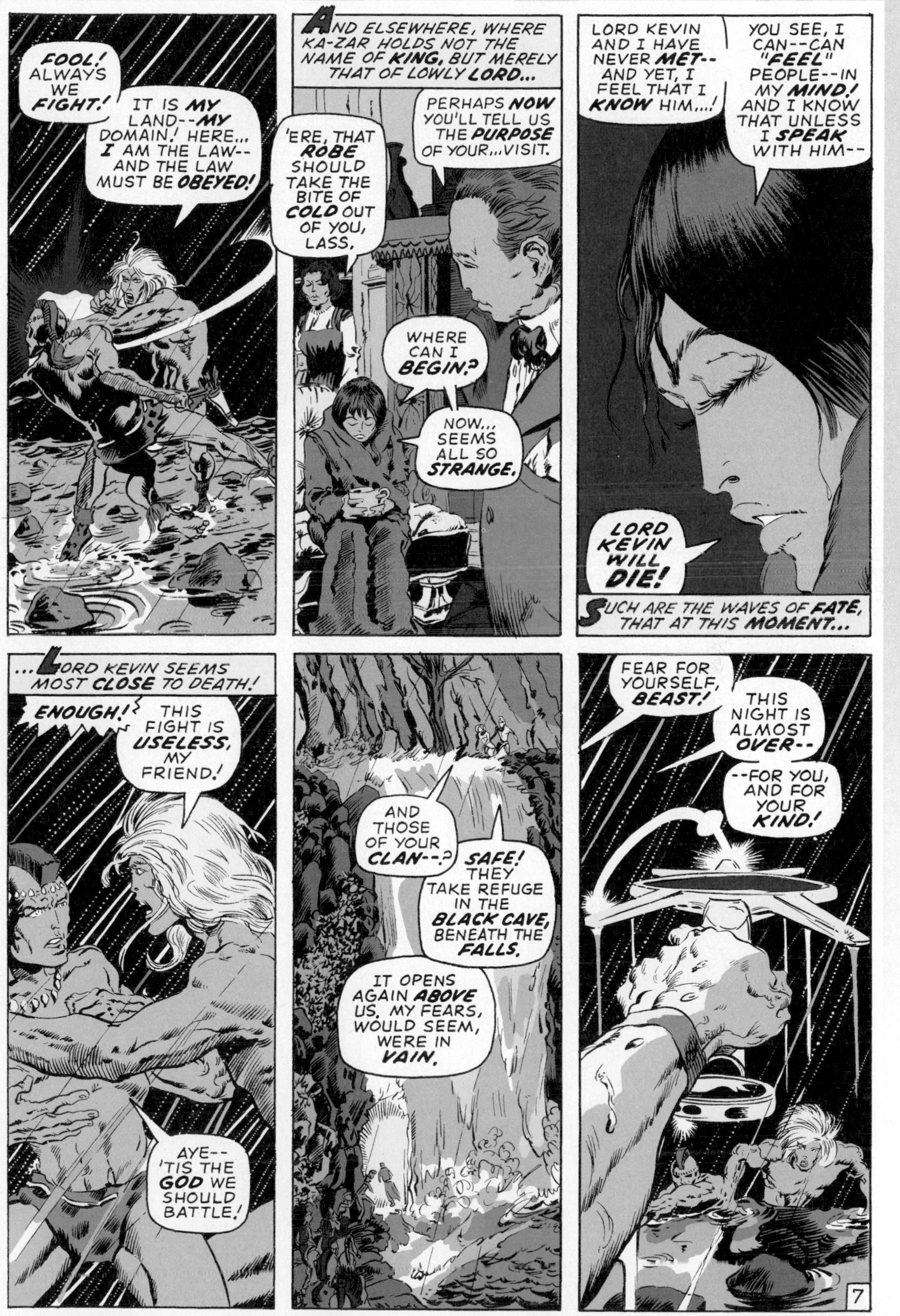
FOOL! ALWAYS WE FIGHT!
IT IS MY LAND--MY DOMAIN! HERE... I AM THE LAW--AND THE LAW MUST BE OBEYED!
AND ELSEWHERE, WHERE KA-ZAR HOLDS NOT THE NAME OF KING, BUT MERELY THAT OF LOWLY LORD...
PERHAPS NOW YOU'LL TELL US THE PURPOSE OF YOUR...VISIT.
'ERE, THAT ROBE SHOULD TAKE THE BITE OF COLD OUT OF YOU, LASS.
WHERE CAN I BEGIN?
NOW... SEEMS ALL SO STRANGE.
LORD KEVIN AND I HAVE NEVER MET--AND YET, I FEEL THAT I KNOW HIM...!
YOU SEE, I CAN--CAN "FEEL" PEOPLE--IN MY MIND! AND I KNOW THAT UNLESS I SPEAK WITH HIM--
LORD KEVIN WILL DIE!
SUCH ARE THE WAVES OF FATE, THAT AT THIS MOMENT...
...LORD KEVIN SEEMS MOST CLOSE TO DEATH!
ENOUGH!
THIS FIGHT IS USELESS, MY FRIEND!
AYE--'TIS THE GOD WE SHOULD BATTLE!
AND THOSE OF YOUR CLAN--?
SAFE! THEY TAKE REFUGE IN THE BLACK CAVE, BENEATH THE FALLS.
IT OPENS AGAIN ABOVE US. MY FEARS, WOULD SEEM, WERE IN VAIN.
FEAR FOR YOURSELF, BEAST!
THIS NIGHT IS ALMOST OVER--
--FOR YOU, AND FOR YOUR KIND!
7

Excerpt from *Astonishing Tales #7*

Writer: Roy Thomas • Artist: Herb Trimpe • Letterer: Artie Simek • Editor: Stan Lee

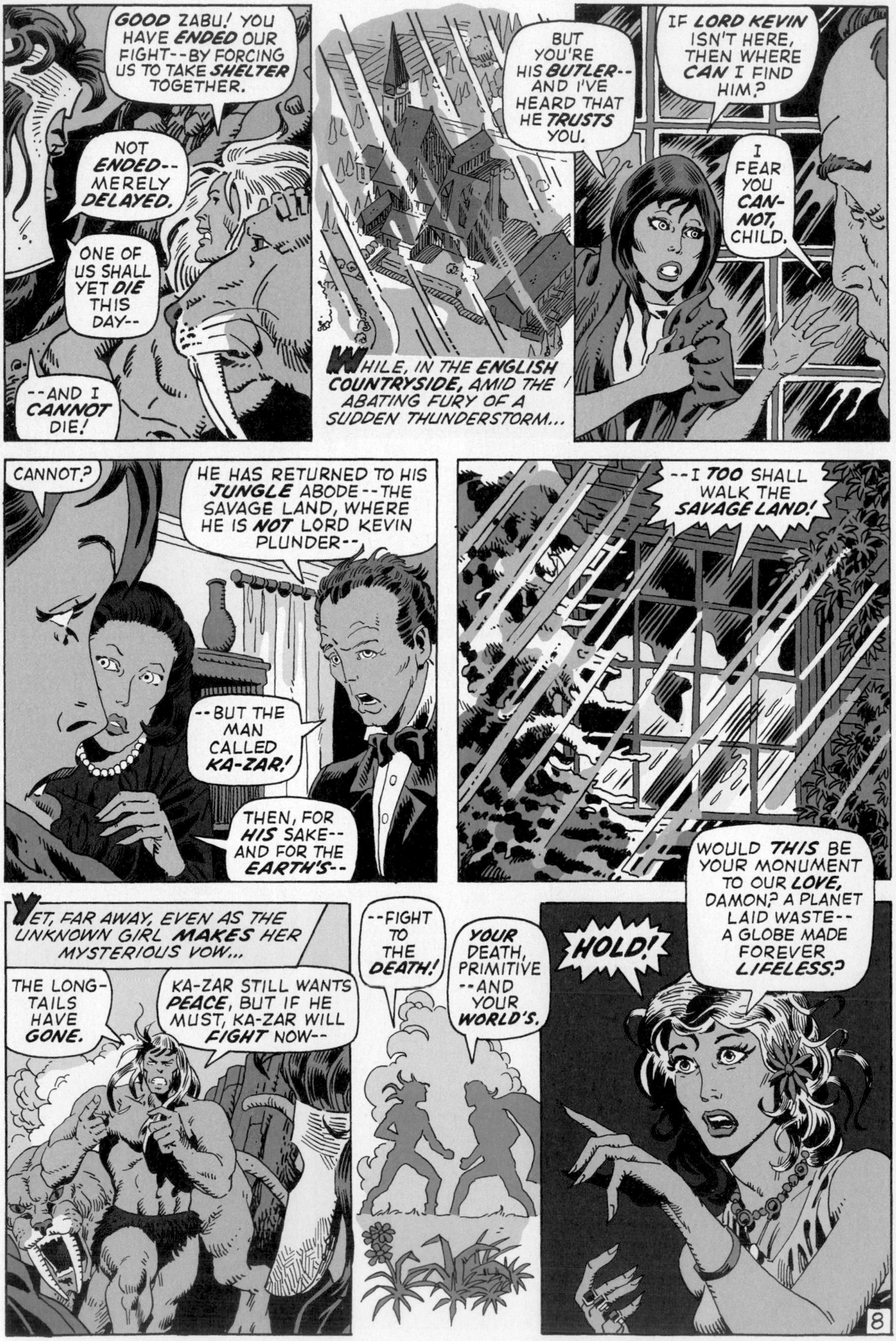

GOOD ZABU! YOU HAVE ENDED OUR FIGHT--BY FORCING US TO TAKE SHELTER TOGETHER.
NOT ENDED-- MERELY DELAYED.
ONE OF US SHALL YET DIE THIS DAY--
--AND I CANNOT DIE!
WHILE, IN THE ENGLISH COUNTRYSIDE, AMID THE ABATING FURY OF A SUDDEN THUNDERSTORM...
BUT YOU'RE HIS BUTLER-- AND I'VE HEARD THAT HE TRUSTS YOU.
IF LORD KEVIN ISN'T HERE, THEN WHERE CAN I FIND HIM?
I FEAR YOU CAN-NOT, CHILD.
CANNOT?
HE HAS RETURNED TO HIS JUNGLE ABODE--THE SAVAGE LAND, WHERE HE IS NOT LORD KEVIN PLUNDER--
--BUT THE MAN CALLED KA-ZAR!
THEN, FOR HIS SAKE-- AND FOR THE EARTH'S--
--I TOO SHALL WALK THE SAVAGE LAND!
YET, FAR AWAY, EVEN AS THE UNKNOWN GIRL MAKES HER MYSTERIOUS VOW...
THE LONG-TAILS HAVE GONE.
KA-ZAR STILL WANTS PEACE, BUT IF HE MUST, KA-ZAR WILL FIGHT NOW--
--FIGHT TO THE DEATH!
YOUR DEATH, PRIMITIVE --AND YOUR WORLD'S.
HOLD!
WOULD THIS BE YOUR MONUMENT TO OUR LOVE, DAMON? A PLANET LAID WASTE-- A GLOBE MADE FOREVER LIFELESS?
8

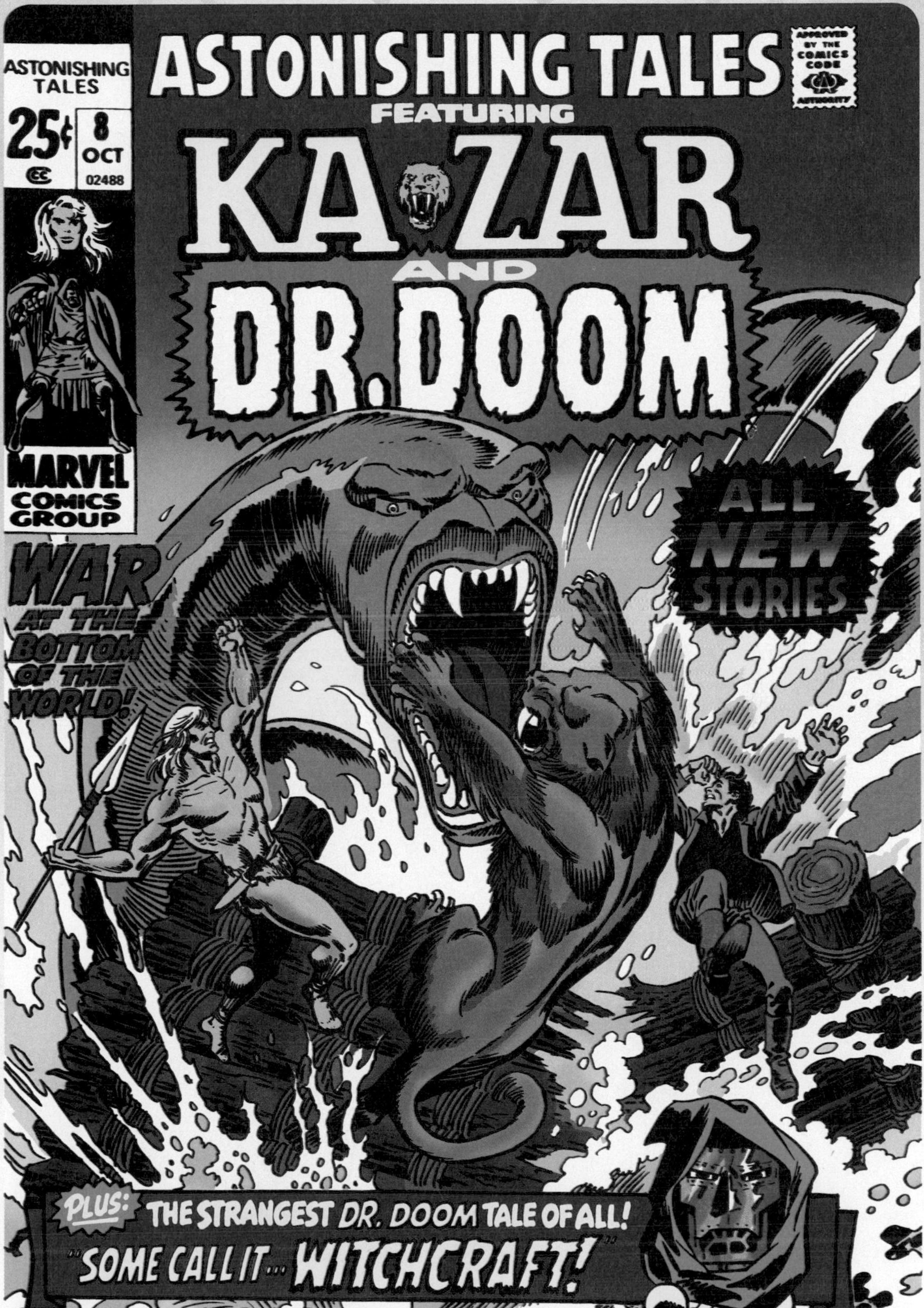

ASTONISHING TALES
25¢
8
OCT
02488
MARVEL COMICS GROUP
ASTONISHING TALES
FEATURING
KA-ZAR
AND
DR. DOOM
ALL NEW STORIES
WAR AT THE BOTTOM OF THE WORLD!
PLUS: THE STRANGEST DR. DOOM TALE OF ALL!
"SOME CALL IT... WITCHCRAFT!"

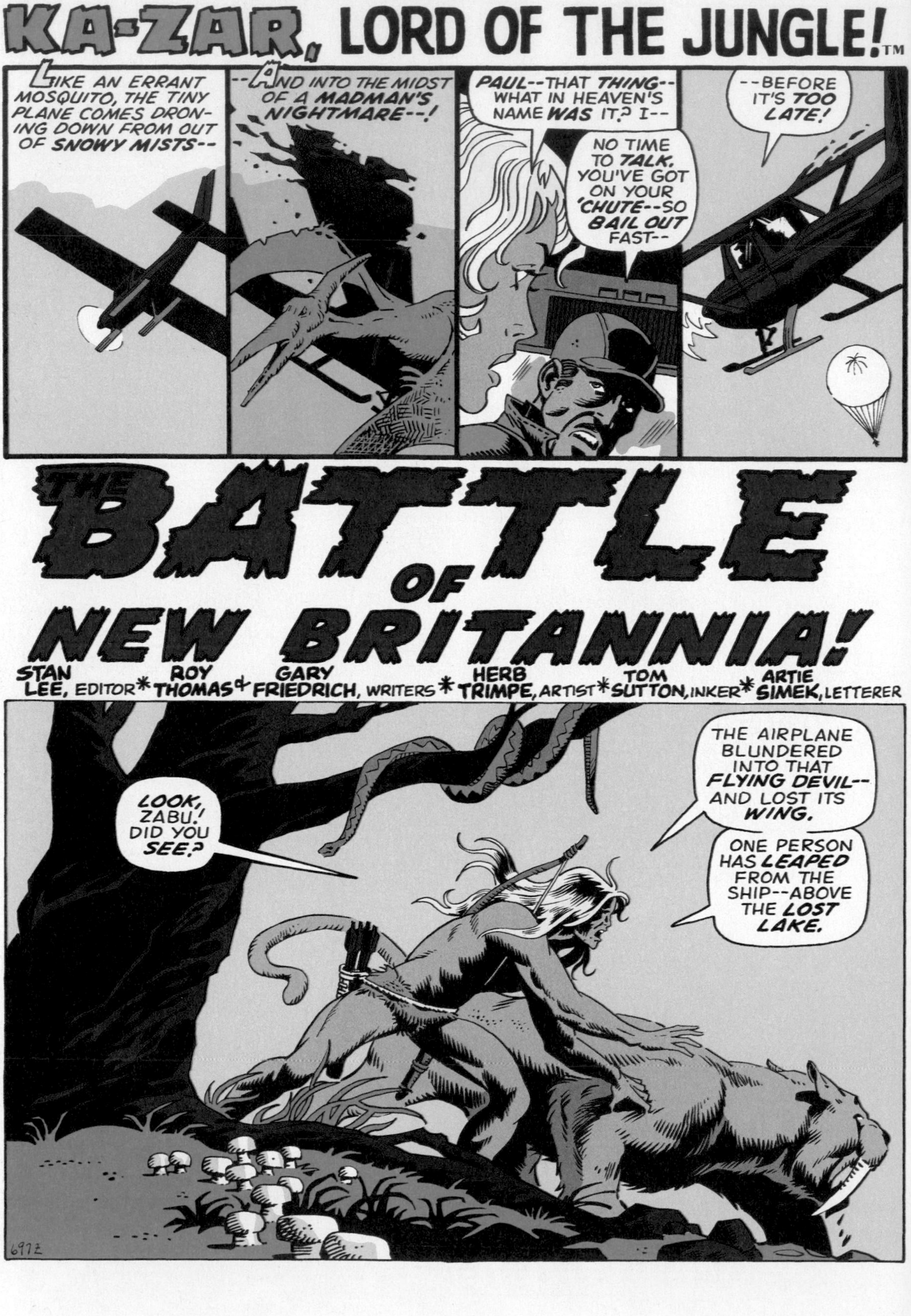
KA-ZAR, LORD OF THE JUNGLE!™
LIKE AN ERRANT MOSQUITO, THE TINY PLANE COMES DRONING DOWN FROM OUT OF SNOWY MISTS--
--AND INTO THE MIDST OF A MADMAN'S NIGHTMARE--!
PAUL--THAT THING--WHAT IN HEAVEN'S NAME WAS IT? I--
NO TIME TO TALK, YOU'VE GOT ON YOUR 'CHUTE--SO BAIL OUT FAST--
--BEFORE IT'S TOO LATE!
THE BATTLE OF NEW BRITANNIA!
STAN LEE, EDITOR * ROY THOMAS & GARY FRIEDRICH, WRITERS * HERB TRIMPE, ARTIST * TOM SUTTON, INKER * ARTIE SIMEK, LETTERER
LOOK, ZABU! DID YOU SEE?
THE AIRPLANE BLUNDERED INTO THAT FLYING DEVIL--AND LOST ITS WING.
ONE PERSON HAS LEAPED FROM THE SHIP--ABOVE THE LOST LAKE.

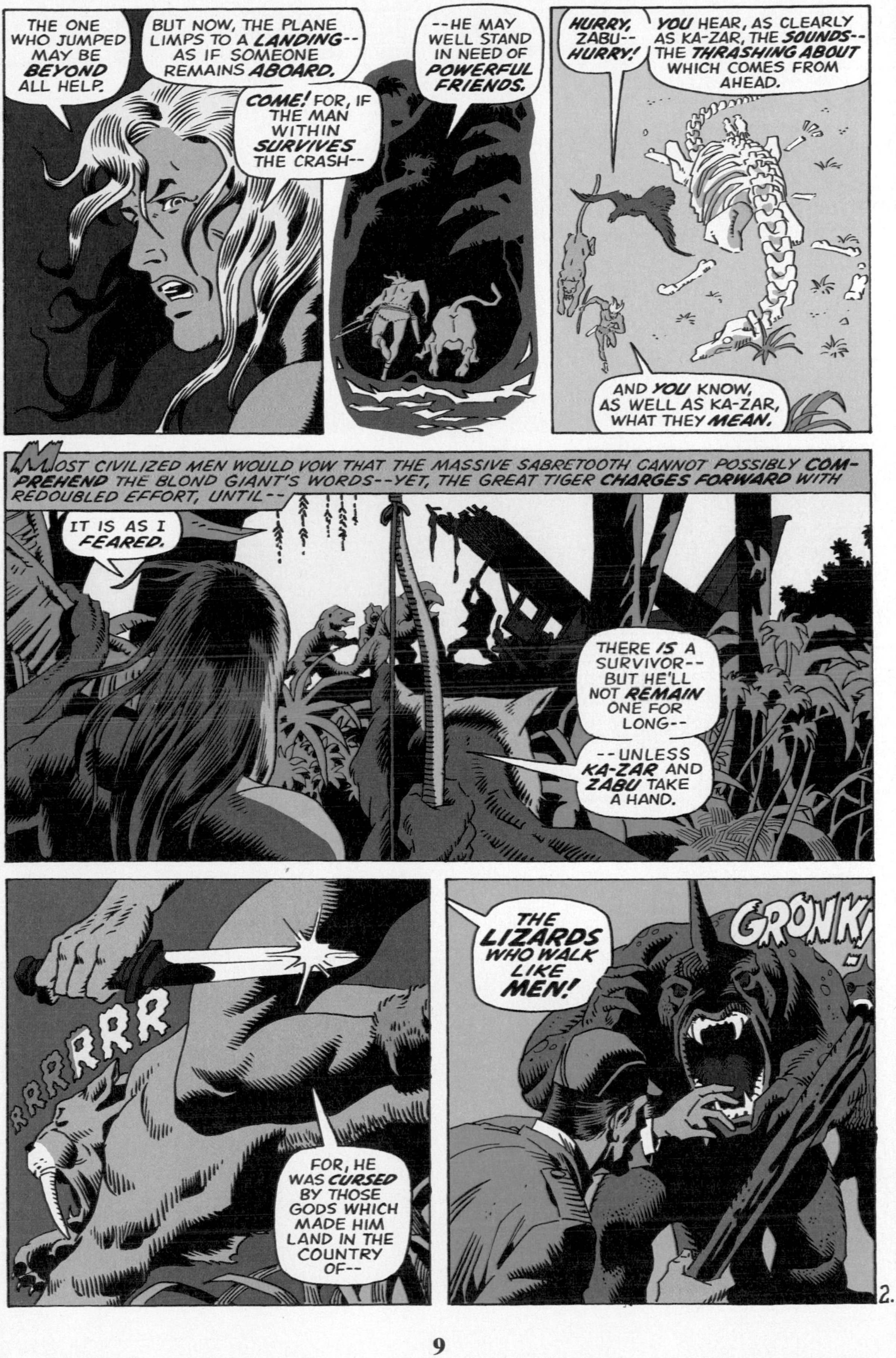
THE ONE WHO JUMPED MAY BE BEYOND ALL HELP.
BUT NOW, THE PLANE LIMPS TO A LANDING-- AS IF SOMEONE REMAINS ABOARD.
COME! FOR, IF THE MAN WITHIN SURVIVES THE CRASH--
--HE MAY WELL STAND IN NEED OF POWERFUL FRIENDS.
HURRY, ZABU-- HURRY!
YOU HEAR, AS CLEARLY AS KA-ZAR, THE SOUNDS-- THE THRASHING ABOUT WHICH COMES FROM AHEAD.
AND YOU KNOW, AS WELL AS KA-ZAR, WHAT THEY MEAN.
MOST CIVILIZED MEN WOULD VOW THAT THE MASSIVE SABRETOOTH CANNOT POSSIBLY COMPREHEND THE BLOND GIANT'S WORDS--YET, THE GREAT TIGER CHARGES FORWARD WITH REDOUBLED EFFORT, UNTIL--
IT IS AS I FEARED.
THERE IS A SURVIVOR-- BUT HE'LL NOT REMAIN ONE FOR LONG--
--UNLESS KA-ZAR AND ZABU TAKE A HAND.
RRRRRRR
FOR, HE WAS CURSED BY THOSE GODS WHICH MADE HIM LAND IN THE COUNTRY OF--
THE LIZARDS WHO WALK LIKE MEN!
GRONK!
2.

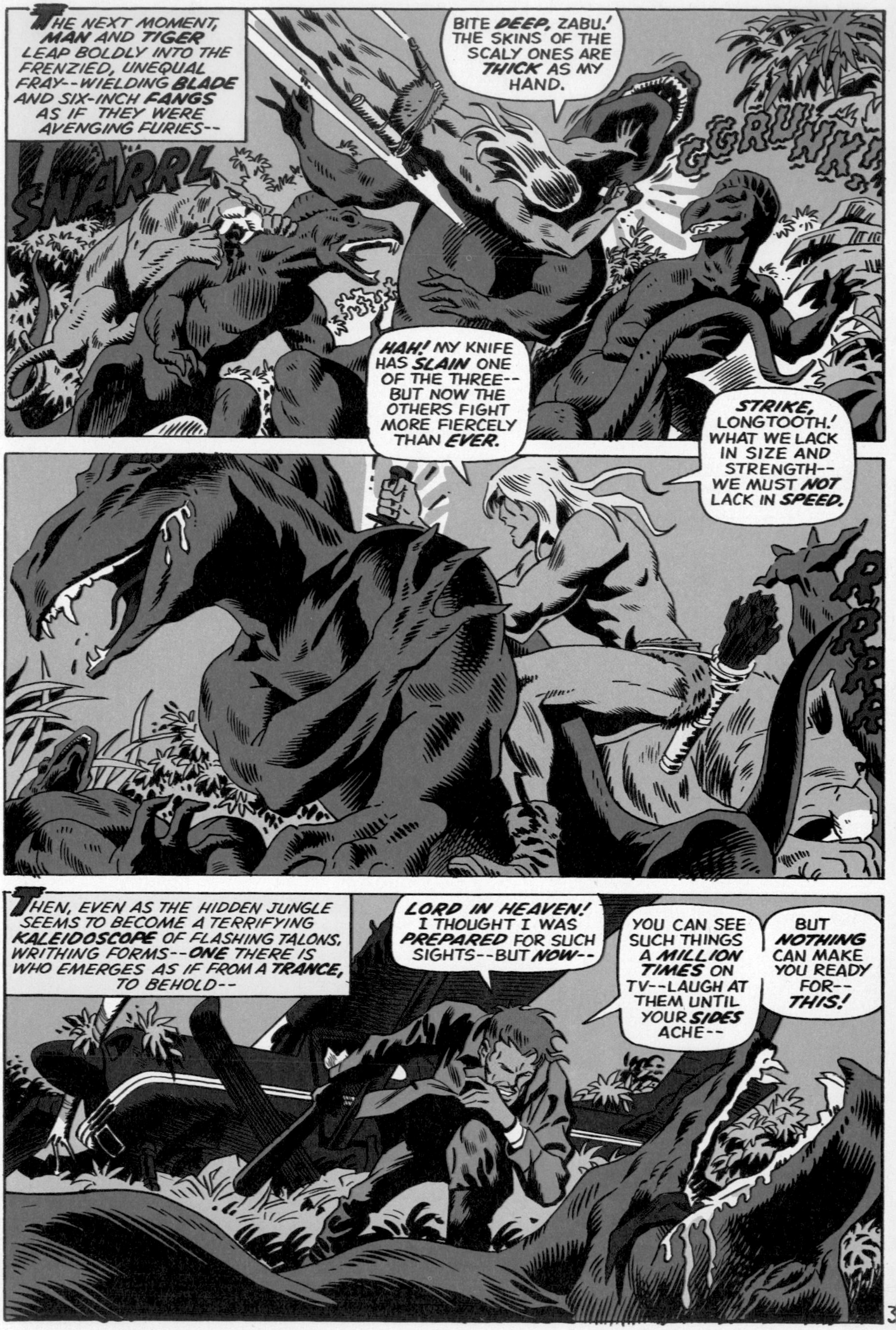

THE NEXT MOMENT, MAN AND TIGER LEAP BOLDLY INTO THE FRENZIED, UNEQUAL FRAY--WIELDING BLADE AND SIX-INCH FANGS AS IF THEY WERE AVENGING FURIES--
BITE DEEP, ZABU! THE SKINS OF THE SCALY ONES ARE THICK AS MY HAND.
SNARRL
GGRUNKK
HAH! MY KNIFE HAS SLAIN ONE OF THE THREE--BUT NOW THE OTHERS FIGHT MORE FIERCELY THAN EVER.
STRIKE, LONGTOOTH! WHAT WE LACK IN SIZE AND STRENGTH--WE MUST NOT LACK IN SPEED.
RRRR
THEN, EVEN AS THE HIDDEN JUNGLE SEEMS TO BECOME A TERRIFYING KALEIDOSCOPE OF FLASHING TALONS, WRITHING FORMS--ONE THERE IS WHO EMERGES AS IF FROM A TRANCE, TO BEHOLD--
LORD IN HEAVEN! I THOUGHT I WAS PREPARED FOR SUCH SIGHTS--BUT NOW--
YOU CAN SEE SUCH THINGS A MILLION TIMES ON TV--LAUGH AT THEM UNTIL YOUR SIDES ACHE--
BUT NOTHING CAN MAKE YOU READY FOR--THIS!
3

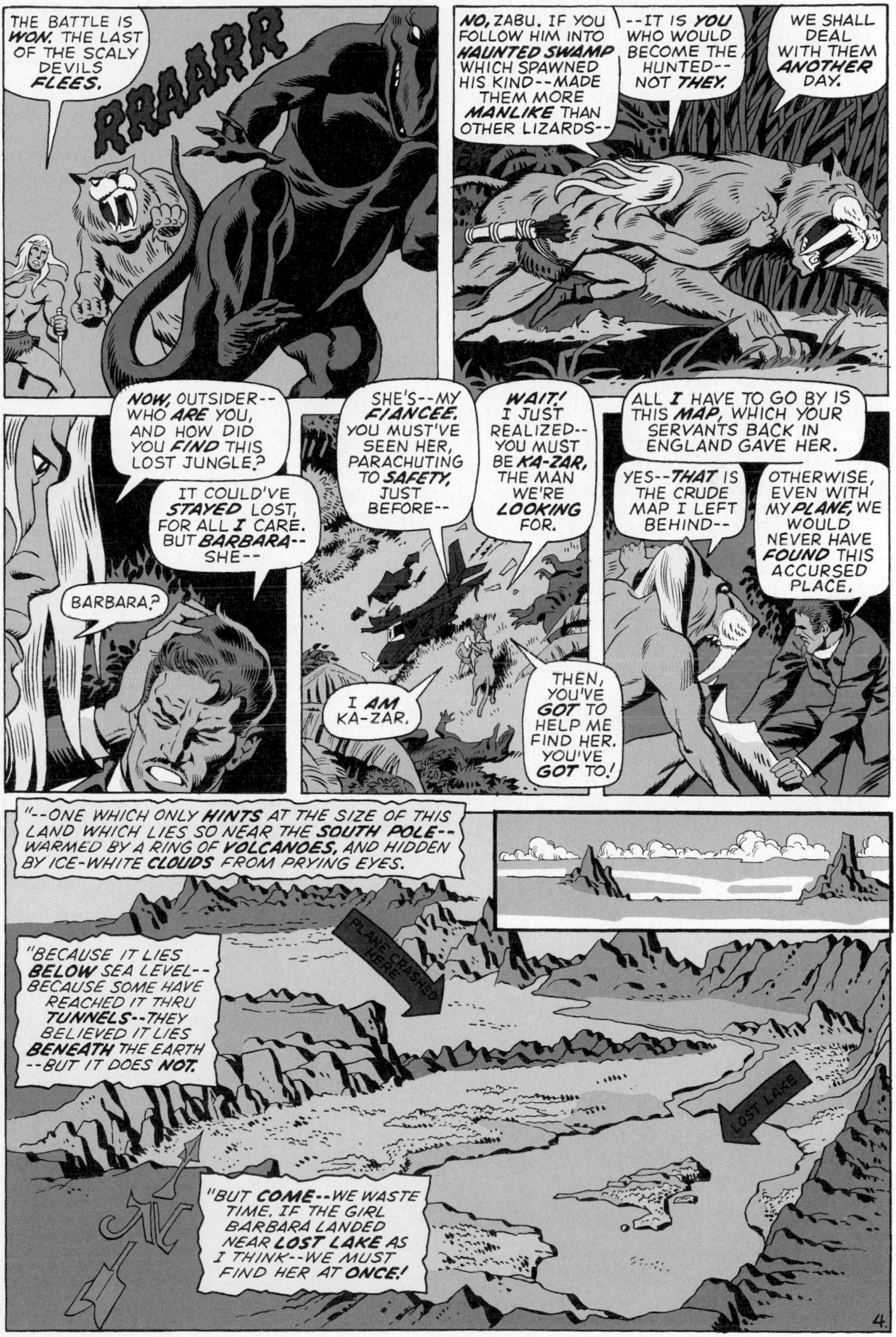
THE BATTLE IS WON. THE LAST OF THE SCALY DEVILS FLEES.
RRAARR
NO, ZABU. IF YOU FOLLOW HIM INTO HAUNTED SWAMP WHICH SPAWNED HIS KIND--MADE THEM MORE MANLIKE THAN OTHER LIZARDS--
--IT IS YOU WHO WOULD BECOME THE HUNTED--NOT THEY.
WE SHALL DEAL WITH THEM ANOTHER DAY.
NOW, OUTSIDER--WHO ARE YOU, AND HOW DID YOU FIND THIS LOST JUNGLE?
IT COULD'VE STAYED LOST, FOR ALL I CARE. BUT BARBARA--SHE--
BARBARA?
SHE'S--MY FIANCEE. YOU MUST'VE SEEN HER, PARACHUTING TO SAFETY, JUST BEFORE--
WAIT! I JUST REALIZED--YOU MUST BE KA-ZAR, THE MAN WE'RE LOOKING FOR.
I AM KA-ZAR.
THEN, YOU'VE GOT TO HELP ME FIND HER. YOU'VE GOT TO!
ALL I HAVE TO GO BY IS THIS MAP, WHICH YOUR SERVANTS BACK IN ENGLAND GAVE HER.
YES--THAT IS THE CRUDE MAP I LEFT BEHIND--
OTHERWISE, EVEN WITH MY PLANE, WE WOULD NEVER HAVE FOUND THIS ACCURSED PLACE.
"--ONE WHICH ONLY HINTS AT THE SIZE OF THIS LAND WHICH LIES SO NEAR THE SOUTH POLE--WARMED BY A RING OF VOLCANOES, AND HIDDEN BY ICE-WHITE CLOUDS FROM PRYING EYES.
PLANE CRASHED HERE
"BECAUSE IT LIES BELOW SEA LEVEL--BECAUSE SOME HAVE REACHED IT THRU TUNNELS--THEY BELIEVED IT LIES BENEATH THE EARTH--BUT IT DOES NOT.
LOST LAKE
N
"BUT COME--WE WASTE TIME. IF THE GIRL BARBARA LANDED NEAR LOST LAKE AS I THINK--WE MUST FIND HER AT ONCE!
4.

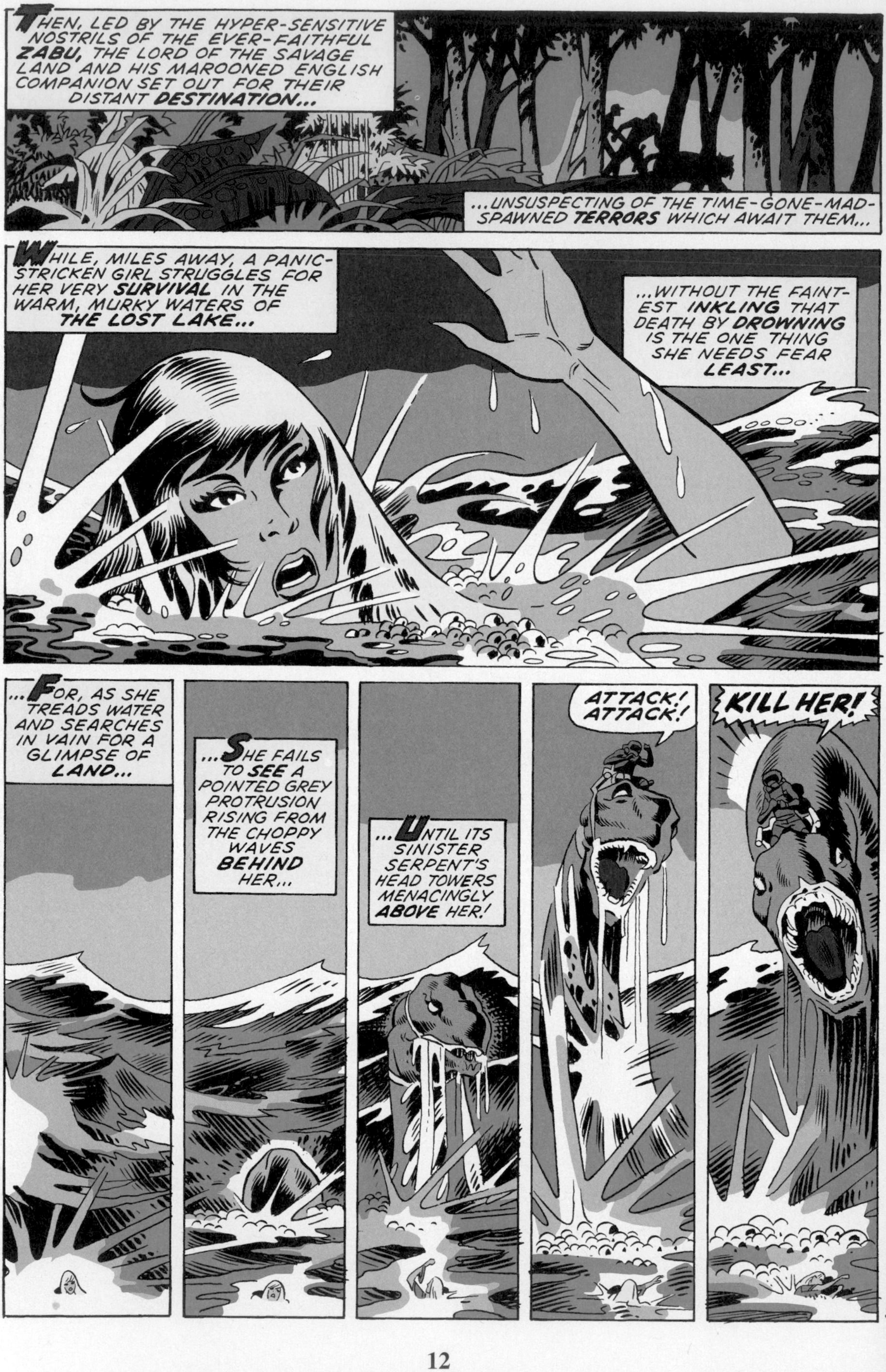
THEN, LED BY THE HYPER-SENSITIVE NOSTRILS OF THE EVER-FAITHFUL ZABU, THE LORD OF THE SAVAGE LAND AND HIS MAROONED ENGLISH COMPANION SET OUT FOR THEIR DISTANT DESTINATION...
...UNSUSPECTING OF THE TIME-GONE-MAD-SPAWNED TERRORS WHICH AWAIT THEM...
WHILE, MILES AWAY, A PANIC-STRICKEN GIRL STRUGGLES FOR HER VERY SURVIVAL IN THE WARM, MURKY WATERS OF THE LOST LAKE...
...WITHOUT THE FAINTEST INKLING THAT DEATH BY DROWNING IS THE ONE THING SHE NEEDS FEAR LEAST...
...FOR, AS SHE TREADS WATER AND SEARCHES IN VAIN FOR A GLIMPSE OF LAND...
...SHE FAILS TO SEE A POINTED GREY PROTRUSION RISING FROM THE CHOPPY WAVES BEHIND HER...
...UNTIL ITS SINISTER SERPENT'S HEAD TOWERS MENACINGLY ABOVE HER!
ATTACK! ATTACK!
KILL HER!

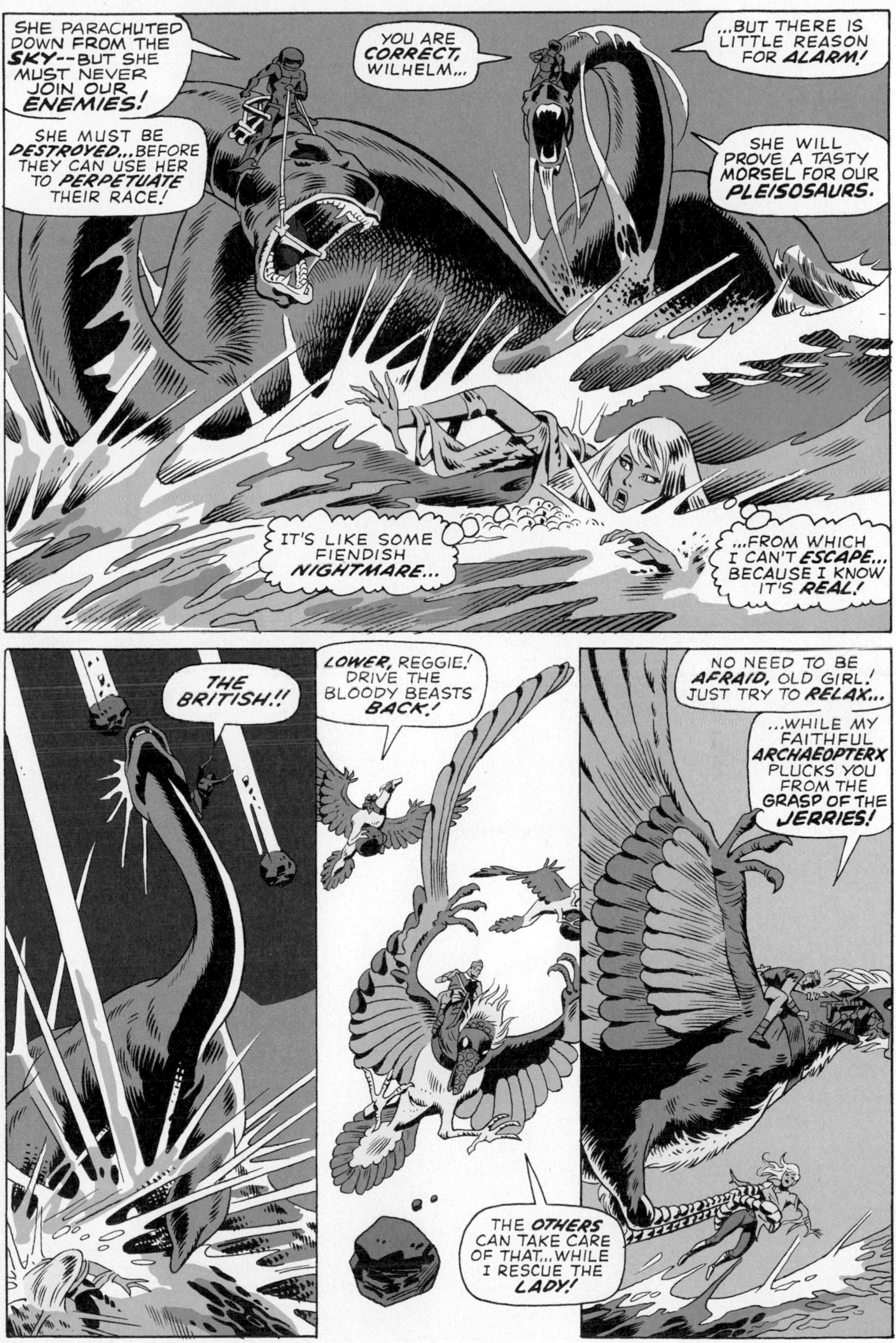
SHE PARACHUTED DOWN FROM THE SKY--BUT SHE MUST NEVER JOIN OUR ENEMIES!
SHE MUST BE DESTROYED...BEFORE THEY CAN USE HER TO PERPETUATE THEIR RACE!
YOU ARE CORRECT, WILHELM...
...BUT THERE IS LITTLE REASON FOR ALARM!
SHE WILL PROVE A TASTY MORSEL FOR OUR PLEISOSAURS.
IT'S LIKE SOME FIENDISH NIGHTMARE...
...FROM WHICH I CAN'T ESCAPE... BECAUSE I KNOW IT'S REAL!
THE BRITISH!!
LOWER, REGGIE! DRIVE THE BLOODY BEASTS BACK!
THE OTHERS CAN TAKE CARE OF THAT...WHILE I RESCUE THE LADY!
NO NEED TO BE AFRAID, OLD GIRL! JUST TRY TO RELAX...
...WHILE MY FAITHFUL ARCHAEOPTERX PLUCKS YOU FROM THE GRASP OF THE JERRIES!
6.

EYES *UPWARD*, CHAPS! *LUFTWAFFE BANDITS* AT TWELVE O'CLOCK!

WE MUST SWEEP THE BRITISH FROM THE *SKIES*...FOR THE GLORY OF THE *FUEHRER!*

UNITS *ONE THROUGH FIVE...*HOLD THE JERRIES OFF UNTIL WE CAN TAKE THE GIRL TO *SAFETY!*

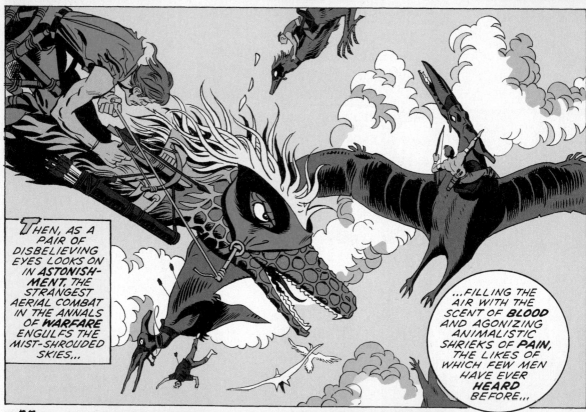

THEN, AS A PAIR OF DISBELIEVING EYES LOOKS ON IN *ASTONISHMENT,* THE STRANGEST AERIAL COMBAT IN THE ANNALS OF *WARFARE* ENGULFS THE MIST-SHROUDED SKIES...

...FILLING THE AIR WITH THE SCENT OF *BLOOD* AND AGONIZING ANIMALISTIC SHRIEKS OF *PAIN,* THE LIKES OF WHICH FEW MEN HAVE EVER *HEARD* BEFORE...

*U*NTIL, AT LAST, THE BATTLE IS *ENDED,* AND THE VANQUISHED LIMP *HOMEWARD,* NURSING THEIR WOUNDS AND LOOKING FORWARD TO *ANOTHER DAY...*

THE GERMANS ARE *BEATEN!* NOW WE RETURN TO *NEW BRITANNIA!*

AM I GOING *MAD...*OR IS THIS SOME INSANE RECREATION OF--*A WAR THAT'S OVER?!*

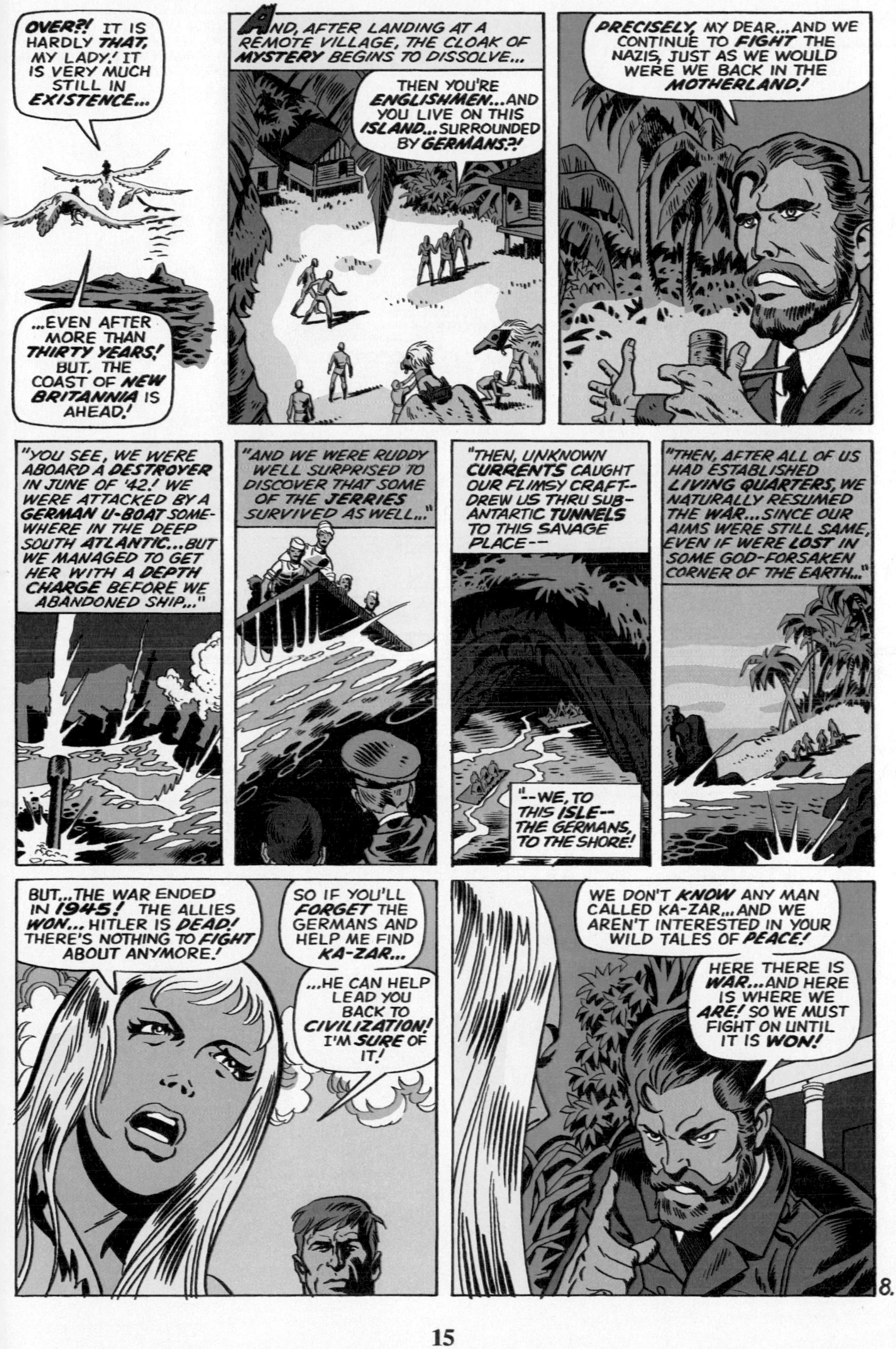
OVER?! IT IS HARDLY THAT, MY LADY! IT IS VERY MUCH STILL IN EXISTENCE...
...EVEN AFTER MORE THAN THIRTY YEARS! BUT, THE COAST OF NEW BRITANNIA IS AHEAD!
AND, AFTER LANDING AT A REMOTE VILLAGE, THE CLOAK OF MYSTERY BEGINS TO DISSOLVE...
THEN YOU'RE ENGLISHMEN...AND YOU LIVE ON THIS ISLAND...SURROUNDED BY GERMANS?!
PRECISELY, MY DEAR...AND WE CONTINUE TO FIGHT THE NAZIS, JUST AS WE WOULD WERE WE BACK IN THE MOTHERLAND!
"YOU SEE, WE WERE ABOARD A DESTROYER IN JUNE OF '42! WE WERE ATTACKED BY A GERMAN U-BOAT SOMEWHERE IN THE DEEP SOUTH ATLANTIC...BUT WE MANAGED TO GET HER WITH A DEPTH CHARGE BEFORE WE ABANDONED SHIP..."
"AND WE WERE RUDDY WELL SURPRISED TO DISCOVER THAT SOME OF THE JERRIES SURVIVED AS WELL..."
"THEN, UNKNOWN CURRENTS CAUGHT OUR FLIMSY CRAFT--DREW US THRU SUB-ANTARTIC TUNNELS TO THIS SAVAGE PLACE--
"--WE, TO THIS ISLE--THE GERMANS, TO THE SHORE!
"THEN, AFTER ALL OF US HAD ESTABLISHED LIVING QUARTERS, WE NATURALLY RESUMED THE WAR...SINCE OUR AIMS WERE STILL SAME, EVEN IF WERE LOST IN SOME GOD-FORSAKEN CORNER OF THE EARTH..."
BUT...THE WAR ENDED IN 1945! THE ALLIES WON... HITLER IS DEAD! THERE'S NOTHING TO FIGHT ABOUT ANYMORE!
SO IF YOU'LL FORGET THE GERMANS AND HELP ME FIND KA-ZAR...
...HE CAN HELP LEAD YOU BACK TO CIVILIZATION! I'M SURE OF IT!
WE DON'T KNOW ANY MAN CALLED KA-ZAR...AND WE AREN'T INTERESTED IN YOUR WILD TALES OF PEACE!
HERE THERE IS WAR...AND HERE IS WHERE WE ARE! SO WE MUST FIGHT ON UNTIL IT IS WON!
8.

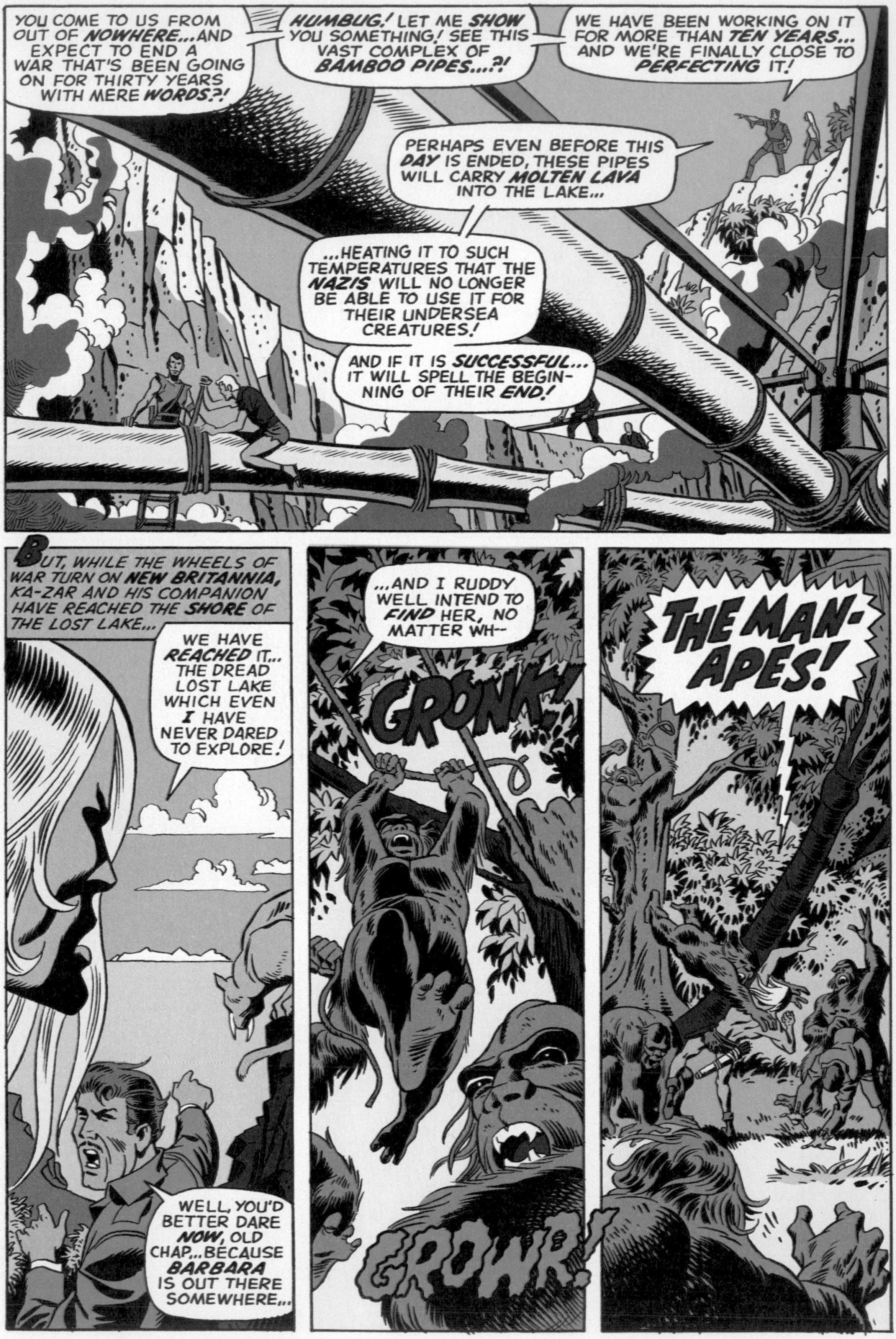

YOU COME TO US FROM OUT OF NOWHERE...AND EXPECT TO END A WAR THAT'S BEEN GOING ON FOR THIRTY YEARS WITH MERE WORDS?!
HUMBUG! LET ME SHOW YOU SOMETHING! SEE THIS VAST COMPLEX OF BAMBOO PIPES...?!
WE HAVE BEEN WORKING ON IT FOR MORE THAN TEN YEARS... AND WE'RE FINALLY CLOSE TO PERFECTING IT!
PERHAPS EVEN BEFORE THIS DAY IS ENDED, THESE PIPES WILL CARRY MOLTEN LAVA INTO THE LAKE...
...HEATING IT TO SUCH TEMPERATURES THAT THE NAZIS WILL NO LONGER BE ABLE TO USE IT FOR THEIR UNDERSEA CREATURES!
AND IF IT IS SUCCESSFUL... IT WILL SPELL THE BEGINNING OF THEIR END!
BUT, WHILE THE WHEELS OF WAR TURN ON NEW BRITANNIA, KA-ZAR AND HIS COMPANION HAVE REACHED THE SHORE OF THE LOST LAKE...
WE HAVE REACHED IT... THE DREAD LOST LAKE WHICH EVEN I HAVE NEVER DARED TO EXPLORE!
WELL, YOU'D BETTER DARE NOW, OLD CHAP...BECAUSE BARBARA IS OUT THERE SOMEWHERE...
...AND I RUDDY WELL INTEND TO FIND HER, NO MATTER WH--
GRONK!
GROWR!
THE MAN-APES!

BUT THE **LORD** OF THE SAVAGE LAND AND HIS **SABRE-TOOTHED** ALLY RECOVER FROM THE SURPRISE ATTACK **INSTANTLY**, CALLING ON AN **EXTRA-SENSE**, HONED TO A RAZOR'S EDGE BY YEARS OF LIVING BY THE LAW OF THE **JUNGLE**...

RROWRR!

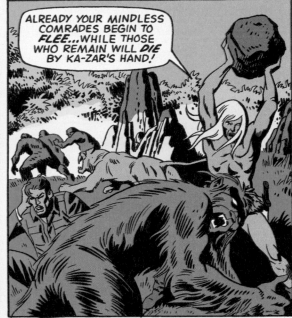

ALREADY YOUR MINDLESS COMRADES BEGIN TO **FLEE**...WHILE THOSE WHO REMAIN WILL **DIE** BY KA-ZAR'S HAND!

THOSE CREATURES WHO WOULD SPILL BLOOD **WANTONLY**... WILL PERISH FROM **LACK** OF IT!

SO SWEARS **KA-ZAR!**

THEIR LEADER HAS **FALLEN**, ZABU...A MERE **SNARL** FROM YOU WILL SEND THE REST OF THEM **SCAMPERING!**

THE BATTLE WITH THE MAN-APES IS **OVER**... BUT FAR **GREATER** CHALLENGES MAY WELL LIE **AHEAD!**

BUT WE WILL NEVER **KNOW**, UNTIL WE EMBARK UPON THESE DANK, FORBIDDEN **WATERS**...

...SO LET US GO **QUICKLY**, BEFORE THIS GRIM FOREBODING CAUSES KA-ZAR TO CHANGE HIS **MIND!**

IT IS THE LONG-HAIRED **ENGLISHMAN** ...THE ONE WE HAVE SEEN ON THE LAKE'S EDGE **BEFORE!**

JAWOHL! BUT THIS TIME HE HAS VENTURED TOO **FAR!**

10.

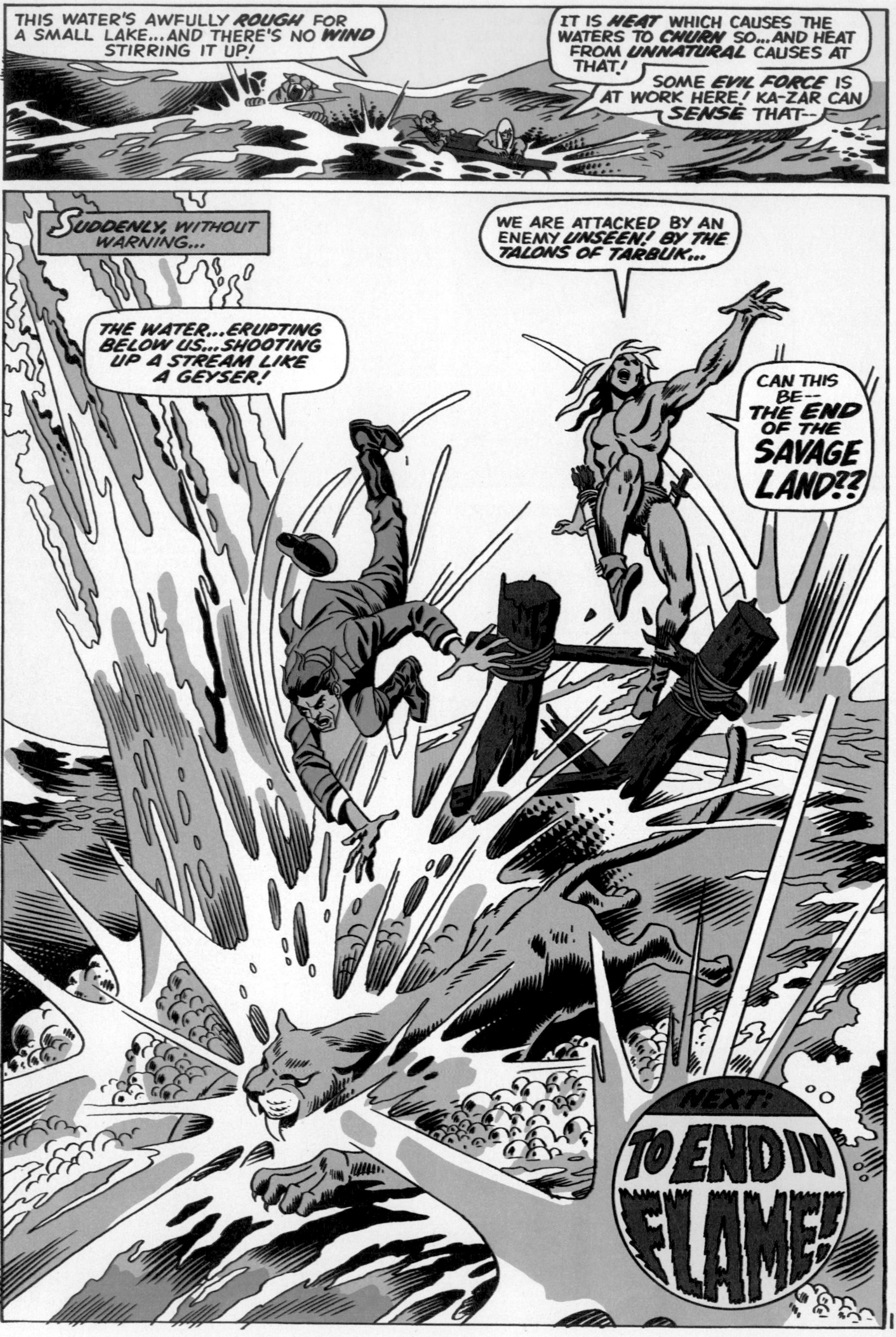
THIS WATER'S AWFULLY ROUGH FOR A SMALL LAKE...AND THERE'S NO WIND STIRRING IT UP!
IT IS HEAT WHICH CAUSES THE WATERS TO CHURN SO...AND HEAT FROM UNNATURAL CAUSES AT THAT!
SOME EVIL FORCE IS AT WORK HERE! KA-ZAR CAN SENSE THAT--
SUDDENLY, WITHOUT WARNING...
WE ARE ATTACKED BY AN ENEMY UNSEEN! BY THE TALONS OF TARBUK...
THE WATER...ERUPTING BELOW US...SHOOTING UP A STREAM LIKE A GEYSER!
CAN THIS BE-- THE END OF THE SAVAGE LAND??
NEXT:
TO END IN FLAME!

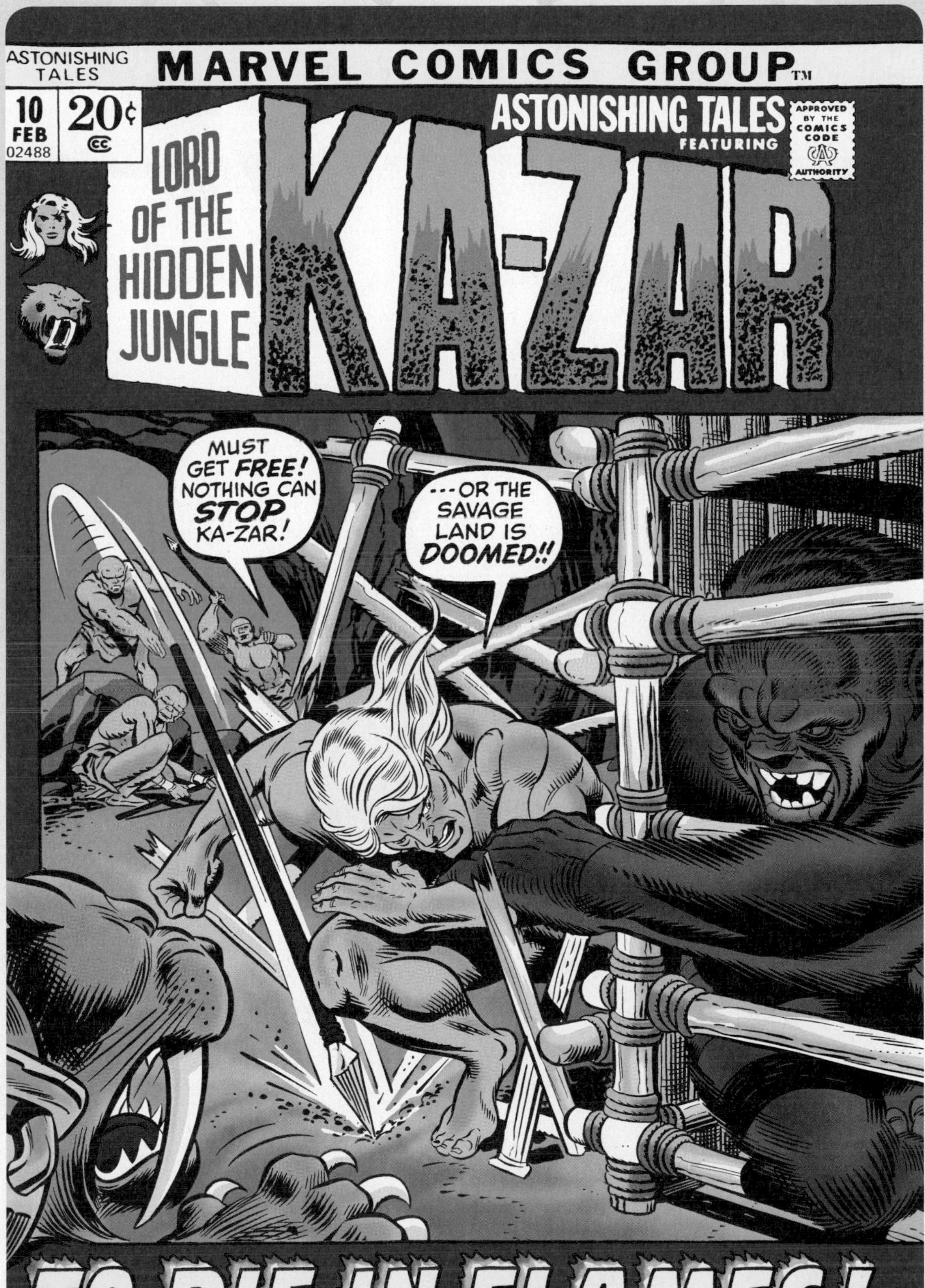
ASTONISHING TALES
MARVEL COMICS GROUP™
10 FEB 02488
20¢
CC
ASTONISHING TALES
FEATURING
APPROVED BY THE COMICS CODE AUTHORITY
LORD OF THE HIDDEN JUNGLE
KA-ZAR
MUST GET FREE! NOTHING CAN STOP KA-ZAR!
---OR THE SAVAGE LAND IS DOOMED!!
TO DIE IN FLAMES!

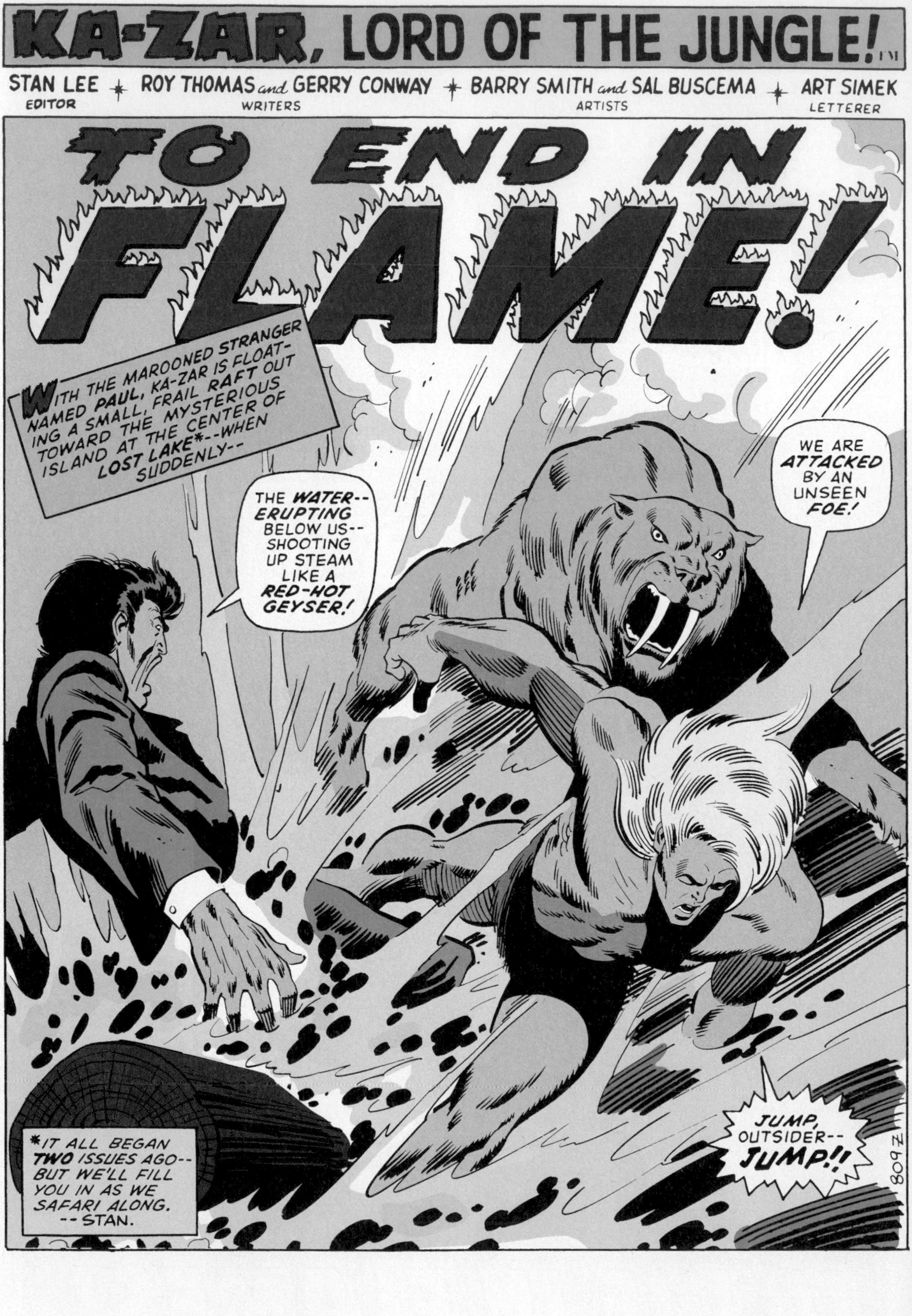
KA-ZAR, LORD OF THE JUNGLE!™
STAN LEE EDITOR ✦ ROY THOMAS and GERRY CONWAY WRITERS ✦ BARRY SMITH and SAL BUSCEMA ARTISTS ✦ ART SIMEK LETTERER
TO END IN FLAME!
WITH THE MAROONED STRANGER NAMED PAUL, KA-ZAR IS FLOATING A SMALL, FRAIL RAFT OUT TOWARD THE MYSTERIOUS ISLAND AT THE CENTER OF LOST LAKE*--WHEN SUDDENLY--
THE WATER--ERUPTING BELOW US--SHOOTING UP STEAM LIKE A RED-HOT GEYSER!
WE ARE ATTACKED BY AN UNSEEN FOE!
*IT ALL BEGAN TWO ISSUES AGO--BUT WE'LL FILL YOU IN AS WE SAFARI ALONG. --STAN.
JUMP, OUTSIDER--JUMP!!

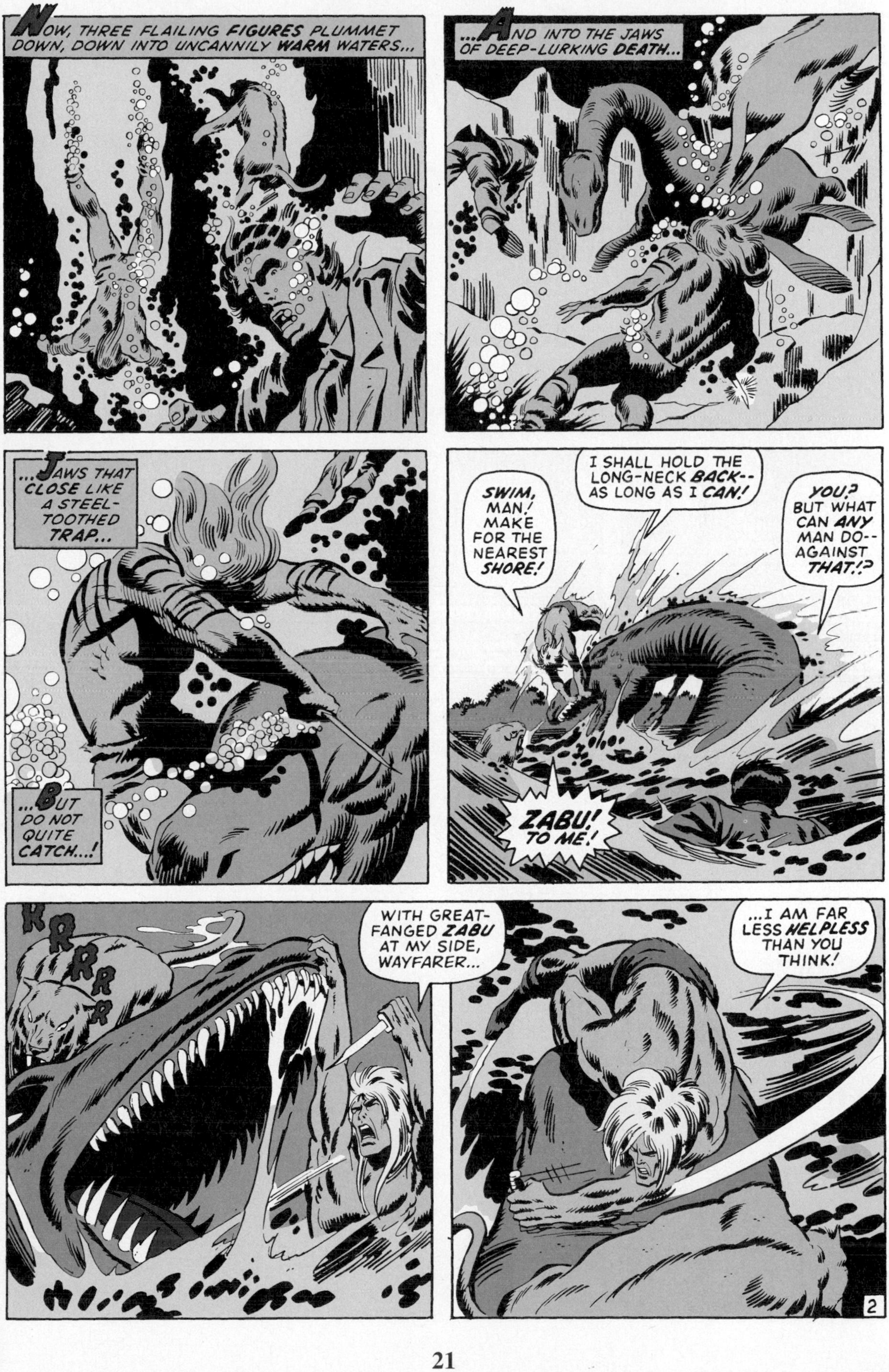
NOW, THREE FLAILING FIGURES PLUMMET DOWN, DOWN INTO UNCANNILY WARM WATERS...
...AND INTO THE JAWS OF DEEP-LURKING DEATH...
...JAWS THAT CLOSE LIKE A STEEL-TOOTHED TRAP...
...BUT DO NOT QUITE CATCH...!
SWIM, MAN! MAKE FOR THE NEAREST SHORE!
I SHALL HOLD THE LONG-NECK BACK-- AS LONG AS I CAN!
YOU?? BUT WHAT CAN ANY MAN DO-- AGAINST THAT!?
ZABU! TO ME!
RRRRR
WITH GREAT-FANGED ZABU AT MY SIDE, WAYFARER...
...I AM FAR LESS HELPLESS THAN YOU THINK!
2

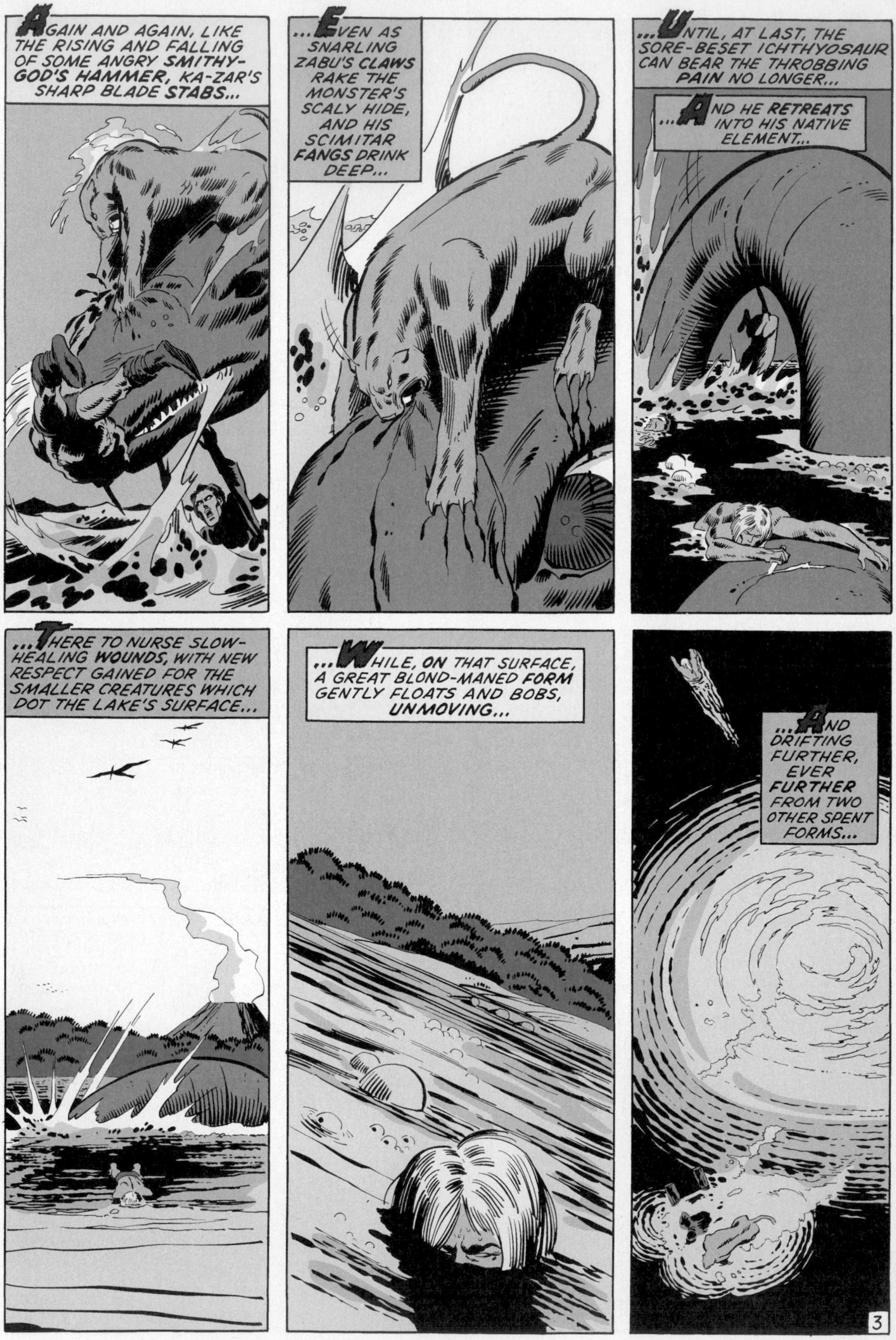
AGAIN AND AGAIN, LIKE THE RISING AND FALLING OF SOME ANGRY SMITHY-GOD'S HAMMER, KA-ZAR'S SHARP BLADE STABS...
...EVEN AS SNARLING ZABU'S CLAWS RAKE THE MONSTER'S SCALY HIDE, AND HIS SCIMITAR FANGS DRINK DEEP...
...UNTIL, AT LAST, THE SORE-BESET ICHTHYOSAUR CAN BEAR THE THROBBING PAIN NO LONGER...
...AND HE RETREATS INTO HIS NATIVE ELEMENT...
...THERE TO NURSE SLOW-HEALING WOUNDS, WITH NEW RESPECT GAINED FOR THE SMALLER CREATURES WHICH DOT THE LAKE'S SURFACE...
...WHILE, ON THAT SURFACE, A GREAT BLOND-MANED FORM GENTLY FLOATS AND BOBS, UNMOVING...
...AND DRIFTING FURTHER, EVER FURTHER FROM TWO OTHER SPENT FORMS...
3

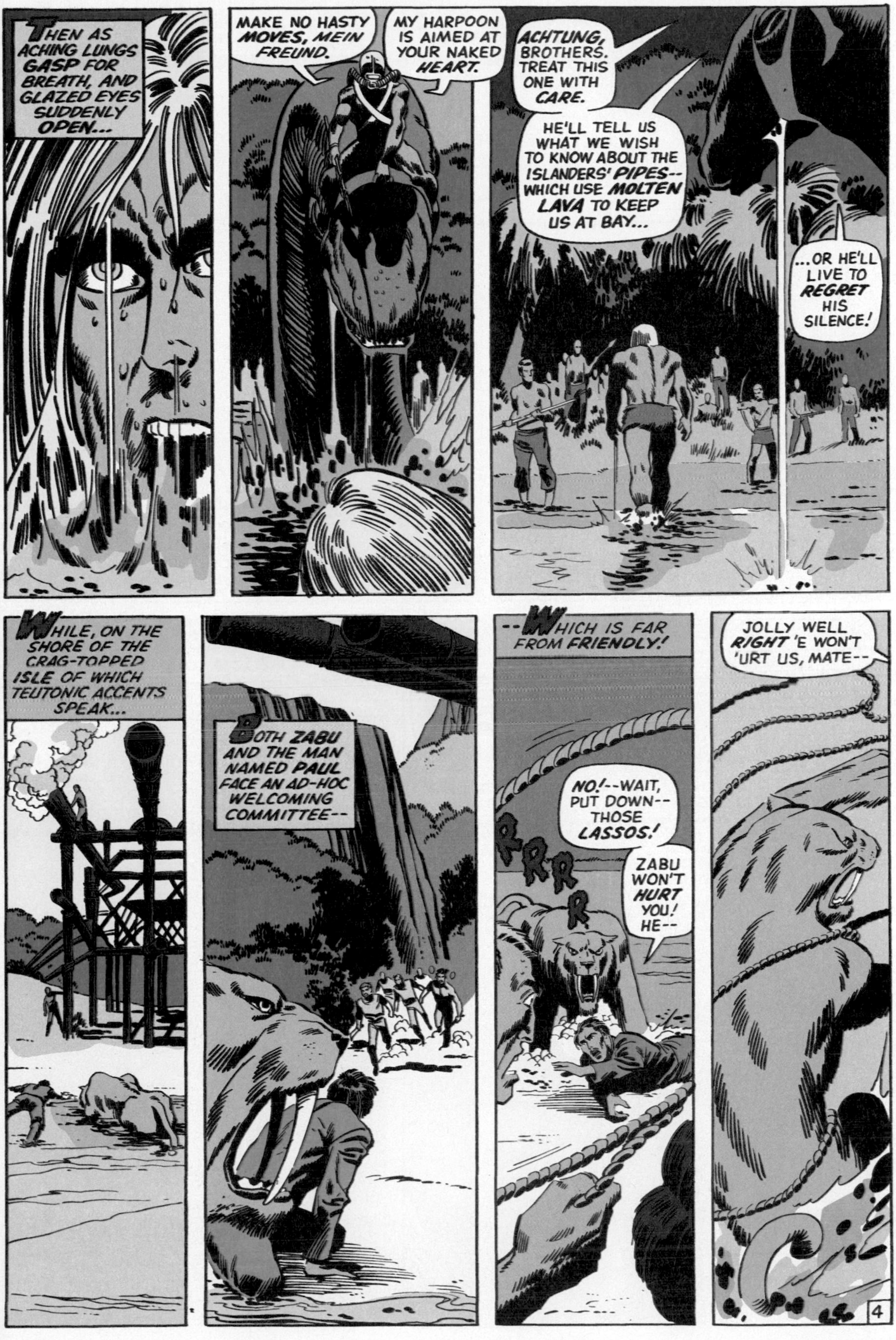
THEN AS ACHING LUNGS GASP FOR BREATH, AND GLAZED EYES SUDDENLY OPEN...
MAKE NO HASTY MOVES, MEIN FREUND.
MY HARPOON IS AIMED AT YOUR NAKED HEART.
ACHTUNG, BROTHERS. TREAT THIS ONE WITH CARE.
HE'LL TELL US WHAT WE WISH TO KNOW ABOUT THE ISLANDERS' PIPES-- WHICH USE MOLTEN LAVA TO KEEP US AT BAY...
...OR HE'LL LIVE TO REGRET HIS SILENCE!
WHILE, ON THE SHORE OF THE CRAG-TOPPED ISLE OF WHICH TEUTONIC ACCENTS SPEAK...
BOTH ZABU AND THE MAN NAMED PAUL FACE AN AD-HOC WELCOMING COMMITTEE--
--WHICH IS FAR FROM FRIENDLY!
NO!--WAIT, PUT DOWN--THOSE LASSOS!
RRRR
ZABU WON'T HURT YOU! HE--
JOLLY WELL RIGHT 'E WON'T 'URT US, MATE--
4

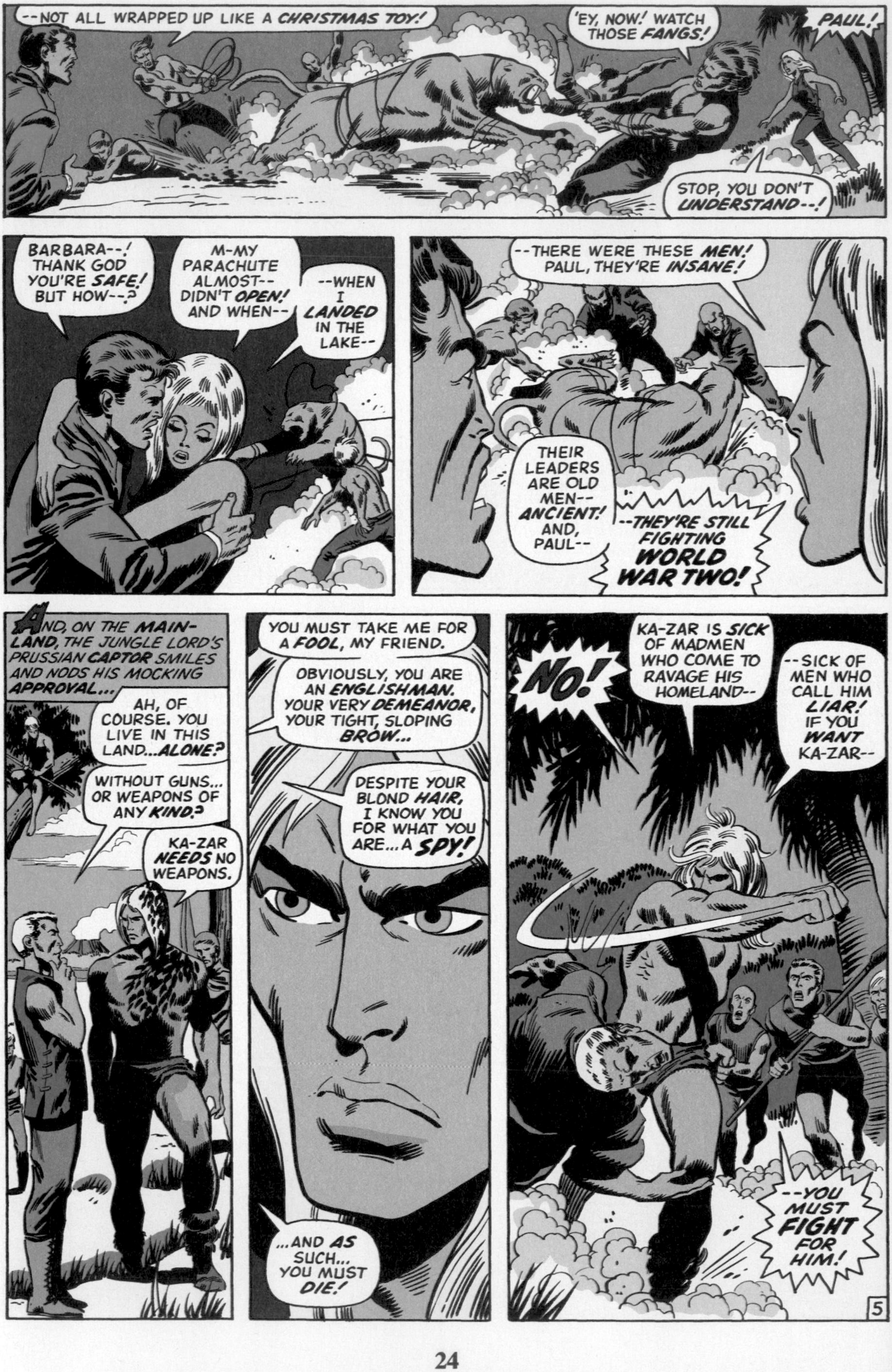
--NOT ALL WRAPPED UP LIKE A CHRISTMAS TOY!
'EY, NOW! WATCH THOSE FANGS!
PAUL!
STOP, YOU DON'T UNDERSTAND--!
BARBARA--! THANK GOD YOU'RE SAFE! BUT HOW--?
M-MY PARACHUTE ALMOST--DIDN'T OPEN! AND WHEN--
--WHEN I LANDED IN THE LAKE--
--THERE WERE THESE MEN! PAUL, THEY'RE INSANE!
THEIR LEADERS ARE OLD MEN--ANCIENT! AND, PAUL--
--THEY'RE STILL FIGHTING WORLD WAR TWO!
AND, ON THE MAINLAND, THE JUNGLE LORD'S PRUSSIAN CAPTOR SMILES AND NODS HIS MOCKING APPROVAL...
AH, OF COURSE. YOU LIVE IN THIS LAND...ALONE?
WITHOUT GUNS... OR WEAPONS OF ANY KIND?
KA-ZAR NEEDS NO WEAPONS.
YOU MUST TAKE ME FOR A FOOL, MY FRIEND.
OBVIOUSLY, YOU ARE AN ENGLISHMAN. YOUR VERY DEMEANOR, YOUR TIGHT, SLOPING BROW...
DESPITE YOUR BLOND HAIR, I KNOW YOU FOR WHAT YOU ARE...A SPY!
...AND AS SUCH... YOU MUST DIE!
NO!
KA-ZAR IS SICK OF MADMEN WHO COME TO RAVAGE HIS HOMELAND--
--SICK OF MEN WHO CALL HIM LIAR! IF YOU WANT KA-ZAR--
--YOU MUST FIGHT FOR HIM!
5

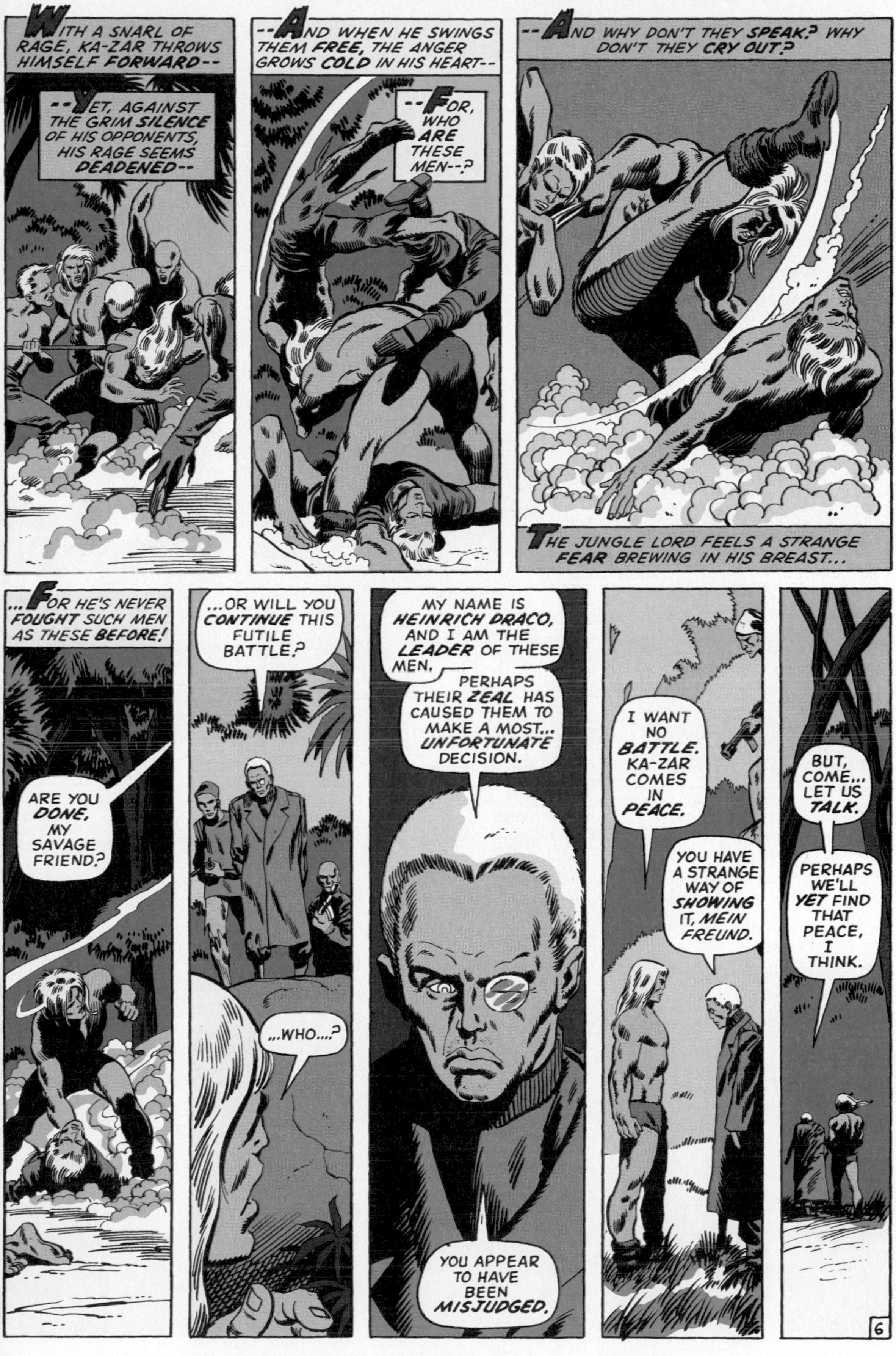
WITH A SNARL OF RAGE, KA-ZAR THROWS HIMSELF FORWARD--
--YET, AGAINST THE GRIM SILENCE OF HIS OPPONENTS, HIS RAGE SEEMS DEADENED--
--AND WHEN HE SWINGS THEM FREE, THE ANGER GROWS COLD IN HIS HEART--
--FOR, WHO ARE THESE MEN--?
--AND WHY DON'T THEY SPEAK? WHY DON'T THEY CRY OUT?
THE JUNGLE LORD FEELS A STRANGE FEAR BREWING IN HIS BREAST...
...FOR HE'S NEVER FOUGHT SUCH MEN AS THESE BEFORE!
ARE YOU DONE, MY SAVAGE FRIEND?
...OR WILL YOU CONTINUE THIS FUTILE BATTLE?
...WHO...?
MY NAME IS HEINRICH DRACO, AND I AM THE LEADER OF THESE MEN.
PERHAPS THEIR ZEAL HAS CAUSED THEM TO MAKE A MOST... UNFORTUNATE DECISION.
YOU APPEAR TO HAVE BEEN MISJUDGED.
I WANT NO BATTLE. KA-ZAR COMES IN PEACE.
YOU HAVE A STRANGE WAY OF SHOWING IT, MEIN FREUND.
BUT, COME... LET US TALK.
PERHAPS WE'LL YET FIND THAT PEACE, I THINK.
6

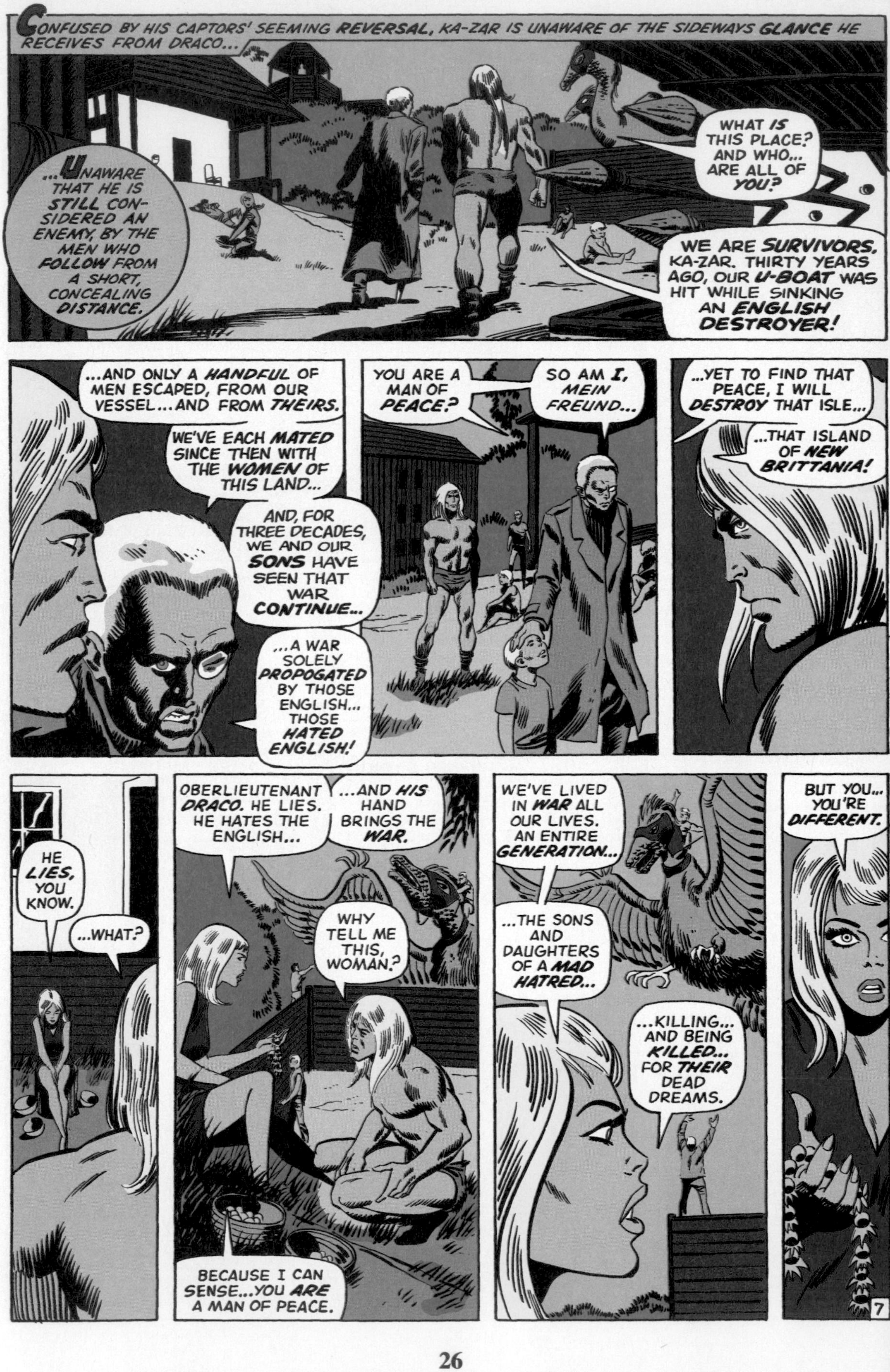
CONFUSED BY HIS CAPTORS' SEEMING REVERSAL, KA-ZAR IS UNAWARE OF THE SIDEWAYS GLANCE HE RECEIVES FROM DRACO...
...UNAWARE THAT HE IS STILL CONSIDERED AN ENEMY, BY THE MEN WHO FOLLOW FROM A SHORT, CONCEALING DISTANCE.
WHAT IS THIS PLACE? AND WHO... ARE ALL OF YOU?
WE ARE SURVIVORS, KA-ZAR. THIRTY YEARS AGO, OUR U-BOAT WAS HIT WHILE SINKING AN ENGLISH DESTROYER!
...AND ONLY A HANDFUL OF MEN ESCAPED, FROM OUR VESSEL... AND FROM THEIRS.
WE'VE EACH MATED SINCE THEN WITH THE WOMEN OF THIS LAND...
AND, FOR THREE DECADES, WE AND OUR SONS HAVE SEEN THAT WAR CONTINUE...
...A WAR SOLELY PROPOGATED BY THOSE ENGLISH... THOSE HATED ENGLISH!
YOU ARE A MAN OF PEACE?
SO AM I, MEIN FREUND...
...YET TO FIND THAT PEACE, I WILL DESTROY THAT ISLE...
...THAT ISLAND OF NEW BRITTANIA!
HE LIES, YOU KNOW.
...WHAT?
OBERLIEUTENANT DRACO. HE LIES. HE HATES THE ENGLISH...
...AND HIS HAND BRINGS THE WAR.
WHY TELL ME THIS, WOMAN?
BECAUSE I CAN SENSE...YOU ARE A MAN OF PEACE.
WE'VE LIVED IN WAR ALL OUR LIVES. AN ENTIRE GENERATION...
...THE SONS AND DAUGHTERS OF A MAD HATRED...
...KILLING... AND BEING KILLED... FOR THEIR DEAD DREAMS.
BUT YOU... YOU'RE DIFFERENT.
7

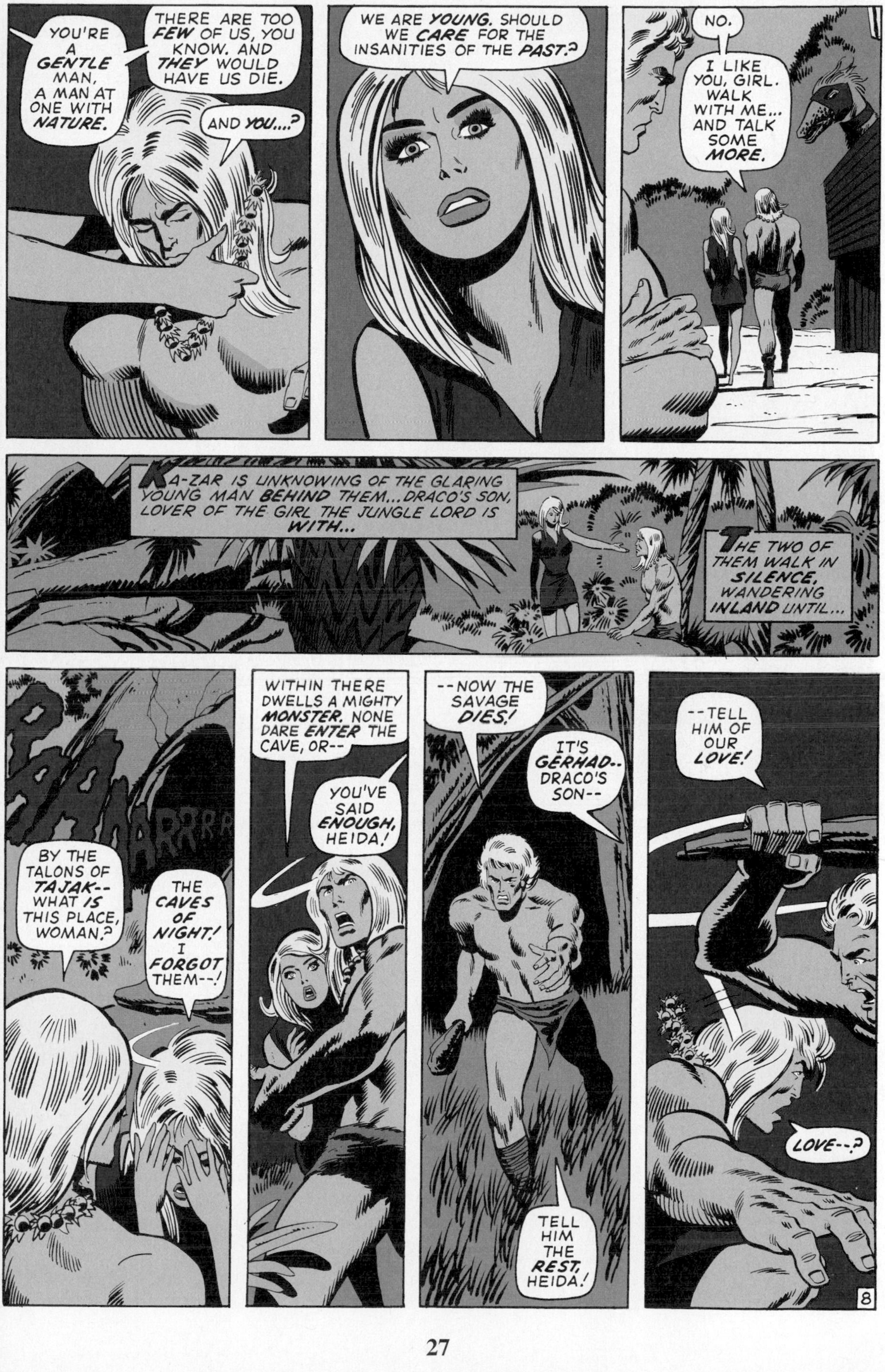
YOU'RE A GENTLE MAN, A MAN AT ONE WITH NATURE.
THERE ARE TOO FEW OF US, YOU KNOW. AND THEY WOULD HAVE US DIE.
AND YOU...?
WE ARE YOUNG. SHOULD WE CARE FOR THE INSANITIES OF THE PAST.?
NO.
I LIKE YOU, GIRL. WALK WITH ME... AND TALK SOME MORE.
KA-ZAR IS UNKNOWING OF THE GLARING YOUNG MAN BEHIND THEM... DRACO'S SON, LOVER OF THE GIRL THE JUNGLE LORD IS WITH...
THE TWO OF THEM WALK IN SILENCE, WANDERING INLAND UNTIL...
RRAAARRRR
BY THE TALONS OF TAJAK-- WHAT IS THIS PLACE, WOMAN.?
THE CAVES OF NIGHT! I FORGOT THEM--!
WITHIN THERE DWELLS A MIGHTY MONSTER. NONE DARE ENTER THE CAVE, OR--
YOU'VE SAID ENOUGH, HEIDA!
--NOW THE SAVAGE DIES!
IT'S GERHAD-- DRACO'S SON--
TELL HIM THE REST, HEIDA!
--TELL HIM OF OUR LOVE!
LOVE--.?
8

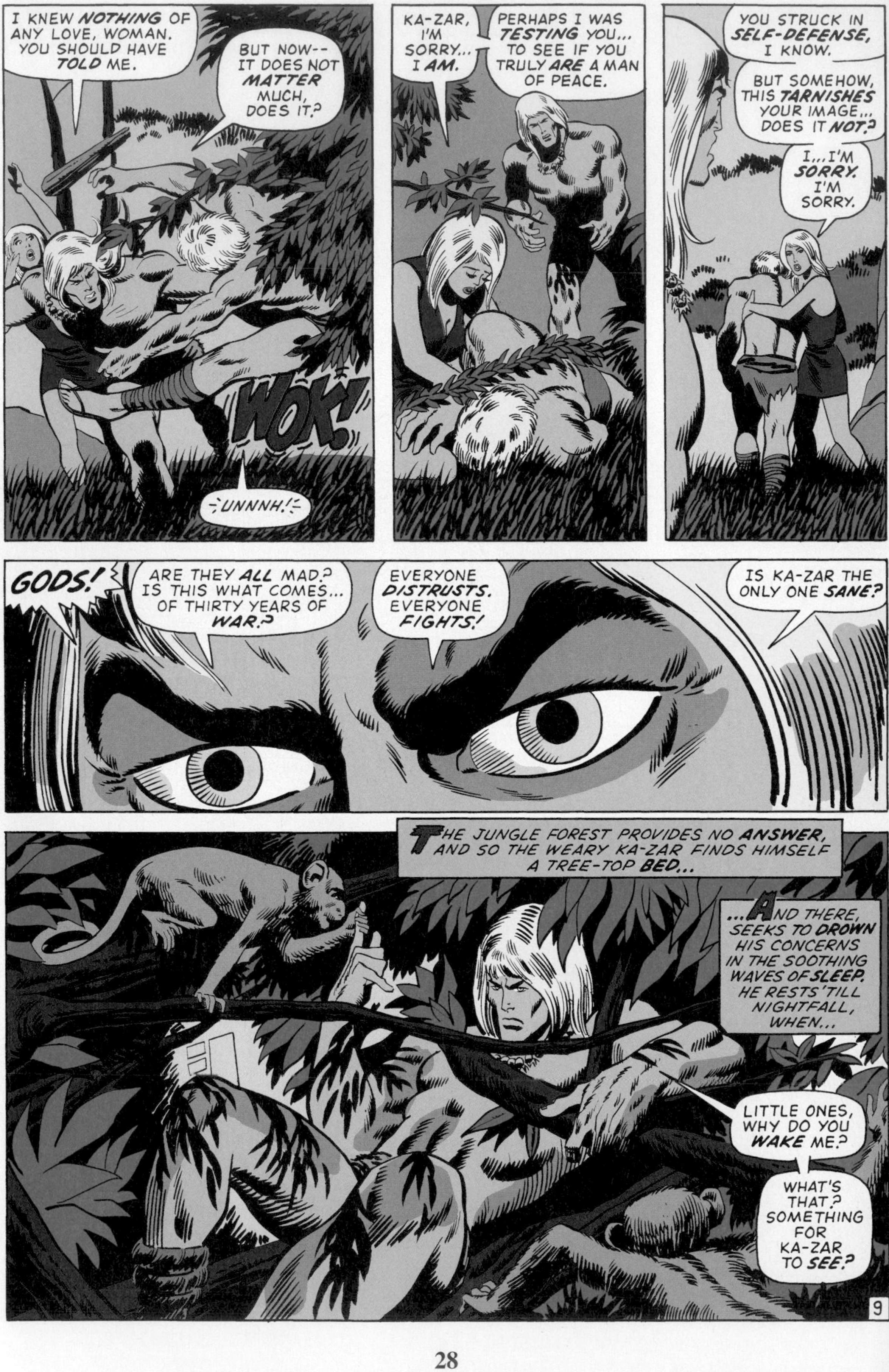
I KNEW NOTHING OF ANY LOVE, WOMAN. YOU SHOULD HAVE TOLD ME.
BUT NOW-- IT DOES NOT MATTER MUCH, DOES IT?
WOK!
UNNNH!
KA-ZAR, I'M SORRY... I AM.
PERHAPS I WAS TESTING YOU... TO SEE IF YOU TRULY ARE A MAN OF PEACE.
YOU STRUCK IN SELF-DEFENSE, I KNOW.
BUT SOMEHOW, THIS TARNISHES YOUR IMAGE... DOES IT NOT?
I...I'M SORRY. I'M SORRY.
GODS!
ARE THEY ALL MAD? IS THIS WHAT COMES... OF THIRTY YEARS OF WAR?
EVERYONE DISTRUSTS. EVERYONE FIGHTS!
IS KA-ZAR THE ONLY ONE SANE?
THE JUNGLE FOREST PROVIDES NO ANSWER, AND SO THE WEARY KA-ZAR FINDS HIMSELF A TREE-TOP BED...
...AND THERE, SEEKS TO DROWN HIS CONCERNS IN THE SOOTHING WAVES OF SLEEP. HE RESTS 'TILL NIGHTFALL, WHEN...
LITTLE ONES, WHY DO YOU WAKE ME?
WHAT'S THAT? SOMETHING FOR KA-ZAR TO SEE?
9

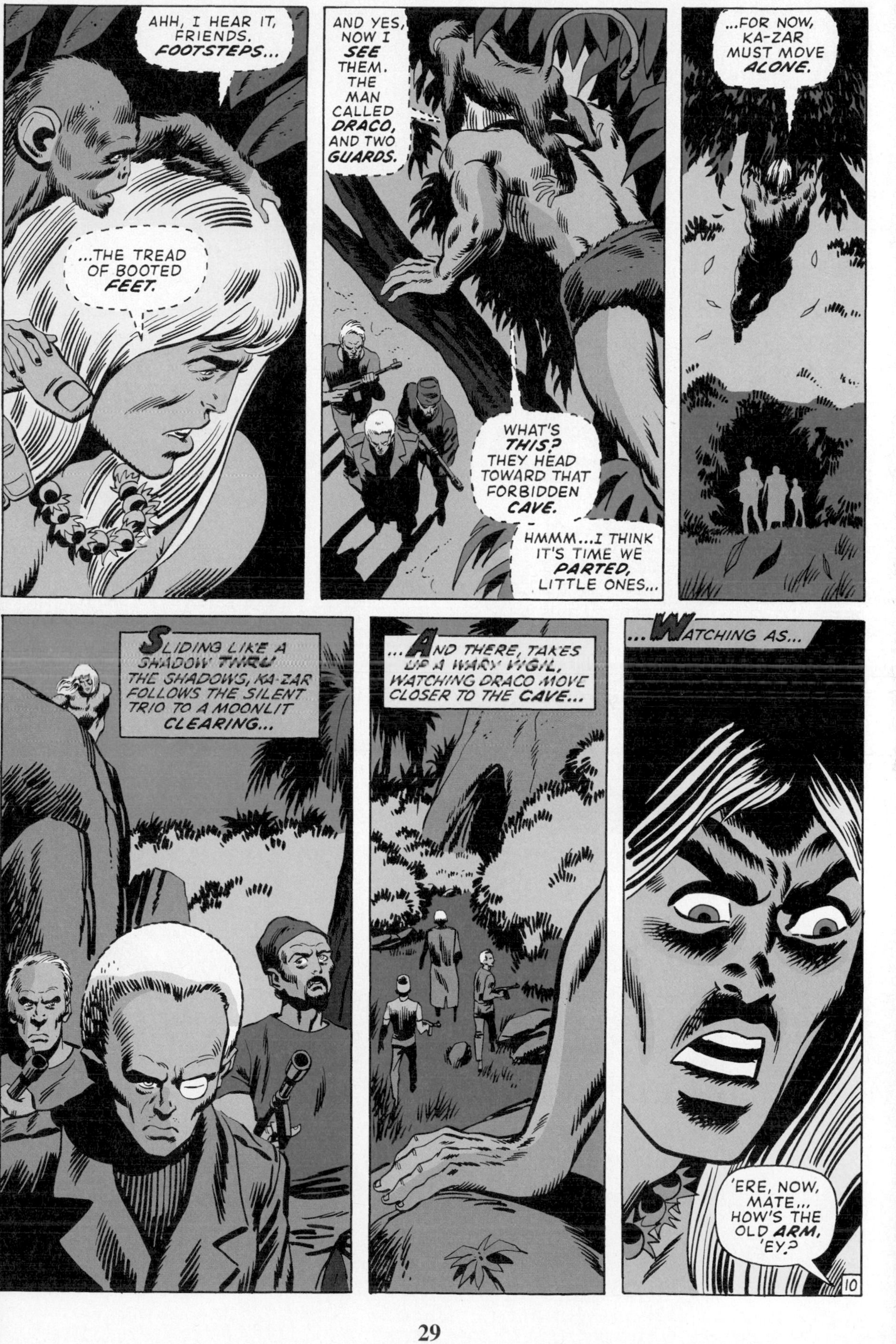
AHH, I HEAR IT, FRIENDS. FOOTSTEPS...
...THE TREAD OF BOOTED FEET.
AND YES, NOW I SEE THEM. THE MAN CALLED DRACO, AND TWO GUARDS.
WHAT'S THIS? THEY HEAD TOWARD THAT FORBIDDEN CAVE.
HMMM...I THINK IT'S TIME WE PARTED, LITTLE ONES...
...FOR NOW, KA-ZAR MUST MOVE ALONE.
SLIDING LIKE A SHADOW THRU THE SHADOWS, KA-ZAR FOLLOWS THE SILENT TRIO TO A MOONLIT CLEARING...
...AND THERE, TAKES UP A WARY VIGIL, WATCHING DRACO MOVE CLOSER TO THE CAVE...
...WATCHING AS...
'ERE, NOW, MATE... HOW'S THE OLD ARM, 'EY?
10

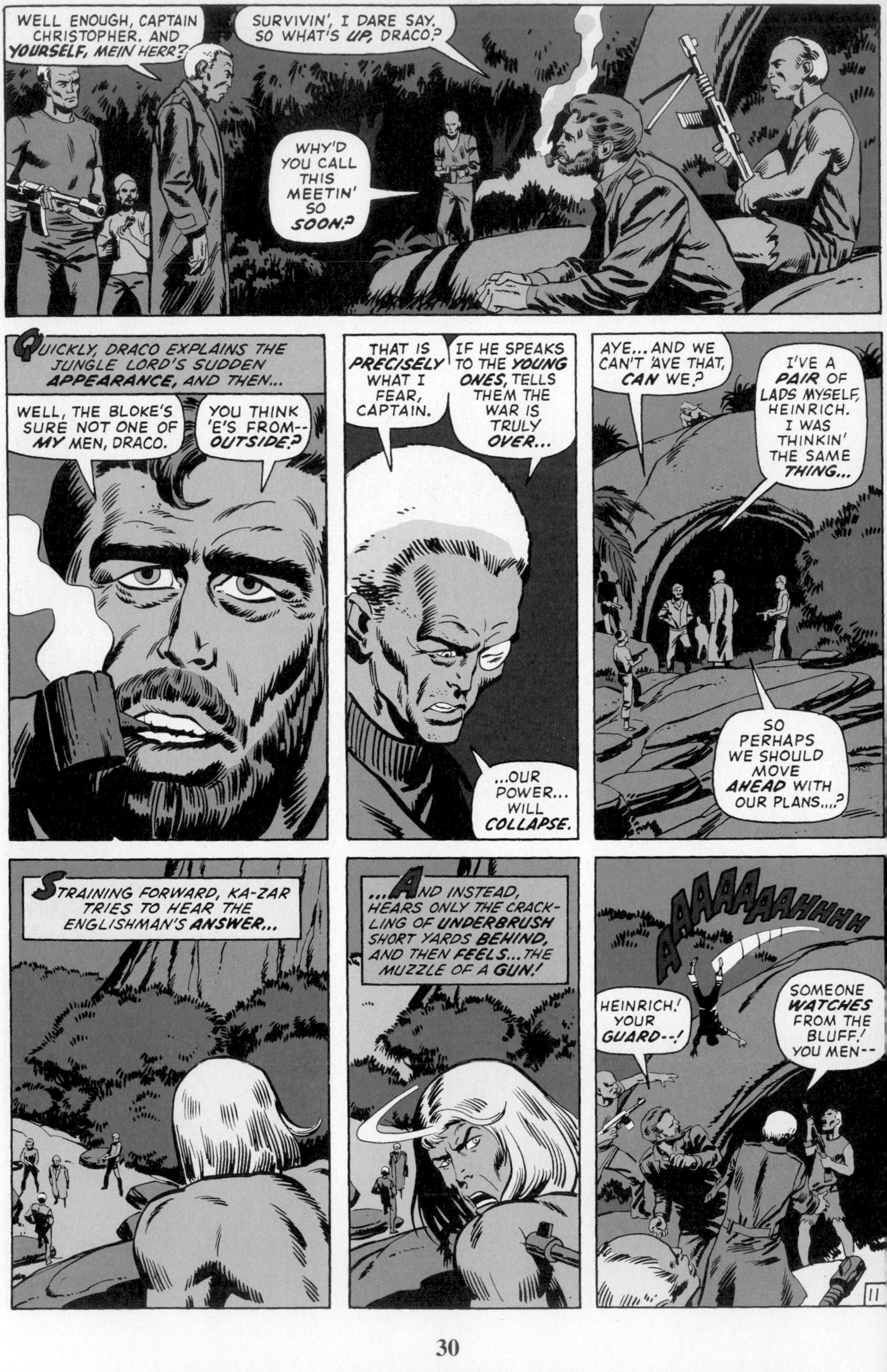

WELL ENOUGH, CAPTAIN CHRISTOPHER. AND YOURSELF, MEIN HERR?
SURVIVIN', I DARE SAY. SO WHAT'S UP, DRACO?
WHY'D YOU CALL THIS MEETIN' SO SOON?
QUICKLY, DRACO EXPLAINS THE JUNGLE LORD'S SUDDEN APPEARANCE, AND THEN...
WELL, THE BLOKE'S SURE NOT ONE OF MY MEN, DRACO.
YOU THINK 'E'S FROM--OUTSIDE?
THAT IS PRECISELY WHAT I FEAR, CAPTAIN.
IF HE SPEAKS TO THE YOUNG ONES, TELLS THEM THE WAR IS TRULY OVER...
...OUR POWER... WILL COLLAPSE.
AYE... AND WE CAN'T 'AVE THAT, CAN WE?
I'VE A PAIR OF LADS MYSELF, HEINRICH. I WAS THINKIN' THE SAME THING...
SO PERHAPS WE SHOULD MOVE AHEAD WITH OUR PLANS...?
STRAINING FORWARD, KA-ZAR TRIES TO HEAR THE ENGLISHMAN'S ANSWER...
...AND INSTEAD, HEARS ONLY THE CRACKLING OF UNDERBRUSH SHORT YARDS BEHIND, AND THEN FEELS... THE MUZZLE OF A GUN!
AAAAAAAHHHHH
HEINRICH! YOUR GUARD--!
SOMEONE WATCHES FROM THE BLUFF! YOU MEN--
11

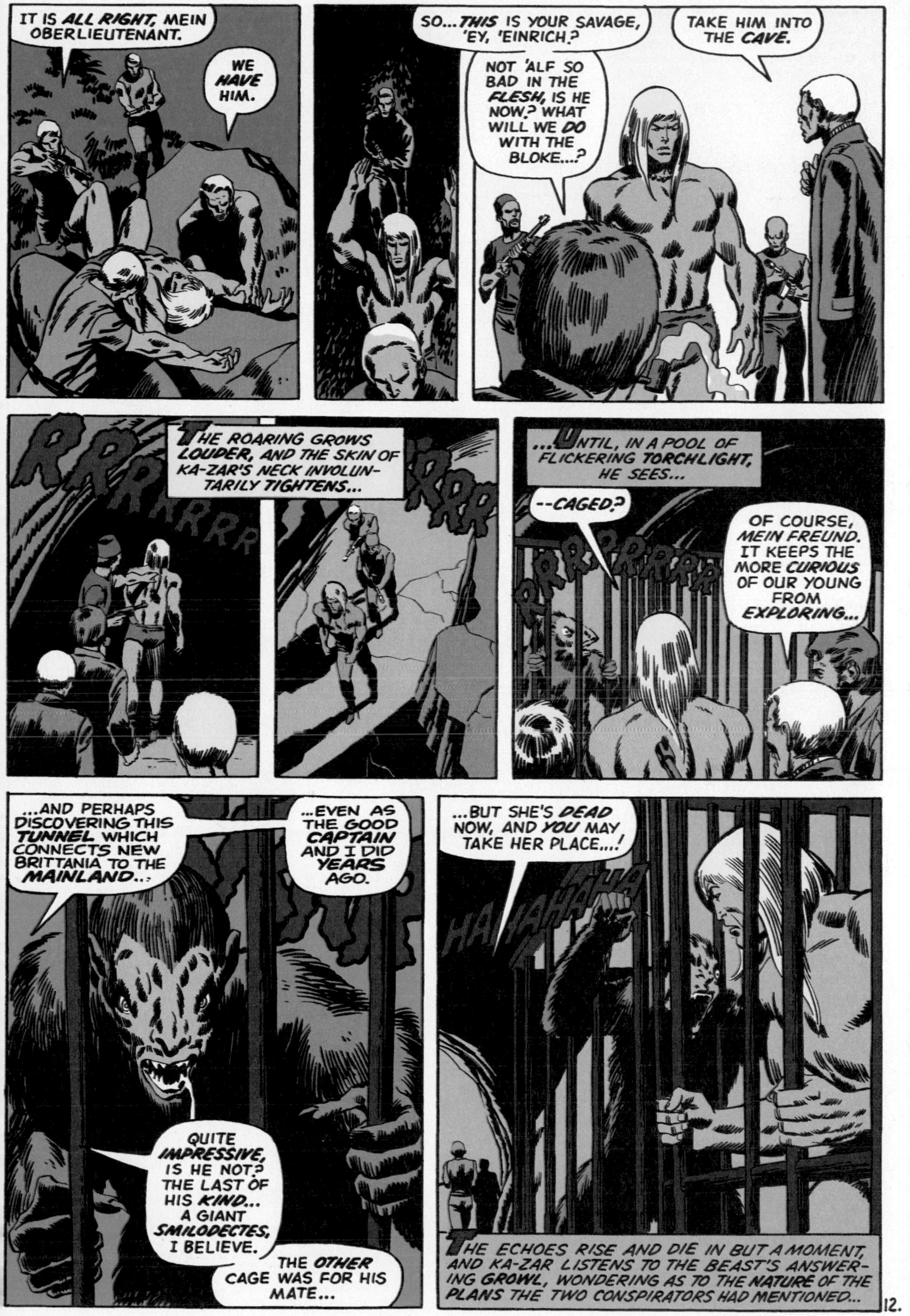
IT IS ALL RIGHT, MEIN OBERLIEUTENANT.
WE HAVE HIM.
SO...THIS IS YOUR SAVAGE, 'EY, 'EINRICH?
NOT 'ALF SO BAD IN THE FLESH, IS HE NOW? WHAT WILL WE DO WITH THE BLOKE...?
TAKE HIM INTO THE CAVE.
RRRRRRRR
THE ROARING GROWS LOUDER, AND THE SKIN OF KA-ZAR'S NECK INVOLUNTARILY TIGHTENS...
RRRR
...UNTIL, IN A POOL OF FLICKERING TORCHLIGHT, HE SEES...
--CAGED?
RRRRRRRRR
OF COURSE, MEIN FREUND. IT KEEPS THE MORE CURIOUS OF OUR YOUNG FROM EXPLORING...
...AND PERHAPS DISCOVERING THIS TUNNEL WHICH CONNECTS NEW BRITTANIA TO THE MAINLAND...
...EVEN AS THE GOOD CAPTAIN AND I DID YEARS AGO.
QUITE IMPRESSIVE, IS HE NOT? THE LAST OF HIS KIND... A GIANT SMILODECTES, I BELIEVE.
THE OTHER CAGE WAS FOR HIS MATE...
...BUT SHE'S DEAD NOW, AND YOU MAY TAKE HER PLACE...!
HAHAHAHAHA
THE ECHOES RISE AND DIE IN BUT A MOMENT, AND KA-ZAR LISTENS TO THE BEAST'S ANSWERING GROWL, WONDERING AS TO THE NATURE OF THE PLANS THE TWO CONSPIRATORS HAD MENTIONED...
12.

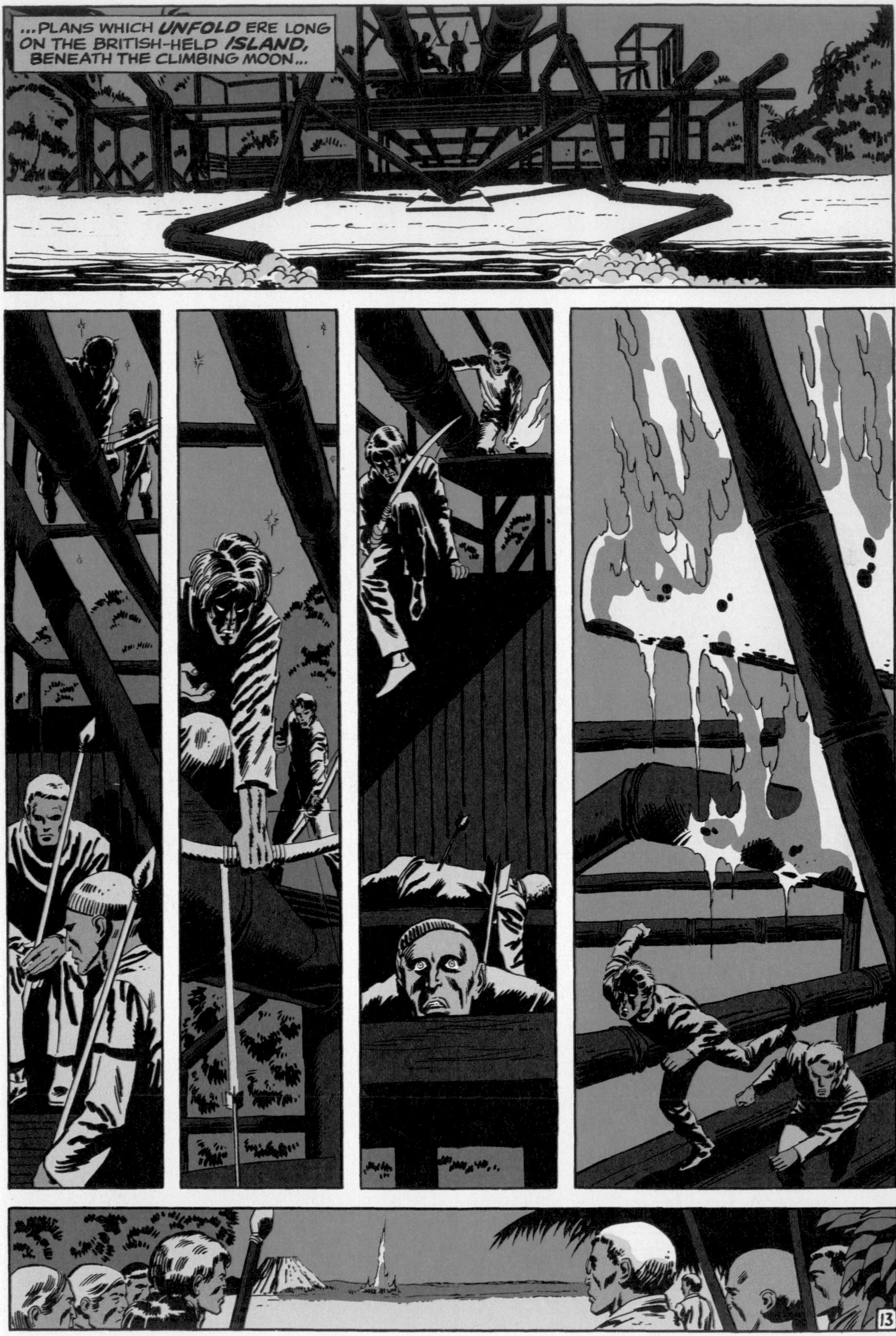
...PLANS WHICH UNFOLD ERE LONG ON THE BRITISH-HELD ISLAND, BENEATH THE CLIMBING MOON...
13

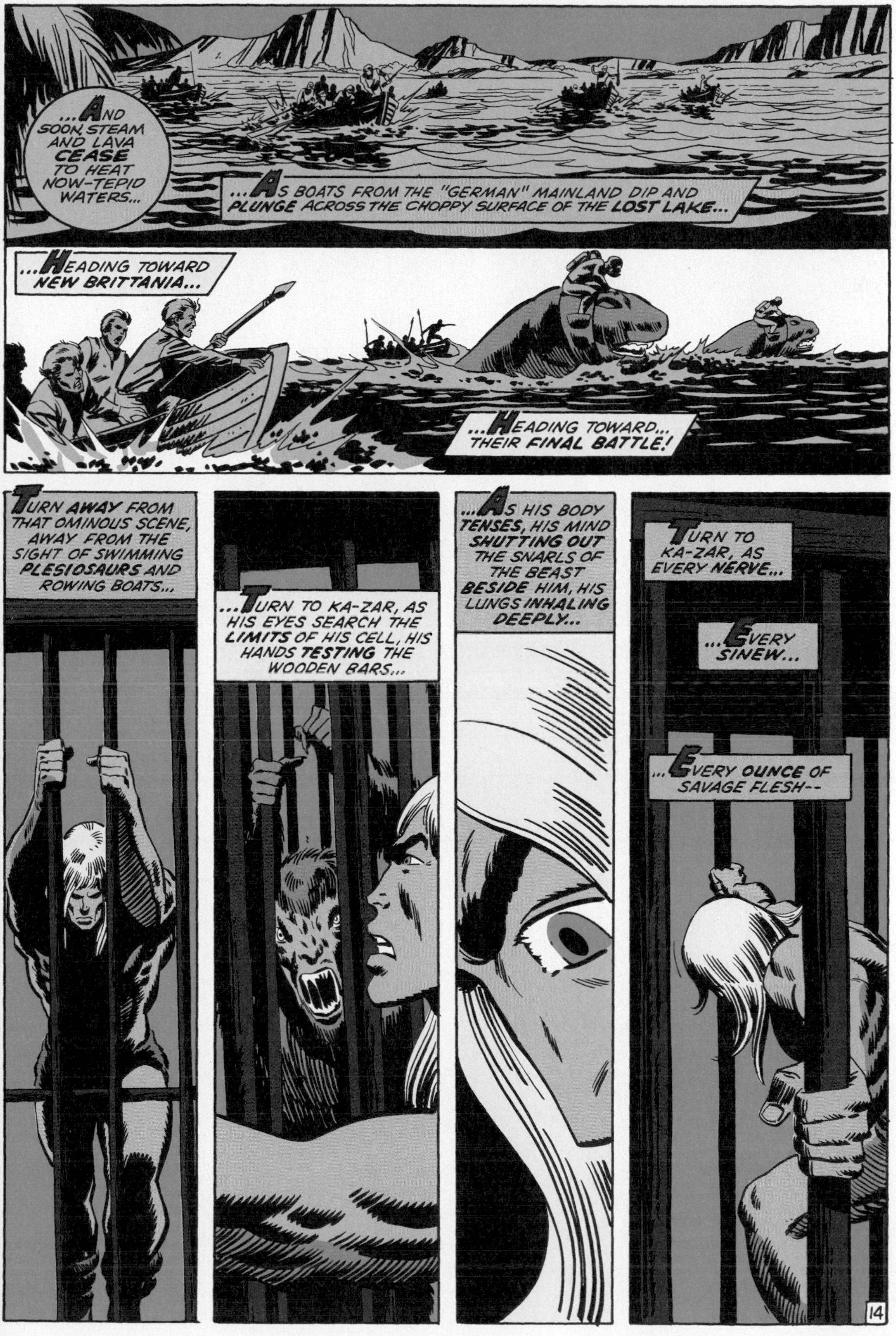
...AND SOON, STEAM AND LAVA CEASE TO HEAT NOW-TEPID WATERS...
...AS BOATS FROM THE "GERMAN" MAINLAND DIP AND PLUNGE ACROSS THE CHOPPY SURFACE OF THE LOST LAKE...
...HEADING TOWARD NEW BRITTANIA...
...HEADING TOWARD... THEIR FINAL BATTLE!
TURN AWAY FROM THAT OMINOUS SCENE, AWAY FROM THE SIGHT OF SWIMMING PLESIOSAURS AND ROWING BOATS...
...TURN TO KA-ZAR, AS HIS EYES SEARCH THE LIMITS OF HIS CELL, HIS HANDS TESTING THE WOODEN BARS...
...AS HIS BODY TENSES, HIS MIND SHUTTING OUT THE SNARLS OF THE BEAST BESIDE HIM, HIS LUNGS INHALING DEEPLY...
TURN TO KA-ZAR, AS EVERY NERVE...
...EVERY SINEW...
...EVERY OUNCE OF SAVAGE FLESH--
14

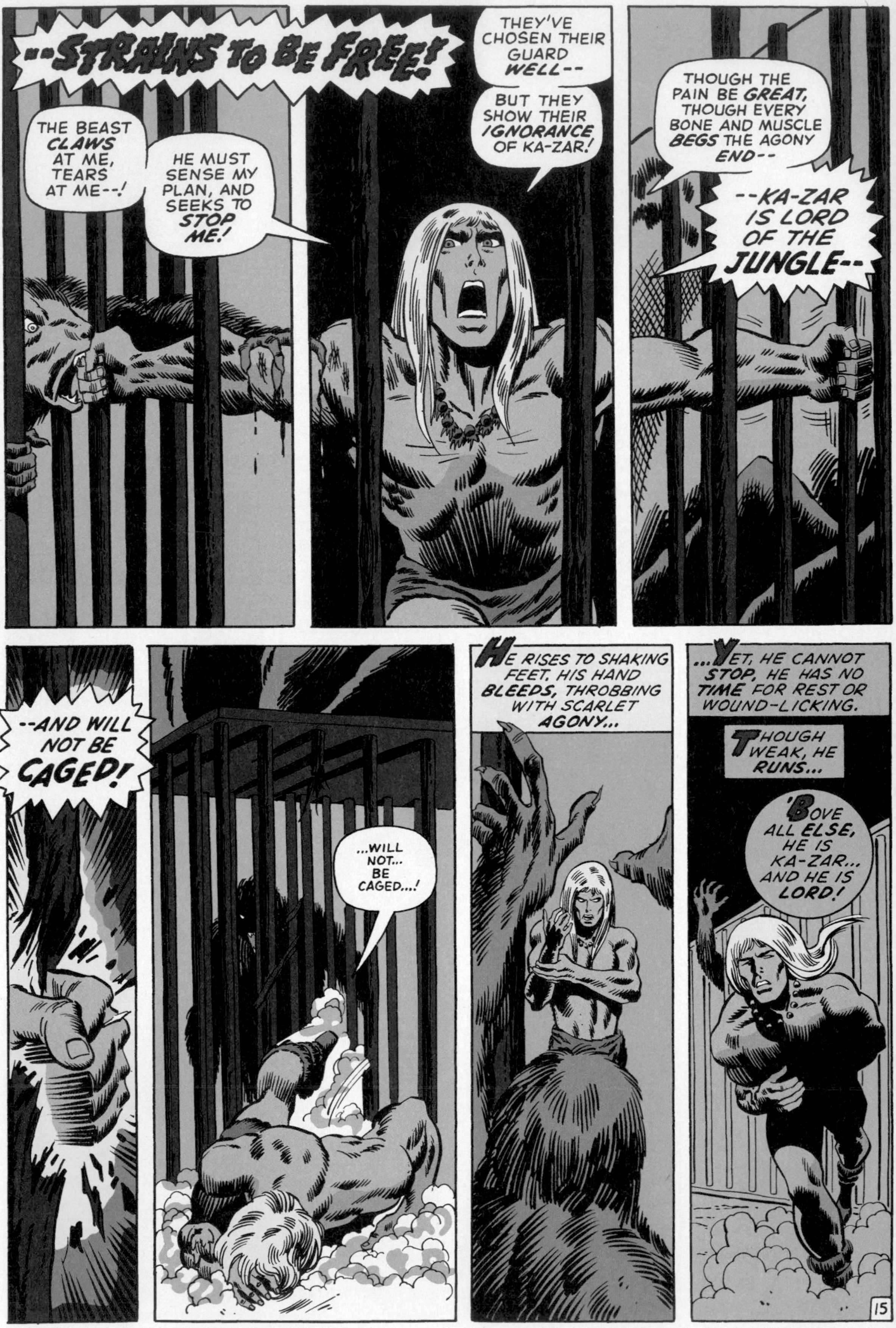
--STRAINS TO BE FREE!
THE BEAST CLAWS AT ME, TEARS AT ME--!
HE MUST SENSE MY PLAN, AND SEEKS TO STOP ME!
THEY'VE CHOSEN THEIR GUARD WELL--
BUT THEY SHOW THEIR IGNORANCE OF KA-ZAR!
THOUGH THE PAIN BE GREAT, THOUGH EVERY BONE AND MUSCLE BEGS THE AGONY END--
--KA-ZAR IS LORD OF THE JUNGLE--
--AND WILL NOT BE CAGED!
...WILL NOT... BE CAGED...!
HE RISES TO SHAKING FEET. HIS HAND BLEEDS, THROBBING WITH SCARLET AGONY...
...YET, HE CANNOT STOP, HE HAS NO TIME FOR REST OR WOUND-LICKING.
THOUGH WEAK, HE RUNS...
'BOVE ALL ELSE, HE IS KA-ZAR... AND HE IS LORD!
15

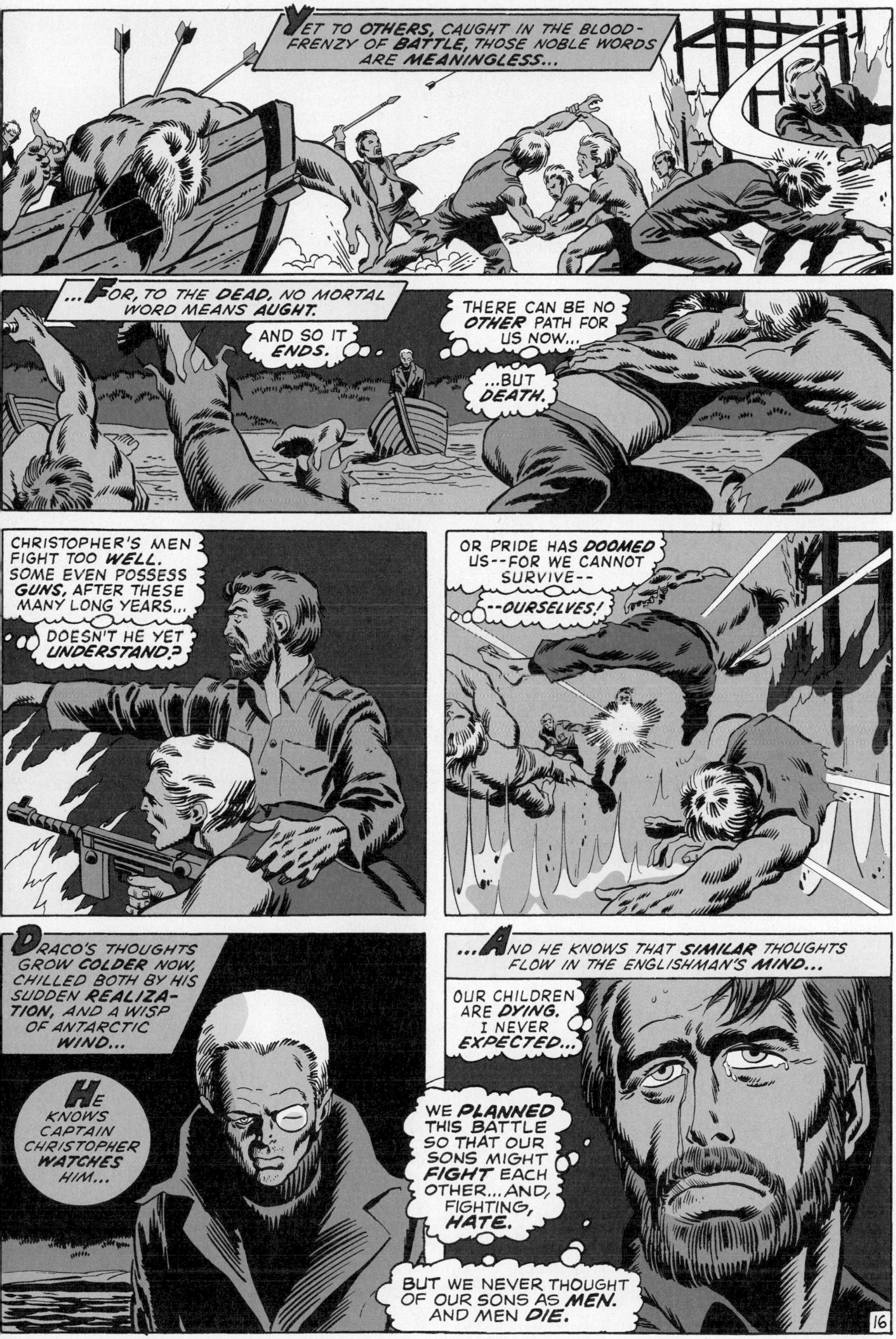
YET TO OTHERS, CAUGHT IN THE BLOOD-FRENZY OF BATTLE, THOSE NOBLE WORDS ARE MEANINGLESS...
...FOR, TO THE DEAD, NO MORTAL WORD MEANS AUGHT.
AND SO IT ENDS.
THERE CAN BE NO OTHER PATH FOR US NOW...
...BUT DEATH.
CHRISTOPHER'S MEN FIGHT TOO WELL. SOME EVEN POSSESS GUNS, AFTER THESE MANY LONG YEARS...
DOESN'T HE YET UNDERSTAND?
OR PRIDE HAS DOOMED US--FOR WE CANNOT SURVIVE--
--OURSELVES!
DRACO'S THOUGHTS GROW COLDER NOW, CHILLED BOTH BY HIS SUDDEN REALIZATION, AND A WISP OF ANTARCTIC WIND...
HE KNOWS CAPTAIN CHRISTOPHER WATCHES HIM...
...AND HE KNOWS THAT SIMILAR THOUGHTS FLOW IN THE ENGLISHMAN'S MIND...
OUR CHILDREN ARE DYING. I NEVER EXPECTED...
WE PLANNED THIS BATTLE SO THAT OUR SONS MIGHT FIGHT EACH OTHER...AND, FIGHTING, HATE.
BUT WE NEVER THOUGHT OF OUR SONS AS MEN. AND MEN DIE.
16

AND ELSE-WHERE...

...A WEAKENED KA-ZAR COMES OUT ON THE BESEIGED ISLE, TO FIND...

ZABU!

THANK THE GODS THEY DIDN'T *KILL* YOU--!

YES, I'M *WOUNDED*, MY FRIEND, BUT YOUR TONGUE DOES ME NO *GOOD*.

WE HAVE *OTHER* THINGS TO DO.

SOON, MIDST DANCING *SHADOWS* AND ANGERED CRIES...

THESE MUST BE THE FIRE TUBES WHICH BURNED THE LAKE WITH *MOLTEN LAVA*, ZABU--*

* A.T. #8, FRENZIED ONES--STAN.

YET NOW, WHILE THEIR MAKERS BATTLE *BELOW*--

--THEY'LL FIND *ANOTHER* USE--

--ONE MORE *FITTING*, EH?

RRRIP

FFWHOOOSH!

AH, YOU *SEE* ME NOW, DO YOU?

THEN *LISTEN* TO KA-ZAR.

LISTEN!

36

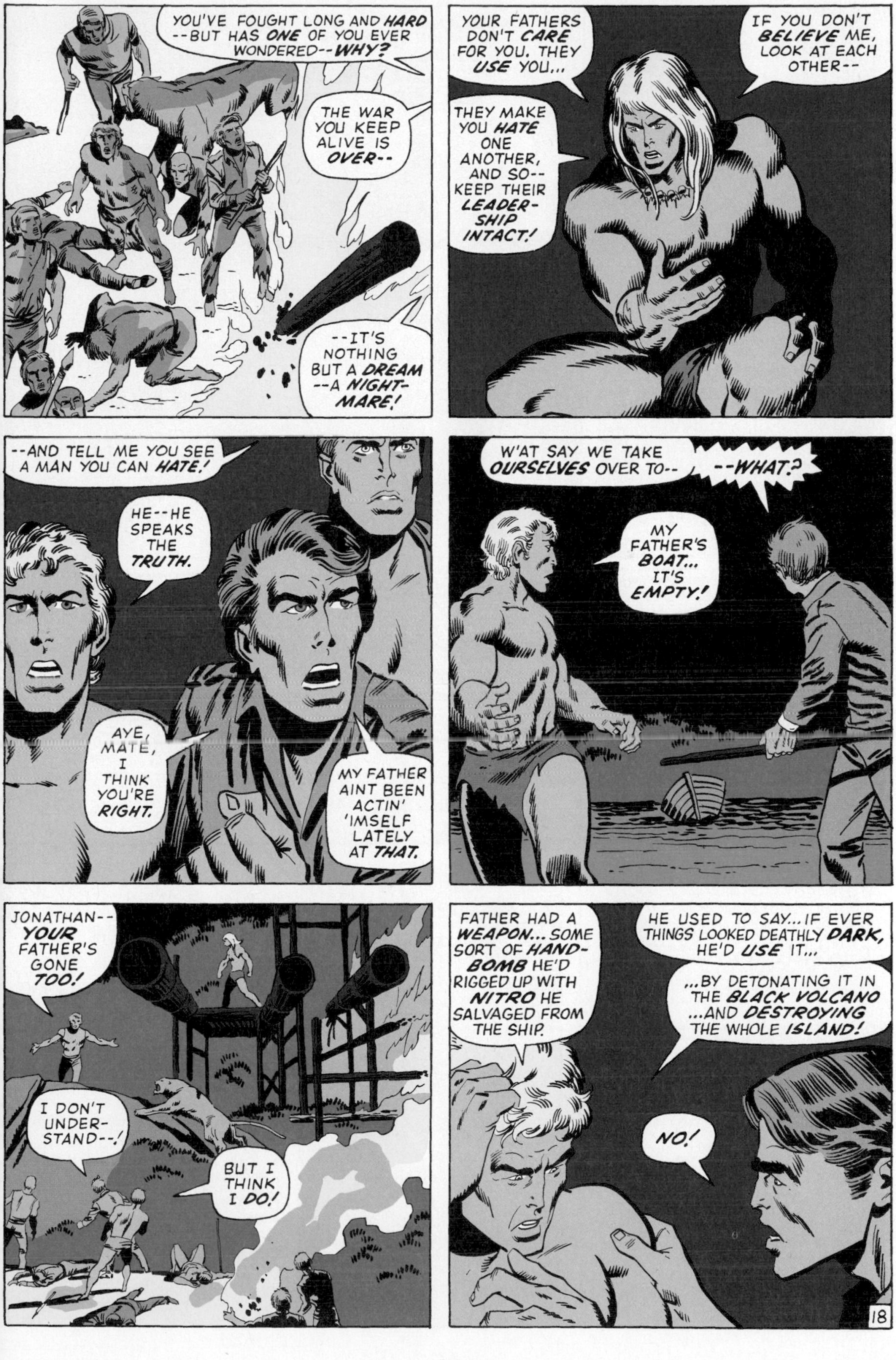
YOU'VE FOUGHT LONG AND HARD --BUT HAS ONE OF YOU EVER WONDERED--WHY?
THE WAR YOU KEEP ALIVE IS OVER--
--IT'S NOTHING BUT A DREAM --A NIGHTMARE!
YOUR FATHERS DON'T CARE FOR YOU. THEY USE YOU...
THEY MAKE YOU HATE ONE ANOTHER, AND SO--KEEP THEIR LEADERSHIP INTACT!
IF YOU DON'T BELIEVE ME, LOOK AT EACH OTHER--
--AND TELL ME YOU SEE A MAN YOU CAN HATE!
HE--HE SPEAKS THE TRUTH.
AYE, MATE, I THINK YOU'RE RIGHT.
MY FATHER AINT BEEN ACTIN' 'IMSELF LATELY AT THAT.
W'AT SAY WE TAKE OURSELVES OVER TO--
--WHAT?
MY FATHER'S BOAT... IT'S EMPTY!
JONATHAN--YOUR FATHER'S GONE TOO!
I DON'T UNDERSTAND--!
BUT I THINK I DO!
FATHER HAD A WEAPON... SOME SORT OF HAND-BOMB HE'D RIGGED UP WITH NITRO HE SALVAGED FROM THE SHIP.
HE USED TO SAY... IF EVER THINGS LOOKED DEATHLY DARK, HE'D USE IT...
...BY DETONATING IT IN THE BLACK VOLCANO ...AND DESTROYING THE WHOLE ISLAND!
NO!
18

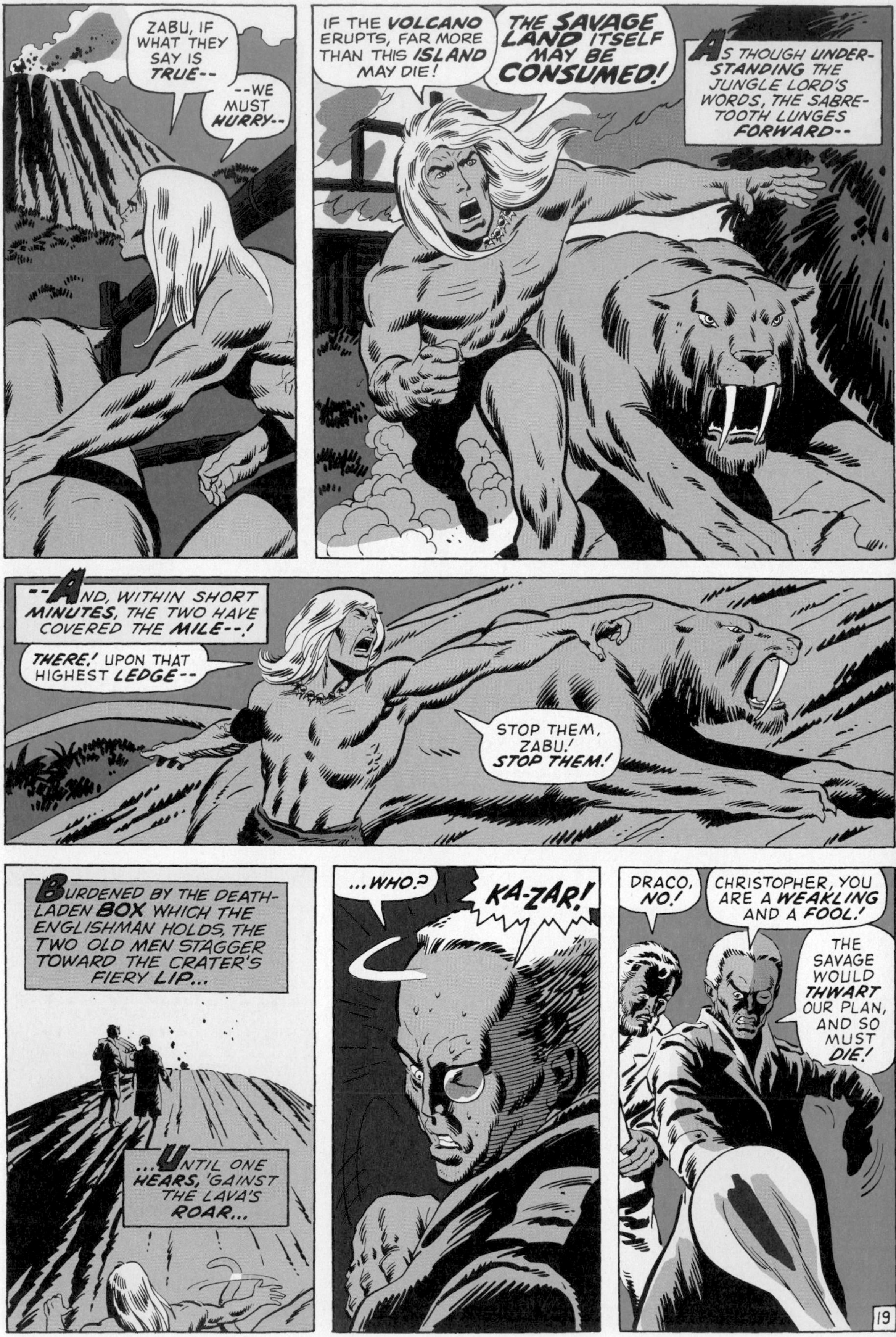
ZABU, IF WHAT THEY SAY IS TRUE--
--WE MUST HURRY--
IF THE VOLCANO ERUPTS, FAR MORE THAN THIS ISLAND MAY DIE!
THE SAVAGE LAND ITSELF MAY BE CONSUMED!
AS THOUGH UNDERSTANDING THE JUNGLE LORD'S WORDS, THE SABRE-TOOTH LUNGES FORWARD--
--AND, WITHIN SHORT MINUTES, THE TWO HAVE COVERED THE MILE--!
THERE! UPON THAT HIGHEST LEDGE--
STOP THEM, ZABU! STOP THEM!
BURDENED BY THE DEATH-LADEN BOX WHICH THE ENGLISHMAN HOLDS, THE TWO OLD MEN STAGGER TOWARD THE CRATER'S FIERY LIP...
...UNTIL ONE HEARS, 'GAINST THE LAVA'S ROAR...
...WHO?
KA-ZAR!
DRACO, NO!
CHRISTOPHER, YOU ARE A WEAKLING AND A FOOL!
THE SAVAGE WOULD THWART OUR PLAN, AND SO MUST DIE!
19

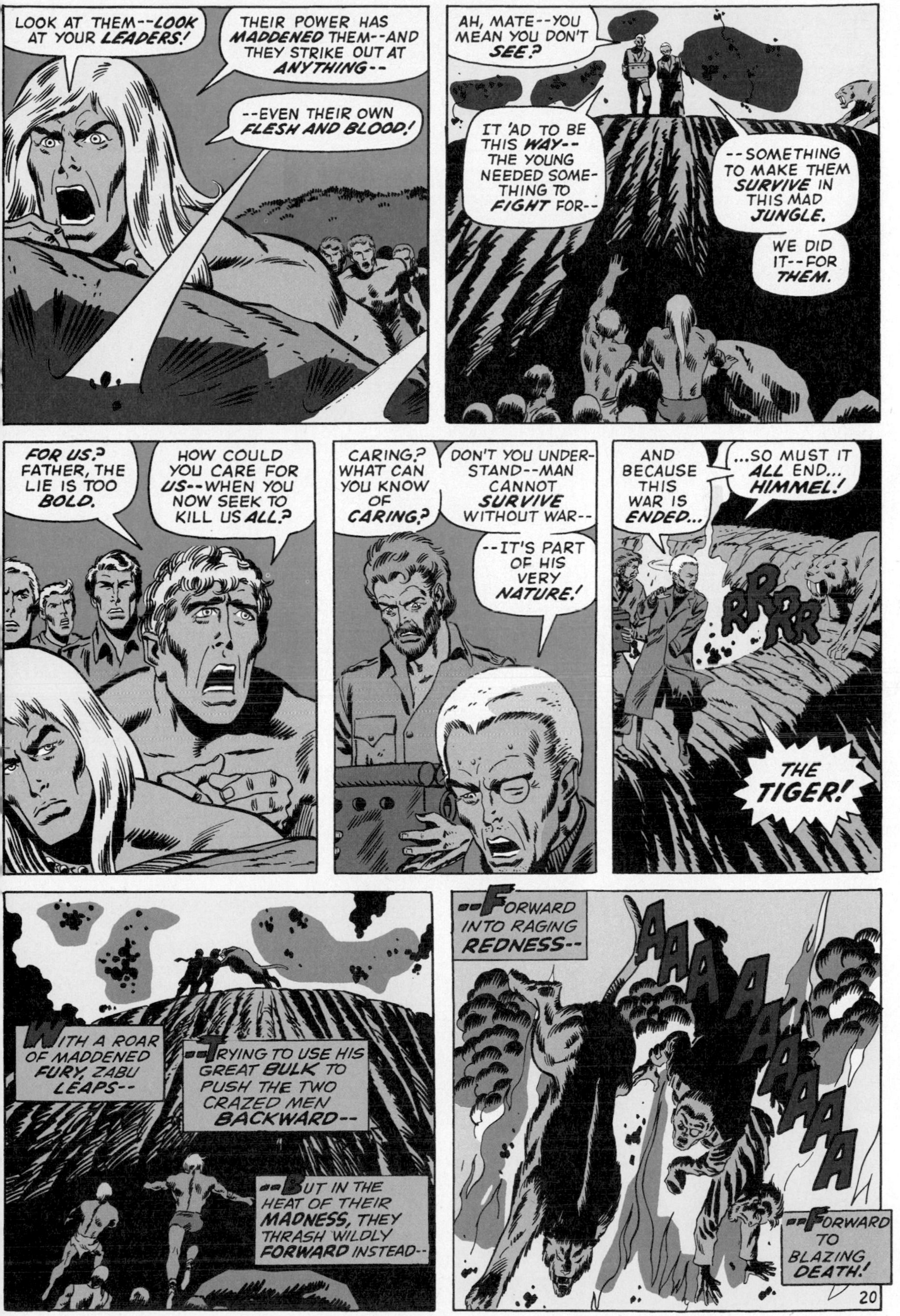

LOOK AT THEM--LOOK AT YOUR LEADERS!
THEIR POWER HAS MADDENED THEM--AND THEY STRIKE OUT AT ANYTHING--
--EVEN THEIR OWN FLESH AND BLOOD!
AH, MATE--YOU MEAN YOU DON'T SEE?
IT 'AD TO BE THIS WAY--THE YOUNG NEEDED SOME-THING TO FIGHT FOR--
--SOMETHING TO MAKE THEM SURVIVE IN THIS MAD JUNGLE.
WE DID IT--FOR THEM.
FOR US? FATHER, THE LIE IS TOO BOLD.
HOW COULD YOU CARE FOR US--WHEN YOU NOW SEEK TO KILL US ALL?
CARING? WHAT CAN YOU KNOW OF CARING?
DON'T YOU UNDER-STAND--MAN CANNOT SURVIVE WITHOUT WAR--
--IT'S PART OF HIS VERY NATURE!
AND BECAUSE THIS WAR IS ENDED...
...SO MUST IT ALL END... HIMMEL!
RRRRR
THE TIGER!
WITH A ROAR OF MADDENED FURY, ZABU LEAPS--
--TRYING TO USE HIS GREAT BULK TO PUSH THE TWO CRAZED MEN BACKWARD--
--BUT IN THE HEAT OF THEIR MADNESS, THEY THRASH WILDLY FORWARD INSTEAD--
--FORWARD INTO RAGING REDNESS--
AAAAAAAAAAAA
--FORWARD TO BLAZING DEATH!
20

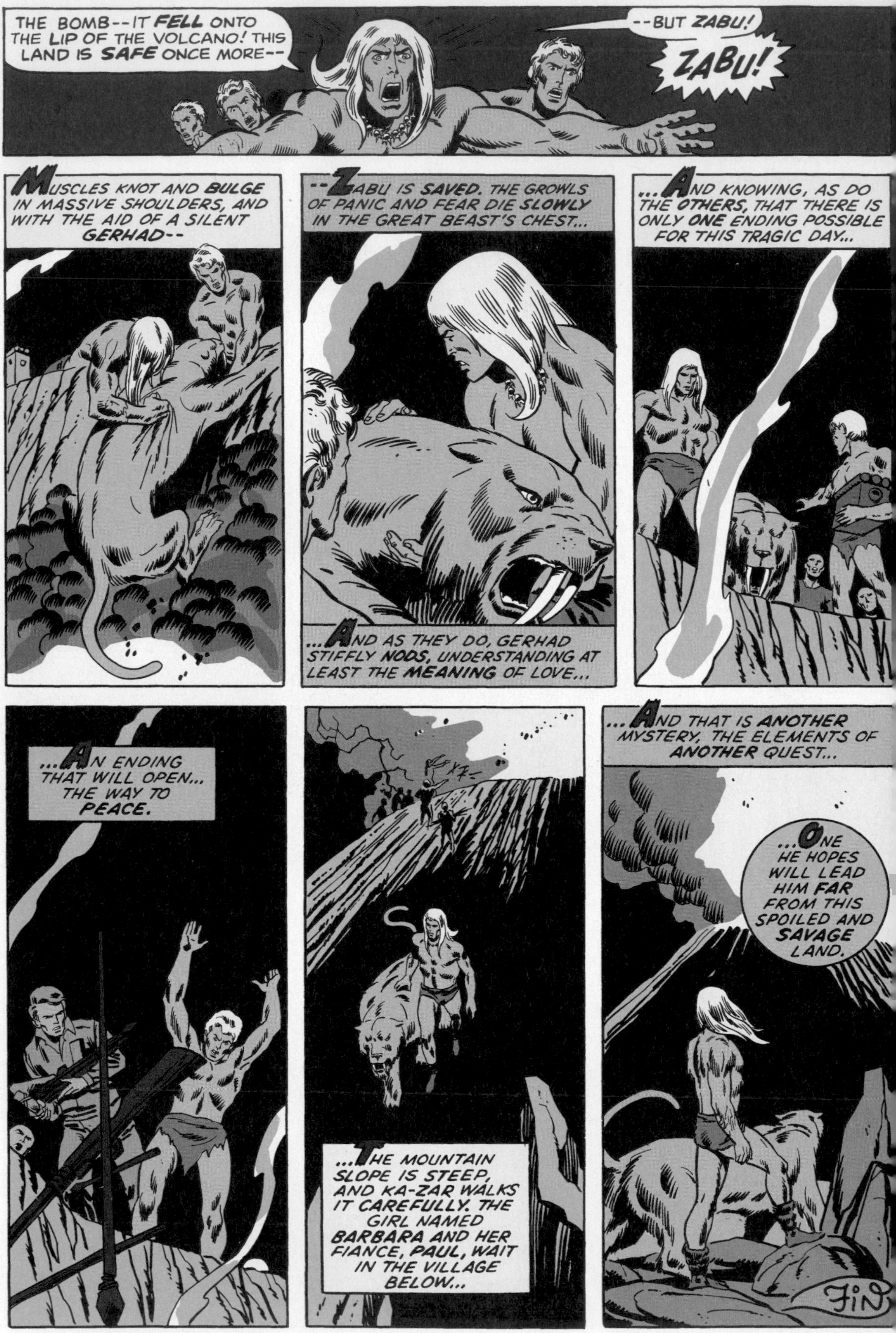
THE BOMB--IT FELL ONTO THE LIP OF THE VOLCANO! THIS LAND IS SAFE ONCE MORE--
--BUT ZABU!
ZABU!
MUSCLES KNOT AND BULGE IN MASSIVE SHOULDERS, AND WITH THE AID OF A SILENT GERHAD--
--ZABU IS SAVED. THE GROWLS OF PANIC AND FEAR DIE SLOWLY IN THE GREAT BEAST'S CHEST...
...AND AS THEY DO, GERHAD STIFFLY NODS, UNDERSTANDING AT LEAST THE MEANING OF LOVE...
...AND KNOWING, AS DO THE OTHERS, THAT THERE IS ONLY ONE ENDING POSSIBLE FOR THIS TRAGIC DAY...
...AN ENDING THAT WILL OPEN... THE WAY TO PEACE.
...THE MOUNTAIN SLOPE IS STEEP, AND KA-ZAR WALKS IT CAREFULLY. THE GIRL NAMED BARBARA AND HER FIANCE, PAUL, WAIT IN THE VILLAGE BELOW...
...AND THAT IS ANOTHER MYSTERY, THE ELEMENTS OF ANOTHER QUEST...
...ONE HE HOPES WILL LEAD HIM FAR FROM THIS SPOILED AND SAVAGE LAND.
FIN

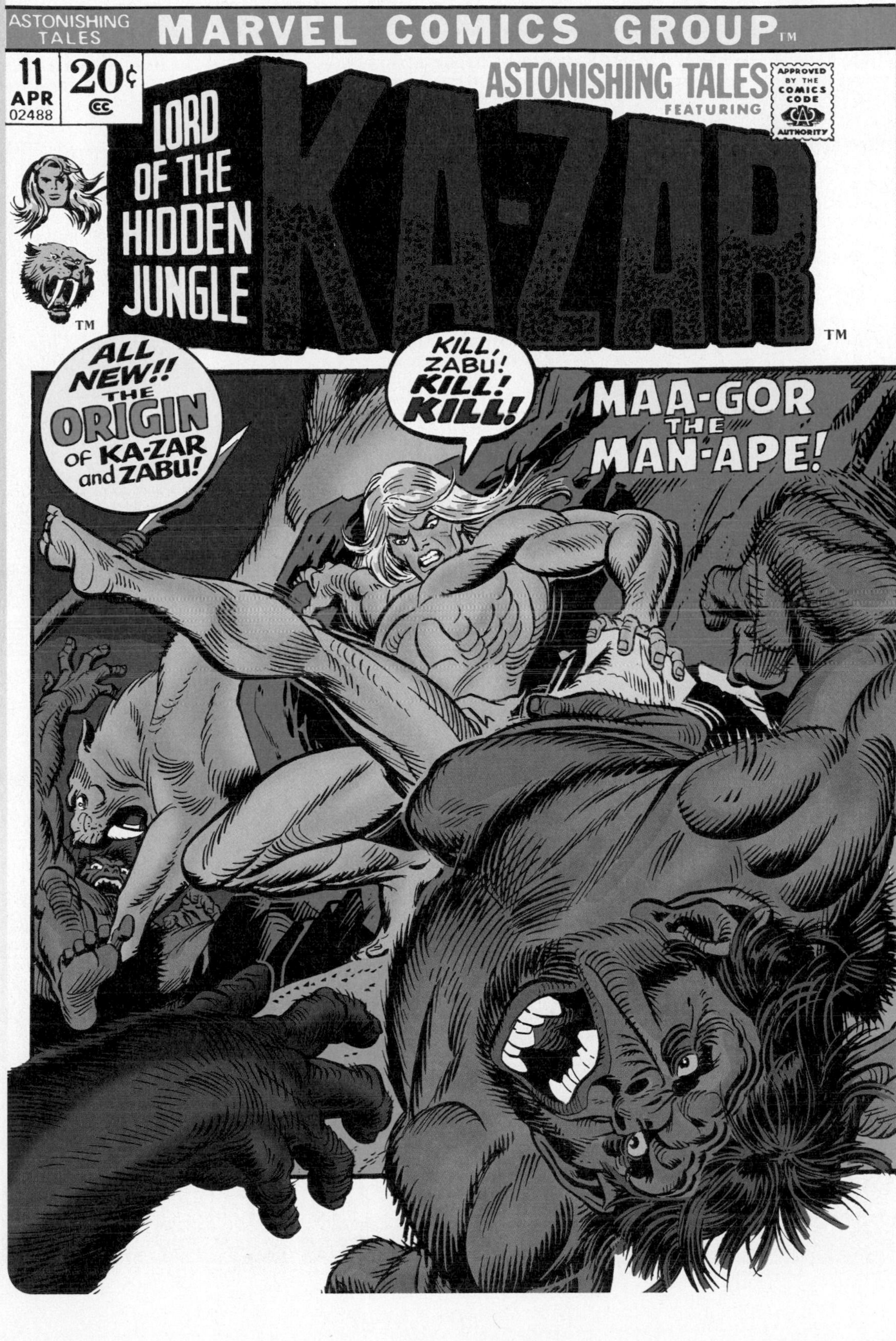
ASTONISHING TALES
MARVEL COMICS GROUP
11
APR
02488
20¢
LORD OF THE HIDDEN JUNGLE
ASTONISHING TALES
FEATURING
APPROVED BY THE COMICS CODE AUTHORITY
KA-ZAR
ALL NEW!! THE ORIGIN OF KA-ZAR and ZABU!
KILL, ZABU! KILL! KILL!
MAA-GOR THE MAN-APE!

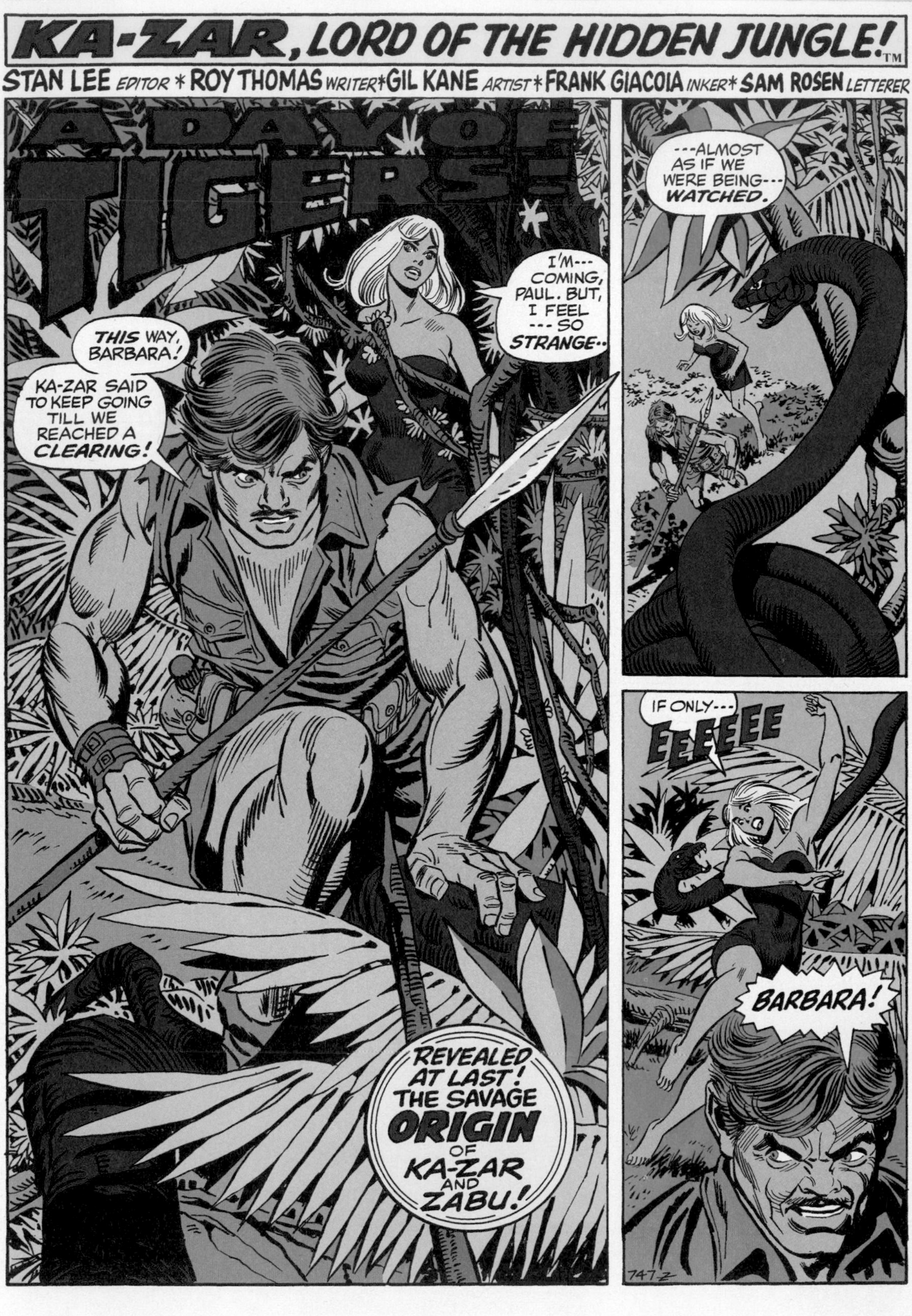
KA-ZAR, LORD OF THE HIDDEN JUNGLE!™
STAN LEE EDITOR * ROY THOMAS WRITER * GIL KANE ARTIST * FRANK GIACOIA INKER * SAM ROSEN LETTERER
A DAY OF TIGERS!
I'M--- COMING, PAUL. BUT, I FEEL --- SO STRANGE..
THIS WAY, BARBARA!
KA-ZAR SAID TO KEEP GOING TILL WE REACHED A CLEARING!
REVEALED AT LAST! THE SAVAGE ORIGIN OF KA-ZAR AND ZABU!
---ALMOST AS IF WE WERE BEING--- WATCHED.
IF ONLY---
EEEEEE
BARBARA!
747-Z

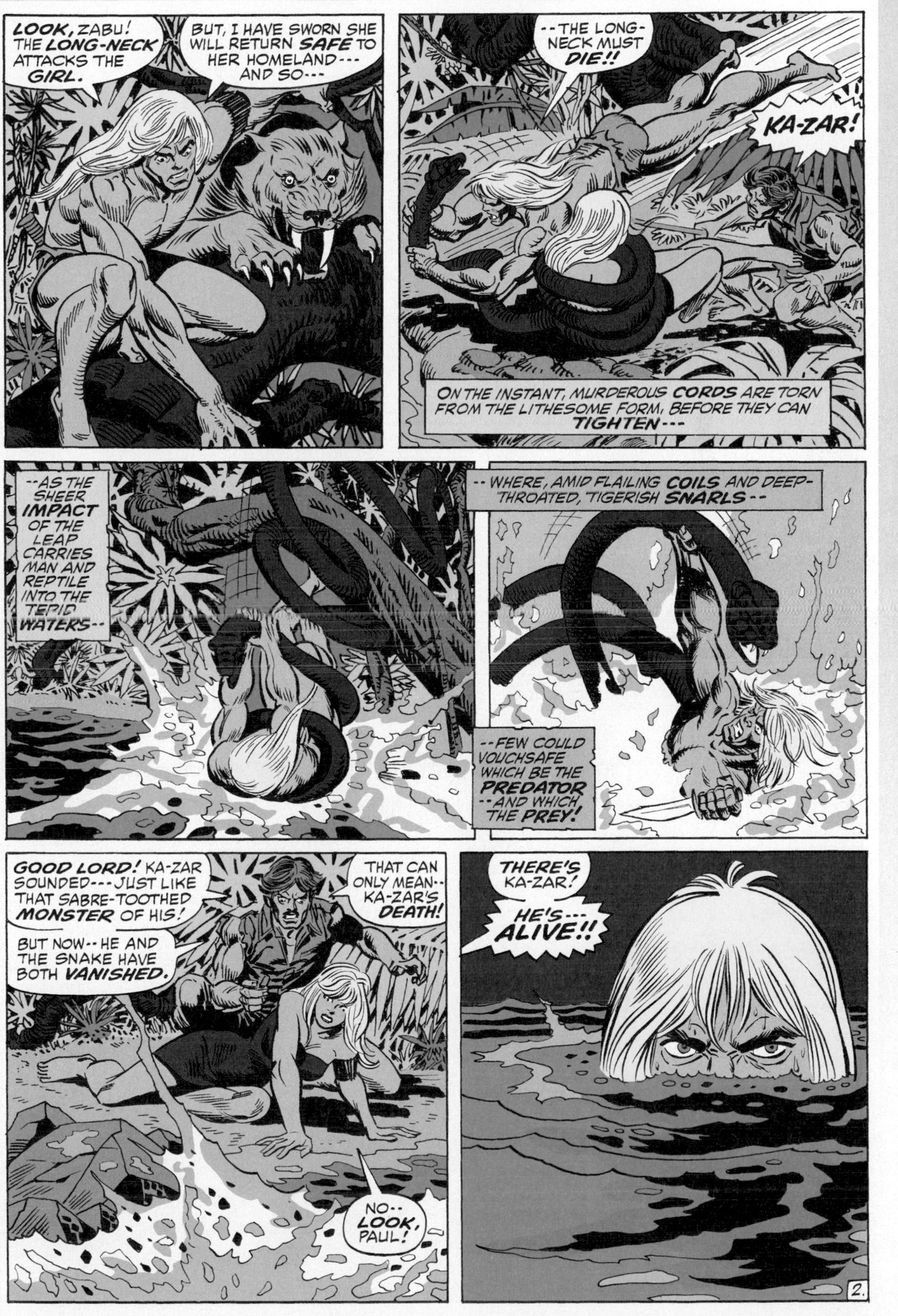

LOOK, ZABU! THE LONG-NECK ATTACKS THE GIRL.
BUT, I HAVE SWORN SHE WILL RETURN SAFE TO HER HOMELAND--- AND SO---
--THE LONG-NECK MUST DIE!!
KA-ZAR!
ON THE INSTANT, MURDEROUS CORDS ARE TORN FROM THE LITHESOME FORM, BEFORE THEY CAN TIGHTEN---
--AS THE SHEER IMPACT OF THE LEAP CARRIES MAN AND REPTILE INTO THE TEPID WATERS--
--WHERE, AMID FLAILING COILS AND DEEP-THROATED, TIGERISH SNARLS--
--FEW COULD VOUCHSAFE WHICH BE THE PREDATOR --AND WHICH, THE PREY!
GOOD LORD! KA-ZAR SOUNDED---JUST LIKE THAT SABRE-TOOTHED MONSTER OF HIS!
THAT CAN ONLY MEAN--KA-ZAR'S DEATH!
BUT NOW--HE AND THE SNAKE HAVE BOTH VANISHED.
NO--LOOK, PAUL!
THERE'S KA-ZAR!
HE'S... ALIVE!!
2.

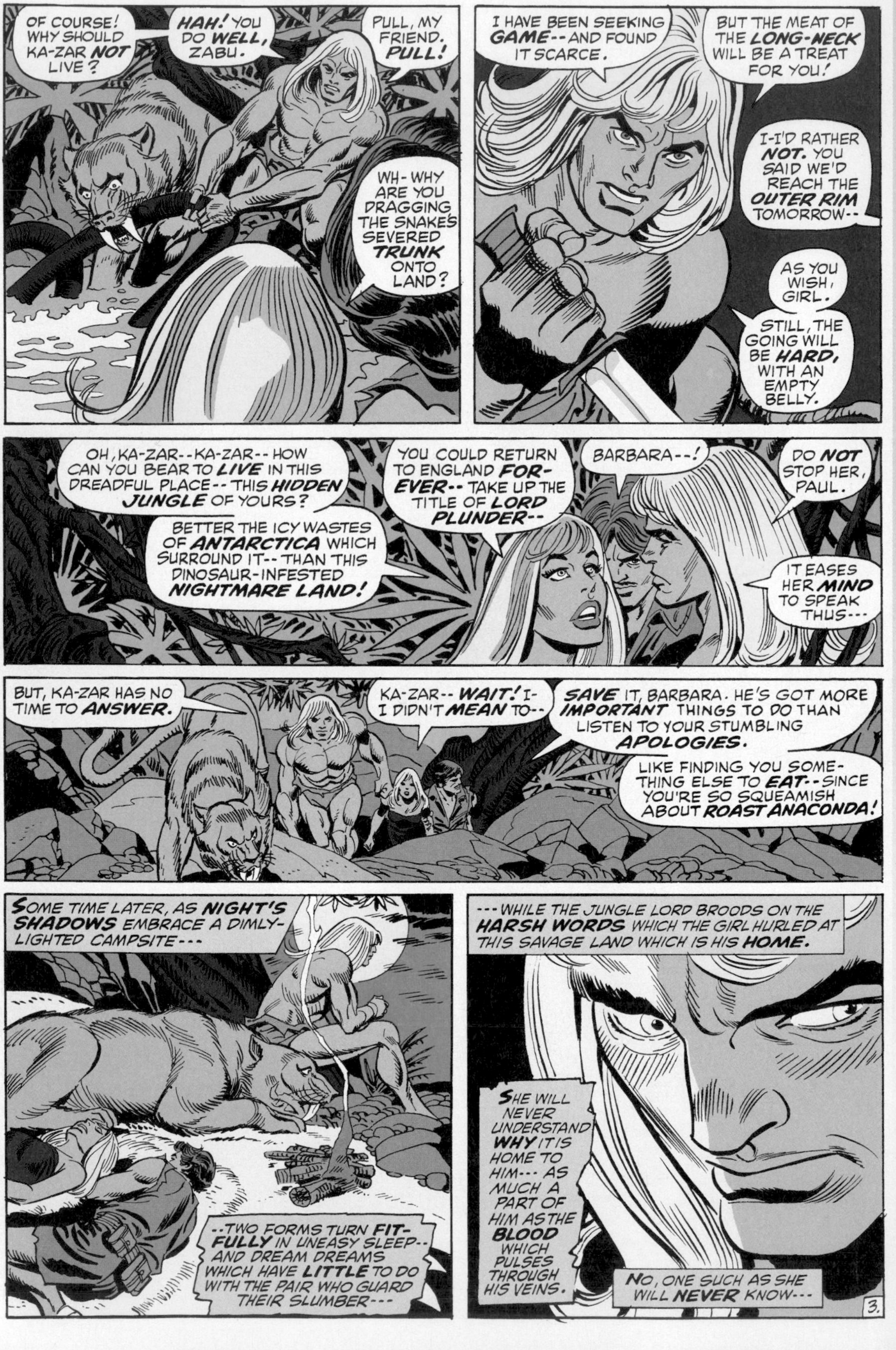

OF COURSE! WHY SHOULD KA-ZAR NOT LIVE?
HAH! YOU DO WELL, ZABU.
PULL, MY FRIEND. PULL!
WH- WHY ARE YOU DRAGGING THE SNAKE'S SEVERED TRUNK ONTO LAND?
I HAVE BEEN SEEKING GAME-- AND FOUND IT SCARCE.
BUT THE MEAT OF THE LONG-NECK WILL BE A TREAT FOR YOU!
I-I'D RATHER NOT. YOU SAID WE'D REACH THE OUTER RIM TOMORROW--
AS YOU WISH, GIRL.
STILL, THE GOING WILL BE HARD, WITH AN EMPTY BELLY.
OH, KA-ZAR--KA-ZAR-- HOW CAN YOU BEAR TO LIVE IN THIS DREADFUL PLACE-- THIS HIDDEN JUNGLE OF YOURS?
BETTER THE ICY WASTES OF ANTARCTICA WHICH SURROUND IT-- THAN THIS DINOSAUR-INFESTED NIGHTMARE LAND!
YOU COULD RETURN TO ENGLAND FOR-EVER-- TAKE UP THE TITLE OF LORD PLUNDER--
BARBARA--!
DO NOT STOP HER, PAUL.
IT EASES HER MIND TO SPEAK THUS---
BUT, KA-ZAR HAS NO TIME TO ANSWER.
KA-ZAR-- WAIT! I- I DIDN'T MEAN TO--
SAVE IT, BARBARA. HE'S GOT MORE IMPORTANT THINGS TO DO THAN LISTEN TO YOUR STUMBLING APOLOGIES.
LIKE FINDING YOU SOME-THING ELSE TO EAT-- SINCE YOU'RE SO SQUEAMISH ABOUT ROAST ANACONDA!
SOME TIME LATER, AS NIGHT'S SHADOWS EMBRACE A DIMLY-LIGHTED CAMPSITE---
--TWO FORMS TURN FIT-FULLY IN UNEASY SLEEP-- AND DREAM DREAMS WHICH HAVE LITTLE TO DO WITH THE PAIR WHO GUARD THEIR SLUMBER---
---WHILE THE JUNGLE LORD BROODS ON THE HARSH WORDS WHICH THE GIRL HURLED AT THIS SAVAGE LAND WHICH IS HIS HOME.
SHE WILL NEVER UNDERSTAND WHY IT IS HOME TO HIM--- AS MUCH A PART OF HIM AS THE BLOOD WHICH PULSES THROUGH HIS VEINS.
NO, ONE SUCH AS SHE WILL NEVER KNOW---
3.

As his two charges slept, Ka-Zar thought back on his past. Decades earlier, his father Robert, Lord Plunder, had traveled to Antarctica in search of a rare element capable of disintegrating metal. Plunder discovered both the hidden Savage Land and a deposit of this "Anti-Metal" during his expedition — but returned home to England to find that his wife had died while he was away, leaving him to raise his young sons Kevin and Parnival alone.

Foreign powers who sought the element's secrets soon threatened Plunder and the children, and Plunder chose to split up his family to hide from them. Parnival was hidden away by Plunder's servant Willis, and Plunder and Kevin fled to the most remote place he knew — back to the Savage Land.

Plunder showed Kevin the location of the Anti-Metal deposit, but the two were attacked by the brutish Man-Ape tribe, whose leader Maa-Gor slew Plunder. Kevin's life was saved when a saber-toothed tiger suddenly attacked Maa-Gor, gouging out his eye. The tiger sought vengeance on the Man-Apes, who had hunted his species to near-extinction. Young Kevin leaped onto the tiger's back and the two fled.

Kevin and the tiger, both all alone in a harsh land, forged an immediate bond. Kevin grew to manhood under the tiger's watchful eye, becoming strong, swift and cunning, and as the two traveled the Savage Land over the years they carved out a legend among its many tribes — becoming known as Ka-Zar, Son of the Tiger, and his faithful companion Zabu.

Meanwhile, Maa-Gor had become embittered, and had spent the years forcing his tribe to hunt for the boy and tiger who took his eye. The Man-Apes' numbers and strength had dwindled dangerously low, but Maa-Gor cared only for revenge. One day, Ka-Zar and Zabu encountered the last remaining Man-Apes, and though he tried several times to reason with them and offer peace, Maa-Gor refused — and threw a spear that badly wounded Zabu.

At this, Ka-Zar snapped and attacked the Man-Apes, causing a rockslide that buried and killed nearly all of them. Maa-Gor was the only survivor, and he and Ka-Zar fought savagely until Ka-Zar ultimately triumphed, beating Maa-Gor senseless. However, rather than avenging his father by killing Maa-Gor, Ka-Zar decided to let him live — for, now that he was the last of his tribe, Maa-Gor would soon know the same loneliness that he had caused Ka-Zar and Zabu.

STILL, IF THE DREAM IS GONE-- THE MEMORY REMAINS.
LET THE OUTSIDERS SLEEP, ZABU.
TOMORROW, WE LEAVE THIS HIDDEN JUNGLE-- WITH THEM.
THEY WILL HAVE MUCH TO TELL US, THEN.
NEXT DAY, AT THE OUTER RIM---
FARE YOU WELL, MY SAVAGE LAND, TILL I RETURN TO YOU.
IF RETURN TO YOU I DO--!
NEXT: A WORLD HE NEVER MADE!

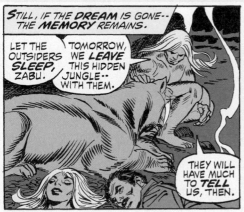

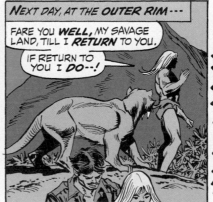

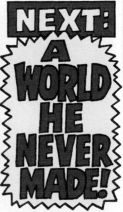

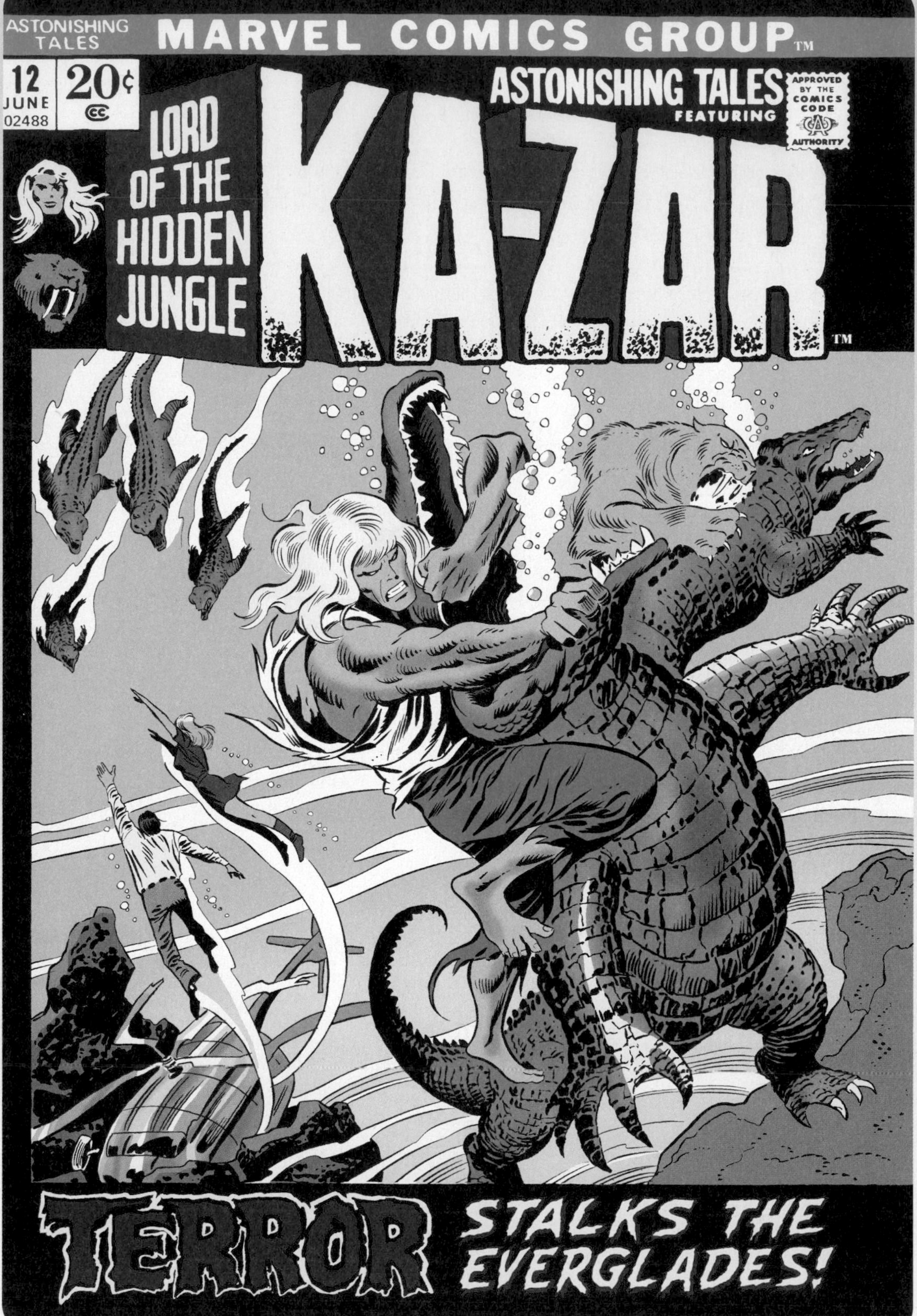

ASTONISHING TALES
MARVEL COMICS GROUP™
12 JUNE 02488
20¢ CC
ASTONISHING TALES FEATURING
APPROVED BY THE COMICS CODE CA AUTHORITY
LORD OF THE HIDDEN JUNGLE
KA-ZAR™
TERROR STALKS THE EVERGLADES!

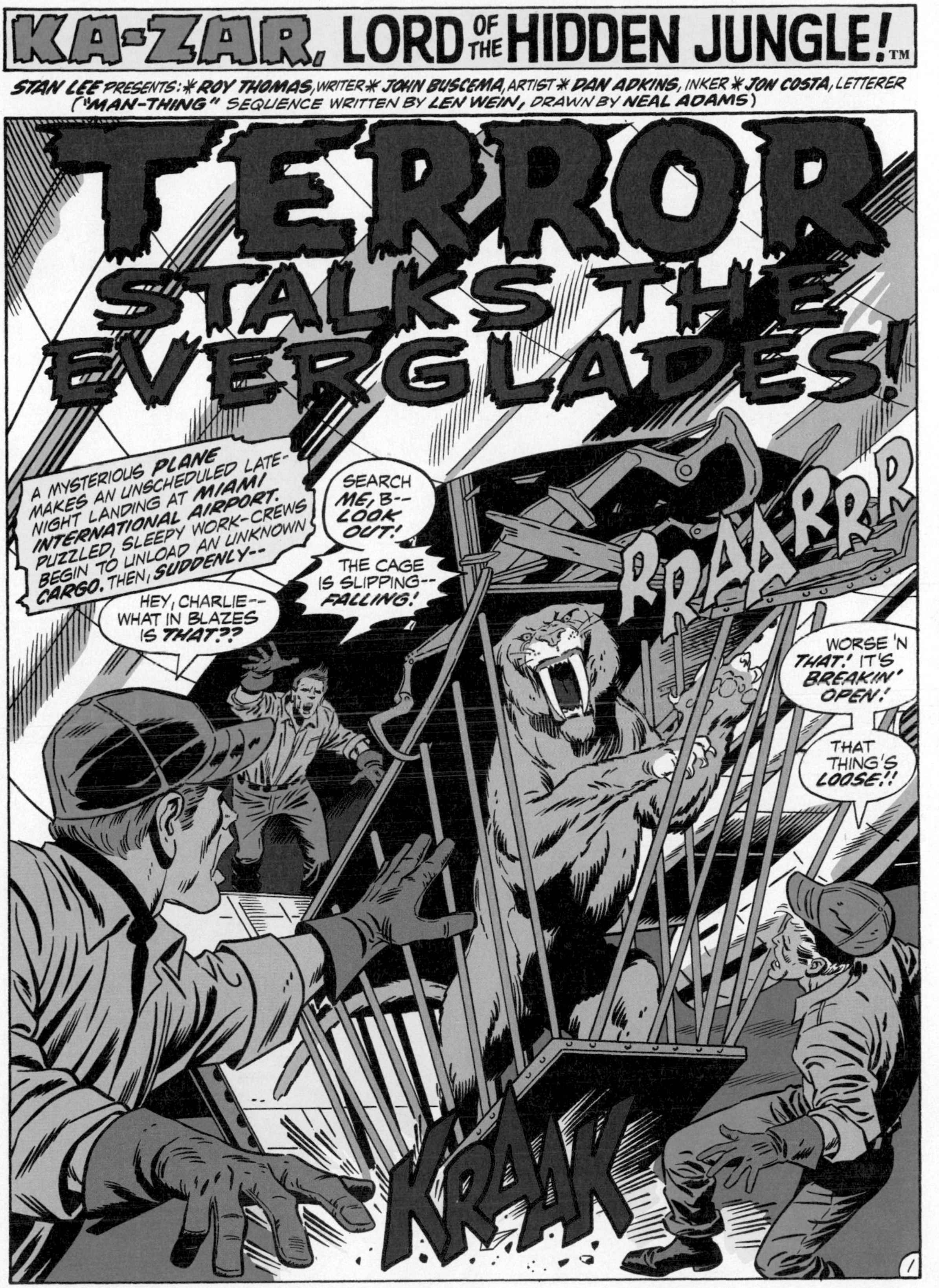
KA-ZAR, LORD OF THE HIDDEN JUNGLE!™
STAN LEE PRESENTS: * ROY THOMAS, WRITER * JOHN BUSCEMA, ARTIST * DAN ADKINS, INKER * JON COSTA, LETTERER
("MAN-THING" SEQUENCE WRITTEN BY LEN WEIN, DRAWN BY NEAL ADAMS)
TERROR STALKS THE EVERGLADES!
A MYSTERIOUS PLANE MAKES AN UNSCHEDULED LATE-NIGHT LANDING AT MIAMI INTERNATIONAL AIRPORT. PUZZLED, SLEEPY WORK-CREWS BEGIN TO UNLOAD AN UNKNOWN CARGO. THEN, SUDDENLY--
HEY, CHARLIE-- WHAT IN BLAZES IS THAT??
SEARCH ME, B-- LOOK OUT!
THE CAGE IS SLIPPING-- FALLING!
RRAARRR
WORSE 'N THAT! IT'S BREAKIN' OPEN!
THAT THING'S LOOSE!!
KRAAK
1

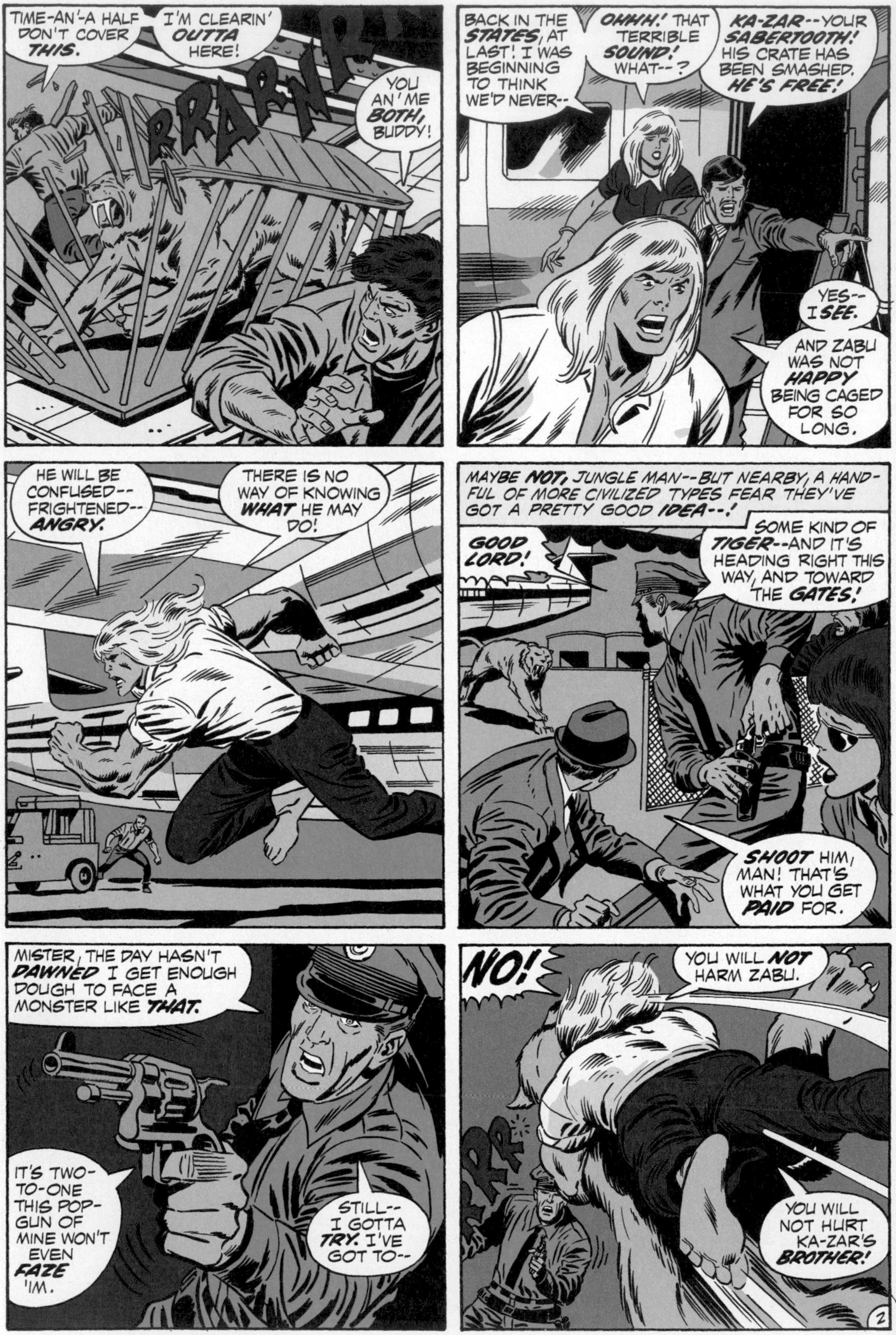
TIME-AN'-A HALF DON'T COVER THIS.
I'M CLEARIN' OUTTA HERE!
RRRARRR
YOU AN' ME BOTH, BUDDY!
BACK IN THE STATES, AT LAST! I WAS BEGINNING TO THINK WE'D NEVER--
OHHH! THAT TERRIBLE SOUND! WHAT--?
KA-ZAR--YOUR SABERTOOTH! HIS CRATE HAS BEEN SMASHED. HE'S FREE!
YES-- I SEE.
AND ZABU WAS NOT HAPPY BEING CAGED FOR SO LONG.
HE WILL BE CONFUSED-- FRIGHTENED-- ANGRY.
THERE IS NO WAY OF KNOWING WHAT HE MAY DO!
MAYBE NOT, JUNGLE MAN--BUT NEARBY, A HANDFUL OF MORE CIVILIZED TYPES FEAR THEY'VE GOT A PRETTY GOOD IDEA--!
GOOD LORD!
SOME KIND OF TIGER--AND IT'S HEADING RIGHT THIS WAY, AND TOWARD THE GATES!
SHOOT HIM, MAN! THAT'S WHAT YOU GET PAID FOR.
MISTER, THE DAY HASN'T DAWNED I GET ENOUGH DOUGH TO FACE A MONSTER LIKE THAT.
IT'S TWO-TO-ONE THIS POP-GUN OF MINE WON'T EVEN FAZE 'IM.
STILL-- I GOTTA TRY. I'VE GOT TO--
NO!
YOU WILL NOT HARM ZABU.
YOU WILL NOT HURT KA-ZAR'S BROTHER!
2

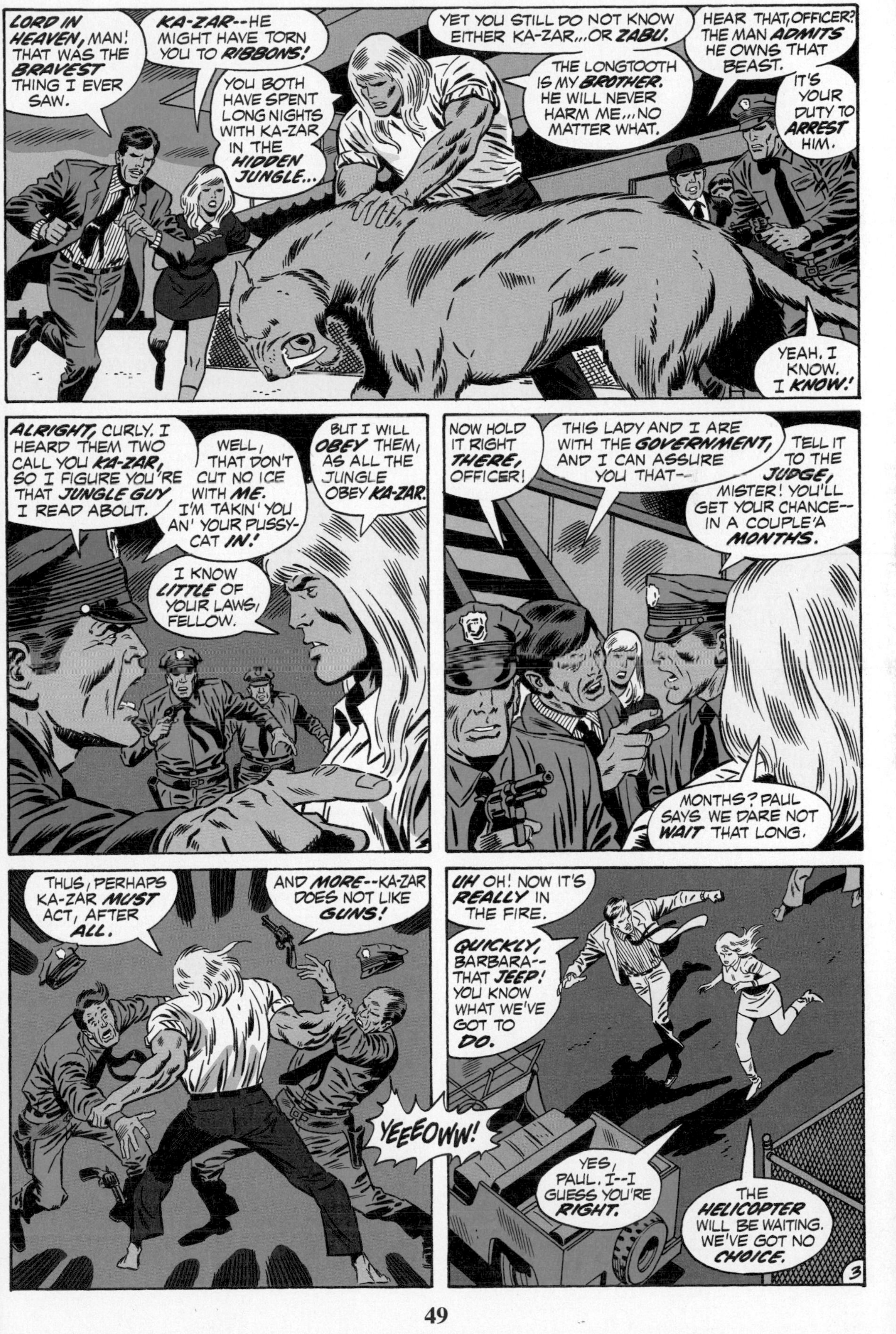
LORD IN HEAVEN, MAN! THAT WAS THE BRAVEST THING I EVER SAW.
KA-ZAR--HE MIGHT HAVE TORN YOU TO RIBBONS!
YOU BOTH HAVE SPENT LONG NIGHTS WITH KA-ZAR IN THE HIDDEN JUNGLE...
YET YOU STILL DO NOT KNOW EITHER KA-ZAR... OR ZABU.
THE LONGTOOTH IS MY BROTHER. HE WILL NEVER HARM ME... NO MATTER WHAT.
HEAR THAT, OFFICER? THE MAN ADMITS HE OWNS THAT BEAST.
IT'S YOUR DUTY TO ARREST HIM.
YEAH. I KNOW. I KNOW!
ALRIGHT, CURLY. I HEARD THEM TWO CALL YOU KA-ZAR, SO I FIGURE YOU'RE THAT JUNGLE GUY I READ ABOUT.
WELL, THAT DON'T CUT NO ICE WITH ME. I'M TAKIN' YOU AN' YOUR PUSSY-CAT IN!
I KNOW LITTLE OF YOUR LAWS, FELLOW.
BUT I WILL OBEY THEM, AS ALL THE JUNGLE OBEY KA-ZAR.
NOW HOLD IT RIGHT THERE, OFFICER!
THIS LADY AND I ARE WITH THE GOVERNMENT, AND I CAN ASSURE YOU THAT--
TELL IT TO THE JUDGE, MISTER! YOU'LL GET YOUR CHANCE-- IN A COUPLE'A MONTHS.
MONTHS? PAUL SAYS WE DARE NOT WAIT THAT LONG.
THUS, PERHAPS KA-ZAR MUST ACT, AFTER ALL.
AND MORE--KA-ZAR DOES NOT LIKE GUNS!
YEEEOWW!
UH OH! NOW IT'S REALLY IN THE FIRE.
QUICKLY, BARBARA--THAT JEEP! YOU KNOW WHAT WE'VE GOT TO DO.
YES, PAUL. I--I GUESS YOU'RE RIGHT.
THE HELICOPTER WILL BE WAITING. WE'VE GOT NO CHOICE.
3

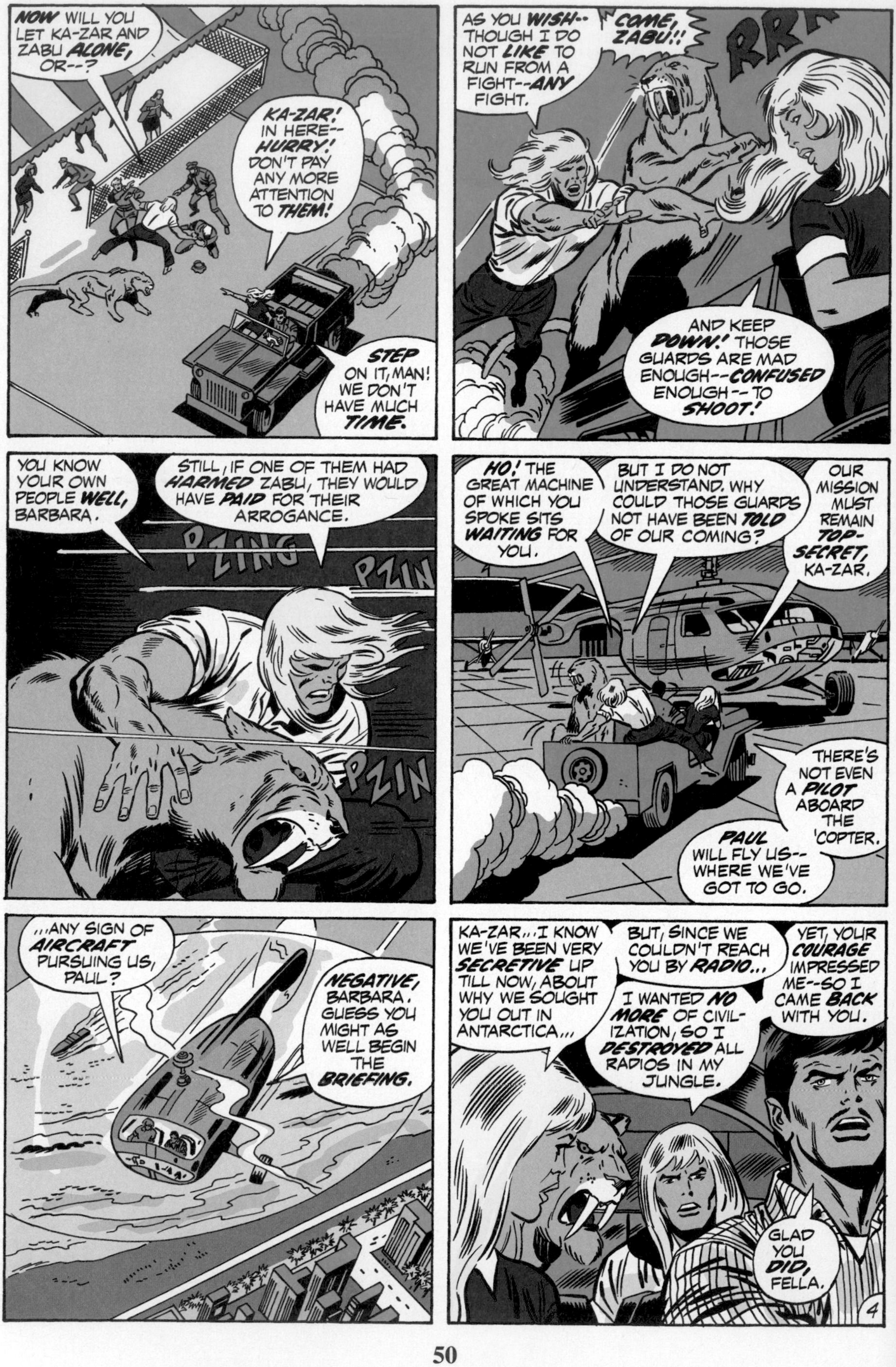
NOW WILL YOU LET KA-ZAR AND ZABU ALONE, OR--?
KA-ZAR! IN HERE--HURRY! DON'T PAY ANY MORE ATTENTION TO THEM!
STEP ON IT, MAN! WE DON'T HAVE MUCH TIME.
AS YOU WISH--THOUGH I DO NOT LIKE TO RUN FROM A FIGHT--ANY FIGHT.
COME, ZABU!!
RRR
AND KEEP DOWN! THOSE GUARDS ARE MAD ENOUGH--CONFUSED ENOUGH--TO SHOOT!
YOU KNOW YOUR OWN PEOPLE WELL, BARBARA.
STILL, IF ONE OF THEM HAD HARMED ZABU, THEY WOULD HAVE PAID FOR THEIR ARROGANCE.
PZING
PZIN
PZIN
HO! THE GREAT MACHINE OF WHICH YOU SPOKE SITS WAITING FOR YOU.
BUT I DO NOT UNDERSTAND. WHY COULD THOSE GUARDS NOT HAVE BEEN TOLD OF OUR COMING?
OUR MISSION MUST REMAIN TOP-SECRET, KA-ZAR.
THERE'S NOT EVEN A PILOT ABOARD THE 'COPTER.
PAUL WILL FLY US--WHERE WE'VE GOT TO GO.
...ANY SIGN OF AIRCRAFT PURSUING US, PAUL?
NEGATIVE, BARBARA. GUESS YOU MIGHT AS WELL BEGIN THE BRIEFING.
KA-ZAR...I KNOW WE'VE BEEN VERY SECRETIVE UP TILL NOW, ABOUT WHY WE SOUGHT YOU OUT IN ANTARCTICA...
BUT, SINCE WE COULDN'T REACH YOU BY RADIO...
I WANTED NO MORE OF CIVIL-IZATION, SO I DESTROYED ALL RADIOS IN MY JUNGLE.
YET, YOUR COURAGE IMPRESSED ME--SO I CAME BACK WITH YOU.
GLAD YOU DID, FELLA.
4

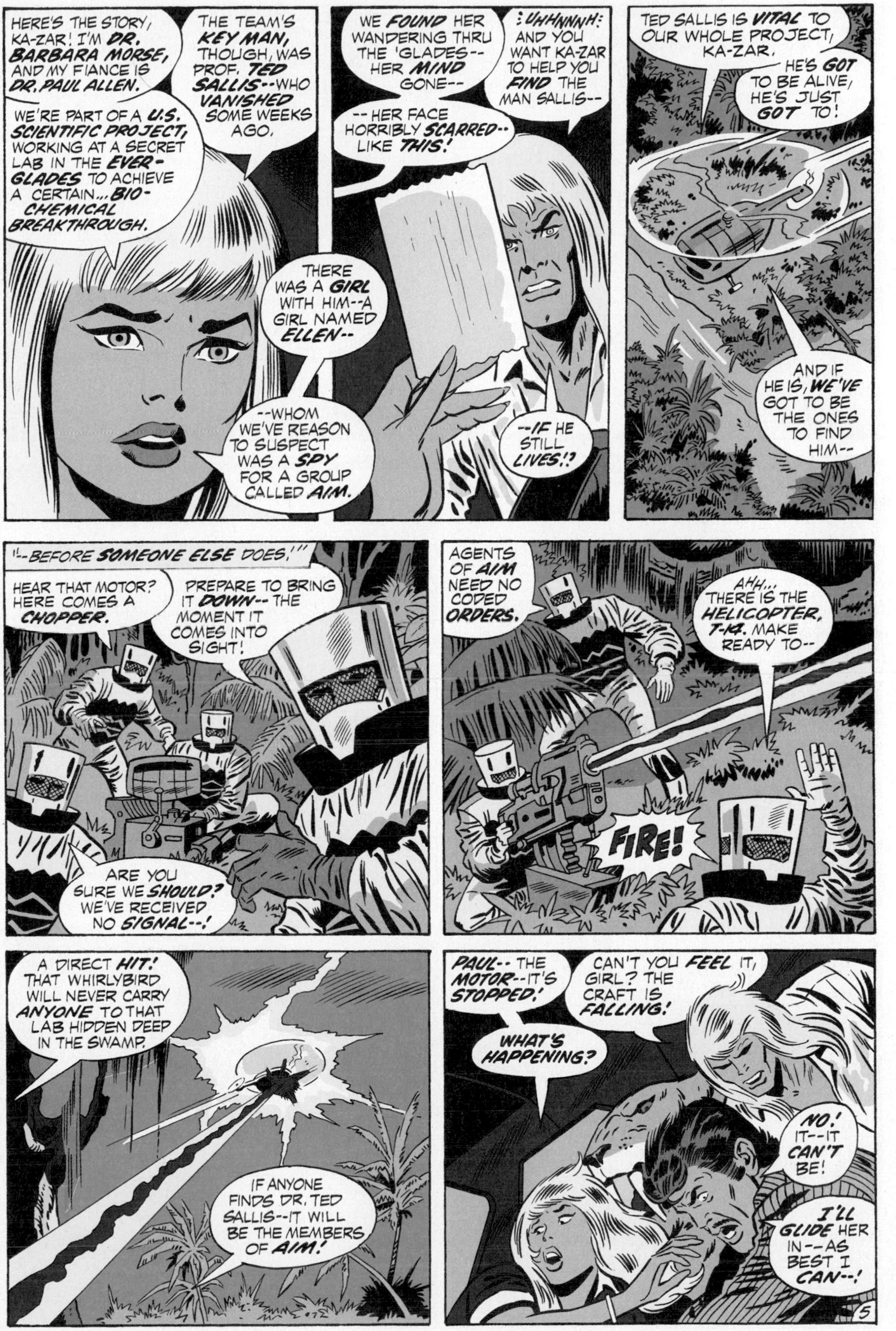
HERE'S THE STORY, KA-ZAR! I'M DR. BARBARA MORSE, AND MY FIANCE IS DR. PAUL ALLEN.
WE'RE PART OF A U.S. SCIENTIFIC PROJECT, WORKING AT A SECRET LAB IN THE EVER-GLADES TO ACHIEVE A CERTAIN... BIO-CHEMICAL BREAKTHROUGH.
THE TEAM'S KEY MAN, THOUGH, WAS PROF. TED SALLIS--WHO VANISHED SOME WEEKS AGO.
THERE WAS A GIRL WITH HIM--A GIRL NAMED ELLEN--
--WHOM WE'VE REASON TO SUSPECT WAS A SPY FOR A GROUP CALLED AIM.
WE FOUND HER WANDERING THRU THE 'GLADES--HER MIND GONE--
--HER FACE HORRIBLY SCARRED--LIKE THIS!
UHHNNNH: AND YOU WANT KA-ZAR TO HELP YOU FIND THE MAN SALLIS--
--IF HE STILL LIVES!?
TED SALLIS IS VITAL TO OUR WHOLE PROJECT, KA-ZAR.
HE'S GOT TO BE ALIVE, HE'S JUST GOT TO!
AND IF HE IS, WE'VE GOT TO BE THE ONES TO FIND HIM--
"--BEFORE SOMEONE ELSE DOES!"
HEAR THAT MOTOR? HERE COMES A CHOPPER.
PREPARE TO BRING IT DOWN--THE MOMENT IT COMES INTO SIGHT!
ARE YOU SURE WE SHOULD? WE'VE RECEIVED NO SIGNAL--!
AGENTS OF AIM NEED NO CODED ORDERS.
AHH... THERE IS THE HELICOPTER, T-14. MAKE READY TO--
FIRE!
A DIRECT HIT! THAT WHIRLYBIRD WILL NEVER CARRY ANYONE TO THAT LAB HIDDEN DEEP IN THE SWAMP.
IF ANYONE FINDS DR. TED SALLIS--IT WILL BE THE MEMBERS OF AIM!
PAUL--THE MOTOR--IT'S STOPPED!
WHAT'S HAPPENING?
CAN'T YOU FEEL IT, GIRL? THE CRAFT IS FALLING!
NO! IT--IT CAN'T BE!
I'LL GLIDE HER IN--AS BEST I CAN--!
5

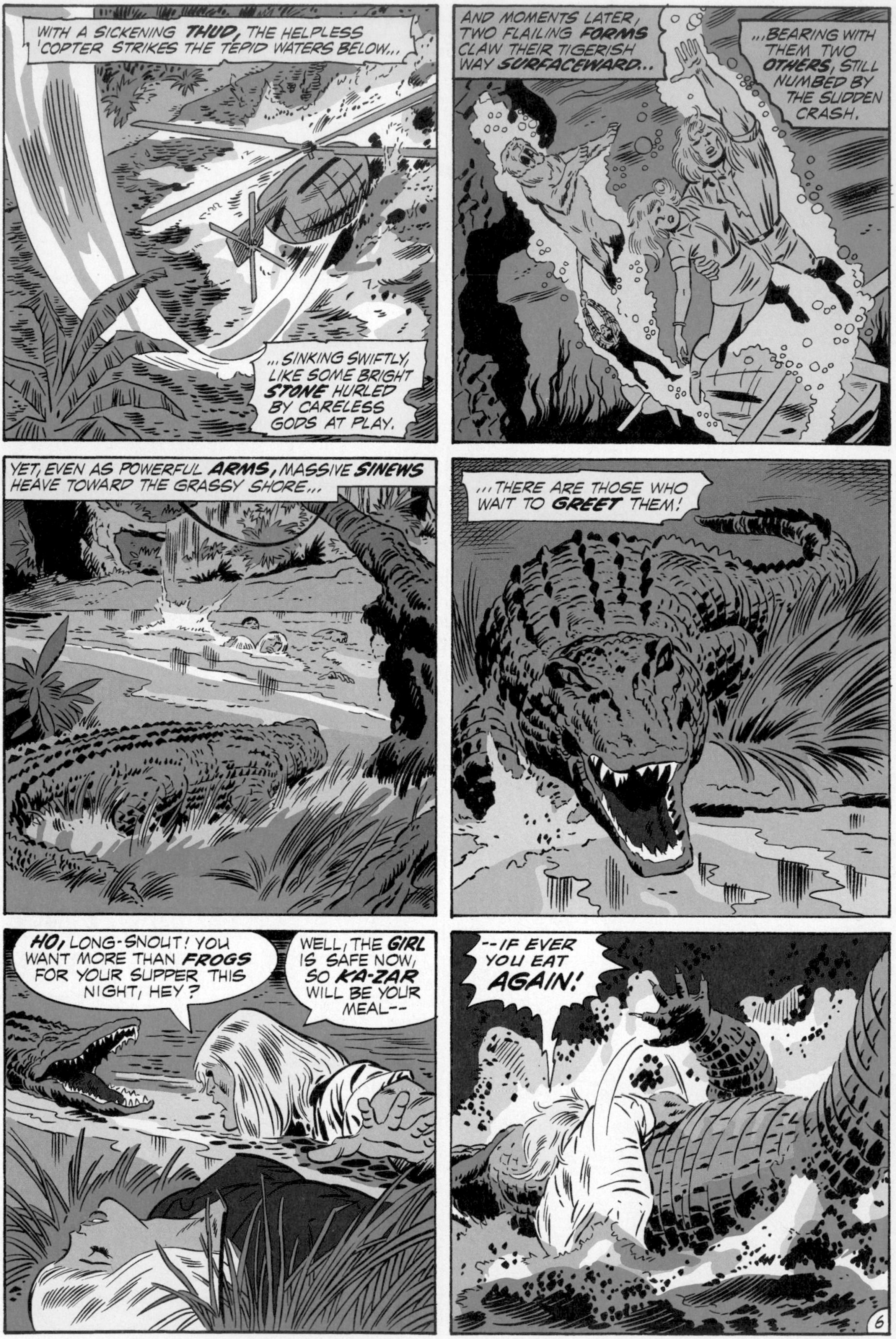
WITH A SICKENING THUD, THE HELPLESS 'COPTER STRIKES THE TEPID WATERS BELOW...
...SINKING SWIFTLY, LIKE SOME BRIGHT STONE HURLED BY CARELESS GODS AT PLAY.
AND MOMENTS LATER, TWO FLAILING FORMS CLAW THEIR TIGERISH WAY SURFACEWARD...
...BEARING WITH THEM TWO OTHERS, STILL NUMBED BY THE SUDDEN CRASH.
YET, EVEN AS POWERFUL ARMS, MASSIVE SINEWS HEAVE TOWARD THE GRASSY SHORE...
...THERE ARE THOSE WHO WAIT TO GREET THEM!
HO, LONG-SNOUT! YOU WANT MORE THAN FROGS FOR YOUR SUPPER THIS NIGHT, HEY?
WELL, THE GIRL IS SAFE NOW, SO KA-ZAR WILL BE YOUR MEAL--
--IF EVER YOU EAT AGAIN!
6

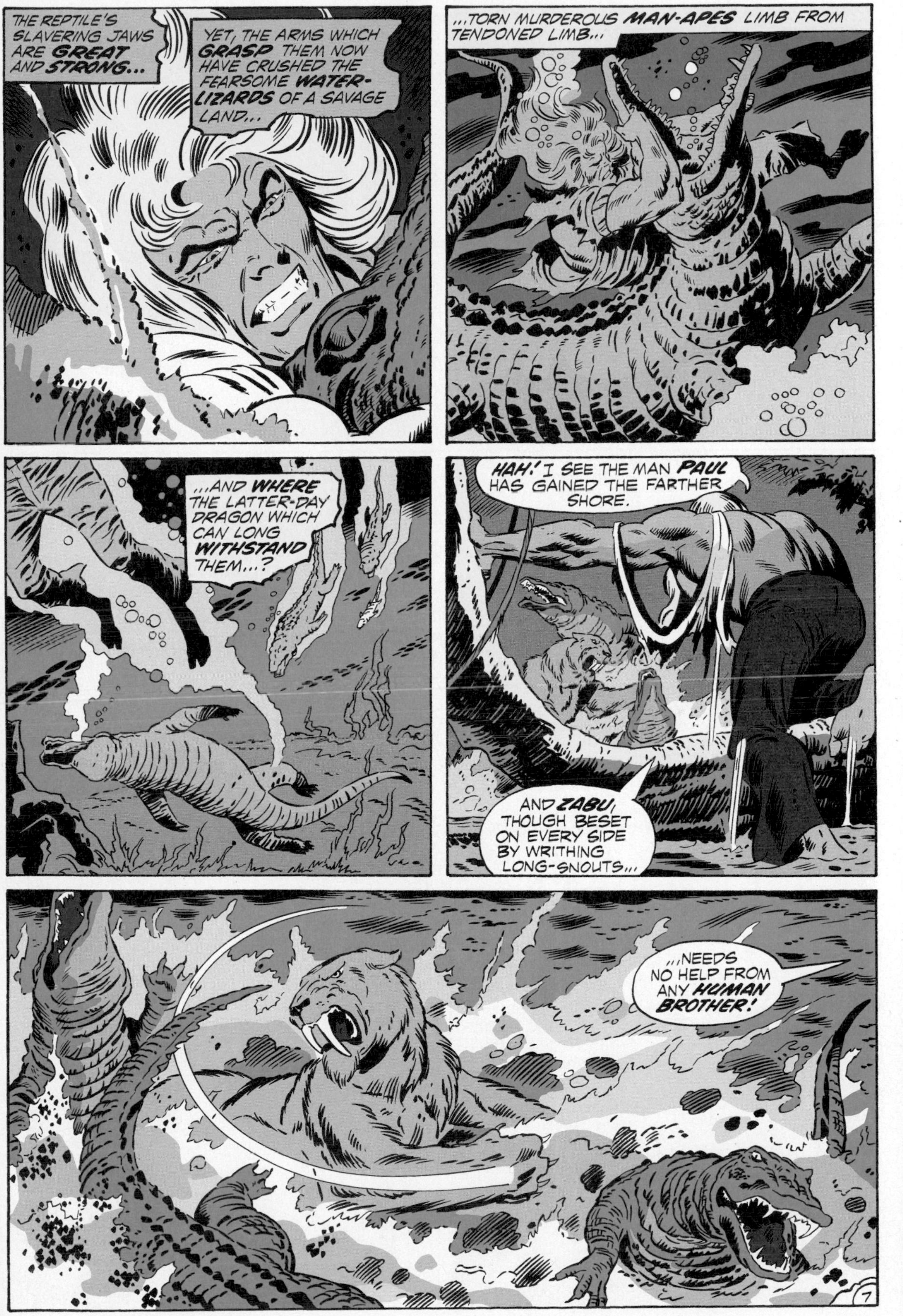
THE REPTILE'S SLAVERING JAWS ARE GREAT AND STRONG...
YET, THE ARMS WHICH GRASP THEM NOW HAVE CRUSHED THE FEARSOME WATER-LIZARDS OF A SAVAGE LAND...
...TORN MURDEROUS MAN-APES LIMB FROM TENDONED LIMB...
...AND WHERE THE LATTER-DAY DRAGON WHICH CAN LONG WITHSTAND THEM...?
HAH! I SEE THE MAN PAUL HAS GAINED THE FARTHER SHORE.
AND ZABU, THOUGH BESET ON EVERY SIDE BY WRITHING LONG-SNOUTS...
...NEEDS NO HELP FROM ANY HUMAN BROTHER!
7

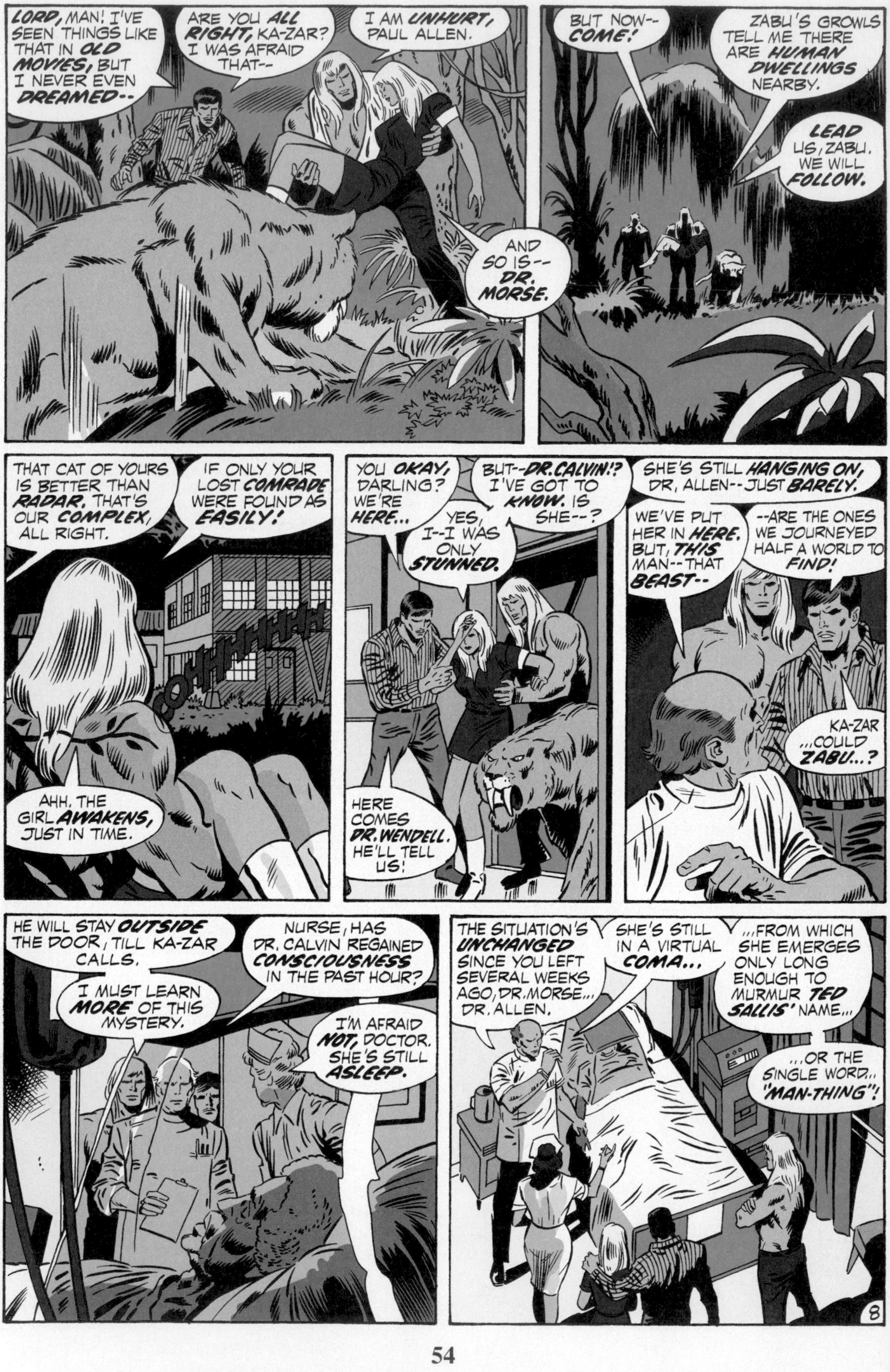

LORD, MAN! I'VE SEEN THINGS LIKE THAT IN OLD MOVIES, BUT I NEVER EVEN DREAMED--
ARE YOU ALL RIGHT, KA-ZAR? I WAS AFRAID THAT--
I AM UNHURT, PAUL ALLEN.
AND SO IS-- DR. MORSE.
BUT NOW-- COME!
ZABU'S GROWLS TELL ME THERE ARE HUMAN DWELLINGS NEARBY.
LEAD US, ZABU. WE WILL FOLLOW.
THAT CAT OF YOURS IS BETTER THAN RADAR. THAT'S OUR COMPLEX, ALL RIGHT.
IF ONLY YOUR LOST COMRADE WERE FOUND AS EASILY!
OOHHHHHHHH
AHH. THE GIRL AWAKENS, JUST IN TIME.
YOU OKAY, DARLING? WE'RE HERE...
YES, I--I WAS ONLY STUNNED.
BUT--DR. CALVIN!? I'VE GOT TO KNOW. IS SHE--?
HERE COMES DR. WENDELL. HE'LL TELL US!
SHE'S STILL HANGING ON, DR. ALLEN--JUST BARELY.
WE'VE PUT HER IN HERE. BUT, THIS MAN--THAT BEAST--
--ARE THE ONES WE JOURNEYED HALF A WORLD TO FIND!
KA-ZAR ...COULD ZABU...?
HE WILL STAY OUTSIDE THE DOOR, TILL KA-ZAR CALLS.
I MUST LEARN MORE OF THIS MYSTERY.
NURSE, HAS DR. CALVIN REGAINED CONSCIOUSNESS IN THE PAST HOUR?
I'M AFRAID NOT, DOCTOR. SHE'S STILL ASLEEP.
THE SITUATION'S UNCHANGED SINCE YOU LEFT SEVERAL WEEKS AGO, DR. MORSE... DR. ALLEN.
SHE'S STILL IN A VIRTUAL COMA...
...FROM WHICH SHE EMERGES ONLY LONG ENOUGH TO MURMUR TED SALLIS' NAME...
...OR THE SINGLE WORD... "MAN-THING"!
8

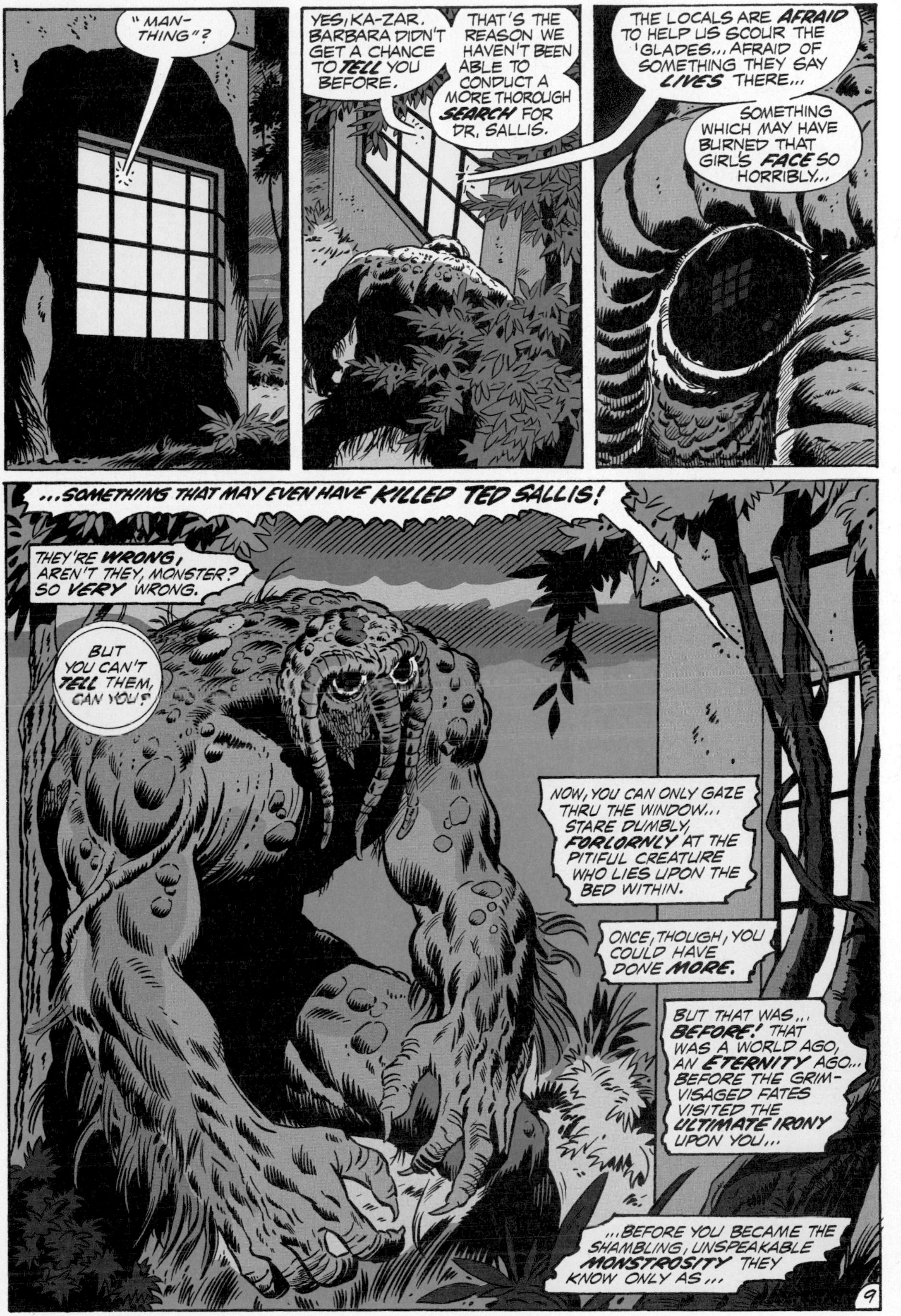
"MAN-THING"?
YES, KA-ZAR. BARBARA DIDN'T GET A CHANCE TO TELL YOU BEFORE.
THAT'S THE REASON WE HAVEN'T BEEN ABLE TO CONDUCT A MORE THOROUGH SEARCH FOR DR. SALLIS.
THE LOCALS ARE AFRAID TO HELP US SCOUR THE 'GLADES... AFRAID OF SOMETHING THEY SAY LIVES THERE...
SOMETHING WHICH MAY HAVE BURNED THAT GIRL'S FACE SO HORRIBLY...
...SOMETHING THAT MAY EVEN HAVE KILLED TED SALLIS!
THEY'RE WRONG, AREN'T THEY, MONSTER? SO VERY WRONG.
BUT YOU CAN'T TELL THEM, CAN YOU?
NOW, YOU CAN ONLY GAZE THRU THE WINDOW... STARE DUMBLY, FORLORNLY AT THE PITIFUL CREATURE WHO LIES UPON THE BED WITHIN.
ONCE, THOUGH, YOU COULD HAVE DONE MORE.
BUT THAT WAS... BEFORE! THAT WAS A WORLD AGO, AN ETERNITY AGO... BEFORE THE GRIM-VISAGED FATES VISITED THE ULTIMATE IRONY UPON YOU...
...BEFORE YOU BECAME THE SHAMBLING, UNSPEAKABLE MONSTROSITY THEY KNOW ONLY AS...
9

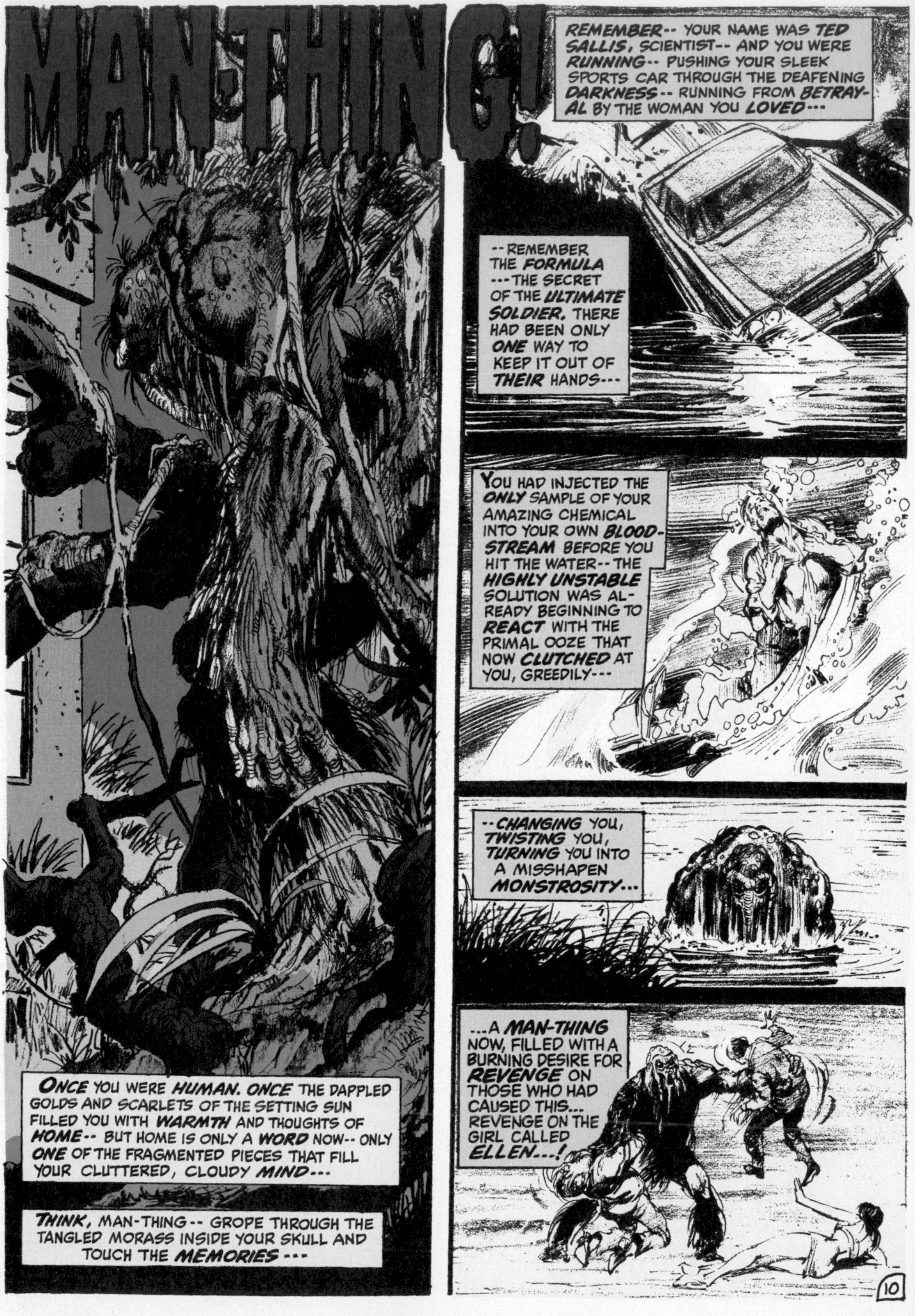
MAN-THING!
REMEMBER-- YOUR NAME WAS TED SALLIS, SCIENTIST-- AND YOU WERE RUNNING-- PUSHING YOUR SLEEK SPORTS CAR THROUGH THE DEAFENING DARKNESS-- RUNNING FROM BETRAYAL BY THE WOMAN YOU LOVED---
--REMEMBER THE FORMULA ---THE SECRET OF THE ULTIMATE SOLDIER. THERE HAD BEEN ONLY ONE WAY TO KEEP IT OUT OF THEIR HANDS---
YOU HAD INJECTED THE ONLY SAMPLE OF YOUR AMAZING CHEMICAL INTO YOUR OWN BLOODSTREAM BEFORE YOU HIT THE WATER-- THE HIGHLY UNSTABLE SOLUTION WAS ALREADY BEGINNING TO REACT WITH THE PRIMAL OOZE THAT NOW CLUTCHED AT YOU, GREEDILY---
--CHANGING YOU, TWISTING YOU, TURNING YOU INTO A MISSHAPEN MONSTROSITY...
...A MAN-THING NOW, FILLED WITH A BURNING DESIRE FOR REVENGE ON THOSE WHO HAD CAUSED THIS... REVENGE ON THE GIRL CALLED ELLEN...!
ONCE YOU WERE HUMAN. ONCE THE DAPPLED GOLDS AND SCARLETS OF THE SETTING SUN FILLED YOU WITH WARMTH AND THOUGHTS OF HOME-- BUT HOME IS ONLY A WORD NOW-- ONLY ONE OF THE FRAGMENTED PIECES THAT FILL YOUR CLUTTERED, CLOUDY MIND---
THINK, MAN-THING-- GROPE THROUGH THE TANGLED MORASS INSIDE YOUR SKULL AND TOUCH THE MEMORIES---
10

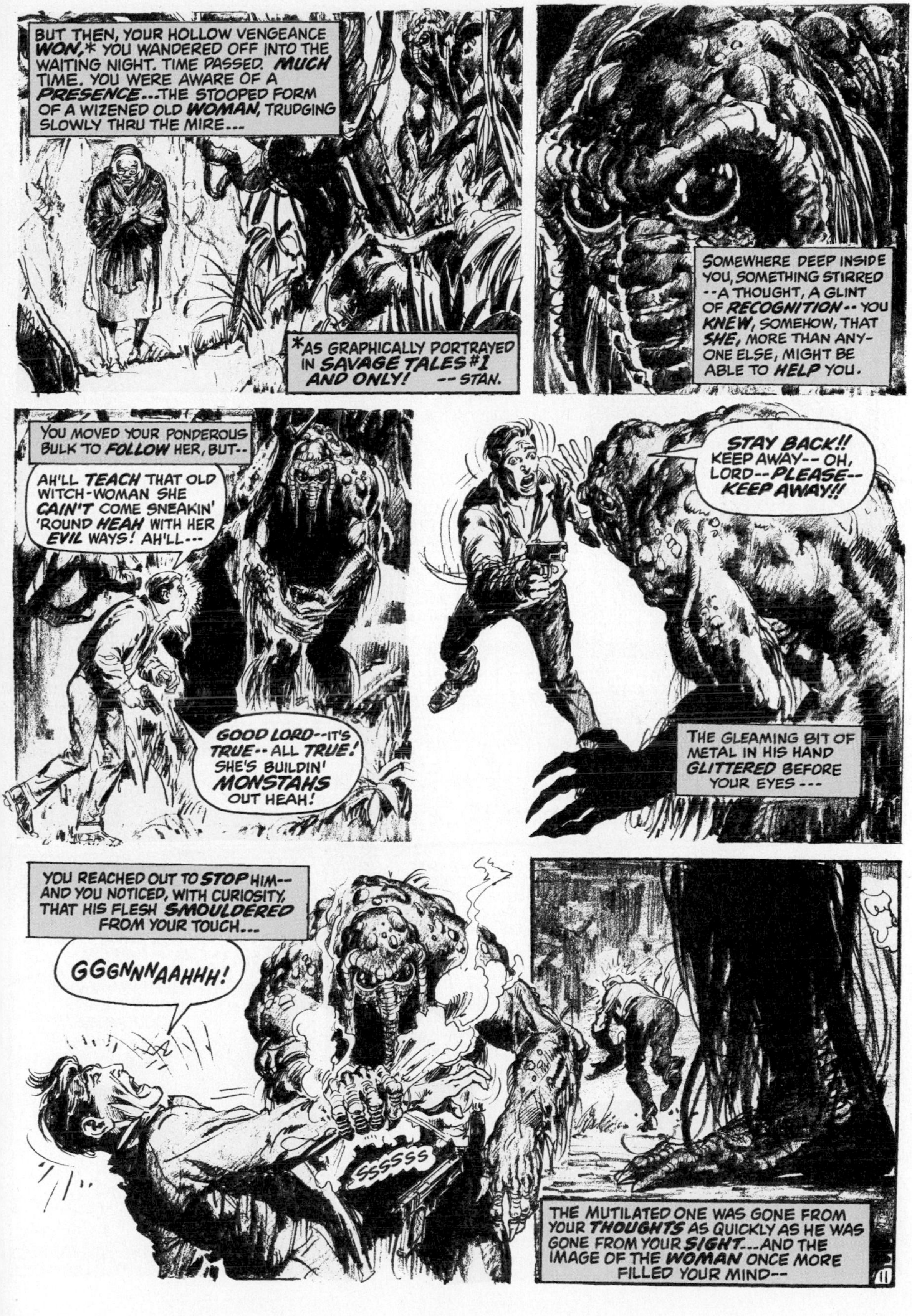
BUT THEN, YOUR HOLLOW VENGEANCE WON,* YOU WANDERED OFF INTO THE WAITING NIGHT. TIME PASSED. MUCH TIME. YOU WERE AWARE OF A PRESENCE...THE STOOPED FORM OF A WIZENED OLD WOMAN, TRUDGING SLOWLY THRU THE MIRE...
*AS GRAPHICALLY PORTRAYED IN SAVAGE TALES #1 AND ONLY! --STAN.
SOMEWHERE DEEP INSIDE YOU, SOMETHING STIRRED --A THOUGHT, A GLINT OF RECOGNITION-- YOU KNEW, SOMEHOW, THAT SHE, MORE THAN ANY-ONE ELSE, MIGHT BE ABLE TO HELP YOU.
YOU MOVED YOUR PONDEROUS BULK TO FOLLOW HER, BUT--
AH'LL TEACH THAT OLD WITCH-WOMAN SHE CAIN'T COME SNEAKIN' 'ROUND HEAH WITH HER EVIL WAYS! AH'LL---
GOOD LORD--IT'S TRUE--ALL TRUE! SHE'S BUILDIN' MONSTAHS OUT HEAH!
STAY BACK!! KEEP AWAY-- OH, LORD--PLEASE-- KEEP AWAY!!
THE GLEAMING BIT OF METAL IN HIS HAND GLITTERED BEFORE YOUR EYES---
YOU REACHED OUT TO STOP HIM-- AND YOU NOTICED, WITH CURIOSITY, THAT HIS FLESH SMOULDERED FROM YOUR TOUCH...
GGGNNNAAHHH!
SSSSSS
THE MUTILATED ONE WAS GONE FROM YOUR THOUGHTS AS QUICKLY AS HE WAS GONE FROM YOUR SIGHT...AND THE IMAGE OF THE WOMAN ONCE MORE FILLED YOUR MIND--
11

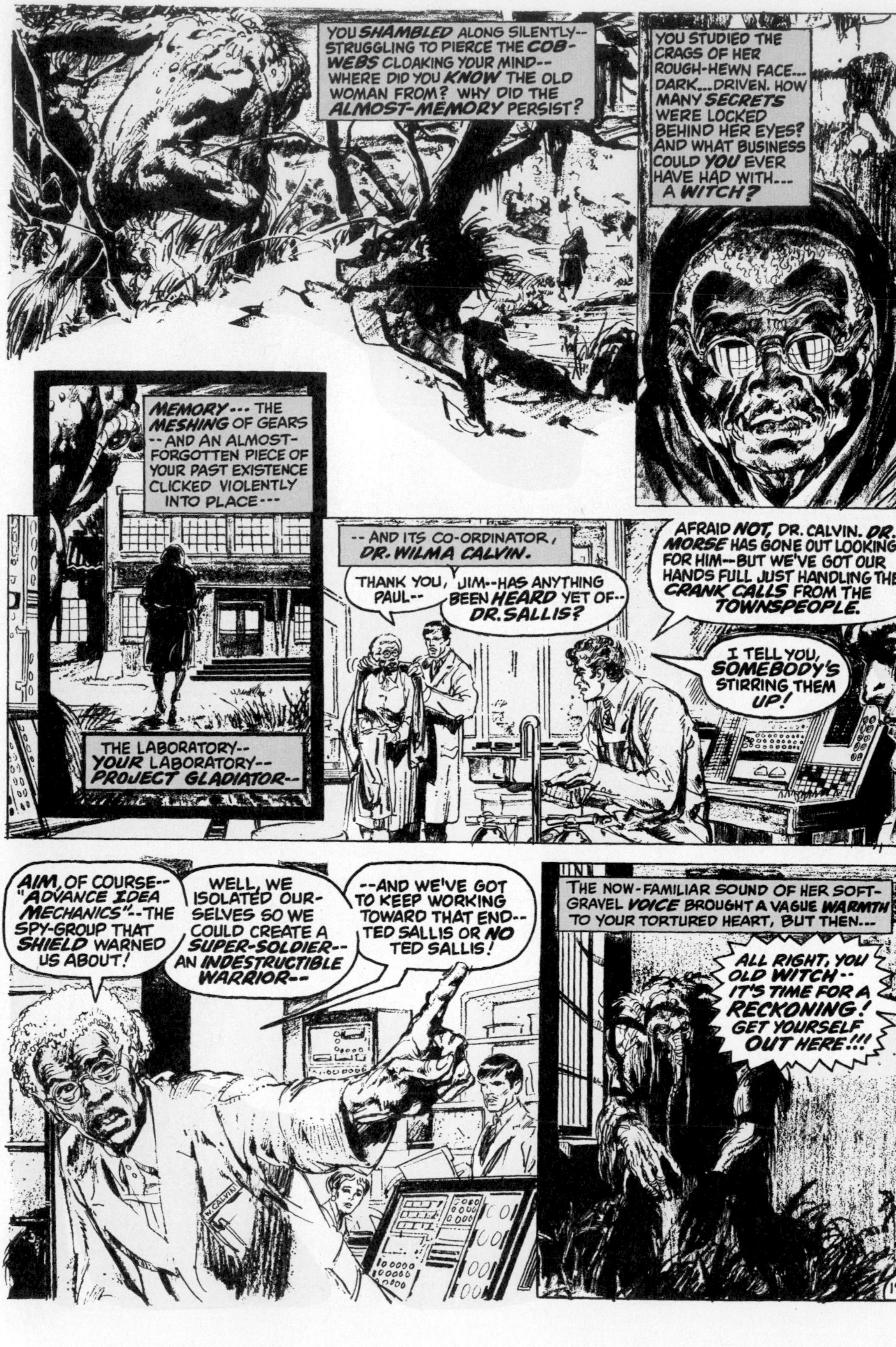
YOU SHAMBLED ALONG SILENTLY--STRUGGLING TO PIERCE THE COB-WEBS CLOAKING YOUR MIND--WHERE DID YOU KNOW THE OLD WOMAN FROM? WHY DID THE ALMOST-MEMORY PERSIST?
YOU STUDIED THE CRAGS OF HER ROUGH-HEWN FACE... DARK...DRIVEN. HOW MANY SECRETS WERE LOCKED BEHIND HER EYES? AND WHAT BUSINESS COULD YOU EVER HAVE HAD WITH... A WITCH?
MEMORY--- THE MESHING OF GEARS --AND AN ALMOST-FORGOTTEN PIECE OF YOUR PAST EXISTENCE CLICKED VIOLENTLY INTO PLACE---
THE LABORATORY--YOUR LABORATORY--PROJECT GLADIATOR--
--AND ITS CO-ORDINATOR, DR. WILMA CALVIN.
THANK YOU, PAUL--
JIM--HAS ANYTHING BEEN HEARD YET OF--DR. SALLIS?
AFRAID NOT, DR. CALVIN. DR. MORSE HAS GONE OUT LOOKING FOR HIM--BUT WE'VE GOT OUR HANDS FULL JUST HANDLING THE CRANK CALLS FROM THE TOWNSPEOPLE.
I TELL YOU, SOMEBODY'S STIRRING THEM UP!
AIM, OF COURSE--"ADVANCE IDEA MECHANICS"--THE SPY-GROUP THAT SHIELD WARNED US ABOUT!
WELL, WE ISOLATED OUR-SELVES SO WE COULD CREATE A SUPER-SOLDIER--AN INDESTRUCTIBLE WARRIOR--
--AND WE'VE GOT TO KEEP WORKING TOWARD THAT END--TED SALLIS OR NO TED SALLIS!
W. CALVIN
THE NOW-FAMILIAR SOUND OF HER SOFT-GRAVEL VOICE BROUGHT A VAGUE WARMTH TO YOUR TORTURED HEART, BUT THEN---
ALL RIGHT, YOU OLD WITCH--IT'S TIME FOR A RECKONING! GET YOURSELF OUT HERE!!!
12

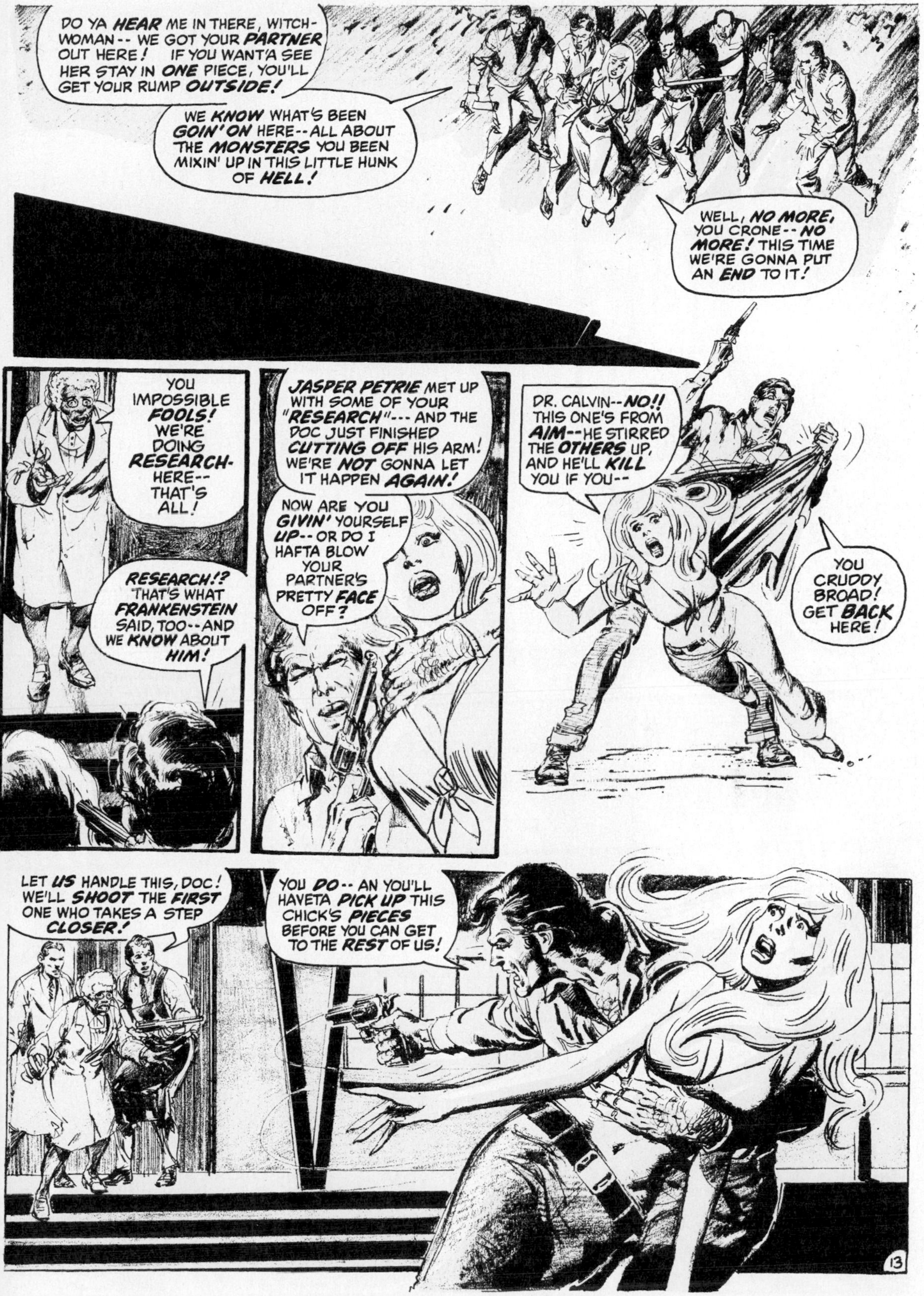
DO YA HEAR ME IN THERE, WITCH-WOMAN-- WE GOT YOUR PARTNER OUT HERE! IF YOU WANT'A SEE HER STAY IN ONE PIECE, YOU'LL GET YOUR RUMP OUTSIDE!
WE KNOW WHAT'S BEEN GOIN' ON HERE--ALL ABOUT THE MONSTERS YOU BEEN MIXIN' UP IN THIS LITTLE HUNK OF HELL!
WELL, NO MORE, YOU CRONE--NO MORE! THIS TIME WE'RE GONNA PUT AN END TO IT!
YOU IMPOSSIBLE FOOLS! WE'RE DOING RESEARCH-HERE--THAT'S ALL!
RESEARCH!? THAT'S WHAT FRANKENSTEIN SAID, TOO--AND WE KNOW ABOUT HIM!
JASPER PETRIE MET UP WITH SOME OF YOUR "RESEARCH"--- AND THE DOC JUST FINISHED CUTTING OFF HIS ARM! WE'RE NOT GONNA LET IT HAPPEN AGAIN!
NOW ARE YOU GIVIN' YOURSELF UP--OR DO I HAFTA BLOW YOUR PARTNER'S PRETTY FACE OFF?
DR. CALVIN--NO!! THIS ONE'S FROM AIM--HE STIRRED THE OTHERS UP, AND HE'LL KILL YOU IF YOU--
YOU CRUDDY BROAD! GET BACK HERE!
LET US HANDLE THIS, DOC! WE'LL SHOOT THE FIRST ONE WHO TAKES A STEP CLOSER!
YOU DO--AN YOU'LL HAVETA PICK UP THIS CHICK'S PIECES BEFORE YOU CAN GET TO THE REST OF US!
13

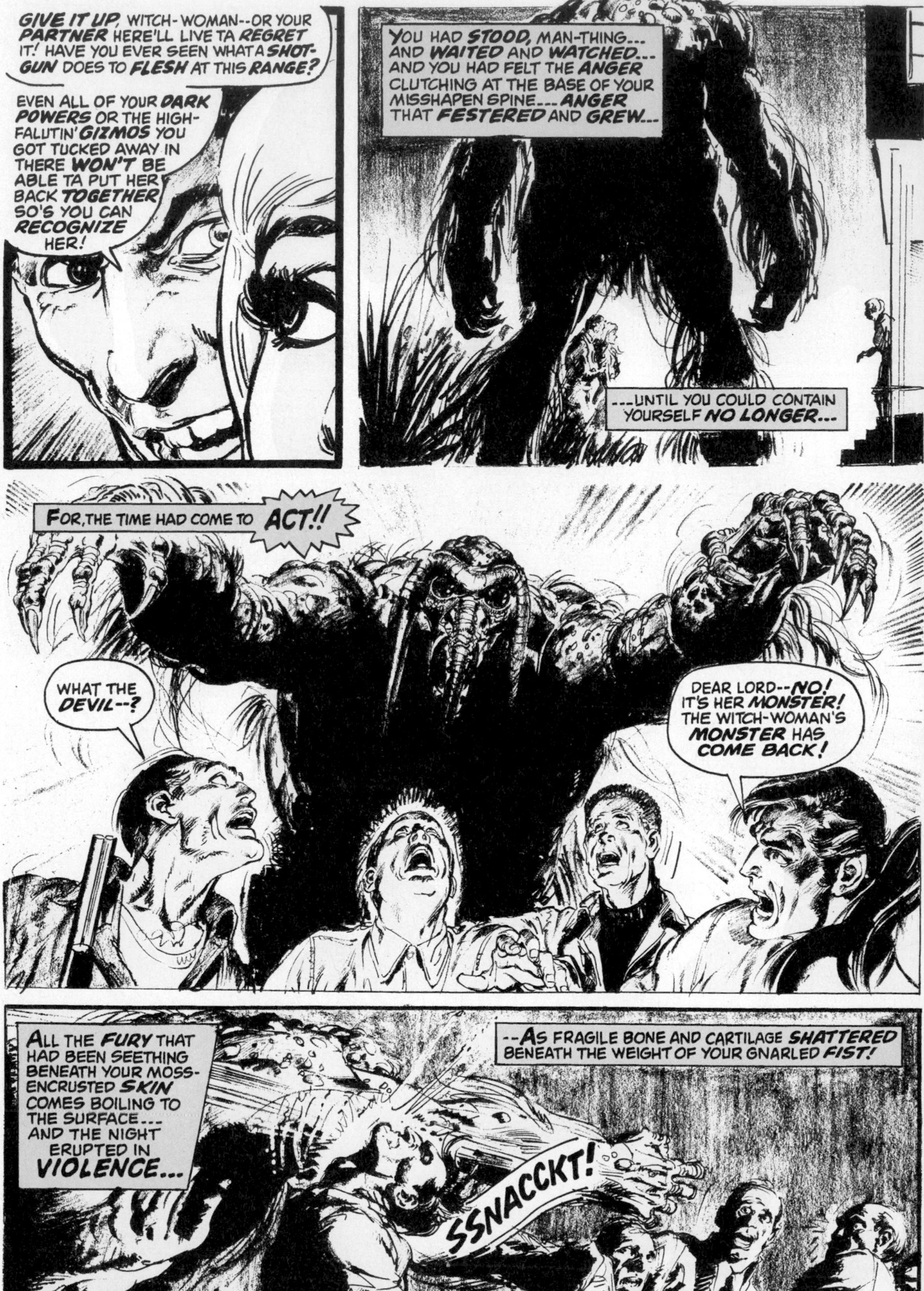
GIVE IT UP, WITCH-WOMAN--OR YOUR PARTNER HERE'LL LIVE TA REGRET IT! HAVE YOU EVER SEEN WHAT A SHOT-GUN DOES TO FLESH AT THIS RANGE?
EVEN ALL OF YOUR DARK POWERS OR THE HIGH-FALUTIN' GIZMOS YOU GOT TUCKED AWAY IN THERE WON'T BE ABLE TA PUT HER BACK TOGETHER SO'S YOU CAN RECOGNIZE HER!
YOU HAD STOOD, MAN-THING... AND WAITED AND WATCHED... AND YOU HAD FELT THE ANGER CLUTCHING AT THE BASE OF YOUR MISSHAPEN SPINE... ANGER THAT FESTERED AND GREW...
...UNTIL YOU COULD CONTAIN YOURSELF NO LONGER...
FOR, THE TIME HAD COME TO ACT!!
WHAT THE DEVIL--?
DEAR LORD--NO! IT'S HER MONSTER! THE WITCH-WOMAN'S MONSTER HAS COME BACK!
ALL THE FURY THAT HAD BEEN SEETHING BENEATH YOUR MOSS-ENCRUSTED SKIN COMES BOILING TO THE SURFACE... AND THE NIGHT ERUPTED IN VIOLENCE...
--AS FRAGILE BONE AND CARTILAGE SHATTERED BENEATH THE WEIGHT OF YOUR GNARLED FIST!
SSNACCKT!
14

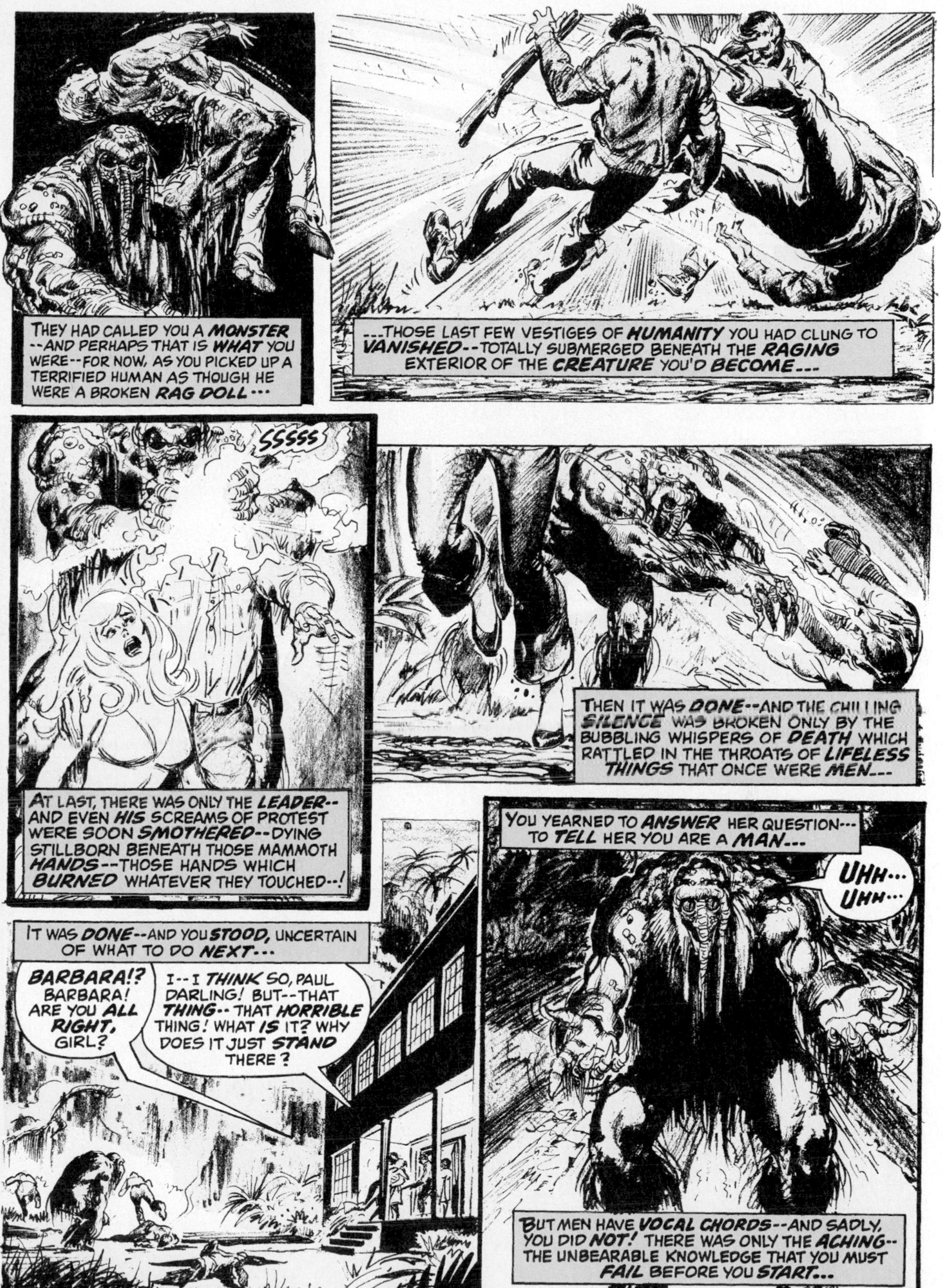

THEY HAD CALLED YOU A MONSTER --AND PERHAPS THAT IS WHAT YOU WERE--FOR NOW, AS YOU PICKED UP A TERRIFIED HUMAN AS THOUGH HE WERE A BROKEN RAG DOLL...
...THOSE LAST FEW VESTIGES OF HUMANITY YOU HAD CLUNG TO VANISHED--TOTALLY SUBMERGED BENEATH THE RAGING EXTERIOR OF THE CREATURE YOU'D BECOME...
SSSSS
AT LAST, THERE WAS ONLY THE LEADER-- AND EVEN HIS SCREAMS OF PROTEST WERE SOON SMOTHERED--DYING STILLBORN BENEATH THOSE MAMMOTH HANDS--THOSE HANDS WHICH BURNED WHATEVER THEY TOUCHED--!
THEN IT WAS DONE--AND THE CHILLING SILENCE WAS BROKEN ONLY BY THE BUBBLING WHISPERS OF DEATH WHICH RATTLED IN THE THROATS OF LIFELESS THINGS THAT ONCE WERE MEN...
IT WAS DONE--AND YOU STOOD, UNCERTAIN OF WHAT TO DO NEXT...
BARBARA!? BARBARA! ARE YOU ALL RIGHT, GIRL?
I--I THINK SO, PAUL DARLING! BUT--THAT THING--THAT HORRIBLE THING! WHAT IS IT? WHY DOES IT JUST STAND THERE?
YOU YEARNED TO ANSWER HER QUESTION--- TO TELL HER YOU ARE A MAN...
UHH... UHH...
BUT MEN HAVE VOCAL CHORDS--AND SADLY, YOU DID NOT! THERE WAS ONLY THE ACHING-- THE UNBEARABLE KNOWLEDGE THAT YOU MUST FAIL BEFORE YOU START...
15

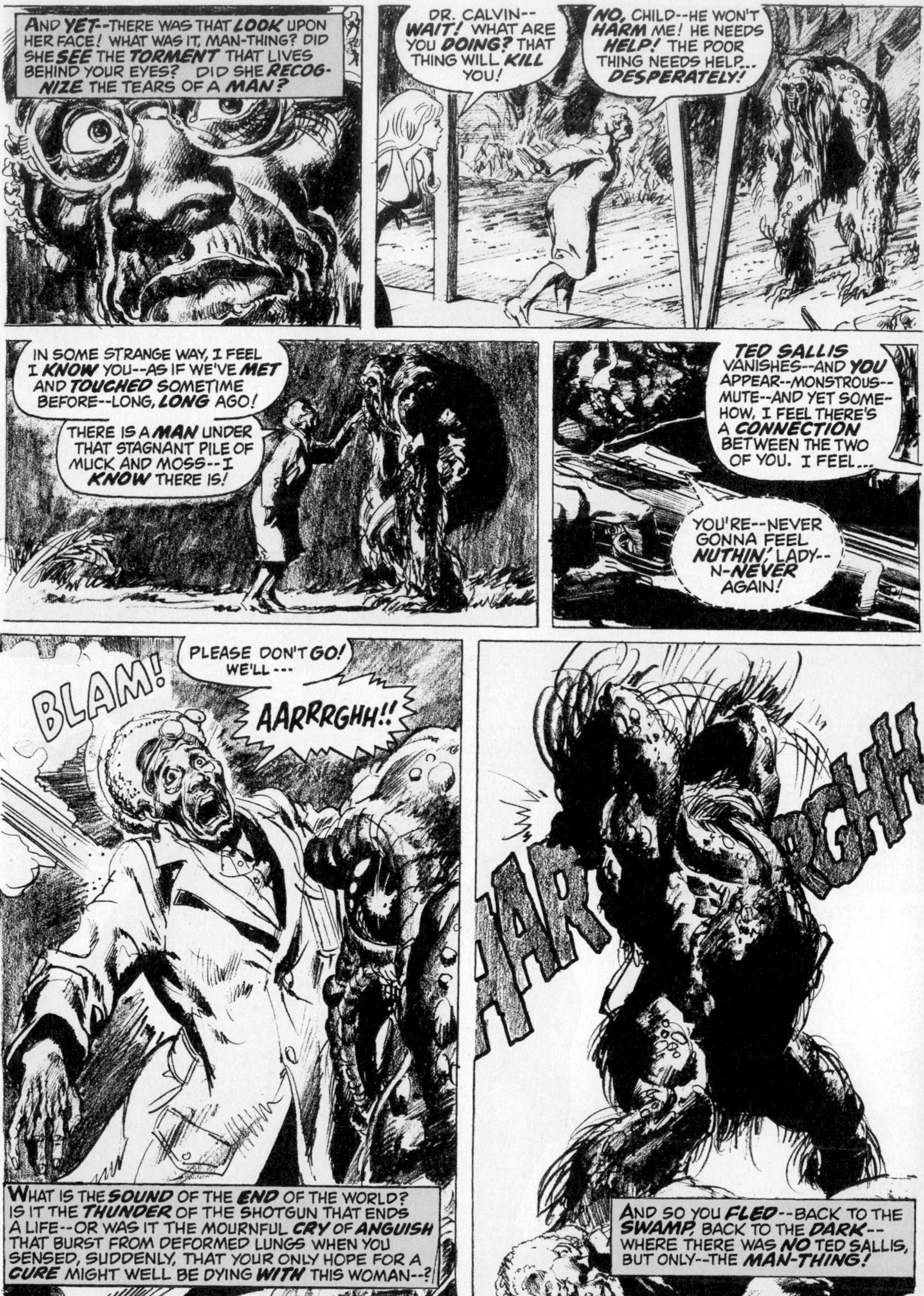

AND YET--THERE WAS THAT LOOK UPON HER FACE! WHAT WAS IT, MAN-THING? DID SHE SEE THE TORMENT THAT LIVES BEHIND YOUR EYES? DID SHE RECOGNIZE THE TEARS OF A MAN?
DR. CALVIN-- WAIT! WHAT ARE YOU DOING? THAT THING WILL KILL YOU!
NO, CHILD--HE WON'T HARM ME! HE NEEDS HELP! THE POOR THING NEEDS HELP... DESPERATELY!
IN SOME STRANGE WAY, I FEEL I KNOW YOU--AS IF WE'VE MET AND TOUCHED SOMETIME BEFORE--LONG, LONG AGO!
THERE IS A MAN UNDER THAT STAGNANT PILE OF MUCK AND MOSS--I KNOW THERE IS!
TED SALLIS VANISHES--AND YOU APPEAR--MONSTROUS--MUTE--AND YET SOMEHOW, I FEEL THERE'S A CONNECTION BETWEEN THE TWO OF YOU. I FEEL...
YOU'RE--NEVER GONNA FEEL NUTHIN', LADY-- N-NEVER AGAIN!
BLAM!
PLEASE DON'T GO! WE'LL ---
AARRRGHH!!
WHAT IS THE SOUND OF THE END OF THE WORLD? IS IT THE THUNDER OF THE SHOTGUN THAT ENDS A LIFE--OR WAS IT THE MOURNFUL CRY OF ANGUISH THAT BURST FROM DEFORMED LUNGS WHEN YOU SENSED, SUDDENLY, THAT YOUR ONLY HOPE FOR A CURE MIGHT WELL BE DYING WITH THIS WOMAN--?
AARRRGHH
AND SO YOU FLED--BACK TO THE SWAMP, BACK TO THE DARK-- WHERE THERE WAS NO TED SALLIS, BUT ONLY--THE MAN-THING!
16

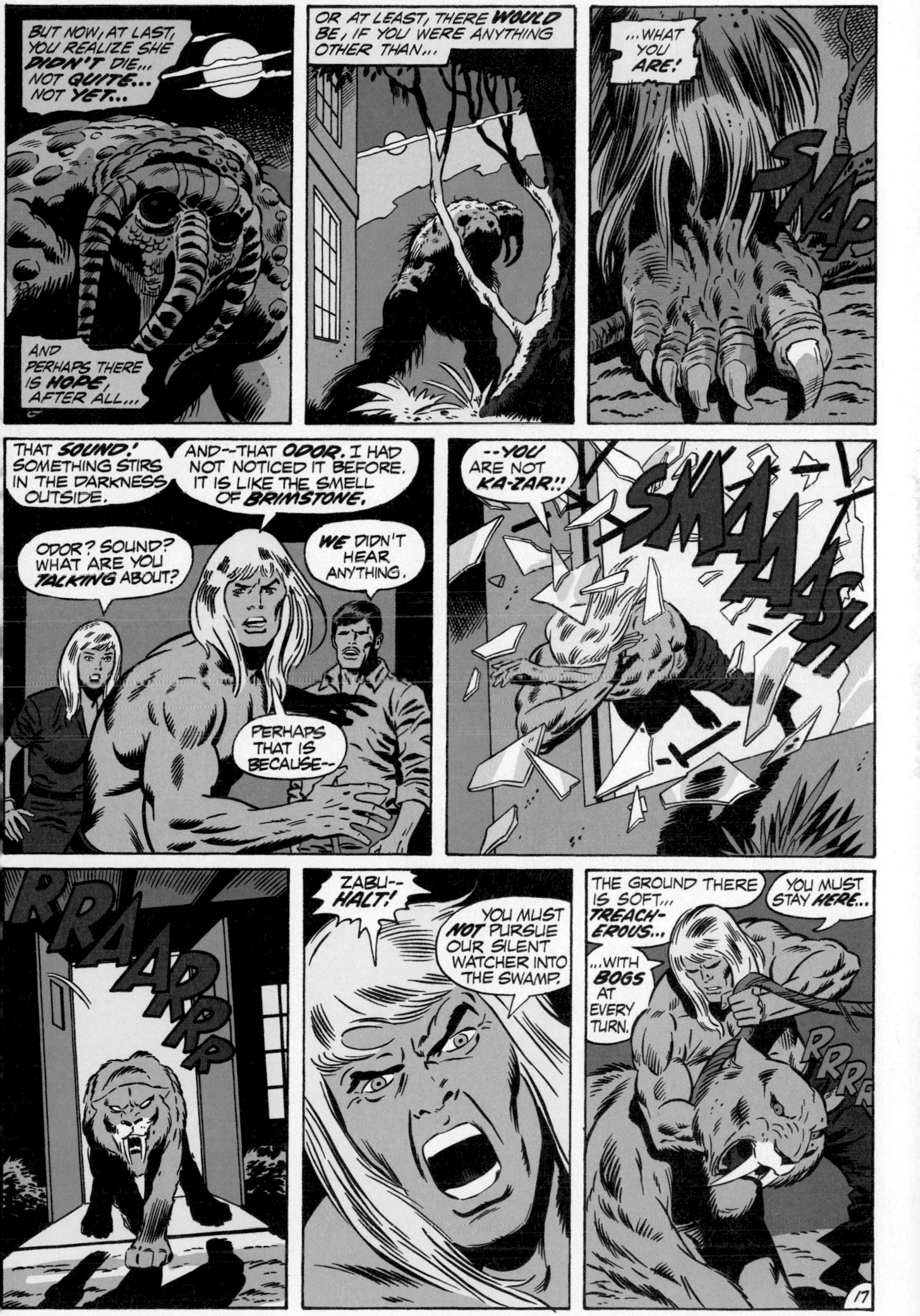
BUT NOW, AT LAST, YOU REALIZE SHE DIDN'T DIE... NOT QUITE... NOT YET...
AND PERHAPS THERE IS HOPE, AFTER ALL...
OR AT LEAST, THERE WOULD BE, IF YOU WERE ANYTHING OTHER THAN...
...WHAT YOU ARE!
SNAP
THAT SOUND! SOMETHING STIRS IN THE DARKNESS OUTSIDE.
AND--THAT ODOR. I HAD NOT NOTICED IT BEFORE. IT IS LIKE THE SMELL OF BRIMSTONE.
ODOR? SOUND? WHAT ARE YOU TALKING ABOUT?
WE DIDN'T HEAR ANYTHING.
PERHAPS THAT IS BECAUSE--
--YOU ARE NOT KA-ZAR!!
SMAAAASH
RRAARRR
ZABU--HALT!
YOU MUST NOT PURSUE OUR SILENT WATCHER INTO THE SWAMP.
THE GROUND THERE IS SOFT... TREACH-EROUS...
...WITH BOGS AT EVERY TURN.
YOU MUST STAY HERE...
RRRR
17

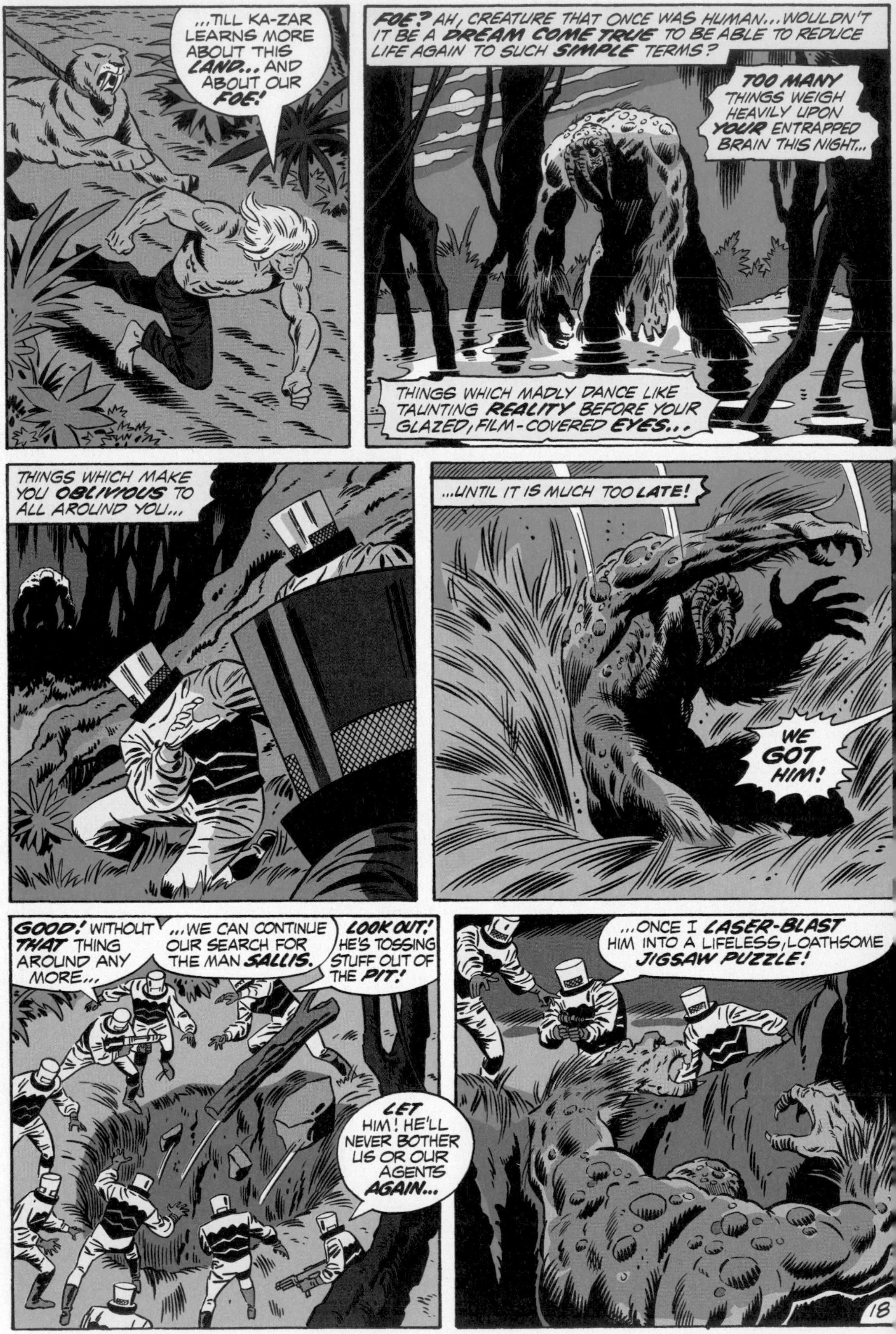
...TILL KA-ZAR LEARNS MORE ABOUT THIS LAND... AND ABOUT OUR FOE!
FOE? AH, CREATURE THAT ONCE WAS HUMAN... WOULDN'T IT BE A DREAM COME TRUE TO BE ABLE TO REDUCE LIFE AGAIN TO SUCH SIMPLE TERMS?
TOO MANY THINGS WEIGH HEAVILY UPON YOUR ENTRAPPED BRAIN THIS NIGHT...
THINGS WHICH MADLY DANCE LIKE TAUNTING REALITY BEFORE YOUR GLAZED, FILM-COVERED EYES...
THINGS WHICH MAKE YOU OBLIVIOUS TO ALL AROUND YOU...
...UNTIL IT IS MUCH TOO LATE!
WE GOT HIM!
GOOD! WITHOUT THAT THING AROUND ANY MORE...
...WE CAN CONTINUE OUR SEARCH FOR THE MAN SALLIS.
LOOK OUT! HE'S TOSSING STUFF OUT OF THE PIT!
LET HIM! HE'LL NEVER BOTHER US OR OUR AGENTS AGAIN...
...ONCE I LASER-BLAST HIM INTO A LIFELESS, LOATHSOME JIGSAW PUZZLE!
18

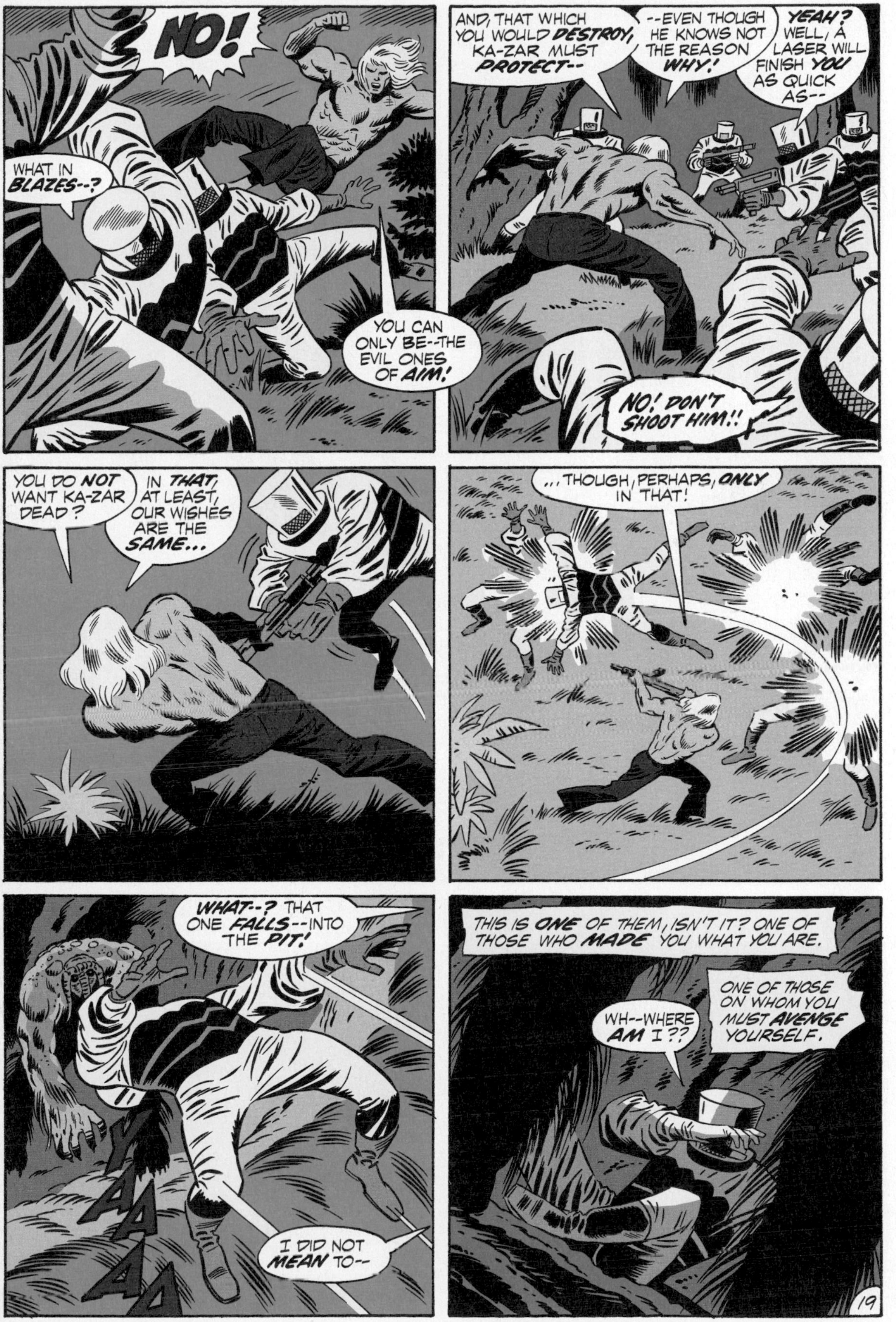
NO!
WHAT IN BLAZES--?
YOU CAN ONLY BE--THE EVIL ONES OF AIM!
AND, THAT WHICH YOU WOULD DESTROY, KA-ZAR MUST PROTECT--
--EVEN THOUGH HE KNOWS NOT THE REASON WHY!
YEAH? WELL, A LASER WILL FINISH YOU AS QUICK AS--
NO! DON'T SHOOT HIM!!
YOU DO NOT WANT KA-ZAR DEAD?
IN THAT, AT LEAST, OUR WISHES ARE THE SAME...
...THOUGH, PERHAPS, ONLY IN THAT!
WHAT--? THAT ONE FALLS--INTO THE PIT!
YAAA
I DID NOT MEAN TO--
THIS IS ONE OF THEM, ISN'T IT? ONE OF THOSE WHO MADE YOU WHAT YOU ARE.
WH--WHERE AM I??
ONE OF THOSE ON WHOM YOU MUST AVENGE YOURSELF.
19

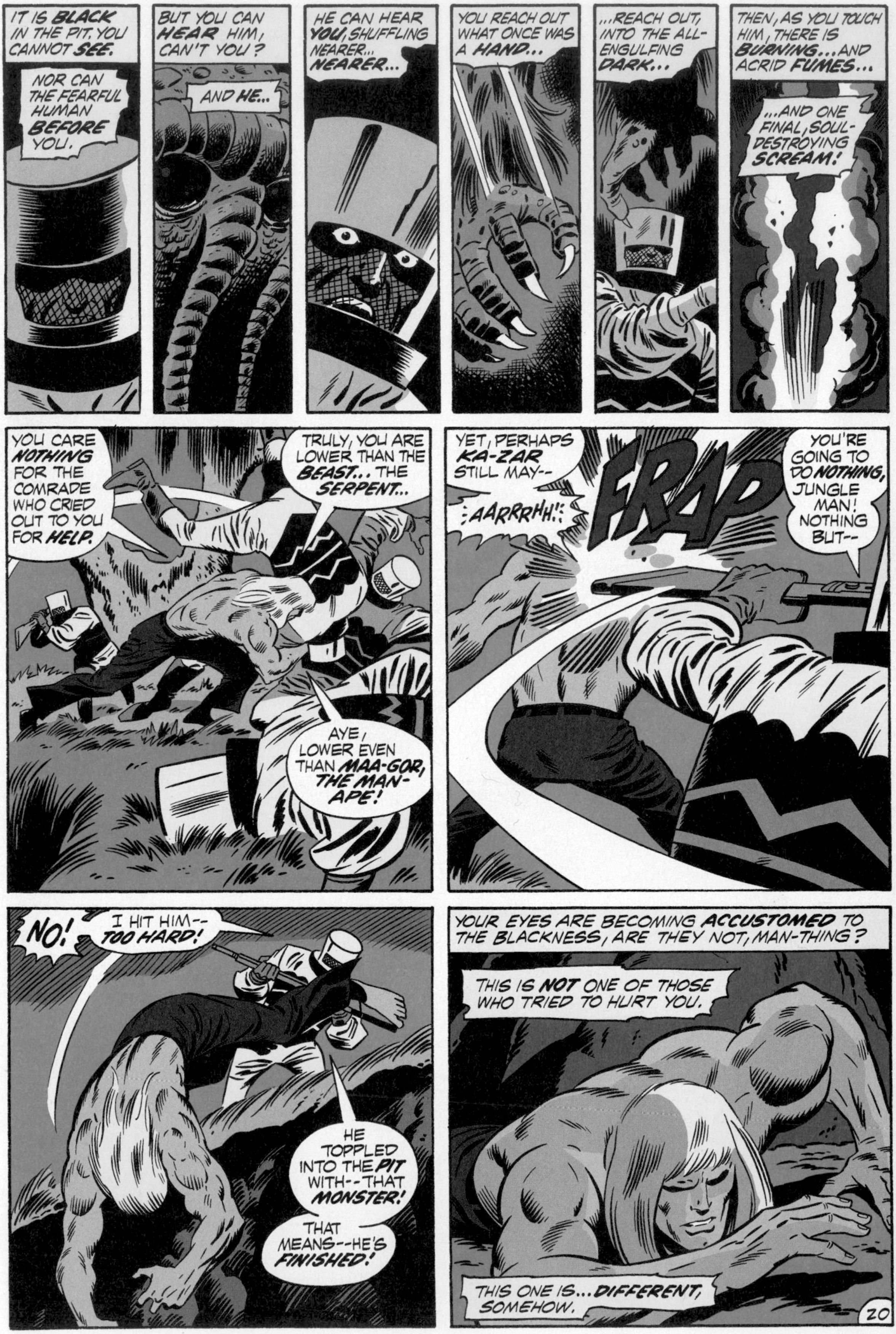
IT IS BLACK IN THE PIT. YOU CANNOT SEE.
NOR CAN THE FEARFUL HUMAN BEFORE YOU.
BUT YOU CAN HEAR HIM, CAN'T YOU?
AND HE...
HE CAN HEAR YOU, SHUFFLING NEARER... NEARER...
YOU REACH OUT WHAT ONCE WAS A HAND...
...REACH OUT, INTO THE ALL-ENGULFING DARK...
THEN, AS YOU TOUCH HIM, THERE IS BURNING... AND ACRID FUMES...
...AND ONE FINAL, SOUL-DESTROYING SCREAM!
YOU CARE NOTHING FOR THE COMRADE WHO CRIED OUT TO YOU FOR HELP.
TRULY, YOU ARE LOWER THAN THE BEAST... THE SERPENT...
AYE, LOWER EVEN THAN MAA-GOR, THE MAN-APE!
YET, PERHAPS KA-ZAR STILL MAY--
AARRRHH!
FRAP
YOU'RE GOING TO DO NOTHING, JUNGLE MAN! NOTHING BUT--
NO!
I HIT HIM-- TOO HARD!
HE TOPPLED INTO THE PIT WITH--THAT MONSTER!
THAT MEANS--HE'S FINISHED!
YOUR EYES ARE BECOMING ACCUSTOMED TO THE BLACKNESS, ARE THEY NOT, MAN-THING?
THIS IS NOT ONE OF THOSE WHO TRIED TO HURT YOU.
THIS ONE IS... DIFFERENT, SOMEHOW.
20

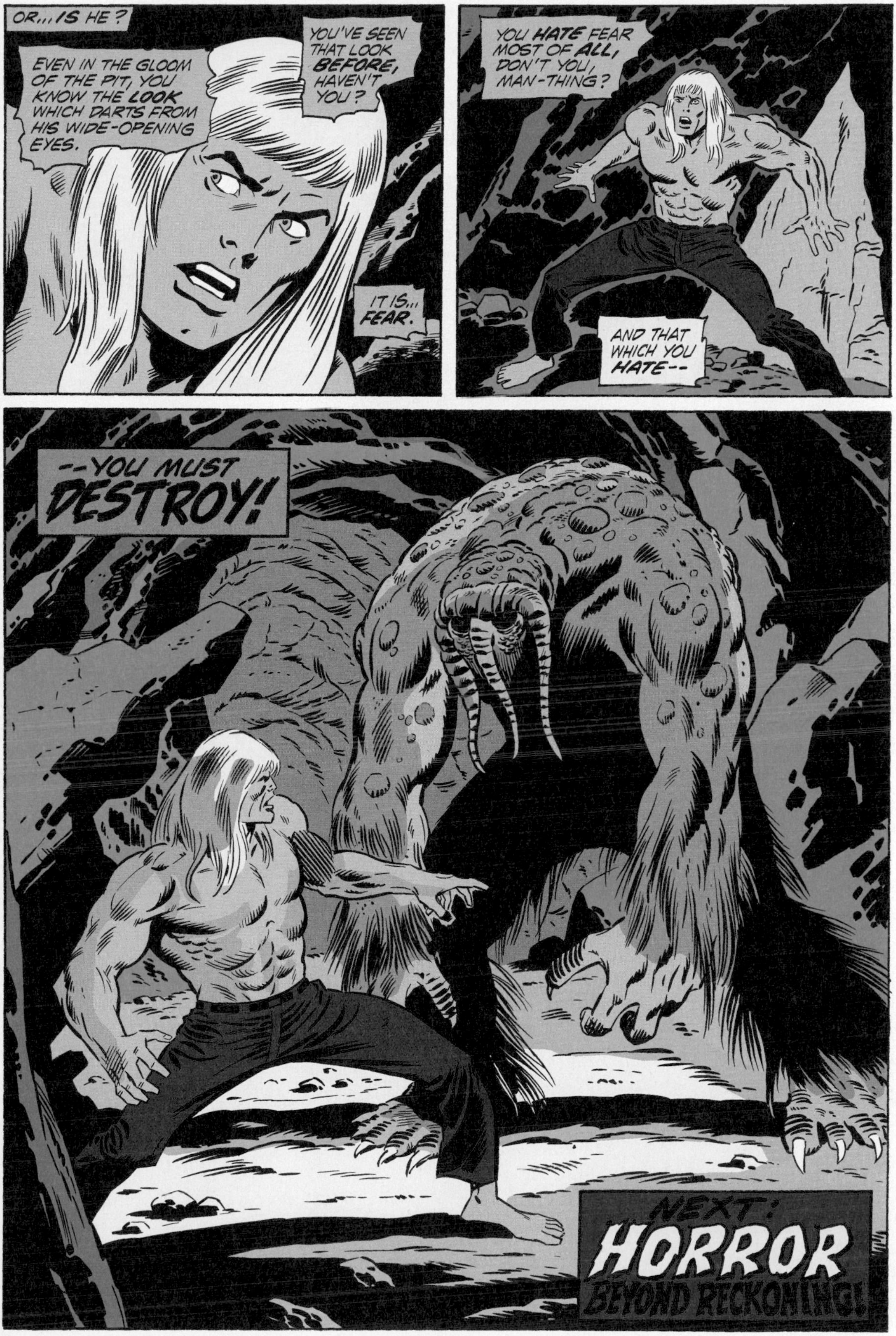

OR... IS HE?
EVEN IN THE GLOOM OF THE PIT, YOU KNOW THE LOOK WHICH DARTS FROM HIS WIDE-OPENING EYES.
YOU'VE SEEN THAT LOOK BEFORE, HAVEN'T YOU?
IT IS... FEAR.
YOU HATE FEAR MOST OF ALL, DON'T YOU, MAN-THING?
AND THAT WHICH YOU HATE--
--YOU MUST DESTROY!
NEXT: HORROR BEYOND RECKONING!

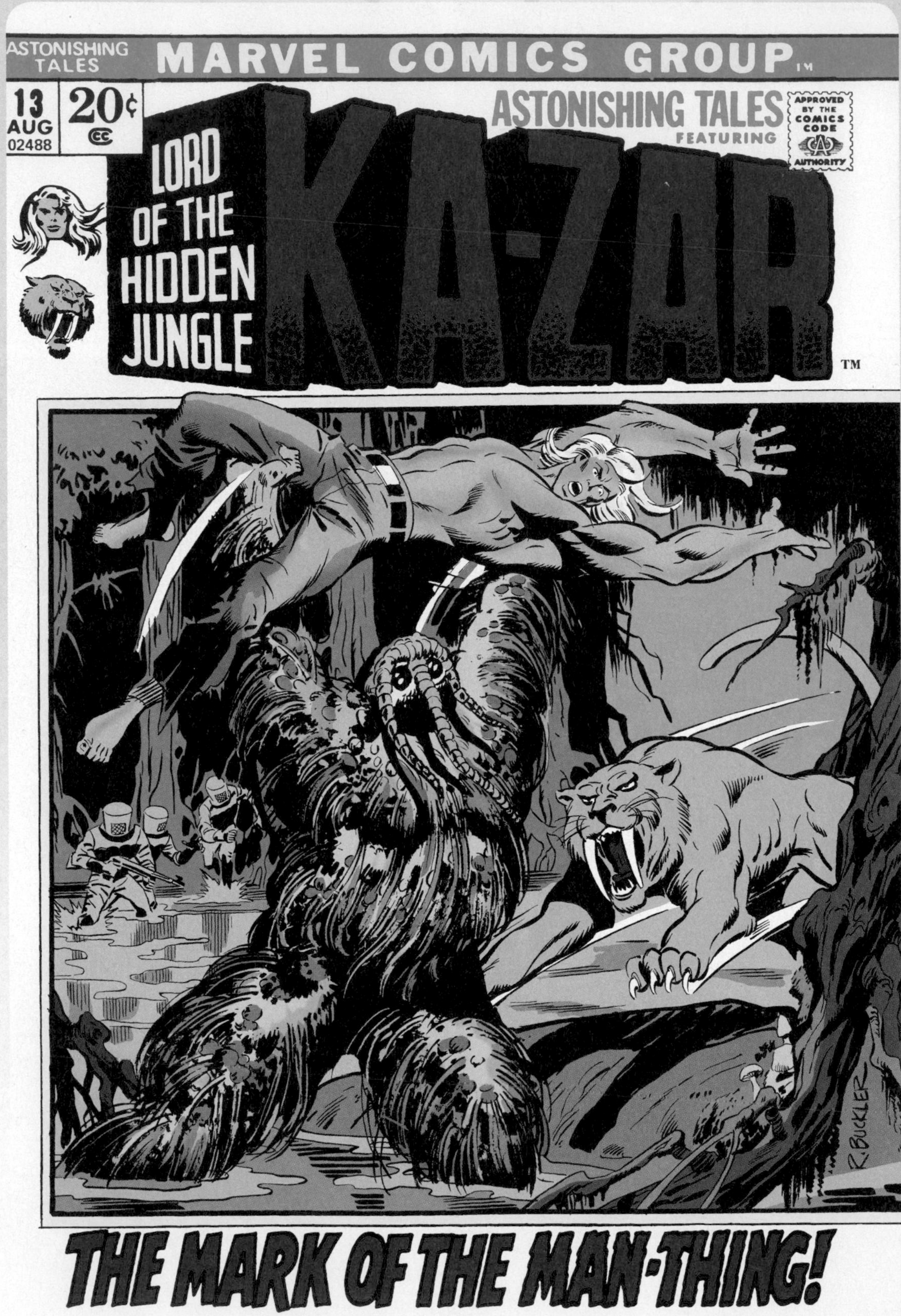
ASTONISHING TALES
MARVEL COMICS GROUP
13 AUG 02488
20¢
ASTONISHING TALES FEATURING
APPROVED BY THE COMICS CODE AUTHORITY
LORD OF THE HIDDEN JUNGLE
KA-ZAR
R. BUCKLER
THE MARK OF THE MAN-THING!

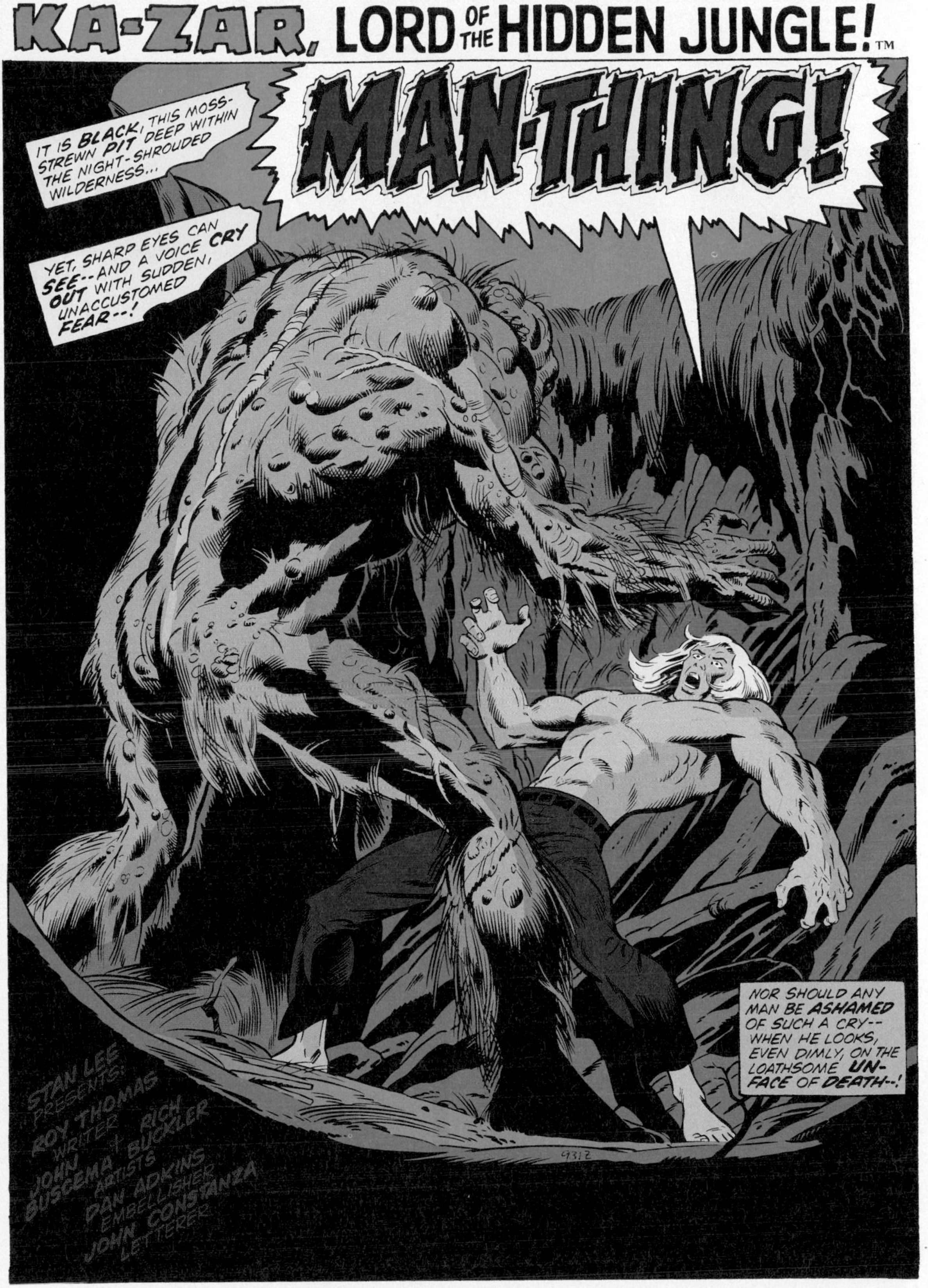
KA-ZAR, LORD OF THE HIDDEN JUNGLE!™
MAN-THING!
IT IS BLACK, THIS MOSS-STREWN PIT DEEP WITHIN THE NIGHT-SHROUDED WILDERNESS...
YET, SHARP EYES CAN SEE--AND A VOICE CRY OUT WITH SUDDEN, UNACCUSTOMED FEAR--!
NOR SHOULD ANY MAN BE ASHAMED OF SUCH A CRY--WHEN HE LOOKS, EVEN DIMLY, ON THE LOATHSOME UN-FACE OF DEATH--!
STAN LEE PRESENTS:
ROY THOMAS WRITER
JOHN BUSCEMA + RICH BUCKLER ARTISTS
DAN ADKINS EMBELLISHER
JOHN CONSTANZA LETTERER

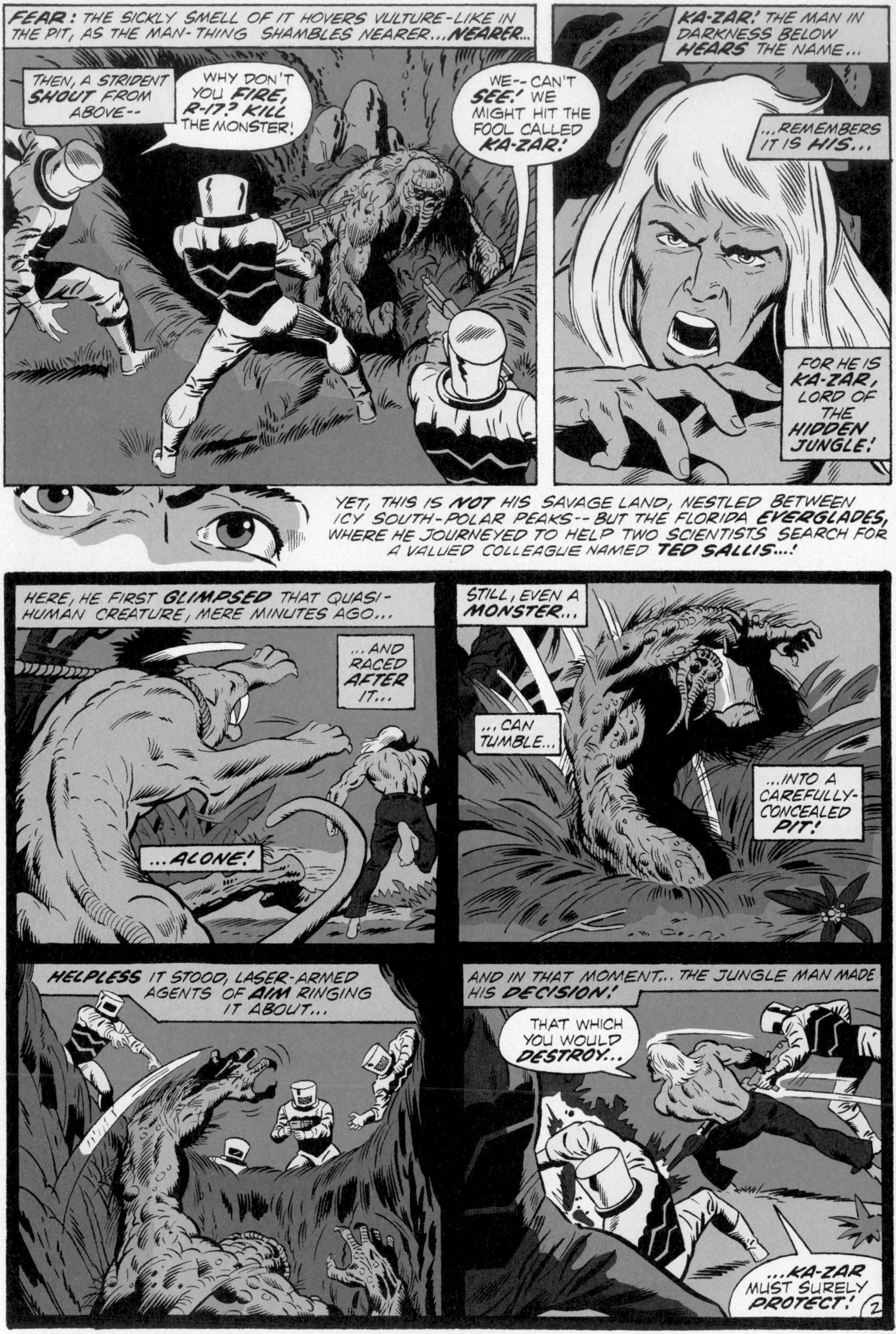
FEAR: THE SICKLY SMELL OF IT HOVERS VULTURE-LIKE IN THE PIT, AS THE MAN-THING SHAMBLES NEARER... NEARER...
THEN, A STRIDENT SHOUT FROM ABOVE--
WHY DON'T YOU FIRE, R-17? KILL THE MONSTER!
WE--CAN'T SEE! WE MIGHT HIT THE FOOL CALLED KA-ZAR!
KA-ZAR! THE MAN IN DARKNESS BELOW HEARS THE NAME...
...REMEMBERS IT IS HIS...
FOR HE IS KA-ZAR, LORD OF THE HIDDEN JUNGLE!
YET, THIS IS NOT HIS SAVAGE LAND, NESTLED BETWEEN ICY SOUTH-POLAR PEAKS--BUT THE FLORIDA EVERGLADES, WHERE HE JOURNEYED TO HELP TWO SCIENTISTS SEARCH FOR A VALUED COLLEAGUE NAMED TED SALLIS...!
HERE, HE FIRST GLIMPSED THAT QUASI-HUMAN CREATURE, MERE MINUTES AGO...
...AND RACED AFTER IT...
...ALONE!
STILL, EVEN A MONSTER...
...CAN TUMBLE...
...INTO A CAREFULLY-CONCEALED PIT!
HELPLESS IT STOOD, LASER-ARMED AGENTS OF AIM RINGING IT ABOUT...
AND IN THAT MOMENT... THE JUNGLE MAN MADE HIS DECISION!
THAT WHICH YOU WOULD DESTROY...
...KA-ZAR MUST SURELY PROTECT!
2

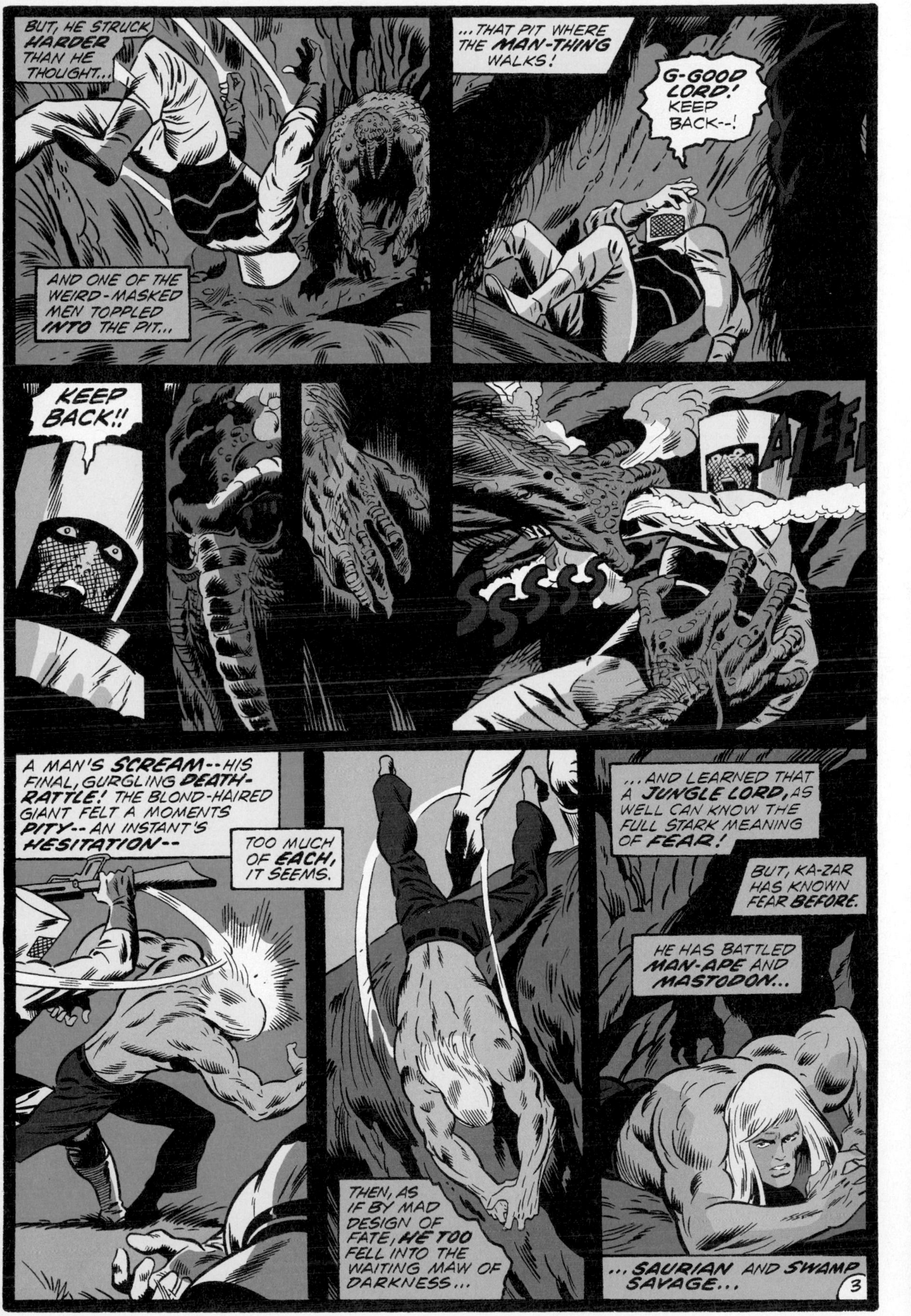
BUT, HE STRUCK HARDER THAN HE THOUGHT...
AND ONE OF THE WEIRD-MASKED MEN TOPPLED INTO THE PIT...
...THAT PIT WHERE THE MAN-THING WALKS!
G-GOOD LORD! KEEP BACK--!
KEEP BACK!!
SSSSS
AIEE
A MAN'S SCREAM--HIS FINAL, GURGLING DEATH-RATTLE! THE BLOND-HAIRED GIANT FELT A MOMENTS PITY--AN INSTANT'S HESITATION--
TOO MUCH OF EACH, IT SEEMS.
THEN, AS IF BY MAD DESIGN OF FATE, HE TOO FELL INTO THE WAITING MAW OF DARKNESS...
...AND LEARNED THAT A JUNGLE LORD, AS WELL CAN KNOW THE FULL STARK MEANING OF FEAR!
BUT, KA-ZAR HAS KNOWN FEAR BEFORE.
HE HAS BATTLED MAN-APE AND MASTODON...
...SAURIAN AND SWAMP SAVAGE...
3

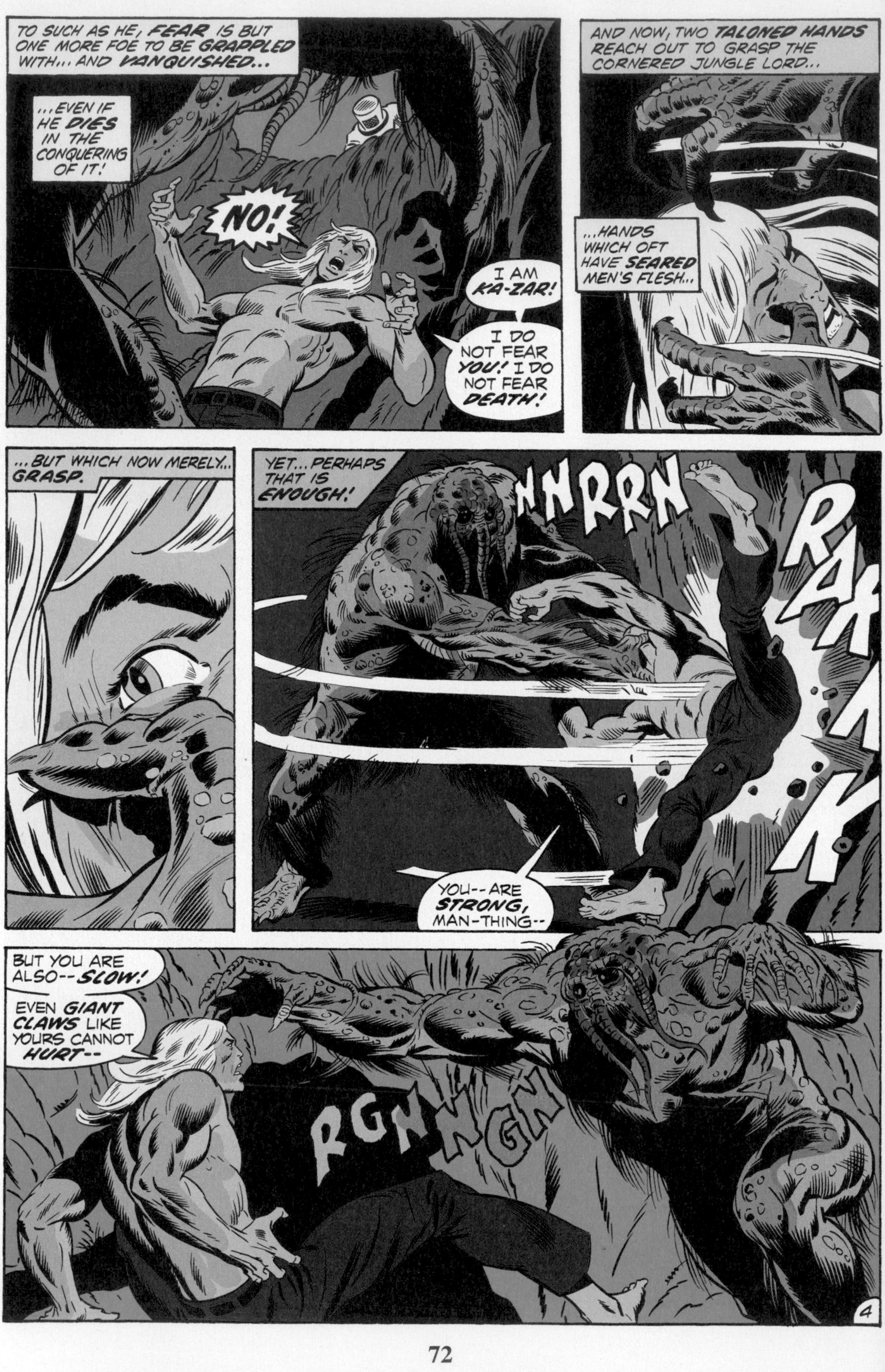
TO SUCH AS HE, FEAR IS BUT ONE MORE FOE TO BE GRAPPLED WITH... AND VANQUISHED...
...EVEN IF HE DIES IN THE CONQUERING OF IT!
NO!
I AM KA-ZAR!
I DO NOT FEAR YOU! I DO NOT FEAR DEATH!
AND NOW, TWO TALONED HANDS REACH OUT TO GRASP THE CORNERED JUNGLE LORD...
...HANDS WHICH OFT HAVE SEARED MEN'S FLESH...
...BUT WHICH NOW MERELY... GRASP.
YET... PERHAPS THAT IS ENOUGH!
NNRRN
RAKK
YOU--ARE STRONG, MAN-THING--
BUT YOU ARE ALSO--SLOW!
EVEN GIANT CLAWS LIKE YOURS CANNOT HURT--
RGNNGN
4

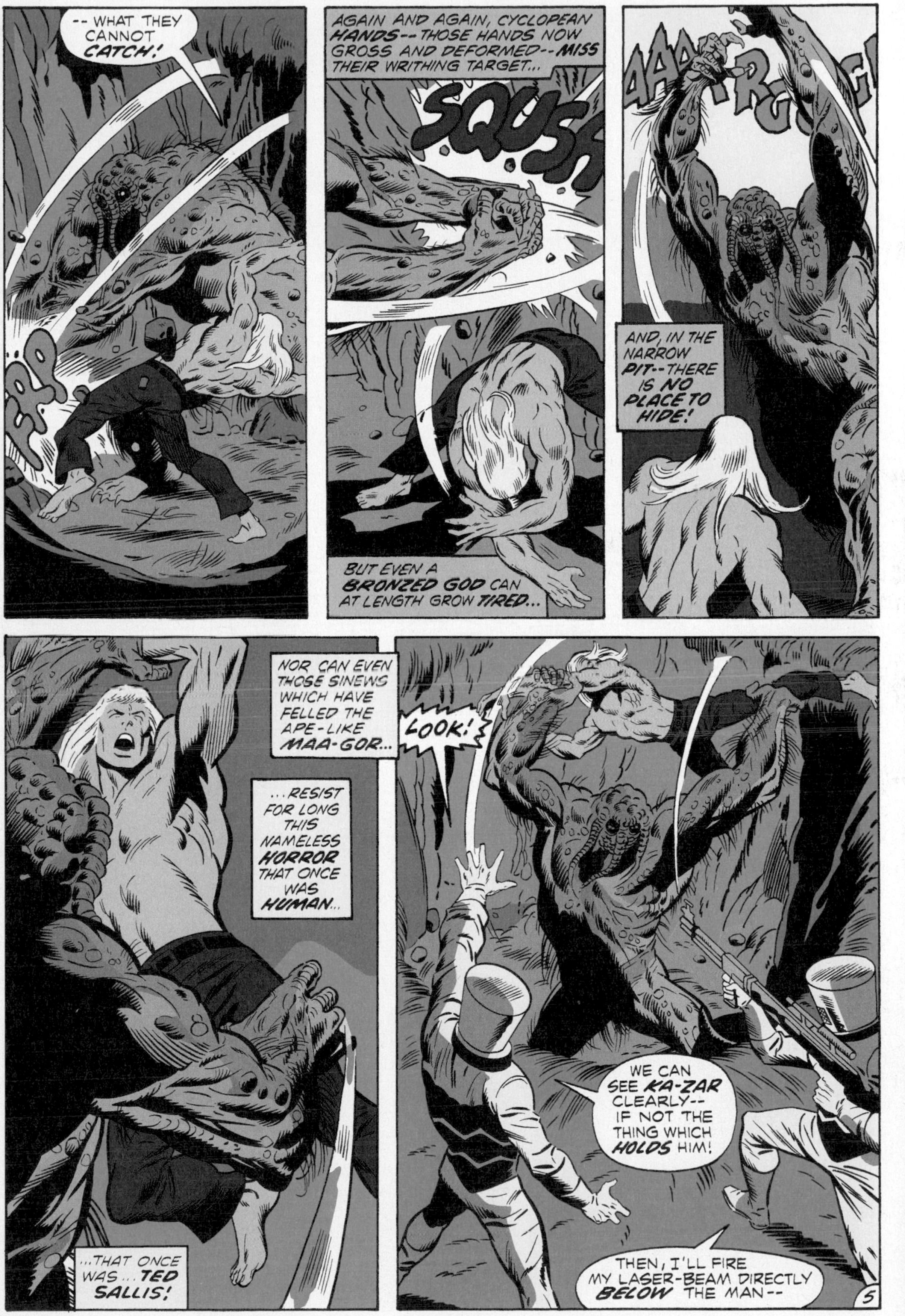
-- WHAT THEY CANNOT CATCH!
AGAIN AND AGAIN, CYCLOPEAN HANDS-- THOSE HANDS NOW GROSS AND DEFORMED-- MISS THEIR WRITHING TARGET...
SQUSH
BUT EVEN A BRONZED GOD CAN AT LENGTH GROW TIRED...
AND, IN THE NARROW PIT-- THERE IS NO PLACE TO HIDE!
NOR CAN EVEN THOSE SINEWS WHICH HAVE FELLED THE APE-LIKE MAA-GOR...
...RESIST FOR LONG THIS NAMELESS HORROR THAT ONCE WAS HUMAN...
...THAT ONCE WAS... TED SALLIS!
LOOK!
WE CAN SEE KA-ZAR CLEARLY-- IF NOT THE THING WHICH HOLDS HIM!
THEN, I'LL FIRE MY LASER-BEAM DIRECTLY BELOW THE MAN--
5

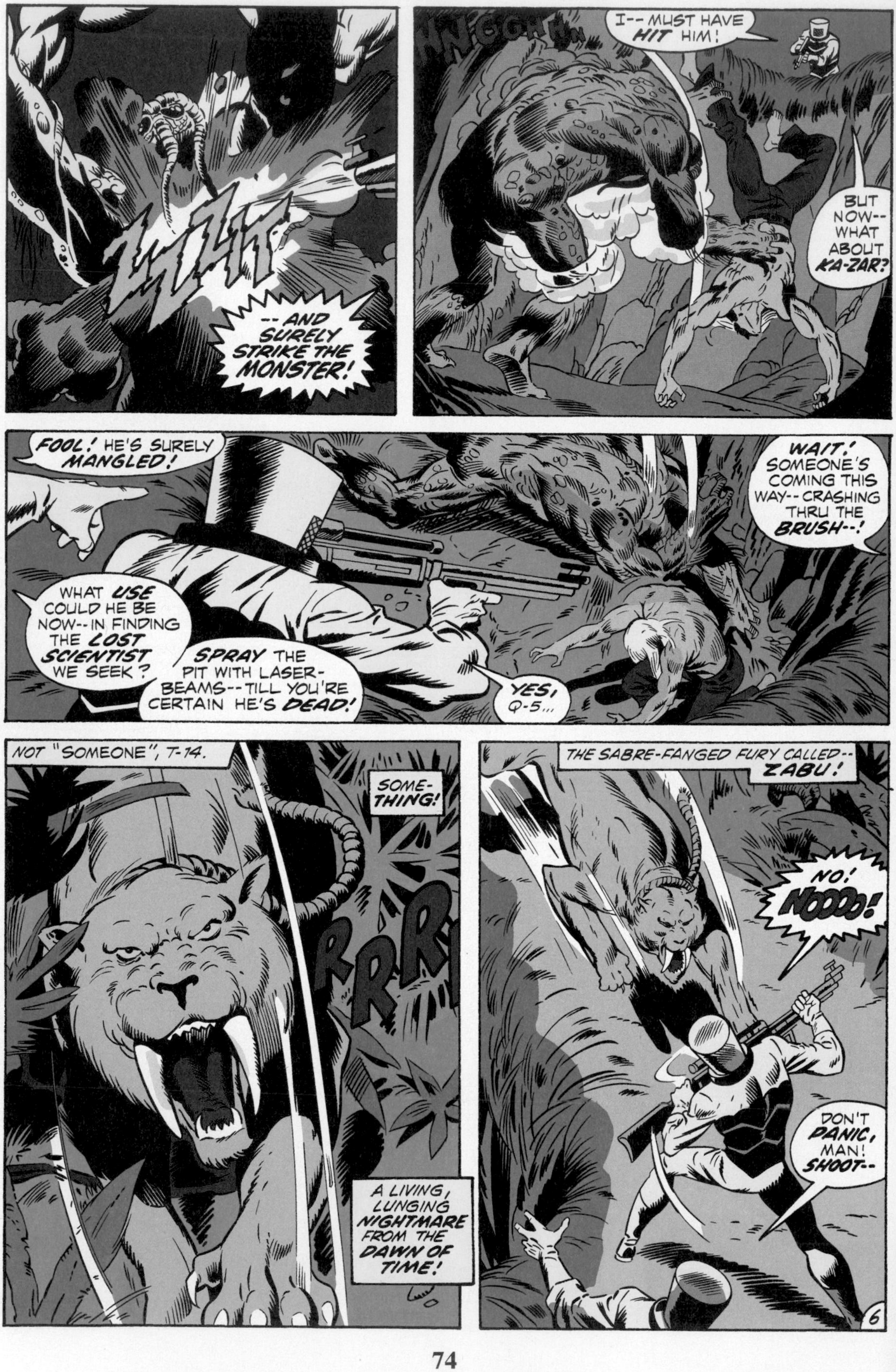
ZZZT
-- AND SURELY STRIKE THE MONSTER!
NNGGHHH
I-- MUST HAVE HIT HIM!
BUT NOW-- WHAT ABOUT KA-ZAR?
FOOL! HE'S SURELY MANGLED!
WHAT USE COULD HE BE NOW-- IN FINDING THE LOST SCIENTIST WE SEEK?
SPRAY THE PIT WITH LASER-BEAMS-- TILL YOU'RE CERTAIN HE'S DEAD!
YES, Q-5...
WAIT! SOMEONE'S COMING THIS WAY-- CRASHING THRU THE BRUSH--!
NOT "SOMEONE", T-14.
SOME-THING!
RRR
A LIVING, LUNGING NIGHTMARE FROM THE DAWN OF TIME!
THE SABRE-FANGED FURY CALLED-- ZABU!
NO! NOOOO!
DON'T PANIC, MAN! SHOOT--
6

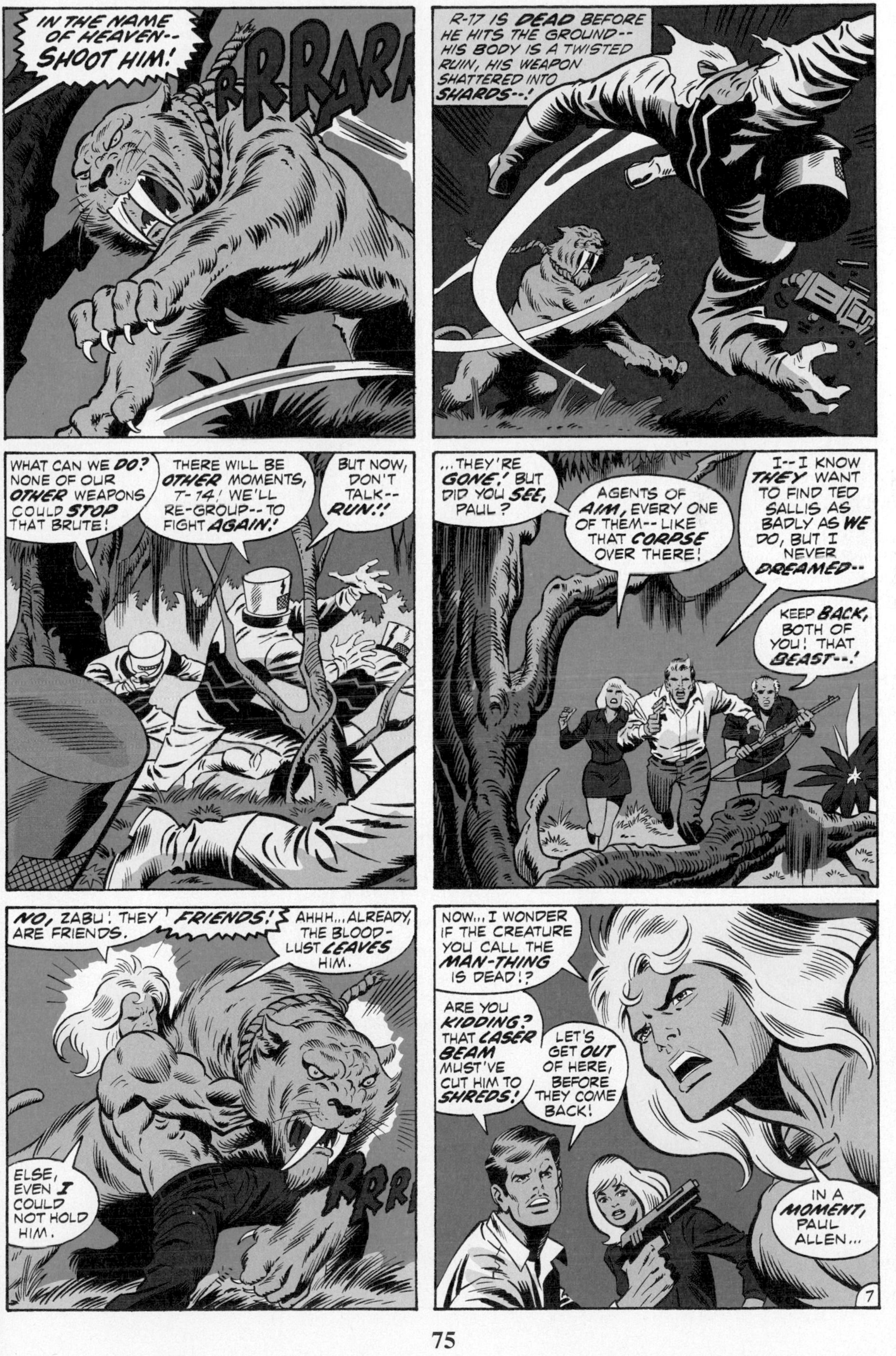
IN THE NAME OF HEAVEN-- SHOOT HIM!
RRRARR
R-17 IS DEAD BEFORE HE HITS THE GROUND-- HIS BODY IS A TWISTED RUIN, HIS WEAPON SHATTERED INTO SHARDS--!
WHAT CAN WE DO? NONE OF OUR OTHER WEAPONS COULD STOP THAT BRUTE!
THERE WILL BE OTHER MOMENTS, T-74! WE'LL RE-GROUP-- TO FIGHT AGAIN!
BUT NOW, DON'T TALK-- RUN!!
...THEY'RE GONE! BUT DID YOU SEE, PAUL?
AGENTS OF AIM, EVERY ONE OF THEM-- LIKE THAT CORPSE OVER THERE!
I--I KNOW THEY WANT TO FIND TED SALLIS AS BADLY AS WE DO, BUT I NEVER DREAMED--
KEEP BACK, BOTH OF YOU! THAT BEAST--!
NO, ZABU! THEY ARE FRIENDS.
FRIENDS!
AHHH...ALREADY, THE BLOOD-LUST LEAVES HIM.
ELSE, EVEN I COULD NOT HOLD HIM.
RRR
NOW... I WONDER IF THE CREATURE YOU CALL THE MAN-THING IS DEAD!?
ARE YOU KIDDING? THAT LASER BEAM MUST'VE CUT HIM TO SHREDS!
LET'S GET OUT OF HERE, BEFORE THEY COME BACK!
IN A MOMENT, PAUL ALLEN...
7

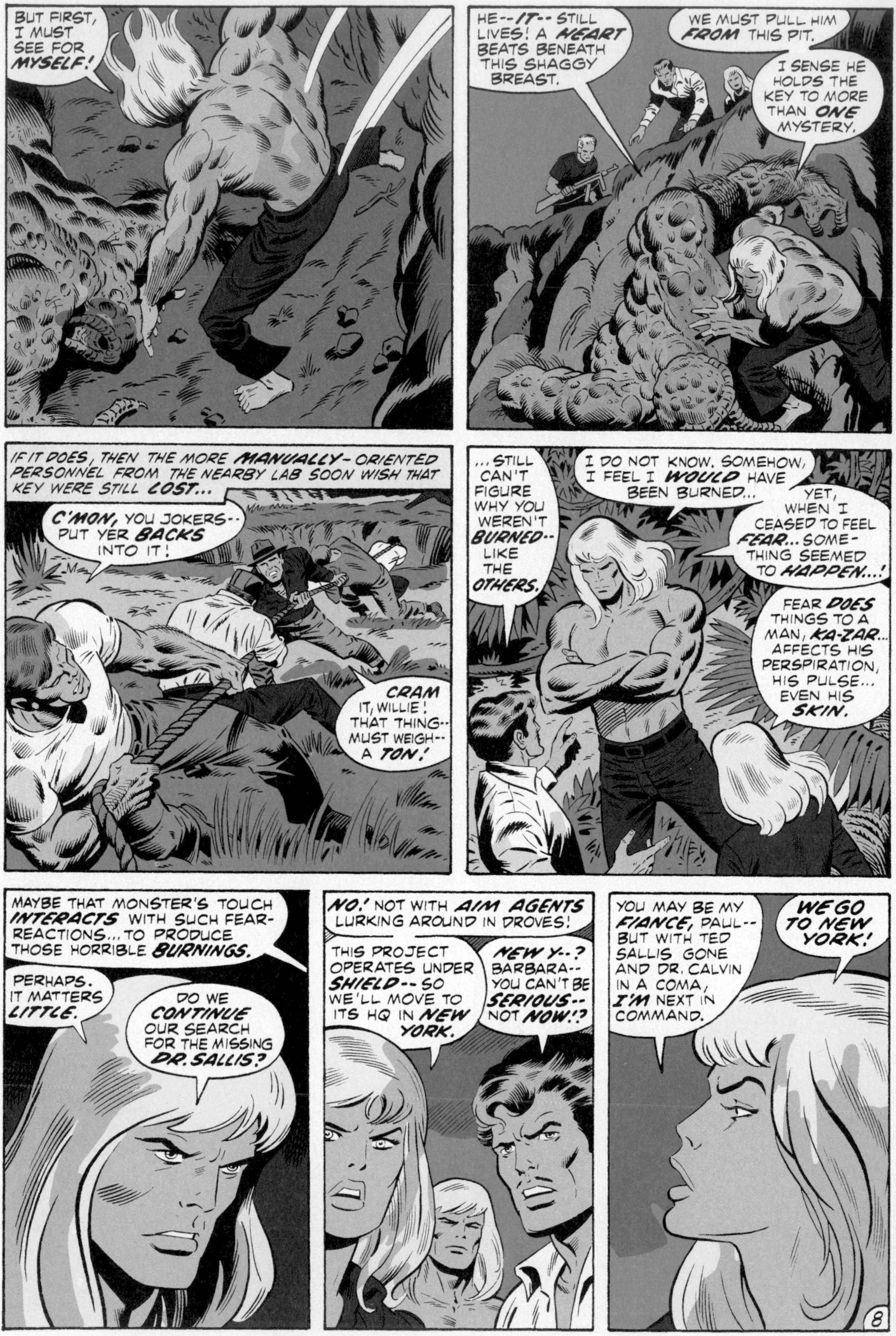
BUT FIRST, I MUST SEE FOR MYSELF!
HE--IT--STILL LIVES! A HEART BEATS BENEATH THIS SHAGGY BREAST.
WE MUST PULL HIM FROM THIS PIT.
I SENSE HE HOLDS THE KEY TO MORE THAN ONE MYSTERY.
IF IT DOES, THEN THE MORE MANUALLY-ORIENTED PERSONNEL FROM THE NEARBY LAB SOON WISH THAT KEY WERE STILL LOST...
C'MON, YOU JOKERS--PUT YER BACKS INTO IT!
CRAM IT, WILLIE! THAT THING--MUST WEIGH--A TON!
...STILL CAN'T FIGURE WHY YOU WEREN'T BURNED--LIKE THE OTHERS.
I DO NOT KNOW. SOMEHOW, I FEEL I WOULD HAVE BEEN BURNED...
YET, WHEN I CEASED TO FEEL FEAR...SOMETHING SEEMED TO HAPPEN...!
FEAR DOES THINGS TO A MAN, KA-ZAR... AFFECTS HIS PERSPIRATION, HIS PULSE... EVEN HIS SKIN.
MAYBE THAT MONSTER'S TOUCH INTERACTS WITH SUCH FEAR-REACTIONS...TO PRODUCE THOSE HORRIBLE BURNINGS.
PERHAPS. IT MATTERS LITTLE.
DO WE CONTINUE OUR SEARCH FOR THE MISSING DR. SALLIS?
NO! NOT WITH AIM AGENTS LURKING AROUND IN DROVES!
THIS PROJECT OPERATES UNDER SHIELD--SO WE'LL MOVE TO ITS HQ IN NEW YORK.
NEW Y--? BARBARA--YOU CAN'T BE SERIOUS--NOT NOW!?
YOU MAY BE MY FIANCE, PAUL--BUT WITH TED SALLIS GONE AND DR. CALVIN IN A COMA, I'M NEXT IN COMMAND.
WE GO TO NEW YORK!
8

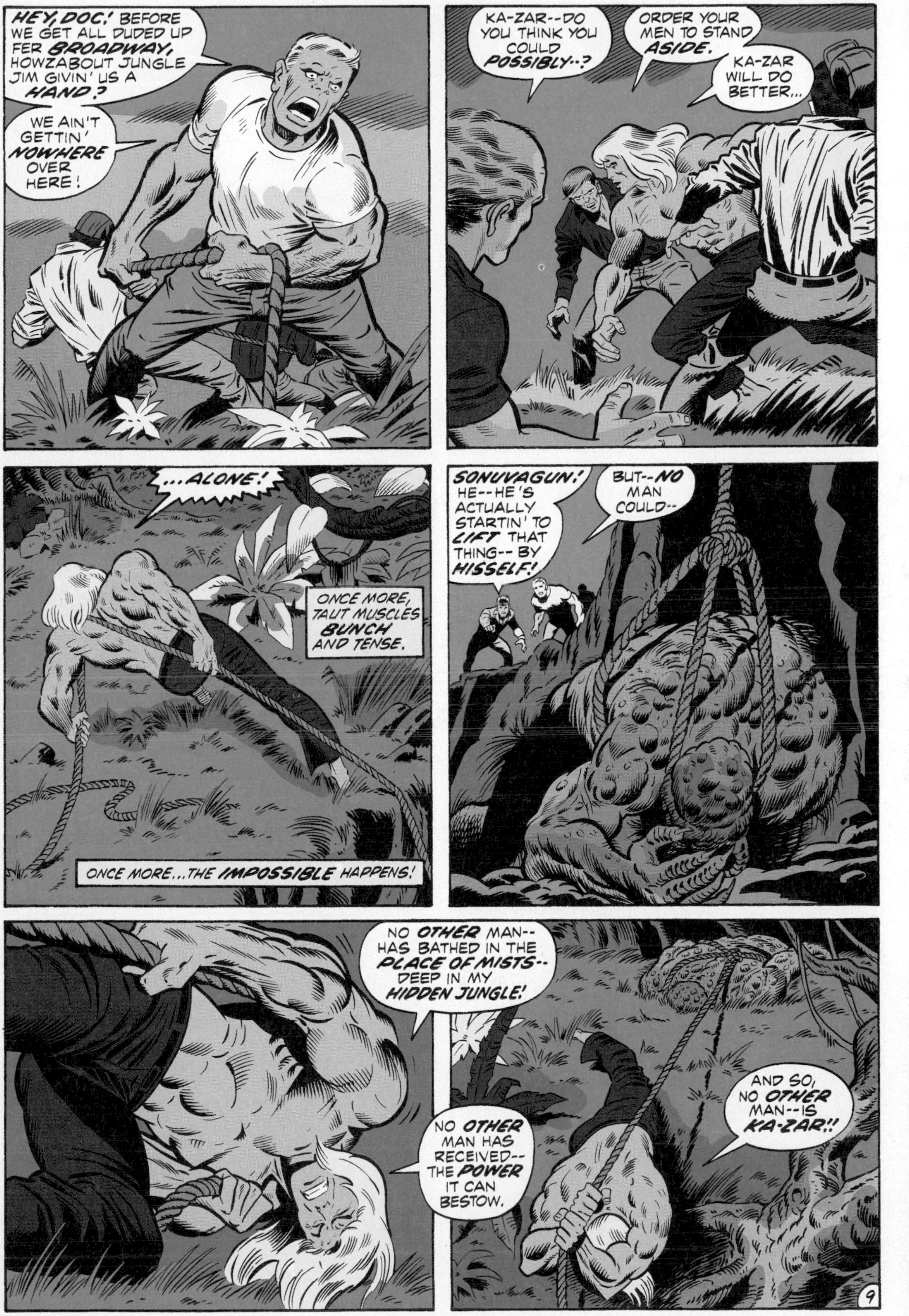
HEY, DOC! BEFORE WE GET ALL DUDED UP FER BROADWAY, HOWZABOUT JUNGLE JIM GIVIN' US A HAND?
WE AIN'T GETTIN' NOWHERE OVER HERE!
KA-ZAR--DO YOU THINK YOU COULD POSSIBLY..?
ORDER YOUR MEN TO STAND ASIDE.
KA-ZAR WILL DO BETTER...
...ALONE!
ONCE MORE, TAUT MUSCLES BUNCH AND TENSE.
ONCE MORE...THE IMPOSSIBLE HAPPENS!
SONUVAGUN! HE--HE'S ACTUALLY STARTIN' TO LIFT THAT THING-- BY HISSELF!
BUT--NO MAN COULD--
NO OTHER MAN--HAS BATHED IN THE PLACE OF MISTS--DEEP IN MY HIDDEN JUNGLE!
NO OTHER MAN HAS RECEIVED--THE POWER IT CAN BESTOW.
AND SO, NO OTHER MAN--IS KA-ZAR!!
9

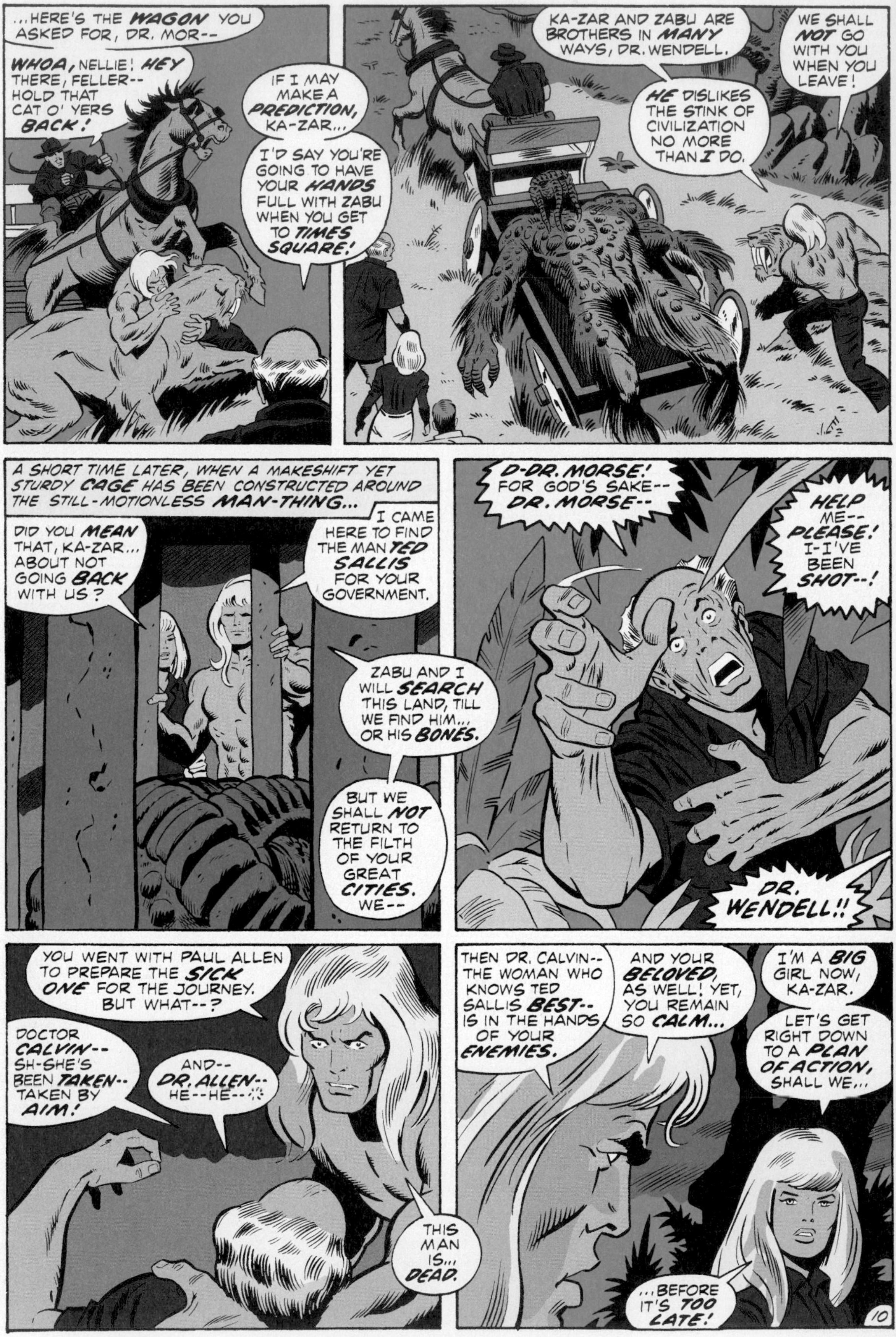
...HERE'S THE WAGON YOU ASKED FOR, DR. MOR--
WHOA, NELLIE! HEY THERE, FELLER-- HOLD THAT CAT O' YERS BACK!
IF I MAY MAKE A PREDICTION, KA-ZAR...
I'D SAY YOU'RE GOING TO HAVE YOUR HANDS FULL WITH ZABU WHEN YOU GET TO TIMES SQUARE!
KA-ZAR AND ZABU ARE BROTHERS IN MANY WAYS, DR. WENDELL.
HE DISLIKES THE STINK OF CIVILIZATION NO MORE THAN I DO.
WE SHALL NOT GO WITH YOU WHEN YOU LEAVE!
A SHORT TIME LATER, WHEN A MAKESHIFT YET STURDY CAGE HAS BEEN CONSTRUCTED AROUND THE STILL-MOTIONLESS MAN-THING...
DID YOU MEAN THAT, KA-ZAR... ABOUT NOT GOING BACK WITH US?
I CAME HERE TO FIND THE MAN TED SALLIS FOR YOUR GOVERNMENT.
ZABU AND I WILL SEARCH THIS LAND, TILL WE FIND HIM... OR HIS BONES.
BUT WE SHALL NOT RETURN TO THE FILTH OF YOUR GREAT CITIES. WE--
D-DR. MORSE! FOR GOD'S SAKE-- DR. MORSE--
HELP ME-- PLEASE! I-I'VE BEEN SHOT--!
DR. WENDELL!!
YOU WENT WITH PAUL ALLEN TO PREPARE THE SICK ONE FOR THE JOURNEY. BUT WHAT--?
DOCTOR CALVIN-- SH-SHE'S BEEN TAKEN-- TAKEN BY AIM!
AND-- DR. ALLEN-- HE--HE--
THIS MAN IS... DEAD.
THEN DR. CALVIN-- THE WOMAN WHO KNOWS TED SALLIS BEST-- IS IN THE HANDS OF YOUR ENEMIES.
AND YOUR BELOVED, AS WELL! YET, YOU REMAIN SO CALM...
I'M A BIG GIRL NOW, KA-ZAR.
LET'S GET RIGHT DOWN TO A PLAN OF ACTION, SHALL WE...
...BEFORE IT'S TOO LATE!
10

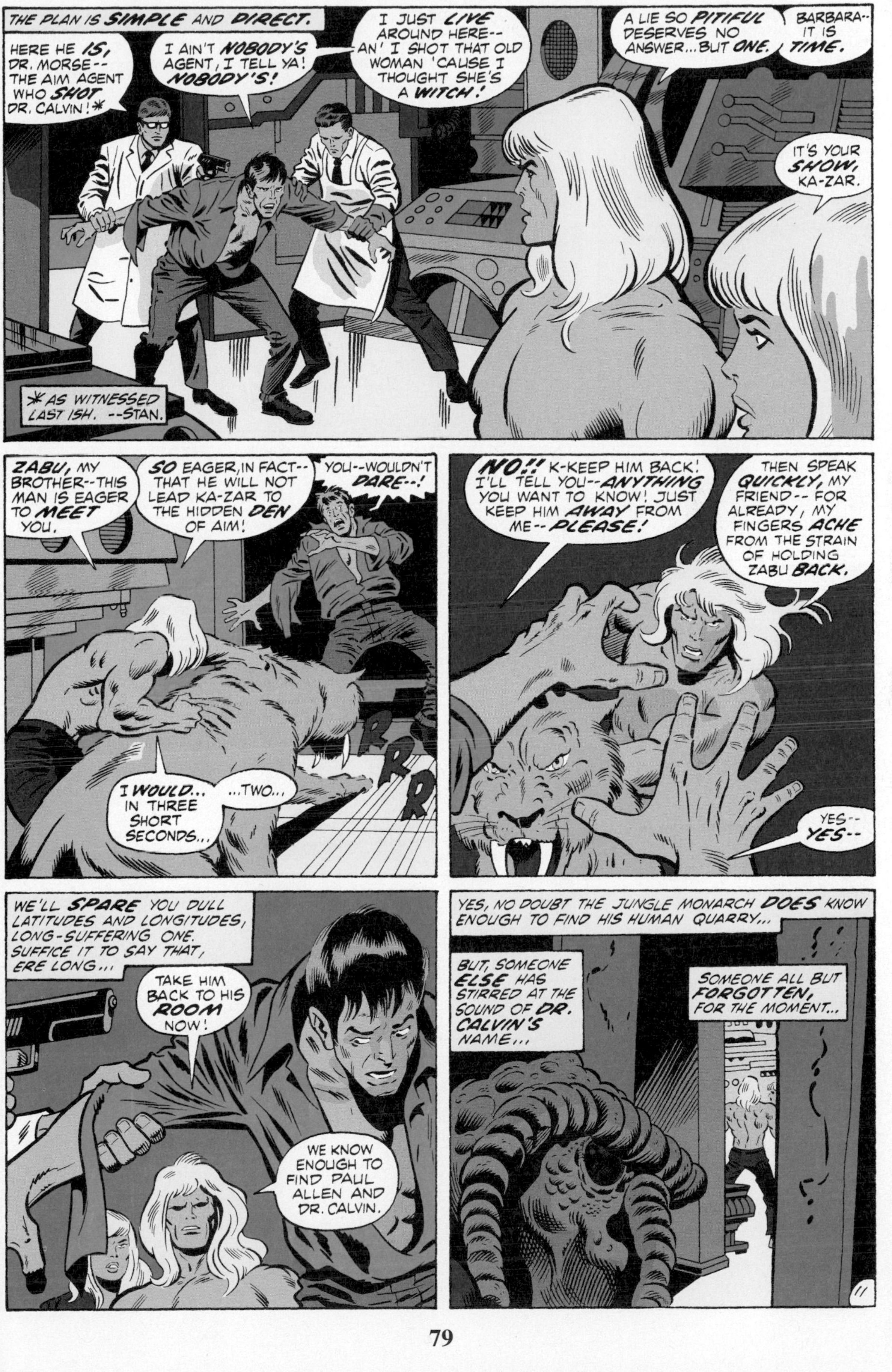
THE PLAN IS SIMPLE AND DIRECT.
HERE HE IS, DR. MORSE-- THE AIM AGENT WHO SHOT DR. CALVIN! *
I AIN'T NOBODY'S AGENT, I TELL YA! NOBODY'S!
I JUST LIVE AROUND HERE-- AN' I SHOT THAT OLD WOMAN 'CAUSE I THOUGHT SHE'S A WITCH!
A LIE SO PITIFUL DESERVES NO ANSWER... BUT ONE.
BARBARA-- IT IS TIME.
IT'S YOUR SHOW, KA-ZAR.
* AS WITNESSED LAST ISH. --STAN.
ZABU, MY BROTHER--THIS MAN IS EAGER TO MEET YOU.
SO EAGER, IN FACT-- THAT HE WILL NOT LEAD KA-ZAR TO THE HIDDEN DEN OF AIM!
YOU--WOULDN'T DARE--!
I WOULD... IN THREE SHORT SECONDS...
...TWO...
RRR
NO!! K-KEEP HIM BACK! I'LL TELL YOU--ANYTHING YOU WANT TO KNOW! JUST KEEP HIM AWAY FROM ME--PLEASE!
THEN SPEAK QUICKLY, MY FRIEND-- FOR ALREADY, MY FINGERS ACHE FROM THE STRAIN OF HOLDING ZABU BACK.
YES-- YES--
WE'LL SPARE YOU DULL LATITUDES AND LONGITUDES, LONG-SUFFERING ONE. SUFFICE IT TO SAY THAT, ERE LONG...
TAKE HIM BACK TO HIS ROOM NOW!
WE KNOW ENOUGH TO FIND PAUL ALLEN AND DR. CALVIN.
YES, NO DOUBT THE JUNGLE MONARCH DOES KNOW ENOUGH TO FIND HIS HUMAN QUARRY...
BUT, SOMEONE ELSE HAS STIRRED AT THE SOUND OF DR. CALVIN'S NAME...
SOMEONE ALL BUT FORGOTTEN, FOR THE MOMENT...
11

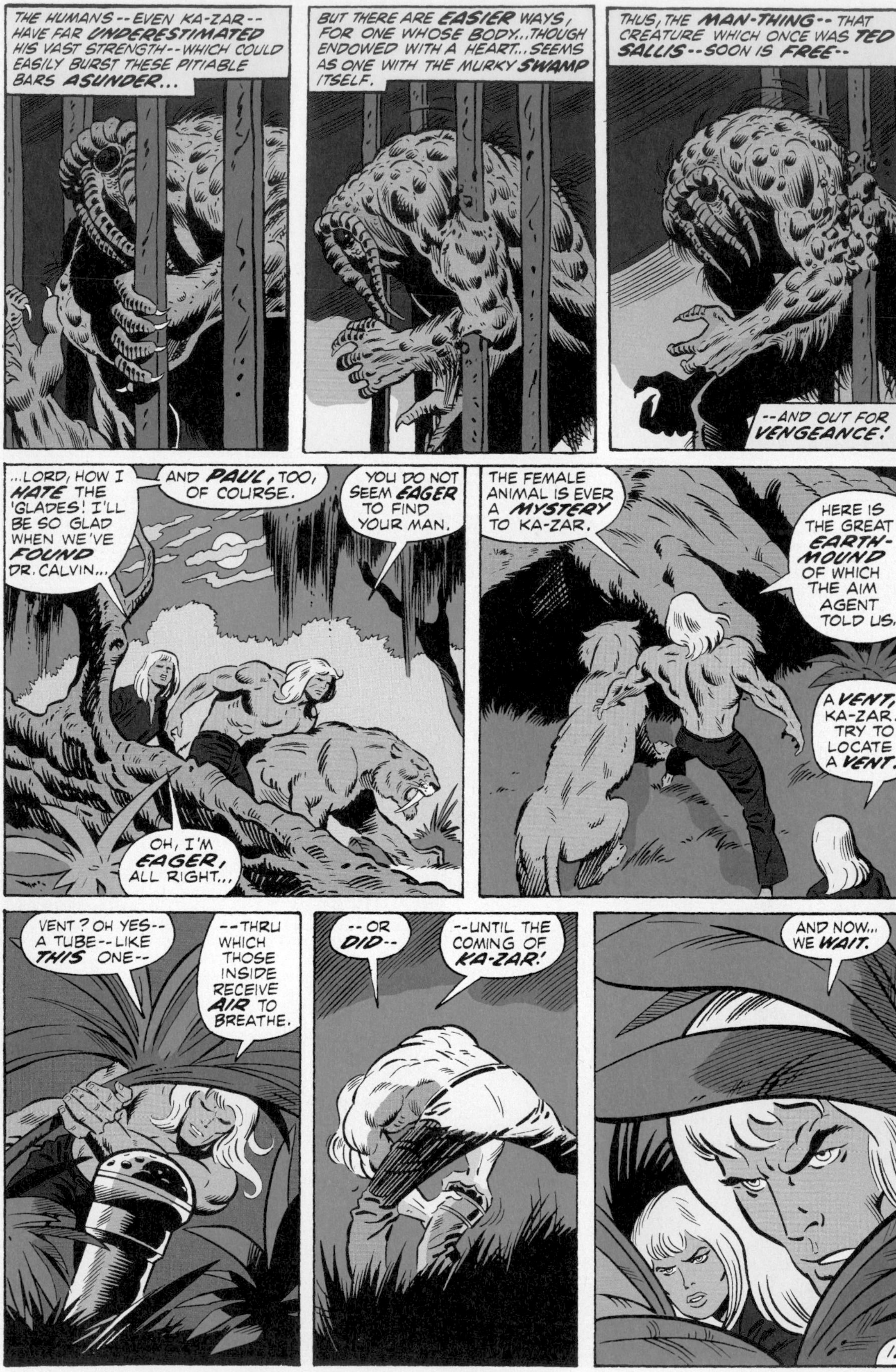
THE HUMANS -- EVEN KA-ZAR -- HAVE FAR UNDERESTIMATED HIS VAST STRENGTH -- WHICH COULD EASILY BURST THESE PITIABLE BARS ASUNDER...
BUT THERE ARE EASIER WAYS, FOR ONE WHOSE BODY... THOUGH ENDOWED WITH A HEART... SEEMS AS ONE WITH THE MURKY SWAMP ITSELF.
THUS, THE MAN-THING -- THAT CREATURE WHICH ONCE WAS TED SALLIS -- SOON IS FREE --
-- AND OUT FOR VENGEANCE!
...LORD, HOW I HATE THE 'GLADES! I'LL BE SO GLAD WHEN WE'VE FOUND DR. CALVIN...
AND PAUL, TOO, OF COURSE.
YOU DO NOT SEEM EAGER TO FIND YOUR MAN.
OH, I'M EAGER, ALL RIGHT...
THE FEMALE ANIMAL IS EVER A MYSTERY TO KA-ZAR.
HERE IS THE GREAT EARTH-MOUND OF WHICH THE AIM AGENT TOLD US...
A VENT, KA-ZAR. TRY TO LOCATE A VENT!
VENT? OH YES -- A TUBE -- LIKE THIS ONE --
-- THRU WHICH THOSE INSIDE RECEIVE AIR TO BREATHE.
-- OR DID --
-- UNTIL THE COMING OF KA-ZAR!
AND NOW... WE WAIT.
12

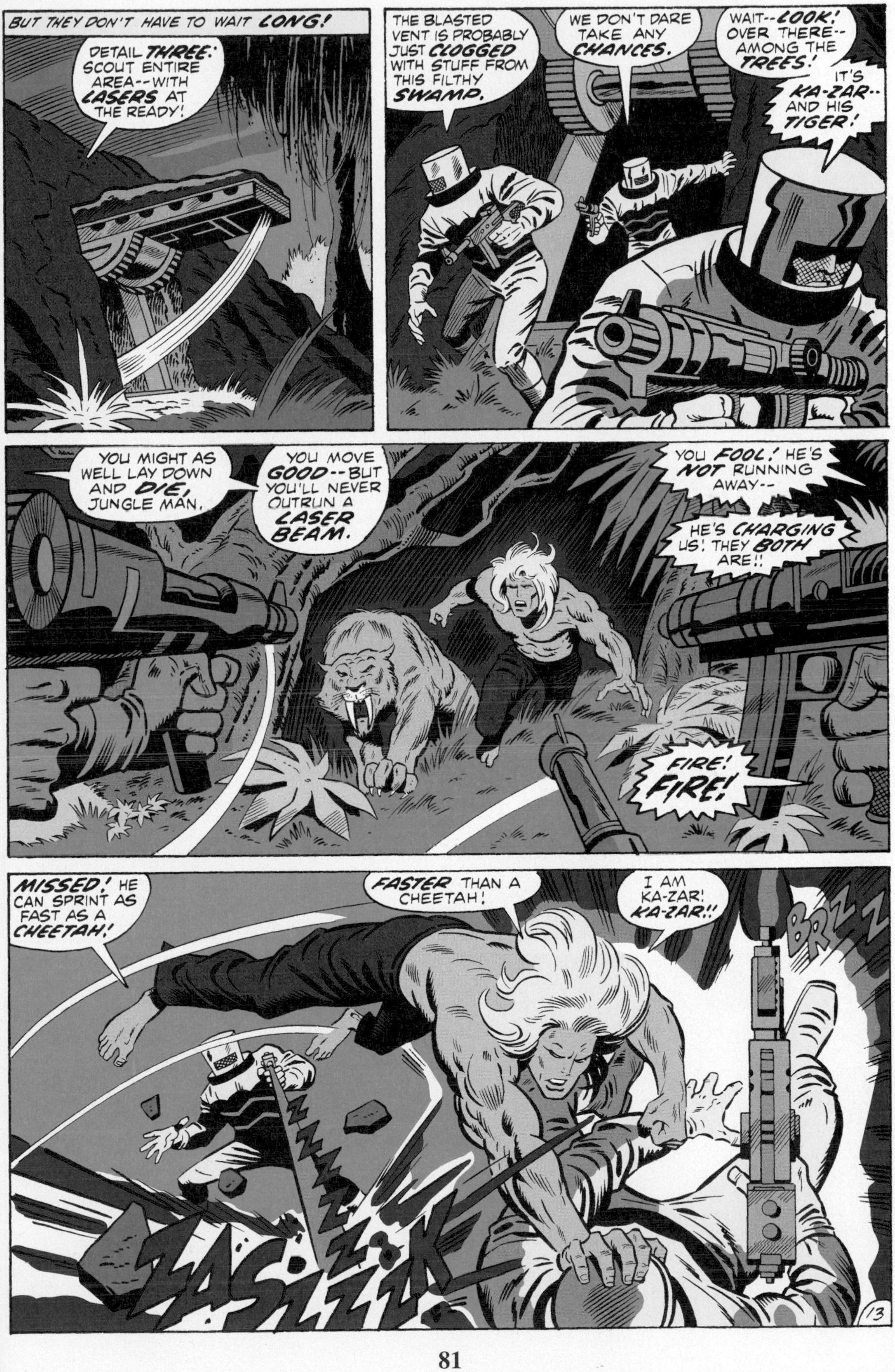
BUT THEY DON'T HAVE TO WAIT LONG!
DETAIL THREE: SCOUT ENTIRE AREA--WITH LASERS AT THE READY!
THE BLASTED VENT IS PROBABLY JUST CLOGGED WITH STUFF FROM THIS FILTHY SWAMP.
WE DON'T DARE TAKE ANY CHANCES.
WAIT--LOOK! OVER THERE--AMONG THE TREES!
IT'S KA-ZAR--AND HIS TIGER!
YOU MIGHT AS WELL LAY DOWN AND DIE, JUNGLE MAN.
YOU MOVE GOOD--BUT YOU'LL NEVER OUTRUN A LASER BEAM.
YOU FOOL! HE'S NOT RUNNING AWAY--
HE'S CHARGING US! THEY BOTH ARE!!
FIRE! FIRE!
MISSED! HE CAN SPRINT AS FAST AS A CHEETAH!
FASTER THAN A CHEETAH!
I AM KA-ZAR! KA-ZAR!!
BRZZZ
ZASZZZK
13

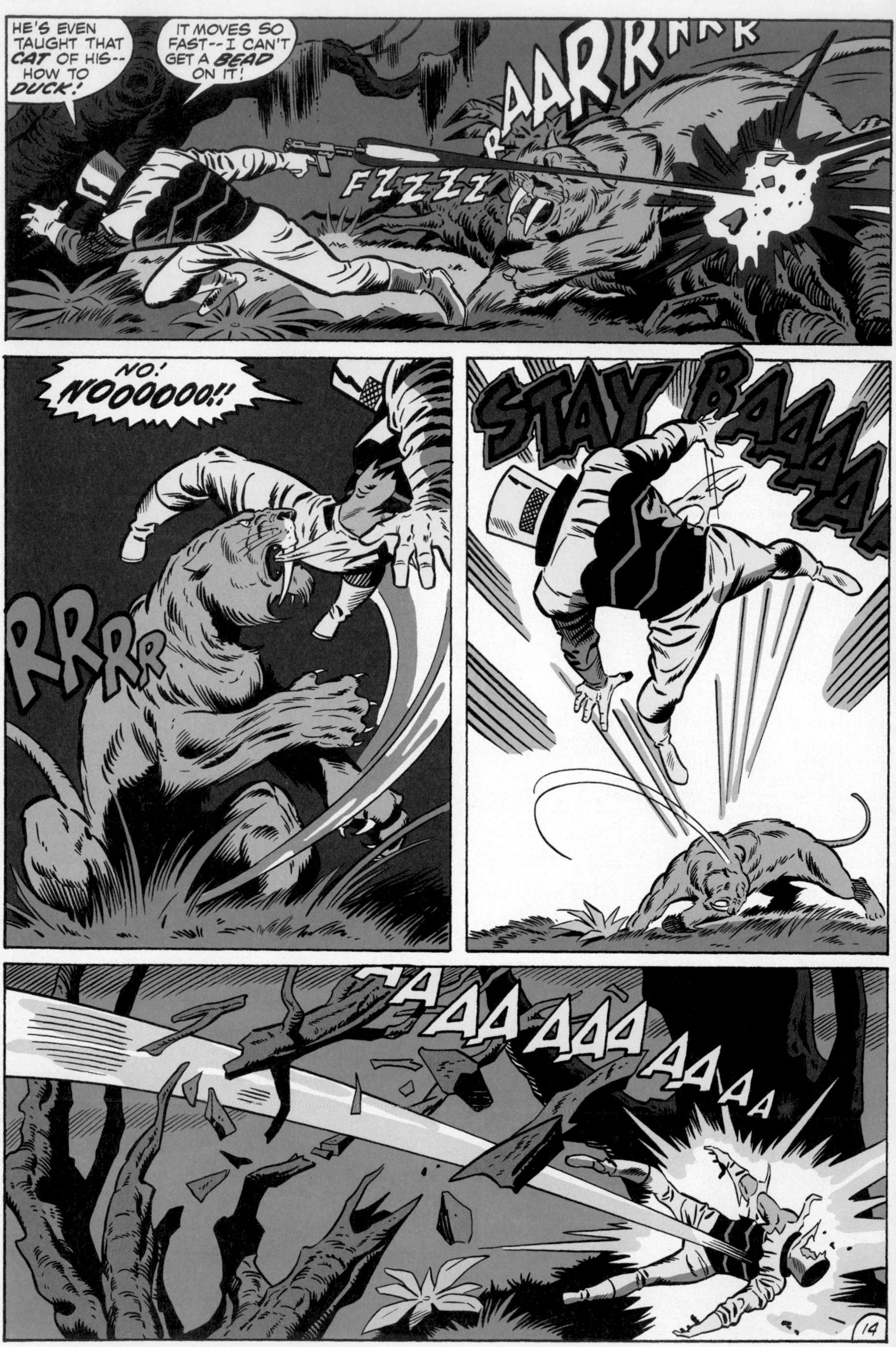
HE'S EVEN TAUGHT THAT CAT OF HIS-- HOW TO DUCK!
IT MOVES SO FAST--I CAN'T GET A BEAD ON IT!
RAARRRRRR
FZZZZZ
NO! NOOOOOO!!
RRRR
STAY BAAAAA
AAAAAAAAAAAA
14

NOW, BUT **ONE** GOLD-GARBED FIGURE **REMAINS!**

ZASST

HOW TEMPTING IT IS TO **PLAY** WITH THIS GUN-WIELDING OAF--TO **TOY** WITH HIM--TO **STALK** HIM, LIKE SOME ANTELOPE OR BOAR!

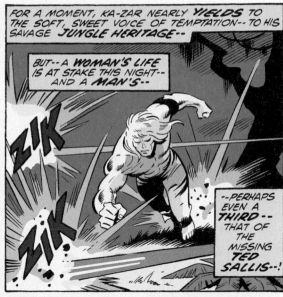

FOR A MOMENT, KA-ZAR NEARLY **YIELDS** TO THE SOFT, SWEET VOICE OF TEMPTATION--TO HIS SAVAGE **JUNGLE HERITAGE**--

BUT--A **WOMAN'S** LIFE IS AT STAKE THIS NIGHT--AND A **MAN'S**--

ZIK ZIK

--PERHAPS EVEN A **THIRD**--THAT OF THE MISSING **TED SALLIS**--!

AND SO--

BPOK!

15

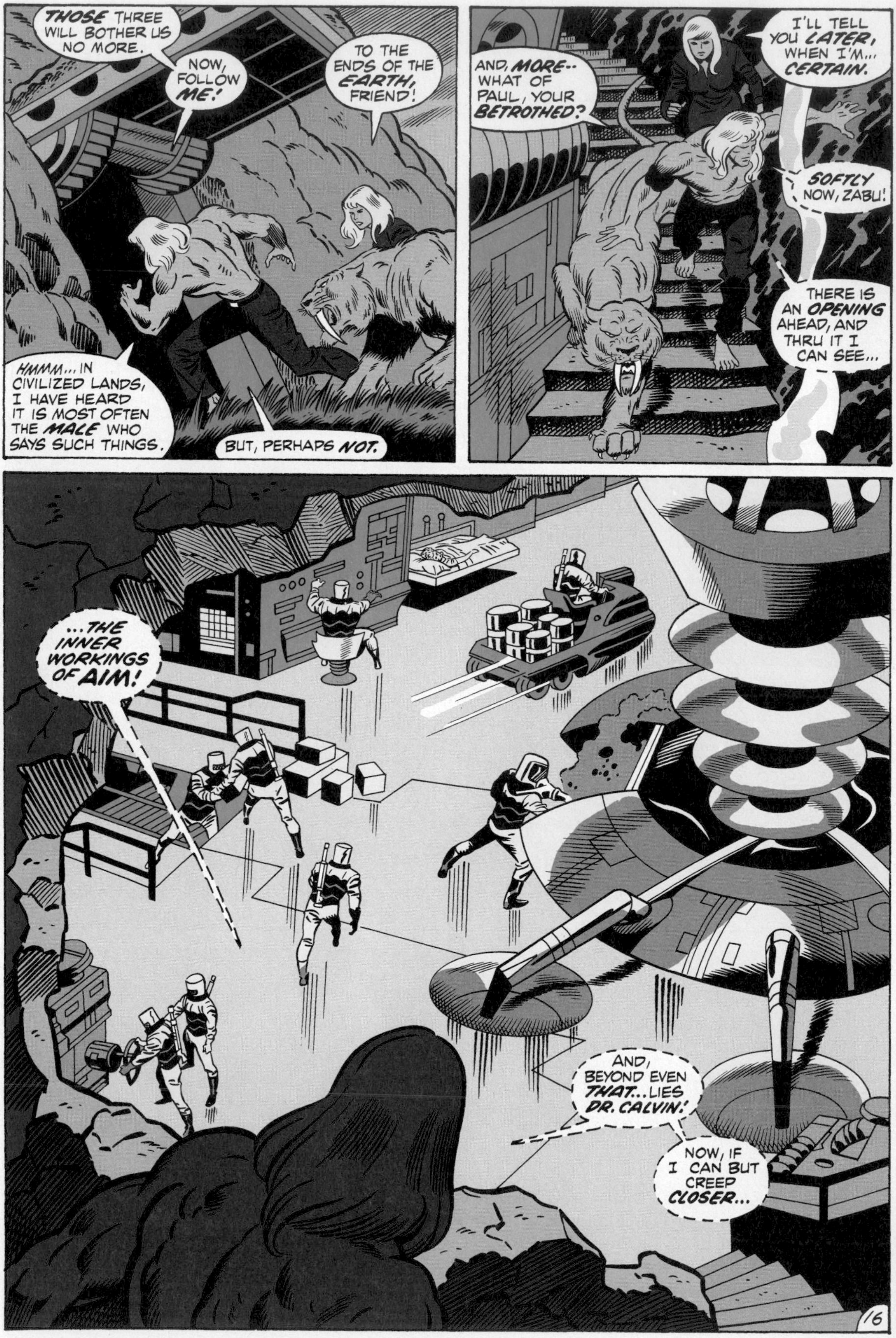

THOSE THREE WILL BOTHER US NO MORE.
NOW, FOLLOW ME!
TO THE ENDS OF THE EARTH, FRIEND!
HMMM... IN CIVILIZED LANDS, I HAVE HEARD IT IS MOST OFTEN THE MALE WHO SAYS SUCH THINGS.
BUT, PERHAPS NOT.
AND, MORE-- WHAT OF PAUL, YOUR BETROTHED?
I'LL TELL YOU LATER, WHEN I'M... CERTAIN.
SOFTLY NOW, ZABU!
THERE IS AN OPENING AHEAD, AND THRU IT I CAN SEE...
...THE INNER WORKINGS OF AIM!
AND, BEYOND EVEN THAT... LIES DR. CALVIN!
NOW, IF I CAN BUT CREEP CLOSER...
16

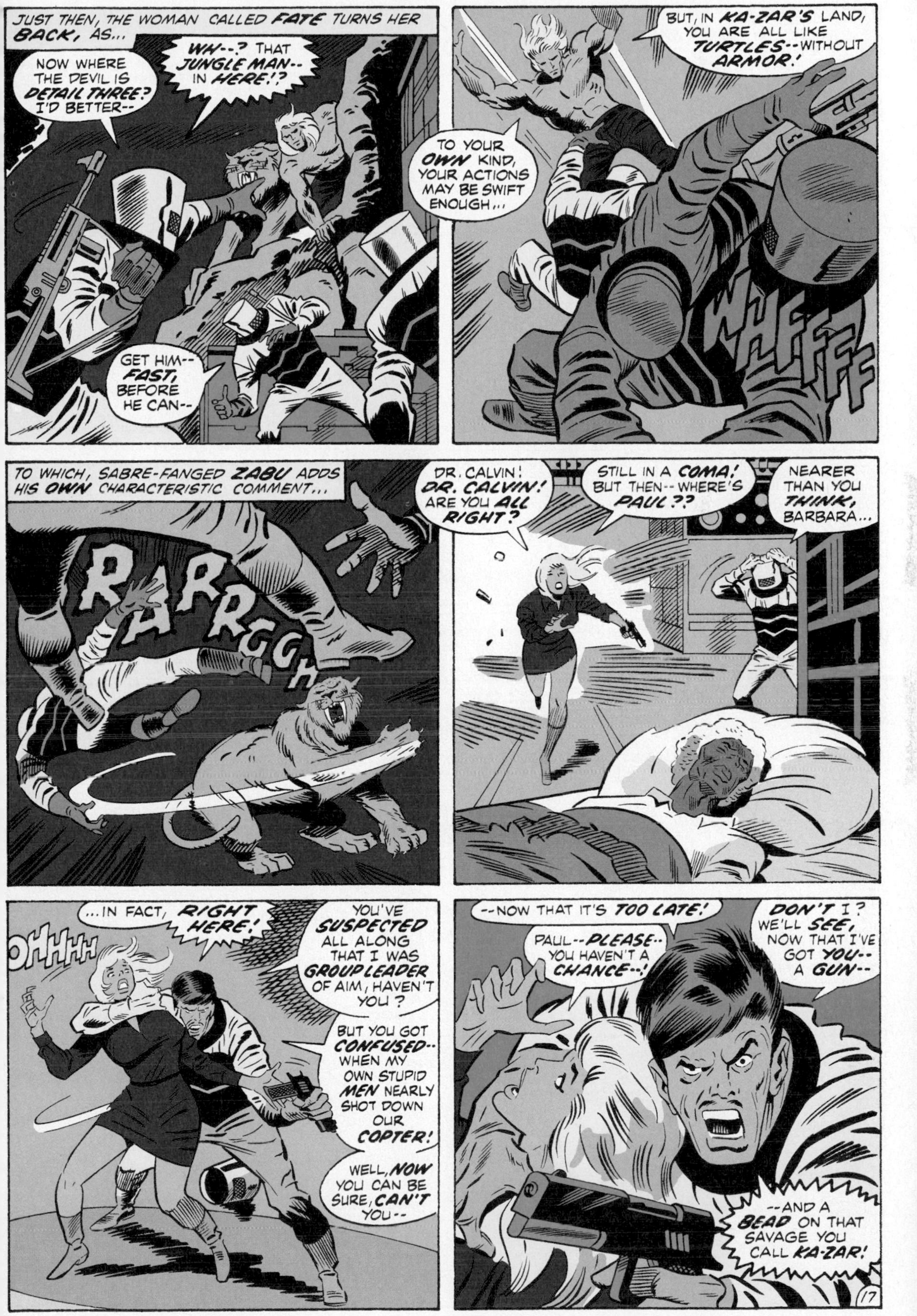
JUST THEN, THE WOMAN CALLED FATE TURNS HER BACK, AS...
NOW WHERE THE DEVIL IS DETAIL THREE? I'D BETTER--
WH--? THAT JUNGLE MAN-- IN HERE!?
GET HIM-- FAST, BEFORE HE CAN--
BUT, IN KA-ZAR'S LAND, YOU ARE ALL LIKE TURTLES--WITHOUT ARMOR!
TO YOUR OWN KIND, YOUR ACTIONS MAY BE SWIFT ENOUGH...
WHFFFF
TO WHICH, SABRE-FANGED ZABU ADDS HIS OWN CHARACTERISTIC COMMENT...
RARRGGH
DR. CALVIN! DR. CALVIN! ARE YOU ALL RIGHT?
STILL IN A COMA! BUT THEN--WHERE'S PAUL??
NEARER THAN YOU THINK, BARBARA...
...IN FACT, RIGHT HERE!
OHHHH
YOU'VE SUSPECTED ALL ALONG THAT I WAS GROUP LEADER OF AIM, HAVEN'T YOU?
BUT YOU GOT CONFUSED-- WHEN MY OWN STUPID MEN NEARLY SHOT DOWN OUR COPTER!
WELL, NOW YOU CAN BE SURE, CAN'T YOU--
--NOW THAT IT'S TOO LATE!
PAUL--PLEASE-- YOU HAVEN'T A CHANCE--!
DON'T I? WE'LL SEE, NOW THAT I'VE GOT YOU-- A GUN--
--AND A BEAD ON THAT SAVAGE YOU CALL KA-ZAR!
17

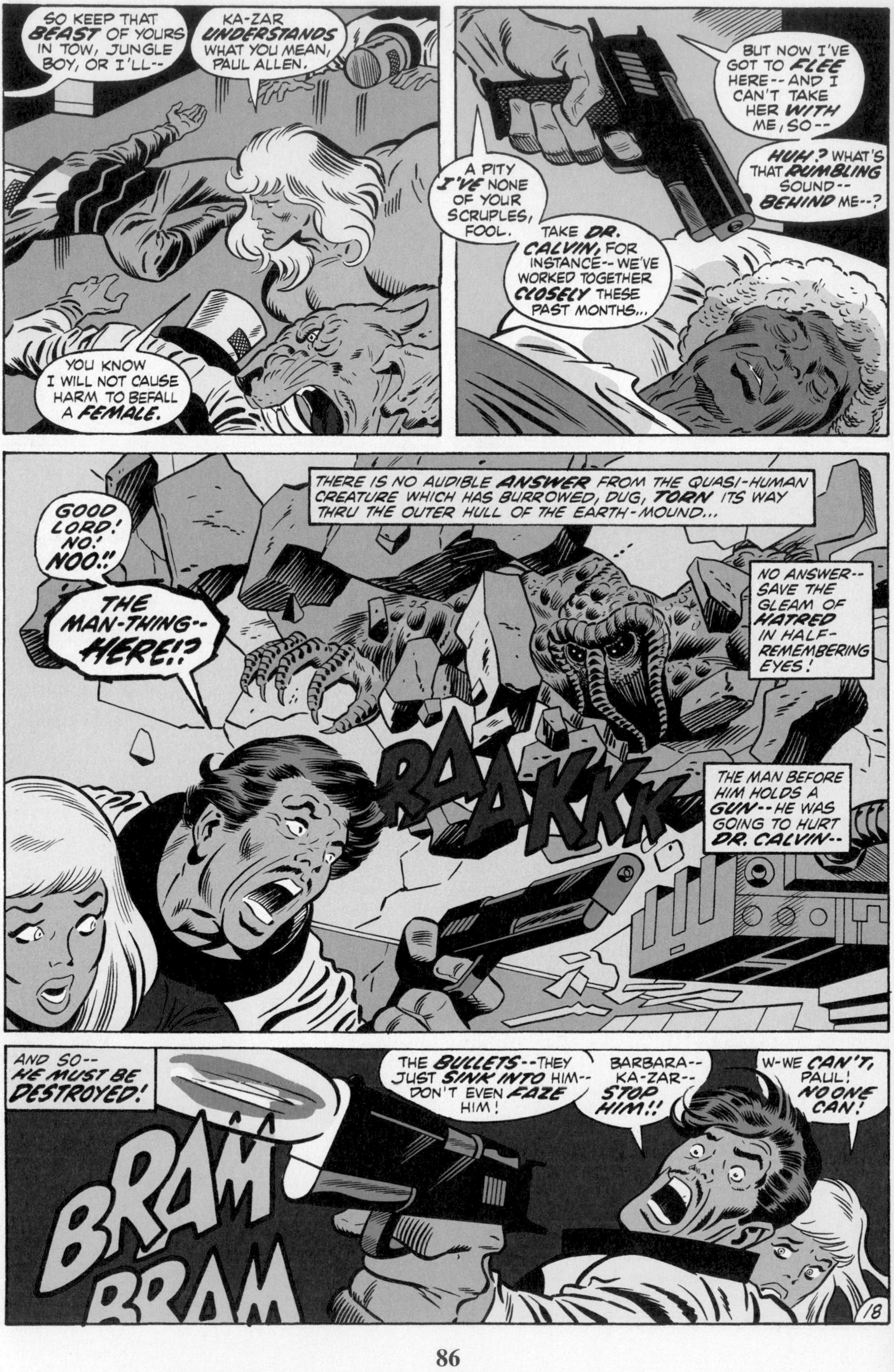
SO KEEP THAT BEAST OF YOURS IN TOW, JUNGLE BOY, OR I'LL--
KA-ZAR UNDERSTANDS WHAT YOU MEAN, PAUL ALLEN.
YOU KNOW I WILL NOT CAUSE HARM TO BEFALL A FEMALE.
A PITY I'VE NONE OF YOUR SCRUPLES, FOOL.
TAKE DR. CALVIN, FOR INSTANCE-- WE'VE WORKED TOGETHER CLOSELY THESE PAST MONTHS...
BUT NOW I'VE GOT TO FLEE HERE-- AND I CAN'T TAKE HER WITH ME, SO--
HUH? WHAT'S THAT RUMBLING SOUND-- BEHIND ME--?
THERE IS NO AUDIBLE ANSWER FROM THE QUASI-HUMAN CREATURE WHICH HAS BURROWED, DUG, TORN ITS WAY THRU THE OUTER HULL OF THE EARTH-MOUND...
GOOD LORD! NO! NOO!!
THE MAN-THING-- HERE!?
NO ANSWER-- SAVE THE GLEAM OF HATRED IN HALF-REMEMBERING EYES!
RAAKKK
THE MAN BEFORE HIM HOLDS A GUN-- HE WAS GOING TO HURT DR. CALVIN--
AND SO-- HE MUST BE DESTROYED!
THE BULLETS--THEY JUST SINK INTO HIM-- DON'T EVEN FAZE HIM!
BARBARA-- KA-ZAR-- STOP HIM!!
W-WE CAN'T, PAUL! NO ONE CAN!
BRAM
BRAM
18

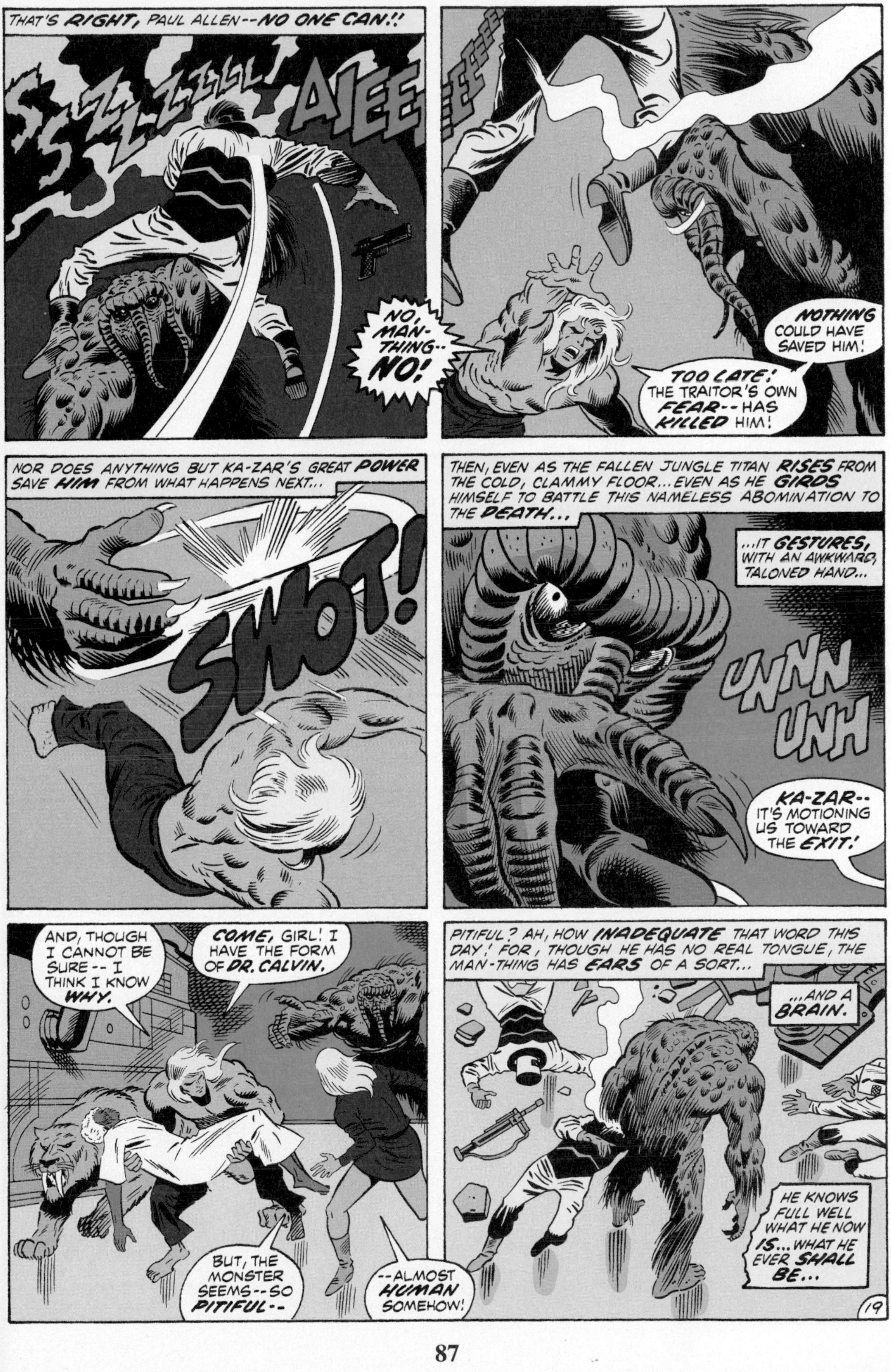
THAT'S RIGHT, PAUL ALLEN--NO ONE CAN!!
S-SZZ-ZZZZLLL!
AIEEEEEEEEEEE
NO, MAN-THING--NO!
NOTHING COULD HAVE SAVED HIM!
TOO LATE! THE TRAITOR'S OWN FEAR--HAS KILLED HIM!
NOR DOES ANYTHING BUT KA-ZAR'S GREAT POWER SAVE HIM FROM WHAT HAPPENS NEXT...
SWOT!
THEN, EVEN AS THE FALLEN JUNGLE TITAN RISES FROM THE COLD, CLAMMY FLOOR... EVEN AS HE GIRDS HIMSELF TO BATTLE THIS NAMELESS ABOMINATION TO THE DEATH...
...IT GESTURES, WITH AN AWKWARD, TALONED HAND...
UNNN UNH
KA-ZAR-- IT'S MOTIONING US TOWARD THE EXIT!
AND, THOUGH I CANNOT BE SURE -- I THINK I KNOW WHY.
COME, GIRL! I HAVE THE FORM OF DR. CALVIN.
BUT, THE MONSTER SEEMS--SO PITIFUL--
--ALMOST HUMAN SOMEHOW!
PITIFUL? AH, HOW INADEQUATE THAT WORD THIS DAY! FOR, THOUGH HE HAS NO REAL TONGUE, THE MAN-THING HAS EARS OF A SORT...
...AND A BRAIN.
HE KNOWS FULL WELL WHAT HE NOW IS... WHAT HE EVER SHALL BE...
19

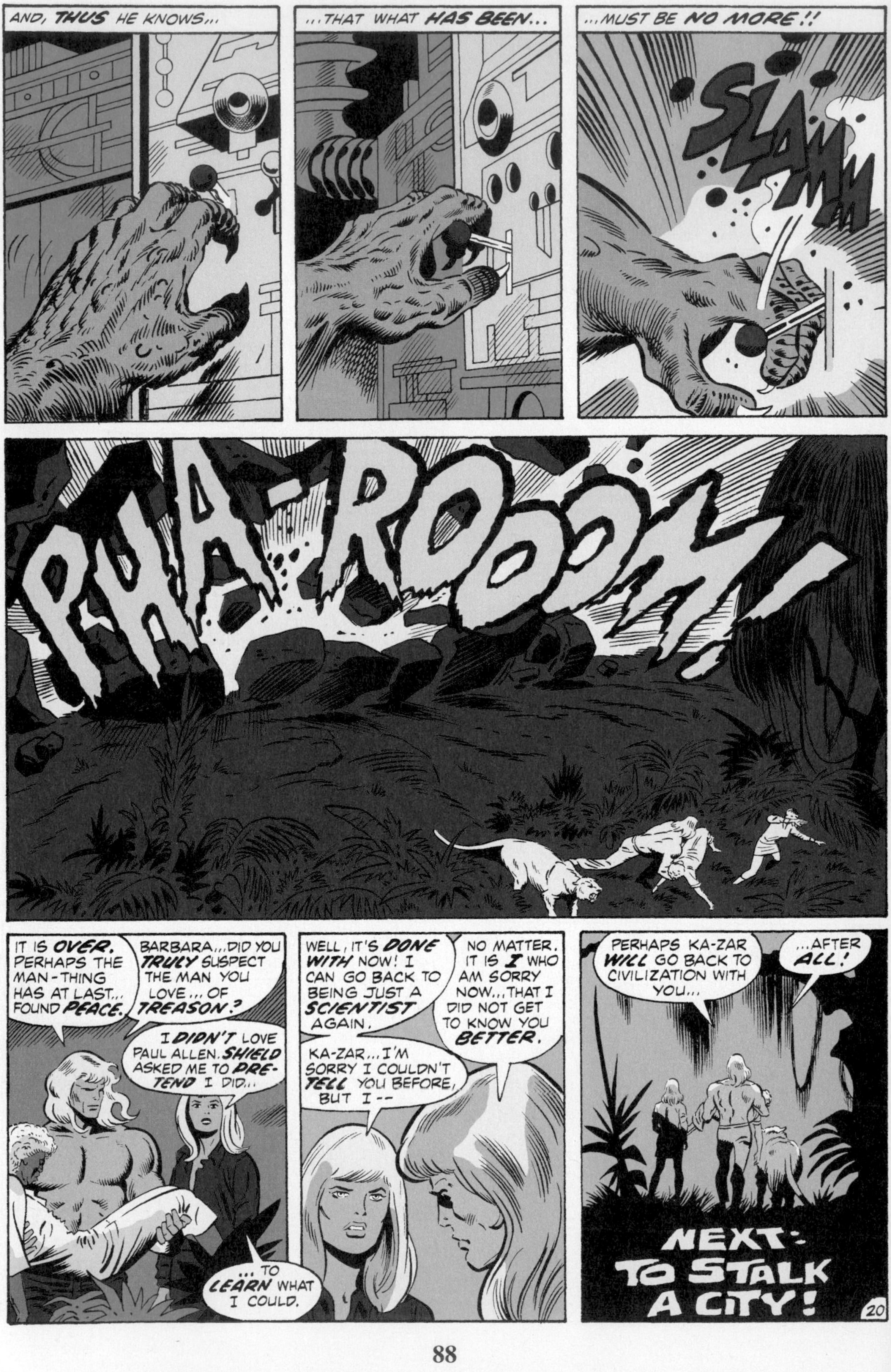
AND, THUS HE KNOWS...
...THAT WHAT HAS BEEN...
...MUST BE NO MORE!!
SLAMM
PHA-ROOOM!
IT IS OVER. PERHAPS THE MAN-THING HAS AT LAST... FOUND PEACE.
BARBARA...DID YOU TRULY SUSPECT THE MAN YOU LOVE... OF TREASON?
I DIDN'T LOVE PAUL ALLEN. SHIELD ASKED ME TO PRETEND I DID...
... TO LEARN WHAT I COULD.
WELL, IT'S DONE WITH NOW! I CAN GO BACK TO BEING JUST A SCIENTIST AGAIN.
KA-ZAR... I'M SORRY I COULDN'T TELL YOU BEFORE, BUT I --
NO MATTER. IT IS I WHO AM SORRY NOW... THAT I DID NOT GET TO KNOW YOU BETTER.
PERHAPS KA-ZAR WILL GO BACK TO CIVILIZATION WITH YOU...
...AFTER ALL!
NEXT: TO STALK A CITY!
20

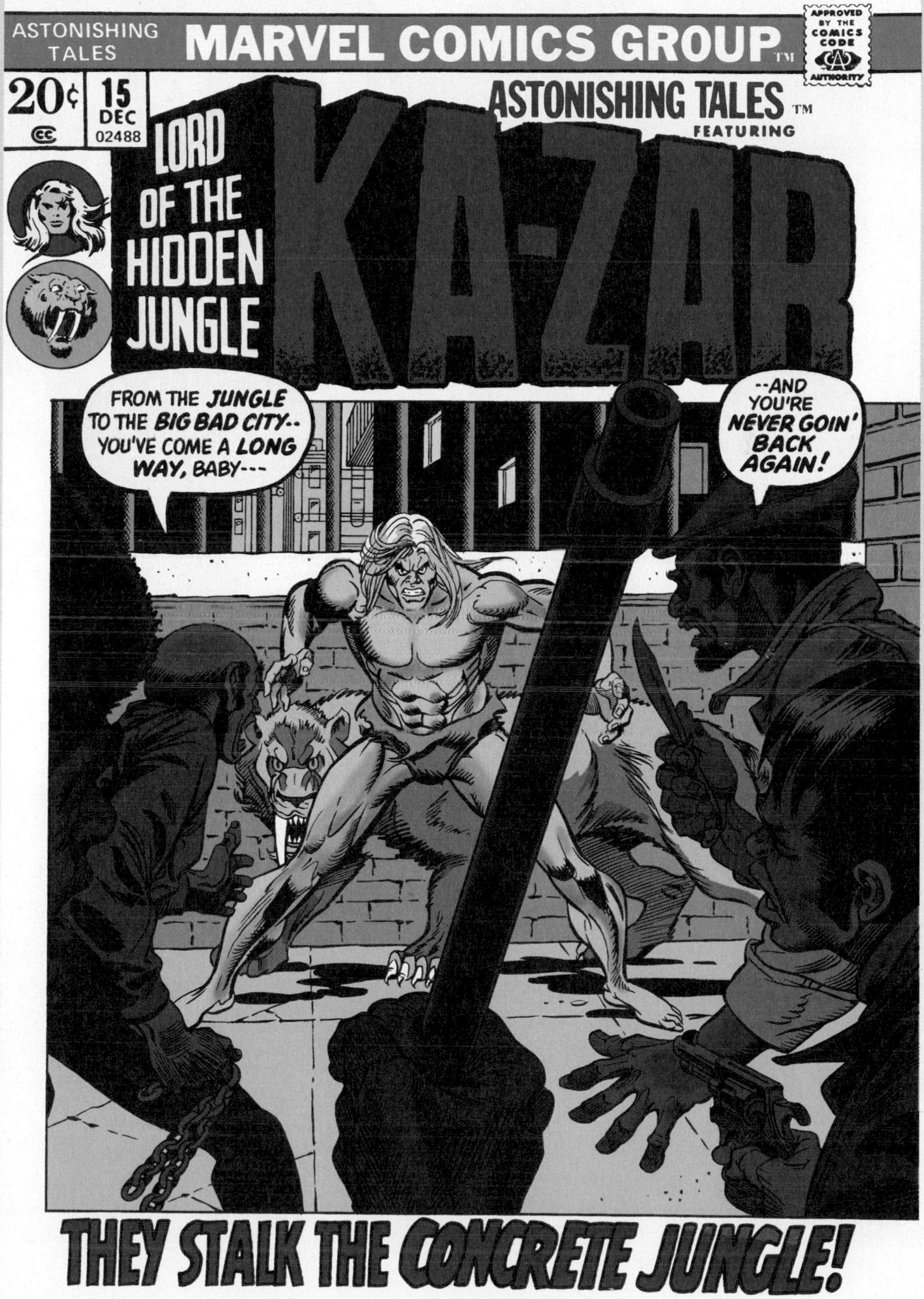

ASTONISHING TALES
MARVEL COMICS GROUP
APPROVED BY THE COMICS CODE AUTHORITY
20¢
15 DEC 02488
ASTONISHING TALES FEATURING
LORD OF THE HIDDEN JUNGLE
KA-ZAR
FROM THE JUNGLE TO THE BIG BAD CITY.. YOU'VE COME A LONG WAY, BABY---
--AND YOU'RE NEVER GOIN' BACK AGAIN!
THEY STALK THE CONCRETE JUNGLE!

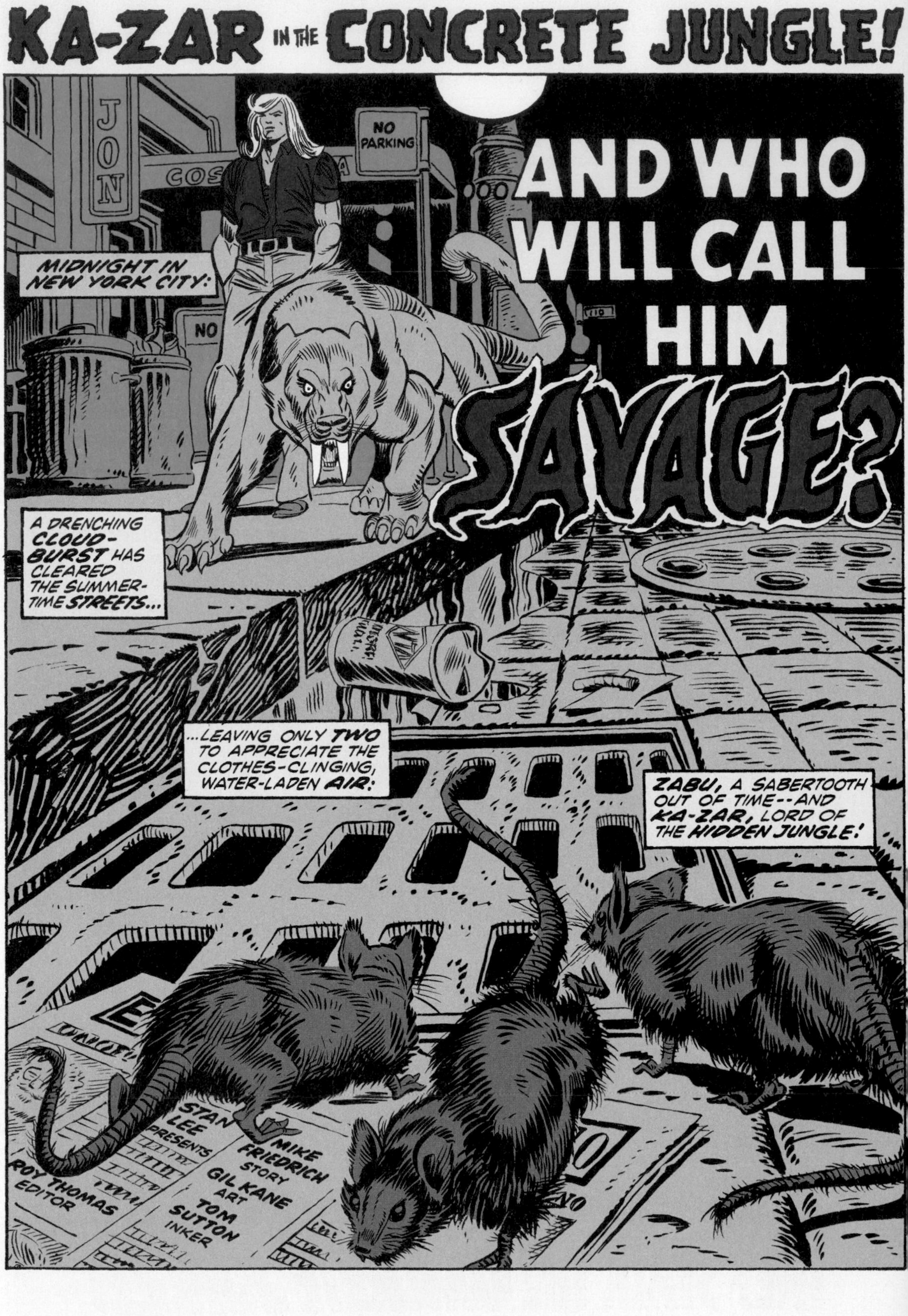
KA-ZAR IN THE CONCRETE JUNGLE!
AND WHO WILL CALL HIM SAVAGE?
MIDNIGHT IN NEW YORK CITY:
A DRENCHING CLOUD-BURST HAS CLEARED THE SUMMER-TIME STREETS...
...LEAVING ONLY TWO TO APPRECIATE THE CLOTHES-CLINGING, WATER-LADEN AIR:
ZABU, A SABERTOOTH OUT OF TIME--AND KA-ZAR, LORD OF THE HIDDEN JUNGLE!
STAN LEE PRESENTS
MIKE FRIEDRICH STORY
GIL KANE ART
TOM SUTTON INKER
ROY THOMAS EDITOR
NO PARKING
JON
NO

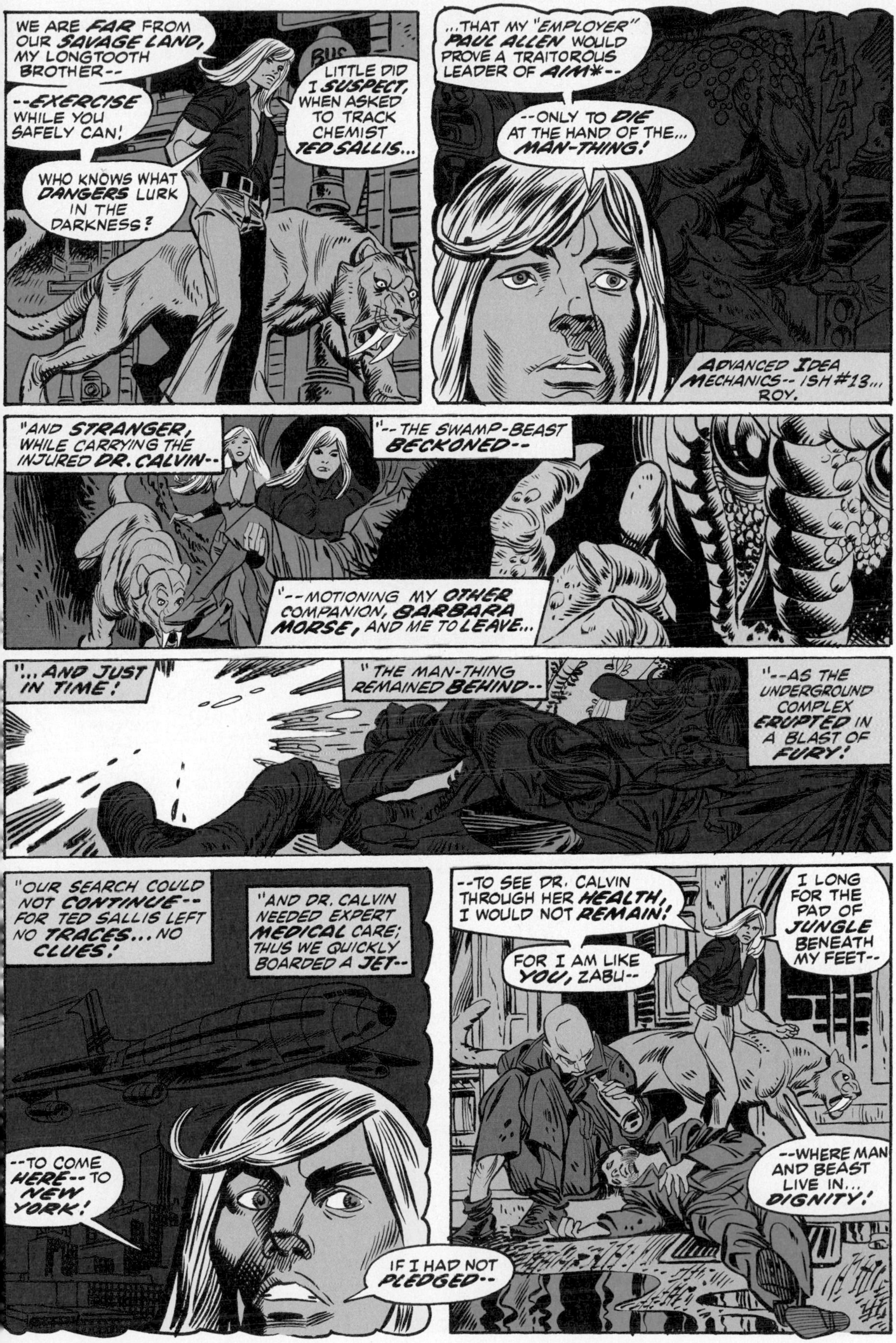
WE ARE FAR FROM OUR SAVAGE LAND, MY LONGTOOTH BROTHER--
--EXERCISE WHILE YOU SAFELY CAN!
WHO KNOWS WHAT DANGERS LURK IN THE DARKNESS?
LITTLE DID I SUSPECT, WHEN ASKED TO TRACK CHEMIST TED SALLIS...
...THAT MY "EMPLOYER" PAUL ALLEN WOULD PROVE A TRAITOROUS LEADER OF AIM*--
--ONLY TO DIE AT THE HAND OF THE... MAN-THING!
ADVANCED IDEA MECHANICS-- ISH #13... ROY.
"AND STRANGER, WHILE CARRYING THE INJURED DR. CALVIN--
"--THE SWAMP-BEAST BECKONED--
"--MOTIONING MY OTHER COMPANION, BARBARA MORSE, AND ME TO LEAVE...
"...AND JUST IN TIME!
"THE MAN-THING REMAINED BEHIND--
"--AS THE UNDERGROUND COMPLEX ERUPTED IN A BLAST OF FURY!
"OUR SEARCH COULD NOT CONTINUE--FOR TED SALLIS LEFT NO TRACES... NO CLUES!
"AND DR. CALVIN NEEDED EXPERT MEDICAL CARE; THUS WE QUICKLY BOARDED A JET--
--TO COME HERE-- TO NEW YORK!
IF I HAD NOT PLEDGED--
--TO SEE DR. CALVIN THROUGH HER HEALTH, I WOULD NOT REMAIN!
FOR I AM LIKE YOU, ZABU--
I LONG FOR THE PAD OF JUNGLE BENEATH MY FEET--
--WHERE MAN AND BEAST LIVE IN... DIGNITY!

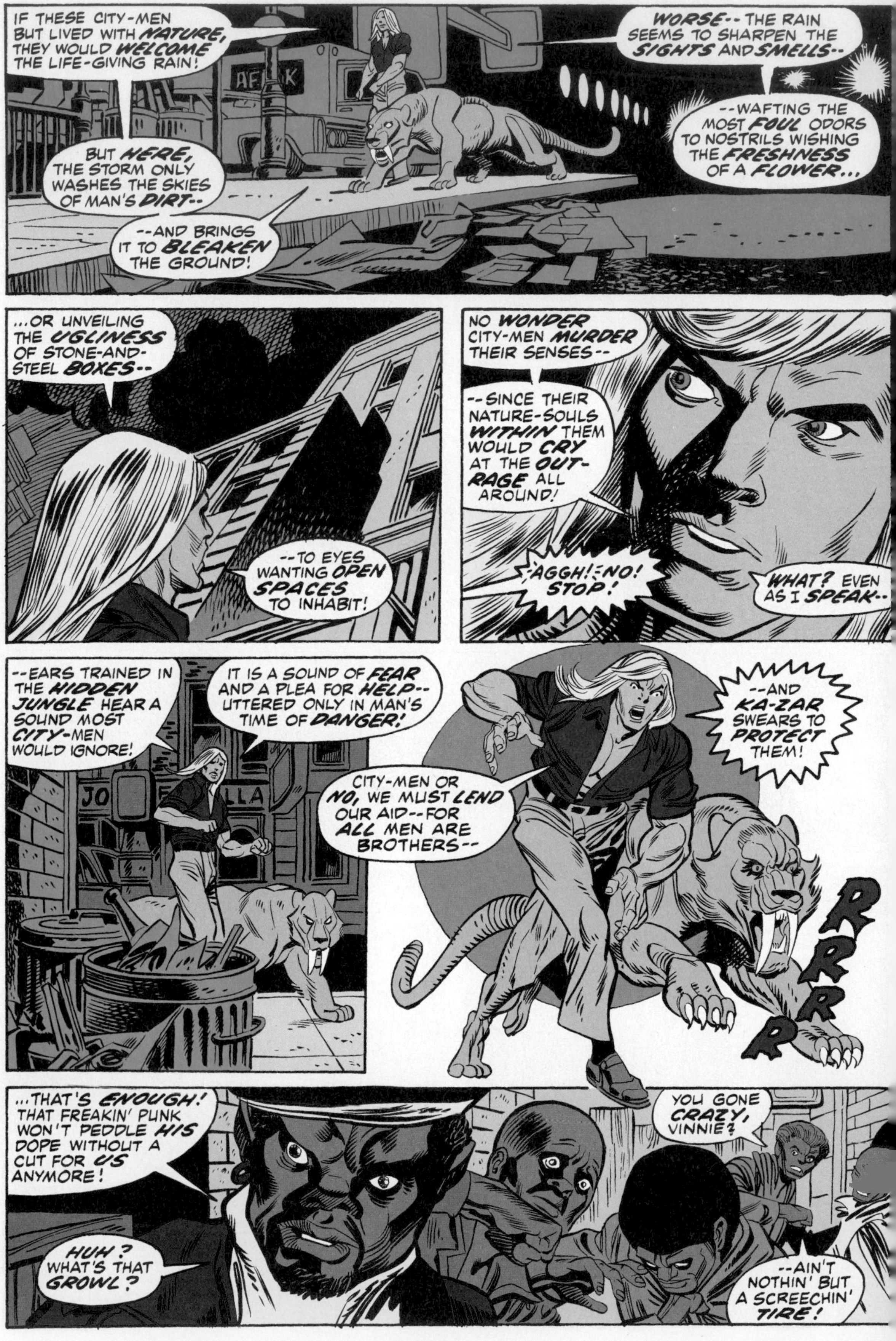
IF THESE CITY-MEN BUT LIVED WITH NATURE, THEY WOULD WELCOME THE LIFE-GIVING RAIN!
BUT HERE, THE STORM ONLY WASHES THE SKIES OF MAN'S DIRT--
--AND BRINGS IT TO BLEAKEN THE GROUND!
WORSE--THE RAIN SEEMS TO SHARPEN THE SIGHTS AND SMELLS--
--WAFTING THE MOST FOUL ODORS TO NOSTRILS WISHING THE FRESHNESS OF A FLOWER...
...OR UNVEILING THE UGLINESS OF STONE-AND-STEEL BOXES--
--TO EYES WANTING OPEN SPACES TO INHABIT!
NO WONDER CITY-MEN MURDER THEIR SENSES--
--SINCE THEIR NATURE-SOULS WITHIN THEM WOULD CRY AT THE OUT-RAGE ALL AROUND!
AGGH! NO! STOP!
WHAT? EVEN AS I SPEAK--
--EARS TRAINED IN THE HIDDEN JUNGLE HEAR A SOUND MOST CITY-MEN WOULD IGNORE!
IT IS A SOUND OF FEAR AND A PLEA FOR HELP--UTTERED ONLY IN MAN'S TIME OF DANGER!
CITY-MEN OR NO, WE MUST LEND OUR AID--FOR ALL MEN ARE BROTHERS--
--AND KA-ZAR SWEARS TO PROTECT THEM!
RRRRR
...THAT'S ENOUGH! THAT FREAKIN' PUNK WON'T PEDDLE HIS DOPE WITHOUT A CUT FOR US ANYMORE!
YOU GONE CRAZY, VINNIE?
HUH? WHAT'S THAT GROWL?
--AIN'T NOTHIN' BUT A SCREECHIN' TIRE!

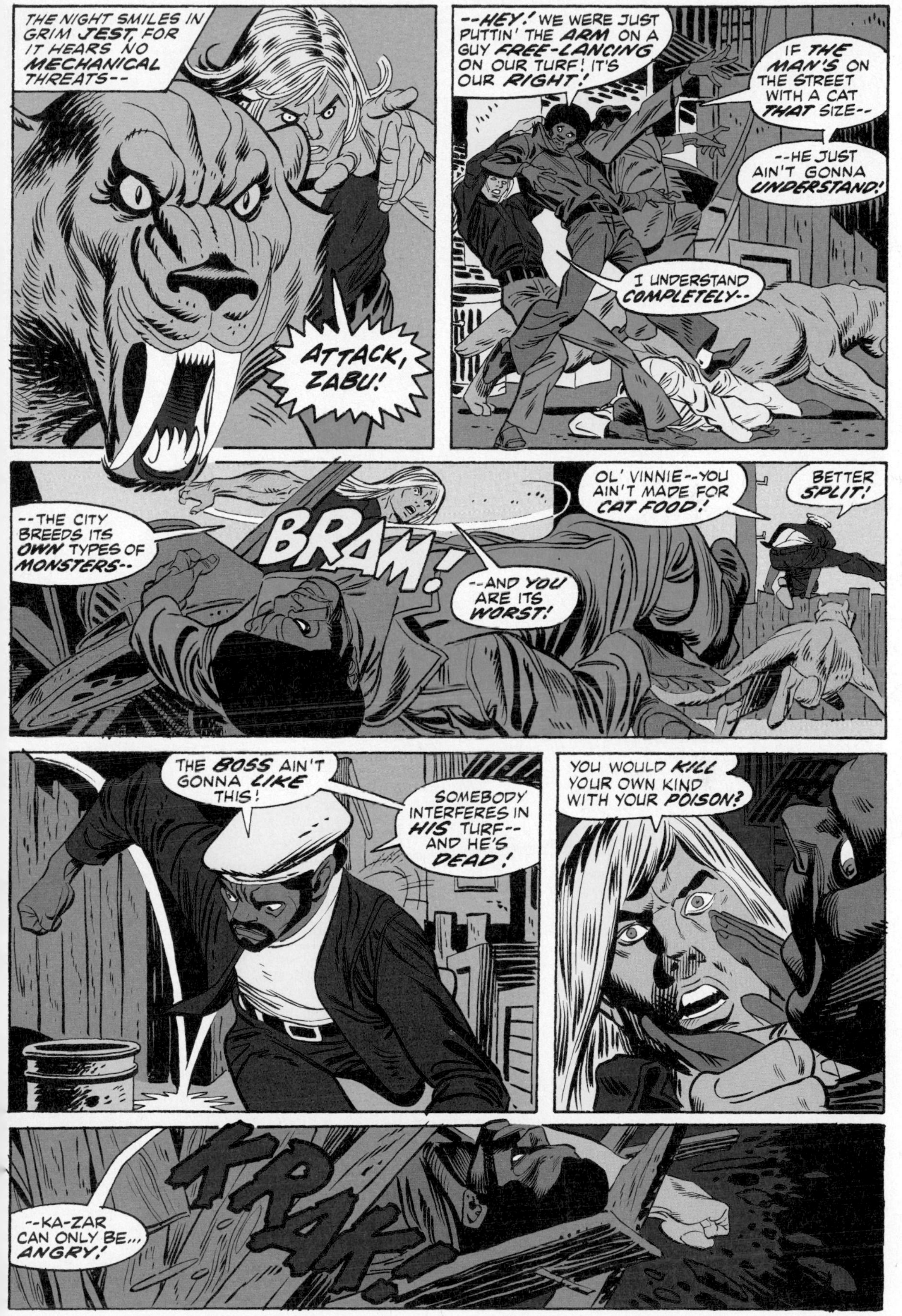
THE NIGHT SMILES IN GRIM JEST, FOR IT HEARS NO MECHANICAL THREATS--
ATTACK, ZABU!
--HEY! WE WERE JUST PUTTIN' THE ARM ON A GUY FREE-LANCING ON OUR TURF! IT'S OUR RIGHT!
IF THE MAN'S ON THE STREET WITH A CAT THAT SIZE--
--HE JUST AIN'T GONNA UNDERSTAND!
I UNDERSTAND COMPLETELY--
--THE CITY BREEDS ITS OWN TYPES OF MONSTERS--
BRAM!
--AND YOU ARE ITS WORST!
OL' VINNIE--YOU AIN'T MADE FOR CAT FOOD!
BETTER SPLIT!
THE BOSS AIN'T GONNA LIKE THIS!
SOMEBODY INTERFERES IN HIS TURF--AND HE'S DEAD!
YOU WOULD KILL YOUR OWN KIND WITH YOUR POISON?
KRAK!
--KA-ZAR CAN ONLY BE... ANGRY!

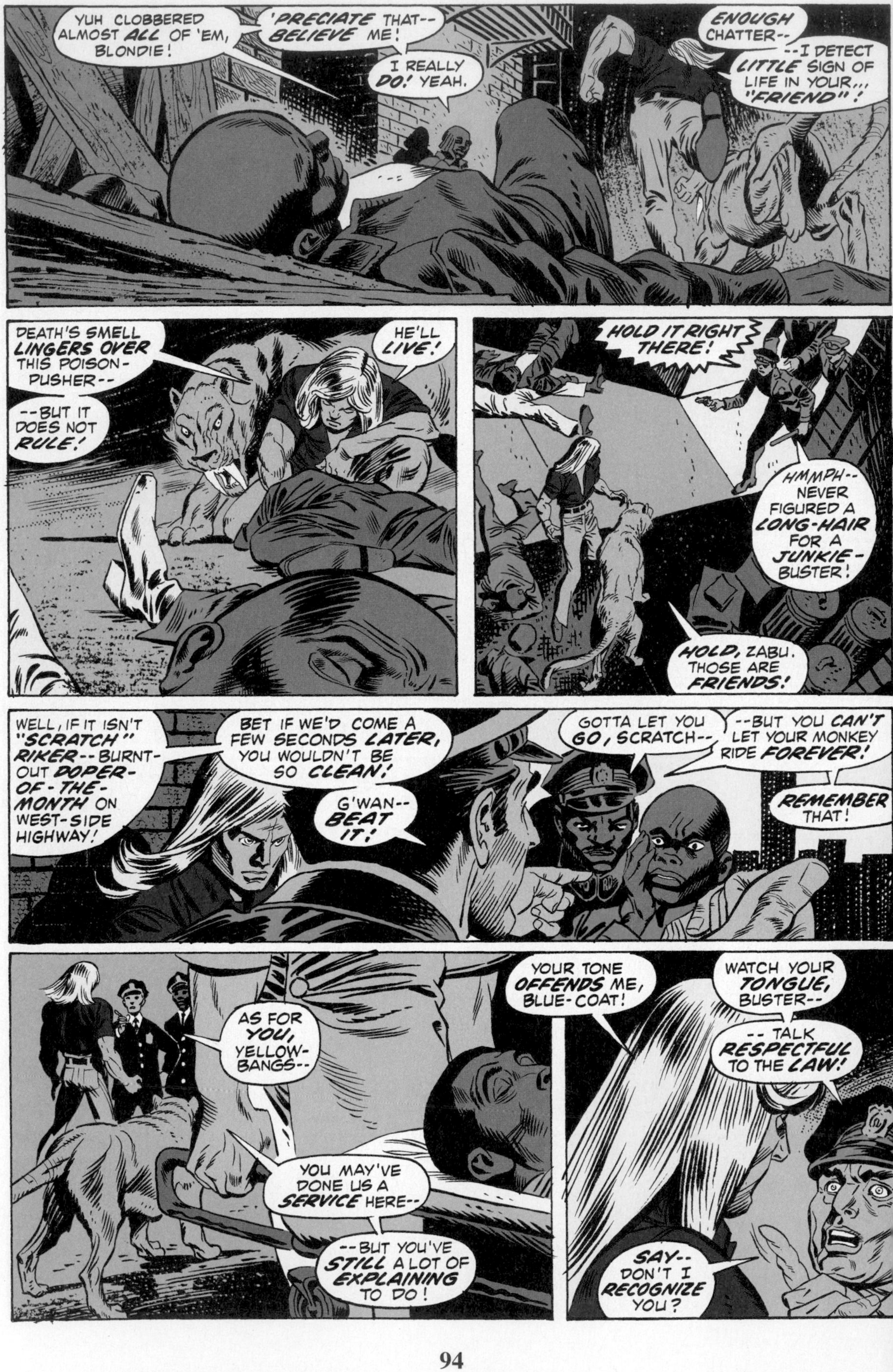

YUH CLOBBERED ALMOST ALL OF 'EM, BLONDIE!
'PRECIATE THAT-- BELIEVE ME!
I REALLY DO! YEAH.
ENOUGH CHATTER--
--I DETECT LITTLE SIGN OF LIFE IN YOUR... "FRIEND"...!
DEATH'S SMELL LINGERS OVER THIS POISON-PUSHER--
--BUT IT DOES NOT RULE!
HE'LL LIVE!
HOLD IT RIGHT THERE!
HMMPH-- NEVER FIGURED A LONG-HAIR FOR A JUNKIE-BUSTER!
HOLD, ZABU. THOSE ARE FRIENDS!
WELL, IF IT ISN'T "SCRATCH" RIKER--BURNT-OUT DOPER-OF-THE-MONTH ON WEST-SIDE HIGHWAY!
BET IF WE'D COME A FEW SECONDS LATER, YOU WOULDN'T BE SO CLEAN!
G'WAN-- BEAT IT!
GOTTA LET YOU GO, SCRATCH--
--BUT YOU CAN'T LET YOUR MONKEY RIDE FOREVER!
REMEMBER THAT!
AS FOR YOU, YELLOW-BANGS--
YOU MAY'VE DONE US A SERVICE HERE--
--BUT YOU'VE STILL A LOT OF EXPLAINING TO DO!
YOUR TONE OFFENDS ME, BLUE-COAT!
WATCH YOUR TONGUE, BUSTER--
--TALK RESPECTFUL TO THE LAW!
SAY-- DON'T I RECOGNIZE YOU?

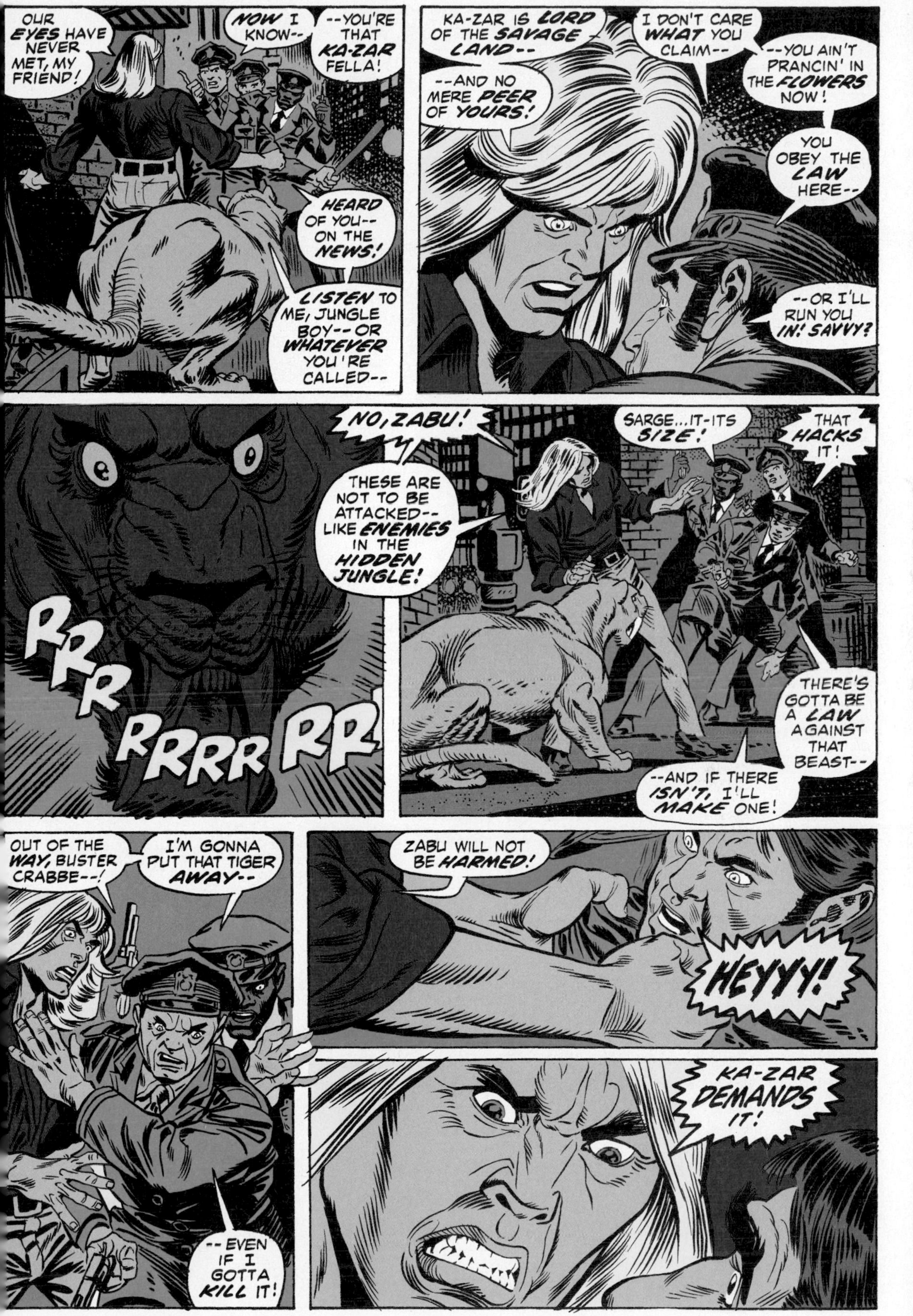
OUR EYES HAVE NEVER MET, MY FRIEND!
NOW I KNOW--
--YOU'RE THAT KA-ZAR FELLA!
HEARD OF YOU--ON THE NEWS!
LISTEN TO ME, JUNGLE BOY--OR WHATEVER YOU'RE CALLED--
KA-ZAR IS LORD OF THE SAVAGE LAND--
--AND NO MERE PEER OF YOURS!
I DON'T CARE WHAT YOU CLAIM--
--YOU AIN'T PRANCIN' IN THE FLOWERS NOW!
YOU OBEY THE LAW HERE--
--OR I'LL RUN YOU IN! SAVVY?
RRR RRRR RR
NO, ZABU!
THESE ARE NOT TO BE ATTACKED--LIKE ENEMIES IN THE HIDDEN JUNGLE!
SARGE...IT-ITS SIZE!
THAT HACKS IT!
THERE'S GOTTA BE A LAW AGAINST THAT BEAST--
--AND IF THERE ISN'T, I'LL MAKE ONE!
OUT OF THE WAY, BUSTER CRABBE--!
I'M GONNA PUT THAT TIGER AWAY--
--EVEN IF I GOTTA KILL IT!
ZABU WILL NOT BE HARMED!
HEYYY!
KA-ZAR DEMANDS IT!

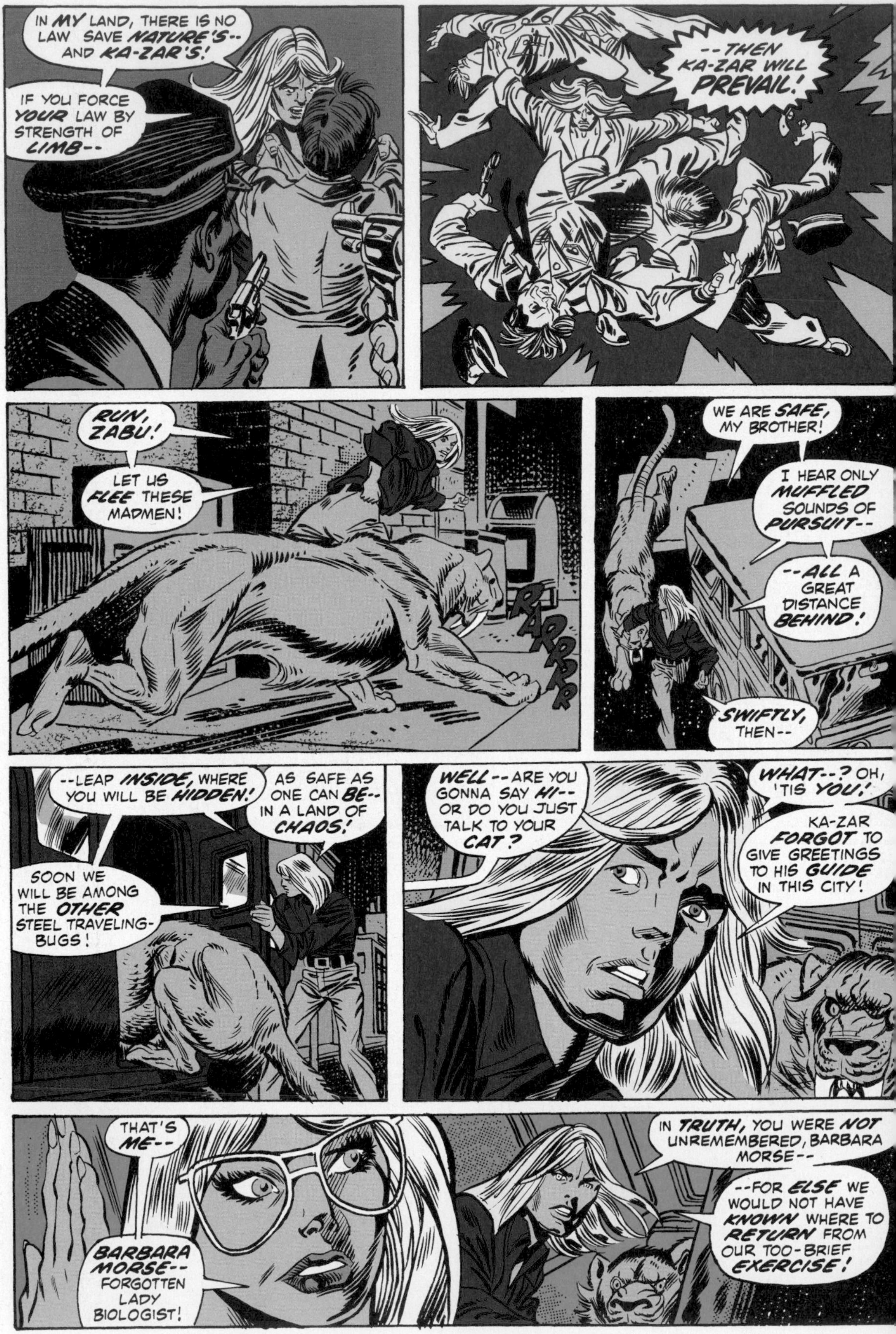
IN MY LAND, THERE IS NO LAW SAVE NATURE'S-- AND KA-ZAR'S!
IF YOU FORCE YOUR LAW BY STRENGTH OF LIMB--
--THEN KA-ZAR WILL PREVAIL!
RUN, ZABU!
LET US FLEE THESE MADMEN!
RARRRR
WE ARE SAFE, MY BROTHER!
I HEAR ONLY MUFFLED SOUNDS OF PURSUIT--
--ALL A GREAT DISTANCE BEHIND!
SWIFTLY, THEN--
--LEAP INSIDE, WHERE YOU WILL BE HIDDEN!
SOON WE WILL BE AMONG THE OTHER STEEL TRAVELING-BUGS!
AS SAFE AS ONE CAN BE-- IN A LAND OF CHAOS!
WELL--ARE YOU GONNA SAY HI-- OR DO YOU JUST TALK TO YOUR CAT?
WHAT--? OH, 'TIS YOU!
KA-ZAR FORGOT TO GIVE GREETINGS TO HIS GUIDE IN THIS CITY!
THAT'S ME--
BARBARA MORSE-- FORGOTTEN LADY BIOLOGIST!
IN TRUTH, YOU WERE NOT UNREMEMBERED, BARBARA MORSE--
--FOR ELSE WE WOULD NOT HAVE KNOWN WHERE TO RETURN FROM OUR TOO-BRIEF EXERCISE!

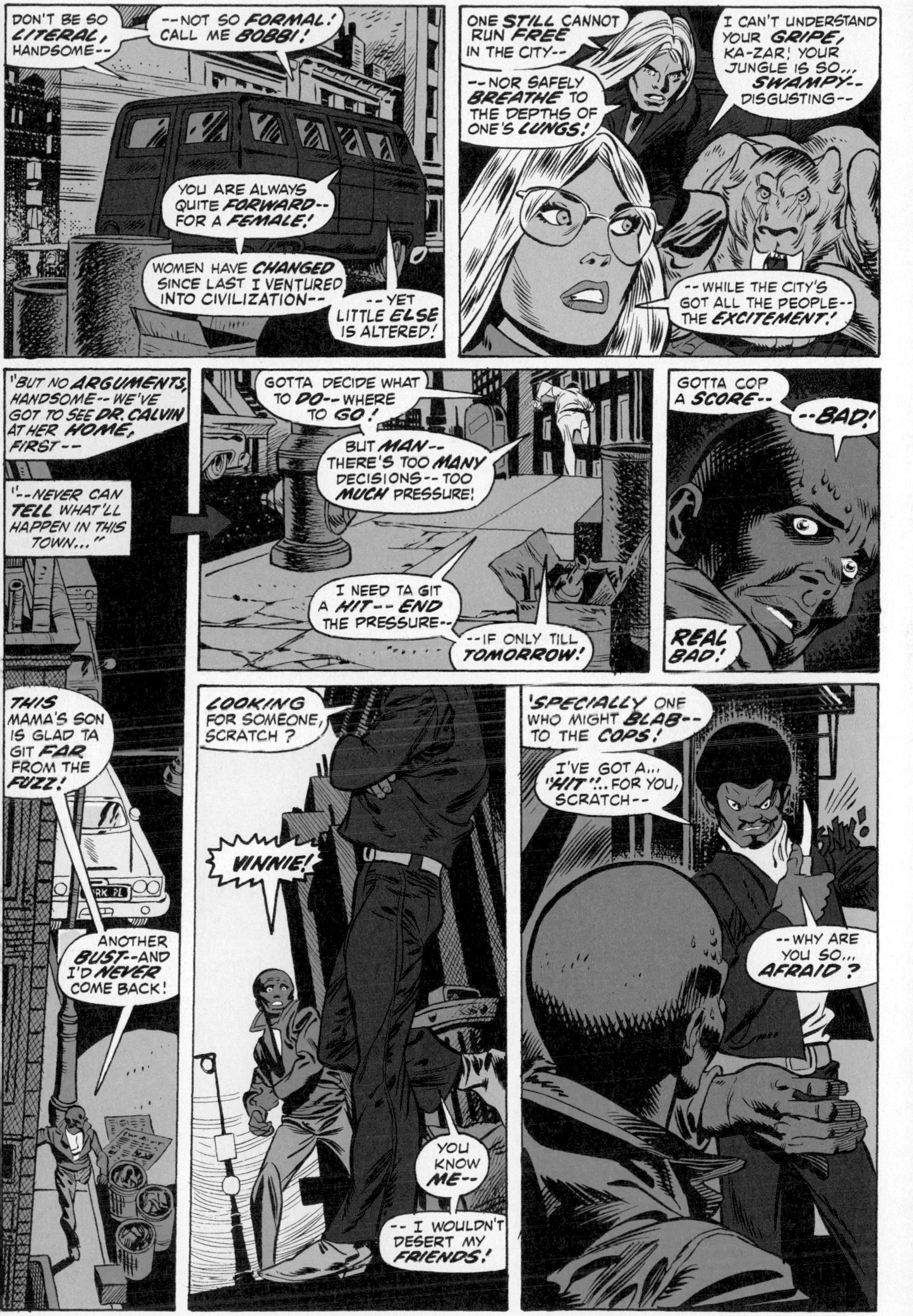

DON'T BE SO LITERAL, HANDSOME--
--NOT SO FORMAL! CALL ME BOBBI!
YOU ARE ALWAYS QUITE FORWARD-- FOR A FEMALE!
WOMEN HAVE CHANGED SINCE LAST I VENTURED INTO CIVILIZATION--
--YET LITTLE ELSE IS ALTERED!
ONE STILL CANNOT RUN FREE IN THE CITY--
--NOR SAFELY BREATHE TO THE DEPTHS OF ONE'S LUNGS!
I CAN'T UNDERSTAND YOUR GRIPE, KA-ZAR! YOUR JUNGLE IS SO... SWAMPY-- DISGUSTING--
--WHILE THE CITY'S GOT ALL THE PEOPLE-- THE EXCITEMENT!
"BUT NO ARGUMENTS, HANDSOME-- WE'VE GOT TO SEE DR. CALVIN AT HER HOME, FIRST--
"--NEVER CAN TELL WHAT'LL HAPPEN IN THIS TOWN..."
GOTTA DECIDE WHAT TO DO-- WHERE TO GO!
BUT MAN-- THERE'S TOO MANY DECISIONS-- TOO MUCH PRESSURE!
I NEED TA GIT A HIT-- END THE PRESSURE--
--IF ONLY TILL TOMORROW!
GOTTA COP A SCORE--
--BAD!
REAL BAD!
THIS MAMA'S SON IS GLAD TA GIT FAR FROM THE FUZZ!
ANOTHER BUST--AND I'D NEVER COME BACK!
LOOKING FOR SOMEONE, SCRATCH?
VINNIE!
YOU KNOW ME--
--I WOULDN'T DESERT MY FRIENDS!
'SPECIALLY ONE WHO MIGHT BLAB-- TO THE COPS!
I'VE GOT A... "HIT"... FOR YOU, SCRATCH--
SNIK!
--WHY ARE YOU SO... AFRAID?

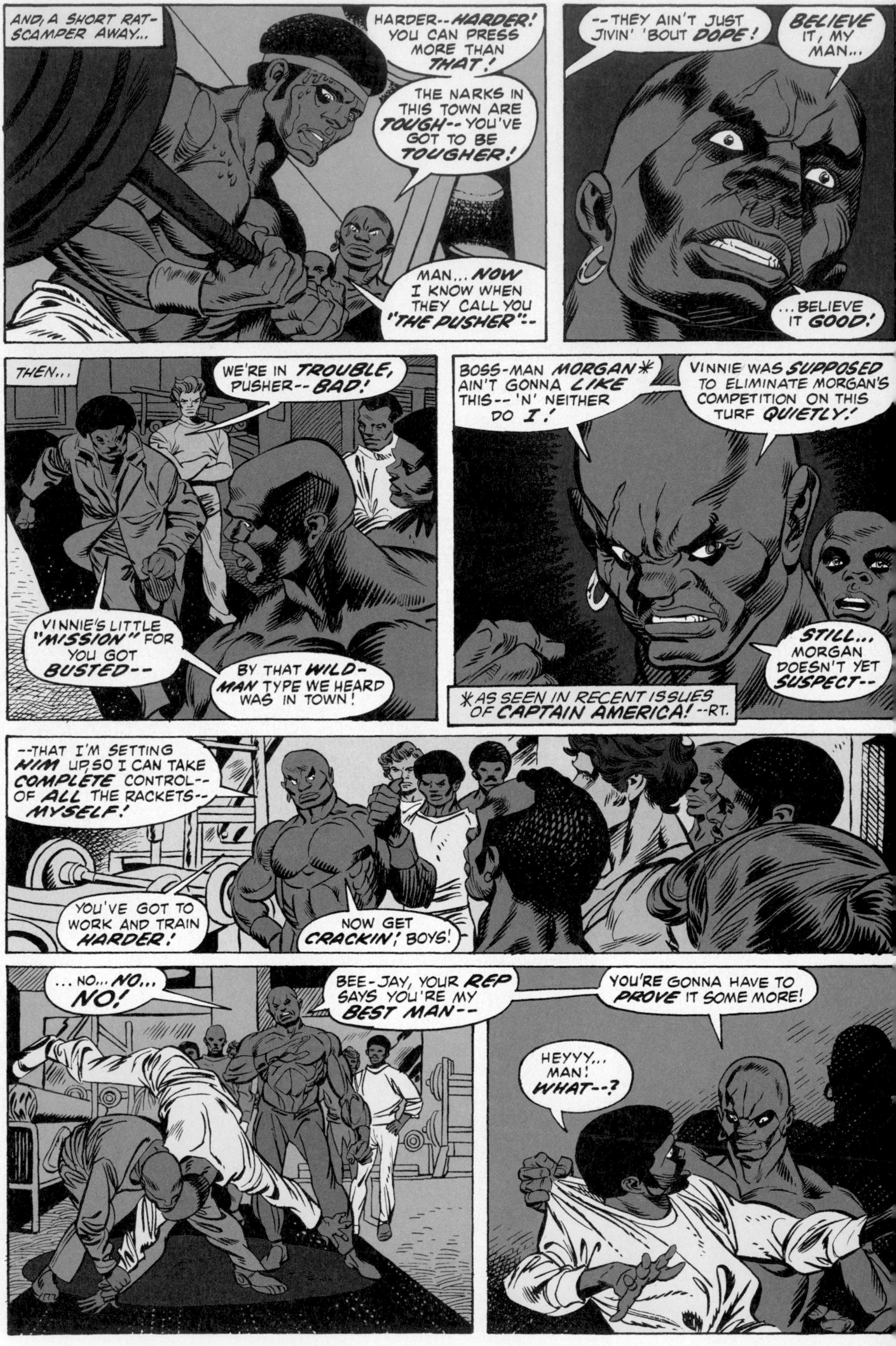
AND, A SHORT RAT-SCAMPER AWAY...
HARDER--HARDER! YOU CAN PRESS MORE THAN THAT!
THE NARKS IN THIS TOWN ARE TOUGH--YOU'VE GOT TO BE TOUGHER!
MAN... NOW I KNOW WHEN THEY CALL YOU "THE PUSHER"--
--THEY AIN'T JUST JIVIN' 'BOUT DOPE!
BELIEVE IT, MY MAN...
...BELIEVE IT GOOD!
THEN...
WE'RE IN TROUBLE, PUSHER--BAD!
VINNIE'S LITTLE "MISSION" FOR YOU GOT BUSTED--
BY THAT WILD-MAN TYPE WE HEARD WAS IN TOWN!
BOSS-MAN MORGAN* AIN'T GONNA LIKE THIS--'N' NEITHER DO I!
VINNIE WAS SUPPOSED TO ELIMINATE MORGAN'S COMPETITION ON THIS TURF QUIETLY!
STILL... MORGAN DOESN'T YET SUSPECT--
*AS SEEN IN RECENT ISSUES OF CAPTAIN AMERICA! --RT.
--THAT I'M SETTING HIM UP, SO I CAN TAKE COMPLETE CONTROL--OF ALL THE RACKETS--MYSELF!
YOU'VE GOT TO WORK AND TRAIN HARDER!
NOW GET CRACKIN', BOYS!
...NO... NO... NO!
BEE-JAY, YOUR REP SAYS YOU'RE MY BEST MAN--
YOU'RE GONNA HAVE TO PROVE IT SOME MORE!
HEYYY... MAN! WHAT--?

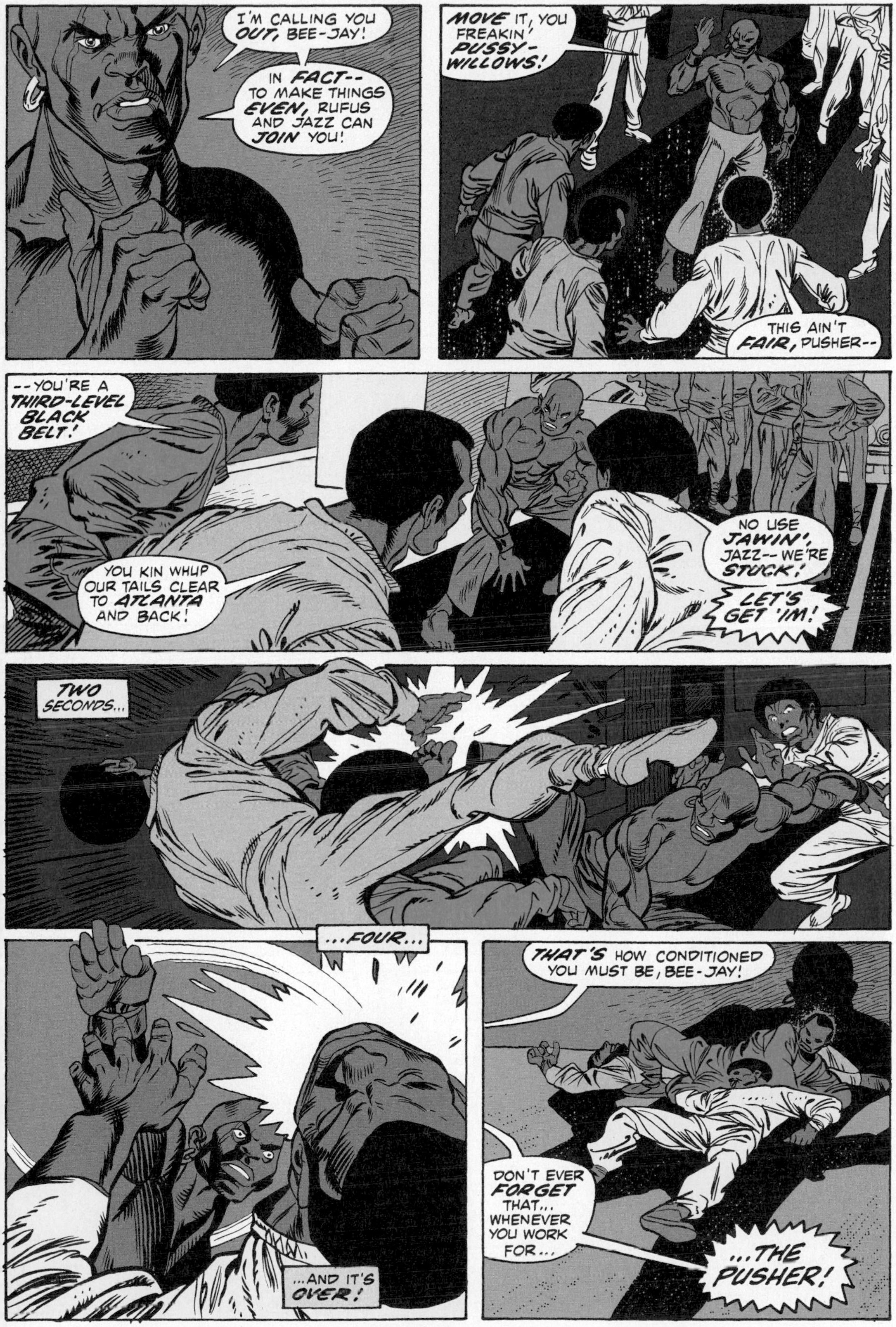

I'M CALLING YOU OUT, BEE-JAY!
IN FACT-- TO MAKE THINGS EVEN, RUFUS AND JAZZ CAN JOIN YOU!
MOVE IT, YOU FREAKIN' PUSSY-WILLOWS!
THIS AIN'T FAIR, PUSHER--
--YOU'RE A THIRD-LEVEL BLACK BELT!
YOU KIN WHUP OUR TAILS CLEAR TO ATLANTA AND BACK!
NO USE JAWIN', JAZZ-- WE'RE STUCK!
LET'S GET 'IM!
TWO SECONDS...
...FOUR...
...AND IT'S OVER!
THAT'S HOW CONDITIONED YOU MUST BE, BEE-JAY!
DON'T EVER FORGET THAT... WHENEVER YOU WORK FOR...
...THE PUSHER!

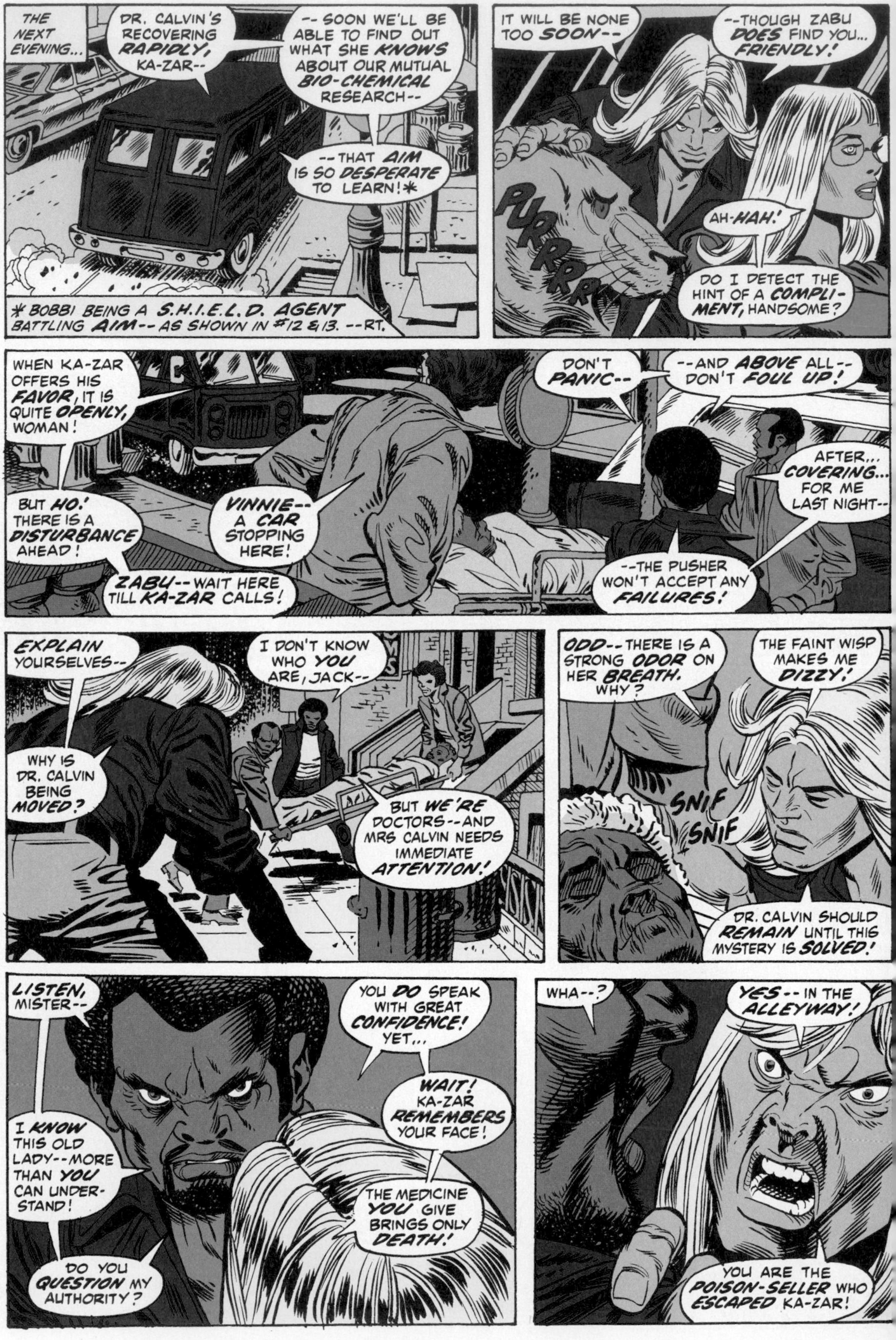
THE NEXT EVENING...
DR. CALVIN'S RECOVERING RAPIDLY, KA-ZAR--
-- SOON WE'LL BE ABLE TO FIND OUT WHAT SHE KNOWS ABOUT OUR MUTUAL BIO-CHEMICAL RESEARCH--
--THAT AIM IS SO DESPERATE TO LEARN!*
*BOBBI BEING A S.H.I.E.L.D. AGENT BATTLING AIM-- AS SHOWN IN #12 & 13. --RT.
IT WILL BE NONE TOO SOON--
--THOUGH ZABU DOES FIND YOU... FRIENDLY!
PURRRR
AH-HAH!
DO I DETECT THE HINT OF A COMPLIMENT, HANDSOME?
WHEN KA-ZAR OFFERS HIS FAVOR, IT IS QUITE OPENLY, WOMAN!
BUT HO! THERE IS A DISTURBANCE AHEAD!
ZABU--WAIT HERE TILL KA-ZAR CALLS!
VINNIE-- A CAR STOPPING HERE!
DON'T PANIC--
--AND ABOVE ALL-- DON'T FOUL UP!
AFTER... COVERING... FOR ME LAST NIGHT--
--THE PUSHER WON'T ACCEPT ANY FAILURES!
EXPLAIN YOURSELVES--
WHY IS DR. CALVIN BEING MOVED?
I DON'T KNOW WHO YOU ARE, JACK--
BUT WE'RE DOCTORS--AND MRS CALVIN NEEDS IMMEDIATE ATTENTION!
ODD--THERE IS A STRONG ODOR ON HER BREATH. WHY?
THE FAINT WISP MAKES ME DIZZY!
SNIF SNIF
DR. CALVIN SHOULD REMAIN UNTIL THIS MYSTERY IS SOLVED!
LISTEN, MISTER--
I KNOW THIS OLD LADY--MORE THAN YOU CAN UNDERSTAND!
DO YOU QUESTION MY AUTHORITY?
YOU DO SPEAK WITH GREAT CONFIDENCE! YET...
WAIT! KA-ZAR REMEMBERS YOUR FACE!
THE MEDICINE YOU GIVE BRINGS ONLY DEATH!
WHA--?
YES--IN THE ALLEYWAY!
YOU ARE THE POISON-SELLER WHO ESCAPED KA-ZAR!

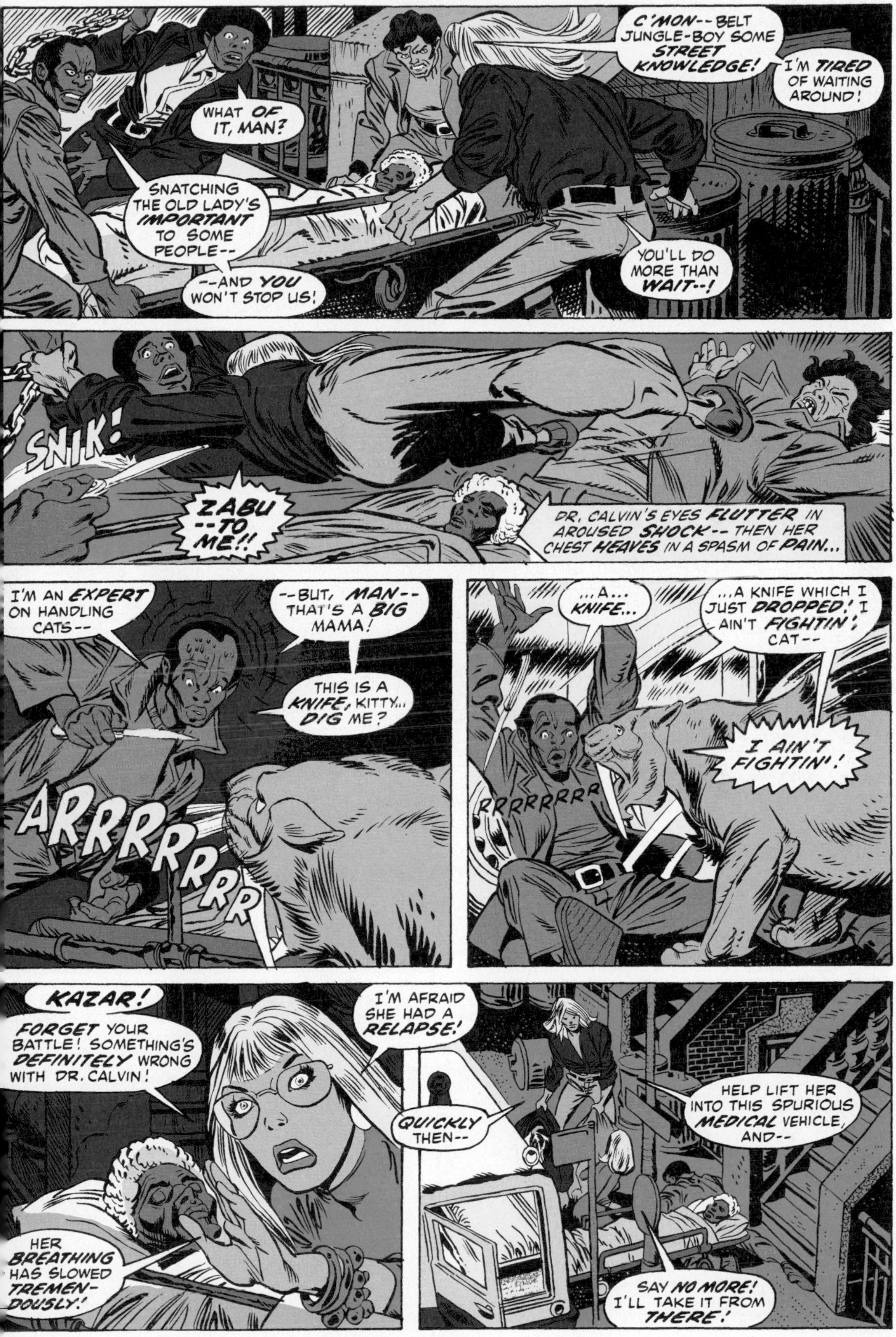
C'MON--BELT JUNGLE-BOY SOME STREET KNOWLEDGE!
I'M TIRED OF WAITING AROUND!
WHAT OF IT, MAN?
SNATCHING THE OLD LADY'S IMPORTANT TO SOME PEOPLE--
--AND YOU WON'T STOP US!
YOU'LL DO MORE THAN WAIT--!
SNIK!
ZABU--TO ME!!
DR. CALVIN'S EYES FLUTTER IN AROUSED SHOCK--THEN HER CHEST HEAVES IN A SPASM OF PAIN...
I'M AN EXPERT ON HANDLING CATS--
--BUT, MAN--THAT'S A BIG MAMA!
THIS IS A KNIFE, KITTY... DIG ME?
ARRRRRRRRR
...A... KNIFE...
...A KNIFE WHICH I JUST DROPPED! I AIN'T FIGHTIN', CAT--
I AIN'T FIGHTIN'!
RRRRRRRR
KAZAR!
FORGET YOUR BATTLE! SOMETHING'S DEFINITELY WRONG WITH DR. CALVIN!
I'M AFRAID SHE HAD A RELAPSE!
QUICKLY THEN--
HER BREATHING HAS SLOWED TREMENDOUSLY!
HELP LIFT HER INTO THIS SPURIOUS MEDICAL VEHICLE, AND--
SAY NO MORE! I'LL TAKE IT FROM THERE!

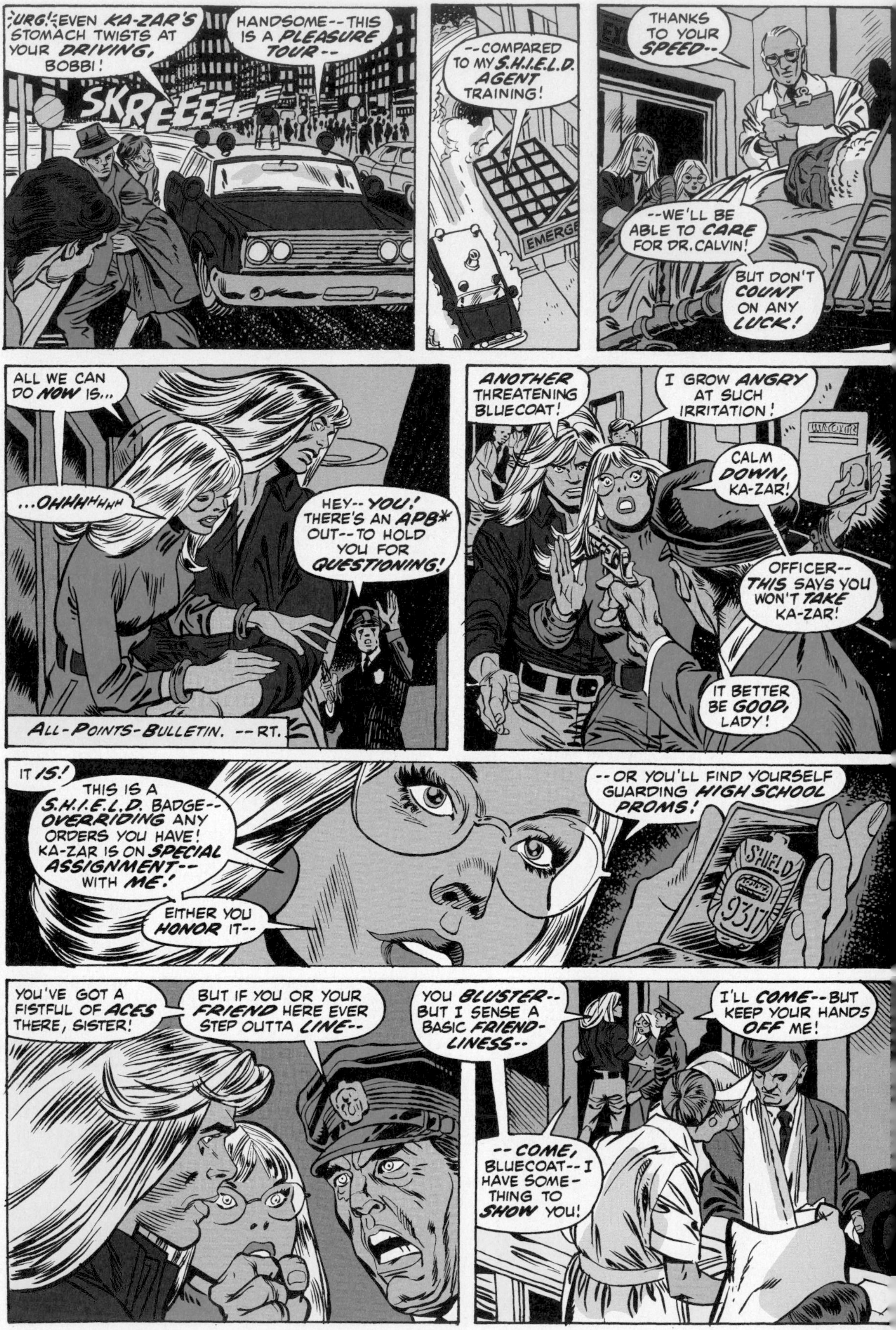
URG! EVEN KA-ZAR'S STOMACH TWISTS AT YOUR DRIVING, BOBBI!
HANDSOME--THIS IS A PLEASURE TOUR--
SKREEEEEEE
--COMPARED TO MY S.H.I.E.L.D. AGENT TRAINING!
EMERGE
THANKS TO YOUR SPEED--
--WE'LL BE ABLE TO CARE FOR DR. CALVIN!
BUT DON'T COUNT ON ANY LUCK!
ALL WE CAN DO NOW IS...
...OHHHHHHH
HEY--YOU! THERE'S AN APB* OUT--TO HOLD YOU FOR QUESTIONING!
*ALL-POINTS-BULLETIN. --RT.
ANOTHER THREATENING BLUECOAT!
I GROW ANGRY AT SUCH IRRITATION!
CALM DOWN, KA-ZAR!
OFFICER--THIS SAYS YOU WON'T TAKE KA-ZAR!
IT BETTER BE GOOD, LADY!
IT IS! THIS IS A S.H.I.E.L.D. BADGE--OVERRIDING ANY ORDERS YOU HAVE! KA-ZAR IS ON SPECIAL ASSIGNMENT--WITH ME!
EITHER YOU HONOR IT--
--OR YOU'LL FIND YOURSELF GUARDING HIGH SCHOOL PROMS!
SHIELD
9317
YOU'VE GOT A FISTFUL OF ACES THERE, SISTER!
BUT IF YOU OR YOUR FRIEND HERE EVER STEP OUTTA LINE--
YOU BLUSTER--BUT I SENSE A BASIC FRIENDLINESS--
--COME, BLUECOAT--I HAVE SOMETHING TO SHOW YOU!
I'LL COME--BUT KEEP YOUR HANDS OFF ME!

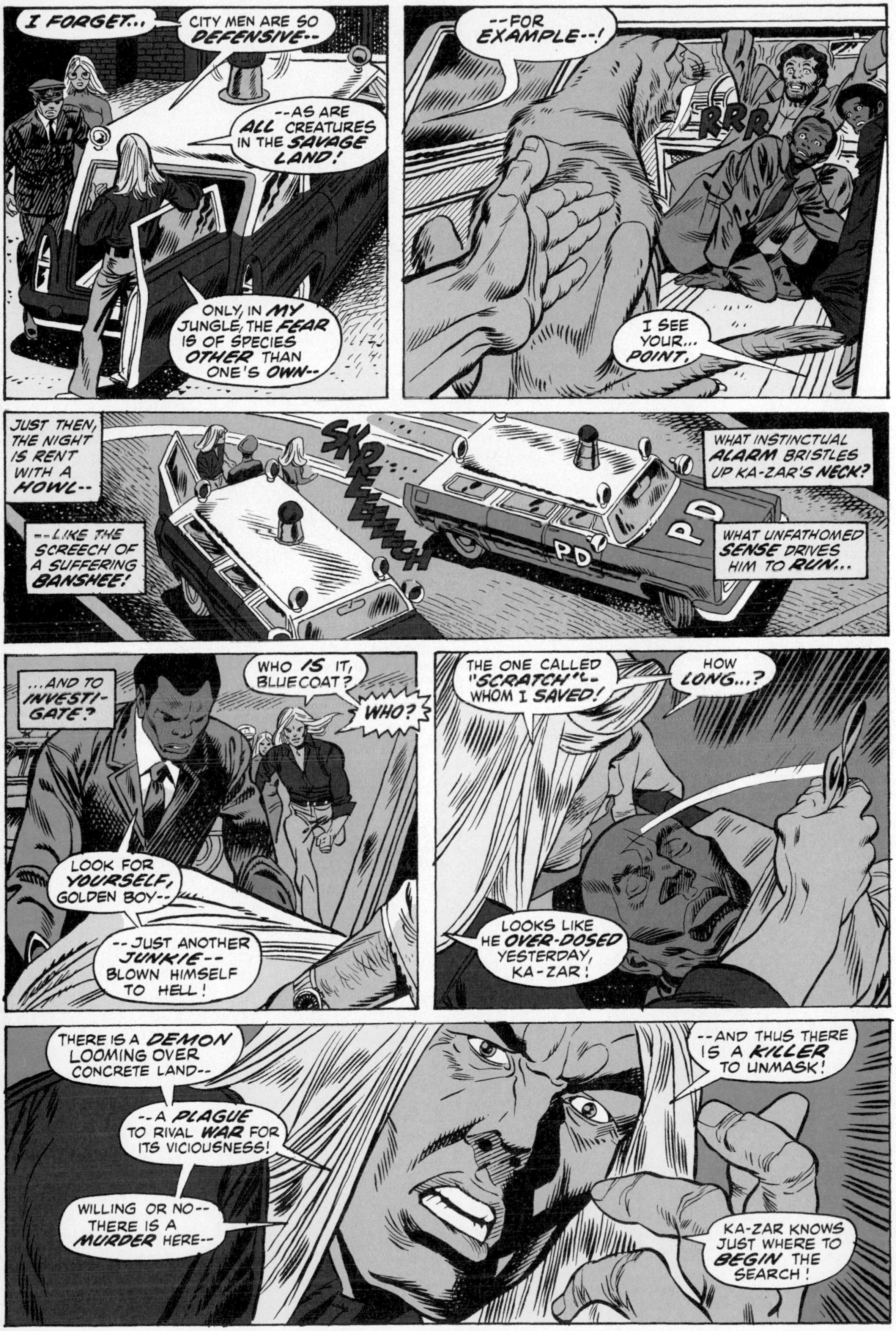
I FORGET...
CITY MEN ARE SO DEFENSIVE--
--AS ARE ALL CREATURES IN THE SAVAGE LAND!
ONLY, IN MY JUNGLE, THE FEAR IS OF SPECIES OTHER THAN ONE'S OWN--
--FOR EXAMPLE--!
RRR
I SEE YOUR... POINT.
JUST THEN, THE NIGHT IS RENT WITH A HOWL--
--LIKE THE SCREECH OF A SUFFERING BANSHEE!
SKREEEEEEECH
PD
PD
WHAT INSTINCTUAL ALARM BRISTLES UP KA-ZAR'S NECK?
WHAT UNFATHOMED SENSE DRIVES HIM TO RUN...
...AND TO INVESTI-GATE?
WHO IS IT, BLUECOAT?
WHO?
LOOK FOR YOURSELF, GOLDEN BOY--
--JUST ANOTHER JUNKIE-- BLOWN HIMSELF TO HELL!
THE ONE CALLED "SCRATCH"-- WHOM I SAVED!
HOW LONG...?
LOOKS LIKE HE OVER-DOSED YESTERDAY, KA-ZAR!
THERE IS A DEMON LOOMING OVER CONCRETE LAND--
--A PLAGUE TO RIVAL WAR FOR ITS VICIOUSNESS!
WILLING OR NO-- THERE IS A MURDER HERE--
--AND THUS THERE IS A KILLER TO UNMASK!
KA-ZAR KNOWS JUST WHERE TO BEGIN THE SEARCH!

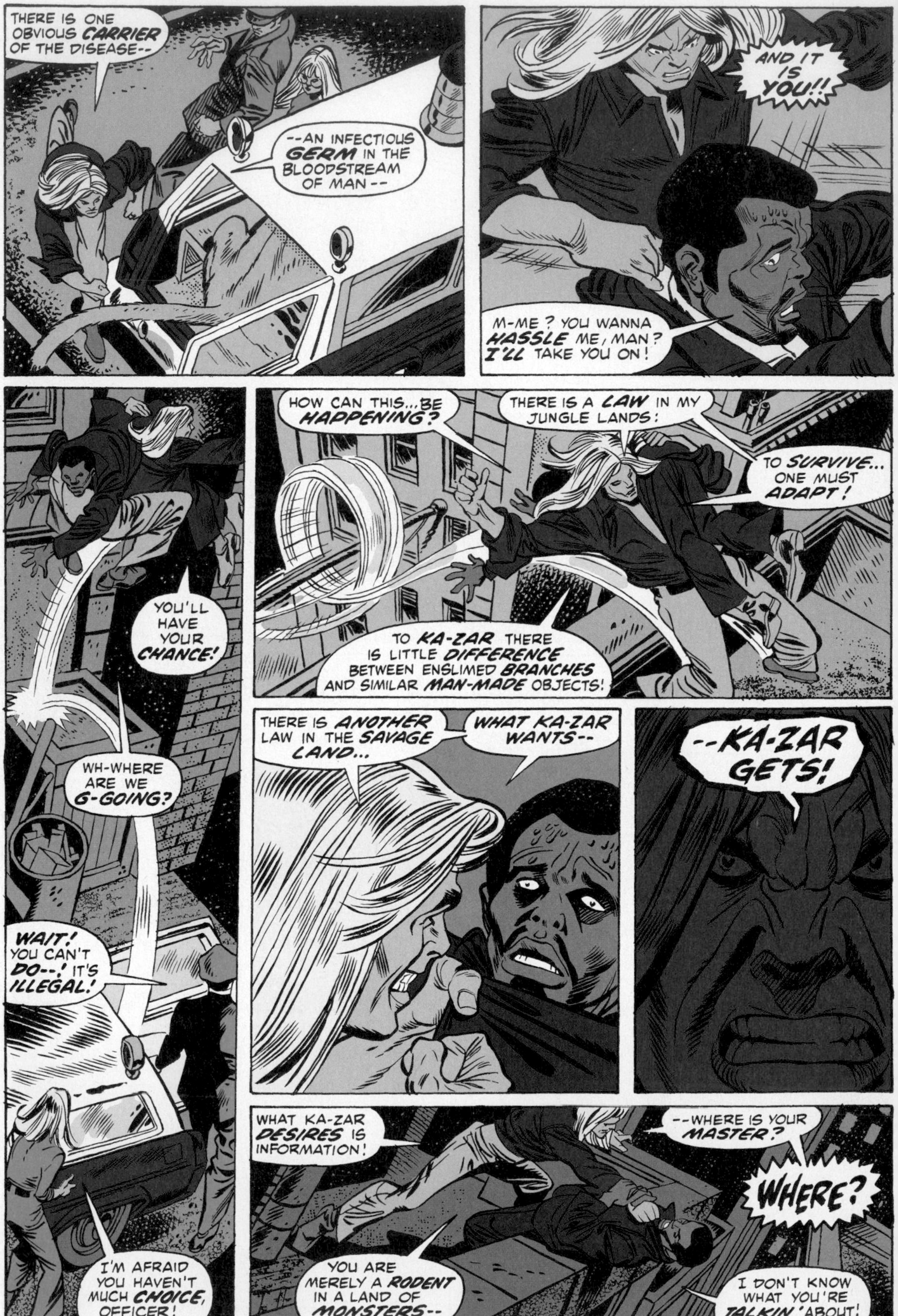
THERE IS ONE OBVIOUS CARRIER OF THE DISEASE--
--AN INFECTIOUS GERM IN THE BLOODSTREAM OF MAN--
AND IT IS YOU!!
M-ME? YOU WANNA HASSLE ME, MAN? I'LL TAKE YOU ON!
YOU'LL HAVE YOUR CHANCE!
WH-WHERE ARE WE G-GOING?
WAIT! YOU CAN'T DO--! IT'S ILLEGAL!
I'M AFRAID YOU HAVEN'T MUCH CHOICE, OFFICER!
HOW CAN THIS... BE HAPPENING?
THERE IS A LAW IN MY JUNGLE LANDS:
TO SURVIVE... ONE MUST ADAPT!
TO KA-ZAR THERE IS LITTLE DIFFERENCE BETWEEN ENSLIMED BRANCHES AND SIMILAR MAN-MADE OBJECTS!
THERE IS ANOTHER LAW IN THE SAVAGE LAND...
WHAT KA-ZAR WANTS--
--KA-ZAR GETS!
WHAT KA-ZAR DESIRES IS INFORMATION!
YOU ARE MERELY A RODENT IN A LAND OF MONSTERS--
--WHERE IS YOUR MASTER?
WHERE?
I DON'T KNOW WHAT YOU'RE TALKIN' ABOUT!

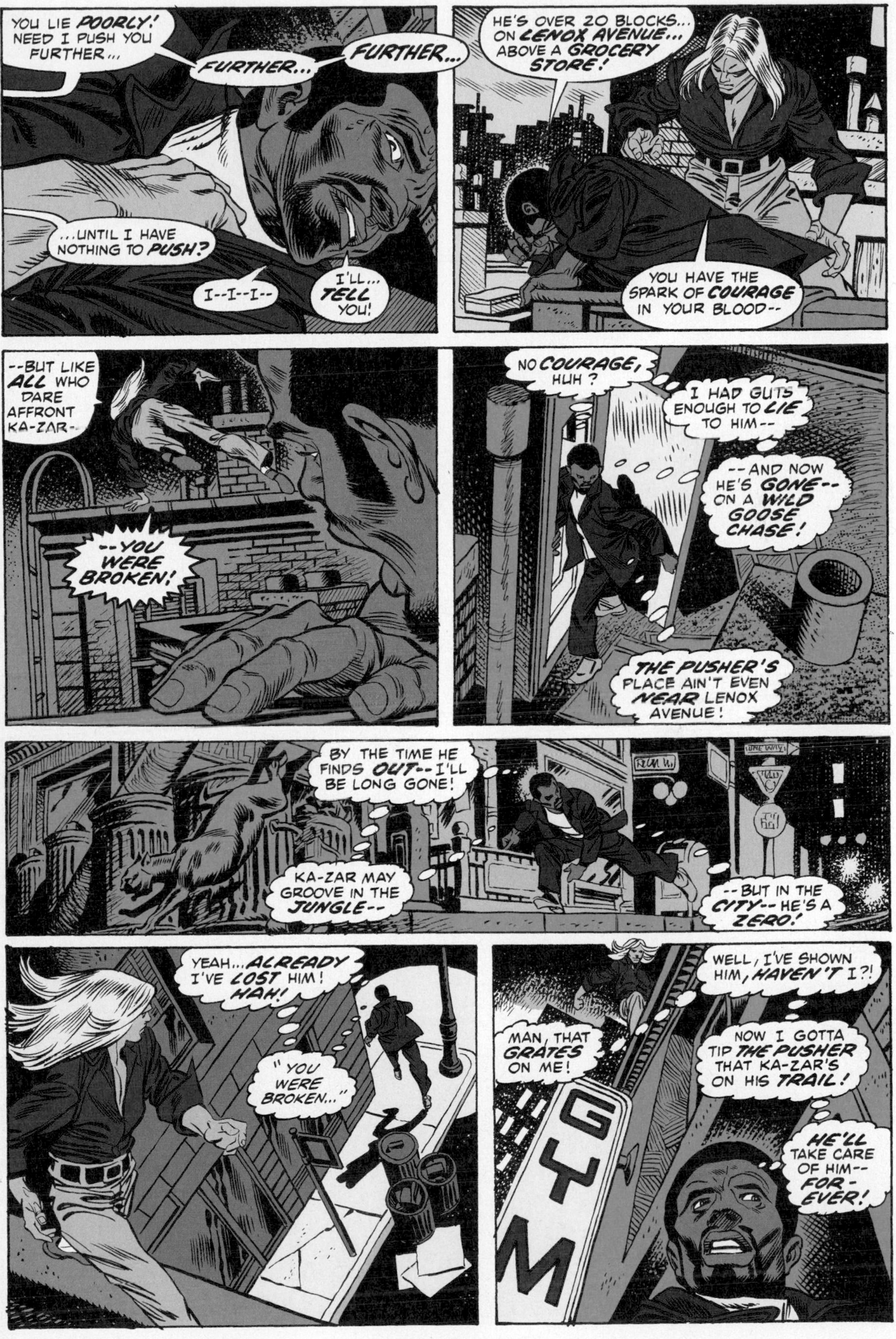

YOU LIE POORLY! NEED I PUSH YOU FURTHER...
FURTHER...
FURTHER...
...UNTIL I HAVE NOTHING TO PUSH?
I--I--I--
I'LL... TELL YOU!
HE'S OVER 20 BLOCKS... ON LENOX AVENUE... ABOVE A GROCERY STORE!
YOU HAVE THE SPARK OF COURAGE IN YOUR BLOOD--
--BUT LIKE ALL WHO DARE AFFRONT KA-ZAR--
--YOU WERE BROKEN!
NO COURAGE, HUH?
I HAD GUTS ENOUGH TO LIE TO HIM--
--AND NOW HE'S GONE--ON A WILD GOOSE CHASE!
THE PUSHER'S PLACE AIN'T EVEN NEAR LENOX AVENUE!
BY THE TIME HE FINDS OUT--I'LL BE LONG GONE!
KA-ZAR MAY GROOVE IN THE JUNGLE--
--BUT IN THE CITY--HE'S A ZERO!
YEAH...ALREADY I'VE LOST HIM! HAH!
"YOU WERE BROKEN..."
WELL, I'VE SHOWN HIM, HAVEN'T I?!
MAN, THAT GRATES ON ME!
NOW I GOTTA TIP THE PUSHER THAT KA-ZAR'S ON HIS TRAIL!
HE'LL TAKE CARE OF HIM--FOR-EVER!
GYM

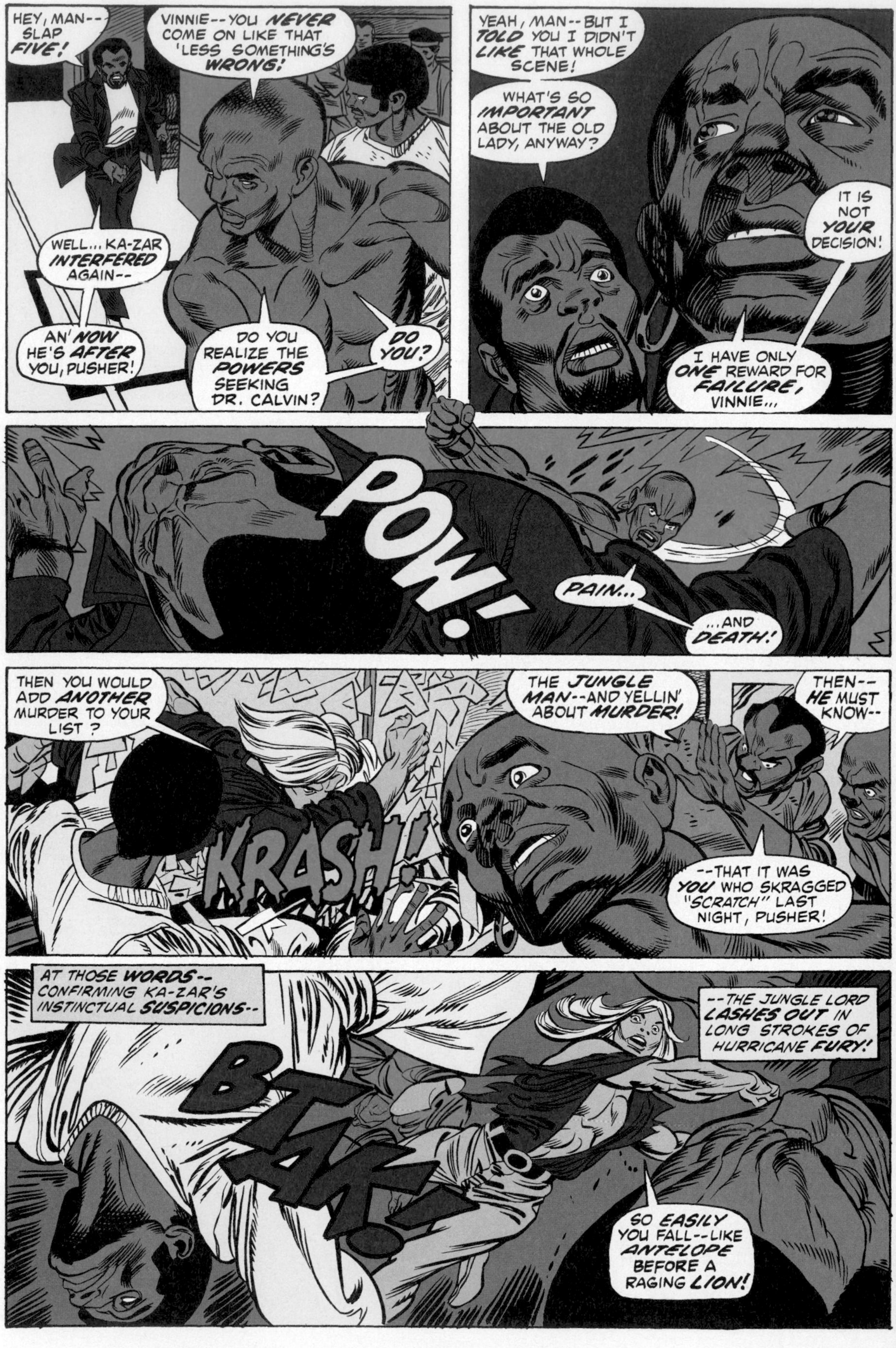
HEY, MAN-- SLAP FIVE!
VINNIE--YOU NEVER COME ON LIKE THAT 'LESS SOMETHING'S WRONG!
WELL... KA-ZAR INTERFERED AGAIN--
AN' NOW HE'S AFTER YOU, PUSHER!
DO YOU REALIZE THE POWERS SEEKING DR. CALVIN?
DO YOU?
YEAH, MAN--BUT I TOLD YOU I DIDN'T LIKE THAT WHOLE SCENE!
WHAT'S SO IMPORTANT ABOUT THE OLD LADY, ANYWAY?
IT IS NOT YOUR DECISION!
I HAVE ONLY ONE REWARD FOR FAILURE, VINNIE...
POW!
PAIN...
...AND DEATH!
THEN YOU WOULD ADD ANOTHER MURDER TO YOUR LIST?
KRASH!
THE JUNGLE MAN--AND YELLIN' ABOUT MURDER!
THEN-- HE MUST KNOW--
--THAT IT WAS YOU WHO SKRAGGED "SCRATCH" LAST NIGHT, PUSHER!
AT THOSE WORDS--CONFIRMING KA-ZAR'S INSTINCTUAL SUSPICIONS--
--THE JUNGLE LORD LASHES OUT IN LONG STROKES OF HURRICANE FURY!
BTAK!
SO EASILY YOU FALL--LIKE ANTELOPE BEFORE A RAGING LION!

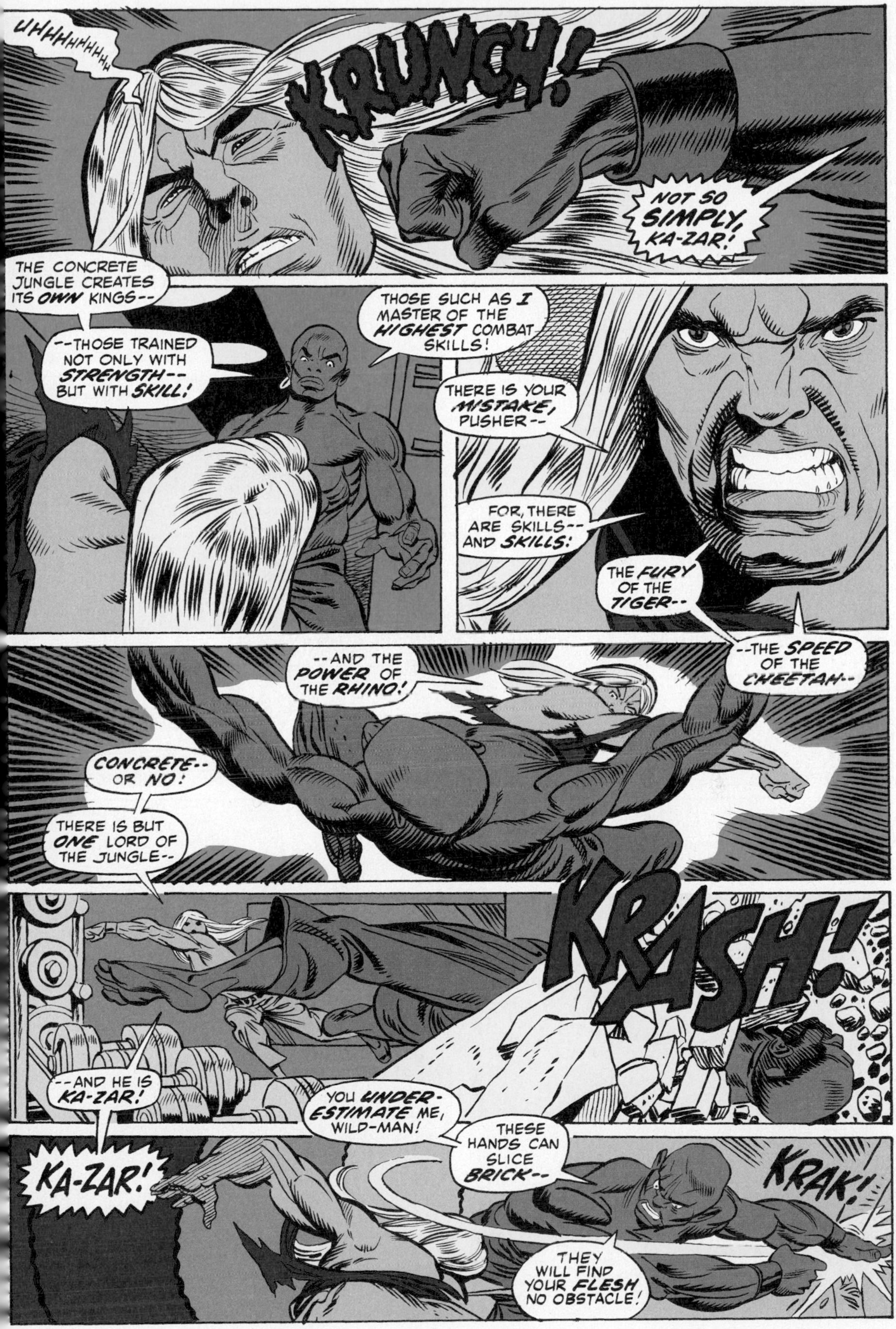
UHHHHHHHHH
KRUNCH!
NOT SO SIMPLY, KA-ZAR!
THE CONCRETE JUNGLE CREATES ITS OWN KINGS--
--THOSE TRAINED NOT ONLY WITH STRENGTH-- BUT WITH SKILL!
THOSE SUCH AS I MASTER OF THE HIGHEST COMBAT SKILLS!
THERE IS YOUR MISTAKE, PUSHER--
FOR, THERE ARE SKILLS-- AND SKILLS:
THE FURY OF THE TIGER--
--THE SPEED OF THE CHEETAH--
--AND THE POWER OF THE RHINO!
CONCRETE-- OR NO:
THERE IS BUT ONE LORD OF THE JUNGLE--
KRASH!
--AND HE IS KA-ZAR!
YOU UNDER-ESTIMATE ME, WILD-MAN!
THESE HANDS CAN SLICE BRICK--
KRAK!
KA-ZAR!
THEY WILL FIND YOUR FLESH NO OBSTACLE!

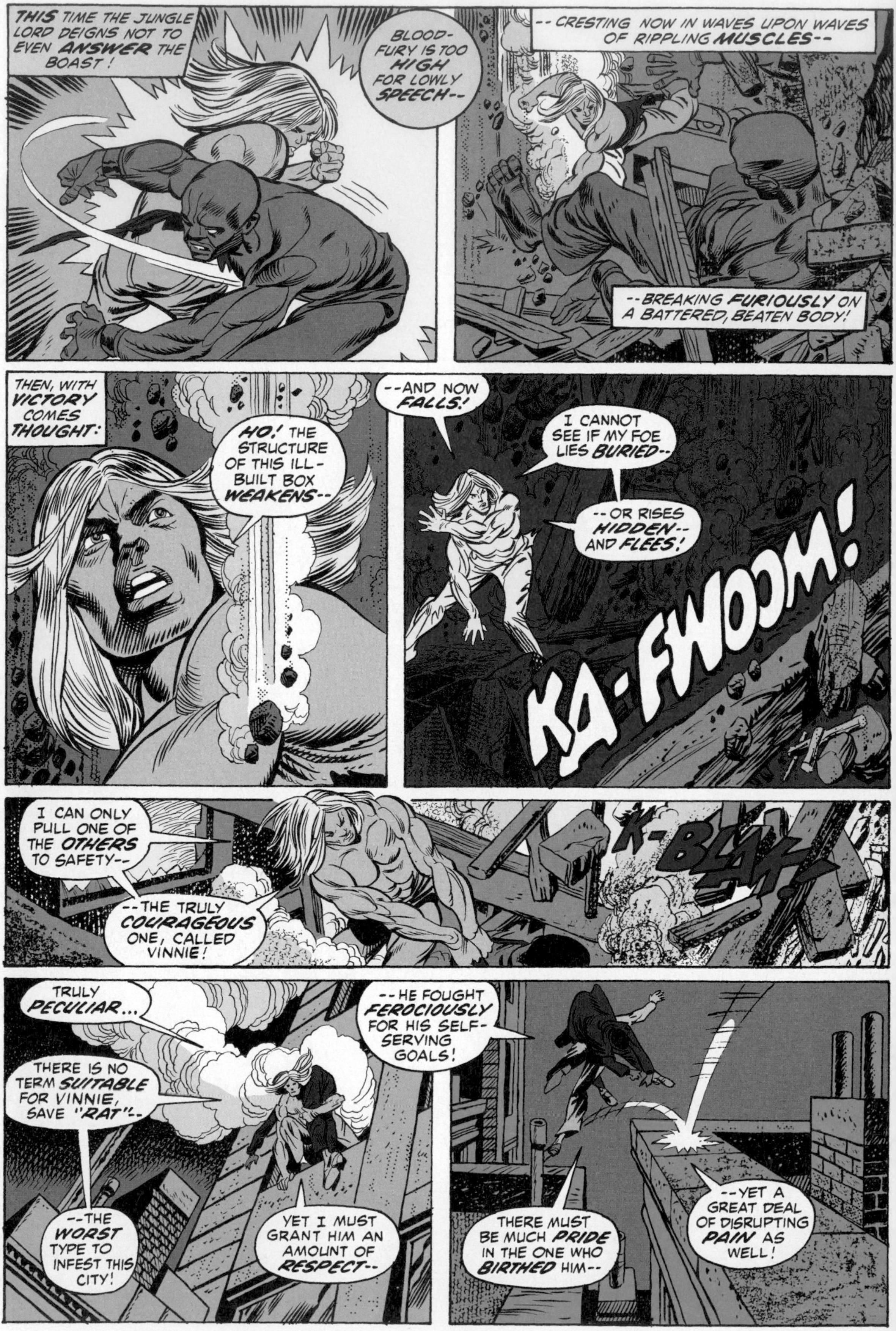
THIS TIME THE JUNGLE LORD DEIGNS NOT TO EVEN ANSWER THE BOAST!
BLOOD-FURY IS TOO HIGH FOR LOWLY SPEECH--
--CRESTING NOW IN WAVES UPON WAVES OF RIPPLING MUSCLES--
--BREAKING FURIOUSLY ON A BATTERED, BEATEN BODY!
THEN, WITH VICTORY COMES THOUGHT:
HO! THE STRUCTURE OF THIS ILL-BUILT BOX WEAKENS--
--AND NOW FALLS!
I CANNOT SEE IF MY FOE LIES BURIED--
--OR RISES HIDDEN--AND FLEES!
KA-FWOOM!
I CAN ONLY PULL ONE OF THE OTHERS TO SAFETY--
--THE TRULY COURAGEOUS ONE, CALLED VINNIE!
K-BLAK!
TRULY PECULIAR...
THERE IS NO TERM SUITABLE FOR VINNIE, SAVE "RAT"--
--THE WORST TYPE TO INFEST THIS CITY!
--HE FOUGHT FEROCIOUSLY FOR HIS SELF-SERVING GOALS!
YET I MUST GRANT HIM AN AMOUNT OF RESPECT--
THERE MUST BE MUCH PRIDE IN THE ONE WHO BIRTHED HIM--
--YET A GREAT DEAL OF DISRUPTING PAIN AS WELL!

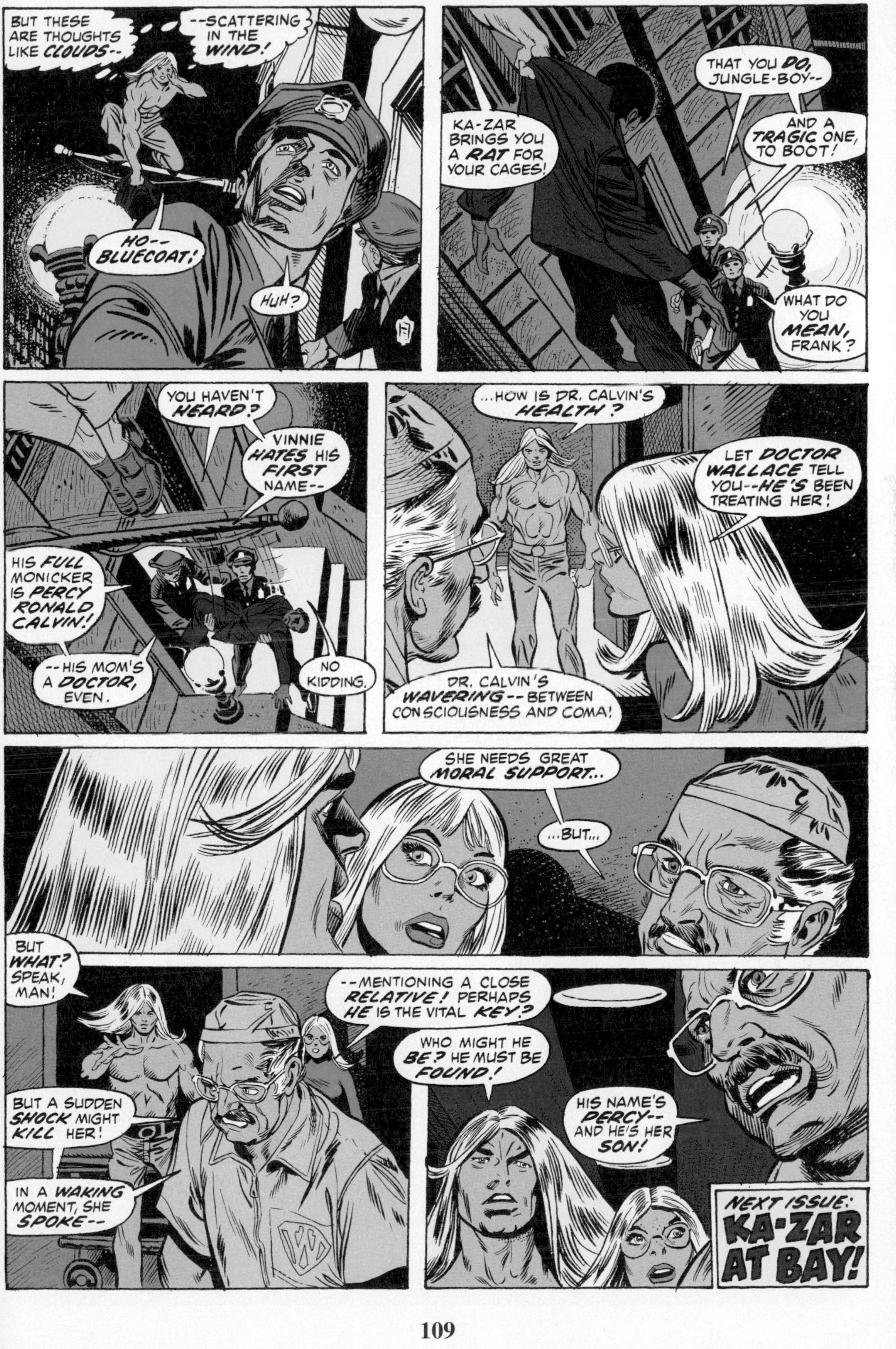
BUT THESE ARE THOUGHTS LIKE CLOUDS--
--SCATTERING IN THE WIND!
HO--BLUECOAT!
HUH?
KA-ZAR BRINGS YOU A RAT FOR YOUR CAGES!
THAT YOU DO, JUNGLE-BOY--
AND A TRAGIC ONE, TO BOOT!
WHAT DO YOU MEAN, FRANK?
YOU HAVEN'T HEARD?
VINNIE HATES HIS FIRST NAME--
HIS FULL MONICKER IS PERCY RONALD CALVIN!
--HIS MOM'S A DOCTOR, EVEN.
NO KIDDING.
...HOW IS DR. CALVIN'S HEALTH?
LET DOCTOR WALLACE TELL YOU--HE'S BEEN TREATING HER!
DR. CALVIN'S WAVERING--BETWEEN CONSCIOUSNESS AND COMA!
SHE NEEDS GREAT MORAL SUPPORT...
...BUT...
BUT WHAT? SPEAK, MAN!
BUT A SUDDEN SHOCK MIGHT KILL HER!
IN A WAKING MOMENT, SHE SPOKE--
--MENTIONING A CLOSE RELATIVE! PERHAPS HE IS THE VITAL KEY?
WHO MIGHT HE BE? HE MUST BE FOUND!
HIS NAME'S PERCY--AND HE'S HER SON!
NEXT ISSUE: KA-ZAR AT BAY!

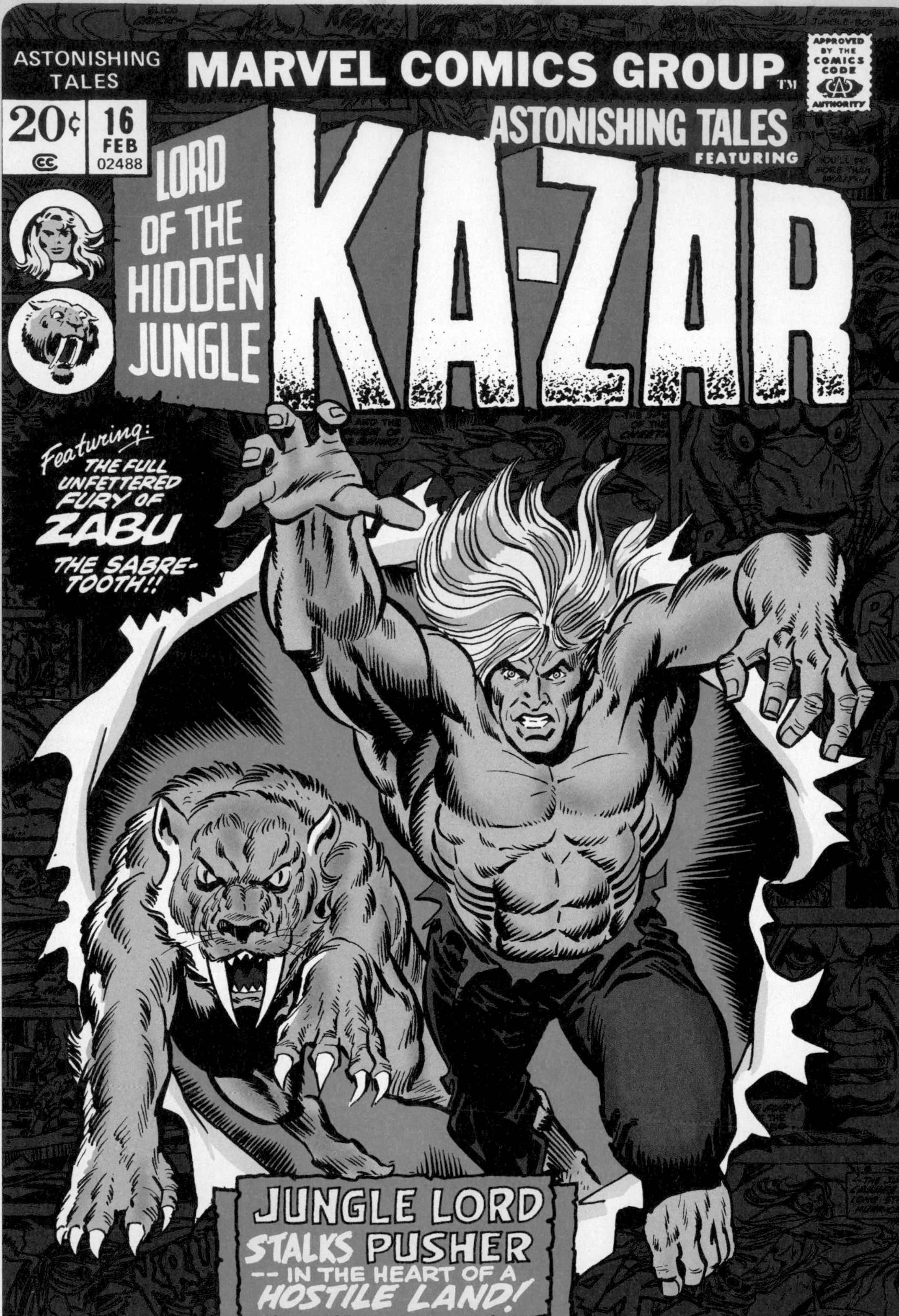
ASTONISHING TALES
MARVEL COMICS GROUP
APPROVED BY THE COMICS CODE AUTHORITY
20¢
16 FEB 02488
ASTONISHING TALES FEATURING
LORD OF THE HIDDEN JUNGLE
KA-ZAR
Featuring: THE FULL UNFETTERED FURY OF ZABU THE SABRE-TOOTH!!
JUNGLE LORD STALKS PUSHER -- IN THE HEART OF A HOSTILE LAND!

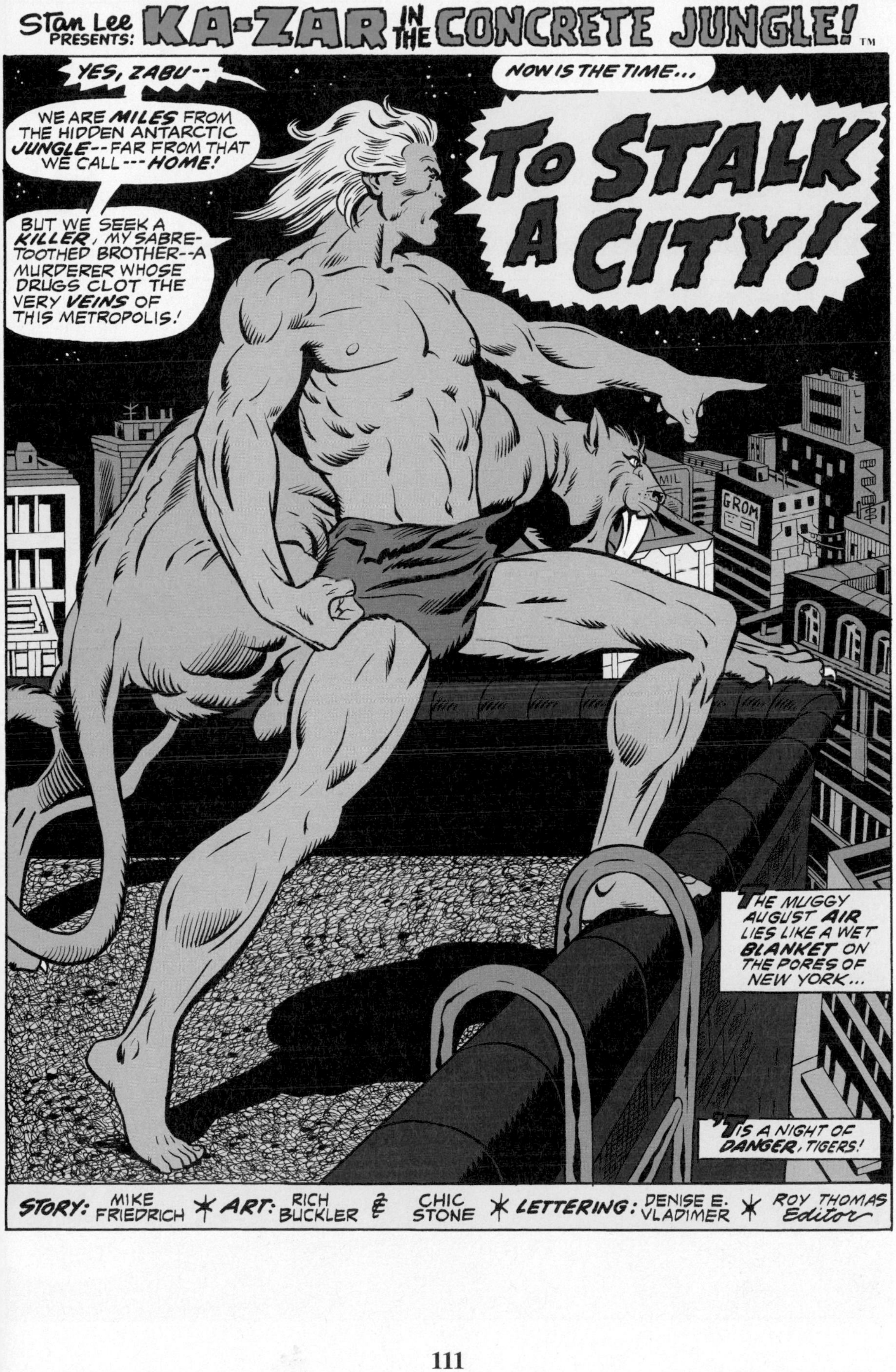
Stan Lee PRESENTS: KA-ZAR IN THE CONCRETE JUNGLE! TM
YES, ZABU--
WE ARE MILES FROM THE HIDDEN ANTARCTIC JUNGLE--FAR FROM THAT WE CALL---HOME!
BUT WE SEEK A KILLER, MY SABRE-TOOTHED BROTHER--A MURDERER WHOSE DRUGS CLOT THE VERY VEINS OF THIS METROPOLIS!
NOW IS THE TIME...
TO STALK A CITY!
MIL
GROM
THE MUGGY AUGUST AIR LIES LIKE A WET BLANKET ON THE PORES OF NEW YORK...
'TIS A NIGHT OF DANGER, TIGERS!
STORY: MIKE FRIEDRICH * ART: RICH BUCKLER & CHIC STONE * LETTERING: DENISE E. VLADIMER * ROY THOMAS Editor

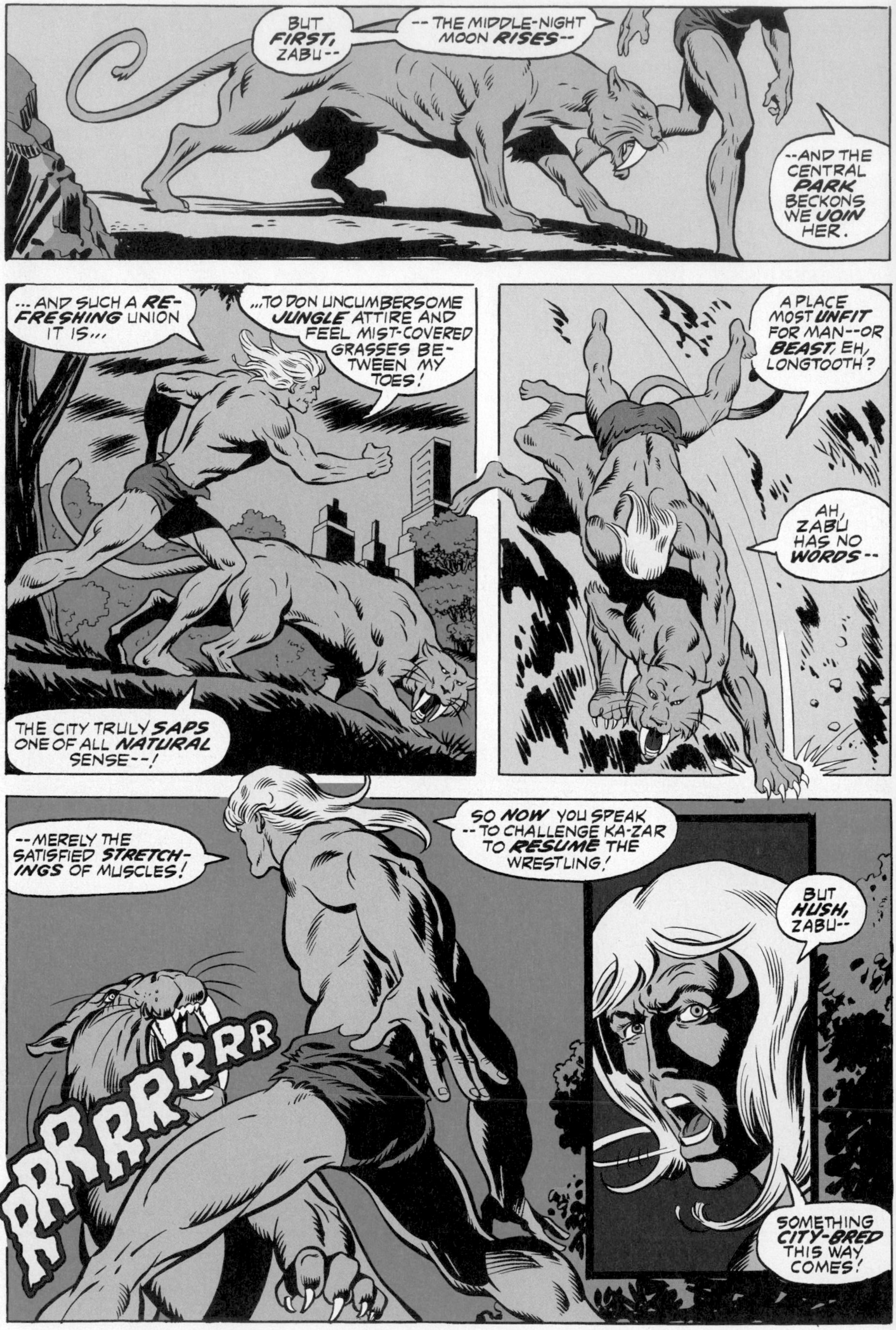

BUT FIRST, ZABU--
--THE MIDDLE-NIGHT MOON RISES--
--AND THE CENTRAL PARK BECKONS WE JOIN HER.
...AND SUCH A REFRESHING UNION IT IS...
...TO DON UNCUMBERSOME JUNGLE ATTIRE AND FEEL MIST-COVERED GRASSES BETWEEN MY TOES!
THE CITY TRULY SAPS ONE OF ALL NATURAL SENSE--!
A PLACE MOST UNFIT FOR MAN--OR BEAST, EH, LONGTOOTH?
AH, ZABU HAS NO WORDS--
--MERELY THE SATISFIED STRETCHINGS OF MUSCLES!
SO NOW YOU SPEAK--TO CHALLENGE KA-ZAR TO RESUME THE WRESTLING!
RRRRRRRR
BUT HUSH, ZABU--
SOMETHING CITY-BRED THIS WAY COMES!

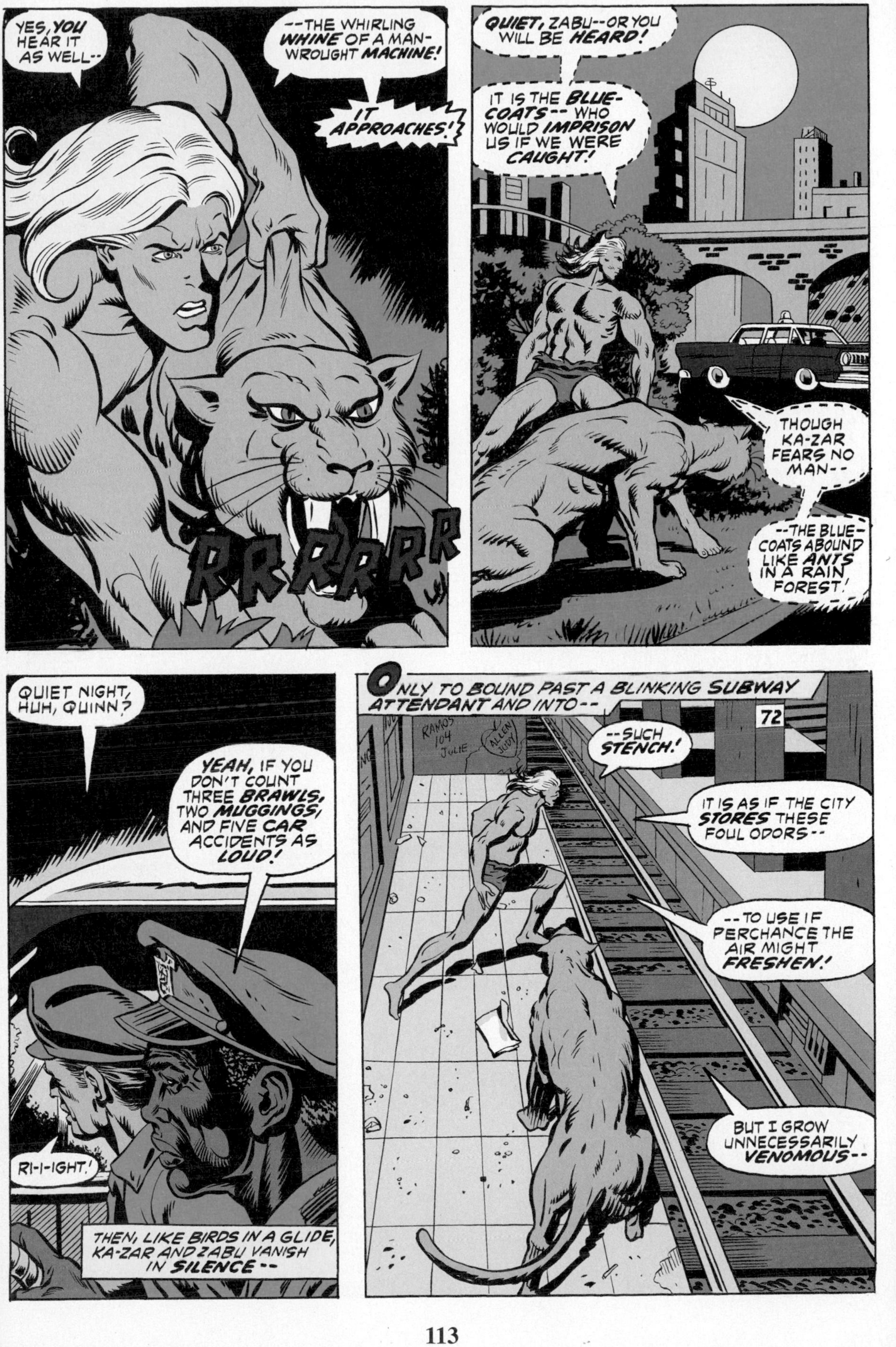
YES, YOU HEAR IT AS WELL--
--THE WHIRLING WHINE OF A MAN-WROUGHT MACHINE!
IT APPROACHES!
RRRRRRR
QUIET, ZABU--OR YOU WILL BE HEARD!
IT IS THE BLUE-COATS-- WHO WOULD IMPRISON US IF WE WERE CAUGHT!
THOUGH KA-ZAR FEARS NO MAN--
--THE BLUE-COATS ABOUND LIKE ANTS IN A RAIN FOREST!
QUIET NIGHT, HUH, QUINN?
YEAH, IF YOU DON'T COUNT THREE BRAWLS, TWO MUGGINGS, AND FIVE CAR ACCIDENTS AS LOUD!
RI-I-IGHT!
THEN, LIKE BIRDS IN A GLIDE, KA-ZAR AND ZABU VANISH IN SILENCE--
ONLY TO BOUND PAST A BLINKING SUBWAY ATTENDANT AND INTO--
72
RAMOS 104
JULIE
ALLEN JUDY
--SUCH STENCH!
IT IS AS IF THE CITY STORES THESE FOUL ODORS--
--TO USE IF PERCHANCE THE AIR MIGHT FRESHEN!
BUT I GROW UNNECESSARILY VENOMOUS--

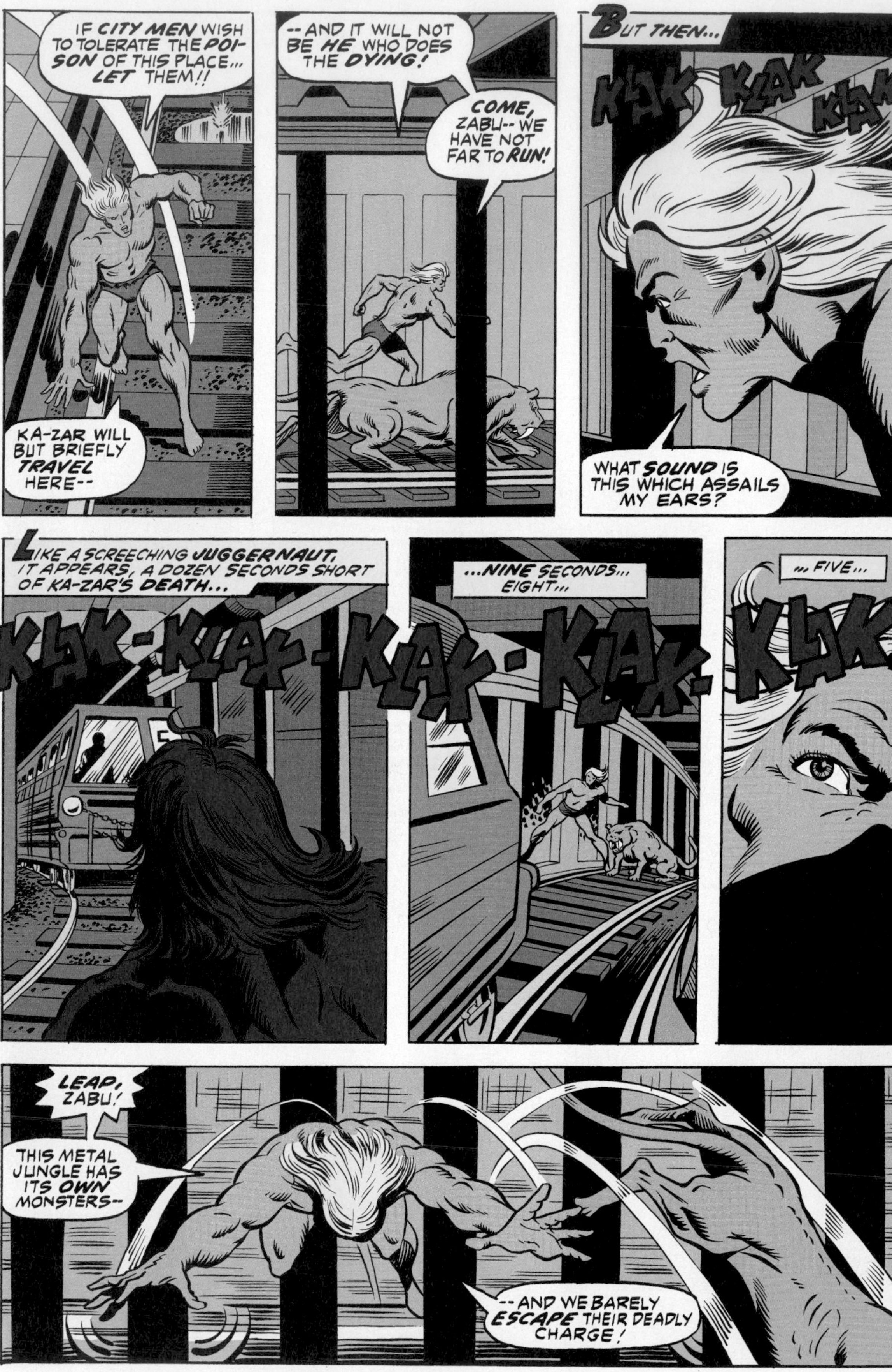
IF CITY MEN WISH TO TOLERATE THE POISON OF THIS PLACE... LET THEM!!
KA-ZAR WILL BUT BRIEFLY TRAVEL HERE--
--AND IT WILL NOT BE HE WHO DOES THE DYING!
COME, ZABU-- WE HAVE NOT FAR TO RUN!
BUT THEN...
KLAK KLAK KLAK
WHAT SOUND IS THIS WHICH ASSAILS MY EARS?
LIKE A SCREECHING JUGGERNAUT, IT APPEARS, A DOZEN SECONDS SHORT OF KA-ZAR'S DEATH...
KLAK-KLAK-KLAK-KLAK-KLAK
...NINE SECONDS... EIGHT...
...FIVE...
LEAP, ZABU!
THIS METAL JUNGLE HAS ITS OWN MONSTERS--
--AND WE BARELY ESCAPE THEIR DEADLY CHARGE!

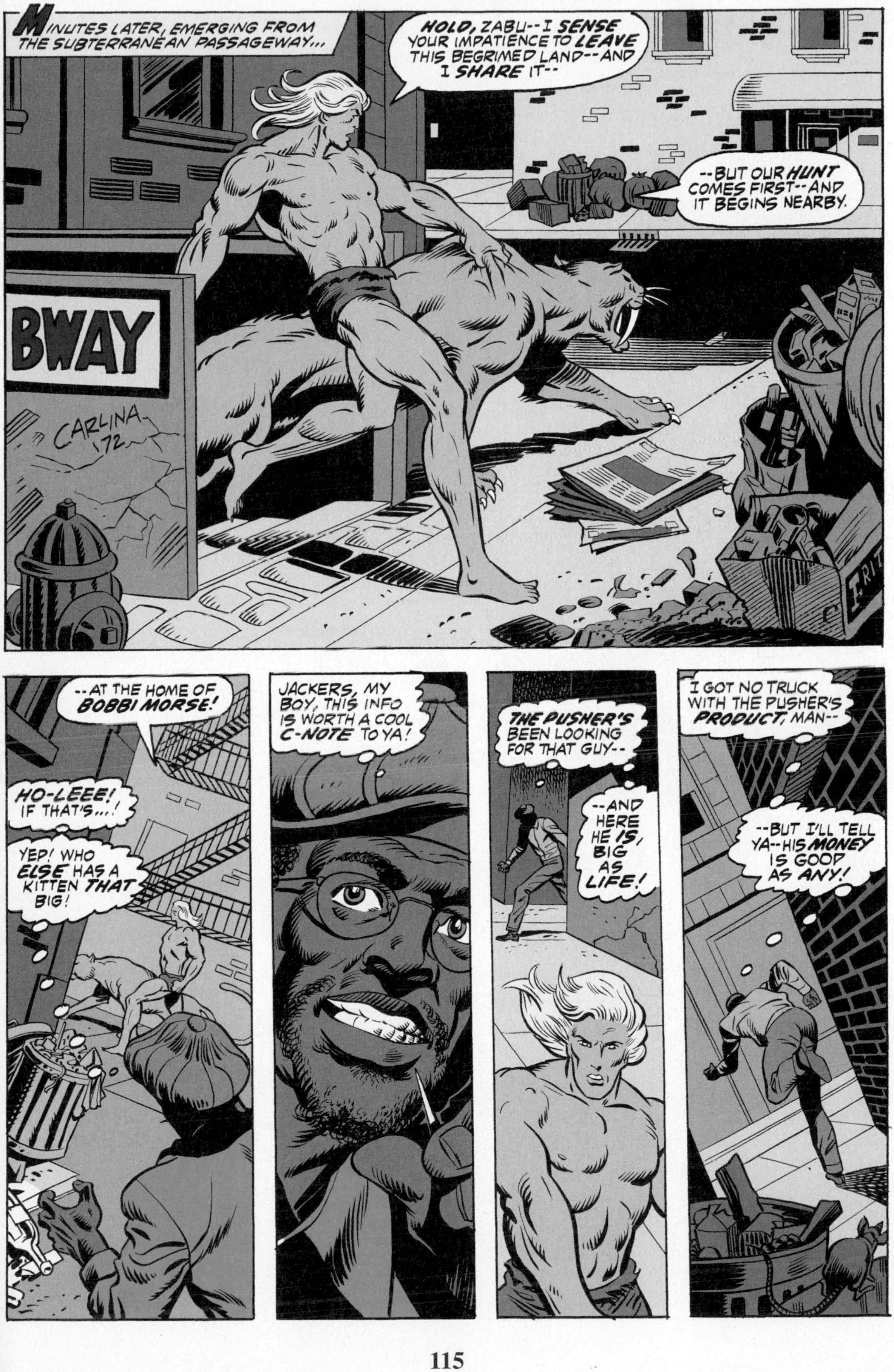
MINUTES LATER, EMERGING FROM THE SUBTERRANEAN PASSAGEWAY...
HOLD, ZABU--I SENSE YOUR IMPATIENCE TO LEAVE THIS BEGRIMED LAND--AND I SHARE IT--
--BUT OUR HUNT COMES FIRST--AND IT BEGINS NEARBY.
BWAY
CARLINA '72
--AT THE HOME OF BOBBI MORSE!
HO-LEEE! IF THAT'S...!
YEP! WHO ELSE HAS A KITTEN THAT BIG!
JACKERS, MY BOY, THIS INFO IS WORTH A COOL C-NOTE TO YA!
THE PUSHER'S BEEN LOOKING FOR THAT GUY--
--AND HERE HE IS, BIG AS LIFE!
I GOT NO TRUCK WITH THE PUSHER'S PRODUCT, MAN--
--BUT I'LL TELL YA--HIS MONEY IS GOOD AS ANY!

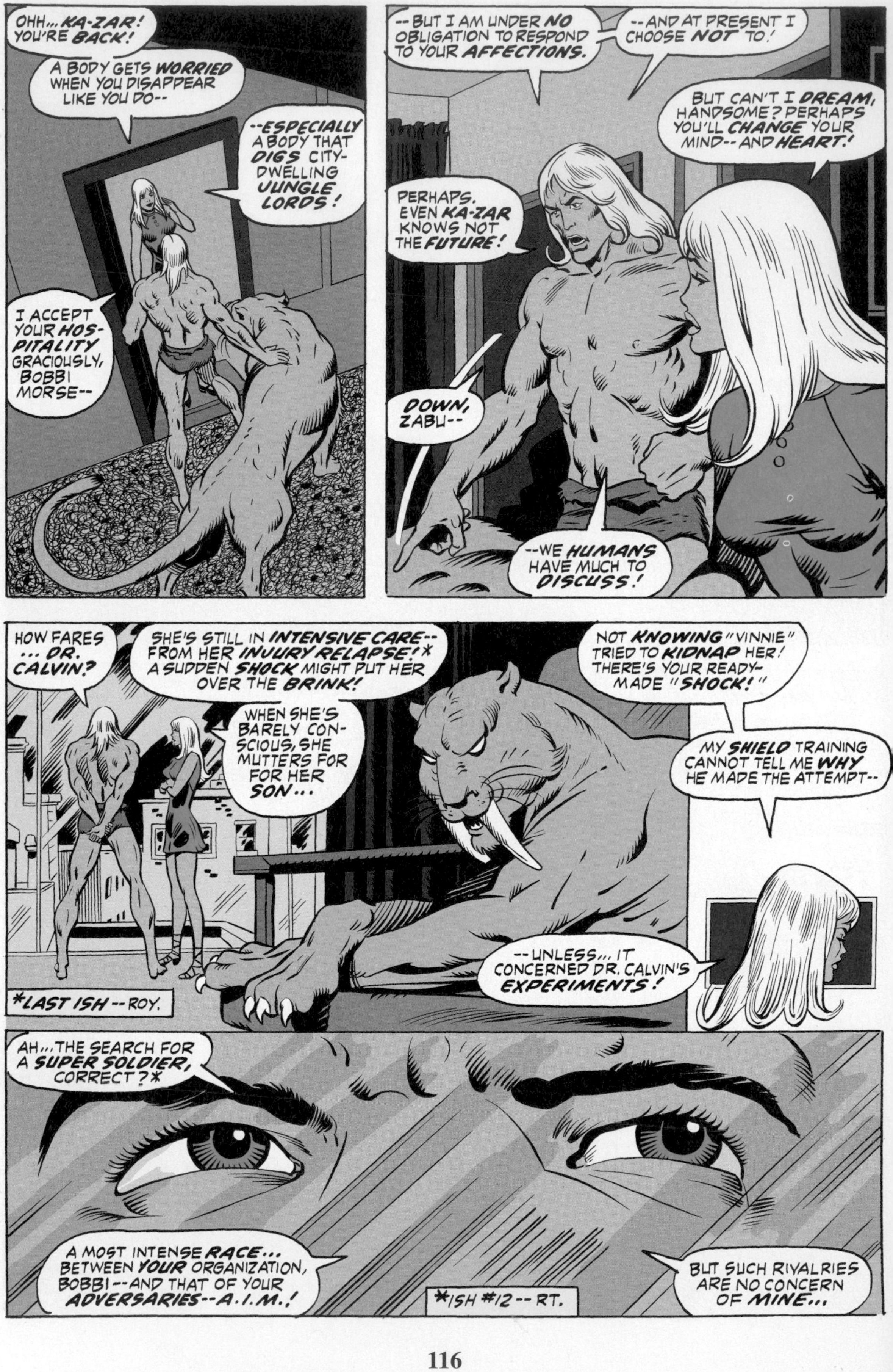
OHH... KA-ZAR! YOU'RE BACK!
A BODY GETS WORRIED WHEN YOU DISAPPEAR LIKE YOU DO--
--ESPECIALLY A BODY THAT DIGS CITY-DWELLING JUNGLE LORDS!
I ACCEPT YOUR HOSPITALITY GRACIOUSLY, BOBBI MORSE--
--BUT I AM UNDER NO OBLIGATION TO RESPOND TO YOUR AFFECTIONS.
--AND AT PRESENT I CHOOSE NOT TO!
BUT CAN'T I DREAM, HANDSOME? PERHAPS YOU'LL CHANGE YOUR MIND-- AND HEART!
PERHAPS. EVEN KA-ZAR KNOWS NOT THE FUTURE!
DOWN, ZABU--
--WE HUMANS HAVE MUCH TO DISCUSS!
HOW FARES ... DR. CALVIN?
SHE'S STILL IN INTENSIVE CARE-- FROM HER INJURY RELAPSE!* A SUDDEN SHOCK MIGHT PUT HER OVER THE BRINK!
WHEN SHE'S BARELY CONSCIOUS, SHE MUTTERS FOR FOR HER SON...
NOT KNOWING "VINNIE" TRIED TO KIDNAP HER! THERE'S YOUR READY-MADE "SHOCK!"
MY SHIELD TRAINING CANNOT TELL ME WHY HE MADE THE ATTEMPT--
--UNLESS... IT CONCERNED DR. CALVIN'S EXPERIMENTS!
*LAST ISH -- ROY.
AH... THE SEARCH FOR A SUPER SOLDIER, CORRECT?*
A MOST INTENSE RACE... BETWEEN YOUR ORGANIZATION, BOBBI --AND THAT OF YOUR ADVERSARIES--A.I.M.!
BUT SUCH RIVALRIES ARE NO CONCERN OF MINE...
*ISH #12 -- RT.

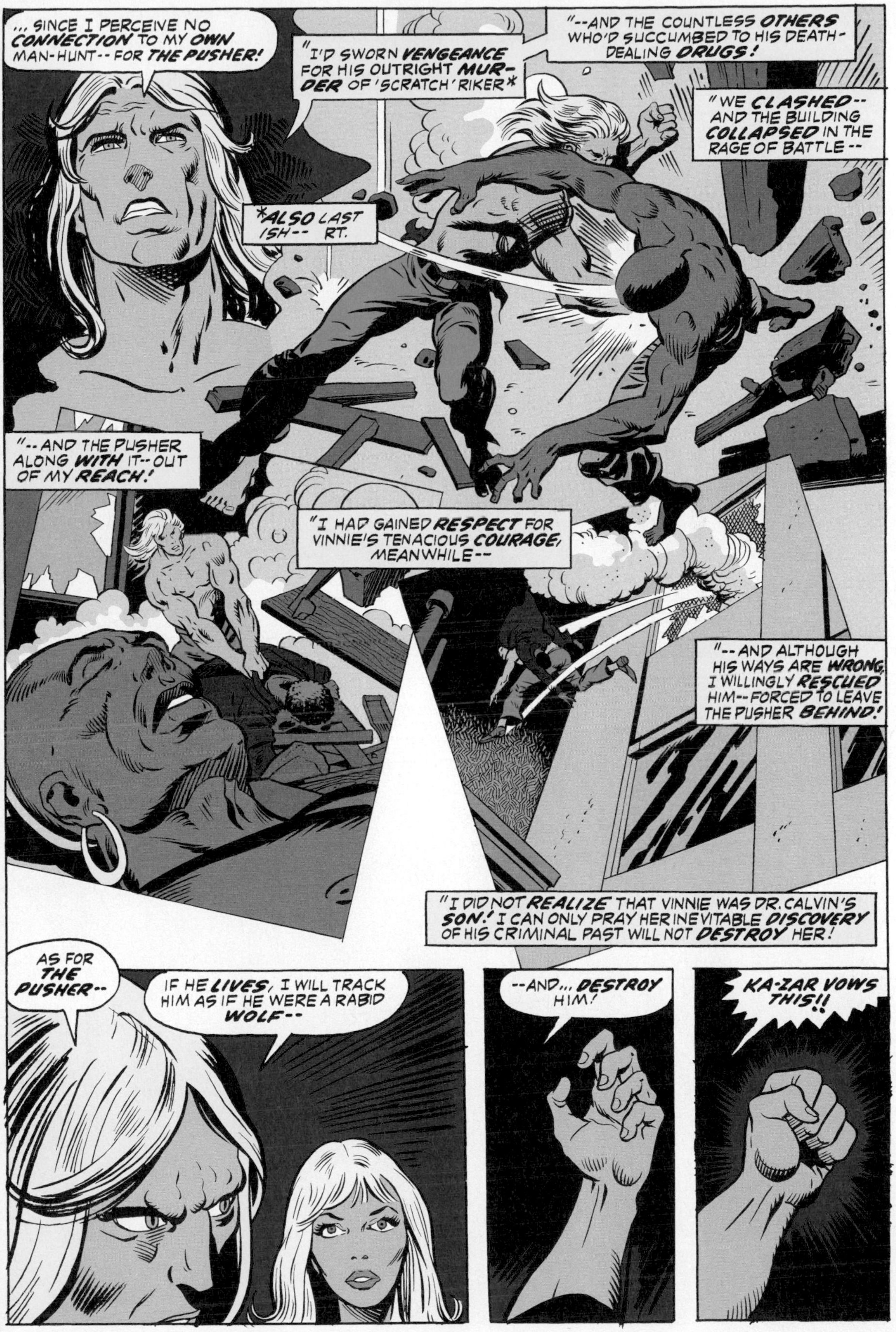
... SINCE I PERCEIVE NO CONNECTION TO MY OWN MAN-HUNT -- FOR THE PUSHER!
"I'D SWORN VENGEANCE FOR HIS OUTRIGHT MURDER OF 'SCRATCH' RIKER*
"--AND THE COUNTLESS OTHERS WHO'D SUCCUMBED TO HIS DEATH-DEALING DRUGS!
"WE CLASHED -- AND THE BUILDING COLLAPSED IN THE RAGE OF BATTLE --
*ALSO LAST ISH -- RT.
"-- AND THE PUSHER ALONG WITH IT -- OUT OF MY REACH!
"I HAD GAINED RESPECT FOR VINNIE'S TENACIOUS COURAGE, MEANWHILE --
"-- AND ALTHOUGH HIS WAYS ARE WRONG, I WILLINGLY RESCUED HIM -- FORCED TO LEAVE THE PUSHER BEHIND!
"I DID NOT REALIZE THAT VINNIE WAS DR. CALVIN'S SON! I CAN ONLY PRAY HER INEVITABLE DISCOVERY OF HIS CRIMINAL PAST WILL NOT DESTROY HER!
AS FOR THE PUSHER --
IF HE LIVES, I WILL TRACK HIM AS IF HE WERE A RABID WOLF --
-- AND... DESTROY HIM!
KA-ZAR VOWS THIS!!

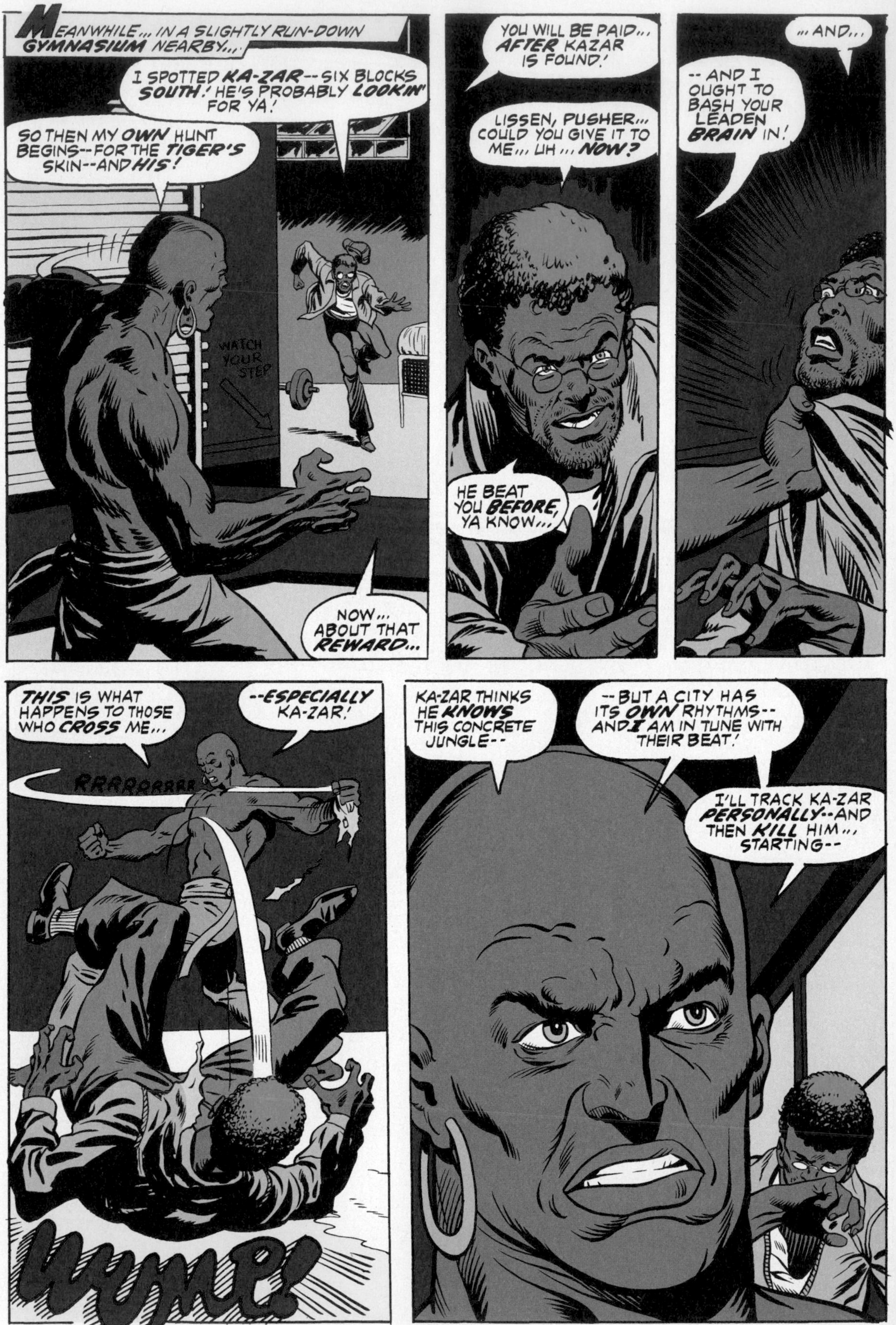
MEANWHILE... IN A SLIGHTLY RUN-DOWN GYMNASIUM NEARBY...
I SPOTTED KA-ZAR--SIX BLOCKS SOUTH! HE'S PROBABLY LOOKIN' FOR YA!
SO THEN MY OWN HUNT BEGINS--FOR THE TIGER'S SKIN--AND HIS!
WATCH YOUR STEP
NOW... ABOUT THAT REWARD...
YOU WILL BE PAID... AFTER KAZAR IS FOUND!
LISSEN, PUSHER... COULD YOU GIVE IT TO ME... UH... NOW?
HE BEAT YOU BEFORE, YA KNOW...
...AND...
--AND I OUGHT TO BASH YOUR LEADEN BRAIN IN!
THIS IS WHAT HAPPENS TO THOSE WHO CROSS ME...
--ESPECIALLY KA-ZAR!
RRRRrrrrr
WUMP!
KA-ZAR THINKS HE KNOWS THIS CONCRETE JUNGLE--
--BUT A CITY HAS ITS OWN RHYTHMS--AND I AM IN TUNE WITH THEIR BEAT!
I'LL TRACK KA-ZAR PERSONALLY--AND THEN KILL HIM... STARTING--

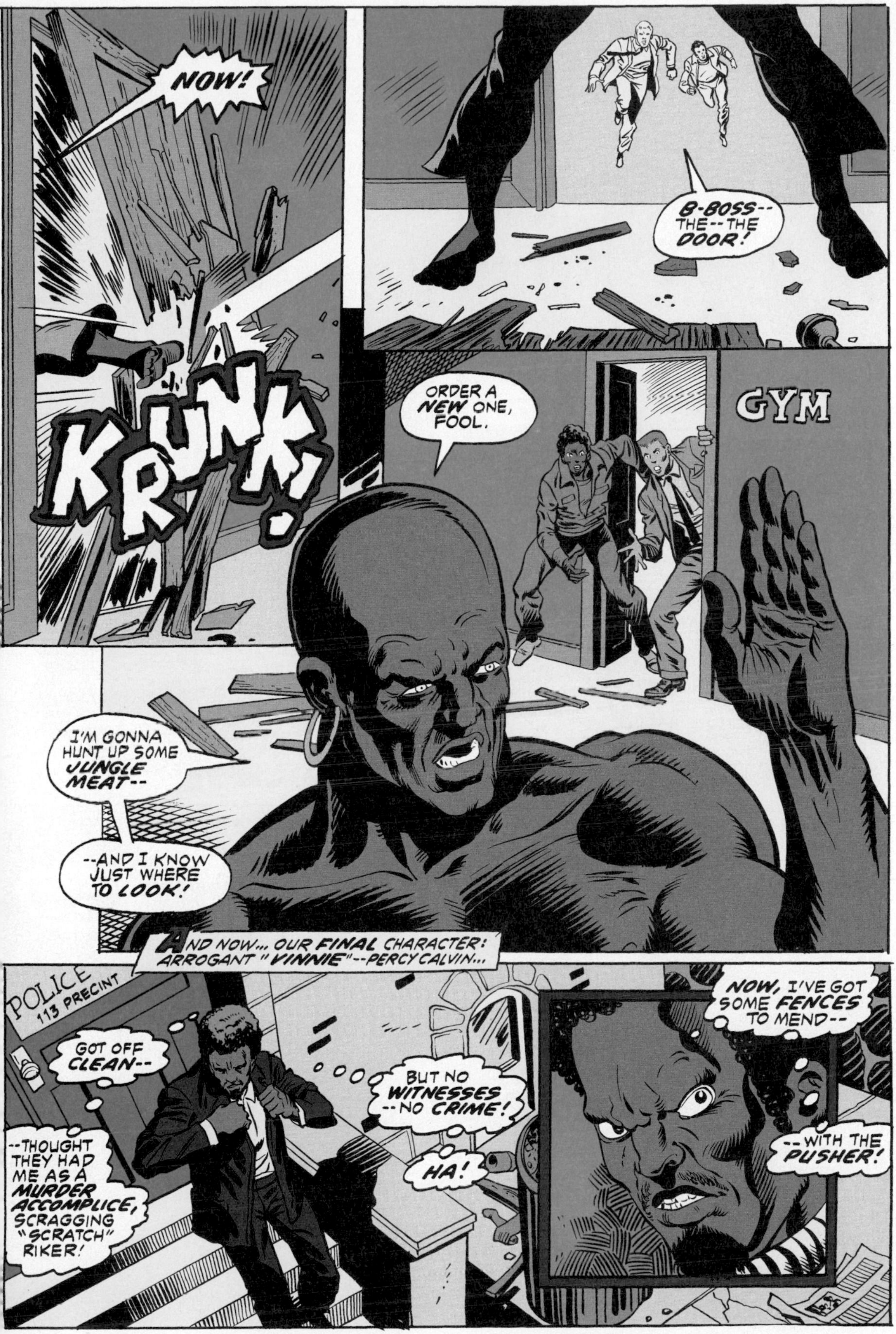
NOW!
KRUNK!
B-BOSS-- THE--THE DOOR!
ORDER A NEW ONE, FOOL.
GYM
I'M GONNA HUNT UP SOME JUNGLE MEAT--
--AND I KNOW JUST WHERE TO LOOK!
AND NOW... OUR FINAL CHARACTER: ARROGANT "VINNIE"--PERCY CALVIN...
POLICE 113 PRECINT
GOT OFF CLEAN--
--THOUGHT THEY HAD ME AS A MURDER ACCOMPLICE, SCRAGGING "SCRATCH" RIKER!
BUT NO WITNESSES --NO CRIME!
HA!
NOW, I'VE GOT SOME FENCES TO MEND--
--WITH THE PUSHER!

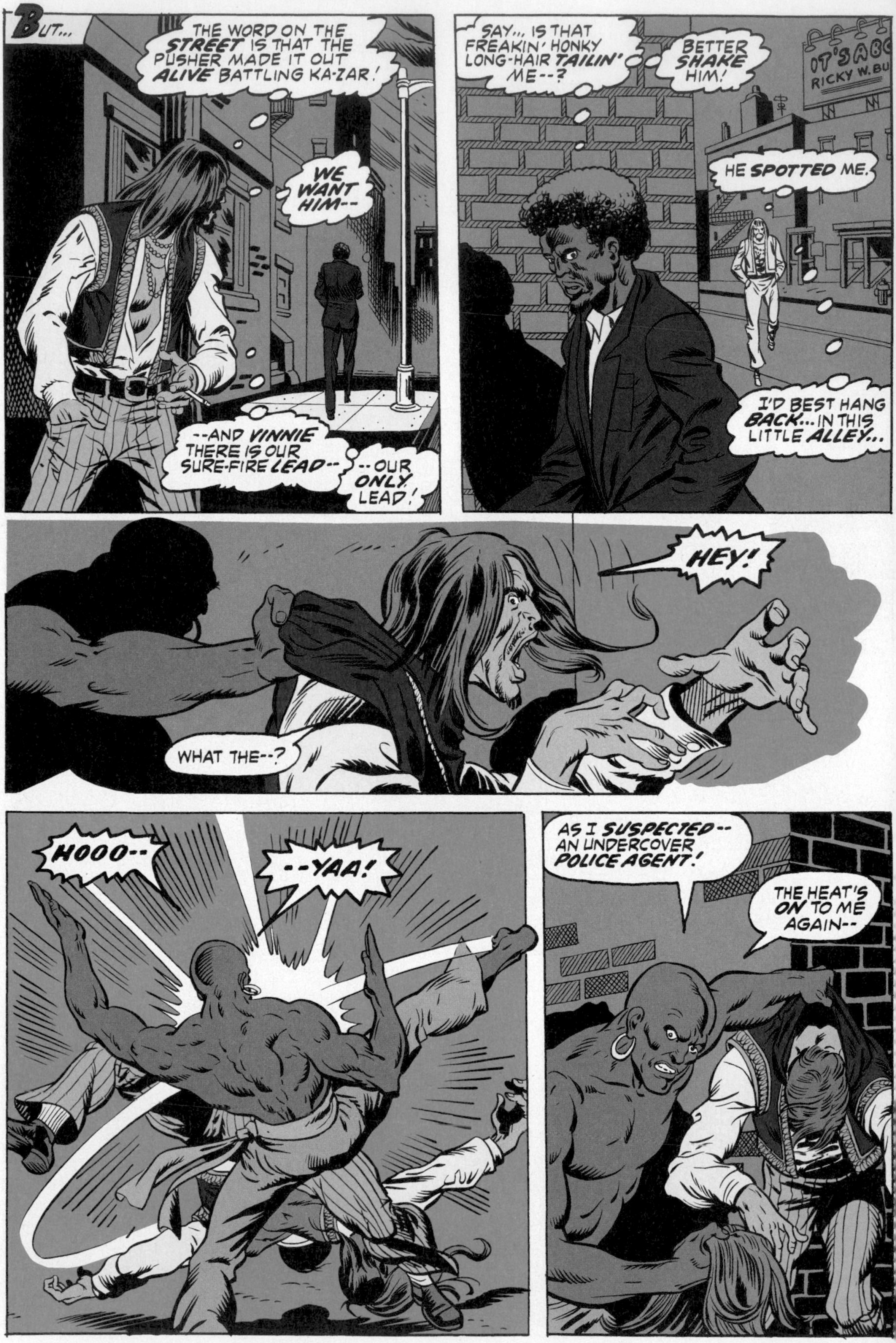
BUT...
THE WORD ON THE STREET IS THAT THE PUSHER MADE IT OUT ALIVE BATTLING KA-ZAR!
WE WANT HIM--
--AND VINNIE THERE IS OUR SURE-FIRE LEAD--
--OUR ONLY LEAD!
SAY... IS THAT FREAKIN' HONKY LONG-HAIR TAILIN' ME--?
BETTER SHAKE HIM!
HE SPOTTED ME.
I'D BEST HANG BACK... IN THIS LITTLE ALLEY...
HEY!
WHAT THE--?
HOOO--
--YAA!
AS I SUSPECTED-- AN UNDERCOVER POLICE AGENT!
THE HEAT'S ON TO ME AGAIN--

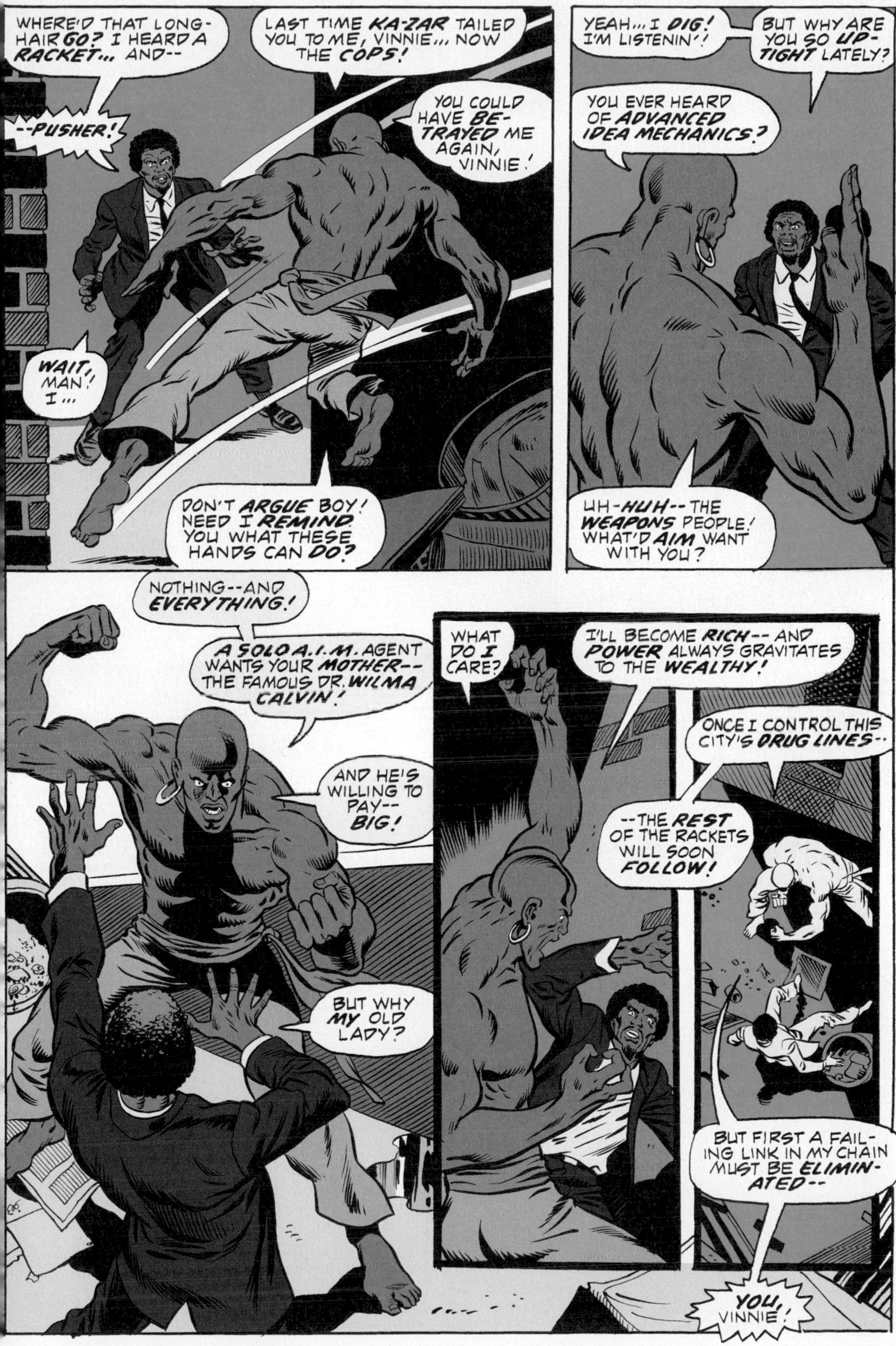
WHERE'D THAT LONG-HAIR GO? I HEARD A RACKET... AND--
LAST TIME KA-ZAR TAILED YOU TO ME, VINNIE... NOW THE COPS!
--PUSHER!
YOU COULD HAVE BE-TRAYED ME AGAIN, VINNIE!
WAIT, MAN! I...
DON'T ARGUE BOY! NEED I REMIND YOU WHAT THESE HANDS CAN DO?
YEAH... I DIG! I'M LISTENIN'!
BUT WHY ARE YOU SO UP-TIGHT LATELY?
YOU EVER HEARD OF ADVANCED IDEA MECHANICS?
UH-HUH-- THE WEAPONS PEOPLE! WHAT'D AIM WANT WITH YOU?
NOTHING--AND EVERYTHING!
A SOLO A.I.M. AGENT WANTS YOUR MOTHER-- THE FAMOUS DR. WILMA CALVIN!
AND HE'S WILLING TO PAY-- BIG!
BUT WHY MY OLD LADY?
WHAT DO I CARE?
I'LL BECOME RICH-- AND POWER ALWAYS GRAVITATES TO THE WEALTHY!
ONCE I CONTROL THIS CITY'S DRUG LINES--
--THE REST OF THE RACKETS WILL SOON FOLLOW!
BUT FIRST A FAIL-ING LINK IN MY CHAIN MUST BE ELIMIN-ATED--
YOU, VINNIE!

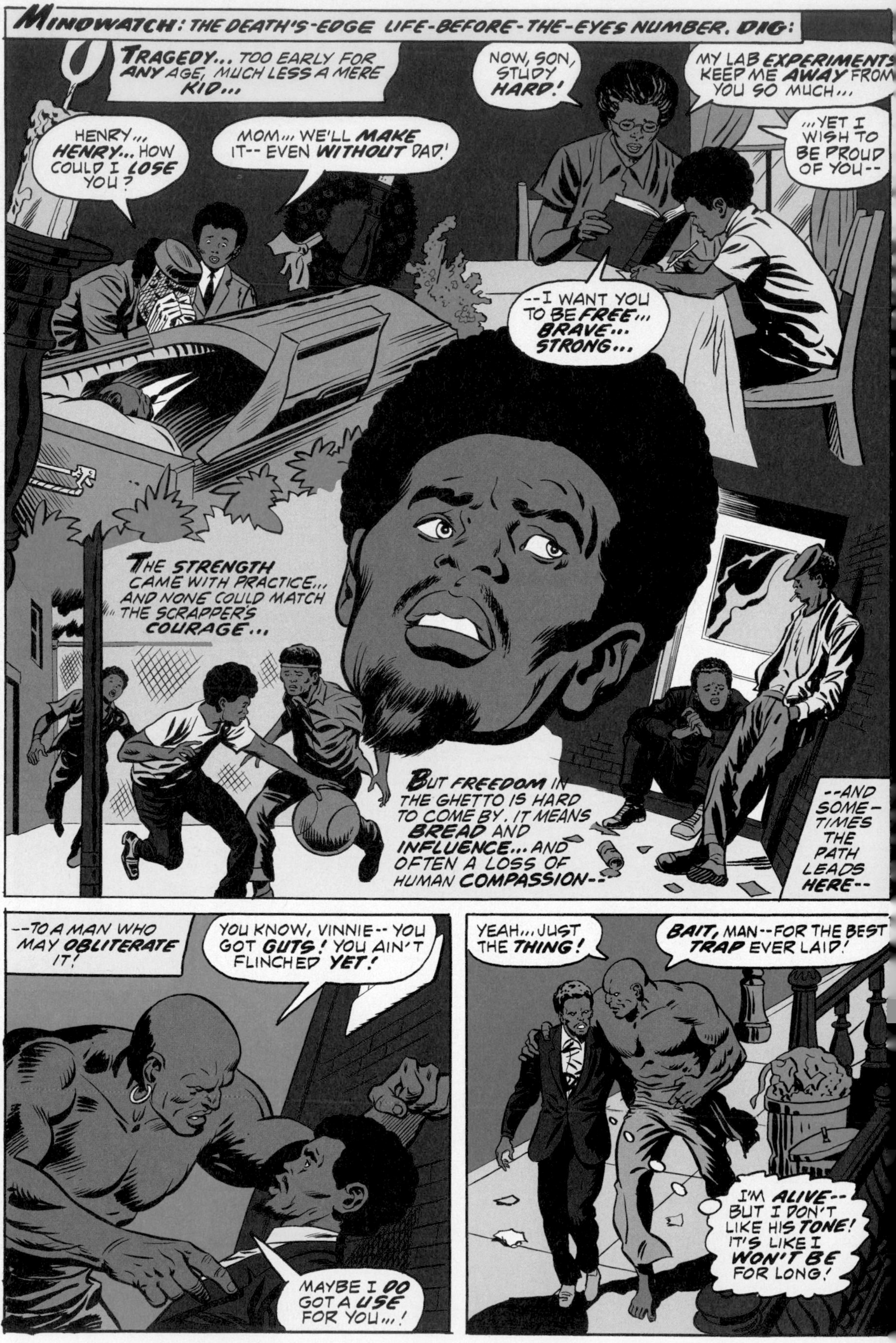
MINDWATCH: THE DEATH'S-EDGE LIFE-BEFORE-THE-EYES NUMBER. DIG:
TRAGEDY... TOO EARLY FOR ANY AGE, MUCH LESS A MERE KID...
HENRY... HENRY... HOW COULD I LOSE YOU?
MOM... WE'LL MAKE IT-- EVEN WITHOUT DAD!
NOW, SON, STUDY HARD!
MY LAB EXPERIMENTS KEEP ME AWAY FROM YOU SO MUCH...
...YET I WISH TO BE PROUD OF YOU--
--I WANT YOU TO BE FREE... BRAVE... STRONG...
THE STRENGTH CAME WITH PRACTICE... AND NONE COULD MATCH THE SCRAPPER'S COURAGE...
BUT FREEDOM IN THE GHETTO IS HARD TO COME BY. IT MEANS BREAD AND INFLUENCE... AND OFTEN A LOSS OF HUMAN COMPASSION--
--AND SOMETIMES THE PATH LEADS HERE--
--TO A MAN WHO MAY OBLITERATE IT!
YOU KNOW, VINNIE-- YOU GOT GUTS! YOU AIN'T FLINCHED YET!
MAYBE I DO GOT A USE FOR YOU...!
YEAH... JUST THE THING!
BAIT, MAN--FOR THE BEST TRAP EVER LAID!
I'M ALIVE-- BUT I DON'T LIKE HIS TONE! IT'S LIKE I WON'T BE FOR LONG!

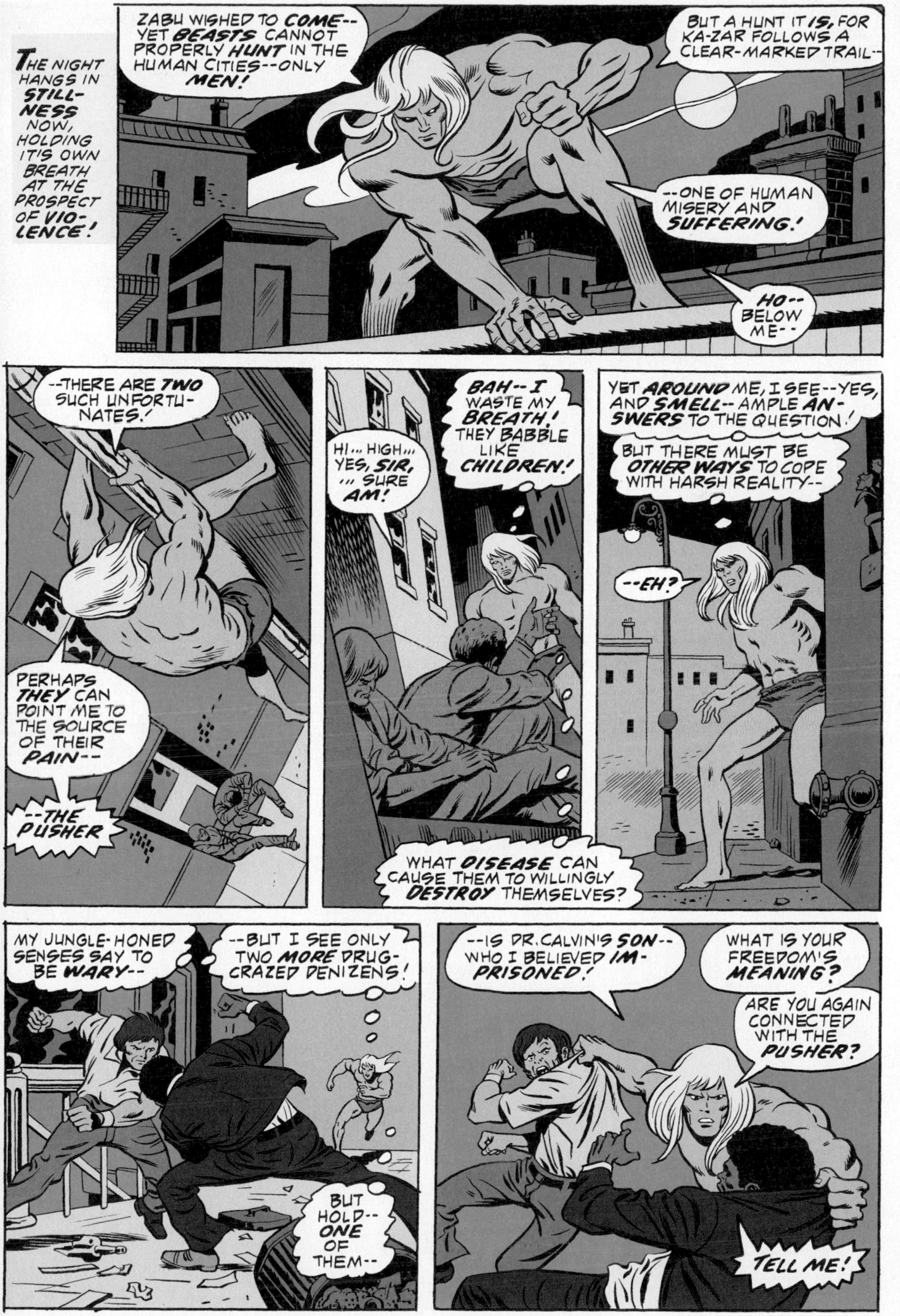
THE NIGHT HANGS IN STILLNESS NOW, HOLDING IT'S OWN BREATH AT THE PROSPECT OF VIOLENCE!
ZABU WISHED TO COME-- YET BEASTS CANNOT PROPERLY HUNT IN THE HUMAN CITIES--ONLY MEN!
BUT A HUNT IT IS, FOR KA-ZAR FOLLOWS A CLEAR-MARKED TRAIL--
--ONE OF HUMAN MISERY AND SUFFERING!
HO-- BELOW ME--
--THERE ARE TWO SUCH UNFORTUNATES!
PERHAPS THEY CAN POINT ME TO THE SOURCE OF THEIR PAIN--
--THE PUSHER
HI... HIGH... YES, SIR, ... SURE AM!
BAH-- I WASTE MY BREATH! THEY BABBLE LIKE CHILDREN!
WHAT DISEASE CAN CAUSE THEM TO WILLINGLY DESTROY THEMSELVES?
YET AROUND ME, I SEE--YES, AND SMELL-- AMPLE ANSWERS TO THE QUESTION!
BUT THERE MUST BE OTHER WAYS TO COPE WITH HARSH REALITY--
--EH?
MY JUNGLE-HONED SENSES SAY TO BE WARY--
--BUT I SEE ONLY TWO MORE DRUG-CRAZED DENIZENS!
BUT HOLD-- ONE OF THEM--
--IS DR. CALVIN'S SON-- WHO I BELIEVED IMPRISONED!
WHAT IS YOUR FREEDOM'S MEANING?
ARE YOU AGAIN CONNECTED WITH THE PUSHER?
TELL ME!

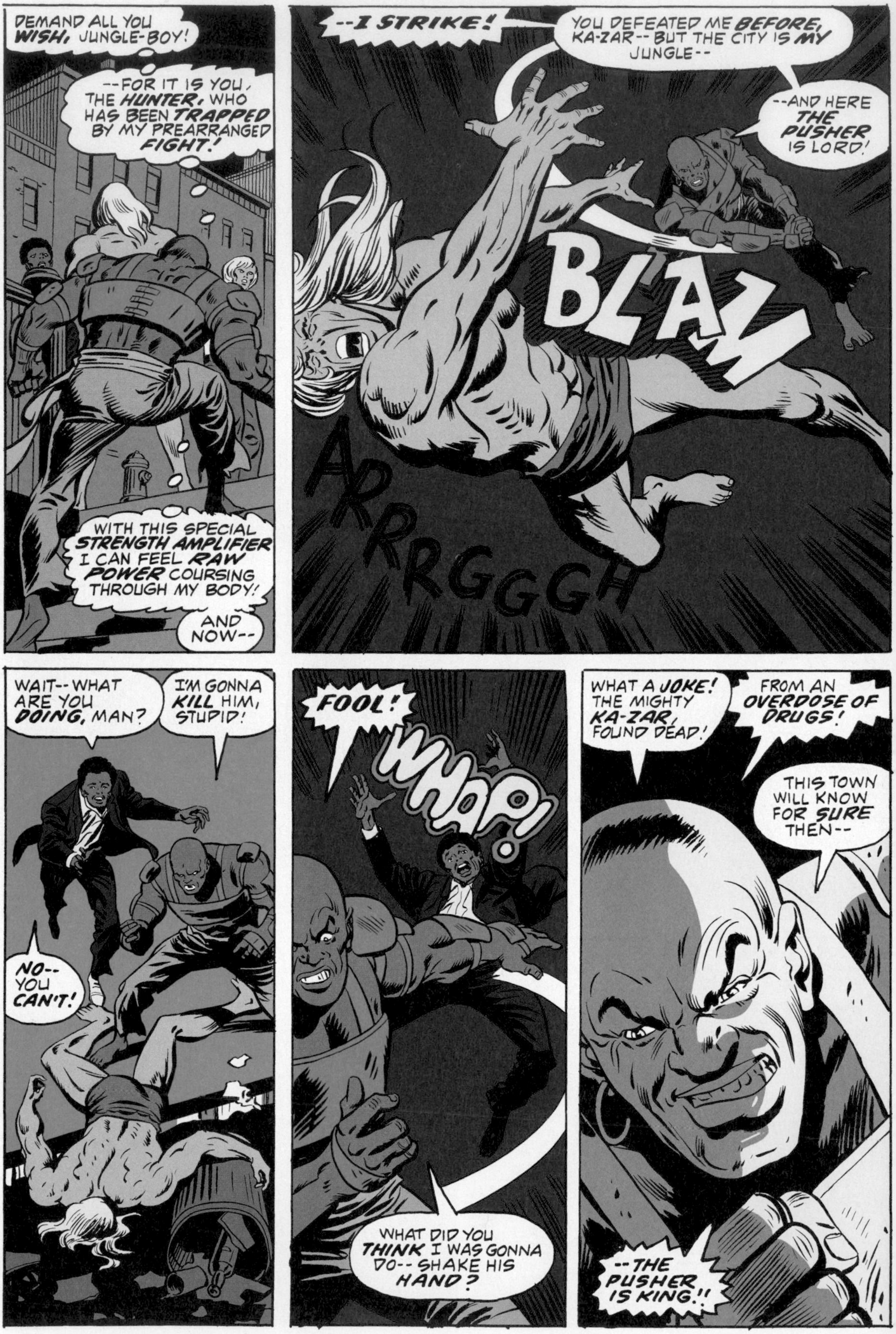
DEMAND ALL YOU WISH, JUNGLE-BOY!
--FOR IT IS YOU, THE HUNTER, WHO HAS BEEN TRAPPED BY MY PREARRANGED FIGHT!
WITH THIS SPECIAL STRENGTH AMPLIFIER I CAN FEEL RAW POWER COURSING THROUGH MY BODY!
AND NOW--
--I STRIKE!
YOU DEFEATED ME BEFORE, KA-ZAR-- BUT THE CITY IS MY JUNGLE--
--AND HERE THE PUSHER IS LORD!
BLAM
ARRRGGGH
WAIT-- WHAT ARE YOU DOING, MAN?
I'M GONNA KILL HIM, STUPID!
NO-- YOU CAN'T!
FOOL!
WHAP!
WHAT DID YOU THINK I WAS GONNA DO-- SHAKE HIS HAND?
WHAT A JOKE! THE MIGHTY KA-ZAR, FOUND DEAD!
FROM AN OVERDOSE OF DRUGS!
THIS TOWN WILL KNOW FOR SURE THEN--
--THE PUSHER IS KING!!

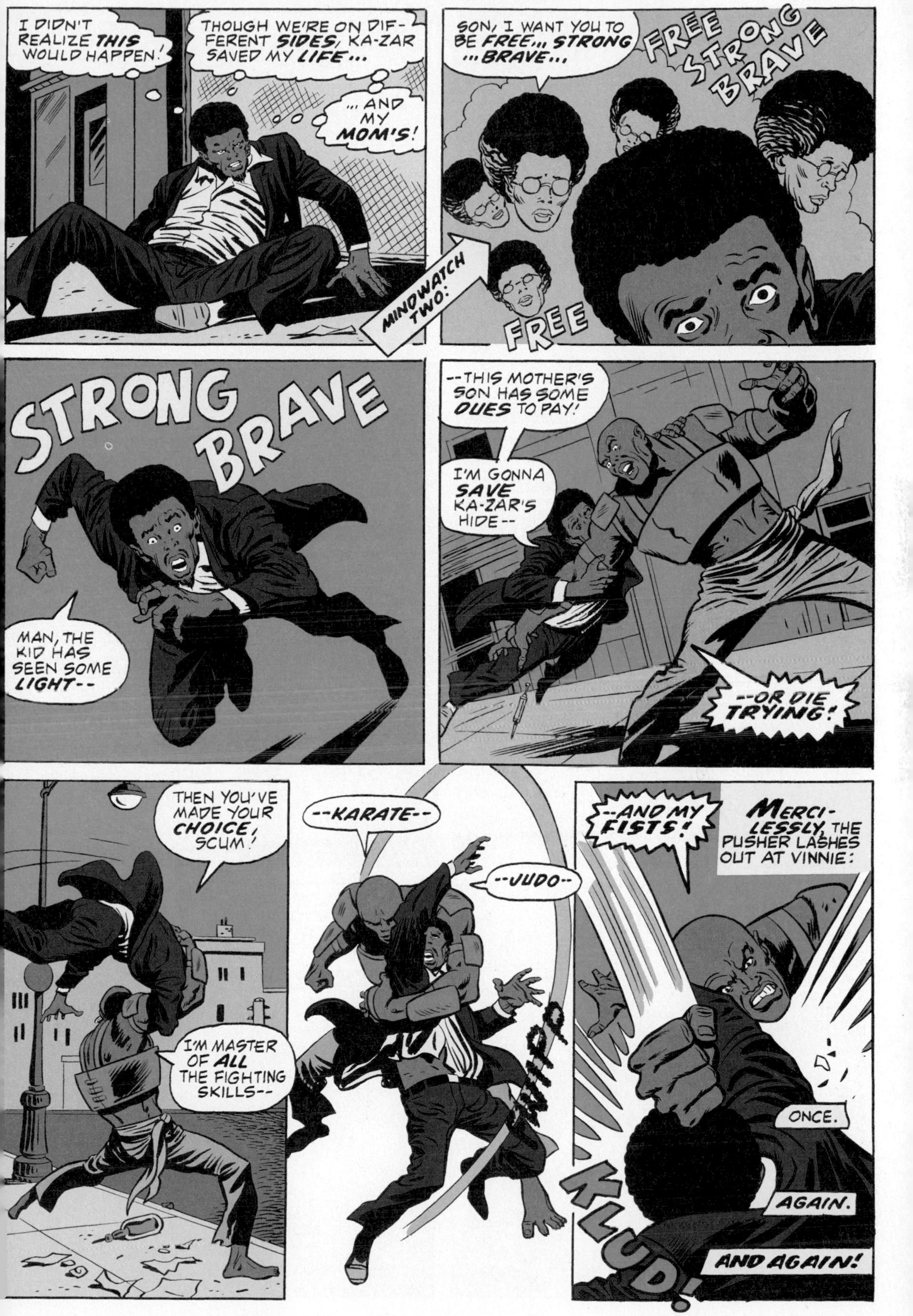
I DIDN'T REALIZE THIS WOULD HAPPEN!
THOUGH WE'RE ON DIF-FERENT SIDES, KA-ZAR SAVED MY LIFE...
...AND MY MOM'S!
MINDWATCH TWO:
SON, I WANT YOU TO BE FREE... STRONG ...BRAVE...
FREE
STRONG
BRAVE
FREE
STRONG
BRAVE
MAN, THE KID HAS SEEN SOME LIGHT--
--THIS MOTHER'S SON HAS SOME DUES TO PAY!
I'M GONNA SAVE KA-ZAR'S HIDE--
--OR DIE TRYING!
THEN YOU'VE MADE YOUR CHOICE, SCUM!
I'M MASTER OF ALL THE FIGHTING SKILLS--
--KARATE--
--JUDO--
WHIPP
--AND MY FISTS!
MERCILESSLY, THE PUSHER LASHES OUT AT VINNIE:
ONCE.
AGAIN.
AND AGAIN!
KLUD!

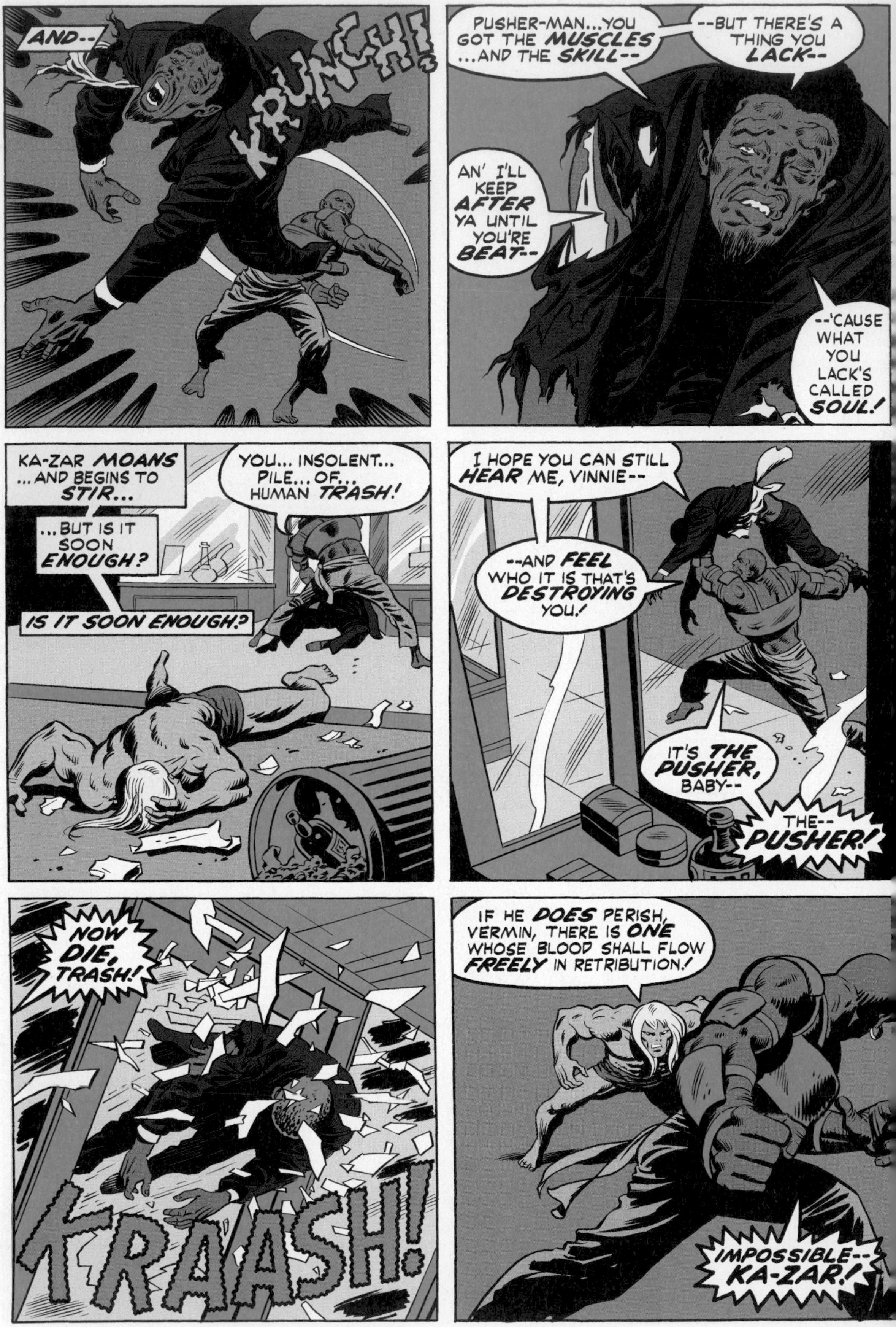
AND--
KRUNCH!
PUSHER-MAN...YOU GOT THE MUSCLES ...AND THE SKILL--
--BUT THERE'S A THING YOU LACK--
AN' I'LL KEEP AFTER YA UNTIL YOU'RE BEAT--
--'CAUSE WHAT YOU LACK'S CALLED SOUL!
KA-ZAR MOANS ...AND BEGINS TO STIR...
...BUT IS IT SOON ENOUGH?
IS IT SOON ENOUGH?
YOU... INSOLENT... PILE... OF... HUMAN TRASH!
I HOPE YOU CAN STILL HEAR ME, VINNIE--
--AND FEEL WHO IT IS THAT'S DESTROYING YOU!
IT'S THE PUSHER, BABY--
THE--PUSHER!
NOW DIE, TRASH!
KRAASH!
IF HE DOES PERISH, VERMIN, THERE IS ONE WHOSE BLOOD SHALL FLOW FREELY IN RETRIBUTION!
IMPOSSIBLE--KA-ZAR!

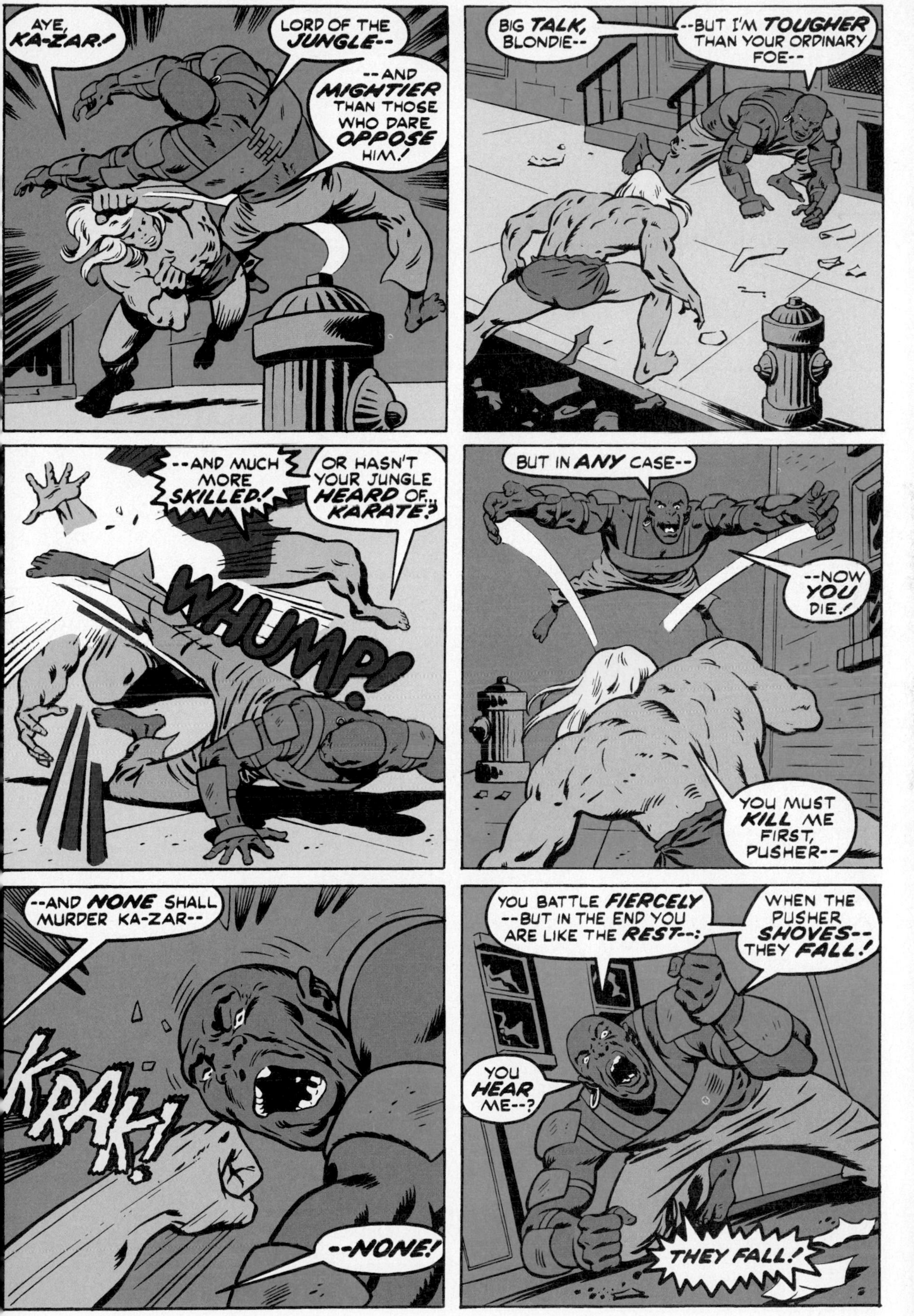
AYE, KA-ZAR!
LORD OF THE JUNGLE--
--AND MIGHTIER THAN THOSE WHO DARE OPPOSE HIM!
BIG TALK, BLONDIE--
--BUT I'M TOUGHER THAN YOUR ORDINARY FOE--
--AND MUCH MORE SKILLED!
OR HASN'T YOUR JUNGLE HEARD OF.. KARATE?
WHUMP!
BUT IN ANY CASE--
--NOW YOU DIE.!
YOU MUST KILL ME FIRST, PUSHER--
--AND NONE SHALL MURDER KA-ZAR--
KRAK!
--NONE!
YOU BATTLE FIERCELY --BUT IN THE END YOU ARE LIKE THE REST--:
WHEN THE PUSHER SHOVES-- THEY FALL!
YOU HEAR ME--?
THEY FALL!

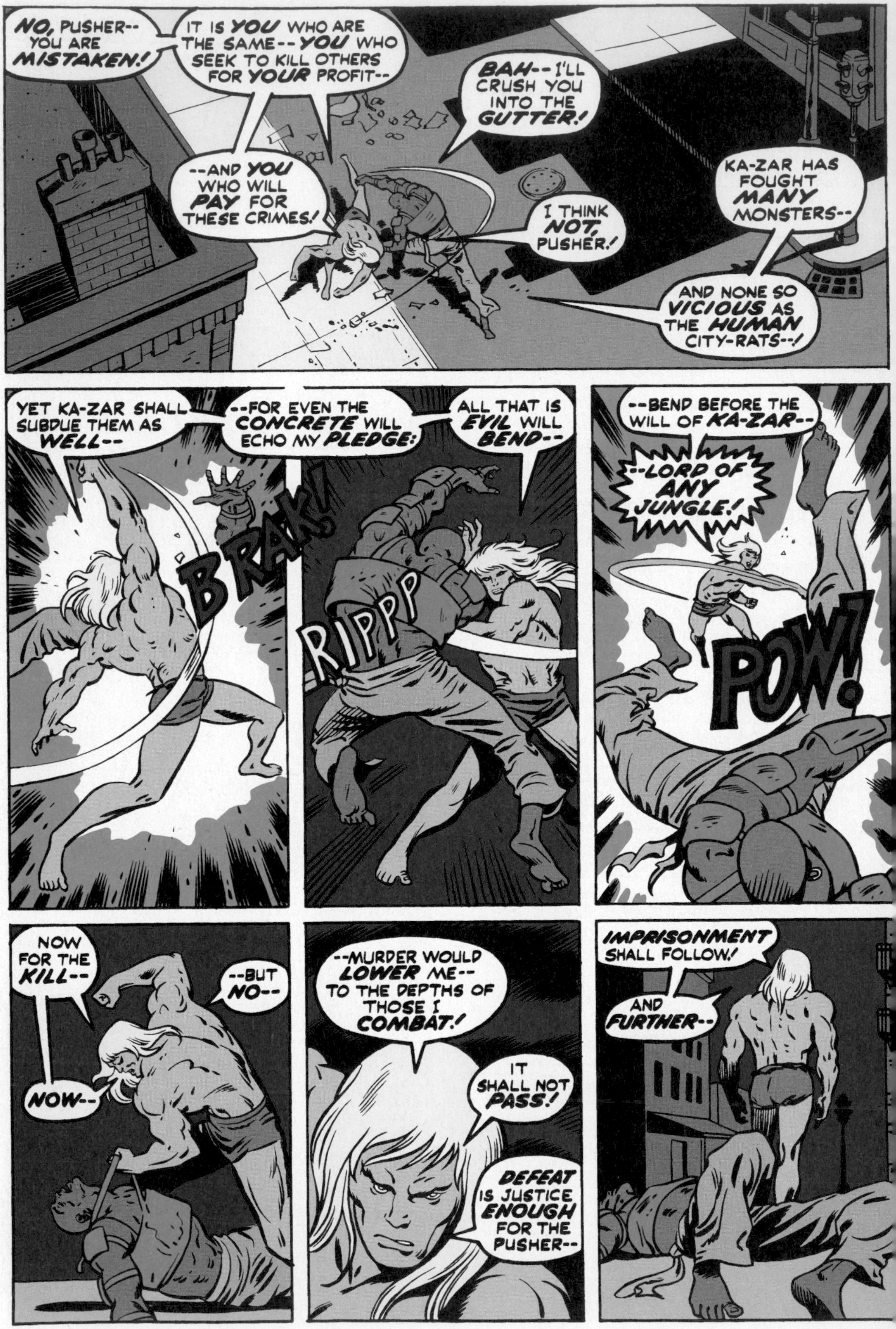
NO, PUSHER-- YOU ARE MISTAKEN!
IT IS YOU WHO ARE THE SAME--YOU WHO SEEK TO KILL OTHERS FOR YOUR PROFIT--
--AND YOU WHO WILL PAY FOR THESE CRIMES!
BAH--I'LL CRUSH YOU INTO THE GUTTER!
I THINK NOT, PUSHER!
KA-ZAR HAS FOUGHT MANY MONSTERS--
AND NONE SO VICIOUS AS THE HUMAN CITY-RATS--!
YET KA-ZAR SHALL SUBDUE THEM AS WELL--
--FOR EVEN THE CONCRETE WILL ECHO MY PLEDGE:
BRAK!
ALL THAT IS EVIL WILL BEND--
RIPPP
--BEND BEFORE THE WILL OF KA-ZAR--
--LORD OF ANY JUNGLE!
POW!
NOW FOR THE KILL--
--BUT NO--
NOW--
--MURDER WOULD LOWER ME-- TO THE DEPTHS OF THOSE I COMBAT!
IT SHALL NOT PASS!
DEFEAT IS JUSTICE ENOUGH FOR THE PUSHER--
IMPRISONMENT SHALL FOLLOW!
AND FURTHER--

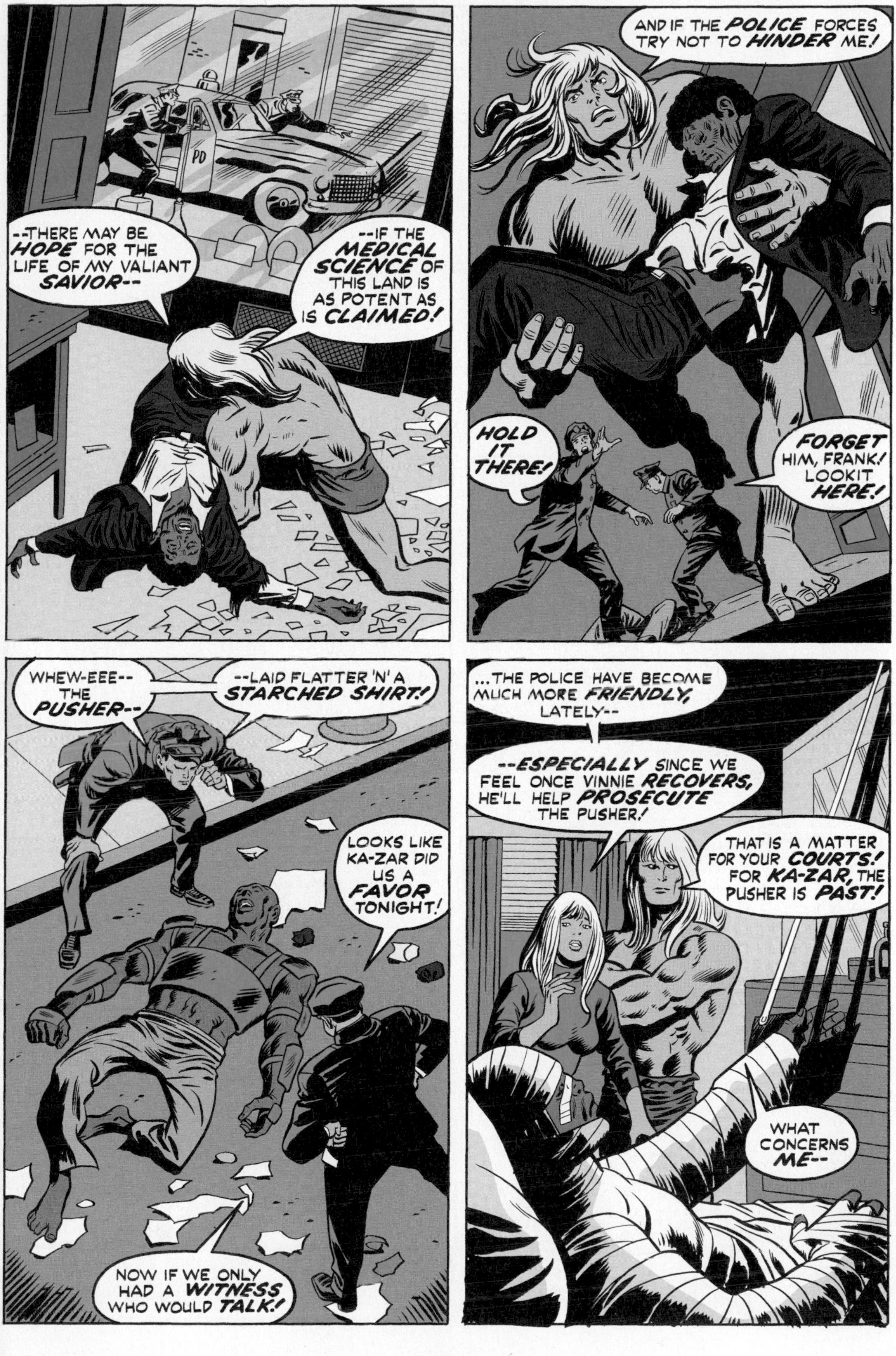
--THERE MAY BE HOPE FOR THE LIFE OF MY VALIANT SAVIOR--
--IF THE MEDICAL SCIENCE OF THIS LAND IS AS POTENT AS IS CLAIMED!
AND IF THE POLICE FORCES TRY NOT TO HINDER ME!
HOLD IT THERE!
FORGET HIM, FRANK! LOOKIT HERE!
WHEW-EEE-- THE PUSHER--
--LAID FLATTER 'N' A STARCHED SHIRT!
LOOKS LIKE KA-ZAR DID US A FAVOR TONIGHT!
NOW IF WE ONLY HAD A WITNESS WHO WOULD TALK!
...THE POLICE HAVE BECOME MUCH MORE FRIENDLY, LATELY--
--ESPECIALLY SINCE WE FEEL ONCE VINNIE RECOVERS, HE'LL HELP PROSECUTE THE PUSHER!
THAT IS A MATTER FOR YOUR COURTS! FOR KA-ZAR, THE PUSHER IS PAST!
WHAT CONCERNS ME--

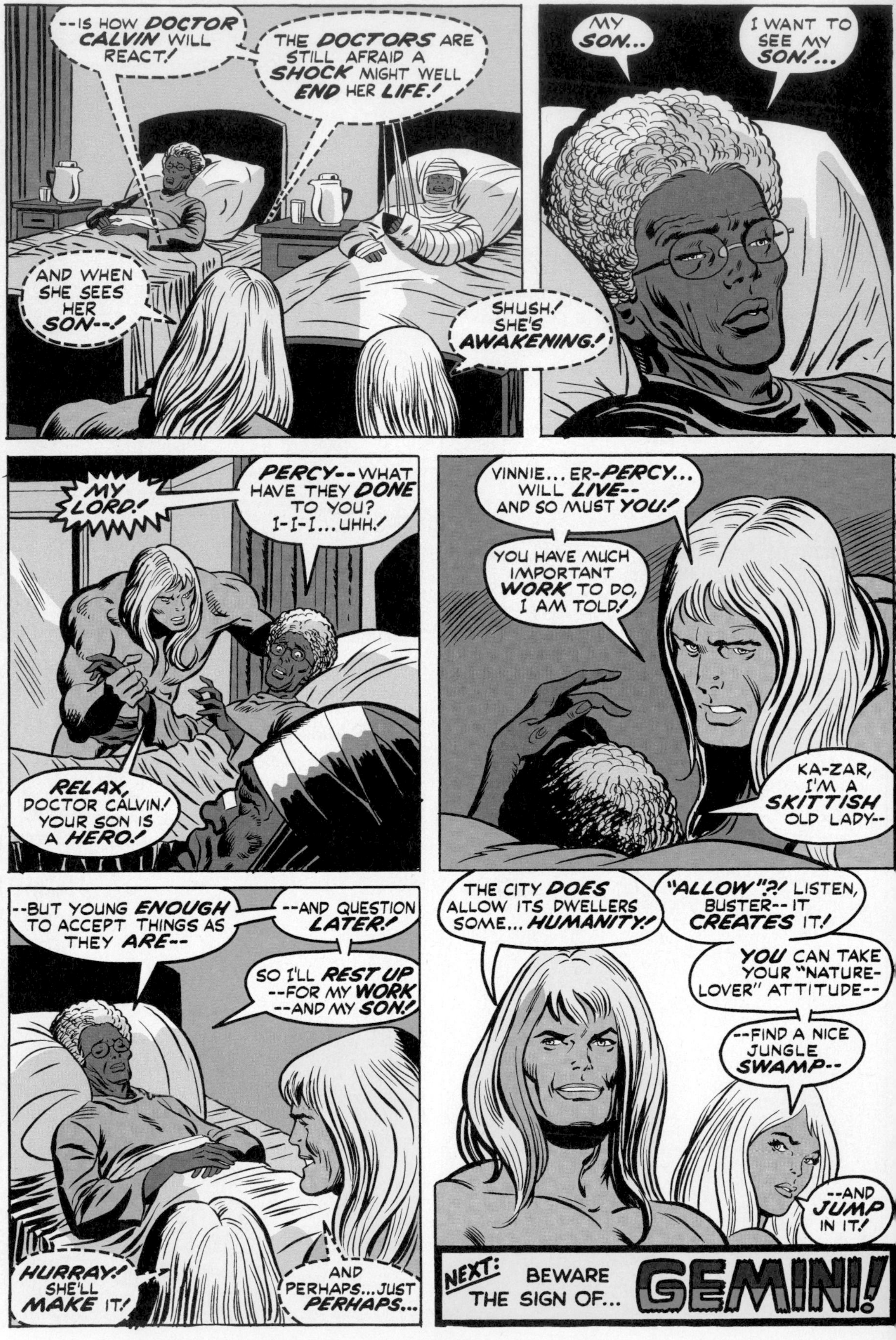
--IS HOW DOCTOR CALVIN WILL REACT!
THE DOCTORS ARE STILL AFRAID A SHOCK MIGHT WELL END HER LIFE!
AND WHEN SHE SEES HER SON--!
SHUSH! SHE'S AWAKENING!
MY SON...
I WANT TO SEE MY SON!...
MY LORD!
PERCY--WHAT HAVE THEY DONE TO YOU? I-I-I...UHH!
RELAX, DOCTOR CALVIN! YOUR SON IS A HERO!
VINNIE... ER-PERCY... WILL LIVE-- AND SO MUST YOU!
YOU HAVE MUCH IMPORTANT WORK TO DO, I AM TOLD!
KA-ZAR, I'M A SKITTISH OLD LADY--
--BUT YOUNG ENOUGH TO ACCEPT THINGS AS THEY ARE--
--AND QUESTION LATER!
SO I'LL REST UP --FOR MY WORK --AND MY SON!
HURRAY! SHE'LL MAKE IT!
AND PERHAPS...JUST PERHAPS...
THE CITY DOES ALLOW ITS DWELLERS SOME... HUMANITY!
"ALLOW"?! LISTEN, BUSTER-- IT CREATES IT!
YOU CAN TAKE YOUR "NATURE-LOVER" ATTITUDE--
--FIND A NICE JUNGLE SWAMP--
--AND JUMP IN IT!
NEXT: BEWARE THE SIGN OF... GEMINI!

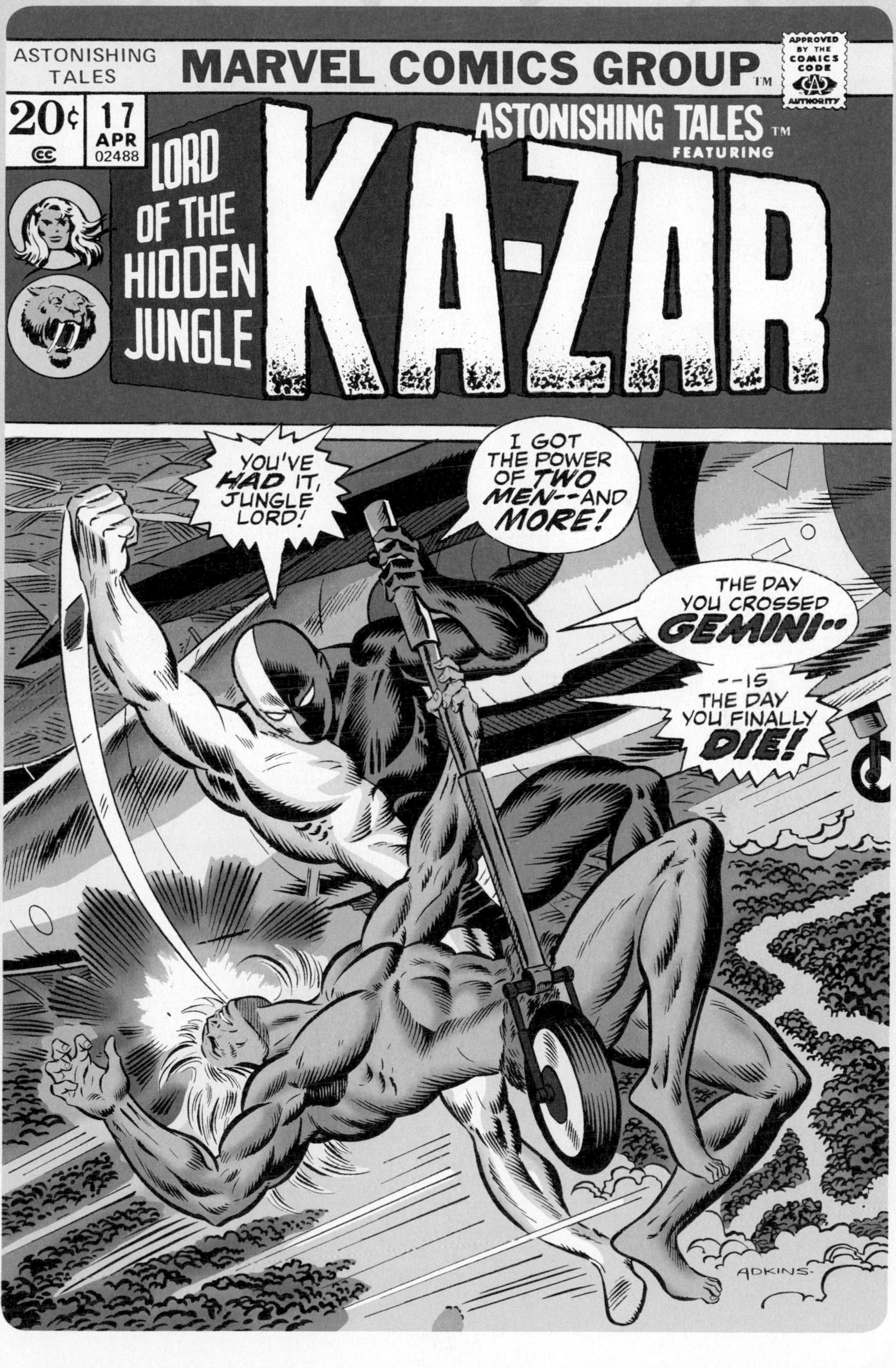

ASTONISHING TALES
MARVEL COMICS GROUP
APPROVED BY THE COMICS CODE AUTHORITY
20¢
17 APR 02488
ASTONISHING TALES FEATURING
LORD OF THE HIDDEN JUNGLE
KA-ZAR
YOU'VE HAD IT, JUNGLE LORD!
I GOT THE POWER OF TWO MEN--AND MORE!
THE DAY YOU CROSSED GEMINI--
--IS THE DAY YOU FINALLY DIE!
ADKINS

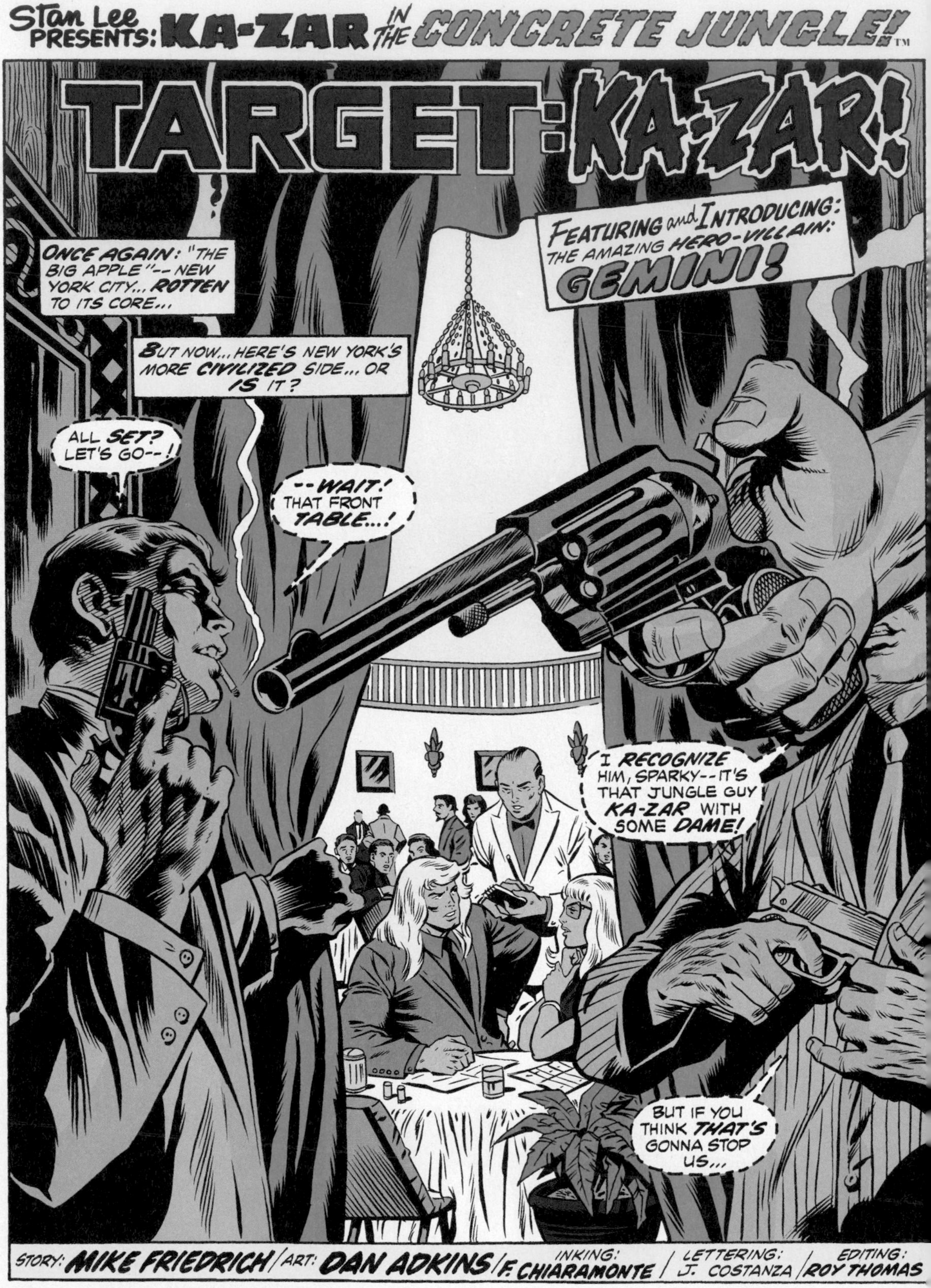
Stan Lee PRESENTS: KA-ZAR IN THE CONCRETE JUNGLE!™
TARGET: KA-ZAR!
FEATURING and INTRODUCING: THE AMAZING HERO-VILLAIN: GEMINI!
ONCE AGAIN: "THE BIG APPLE"-- NEW YORK CITY... ROTTEN TO ITS CORE...
BUT NOW... HERE'S NEW YORK'S MORE CIVILIZED SIDE... OR IS IT?
ALL SET? LET'S GO--!
--WAIT! THAT FRONT TABLE...!
I RECOGNIZE HIM, SPARKY-- IT'S THAT JUNGLE GUY KA-ZAR WITH SOME DAME!
BUT IF YOU THINK THAT'S GONNA STOP US...
STORY: MIKE FRIEDRICH / ART: DAN ADKINS / INKING: F. CHIARAMONTE / LETTERING: J. COSTANZA / EDITING: ROY THOMAS

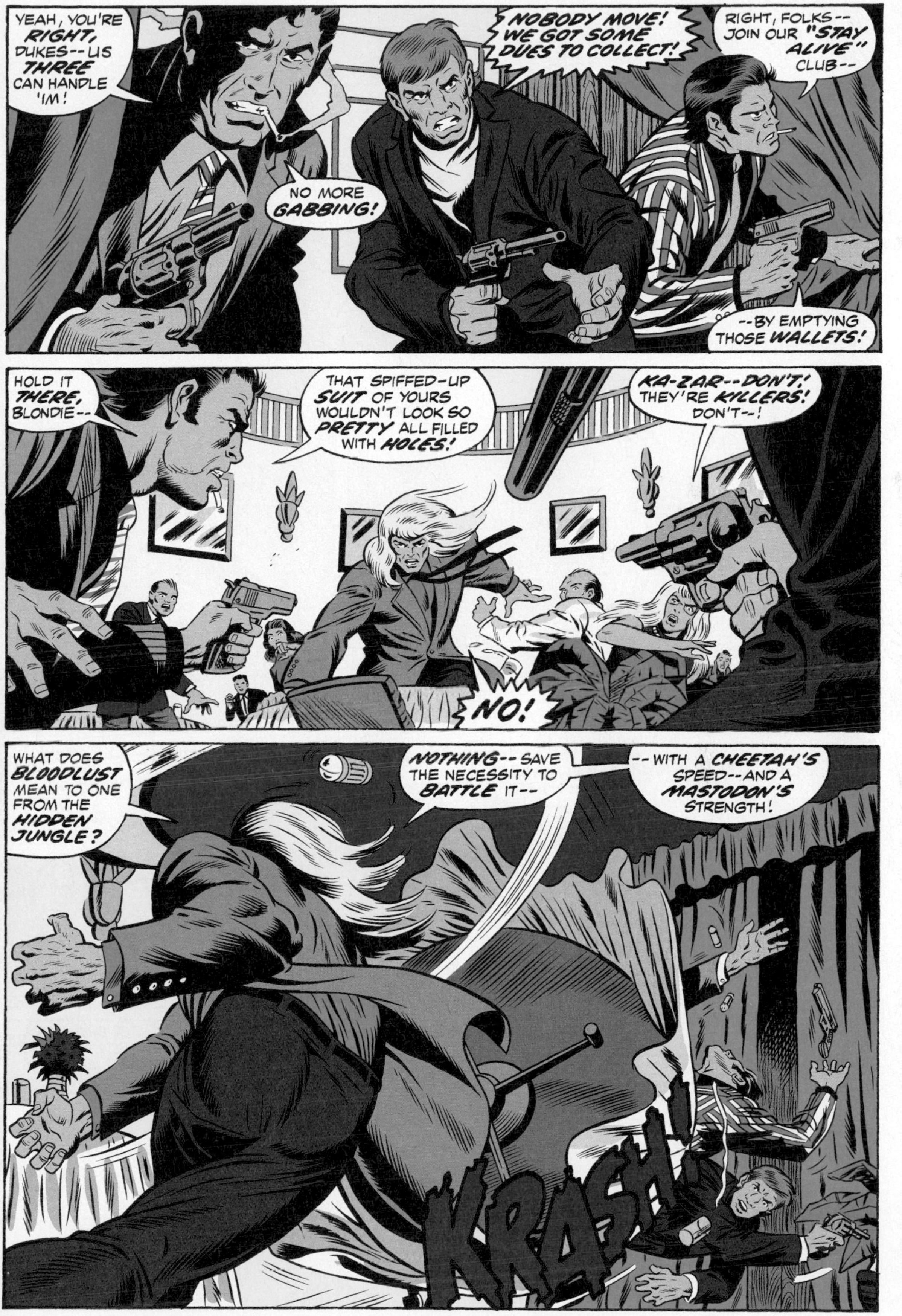
YEAH, YOU'RE RIGHT, DUKES--US THREE CAN HANDLE 'IM!
NO MORE GABBING!
NOBODY MOVE! WE GOT SOME DUES TO COLLECT!
RIGHT, FOLKS--JOIN OUR "STAY ALIVE" CLUB--
--BY EMPTYING THOSE WALLETS!
HOLD IT THERE, BLONDIE--
THAT SPIFFED-UP SUIT OF YOURS WOULDN'T LOOK SO PRETTY ALL FILLED WITH HOLES!
KA-ZAR--DON'T! THEY'RE KILLERS! DON'T--!
NO!
WHAT DOES BLOODLUST MEAN TO ONE FROM THE HIDDEN JUNGLE?
NOTHING--SAVE THE NECESSITY TO BATTLE IT--
--WITH A CHEETAH'S SPEED--AND A MASTODON'S STRENGTH!
KRASH!

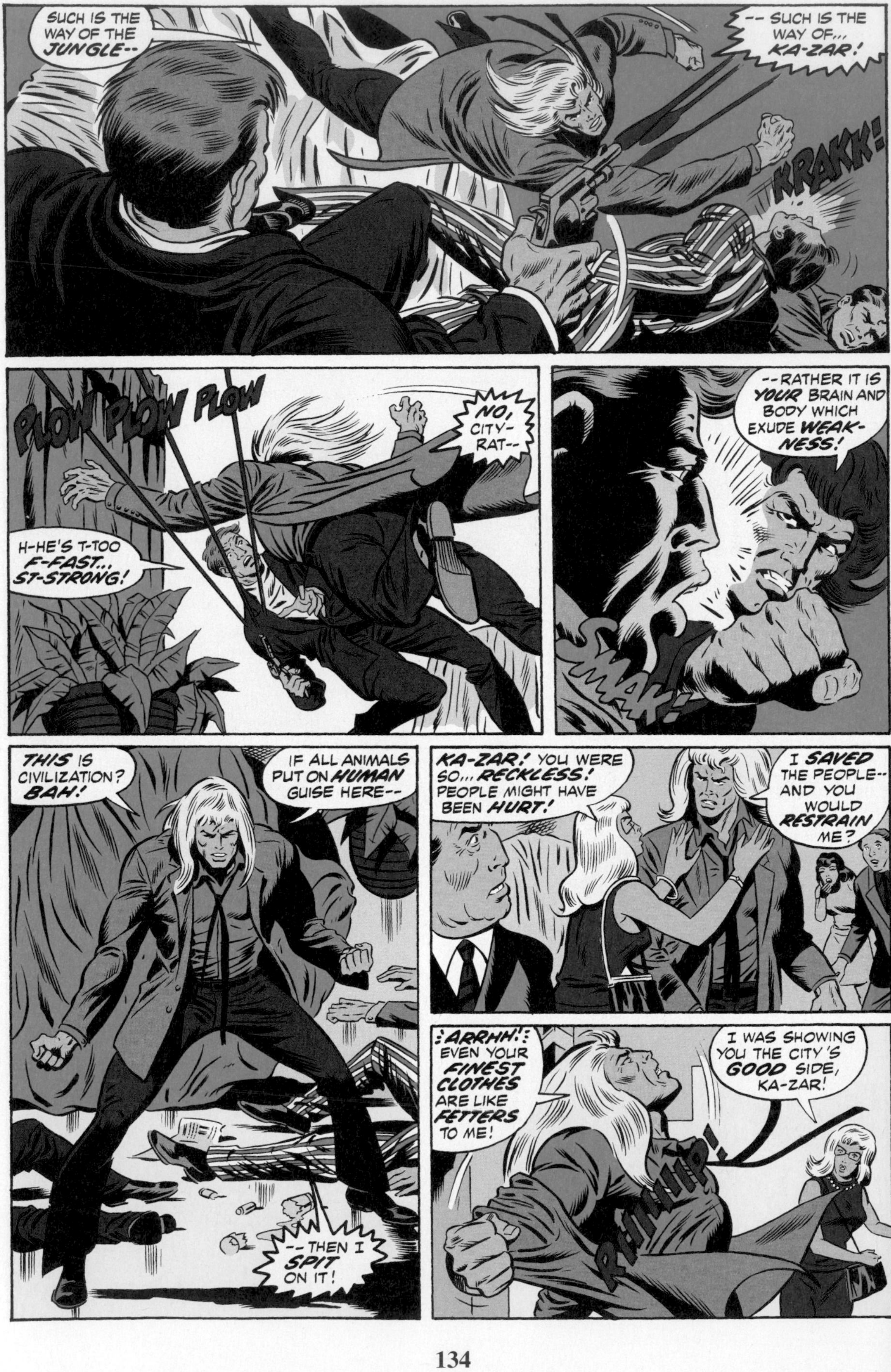
SUCH IS THE WAY OF THE JUNGLE--
-- SUCH IS THE WAY OF... KA-ZAR!
KRAKK!
PLOW PLOW PLOW PLOW
NO, CITY-RAT--
H-HE'S T-TOO F-FAST... ST-STRONG!
--RATHER IT IS YOUR BRAIN AND BODY WHICH EXUDE WEAKNESS!
SMAK!
THIS IS CIVILIZATION? BAH!
IF ALL ANIMALS PUT ON HUMAN GUISE HERE--
--THEN I SPIT ON IT!
KA-ZAR! YOU WERE SO... RECKLESS! PEOPLE MIGHT HAVE BEEN HURT!
I SAVED THE PEOPLE--AND YOU WOULD RESTRAIN ME?
ARRHH! EVEN YOUR FINEST CLOTHES ARE LIKE FETTERS TO ME!
I WAS SHOWING YOU THE CITY'S GOOD SIDE, KA-ZAR!
RIIIIIP!

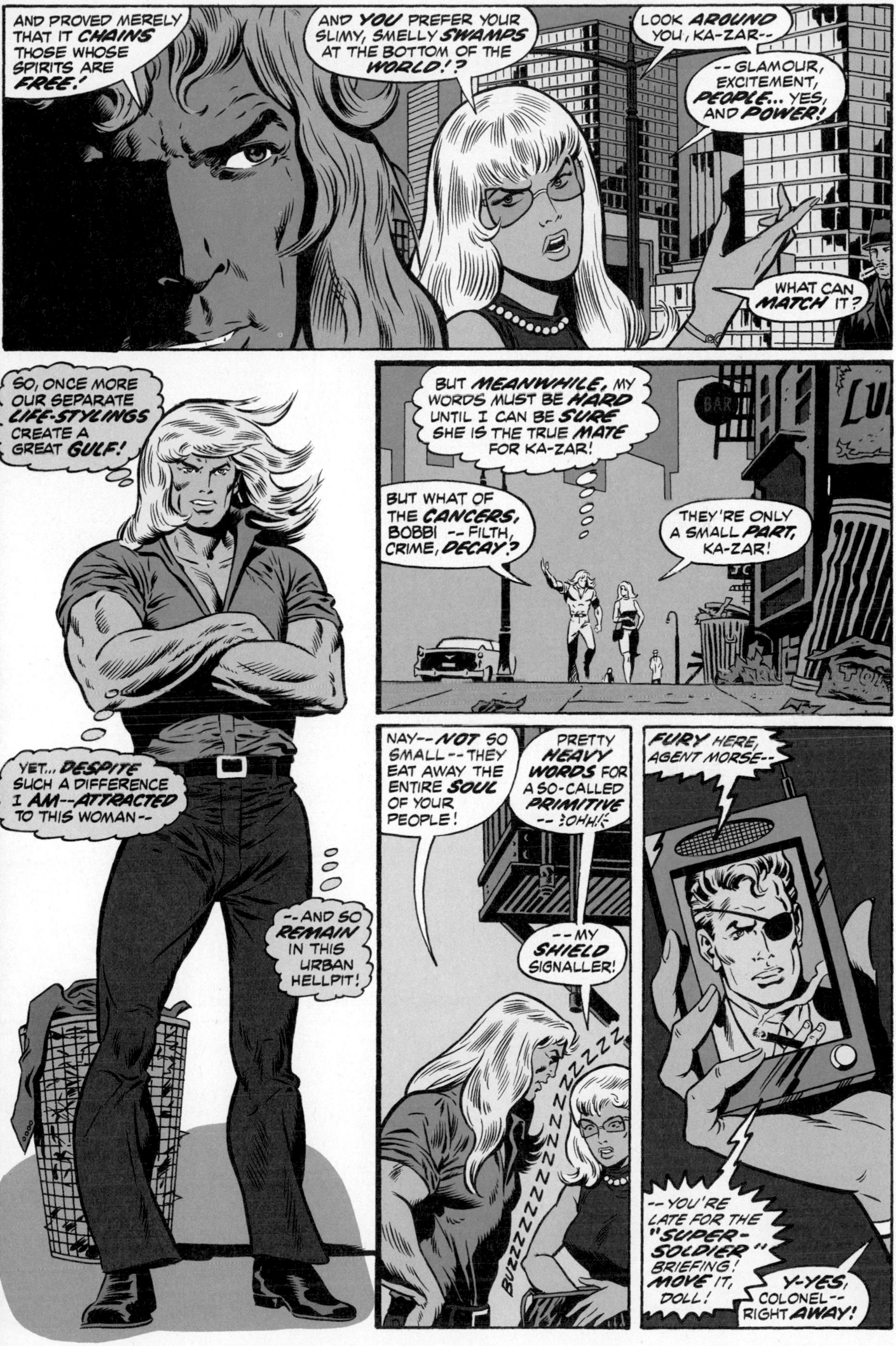

AND PROVED MERELY THAT IT CHAINS THOSE WHOSE SPIRITS ARE FREE!
AND YOU PREFER YOUR SLIMY, SMELLY SWAMPS AT THE BOTTOM OF THE WORLD!?
LOOK AROUND YOU, KA-ZAR--
--GLAMOUR, EXCITEMENT, PEOPLE... YES, AND POWER!
WHAT CAN MATCH IT?
SO, ONCE MORE OUR SEPARATE LIFE-STYLINGS CREATE A GREAT GULF!
YET... DESPITE SUCH A DIFFERENCE I AM--ATTRACTED TO THIS WOMAN--
--AND SO REMAIN IN THIS URBAN HELLPIT!
BUT MEANWHILE, MY WORDS MUST BE HARD UNTIL I CAN BE SURE SHE IS THE TRUE MATE FOR KA-ZAR!
BUT WHAT OF THE CANCERS, BOBBI --FILTH, CRIME, DECAY?
THEY'RE ONLY A SMALL PART, KA-ZAR!
BAR
NAY--NOT SO SMALL--THEY EAT AWAY THE ENTIRE SOUL OF YOUR PEOPLE!
PRETTY HEAVY WORDS FOR A SO-CALLED PRIMITIVE --OHH!
--MY SHIELD SIGNALLER!
BUZZZZZZZZZZZZZZ
FURY HERE, AGENT MORSE--
--YOU'RE LATE FOR THE "SUPER-SOLDIER" BRIEFING! MOVE IT, DOLL!
Y-YES, COLONEL--RIGHT AWAY!

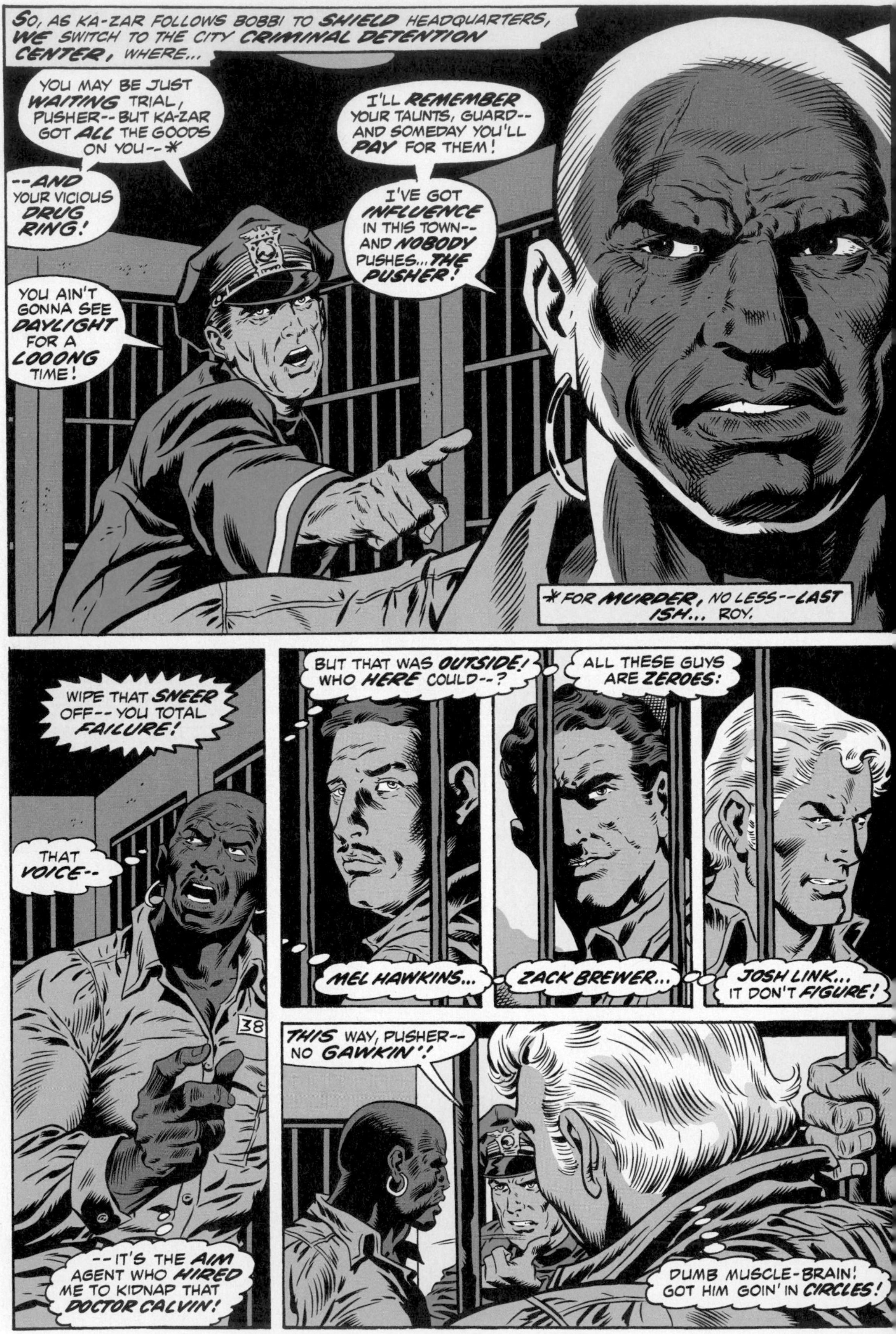
SO, AS KA-ZAR FOLLOWS BOBBI TO SHIELD HEADQUARTERS, WE SWITCH TO THE CITY CRIMINAL DETENTION CENTER, WHERE...
YOU MAY BE JUST WAITING TRIAL, PUSHER-- BUT KA-ZAR GOT ALL THE GOODS ON YOU--*
--AND YOUR VICIOUS DRUG RING!
YOU AIN'T GONNA SEE DAYLIGHT FOR A LOOONG TIME!
I'LL REMEMBER YOUR TAUNTS, GUARD-- AND SOMEDAY YOU'LL PAY FOR THEM!
I'VE GOT INFLUENCE IN THIS TOWN-- AND NOBODY PUSHES... THE PUSHER!
*FOR MURDER, NO LESS--LAST ISH... ROY.
WIPE THAT SNEER OFF-- YOU TOTAL FAILURE!
THAT VOICE--
38
--IT'S THE AIM AGENT WHO HIRED ME TO KIDNAP THAT DOCTOR CALVIN!
BUT THAT WAS OUTSIDE! WHO HERE COULD--?
ALL THESE GUYS ARE ZEROES:
MEL HAWKINS...
ZACK BREWER...
JOSH LINK... IT DON'T FIGURE!
THIS WAY, PUSHER-- NO GAWKIN'!
DUMB MUSCLE-BRAIN! GOT HIM GOIN' IN CIRCLES!

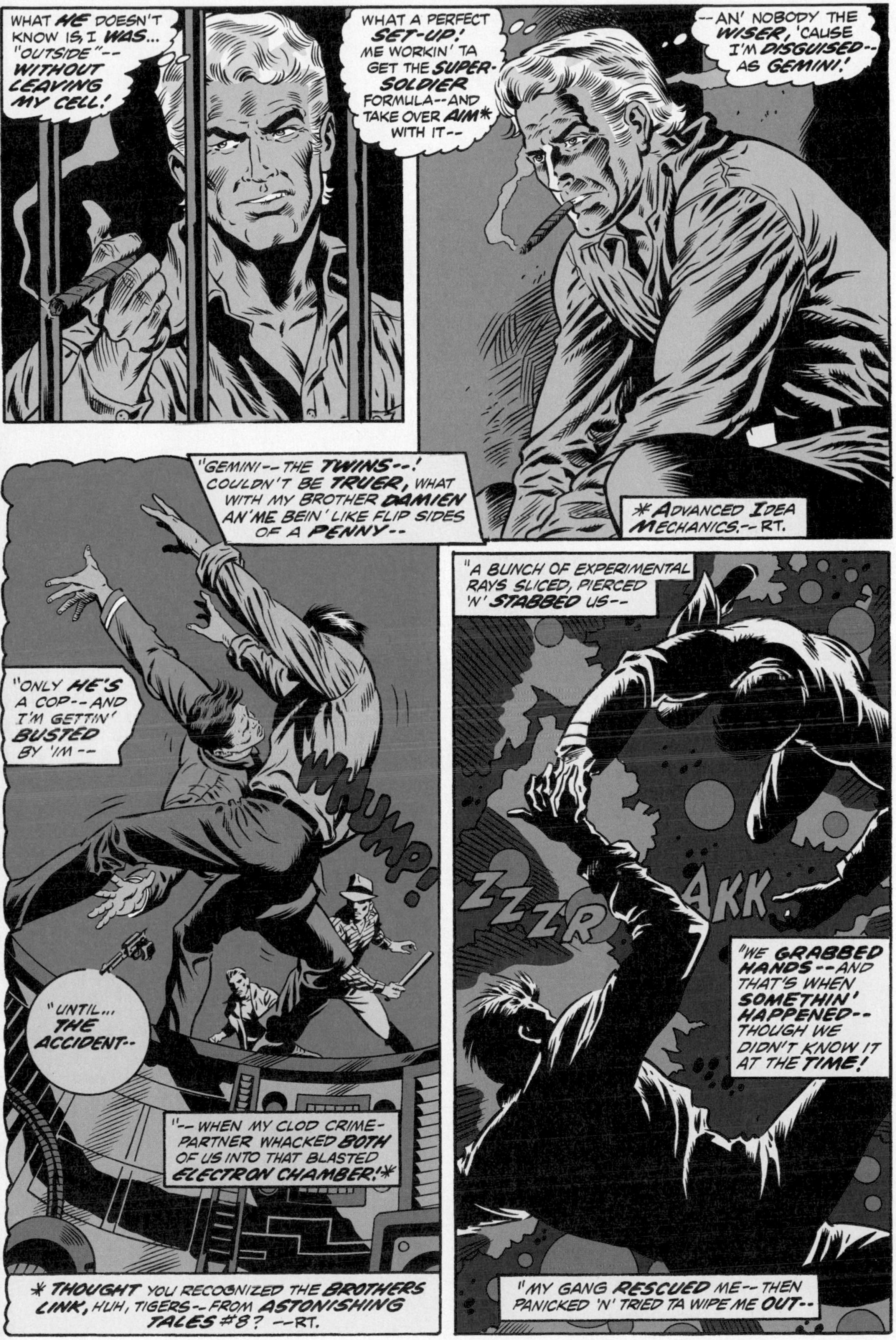
WHAT HE DOESN'T KNOW IS, I WAS... "OUTSIDE"-- WITHOUT LEAVING MY CELL!
WHAT A PERFECT SET-UP! ME WORKIN' TA GET THE SUPER-SOLDIER FORMULA--AND TAKE OVER AIM* WITH IT--
--AN' NOBODY THE WISER, 'CAUSE I'M DISGUISED--AS GEMINI!'
"GEMINI--THE TWINS--! COULDN'T BE TRUER, WHAT WITH MY BROTHER DAMIEN AN' ME BEIN' LIKE FLIP SIDES OF A PENNY--
*ADVANCED IDEA MECHANICS.--RT.
"ONLY HE'S A COP--AND I'M GETTIN' BUSTED BY 'IM--
WHUMP!
"UNTIL... THE ACCIDENT--
"--WHEN MY CLOD CRIME-PARTNER WHACKED BOTH OF US INTO THAT BLASTED ELECTRON CHAMBER!*
*THOUGHT YOU RECOGNIZED THE BROTHERS LINK, HUH, TIGERS--FROM ASTONISHING TALES #8? --RT.
"A BUNCH OF EXPERIMENTAL RAYS SLICED, PIERCED 'N' STABBED US--
ZZZZR
AKK
"WE GRABBED HANDS--AND THAT'S WHEN SOMETHIN' HAPPENED--THOUGH WE DIDN'T KNOW IT AT THE TIME!
"MY GANG RESCUED ME--THEN PANICKED 'N' TRIED TA WIPE ME OUT--

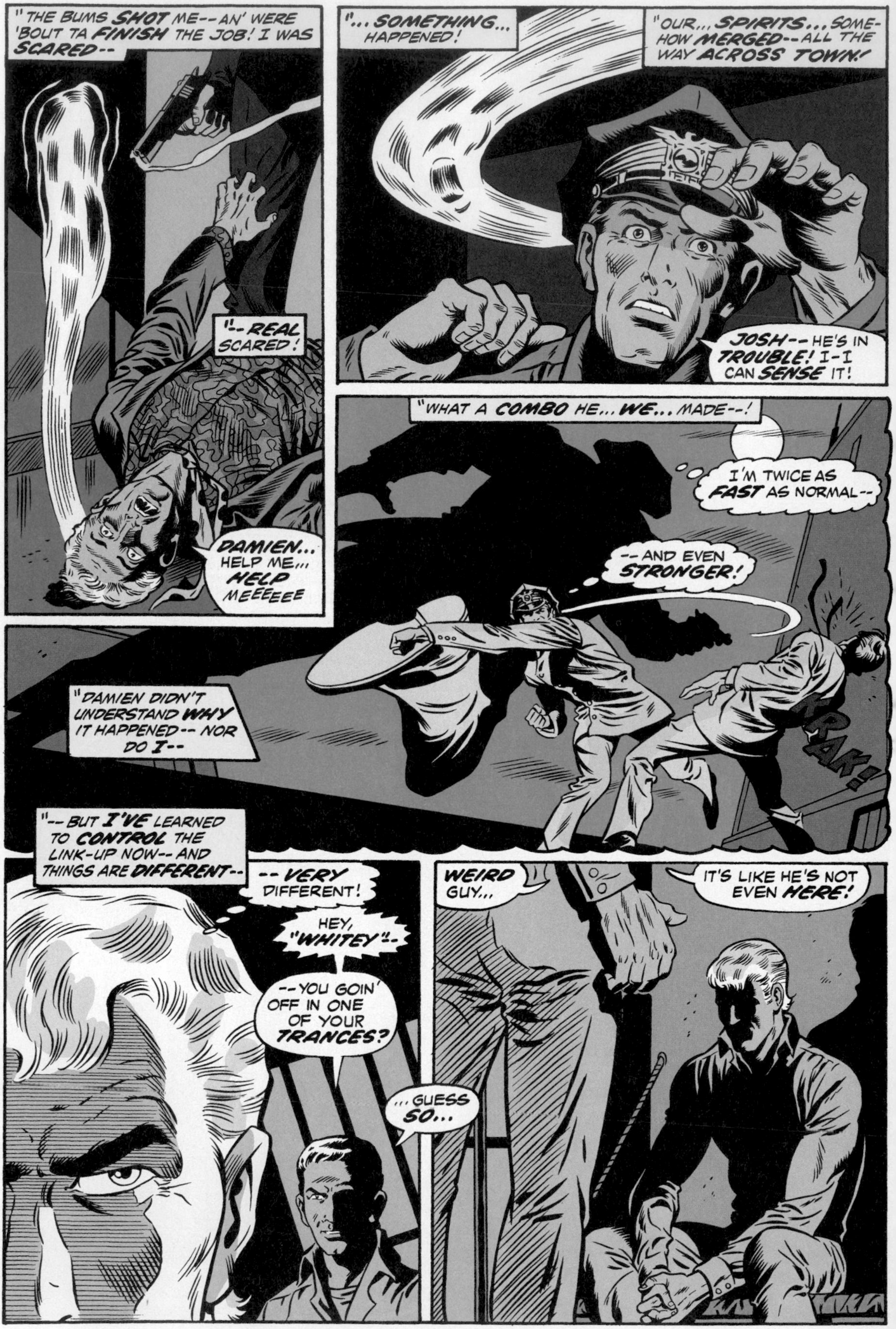
"THE BUMS SHOT ME--AN' WERE 'BOUT TA FINISH THE JOB! I WAS SCARED--
"--REAL SCARED!
DAMIEN... HELP ME... HELP MEEEEEEE
"...SOMETHING... HAPPENED!
"OUR... SPIRITS... SOMEHOW MERGED--ALL THE WAY ACROSS TOWN!
JOSH--HE'S IN TROUBLE! I-I CAN SENSE IT!
"WHAT A COMBO HE... WE... MADE--!
I'M TWICE AS FAST AS NORMAL--
--AND EVEN STRONGER!
"DAMIEN DIDN'T UNDERSTAND WHY IT HAPPENED--NOR DO I--
KRAK!
"--BUT I'VE LEARNED TO CONTROL THE LINK-UP NOW--AND THINGS ARE DIFFERENT--
--VERY DIFFERENT!
HEY, "WHITEY"--
--YOU GOIN' OFF IN ONE OF YOUR TRANCES?
...GUESS SO...
WEIRD GUY...
IT'S LIKE HE'S NOT EVEN HERE!

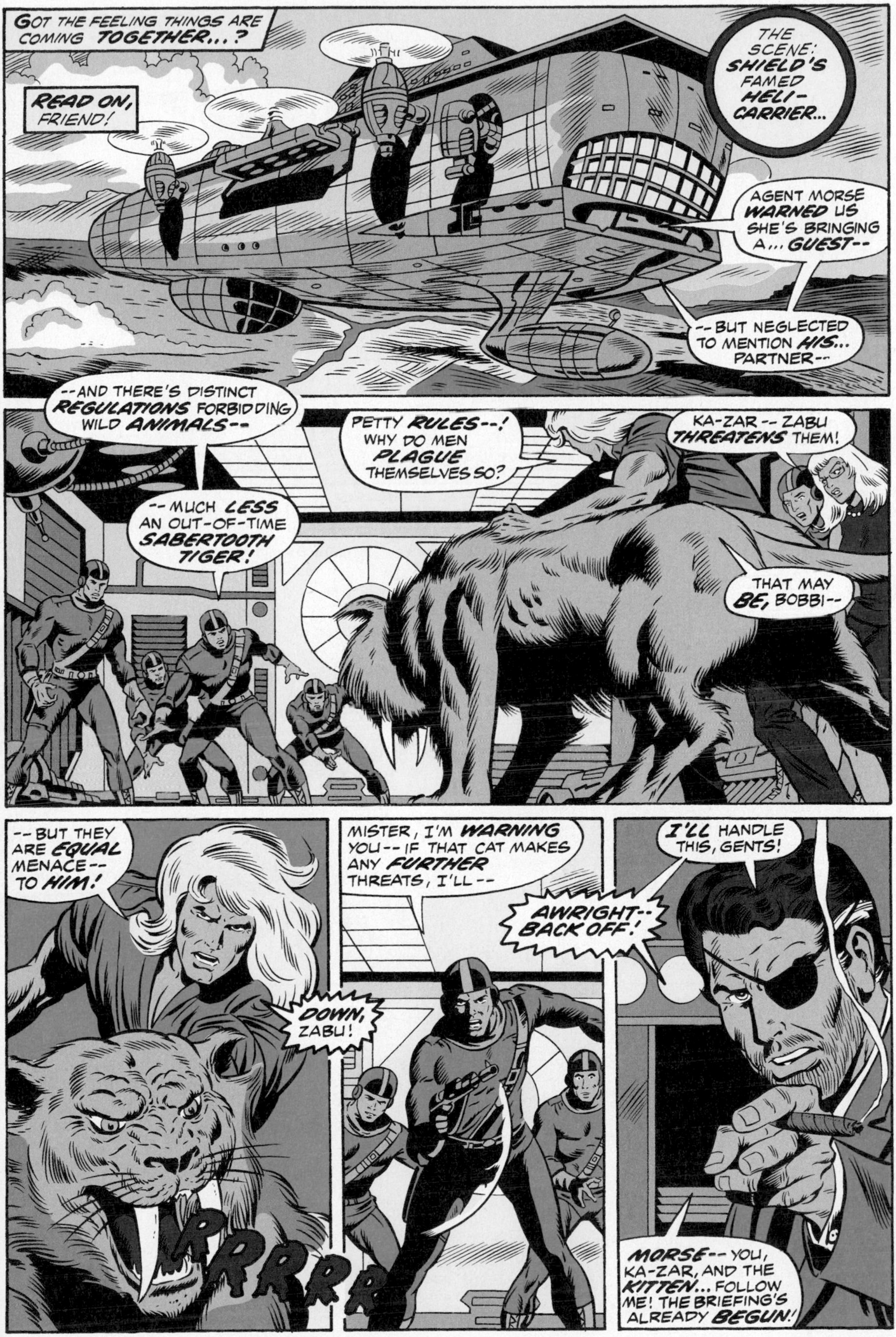
GOT THE FEELING THINGS ARE COMING TOGETHER...?
READ ON, FRIEND!
THE SCENE: SHIELD'S FAMED HELI-CARRIER...
AGENT MORSE WARNED US SHE'S BRINGING A... GUEST--
--BUT NEGLECTED TO MENTION HIS... PARTNER--
--AND THERE'S DISTINCT REGULATIONS FORBIDDING WILD ANIMALS--
--MUCH LESS AN OUT-OF-TIME SABERTOOTH TIGER!
PETTY RULES--! WHY DO MEN PLAGUE THEMSELVES SO?
KA-ZAR--ZABU THREATENS THEM!
THAT MAY BE, BOBBI--
--BUT THEY ARE EQUAL MENACE--TO HIM!
DOWN, ZABU!
RRRRR
MISTER, I'M WARNING YOU--IF THAT CAT MAKES ANY FURTHER THREATS, I'LL--
AWRIGHT--BACK OFF!
I'LL HANDLE THIS, GENTS!
MORSE--YOU, KA-ZAR, AND THE KITTEN... FOLLOW ME! THE BRIEFING'S ALREADY BEGUN!

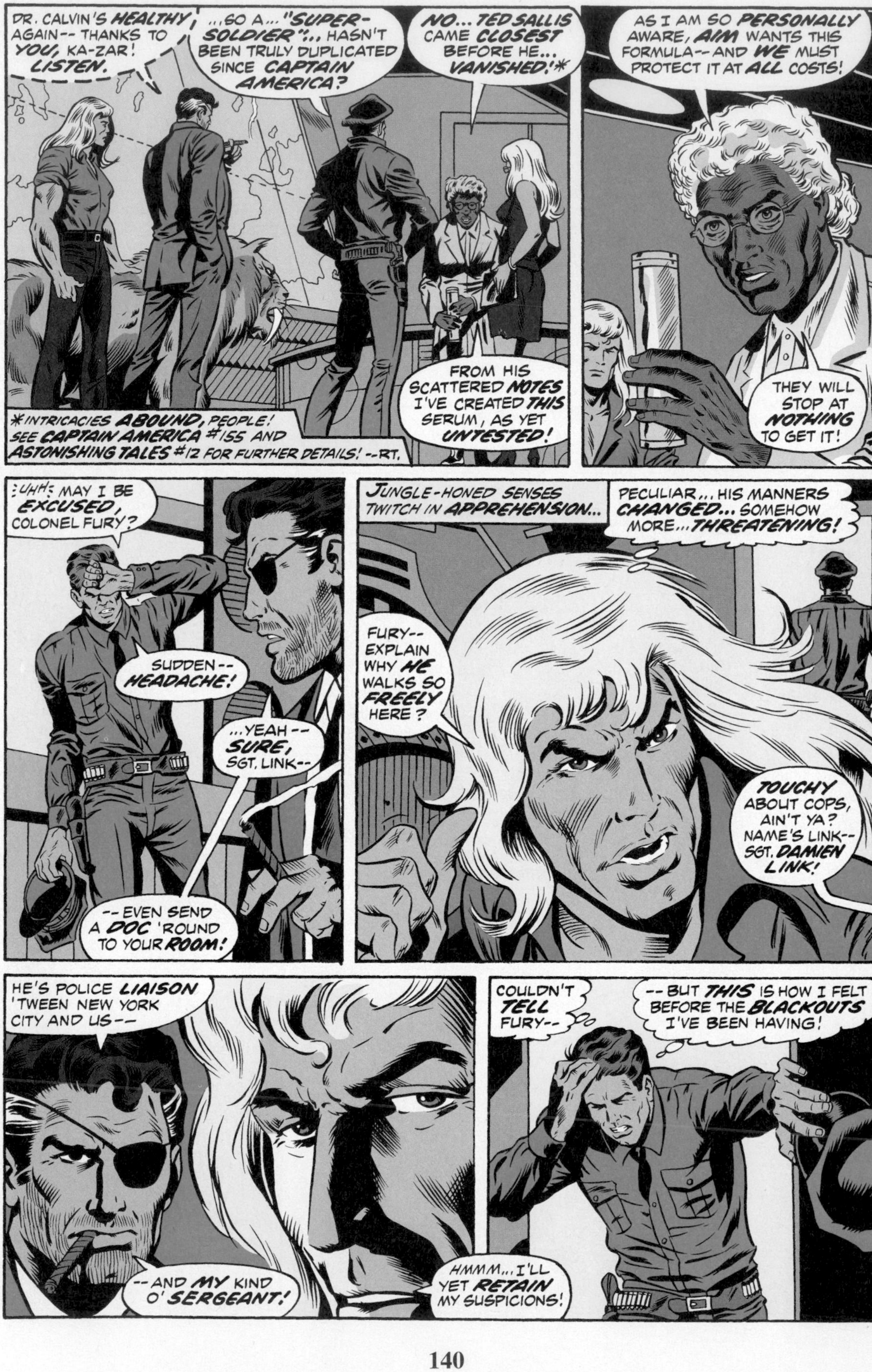
DR. CALVIN'S HEALTHY AGAIN-- THANKS TO YOU, KA-ZAR! LISTEN.
...SO A..."SUPER-SOLDIER"... HASN'T BEEN TRULY DUPLICATED SINCE CAPTAIN AMERICA?
NO...TED SALLIS CAME CLOSEST BEFORE HE... VANISHED!*
FROM HIS SCATTERED NOTES I'VE CREATED THIS SERUM, AS YET UNTESTED!
*INTRICACIES ABOUND, PEOPLE! SEE CAPTAIN AMERICA #155 AND ASTONISHING TALES #12 FOR FURTHER DETAILS! --RT.
AS I AM SO PERSONALLY AWARE, AIM WANTS THIS FORMULA--AND WE MUST PROTECT IT AT ALL COSTS!
THEY WILL STOP AT NOTHING TO GET IT!
UHH: MAY I BE EXCUSED, COLONEL FURY?
SUDDEN-- HEADACHE!
...YEAH-- SURE, SGT. LINK--
--EVEN SEND A DOC 'ROUND TO YOUR ROOM!
JUNGLE-HONED SENSES TWITCH IN APPREHENSION...
PECULIAR... HIS MANNERS CHANGED... SOMEHOW MORE... THREATENING!
FURY-- EXPLAIN WHY HE WALKS SO FREELY HERE?
TOUCHY ABOUT COPS, AIN'T YA? NAME'S LINK-- SGT. DAMIEN LINK!
HE'S POLICE LIAISON 'TWEEN NEW YORK CITY AND US--
--AND MY KIND O' SERGEANT!
HMMM... I'LL YET RETAIN MY SUSPICIONS!
COULDN'T TELL FURY--
--BUT THIS IS HOW I FELT BEFORE THE BLACKOUTS I'VE BEEN HAVING!

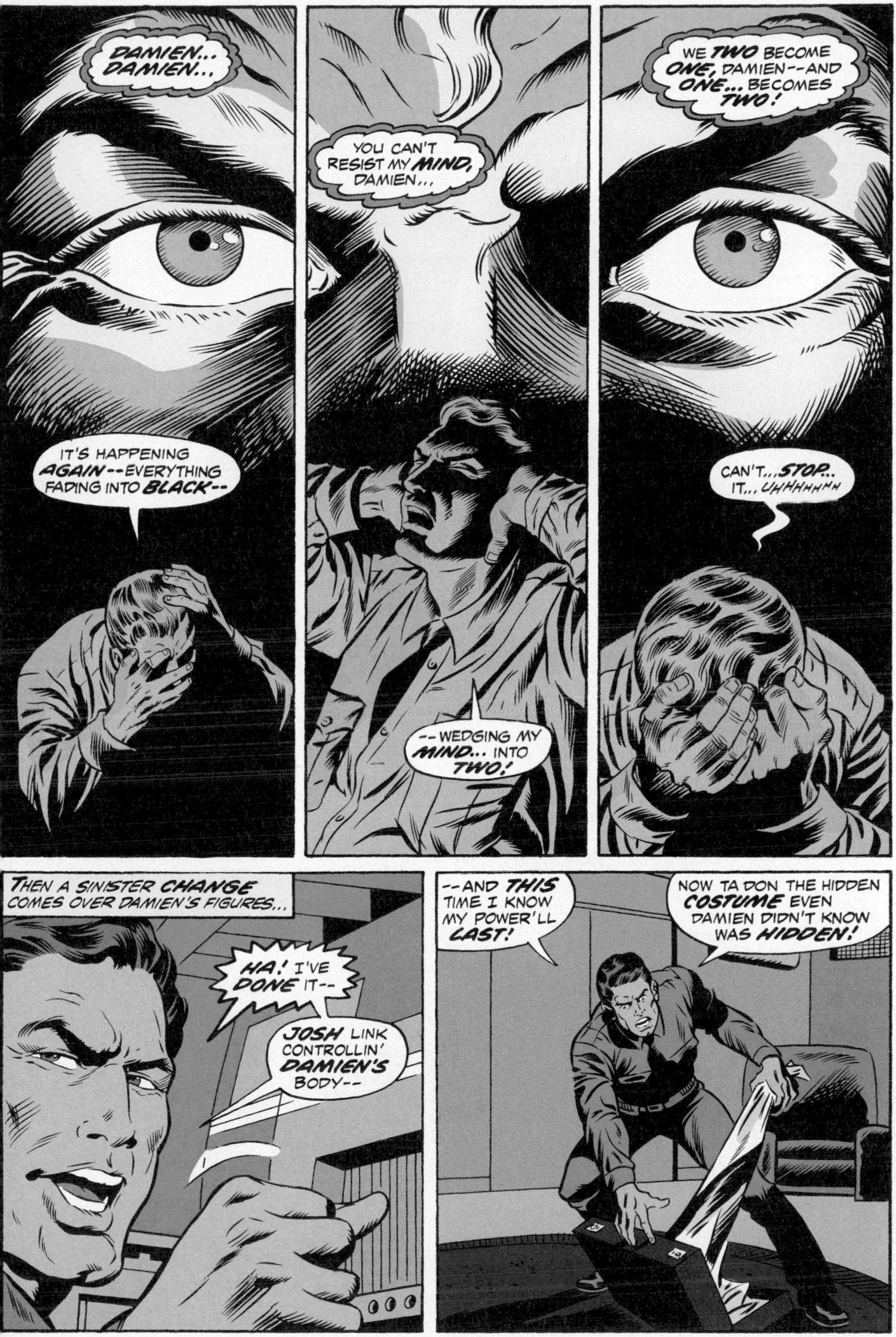
DAMIEN... DAMIEN...
YOU CAN'T RESIST MY MIND, DAMIEN...
WE TWO BECOME ONE, DAMIEN--AND ONE... BECOMES TWO!
IT'S HAPPENING AGAIN--EVERYTHING FADING INTO BLACK--
--WEDGING MY MIND... INTO TWO!
CAN'T... STOP... IT... UHHHHHHH
THEN A SINISTER CHANGE COMES OVER DAMIEN'S FIGURES...
HA! I'VE DONE IT--
JOSH LINK CONTROLLIN' DAMIEN'S BODY--
--AND THIS TIME I KNOW MY POWER'LL LAST!
NOW TA DON THE HIDDEN COSTUME EVEN DAMIEN DIDN'T KNOW WAS HIDDEN!

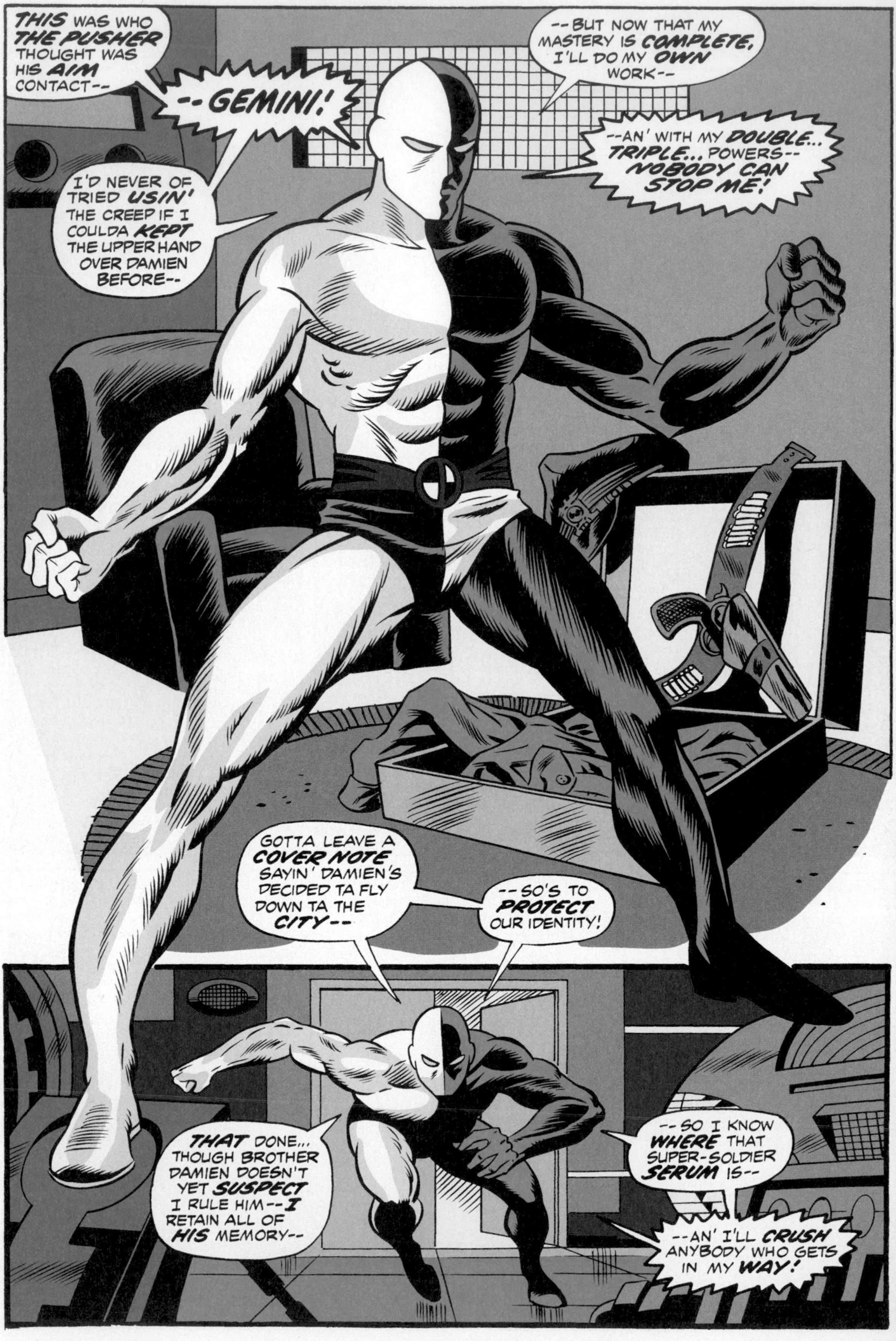
THIS WAS WHO THE PUSHER THOUGHT WAS HIS AIM CONTACT--
--GEMINI!
I'D NEVER OF TRIED USIN' THE CREEP IF I COULDA KEPT THE UPPER HAND OVER DAMIEN BEFORE--
--BUT NOW THAT MY MASTERY IS COMPLETE, I'LL DO MY OWN WORK--
--AN' WITH MY DOUBLE... TRIPLE... POWERS--NOBODY CAN STOP ME!
GOTTA LEAVE A COVER NOTE SAYIN' DAMIEN'S DECIDED TA FLY DOWN TA THE CITY--
--SO'S TO PROTECT OUR IDENTITY!
THAT DONE... THOUGH BROTHER DAMIEN DOESN'T YET SUSPECT I RULE HIM--I RETAIN ALL OF HIS MEMORY--
--SO I KNOW WHERE THAT SUPER-SOLDIER SERUM IS--
--AN' I'LL CRUSH ANYBODY WHO GETS IN MY WAY!

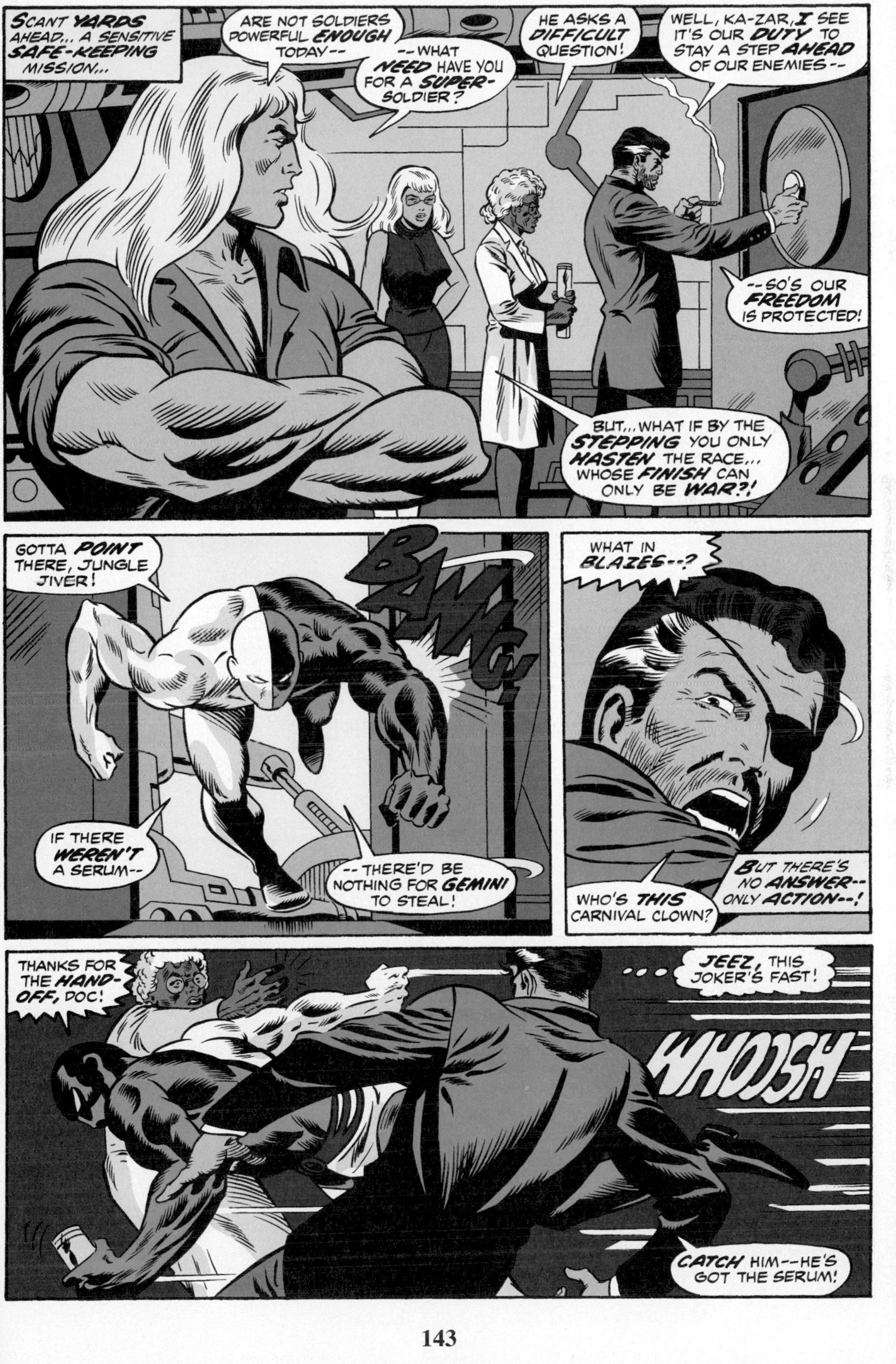
SCANT YARDS AHEAD... A SENSITIVE SAFE-KEEPING MISSION...
ARE NOT SOLDIERS POWERFUL ENOUGH TODAY--
--WHAT NEED HAVE YOU FOR A SUPER-SOLDIER?
HE ASKS A DIFFICULT QUESTION!
WELL, KA-ZAR, I SEE IT'S OUR DUTY TO STAY A STEP AHEAD OF OUR ENEMIES--
--SO'S OUR FREEDOM IS PROTECTED!
BUT... WHAT IF BY THE STEPPING YOU ONLY HASTEN THE RACE... WHOSE FINISH CAN ONLY BE WAR?!
GOTTA POINT THERE, JUNGLE JIVER!
BANG!
IF THERE WEREN'T A SERUM--
--THERE'D BE NOTHING FOR GEMINI TO STEAL!
WHAT IN BLAZES--?
WHO'S THIS CARNIVAL CLOWN?
BUT THERE'S NO ANSWER--ONLY ACTION--!
THANKS FOR THE HAND-OFF, DOC!
...JEEZ, THIS JOKER'S FAST!
WHOOSH
CATCH HIM--HE'S GOT THE SERUM!

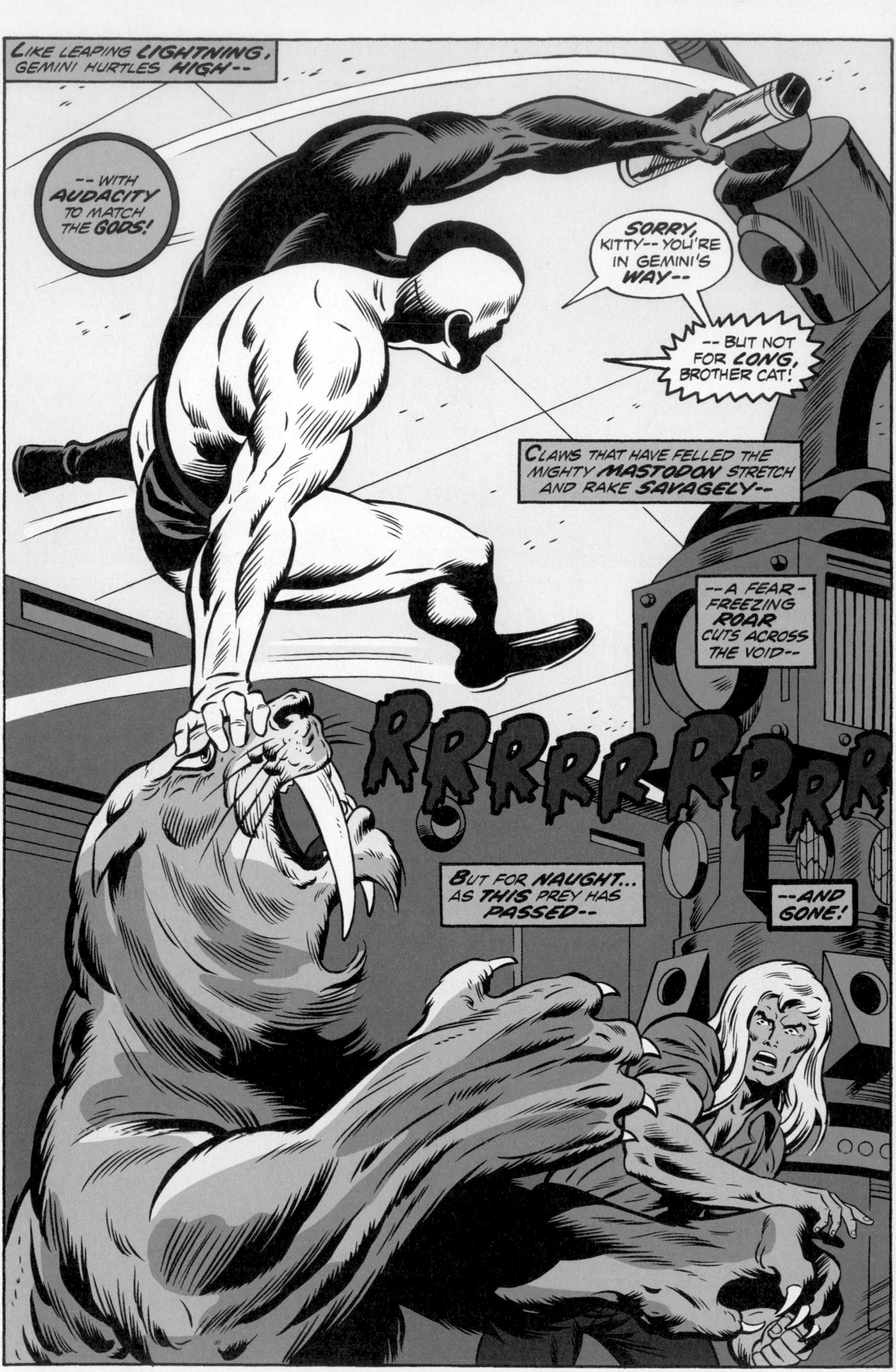

LIKE LEAPING LIGHTNING, GEMINI HURTLES HIGH--
-- WITH AUDACITY TO MATCH THE GODS!
SORRY, KITTY-- YOU'RE IN GEMINI'S WAY--
-- BUT NOT FOR LONG, BROTHER CAT!
CLAWS THAT HAVE FELLED THE MIGHTY MASTODON STRETCH AND RAKE SAVAGELY--
--A FEAR-FREEZING ROAR CUTS ACROSS THE VOID--
RRRRRRRRRR
BUT FOR NAUGHT... AS THIS PREY HAS PASSED--
--AND GONE!

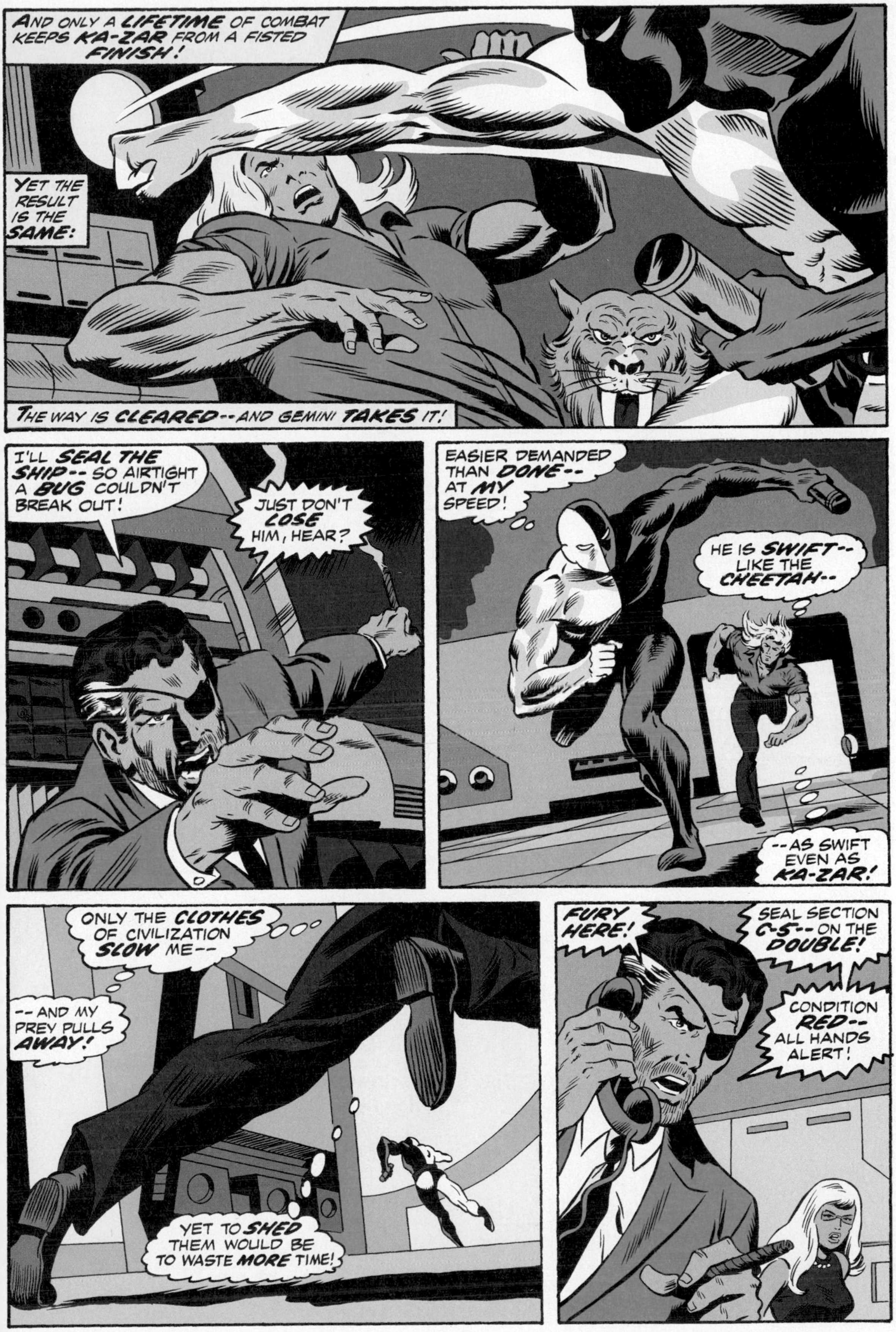
AND ONLY A LIFETIME OF COMBAT KEEPS KA-ZAR FROM A FISTED FINISH!
YET THE RESULT IS THE SAME:
THE WAY IS CLEARED--AND GEMINI TAKES IT!
I'LL SEAL THE SHIP--SO AIRTIGHT A BUG COULDN'T BREAK OUT!
JUST DON'T LOSE HIM, HEAR?
EASIER DEMANDED THAN DONE--AT MY SPEED!
HE IS SWIFT--LIKE THE CHEETAH--
--AS SWIFT EVEN AS KA-ZAR!
ONLY THE CLOTHES OF CIVILIZATION SLOW ME--
--AND MY PREY PULLS AWAY!
YET TO SHED THEM WOULD BE TO WASTE MORE TIME!
FURY HERE!
SEAL SECTION C-5--ON THE DOUBLE!
CONDITION RED--ALL HANDS ALERT!

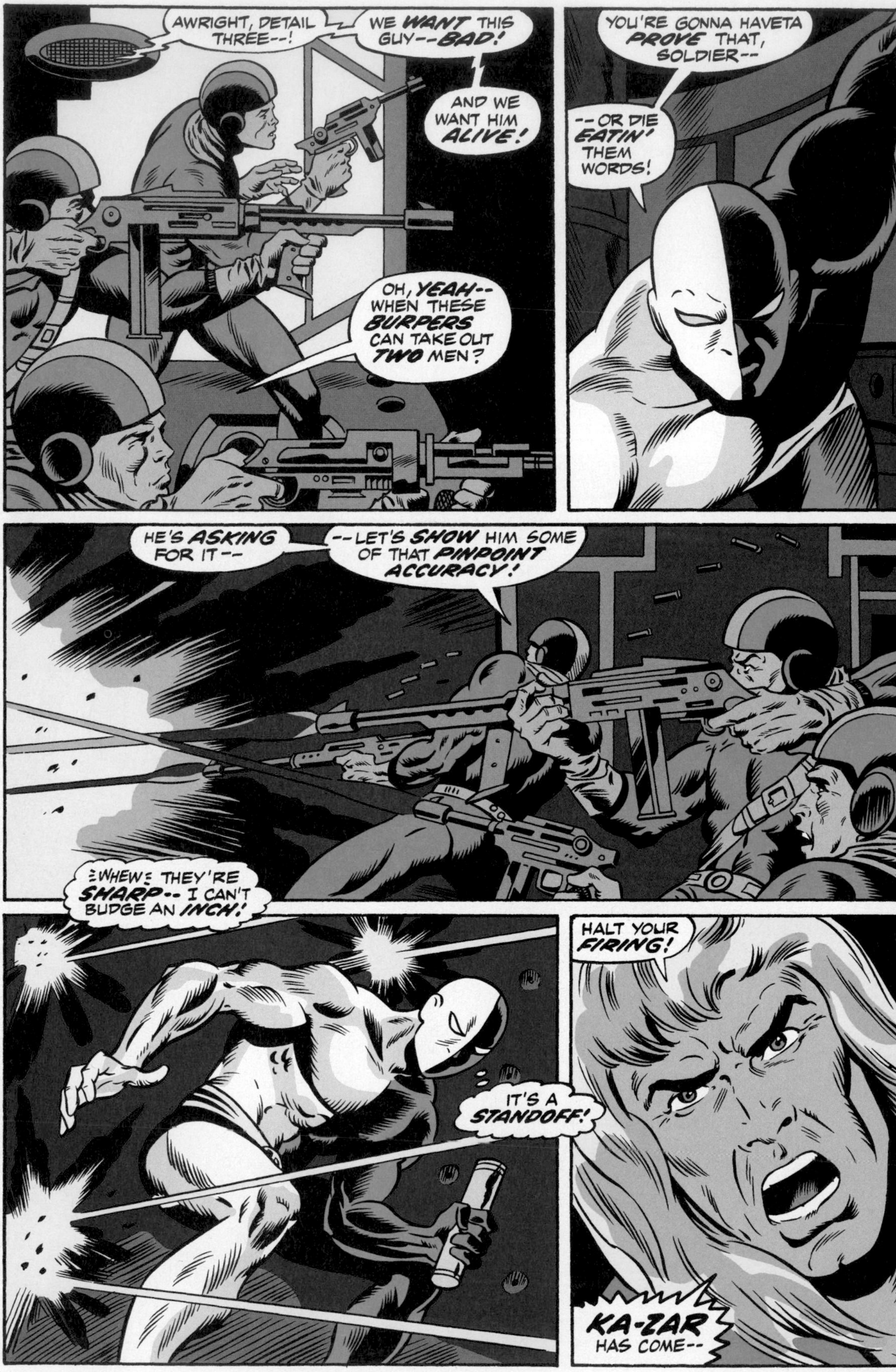
AWRIGHT, DETAIL THREE--!
WE WANT THIS GUY--BAD!
AND WE WANT HIM ALIVE!
OH, YEAH--WHEN THESE BURPERS CAN TAKE OUT TWO MEN?
YOU'RE GONNA HAVETA PROVE THAT, SOLDIER--
--OR DIE EATIN' THEM WORDS!
HE'S ASKING FOR IT--
--LET'S SHOW HIM SOME OF THAT PINPOINT ACCURACY!
WHEW! THEY'RE SHARP-- I CAN'T BUDGE AN INCH!
IT'S A STANDOFF!
HALT YOUR FIRING!
KA-ZAR HAS COME--

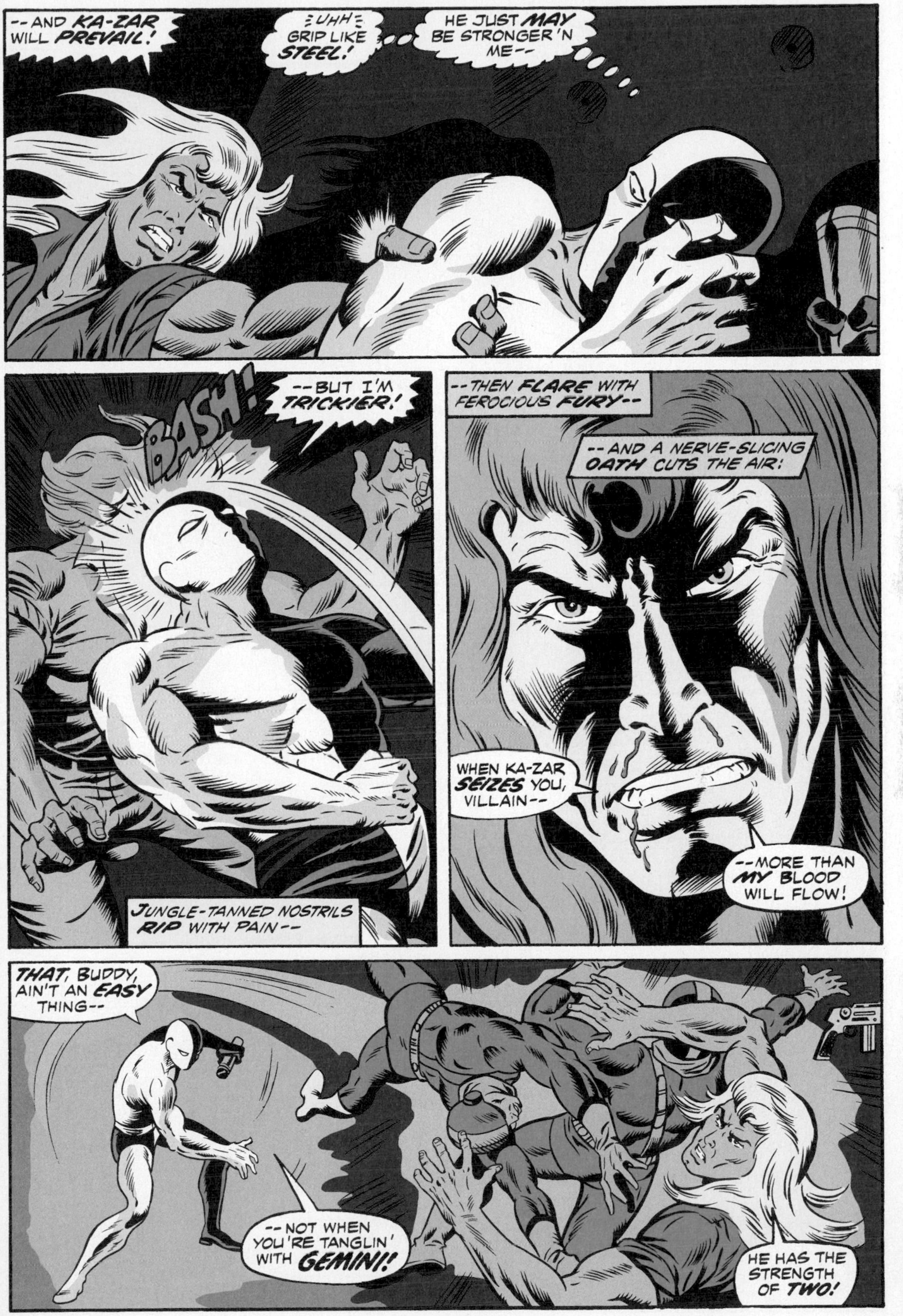
--AND KA-ZAR WILL PREVAIL!
UHH GRIP LIKE STEEL!
HE JUST MAY BE STRONGER'N ME--
BASH!
--BUT I'M TRICKIER!
JUNGLE-TANNED NOSTRILS RIP WITH PAIN--
--THEN FLARE WITH FEROCIOUS FURY--
--AND A NERVE-SLICING OATH CUTS THE AIR:
WHEN KA-ZAR SEIZES YOU, VILLAIN--
--MORE THAN MY BLOOD WILL FLOW!
THAT, BUDDY, AIN'T AN EASY THING--
--NOT WHEN YOU'RE TANGLIN' WITH GEMINI!
HE HAS THE STRENGTH OF TWO!

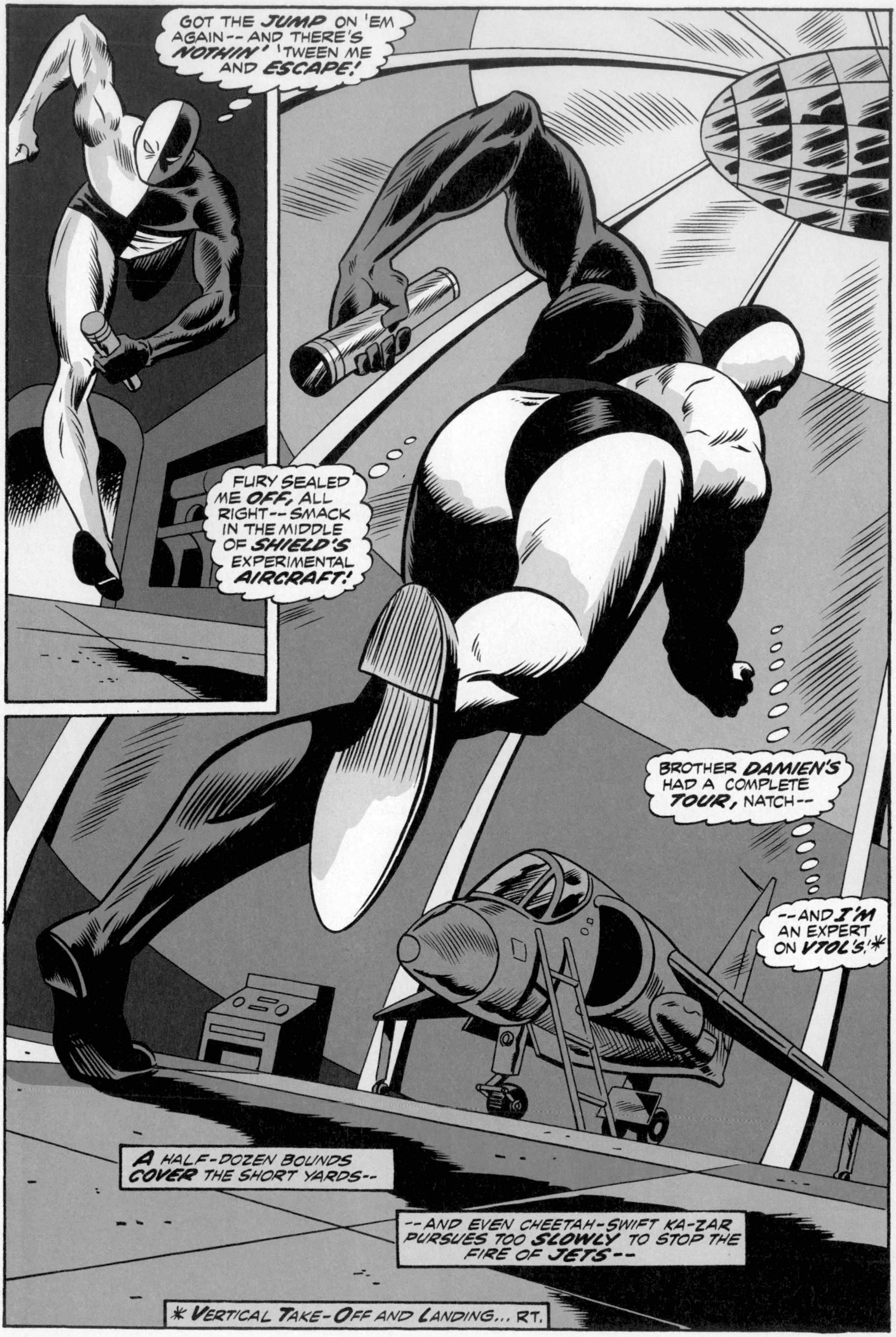
GOT THE JUMP ON 'EM AGAIN-- AND THERE'S NOTHIN' 'TWEEN ME AND ESCAPE!
FURY SEALED ME OFF, ALL RIGHT-- SMACK IN THE MIDDLE OF SHIELD'S EXPERIMENTAL AIRCRAFT!
BROTHER DAMIEN'S HAD A COMPLETE TOUR, NATCH--
--AND I'M AN EXPERT ON VTOL'S!*
A HALF-DOZEN BOUNDS COVER THE SHORT YARDS--
--AND EVEN CHEETAH-SWIFT KA-ZAR PURSUES TOO SLOWLY TO STOP THE FIRE OF JETS--
* VERTICAL TAKE-OFF AND LANDING... RT.

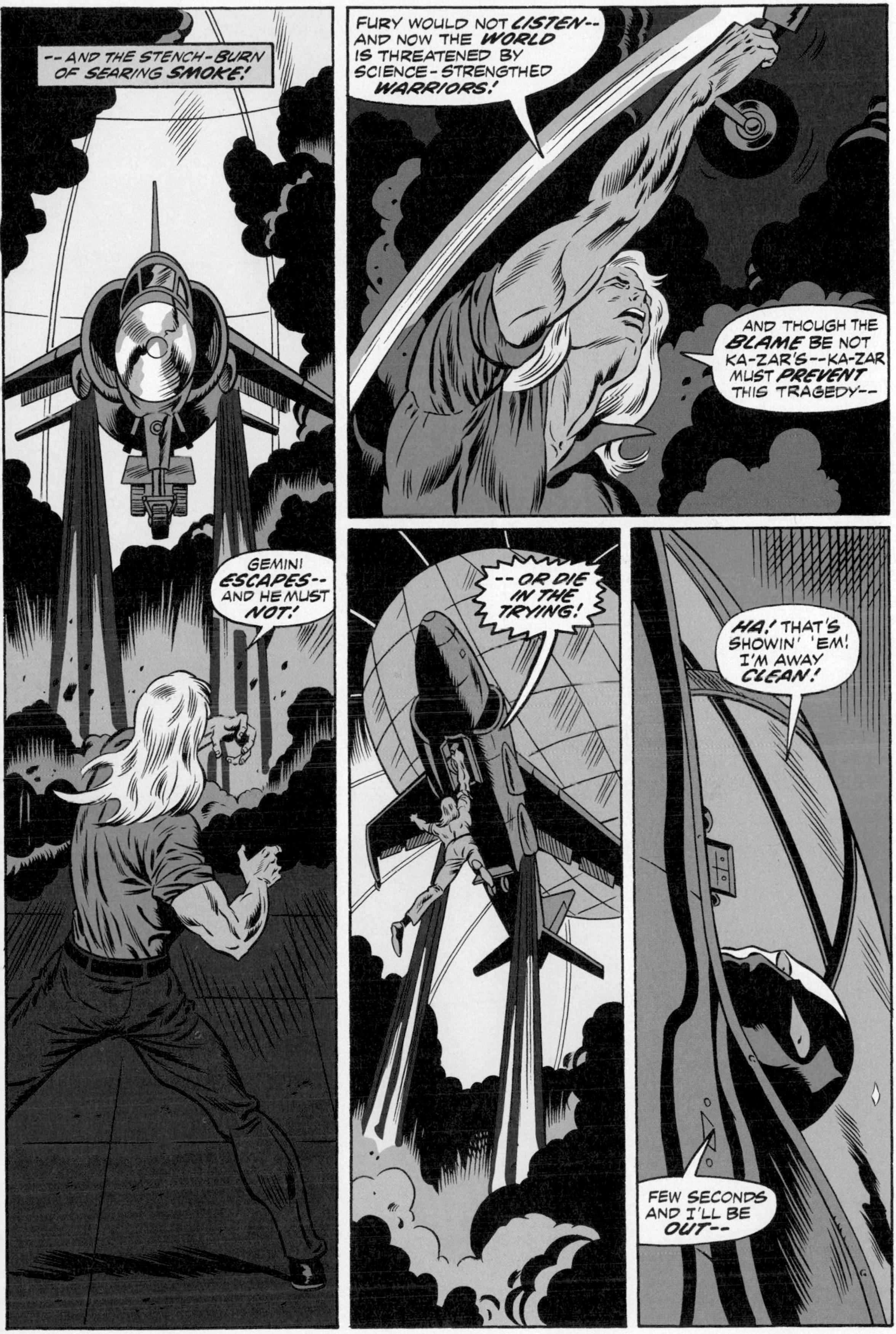
--AND THE STENCH-BURN OF SEARING SMOKE!
GEMINI ESCAPES--AND HE MUST NOT!
FURY WOULD NOT LISTEN--AND NOW THE WORLD IS THREATENED BY SCIENCE-STRENGTHED WARRIORS!
AND THOUGH THE BLAME BE NOT KA-ZAR'S--KA-ZAR MUST PREVENT THIS TRAGEDY--
--OR DIE IN THE TRYING!
HA! THAT'S SHOWIN' 'EM! I'M AWAY CLEAN!
FEW SECONDS AND I'LL BE OUT--

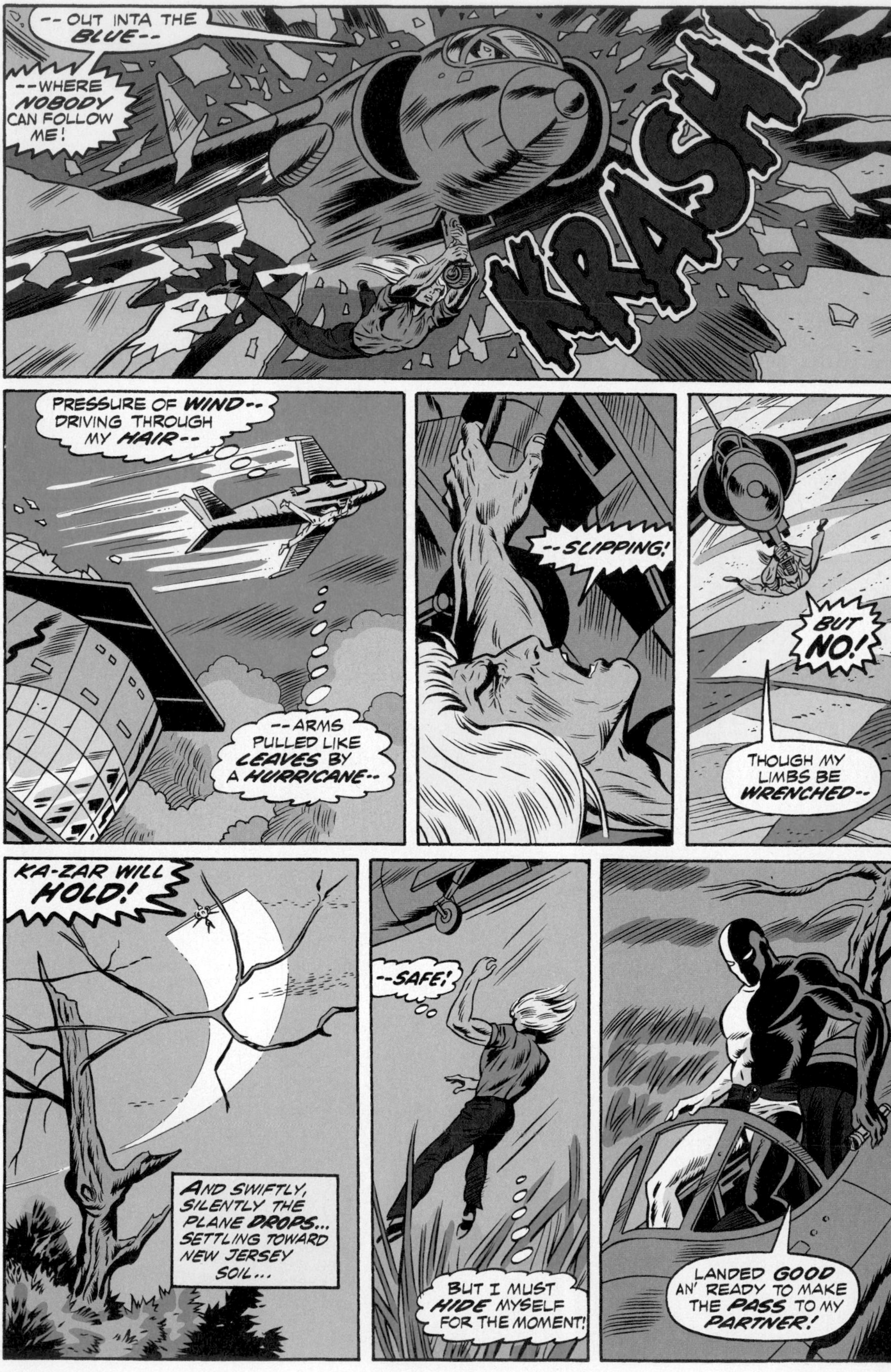
--OUT INTA THE BLUE--
--WHERE NOBODY CAN FOLLOW ME!
KRASH!
PRESSURE OF WIND--DRIVING THROUGH MY HAIR--
--ARMS PULLED LIKE LEAVES BY A HURRICANE--
--SLIPPING!
BUT NO!
THOUGH MY LIMBS BE WRENCHED--
KA-ZAR WILL HOLD!
AND SWIFTLY, SILENTLY THE PLANE DROPS... SETTLING TOWARD NEW JERSEY SOIL...
--SAFE!
BUT I MUST HIDE MYSELF FOR THE MOMENT!
LANDED GOOD AN' READY TO MAKE THE PASS TO MY PARTNER!

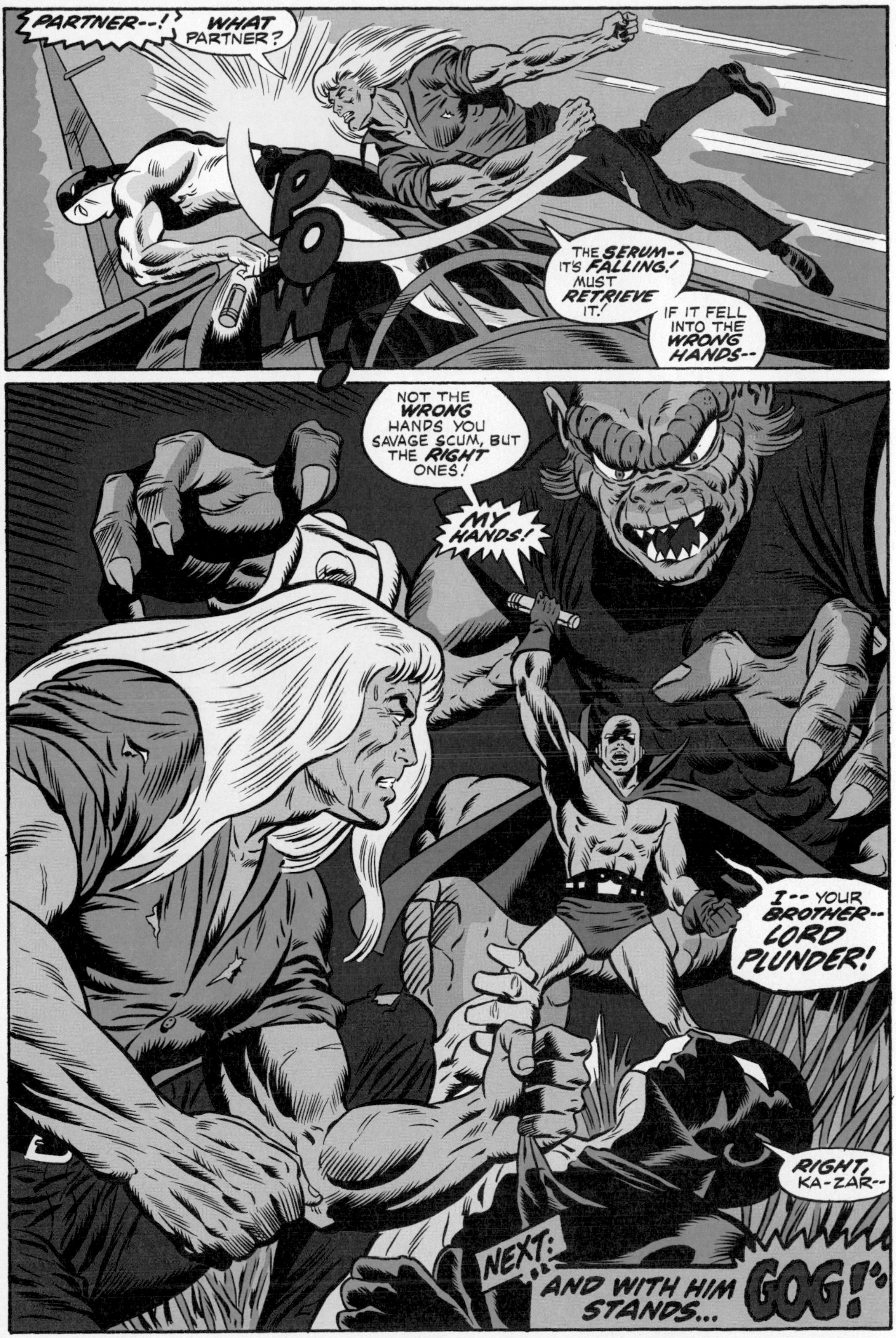
PARTNER--! WHAT PARTNER?
POW!
THE SERUM-- IT'S FALLING! MUST RETRIEVE IT!
IF IT FELL INTO THE WRONG HANDS--
NOT THE WRONG HANDS YOU SAVAGE SCUM, BUT THE RIGHT ONES!
MY HANDS!
I-- YOUR BROTHER-- LORD PLUNDER!
RIGHT, KA-ZAR--
NEXT:
AND WITH HIM STANDS... GOG!

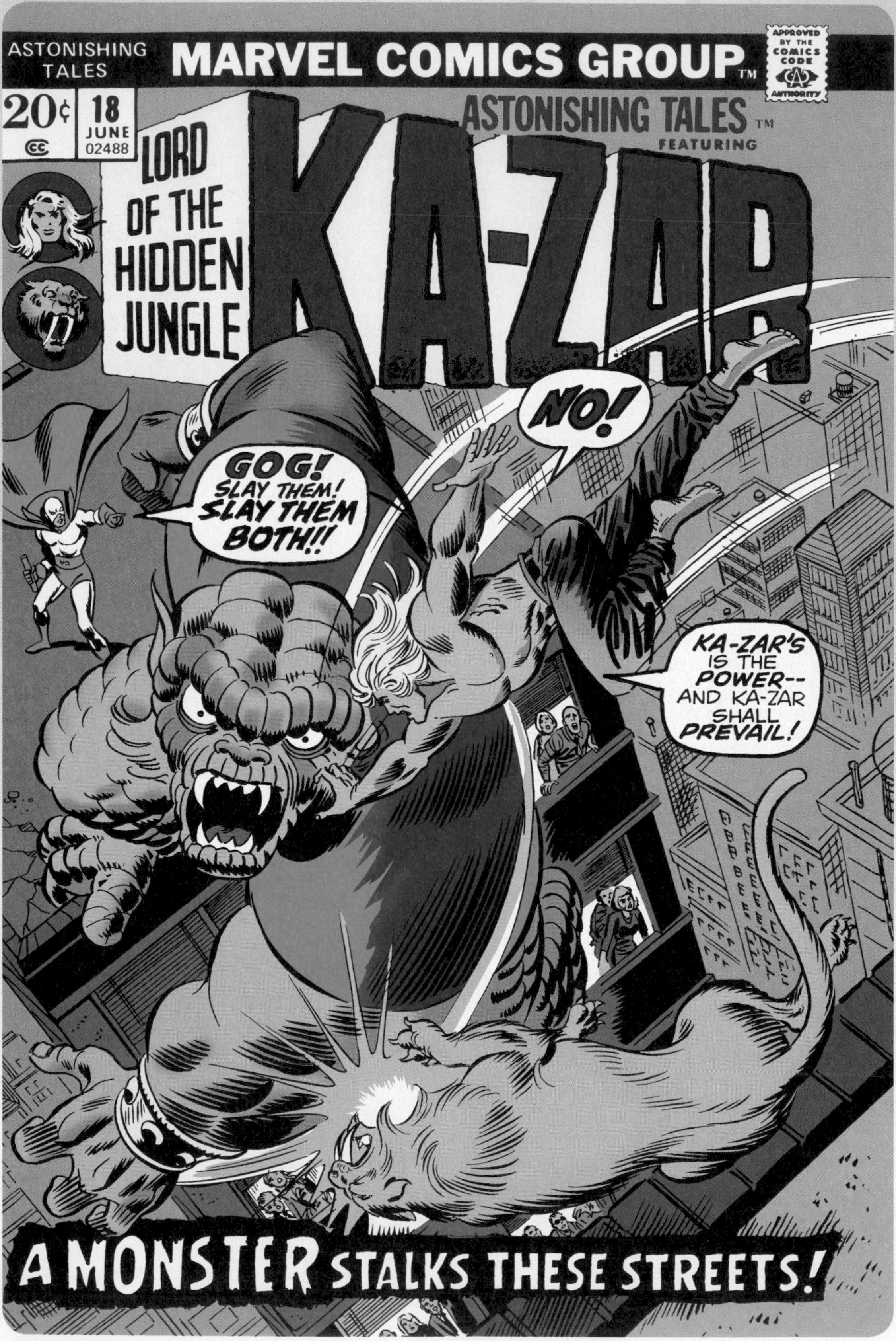
ASTONISHING TALES
MARVEL COMICS GROUP TM
APPROVED BY THE COMICS CODE AUTHORITY
20¢
18
JUNE
02488
ASTONISHING TALES TM
FEATURING
LORD OF THE HIDDEN JUNGLE
KA-ZAR
NO!
GOG! SLAY THEM! SLAY THEM BOTH!!
KA-ZAR'S IS THE POWER-- AND KA-ZAR SHALL PREVAIL!
A MONSTER STALKS THESE STREETS!

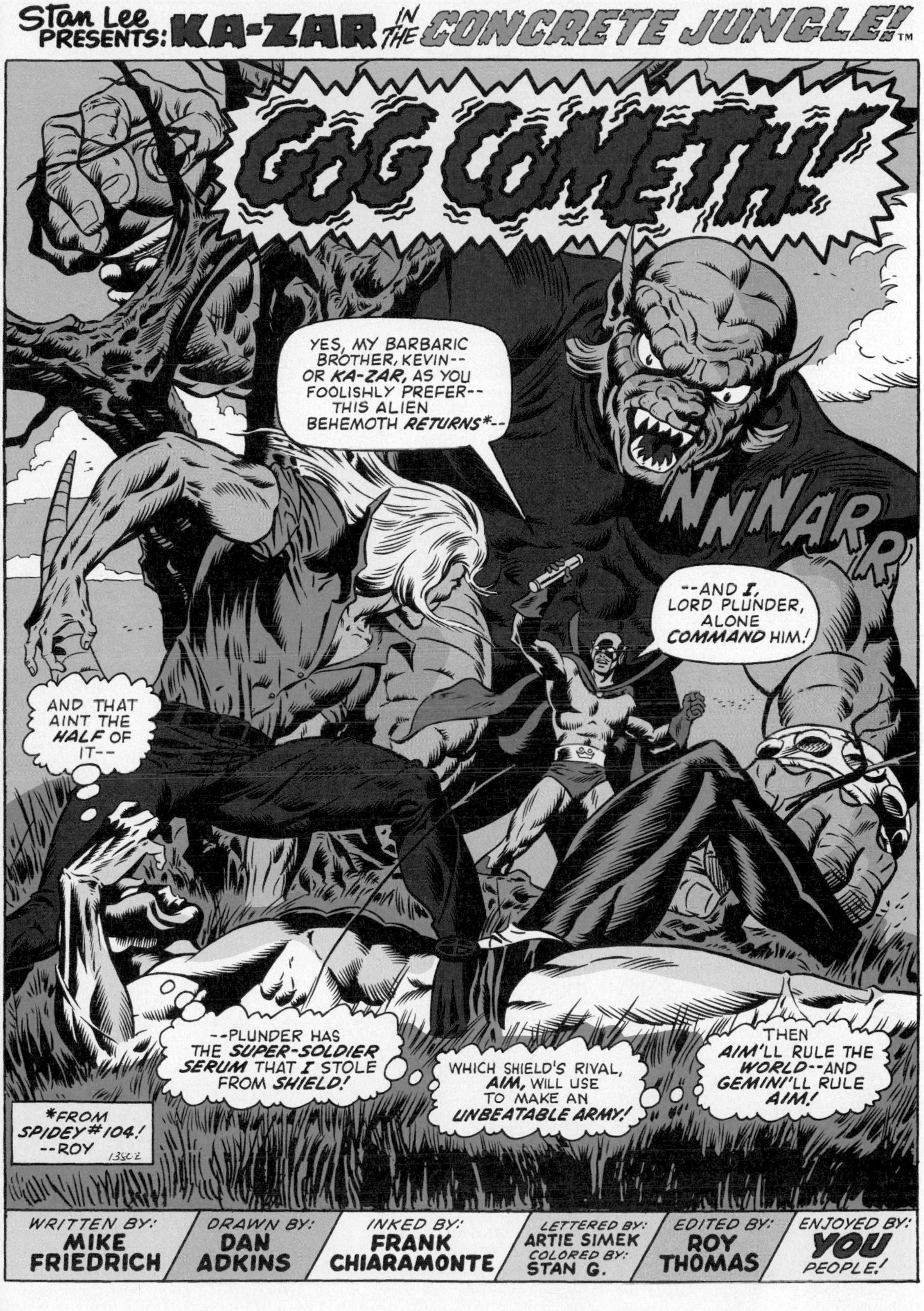
Stan Lee PRESENTS: KA-ZAR IN THE CONCRETE JUNGLE!™
GOG COMETH!
YES, MY BARBARIC BROTHER, KEVIN-- OR KA-ZAR, AS YOU FOOLISHLY PREFER-- THIS ALIEN BEHEMOTH RETURNS*--
NNNARR
--AND I, LORD PLUNDER, ALONE COMMAND HIM!
AND THAT AINT THE HALF OF IT--
--PLUNDER HAS THE SUPER-SOLDIER SERUM THAT I STOLE FROM SHIELD!
WHICH SHIELD'S RIVAL, AIM, WILL USE TO MAKE AN UNBEATABLE ARMY!
THEN AIM'LL RULE THE WORLD--AND GEMINI'LL RULE AIM!
*FROM SPIDEY #104! --ROY
WRITTEN BY: MIKE FRIEDRICH
DRAWN BY: DAN ADKINS
INKED BY: FRANK CHIARAMONTE
LETTERED BY: ARTIE SIMEK COLORED BY: STAN G.
EDITED BY: ROY THOMAS
ENJOYED BY: YOU PEOPLE!

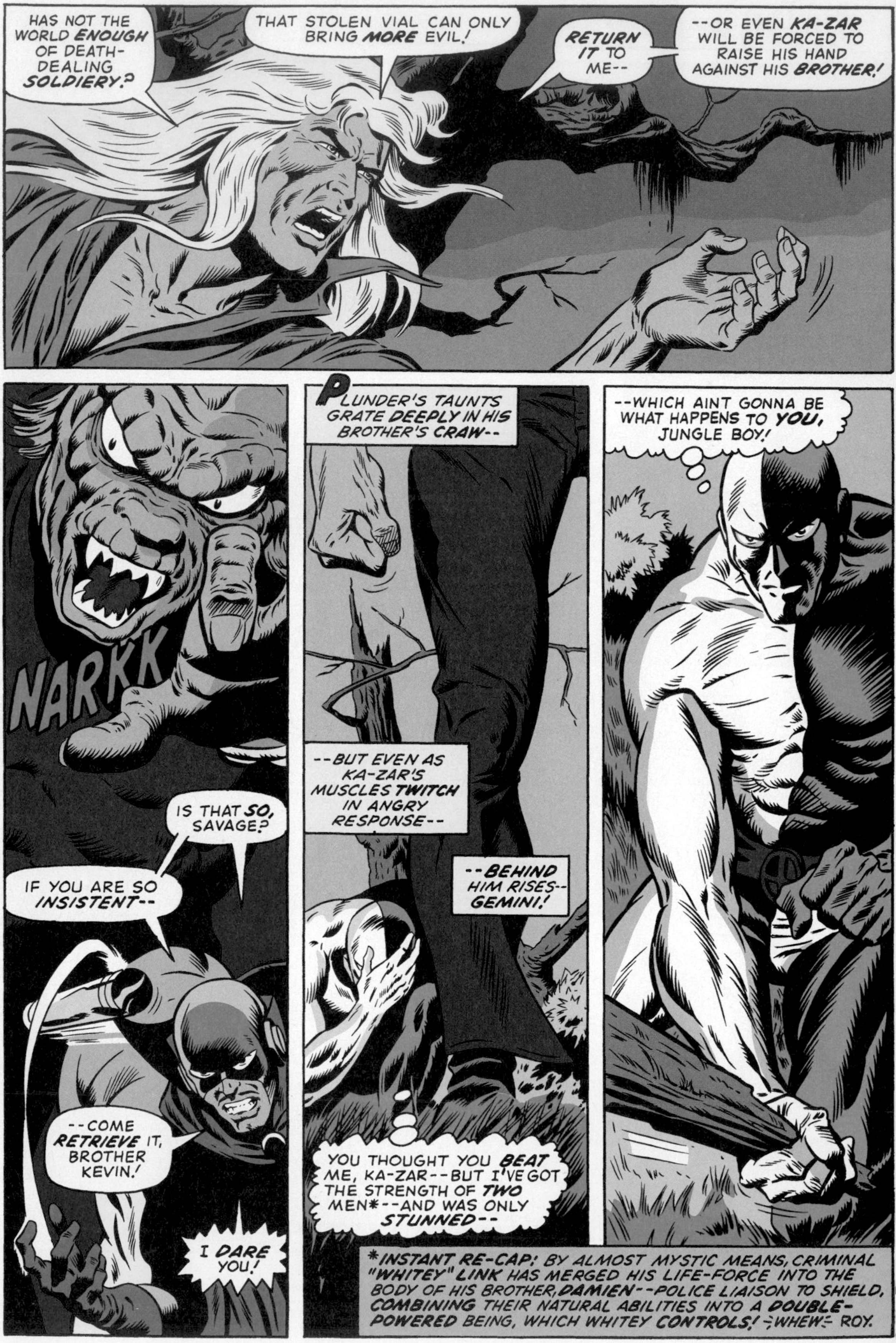
HAS NOT THE WORLD ENOUGH OF DEATH-DEALING SOLDIERY?
THAT STOLEN VIAL CAN ONLY BRING MORE EVIL!
RETURN IT TO ME--
--OR EVEN KA-ZAR WILL BE FORCED TO RAISE HIS HAND AGAINST HIS BROTHER!
NARKK
IS THAT SO, SAVAGE?
IF YOU ARE SO INSISTENT--
--COME RETRIEVE IT, BROTHER KEVIN!
I DARE YOU!
PLUNDER'S TAUNTS GRATE DEEPLY IN HIS BROTHER'S CRAW--
--BUT EVEN AS KA-ZAR'S MUSCLES TWITCH IN ANGRY RESPONSE--
--BEHIND HIM RISES-- GEMINI!
--WHICH AINT GONNA BE WHAT HAPPENS TO YOU, JUNGLE BOY!
YOU THOUGHT YOU BEAT ME, KA-ZAR--BUT I'VE GOT THE STRENGTH OF TWO MEN*--AND WAS ONLY STUNNED--
*INSTANT RE-CAP: BY ALMOST MYSTIC MEANS, CRIMINAL "WHITEY" LINK HAS MERGED HIS LIFE-FORCE INTO THE BODY OF HIS BROTHER, DAMIEN--POLICE LIAISON TO SHIELD, COMBINING THEIR NATURAL ABILITIES INTO A DOUBLE-POWERED BEING, WHICH WHITEY CONTROLS! -WHEW- ROY.

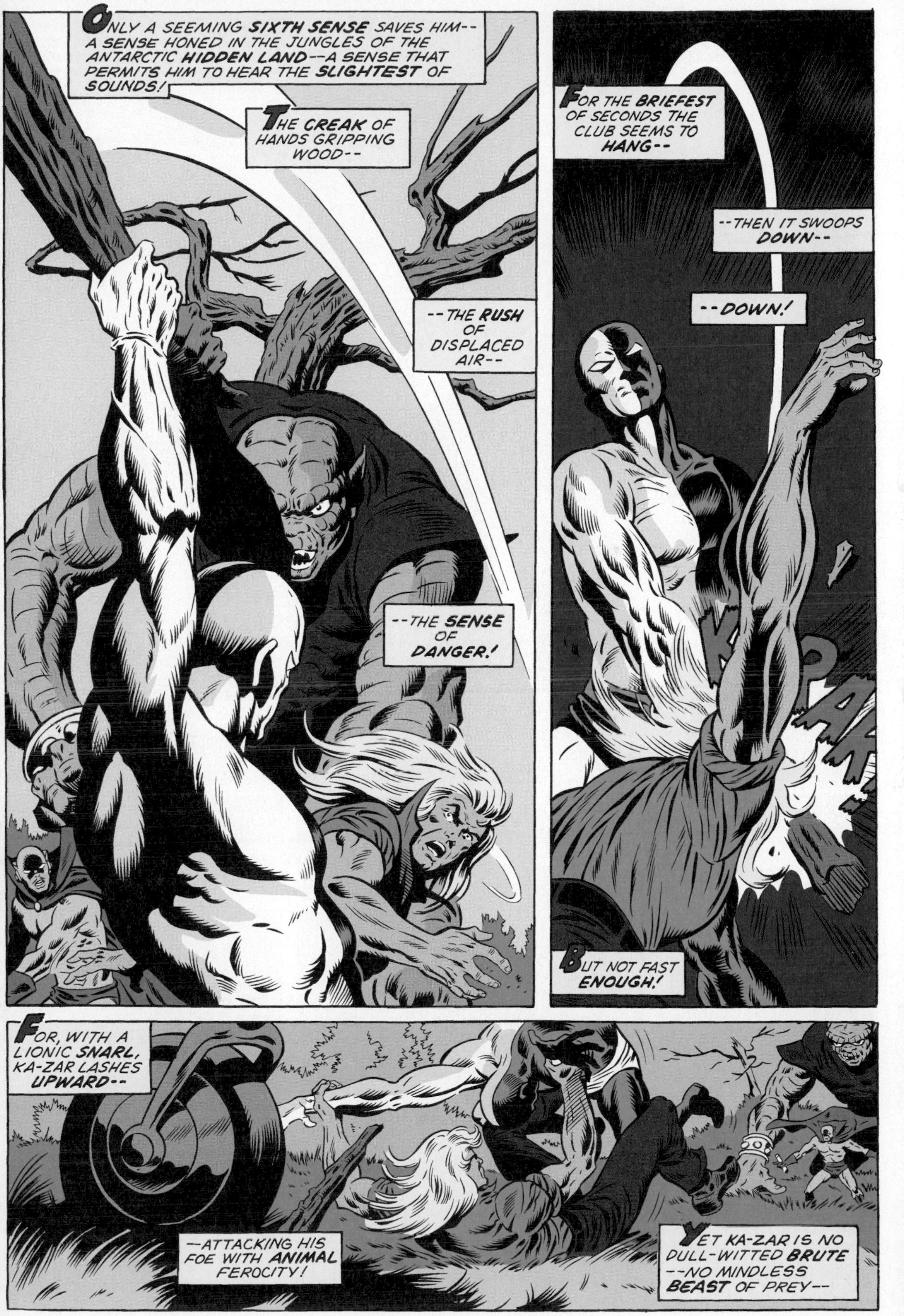
ONLY A SEEMING SIXTH SENSE SAVES HIM-- A SENSE HONED IN THE JUNGLES OF THE ANTARCTIC HIDDEN LAND--A SENSE THAT PERMITS HIM TO HEAR THE SLIGHTEST OF SOUNDS!
THE CREAK OF HANDS GRIPPING WOOD--
--THE RUSH OF DISPLACED AIR--
--THE SENSE OF DANGER!
FOR THE BRIEFEST OF SECONDS THE CLUB SEEMS TO HANG--
--THEN IT SWOOPS DOWN--
--DOWN!
BUT NOT FAST ENOUGH!
FOR, WITH A LIONIC SNARL, KA-ZAR LASHES UPWARD--
--ATTACKING HIS FOE WITH ANIMAL FEROCITY!
YET KA-ZAR IS NO DULL-WITTED BRUTE --NO MINDLESS BEAST OF PREY--

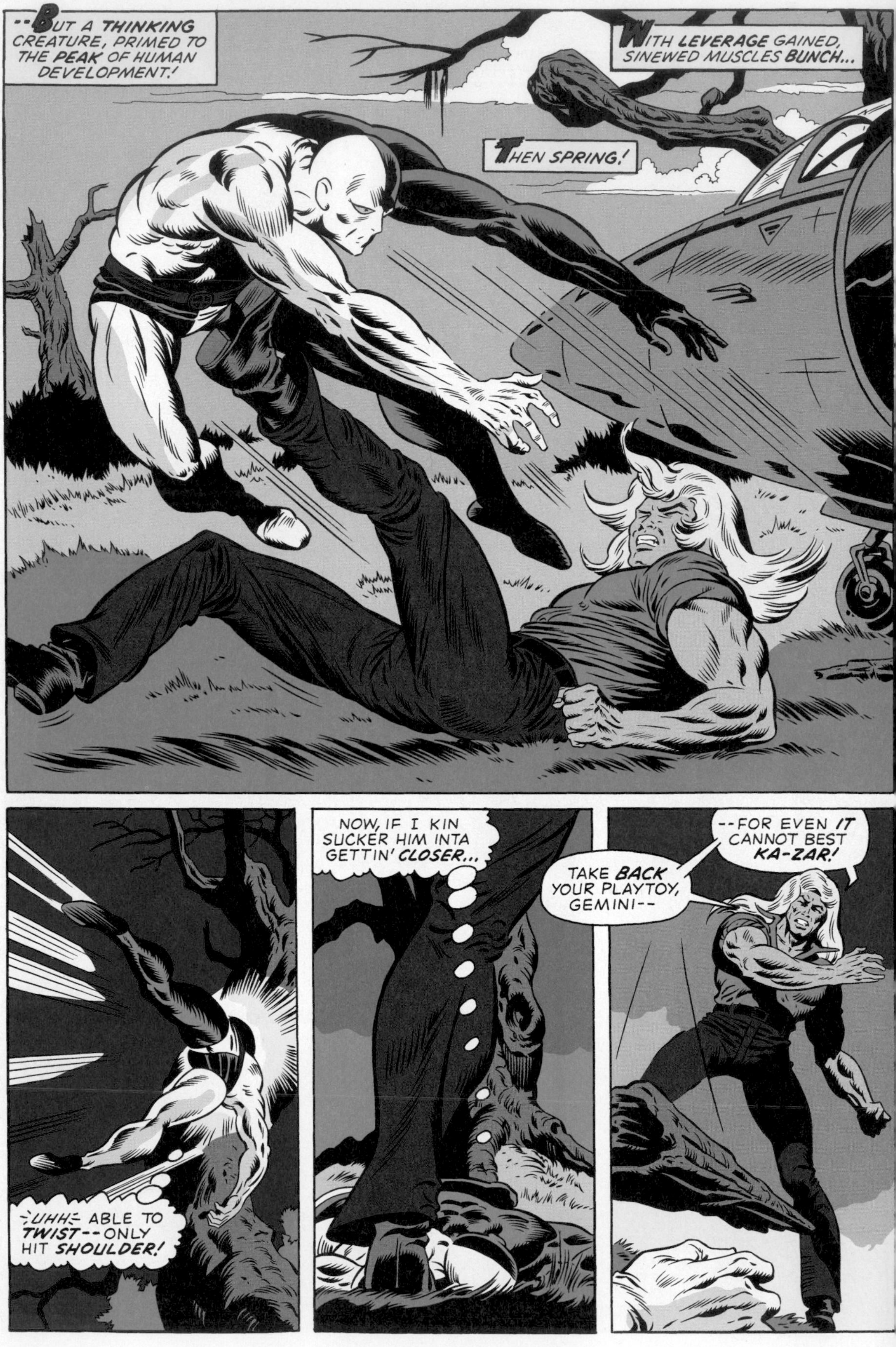
--BUT A THINKING CREATURE, PRIMED TO THE PEAK OF HUMAN DEVELOPMENT!
WITH LEVERAGE GAINED, SINEWED MUSCLES BUNCH...
THEN SPRING!
-UHH- ABLE TO TWIST--ONLY HIT SHOULDER!
NOW, IF I KIN SUCKER HIM INTA GETTIN' CLOSER...
TAKE BACK YOUR PLAYTOY, GEMINI--
--FOR EVEN IT CANNOT BEST KA-ZAR!

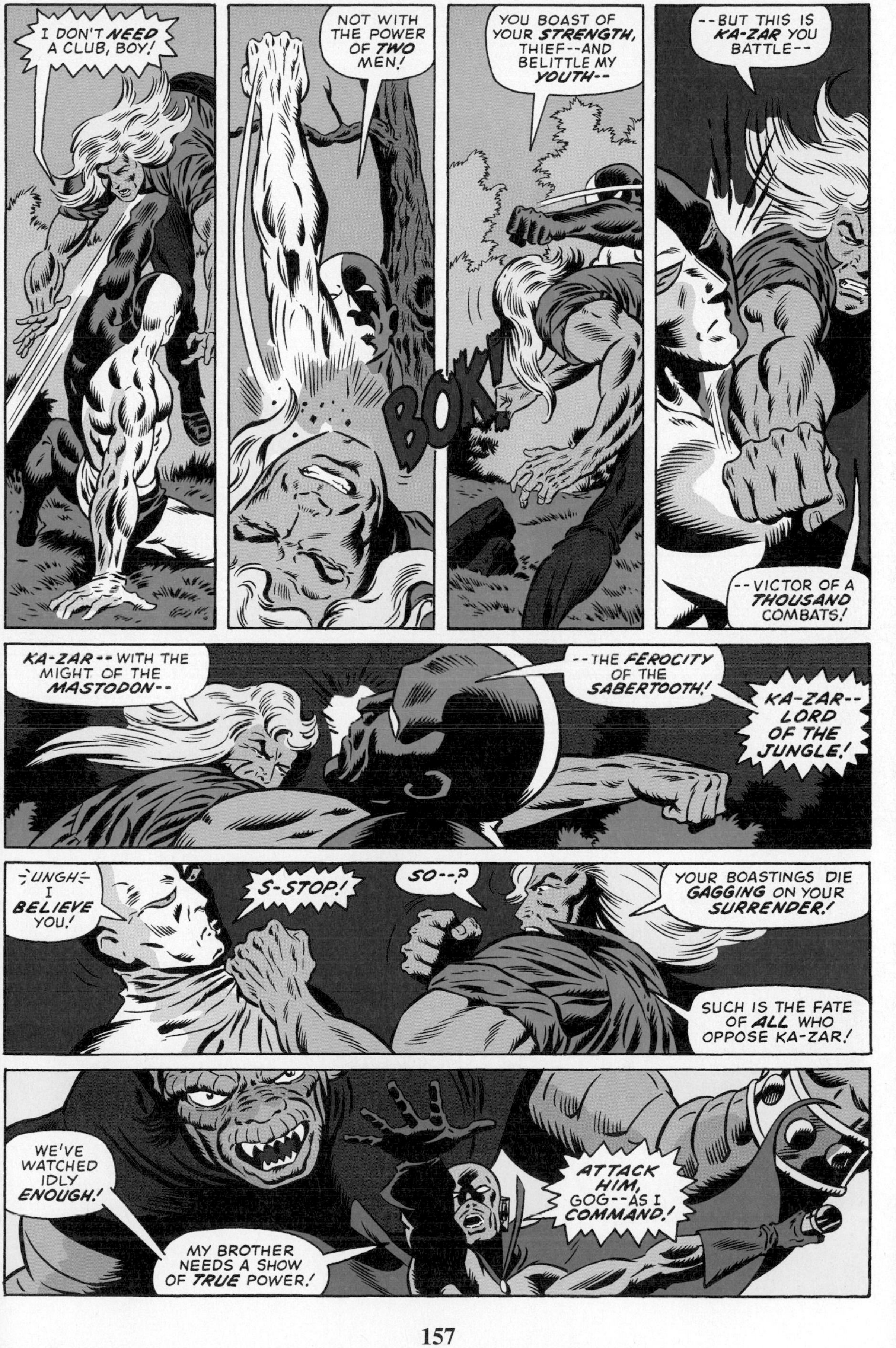

I DON'T NEED A CLUB, BOY!
NOT WITH THE POWER OF TWO MEN!
YOU BOAST OF YOUR STRENGTH, THIEF--AND BELITTLE MY YOUTH--
BOK!
--BUT THIS IS KA-ZAR YOU BATTLE--
--VICTOR OF A THOUSAND COMBATS!
KA-ZAR--WITH THE MIGHT OF THE MASTODON--
--THE FEROCITY OF THE SABERTOOTH!
KA-ZAR--LORD OF THE JUNGLE!
UNGH-- I BELIEVE YOU!
S-STOP!
SO--?
YOUR BOASTINGS DIE GAGGING ON YOUR SURRENDER!
SUCH IS THE FATE OF ALL WHO OPPOSE KA-ZAR!
WE'VE WATCHED IDLY ENOUGH!
MY BROTHER NEEDS A SHOW OF TRUE POWER!
ATTACK HIM, GOG--AS I COMMAND!

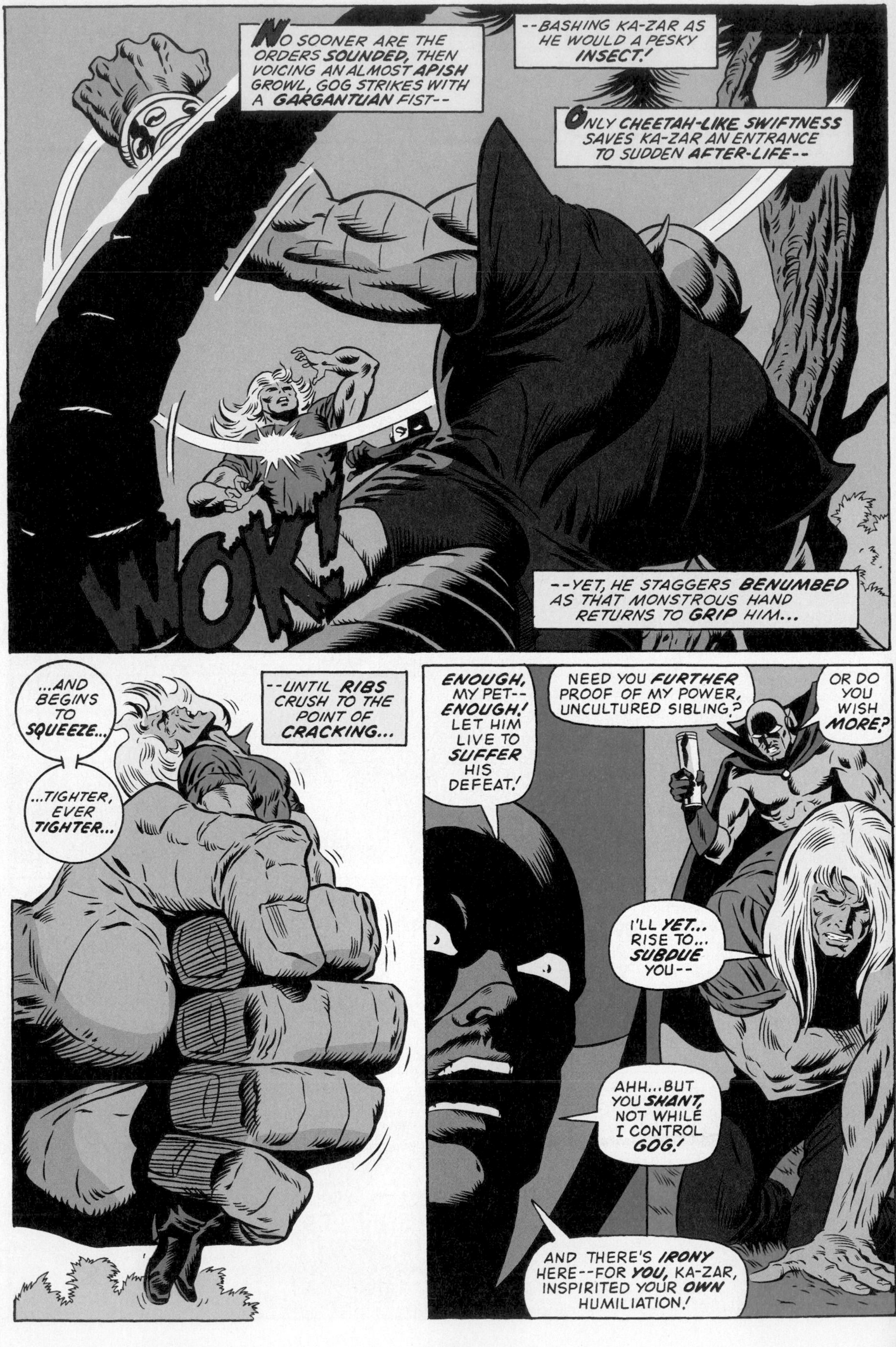

NO SOONER ARE THE ORDERS SOUNDED, THEN VOICING AN ALMOST APISH GROWL, GOG STRIKES WITH A GARGANTUAN FIST--
--BASHING KA-ZAR AS HE WOULD A PESKY INSECT!
ONLY CHEETAH-LIKE SWIFTNESS SAVES KA-ZAR AN ENTRANCE TO SUDDEN AFTER-LIFE--
WOK!
--YET, HE STAGGERS BENUMBED AS THAT MONSTROUS HAND RETURNS TO GRIP HIM...
...AND BEGINS TO SQUEEZE...
...TIGHTER, EVER TIGHTER...
--UNTIL RIBS CRUSH TO THE POINT OF CRACKING...
ENOUGH, MY PET-- ENOUGH! LET HIM LIVE TO SUFFER HIS DEFEAT!
NEED YOU FURTHER PROOF OF MY POWER, UNCULTURED SIBLING?
OR DO YOU WISH MORE?
I'LL YET... RISE TO... SUBDUE YOU--
AHH...BUT YOU SHANT, NOT WHILE I CONTROL GOG!
AND THERE'S IRONY HERE--FOR YOU, KA-ZAR, INSPIRITED YOUR OWN HUMILIATION!

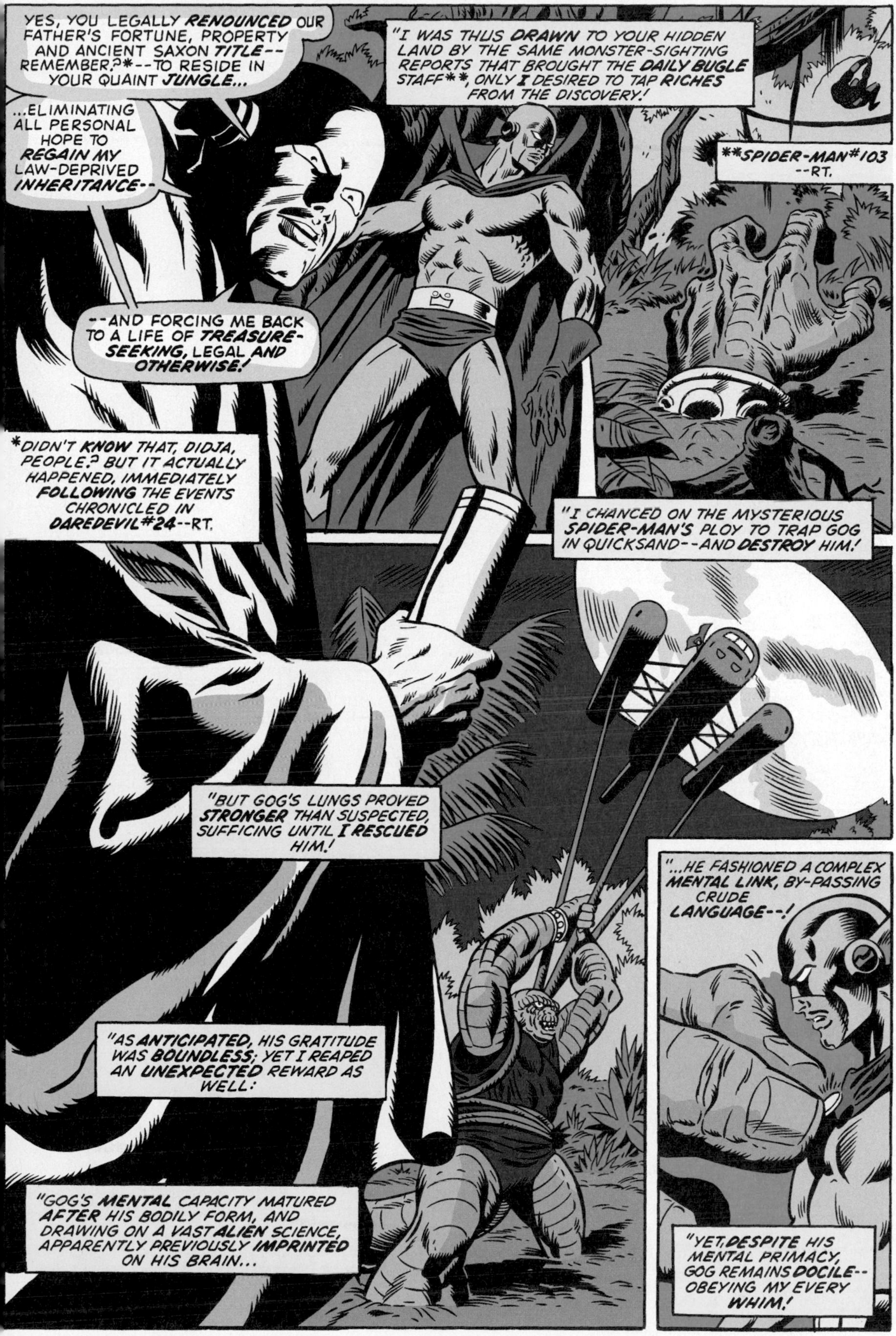
YES, YOU LEGALLY RENOUNCED OUR FATHER'S FORTUNE, PROPERTY AND ANCIENT SAXON TITLE-- REMEMBER?*--TO RESIDE IN YOUR QUAINT JUNGLE...
...ELIMINATING ALL PERSONAL HOPE TO REGAIN MY LAW-DEPRIVED INHERITANCE--
--AND FORCING ME BACK TO A LIFE OF TREASURE-SEEKING, LEGAL AND OTHERWISE!
*DIDN'T KNOW THAT, DIDJA, PEOPLE? BUT IT ACTUALLY HAPPENED, IMMEDIATELY FOLLOWING THE EVENTS CHRONICLED IN DAREDEVIL #24--RT.
"I WAS THUS DRAWN TO YOUR HIDDEN LAND BY THE SAME MONSTER-SIGHTING REPORTS THAT BROUGHT THE DAILY BUGLE STAFF**, ONLY I DESIRED TO TAP RICHES FROM THE DISCOVERY!
**SPIDER-MAN #103 --RT.
"I CHANCED ON THE MYSTERIOUS SPIDER-MAN'S PLOY TO TRAP GOG IN QUICKSAND--AND DESTROY HIM!
"BUT GOG'S LUNGS PROVED STRONGER THAN SUSPECTED, SUFFICING UNTIL I RESCUED HIM!
"AS ANTICIPATED, HIS GRATITUDE WAS BOUNDLESS; YET I REAPED AN UNEXPECTED REWARD AS WELL:
"GOG'S MENTAL CAPACITY MATURED AFTER HIS BODILY FORM, AND DRAWING ON A VAST ALIEN SCIENCE, APPARENTLY PREVIOUSLY IMPRINTED ON HIS BRAIN...
"...HE FASHIONED A COMPLEX MENTAL LINK, BY-PASSING CRUDE LANGUAGE--!
"YET, DESPITE HIS MENTAL PRIMACY, GOG REMAINS DOCILE-- OBEYING MY EVERY WHIM!

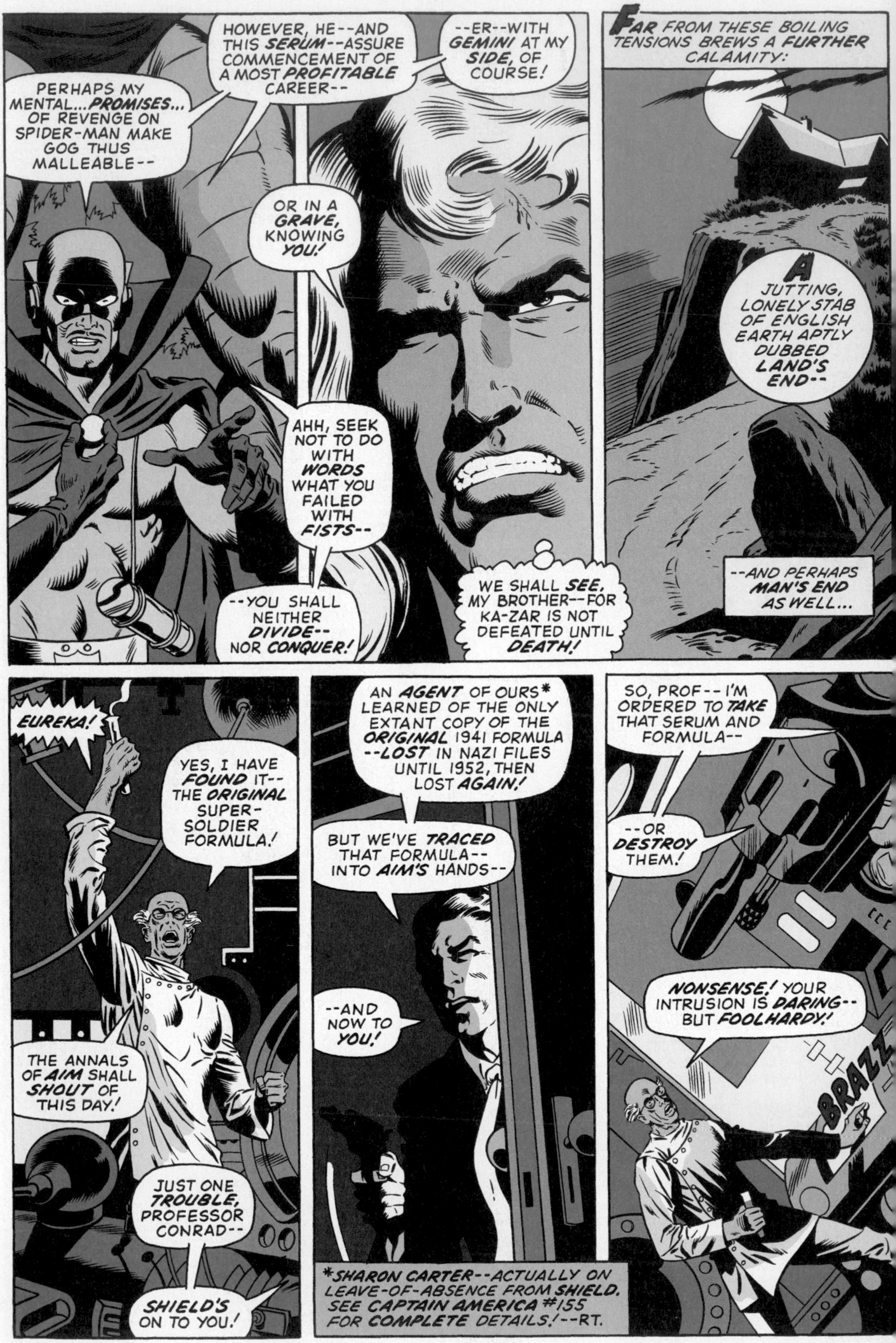
PERHAPS MY MENTAL... PROMISES... OF REVENGE ON SPIDER-MAN MAKE GOG THUS MALLEABLE--
HOWEVER, HE--AND THIS SERUM--ASSURE COMMENCEMENT OF A MOST PROFITABLE CAREER--
--ER--WITH GEMINI AT MY SIDE, OF COURSE!
OR IN A GRAVE, KNOWING YOU!
AHH, SEEK NOT TO DO WITH WORDS WHAT YOU FAILED WITH FISTS--
--YOU SHALL NEITHER DIVIDE--NOR CONQUER!
WE SHALL SEE, MY BROTHER--FOR KA-ZAR IS NOT DEFEATED UNTIL DEATH!
FAR FROM THESE BOILING TENSIONS BREWS A FURTHER CALAMITY:
A JUTTING, LONELY STAB OF ENGLISH EARTH APTLY DUBBED LAND'S END--
--AND PERHAPS MAN'S END AS WELL...
EUREKA!
YES, I HAVE FOUND IT--THE ORIGINAL SUPER-SOLDIER FORMULA!
THE ANNALS OF AIM SHALL SHOUT OF THIS DAY!
JUST ONE TROUBLE, PROFESSOR CONRAD--
SHIELD'S ON TO YOU!
AN AGENT OF OURS* LEARNED OF THE ONLY EXTANT COPY OF THE ORIGINAL 1941 FORMULA--LOST IN NAZI FILES UNTIL 1952, THEN LOST AGAIN!
BUT WE'VE TRACED THAT FORMULA--INTO AIM'S HANDS--
--AND NOW TO YOU!
*SHARON CARTER--ACTUALLY ON LEAVE-OF-ABSENCE FROM SHIELD. SEE CAPTAIN AMERICA #155 FOR COMPLETE DETAILS!--RT.
SO, PROF--I'M ORDERED TO TAKE THAT SERUM AND FORMULA--
--OR DESTROY THEM!
NONSENSE! YOUR INTRUSION IS DARING--BUT FOOLHARDY!
BRAZZ

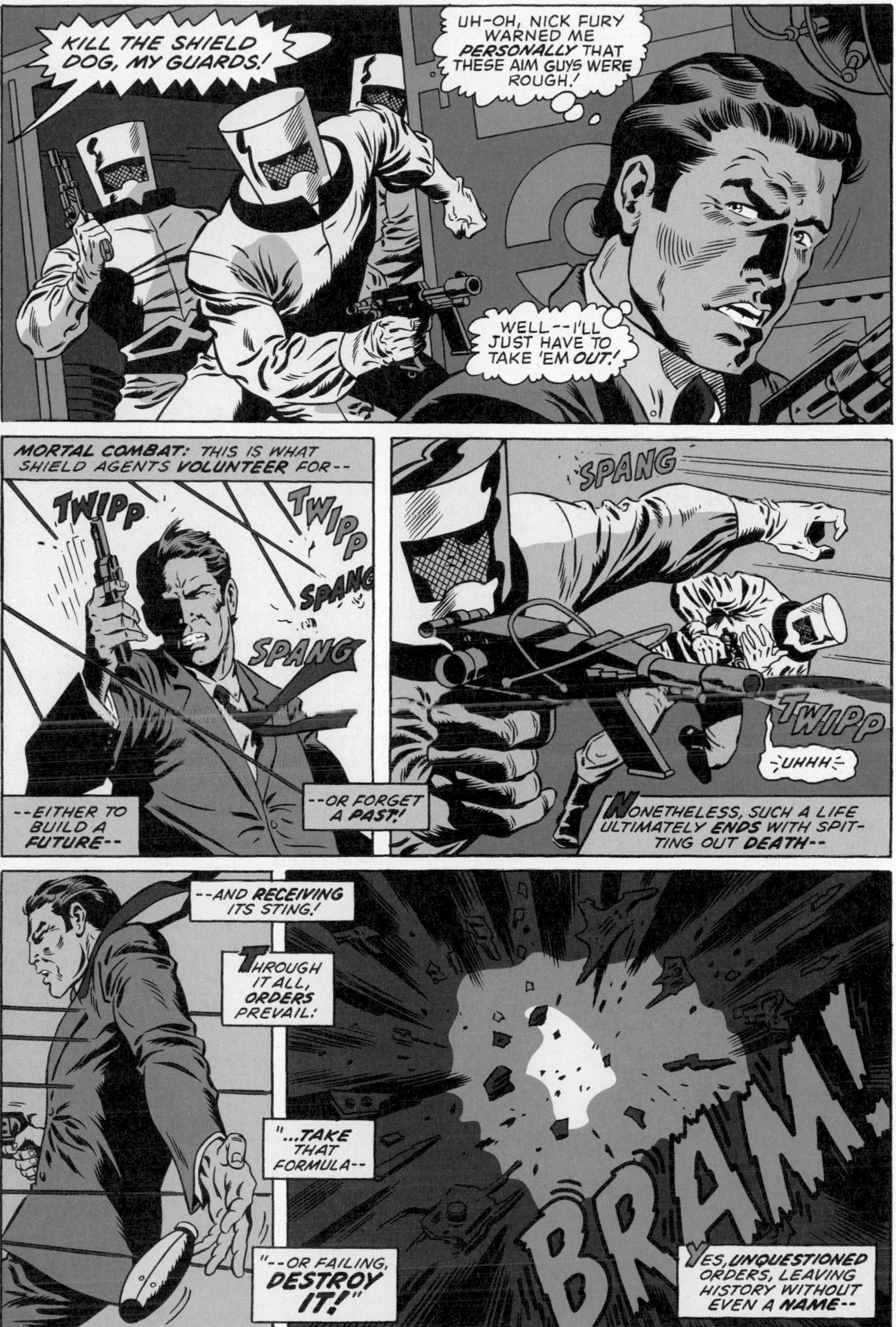
KILL THE SHIELD DOG, MY GUARDS!
UH-OH, NICK FURY WARNED ME PERSONALLY THAT THESE AIM GUYS WERE ROUGH!
WELL--I'LL JUST HAVE TO TAKE 'EM OUT!
MORTAL COMBAT: THIS IS WHAT SHIELD AGENTS VOLUNTEER FOR--
TWIPP
TWIPP
SPANG
SPANG
--EITHER TO BUILD A FUTURE--
--OR FORGET A PAST!
SPANG
TWIPP
UHHH
NONETHELESS, SUCH A LIFE ULTIMATELY ENDS WITH SPITTING OUT DEATH--
--AND RECEIVING ITS STING!
THROUGH IT ALL, ORDERS PREVAIL:
"...TAKE THAT FORMULA--
"--OR FAILING, DESTROY IT!"
BRAM!
YES, UNQUESTIONED ORDERS, LEAVING HISTORY WITHOUT EVEN A NAME--

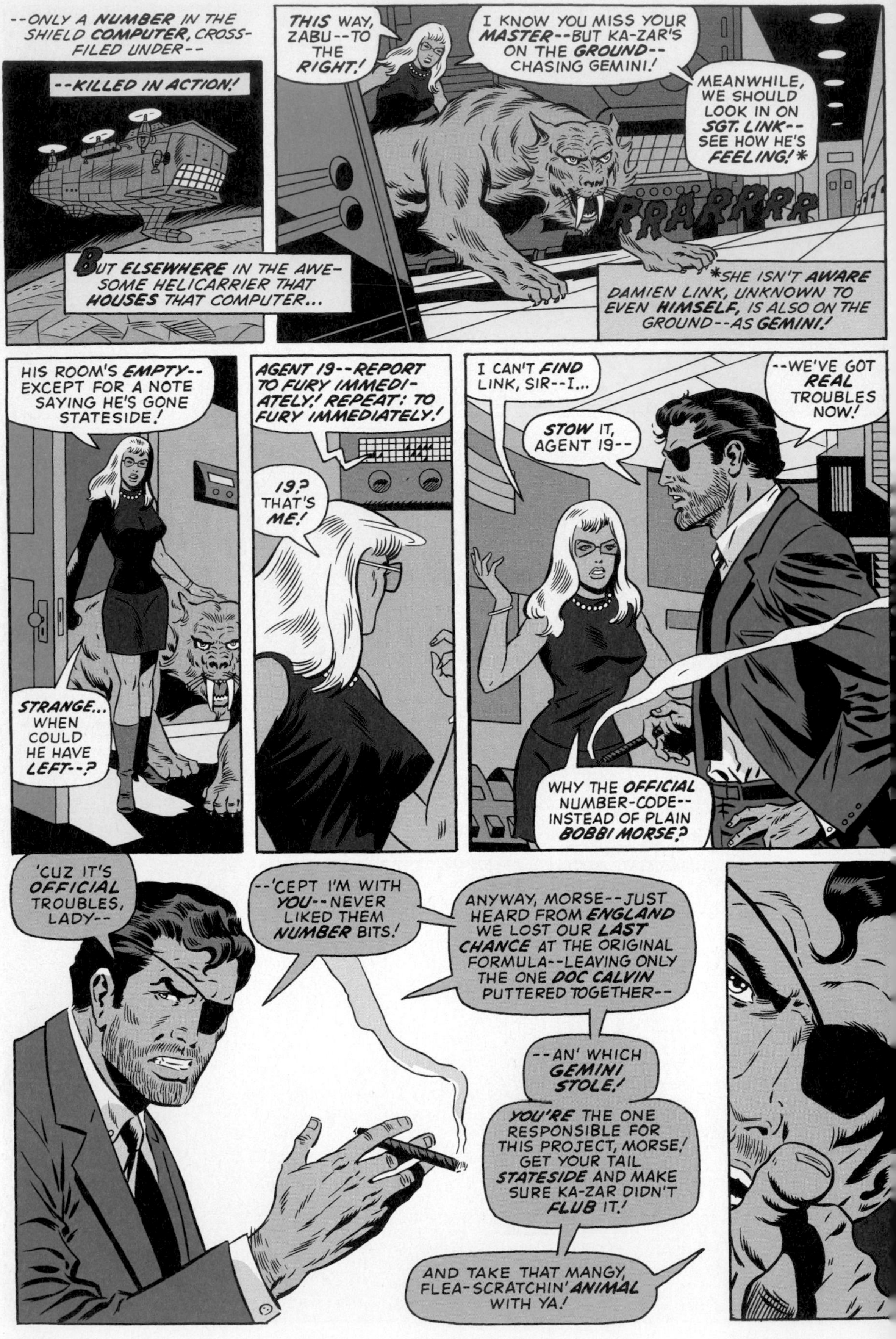
--ONLY A NUMBER IN THE SHIELD COMPUTER, CROSS-FILED UNDER--
--KILLED IN ACTION!
BUT ELSEWHERE IN THE AWESOME HELICARRIER THAT HOUSES THAT COMPUTER...
THIS WAY, ZABU--TO THE RIGHT!
I KNOW YOU MISS YOUR MASTER--BUT KA-ZAR'S ON THE GROUND--CHASING GEMINI!
MEANWHILE, WE SHOULD LOOK IN ON SGT. LINK--SEE HOW HE'S FEELING!*
RRARRRRR
*SHE ISN'T AWARE DAMIEN LINK, UNKNOWN TO EVEN HIMSELF, IS ALSO ON THE GROUND--AS GEMINI!
HIS ROOM'S EMPTY--EXCEPT FOR A NOTE SAYING HE'S GONE STATESIDE!
STRANGE... WHEN COULD HE HAVE LEFT--?
AGENT 19--REPORT TO FURY IMMEDIATELY! REPEAT: TO FURY IMMEDIATELY!
19? THAT'S ME!
I CAN'T FIND LINK, SIR--I...
STOW IT, AGENT 19--
--WE'VE GOT REAL TROUBLES NOW!
WHY THE OFFICIAL NUMBER-CODE--INSTEAD OF PLAIN BOBBI MORSE?
'CUZ IT'S OFFICIAL TROUBLES, LADY--
--'CEPT I'M WITH YOU--NEVER LIKED THEM NUMBER BITS!
ANYWAY, MORSE--JUST HEARD FROM ENGLAND WE LOST OUR LAST CHANCE AT THE ORIGINAL FORMULA--LEAVING ONLY THE ONE DOC CALVIN PUTTERED TOGETHER--
--AN' WHICH GEMINI STOLE!
YOU'RE THE ONE RESPONSIBLE FOR THIS PROJECT, MORSE! GET YOUR TAIL STATESIDE AND MAKE SURE KA-ZAR DIDN'T FLUB IT!
AND TAKE THAT MANGY, FLEA-SCRATCHIN' ANIMAL WITH YA!

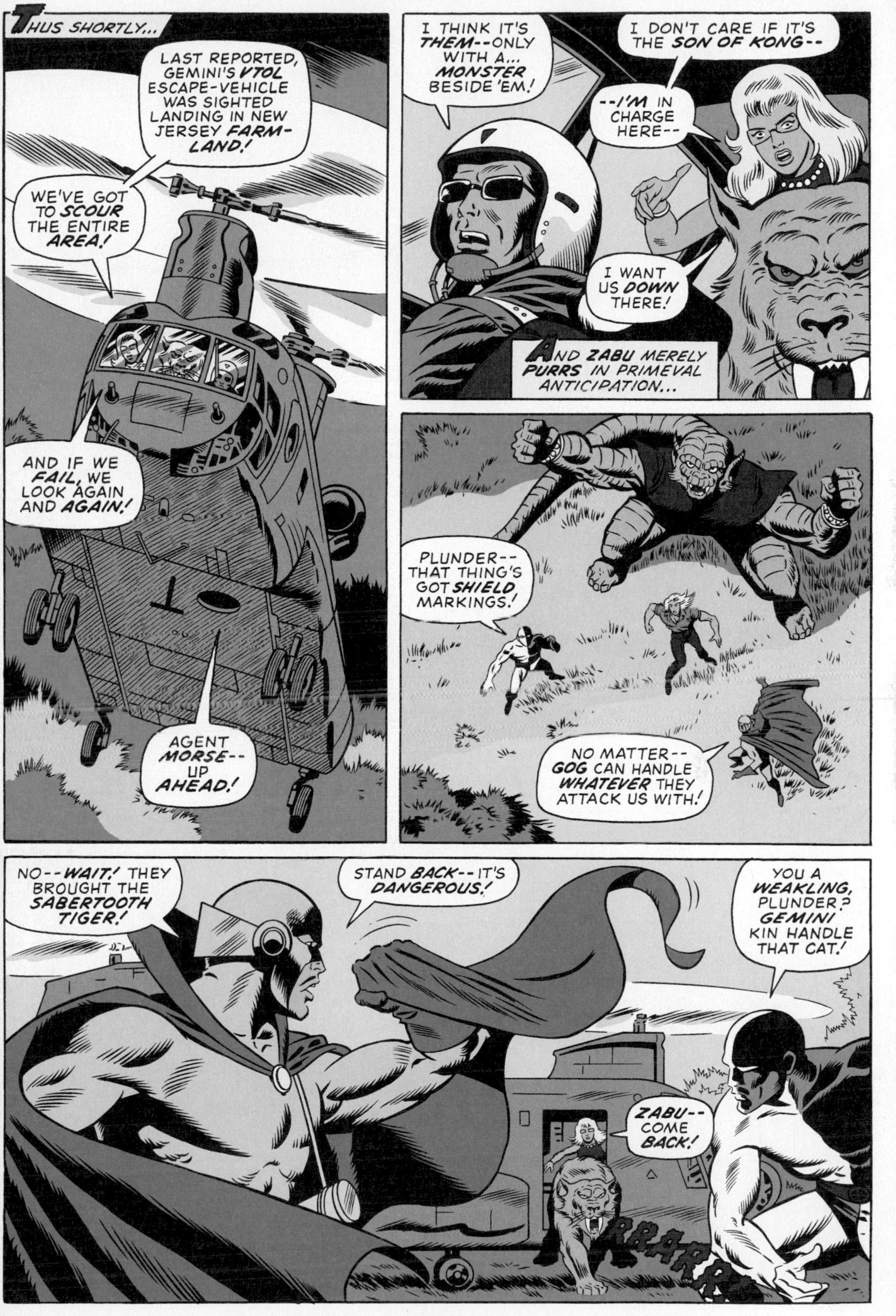
THUS SHORTLY...
LAST REPORTED, GEMINI'S VTOL ESCAPE-VEHICLE WAS SIGHTED LANDING IN NEW JERSEY FARM-LAND!
WE'VE GOT TO SCOUR THE ENTIRE AREA!
AND IF WE FAIL, WE LOOK AGAIN AND AGAIN!
AGENT MORSE-- UP AHEAD!
I THINK IT'S THEM--ONLY WITH A... MONSTER BESIDE 'EM!
I DON'T CARE IF IT'S THE SON OF KONG--
--I'M IN CHARGE HERE--
I WANT US DOWN THERE!
AND ZABU MERELY PURRS IN PRIMEVAL ANTICIPATION...
PLUNDER-- THAT THING'S GOT SHIELD MARKINGS!
NO MATTER-- GOG CAN HANDLE WHATEVER THEY ATTACK US WITH!
NO--WAIT! THEY BROUGHT THE SABERTOOTH TIGER!
STAND BACK--IT'S DANGEROUS!
YOU A WEAKLING, PLUNDER? GEMINI KIN HANDLE THAT CAT!
ZABU-- COME BACK!
RRAARRR

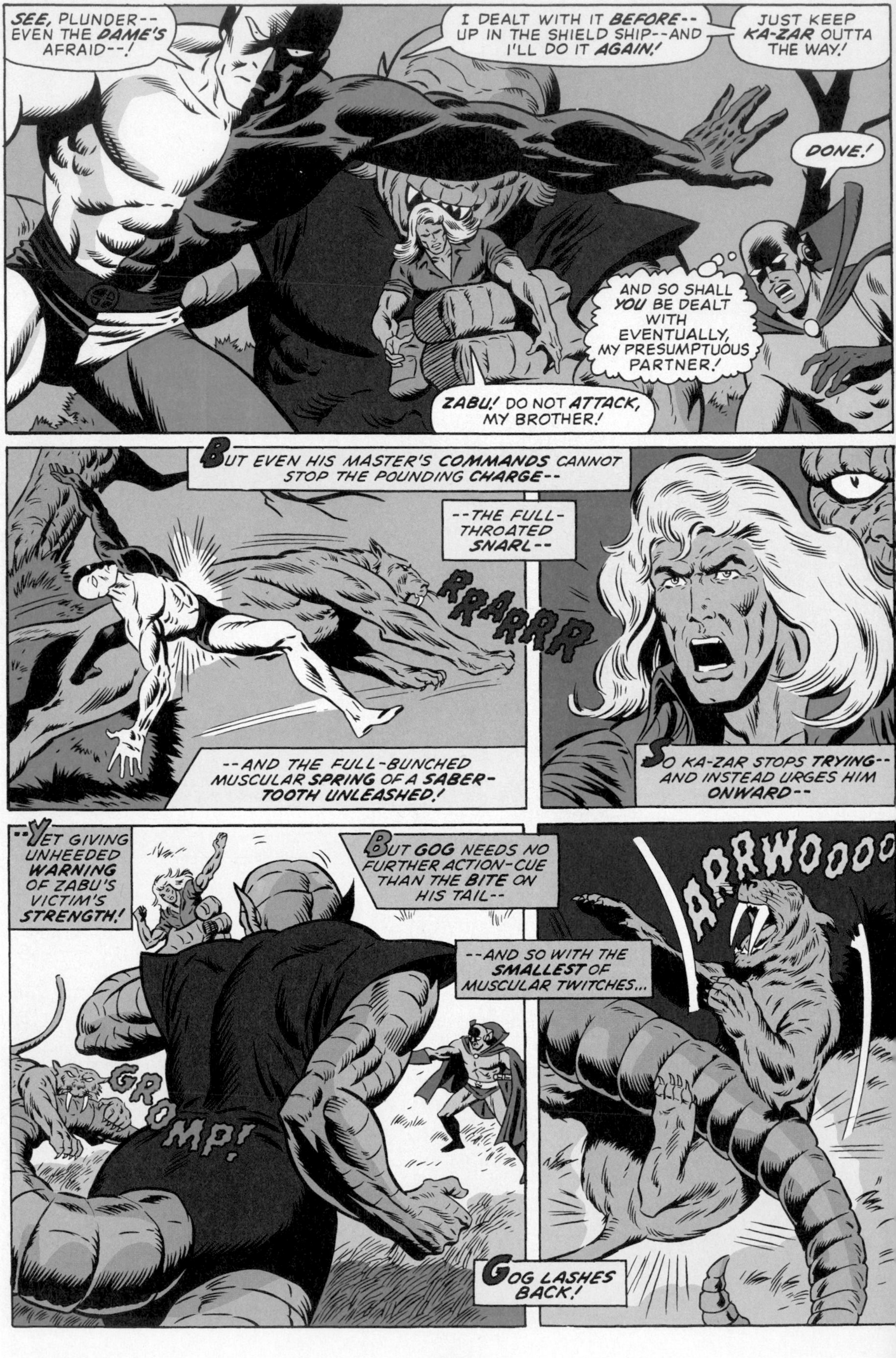
SEE, PLUNDER-- EVEN THE DAME'S AFRAID--!
I DEALT WITH IT BEFORE-- UP IN THE SHIELD SHIP--AND I'LL DO IT AGAIN!
JUST KEEP KA-ZAR OUTTA THE WAY!
DONE!
AND SO SHALL YOU BE DEALT WITH EVENTUALLY, MY PRESUMPTUOUS PARTNER!
ZABU! DO NOT ATTACK, MY BROTHER!
BUT EVEN HIS MASTER'S COMMANDS CANNOT STOP THE POUNDING CHARGE--
--THE FULL-THROATED SNARL--
RRARRRR
--AND THE FULL-BUNCHED MUSCULAR SPRING OF A SABER-TOOTH UNLEASHED!
SO KA-ZAR STOPS TRYING-- AND INSTEAD URGES HIM ONWARD--
--YET GIVING UNHEEDED WARNING OF ZABU'S VICTIM'S STRENGTH!
BUT GOG NEEDS NO FURTHER ACTION-CUE THAN THE BITE ON HIS TAIL--
GROMP!
APRWOOOO
--AND SO WITH THE SMALLEST OF MUSCULAR TWITCHES...
GOG LASHES BACK!

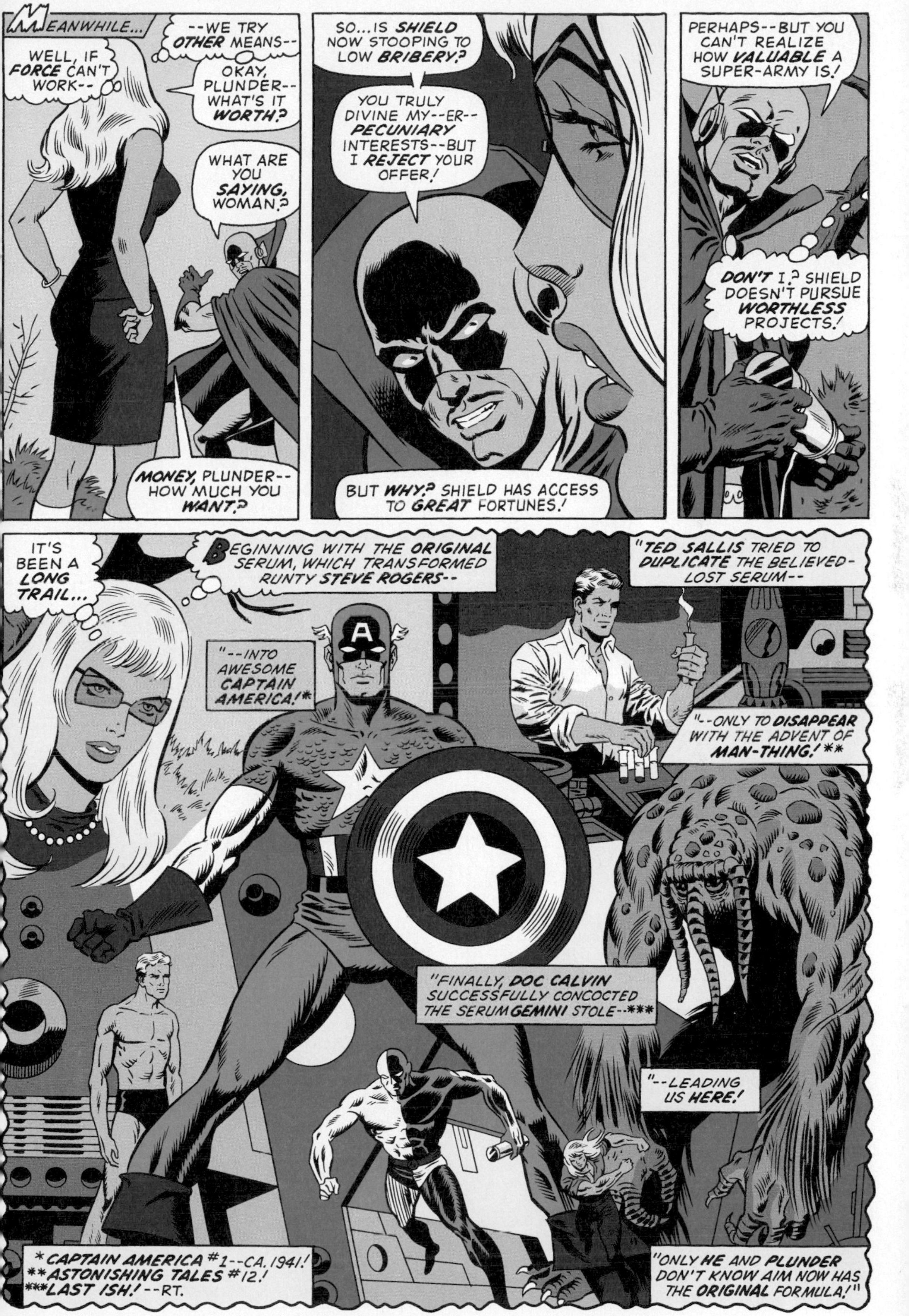
MEANWHILE...
WELL, IF FORCE CAN'T WORK--
--WE TRY OTHER MEANS--
OKAY, PLUNDER--WHAT'S IT WORTH?
WHAT ARE YOU SAYING, WOMAN?
MONEY, PLUNDER--HOW MUCH YOU WANT?
SO...IS SHIELD NOW STOOPING TO LOW BRIBERY?
YOU TRULY DIVINE MY--ER--PECUNIARY INTERESTS--BUT I REJECT YOUR OFFER!
BUT WHY? SHIELD HAS ACCESS TO GREAT FORTUNES!
PERHAPS--BUT YOU CAN'T REALIZE HOW VALUABLE A SUPER-ARMY IS!
DON'T I? SHIELD DOESN'T PURSUE WORTHLESS PROJECTS!
IT'S BEEN A LONG TRAIL...
BEGINNING WITH THE ORIGINAL SERUM, WHICH TRANSFORMED RUNTY STEVE ROGERS--
"--INTO AWESOME CAPTAIN AMERICA!*
"TED SALLIS TRIED TO DUPLICATE THE BELIEVED-LOST SERUM--
"--ONLY TO DISAPPEAR WITH THE ADVENT OF MAN-THING!**
"FINALLY, DOC CALVIN SUCCESSFULLY CONCOCTED THE SERUM GEMINI STOLE--***
"--LEADING US HERE!
*CAPTAIN AMERICA #1--CA. 1941!
**ASTONISHING TALES #12!
***LAST ISH! --RT.
"ONLY HE AND PLUNDER DON'T KNOW AIM NOW HAS THE ORIGINAL FORMULA!"

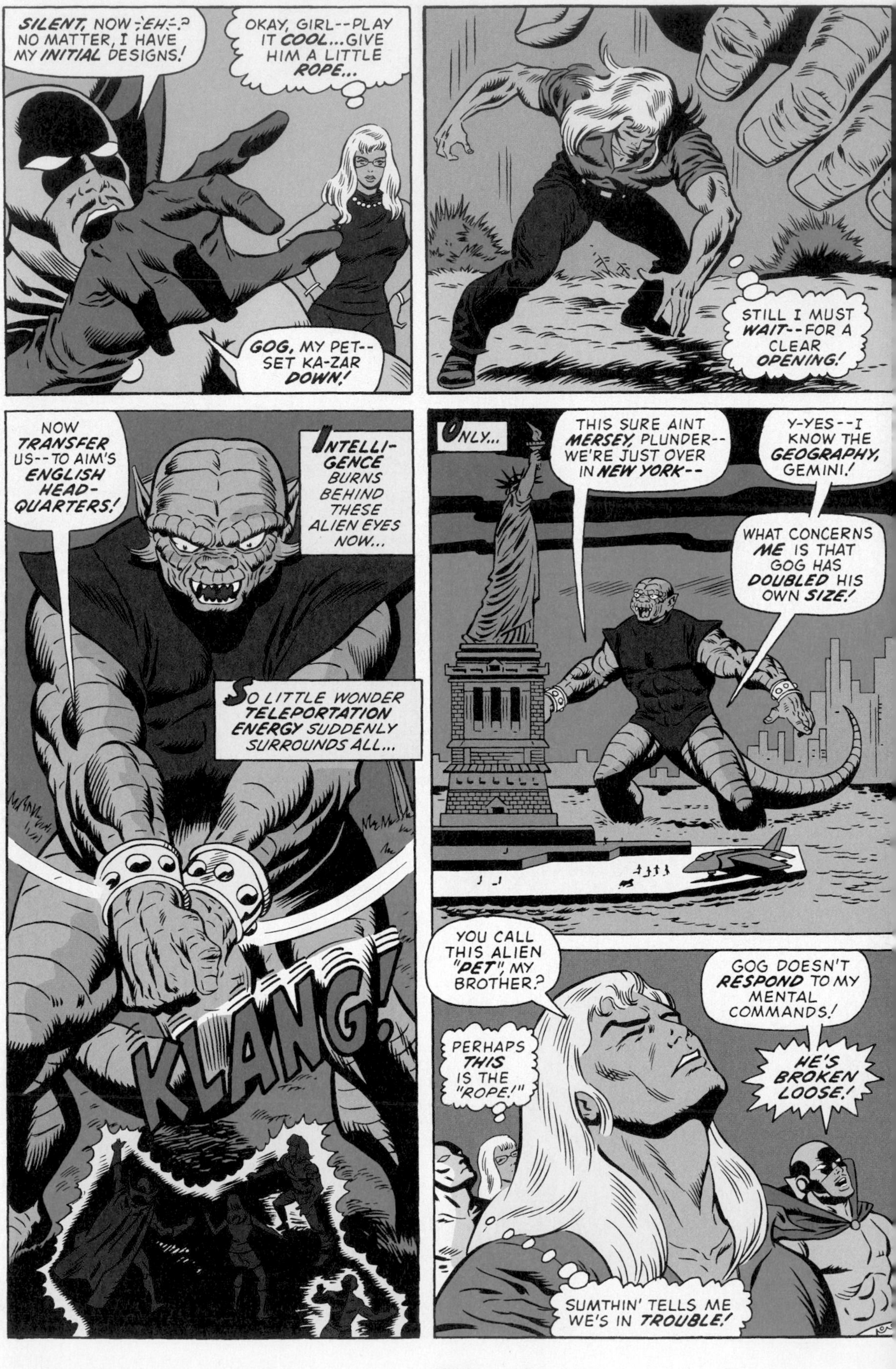
SILENT, NOW -EH-? NO MATTER, I HAVE MY INITIAL DESIGNS!
OKAY, GIRL--PLAY IT COOL...GIVE HIM A LITTLE ROPE...
GOG, MY PET--SET KA-ZAR DOWN!
STILL I MUST WAIT--FOR A CLEAR OPENING!
NOW TRANSFER US--TO AIM'S ENGLISH HEAD-QUARTERS!
INTELLI-GENCE BURNS BEHIND THESE ALIEN EYES NOW...
SO LITTLE WONDER TELEPORTATION ENERGY SUDDENLY SURROUNDS ALL...
KLANG!
ONLY...
THIS SURE AINT MERSEY, PLUNDER--WE'RE JUST OVER IN NEW YORK--
Y-YES--I KNOW THE GEOGRAPHY, GEMINI!
WHAT CONCERNS ME IS THAT GOG HAS DOUBLED HIS OWN SIZE!
YOU CALL THIS ALIEN "PET", MY BROTHER?
GOG DOESN'T RESPOND TO MY MENTAL COMMANDS!
PERHAPS THIS IS THE "ROPE!"
HE'S BROKEN LOOSE!
SUMTHIN' TELLS ME WE'S IN TROUBLE!

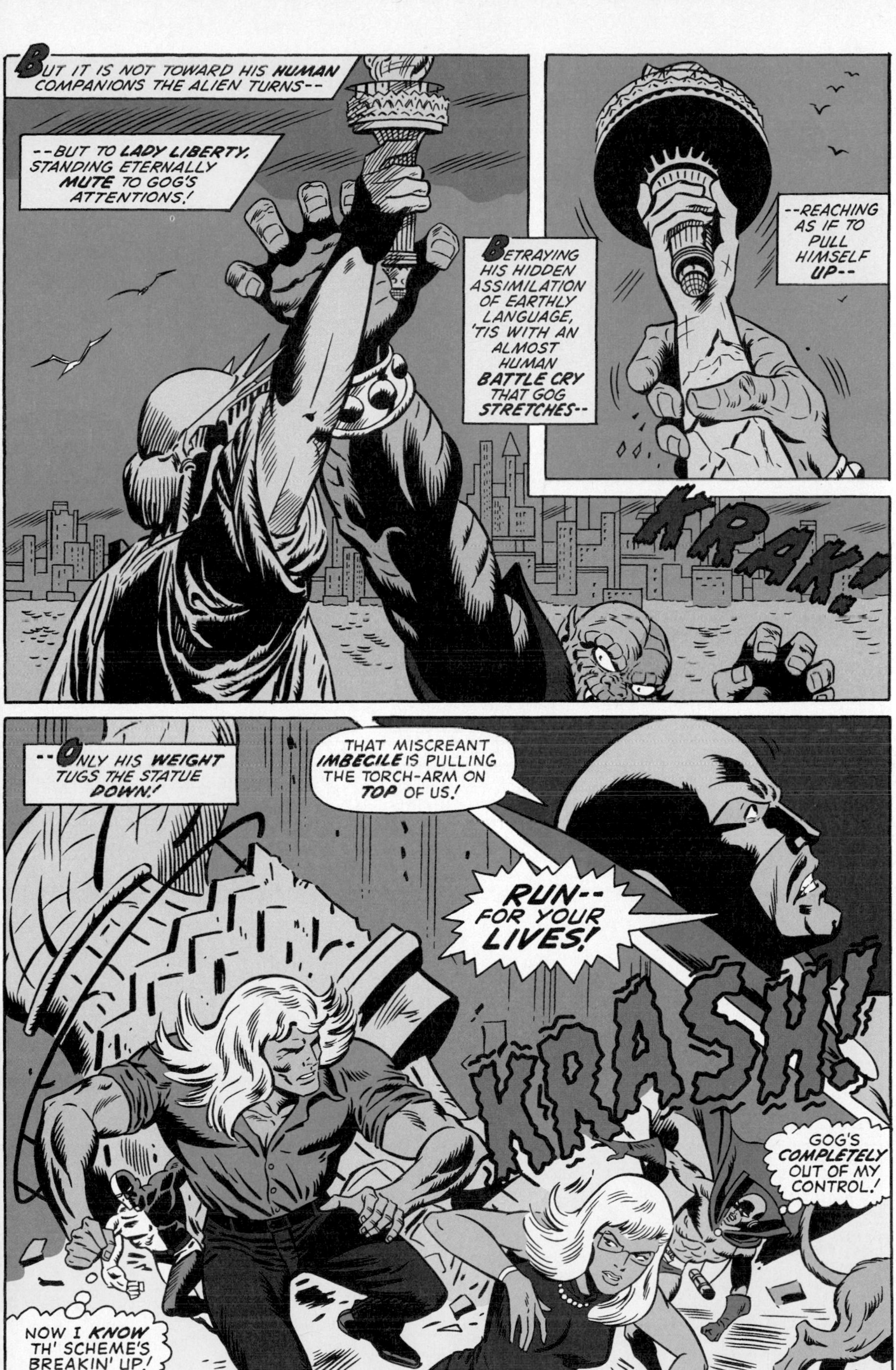
BUT IT IS NOT TOWARD HIS HUMAN COMPANIONS THE ALIEN TURNS--
--BUT TO LADY LIBERTY, STANDING ETERNALLY MUTE TO GOG'S ATTENTIONS!
BETRAYING HIS HIDDEN ASSIMILATION OF EARTHLY LANGUAGE, 'TIS WITH AN ALMOST HUMAN BATTLE CRY THAT GOG STRETCHES--
--REACHING AS IF TO PULL HIMSELF UP--
KRAK!
--ONLY HIS WEIGHT TUGS THE STATUE DOWN!
THAT MISCREANT IMBECILE IS PULLING THE TORCH-ARM ON TOP OF US!
RUN-- FOR YOUR LIVES!
KRASH!
GOG'S COMPLETELY OUT OF MY CONTROL!
NOW I KNOW TH' SCHEME'S BREAKIN' UP!

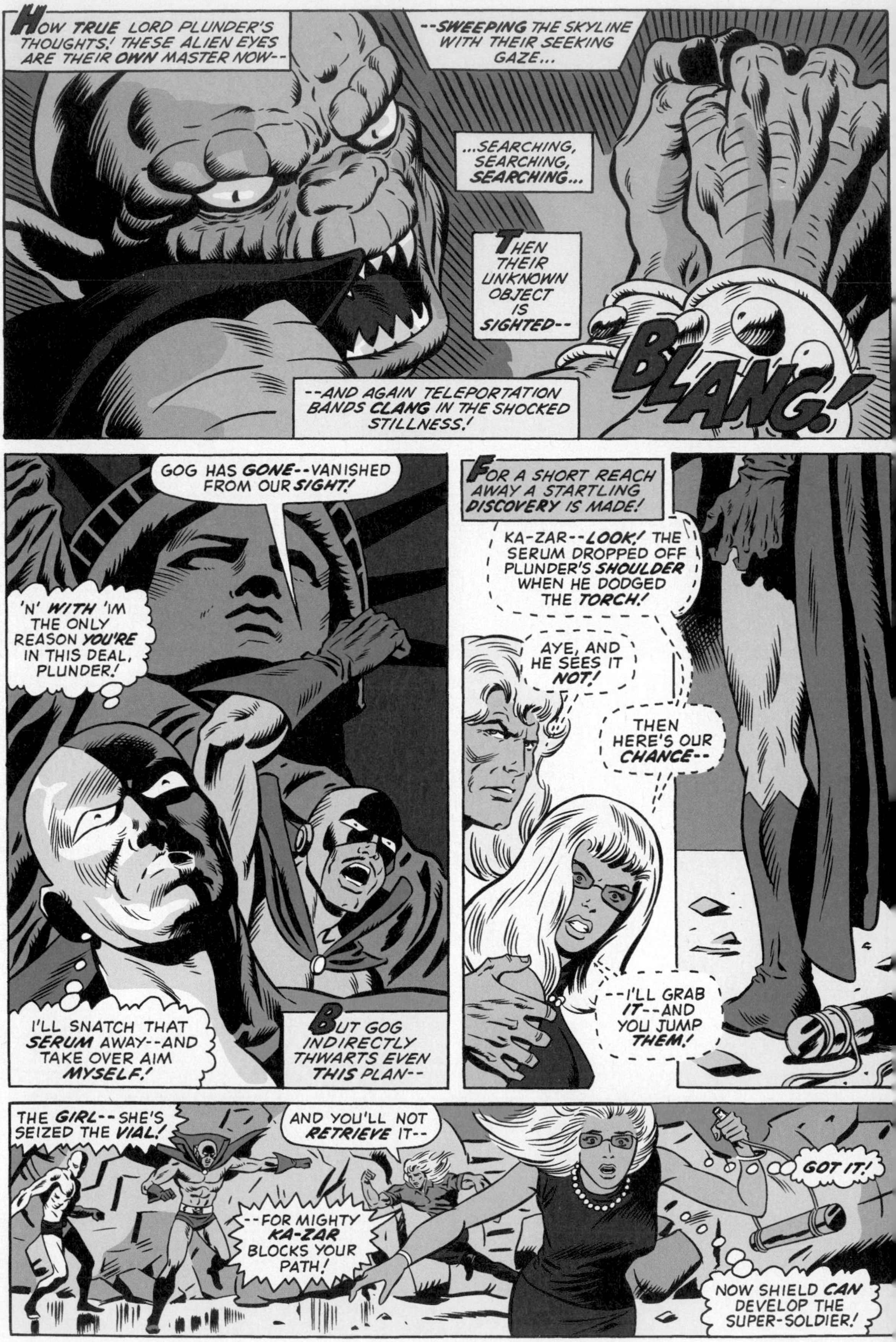
HOW TRUE LORD PLUNDER'S THOUGHTS! THESE ALIEN EYES ARE THEIR OWN MASTER NOW--
--SWEEPING THE SKYLINE WITH THEIR SEEKING GAZE...
...SEARCHING, SEARCHING, SEARCHING...
THEN THEIR UNKNOWN OBJECT IS SIGHTED--
--AND AGAIN TELEPORTATION BANDS CLANG IN THE SHOCKED STILLNESS!
BLANG!
GOG HAS GONE--VANISHED FROM OUR SIGHT!
'N' WITH 'IM THE ONLY REASON YOU'RE IN THIS DEAL, PLUNDER!
I'LL SNATCH THAT SERUM AWAY--AND TAKE OVER AIM MYSELF!
BUT GOG INDIRECTLY THWARTS EVEN THIS PLAN--
FOR A SHORT REACH AWAY A STARTLING DISCOVERY IS MADE!
KA-ZAR--LOOK! THE SERUM DROPPED OFF PLUNDER'S SHOULDER WHEN HE DODGED THE TORCH!
AYE, AND HE SEES IT NOT!
THEN HERE'S OUR CHANCE--
--I'LL GRAB IT--AND YOU JUMP THEM!
THE GIRL--SHE'S SEIZED THE VIAL!
AND YOU'LL NOT RETRIEVE IT--
--FOR MIGHTY KA-ZAR BLOCKS YOUR PATH!
GOT IT!
NOW SHIELD CAN DEVELOP THE SUPER-SOLDIER!

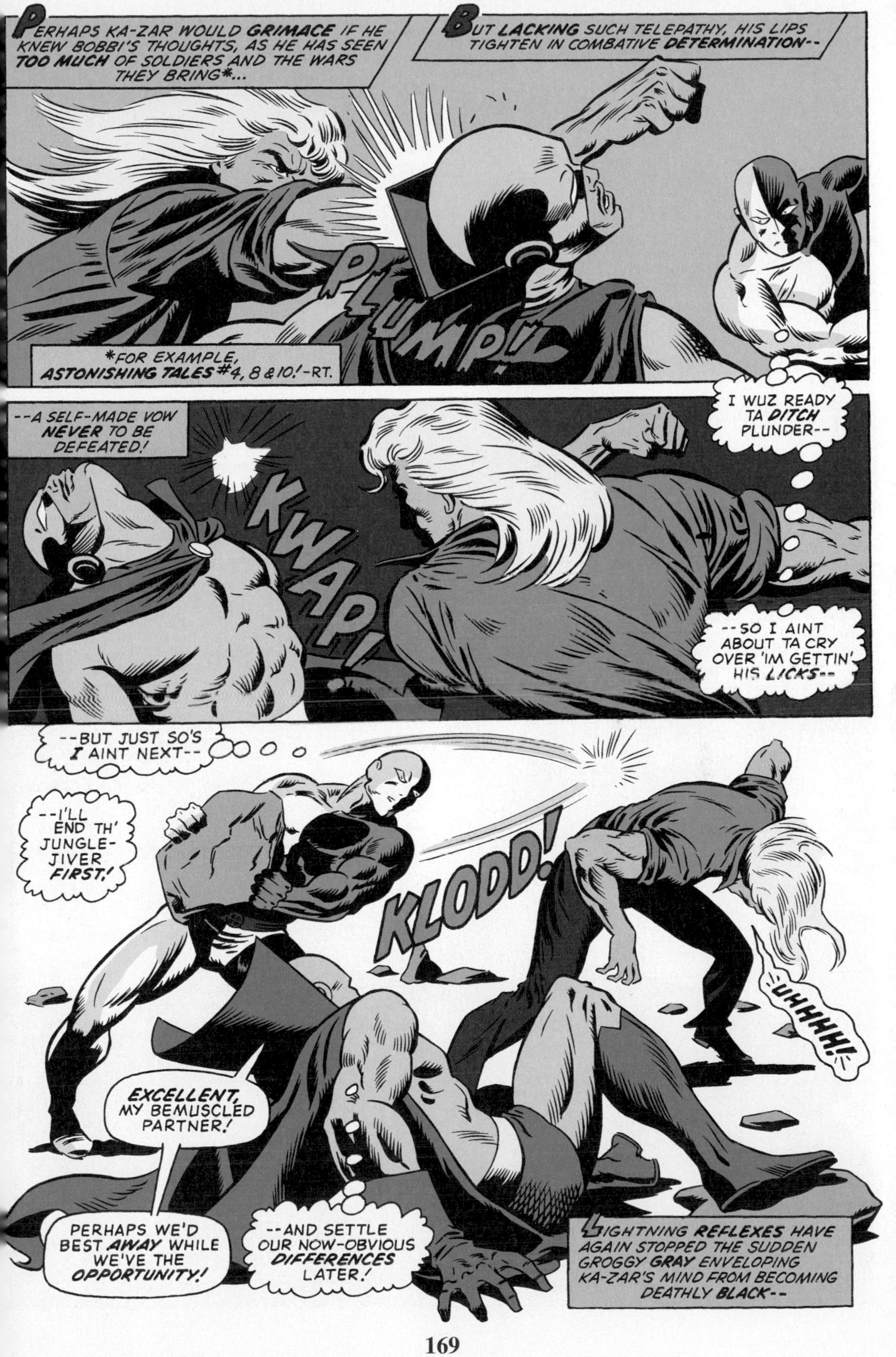

PERHAPS KA-ZAR WOULD GRIMACE IF HE KNEW BOBBI'S THOUGHTS, AS HE HAS SEEN TOO MUCH OF SOLDIERS AND THE WARS THEY BRING*...
BUT LACKING SUCH TELEPATHY, HIS LIPS TIGHTEN IN COMBATIVE DETERMINATION--
PLUMP!!
*FOR EXAMPLE, ASTONISHING TALES #4, 8 & 10! -RT.
--A SELF-MADE VOW NEVER TO BE DEFEATED!
I WUZ READY TA DITCH PLUNDER--
KWAP!
--SO I AINT ABOUT TA CRY OVER 'IM GETTIN' HIS LICKS--
--BUT JUST SO'S I AINT NEXT--
--I'LL END TH' JUNGLE-JIVER FIRST!
KLODD!
UHHHHH!
EXCELLENT, MY BEMUSCLED PARTNER!
PERHAPS WE'D BEST AWAY WHILE WE'VE THE OPPORTUNITY!
--AND SETTLE OUR NOW-OBVIOUS DIFFERENCES LATER!
LIGHTNING REFLEXES HAVE AGAIN STOPPED THE SUDDEN GROGGY GRAY ENVELOPING KA-ZAR'S MIND FROM BECOMING DEATHLY BLACK--

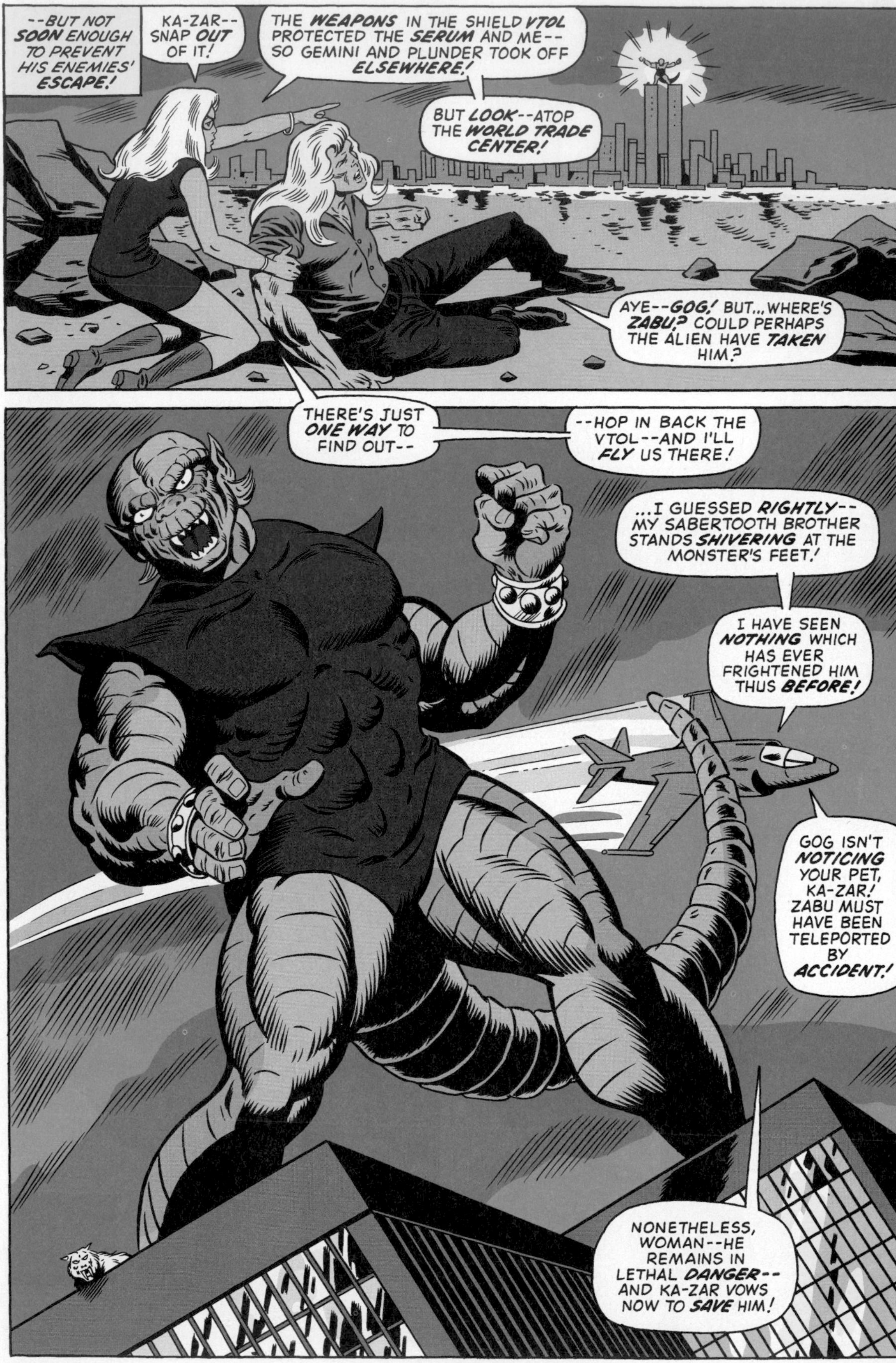
--BUT NOT SOON ENOUGH TO PREVENT HIS ENEMIES' ESCAPE!
KA-ZAR--SNAP OUT OF IT!
THE WEAPONS IN THE SHIELD VTOL PROTECTED THE SERUM AND ME--SO GEMINI AND PLUNDER TOOK OFF ELSEWHERE!
BUT LOOK--ATOP THE WORLD TRADE CENTER!
AYE--GOG! BUT...WHERE'S ZABU? COULD PERHAPS THE ALIEN HAVE TAKEN HIM?
THERE'S JUST ONE WAY TO FIND OUT--
--HOP IN BACK THE VTOL--AND I'LL FLY US THERE!
...I GUESSED RIGHTLY--MY SABERTOOTH BROTHER STANDS SHIVERING AT THE MONSTER'S FEET!
I HAVE SEEN NOTHING WHICH HAS EVER FRIGHTENED HIM THUS BEFORE!
GOG ISN'T NOTICING YOUR PET, KA-ZAR! ZABU MUST HAVE BEEN TELEPORTED BY ACCIDENT!
NONETHELESS, WOMAN--HE REMAINS IN LETHAL DANGER--AND KA-ZAR VOWS NOW TO SAVE HIM!

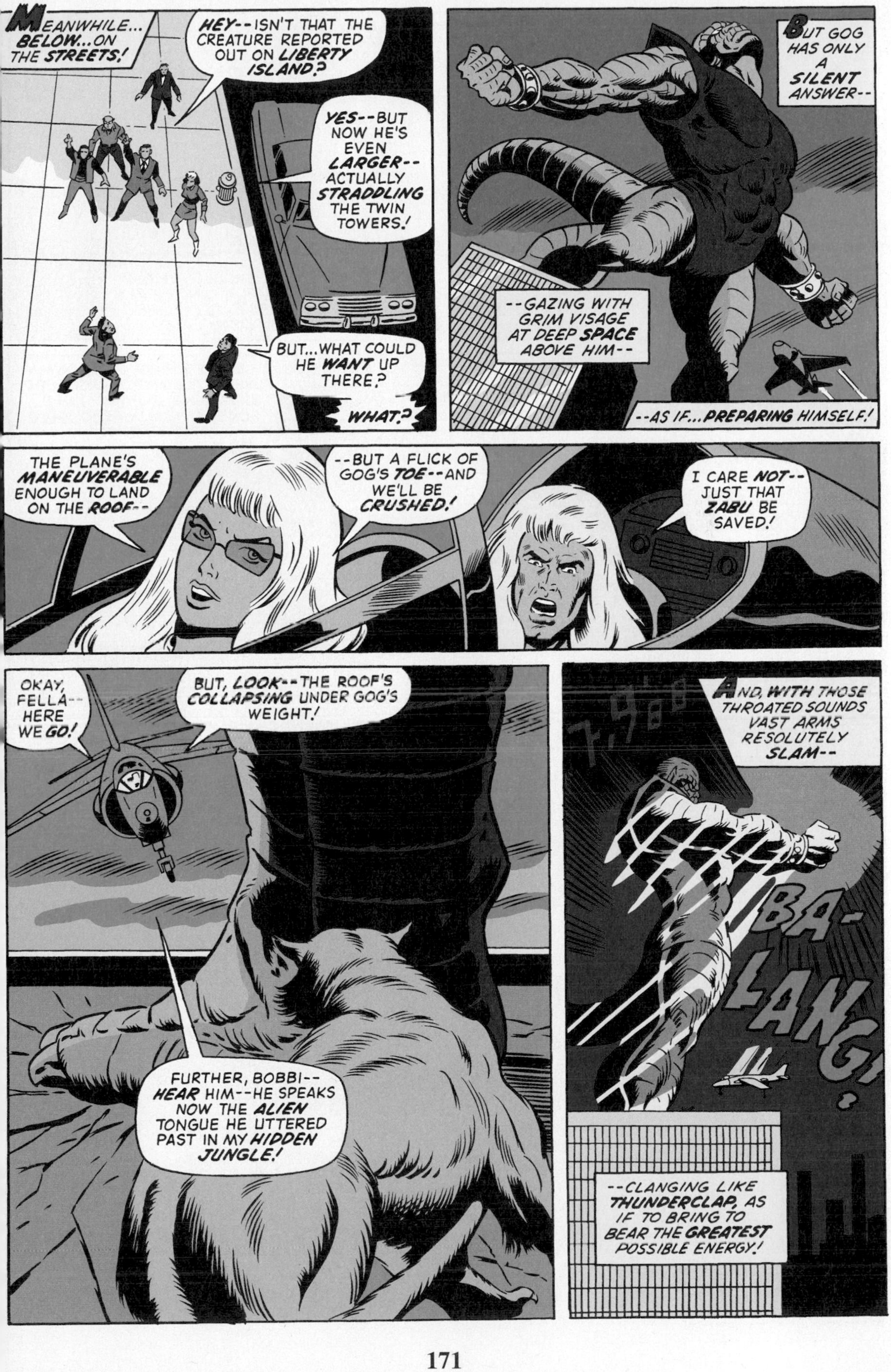
MEANWHILE... BELOW...ON THE STREETS!
HEY--ISN'T THAT THE CREATURE REPORTED OUT ON LIBERTY ISLAND?
YES--BUT NOW HE'S EVEN LARGER--ACTUALLY STRADDLING THE TWIN TOWERS!
BUT...WHAT COULD HE WANT UP THERE?
WHAT?
BUT GOG HAS ONLY A SILENT ANSWER--
--GAZING WITH GRIM VISAGE AT DEEP SPACE ABOVE HIM--
--AS IF...PREPARING HIMSELF!
THE PLANE'S MANEUVERABLE ENOUGH TO LAND ON THE ROOF--
--BUT A FLICK OF GOG'S TOE--AND WE'LL BE CRUSHED!
I CARE NOT--JUST THAT ZABU BE SAVED!
OKAY, FELLA--HERE WE GO!
BUT, LOOK--THE ROOF'S COLLAPSING UNDER GOG'S WEIGHT!
FURTHER, BOBBI--HEAR HIM--HE SPEAKS NOW THE ALIEN TONGUE HE UTTERED PAST IN MY HIDDEN JUNGLE!
AND, WITH THOSE THROATED SOUNDS VAST ARMS RESOLUTELY SLAM--
BA-LANG!
--CLANGING LIKE THUNDERCLAP, AS IF TO BRING TO BEAR THE GREATEST POSSIBLE ENERGY!

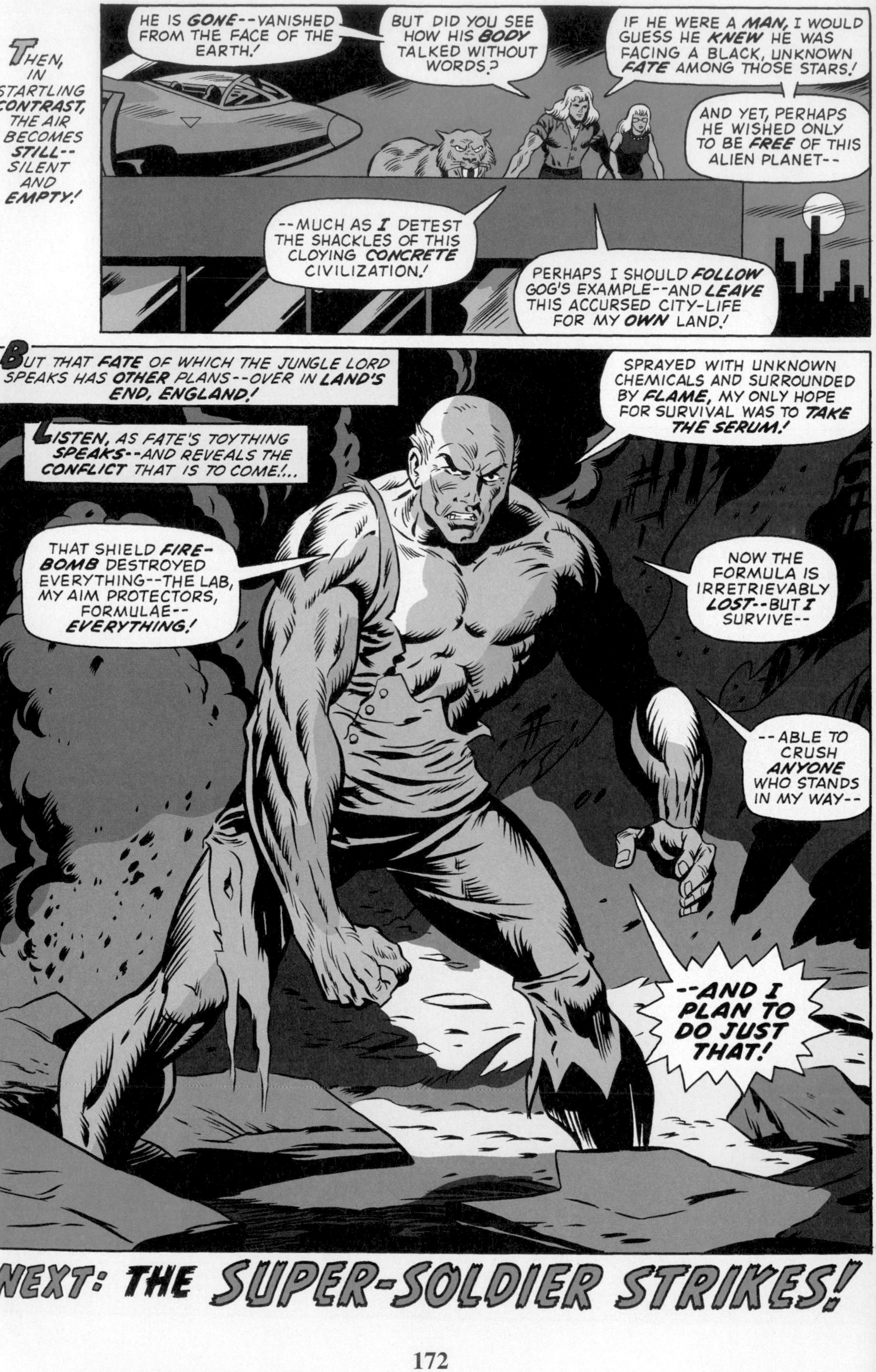
THEN, IN STARTLING CONTRAST, THE AIR BECOMES STILL--SILENT AND EMPTY!
HE IS GONE--VANISHED FROM THE FACE OF THE EARTH!
BUT DID YOU SEE HOW HIS BODY TALKED WITHOUT WORDS?
IF HE WERE A MAN, I WOULD GUESS HE KNEW HE WAS FACING A BLACK, UNKNOWN FATE AMONG THOSE STARS!
AND YET, PERHAPS HE WISHED ONLY TO BE FREE OF THIS ALIEN PLANET--
--MUCH AS I DETEST THE SHACKLES OF THIS CLOYING CONCRETE CIVILIZATION!
PERHAPS I SHOULD FOLLOW GOG'S EXAMPLE--AND LEAVE THIS ACCURSED CITY-LIFE FOR MY OWN LAND!
BUT THAT FATE OF WHICH THE JUNGLE LORD SPEAKS HAS OTHER PLANS--OVER IN LAND'S END, ENGLAND!
LISTEN, AS FATE'S TOYTHING SPEAKS--AND REVEALS THE CONFLICT THAT IS TO COME!...
SPRAYED WITH UNKNOWN CHEMICALS AND SURROUNDED BY FLAME, MY ONLY HOPE FOR SURVIVAL WAS TO TAKE THE SERUM!
THAT SHIELD FIRE-BOMB DESTROYED EVERYTHING--THE LAB, MY AIM PROTECTORS, FORMULAE--EVERYTHING!
NOW THE FORMULA IS IRRETRIEVABLY LOST--BUT I SURVIVE--
--ABLE TO CRUSH ANYONE WHO STANDS IN MY WAY--
--AND I PLAN TO DO JUST THAT!
NEXT: THE SUPER-SOLDIER STRIKES!

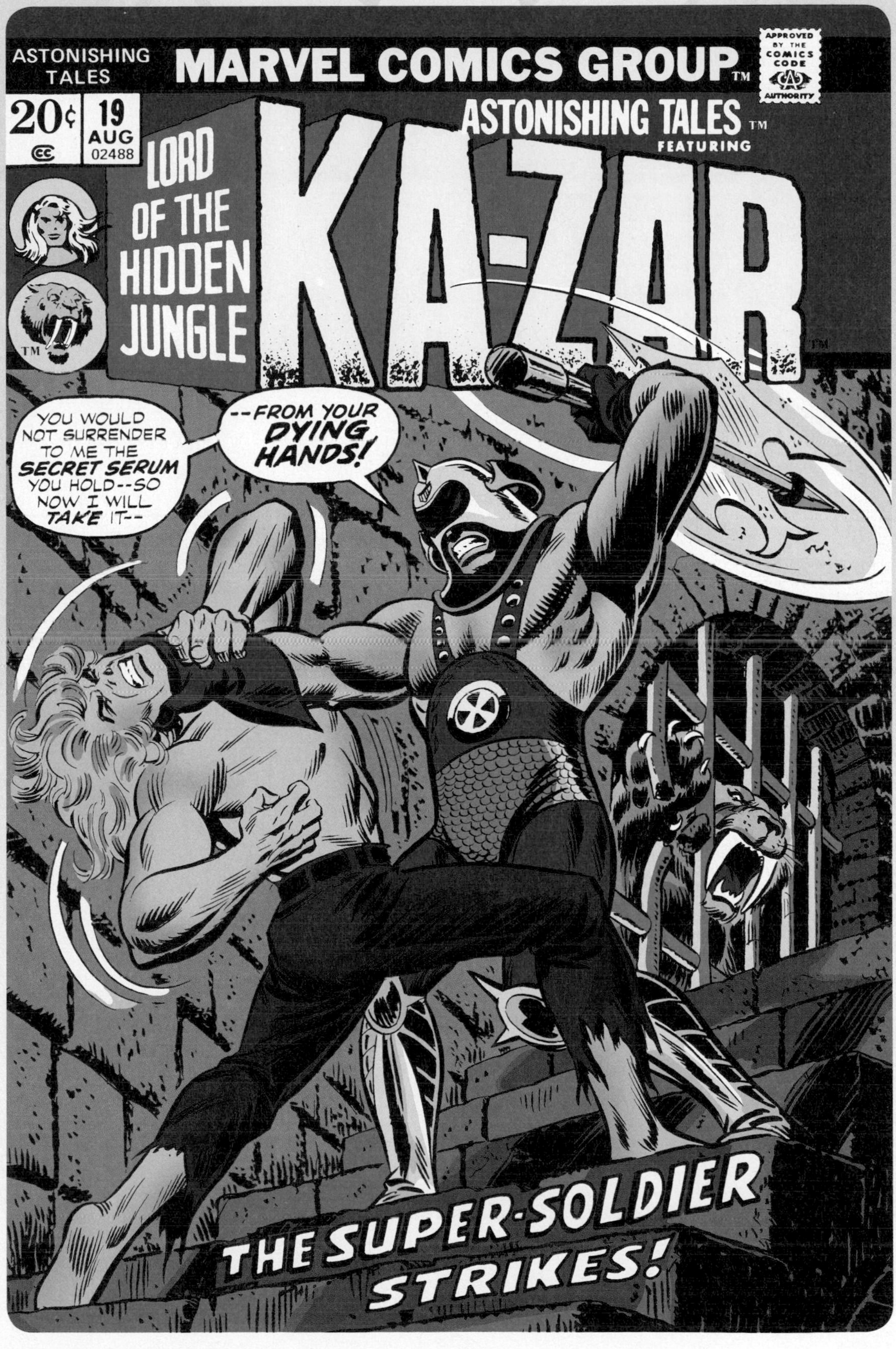

ASTONISHING TALES
MARVEL COMICS GROUP™
APPROVED BY THE COMICS CODE AUTHORITY
20¢
19 AUG 02488
ASTONISHING TALES™ FEATURING
LORD OF THE HIDDEN JUNGLE
KA-ZAR™
YOU WOULD NOT SURRENDER TO ME THE SECRET SERUM YOU HOLD--SO NOW I WILL TAKE IT--
--FROM YOUR DYING HANDS!
THE SUPER-SOLDIER STRIKES!

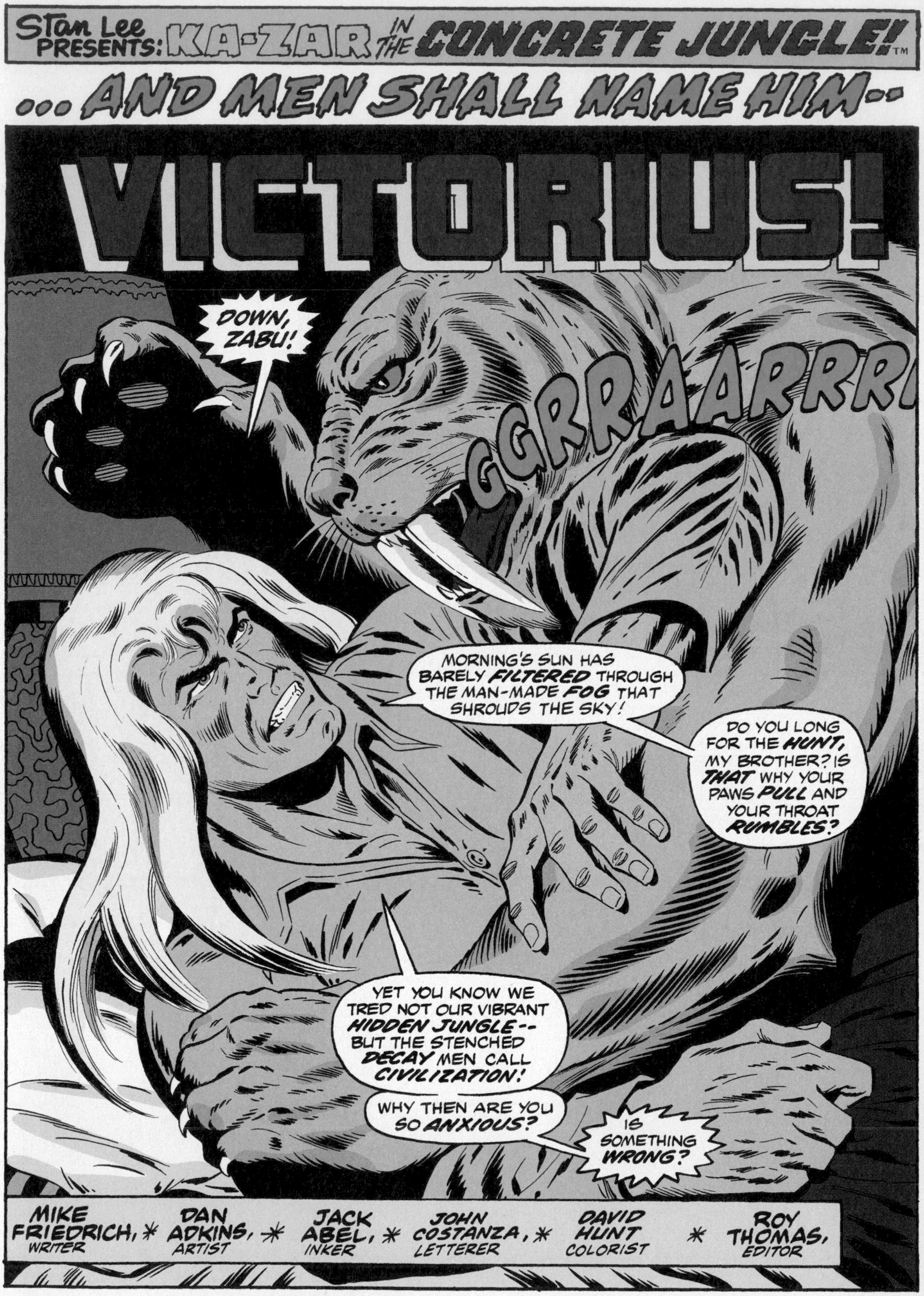

STAN LEE PRESENTS: KA-ZAR IN THE CONCRETE JUNGLE! ™
...AND MEN SHALL NAME HIM--
VICTORIUS!
DOWN, ZABU!
GGRRAARRR
MORNING'S SUN HAS BARELY FILTERED THROUGH THE MAN-MADE FOG THAT SHROUDS THE SKY!
DO YOU LONG FOR THE HUNT, MY BROTHER? IS THAT WHY YOUR PAWS PULL AND YOUR THROAT RUMBLES?
YET YOU KNOW WE TRED NOT OUR VIBRANT HIDDEN JUNGLE-- BUT THE STENCHED DECAY MEN CALL CIVILIZATION!
WHY THEN ARE YOU SO ANXIOUS?
IS SOMETHING WRONG?
MIKE FRIEDRICH, WRITER * DAN ADKINS, ARTIST * JACK ABEL, INKER * JOHN COSTANZA, LETTERER * DAVID HUNT COLORIST * ROY THOMAS, EDITOR

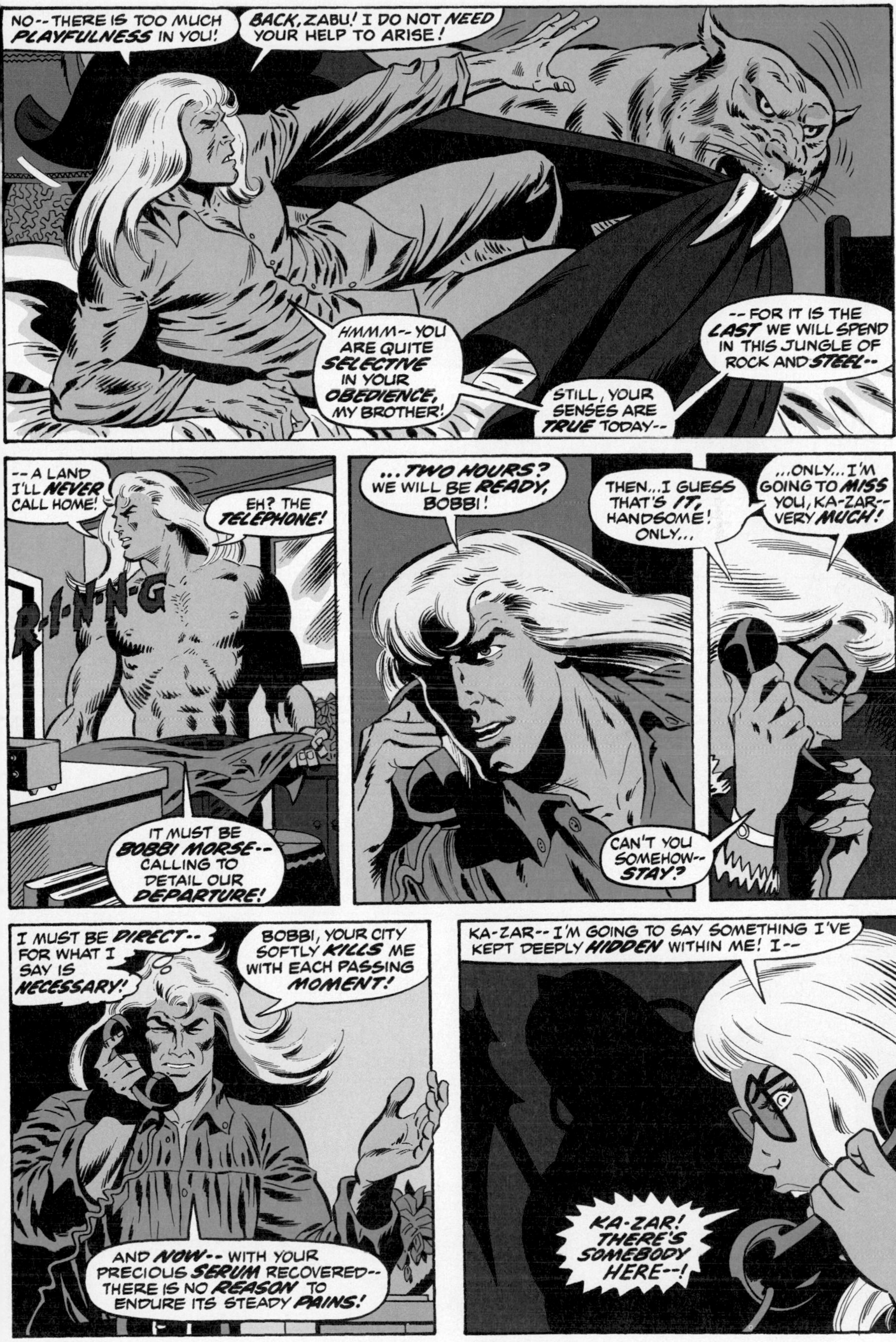

NO--THERE IS TOO MUCH PLAYFULNESS IN YOU!
BACK, ZABU! I DO NOT NEED YOUR HELP TO ARISE!
HMMM--YOU ARE QUITE SELECTIVE IN YOUR OBEDIENCE, MY BROTHER!
STILL, YOUR SENSES ARE TRUE TODAY--
--FOR IT IS THE LAST WE WILL SPEND IN THIS JUNGLE OF ROCK AND STEEL--
--A LAND I'LL NEVER CALL HOME!
EH? THE TELEPHONE!
R-I-N-N-G
IT MUST BE BOBBI MORSE--CALLING TO DETAIL OUR DEPARTURE!
...TWO HOURS? WE WILL BE READY, BOBBI!
THEN...I GUESS THAT'S IT, HANDSOME! ONLY...
...ONLY...I'M GOING TO MISS YOU, KA-ZAR--VERY MUCH!
CAN'T YOU SOMEHOW--STAY?
I MUST BE DIRECT--FOR WHAT I SAY IS NECESSARY!
BOBBI, YOUR CITY SOFTLY KILLS ME WITH EACH PASSING MOMENT!
AND NOW--WITH YOUR PRECIOUS SERUM RECOVERED--THERE IS NO REASON TO ENDURE ITS STEADY PAINS!
KA-ZAR--I'M GOING TO SAY SOMETHING I'VE KEPT DEEPLY HIDDEN WITHIN ME! I--
KA-ZAR! THERE'S SOMEBODY HERE--!

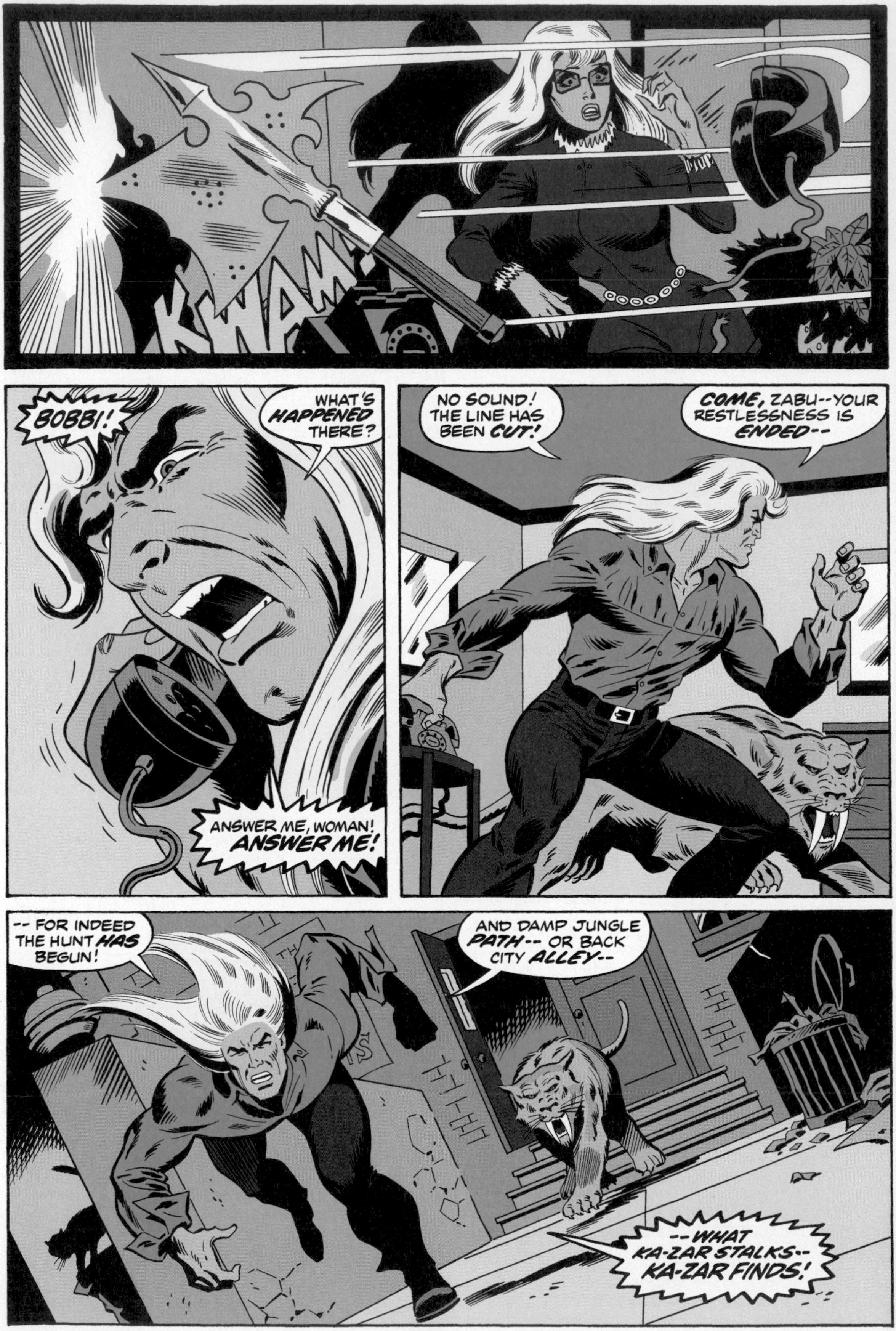
KWAM
BOBBI!
WHAT'S HAPPENED THERE?
ANSWER ME, WOMAN! ANSWER ME!
NO SOUND! THE LINE HAS BEEN CUT!
COME, ZABU--YOUR RESTLESSNESS IS ENDED--
-- FOR INDEED THE HUNT HAS BEGUN!
AND DAMP JUNGLE PATH-- OR BACK CITY ALLEY--
--WHAT KA-ZAR STALKS-- KA-ZAR FINDS!

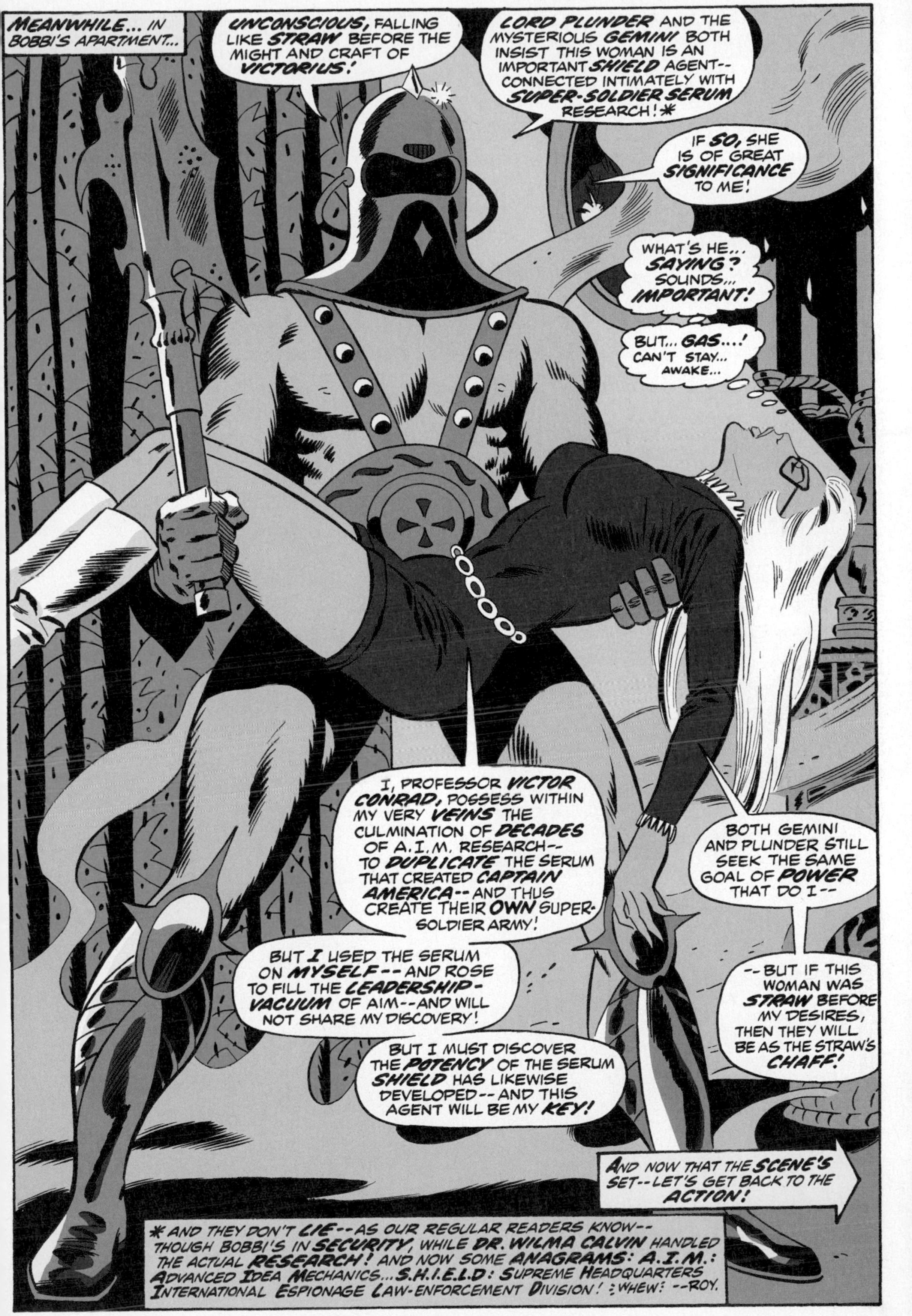
MEANWHILE... IN BOBBI'S APARTMENT...
UNCONSCIOUS, FALLING LIKE STRAW BEFORE THE MIGHT AND CRAFT OF VICTORIUS!
LORD PLUNDER AND THE MYSTERIOUS GEMINI BOTH INSIST THIS WOMAN IS AN IMPORTANT SHIELD AGENT-- CONNECTED INTIMATELY WITH SUPER-SOLDIER SERUM RESEARCH! *
IF SO, SHE IS OF GREAT SIGNIFICANCE TO ME!
WHAT'S HE... SAYING? SOUNDS... IMPORTANT!
BUT... GAS...! CAN'T STAY... AWAKE...
I, PROFESSOR VICTOR CONRAD, POSSESS WITHIN MY VERY VEINS THE CULMINATION OF DECADES OF A.I.M. RESEARCH-- TO DUPLICATE THE SERUM THAT CREATED CAPTAIN AMERICA-- AND THUS CREATE THEIR OWN SUPER-SOLDIER ARMY!
BUT I USED THE SERUM ON MYSELF-- AND ROSE TO FILL THE LEADERSHIP-VACUUM OF AIM-- AND WILL NOT SHARE MY DISCOVERY!
BUT I MUST DISCOVER THE POTENCY OF THE SERUM SHIELD HAS LIKEWISE DEVELOPED-- AND THIS AGENT WILL BE MY KEY!
BOTH GEMINI AND PLUNDER STILL SEEK THE SAME GOAL OF POWER THAT DO I--
--BUT IF THIS WOMAN WAS STRAW BEFORE MY DESIRES, THEN THEY WILL BE AS THE STRAW'S CHAFF!
AND NOW THAT THE SCENE'S SET-- LET'S GET BACK TO THE ACTION!
* AND THEY DON'T LIE-- AS OUR REGULAR READERS KNOW-- THOUGH BOBBI'S IN SECURITY, WHILE DR. WILMA CALVIN HANDLED THE ACTUAL RESEARCH! AND NOW SOME ANAGRAMS: A.I.M.: ADVANCED IDEA MECHANICS... S.H.I.E.L.D: SUPREME HEADQUARTERS INTERNATIONAL ESPIONAGE LAW-ENFORCEMENT DIVISION! :WHEW: --ROY.

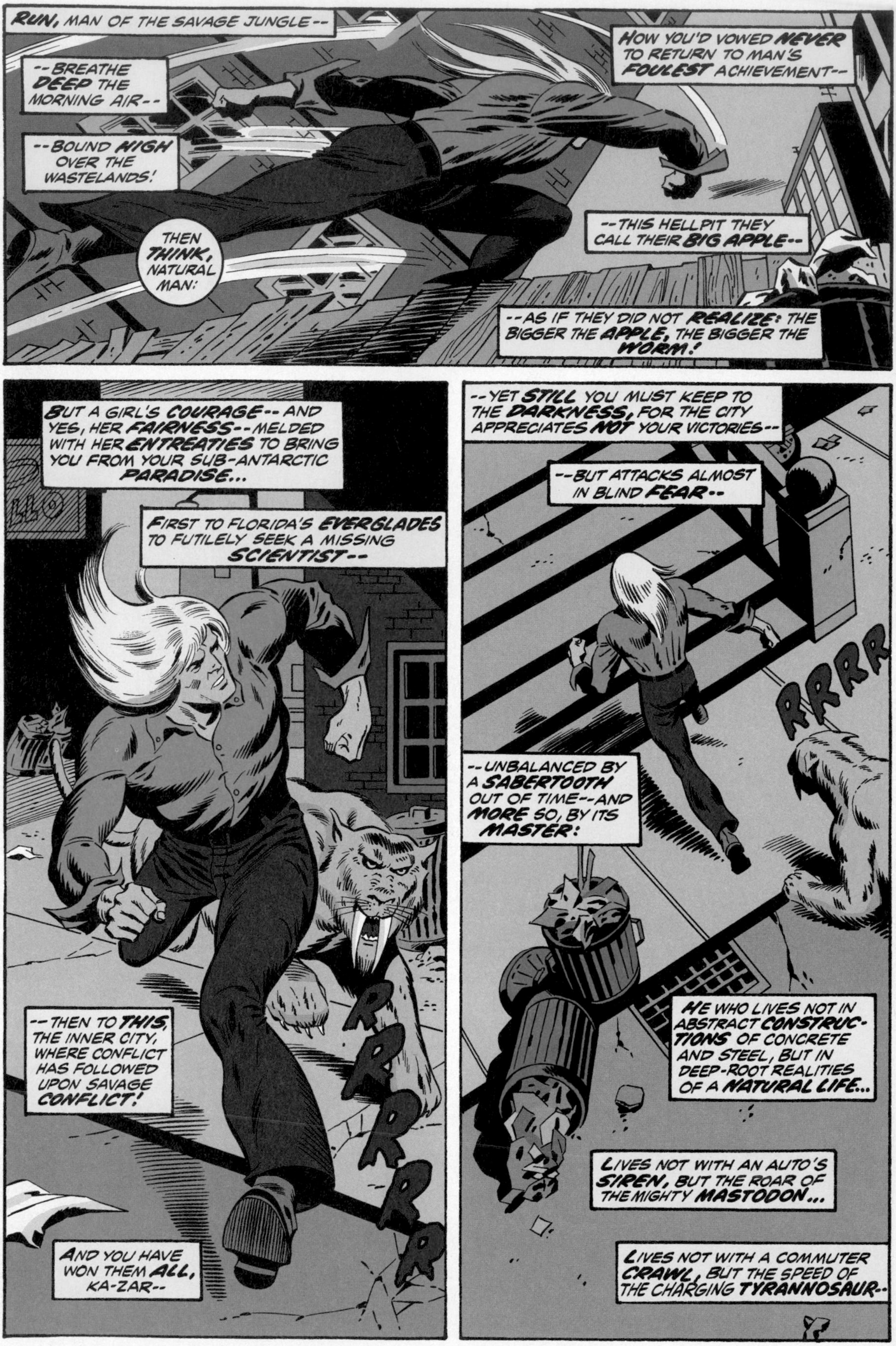
RUN, MAN OF THE SAVAGE JUNGLE--
--BREATHE DEEP THE MORNING AIR--
--BOUND HIGH OVER THE WASTELANDS!
THEN THINK, NATURAL MAN:
HOW YOU'D VOWED NEVER TO RETURN TO MAN'S FOULEST ACHIEVEMENT--
--THIS HELLPIT THEY CALL THEIR BIG APPLE--
--AS IF THEY DID NOT REALIZE: THE BIGGER THE APPLE, THE BIGGER THE WORM!
BUT A GIRL'S COURAGE--AND YES, HER FAIRNESS--MELDED WITH HER ENTREATIES TO BRING YOU FROM YOUR SUB-ANTARCTIC PARADISE...
FIRST TO FLORIDA'S EVERGLADES TO FUTILELY SEEK A MISSING SCIENTIST--
--THEN TO THIS, THE INNER CITY, WHERE CONFLICT HAS FOLLOWED UPON SAVAGE CONFLICT!
RRRRRR
AND YOU HAVE WON THEM ALL, KA-ZAR--
--YET STILL YOU MUST KEEP TO THE DARKNESS, FOR THE CITY APPRECIATES NOT YOUR VICTORIES--
--BUT ATTACKS ALMOST IN BLIND FEAR--
RRRR
--UNBALANCED BY A SABERTOOTH OUT OF TIME--AND MORE SO, BY ITS MASTER:
HE WHO LIVES NOT IN ABSTRACT CONSTRUCTIONS OF CONCRETE AND STEEL, BUT IN DEEP-ROOT REALITIES OF A NATURAL LIFE...
LIVES NOT WITH AN AUTO'S SIREN, BUT THE ROAR OF THE MIGHTY MASTODON...
LIVES NOT WITH A COMMUTER CRAWL, BUT THE SPEED OF THE CHARGING TYRANNOSAUR--

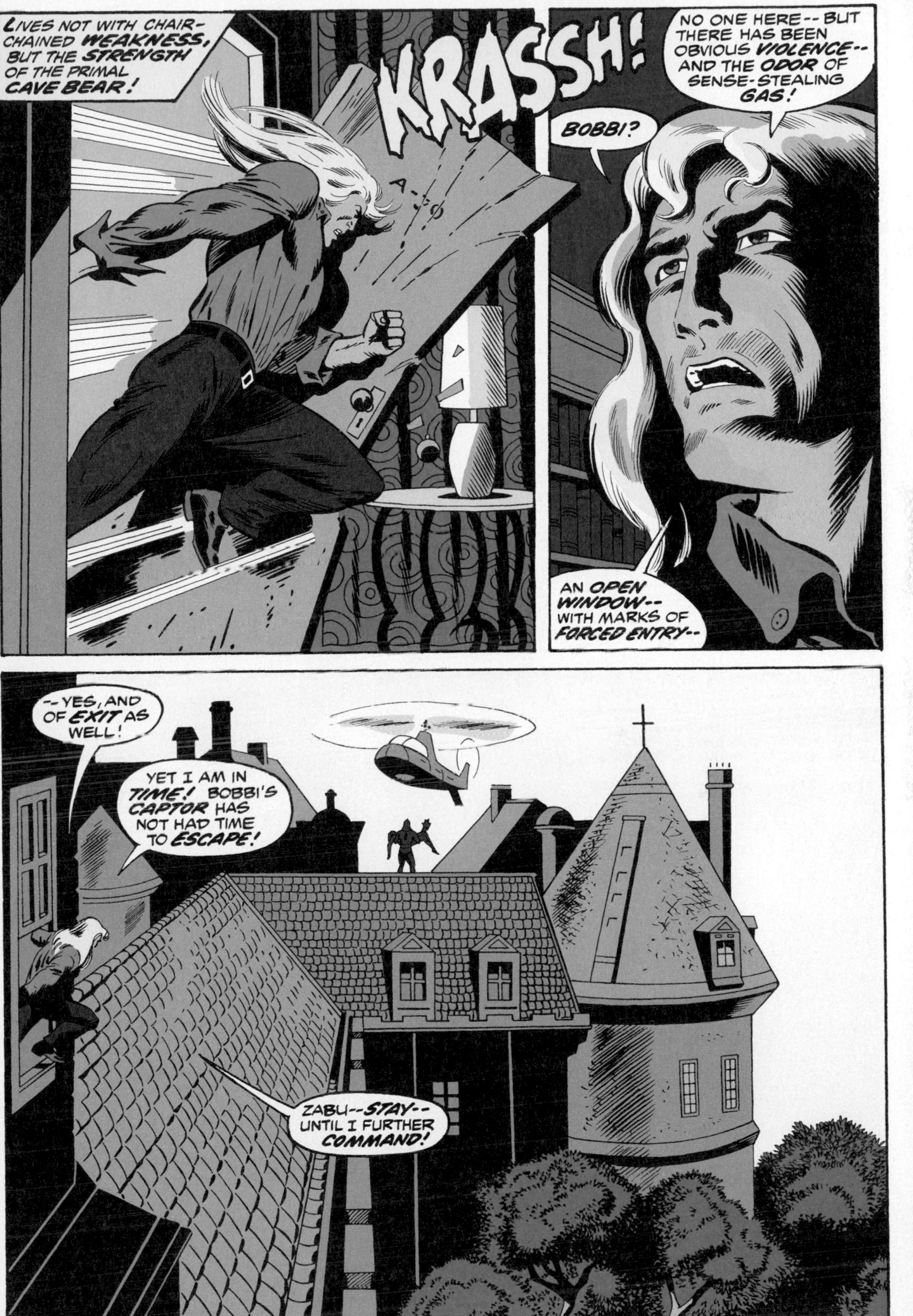
LIVES NOT WITH CHAIR-CHAINED WEAKNESS, BUT THE STRENGTH OF THE PRIMAL CAVE BEAR!
KRASSH!
NO ONE HERE-- BUT THERE HAS BEEN OBVIOUS VIOLENCE-- AND THE ODOR OF SENSE-STEALING GAS!
BOBBI?
AN OPEN WINDOW-- WITH MARKS OF FORCED ENTRY--
--YES, AND OF EXIT AS WELL!
YET I AM IN TIME! BOBBI'S CAPTOR HAS NOT HAD TIME TO ESCAPE!
ZABU--STAY-- UNTIL I FURTHER COMMAND!

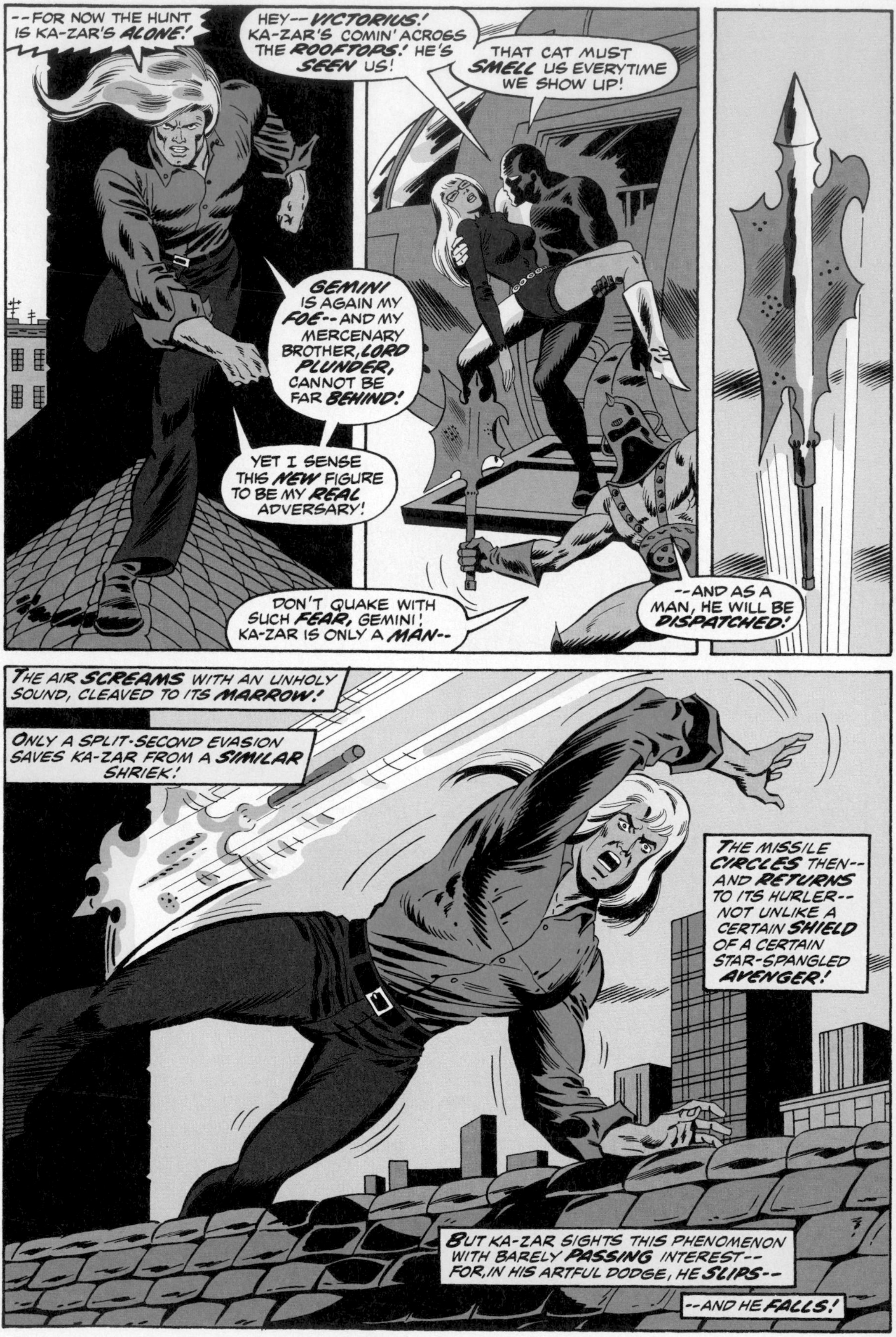
--FOR NOW THE HUNT IS KA-ZAR'S ALONE!
HEY--VICTORIUS! KA-ZAR'S COMIN' ACROSS THE ROOFTOPS! HE'S SEEN US!
THAT CAT MUST SMELL US EVERYTIME WE SHOW UP!
GEMINI IS AGAIN MY FOE--AND MY MERCENARY BROTHER, LORD PLUNDER, CANNOT BE FAR BEHIND!
YET I SENSE THIS NEW FIGURE TO BE MY REAL ADVERSARY!
DON'T QUAKE WITH SUCH FEAR, GEMINI! KA-ZAR IS ONLY A MAN--
--AND AS A MAN, HE WILL BE DISPATCHED!
THE AIR SCREAMS WITH AN UNHOLY SOUND, CLEAVED TO ITS MARROW!
ONLY A SPLIT-SECOND EVASION SAVES KA-ZAR FROM A SIMILAR SHRIEK!
THE MISSILE CIRCLES THEN--AND RETURNS TO ITS HURLER--NOT UNLIKE A CERTAIN SHIELD OF A CERTAIN STAR-SPANGLED AVENGER!
BUT KA-ZAR SIGHTS THIS PHENOMENON WITH BARELY PASSING INTEREST--FOR, IN HIS ARTFUL DODGE, HE SLIPS--
--AND HE FALLS!

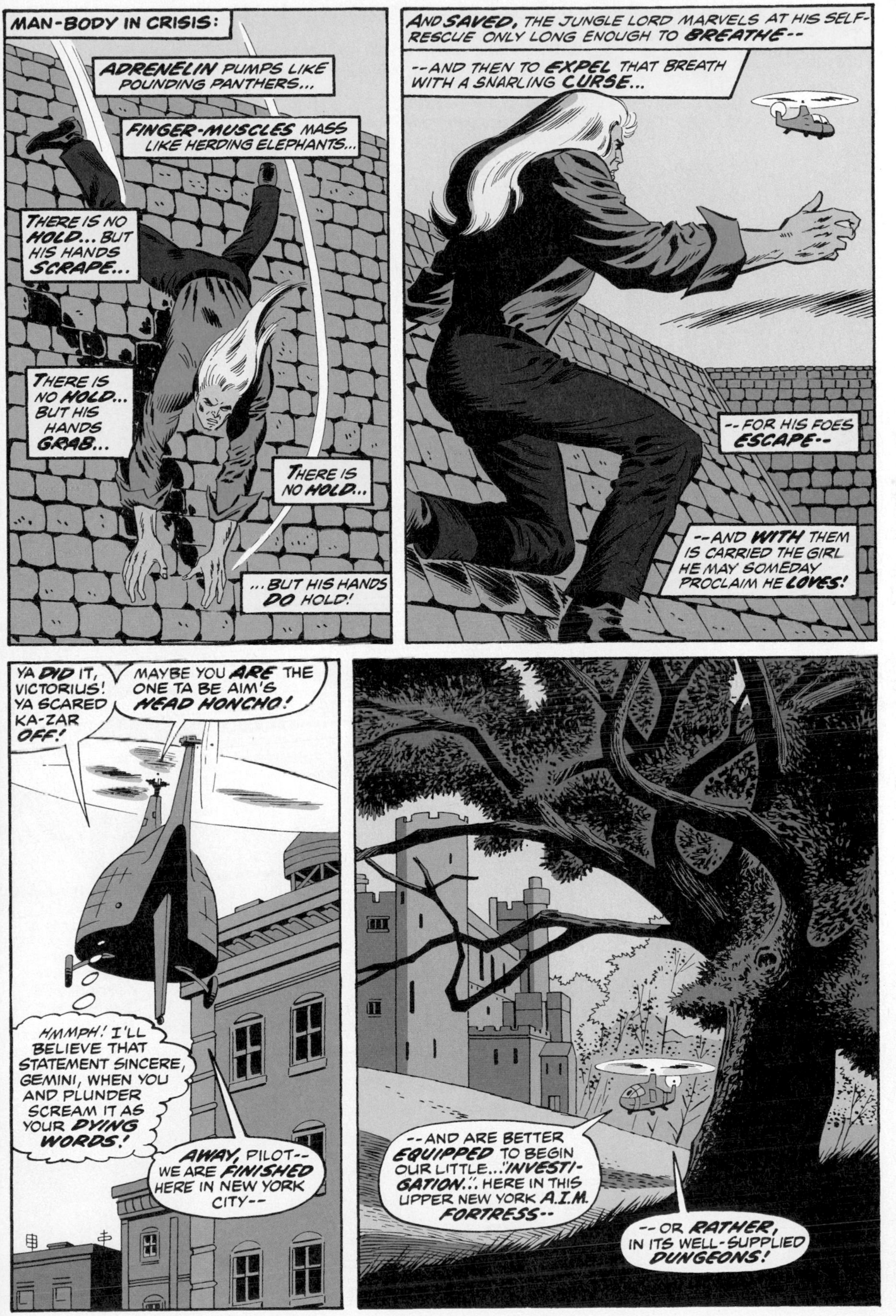
MAN-BODY IN CRISIS:
ADRENELIN PUMPS LIKE POUNDING PANTHERS...
FINGER-MUSCLES MASS LIKE HERDING ELEPHANTS...
THERE IS NO HOLD... BUT HIS HANDS SCRAPE...
THERE IS NO HOLD... BUT HIS HANDS GRAB...
THERE IS NO HOLD...
...BUT HIS HANDS DO HOLD!
AND SAVED, THE JUNGLE LORD MARVELS AT HIS SELF-RESCUE ONLY LONG ENOUGH TO BREATHE--
--AND THEN TO EXPEL THAT BREATH WITH A SNARLING CURSE...
--FOR HIS FOES ESCAPE--
--AND WITH THEM IS CARRIED THE GIRL HE MAY SOMEDAY PROCLAIM HE LOVES!
YA DID IT, VICTORIUS! YA SCARED KA-ZAR OFF!
MAYBE YOU ARE THE ONE TA BE AIM'S HEAD HONCHO!
HMMPH! I'LL BELIEVE THAT STATEMENT SINCERE, GEMINI, WHEN YOU AND PLUNDER SCREAM IT AS YOUR DYING WORDS!
AWAY, PILOT-- WE ARE FINISHED HERE IN NEW YORK CITY--
--AND ARE BETTER EQUIPPED TO BEGIN OUR LITTLE...'INVESTI-GATION.'.. HERE IN THIS UPPER NEW YORK A.I.M. FORTRESS--
--OR RATHER, IN ITS WELL-SUPPLIED DUNGEONS!

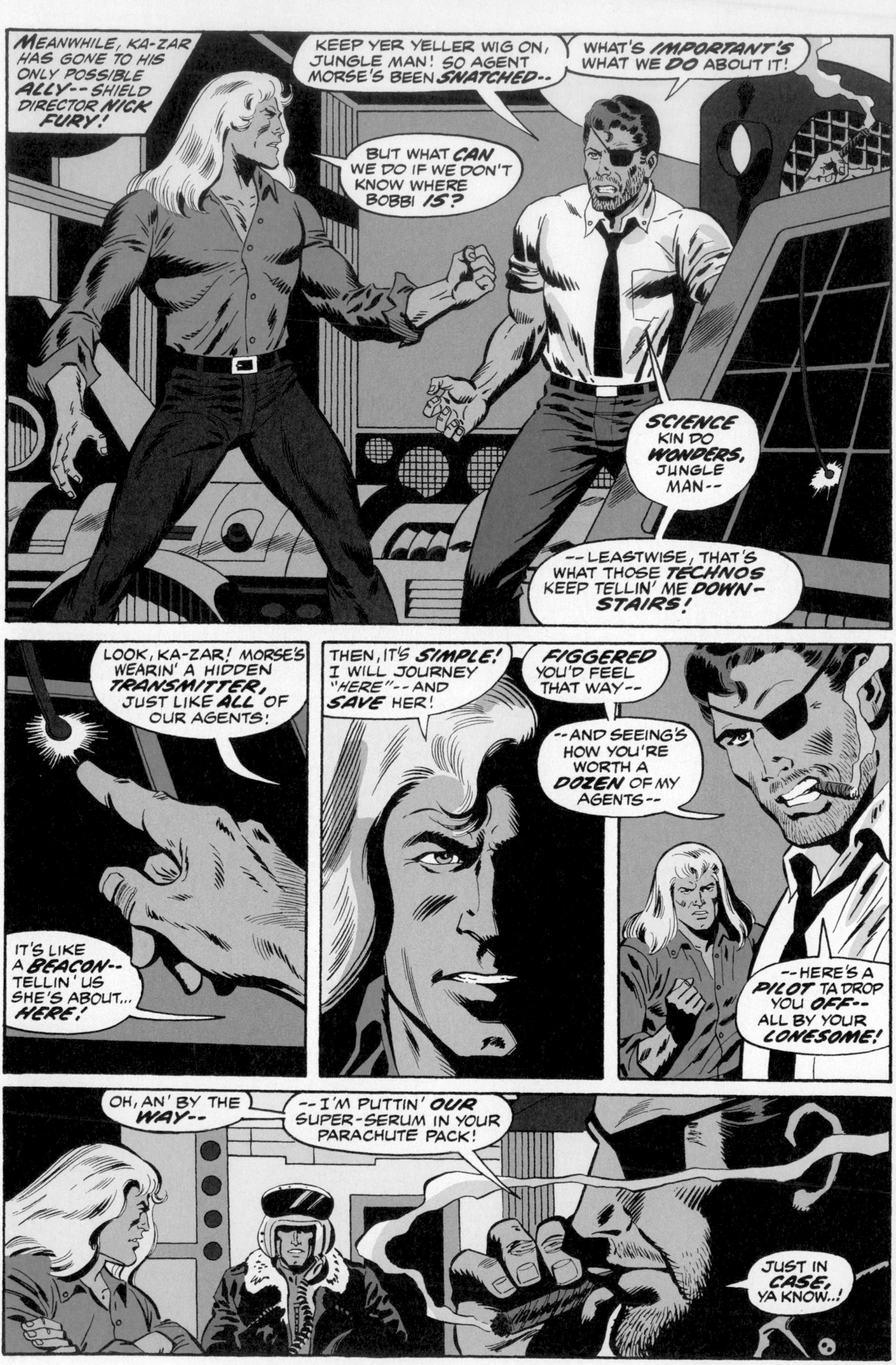
MEANWHILE, KA-ZAR HAS GONE TO HIS ONLY POSSIBLE ALLY-- SHIELD DIRECTOR NICK FURY!
KEEP YER YELLER WIG ON, JUNGLE MAN! SO AGENT MORSE'S BEEN SNATCHED--
WHAT'S IMPORTANT'S WHAT WE DO ABOUT IT!
BUT WHAT CAN WE DO IF WE DON'T KNOW WHERE BOBBI IS?
SCIENCE KIN DO WONDERS, JUNGLE MAN--
--LEASTWISE, THAT'S WHAT THOSE TECHNOS KEEP TELLIN' ME DOWN-STAIRS!
LOOK, KA-ZAR! MORSE'S WEARIN' A HIDDEN TRANSMITTER, JUST LIKE ALL OF OUR AGENTS!
IT'S LIKE A BEACON-- TELLIN' US SHE'S ABOUT... HERE!
THEN, IT'S SIMPLE! I WILL JOURNEY "HERE"-- AND SAVE HER!
FIGGERED YOU'D FEEL THAT WAY--
--AND SEEING'S HOW YOU'RE WORTH A DOZEN OF MY AGENTS--
--HERE'S A PILOT TA DROP YOU OFF-- ALL BY YOUR LONESOME!
OH, AN' BY THE WAY--
--I'M PUTTIN' OUR SUPER-SERUM IN YOUR PARACHUTE PACK!
JUST IN CASE, YA KNOW...!

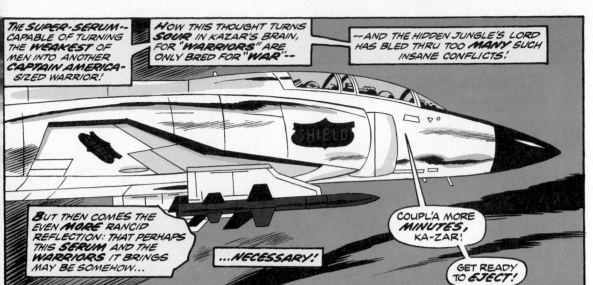

THE SUPER-SERUM-- CAPABLE OF TURNING THE WEAKEST OF MEN INTO ANOTHER CAPTAIN AMERICA-SIZED WARRIOR!

HOW THIS THOUGHT TURNS SOUR IN KAZAR'S BRAIN, FOR "WARRIORS" ARE ONLY BRED FOR "WAR"--

--AND THE HIDDEN JUNGLE'S LORD HAS BLED THRU TOO MANY SUCH INSANE CONFLICTS!

BUT THEN COMES THE EVEN MORE RANCID REFLECTION: THAT PERHAPS THIS SERUM AND THE WARRIORS IT BRINGS MAY BE SOMEHOW...

...NECESSARY!

COUPL'A MORE MINUTES, KA-ZAR!

GET READY TO EJECT!

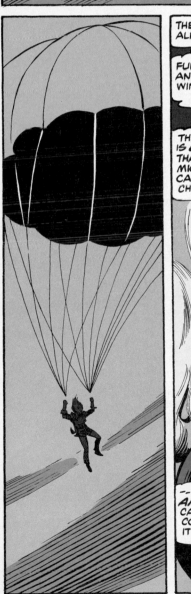

THESE SILKS ARE STRANGE-- ALREADY I PULL OFF MY TARGET!

FURY SAID TO TUG-- AND FORCE THE WINDS TO DO MY BIDDING!

THE THOUGHT IS WONDROUS THAT THE MIGHTY WINDS CAN BE THUS CHARGED--

--BUT IF ANYONE BE CAPABLE OF SUCH COMMANDING-- IT IS KA-ZAR--!

KA-ZAR-- WHO IS LORD OF ALL HE SURVEYS!

AND LO-- THE WINDS DO BEND THEIR KNEES BEFORE ME! THE CASTLE FORTRESS I SEEK LIES BELOW ME!

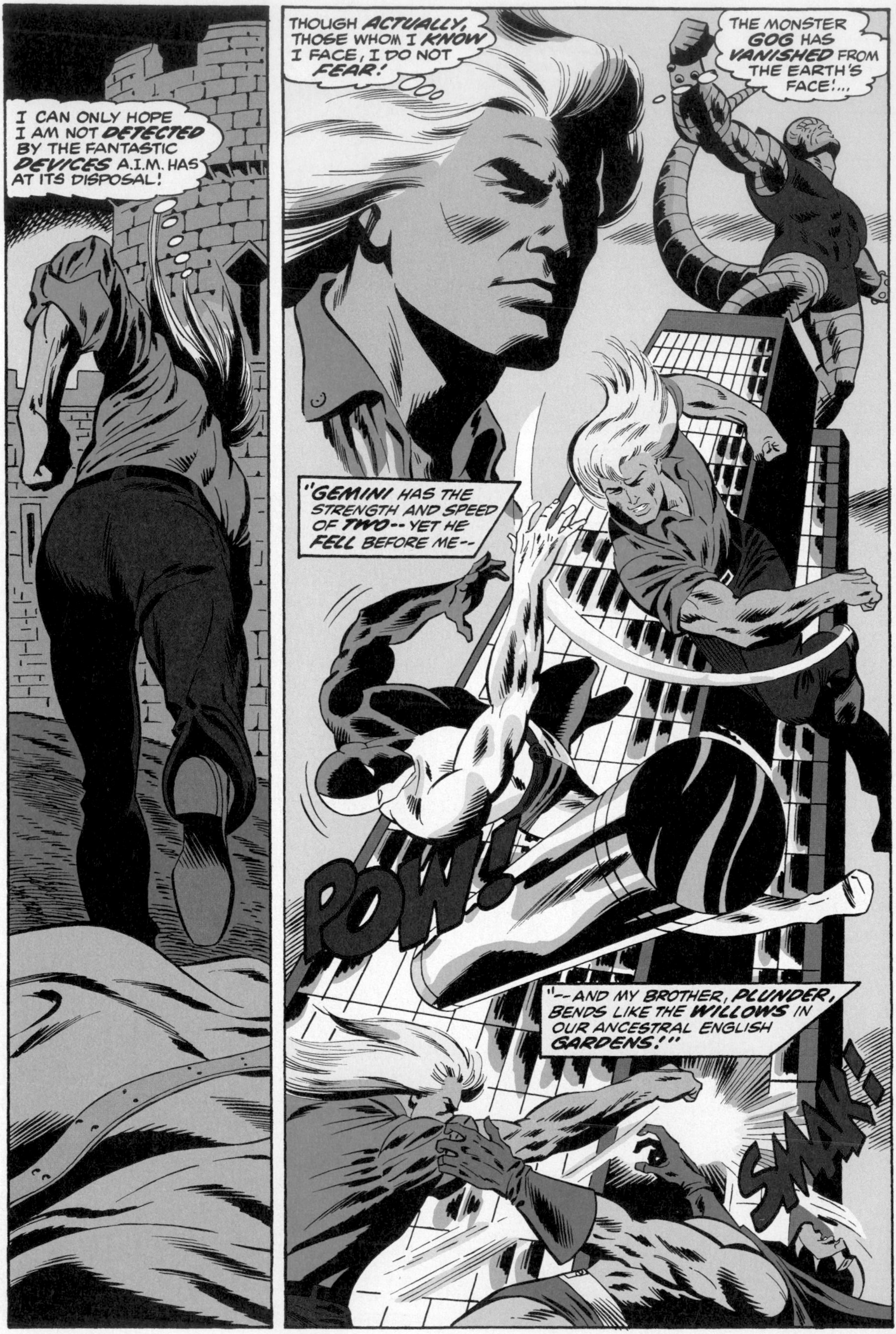
I CAN ONLY HOPE I AM NOT DETECTED BY THE FANTASTIC DEVICES A.I.M. HAS AT ITS DISPOSAL!
THOUGH ACTUALLY, THOSE WHOM I KNOW I FACE, I DO NOT FEAR!
THE MONSTER GOG HAS VANISHED FROM THE EARTH'S FACE!...
"GEMINI HAS THE STRENGTH AND SPEED OF TWO--YET HE FELL BEFORE ME--
POW!
"--AND MY BROTHER, PLUNDER, BENDS LIKE THE WILLOWS IN OUR ANCESTRAL ENGLISH GARDENS!"
SMAK!

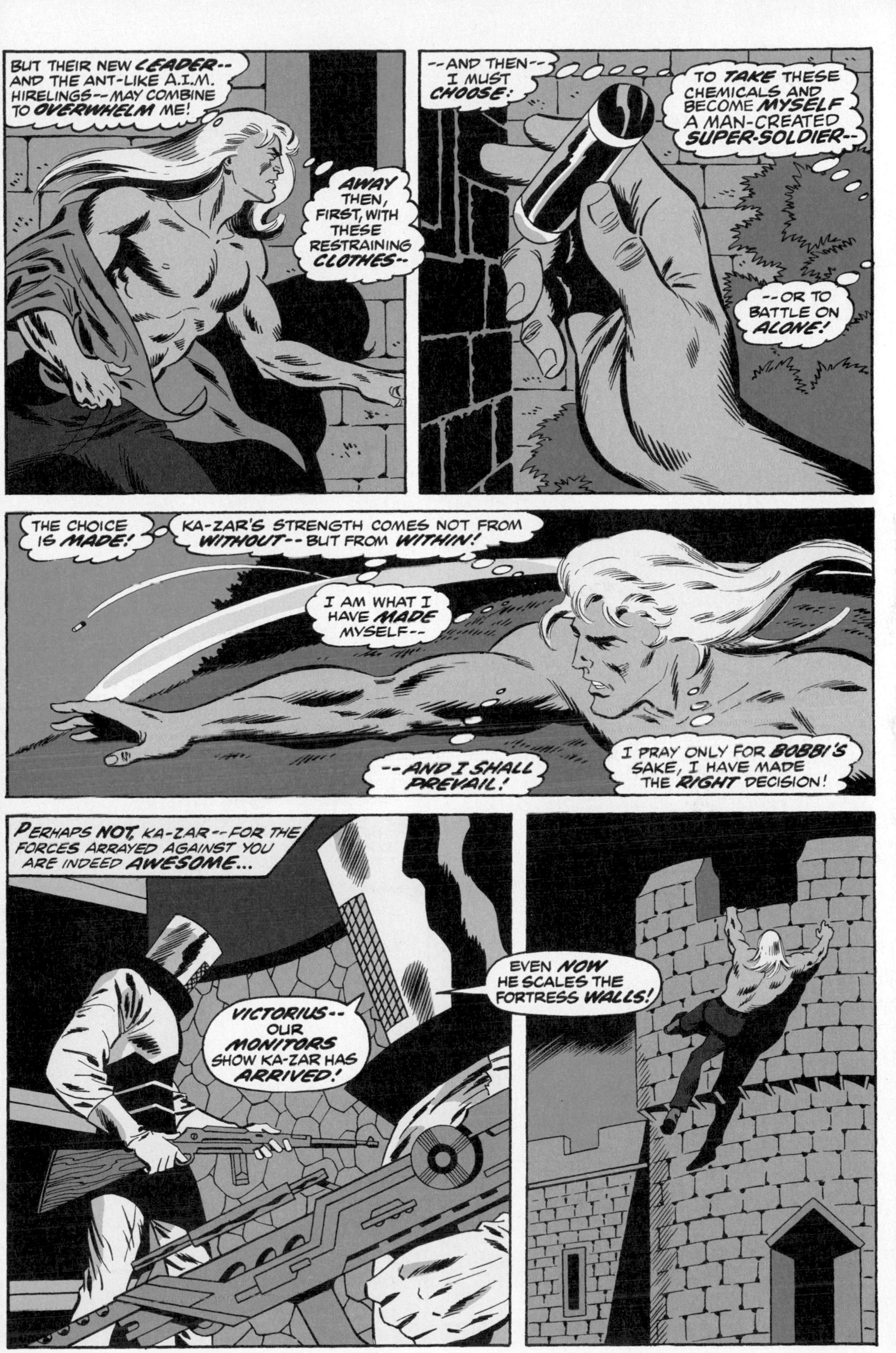
BUT THEIR NEW LEADER-- AND THE ANT-LIKE A.I.M. HIRELINGS--MAY COMBINE TO OVERWHELM ME!
AWAY THEN, FIRST, WITH THESE RESTRAINING CLOTHES--
--AND THEN-- I MUST CHOOSE:
TO TAKE THESE CHEMICALS AND BECOME MYSELF A MAN-CREATED SUPER-SOLDIER--
--OR TO BATTLE ON ALONE!
THE CHOICE IS MADE!
KA-ZAR'S STRENGTH COMES NOT FROM WITHOUT--BUT FROM WITHIN!
I AM WHAT I HAVE MADE MYSELF--
--AND I SHALL PREVAIL!
I PRAY ONLY FOR BOBBI'S SAKE, I HAVE MADE THE RIGHT DECISION!
PERHAPS NOT, KA-ZAR--FOR THE FORCES ARRAYED AGAINST YOU ARE INDEED AWESOME...
VICTORIUS-- OUR MONITORS SHOW KA-ZAR HAS ARRIVED!
EVEN NOW HE SCALES THE FORTRESS WALLS!

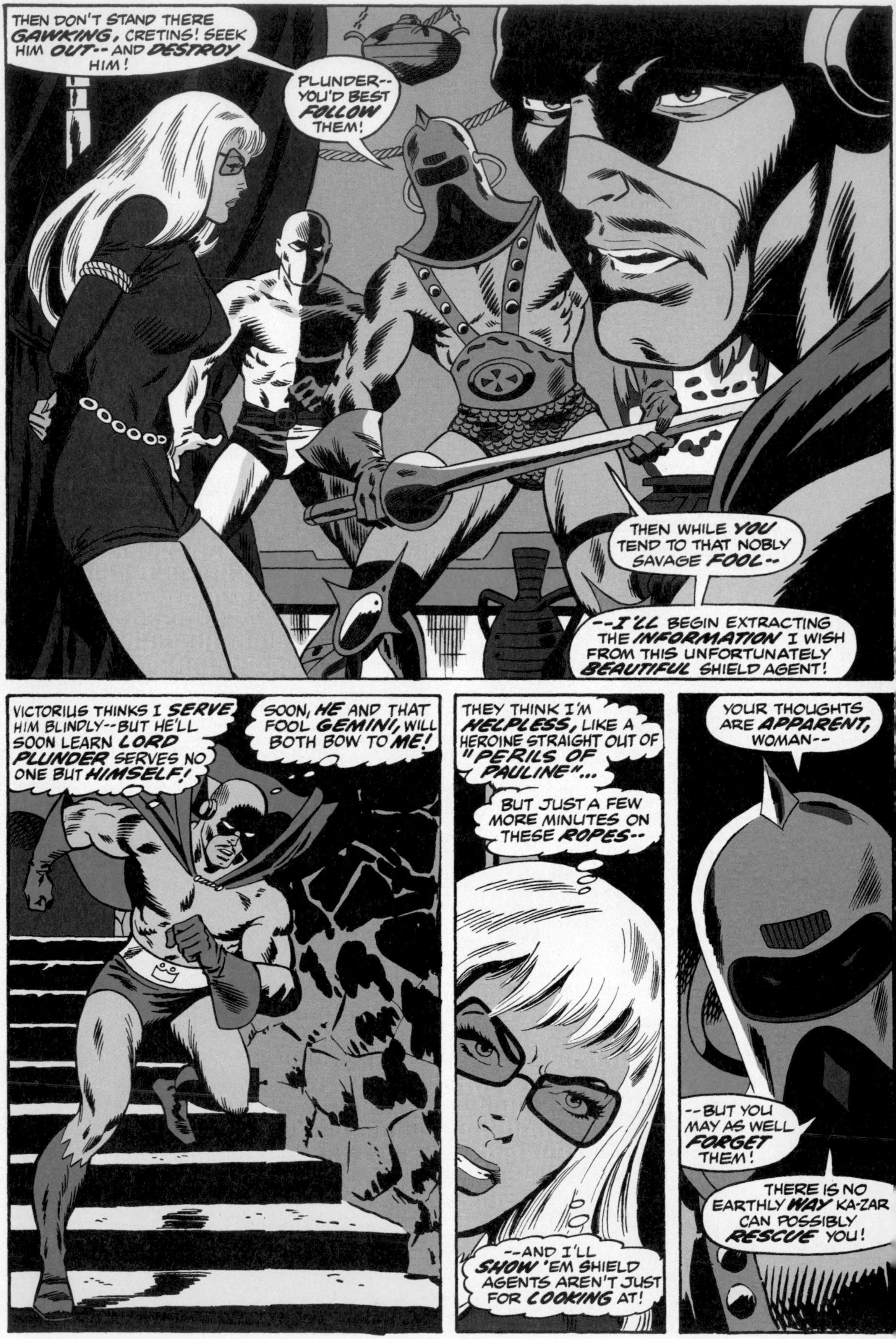
THEN DON'T STAND THERE GAWKING, CRETINS! SEEK HIM OUT-- AND DESTROY HIM!
PLUNDER-- YOU'D BEST FOLLOW THEM!
THEN WHILE YOU TEND TO THAT NOBLY SAVAGE FOOL--
--I'LL BEGIN EXTRACTING THE INFORMATION I WISH FROM THIS UNFORTUNATELY BEAUTIFUL SHIELD AGENT!
VICTORIUS THINKS I SERVE HIM BLINDLY--BUT HE'LL SOON LEARN LORD PLUNDER SERVES NO ONE BUT HIMSELF!
SOON, HE AND THAT FOOL GEMINI, WILL BOTH BOW TO ME!
THEY THINK I'M HELPLESS, LIKE A HEROINE STRAIGHT OUT OF "PERILS OF PAULINE"...
BUT JUST A FEW MORE MINUTES ON THESE ROPES--
--AND I'LL SHOW 'EM SHIELD AGENTS AREN'T JUST FOR LOOKING AT!
YOUR THOUGHTS ARE APPARENT, WOMAN--
--BUT YOU MAY AS WELL FORGET THEM!
THERE IS NO EARTHLY WAY KA-ZAR CAN POSSIBLY RESCUE YOU!

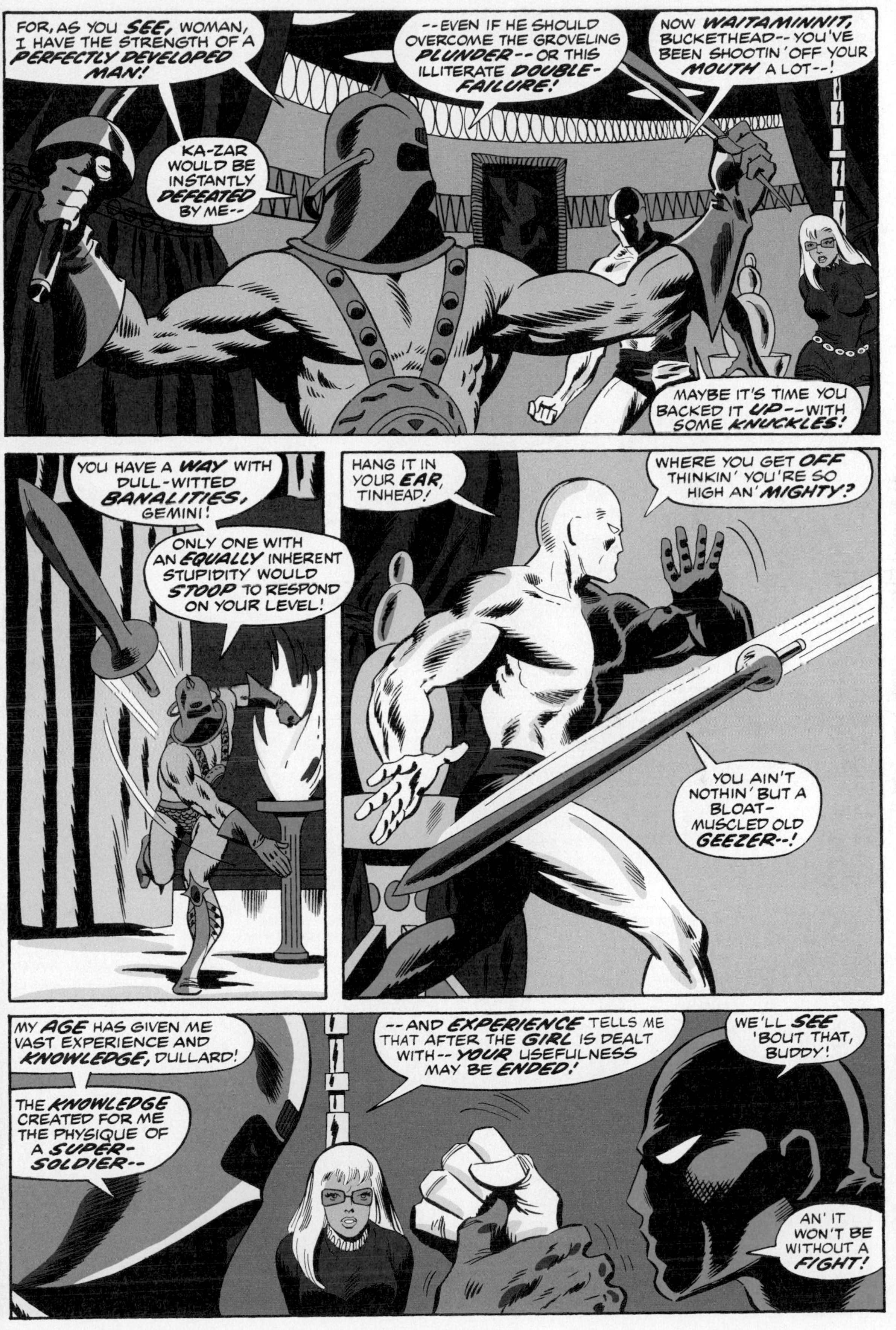

FOR, AS YOU SEE, WOMAN, I HAVE THE STRENGTH OF A PERFECTLY DEVELOPED MAN!
KA-ZAR WOULD BE INSTANTLY DEFEATED BY ME--
--EVEN IF HE SHOULD OVERCOME THE GROVELING PLUNDER--OR THIS ILLITERATE DOUBLE-FAILURE!
NOW WAITAMINNIT, BUCKETHEAD--YOU'VE BEEN SHOOTIN' OFF YOUR MOUTH A LOT--!
MAYBE IT'S TIME YOU BACKED IT UP--WITH SOME KNUCKLES!
YOU HAVE A WAY WITH DULL-WITTED BANALITIES, GEMINI!
ONLY ONE WITH AN EQUALLY INHERENT STUPIDITY WOULD STOOP TO RESPOND ON YOUR LEVEL!
HANG IT IN YOUR EAR, TINHEAD!
WHERE YOU GET OFF THINKIN' YOU'RE SO HIGH AN' MIGHTY?
YOU AIN'T NOTHIN' BUT A BLOAT-MUSCLED OLD GEEZER--!
MY AGE HAS GIVEN ME VAST EXPERIENCE AND KNOWLEDGE, DULLARD!
THE KNOWLEDGE CREATED FOR ME THE PHYSIQUE OF A SUPER-SOLDIER--
--AND EXPERIENCE TELLS ME THAT AFTER THE GIRL IS DEALT WITH--YOUR USEFULNESS MAY BE ENDED!
WE'LL SEE 'BOUT THAT, BUDDY!
AN' IT WON'T BE WITHOUT A FIGHT!

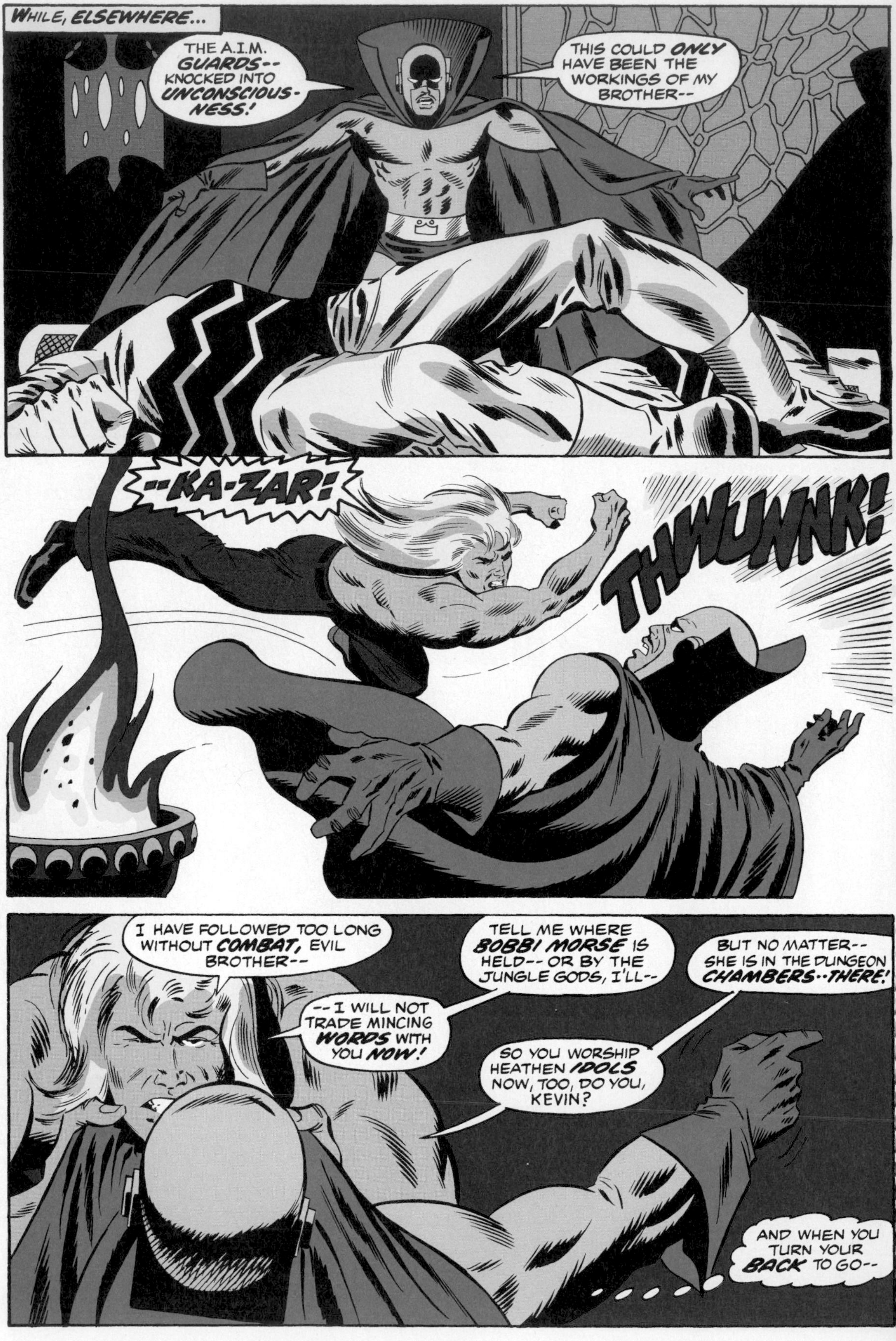
WHILE, ELSEWHERE...
THE A.I.M. GUARDS-- KNOCKED INTO UNCONSCIOUS-NESS!
THIS COULD ONLY HAVE BEEN THE WORKINGS OF MY BROTHER--
--KA-ZAR!
THWUNNK!
I HAVE FOLLOWED TOO LONG WITHOUT COMBAT, EVIL BROTHER--
--I WILL NOT TRADE MINCING WORDS WITH YOU NOW!
TELL ME WHERE BOBBI MORSE IS HELD-- OR BY THE JUNGLE GODS, I'LL--
SO YOU WORSHIP HEATHEN IDOLS NOW, TOO, DO YOU, KEVIN?
BUT NO MATTER-- SHE IS IN THE DUNGEON CHAMBERS--THERE!
AND WHEN YOU TURN YOUR BACK TO GO--

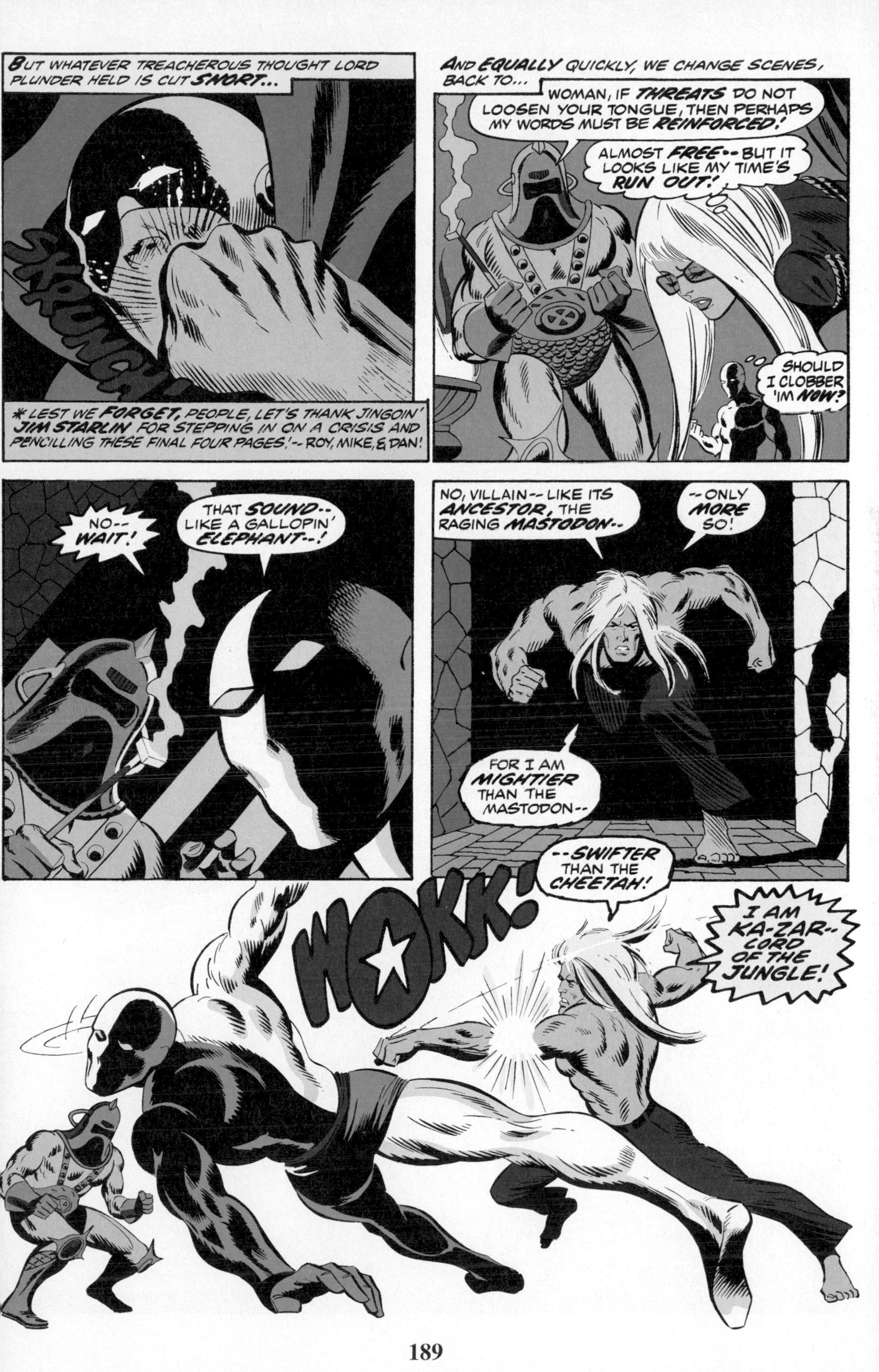
BUT WHATEVER TREACHEROUS THOUGHT LORD PLUNDER HELD IS CUT SHORT...
SKRUNCH!
*LEST WE FORGET, PEOPLE, LET'S THANK JINGOIN' JIM STARLIN FOR STEPPING IN ON A CRISIS AND PENCILLING THESE FINAL FOUR PAGES.'-- ROY, MIKE, & DAN!
AND EQUALLY QUICKLY, WE CHANGE SCENES, BACK TO...
WOMAN, IF THREATS DO NOT LOOSEN YOUR TONGUE, THEN PERHAPS MY WORDS MUST BE REINFORCED!
ALMOST FREE-- BUT IT LOOKS LIKE MY TIME'S RUN OUT!
SHOULD I CLOBBER 'IM NOW?
NO-- WAIT!
THAT SOUND-- LIKE A GALLOPIN' ELEPHANT--!
NO, VILLAIN-- LIKE ITS ANCESTOR, THE RAGING MASTODON--
--ONLY MORE SO!
FOR I AM MIGHTIER THAN THE MASTODON--
--SWIFTER THAN THE CHEETAH!
WOKK!
I AM KA-ZAR-- LORD OF THE JUNGLE!

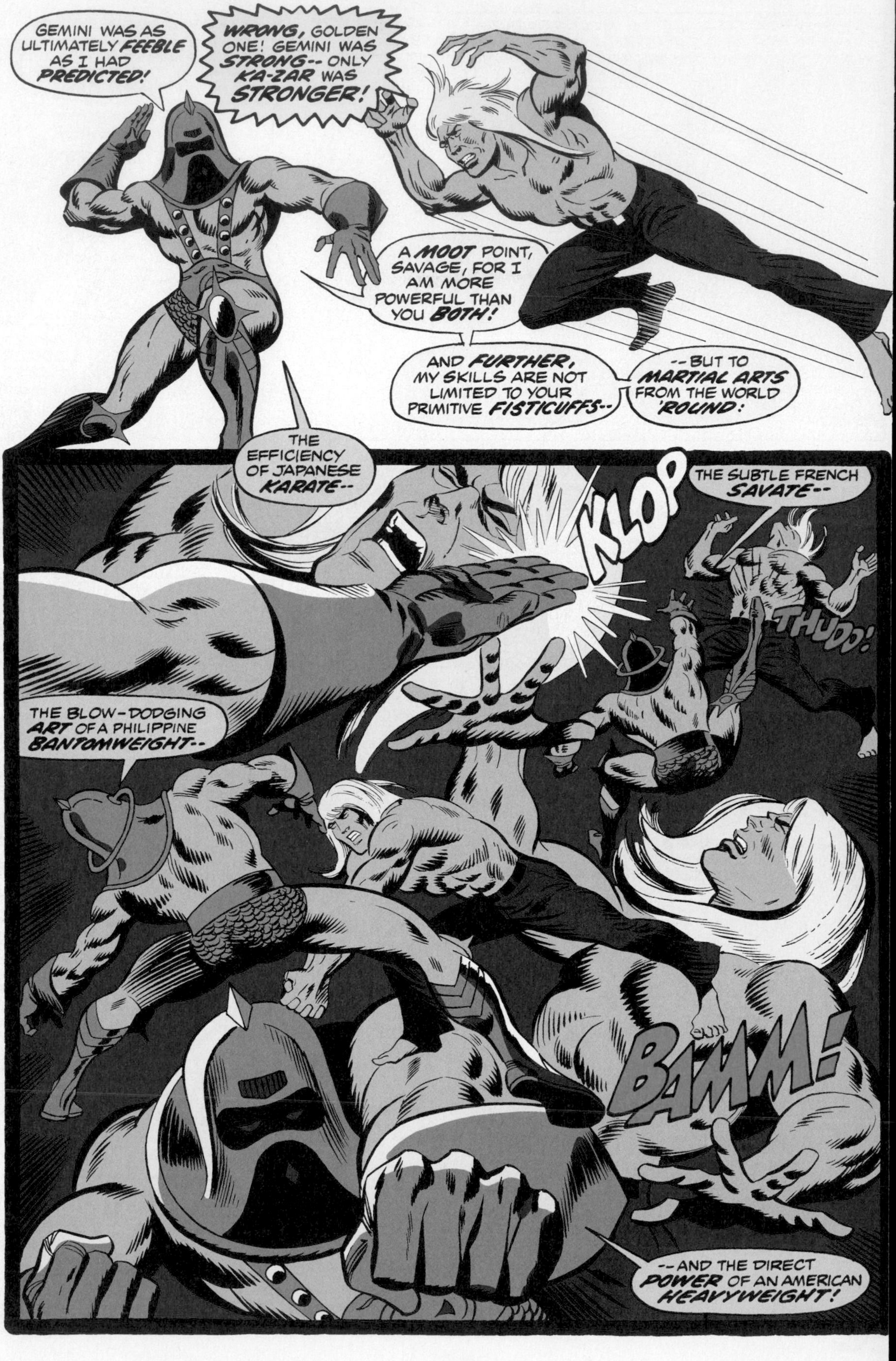

GEMINI WAS AS ULTIMATELY FEEBLE AS I HAD PREDICTED!
WRONG, GOLDEN ONE! GEMINI WAS STRONG-- ONLY KA-ZAR WAS STRONGER!
A MOOT POINT, SAVAGE, FOR I AM MORE POWERFUL THAN YOU BOTH!
AND FURTHER, MY SKILLS ARE NOT LIMITED TO YOUR PRIMITIVE FISTICUFFS--
--BUT TO MARTIAL ARTS FROM THE WORLD 'ROUND:
THE EFFICIENCY OF JAPANESE KARATE--
KLOP
THE SUBTLE FRENCH SAVATE--
THUDD!
THE BLOW-DODGING ART OF A PHILIPPINE BANTOMWEIGHT--
BAMM!
--AND THE DIRECT POWER OF AN AMERICAN HEAVYWEIGHT!

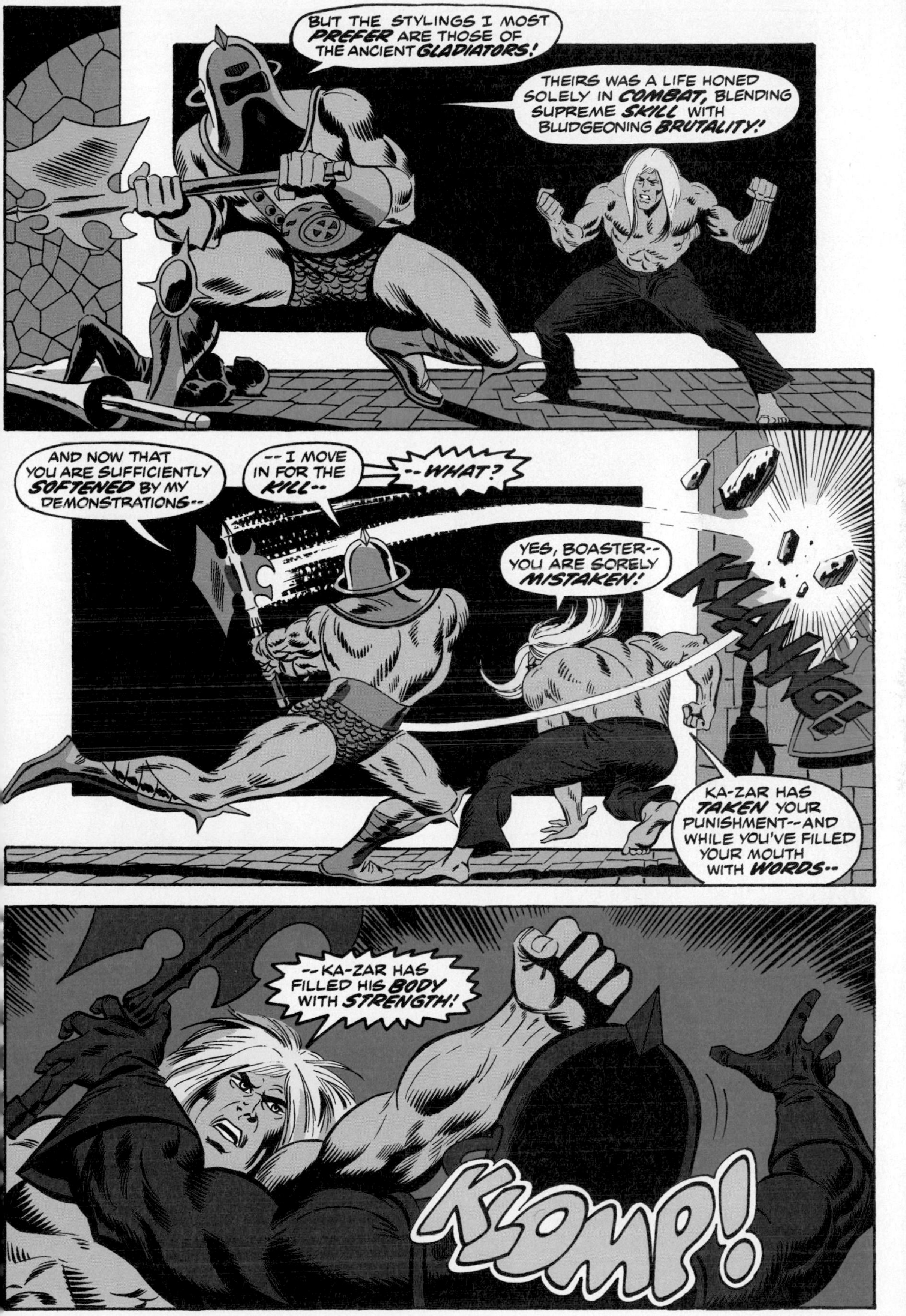
BUT THE STYLINGS I MOST PREFER ARE THOSE OF THE ANCIENT GLADIATORS!
THEIRS WAS A LIFE HONED SOLELY IN COMBAT, BLENDING SUPREME SKILL WITH BLUDGEONING BRUTALITY!
AND NOW THAT YOU ARE SUFFICIENTLY SOFTENED BY MY DEMONSTRATIONS--
--I MOVE IN FOR THE KILL--
--WHAT?
YES, BOASTER-- YOU ARE SORELY MISTAKEN!
KLANG!
KA-ZAR HAS TAKEN YOUR PUNISHMENT--AND WHILE YOU'VE FILLED YOUR MOUTH WITH WORDS--
--KA-ZAR HAS FILLED HIS BODY WITH STRENGTH!
KLOMP!

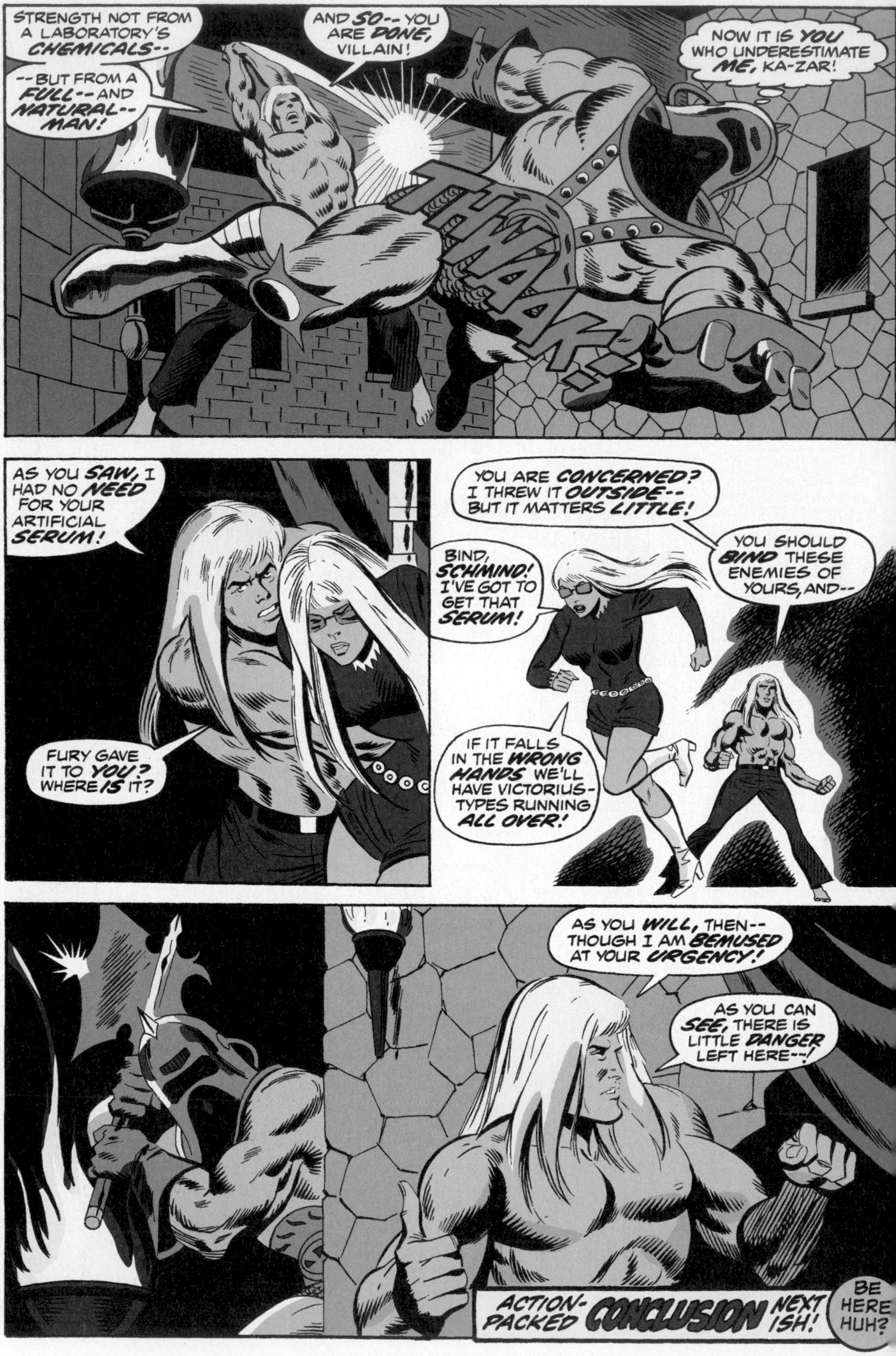
STRENGTH NOT FROM A LABORATORY'S CHEMICALS--
--BUT FROM A FULL--AND NATURAL--MAN!
AND SO--YOU ARE DONE, VILLAIN!
NOW IT IS YOU WHO UNDERESTIMATE ME, KA-ZAR!
THWAK!
AS YOU SAW, I HAD NO NEED FOR YOUR ARTIFICIAL SERUM!
FURY GAVE IT TO YOU? WHERE IS IT?
YOU ARE CONCERNED? I THREW IT OUTSIDE--BUT IT MATTERS LITTLE!
BIND, SCHMIND! I'VE GOT TO GET THAT SERUM!
YOU SHOULD BIND THESE ENEMIES OF YOURS, AND--
IF IT FALLS IN THE WRONG HANDS WE'LL HAVE VICTORIUS-TYPES RUNNING ALL OVER!
AS YOU WILL, THEN--THOUGH I AM BEMUSED AT YOUR URGENCY!
AS YOU CAN SEE, THERE IS LITTLE DANGER LEFT HERE--!
ACTION-PACKED CONCLUSION NEXT ISH!
BE HERE HUH?

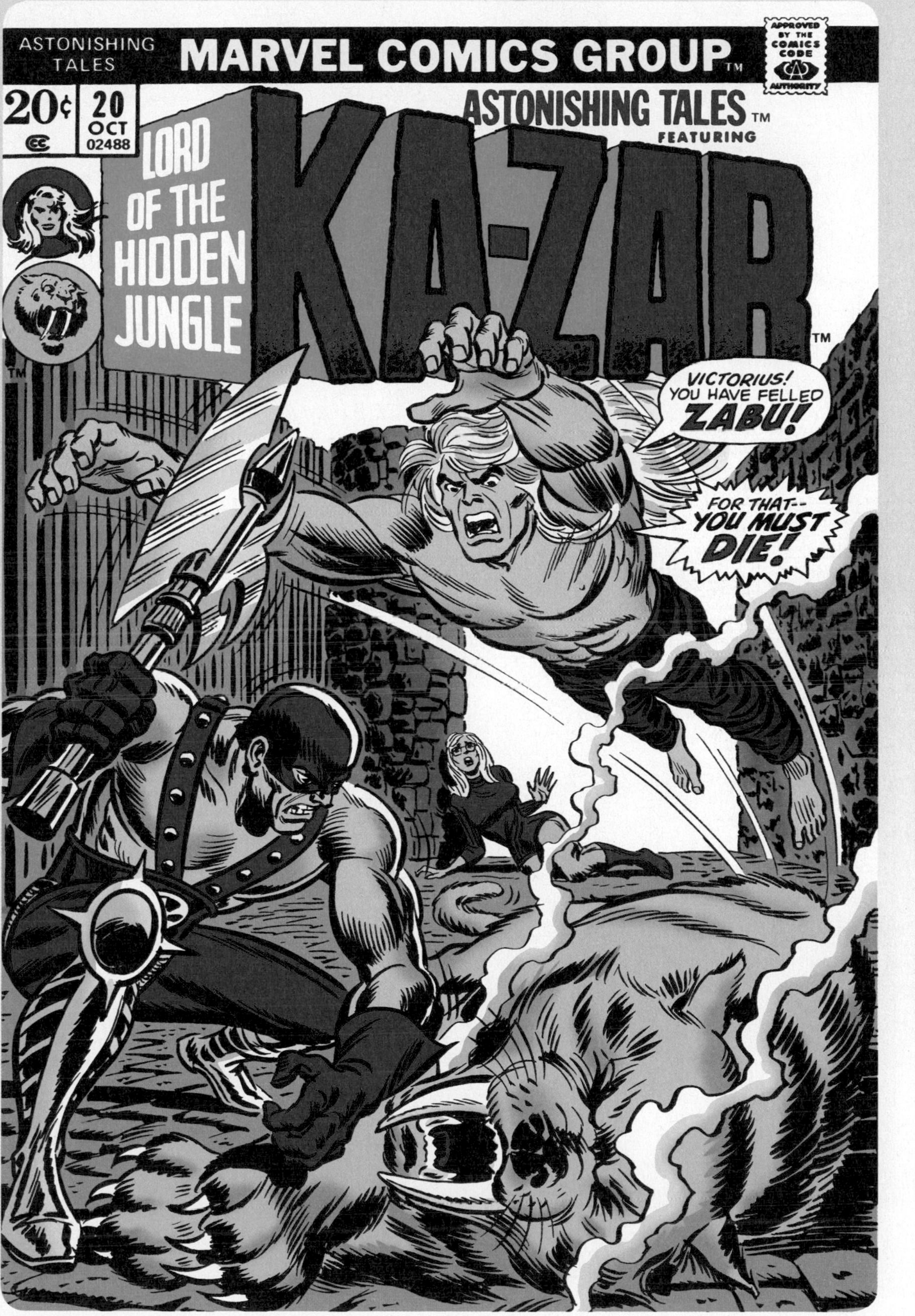
ASTONISHING TALES
MARVEL COMICS GROUP
APPROVED BY THE COMICS CODE AUTHORITY
20¢
20 OCT 02488
ASTONISHING TALES
FEATURING
LORD OF THE HIDDEN JUNGLE
KA-ZAR
VICTORIUS! YOU HAVE FELLED ZABU!
FOR THAT-- YOU MUST DIE!

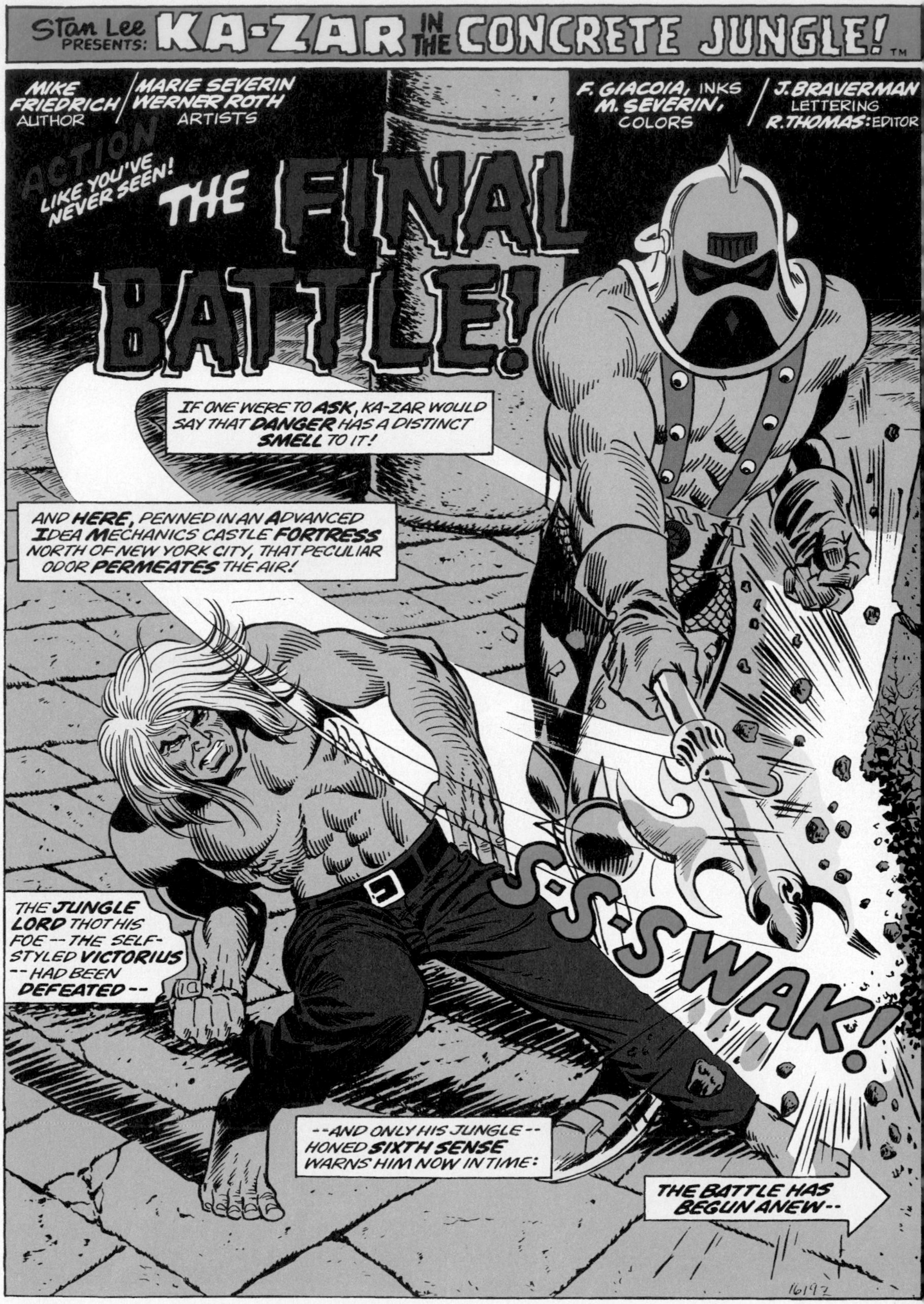
Stan Lee PRESENTS: KA-ZAR IN THE CONCRETE JUNGLE!
MIKE FRIEDRICH AUTHOR
MARIE SEVERIN WERNER ROTH ARTISTS
F. GIACOIA, INKS M. SEVERIN, COLORS
J. BRAVERMAN LETTERING R. THOMAS: EDITOR
ACTION LIKE YOU'VE NEVER SEEN!
THE FINAL BATTLE!
IF ONE WERE TO ASK, KA-ZAR WOULD SAY THAT DANGER HAS A DISTINCT SMELL TO IT!
AND HERE, PENNED IN AN ADVANCED IDEA MECHANICS CASTLE FORTRESS NORTH OF NEW YORK CITY, THAT PECULIAR ODOR PERMEATES THE AIR!
THE JUNGLE LORD THOT HIS FOE -- THE SELF-STYLED VICTORIUS -- HAD BEEN DEFEATED --
S-S-S-SWAK!
--AND ONLY HIS JUNGLE-- HONED SIXTH SENSE WARNS HIM NOW IN TIME:
THE BATTLE HAS BEGUN ANEW--
16192

--AND, WITH LIONIC **FURY**, KA-ZAR RESUMES THE **ATTACK!**

KRAM!

I UNDERESTIMATED YOUR ENDURANCE, VICTORIUS--

--BUT IT MATTERS **NOT!**

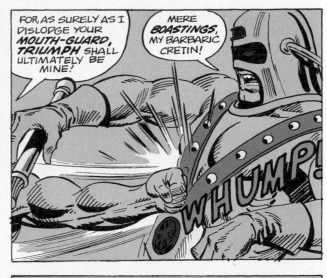

FOR, AS SURELY AS I DISLODGE YOUR **MOUTH-GUARD**, **TRIUMPH** SHALL ULTIMATELY BE MINE!

MERE **BOASTINGS**, MY BARBARIC CRETIN!

WHUMP!

OBSERVE--

MY IMPERVIOUS **BATTLE-AXE** SLIPS FROM MY **RIGHT** HAND --

--INTO THE SMOOTH GRASP OF MY **LEFT!**

LIKE THE ANCIENT **GLADIATORS** THAT I SO MUCH **ADMIRE**, MY COORDINATION MUST BE DEATHLY **PERFECT**--

AND SO IT **IS!**

AYE, YOUR MOVEMENTS ARE **INDEED** SMOOTH AND **SWIFT!**

BUT THE BLOOD OF THE **CHEETAH** FLOWS IN KA-ZAR'S VEINS --

AND **NONE** IS FASTER THAN **HE!**

BUT KA-ZAR FIGHTS NOT MERELY WITH **WORDS**--

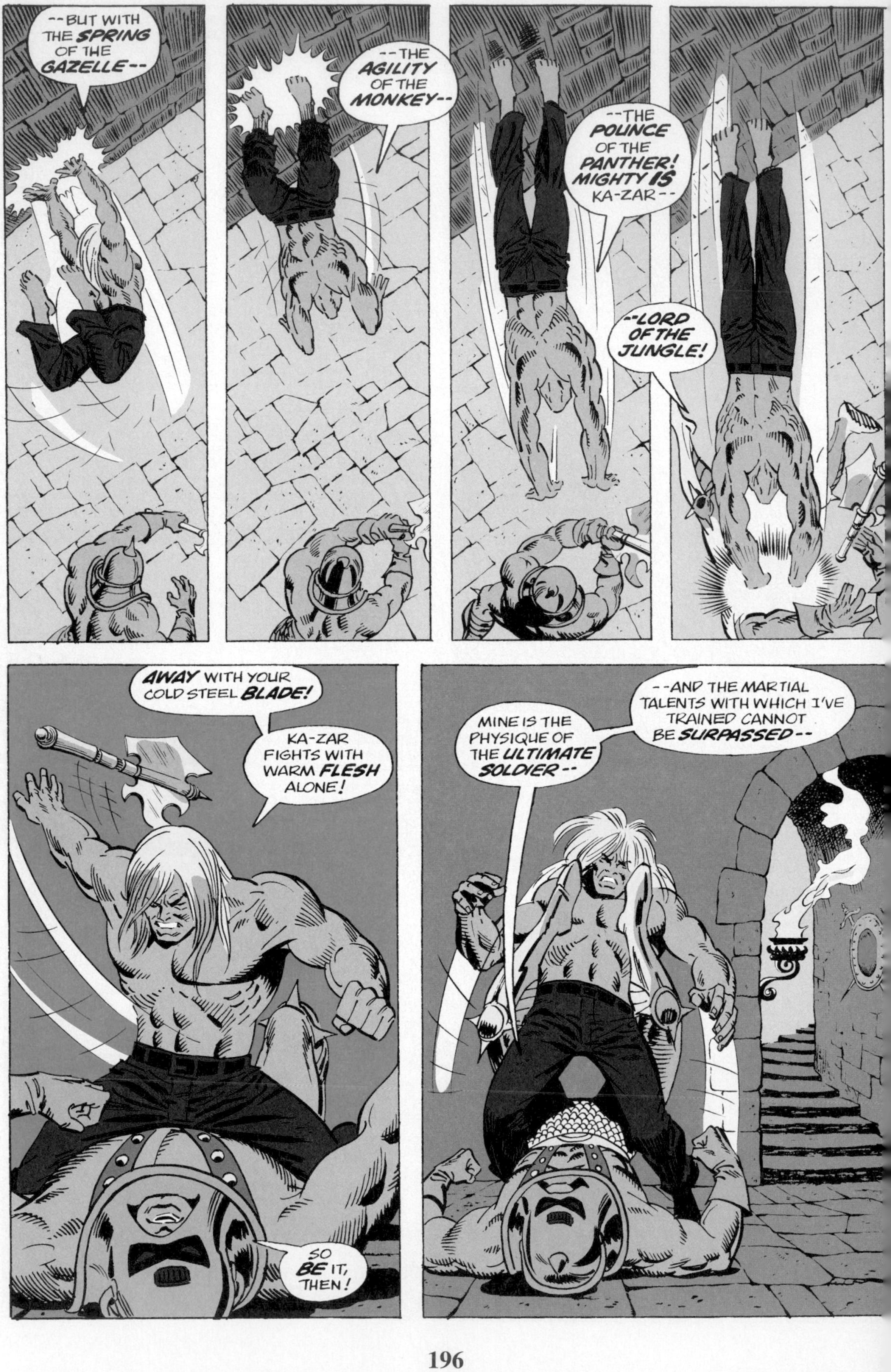
--BUT WITH THE SPRING OF THE GAZELLE--
--THE AGILITY OF THE MONKEY--
--THE POUNCE OF THE PANTHER! MIGHTY IS KA-ZAR--
--LORD OF THE JUNGLE!
AWAY WITH YOUR COLD STEEL BLADE!
KA-ZAR FIGHTS WITH WARM FLESH ALONE!
SO BE IT, THEN!
MINE IS THE PHYSIQUE OF THE ULTIMATE SOLDIER--
--AND THE MARTIAL TALENTS WITH WHICH I'VE TRAINED CANNOT BE SURPASSED--

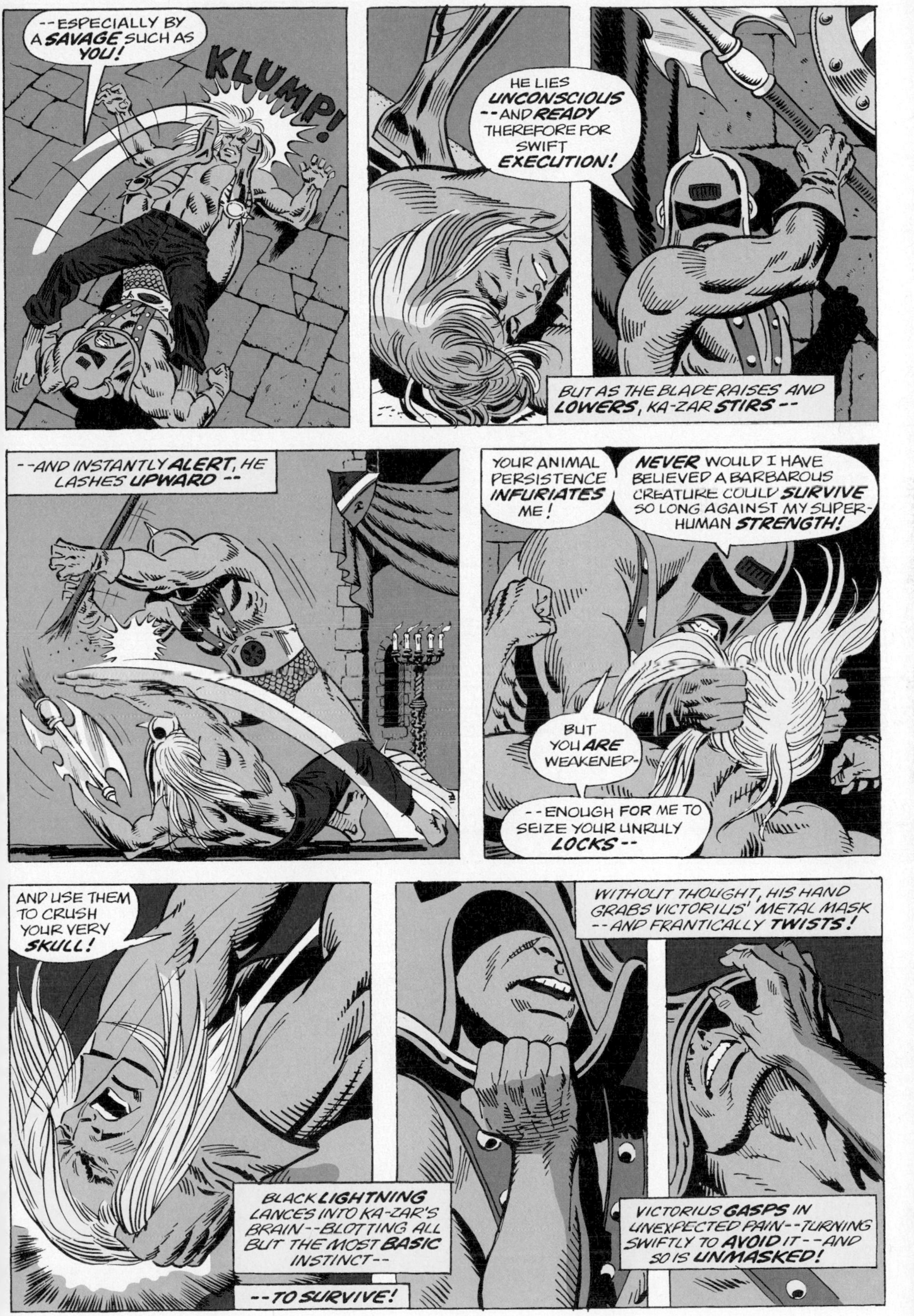
--ESPECIALLY BY A SAVAGE SUCH AS YOU!
KLUMP!
HE LIES UNCONSCIOUS --AND READY THEREFORE FOR SWIFT EXECUTION!
BUT AS THE BLADE RAISES AND LOWERS, KA-ZAR STIRS--
--AND INSTANTLY ALERT, HE LASHES UPWARD--
YOUR ANIMAL PERSISTENCE INFURIATES ME!
NEVER WOULD I HAVE BELIEVED A BARBAROUS CREATURE COULD SURVIVE SO LONG AGAINST MY SUPER-HUMAN STRENGTH!
BUT YOU ARE WEAKENED-
--ENOUGH FOR ME TO SEIZE YOUR UNRULY LOCKS--
AND USE THEM TO CRUSH YOUR VERY SKULL!
BLACK LIGHTNING LANCES INTO KA-ZAR'S BRAIN--BLOTTING ALL BUT THE MOST BASIC INSTINCT--
--TO SURVIVE!
WITHOUT THOUGHT, HIS HAND GRABS VICTORIUS' METAL MASK --AND FRANTICALLY TWISTS!
VICTORIUS GASPS IN UNEXPECTED PAIN--TURNING SWIFTLY TO AVOID IT--AND SO IS UNMASKED!

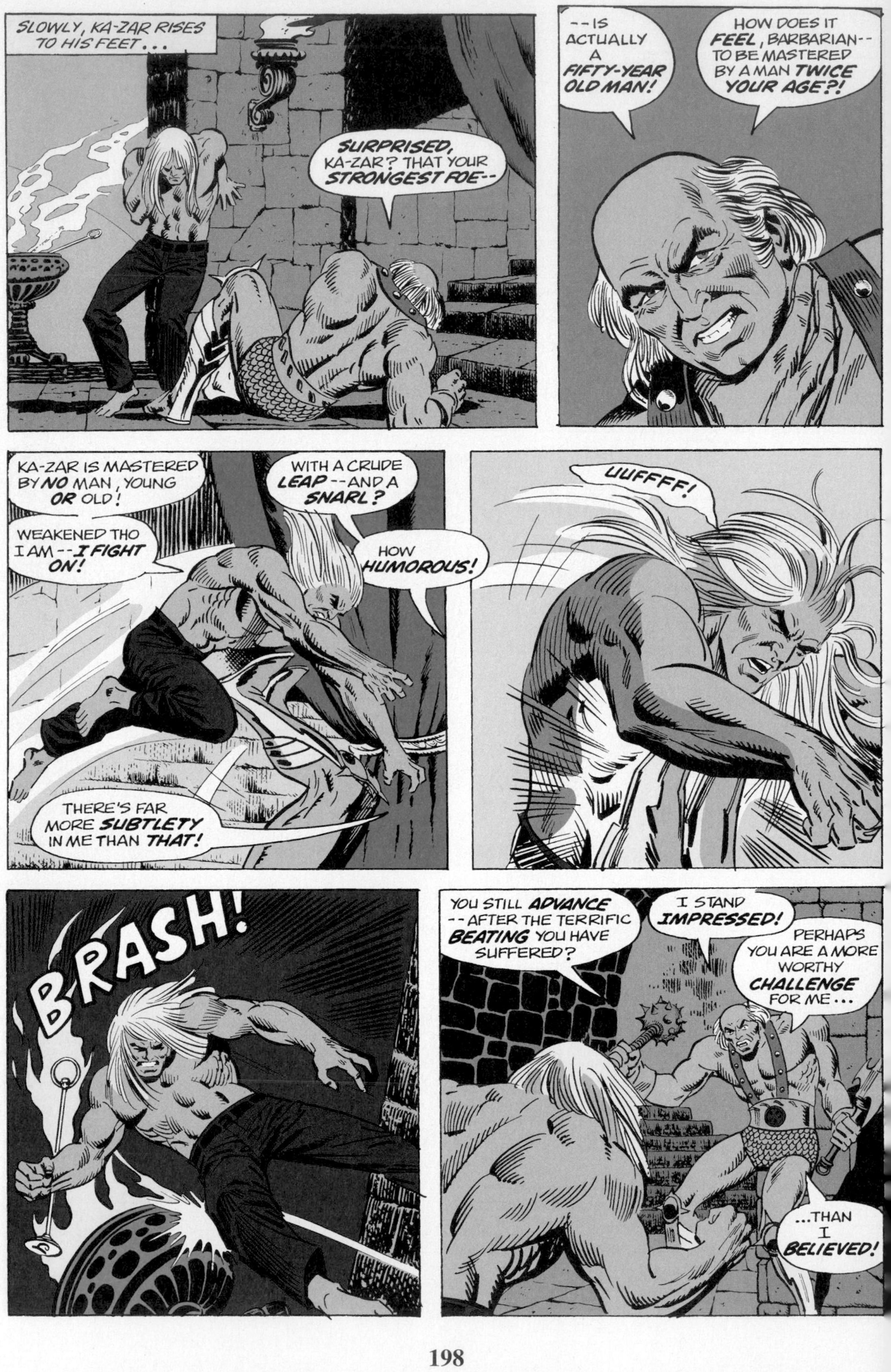

SLOWLY, KA-ZAR RISES TO HIS FEET...
SURPRISED, KA-ZAR? THAT YOUR STRONGEST FOE--
--IS ACTUALLY A FIFTY-YEAR OLD MAN!
HOW DOES IT FEEL, BARBARIAN--TO BE MASTERED BY A MAN TWICE YOUR AGE?!
KA-ZAR IS MASTERED BY NO MAN, YOUNG OR OLD!
WEAKENED THO I AM--I FIGHT ON!
WITH A CRUDE LEAP--AND A SNARL?
HOW HUMOROUS!
THERE'S FAR MORE SUBTLETY IN ME THAN THAT!
UUFFFF!
BRASH!
YOU STILL ADVANCE--AFTER THE TERRIFIC BEATING YOU HAVE SUFFERED?
I STAND IMPRESSED!
PERHAPS YOU ARE A MORE WORTHY CHALLENGE FOR ME...
...THAN I BELIEVED!

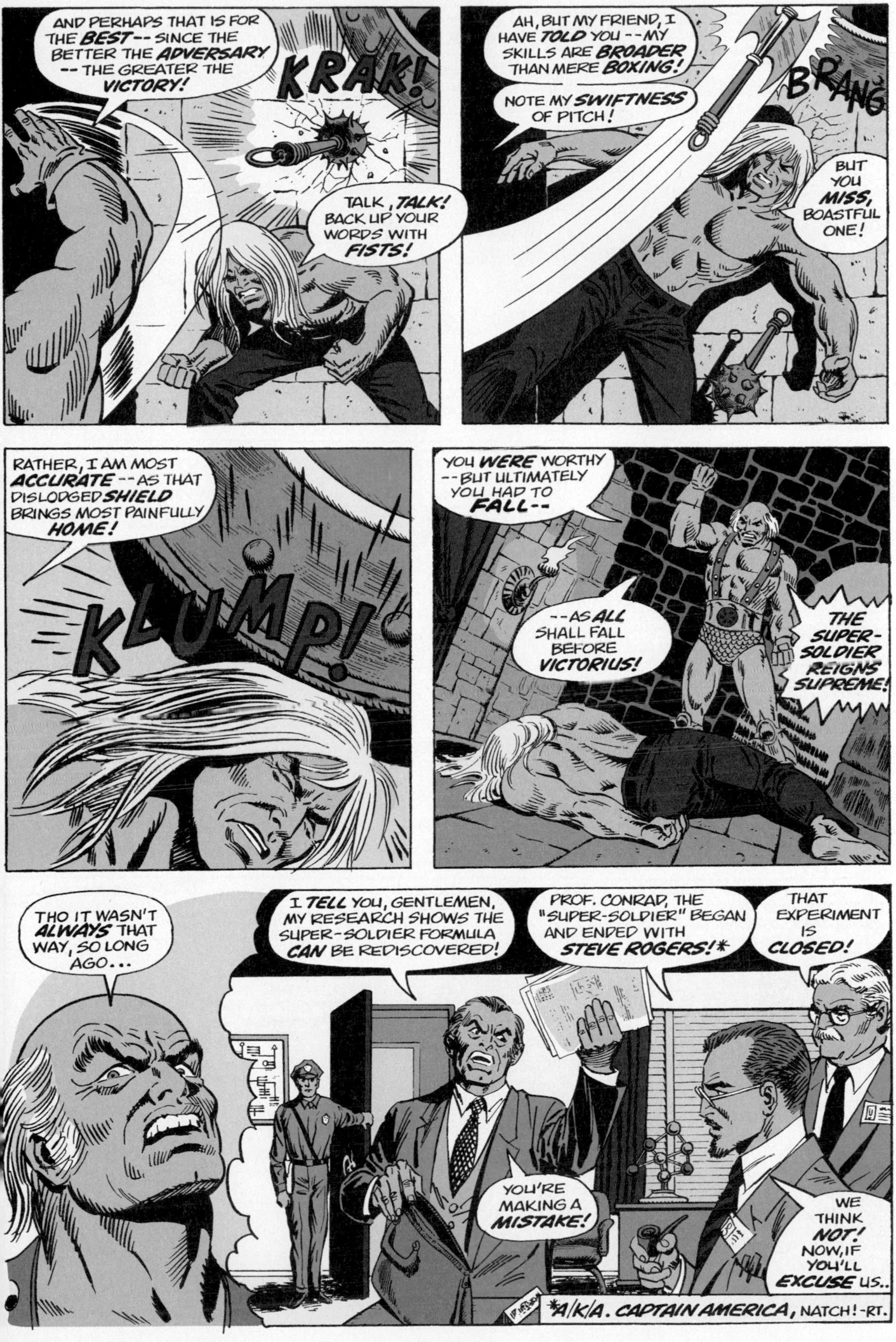
AND PERHAPS THAT IS FOR THE BEST -- SINCE THE BETTER THE ADVERSARY -- THE GREATER THE VICTORY!
KRAK!
TALK, TALK! BACK UP YOUR WORDS WITH FISTS!
AH, BUT MY FRIEND, I HAVE TOLD YOU -- MY SKILLS ARE BROADER THAN MERE BOXING!
NOTE MY SWIFTNESS OF PITCH!
BRANG
BUT YOU MISS, BOASTFUL ONE!
RATHER, I AM MOST ACCURATE -- AS THAT DISLODGED SHIELD BRINGS MOST PAINFULLY HOME!
KLUMP!
YOU WERE WORTHY -- BUT ULTIMATELY YOU HAD TO FALL--
--AS ALL SHALL FALL BEFORE VICTORIUS!
THE SUPER-SOLDIER REIGNS SUPREME!
THO IT WASN'T ALWAYS THAT WAY, SO LONG AGO...
I TELL YOU, GENTLEMEN, MY RESEARCH SHOWS THE SUPER-SOLDIER FORMULA CAN BE REDISCOVERED!
PROF. CONRAD, THE "SUPER-SOLDIER" BEGAN AND ENDED WITH STEVE ROGERS!*
THAT EXPERIMENT IS CLOSED!
YOU'RE MAKING A MISTAKE!
WE THINK NOT! NOW, IF YOU'LL EXCUSE US..
*A/K/A. CAPTAIN AMERICA, NATCH! -RT.

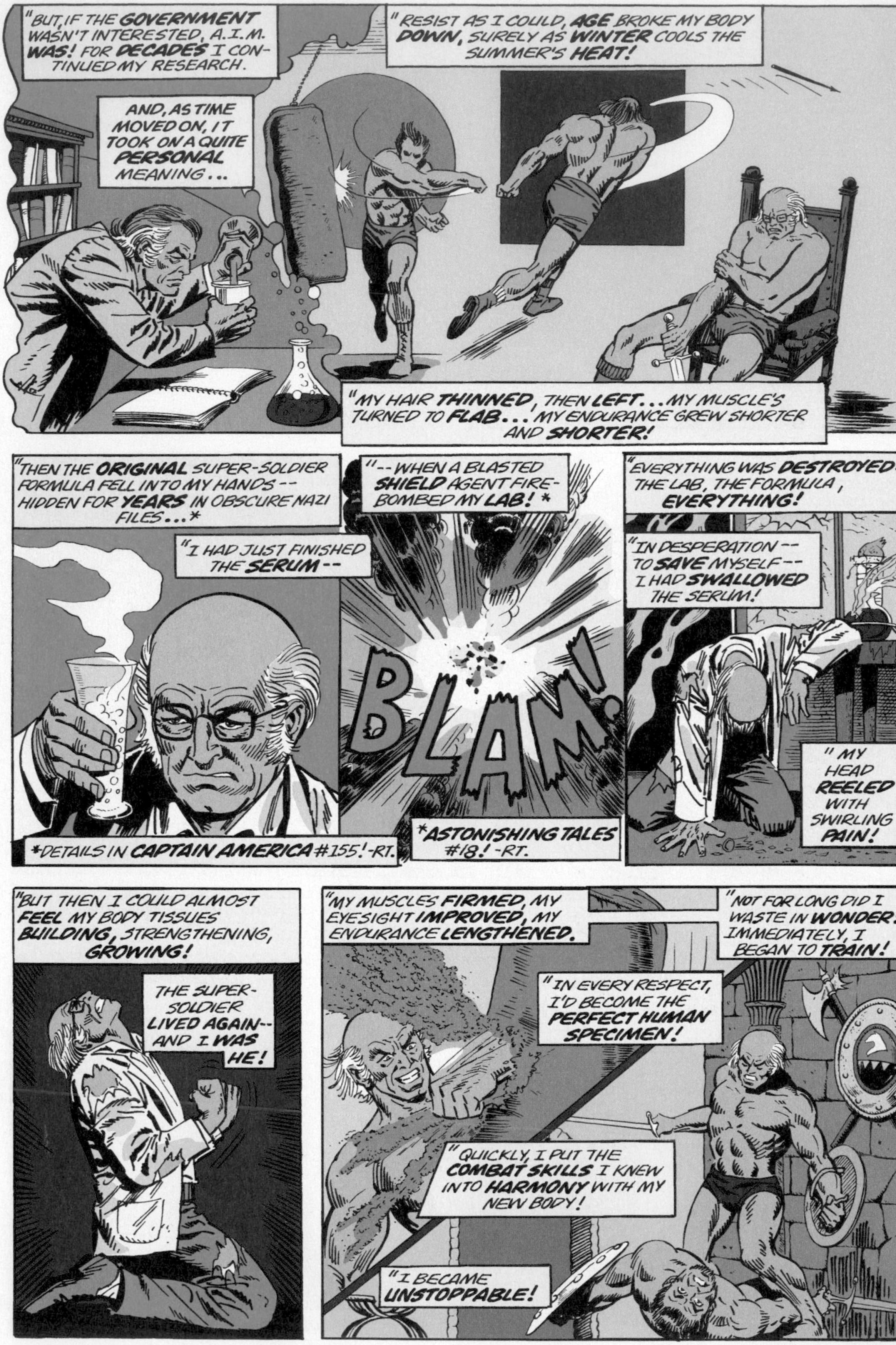
"BUT, IF THE GOVERNMENT WASN'T INTERESTED, A.I.M. WAS! FOR DECADES I CONTINUED MY RESEARCH.
AND, AS TIME MOVED ON, IT TOOK ON A QUITE PERSONAL MEANING...
"RESIST AS I COULD, AGE BROKE MY BODY DOWN, SURELY AS WINTER COOLS THE SUMMER'S HEAT!
"MY HAIR THINNED, THEN LEFT... MY MUSCLE'S TURNED TO FLAB... MY ENDURANCE GREW SHORTER AND SHORTER!
"THEN THE ORIGINAL SUPER-SOLDIER FORMULA FELL INTO MY HANDS -- HIDDEN FOR YEARS IN OBSCURE NAZI FILES...*
"I HAD JUST FINISHED THE SERUM --
*DETAILS IN CAPTAIN AMERICA #155! -RT.
"-- WHEN A BLASTED SHIELD AGENT FIRE-BOMBED MY LAB! *
BLAM!
*ASTONISHING TALES #18! -RT.
"EVERYTHING WAS DESTROYED: THE LAB, THE FORMULA, EVERYTHING!
"IN DESPERATION -- TO SAVE MYSELF -- I HAD SWALLOWED THE SERUM!
"MY HEAD REELED WITH SWIRLING PAIN!
"BUT THEN I COULD ALMOST FEEL MY BODY TISSUES BUILDING, STRENGTHENING, GROWING!
THE SUPER-SOLDIER LIVED AGAIN-- AND I WAS HE!
"MY MUSCLES FIRMED, MY EYESIGHT IMPROVED, MY ENDURANCE LENGTHENED.
"IN EVERY RESPECT, I'D BECOME THE PERFECT HUMAN SPECIMEN!
"NOT FOR LONG DID I WASTE IN WONDER! IMMEDIATELY, I BEGAN TO TRAIN!
"QUICKLY, I PUT THE COMBAT SKILLS I KNEW INTO HARMONY WITH MY NEW BODY!
"I BECAME UNSTOPPABLE!

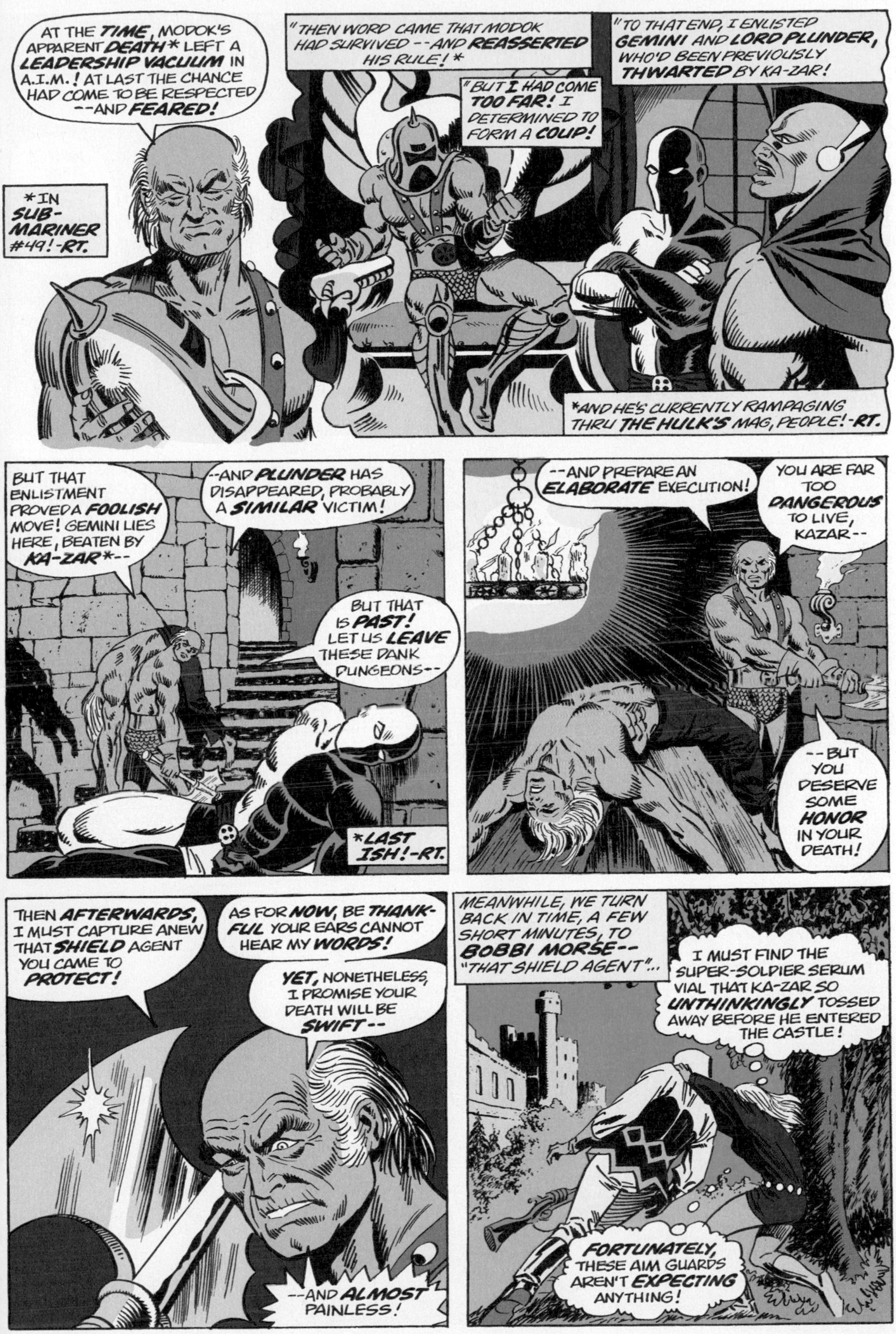
AT THE TIME, MODOK'S APPARENT DEATH* LEFT A LEADERSHIP VACUUM IN A.I.M.! AT LAST THE CHANCE HAD COME TO BE RESPECTED --AND FEARED!
*IN SUB-MARINER #49! -RT.
"THEN WORD CAME THAT MODOK HAD SURVIVED --AND REASSERTED HIS RULE! *
"BUT I HAD COME TOO FAR! I DETERMINED TO FORM A COUP!
"TO THAT END, I ENLISTED GEMINI AND LORD PLUNDER, WHO'D BEEN PREVIOUSLY THWARTED BY KA-ZAR!
*AND HE'S CURRENTLY RAMPAGING THRU THE HULK'S MAG, PEOPLE! -RT.
BUT THAT ENLISTMENT PROVED A FOOLISH MOVE! GEMINI LIES HERE, BEATEN BY KA-ZAR*--
--AND PLUNDER HAS DISAPPEARED, PROBABLY A SIMILAR VICTIM!
BUT THAT IS PAST! LET US LEAVE THESE DANK DUNGEONS--
*LAST ISH! -RT.
--AND PREPARE AN ELABORATE EXECUTION!
YOU ARE FAR TOO DANGEROUS TO LIVE, KAZAR--
--BUT YOU DESERVE SOME HONOR IN YOUR DEATH!
THEN AFTERWARDS, I MUST CAPTURE ANEW THAT SHIELD AGENT YOU CAME TO PROTECT!
AS FOR NOW, BE THANKFUL YOUR EARS CANNOT HEAR MY WORDS!
YET, NONETHELESS, I PROMISE YOUR DEATH WILL BE SWIFT--
--AND ALMOST PAINLESS!
MEANWHILE, WE TURN BACK IN TIME, A FEW SHORT MINUTES, TO BOBBI MORSE-- "THAT SHIELD AGENT"...
I MUST FIND THE SUPER-SOLDIER SERUM VIAL THAT KA-ZAR SO UNTHINKINGLY TOSSED AWAY BEFORE HE ENTERED THE CASTLE!
FORTUNATELY, THESE AIM GUARDS AREN'T EXPECTING ANYTHING!

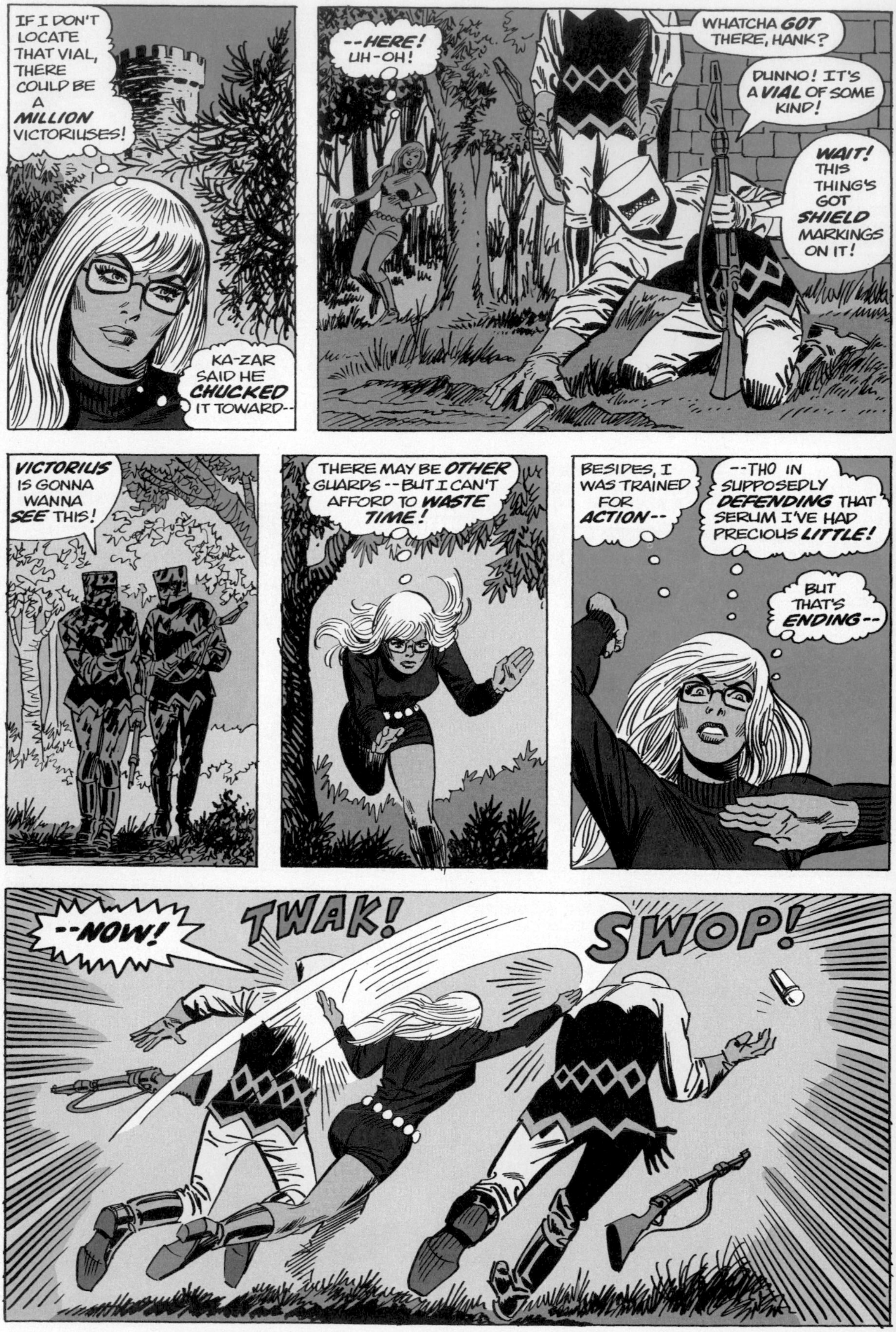
IF I DON'T LOCATE THAT VIAL, THERE COULD BE A MILLION VICTORIUSES!
KA-ZAR SAID HE CHUCKED IT TOWARD--
--HERE! UH-OH!
WHATCHA GOT THERE, HANK?
DUNNO! IT'S A VIAL OF SOME KIND!
WAIT! THIS THING'S GOT SHIELD MARKINGS ON IT!
VICTORIUS IS GONNA WANNA SEE THIS!
THERE MAY BE OTHER GUARDS--BUT I CAN'T AFFORD TO WASTE TIME!
BESIDES, I WAS TRAINED FOR ACTION--
--THO IN SUPPOSEDLY DEFENDING THAT SERUM I'VE HAD PRECIOUS LITTLE!
BUT THAT'S ENDING--
--NOW!
TWAK!
SWOP!

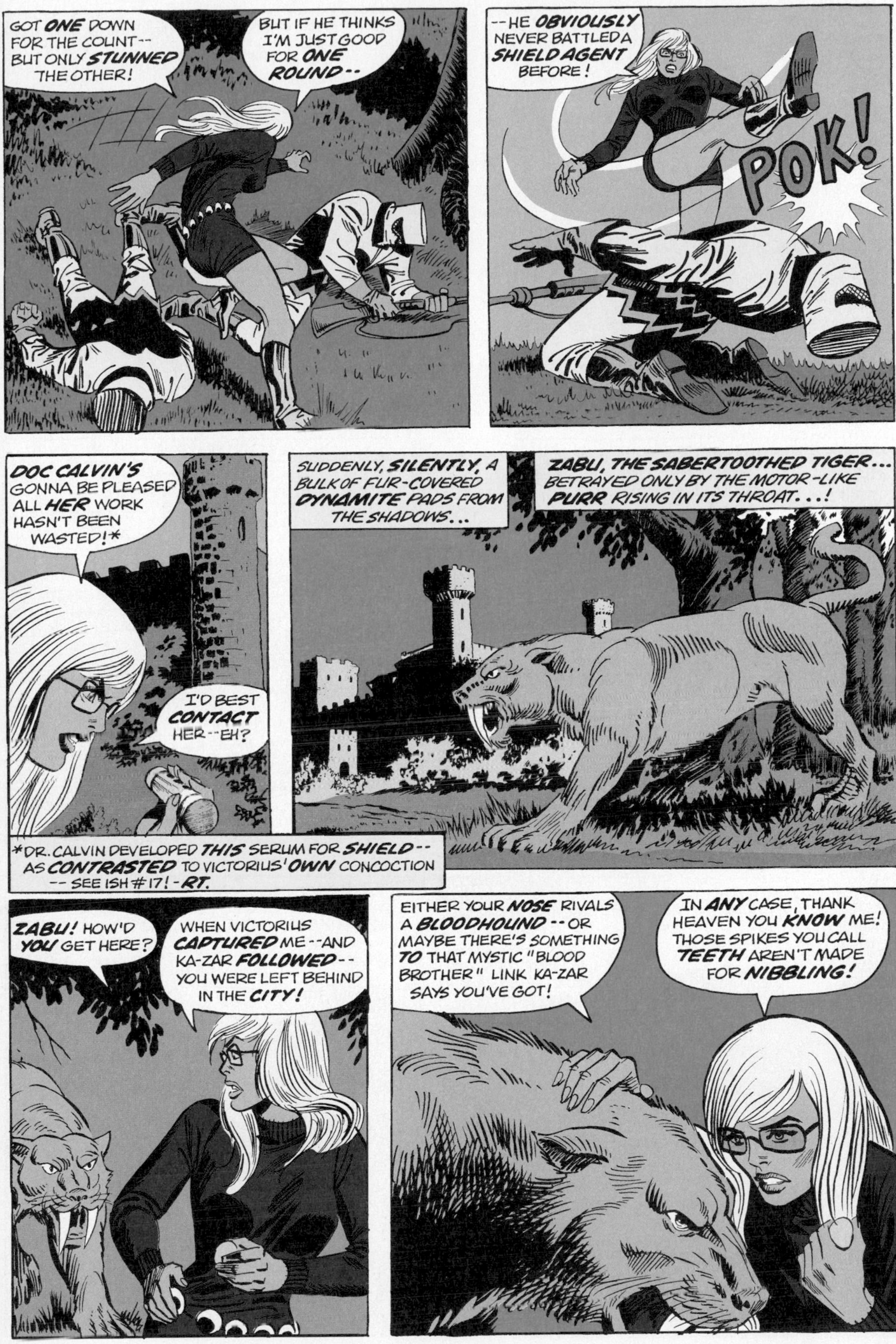
GOT ONE DOWN FOR THE COUNT-- BUT ONLY STUNNED THE OTHER!
BUT IF HE THINKS I'M JUST GOOD FOR ONE ROUND--
--HE OBVIOUSLY NEVER BATTLED A SHIELD AGENT BEFORE!
POK!
DOC CALVIN'S GONNA BE PLEASED ALL HER WORK HASN'T BEEN WASTED!*
I'D BEST CONTACT HER--EH?
SUDDENLY, SILENTLY, A BULK OF FUR-COVERED DYNAMITE PADS FROM THE SHADOWS...
ZABU, THE SABERTOOTHED TIGER... BETRAYED ONLY BY THE MOTOR-LIKE PURR RISING IN ITS THROAT...!
*DR. CALVIN DEVELOPED THIS SERUM FOR SHIELD-- AS CONTRASTED TO VICTORIUS' OWN CONCOCTION -- SEE ISH #17! -RT.
ZABU! HOW'D YOU GET HERE?
WHEN VICTORIUS CAPTURED ME--AND KA-ZAR FOLLOWED-- YOU WERE LEFT BEHIND IN THE CITY!
EITHER YOUR NOSE RIVALS A BLOODHOUND--OR MAYBE THERE'S SOMETHING TO THAT MYSTIC "BLOOD BROTHER" LINK KA-ZAR SAYS YOU'VE GOT!
IN ANY CASE, THANK HEAVEN YOU KNOW ME! THOSE SPIKES YOU CALL TEETH AREN'T MADE FOR NIBBLING!

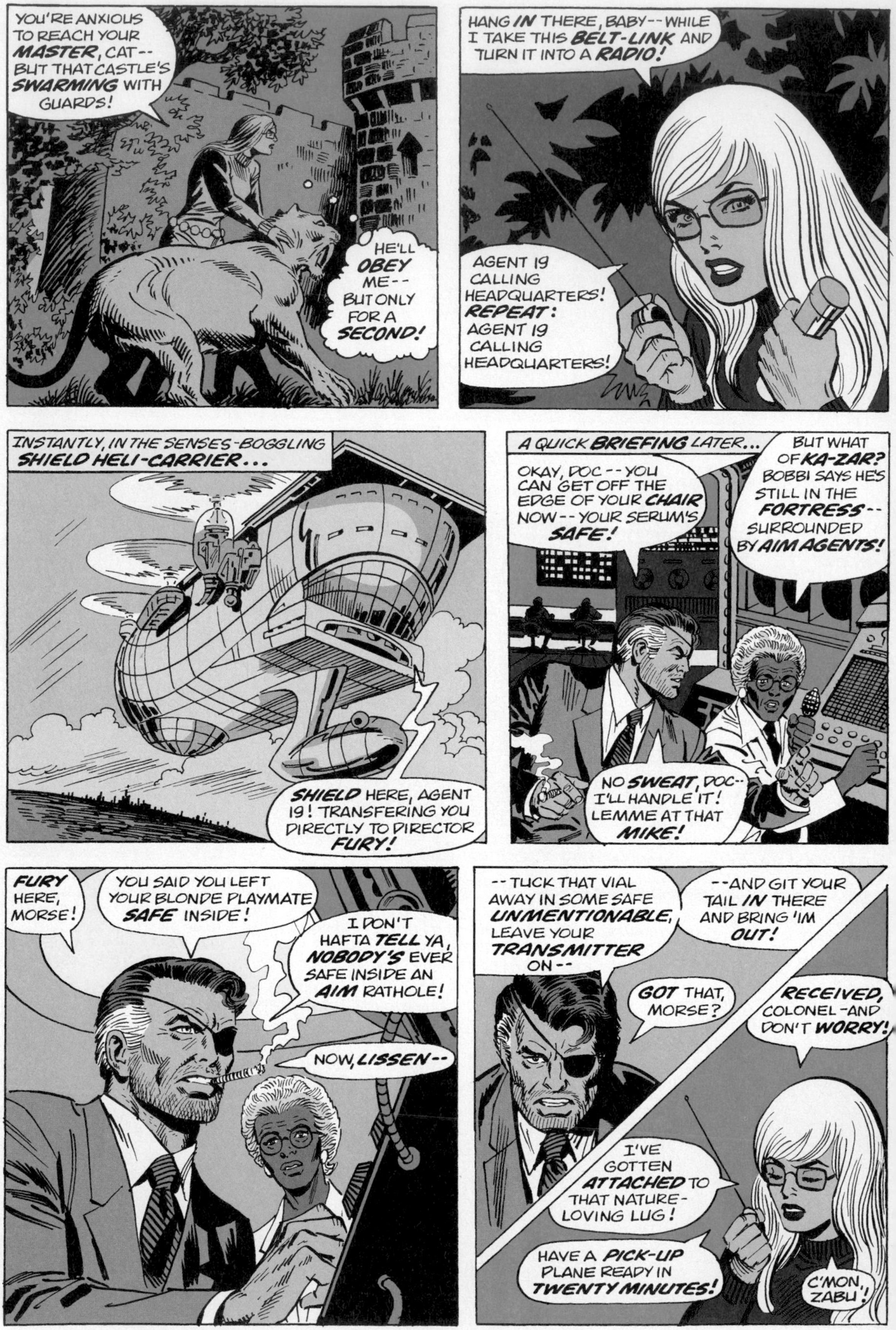
YOU'RE ANXIOUS TO REACH YOUR MASTER, CAT-- BUT THAT CASTLE'S SWARMING WITH GUARDS!
HE'LL OBEY ME-- BUT ONLY FOR A SECOND!
HANG IN THERE, BABY-- WHILE I TAKE THIS BELT-LINK AND TURN IT INTO A RADIO!
AGENT 19 CALLING HEADQUARTERS! REPEAT: AGENT 19 CALLING HEADQUARTERS!
INSTANTLY, IN THE SENSES-BOGGLING SHIELD HELI-CARRIER...
SHIELD HERE, AGENT 19! TRANSFERING YOU DIRECTLY TO DIRECTOR FURY!
A QUICK BRIEFING LATER...
OKAY, DOC--YOU CAN GET OFF THE EDGE OF YOUR CHAIR NOW--YOUR SERUM'S SAFE!
BUT WHAT OF KA-ZAR? BOBBI SAYS HE'S STILL IN THE FORTRESS-- SURROUNDED BY AIM AGENTS!
NO SWEAT, DOC-- I'LL HANDLE IT! LEMME AT THAT MIKE!
FURY HERE, MORSE!
YOU SAID YOU LEFT YOUR BLONDE PLAYMATE SAFE INSIDE!
I DON'T HAFTA TELL YA, NOBODY'S EVER SAFE INSIDE AN AIM RATHOLE!
NOW, LISSEN--
--TUCK THAT VIAL AWAY IN SOME SAFE UNMENTIONABLE, LEAVE YOUR TRANSMITTER ON--
--AND GIT YOUR TAIL IN THERE AND BRING 'IM OUT!
GOT THAT, MORSE?
RECEIVED, COLONEL -AND DON'T WORRY!
I'VE GOTTEN ATTACHED TO THAT NATURE-LOVING LUG!
HAVE A PICK-UP PLANE READY IN TWENTY MINUTES!
C'MON, ZABU!

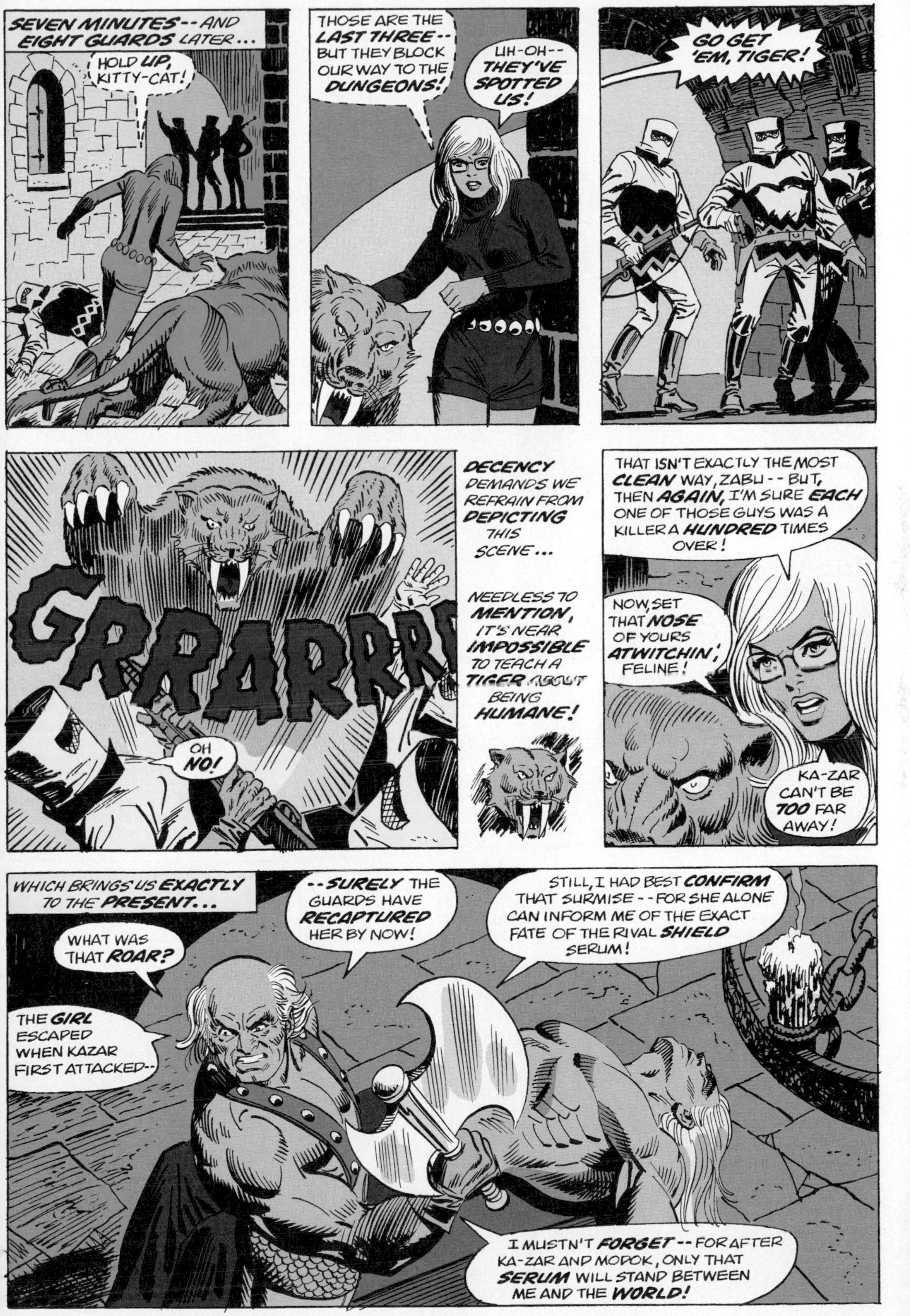
SEVEN MINUTES--AND EIGHT GUARDS LATER...
HOLD UP, KITTY-CAT!
THOSE ARE THE LAST THREE--BUT THEY BLOCK OUR WAY TO THE DUNGEONS!
UH-OH--THEY'VE SPOTTED US!
GO GET 'EM, TIGER!
GRRARRRR
OH NO!
DECENCY DEMANDS WE REFRAIN FROM DEPICTING THIS SCENE...
NEEDLESS TO MENTION, IT'S NEAR IMPOSSIBLE TO TEACH A TIGER ABOUT BEING HUMANE!
THAT ISN'T EXACTLY THE MOST CLEAN WAY, ZABU--BUT, THEN AGAIN, I'M SURE EACH ONE OF THOSE GUYS WAS A KILLER A HUNDRED TIMES OVER!
NOW, SET THAT NOSE OF YOURS ATWITCHIN', FELINE!
KA-ZAR CAN'T BE TOO FAR AWAY!
WHICH BRINGS US EXACTLY TO THE PRESENT...
WHAT WAS THAT ROAR?
--SURELY THE GUARDS HAVE RECAPTURED HER BY NOW!
STILL, I HAD BEST CONFIRM THAT SURMISE--FOR SHE ALONE CAN INFORM ME OF THE EXACT FATE OF THE RIVAL SHIELD SERUM!
THE GIRL ESCAPED WHEN KAZAR FIRST ATTACKED--
I MUSTN'T FORGET--FOR AFTER KA-ZAR AND MODOK, ONLY THAT SERUM WILL STAND BETWEEN ME AND THE WORLD!

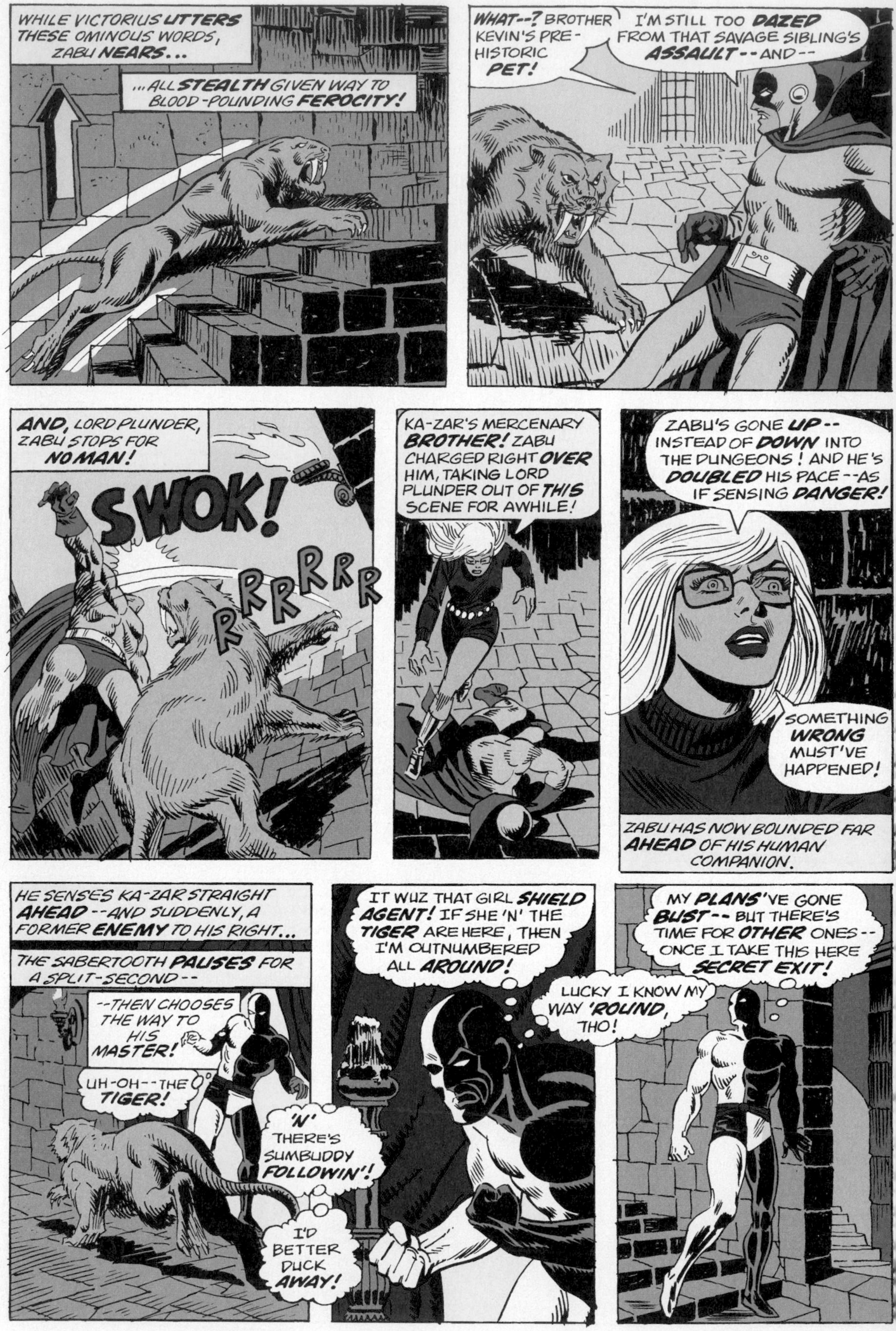
WHILE VICTORIUS UTTERS THESE OMINOUS WORDS, ZABU NEARS...
...ALL STEALTH GIVEN WAY TO BLOOD-POUNDING FEROCITY!
WHAT--? BROTHER KEVIN'S PRE-HISTORIC PET!
I'M STILL TOO DAZED FROM THAT SAVAGE SIBLING'S ASSAULT--AND--
AND, LORD PLUNDER, ZABU STOPS FOR NO MAN!
SWOK!
RRRRRRR
KA-ZAR'S MERCENARY BROTHER! ZABU CHARGED RIGHT OVER HIM, TAKING LORD PLUNDER OUT OF THIS SCENE FOR AWHILE!
ZABU'S GONE UP-- INSTEAD OF DOWN INTO THE DUNGEONS! AND HE'S DOUBLED HIS PACE--AS IF SENSING DANGER!
SOMETHING WRONG MUST'VE HAPPENED!
ZABU HAS NOW BOUNDED FAR AHEAD OF HIS HUMAN COMPANION.
HE SENSES KA-ZAR STRAIGHT AHEAD--AND SUDDENLY, A FORMER ENEMY TO HIS RIGHT...
THE SABERTOOTH PAUSES FOR A SPLIT-SECOND--
--THEN CHOOSES THE WAY TO HIS MASTER!
UH-OH--THE TIGER!
'N' THERE'S SUMBUDDY FOLLOWIN'!
I'D BETTER DUCK AWAY!
IT WUZ THAT GIRL SHIELD AGENT! IF SHE 'N' THE TIGER ARE HERE, THEN I'M OUTNUMBERED ALL AROUND!
LUCKY I KNOW MY WAY 'ROUND, THO!
MY PLANS'VE GONE BUST-- BUT THERE'S TIME FOR OTHER ONES-- ONCE I TAKE THIS HERE SECRET EXIT!

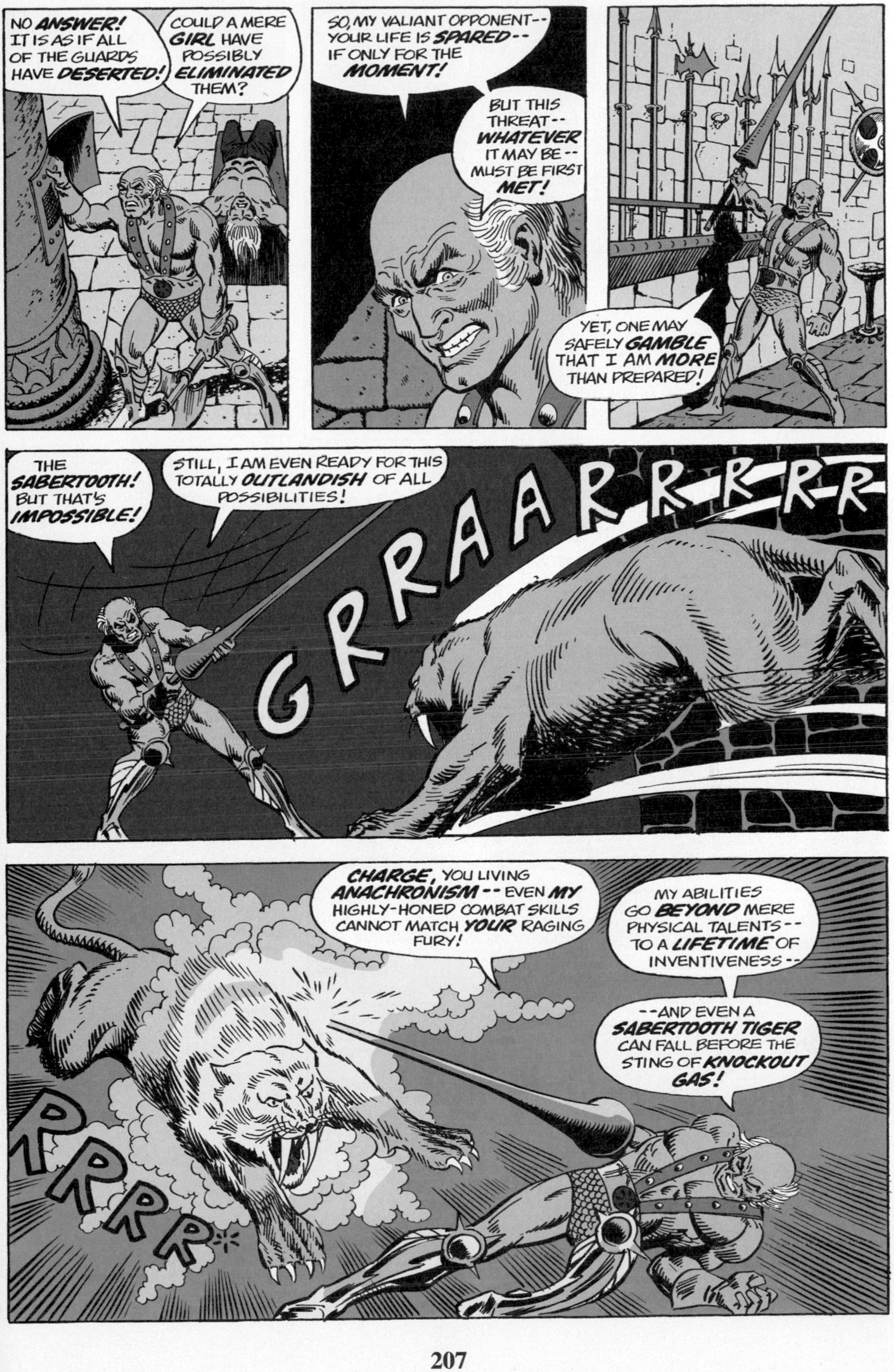
NO ANSWER! IT IS AS IF ALL OF THE GUARDS HAVE DESERTED!
COULD A MERE GIRL HAVE POSSIBLY ELIMINATED THEM?
SO, MY VALIANT OPPONENT-- YOUR LIFE IS SPARED-- IF ONLY FOR THE MOMENT!
BUT THIS THREAT-- WHATEVER IT MAY BE-- MUST BE FIRST MET!
YET, ONE MAY SAFELY GAMBLE THAT I AM MORE THAN PREPARED!
THE SABERTOOTH! BUT THAT'S IMPOSSIBLE!
STILL, I AM EVEN READY FOR THIS TOTALLY OUTLANDISH OF ALL POSSIBILITIES!
GRRAARRRRR
CHARGE, YOU LIVING ANACHRONISM-- EVEN MY HIGHLY-HONED COMBAT SKILLS CANNOT MATCH YOUR RAGING FURY!
MY ABILITIES GO BEYOND MERE PHYSICAL TALENTS-- TO A LIFETIME OF INVENTIVENESS--
--AND EVEN A SABERTOOTH TIGER CAN FALL BEFORE THE STING OF KNOCKOUT GAS!
RRRR

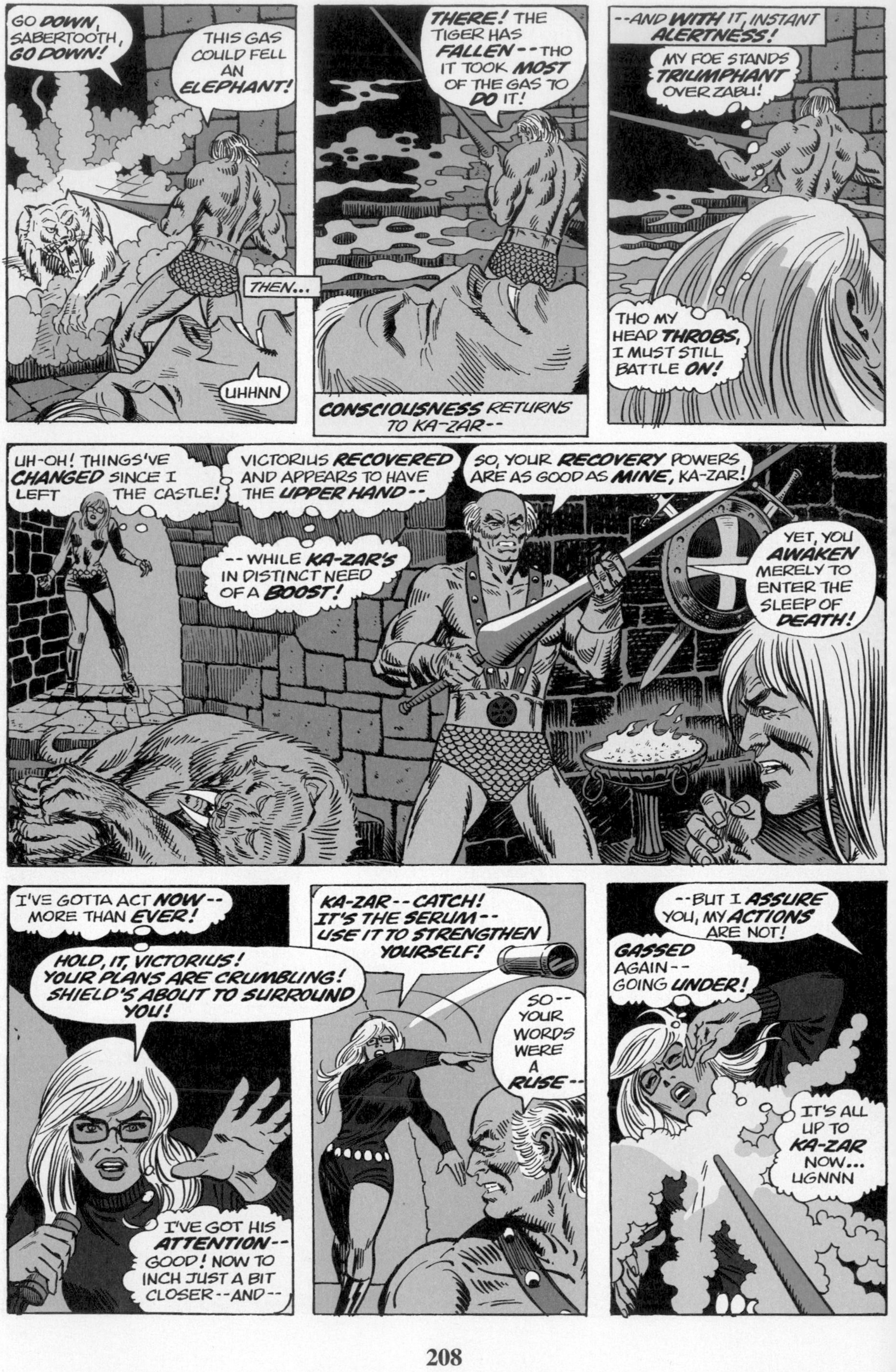

GO DOWN, SABERTOOTH, GO DOWN!
THIS GAS COULD FELL AN ELEPHANT!
THEN...
UHHNN
THERE! THE TIGER HAS FALLEN--THO IT TOOK MOST OF THE GAS TO DO IT!
CONSCIOUSNESS RETURNS TO KA-ZAR--
--AND WITH IT, INSTANT ALERTNESS!
MY FOE STANDS TRIUMPHANT OVER ZABU!
THO MY HEAD THROBS, I MUST STILL BATTLE ON!
UH-OH! THINGS'VE CHANGED SINCE I LEFT THE CASTLE!
VICTORIUS RECOVERED AND APPEARS TO HAVE THE UPPER HAND--
--WHILE KA-ZAR'S IN DISTINCT NEED OF A BOOST!
SO, YOUR RECOVERY POWERS ARE AS GOOD AS MINE, KA-ZAR!
YET, YOU AWAKEN MERELY TO ENTER THE SLEEP OF DEATH!
I'VE GOTTA ACT NOW--MORE THAN EVER!
HOLD, IT, VICTORIUS! YOUR PLANS ARE CRUMBLING! SHIELD'S ABOUT TO SURROUND YOU!
I'VE GOT HIS ATTENTION--GOOD! NOW TO INCH JUST A BIT CLOSER--AND--
KA-ZAR--CATCH! IT'S THE SERUM--USE IT TO STRENGTHEN YOURSELF!
SO--YOUR WORDS WERE A RUSE--
--BUT I ASSURE YOU, MY ACTIONS ARE NOT!
GASSED AGAIN--GOING UNDER!
IT'S ALL UP TO KA-ZAR NOW... UGNNN

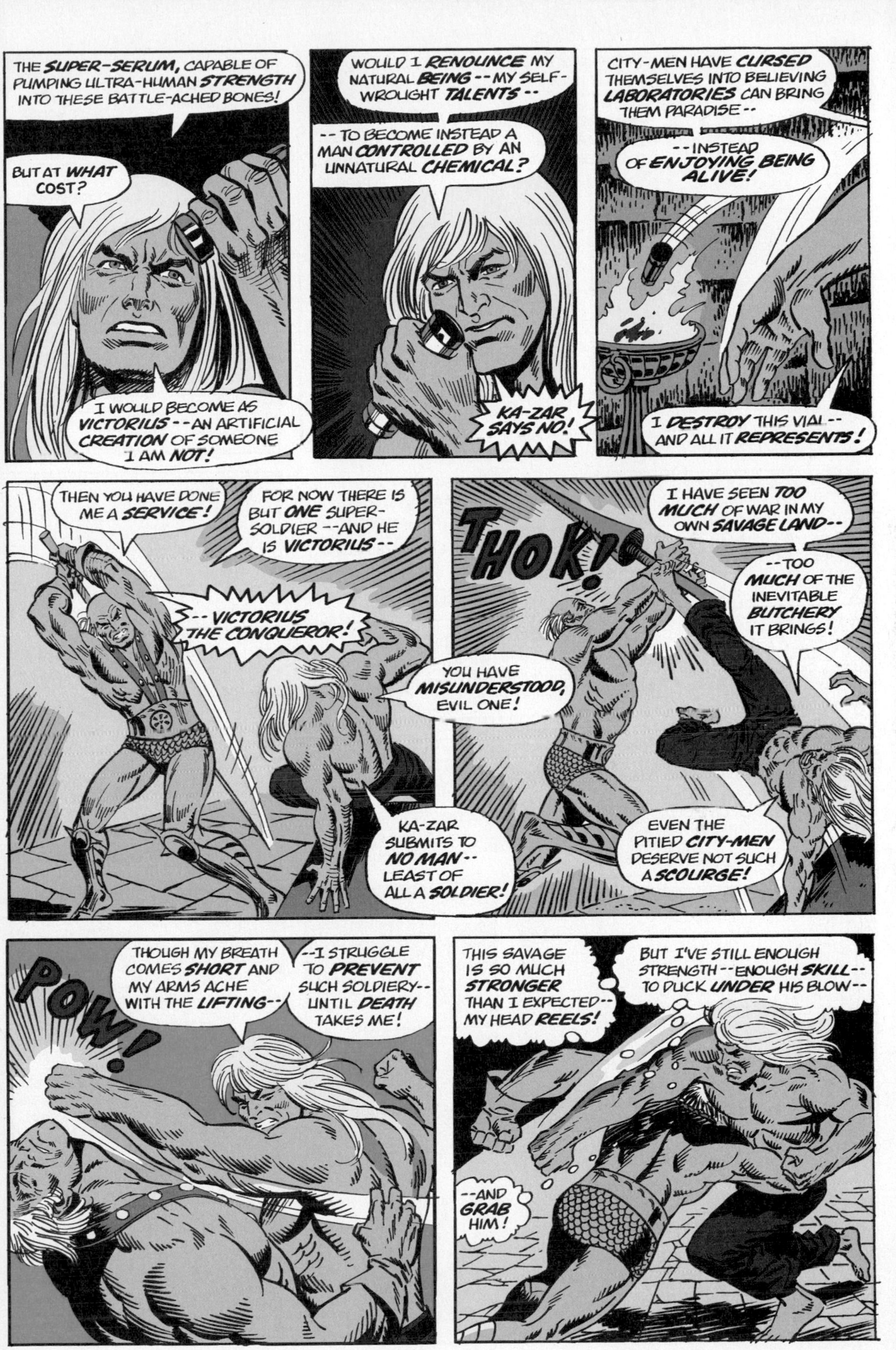
THE SUPER-SERUM, CAPABLE OF PUMPING ULTRA-HUMAN STRENGTH INTO THESE BATTLE-ACHED BONES!
BUT AT WHAT COST?
I WOULD BECOME AS VICTORIUS--AN ARTIFICIAL CREATION OF SOMEONE I AM NOT!
WOULD I RENOUNCE MY NATURAL BEING--MY SELF-WROUGHT TALENTS--
--TO BECOME INSTEAD A MAN CONTROLLED BY AN UNNATURAL CHEMICAL?
KA-ZAR SAYS NO!
CITY-MEN HAVE CURSED THEMSELVES INTO BELIEVING LABORATORIES CAN BRING THEM PARADISE--
--INSTEAD OF ENJOYING BEING ALIVE!
I DESTROY THIS VIAL--AND ALL IT REPRESENTS!
THEN YOU HAVE DONE ME A SERVICE!
FOR NOW THERE IS BUT ONE SUPER-SOLDIER--AND HE IS VICTORIUS--
--VICTORIUS THE CONQUEROR!
YOU HAVE MISUNDERSTOOD, EVIL ONE!
KA-ZAR SUBMITS TO NO MAN--LEAST OF ALL A SOLDIER!
THOK!
I HAVE SEEN TOO MUCH OF WAR IN MY OWN SAVAGE LAND--
--TOO MUCH OF THE INEVITABLE BUTCHERY IT BRINGS!
EVEN THE PITIED CITY-MEN DESERVE NOT SUCH A SCOURGE!
POW!
THOUGH MY BREATH COMES SHORT AND MY ARMS ACHE WITH THE LIFTING--
--I STRUGGLE TO PREVENT SUCH SOLDIERY--UNTIL DEATH TAKES ME!
THIS SAVAGE IS SO MUCH STRONGER THAN I EXPECTED--MY HEAD REELS!
BUT I'VE STILL ENOUGH STRENGTH--ENOUGH SKILL--TO DUCK UNDER HIS BLOW--
--AND GRAB HIM!

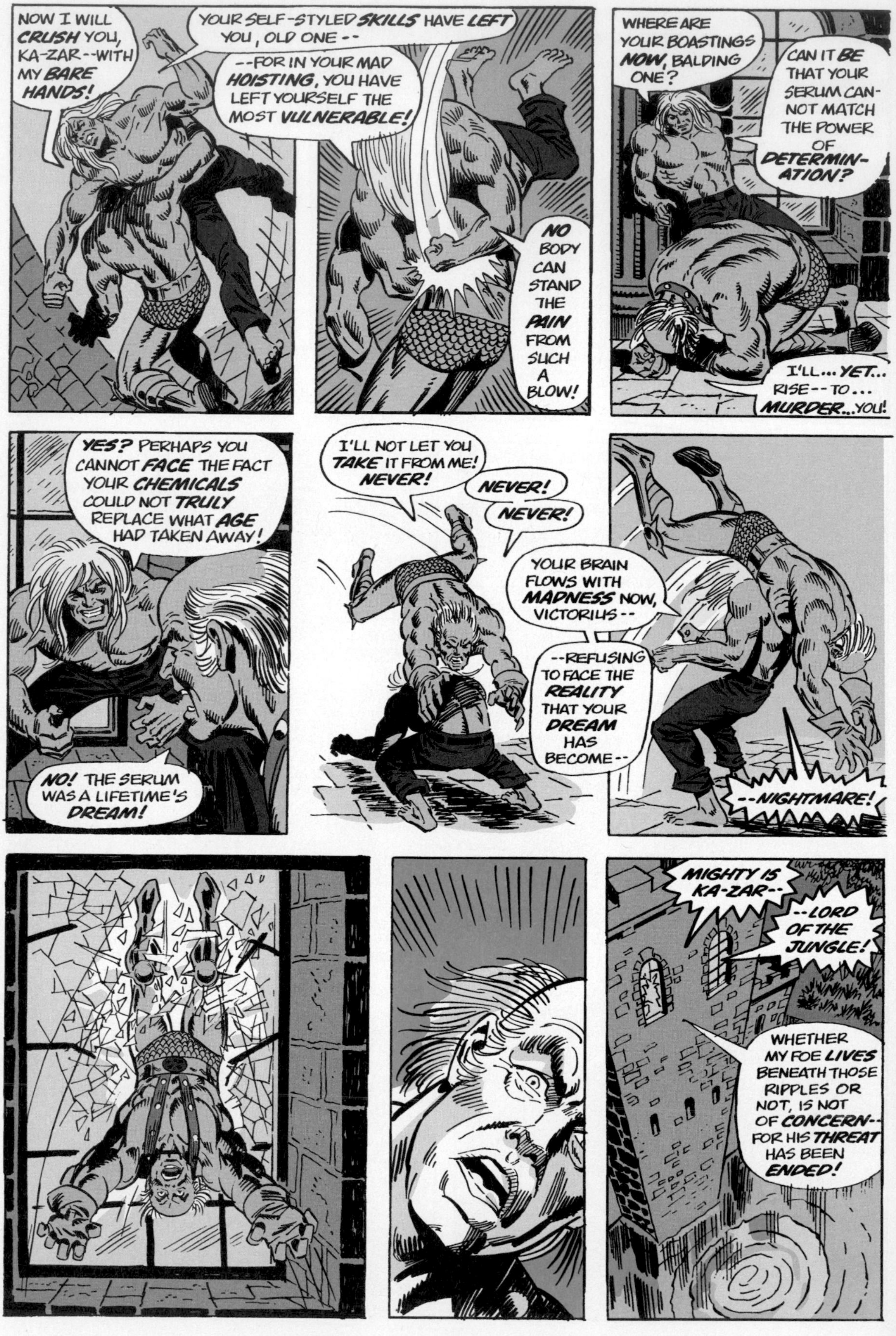
NOW I WILL CRUSH YOU, KA-ZAR--WITH MY BARE HANDS!
YOUR SELF-STYLED SKILLS HAVE LEFT YOU, OLD ONE--
--FOR IN YOUR MAD HOISTING, YOU HAVE LEFT YOURSELF THE MOST VULNERABLE!
NO BODY CAN STAND THE PAIN FROM SUCH A BLOW!
WHERE ARE YOUR BOASTINGS NOW, BALDING ONE?
CAN IT BE THAT YOUR SERUM CANNOT MATCH THE POWER OF DETERMINATION?
I'LL... YET... RISE--TO... MURDER... YOU!
YES? PERHAPS YOU CANNOT FACE THE FACT YOUR CHEMICALS COULD NOT TRULY REPLACE WHAT AGE HAD TAKEN AWAY!
NO! THE SERUM WAS A LIFETIME'S DREAM!
I'LL NOT LET YOU TAKE IT FROM ME! NEVER!
NEVER!
NEVER!
YOUR BRAIN FLOWS WITH MADNESS NOW, VICTORIUS--
--REFUSING TO FACE THE REALITY THAT YOUR DREAM HAS BECOME--
--NIGHTMARE!
MIGHTY IS KA-ZAR--
--LORD OF THE JUNGLE!
WHETHER MY FOE LIVES BENEATH THOSE RIPPLES OR NOT, IS NOT OF CONCERN--FOR HIS THREAT HAS BEEN ENDED!

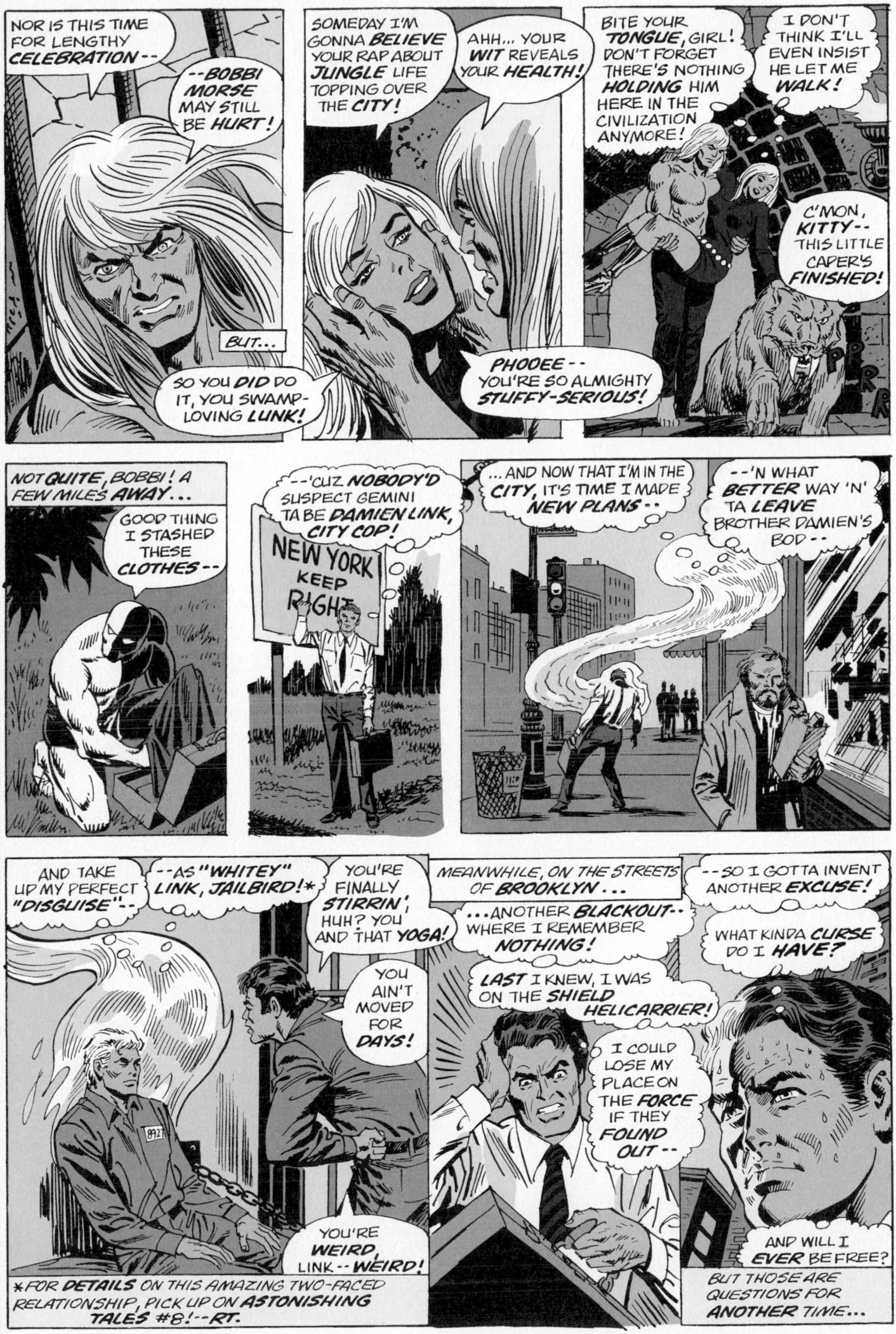

NOR IS THIS TIME FOR LENGTHY CELEBRATION--
--BOBBI MORSE MAY STILL BE HURT!
BUT...
SO YOU DID DO IT, YOU SWAMP-LOVING LUNK!
SOMEDAY I'M GONNA BELIEVE YOUR RAP ABOUT JUNGLE LIFE TOPPING OVER THE CITY!
AHH... YOUR WIT REVEALS YOUR HEALTH!
PHOOEE-- YOU'RE SO ALMIGHTY STUFFY-SERIOUS!
BITE YOUR TONGUE, GIRL! DON'T FORGET THERE'S NOTHING HOLDING HIM HERE IN THE CIVILIZATION ANYMORE!
I DON'T THINK I'LL EVEN INSIST HE LET ME WALK!
C'MON, KITTY-- THIS LITTLE CAPER'S FINISHED!
PRRR
NOT QUITE, BOBBI! A FEW MILES AWAY...
GOOD THING I STASHED THESE CLOTHES--
--'CUZ NOBODY'D SUSPECT GEMINI TA BE DAMIEN LINK, CITY COP!
NEW YORK KEEP RIGHT
...AND NOW THAT I'M IN THE CITY, IT'S TIME I MADE NEW PLANS--
--'N WHAT BETTER WAY 'N' TA LEAVE BROTHER DAMIEN'S BOD--
AND TAKE UP MY PERFECT "DISGUISE"--
--AS "WHITEY" LINK, JAILBIRD!*
YOU'RE FINALLY STIRRIN', HUH? YOU AND THAT YOGA!
YOU AIN'T MOVED FOR DAYS!
YOU'RE WEIRD, LINK--WEIRD!
*FOR DETAILS ON THIS AMAZING TWO-FACED RELATIONSHIP, PICK UP ON ASTONISHING TALES #8!--RT.
MEANWHILE, ON THE STREETS OF BROOKLYN...
...ANOTHER BLACKOUT-- WHERE I REMEMBER NOTHING!
LAST I KNEW, I WAS ON THE SHIELD HELICARRIER!
I COULD LOSE MY PLACE ON THE FORCE IF THEY FOUND OUT--
--SO I GOTTA INVENT ANOTHER EXCUSE!
WHAT KINDA CURSE DO I HAVE?
AND WILL I EVER BE FREE?
BUT THOSE ARE QUESTIONS FOR ANOTHER TIME...

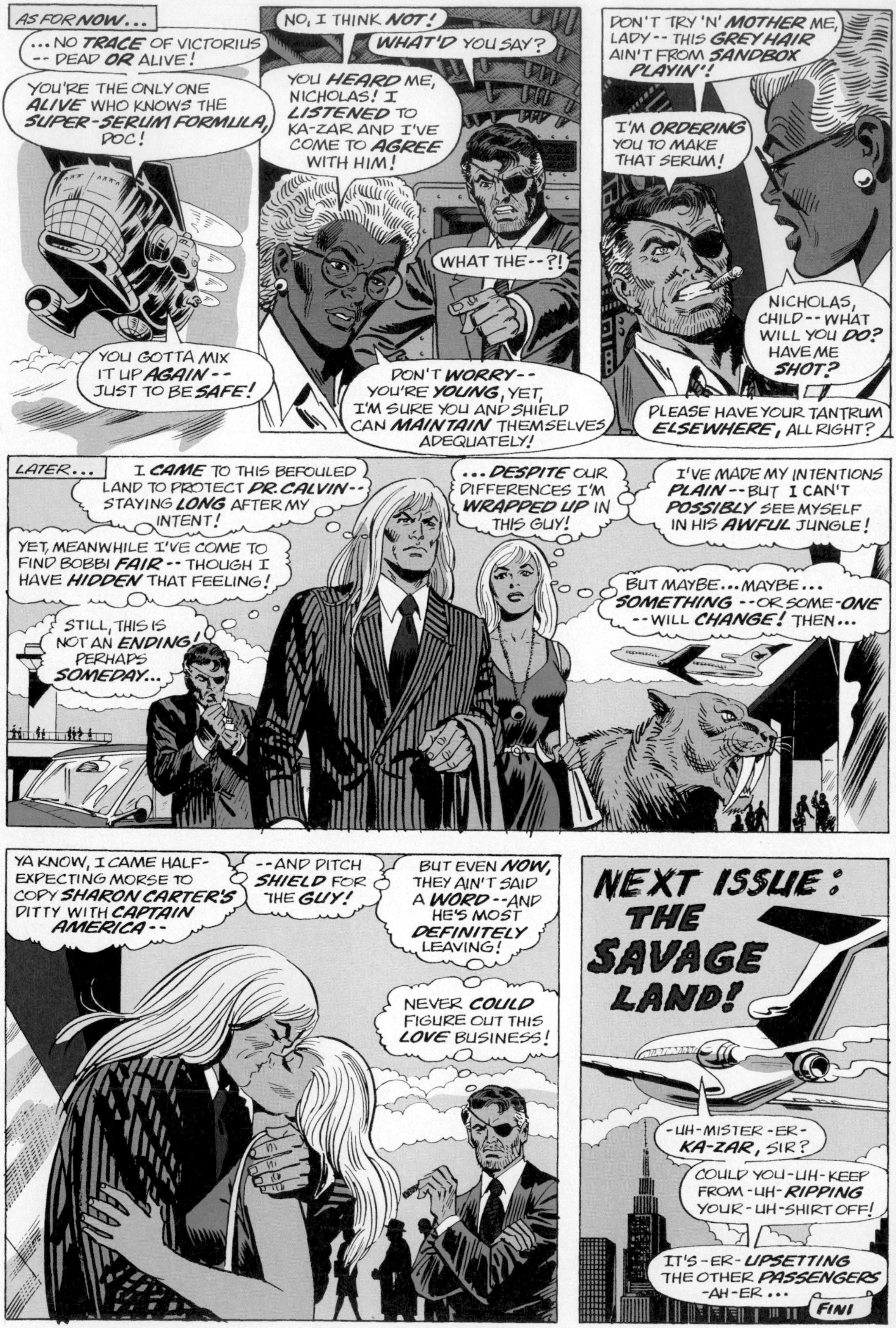
AS FOR NOW...
...NO TRACE OF VICTORIUS -- DEAD OR ALIVE!
YOU'RE THE ONLY ONE ALIVE WHO KNOWS THE SUPER-SERUM FORMULA, DOC!
YOU GOTTA MIX IT UP AGAIN -- JUST TO BE SAFE!
NO, I THINK NOT!
WHAT'D YOU SAY?
YOU HEARD ME, NICHOLAS! I LISTENED TO KA-ZAR AND I'VE COME TO AGREE WITH HIM!
WHAT THE--?!
DON'T WORRY-- YOU'RE YOUNG, YET, I'M SURE YOU AND SHIELD CAN MAINTAIN THEMSELVES ADEQUATELY!
DON'T TRY 'N' MOTHER ME, LADY -- THIS GREY HAIR AIN'T FROM SANDBOX PLAYIN'!
I'M ORDERING YOU TO MAKE THAT SERUM!
NICHOLAS, CHILD -- WHAT WILL YOU DO? HAVE ME SHOT?
PLEASE HAVE YOUR TANTRUM ELSEWHERE, ALL RIGHT?
LATER...
I CAME TO THIS BEFOULED LAND TO PROTECT DR. CALVIN -- STAYING LONG AFTER MY INTENT!
YET, MEANWHILE I'VE COME TO FIND BOBBI FAIR -- THOUGH I HAVE HIDDEN THAT FEELING!
STILL, THIS IS NOT AN ENDING! PERHAPS SOMEDAY...
...DESPITE OUR DIFFERENCES I'M WRAPPED UP IN THIS GUY!
I'VE MADE MY INTENTIONS PLAIN -- BUT I CAN'T POSSIBLY SEE MYSELF IN HIS AWFUL JUNGLE!
BUT MAYBE... MAYBE... SOMETHING --OR SOME-ONE -- WILL CHANGE! THEN...
YA KNOW, I CAME HALF-EXPECTING MORSE TO COPY SHARON CARTER'S DITTY WITH CAPTAIN AMERICA --
--AND PITCH SHIELD FOR THE GUY!
BUT EVEN NOW, THEY AIN'T SAID A WORD -- AND HE'S MOST DEFINITELY LEAVING!
NEVER COULD FIGURE OUT THIS LOVE BUSINESS!
NEXT ISSUE: THE SAVAGE LAND!
-UH-MISTER-ER-KA-ZAR, SIR?
COULD YOU-UH-KEEP FROM-UH-RIPPING YOUR-UH-SHIRT OFF!
IT'S-ER-UPSETTING THE OTHER PASSENGERS -AH-ER...
FINI

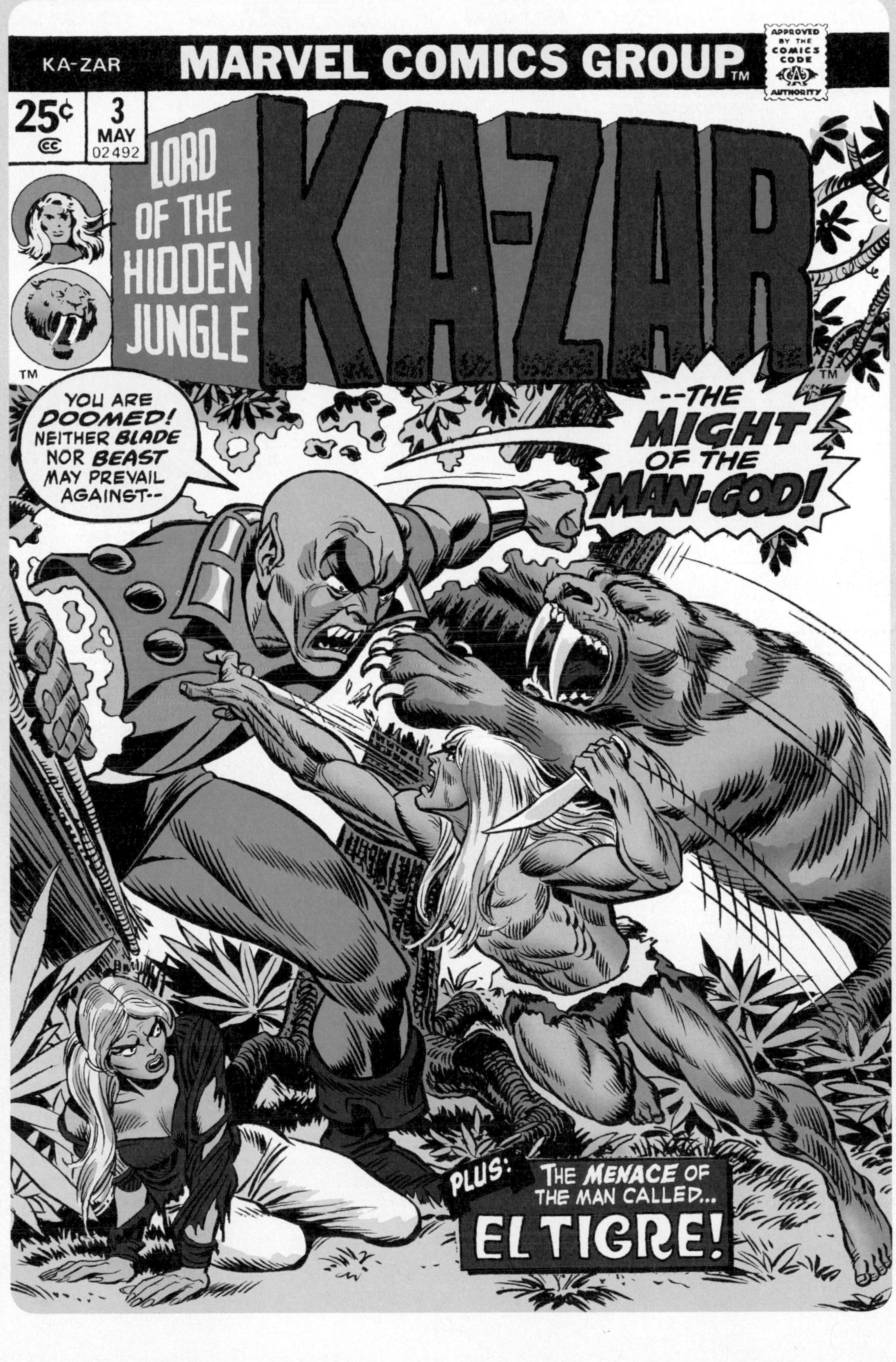
KA-ZAR
MARVEL COMICS GROUP
APPROVED BY THE COMICS CODE AUTHORITY
25¢
3
MAY
02492
LORD OF THE HIDDEN JUNGLE
KA-ZAR
YOU ARE DOOMED! NEITHER BLADE NOR BEAST MAY PREVAIL AGAINST--
--THE MIGHT OF THE MAN-GOD!
PLUS: THE MENACE OF THE MAN CALLED... EL TIGRE!

STAN LEE PRESENTS: **KA-ZAR**, LORD OF THE HIDDEN JUNGLE!™

MIKE FRIEDRICH — AUTHOR • DON HECK — ARTIST • MIKE ROYER — INKER • TOM ORZECHOWSKI — LETTERER • LINDA LESSMANN — COLORIST • ROY THOMAS — EDITOR

THE SAVAGE LAND... AN ISLAND OF TROPICAL *BEAUTY* MIDST THE ANTARCTIC SNOWS... AN *UNEXPLOITED* WONDERLAND OF DINOSAURS AND MEN--

--UNEXPLOITED, THAT IS, UNTIL THE...

NIGHT OF THE MAN-GOD!

BUT *FIRST* IN VIEW THIS EVE, PERHAPS SIGNIFI-CANTLY, IS A MURDER-MINDED SNAKE!

ZABU-- WE ARE ATTACKED!

YET YOUR *SHOULDER* IS NOT YET *HEALED* FROM YOUR *WOUND!**

*SEEN *LAST* ISSUE! --ROY.

RUN, TIGER-BROTHER, *RUN!*

BUT THE WARNING COMES TOO LATE...

RRRRRR

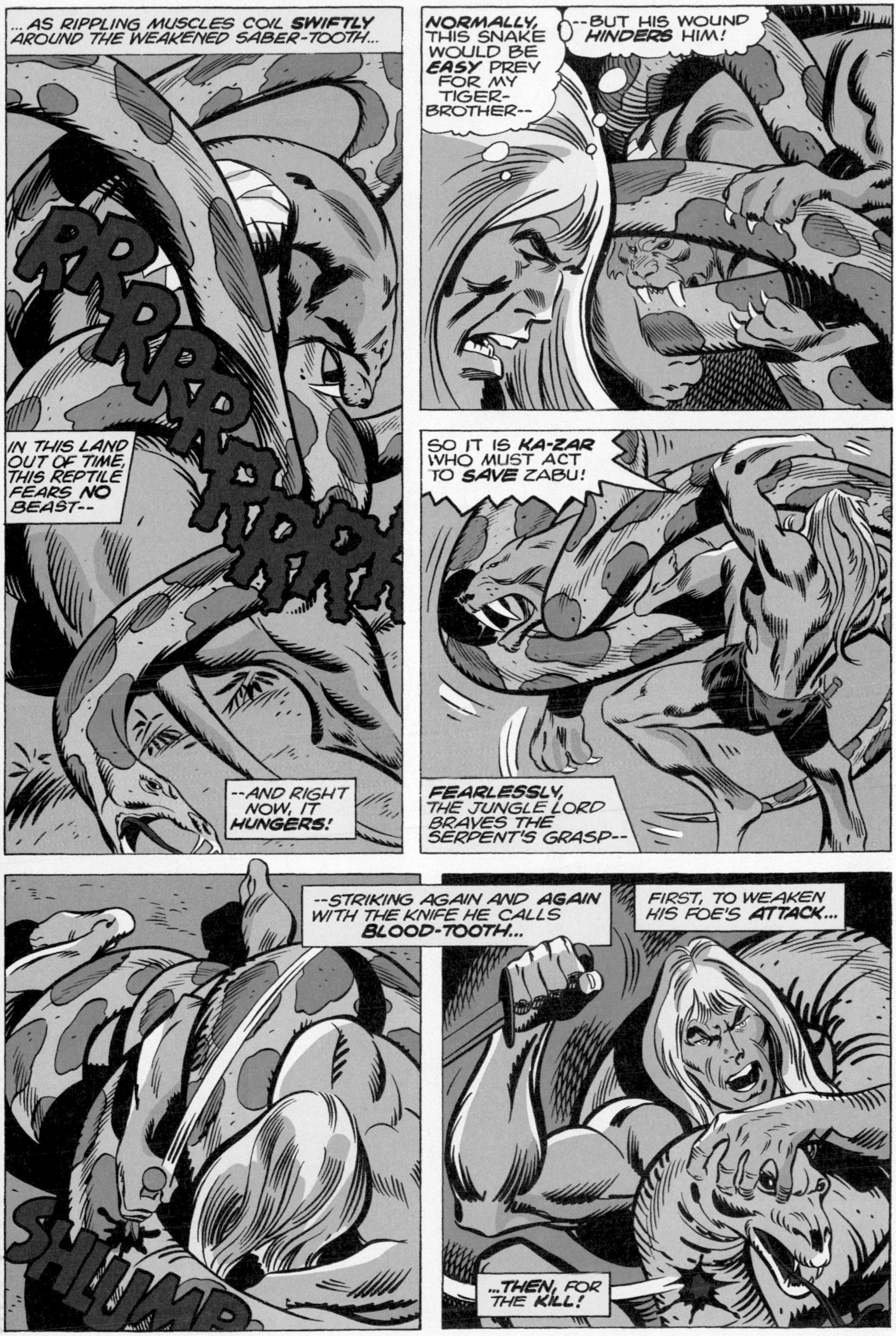
...AS RIPPLING MUSCLES COIL SWIFTLY AROUND THE WEAKENED SABER-TOOTH...
RRRRRRRRRAAAAHH
IN THIS LAND OUT OF TIME, THIS REPTILE FEARS NO BEAST--
--AND RIGHT NOW, IT HUNGERS!
NORMALLY, THIS SNAKE WOULD BE EASY PREY FOR MY TIGER-BROTHER--
--BUT HIS WOUND HINDERS HIM!
SO IT IS KA-ZAR WHO MUST ACT TO SAVE ZABU!
FEARLESSLY, THE JUNGLE LORD BRAVES THE SERPENT'S GRASP--
--STRIKING AGAIN AND AGAIN WITH THE KNIFE HE CALLS BLOOD-TOOTH...
SHLUMP
FIRST, TO WEAKEN HIS FOE'S ATTACK...
...THEN, FOR THE KILL!

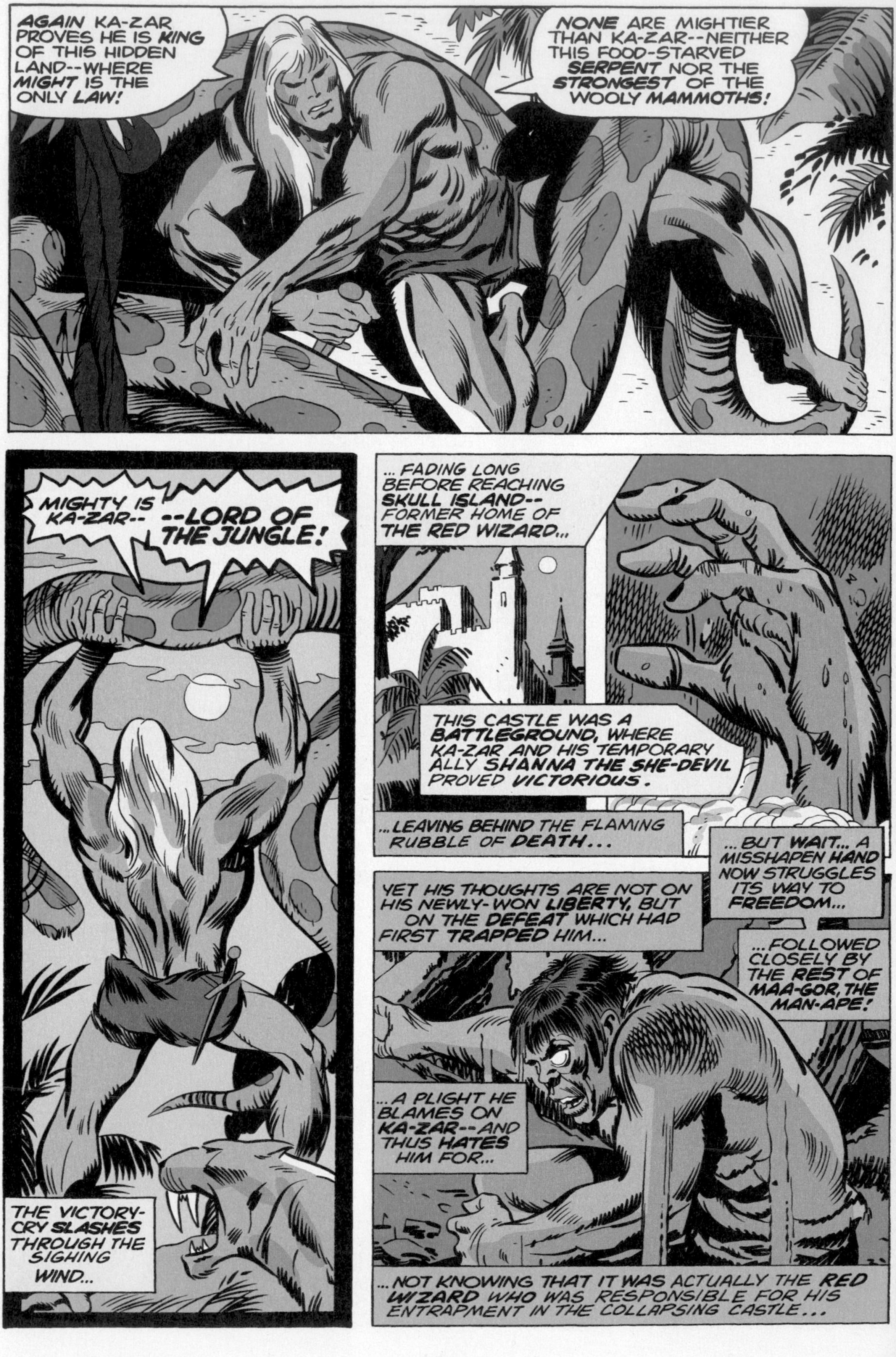

AGAIN KA-ZAR PROVES HE IS KING OF THIS HIDDEN LAND--WHERE MIGHT IS THE ONLY LAW!
NONE ARE MIGHTIER THAN KA-ZAR--NEITHER THIS FOOD-STARVED SERPENT NOR THE STRONGEST OF THE WOOLY MAMMOTHS!
MIGHTY IS KA-ZAR--
--LORD OF THE JUNGLE!
THE VICTORY-CRY SLASHES THROUGH THE SIGHING WIND...
...FADING LONG BEFORE REACHING SKULL ISLAND--FORMER HOME OF THE RED WIZARD...
THIS CASTLE WAS A BATTLEGROUND, WHERE KA-ZAR AND HIS TEMPORARY ALLY SHANNA THE SHE-DEVIL PROVED VICTORIOUS.
...LEAVING BEHIND THE FLAMING RUBBLE OF DEATH...
...BUT WAIT... A MISSHAPEN HAND NOW STRUGGLES ITS WAY TO FREEDOM...
...FOLLOWED CLOSELY BY THE REST OF MAA-GOR, THE MAN-APE!
YET HIS THOUGHTS ARE NOT ON HIS NEWLY-WON LIBERTY, BUT ON THE DEFEAT WHICH HAD FIRST TRAPPED HIM...
...A PLIGHT HE BLAMES ON KA-ZAR--AND THUS HATES HIM FOR...
...NOT KNOWING THAT IT WAS ACTUALLY THE RED WIZARD WHO WAS RESPONSIBLE FOR HIS ENTRAPMENT IN THE COLLAPSING CASTLE...

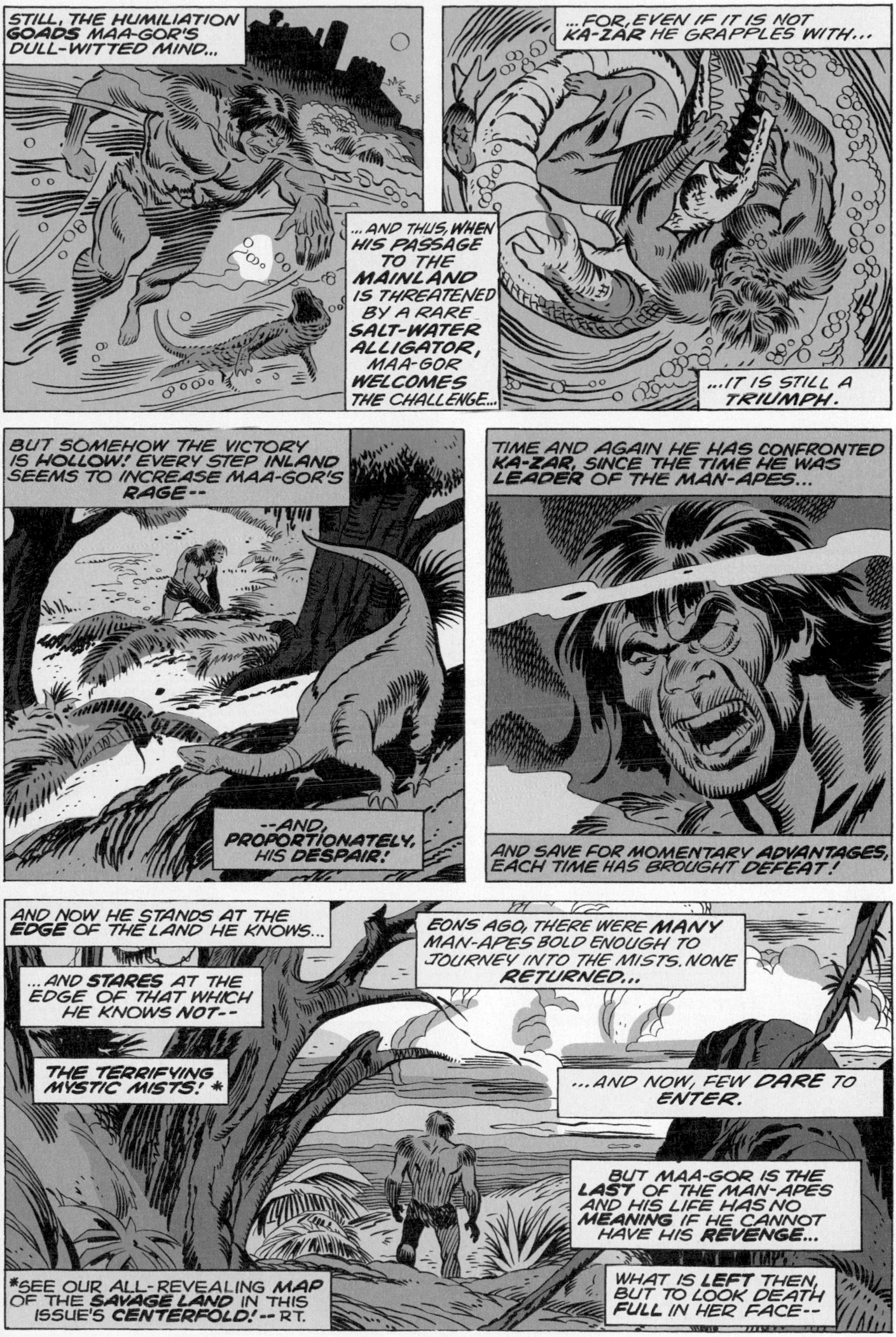
STILL, THE HUMILIATION GOADS MAA-GOR'S DULL-WITTED MIND...
...AND THUS, WHEN HIS PASSAGE TO THE MAINLAND IS THREATENED BY A RARE SALT-WATER ALLIGATOR, MAA-GOR WELCOMES THE CHALLENGE...
...FOR, EVEN IF IT IS NOT KA-ZAR HE GRAPPLES WITH...
...IT IS STILL A TRIUMPH.
BUT SOMEHOW THE VICTORY IS HOLLOW! EVERY STEP INLAND SEEMS TO INCREASE MAA-GOR'S RAGE--
--AND, PROPORTIONATELY, HIS DESPAIR!
TIME AND AGAIN HE HAS CONFRONTED KA-ZAR, SINCE THE TIME HE WAS LEADER OF THE MAN-APES...
AND SAVE FOR MOMENTARY ADVANTAGES, EACH TIME HAS BROUGHT DEFEAT!
AND NOW HE STANDS AT THE EDGE OF THE LAND HE KNOWS...
...AND STARES AT THE EDGE OF THAT WHICH HE KNOWS NOT--
THE TERRIFYING MYSTIC MISTS! *
EONS AGO, THERE WERE MANY MAN-APES BOLD ENOUGH TO JOURNEY INTO THE MISTS. NONE RETURNED...
...AND NOW, FEW DARE TO ENTER.
BUT MAA-GOR IS THE LAST OF THE MAN-APES AND HIS LIFE HAS NO MEANING IF HE CANNOT HAVE HIS REVENGE...
WHAT IS LEFT THEN, BUT TO LOOK DEATH FULL IN HER FACE--
*SEE OUR ALL-REVEALING MAP OF THE SAVAGE LAND IN THIS ISSUE'S CENTERFOLD! --RT.

--AND LEAP INTO HER *RAVISHING* ARMS?

BUT THESE ARE *SPECIAL* MISTS--UNLIKE ANY *OTHERS* IN THE *WORLD.*

THESE ARE THE MISTS THAT KEEP *ZABU YOUNG*--

--AND MAKE *KA-ZAR* THE STRONG-MUSCLED TITAN HE IS...

...AND NOW THEY CHANGE *MAA-GOR*...

HE STANDS *ERECT,* SLEEK AND *POWERFUL*--MUCH LIKE A MAN--

--YET SO MUCH *MORE!*

BUT *ONE* THING STILL RE-MAINS THE *SAME*--

--HIS *HATRED!*

KA-ZAR! IT WAS *HE* WHO DROVE ME TO THIS-- WHO *FORCED* THIS TRANS-FORMATION UPON ME!

GROK!

THAT *GRANITE*-- I SMASHED IT WITH MY *BARE* HAND!

AND MY *MIND*-- GRASPING LANGUAGE-- *CONCEPTS*-- I NEVER *DREAMED* POSSIBLE!

SLOWLY MAA-GOR'S SEETHING EMOTIONS *COOL*--

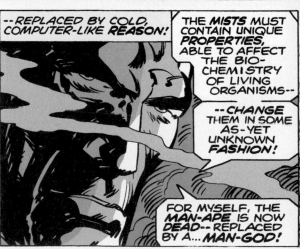

--REPLACED BY COLD, COMPUTER-LIKE *REASON!*

THE *MISTS* MUST CONTAIN UNIQUE *PROPERTIES,* ABLE TO AFFECT THE BIO-CHEMISTRY OF LIVING ORGANISMS--

--CHANGE THEM IN SOME AS-YET UNKNOWN *FASHION!*

FOR MYSELF, THE *MAN-APE* IS NOW *DEAD*--REPLACED BY A...*MAN-GOD!*

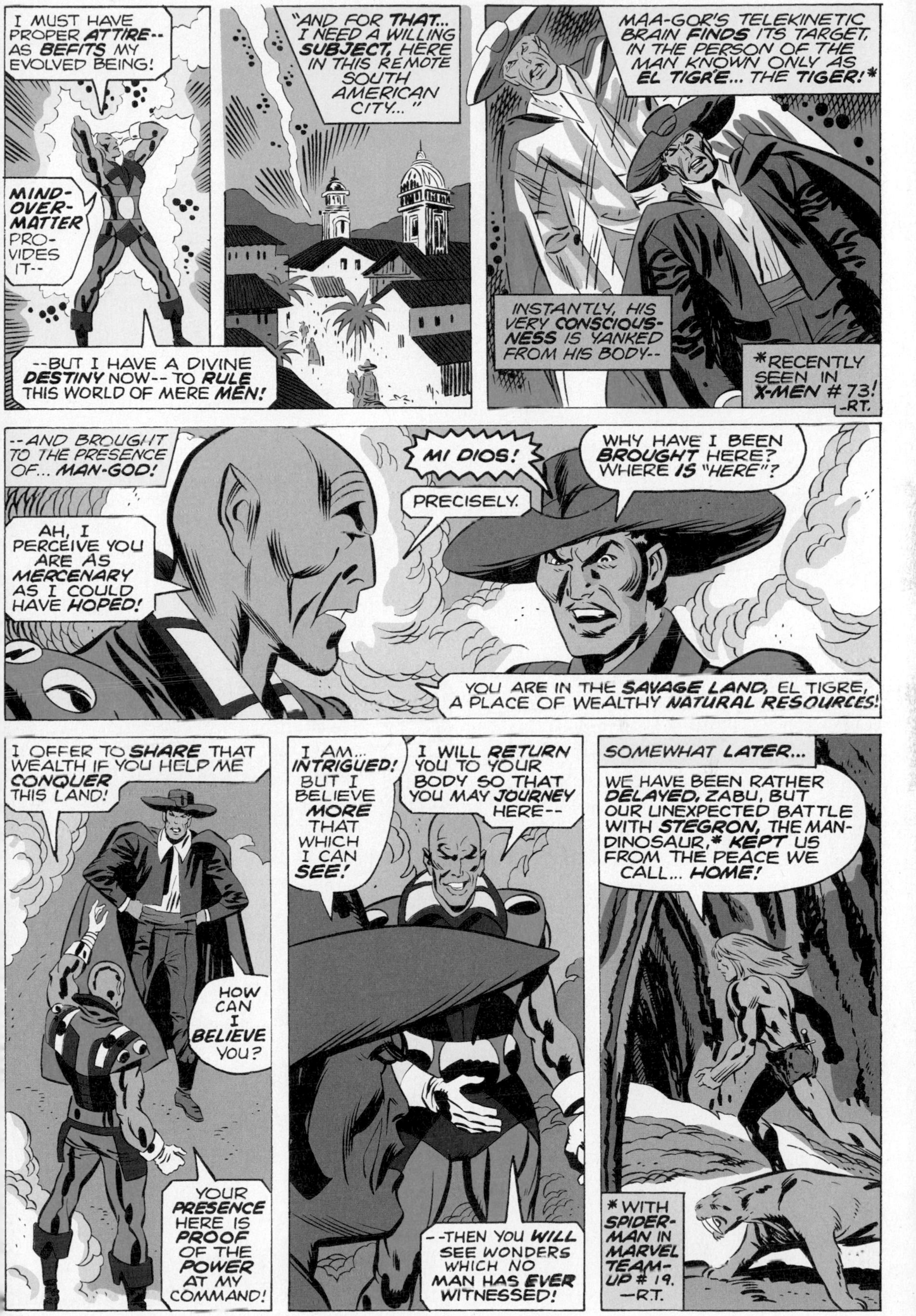
I MUST HAVE PROPER ATTIRE-- AS BEFITS MY EVOLVED BEING!
MIND-OVER-MATTER PROVIDES IT--
--BUT I HAVE A DIVINE DESTINY NOW-- TO RULE THIS WORLD OF MERE MEN!
"AND FOR THAT... I NEED A WILLING SUBJECT, HERE IN THIS REMOTE SOUTH AMERICAN CITY..."
MAA-GOR'S TELEKINETIC BRAIN FINDS ITS TARGET, IN THE PERSON OF THE MAN KNOWN ONLY AS EL TIGRE... THE TIGER!*
INSTANTLY, HIS VERY CONSCIOUSNESS IS YANKED FROM HIS BODY--
*RECENTLY SEEN IN X-MEN #73! -RT.
--AND BROUGHT TO THE PRESENCE OF... MAN-GOD!
MI DIOS!
WHY HAVE I BEEN BROUGHT HERE? WHERE IS "HERE"?
PRECISELY.
AH, I PERCEIVE YOU ARE AS MERCENARY AS I COULD HAVE HOPED!
YOU ARE IN THE SAVAGE LAND, EL TIGRE, A PLACE OF WEALTHY NATURAL RESOURCES!
I OFFER TO SHARE THAT WEALTH IF YOU HELP ME CONQUER THIS LAND!
HOW CAN I BELIEVE YOU?
YOUR PRESENCE HERE IS PROOF OF THE POWER AT MY COMMAND!
I AM... INTRIGUED! BUT I BELIEVE MORE THAT WHICH I CAN SEE!
I WILL RETURN YOU TO YOUR BODY SO THAT YOU MAY JOURNEY HERE--
--THEN YOU WILL SEE WONDERS WHICH NO MAN HAS EVER WITNESSED!
SOMEWHAT LATER...
WE HAVE BEEN RATHER DELAYED, ZABU, BUT OUR UNEXPECTED BATTLE WITH STEGRON, THE MAN-DINOSAUR,* KEPT US FROM THE PEACE WE CALL... HOME!
*WITH SPIDER-MAN IN MARVEL TEAM-UP #19. —R.T.

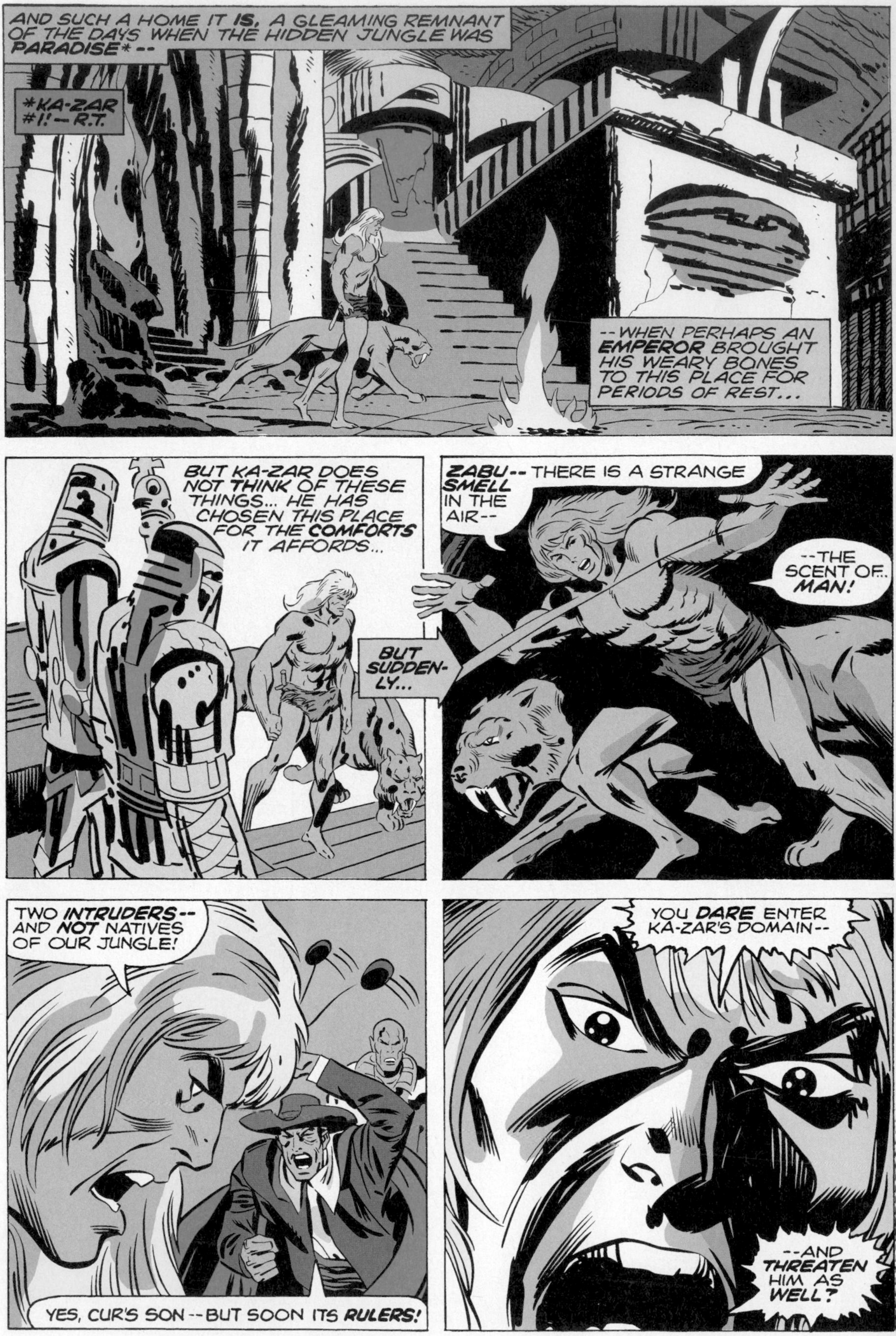

AND SUCH A HOME IT IS, A GLEAMING REMNANT OF THE DAYS WHEN THE HIDDEN JUNGLE WAS PARADISE* --
*KA-ZAR #1! -- R.T.
-- WHEN PERHAPS AN EMPEROR BROUGHT HIS WEARY BONES TO THIS PLACE FOR PERIODS OF REST...
BUT KA-ZAR DOES NOT THINK OF THESE THINGS... HE HAS CHOSEN THIS PLACE FOR THE COMFORTS IT AFFORDS...
BUT SUDDEN-LY...
ZABU -- THERE IS A STRANGE SMELL IN THE AIR --
-- THE SCENT OF... MAN!
TWO INTRUDERS -- AND NOT NATIVES OF OUR JUNGLE!
YES, CUR'S SON -- BUT SOON ITS RULERS!
YOU DARE ENTER KA-ZAR'S DOMAIN --
-- AND THREATEN HIM AS WELL?

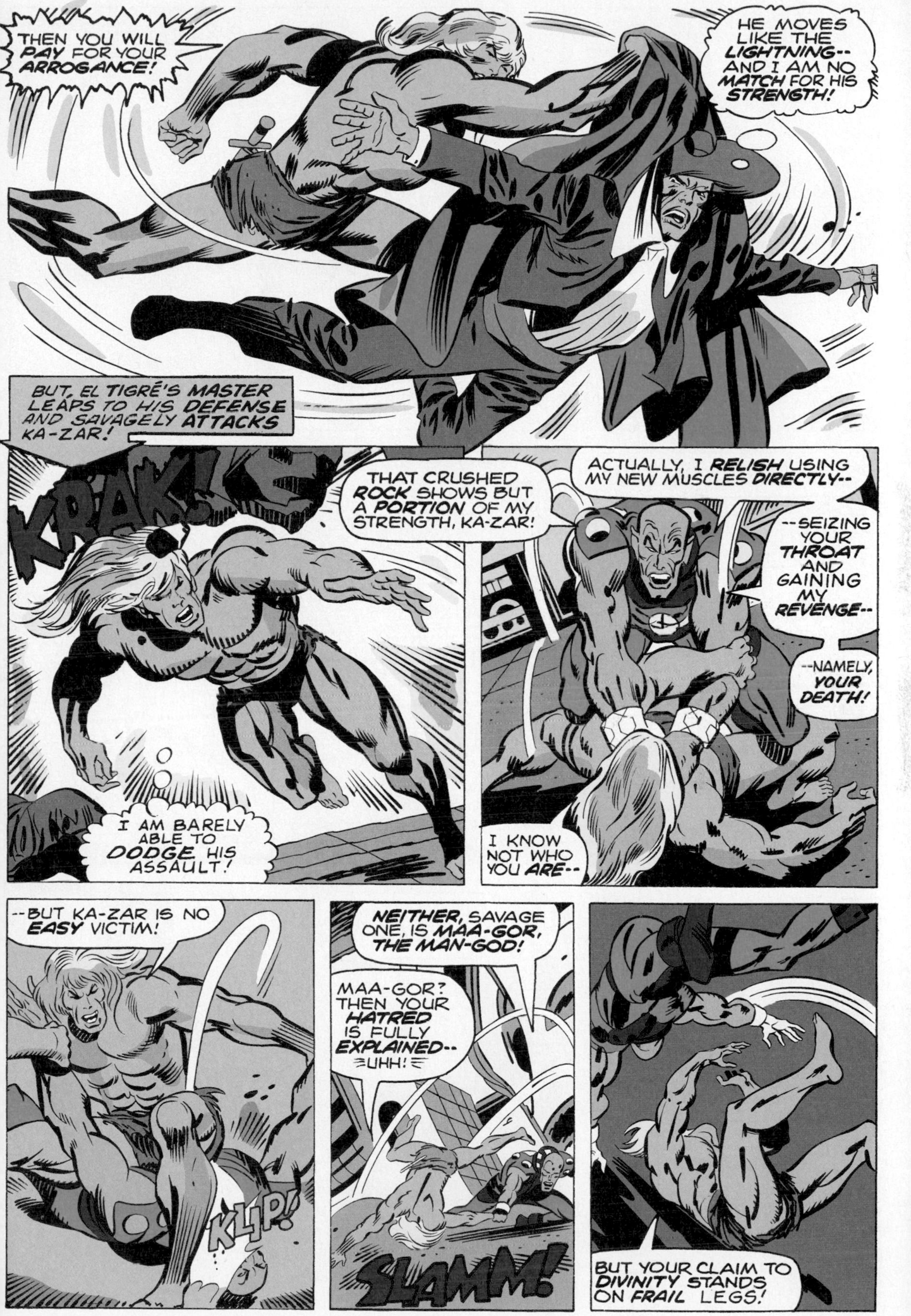
THEN YOU WILL PAY FOR YOUR ARROGANCE!
HE MOVES LIKE THE LIGHTNING-- AND I AM NO MATCH FOR HIS STRENGTH!
BUT, EL TIGRÉ'S MASTER LEAPS TO HIS DEFENSE AND SAVAGELY ATTACKS KA-ZAR!
KRAK!
THAT CRUSHED ROCK SHOWS BUT A PORTION OF MY STRENGTH, KA-ZAR!
I AM BARELY ABLE TO DODGE HIS ASSAULT!
ACTUALLY, I RELISH USING MY NEW MUSCLES DIRECTLY--
--SEIZING YOUR THROAT AND GAINING MY REVENGE--
--NAMELY, YOUR DEATH!
I KNOW NOT WHO YOU ARE--
--BUT KA-ZAR IS NO EASY VICTIM!
KLIP!
NEITHER, SAVAGE ONE, IS MAA-GOR, THE MAN-GOD!
MAA-GOR? THEN YOUR HATRED IS FULLY EXPLAINED-- UHH!
SLAMM!
BUT YOUR CLAIM TO DIVINITY STANDS ON FRAIL LEGS!

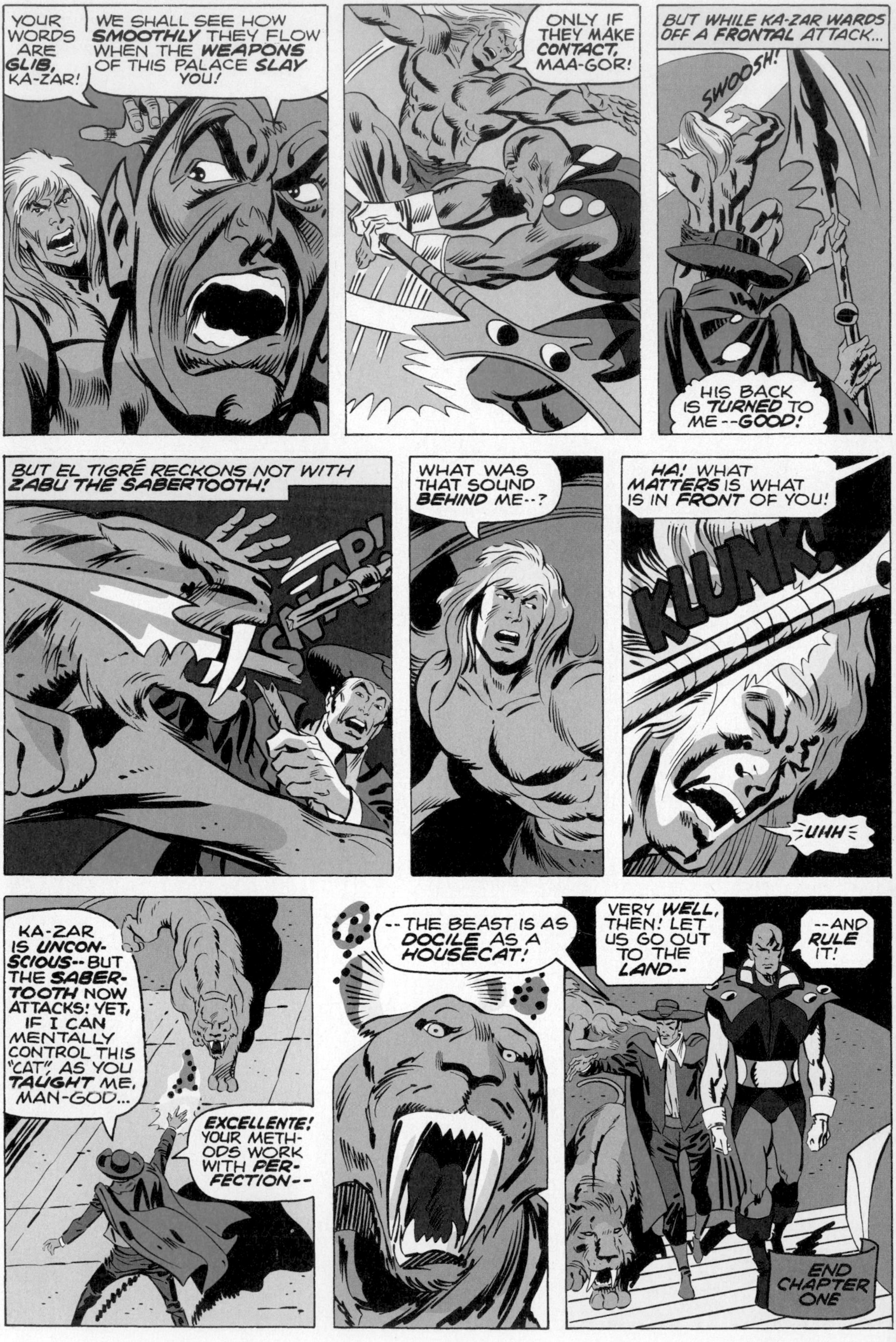
YOUR WORDS ARE GLIB, KA-ZAR!
WE SHALL SEE HOW SMOOTHLY THEY FLOW WHEN THE WEAPONS OF THIS PALACE SLAY YOU!
ONLY IF THEY MAKE CONTACT, MAA-GOR!
BUT WHILE KA-ZAR WARDS OFF A FRONTAL ATTACK...
SWOOSH!
HIS BACK IS TURNED TO ME--GOOD!
BUT EL TIGRÉ RECKONS NOT WITH ZABU THE SABERTOOTH!
SNAP!
WHAT WAS THAT SOUND BEHIND ME--?
HA! WHAT MATTERS IS WHAT IS IN FRONT OF YOU!
KLUNK!
UHH
KA-ZAR IS UNCONSCIOUS--BUT THE SABERTOOTH NOW ATTACKS! YET, IF I CAN MENTALLY CONTROL THIS "CAT", AS YOU TAUGHT ME, MAN-GOD...
EXCELLENTE! YOUR METHODS WORK WITH PERFECTION--
--THE BEAST IS AS DOCILE AS A HOUSECAT!
VERY WELL, THEN! LET US GO OUT TO THE LAND--
--AND RULE IT!
END CHAPTER ONE

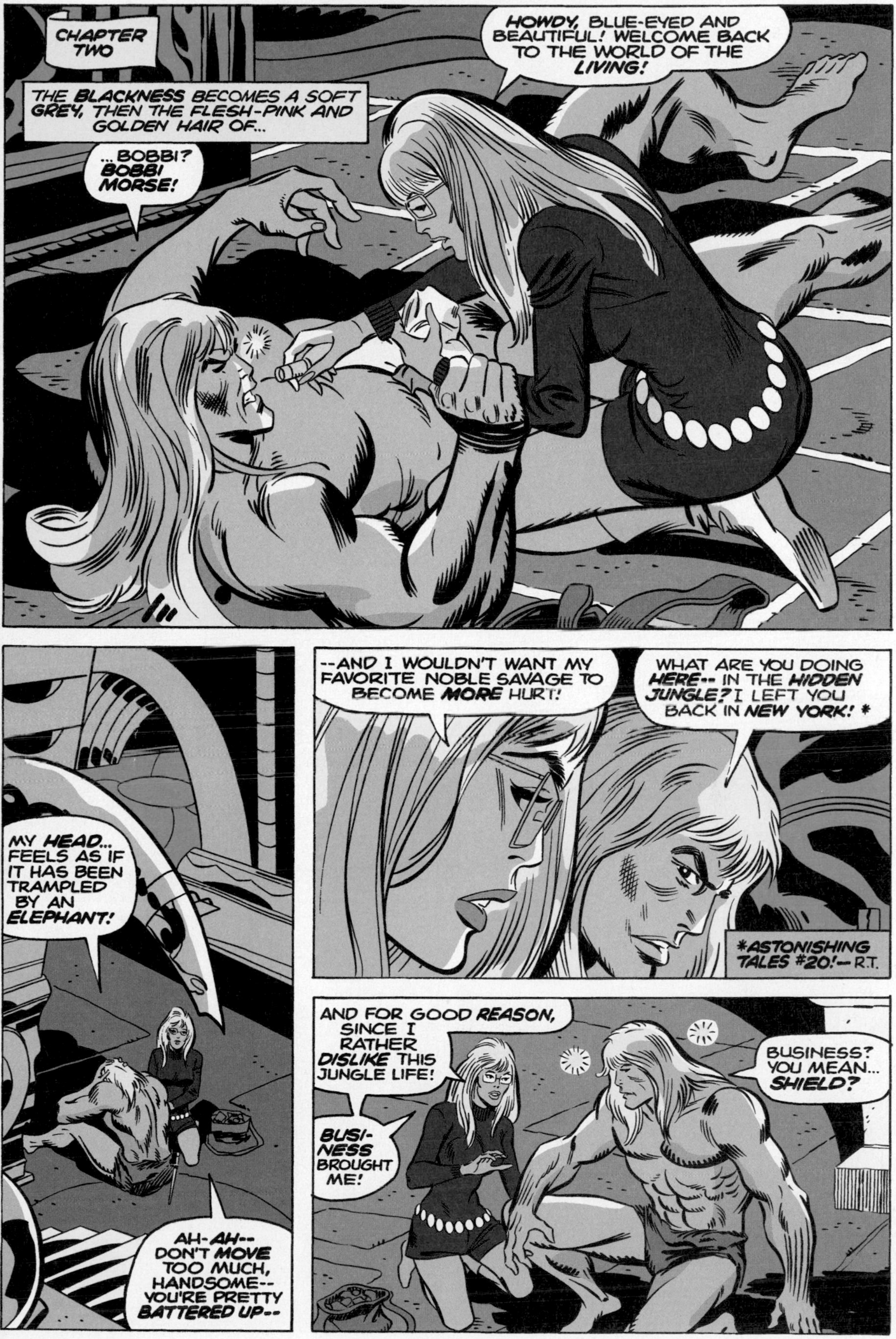
CHAPTER TWO
THE BLACKNESS BECOMES A SOFT GREY, THEN THE FLESH-PINK AND GOLDEN HAIR OF...
HOWDY, BLUE-EYED AND BEAUTIFUL! WELCOME BACK TO THE WORLD OF THE LIVING!
...BOBBI? BOBBI MORSE!
MY HEAD... FEELS AS IF IT HAS BEEN TRAMPLED BY AN ELEPHANT!
AH-AH-- DON'T MOVE TOO MUCH, HANDSOME-- YOU'RE PRETTY BATTERED UP--
--AND I WOULDN'T WANT MY FAVORITE NOBLE SAVAGE TO BECOME MORE HURT!
WHAT ARE YOU DOING HERE-- IN THE HIDDEN JUNGLE? I LEFT YOU BACK IN NEW YORK! *
*ASTONISHING TALES #20!--R.T.
AND FOR GOOD REASON, SINCE I RATHER DISLIKE THIS JUNGLE LIFE!
BUSI-NESS BROUGHT ME!
BUSINESS? YOU MEAN... SHIELD?

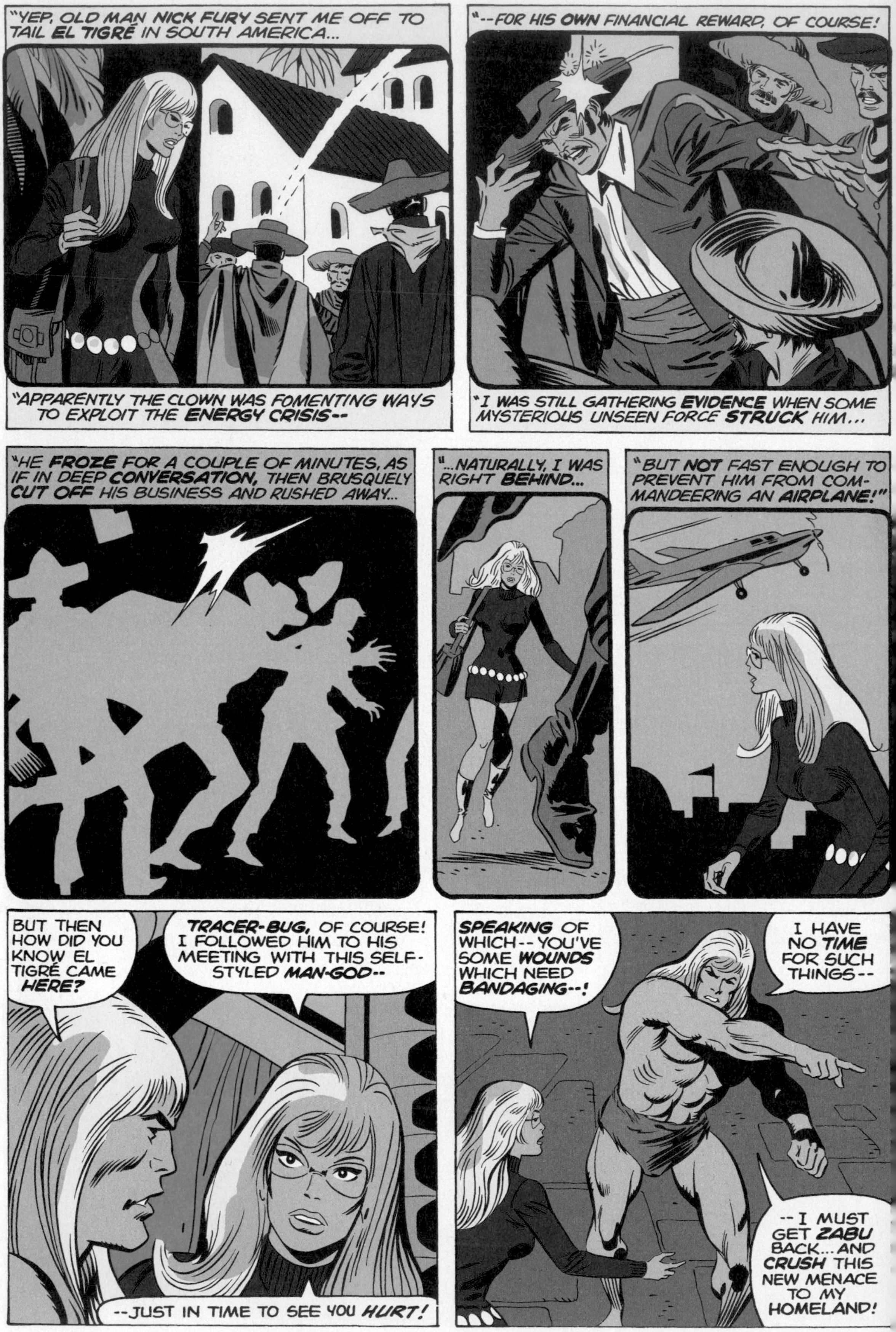
"YEP, OLD MAN NICK FURY SENT ME OFF TO TAIL EL TIGRÉ IN SOUTH AMERICA...
"APPARENTLY THE CLOWN WAS FOMENTING WAYS TO EXPLOIT THE ENERGY CRISIS--
"--FOR HIS OWN FINANCIAL REWARD, OF COURSE!
"I WAS STILL GATHERING EVIDENCE WHEN SOME MYSTERIOUS UNSEEN FORCE STRUCK HIM...
"HE FROZE FOR A COUPLE OF MINUTES, AS IF IN DEEP CONVERSATION, THEN BRUSQUELY CUT OFF HIS BUSINESS AND RUSHED AWAY...
"...NATURALLY, I WAS RIGHT BEHIND...
"BUT NOT FAST ENOUGH TO PREVENT HIM FROM COMMANDEERING AN AIRPLANE!"
BUT THEN HOW DID YOU KNOW EL TIGRÉ CAME HERE?
TRACER-BUG, OF COURSE! I FOLLOWED HIM TO HIS MEETING WITH THIS SELF-STYLED MAN-GOD--
--JUST IN TIME TO SEE YOU HURT!
SPEAKING OF WHICH--YOU'VE SOME WOUNDS WHICH NEED BANDAGING--!
I HAVE NO TIME FOR SUCH THINGS--
--I MUST GET ZABU BACK...AND CRUSH THIS NEW MENACE TO MY HOMELAND!

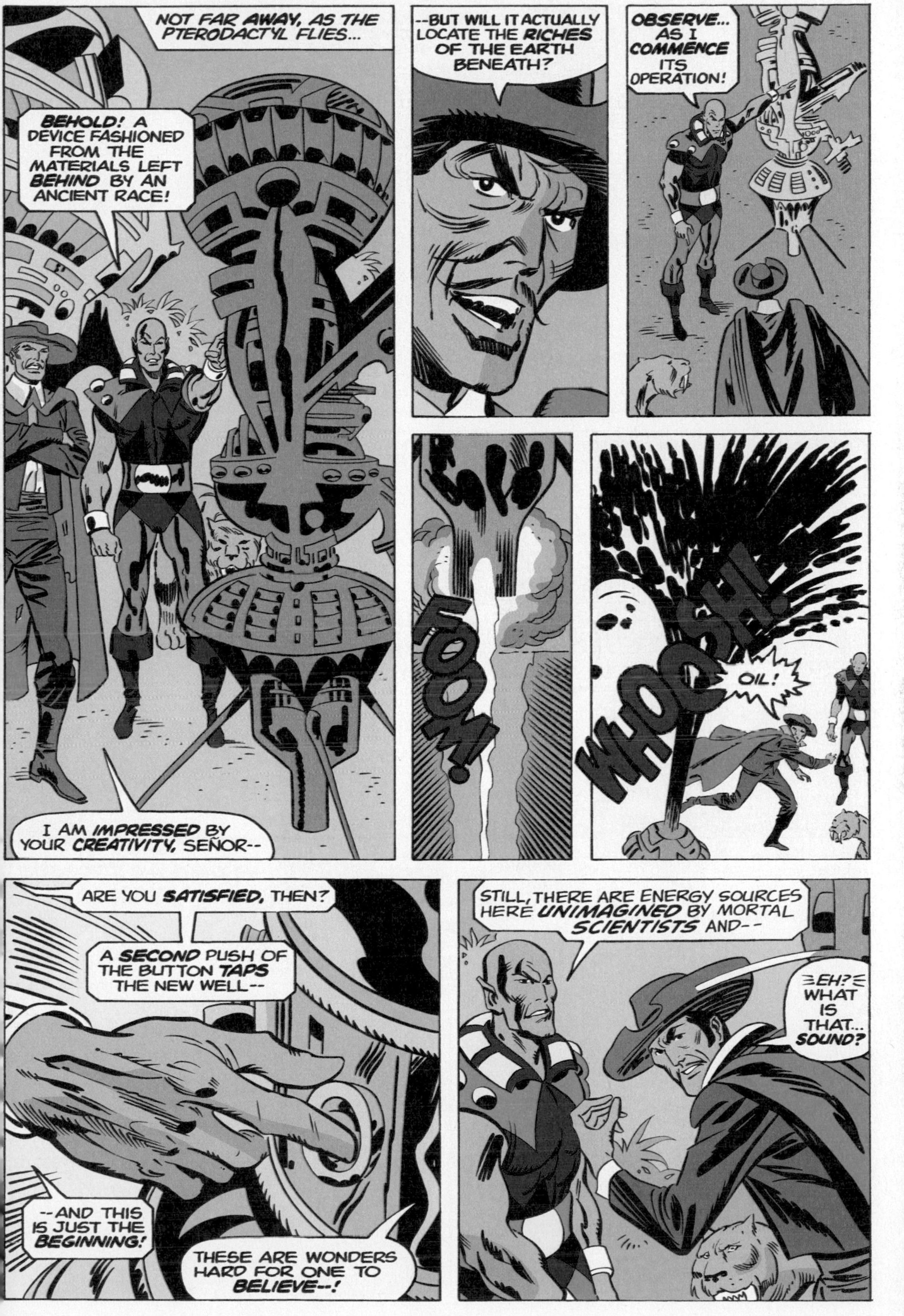
NOT FAR AWAY, AS THE PTERODACTYL FLIES...
BEHOLD! A DEVICE FASHIONED FROM THE MATERIALS LEFT BEHIND BY AN ANCIENT RACE!
I AM IMPRESSED BY YOUR CREATIVITY, SEÑOR--
--BUT WILL IT ACTUALLY LOCATE THE RICHES OF THE EARTH BENEATH?
OBSERVE... AS I COMMENCE ITS OPERATION!
FOOM!
WHOOSH!
OIL!
ARE YOU SATISFIED, THEN?
A SECOND PUSH OF THE BUTTON TAPS THE NEW WELL--
--AND THIS IS JUST THE BEGINNING!
THESE ARE WONDERS HARD FOR ONE TO BELIEVE--!
STILL, THERE ARE ENERGY SOURCES HERE UNIMAGINED BY MORTAL SCIENTISTS AND--
EH? WHAT IS THAT... SOUND?

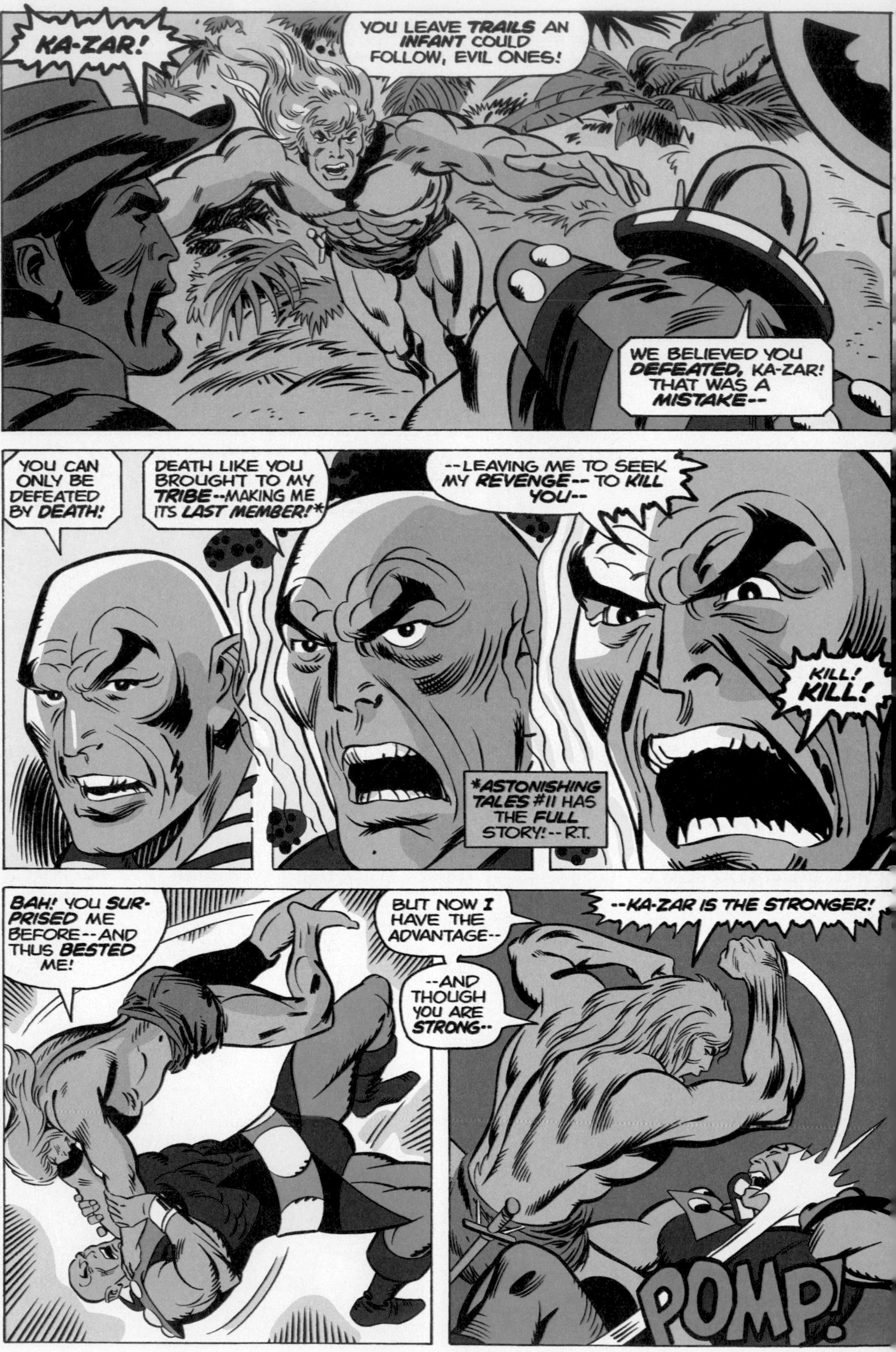
KA-ZAR!
YOU LEAVE TRAILS AN INFANT COULD FOLLOW, EVIL ONES!
WE BELIEVED YOU DEFEATED, KA-ZAR! THAT WAS A MISTAKE--
YOU CAN ONLY BE DEFEATED BY DEATH!
DEATH LIKE YOU BROUGHT TO MY TRIBE--MAKING ME ITS LAST MEMBER!*
--LEAVING ME TO SEEK MY REVENGE-- TO KILL YOU--
KILL! KILL!
*ASTONISHING TALES #11 HAS THE FULL STORY! --R.T.
BAH! YOU SURPRISED ME BEFORE--AND THUS BESTED ME!
BUT NOW I HAVE THE ADVANTAGE--
--AND THOUGH YOU ARE STRONG--
--KA-ZAR IS THE STRONGER!
POMP!

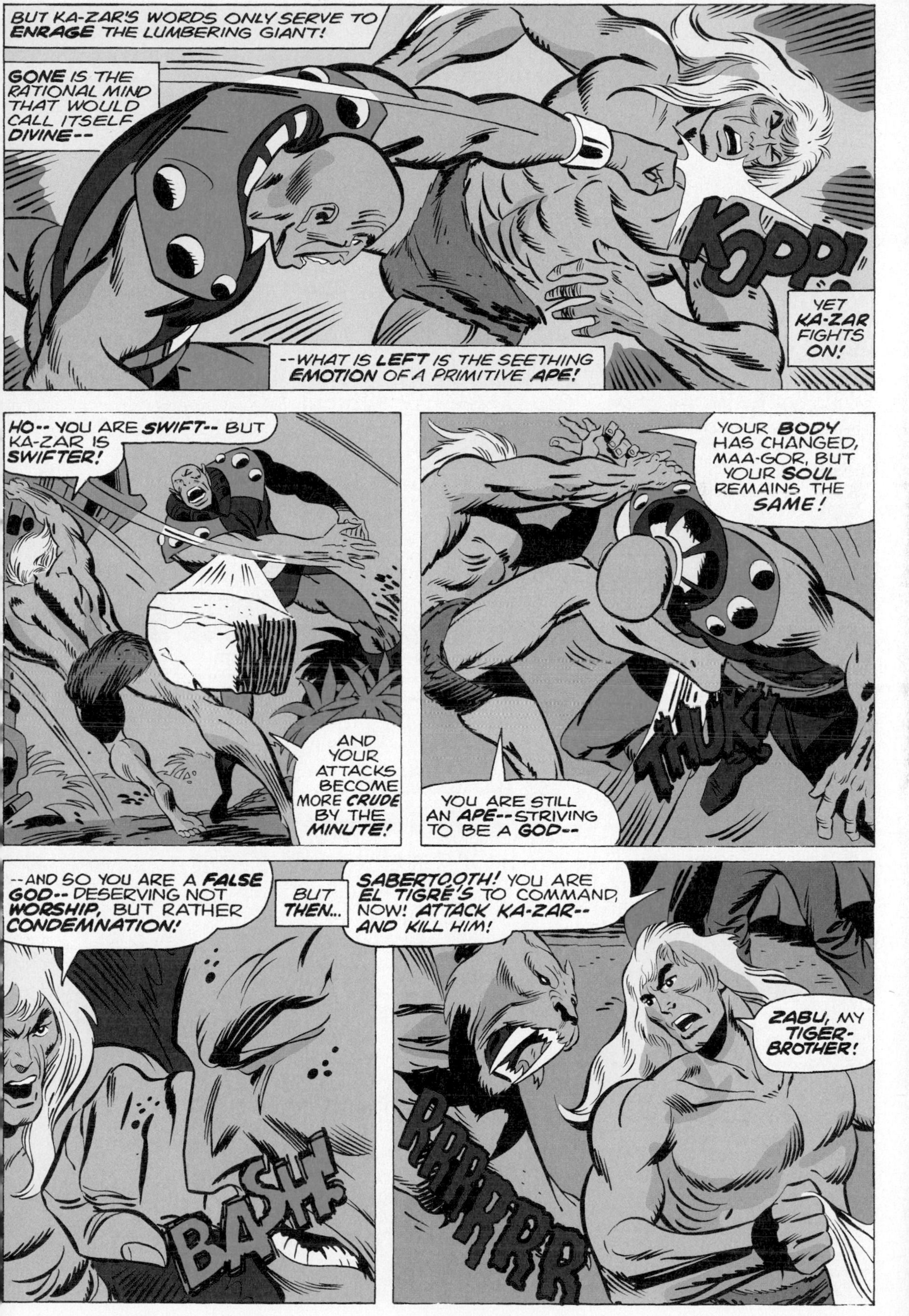
BUT KA-ZAR'S WORDS ONLY SERVE TO ENRAGE THE LUMBERING GIANT!
GONE IS THE RATIONAL MIND THAT WOULD CALL ITSELF DIVINE--
KOPP!
--WHAT IS LEFT IS THE SEETHING EMOTION OF A PRIMITIVE APE!
YET KA-ZAR FIGHTS ON!
HO-- YOU ARE SWIFT-- BUT KA-ZAR IS SWIFTER!
AND YOUR ATTACKS BECOME MORE CRUDE BY THE MINUTE!
YOUR BODY HAS CHANGED, MAA-GOR, BUT YOUR SOUL REMAINS THE SAME!
THUK!
YOU ARE STILL AN APE--STRIVING TO BE A GOD--
--AND SO YOU ARE A FALSE GOD-- DESERVING NOT WORSHIP, BUT RATHER CONDEMNATION!
BASH
BUT THEN...
SABERTOOTH! YOU ARE EL TIGRÉ'S TO COMMAND, NOW! ATTACK KA-ZAR-- AND KILL HIM!
ZABU, MY TIGER-BROTHER!
RRRRRRR

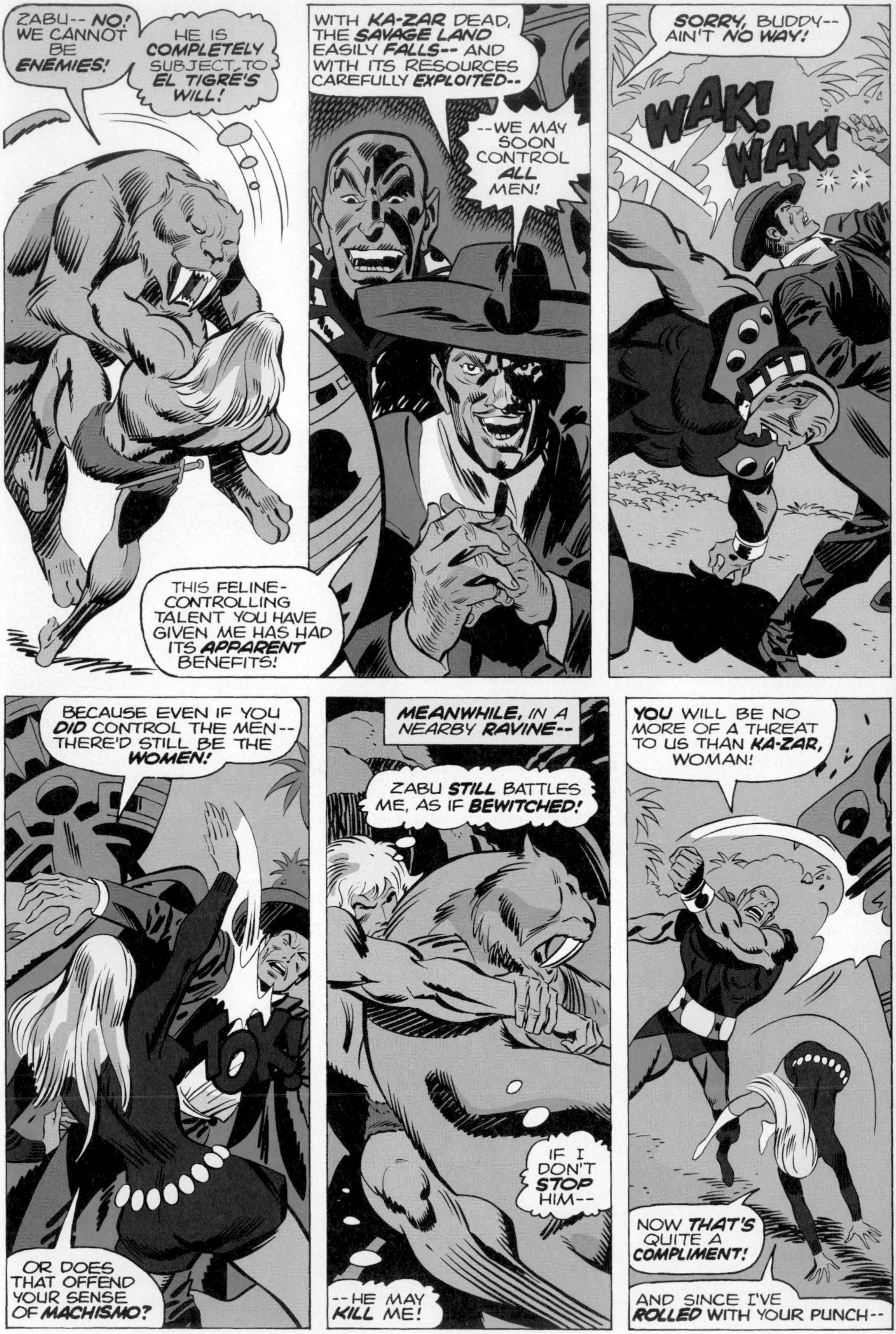
ZABU-- NO! WE CANNOT BE ENEMIES!
HE IS COMPLETELY SUBJECT TO EL TIGRÉ'S WILL!
THIS FELINE-CONTROLLING TALENT YOU HAVE GIVEN ME HAS HAD ITS APPARENT BENEFITS!
WITH KA-ZAR DEAD, THE SAVAGE LAND EASILY FALLS-- AND WITH ITS RESOURCES CAREFULLY EXPLOITED--
--WE MAY SOON CONTROL ALL MEN!
SORRY, BUDDY-- AIN'T NO WAY!
WAK! WAK!
BECAUSE EVEN IF YOU DID CONTROL THE MEN-- THERE'D STILL BE THE WOMEN!
TOK!
OR DOES THAT OFFEND YOUR SENSE OF MACHISMO?
MEANWHILE, IN A NEARBY RAVINE--
ZABU STILL BATTLES ME, AS IF BEWITCHED!
IF I DON'T STOP HIM--
--HE MAY KILL ME!
YOU WILL BE NO MORE OF A THREAT TO US THAN KA-ZAR, WOMAN!
NOW THAT'S QUITE A COMPLIMENT!
AND SINCE I'VE ROLLED WITH YOUR PUNCH--

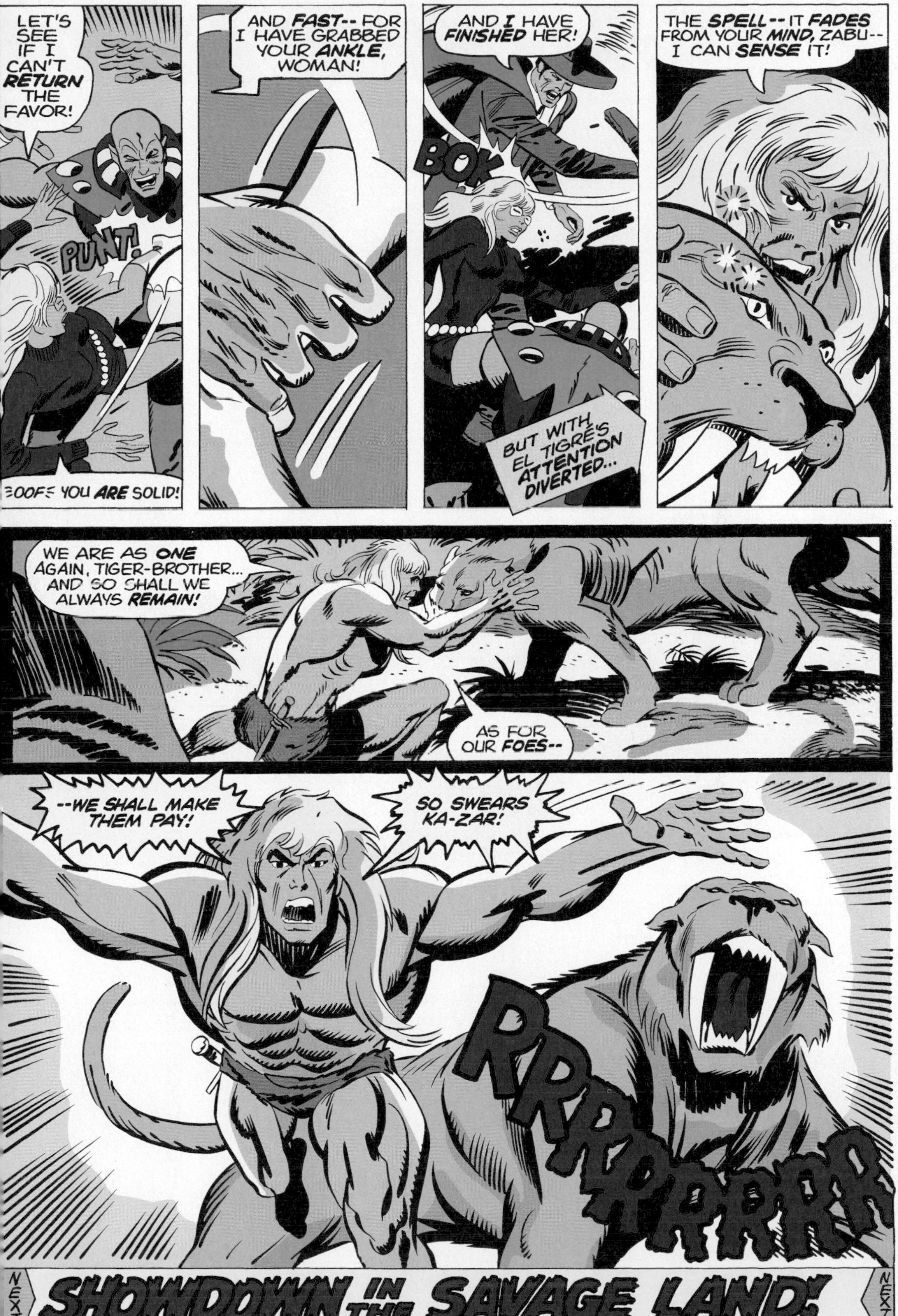

LET'S SEE IF I CAN'T RETURN THE FAVOR!
PUNT!
OOF! YOU ARE SOLID!
AND FAST-- FOR I HAVE GRABBED YOUR ANKLE, WOMAN!
AND I HAVE FINISHED HER!
BOK
BUT WITH EL TIGRE'S ATTENTION DIVERTED...
THE SPELL-- IT FADES FROM YOUR MIND, ZABU-- I CAN SENSE IT!
WE ARE AS ONE AGAIN, TIGER-BROTHER... AND SO SHALL WE ALWAYS REMAIN!
AS FOR OUR FOES--
--WE SHALL MAKE THEM PAY!
SO SWEARS KA-ZAR!
RRRRRRRRRR
NEXT
SHOWDOWN IN THE SAVAGE LAND!
NEXT

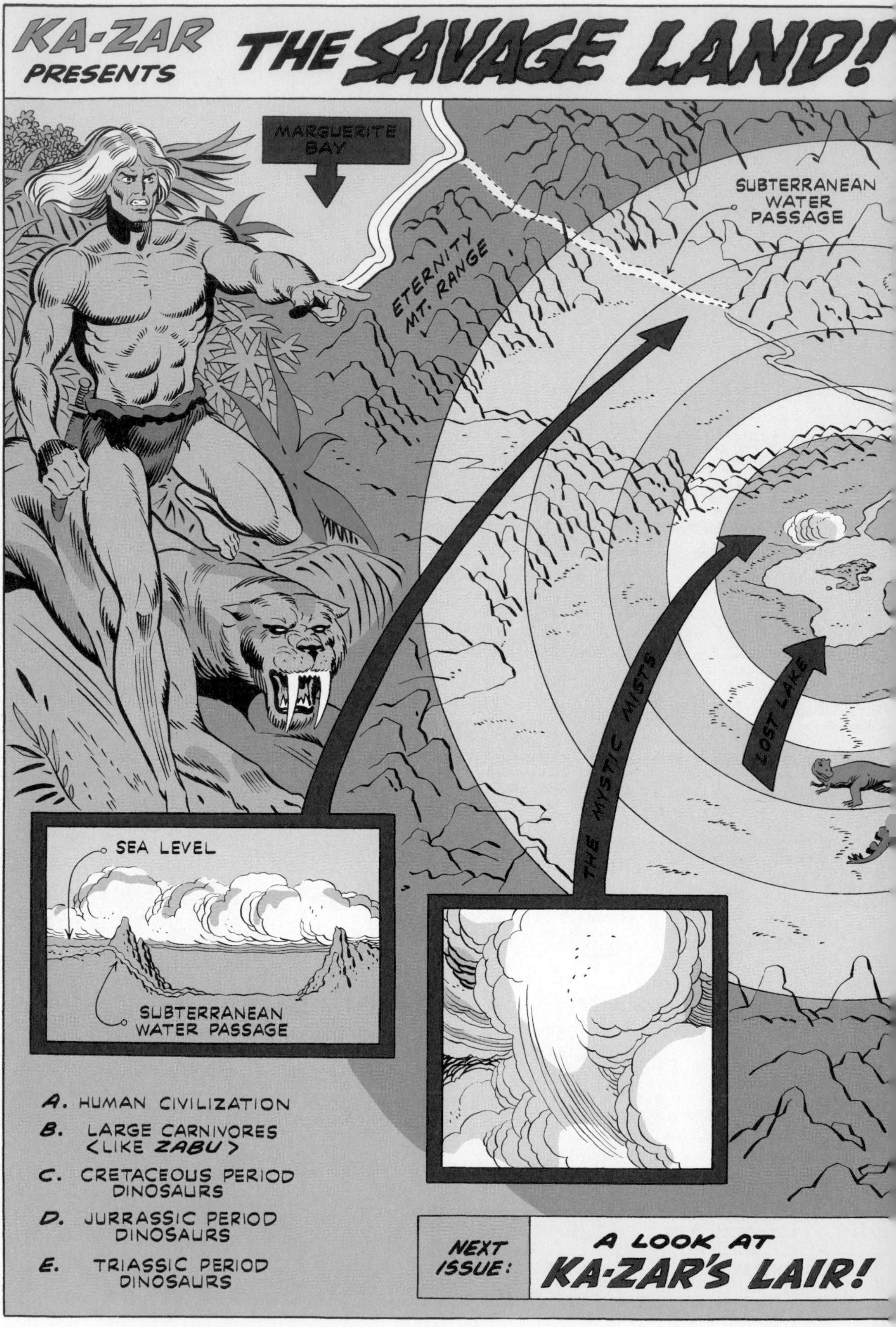
KA-ZAR PRESENTS
THE SAVAGE LAND!
MARGUERITE BAY
ETERNITY MT. RANGE
SUBTERRANEAN WATER PASSAGE
THE MYSTIC MISTS
LOST LAKE
SEA LEVEL
SUBTERRANEAN WATER PASSAGE
A. HUMAN CIVILIZATION
B. LARGE CARNIVORES (LIKE ZABU)
C. CRETACEOUS PERIOD DINOSAURS
D. JURRASSIC PERIOD DINOSAURS
E. TRIASSIC PERIOD DINOSAURS
NEXT ISSUE: A LOOK AT KA-ZAR'S LAIR!

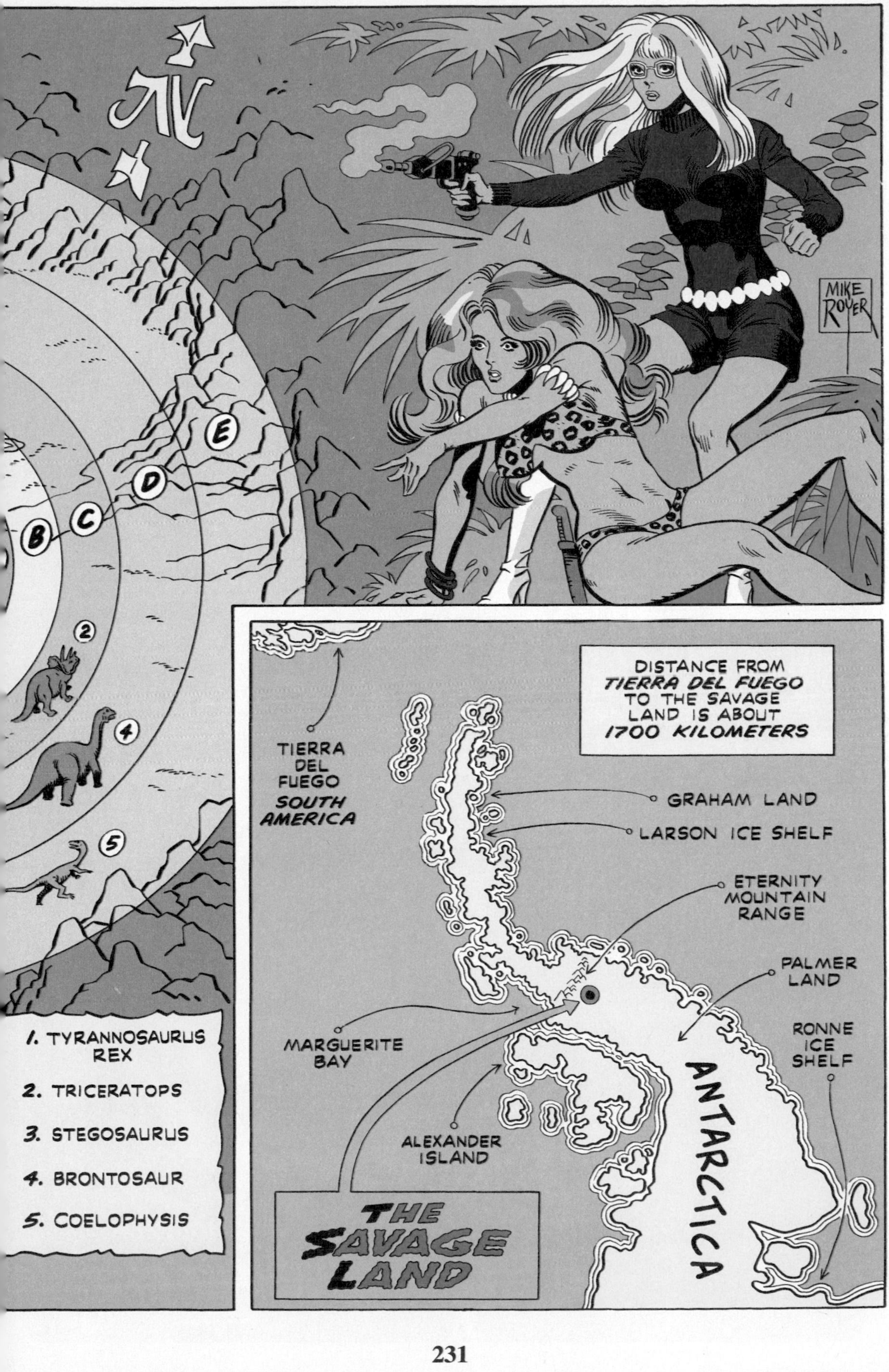

MIKE ROYER
E
D
C
B
2
4
5
1. TYRANNOSAURUS REX
2. TRICERATOPS
3. STEGOSAURUS
4. BRONTOSAUR
5. COELOPHYSIS
DISTANCE FROM TIERRA DEL FUEGO TO THE SAVAGE LAND IS ABOUT 1700 KILOMETERS
TIERRA DEL FUEGO SOUTH AMERICA
GRAHAM LAND
LARSON ICE SHELF
ETERNITY MOUNTAIN RANGE
PALMER LAND
RONNE ICE SHELF
MARGUERITE BAY
ALEXANDER ISLAND
ANTARCTICA
THE SAVAGE LAND

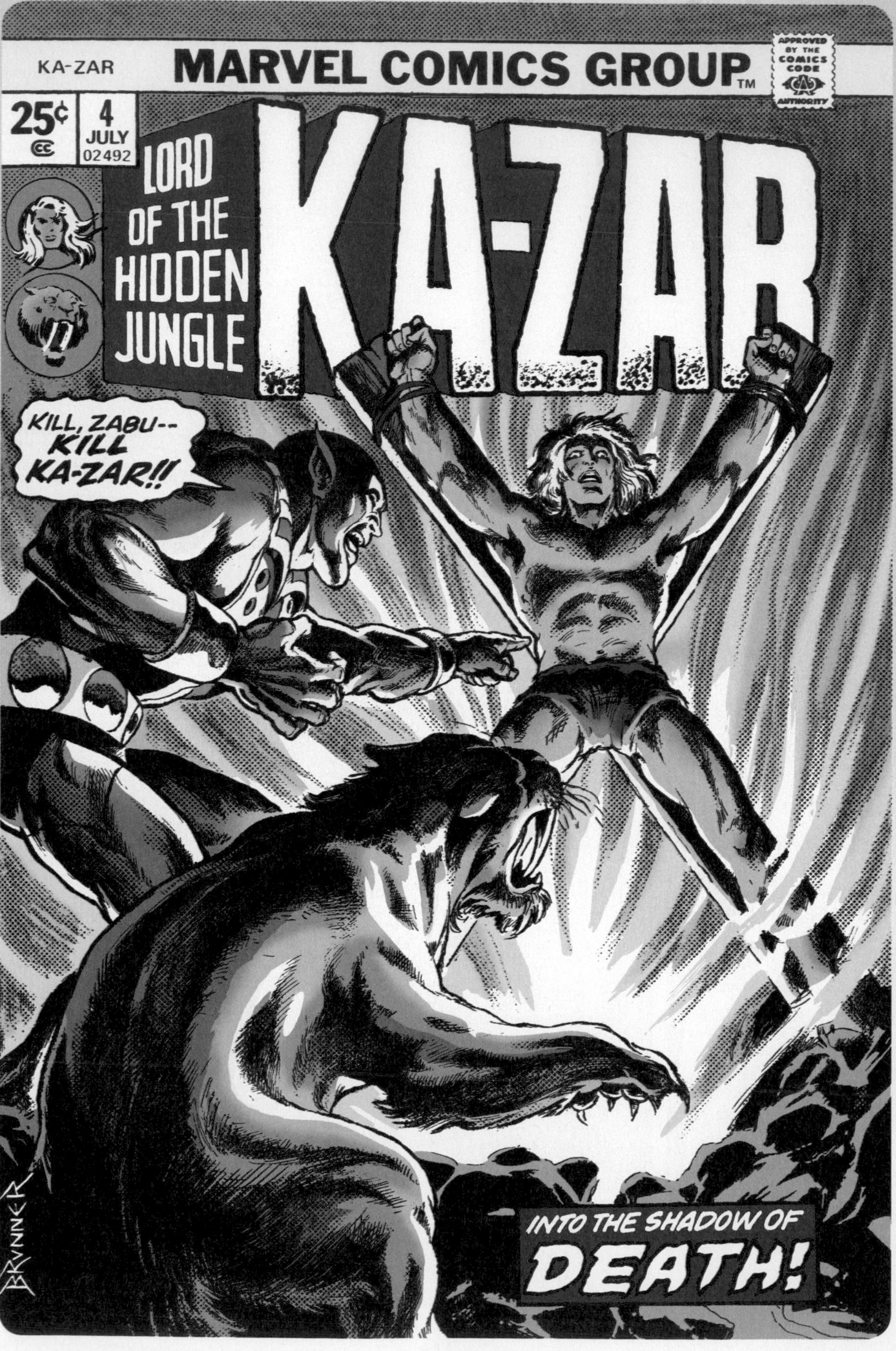
KA-ZAR
MARVEL COMICS GROUP™
APPROVED BY THE COMICS CODE AUTHORITY
25¢
CC
4
JULY
02492
LORD OF THE HIDDEN JUNGLE
KA-ZAR
KILL, ZABU-- KILL KA-ZAR!!
INTO THE SHADOW OF DEATH!
BRUNNER

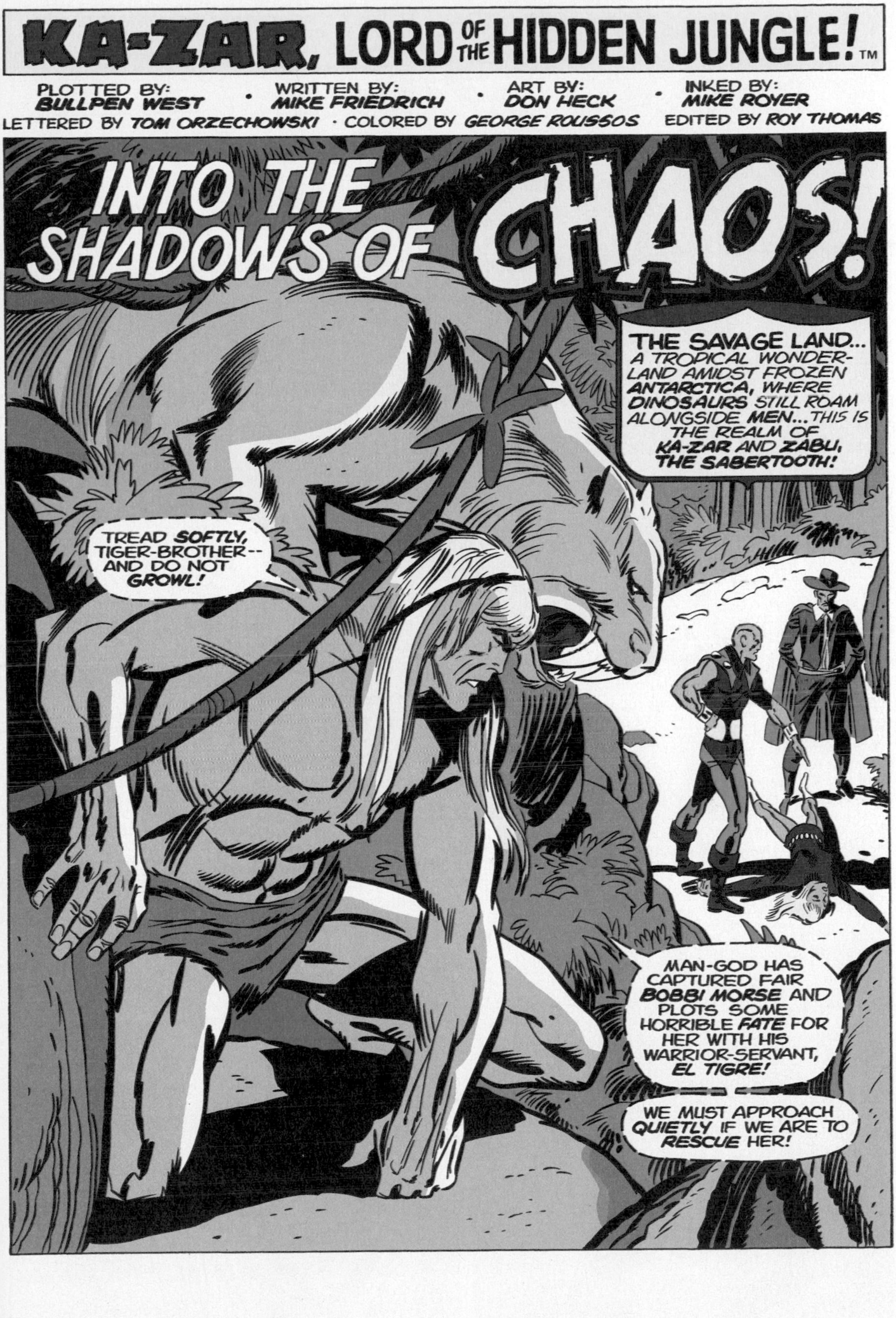

KA-ZAR, LORD OF THE HIDDEN JUNGLE! TM
PLOTTED BY: BULLPEN WEST · WRITTEN BY: MIKE FRIEDRICH · ART BY: DON HECK · INKED BY: MIKE ROYER
LETTERED BY TOM ORZECHOWSKI · COLORED BY GEORGE ROUSSOS · EDITED BY ROY THOMAS
INTO THE SHADOWS OF CHAOS!
THE SAVAGE LAND... A TROPICAL WONDER-LAND AMIDST FROZEN ANTARCTICA, WHERE DINOSAURS STILL ROAM ALONGSIDE MEN... THIS IS THE REALM OF KA-ZAR AND ZABU, THE SABERTOOTH!
TREAD SOFTLY, TIGER-BROTHER-- AND DO NOT GROWL!
MAN-GOD HAS CAPTURED FAIR BOBBI MORSE AND PLOTS SOME HORRIBLE FATE FOR HER WITH HIS WARRIOR-SERVANT, EL TIGRE!
WE MUST APPROACH QUIETLY IF WE ARE TO RESCUE HER!

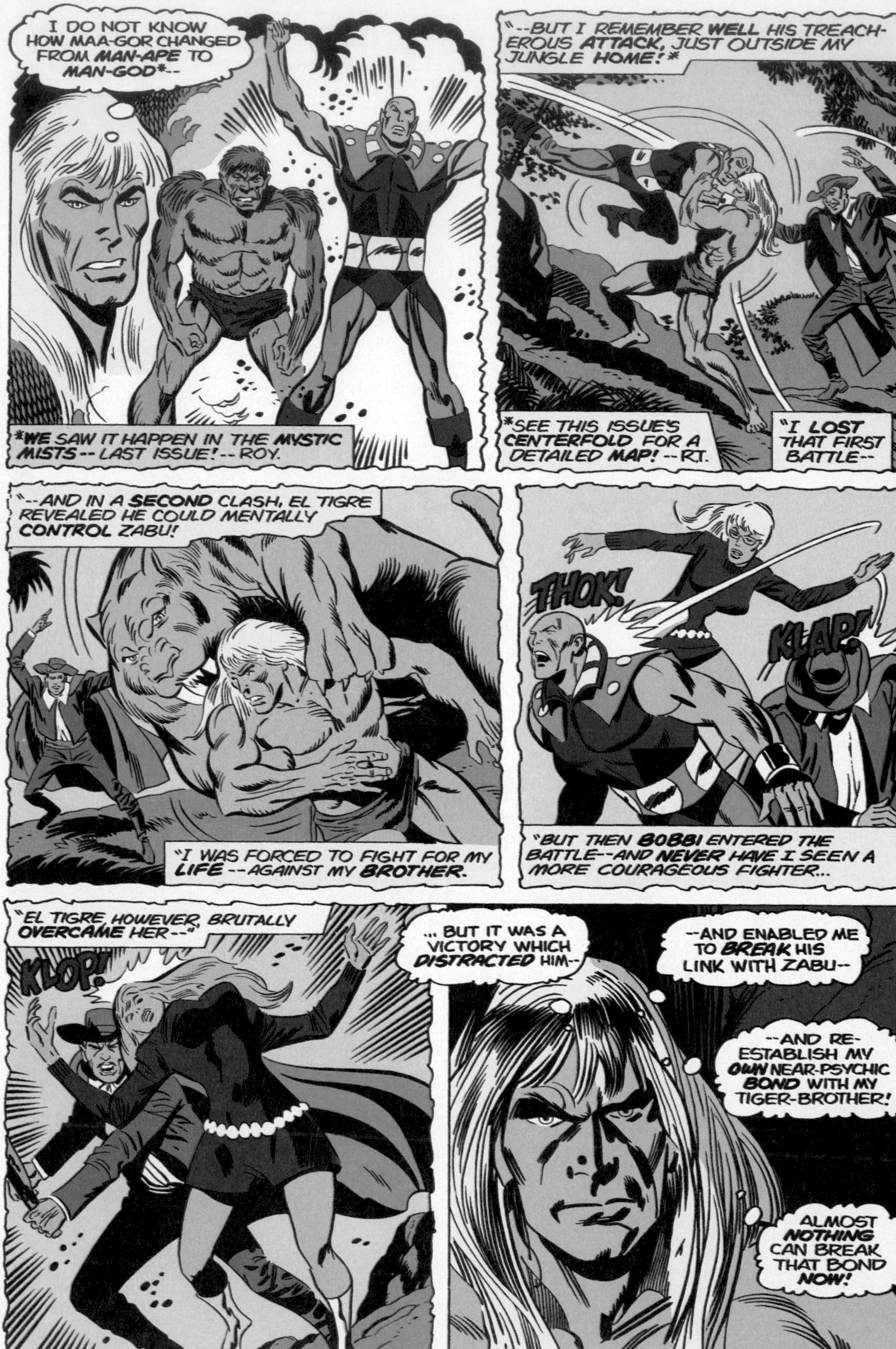
I DO NOT KNOW HOW MAA-GOR CHANGED FROM MAN-APE TO MAN-GOD*--
*WE SAW IT HAPPEN IN THE MYSTIC MISTS -- LAST ISSUE! -- ROY.
"--BUT I REMEMBER WELL HIS TREACHEROUS ATTACK, JUST OUTSIDE MY JUNGLE HOME!*
*SEE THIS ISSUE'S CENTERFOLD FOR A DETAILED MAP! -- RT.
"I LOST THAT FIRST BATTLE--
"--AND IN A SECOND CLASH, EL TIGRE REVEALED HE COULD MENTALLY CONTROL ZABU!
"I WAS FORCED TO FIGHT FOR MY LIFE -- AGAINST MY BROTHER.
THOK!
KLAP!
"BUT THEN BOBBI ENTERED THE BATTLE--AND NEVER HAVE I SEEN A MORE COURAGEOUS FIGHTER...
"EL TIGRE, HOWEVER, BRUTALLY OVERCAME HER--"
KLOP!
... BUT IT WAS A VICTORY WHICH DISTRACTED HIM--
--AND ENABLED ME TO BREAK HIS LINK WITH ZABU--
--AND RE-ESTABLISH MY OWN NEAR-PSYCHIC BOND WITH MY TIGER-BROTHER!
ALMOST NOTHING CAN BREAK THAT BOND NOW!

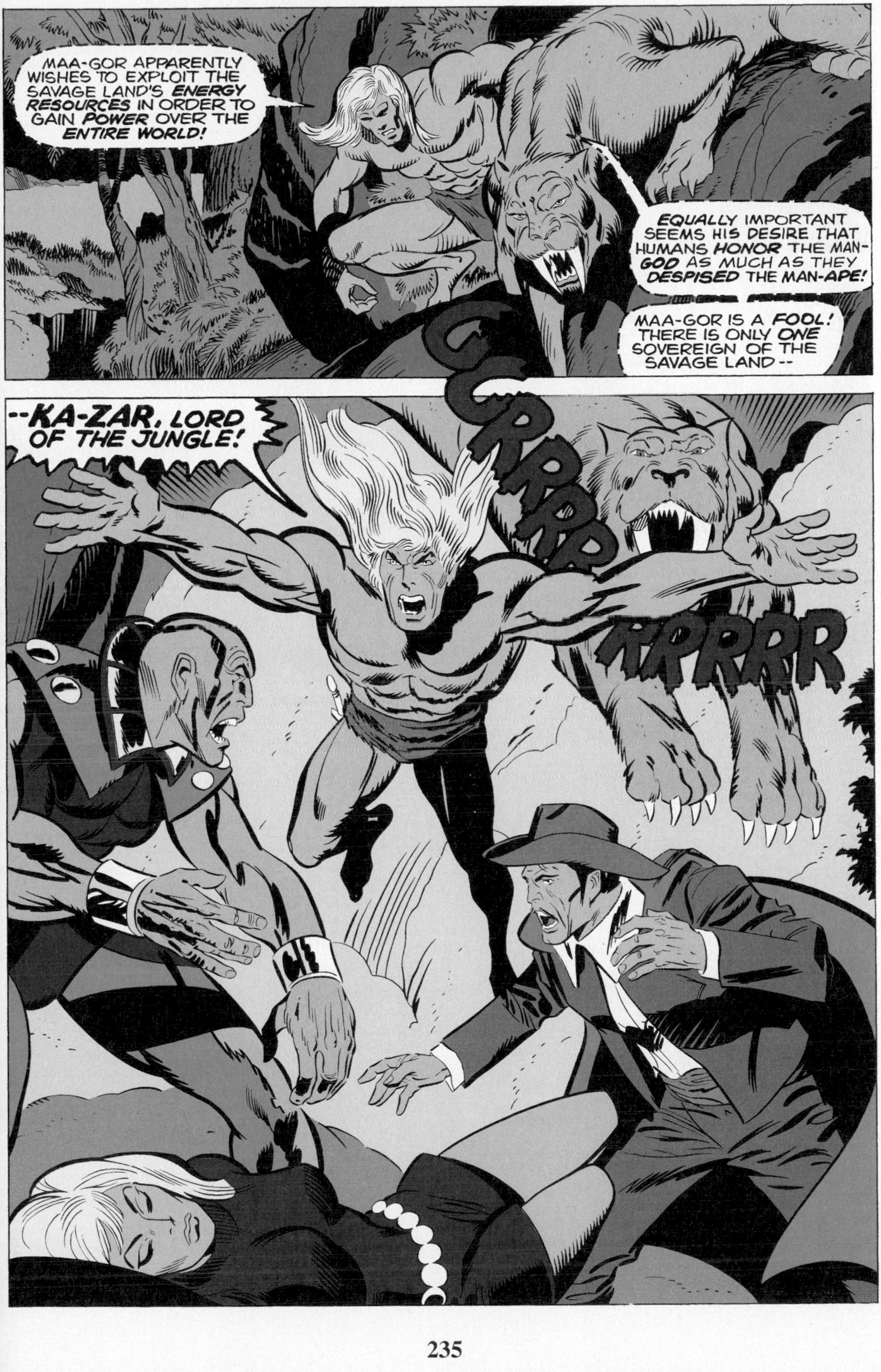

MAA-GOR APPARENTLY WISHES TO EXPLOIT THE SAVAGE LAND'S ENERGY RESOURCES IN ORDER TO GAIN POWER OVER THE ENTIRE WORLD!
EQUALLY IMPORTANT SEEMS HIS DESIRE THAT HUMANS HONOR THE MAN-GOD AS MUCH AS THEY DESPISED THE MAN-APE!
MAA-GOR IS A FOOL! THERE IS ONLY ONE SOVEREIGN OF THE SAVAGE LAND --
GURRRR
--KA-ZAR, LORD OF THE JUNGLE!
RRRRRR

I WOULD HAVE BELIEVED YOU *DEAD* BY NOW, KA-ZAR! YOU MUST HAVE MADE A *MIRACULOUS* ESCAPE!

HAVE YOU NOT YET *LEARNED* THAT I AM NOW YOUR *SUPERIOR?*

YOUR WORDS CARRY NO *EMOTION*, MAA-GOR, AS IF THEY WERE FULL OF *LOGIC!*

BUT *ANYONE* COULD REASON THAT KA-ZAR BOWS TO *NO-ONE!*

AND NEITHER DOES *ZABU*, IT SEEMS!

MY MENTAL *POWER* OVER THE SABER-TOOTH APPEARS *LOST!*

GRRRRR

PUNK!

BUT AS THE MAN-GOD LANDS A STUNNING KICK TO KA-ZAR'S *SKULL*--

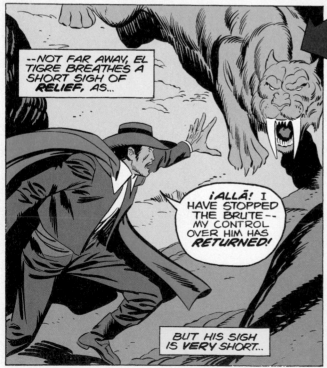

--NOT FAR AWAY, EL TIGRE BREATHES A SHORT SIGH OF *RELIEF*, AS...

¡ALLÁ! I HAVE STOPPED THE BRUTE-- MY CONTROL OVER HIM HAS *RETURNED!*

BUT HIS SIGH IS *VERY SHORT*...

...SINCE EL TIGRE DOESN'T KNOW IT WAS ONLY KA-ZAR'S *GROGGINESS* THAT ALLOWED THAT MOMENTARY CONTROL...

AND SO NOW...

¡DIABLOS! I HAVE ONLY SAVED MY-SELF FOR A *SECOND*--

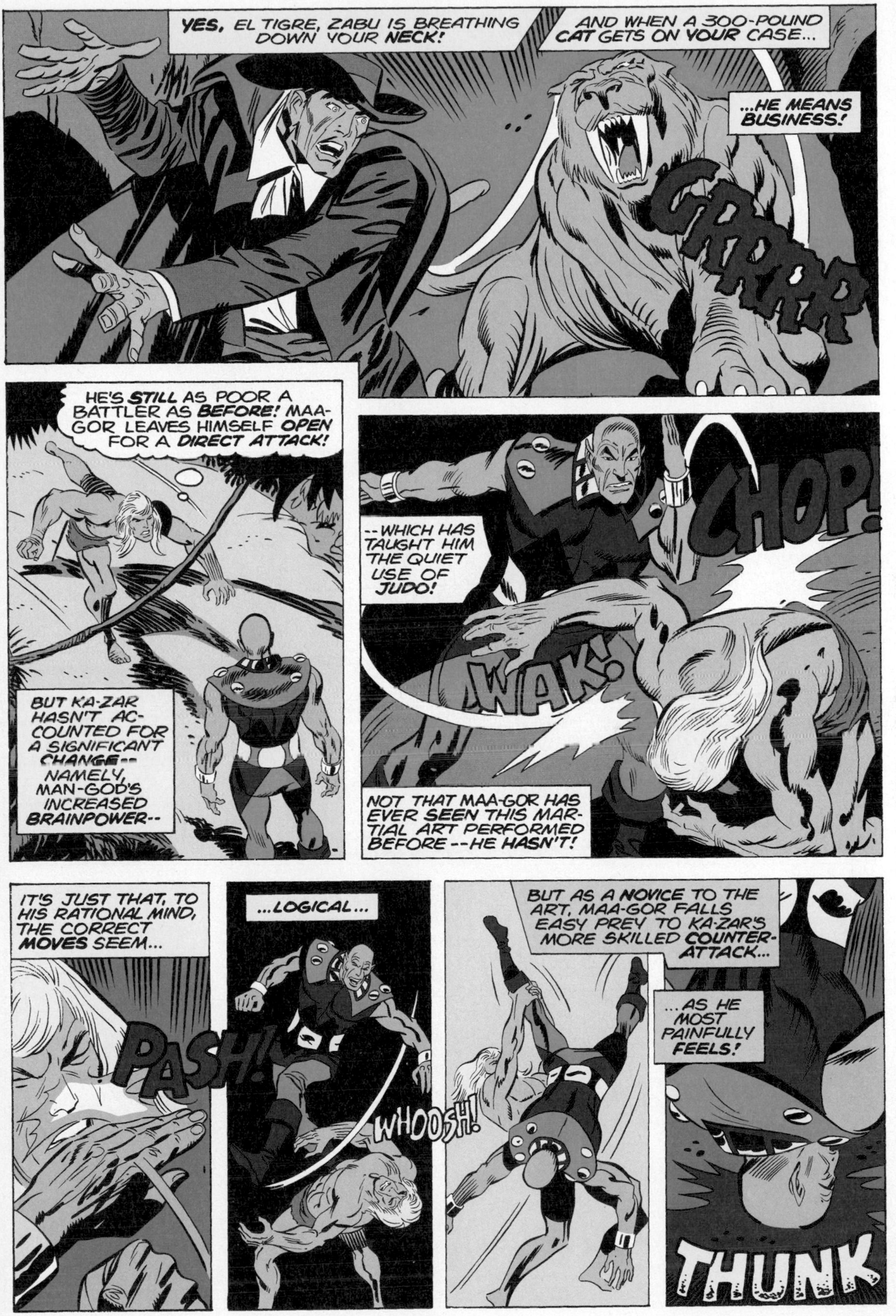
YES, EL TIGRE, ZABU IS BREATHING DOWN YOUR NECK!
AND WHEN A 300-POUND CAT GETS ON YOUR CASE...
...HE MEANS BUSINESS!
GRRRR
HE'S STILL AS POOR A BATTLER AS BEFORE! MAA-GOR LEAVES HIMSELF OPEN FOR A DIRECT ATTACK!
BUT KA-ZAR HASN'T ACCOUNTED FOR A SIGNIFICANT CHANGE-- NAMELY, MAN-GOD'S INCREASED BRAINPOWER--
--WHICH HAS TAUGHT HIM THE QUIET USE OF JUDO!
CHOP!
WAK!
NOT THAT MAA-GOR HAS EVER SEEN THIS MARTIAL ART PERFORMED BEFORE --HE HASN'T!
IT'S JUST THAT, TO HIS RATIONAL MIND, THE CORRECT MOVES SEEM...
PASH!
...LOGICAL...
WHOOSH!
BUT AS A NOVICE TO THE ART, MAA-GOR FALLS EASY PREY TO KA-ZAR'S MORE SKILLED COUNTER-ATTACK...
...AS HE MOST PAINFULLY FEELS!
THUNK

YES, FEELS!

MAA-GOR'S *PAIN* ACTS AS A *STEAM-ROLLER* THRU HIS LOGIC, PAVING A PATH STRAIGHT TO THE *EMOTION* DEEP WITHIN... THE HATE--!

--AND IT *CHANGES* HIM!

OUT COMES THE *MONSTER* THAT REMEMBERS EACH *DEFEAT* AT KA-ZAR'S HANDS!

IT IS THE *HATE* THAT DRIVES MAA-GOR NOW--

CHOK!

--AND IT BRINGS TO THE FORE UNTHINKING *BRUTE FORCE!*

I HAD *SEEN* THIS CHANGE COME OVER MAA-GOR *BEFORE*--

--BUT I WAS STILL CAUGHT *OFF-GUARD*-- ϶UHH!϶

BASH!

THERE CAN ONLY BE *ONE FATE* FOR YOU, KA-ZAR--

DEATH!

DEATH!

DEATH!

THEN AS KA-ZAR *CRUMPLES* AT MAN-GOD'S FEET...

...MAA-GOR'S EMOTION WASHES AWAY LIKE A DEPARTING *TIDE*...

NO... NO... I DO NOT *TRULY* WISH TO SO *PRIVATELY* MURDER KA-ZAR!

I HAVE A MORE *APPROPRIATE* PLAN!

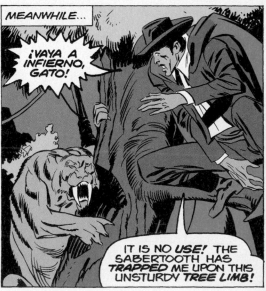

MEANWHILE...

¡VAYA A INFIERNO, GATO!

IT IS NO *USE!* THE *SABERTOOTH* HAS *TRAPPED* ME UPON THIS UNSTURDY *TREE LIMB!*

238

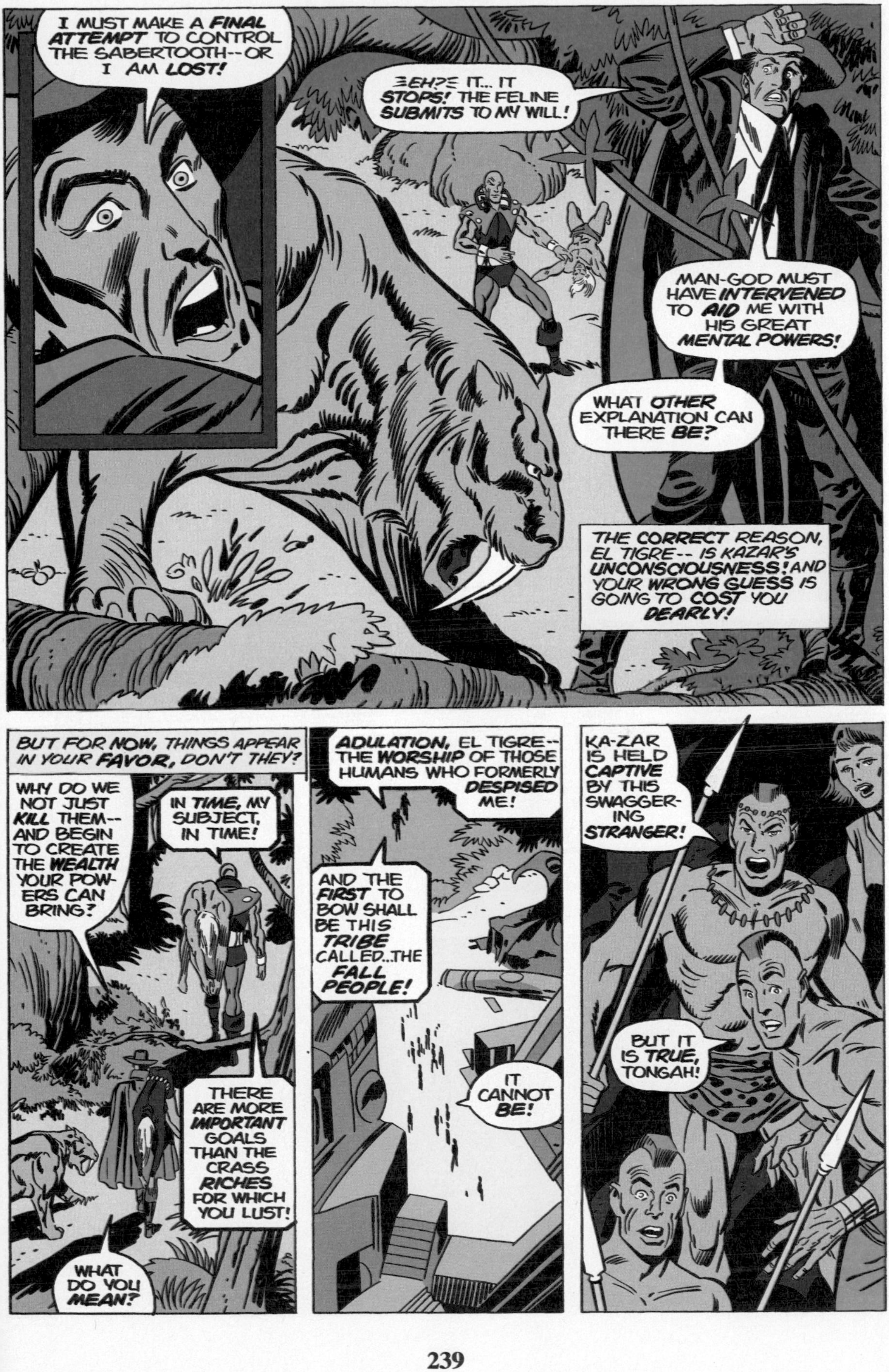
I MUST MAKE A FINAL ATTEMPT TO CONTROL THE SABERTOOTH--OR I AM LOST!
EH? IT... IT STOPS! THE FELINE SUBMITS TO MY WILL!
MAN-GOD MUST HAVE INTERVENED TO AID ME WITH HIS GREAT MENTAL POWERS!
WHAT OTHER EXPLANATION CAN THERE BE?
THE CORRECT REASON, EL TIGRE-- IS KAZAR'S UNCONSCIOUSNESS! AND YOUR WRONG GUESS IS GOING TO COST YOU DEARLY!
BUT FOR NOW, THINGS APPEAR IN YOUR FAVOR, DON'T THEY?
WHY DO WE NOT JUST KILL THEM-- AND BEGIN TO CREATE THE WEALTH YOUR POWERS CAN BRING?
IN TIME, MY SUBJECT, IN TIME!
THERE ARE MORE IMPORTANT GOALS THAN THE CRASS RICHES FOR WHICH YOU LUST!
WHAT DO YOU MEAN?
ADULATION, EL TIGRE-- THE WORSHIP OF THOSE HUMANS WHO FORMERLY DESPISED ME!
AND THE FIRST TO BOW SHALL BE THIS TRIBE CALLED...THE FALL PEOPLE!
IT CANNOT BE!
KA-ZAR IS HELD CAPTIVE BY THIS SWAGGERING STRANGER!
BUT IT IS TRUE, TONGAH!

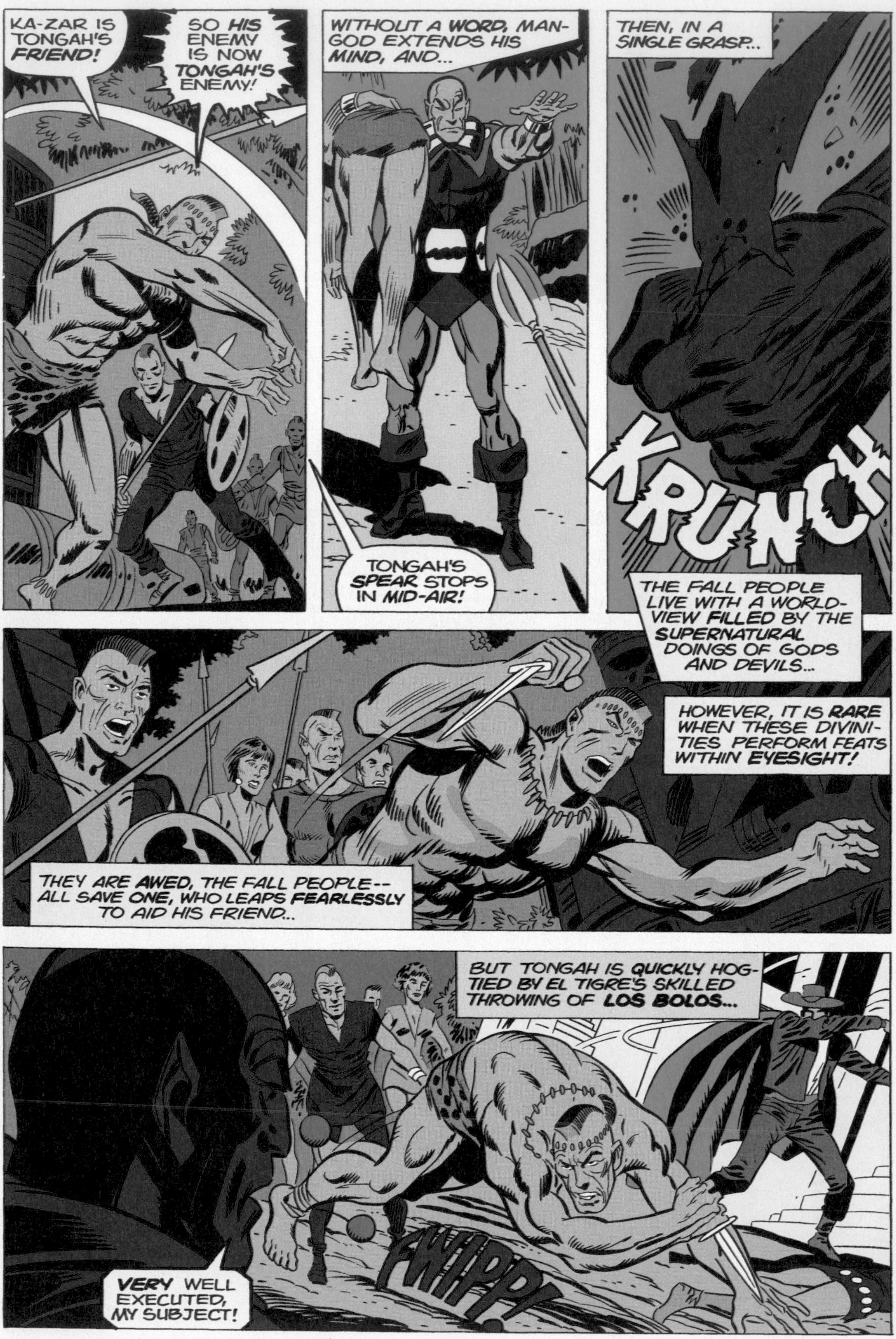
KA-ZAR IS TONGAH'S FRIEND!
SO HIS ENEMY IS NOW TONGAH'S ENEMY!
WITHOUT A WORD, MAN-GOD EXTENDS HIS MIND, AND...
TONGAH'S SPEAR STOPS IN MID-AIR!
THEN, IN A SINGLE GRASP...
KRUNCH
THE FALL PEOPLE LIVE WITH A WORLD-VIEW FILLED BY THE SUPERNATURAL DOINGS OF GODS AND DEVILS...
HOWEVER, IT IS RARE WHEN THESE DIVINITIES PERFORM FEATS WITHIN EYESIGHT!
THEY ARE AWED, THE FALL PEOPLE-- ALL SAVE ONE, WHO LEAPS FEARLESSLY TO AID HIS FRIEND...
BUT TONGAH IS QUICKLY HOG-TIED BY EL TIGRE'S SKILLED THROWING OF LOS BOLOS...
VERY WELL EXECUTED, MY SUBJECT!
FWIPP!

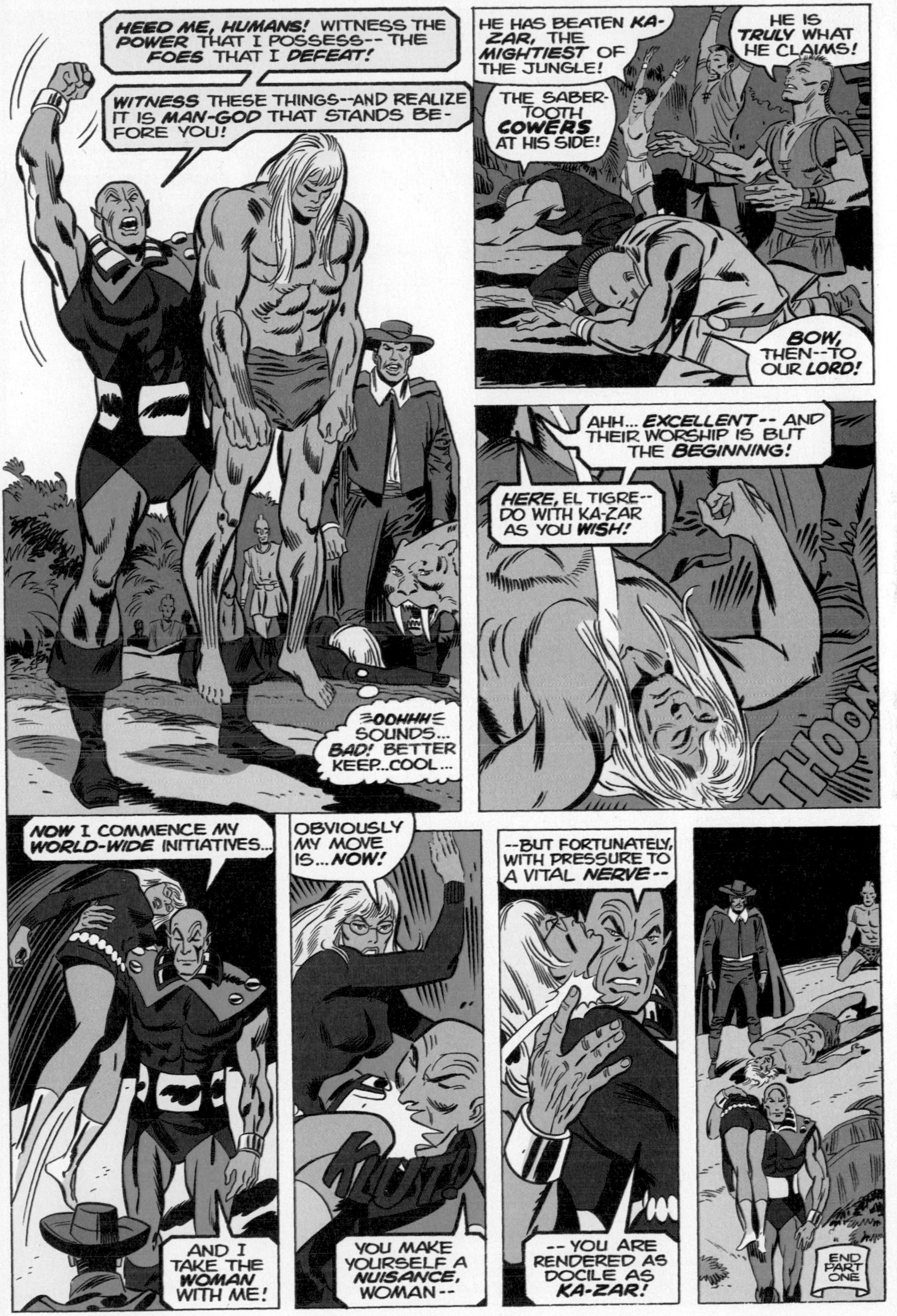
HEED ME, HUMANS! WITNESS THE POWER THAT I POSSESS-- THE FOES THAT I DEFEAT!
WITNESS THESE THINGS--AND REALIZE IT IS MAN-GOD THAT STANDS BE-FORE YOU!
OOHHH SOUNDS... BAD! BETTER KEEP...COOL...
HE HAS BEATEN KA-ZAR, THE MIGHTIEST OF THE JUNGLE!
THE SABER-TOOTH COWERS AT HIS SIDE!
HE IS TRULY WHAT HE CLAIMS!
BOW, THEN--TO OUR LORD!
AHH... EXCELLENT-- AND THEIR WORSHIP IS BUT THE BEGINNING!
HERE, EL TIGRE-- DO WITH KA-ZAR AS YOU WISH!
THOOM
NOW I COMMENCE MY WORLD-WIDE INITIATIVES...
AND I TAKE THE WOMAN WITH ME!
OBVIOUSLY MY MOVE IS...NOW!
KLUT!
YOU MAKE YOURSELF A NUISANCE, WOMAN--
--BUT FORTUNATELY, WITH PRESSURE TO A VITAL NERVE--
--YOU ARE RENDERED AS DOCILE AS KA-ZAR!
END PART ONE

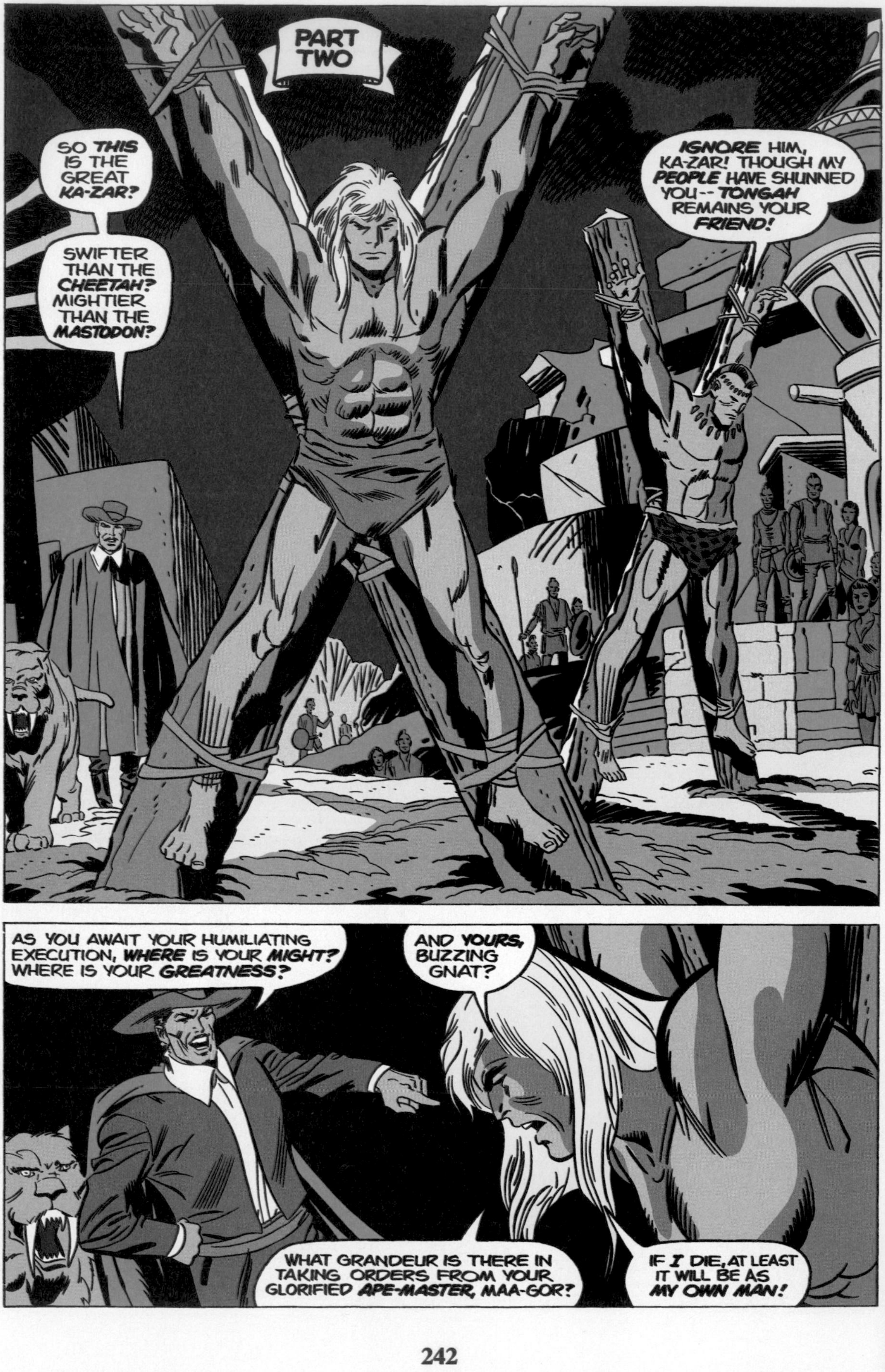
PART TWO
SO THIS IS THE GREAT KA-ZAR?
SWIFTER THAN THE CHEETAH? MIGHTIER THAN THE MASTODON?
IGNORE HIM, KA-ZAR! THOUGH MY PEOPLE HAVE SHUNNED YOU-- TONGAH REMAINS YOUR FRIEND!
AS YOU AWAIT YOUR HUMILIATING EXECUTION, WHERE IS YOUR MIGHT? WHERE IS YOUR GREATNESS?
AND YOURS, BUZZING GNAT?
WHAT GRANDEUR IS THERE IN TAKING ORDERS FROM YOUR GLORIFIED APE-MASTER, MAA-GOR?
IF I DIE, AT LEAST IT WILL BE AS MY OWN MAN!

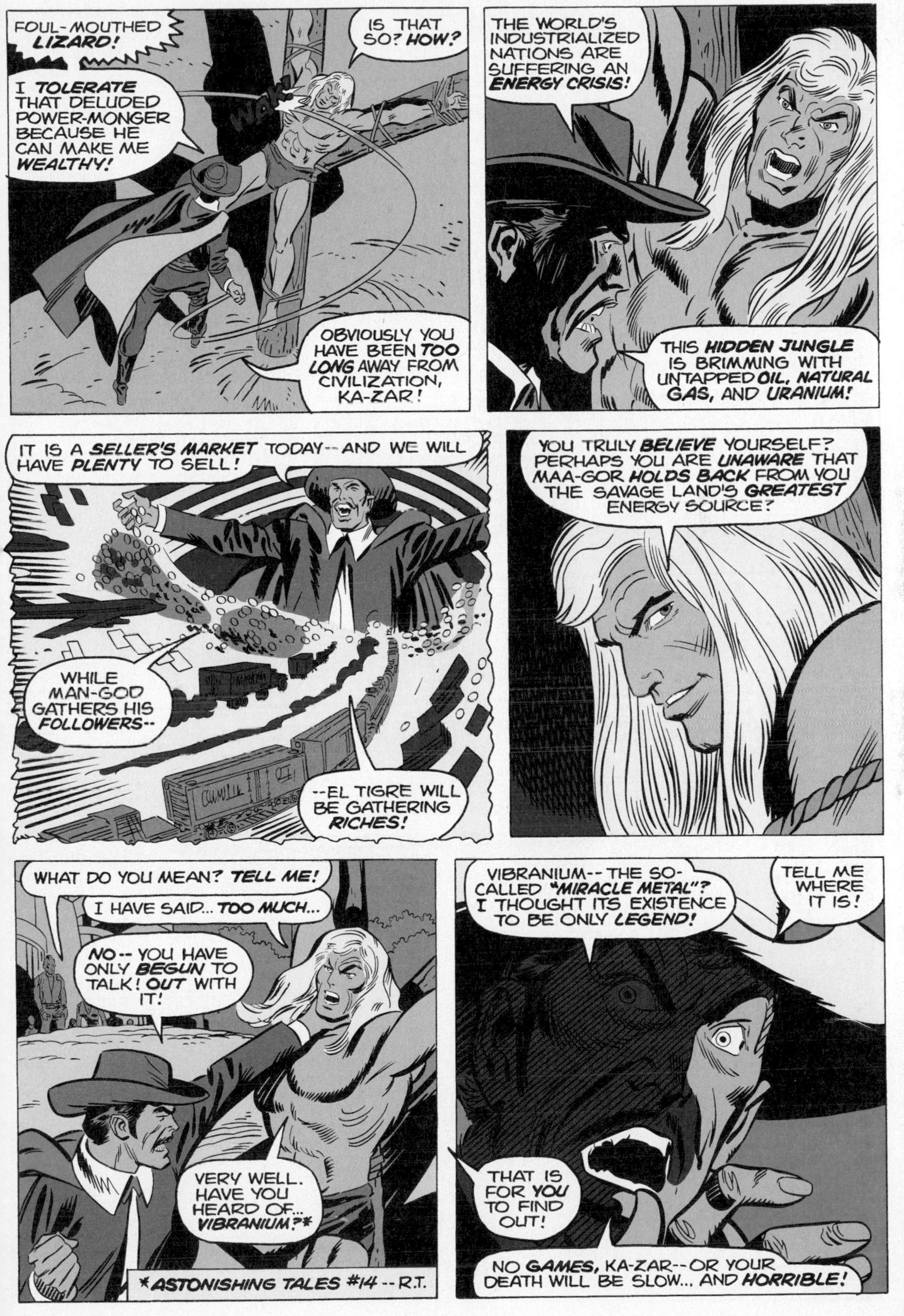

FOUL-MOUTHED LIZARD!
IS THAT SO? HOW?
I TOLERATE THAT DELUDED POWER-MONGER BECAUSE HE CAN MAKE ME WEALTHY!
WAK!
OBVIOUSLY YOU HAVE BEEN TOO LONG AWAY FROM CIVILIZATION, KA-ZAR!
THE WORLD'S INDUSTRIALIZED NATIONS ARE SUFFERING AN ENERGY CRISIS!
THIS HIDDEN JUNGLE IS BRIMMING WITH UNTAPPED OIL, NATURAL GAS, AND URANIUM!
IT IS A SELLER'S MARKET TODAY-- AND WE WILL HAVE PLENTY TO SELL!
WHILE MAN-GOD GATHERS HIS FOLLOWERS--
--EL TIGRE WILL BE GATHERING RICHES!
YOU TRULY BELIEVE YOURSELF? PERHAPS YOU ARE UNAWARE THAT MAA-GOR HOLDS BACK FROM YOU THE SAVAGE LAND'S GREATEST ENERGY SOURCE?
WHAT DO YOU MEAN? TELL ME!
I HAVE SAID... TOO MUCH...
NO-- YOU HAVE ONLY BEGUN TO TALK! OUT WITH IT!
VERY WELL. HAVE YOU HEARD OF... VIBRANIUM?*
*ASTONISHING TALES #14 -- R.T.
VIBRANIUM-- THE SO-CALLED "MIRACLE METAL"? I THOUGHT ITS EXISTENCE TO BE ONLY LEGEND!
TELL ME WHERE IT IS!
THAT IS FOR YOU TO FIND OUT!
NO GAMES, KA-ZAR-- OR YOUR DEATH WILL BE SLOW... AND HORRIBLE!

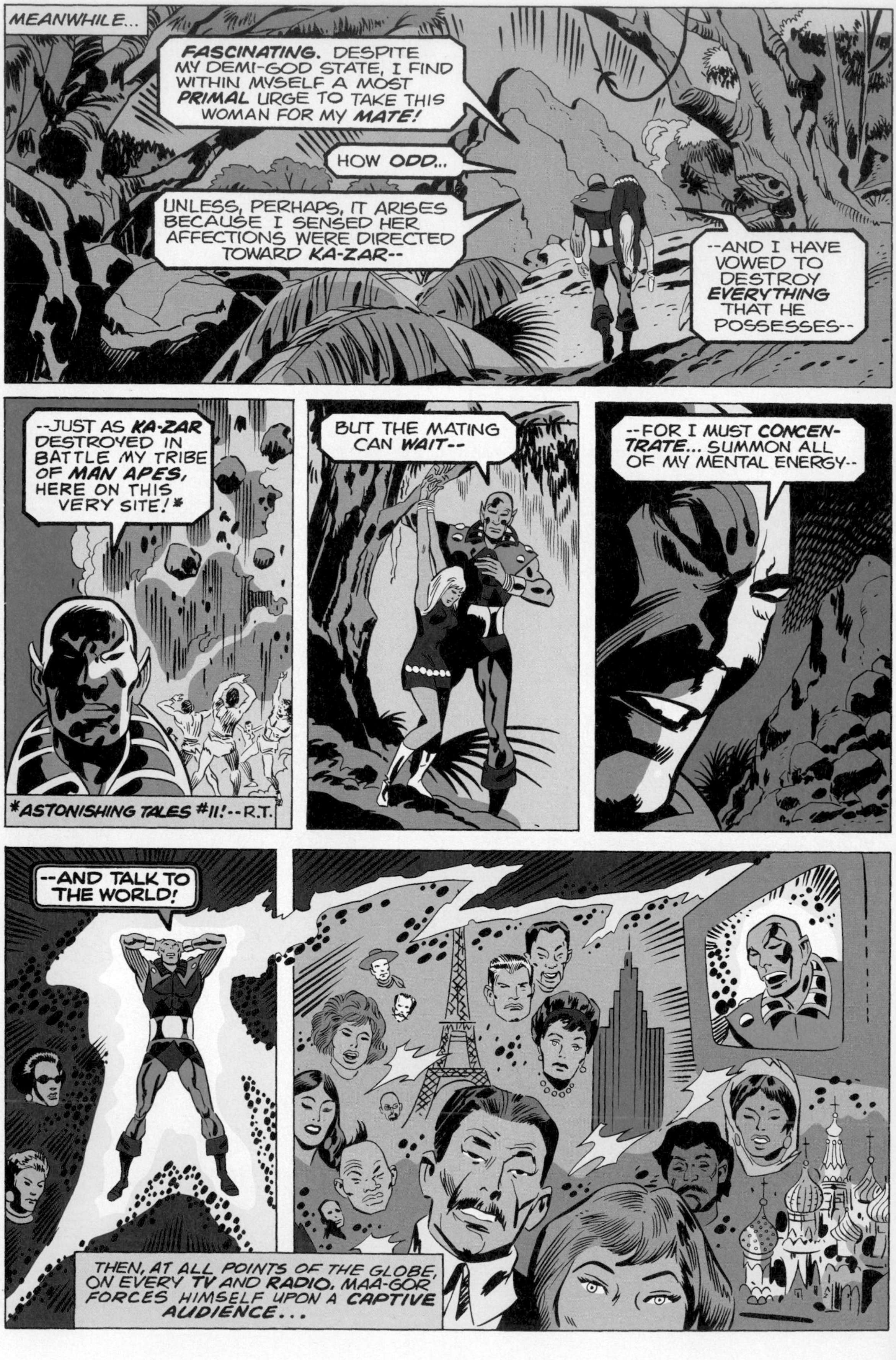
MEANWHILE...
FASCINATING. DESPITE MY DEMI-GOD STATE, I FIND WITHIN MYSELF A MOST PRIMAL URGE TO TAKE THIS WOMAN FOR MY MATE!
HOW ODD...
UNLESS, PERHAPS, IT ARISES BECAUSE I SENSED HER AFFECTIONS WERE DIRECTED TOWARD KA-ZAR--
--AND I HAVE VOWED TO DESTROY EVERYTHING THAT HE POSSESSES--
--JUST AS KA-ZAR DESTROYED IN BATTLE MY TRIBE OF MAN APES, HERE ON THIS VERY SITE!*
*ASTONISHING TALES #11!--R.T.
BUT THE MATING CAN WAIT--
--FOR I MUST CONCEN-TRATE... SUMMON ALL OF MY MENTAL ENERGY--
--AND TALK TO THE WORLD!
THEN, AT ALL POINTS OF THE GLOBE, ON EVERY TV AND RADIO, MAA-GOR FORCES HIMSELF UPON A CAPTIVE AUDIENCE...

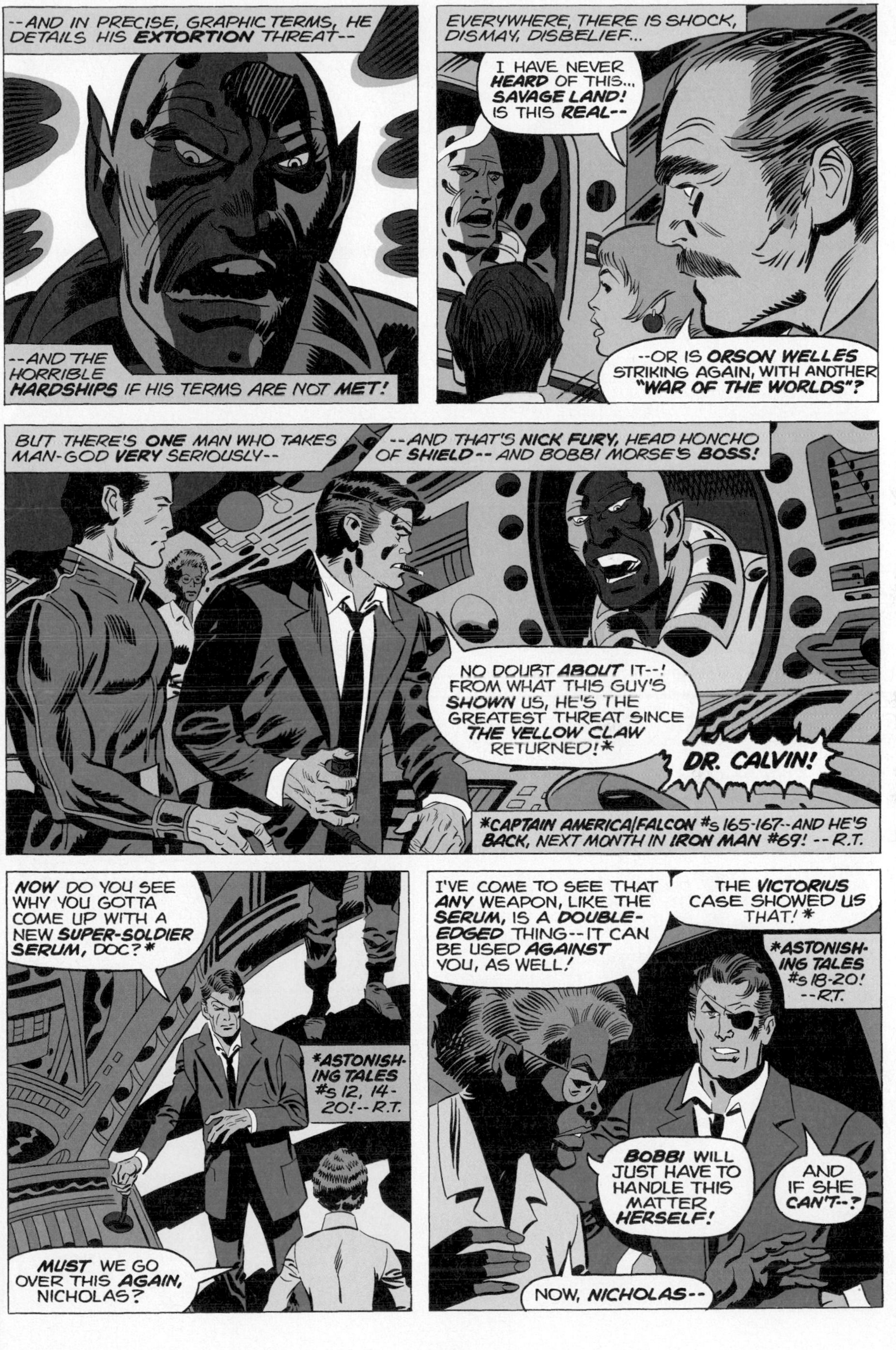
--AND IN PRECISE, GRAPHIC TERMS, HE DETAILS HIS EXTORTION THREAT--
--AND THE HORRIBLE HARDSHIPS IF HIS TERMS ARE NOT MET!
EVERYWHERE, THERE IS SHOCK, DISMAY, DISBELIEF...
I HAVE NEVER HEARD OF THIS... SAVAGE LAND! IS THIS REAL--
--OR IS ORSON WELLES STRIKING AGAIN, WITH ANOTHER "WAR OF THE WORLDS"?
BUT THERE'S ONE MAN WHO TAKES MAN-GOD VERY SERIOUSLY--
--AND THAT'S NICK FURY, HEAD HONCHO OF SHIELD-- AND BOBBI MORSE'S BOSS!
NO DOUBT ABOUT IT--! FROM WHAT THIS GUY'S SHOWN US, HE'S THE GREATEST THREAT SINCE THE YELLOW CLAW RETURNED!*
DR. CALVIN!
*CAPTAIN AMERICA/FALCON #s 165-167--AND HE'S BACK, NEXT MONTH IN IRON MAN #69! --R.T.
NOW DO YOU SEE WHY YOU GOTTA COME UP WITH A NEW SUPER-SOLDIER SERUM, DOC?*
*ASTONISHING TALES #s 12, 14-20!--R.T.
MUST WE GO OVER THIS AGAIN, NICHOLAS?
I'VE COME TO SEE THAT ANY WEAPON, LIKE THE SERUM, IS A DOUBLE-EDGED THING--IT CAN BE USED AGAINST YOU, AS WELL!
THE VICTORIUS CASE SHOWED US THAT!*
*ASTONISHING TALES #s 18-20! --R.T.
BOBBI WILL JUST HAVE TO HANDLE THIS MATTER HERSELF!
AND IF SHE CAN'T--?
NOW, NICHOLAS--

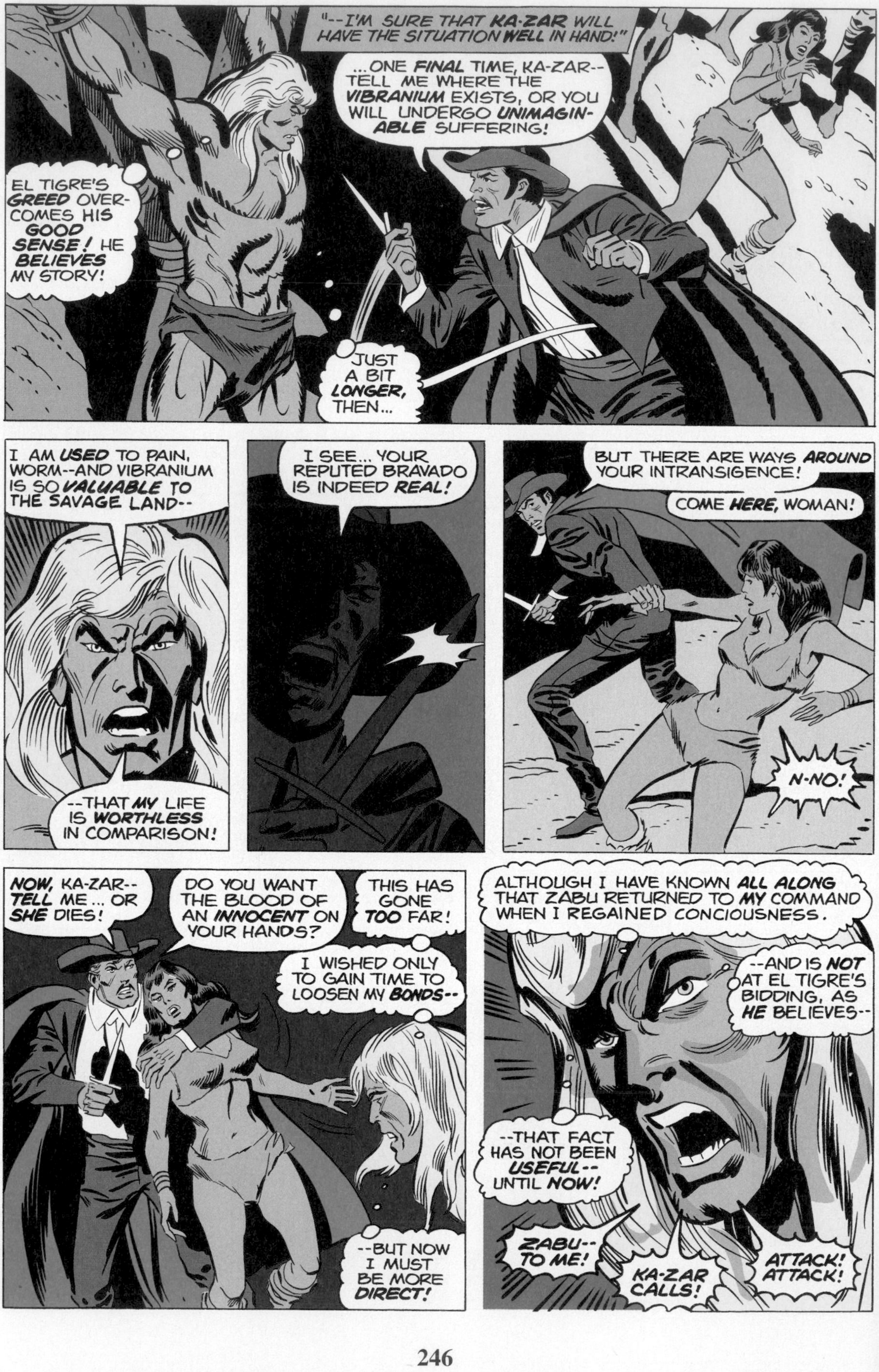
"--I'M SURE THAT KA-ZAR WILL HAVE THE SITUATION WELL IN HAND!"
...ONE FINAL TIME, KA-ZAR--TELL ME WHERE THE VIBRANIUM EXISTS, OR YOU WILL UNDERGO UNIMAGIN-ABLE SUFFERING!
EL TIGRE'S GREED OVER-COMES HIS GOOD SENSE! HE BELIEVES MY STORY!
JUST A BIT LONGER, THEN...
I AM USED TO PAIN, WORM--AND VIBRANIUM IS SO VALUABLE TO THE SAVAGE LAND--
--THAT MY LIFE IS WORTHLESS IN COMPARISON!
I SEE... YOUR REPUTED BRAVADO IS INDEED REAL!
BUT THERE ARE WAYS AROUND YOUR INTRANSIGENCE!
COME HERE, WOMAN!
N-NO!
NOW, KA-ZAR--TELL ME... OR SHE DIES!
DO YOU WANT THE BLOOD OF AN INNOCENT ON YOUR HANDS?
THIS HAS GONE TOO FAR!
I WISHED ONLY TO GAIN TIME TO LOOSEN MY BONDS--
--BUT NOW I MUST BE MORE DIRECT!
ALTHOUGH I HAVE KNOWN ALL ALONG THAT ZABU RETURNED TO MY COMMAND WHEN I REGAINED CONCIOUSNESS.
--AND IS NOT AT EL TIGRE'S BIDDING, AS HE BELIEVES--
--THAT FACT HAS NOT BEEN USEFUL--UNTIL NOW!
ZABU--TO ME!
KA-ZAR CALLS!
ATTACK! ATTACK!

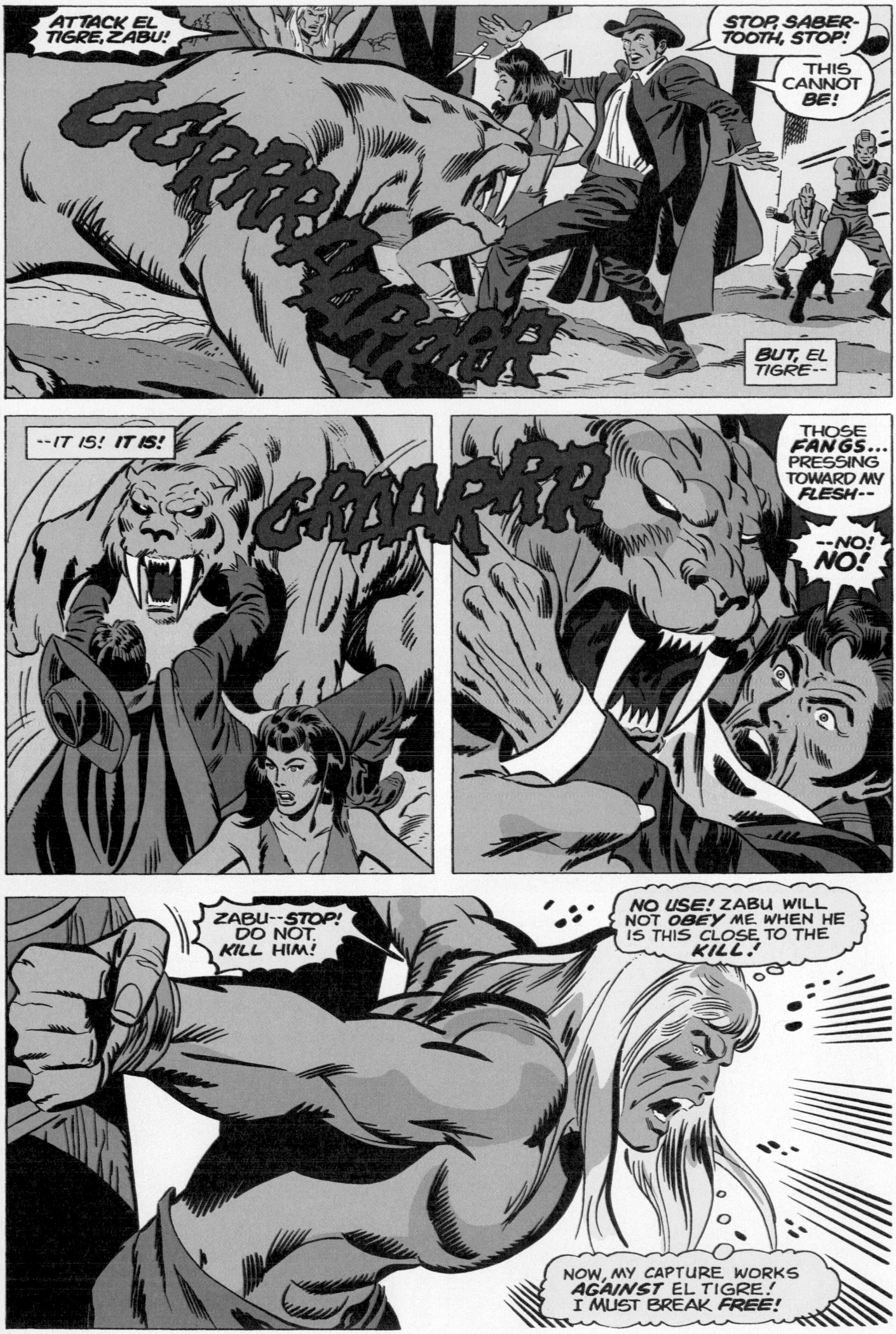
ATTACK EL TIGRE, ZABU!
STOP, SABER-TOOTH, STOP!
THIS CANNOT BE!
GGRRRAARRRR
BUT, EL TIGRE--
--IT IS! IT IS!
GRAARRR
THOSE FANGS... PRESSING TOWARD MY FLESH--
--NO! NO!
ZABU--STOP! DO NOT KILL HIM!
NO USE! ZABU WILL NOT OBEY ME WHEN HE IS THIS CLOSE TO THE KILL!
NOW, MY CAPTURE WORKS AGAINST EL TIGRE! I MUST BREAK FREE!

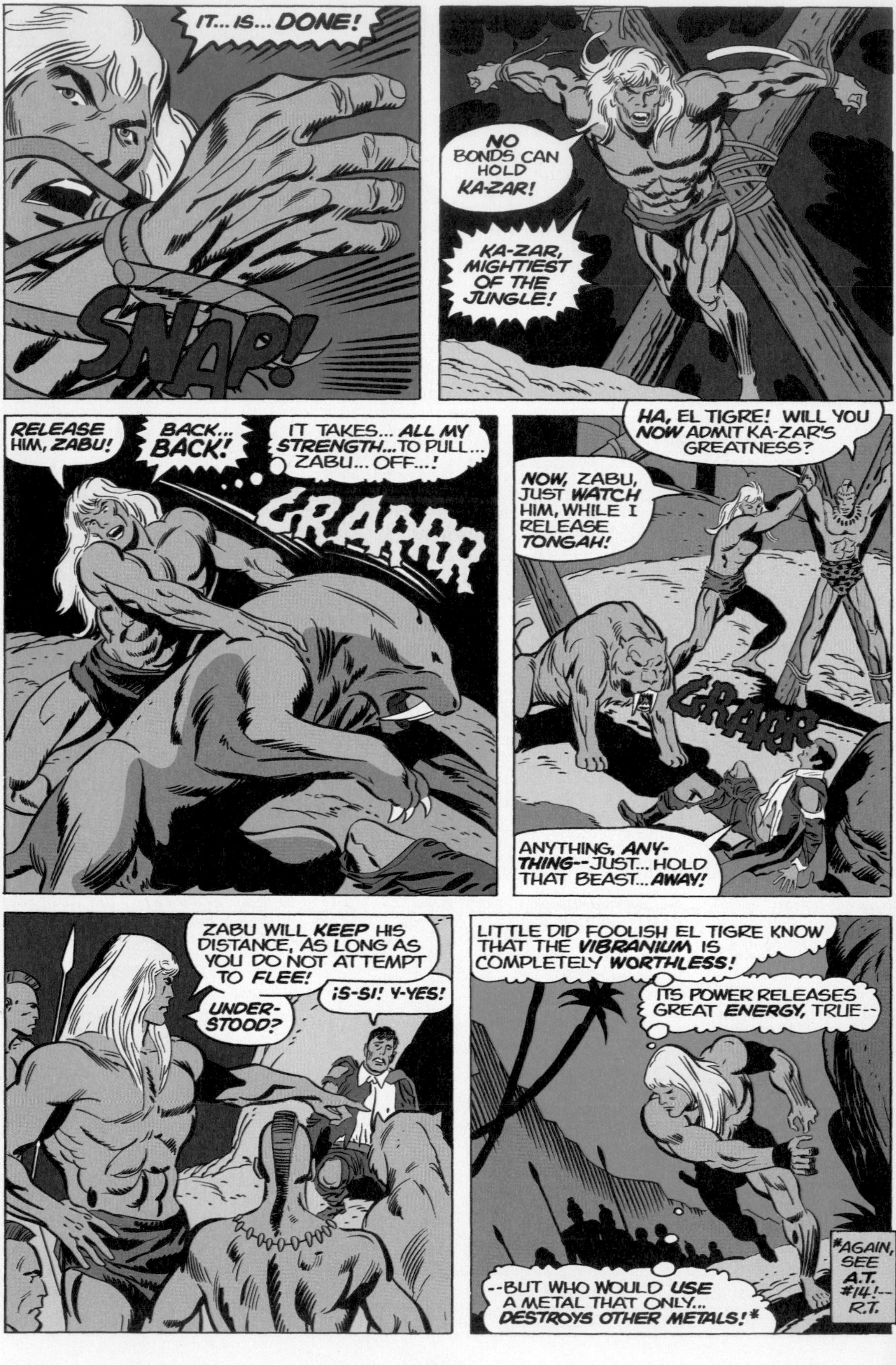
IT... IS... DONE!
SNAP!
NO BONDS CAN HOLD KA-ZAR!
KA-ZAR, MIGHTIEST OF THE JUNGLE!
RELEASE HIM, ZABU!
BACK... BACK!
IT TAKES... ALL MY STRENGTH... TO PULL... ZABU... OFF...!
GRARRR
HA, EL TIGRE! WILL YOU NOW ADMIT KA-ZAR'S GREATNESS?
NOW, ZABU, JUST WATCH HIM, WHILE I RELEASE TONGAH!
GRARR
ANYTHING, ANY-THING-- JUST... HOLD THAT BEAST... AWAY!
ZABU WILL KEEP HIS DISTANCE, AS LONG AS YOU DO NOT ATTEMPT TO FLEE!
UNDER-STOOD?
¡S-SI! Y-YES!
LITTLE DID FOOLISH EL TIGRE KNOW THAT THE VIBRANIUM IS COMPLETELY WORTHLESS!
ITS POWER RELEASES GREAT ENERGY, TRUE--
--BUT WHO WOULD USE A METAL THAT ONLY... DESTROYS OTHER METALS!*
*AGAIN, SEE A.T. #14!-- R.T.

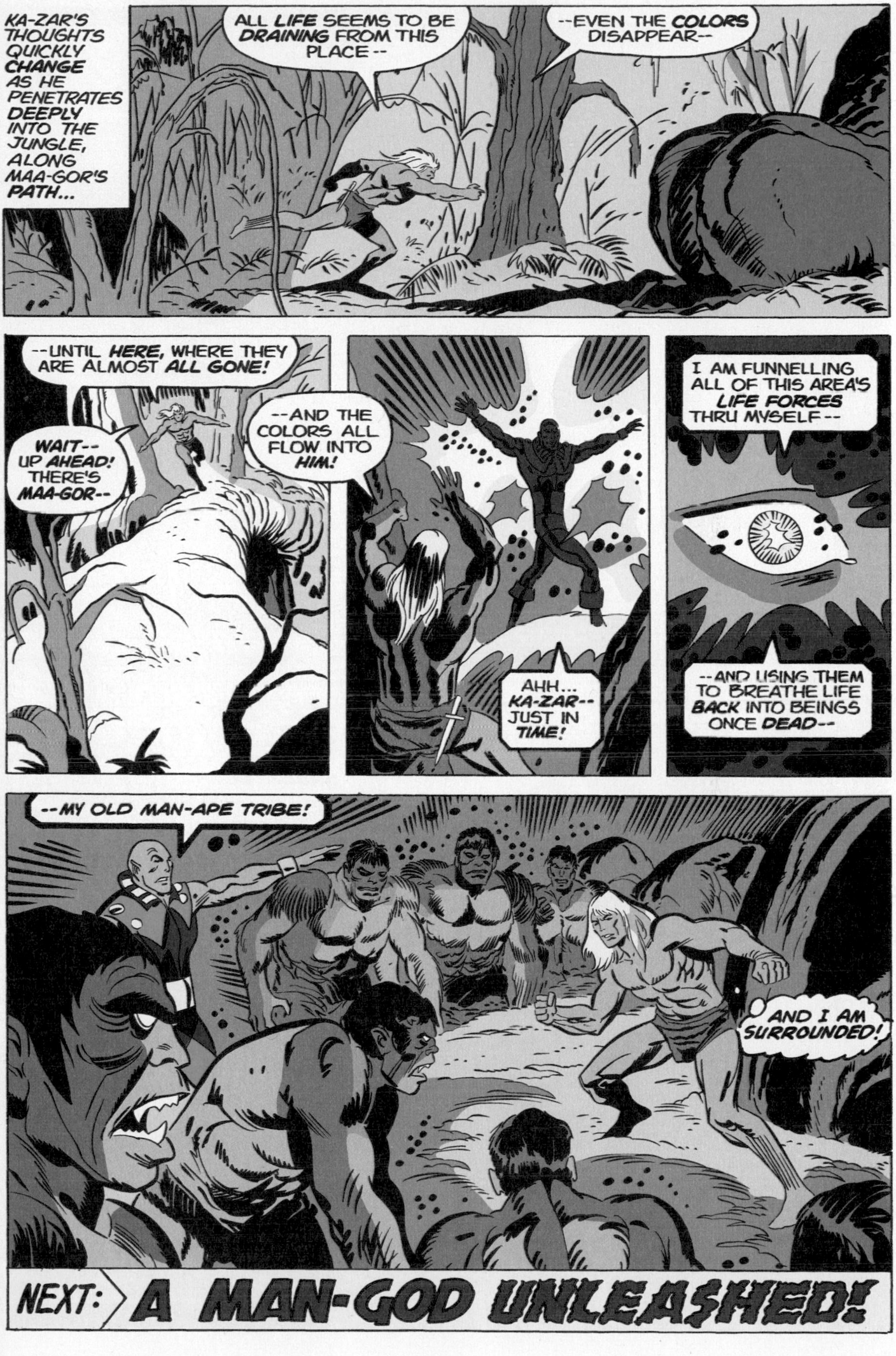
KA-ZAR'S THOUGHTS QUICKLY CHANGE AS HE PENETRATES DEEPLY INTO THE JUNGLE, ALONG MAA-GOR'S PATH...
ALL LIFE SEEMS TO BE DRAINING FROM THIS PLACE --
--EVEN THE COLORS DISAPPEAR--
--UNTIL HERE, WHERE THEY ARE ALMOST ALL GONE!
WAIT-- UP AHEAD! THERE'S MAA-GOR--
--AND THE COLORS ALL FLOW INTO HIM!
AHH... KA-ZAR-- JUST IN TIME!
I AM FUNNELLING ALL OF THIS AREA'S LIFE FORCES THRU MYSELF--
--AND USING THEM TO BREATHE LIFE BACK INTO BEINGS ONCE DEAD--
--MY OLD MAN-APE TRIBE!
AND I AM SURROUNDED!
NEXT: A MAN-GOD UNLEASHED!

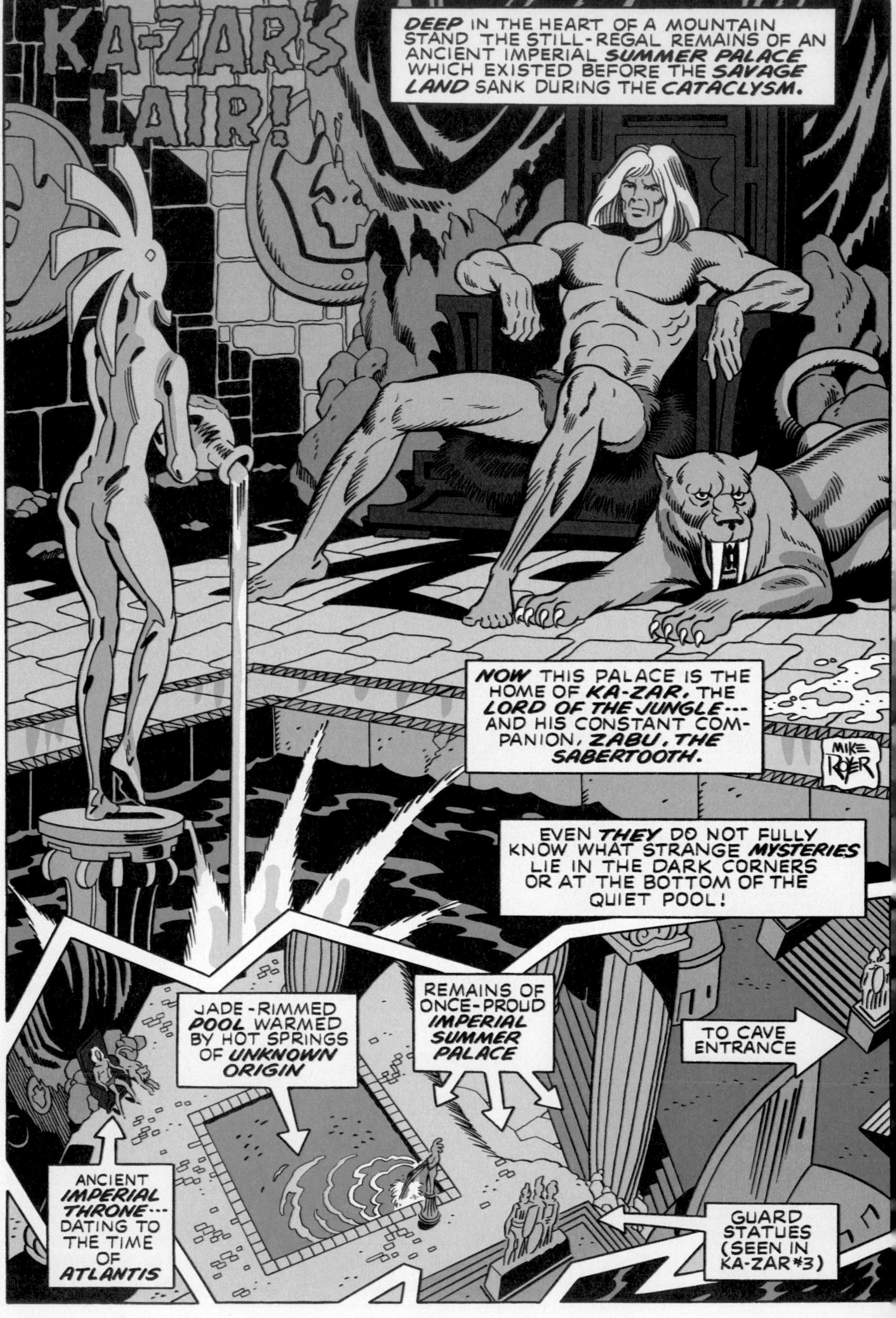
KA-ZAR'S LAIR!
DEEP IN THE HEART OF A MOUNTAIN STAND THE STILL-REGAL REMAINS OF AN ANCIENT IMPERIAL SUMMER PALACE WHICH EXISTED BEFORE THE SAVAGE LAND SANK DURING THE CATACLYSM.
NOW THIS PALACE IS THE HOME OF KA-ZAR, THE LORD OF THE JUNGLE--- AND HIS CONSTANT COMPANION, ZABU, THE SABERTOOTH.
MIKE ROYER
EVEN THEY DO NOT FULLY KNOW WHAT STRANGE MYSTERIES LIE IN THE DARK CORNERS OR AT THE BOTTOM OF THE QUIET POOL!
JADE-RIMMED POOL WARMED BY HOT SPRINGS OF UNKNOWN ORIGIN
REMAINS OF ONCE-PROUD IMPERIAL SUMMER PALACE
TO CAVE ENTRANCE
ANCIENT IMPERIAL THRONE--- DATING TO THE TIME OF ATLANTIS
GUARD STATUES (SEEN IN KA-ZAR #3)

KA-ZAR
MARVEL COMICS GROUP
APPROVED BY THE COMICS CODE AUTHORITY
25¢
5
SEPT
02492
LORD OF THE HIDDEN JUNGLE
KA-ZAR
STRIKE, ZABU! STRIKE!
THIS DAY, THE MAN-APES MUST DIE!!
KA-ZAR AT BAY!

KA-ZAR! Heir to English aristocracy—raised since childhood in THE SAVAGE LAND, where his father was killed by the barbaric Man-Apes! KA-ZAR! A youth left stranded in this hidden land, where he grew to manhood under the protection of ZABU, THE SABRETOOTH!

STAN LEE PRESENTS: KA-ZAR, LORD OF THE HIDDEN JUNGLE!™

A MAN-GOD UNLEASHED!

MY HATED ENEMIES-- THE MAN-APES-- HAVE RETURNED TO LIFE!

I AM SURROUNDED BY THEM-- WITHOUT ANY CHANCE FOR ESCAPE!

PLOTTED BY: BULLPEN WEST		SCRIPTED BY: MIKE FRIEDRICH		DRAWN BY: DON HECK
M. ESPOSITO inking	TOM ORZ lettering	L. LESSMANN coloring		ROY THOMAS editing

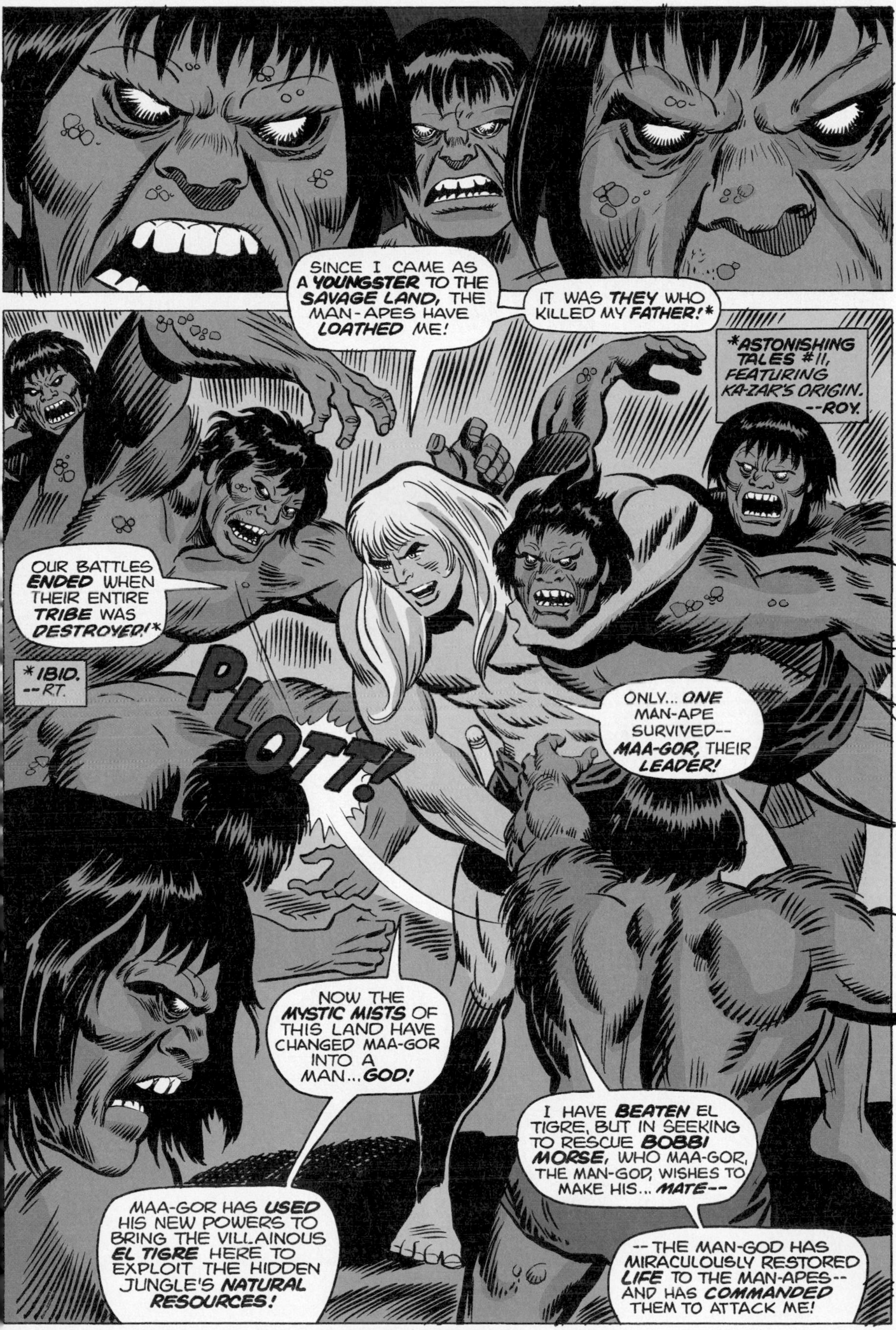
SINCE I CAME AS A YOUNGSTER TO THE SAVAGE LAND, THE MAN-APES HAVE LOATHED ME!
IT WAS THEY WHO KILLED MY FATHER!*
*ASTONISHING TALES #11, FEATURING KA-ZAR'S ORIGIN. --ROY.
OUR BATTLES ENDED WHEN THEIR ENTIRE TRIBE WAS DESTROYED!*
*IBID. --RT.
PLOTT!
ONLY... ONE MAN-APE SURVIVED-- MAA-GOR, THEIR LEADER!
NOW THE MYSTIC MISTS OF THIS LAND HAVE CHANGED MAA-GOR INTO A MAN...GOD!
MAA-GOR HAS USED HIS NEW POWERS TO BRING THE VILLAINOUS EL TIGRE HERE TO EXPLOIT THE HIDDEN JUNGLE'S NATURAL RESOURCES!
I HAVE BEATEN EL TIGRE, BUT IN SEEKING TO RESCUE BOBBI MORSE, WHO MAA-GOR, THE MAN-GOD, WISHES TO MAKE HIS... MATE--
-- THE MAN-GOD HAS MIRACULOUSLY RESTORED LIFE TO THE MAN-APES-- AND HAS COMMANDED THEM TO ATTACK ME!

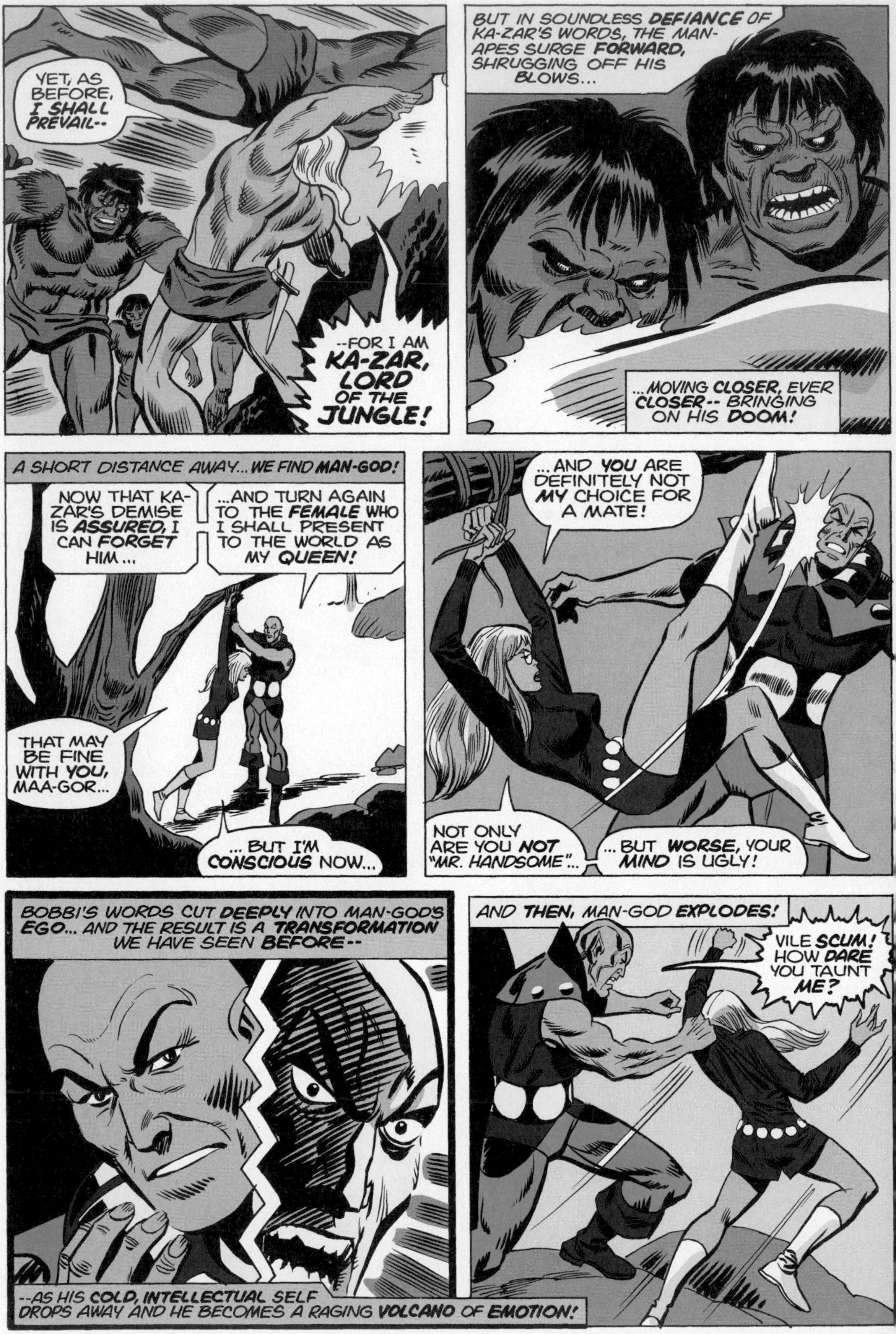
YET, AS BEFORE, I SHALL PREVAIL--
--FOR I AM KA-ZAR, LORD OF THE JUNGLE!
BUT IN SOUNDLESS DEFIANCE OF KA-ZAR'S WORDS, THE MAN-APES SURGE FORWARD, SHRUGGING OFF HIS BLOWS...
...MOVING CLOSER, EVER CLOSER-- BRINGING ON HIS DOOM!
A SHORT DISTANCE AWAY... WE FIND MAN-GOD!
NOW THAT KA-ZAR'S DEMISE IS ASSURED, I CAN FORGET HIM...
...AND TURN AGAIN TO THE FEMALE WHO I SHALL PRESENT TO THE WORLD AS MY QUEEN!
THAT MAY BE FINE WITH YOU, MAA-GOR...
... BUT I'M CONSCIOUS NOW...
...AND YOU ARE DEFINITELY NOT MY CHOICE FOR A MATE!
NOT ONLY ARE YOU NOT "MR. HANDSOME"...
... BUT WORSE, YOUR MIND IS UGLY!
BOBBI'S WORDS CUT DEEPLY INTO MAN-GOD'S EGO... AND THE RESULT IS A TRANSFORMATION WE HAVE SEEN BEFORE--
--AS HIS COLD, INTELLECTUAL SELF DROPS AWAY AND HE BECOMES A RAGING VOLCANO OF EMOTION!
AND THEN, MAN-GOD EXPLODES!
VILE SCUM! HOW DARE YOU TAUNT ME?

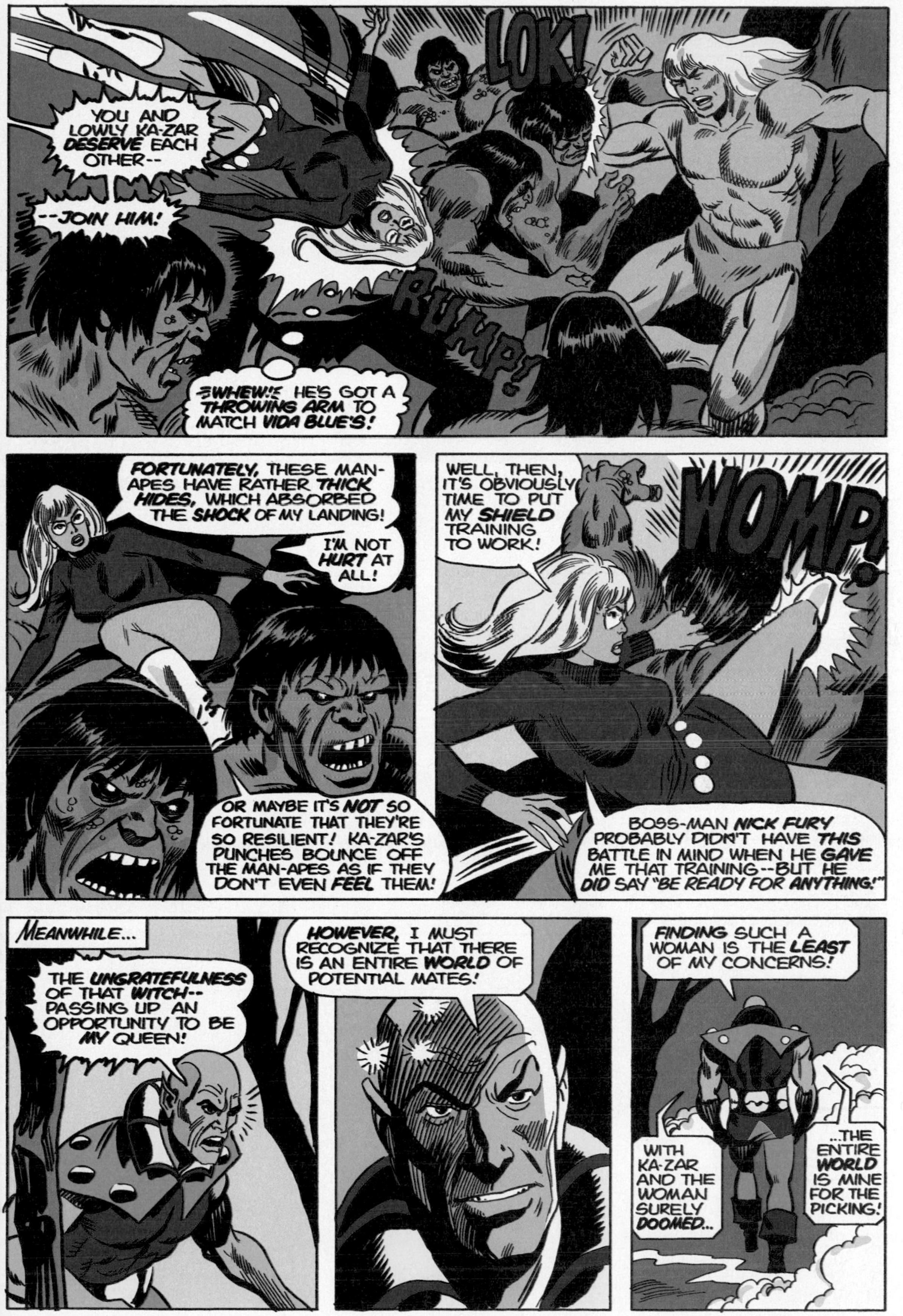

YOU AND LOWLY KA-ZAR DESERVE EACH OTHER--
--JOIN HIM!
LOK!
RUMP!
WHEW! HE'S GOT A THROWING ARM TO MATCH VIDA BLUE'S!
FORTUNATELY, THESE MAN-APES HAVE RATHER THICK HIDES, WHICH ABSORBED THE SHOCK OF MY LANDING!
I'M NOT HURT AT ALL!
OR MAYBE IT'S NOT SO FORTUNATE THAT THEY'RE SO RESILIENT! KA-ZAR'S PUNCHES BOUNCE OFF THE MAN-APES AS IF THEY DON'T EVEN FEEL THEM!
WELL, THEN, IT'S OBVIOUSLY TIME TO PUT MY SHIELD TRAINING TO WORK!
WOMP!
BOSS-MAN NICK FURY PROBABLY DIDN'T HAVE THIS BATTLE IN MIND WHEN HE GAVE ME THAT TRAINING--BUT HE DID SAY "BE READY FOR ANYTHING!"
MEANWHILE...
THE UNGRATEFULNESS OF THAT WITCH-- PASSING UP AN OPPORTUNITY TO BE MY QUEEN!
HOWEVER, I MUST RECOGNIZE THAT THERE IS AN ENTIRE WORLD OF POTENTIAL MATES!
FINDING SUCH A WOMAN IS THE LEAST OF MY CONCERNS!
WITH KA-ZAR AND THE WOMAN SURELY DOOMED...
...THE ENTIRE WORLD IS MINE FOR THE PICKING!

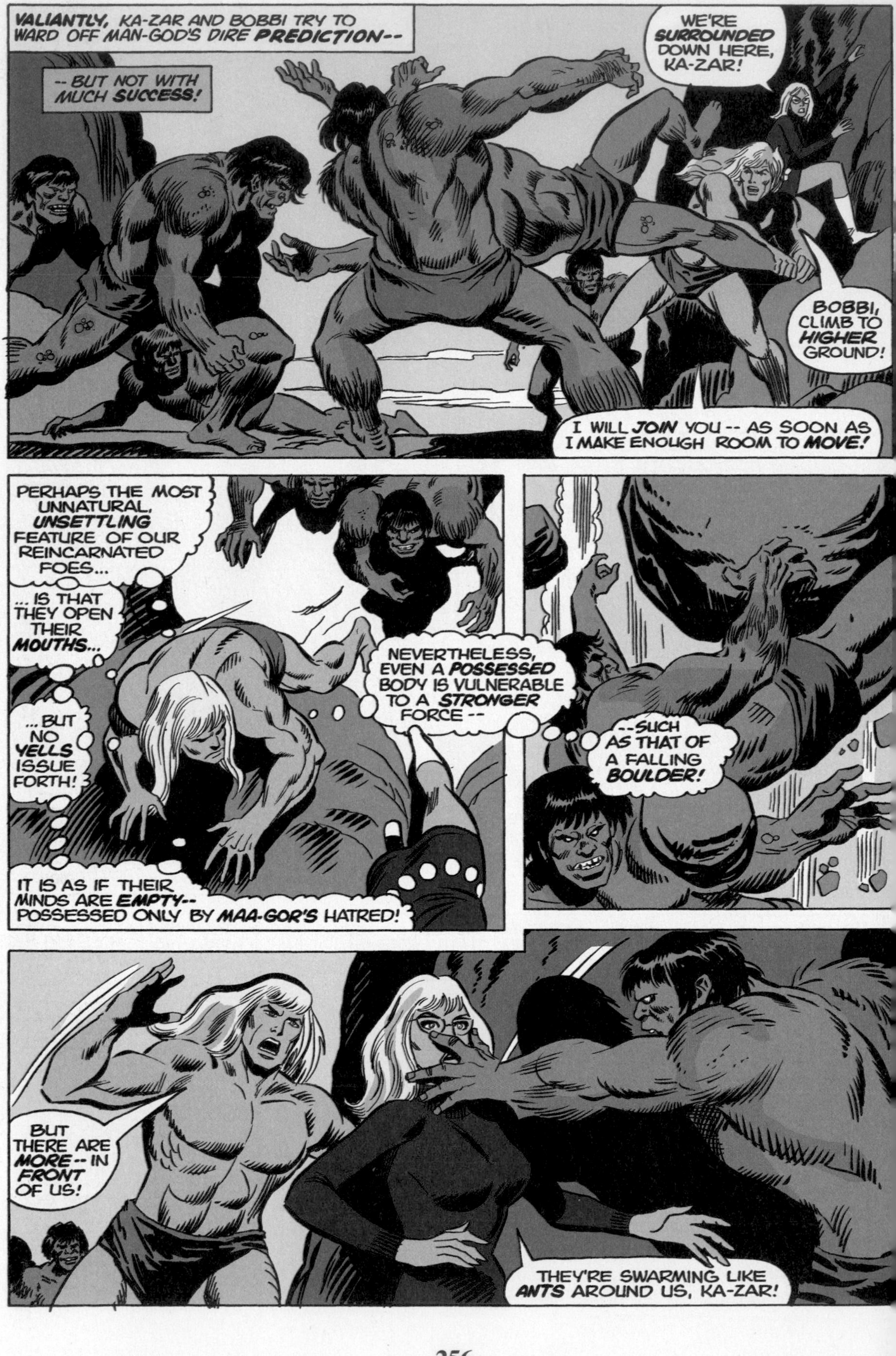
VALIANTLY, KA-ZAR AND BOBBI TRY TO WARD OFF MAN-GOD'S DIRE PREDICTION--
-- BUT NOT WITH MUCH SUCCESS!
WE'RE SURROUNDED DOWN HERE, KA-ZAR!
BOBBI, CLIMB TO HIGHER GROUND!
I WILL JOIN YOU -- AS SOON AS I MAKE ENOUGH ROOM TO MOVE!
PERHAPS THE MOST UNNATURAL, UNSETTLING FEATURE OF OUR REINCARNATED FOES...
... IS THAT THEY OPEN THEIR MOUTHS...
... BUT NO YELLS ISSUE FORTH!
IT IS AS IF THEIR MINDS ARE EMPTY-- POSSESSED ONLY BY MAA-GOR'S HATRED!
NEVERTHELESS, EVEN A POSSESSED BODY IS VULNERABLE TO A STRONGER FORCE --
--SUCH AS THAT OF A FALLING BOULDER!
BUT THERE ARE MORE-- IN FRONT OF US!
THEY'RE SWARMING LIKE ANTS AROUND US, KA-ZAR!

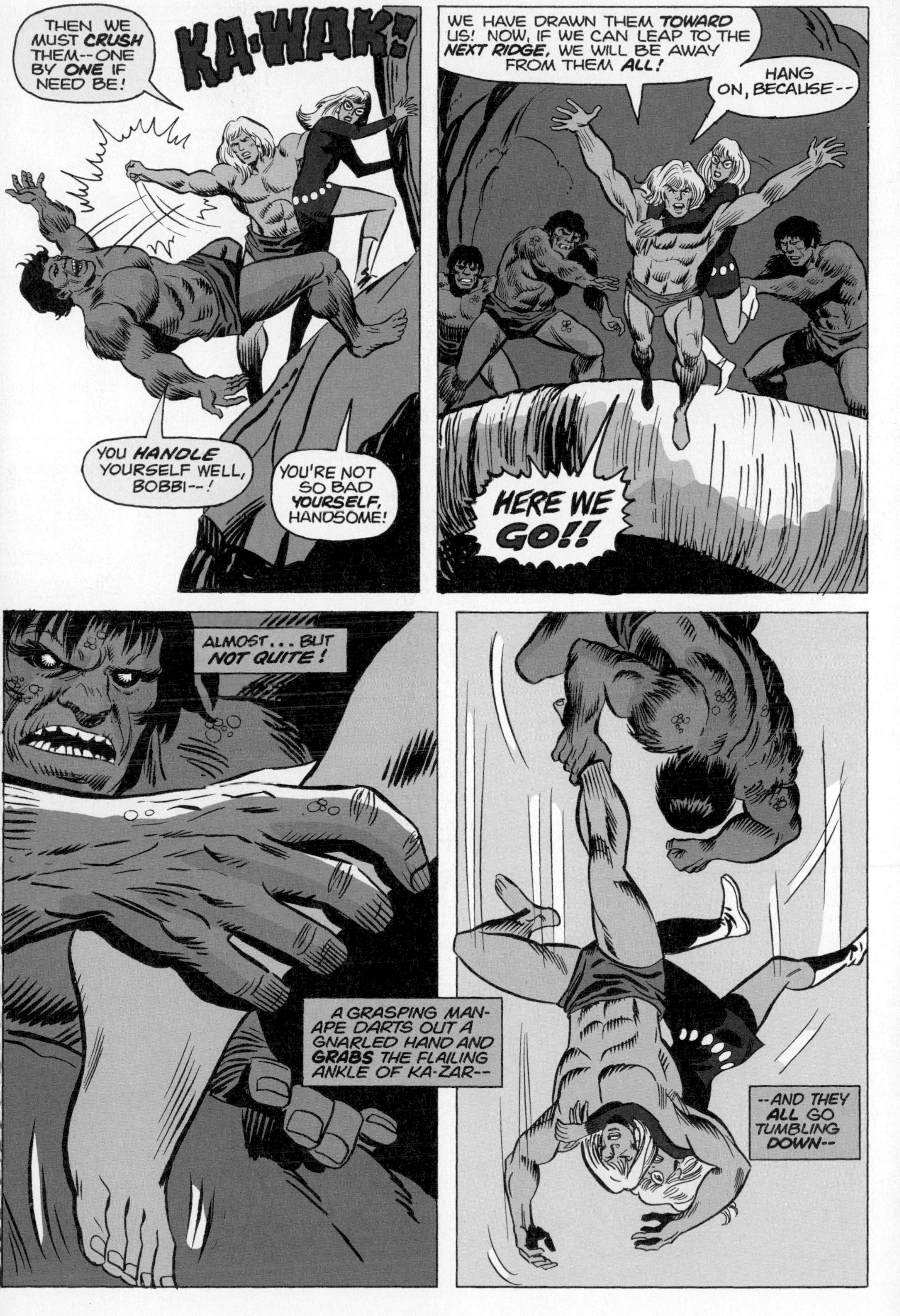

THEN WE MUST CRUSH THEM--ONE BY ONE IF NEED BE!
KA-WAK!
YOU HANDLE YOURSELF WELL, BOBBI--!
YOU'RE NOT SO BAD YOURSELF, HANDSOME!
WE HAVE DRAWN THEM TOWARD US! NOW, IF WE CAN LEAP TO THE NEXT RIDGE, WE WILL BE AWAY FROM THEM ALL!
HANG ON, BECAUSE--
HERE WE GO!!
ALMOST... BUT NOT QUITE!
A GRASPING MAN-APE DARTS OUT A GNARLED HAND AND GRABS THE FLAILING ANKLE OF KA-ZAR--
--AND THEY ALL GO TUMBLING DOWN--

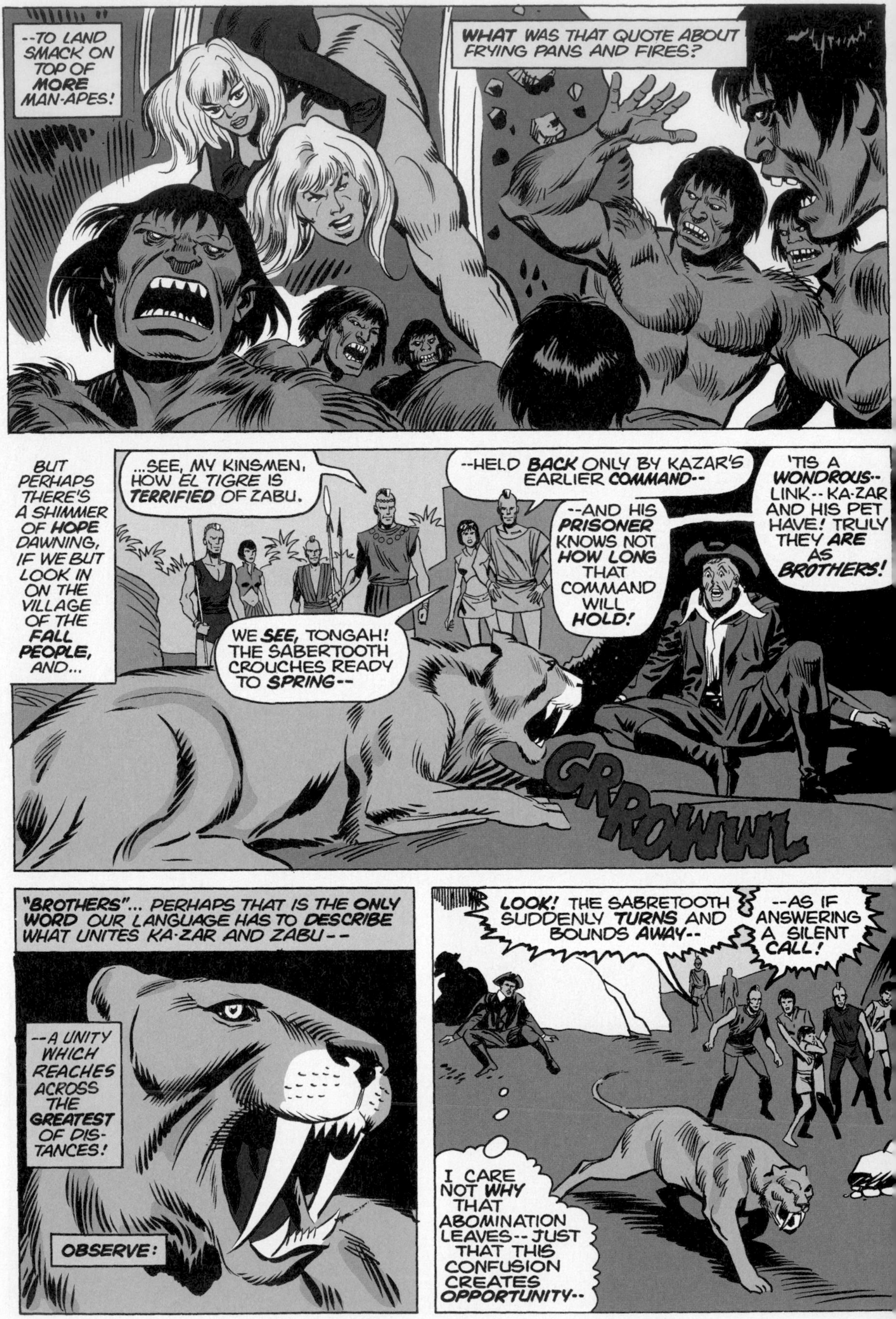
--TO LAND SMACK ON TOP OF MORE MAN-APES!
WHAT WAS THAT QUOTE ABOUT FRYING PANS AND FIRES?
BUT PERHAPS THERE'S A SHIMMER OF HOPE DAWNING, IF WE BUT LOOK IN ON THE VILLAGE OF THE FALL PEOPLE, AND...
...SEE, MY KINSMEN, HOW EL TIGRE IS TERRIFIED OF ZABU.
WE SEE, TONGAH! THE SABERTOOTH CROUCHES READY TO SPRING--
--HELD BACK ONLY BY KAZAR'S EARLIER COMMAND--
--AND HIS PRISONER KNOWS NOT HOW LONG THAT COMMAND WILL HOLD!
'TIS A WONDROUS-- LINK-- KA-ZAR AND HIS PET HAVE! TRULY THEY ARE AS BROTHERS!
GRROWWL
"BROTHERS"... PERHAPS THAT IS THE ONLY WORD OUR LANGUAGE HAS TO DESCRIBE WHAT UNITES KA-ZAR AND ZABU--
--A UNITY WHICH REACHES ACROSS THE GREATEST OF DISTANCES!
OBSERVE:
LOOK! THE SABRETOOTH SUDDENLY TURNS AND BOUNDS AWAY--
--AS IF ANSWERING A SILENT CALL!
I CARE NOT WHY THAT ABOMINATION LEAVES-- JUST THAT THIS CONFUSION CREATES OPPORTUNITY--

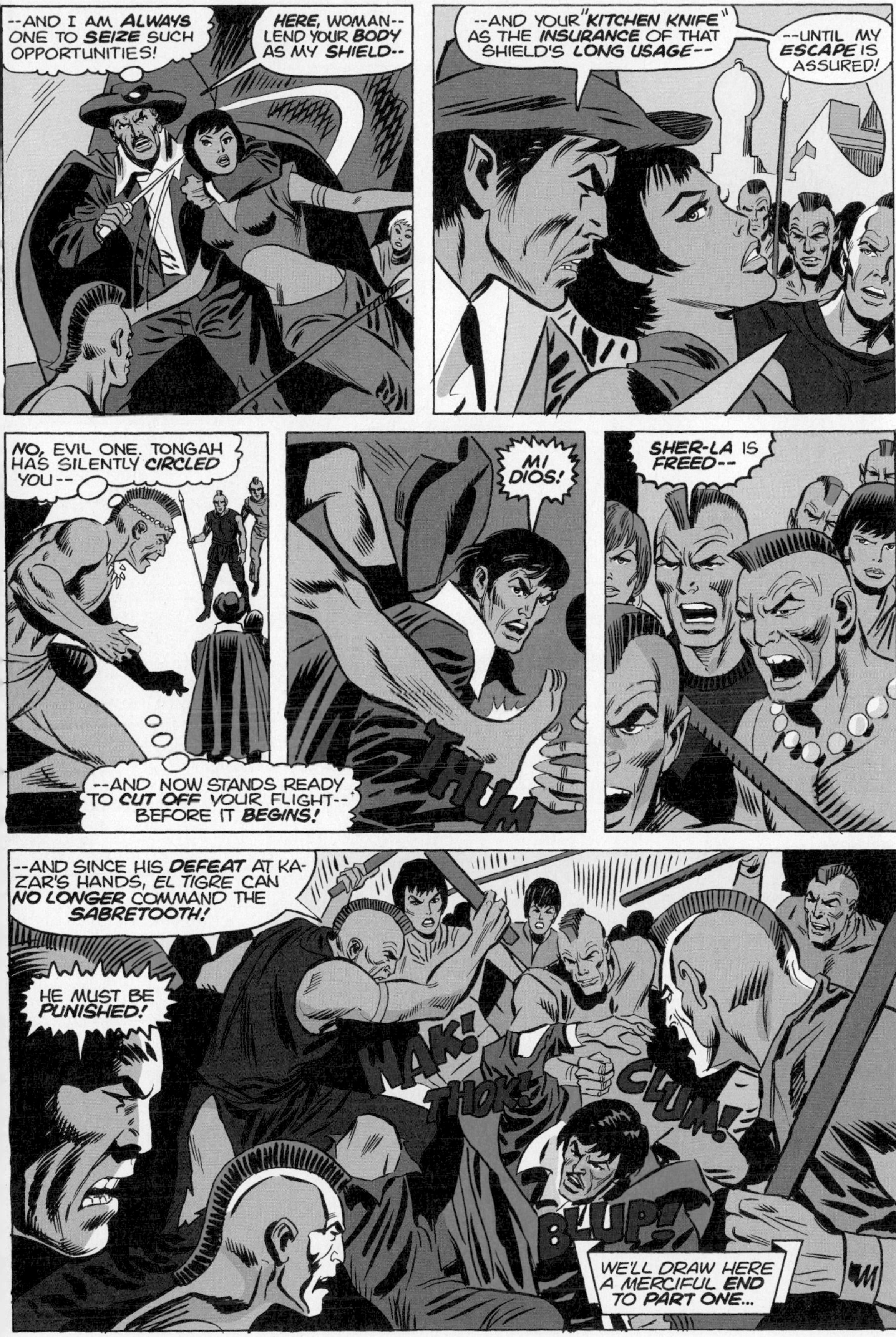
--AND I AM ALWAYS ONE TO SEIZE SUCH OPPORTUNITIES!
HERE, WOMAN-- LEND YOUR BODY AS MY SHIELD--
--AND YOUR "KITCHEN KNIFE" AS THE INSURANCE OF THAT SHIELD'S LONG USAGE--
--UNTIL MY ESCAPE IS ASSURED!
NO, EVIL ONE. TONGAH HAS SILENTLY CIRCLED YOU--
--AND NOW STANDS READY TO CUT OFF YOUR FLIGHT-- BEFORE IT BEGINS!
MI DIOS!
THUM
SHER-LA IS FREED--
--AND SINCE HIS DEFEAT AT KA-ZAR'S HANDS, EL TIGRE CAN NO LONGER COMMAND THE SABRETOOTH!
HE MUST BE PUNISHED!
HAK!
THOK!
CLUM!
BLUP!
WE'LL DRAW HERE A MERCIFUL END TO PART ONE...

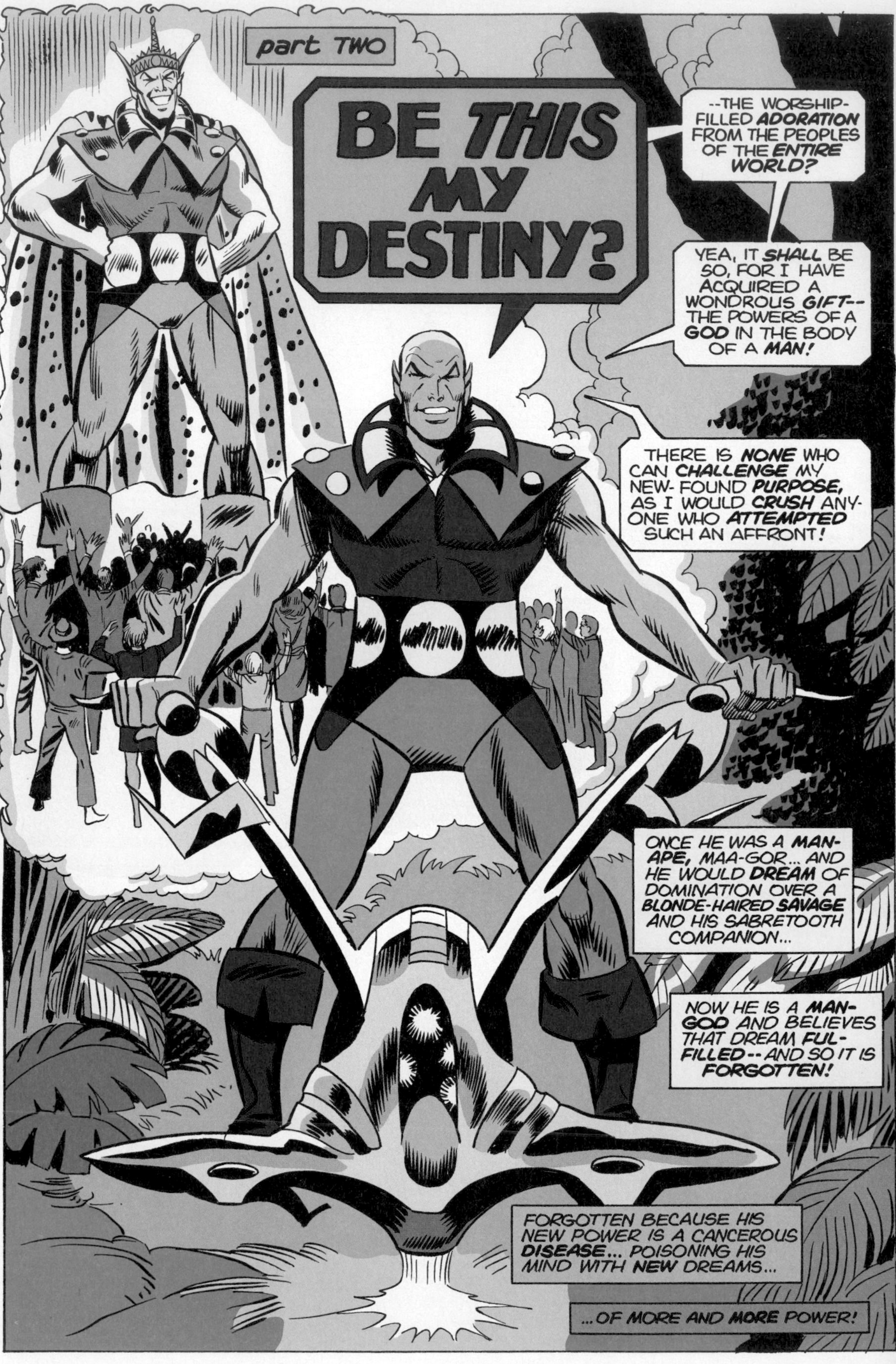
part TWO
BE THIS MY DESTINY?
--THE WORSHIP-FILLED ADORATION FROM THE PEOPLES OF THE ENTIRE WORLD?
YEA, IT SHALL BE SO, FOR I HAVE ACQUIRED A WONDROUS GIFT-- THE POWERS OF A GOD IN THE BODY OF A MAN!
THERE IS NONE WHO CAN CHALLENGE MY NEW-FOUND PURPOSE, AS I WOULD CRUSH ANYONE WHO ATTEMPTED SUCH AN AFFRONT!
ONCE HE WAS A MAN-APE, MAA-GOR... AND HE WOULD DREAM OF DOMINATION OVER A BLONDE-HAIRED SAVAGE AND HIS SABRETOOTH COMPANION...
NOW HE IS A MAN-GOD AND BELIEVES THAT DREAM FULFILLED--AND SO IT IS FORGOTTEN!
FORGOTTEN BECAUSE HIS NEW POWER IS A CANCEROUS DISEASE... POISONING HIS MIND WITH NEW DREAMS...
...OF MORE AND MORE POWER!

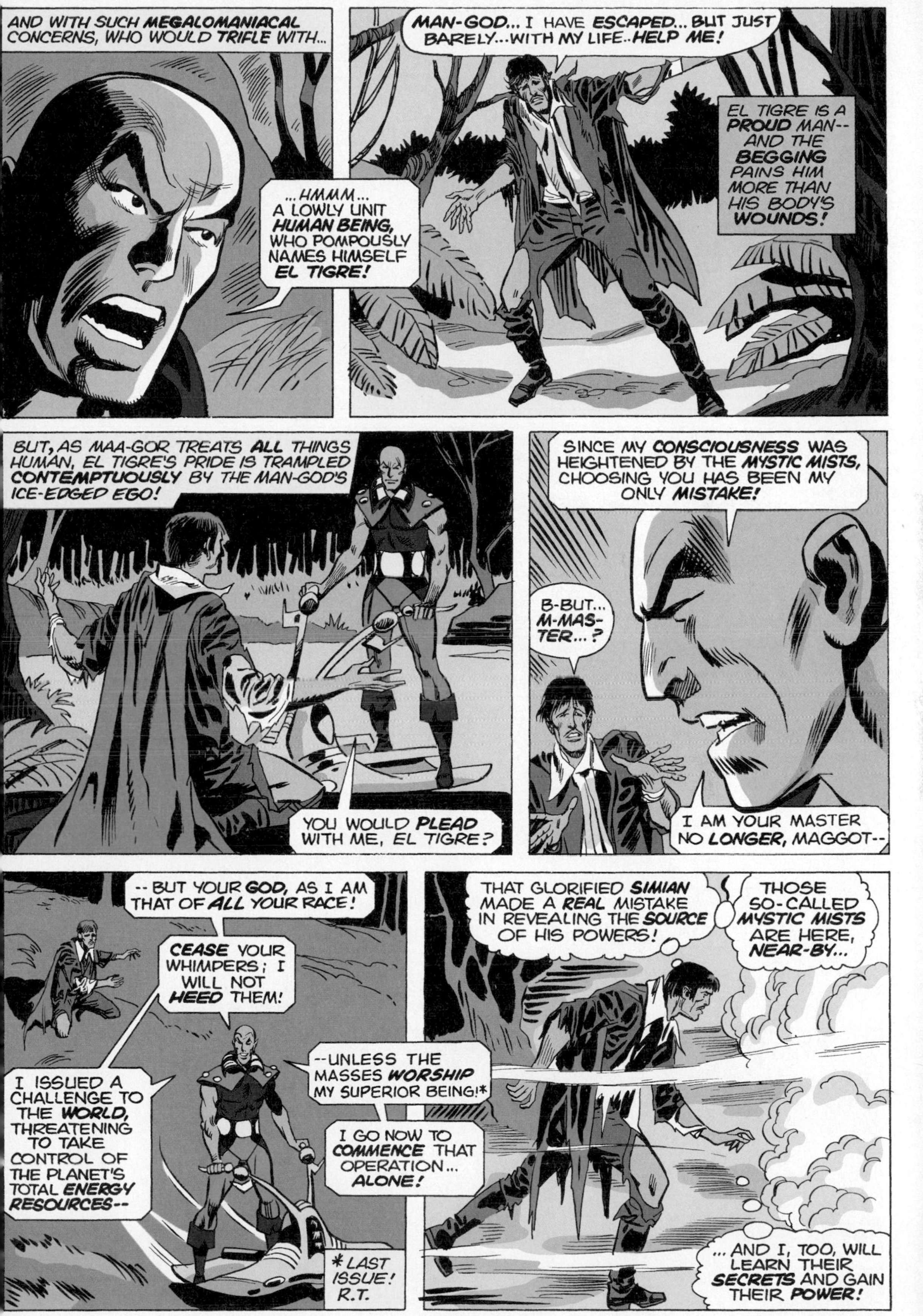
AND WITH SUCH MEGALOMANIACAL CONCERNS, WHO WOULD TRIFLE WITH...
...HMMM... A LOWLY UNIT HUMAN BEING, WHO POMPOUSLY NAMES HIMSELF EL TIGRE!
MAN-GOD... I HAVE ESCAPED... BUT JUST BARELY... WITH MY LIFE.. HELP ME!
EL TIGRE IS A PROUD MAN-- AND THE BEGGING PAINS HIM MORE THAN HIS BODY'S WOUNDS!
BUT, AS MAA-GOR TREATS ALL THINGS HUMAN, EL TIGRE'S PRIDE IS TRAMPLED CONTEMPTUOUSLY BY THE MAN-GOD'S ICE-EDGED EGO!
YOU WOULD PLEAD WITH ME, EL TIGRE?
SINCE MY CONSCIOUSNESS WAS HEIGHTENED BY THE MYSTIC MISTS, CHOOSING YOU HAS BEEN MY ONLY MISTAKE!
B-BUT... M-MAS-TER...?
I AM YOUR MASTER NO LONGER, MAGGOT--
-- BUT YOUR GOD, AS I AM THAT OF ALL YOUR RACE!
CEASE YOUR WHIMPERS; I WILL NOT HEED THEM!
I ISSUED A CHALLENGE TO THE WORLD, THREATENING TO TAKE CONTROL OF THE PLANET'S TOTAL ENERGY RESOURCES--
--UNLESS THE MASSES WORSHIP MY SUPERIOR BEING!*
I GO NOW TO COMMENCE THAT OPERATION... ALONE!
*LAST ISSUE! R.T.
THAT GLORIFIED SIMIAN MADE A REAL MISTAKE IN REVEALING THE SOURCE OF HIS POWERS!
THOSE SO-CALLED MYSTIC MISTS ARE HERE, NEAR-BY...
...AND I, TOO, WILL LEARN THEIR SECRETS AND GAIN THEIR POWER!

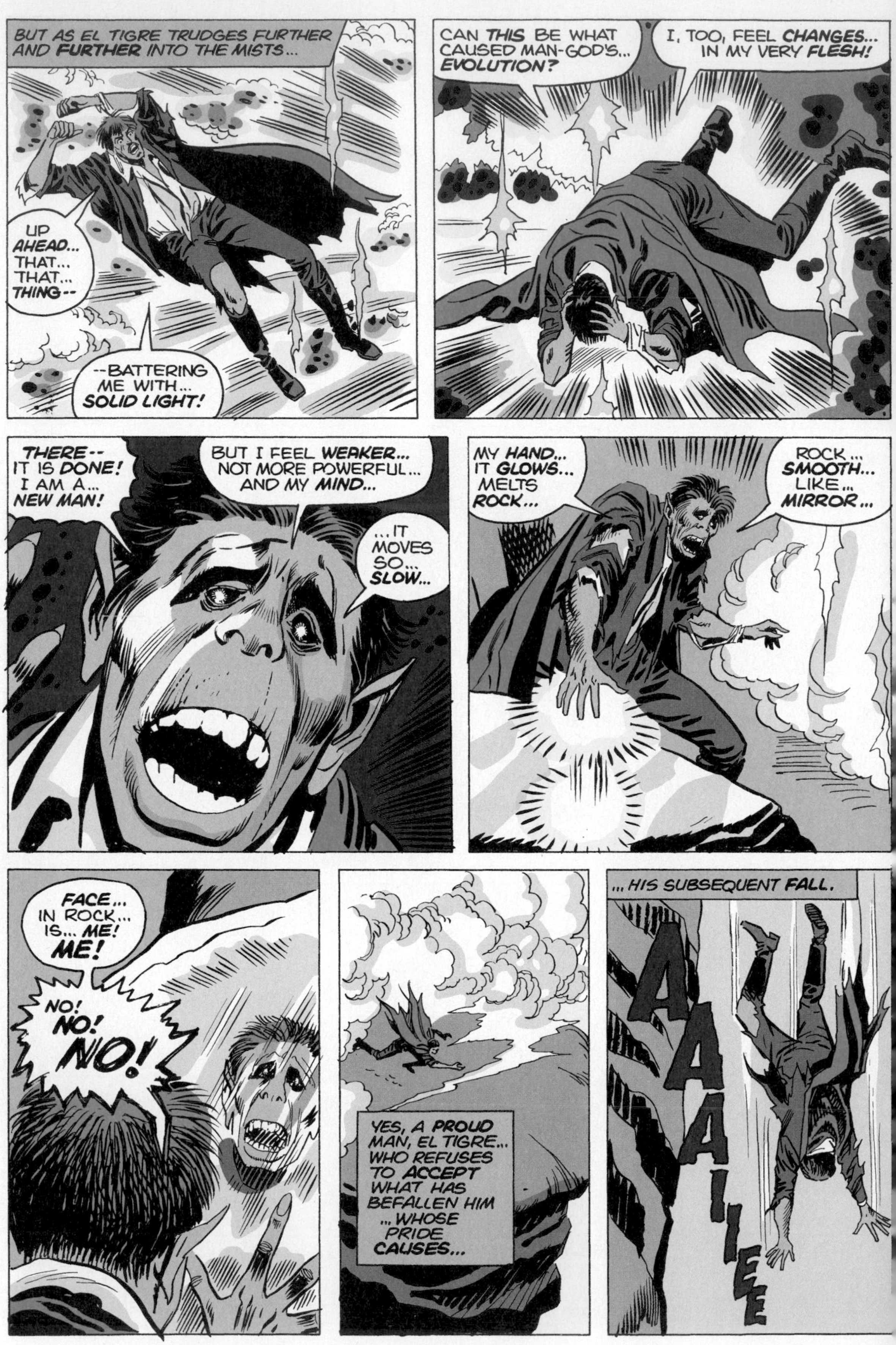
BUT AS EL TIGRE TRUDGES FURTHER AND FURTHER INTO THE MISTS...
UP AHEAD... THAT... THAT... THING--
--BATTERING ME WITH... SOLID LIGHT!
CAN THIS BE WHAT CAUSED MAN-GOD'S... EVOLUTION?
I, TOO, FEEL CHANGES... IN MY VERY FLESH!
THERE-- IT IS DONE! I AM A... NEW MAN!
BUT I FEEL WEAKER... NOT MORE POWERFUL... AND MY MIND...
...IT MOVES SO... SLOW...
MY HAND... IT GLOWS... MELTS ROCK...
ROCK... SMOOTH... LIKE... MIRROR...
FACE... IN ROCK... IS... ME! ME!
NO! NO! NO!
YES, A PROUD MAN, EL TIGRE... WHO REFUSES TO ACCEPT WHAT HAS BEFALLEN HIM ...WHOSE PRIDE CAUSES...
... HIS SUBSEQUENT FALL.
AAAIIEE

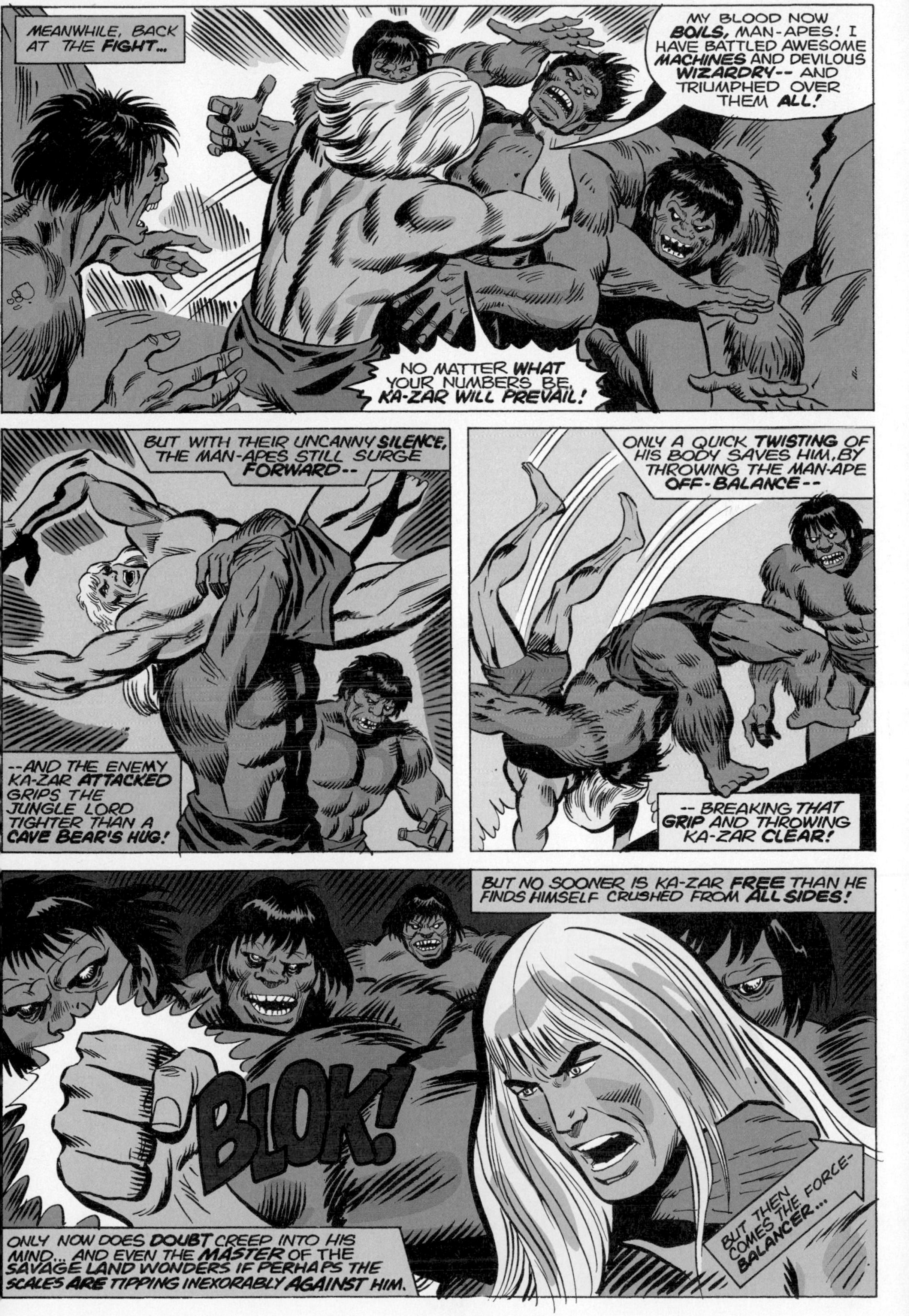
MEANWHILE, BACK AT THE FIGHT...
MY BLOOD NOW BOILS, MAN-APES! I HAVE BATTLED AWESOME MACHINES AND DEVILOUS WIZARDRY-- AND TRIUMPHED OVER THEM ALL!
NO MATTER WHAT YOUR NUMBERS BE, KA-ZAR WILL PREVAIL!
BUT WITH THEIR UNCANNY SILENCE, THE MAN-APES STILL SURGE FORWARD--
--AND THE ENEMY KA-ZAR ATTACKED GRIPS THE JUNGLE LORD TIGHTER THAN A CAVE BEAR'S HUG!
ONLY A QUICK TWISTING OF HIS BODY SAVES HIM, BY THROWING THE MAN-APE OFF-BALANCE--
-- BREAKING THAT GRIP AND THROWING KA-ZAR CLEAR!
BUT NO SOONER IS KA-ZAR FREE THAN HE FINDS HIMSELF CRUSHED FROM ALL SIDES!
BLOK!
ONLY NOW DOES DOUBT CREEP INTO HIS MIND... AND EVEN THE MASTER OF THE SAVAGE LAND WONDERS IF PERHAPS THE SCALES ARE TIPPING INEXORABLY AGAINST HIM.
BUT THEN COMES THE FORCE-BALANCER...

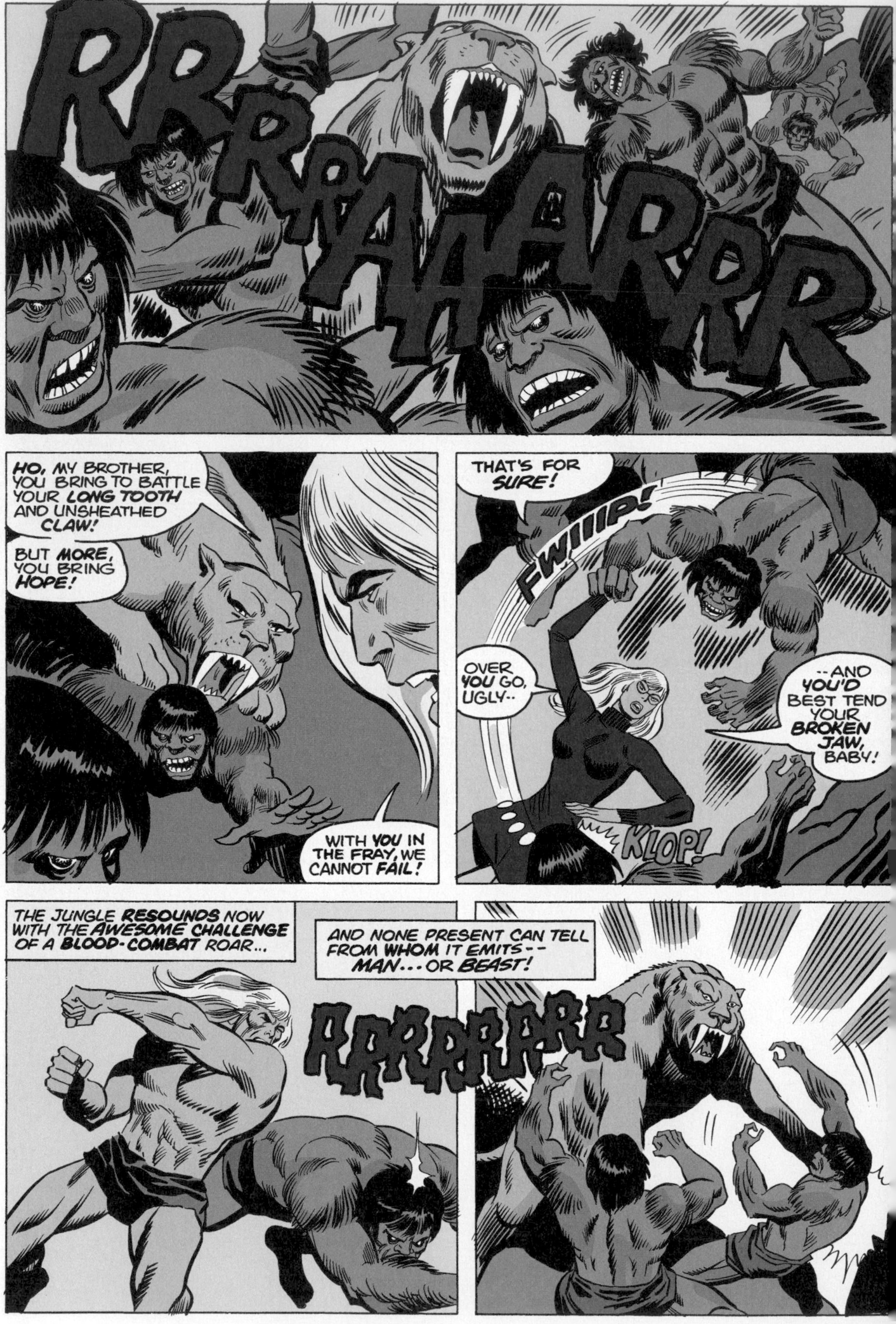
RRRRAAARRRR
HO, MY BROTHER, YOU BRING TO BATTLE YOUR LONG TOOTH AND UNSHEATHED CLAW!
BUT MORE, YOU BRING HOPE!
WITH YOU IN THE FRAY, WE CANNOT FAIL!
THAT'S FOR SURE!
FWIIIP!
OVER YOU GO, UGLY--
--AND YOU'D BEST TEND YOUR BROKEN JAW, BABY!
KLOP!
THE JUNGLE RESOUNDS NOW WITH THE AWESOME CHALLENGE OF A BLOOD-COMBAT ROAR...
AND NONE PRESENT CAN TELL FROM WHOM IT EMITS-- MAN...OR BEAST!
RRRRRRRR

HMM...THE DECEASED BODY OF *EL TIGRE!*

THE PYROTECHNICS I OBSERVED HAVE INDEED PROVEN *WORTH* MY RETURN TO *INVESTIGATE.*

LET ME *ANALYZE* THE SITUATION.

HIS BODY LIES *BELOW* THE LAND OF THE *MYSTIC MISTS...*

...AND THE SKELETAL AND CELLULAR STRUCTURES INDICATE AN *EVOLVED* STATE FROM HIS EARLIER *HUMAN* FORM.

IT IS AS IF *HE* EVOLVED IN THE MISTS AS *I* DID-- ONLY DOWN A *DIFFERENT PATH!*

STILL, THIS INDICATES A HERETOFORE UNCONCEIVED *POSSIBILITY*--THAT THE MISTS ARE THE *CENTRAL CAUSE* OF THIS HIDDEN JUNGLE'S ANACHRONISTIC EVOLUTIONARY STATUS QUO--

--WHEREIN *DINOSAURS* YET LIVE...ALONGSIDE *MEN.*

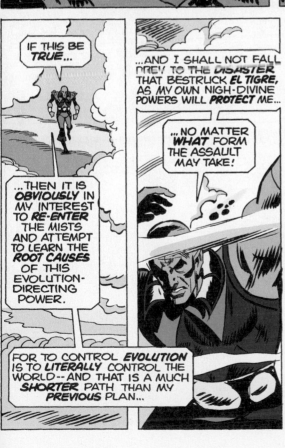

IF THIS BE *TRUE...*

...THEN IT IS *OBVIOUSLY* IN MY INTEREST TO *RE-ENTER* THE MISTS AND ATTEMPT TO LEARN THE *ROOT CAUSES* OF THIS EVOLUTION-DIRECTING POWER.

FOR TO CONTROL *EVOLUTION* IS TO *LITERALLY* CONTROL THE WORLD--AND THAT IS A MUCH *SHORTER* PATH THAN MY *PREVIOUS* PLAN...

...AND I SHALL NOT FALL PREY TO THE *DISASTER* THAT BESTRUCK *EL TIGRE,* AS MY OWN NIGH-DIVINE POWERS WILL *PROTECT* ME...

...NO MATTER *WHAT* FORM THE ASSAULT MAY TAKE!

AHH..., I APPEAR TO HAVE *LOCATED* SOMETHING--A BATTERING ATTACK OF PULSING *SOLID LIGHT...*

...BUT I EASILY PRESS FORWARD *AGAINST* IT!

I *SEE* NOW... IT EMANATES FROM *ONE TANGIBLE SOURCE*--JUST *AHEAD* OF ME--

--A...MACHINE!!

ALIEN IN APPEARANCE-- AND OF APPARENT AWESOME POWER!

COULD SOME ALIEN INTELLIGENCE OF EONS PAST HAVE PLANTED IT HERE... PERHAPS AS A BIO-EVOLUTIONARY EXPERIMENT?

HERE AT ITS CORE, ITS SOLID LIGHT FORCES PUSH AGAINST ME LIKE A TORNADO!

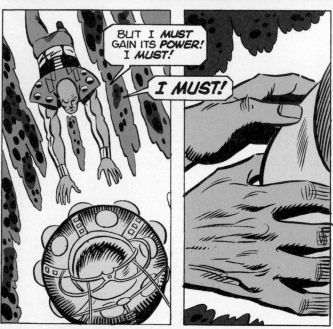

BUT I MUST GAIN ITS POWER! I MUST!

I MUST!

WHY... IT HAS SPLIT US INTO TWO BEINGS!

THAT IS SELF-EVIDENT, FOOL!

YOU HAVE YOUR DAMNABLE COLD LOGIC, WHILE I RETAIN ONLY THE FEELING!

YOU MEAN... YOUR INSANE HATRED-- ≡UHH!≡

QUIET, YOU CALCULATING INCOMPETENT!

OBVIOUSLY, ONE OF US MUST DISAPPEAR! WE MUST REASON A WAY--

NO! I WILL FORCE A WAY--

THUD

--WITH YOUR DEATH!

SHUP

I HAVE WON! --NOW I AM INVINCIBLE!

WRONG!

I HAVE *DESTROYED* THAT LOGIC WHICH *RESTRAINED* ME! NOW I AM *UN-LEASHED*--

REPORT: CONTACT WITH REPORTER ORGANISM SUSTAINED EXTREME IMBALANCE STATE OF PSYCHO / PHYSICAL SCHIZOPHRENIA.

CONTINUING: ORGANISM RESPONDED WITH FURTHER IMBALANCE, CREATING TOTAL DISHARMONY.

CONTINUING: BALANCE RESTORED BY INTERJECTION OF REPORTER. END REPORT. CONTINUING OPERATIONS.

...*HOW LONG* CAN THESE MAN-APES CONTINUE THEIR *ATTACKS*? THEY ARE *TIRELESS*!

WAIT, KA-ZAR-- *LOOK*! THEY'VE GONE *LIMP*-- THEY'RE NOT *ATTACKING* ANYMORE!

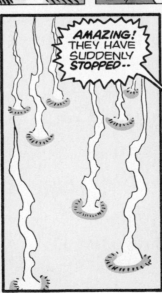

AMAZING! THEY HAVE SUDDENLY *STOPPED*--

--AS IF THEY *LOST* THE LIFE-FORCE THAT WAS *DRIVING* THEM-- AND THEN RETURNED TO THE *DUST* FROM WHICH THEY *CAME*!

YA-KNOW, HANDSOME, I GOT A FEELING THIS ADVENTURE IS *TOTALLY* CLOSED!

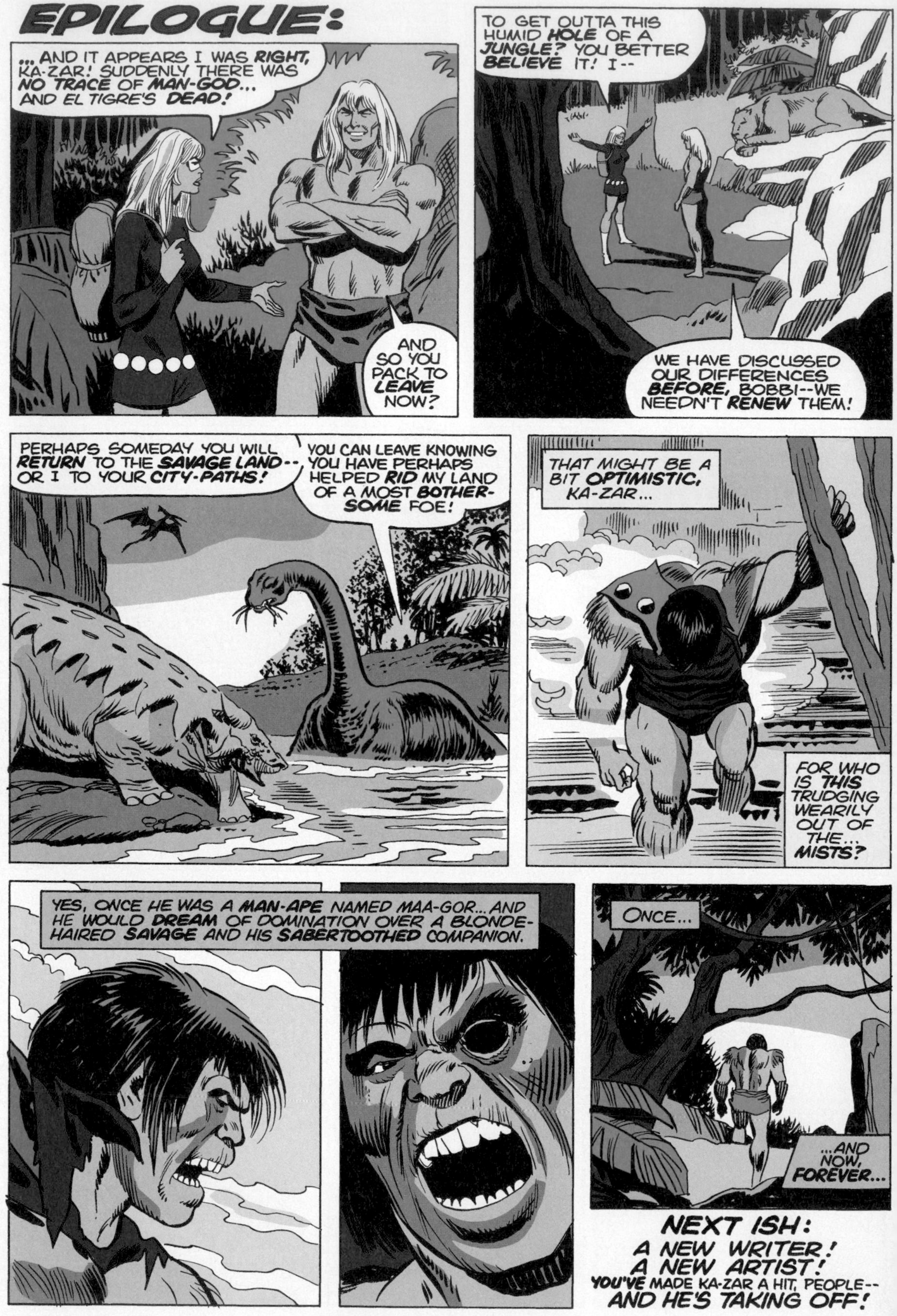
EPILOGUE:
...AND IT APPEARS I WAS RIGHT, KA-ZAR! SUDDENLY THERE WAS NO TRACE OF MAN-GOD... AND EL TIGRE'S DEAD!
AND SO YOU PACK TO LEAVE NOW?
TO GET OUTTA THIS HUMID HOLE OF A JUNGLE? YOU BETTER BELIEVE IT! I--
WE HAVE DISCUSSED OUR DIFFERENCES BEFORE, BOBBI--WE NEEDN'T RENEW THEM!
PERHAPS SOMEDAY YOU WILL RETURN TO THE SAVAGE LAND--OR I TO YOUR CITY-PATHS!
YOU CAN LEAVE KNOWING YOU HAVE PERHAPS HELPED RID MY LAND OF A MOST BOTHER-SOME FOE!
THAT MIGHT BE A BIT OPTIMISTIC, KA-ZAR...
FOR WHO IS THIS TRUDGING WEARILY OUT OF THE... MISTS?
YES, ONCE HE WAS A MAN-APE NAMED MAA-GOR... AND HE WOULD DREAM OF DOMINATION OVER A BLONDE-HAIRED SAVAGE AND HIS SABERTOOTHED COMPANION.
ONCE...
...AND NOW, FOREVER...
NEXT ISH:
A NEW WRITER!
A NEW ARTIST!
YOU'VE MADE KA-ZAR A HIT, PEOPLE--
--AND HE'S TAKING OFF!

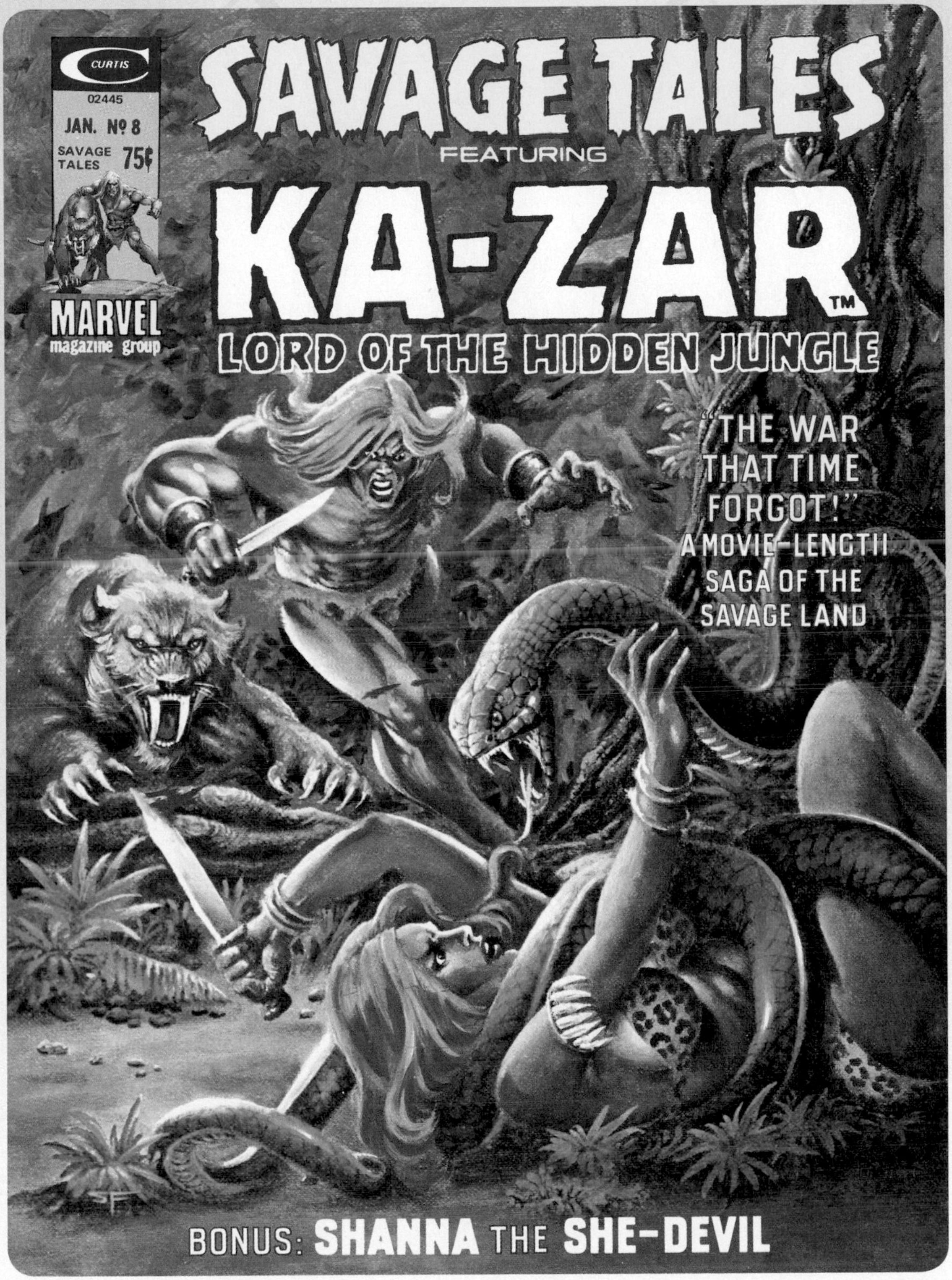

CURTIS
02445
JAN. Nº 8
SAVAGE TALES 75¢
MARVEL
magazine group
SAVAGE TALES
FEATURING
KA-ZAR™
LORD OF THE HIDDEN JUNGLE
"THE WAR THAT TIME FORGOT!"
A MOVIE-LENGTH SAGA OF THE SAVAGE LAND
BONUS: SHANNA THE SHE-DEVIL

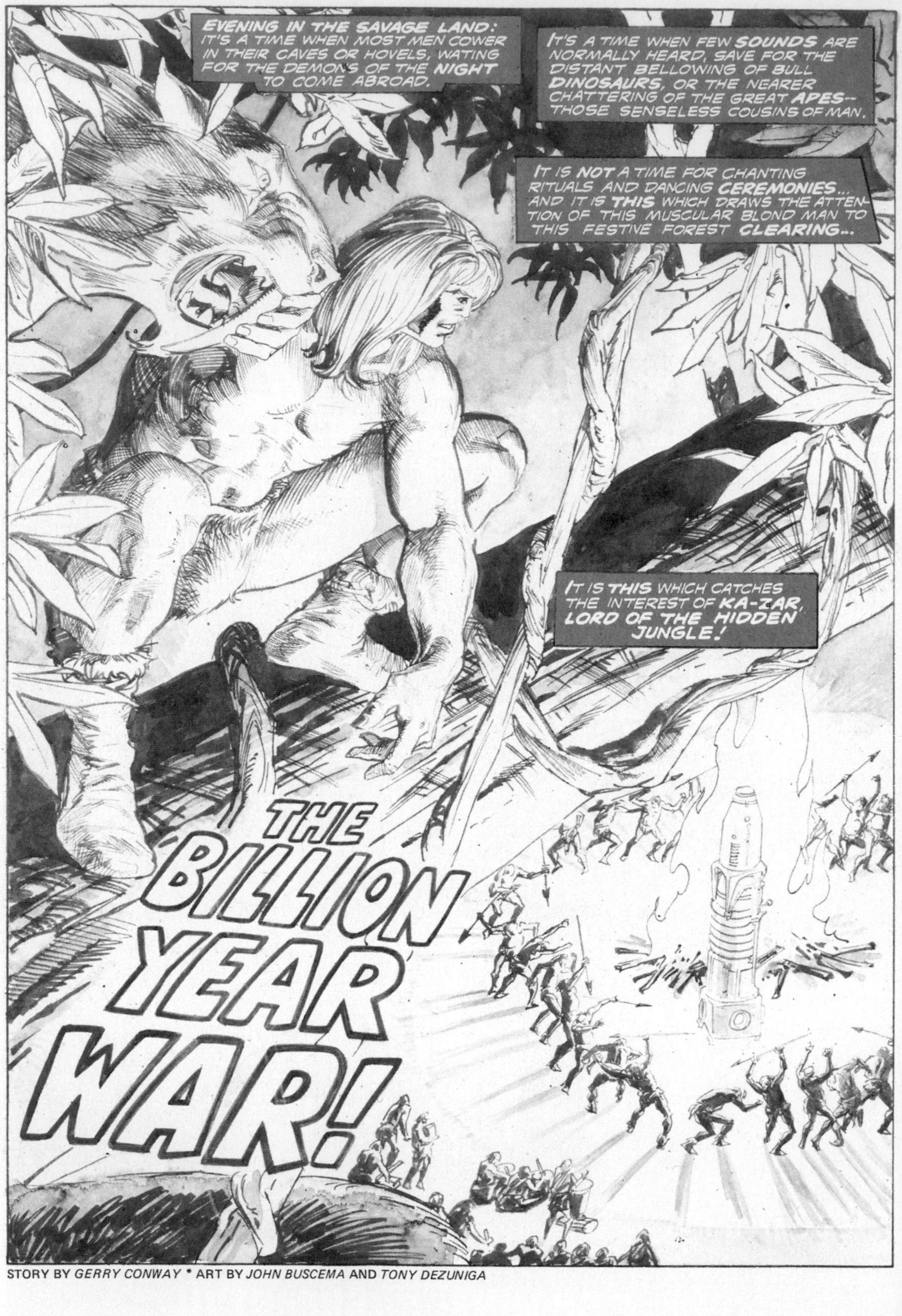
EVENING IN THE SAVAGE LAND: IT'S A TIME WHEN MOST MEN COWER IN THEIR CAVES OR HOVELS, WATING FOR THE DEMONS OF THE NIGHT TO COME ABROAD.
IT'S A TIME WHEN FEW SOUNDS ARE NORMALLY HEARD, SAVE FOR THE DISTANT BELLOWING OF BULL DINOSAURS, OR THE NEARER CHATTERING OF THE GREAT APES-- THOSE SENSELESS COUSINS OF MAN.
IT IS NOT A TIME FOR CHANTING RITUALS AND DANCING CEREMONIES... AND IT IS THIS WHICH DRAWS THE ATTENTION OF THIS MUSCULAR BLOND MAN TO THIS FESTIVE FOREST CLEARING...
IT IS THIS WHICH CATCHES THE INTEREST OF KA-ZAR, LORD OF THE HIDDEN JUNGLE!
THE BILLION YEAR WAR!
STORY BY *GERRY CONWAY* * ART BY *JOHN BUSCEMA* AND *TONY DEZUNIGA*

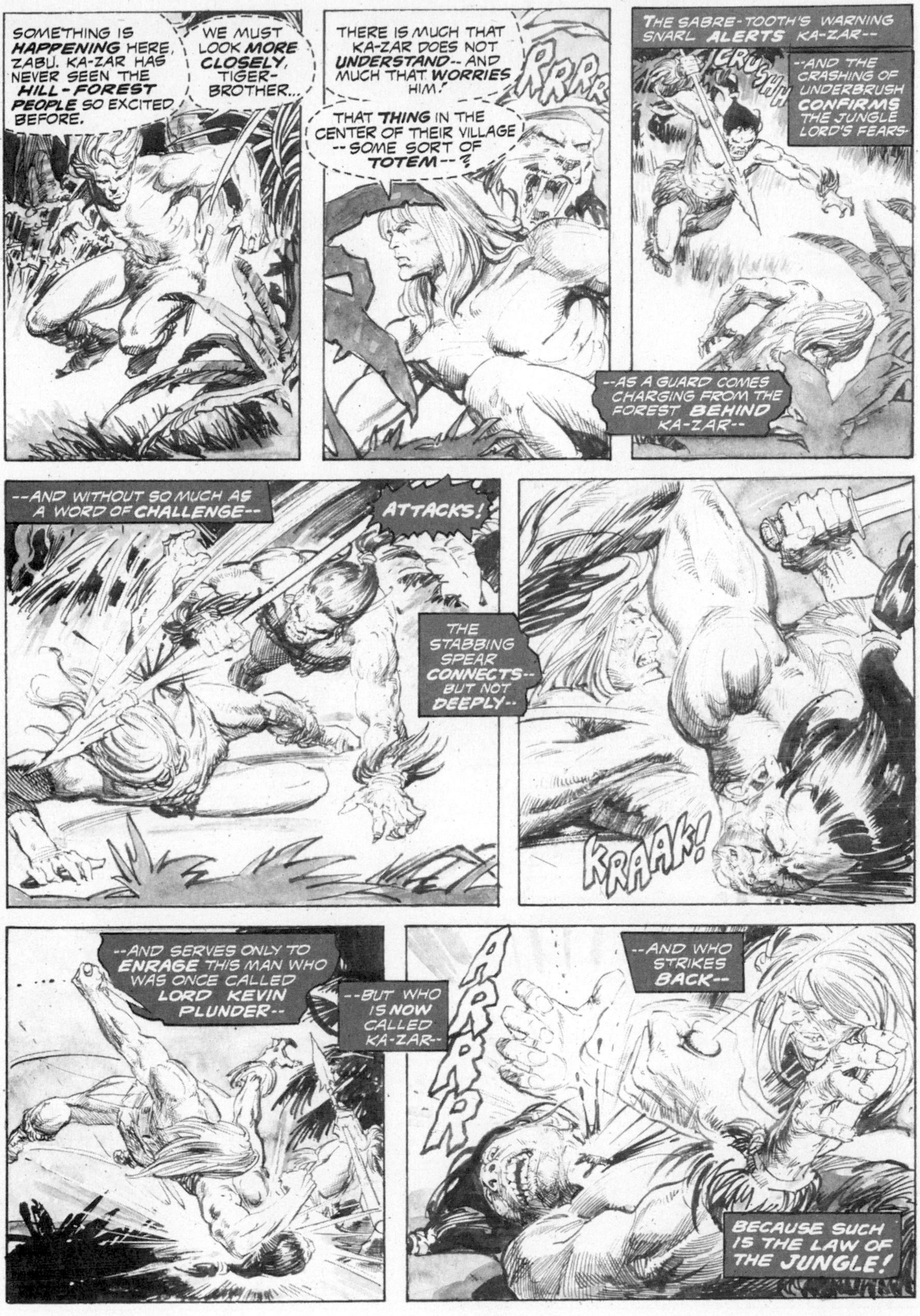
SOMETHING IS HAPPENING HERE, ZABU. KA-ZAR HAS NEVER SEEN THE HILL-FOREST PEOPLE SO EXCITED BEFORE.
WE MUST LOOK MORE CLOSELY, TIGER-BROTHER...
THERE IS MUCH THAT KA-ZAR DOES NOT UNDERSTAND-- AND MUCH THAT WORRIES HIM.
RRRR
THAT THING IN THE CENTER OF THEIR VILLAGE --SOME SORT OF TOTEM--?
THE SABRE-TOOTH'S WARNING SNARL ALERTS KA-ZAR--
CRUSH
--AND THE CRASHING OF UNDERBRUSH CONFIRMS THE JUNGLE LORD'S FEARS--
--AS A GUARD COMES CHARGING FROM THE FOREST BEHIND KA-ZAR--
--AND WITHOUT SO MUCH AS A WORD OF CHALLENGE--
ATTACKS!
THE STABBING SPEAR CONNECTS-- BUT NOT DEEPLY--
KRAAK!
--AND SERVES ONLY TO ENRAGE THIS MAN WHO WAS ONCE CALLED LORD KEVIN PLUNDER--
--BUT WHO IS NOW CALLED KA-ZAR--
ARRRRR
--AND WHO STRIKES BACK--
BECAUSE SUCH IS THE LAW OF THE JUNGLE!

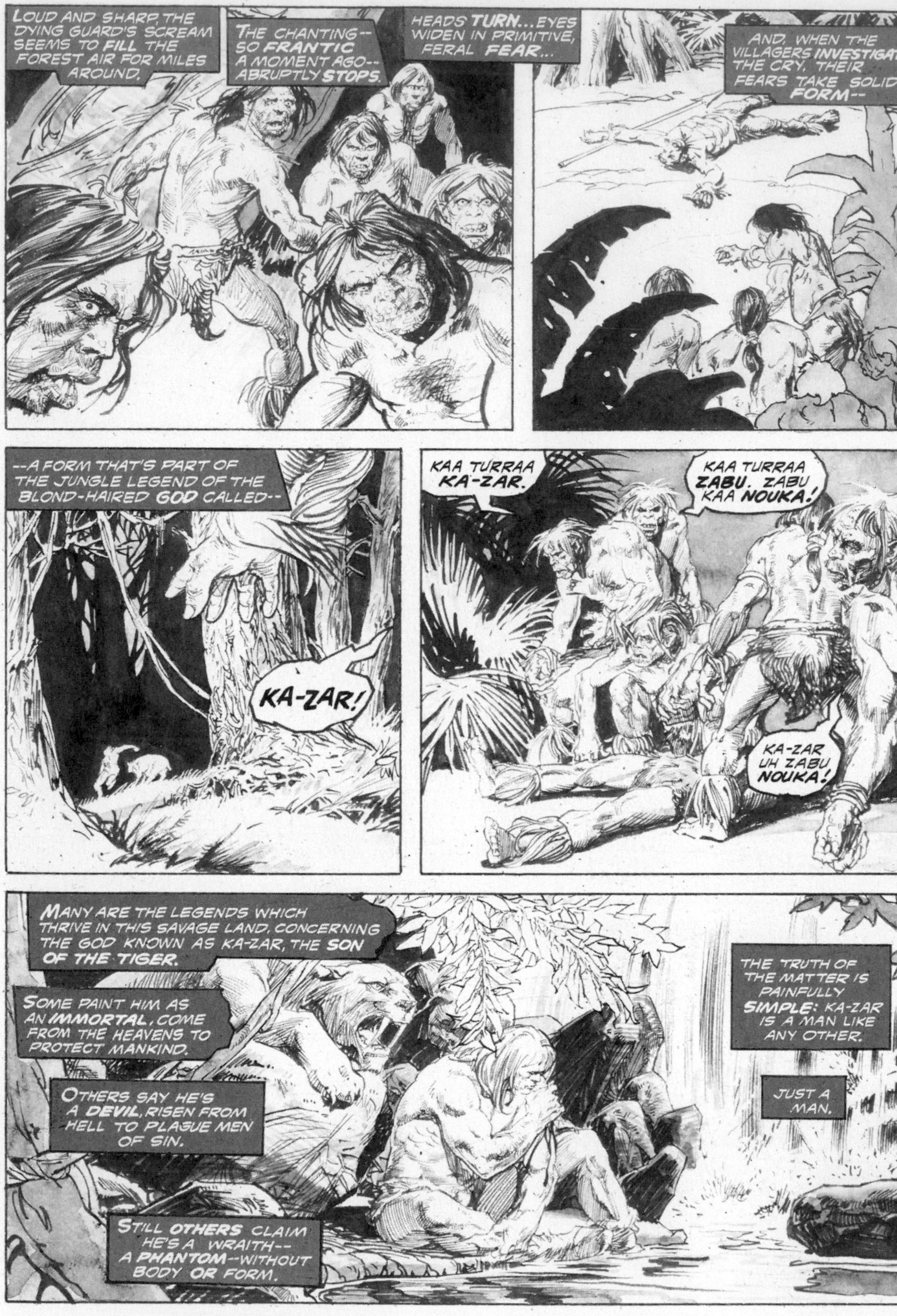
Loud and sharp, the dying guard's scream seems to fill the forest air for miles around.
The chanting--so frantic a moment ago--abruptly stops.
Heads turn...eyes widen in primitive, feral fear...
And, when the villagers investigate the cry, their fears take solid form--
--A form that's part of the jungle legend of the blond-haired god called--
KA-ZAR!
KAA TURRAA KA-ZAR.
KAA TURRAA ZABU. ZABU KAA NOUKA!
KA-ZAR UH ZABU NOUKA!
Many are the legends which thrive in this savage land, concerning the god known as Ka-Zar, the son of the tiger.
Some paint him as an immortal, come from the heavens to protect mankind.
Others say he's a devil, risen from hell to plague men of sin.
Still others claim he's a wraith--a phantom--without body or form.
The truth of the matter is painfully simple: Ka-Zar is a man like any other.
Just a man.

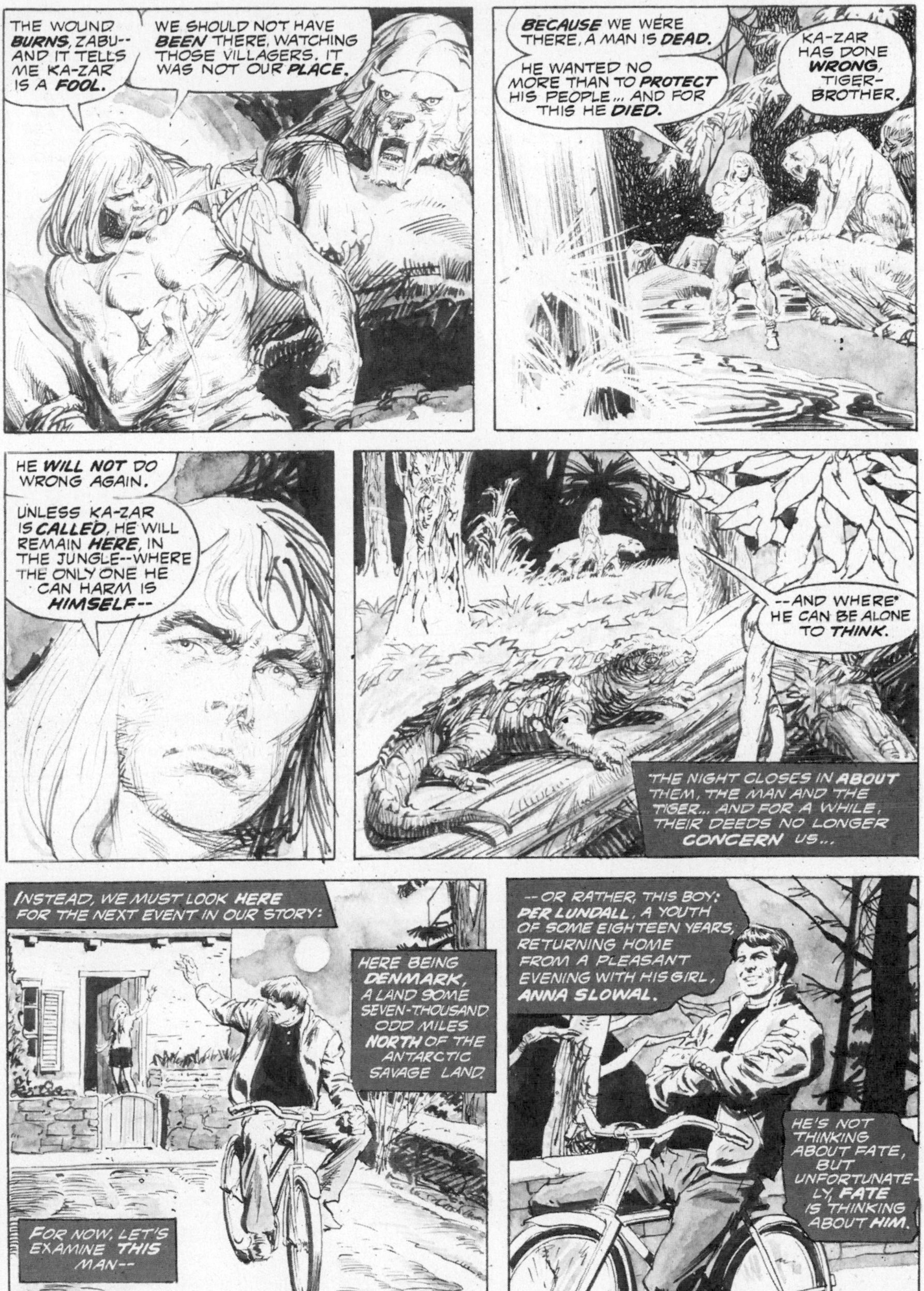
THE WOUND BURNS, ZABU-- AND IT TELLS ME KA-ZAR IS A FOOL.
WE SHOULD NOT HAVE BEEN THERE, WATCHING THOSE VILLAGERS. IT WAS NOT OUR PLACE.
BECAUSE WE WERE THERE, A MAN IS DEAD.
HE WANTED NO MORE THAN TO PROTECT HIS PEOPLE... AND FOR THIS HE DIED.
KA-ZAR HAS DONE WRONG, TIGER-BROTHER.
HE WILL NOT DO WRONG AGAIN.
UNLESS KA-ZAR IS CALLED, HE WILL REMAIN HERE, IN THE JUNGLE--WHERE THE ONLY ONE HE CAN HARM IS HIMSELF--
--AND WHERE HE CAN BE ALONE TO THINK.
THE NIGHT CLOSES IN ABOUT THEM, THE MAN AND THE TIGER... AND FOR A WHILE, THEIR DEEDS NO LONGER CONCERN US...
INSTEAD, WE MUST LOOK HERE FOR THE NEXT EVENT IN OUR STORY:
HERE BEING DENMARK, A LAND SOME SEVEN-THOUSAND ODD MILES NORTH OF THE ANTARCTIC SAVAGE LAND.
FOR NOW, LET'S EXAMINE THIS MAN--
--OR RATHER, THIS BOY: PER LUNDALL, A YOUTH OF SOME EIGHTEEN YEARS, RETURNING HOME FROM A PLEASANT EVENING WITH HIS GIRL, ANNA SLOWAL.
HE'S NOT THINKING ABOUT FATE, BUT UNFORTUNATE-LY, FATE IS THINKING ABOUT HIM.

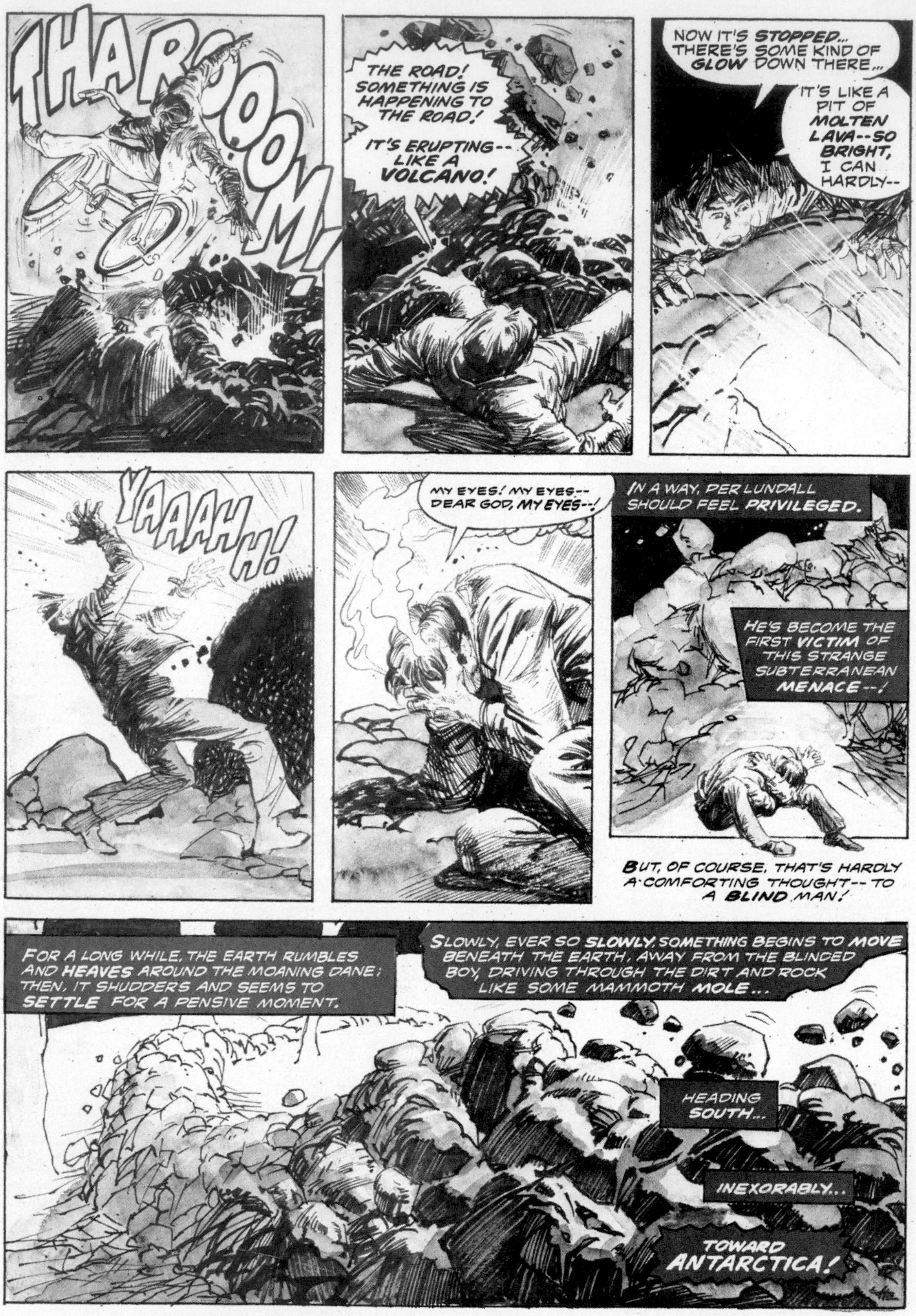
THAROOOOM!
THE ROAD! SOMETHING IS HAPPENING TO THE ROAD!
IT'S ERUPTING-- LIKE A VOLCANO!
NOW IT'S STOPPED... THERE'S SOME KIND OF GLOW DOWN THERE...
IT'S LIKE A PIT OF MOLTEN LAVA--SO BRIGHT, I CAN HARDLY--
YAAAHH!
MY EYES! MY EYES-- DEAR GOD, MY EYES--!
IN A WAY, PER LUNDALL SHOULD FEEL PRIVILEGED.
HE'S BECOME THE FIRST VICTIM OF THIS STRANGE SUBTERRANEAN MENACE--!
BUT, OF COURSE, THAT'S HARDLY A COMFORTING THOUGHT-- TO A BLIND MAN!
FOR A LONG WHILE, THE EARTH RUMBLES AND HEAVES AROUND THE MOANING DANE; THEN, IT SHUDDERS AND SEEMS TO SETTLE FOR A PENSIVE MOMENT.
SLOWLY, EVER SO SLOWLY, SOMETHING BEGINS TO MOVE BENEATH THE EARTH, AWAY FROM THE BLINDED BOY, DRIVING THROUGH THE DIRT AND ROCK LIKE SOME MAMMOTH MOLE...
HEADING SOUTH...
INEXORABLY...
TOWARD ANTARCTICA!

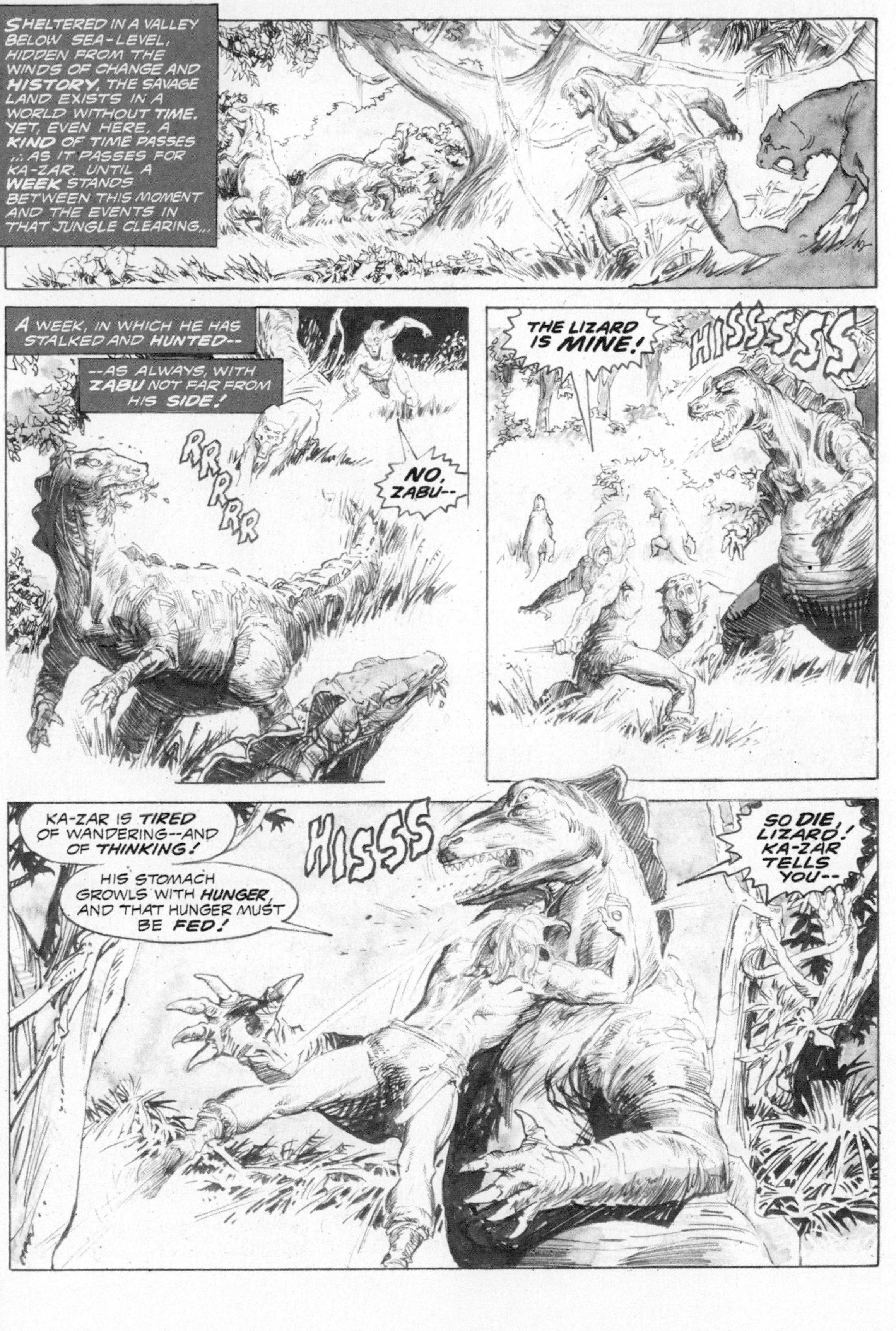
SHELTERED IN A VALLEY BELOW SEA-LEVEL, HIDDEN FROM THE WINDS OF CHANGE AND HISTORY, THE SAVAGE LAND EXISTS IN A WORLD WITHOUT TIME. YET, EVEN HERE, A KIND OF TIME PASSES ... AS IT PASSES FOR KA-ZAR, UNTIL A WEEK STANDS BETWEEN THIS MOMENT AND THE EVENTS IN THAT JUNGLE CLEARING...
A WEEK, IN WHICH HE HAS STALKED AND HUNTED--
--AS ALWAYS, WITH ZABU NOT FAR FROM HIS SIDE!
RRRRR
NO, ZABU--
THE LIZARD IS MINE!
HISSSSSS
KA-ZAR IS TIRED OF WANDERING--AND OF THINKING!
HIS STOMACH GROWLS WITH HUNGER, AND THAT HUNGER MUST BE FED!
HISSS
SO DIE, LIZARD! KA-ZAR TELLS YOU--

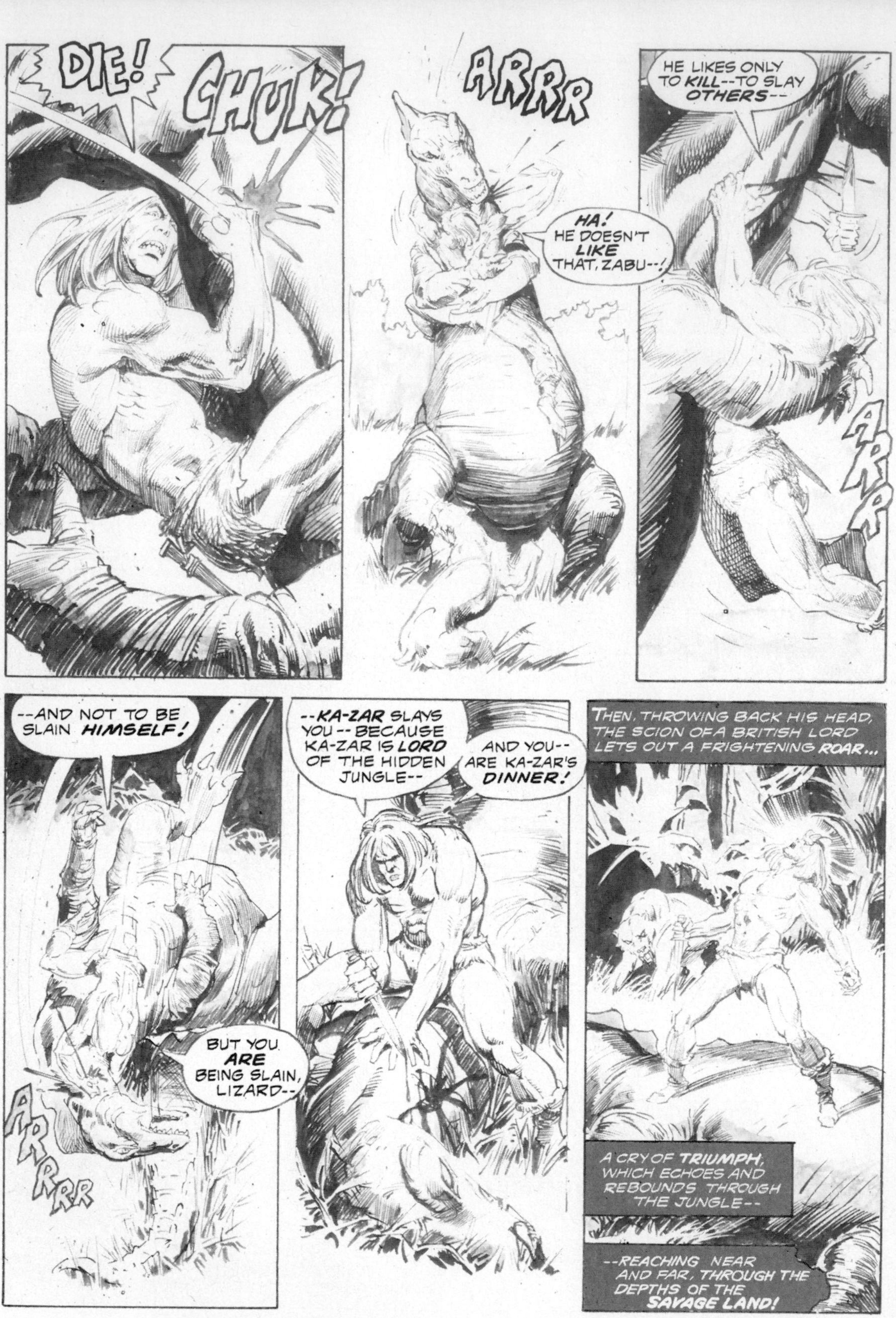
DIE!
CHUK!
ARRR
HA! HE DOESN'T LIKE THAT, ZABU--!
HE LIKES ONLY TO KILL--TO SLAY OTHERS--
ARRR
--AND NOT TO BE SLAIN HIMSELF!
BUT YOU ARE BEING SLAIN, LIZARD--
ARRRR
--KA-ZAR SLAYS YOU--BECAUSE KA-ZAR IS LORD OF THE HIDDEN JUNGLE--
AND YOU--ARE KA-ZAR'S DINNER!
THEN, THROWING BACK HIS HEAD, THE SCION OF A BRITISH LORD LETS OUT A FRIGHTENING ROAR...
A CRY OF TRIUMPH, WHICH ECHOES AND REBOUNDS THROUGH THE JUNGLE--
--REACHING NEAR AND FAR, THROUGH THE DEPTHS OF THE SAVAGE LAND!

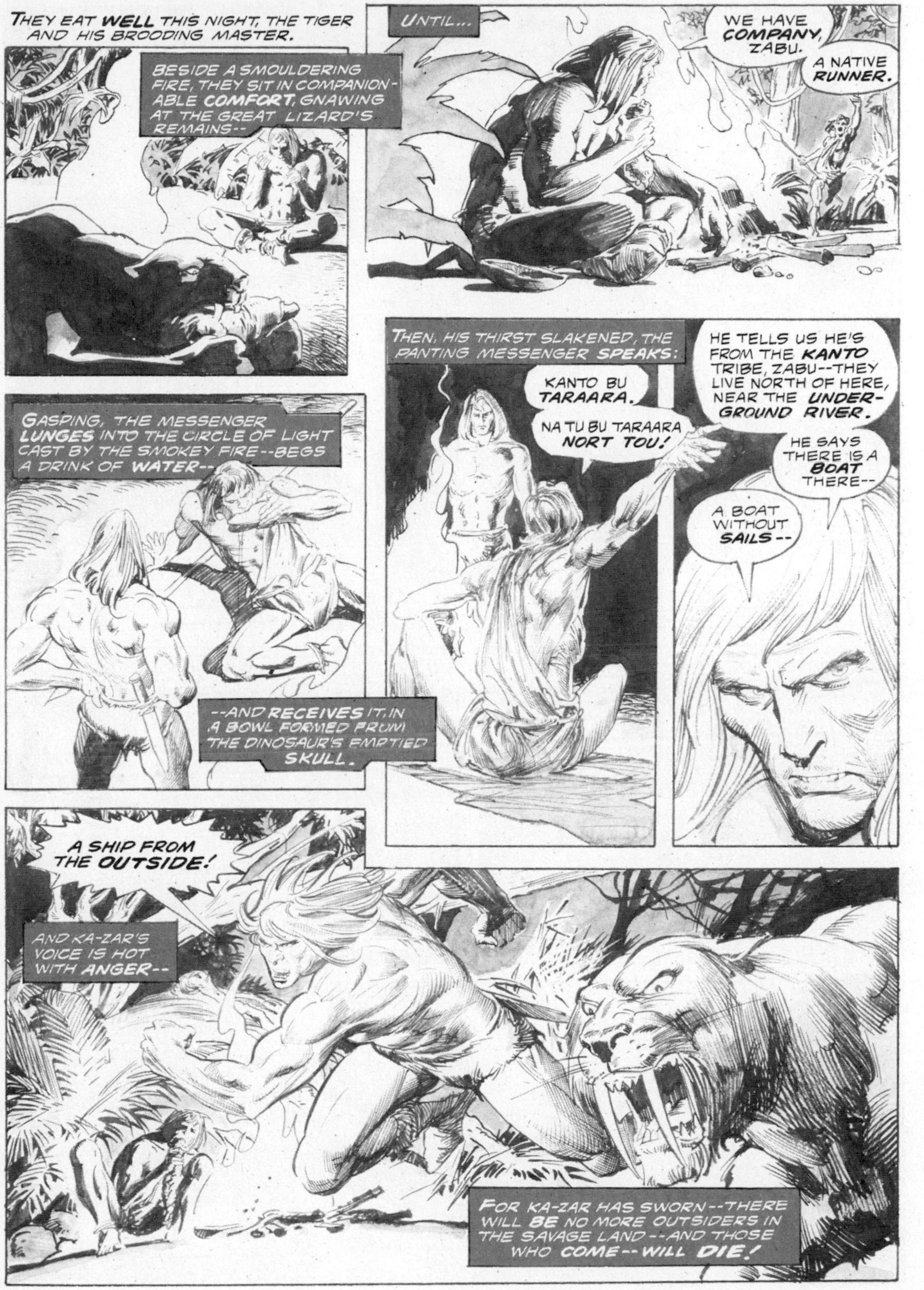
THEY EAT WELL THIS NIGHT, THE TIGER AND HIS BROODING MASTER.
BESIDE A SMOULDERING FIRE, THEY SIT IN COMPANIONABLE COMFORT, GNAWING AT THE GREAT LIZARD'S REMAINS--
UNTIL...
WE HAVE COMPANY, ZABU.
A NATIVE RUNNER.
GASPING, THE MESSENGER LUNGES INTO THE CIRCLE OF LIGHT CAST BY THE SMOKEY FIRE--BEGS A DRINK OF WATER--
--AND RECEIVES IT, IN A BOWL FORMED FROM THE DINOSAUR'S EMPTIED SKULL.
THEN, HIS THIRST SLAKENED, THE PANTING MESSENGER SPEAKS:
KANTO BU TARAARA.
NA TU BU TARAARA NORT TOU!
HE TELLS US HE'S FROM THE KANTO TRIBE, ZABU--THEY LIVE NORTH OF HERE, NEAR THE UNDERGROUND RIVER.
HE SAYS THERE IS A BOAT THERE--
A BOAT WITHOUT SAILS--
A SHIP FROM THE OUTSIDE!
AND KA-ZAR'S VOICE IS HOT WITH ANGER--
FOR KA-ZAR HAS SWORN--THERE WILL BE NO MORE OUTSIDERS IN THE SAVAGE LAND--AND THOSE WHO COME--WILL DIE!

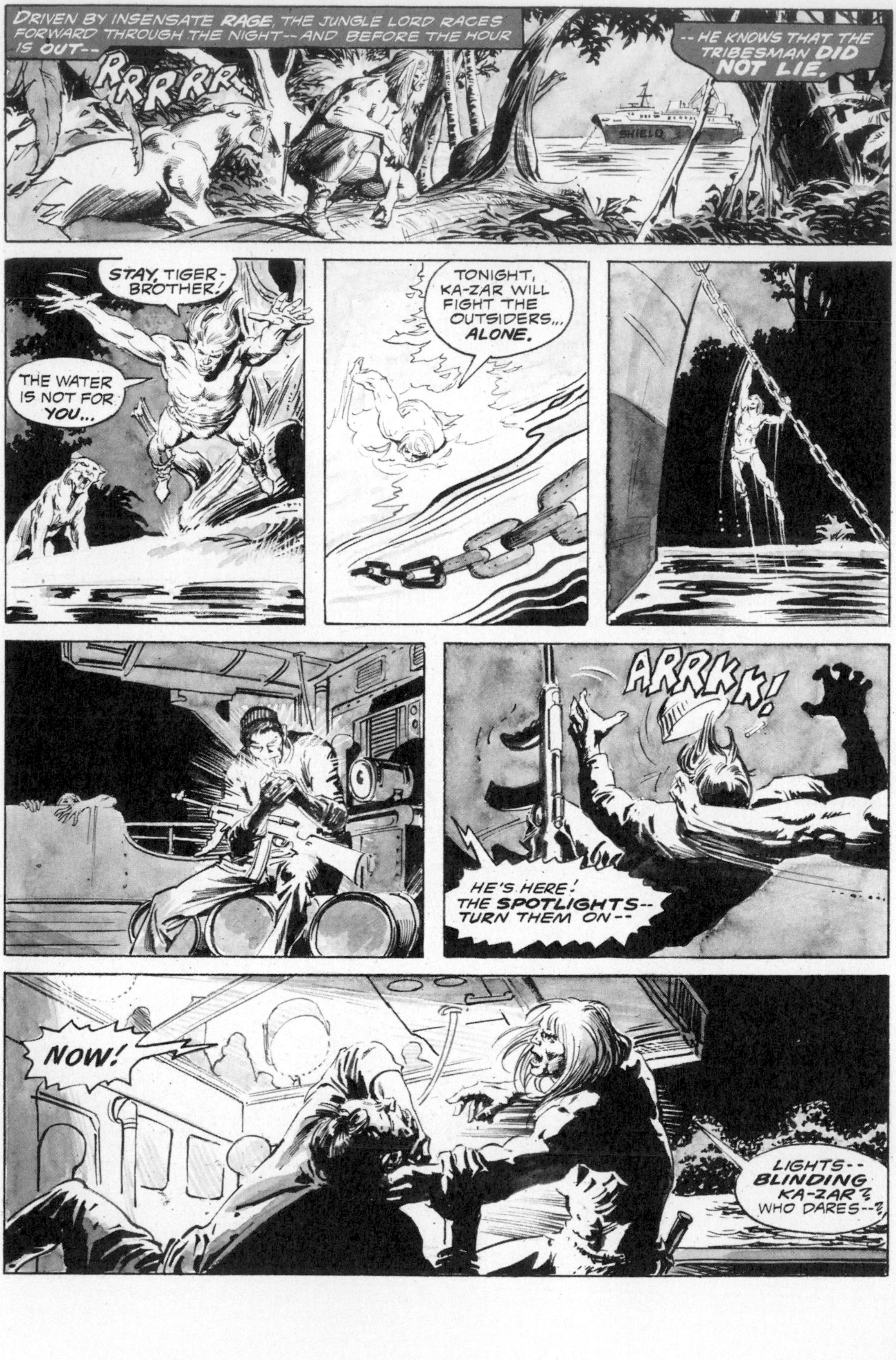
DRIVEN BY INSENSATE RAGE, THE JUNGLE LORD RACES FORWARD THROUGH THE NIGHT--AND BEFORE THE HOUR IS OUT--
RRRRRR
--HE KNOWS THAT THE TRIBESMAN DID NOT LIE.
SHIELD
STAY, TIGER-BROTHER!
THE WATER IS NOT FOR YOU...
TONIGHT, KA-ZAR WILL FIGHT THE OUTSIDERS... ALONE.
ARRKK!
HE'S HERE! THE SPOTLIGHTS-- TURN THEM ON--
NOW!
LIGHTS--BLINDING KA-ZAR? WHO DARES--?!

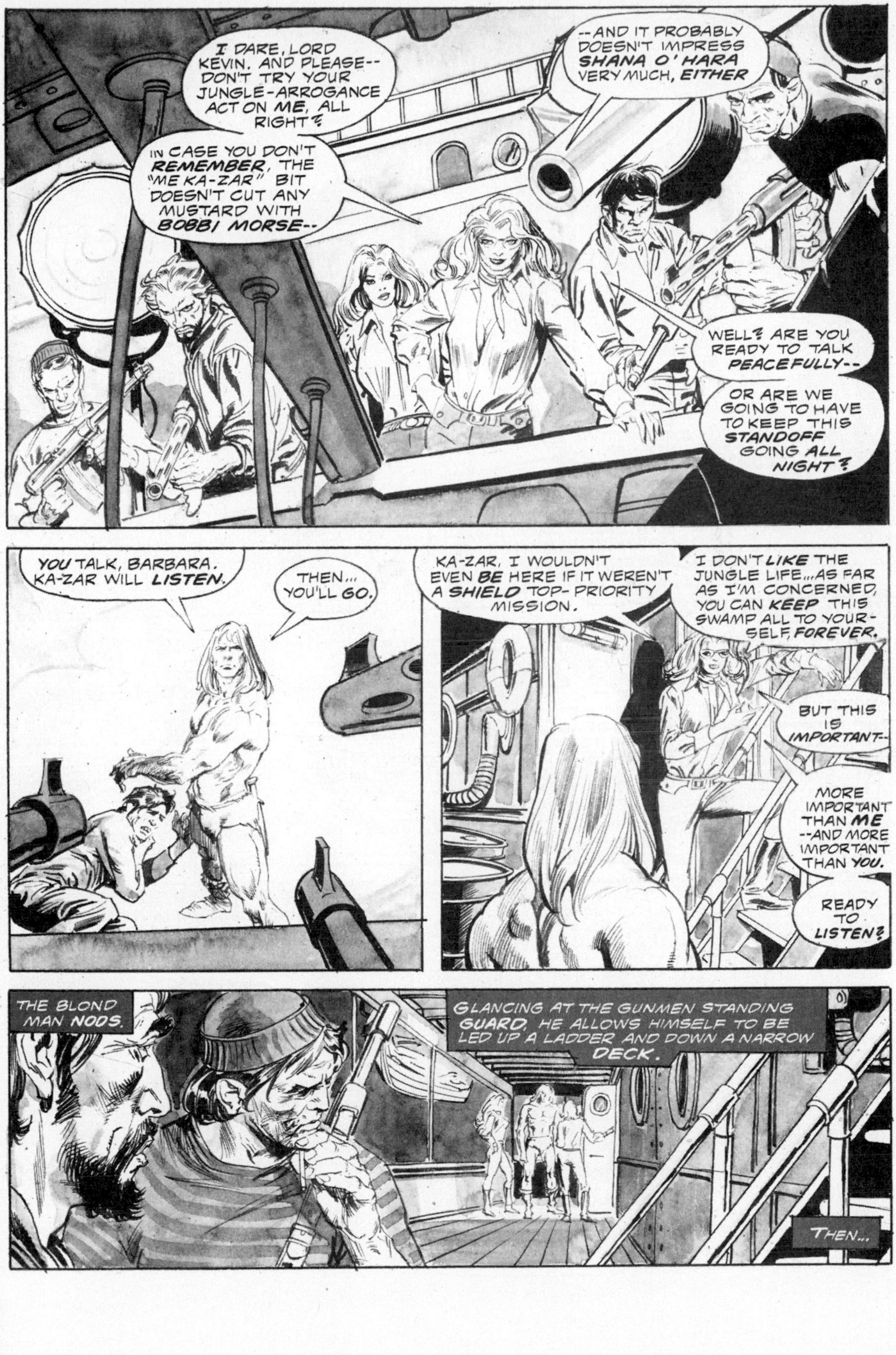
I DARE, LORD KEVIN. AND PLEASE-- DON'T TRY YOUR JUNGLE-ARROGANCE ACT ON ME, ALL RIGHT?
IN CASE YOU DON'T REMEMBER, THE "ME KA-ZAR" BIT DOESN'T CUT ANY MUSTARD WITH BOBBI MORSE--
--AND IT PROBABLY DOESN'T IMPRESS SHANA O'HARA VERY MUCH, EITHER
WELL? ARE YOU READY TO TALK PEACEFULLY--
OR ARE WE GOING TO HAVE TO KEEP THIS STANDOFF GOING ALL NIGHT?
YOU TALK, BARBARA. KA-ZAR WILL LISTEN.
THEN... YOU'LL GO.
KA-ZAR, I WOULDN'T EVEN BE HERE IF IT WEREN'T A SHIELD TOP-PRIORITY MISSION.
I DON'T LIKE THE JUNGLE LIFE... AS FAR AS I'M CONCERNED, YOU CAN KEEP THIS SWAMP ALL TO YOURSELF, FOREVER.
BUT THIS IS IMPORTANT--
MORE IMPORTANT THAN ME --AND MORE IMPORTANT THAN YOU.
READY TO LISTEN?
THE BLOND MAN NODS.
GLANCING AT THE GUNMEN STANDING GUARD, HE ALLOWS HIMSELF TO BE LED UP A LADDER AND DOWN A NARROW DECK.
THEN...

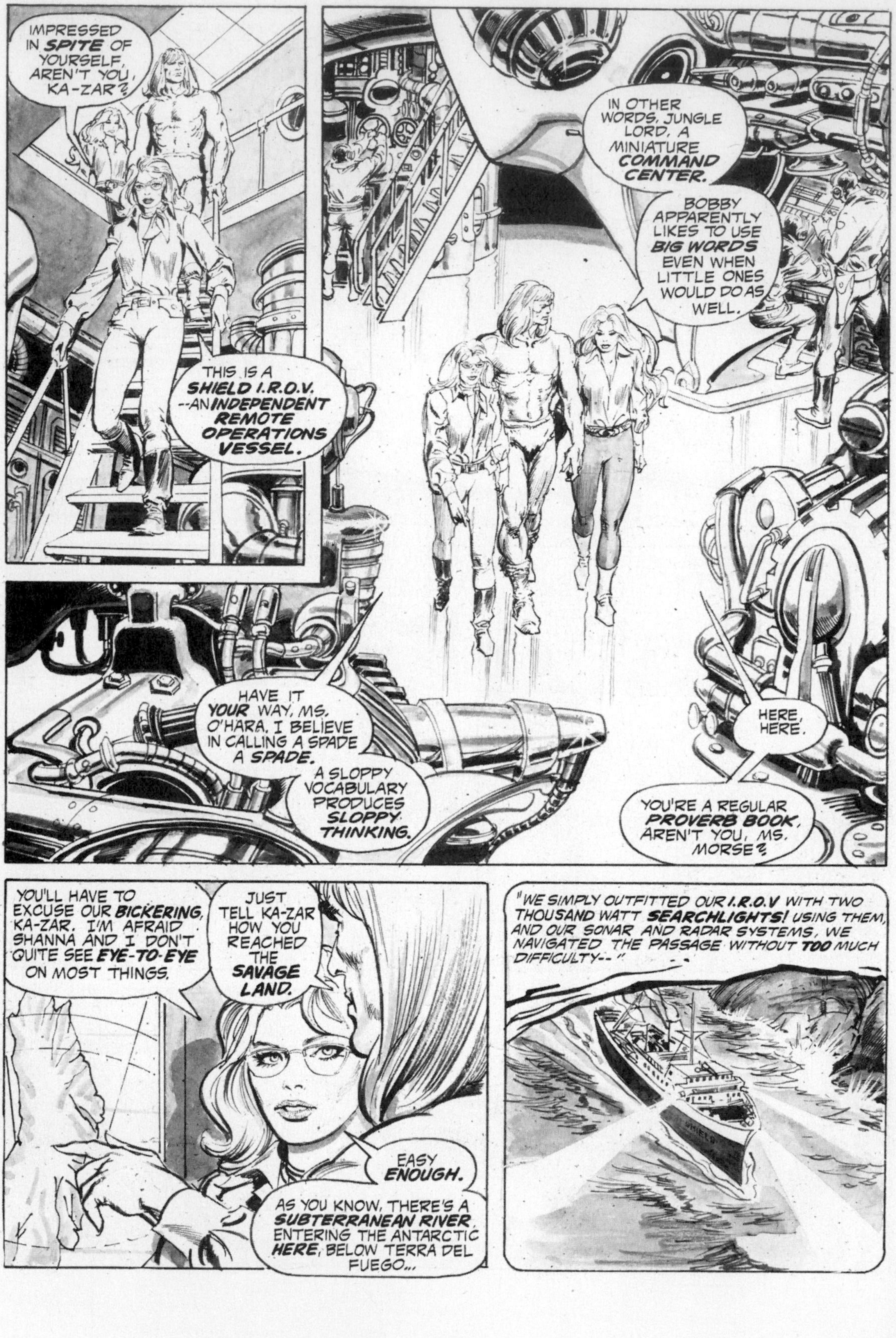
IMPRESSED IN SPITE OF YOURSELF, AREN'T YOU, KA-ZAR?
THIS IS A SHIELD I.R.O.V. --AN INDEPENDENT REMOTE OPERATIONS VESSEL.
IN OTHER WORDS, JUNGLE LORD, A MINIATURE COMMAND CENTER.
BOBBY APPARENTLY LIKES TO USE BIG WORDS EVEN WHEN LITTLE ONES WOULD DO AS WELL.
HAVE IT YOUR WAY, MS. O'HARA. I BELIEVE IN CALLING A SPADE A SPADE.
A SLOPPY VOCABULARY PRODUCES SLOPPY THINKING.
HERE, HERE.
YOU'RE A REGULAR PROVERB BOOK, AREN'T YOU, MS. MORSE?
YOU'LL HAVE TO EXCUSE OUR BICKERING, KA-ZAR. I'M AFRAID SHANNA AND I DON'T QUITE SEE EYE-TO-EYE ON MOST THINGS.
JUST TELL KA-ZAR HOW YOU REACHED THE SAVAGE LAND.
EASY ENOUGH.
AS YOU KNOW, THERE'S A SUBTERRANEAN RIVER ENTERING THE ANTARCTIC HERE, BELOW TERRA DEL FUEGO...
"WE SIMPLY OUTFITTED OUR I.R.O.V WITH TWO THOUSAND WATT SEARCHLIGHTS! USING THEM, AND OUR SONAR AND RADAR SYSTEMS, WE NAVIGATED THE PASSAGE WITHOUT TOO MUCH DIFFICULTY--"
SHIELD

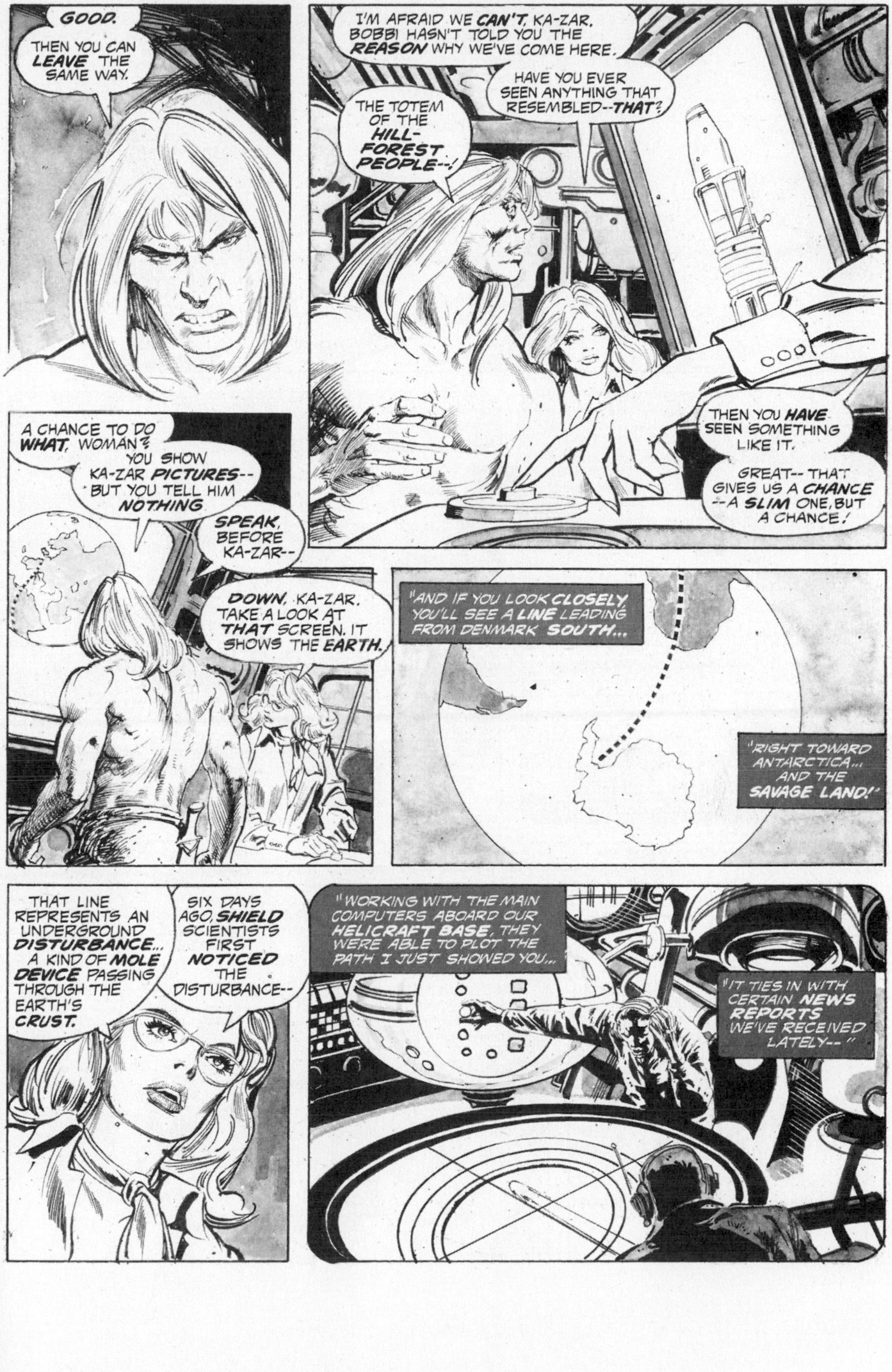
GOOD.
THEN YOU CAN LEAVE THE SAME WAY.
I'M AFRAID WE CAN'T, KA-ZAR. BOBBI HASN'T TOLD YOU THE REASON WHY WE'VE COME HERE.
HAVE YOU EVER SEEN ANYTHING THAT RESEMBLED--THAT?
THE TOTEM OF THE HILL-FOREST PEOPLE--!
THEN YOU HAVE SEEN SOMETHING LIKE IT.
GREAT-- THAT GIVES US A CHANCE --A SLIM ONE, BUT A CHANCE!
A CHANCE TO DO WHAT, WOMAN?
YOU SHOW KA-ZAR PICTURES-- BUT YOU TELL HIM NOTHING.
SPEAK, BEFORE KA-ZAR--
DOWN, KA-ZAR. TAKE A LOOK AT THAT SCREEN. IT SHOWS THE EARTH.
"AND IF YOU LOOK CLOSELY, YOU'LL SEE A LINE LEADING FROM DENMARK SOUTH...
"RIGHT TOWARD ANTARCTICA... AND THE SAVAGE LAND!"
THAT LINE REPRESENTS AN UNDERGROUND DISTURBANCE... A KIND OF MOLE DEVICE PASSING THROUGH THE EARTH'S CRUST.
SIX DAYS AGO, SHIELD SCIENTISTS FIRST NOTICED THE DISTURBANCE--
"WORKING WITH THE MAIN COMPUTERS ABOARD OUR HELICRAFT BASE, THEY WERE ABLE TO PLOT THE PATH I JUST SHOWED YOU...
"IT TIES IN WITH CERTAIN NEWS REPORTS WE'VE RECEIVED LATELY--"

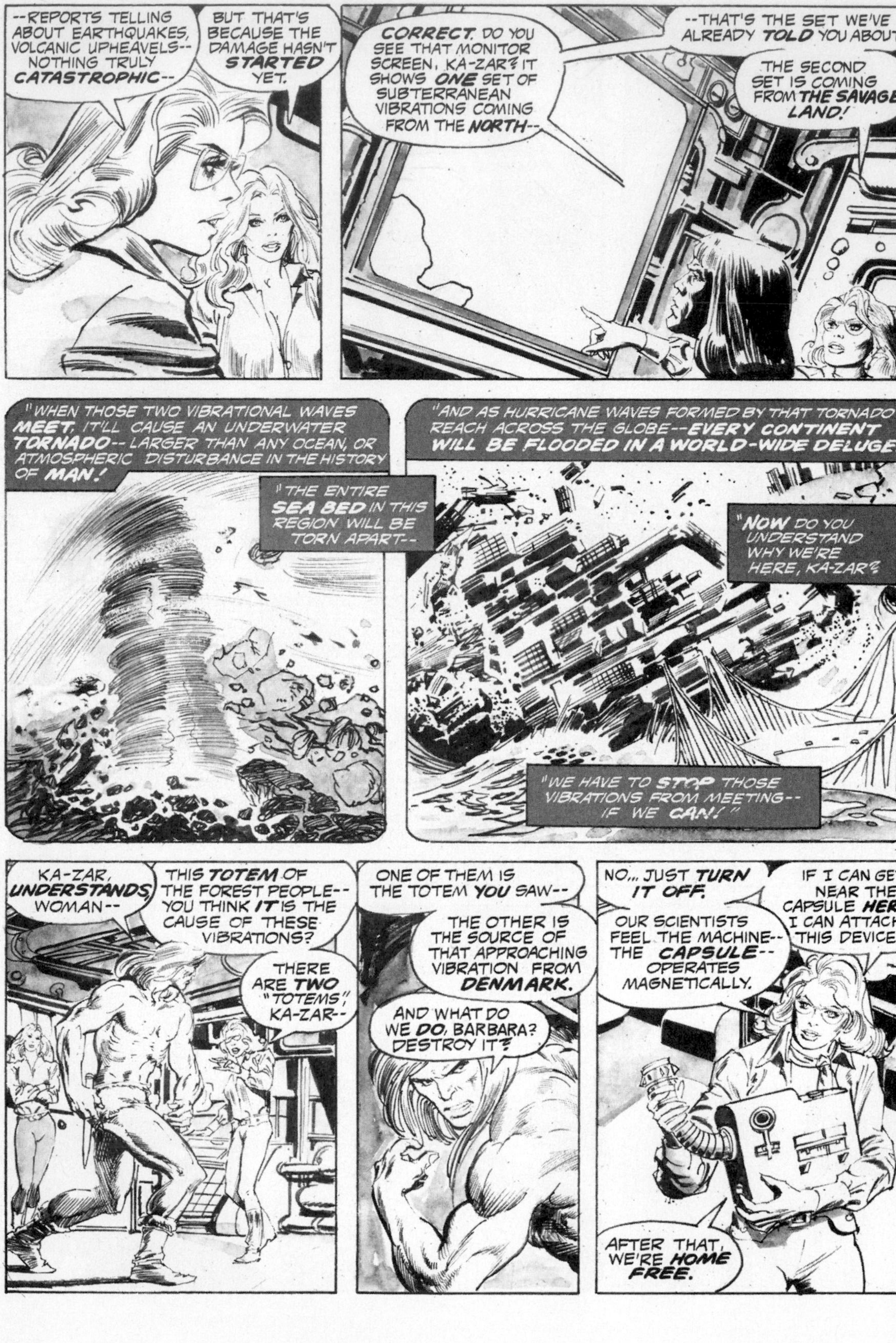
--REPORTS TELLING ABOUT EARTHQUAKES, VOLCANIC UPHEAVELS-- NOTHING TRULY CATASTROPHIC--
BUT THAT'S BECAUSE THE DAMAGE HASN'T STARTED YET.
CORRECT. DO YOU SEE THAT MONITOR SCREEN, KA-ZAR? IT SHOWS ONE SET OF SUBTERRANEAN VIBRATIONS COMING FROM THE NORTH--
--THAT'S THE SET WE'VE ALREADY TOLD YOU ABOUT.
THE SECOND SET IS COMING FROM THE SAVAGE LAND!
"WHEN THOSE TWO VIBRATIONAL WAVES MEET, IT'LL CAUSE AN UNDERWATER TORNADO-- LARGER THAN ANY OCEAN, OR ATMOSPHERIC DISTURBANCE IN THE HISTORY OF MAN!
"THE ENTIRE SEA BED IN THIS REGION WILL BE TORN APART--
"AND AS HURRICANE WAVES FORMED BY THAT TORNADO REACH ACROSS THE GLOBE--EVERY CONTINENT WILL BE FLOODED IN A WORLD-WIDE DELUGE!
"NOW DO YOU UNDERSTAND WHY WE'RE HERE, KA-ZAR?
"WE HAVE TO STOP THOSE VIBRATIONS FROM MEETING-- IF WE CAN!"
KA-ZAR, UNDERSTANDS, WOMAN--
THIS TOTEM OF THE FOREST PEOPLE-- YOU THINK IT IS THE CAUSE OF THESE VIBRATIONS?
THERE ARE TWO "TOTEMS," KA-ZAR--
ONE OF THEM IS THE TOTEM YOU SAW--
THE OTHER IS THE SOURCE OF THAT APPROACHING VIBRATION FROM DENMARK.
AND WHAT DO WE DO, BARBARA? DESTROY IT?
NO... JUST TURN IT OFF.
OUR SCIENTISTS FEEL THE MACHINE-- THE CAPSULE-- OPERATES MAGNETICALLY.
IF I CAN GET NEAR THE CAPSULE HERE, I CAN ATTACH THIS DEVICE--
AFTER THAT, WE'RE HOME FREE.

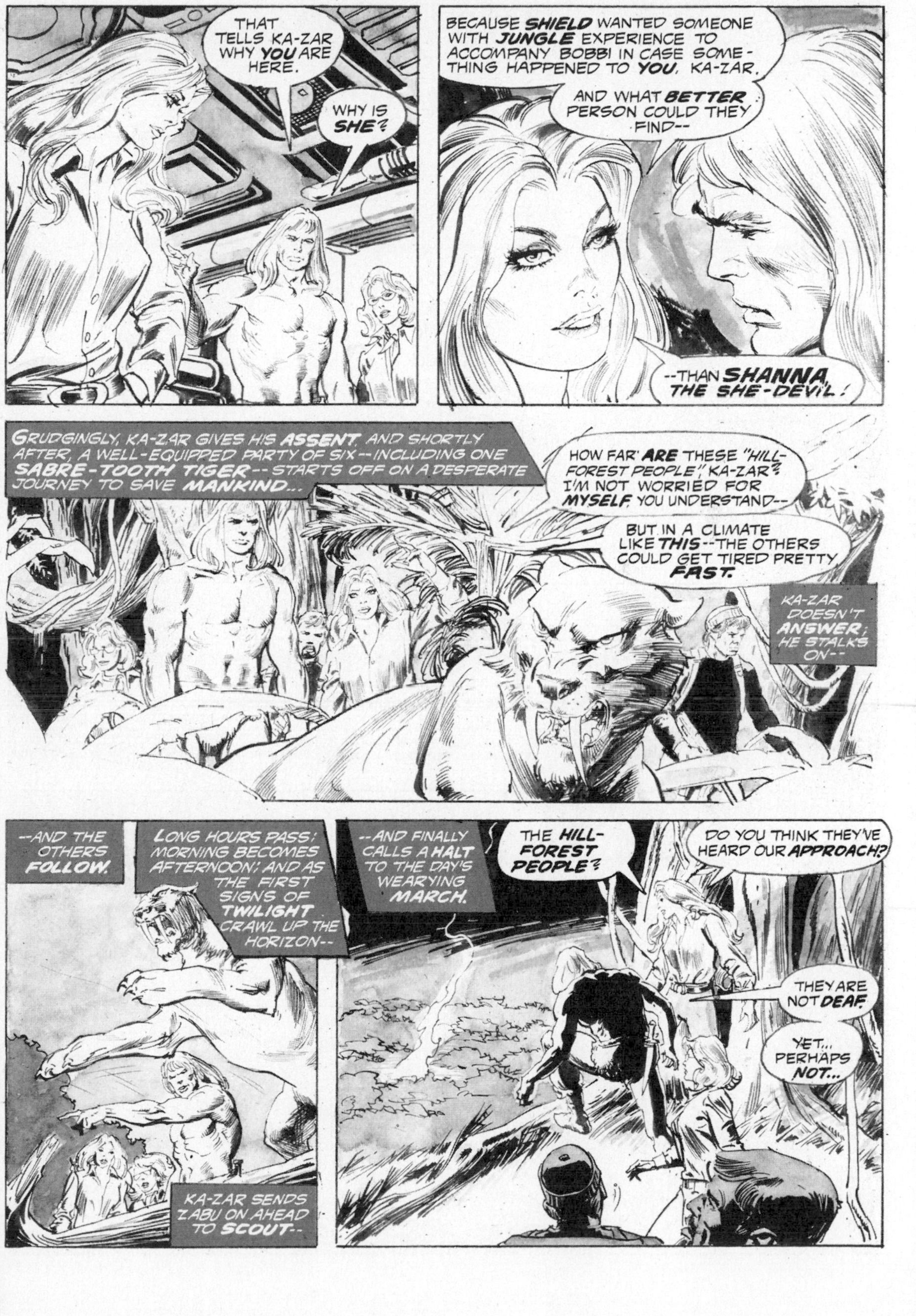

THAT TELLS KA-ZAR WHY YOU ARE HERE.
WHY IS SHE?
BECAUSE SHIELD WANTED SOMEONE WITH JUNGLE EXPERIENCE TO ACCOMPANY BOBBI IN CASE SOMETHING HAPPENED TO YOU, KA-ZAR.
AND WHAT BETTER PERSON COULD THEY FIND--
--THAN SHANNA, THE SHE-DEVIL!
GRUDGINGLY, KA-ZAR GIVES HIS ASSENT, AND SHORTLY AFTER, A WELL-EQUIPPED PARTY OF SIX--INCLUDING ONE SABRE-TOOTH TIGER--STARTS OFF ON A DESPERATE JOURNEY TO SAVE MANKIND...
HOW FAR ARE THESE "HILL-FOREST PEOPLE," KA-ZAR? I'M NOT WORRIED FOR MYSELF, YOU UNDERSTAND--
BUT IN A CLIMATE LIKE THIS--THE OTHERS COULD GET TIRED PRETTY FAST.
KA-ZAR DOESN'T ANSWER; HE STALKS ON--
--AND THE OTHERS FOLLOW.
LONG HOURS PASS: MORNING BECOMES AFTERNOON; AND AS THE FIRST SIGNS OF TWILIGHT CRAWL UP THE HORIZON--
KA-ZAR SENDS ZABU ON AHEAD TO SCOUT--
--AND FINALLY CALLS A HALT TO THE DAY'S WEARYING MARCH.
THE HILL-FOREST PEOPLE?
DO YOU THINK THEY'VE HEARD OUR APPROACH?
THEY ARE NOT DEAF.
YET... PERHAPS NOT...

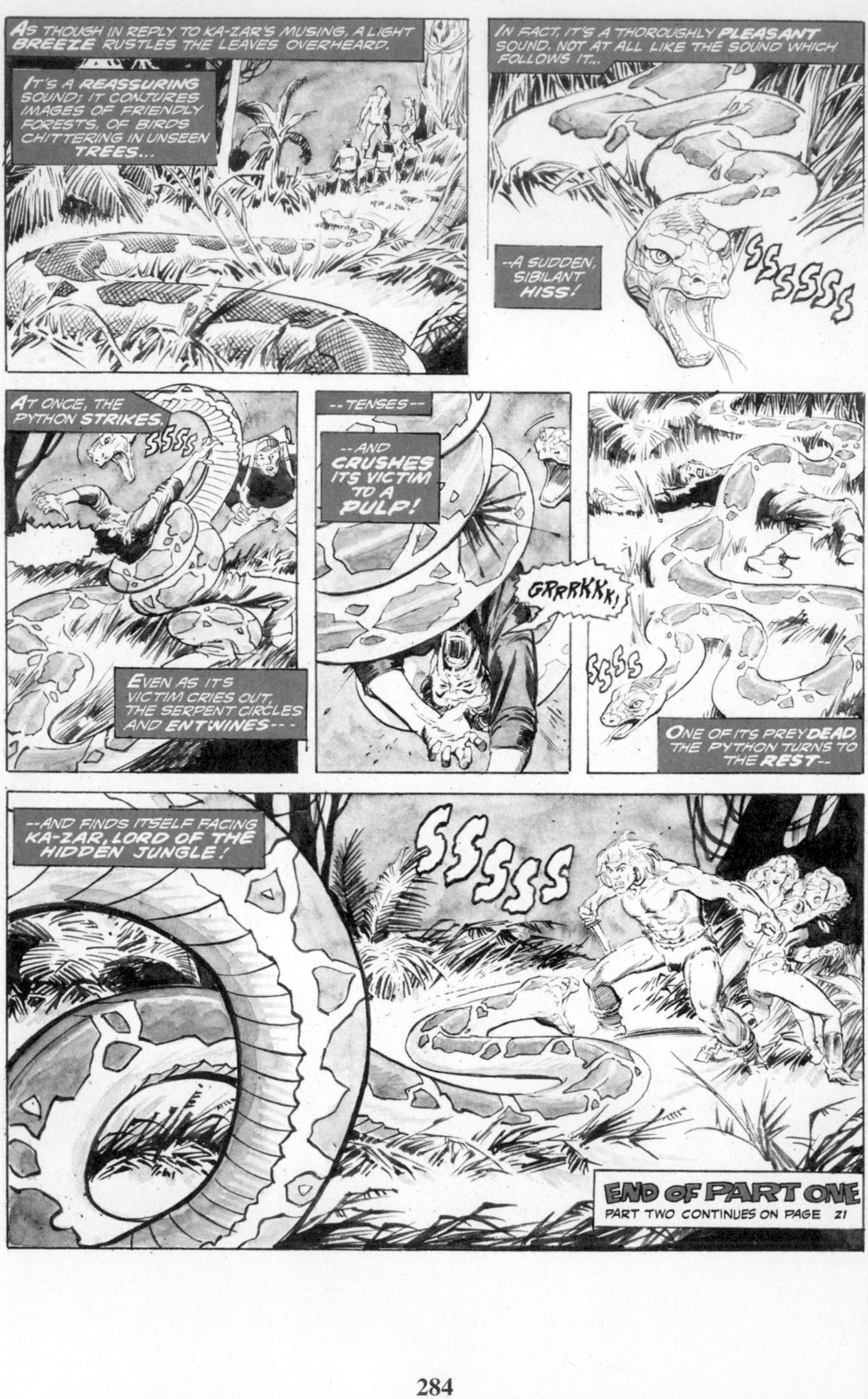
AS THOUGH IN REPLY TO KA-ZAR'S MUSING, A LIGHT BREEZE RUSTLES THE LEAVES OVERHEARD.
IT'S A REASSURING SOUND; IT CONJURES IMAGES OF FRIENDLY FORESTS, OF BIRDS CHITTERING IN UNSEEN TREES...
IN FACT, IT'S A THOROUGHLY PLEASANT SOUND, NOT AT ALL LIKE THE SOUND WHICH FOLLOWS IT...
--A SUDDEN, SIBILANT HISS!
SSSSSS
AT ONCE, THE PYTHON STRIKES.
SSSS
EVEN AS ITS VICTIM CRIES OUT, THE SERPENT CIRCLES AND ENTWINES---
--TENSES--
--AND CRUSHES ITS VICTIM TO A PULP!
GRRRKKK!
SSSS
ONE OF ITS PREY DEAD, THE PYTHON TURNS TO THE REST--
--AND FINDS ITSELF FACING KA-ZAR, LORD OF THE HIDDEN JUNGLE!
SSSSS
END OF PART ONE
PART TWO CONTINUES ON PAGE 21

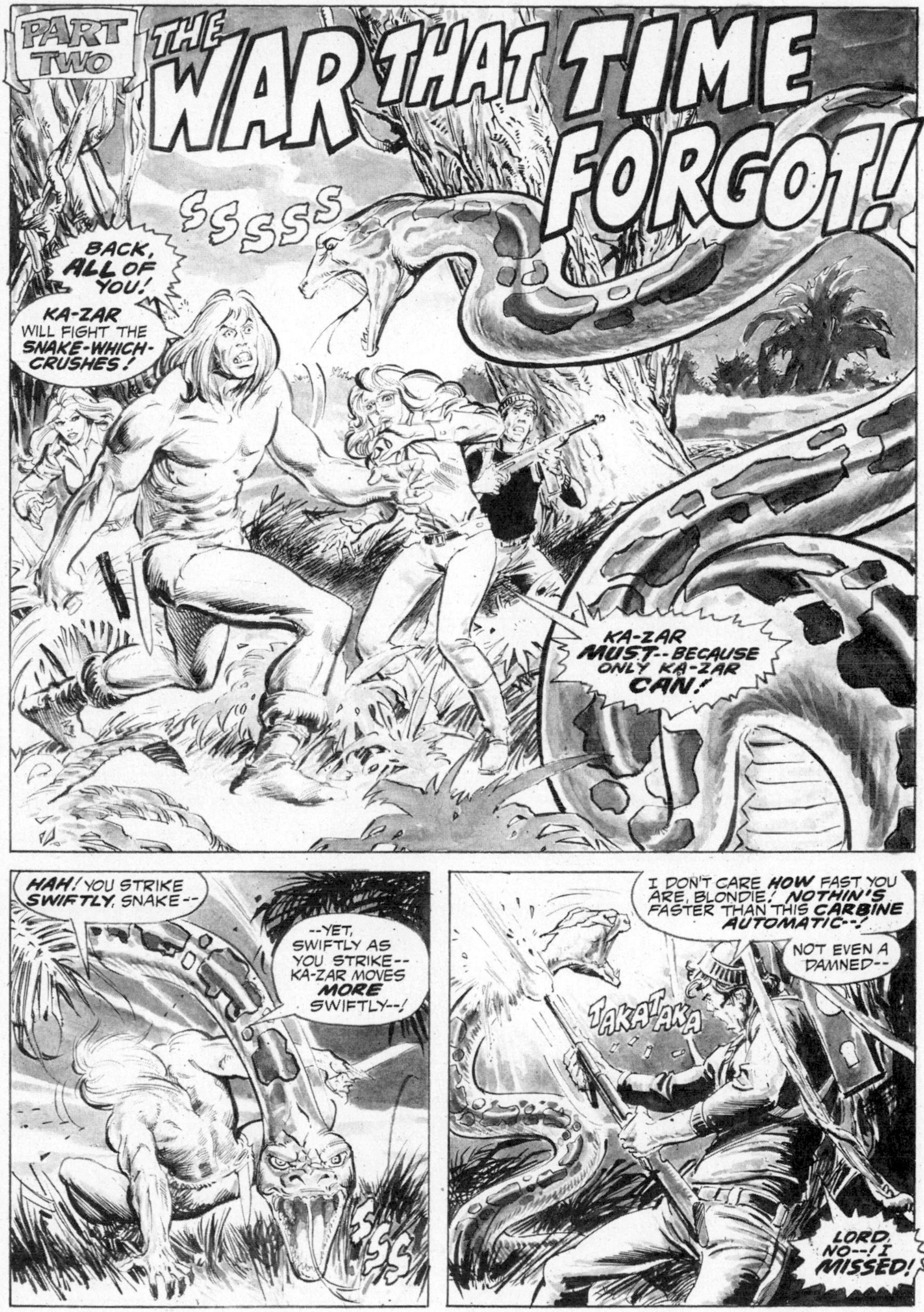
PART TWO
THE WAR THAT TIME FORGOT!
SSSSS
BACK, ALL OF YOU!
KA-ZAR WILL FIGHT THE SNAKE-WHICH-CRUSHES!
KA-ZAR MUST--BECAUSE ONLY KA-ZAR CAN!
HAH! YOU STRIKE SWIFTLY, SNAKE--
--YET, SWIFTLY AS YOU STRIKE--KA-ZAR MOVES MORE SWIFTLY--!
SSS
I DON'T CARE HOW FAST YOU ARE, BLONDIE! NOTHIN'S FASTER THAN THIS CARBINE AUTOMATIC--!
NOT EVEN A DAMNED--
TAKATAKA
LORD, NO--! I MISSED!

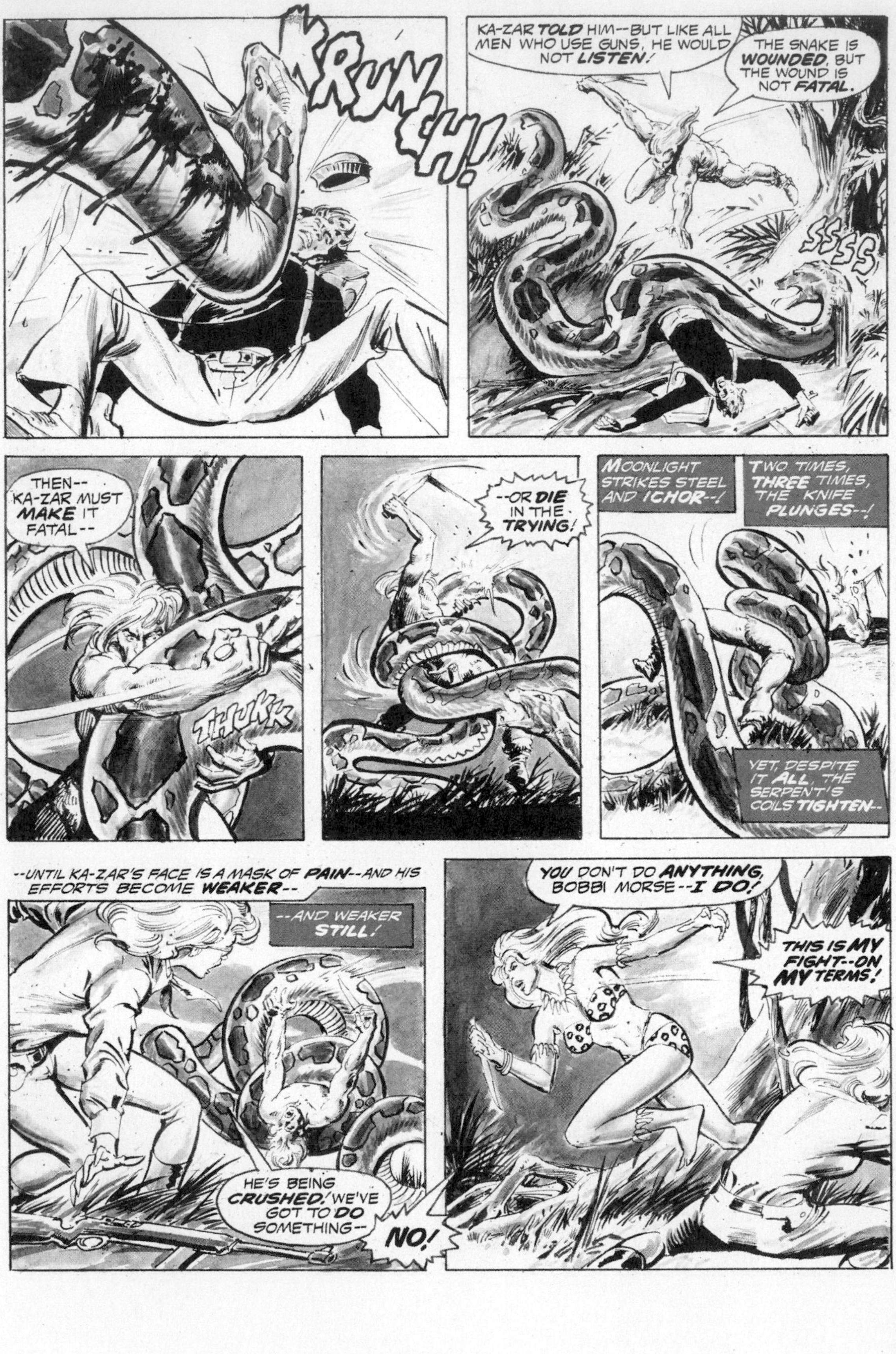

KRUNCH!
KA-ZAR TOLD HIM--BUT LIKE ALL MEN WHO USE GUNS, HE WOULD NOT LISTEN!
THE SNAKE IS WOUNDED, BUT THE WOUND IS NOT FATAL.
SSSS
THEN-- KA-ZAR MUST MAKE IT FATAL--
THUKK
--OR DIE IN THE TRYING!
MOONLIGHT STRIKES STEEL AND ICHOR--!
TWO TIMES, THREE TIMES, THE KNIFE PLUNGES--!
YET, DESPITE IT ALL, THE SERPENT'S COILS TIGHTEN--
--UNTIL KA-ZAR'S FACE IS A MASK OF PAIN--AND HIS EFFORTS BECOME WEAKER--
--AND WEAKER STILL!
HE'S BEING CRUSHED! WE'VE GOT TO DO SOMETHING--
NO!
YOU DON'T DO ANYTHING, BOBBI MORSE--I DO!
THIS IS MY FIGHT--ON MY TERMS!

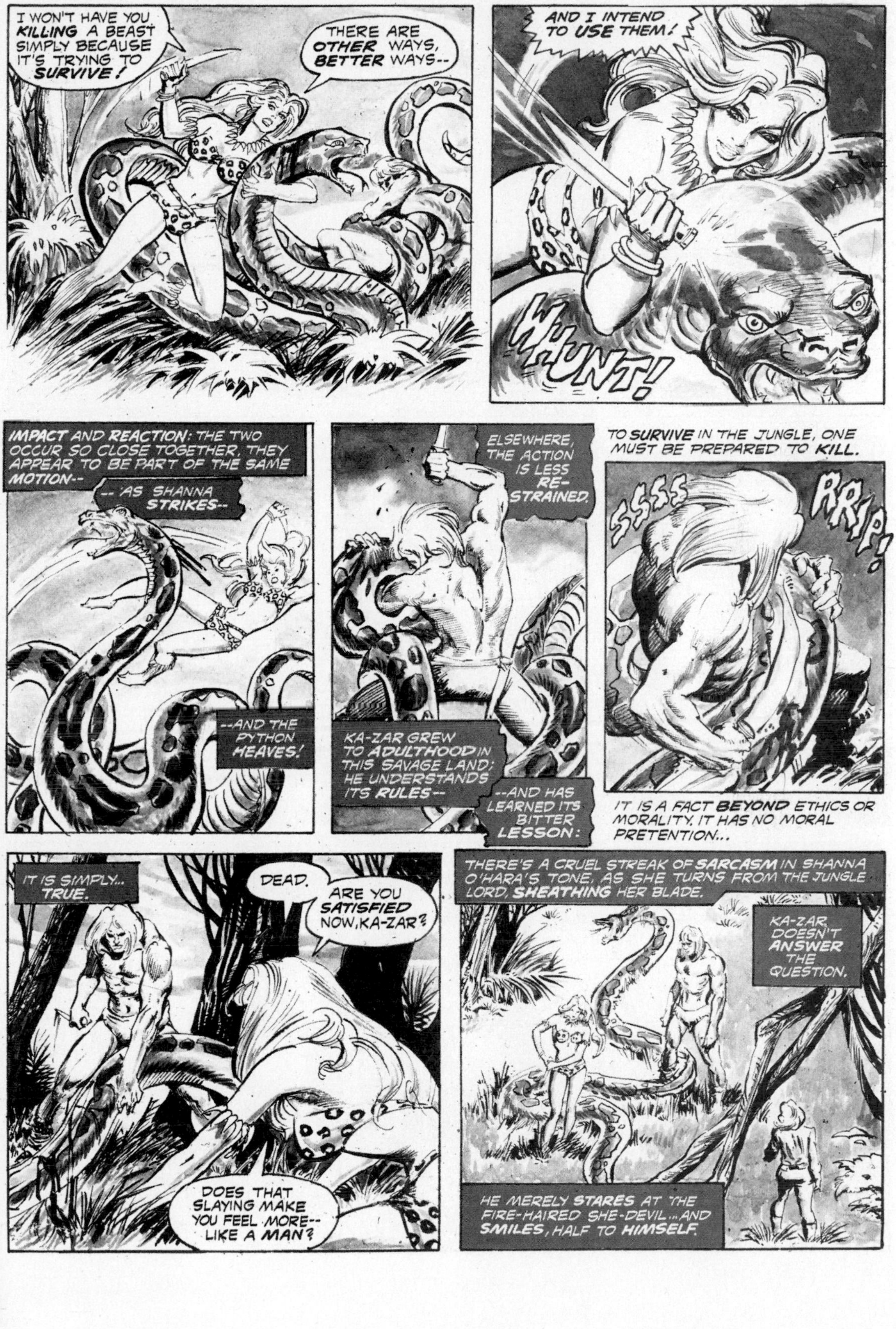
I WON'T HAVE YOU KILLING A BEAST SIMPLY BECAUSE IT'S TRYING TO SURVIVE!
THERE ARE OTHER WAYS, BETTER WAYS--
AND I INTEND TO USE THEM!
WHUNT!
IMPACT AND REACTION: THE TWO OCCUR SO CLOSE TOGETHER, THEY APPEAR TO BE PART OF THE SAME MOTION--
--AS SHANNA STRIKES--
--AND THE PYTHON HEAVES!
ELSEWHERE, THE ACTION IS LESS RE-STRAINED.
KA-ZAR GREW TO ADULTHOOD IN THIS SAVAGE LAND; HE UNDERSTANDS ITS RULES--
--AND HAS LEARNED ITS BITTER LESSON:
TO SURVIVE IN THE JUNGLE, ONE MUST BE PREPARED TO KILL.
SSSS
RRIP!
IT IS A FACT BEYOND ETHICS OR MORALITY. IT HAS NO MORAL PRETENTION...
IT IS SIMPLY... TRUE.
DEAD.
ARE YOU SATISFIED NOW, KA-ZAR?
DOES THAT SLAYING MAKE YOU FEEL MORE--LIKE A MAN?
THERE'S A CRUEL STREAK OF SARCASM IN SHANNA O'HARA'S TONE, AS SHE TURNS FROM THE JUNGLE LORD, SHEATHING HER BLADE.
KA-ZAR, DOESN'T ANSWER THE QUESTION.
HE MERELY STARES AT THE FIRE-HAIRED SHE-DEVIL... AND SMILES, HALF TO HIMSELF.

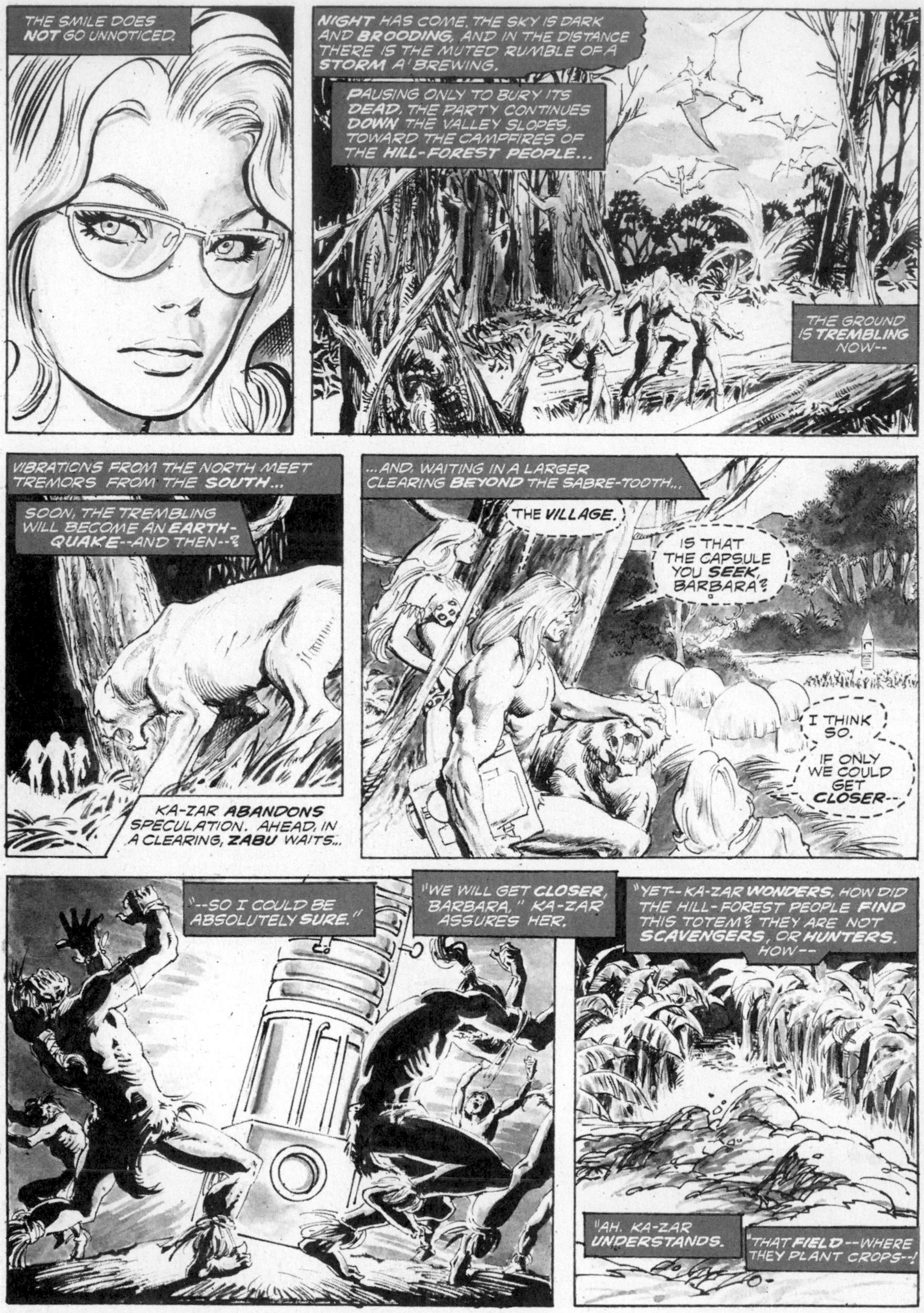
THE SMILE DOES NOT GO UNNOTICED.
NIGHT HAS COME. THE SKY IS DARK AND BROODING, AND IN THE DISTANCE THERE IS THE MUTED RUMBLE OF A STORM A' BREWING.
PAUSING ONLY TO BURY ITS DEAD, THE PARTY CONTINUES DOWN THE VALLEY SLOPES, TOWARD THE CAMPFIRES OF THE HILL-FOREST PEOPLE...
THE GROUND IS TREMBLING NOW--
VIBRATIONS FROM THE NORTH MEET TREMORS FROM THE SOUTH...
SOON, THE TREMBLING WILL BECOME AN EARTH-QUAKE--AND THEN--?
KA-ZAR ABANDONS SPECULATION. AHEAD, IN A CLEARING, ZABU WAITS...
...AND, WAITING IN A LARGER CLEARING BEYOND THE SABRE-TOOTH...
THE VILLAGE.
IS THAT THE CAPSULE YOU SEEK, BARBARA?
I THINK SO.
IF ONLY WE COULD GET CLOSER--
"--SO I COULD BE ABSOLUTELY SURE."
"WE WILL GET CLOSER, BARBARA," KA-ZAR ASSURES HER.
"YET--KA-ZAR WONDERS, HOW DID THE HILL-FOREST PEOPLE FIND THIS TOTEM? THEY ARE NOT SCAVENGERS, OR HUNTERS. HOW--
"AH. KA-ZAR UNDERSTANDS.
"THAT FIELD--WHERE THEY PLANT CROPS--!

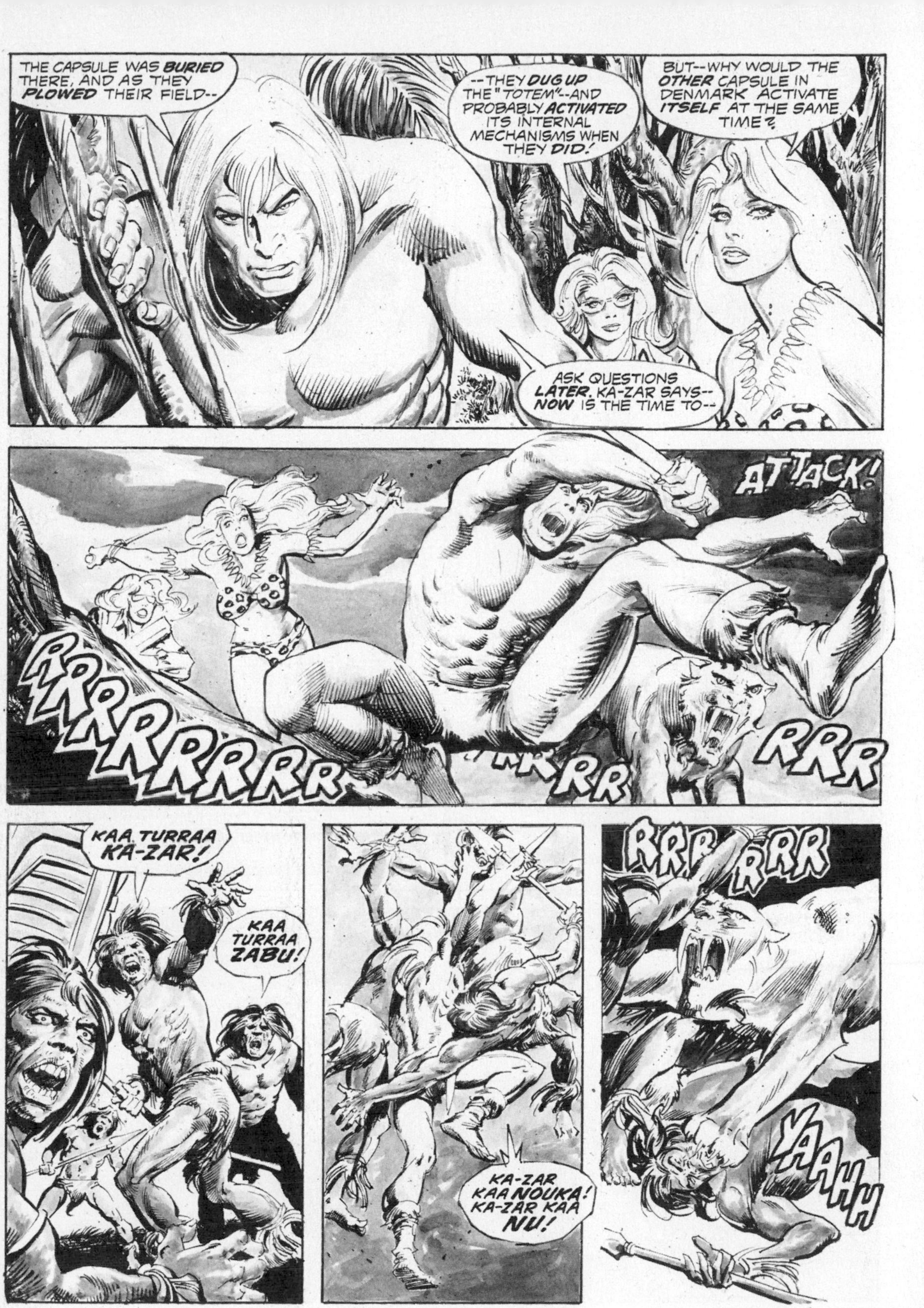

THE CAPSULE WAS BURIED THERE, AND AS THEY PLOWED THEIR FIELD--
--THEY DUG UP THE "TOTEM"--AND PROBABLY ACTIVATED ITS INTERNAL MECHANISMS WHEN THEY DID!
BUT--WHY WOULD THE OTHER CAPSULE IN DENMARK ACTIVATE ITSELF AT THE SAME TIME?
ASK QUESTIONS LATER. KA-ZAR SAYS--NOW IS THE TIME TO--
ATTACK!
RRRRRRRRRR
RRR
RRR
KAA TURRAA KA-ZAR!
KAA TURRAA ZABU!
KA-ZAR KAA NOUKA! KA-ZAR KAA NU!
RRRRRRR
YAAHH

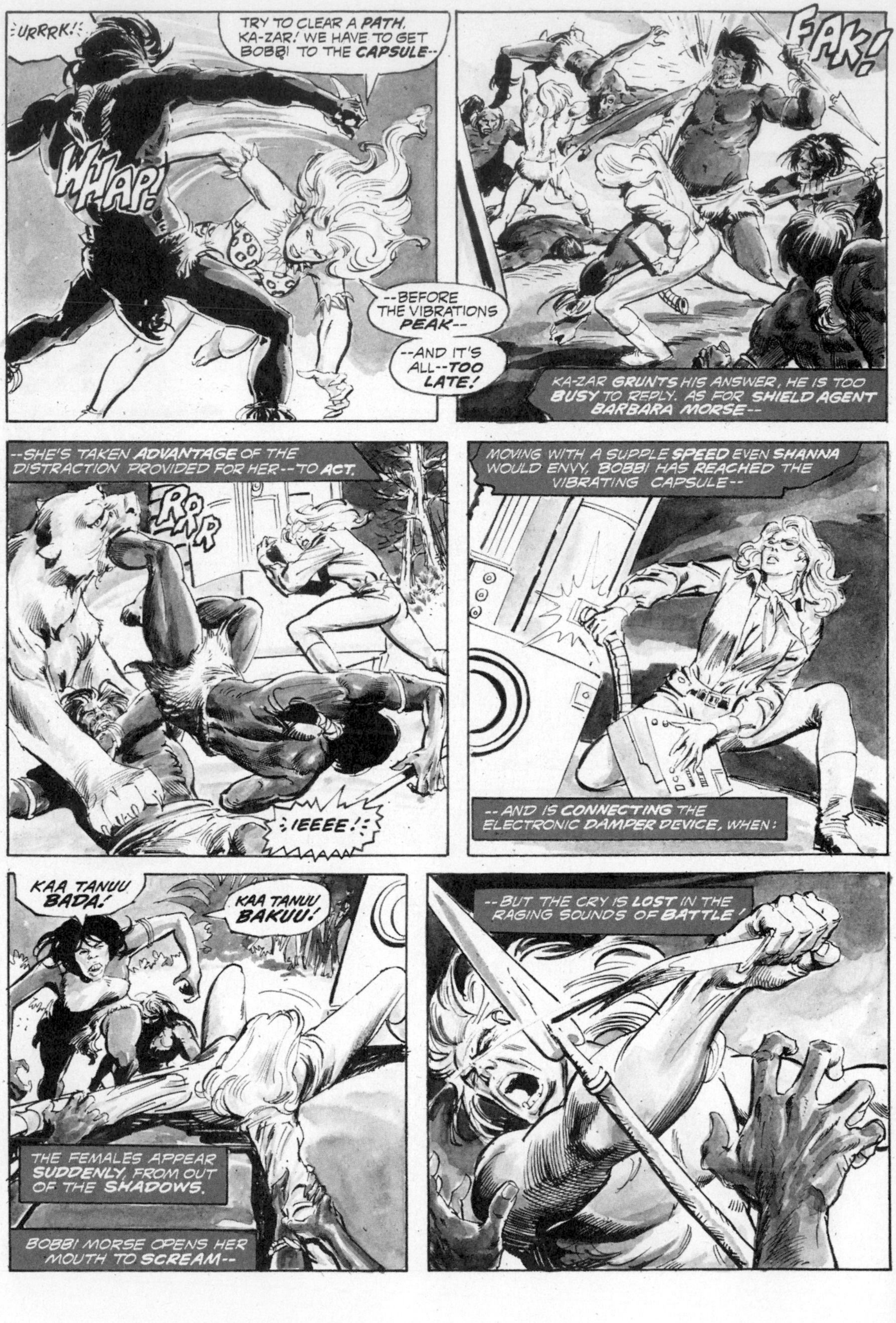
URRRK!
TRY TO CLEAR A PATH, KA-ZAR! WE HAVE TO GET BOBBI TO THE CAPSULE--
WHAP!
--BEFORE THE VIBRATIONS PEAK--
--AND IT'S ALL--TOO LATE!
FAK!
KA-ZAR GRUNTS HIS ANSWER, HE IS TOO BUSY TO REPLY. AS FOR SHIELD AGENT BARBARA MORSE--
--SHE'S TAKEN ADVANTAGE OF THE DISTRACTION PROVIDED FOR HER--TO ACT.
RRR
IEEEE!
MOVING WITH A SUPPLE SPEED EVEN SHANNA WOULD ENVY, BOBBI HAS REACHED THE VIBRATING CAPSULE--
--AND IS CONNECTING THE ELECTRONIC DAMPER DEVICE, WHEN:
KAA TANUU BADA!
KAA TANUU BAKUU!
THE FEMALES APPEAR SUDDENLY, FROM OUT OF THE SHADOWS.
BOBBI MORSE OPENS HER MOUTH TO SCREAM--
--BUT THE CRY IS LOST IN THE RAGING SOUNDS OF BATTLE!

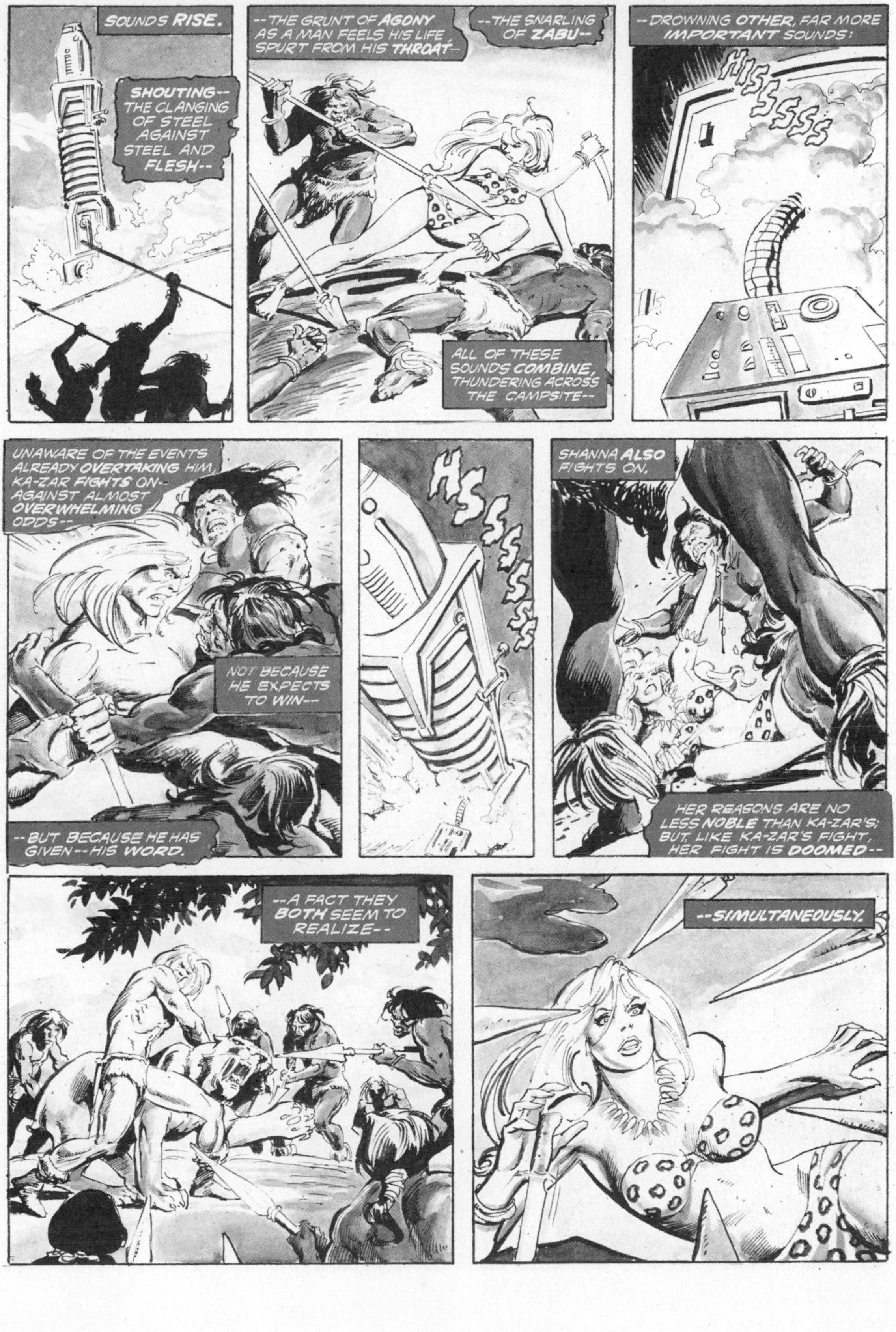
SOUNDS RISE.
SHOUTING-- THE CLANGING OF STEEL AGAINST STEEL AND FLESH--
--THE GRUNT OF AGONY AS A MAN FEELS HIS LIFE SPURT FROM HIS THROAT--
--THE SNARLING OF ZABU--
ALL OF THESE SOUNDS COMBINE, THUNDERING ACROSS THE CAMPSITE--
--DROWNING OTHER, FAR MORE IMPORTANT SOUNDS:
HISSSSSS
UNAWARE OF THE EVENTS ALREADY OVERTAKING HIM, KA-ZAR FIGHTS ON-- AGAINST ALMOST OVERWHELMING ODDS--
NOT BECAUSE HE EXPECTS TO WIN--
--BUT BECAUSE HE HAS GIVEN--HIS WORD.
HSSSSSS
SHANNA ALSO FIGHTS ON.
HER REASONS ARE NO LESS NOBLE THAN KA-ZAR'S; BUT, LIKE KA-ZAR'S FIGHT, HER FIGHT IS DOOMED--
--A FACT THEY BOTH SEEM TO REALIZE--
--SIMULTANEOUSLY.

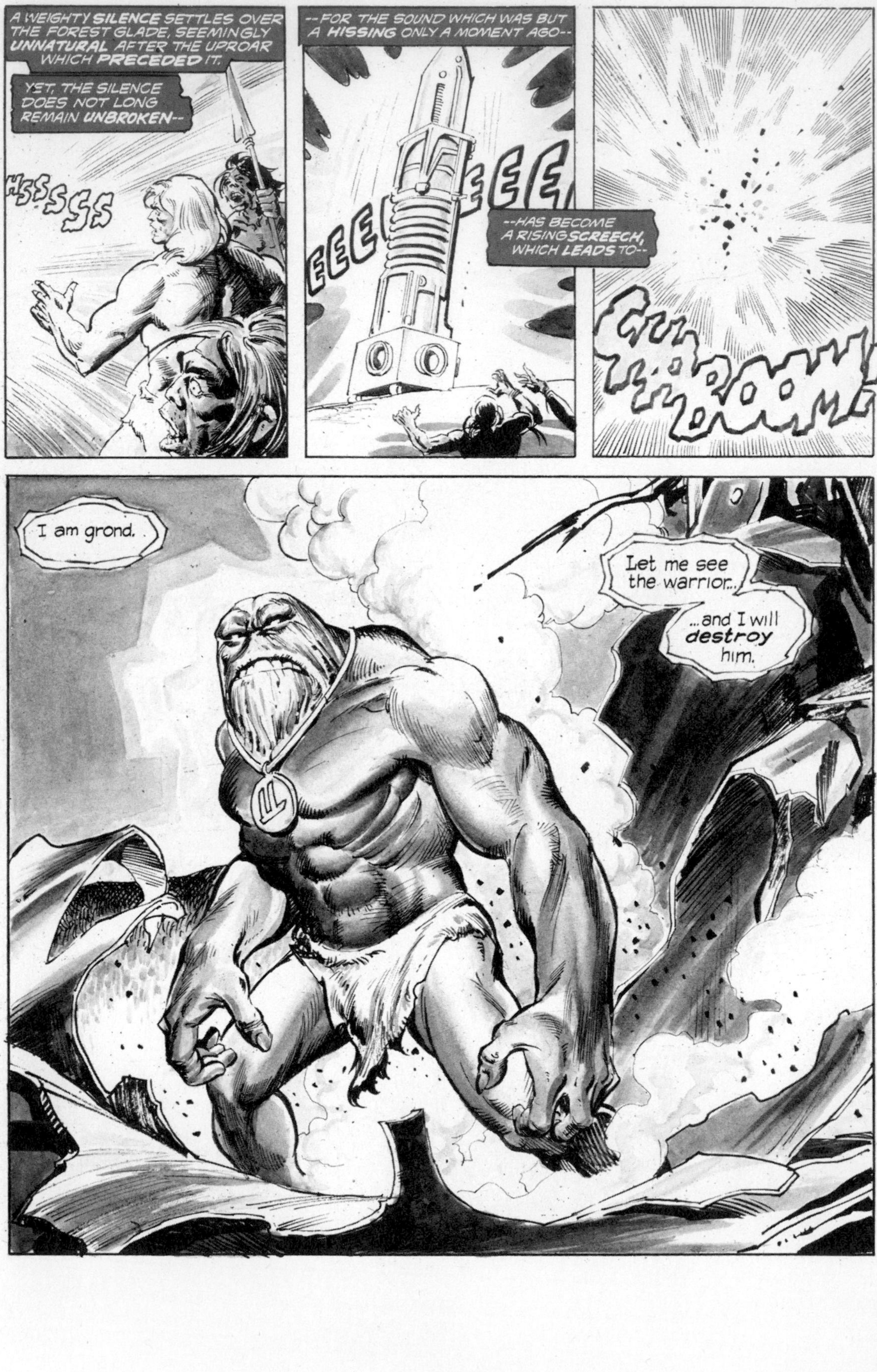
A WEIGHTY SILENCE SETTLES OVER THE FOREST GLADE, SEEMINGLY UNNATURAL AFTER THE UPROAR WHICH PRECEDED IT.
YET, THE SILENCE DOES NOT LONG REMAIN UNBROKEN--
HSSSSSS
--FOR THE SOUND WHICH WAS BUT A HISSING ONLY A MOMENT AGO--
EEEEEEE
--HAS BECOME A RISING SCREECH, WHICH LEADS TO--
CHUDOOOM!
I am grond.
Let me see the warrior...
...and I will destroy him.

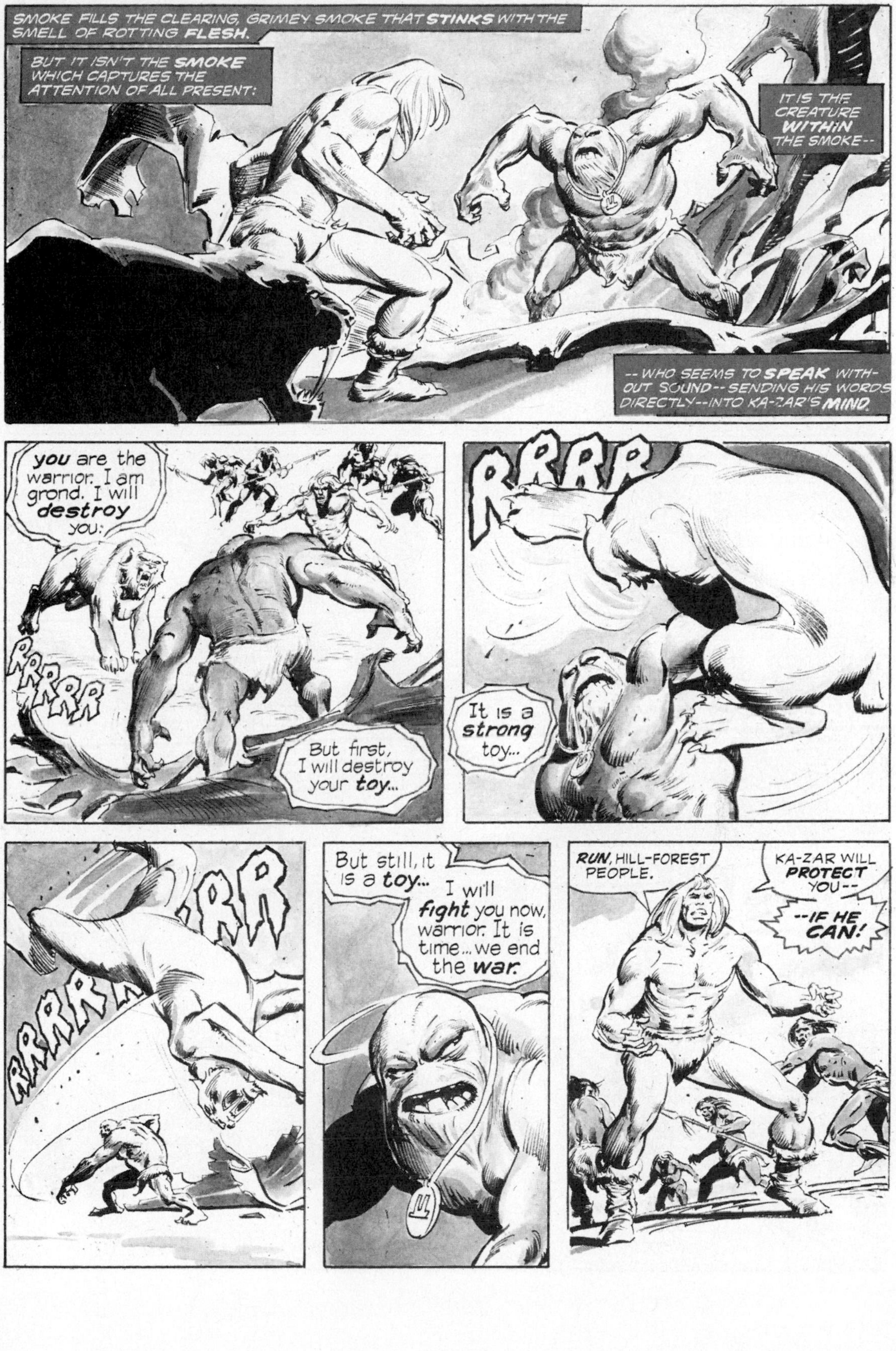
SMOKE FILLS THE CLEARING, GRIMEY SMOKE THAT STINKS WITH THE SMELL OF ROTTING FLESH.
BUT IT ISN'T THE SMOKE WHICH CAPTURES THE ATTENTION OF ALL PRESENT:
IT IS THE CREATURE WITHIN THE SMOKE--
-- WHO SEEMS TO SPEAK WITH-OUT SOUND-- SENDING HIS WORDS DIRECTLY--INTO KA-ZAR'S MIND.
you are the warrior. I am grond. I will destroy you.
RRRRR
But first, I will destroy your toy...
RRRR
It is a strong toy...
RRRRRR
But still, it is a toy...
I will fight you now, warrior. It is time... we end the war.
RUN, HILL-FOREST PEOPLE.
KA-ZAR WILL PROTECT YOU--
--IF HE CAN!

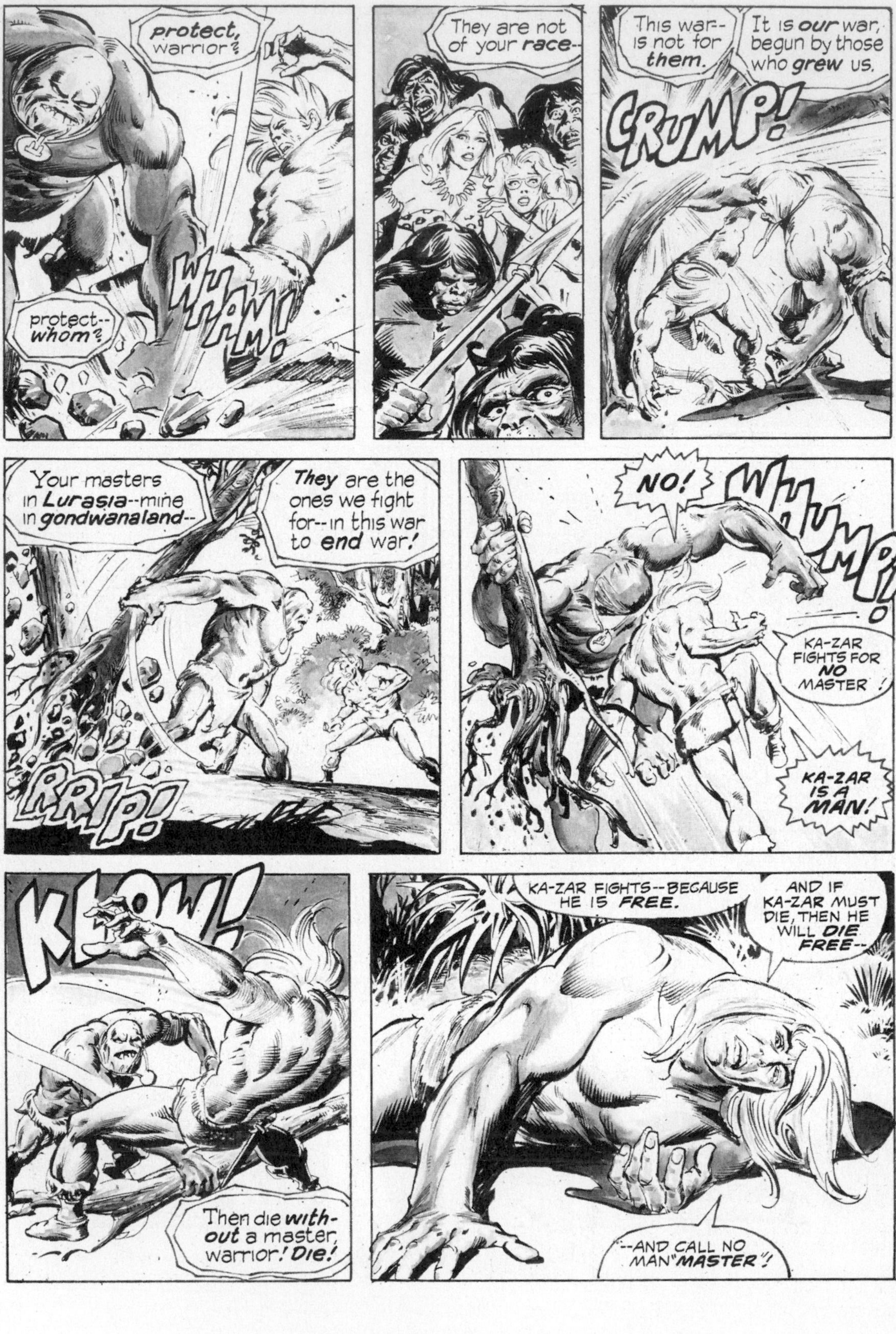
protect, warrior?
WHAM!
protect-- whom?
They are not of your race--
This war-- is not for them.
It is our war, begun by those who grew us.
CRUMP!
Your masters in Lurasia--mine in gondwanaland--
They are the ones we fight for--in this war to end war!
RRIP!
NO!
WHUMP!
KA-ZAR FIGHTS FOR NO MASTER!
KA-ZAR IS A MAN!
KLOW!
Then die without a master, warrior! Die!
KA-ZAR FIGHTS--BECAUSE HE IS FREE.
AND IF KA-ZAR MUST DIE, THEN HE WILL DIE FREE--
--AND CALL NO MAN "MASTER"!

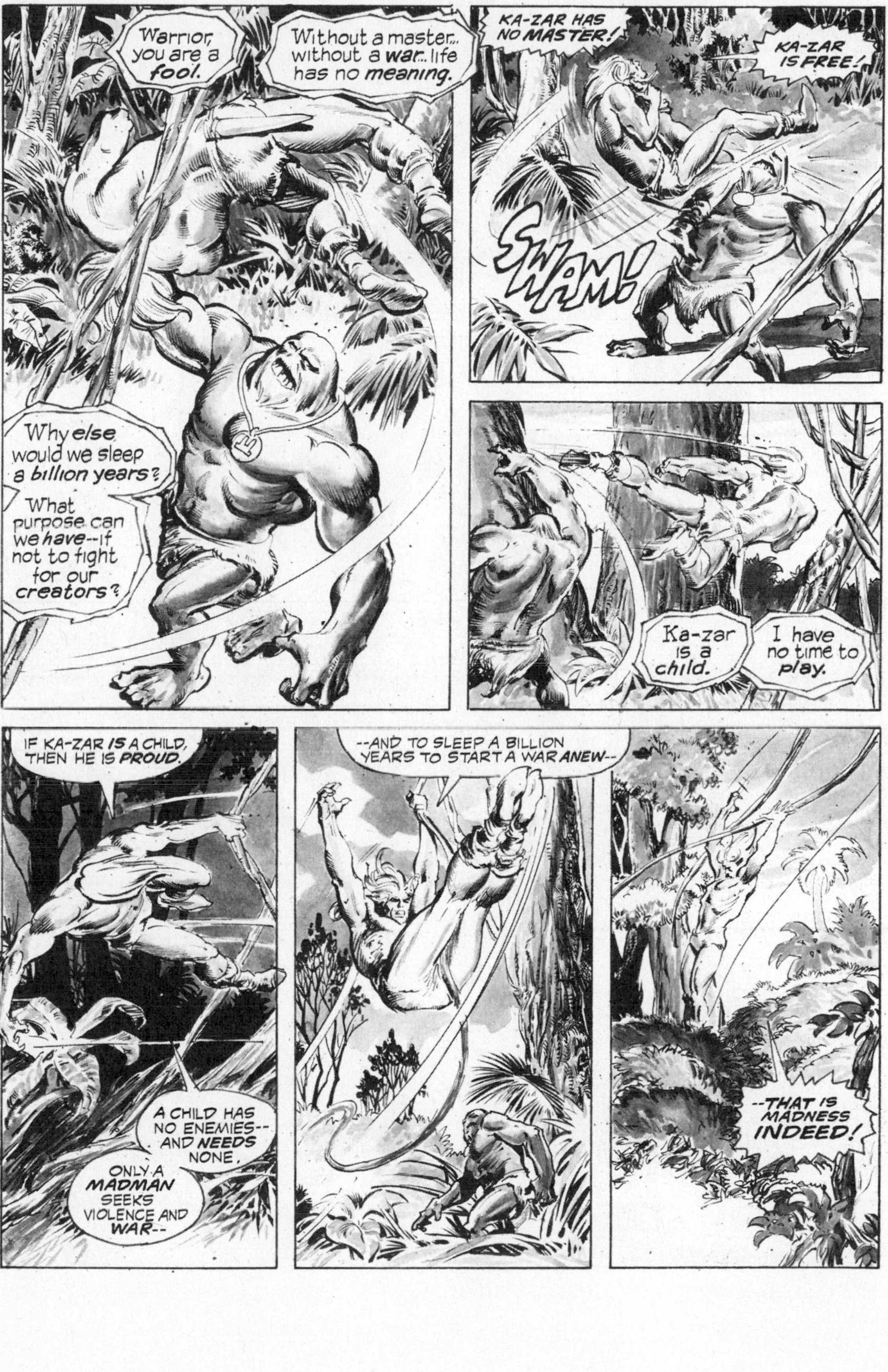
Warrior, you are a fool.
Without a master... without a war... life has no meaning.
KA-ZAR HAS NO MASTER!
KA-ZAR IS FREE!
SWAM!
Why else would we sleep a billion years?
What purpose can we have--if not to fight for our creators?
Ka-zar is a child.
I have no time to play.
IF KA-ZAR IS A CHILD, THEN HE IS PROUD.
A CHILD HAS NO ENEMIES-- AND NEEDS NONE.
ONLY A MADMAN SEEKS VIOLENCE AND WAR--
--AND TO SLEEP A BILLION YEARS TO START A WAR ANEW--
--THAT IS MADNESS INDEED!

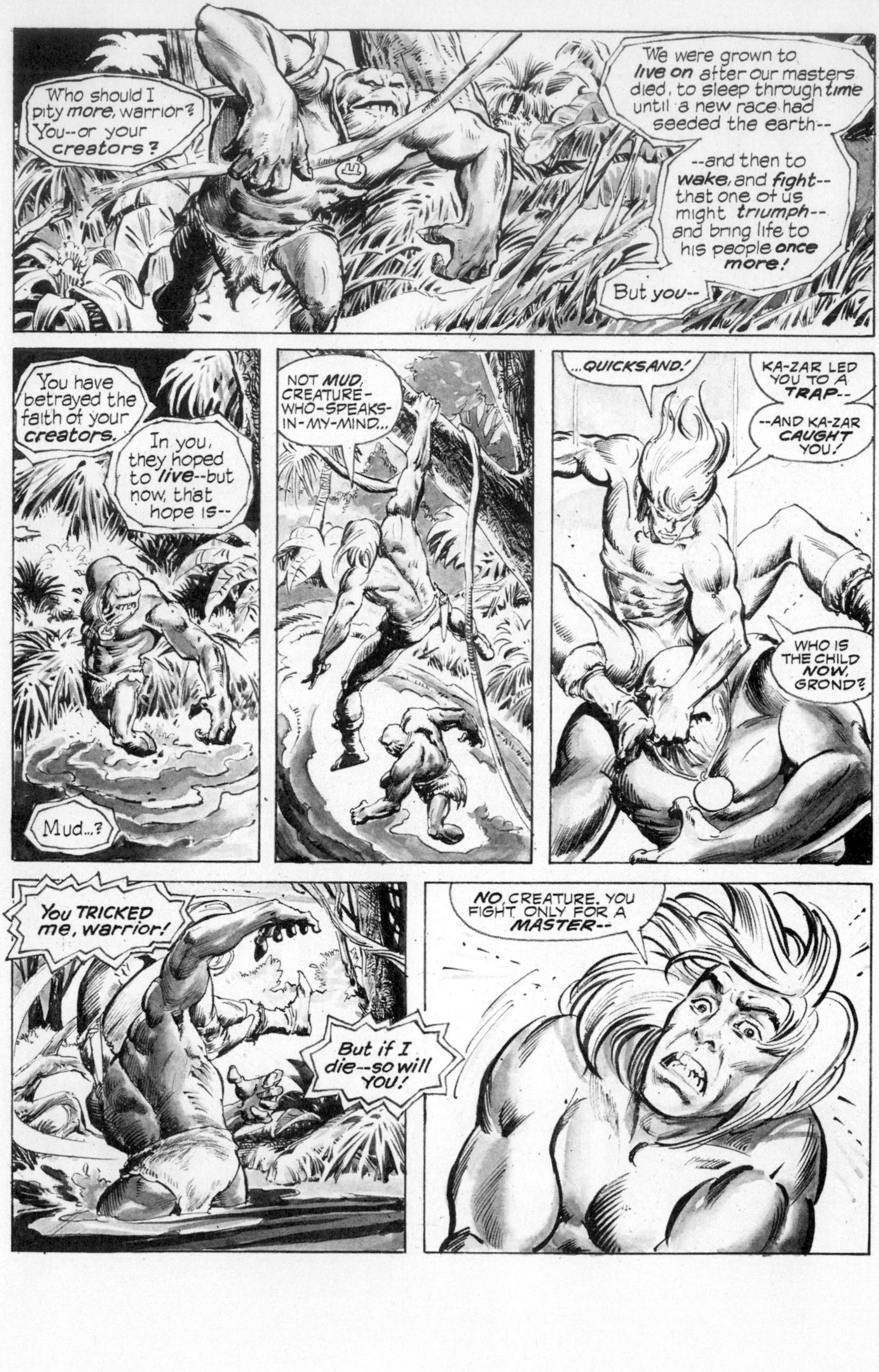
Who should I pity more, warrior? You--or your creators?
We were grown to live on after our masters died, to sleep through time until a new race had seeded the earth--
--and then to wake, and fight--that one of us might triumph--and bring life to his people once more!
But you--
You have betrayed the faith of your creators.
In you, they hoped to live--but now, that hope is--
Mud...?
NOT MUD, CREATURE-WHO-SPEAKS-IN-MY-MIND...
...QUICKSAND!
KA-ZAR LED YOU TO A TRAP--
--AND KA-ZAR CAUGHT YOU!
WHO IS THE CHILD NOW, GROND?
You TRICKED me, warrior!
But if I die--so will YOU!
NO, CREATURE. YOU FIGHT ONLY FOR A MASTER--

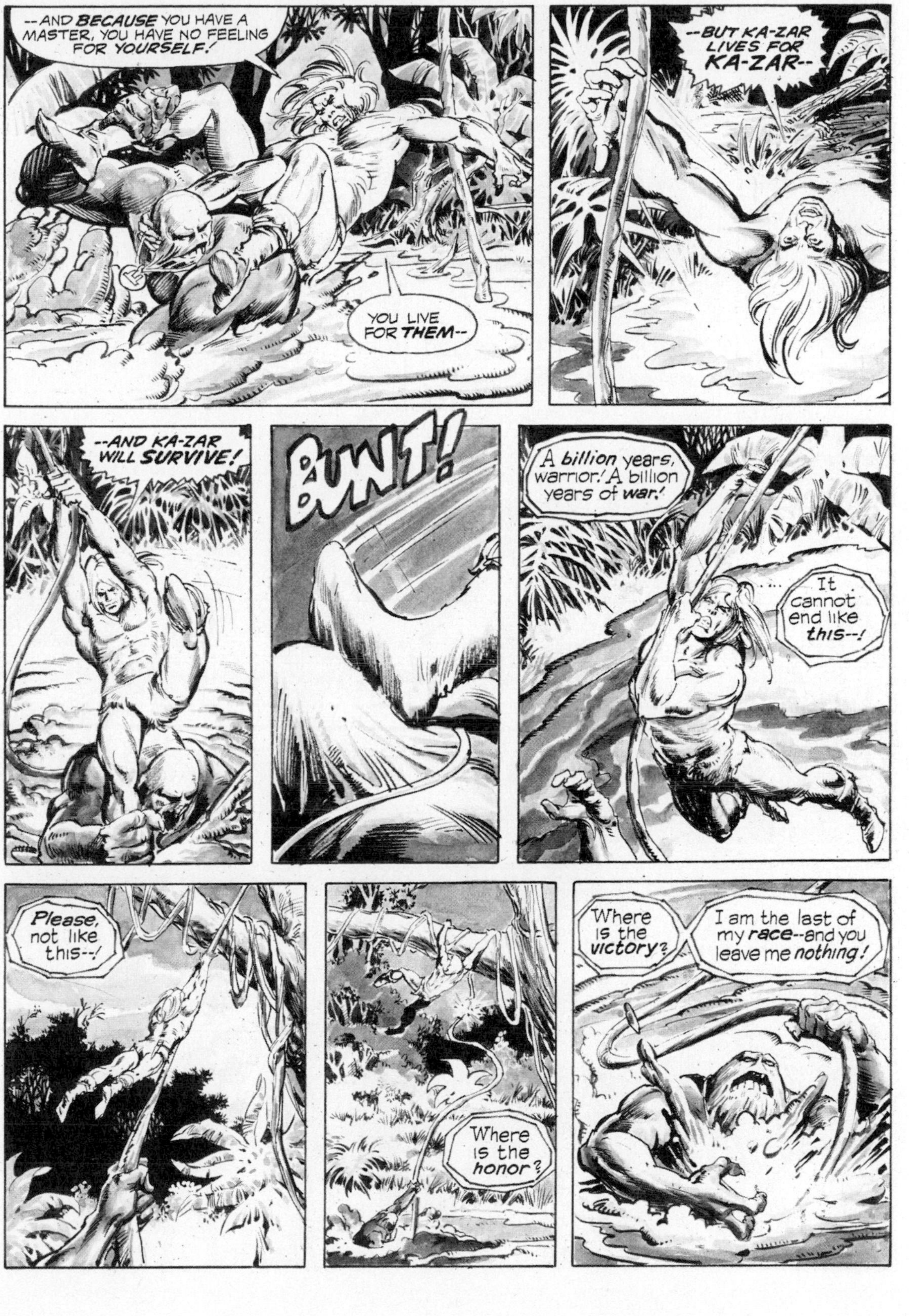
--AND BECAUSE YOU HAVE A MASTER, YOU HAVE NO FEELING FOR YOURSELF!
YOU LIVE FOR THEM--
--BUT KA-ZAR LIVES FOR KA-ZAR--
--AND KA-ZAR WILL SURVIVE!
BUNT!
A billion years, warrior! A billion years of war!
...It cannot end like this--!
Please, not like this--!
Where is the honor?
Where is the victory?
I am the last of my race--and you leave me nothing!

Not even honest *defeat...*

Only...

destruction...

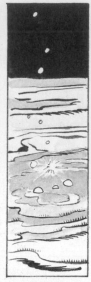

HIS FACE IS COLD AND WITHOUT *EXPRESSION,* THOUGH PERHAPS HIS EYES *NARROW* SLIGHTLY WHEN HE RETURNS TO THE NATIVE CAMP-SITE--

--TO FIND THE HILL-FOREST PEOPLE WORSHIPPING A *NEW* GOD, AS THEY WORSHIPPED THE *OLD.*

YOU REALIZE WHAT'S *HAPPENED* HERE, DON'T YOU, KA-ZAR?

A WAR--BETWEEN *OUR* AGE AND THE *PAST.*

I DON'T THINK KA-ZAR WANTS TO *TALK* ABOUT IT, BOBBI.

IN FACT--

--I'VE A FEELING WE'VE USED UP OUR *WELCOME.*

IT'S TIME WE *ALL* WENT *HOME.*

EPILOGUE:

A FEW DAYS *LATER,* SEVERAL MILES OFF THE ICY COAST OF *ANTARCTICA...*

THAT'S THE OTHER *CAPSULE,* ALL RIGHT.

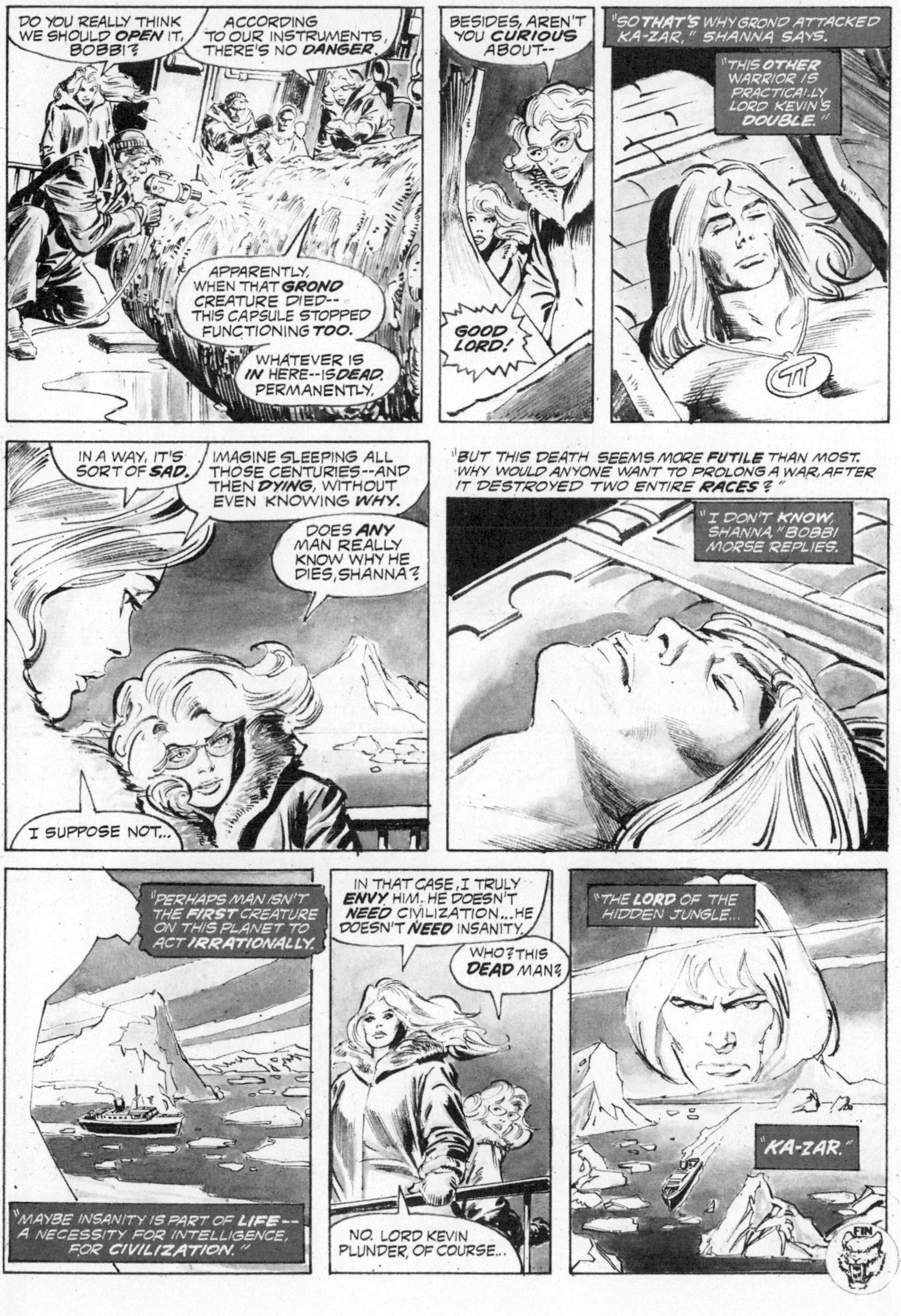
DO YOU REALLY THINK WE SHOULD OPEN IT, BOBBI?
ACCORDING TO OUR INSTRUMENTS, THERE'S NO DANGER.
APPARENTLY, WHEN THAT GROND CREATURE DIED-- THIS CAPSULE STOPPED FUNCTIONING TOO.
WHATEVER IS IN HERE--IS DEAD. PERMANENTLY.
BESIDES, AREN'T YOU CURIOUS ABOUT--
GOOD LORD!
"SO THAT'S WHY GROND ATTACKED KA-ZAR," SHANNA SAYS.
"THIS OTHER WARRIOR IS PRACTICALLY LORD KEVIN'S DOUBLE."
IN A WAY, IT'S SORT OF SAD.
IMAGINE SLEEPING ALL THOSE CENTURIES--AND THEN DYING, WITHOUT EVEN KNOWING WHY.
DOES ANY MAN REALLY KNOW WHY HE DIES, SHANNA?
I SUPPOSE NOT...
"BUT THIS DEATH SEEMS MORE FUTILE THAN MOST. WHY WOULD ANYONE WANT TO PROLONG A WAR, AFTER IT DESTROYED TWO ENTIRE RACES?"
"I DON'T KNOW, SHANNA," BOBBI MORSE REPLIES.
"PERHAPS MAN ISN'T THE FIRST CREATURE ON THIS PLANET TO ACT IRRATIONALLY.
"MAYBE INSANITY IS PART OF LIFE-- A NECESSITY FOR INTELLIGENCE, FOR CIVILIZATION."
IN THAT CASE, I TRULY ENVY HIM. HE DOESN'T NEED CIVILIZATION... HE DOESN'T NEED INSANITY.
WHO? THIS DEAD MAN?
NO. LORD KEVIN PLUNDER, OF COURSE...
"THE LORD OF THE HIDDEN JUNGLE...
"KA-ZAR."
FIN

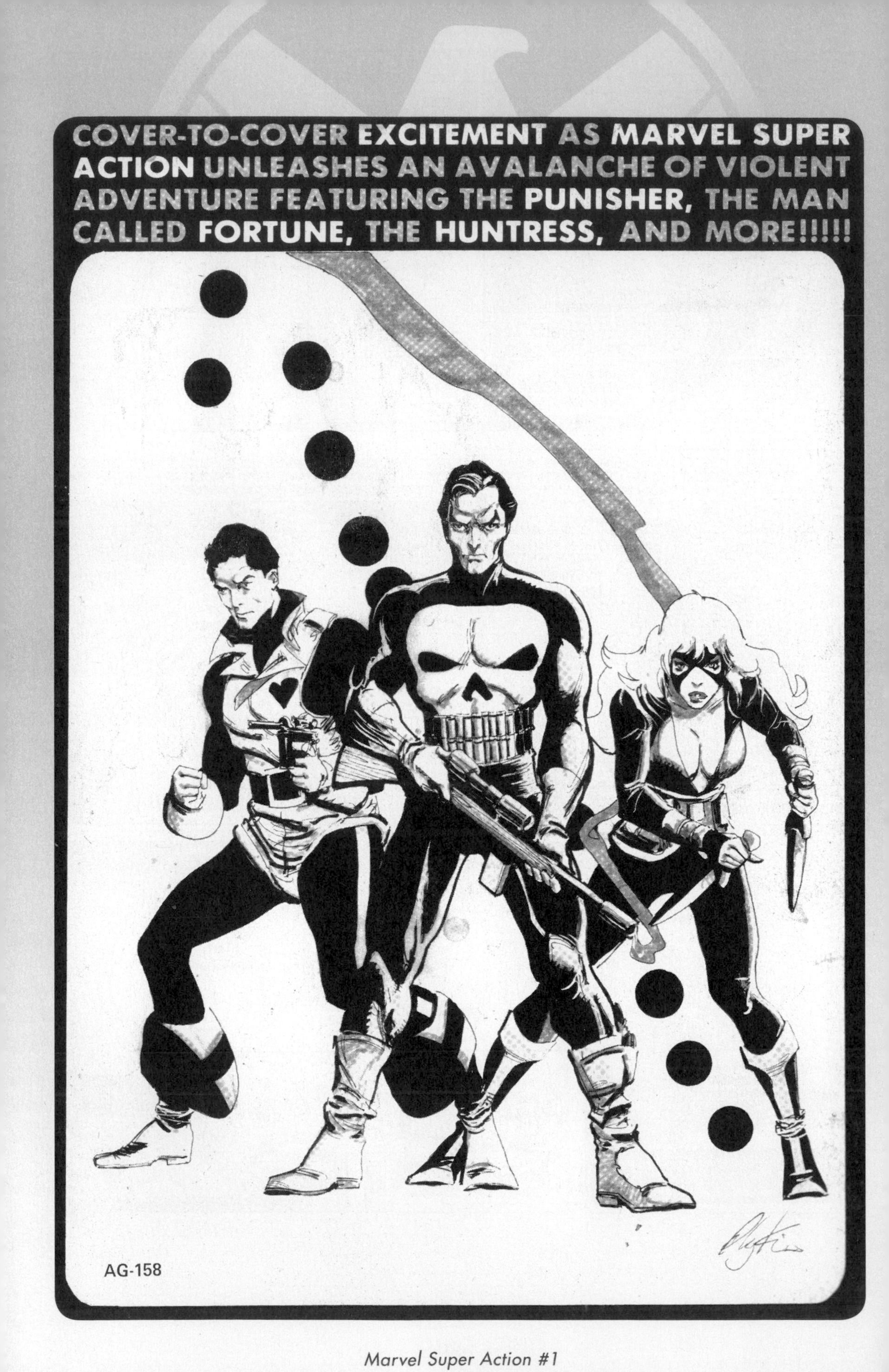
COVER-TO-COVER EXCITEMENT AS MARVEL SUPER ACTION UNLEASHES AN AVALANCHE OF VIOLENT ADVENTURE FEATURING THE PUNISHER, THE MAN CALLED FORTUNE, THE HUNTRESS, AND MORE!!!!!
AG-158

Marvel Super Action #1

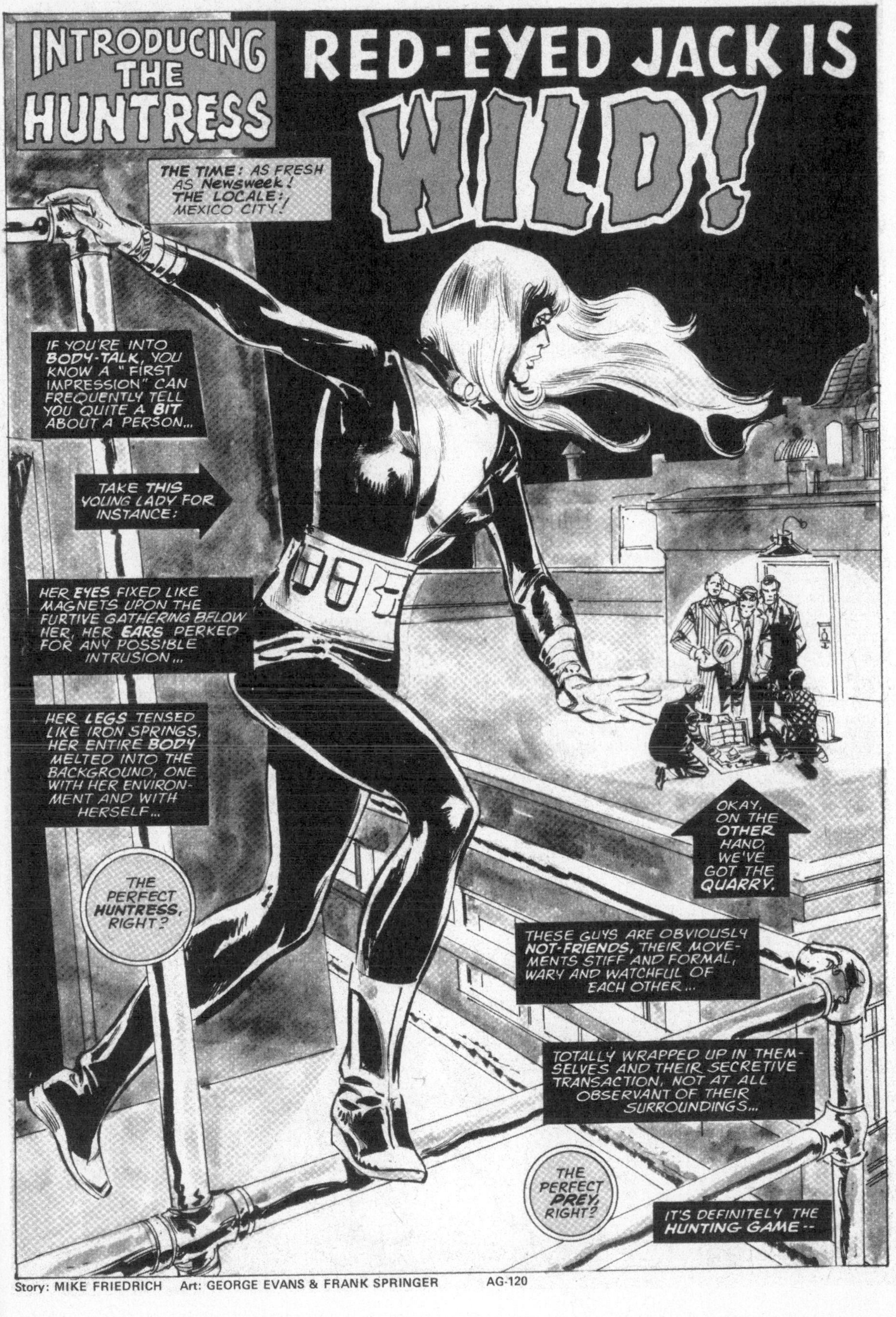

INTRODUCING THE HUNTRESS
RED-EYED JACK IS WILD!
THE TIME: AS FRESH AS Newsweek! THE LOCALE: MEXICO CITY!
IF YOU'RE INTO BODY-TALK, YOU KNOW A "FIRST IMPRESSION" CAN FREQUENTLY TELL YOU QUITE A BIT ABOUT A PERSON...
TAKE THIS YOUNG LADY FOR INSTANCE:
HER EYES FIXED LIKE MAGNETS UPON THE FURTIVE GATHERING BELOW HER, HER EARS PERKED FOR ANY POSSIBLE INTRUSION...
HER LEGS TENSED LIKE IRON SPRINGS, HER ENTIRE BODY MELTED INTO THE BACKGROUND, ONE WITH HER ENVIRONMENT AND WITH HERSELF...
THE PERFECT HUNTRESS, RIGHT?
OKAY, ON THE OTHER HAND, WE'VE GOT THE QUARRY.
THESE GUYS ARE OBVIOUSLY NOT-FRIENDS, THEIR MOVEMENTS STIFF AND FORMAL, WARY AND WATCHFUL OF EACH OTHER...
TOTALLY WRAPPED UP IN THEMSELVES AND THEIR SECRETIVE TRANSACTION, NOT AT ALL OBSERVANT OF THEIR SURROUNDINGS...
THE PERFECT PREY, RIGHT?
IT'S DEFINITELY THE HUNTING GAME--

Story: MIKE FRIEDRICH Art: GEORGE EVANS & FRANK SPRINGER AG-120

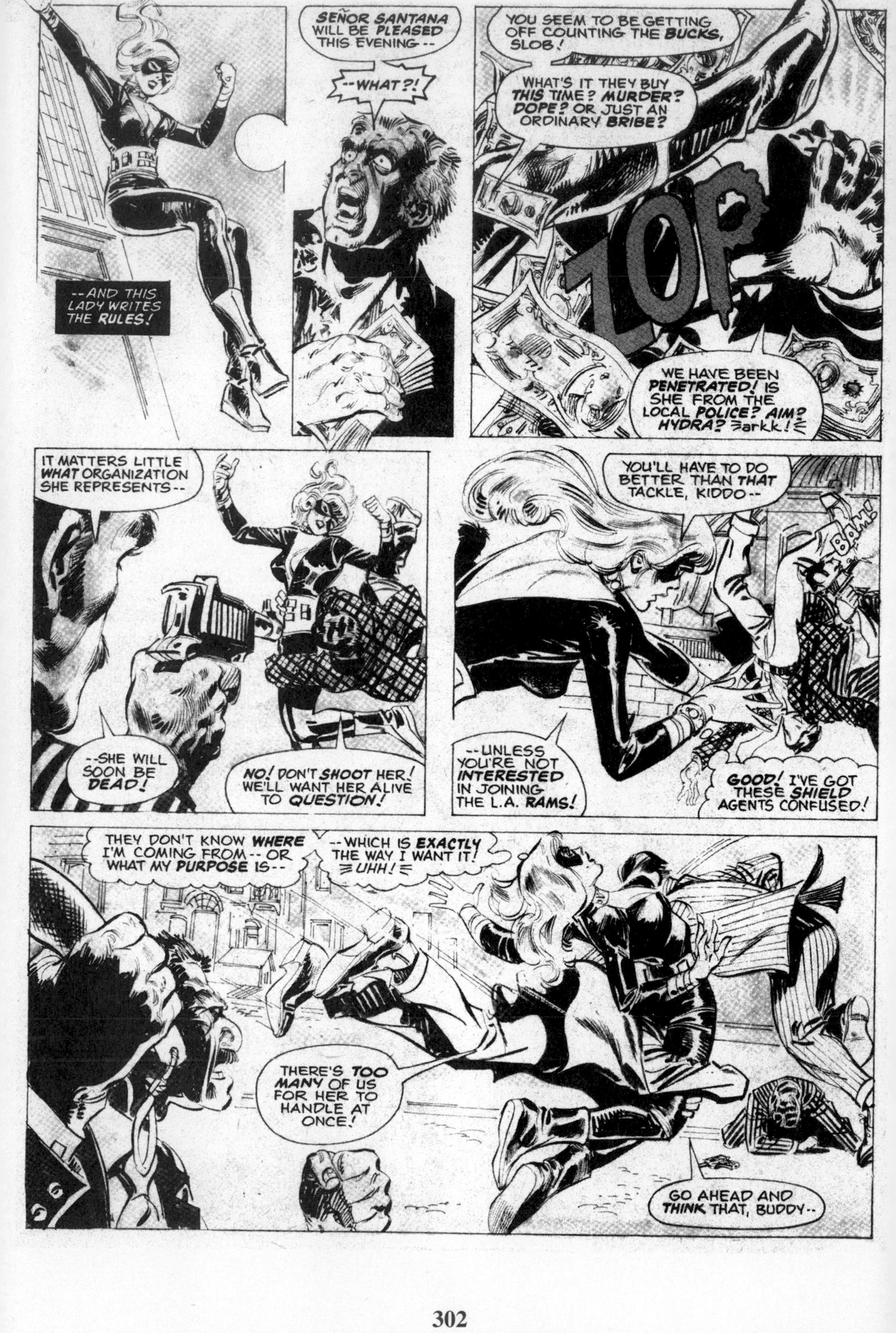

--AND THIS LADY WRITES THE RULES!
SEÑOR SANTANA WILL BE PLEASED THIS EVENING--
--WHAT?!
YOU SEEM TO BE GETTING OFF COUNTING THE BUCKS, SLOB!
WHAT'S IT THEY BUY THIS TIME? MURDER? DOPE? OR JUST AN ORDINARY BRIBE?
ZOP
WE HAVE BEEN PENETRATED! IS SHE FROM THE LOCAL POLICE? AIM? HYDRA? ≡arkk!≡
IT MATTERS LITTLE WHAT ORGANIZATION SHE REPRESENTS--
--SHE WILL SOON BE DEAD!
NO! DON'T SHOOT HER! WE'LL WANT HER ALIVE TO QUESTION!
YOU'LL HAVE TO DO BETTER THAN THAT TACKLE, KIDDO--
--UNLESS YOU'RE NOT INTERESTED IN JOINING THE L.A. RAMS!
GOOD! I'VE GOT THESE SHIELD AGENTS CONFUSED!
THEY DON'T KNOW WHERE I'M COMING FROM--OR WHAT MY PURPOSE IS--
--WHICH IS EXACTLY THE WAY I WANT IT! UHH!
THERE'S TOO MANY OF US FOR HER TO HANDLE AT ONCE!
GO AHEAD AND THINK THAT, BUDDY--

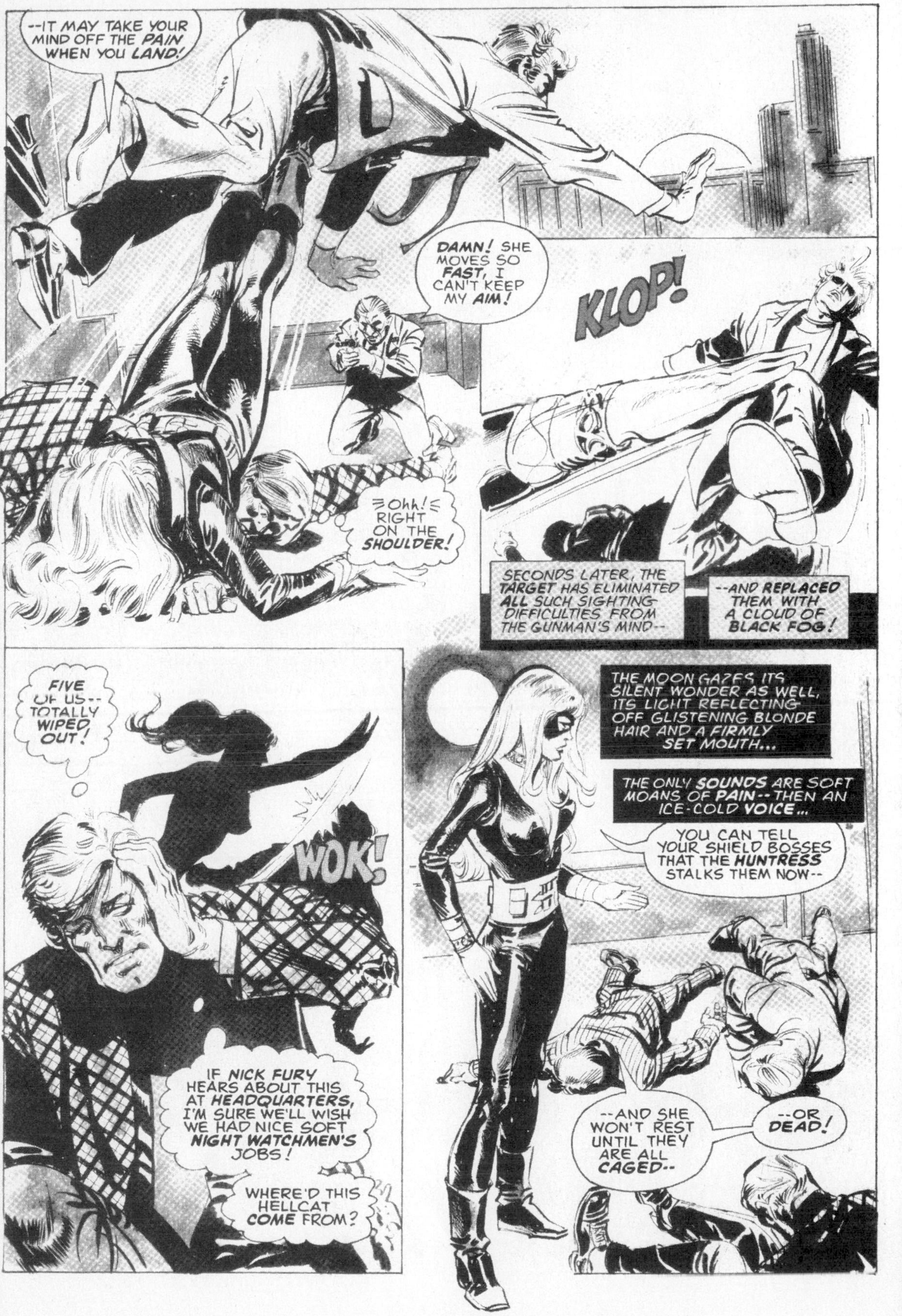
--IT MAY TAKE YOUR MIND OFF THE PAIN WHEN YOU LAND!
DAMN! SHE MOVES SO FAST, I CAN'T KEEP MY AIM!
OHH! RIGHT ON THE SHOULDER!
KLOP!
SECONDS LATER, THE TARGET HAS ELIMINATED ALL SUCH SIGHTING DIFFICULTIES FROM THE GUNMAN'S MIND--
--AND REPLACED THEM WITH A CLOUD OF BLACK FOG!
FIVE OF US-- TOTALLY WIPED OUT!
WOK!
IF NICK FURY HEARS ABOUT THIS AT HEADQUARTERS, I'M SURE WE'LL WISH WE HAD NICE SOFT NIGHT WATCHMEN'S JOBS!
WHERE'D THIS HELLCAT COME FROM?
THE MOON GAZES ITS SILENT WONDER AS WELL, ITS LIGHT REFLECTING OFF GLISTENING BLONDE HAIR AND A FIRMLY SET MOUTH...
THE ONLY SOUNDS ARE SOFT MOANS OF PAIN--THEN AN ICE-COLD VOICE...
YOU CAN TELL YOUR SHIELD BOSSES THAT THE HUNTRESS STALKS THEM NOW--
--AND SHE WON'T REST UNTIL THEY ARE ALL CAGED--
--OR DEAD!

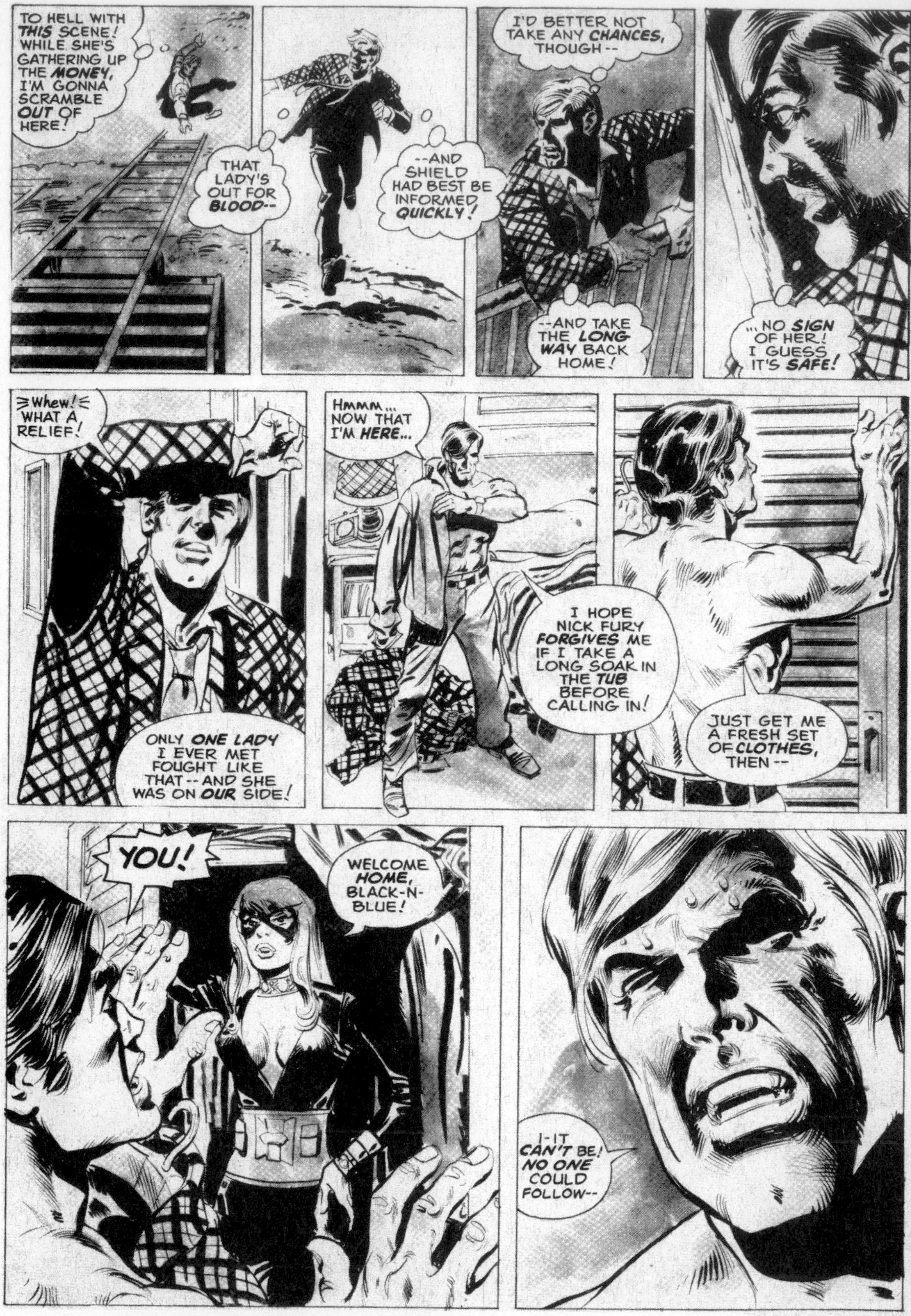
TO HELL WITH THIS SCENE! WHILE SHE'S GATHERING UP THE MONEY, I'M GONNA SCRAMBLE OUT OF HERE!
THAT LADY'S OUT FOR BLOOD--
--AND SHIELD HAD BEST BE INFORMED QUICKLY!
I'D BETTER NOT TAKE ANY CHANCES, THOUGH --
--AND TAKE THE LONG WAY BACK HOME!
...NO SIGN OF HER! I GUESS IT'S SAFE!
Whew! WHAT A RELIEF!
ONLY ONE LADY I EVER MET FOUGHT LIKE THAT--AND SHE WAS ON OUR SIDE!
Hmmm... NOW THAT I'M HERE...
I HOPE NICK FURY FORGIVES ME IF I TAKE A LONG SOAK IN THE TUB BEFORE CALLING IN!
JUST GET ME A FRESH SET OF CLOTHES, THEN --
YOU!
WELCOME HOME, BLACK-N-BLUE!
I-IT CAN'T BE! NO ONE COULD FOLLOW--

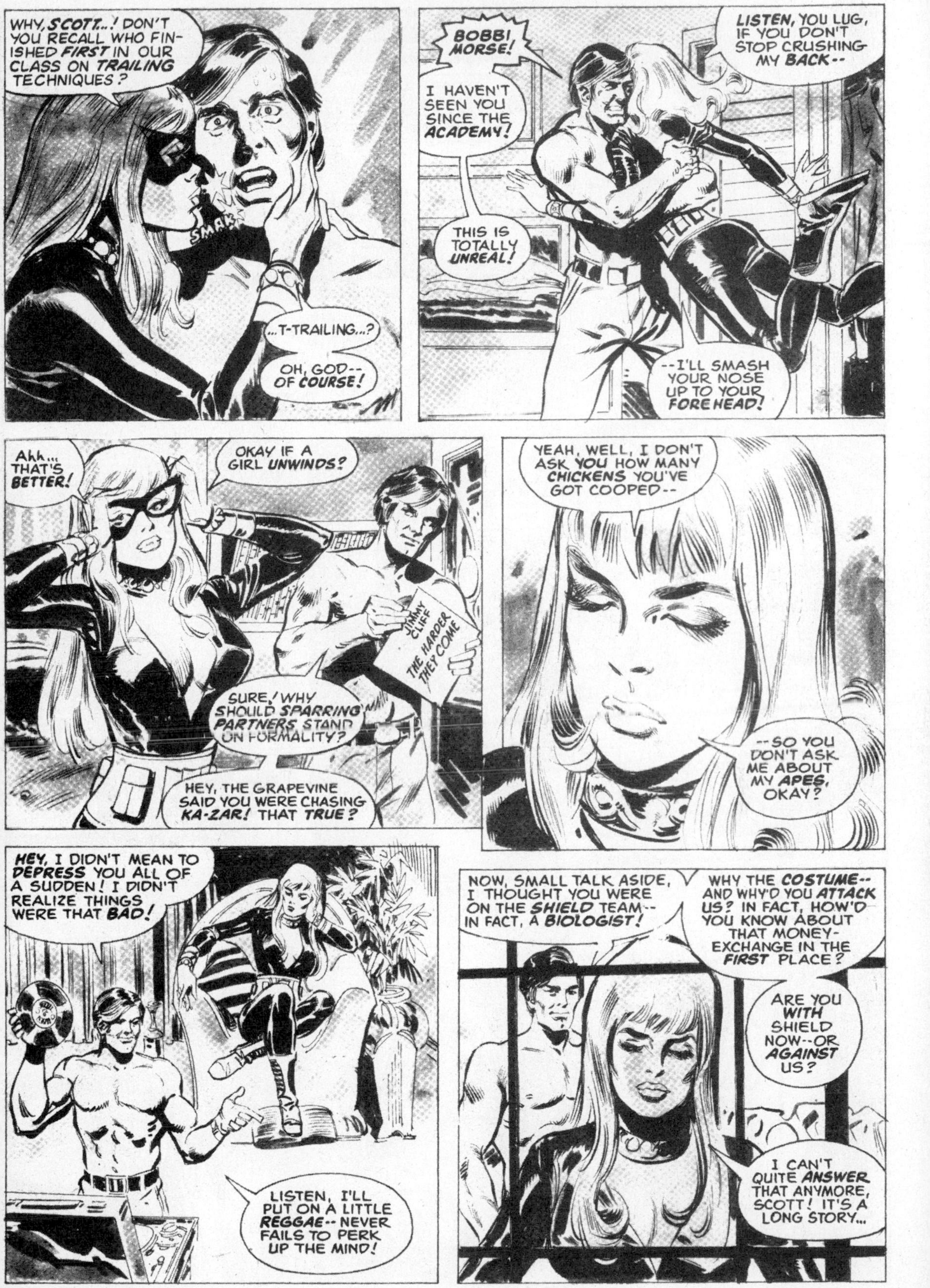
WHY, SCOTT...! DON'T YOU RECALL WHO FINISHED FIRST IN OUR CLASS ON TRAILING TECHNIQUES?
SMAK
...T-TRAILING...?
OH, GOD-- OF COURSE!
BOBBI MORSE!
I HAVEN'T SEEN YOU SINCE THE ACADEMY!
THIS IS TOTALLY UNREAL!
LISTEN, YOU LUG, IF YOU DON'T STOP CRUSHING MY BACK--
--I'LL SMASH YOUR NOSE UP TO YOUR FOREHEAD!
Ahh... THAT'S BETTER!
OKAY IF A GIRL UNWINDS?
JIMMY CLIFF
THE HARDER THEY COME
SURE! WHY SHOULD SPARRING PARTNERS STAND ON FORMALITY?
HEY, THE GRAPEVINE SAID YOU WERE CHASING KA-ZAR! THAT TRUE?
YEAH, WELL, I DON'T ASK YOU HOW MANY CHICKENS YOU'VE GOT COOPED--
--SO YOU DON'T ASK ME ABOUT MY APES, OKAY?
HEY, I DIDN'T MEAN TO DEPRESS YOU ALL OF A SUDDEN! I DIDN'T REALIZE THINGS WERE THAT BAD!
LISTEN, I'LL PUT ON A LITTLE REGGAE--NEVER FAILS TO PERK UP THE MIND!
NOW, SMALL TALK ASIDE, I THOUGHT YOU WERE ON THE SHIELD TEAM--IN FACT, A BIOLOGIST!
WHY THE COSTUME--AND WHY'D YOU ATTACK US? IN FACT, HOW'D YOU KNOW ABOUT THAT MONEY-EXCHANGE IN THE FIRST PLACE?
ARE YOU WITH SHIELD NOW--OR AGAINST US?
I CAN'T QUITE ANSWER THAT ANYMORE, SCOTT! IT'S A LONG STORY...

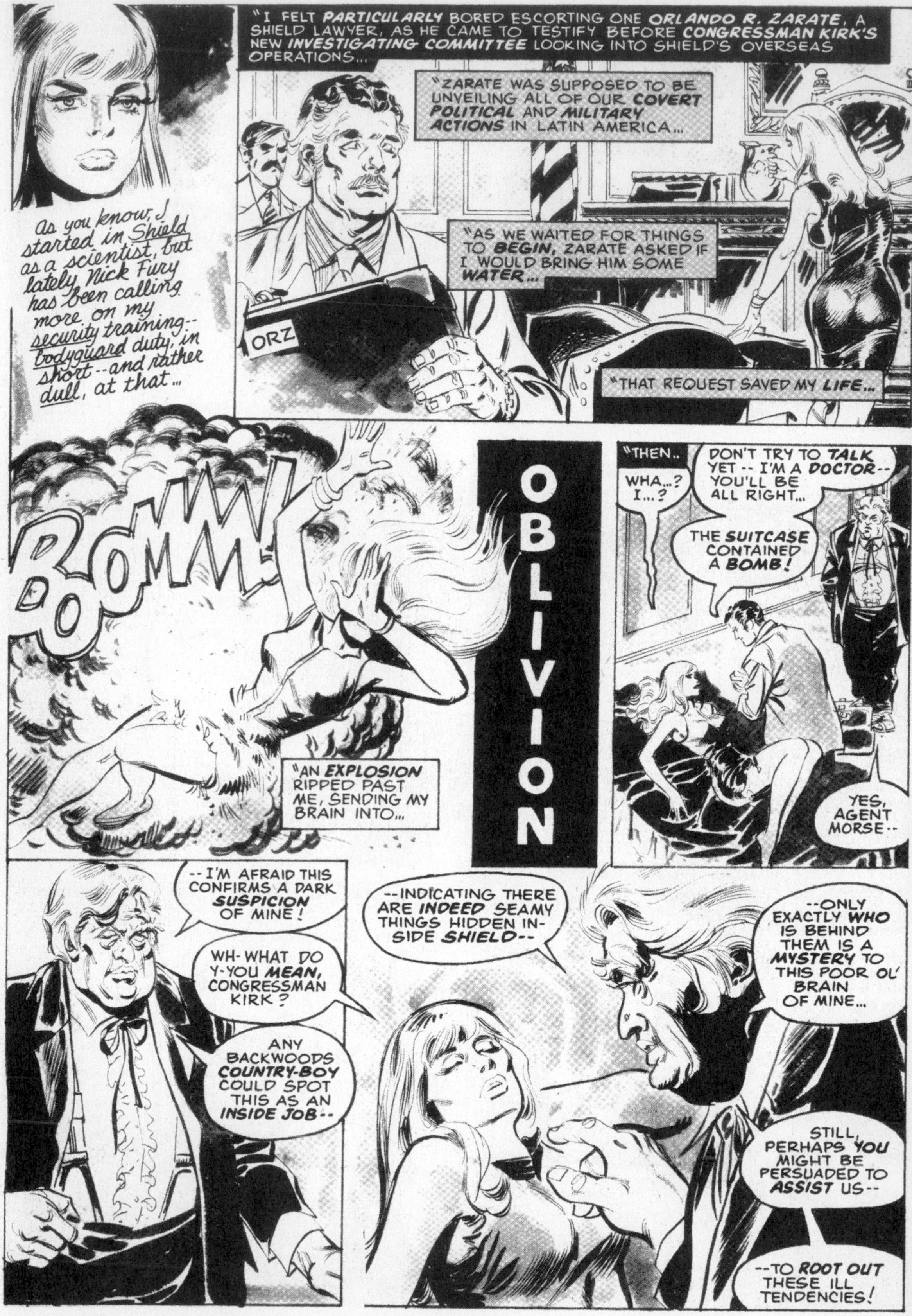
"I FELT PARTICULARLY BORED ESCORTING ONE ORLANDO R. ZARATE, A SHIELD LAWYER, AS HE CAME TO TESTIFY BEFORE CONGRESSMAN KIRK'S NEW INVESTIGATING COMMITTEE LOOKING INTO SHIELD'S OVERSEAS OPERATIONS...
As you know, I started in Shield as a scientist, but lately Nick Fury has been calling more on my security training-- bodyguard duty, in short--and rather dull, at that...
"ZARATE WAS SUPPOSED TO BE UNVEILING ALL OF OUR COVERT POLITICAL AND MILITARY ACTIONS IN LATIN AMERICA...
"AS WE WAITED FOR THINGS TO BEGIN, ZARATE ASKED IF I WOULD BRING HIM SOME WATER...
ORZ
"THAT REQUEST SAVED MY LIFE...
BOOMM!
"AN EXPLOSION RIPPED PAST ME, SENDING MY BRAIN INTO...
OBLIVION
"THEN..
WHA...? I...?
DON'T TRY TO TALK YET -- I'M A DOCTOR-- YOU'LL BE ALL RIGHT...
THE SUITCASE CONTAINED A BOMB!
YES, AGENT MORSE--
--I'M AFRAID THIS CONFIRMS A DARK SUSPICION OF MINE!
WH-WHAT DO Y-YOU MEAN, CONGRESSMAN KIRK?
ANY BACKWOODS COUNTRY-BOY COULD SPOT THIS AS AN INSIDE JOB--
--INDICATING THERE ARE INDEED SEAMY THINGS HIDDEN INSIDE SHIELD--
--ONLY EXACTLY WHO IS BEHIND THEM IS A MYSTERY TO THIS POOR OL' BRAIN OF MINE...
STILL, PERHAPS YOU MIGHT BE PERSUADED TO ASSIST US--
--TO ROOT OUT THESE ILL TENDENCIES!

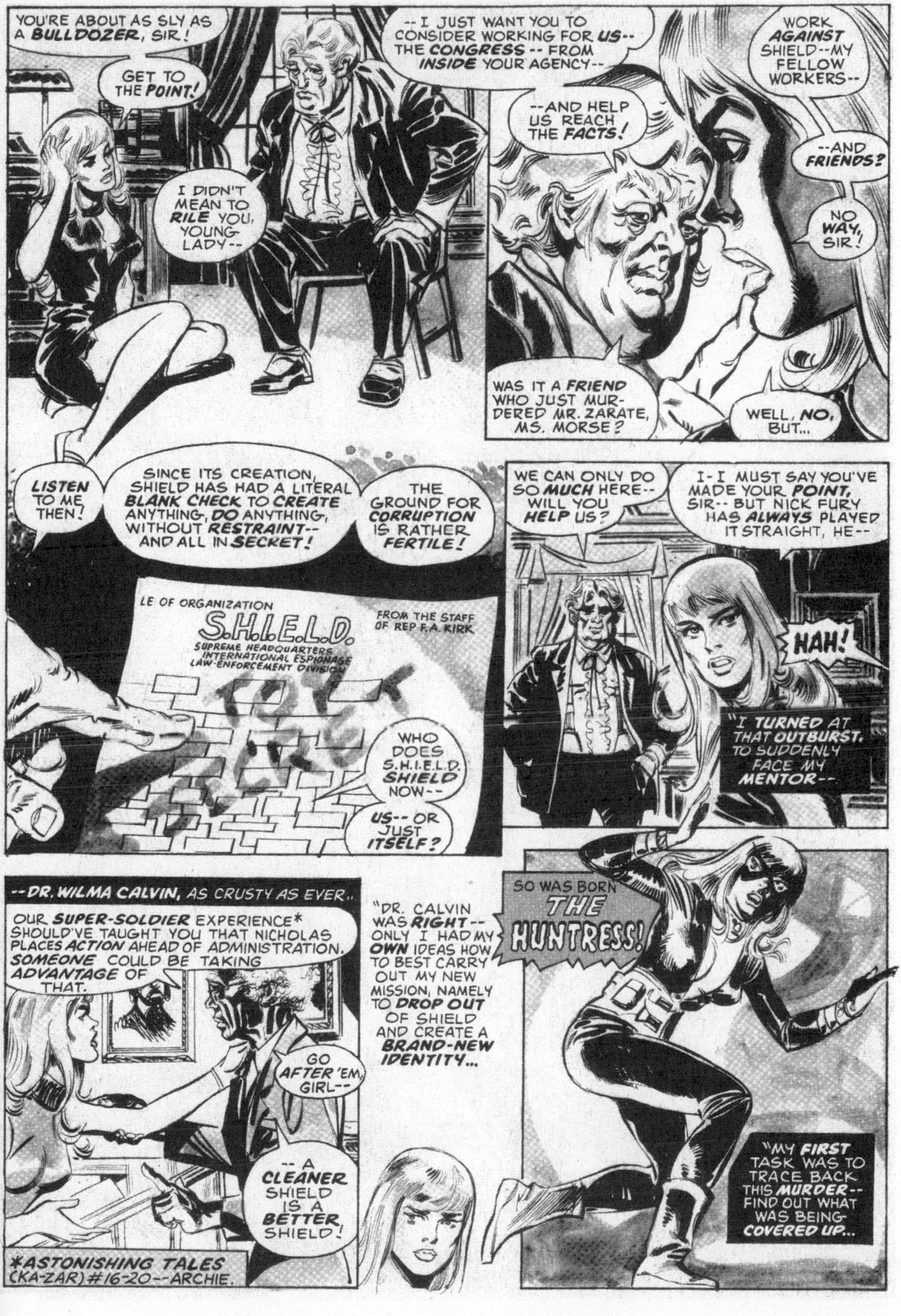
YOU'RE ABOUT AS SLY AS A BULLDOZER, SIR!
GET TO THE POINT!
I DIDN'T MEAN TO RILE YOU, YOUNG LADY--
--I JUST WANT YOU TO CONSIDER WORKING FOR US-- THE CONGRESS -- FROM INSIDE YOUR AGENCY--
--AND HELP US REACH THE FACTS!
WORK AGAINST SHIELD--MY FELLOW WORKERS--
--AND FRIENDS?
NO WAY, SIR!
WAS IT A FRIEND WHO JUST MURDERED MR. ZARATE, MS. MORSE?
WELL, NO, BUT...
LISTEN TO ME THEN!
SINCE ITS CREATION, SHIELD HAS HAD A LITERAL BLANK CHECK TO CREATE ANYTHING, DO ANYTHING, WITHOUT RESTRAINT-- AND ALL IN SECRET!
THE GROUND FOR CORRUPTION IS RATHER FERTILE!
LE OF ORGANIZATION
S.H.I.E.L.D.
SUPREME HEADQUARTERS INTERNATIONAL ESPIONAGE LAW-ENFORCEMENT DIVISION
FROM THE STAFF OF REP F.A. KIRK
WHO DOES S.H.I.E.L.D. SHIELD NOW--
US-- OR JUST ITSELF?
WE CAN ONLY DO SO MUCH HERE-- WILL YOU HELP US?
I-I MUST SAY YOU'VE MADE YOUR POINT, SIR-- BUT NICK FURY HAS ALWAYS PLAYED IT STRAIGHT, HE--
HAH!
"I TURNED AT THAT OUTBURST, TO SUDDENLY FACE MY MENTOR--
--DR. WILMA CALVIN, AS CRUSTY AS EVER..
OUR SUPER-SOLDIER EXPERIENCE* SHOULD'VE TAUGHT YOU THAT NICHOLAS PLACES ACTION AHEAD OF ADMINISTRATION. SOMEONE COULD BE TAKING ADVANTAGE OF THAT.
GO AFTER 'EM, GIRL--
-- A CLEANER SHIELD IS A BETTER SHIELD!
*ASTONISHING TALES (KA-ZAR) #16-20--ARCHIE.
"DR. CALVIN WAS RIGHT-- ONLY I HAD MY OWN IDEAS HOW TO BEST CARRY OUT MY NEW MISSION, NAMELY TO DROP OUT OF SHIELD AND CREATE A BRAND-NEW IDENTITY...
SO WAS BORN THE HUNTRESS!
"MY FIRST TASK WAS TO TRACE BACK THIS MURDER-- FIND OUT WHAT WAS BEING COVERED UP...

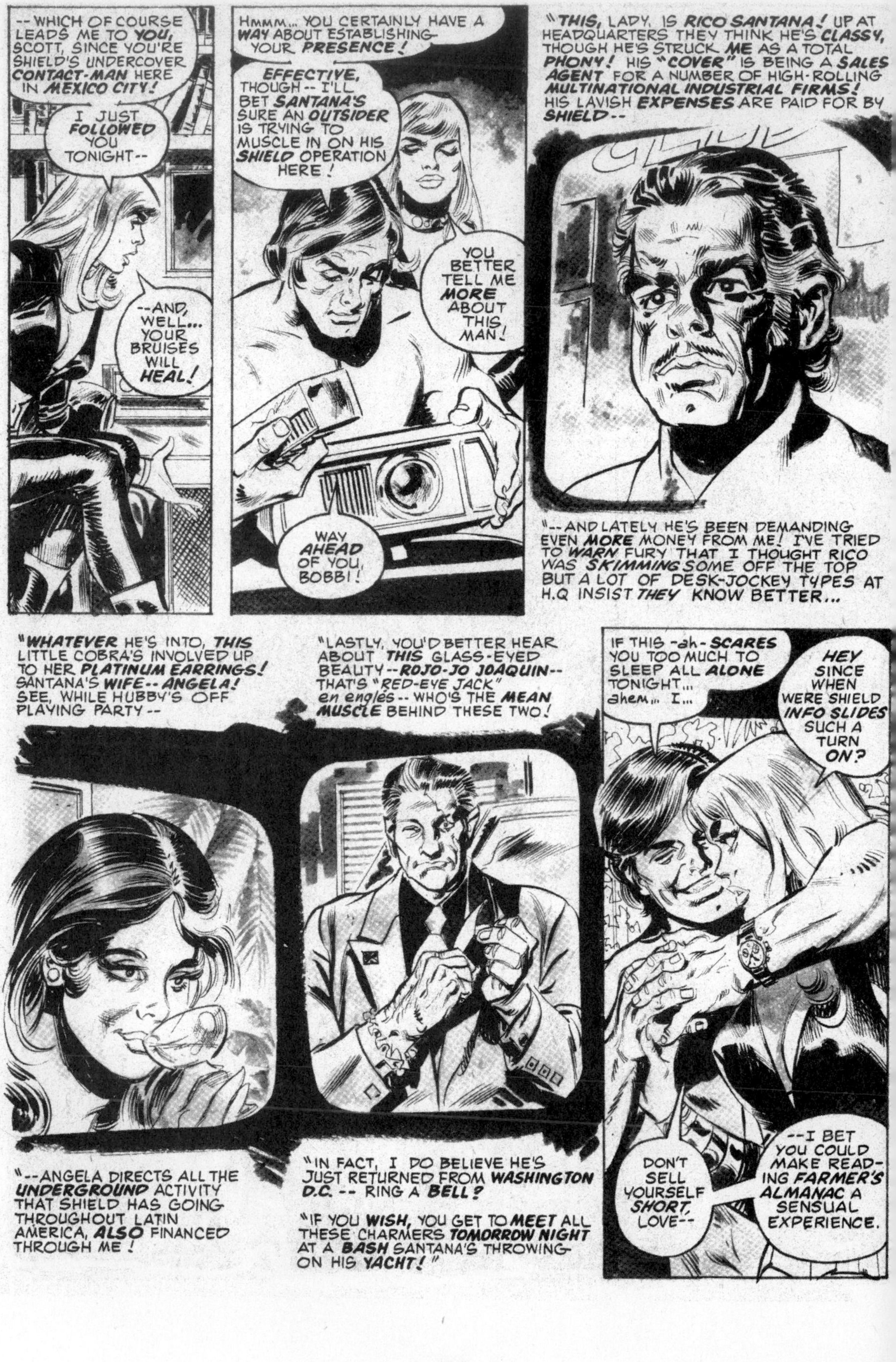
--WHICH OF COURSE LEADS ME TO YOU, SCOTT, SINCE YOU'RE SHIELD'S UNDERCOVER CONTACT-MAN HERE IN MEXICO CITY!
I JUST FOLLOWED YOU TONIGHT--
--AND, WELL... YOUR BRUISES WILL HEAL!
HMMM... YOU CERTAINLY HAVE A WAY ABOUT ESTABLISHING YOUR PRESENCE!
EFFECTIVE, THOUGH -- I'LL BET SANTANA'S SURE AN OUTSIDER IS TRYING TO MUSCLE IN ON HIS SHIELD OPERATION HERE!
YOU BETTER TELL ME MORE ABOUT THIS MAN!
WAY AHEAD OF YOU, BOBBI!
"THIS, LADY, IS RICO SANTANA! UP AT HEADQUARTERS THEY THINK HE'S CLASSY, THOUGH HE'S STRUCK ME AS A TOTAL PHONY! HIS "COVER" IS BEING A SALES AGENT FOR A NUMBER OF HIGH-ROLLING MULTINATIONAL INDUSTRIAL FIRMS! HIS LAVISH EXPENSES ARE PAID FOR BY SHIELD--
"--AND LATELY HE'S BEEN DEMANDING EVEN MORE MONEY FROM ME! I'VE TRIED TO WARN FURY THAT I THOUGHT RICO WAS SKIMMING SOME OFF THE TOP BUT A LOT OF DESK-JOCKEY TYPES AT H.Q INSIST THEY KNOW BETTER...
"WHATEVER HE'S INTO, THIS LITTLE COBRA'S INVOLVED UP TO HER PLATINUM EARRINGS! SANTANA'S WIFE-- ANGELA! SEE, WHILE HUBBY'S OFF PLAYING PARTY --
"--ANGELA DIRECTS ALL THE UNDERGROUND ACTIVITY THAT SHIELD HAS GOING THROUGHOUT LATIN AMERICA, ALSO FINANCED THROUGH ME!
"LASTLY, YOU'D BETTER HEAR ABOUT THIS GLASS-EYED BEAUTY --ROJO-JO JOAQUIN-- THAT'S "RED-EYE JACK" en englés-- WHO'S THE MEAN MUSCLE BEHIND THESE TWO!
"IN FACT, I DO BELIEVE HE'S JUST RETURNED FROM WASHINGTON D.C. -- RING A BELL?
"IF YOU WISH, YOU GET TO MEET ALL THESE CHARMERS TOMORROW NIGHT AT A BASH SANTANA'S THROWING ON HIS YACHT!"
IF THIS -ah- SCARES YOU TOO MUCH TO SLEEP ALL ALONE TONIGHT... ahem... I...
HEY SINCE WHEN WERE SHIELD INFO SLIDES SUCH A TURN ON?
DON'T SELL YOURSELF SHORT, LOVE--
--I BET YOU COULD MAKE READING FARMER'S ALMANAC A SENSUAL EXPERIENCE.

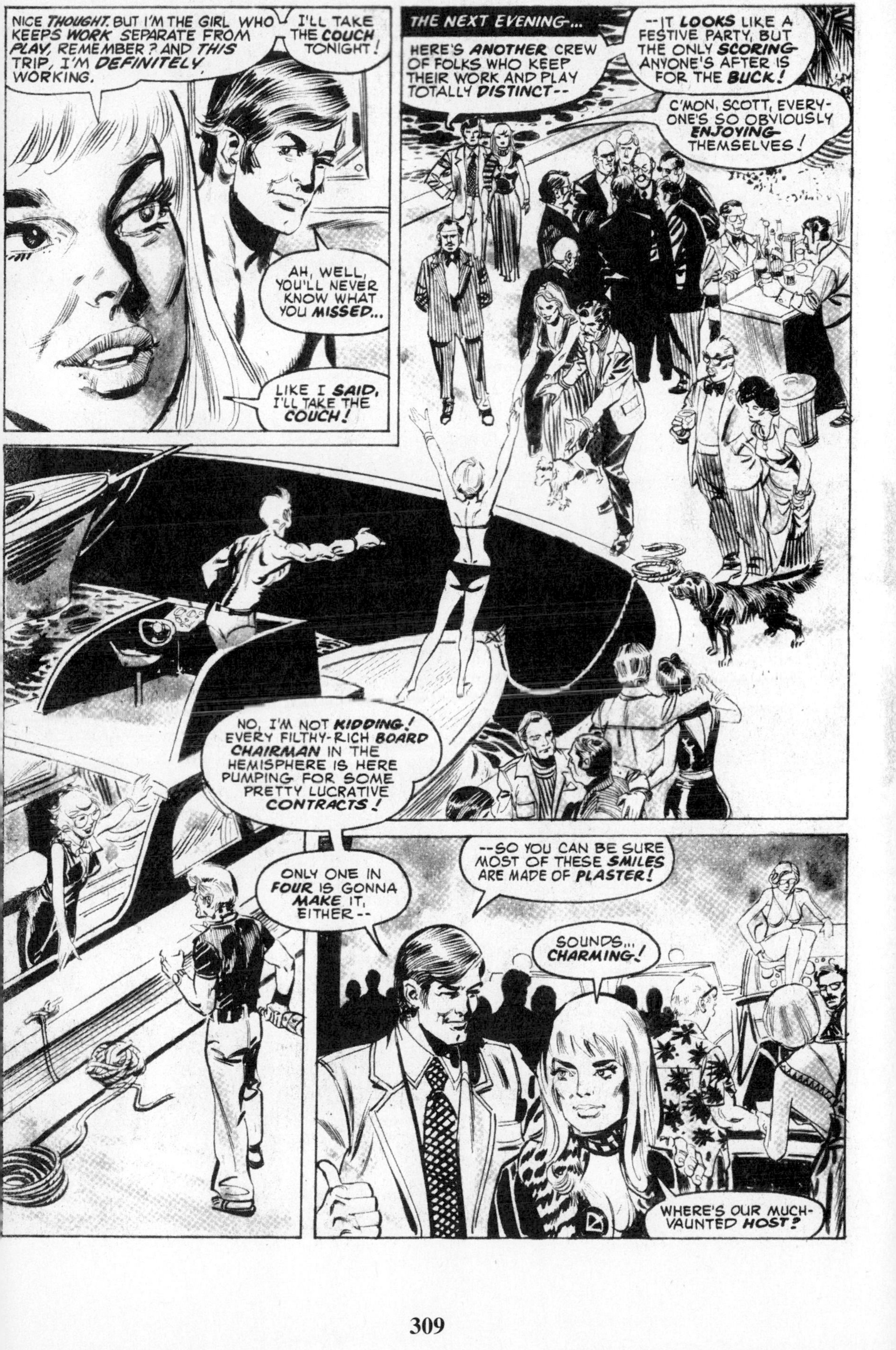
NICE THOUGHT. BUT I'M THE GIRL WHO KEEPS WORK SEPARATE FROM PLAY, REMEMBER? AND THIS TRIP, I'M DEFINITELY WORKING.
I'LL TAKE THE COUCH TONIGHT!
AH, WELL, YOU'LL NEVER KNOW WHAT YOU MISSED...
LIKE I SAID, I'LL TAKE THE COUCH!
THE NEXT EVENING...
HERE'S ANOTHER CREW OF FOLKS WHO KEEP THEIR WORK AND PLAY TOTALLY DISTINCT--
--IT LOOKS LIKE A FESTIVE PARTY, BUT THE ONLY SCORING ANYONE'S AFTER IS FOR THE BUCK!
C'MON, SCOTT, EVERYONE'S SO OBVIOUSLY ENJOYING THEMSELVES!
NO, I'M NOT KIDDING! EVERY FILTHY-RICH BOARD CHAIRMAN IN THE HEMISPHERE IS HERE PUMPING FOR SOME PRETTY LUCRATIVE CONTRACTS!
ONLY ONE IN FOUR IS GONNA MAKE IT, EITHER--
--SO YOU CAN BE SURE MOST OF THESE SMILES ARE MADE OF PLASTER!
SOUNDS... CHARMING!
WHERE'S OUR MUCH-VAUNTED HOST?

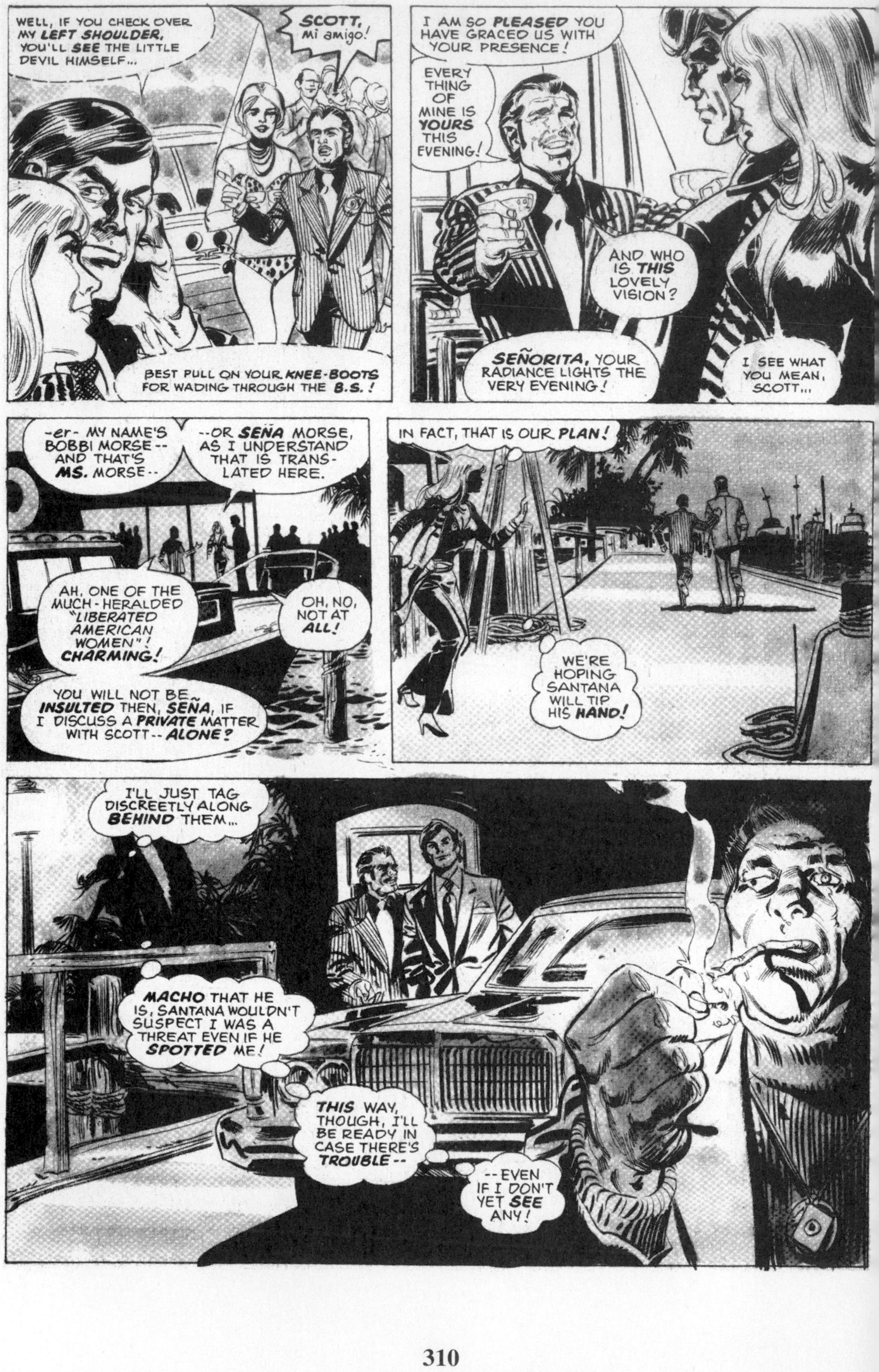
WELL, IF YOU CHECK OVER MY LEFT SHOULDER, YOU'LL SEE THE LITTLE DEVIL HIMSELF...
SCOTT, mi amigo!
BEST PULL ON YOUR KNEE-BOOTS FOR WADING THROUGH THE B.S.!
I AM SO PLEASED YOU HAVE GRACED US WITH YOUR PRESENCE!
EVERY THING OF MINE IS YOURS THIS EVENING!
AND WHO IS THIS LOVELY VISION?
SEÑORITA, YOUR RADIANCE LIGHTS THE VERY EVENING!
I SEE WHAT YOU MEAN, SCOTT...
-er- MY NAME'S BOBBI MORSE -- AND THAT'S MS. MORSE --
--OR SEÑA MORSE, AS I UNDERSTAND THAT IS TRANSLATED HERE.
AH, ONE OF THE MUCH-HERALDED "LIBERATED AMERICAN WOMEN"! CHARMING!
OH, NO, NOT AT ALL!
YOU WILL NOT BE INSULTED THEN, SEÑA, IF I DISCUSS A PRIVATE MATTER WITH SCOTT -- ALONE?
IN FACT, THAT IS OUR PLAN!
WE'RE HOPING SANTANA WILL TIP HIS HAND!
I'LL JUST TAG DISCREETLY ALONG BEHIND THEM...
MACHO THAT HE IS, SANTANA WOULDN'T SUSPECT I WAS A THREAT EVEN IF HE SPOTTED ME!
THIS WAY, THOUGH, I'LL BE READY IN CASE THERE'S TROUBLE --
-- EVEN IF I DON'T YET SEE ANY!

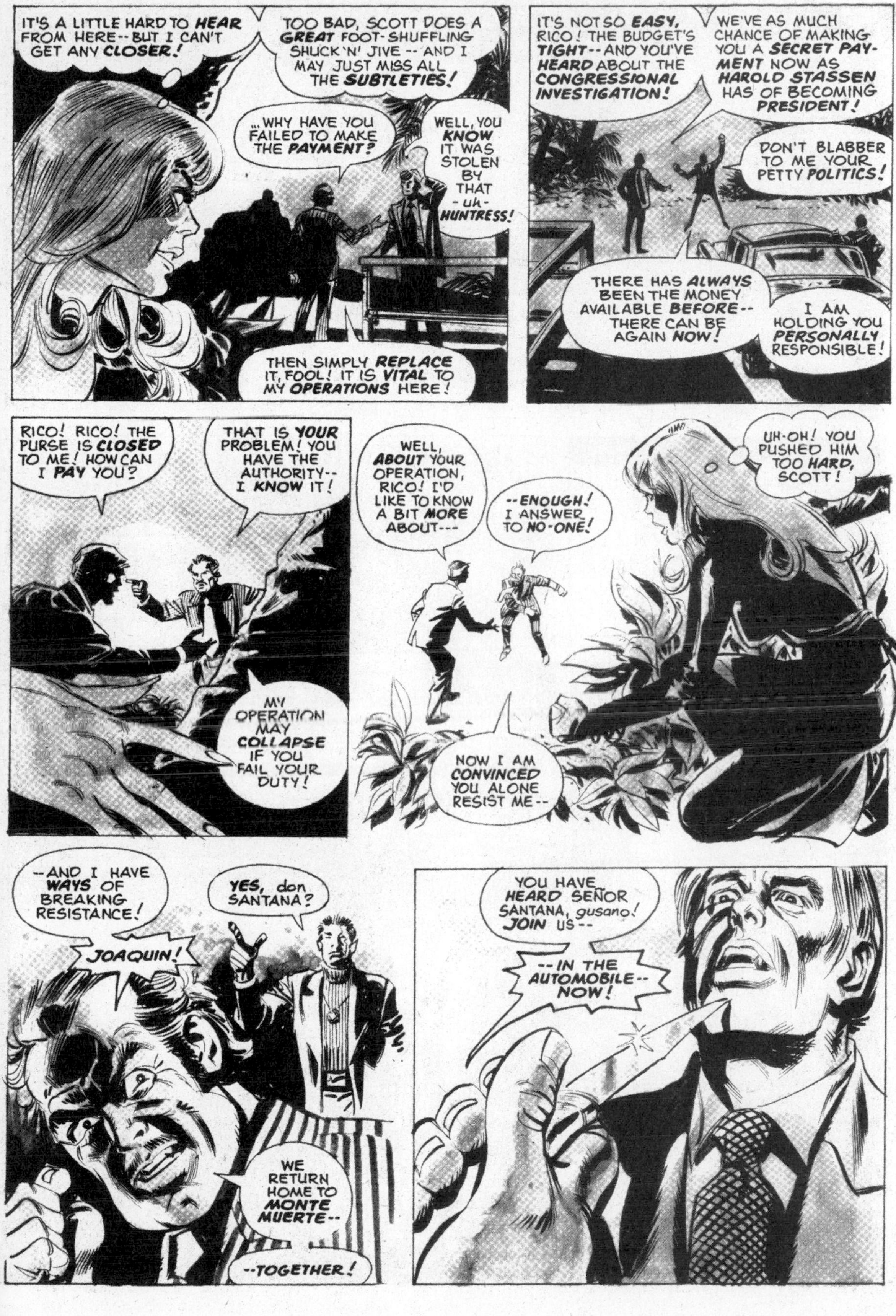

IT'S A LITTLE HARD TO HEAR FROM HERE--BUT I CAN'T GET ANY CLOSER!
TOO BAD, SCOTT DOES A GREAT FOOT-SHUFFLING SHUCK 'N' JIVE -- AND I MAY JUST MISS ALL THE SUBTLETIES!
...WHY HAVE YOU FAILED TO MAKE THE PAYMENT?
WELL, YOU KNOW IT WAS STOLEN BY THAT -uh- HUNTRESS!
THEN SIMPLY REPLACE IT, FOOL! IT IS VITAL TO MY OPERATIONS HERE!
IT'S NOT SO EASY, RICO! THE BUDGET'S TIGHT--AND YOU'VE HEARD ABOUT THE CONGRESSIONAL INVESTIGATION!
WE'VE AS MUCH CHANCE OF MAKING YOU A SECRET PAYMENT NOW AS HAROLD STASSEN HAS OF BECOMING PRESIDENT!
DON'T BLABBER TO ME YOUR PETTY POLITICS!
THERE HAS ALWAYS BEEN THE MONEY AVAILABLE BEFORE--THERE CAN BE AGAIN NOW!
I AM HOLDING YOU PERSONALLY RESPONSIBLE!
RICO! RICO! THE PURSE IS CLOSED TO ME! HOW CAN I PAY YOU?
THAT IS YOUR PROBLEM! YOU HAVE THE AUTHORITY--I KNOW IT!
MY OPERATION MAY COLLAPSE IF YOU FAIL YOUR DUTY!
WELL, ABOUT YOUR OPERATION, RICO! I'D LIKE TO KNOW A BIT MORE ABOUT---
--ENOUGH! I ANSWER TO NO-ONE!
UH-OH! YOU PUSHED HIM TOO HARD, SCOTT!
NOW I AM CONVINCED YOU ALONE RESIST ME--
--AND I HAVE WAYS OF BREAKING RESISTANCE!
JOAQUIN!
YES, don SANTANA?
WE RETURN HOME TO MONTE MUERTE--
--TOGETHER!
YOU HAVE HEARD SEÑOR SANTANA, gusano! JOIN US--
--IN THE AUTOMOBILE--NOW!

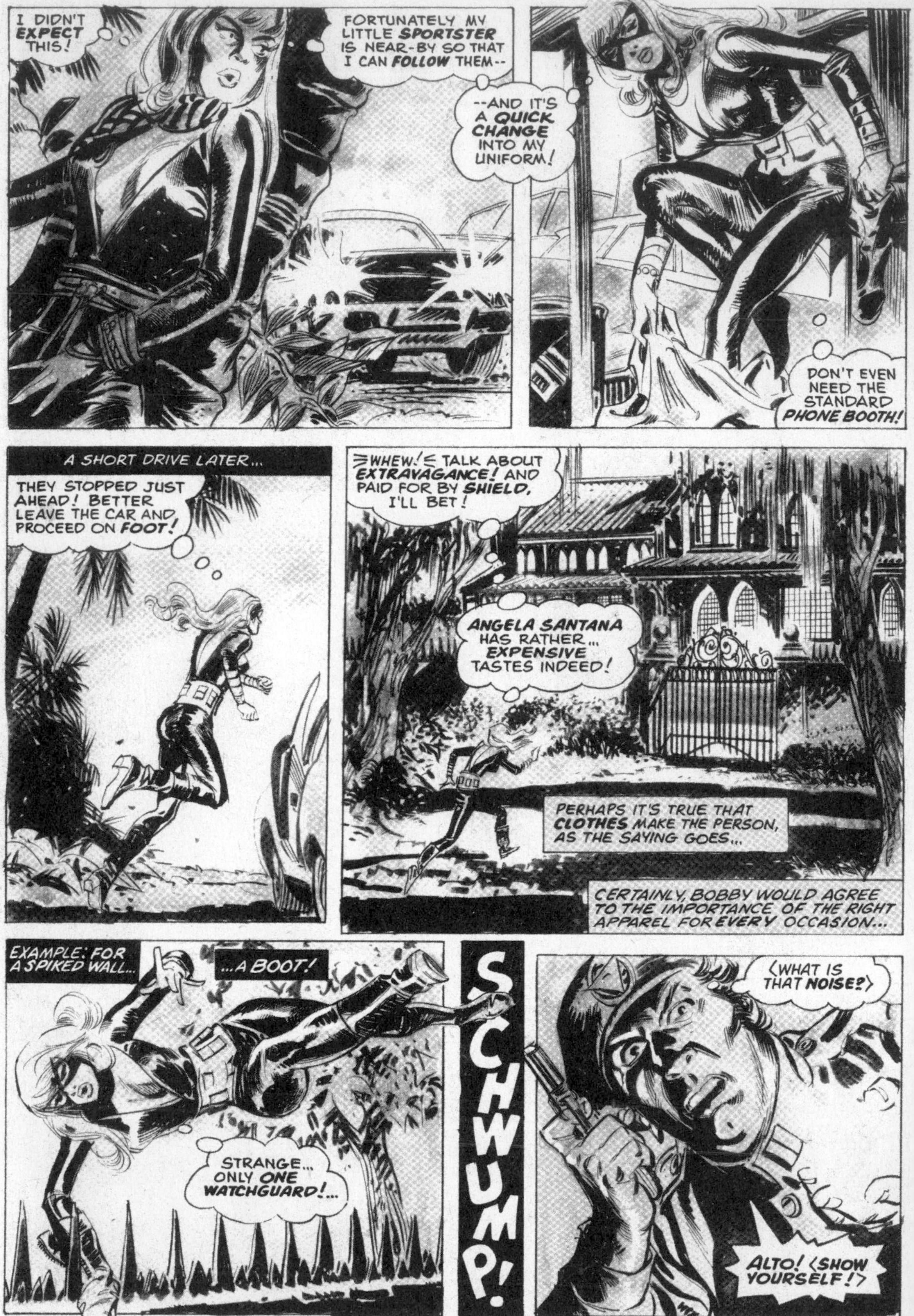
I DIDN'T EXPECT THIS!
FORTUNATELY MY LITTLE SPORTSTER IS NEAR-BY SO THAT I CAN FOLLOW THEM--
--AND IT'S A QUICK CHANGE INTO MY UNIFORM!
DON'T EVEN NEED THE STANDARD PHONE BOOTH!
A SHORT DRIVE LATER...
THEY STOPPED JUST AHEAD! BETTER LEAVE THE CAR AND PROCEED ON FOOT!
WHEW! TALK ABOUT EXTRAVAGANCE! AND PAID FOR BY SHIELD, I'LL BET!
ANGELA SANTANA HAS RATHER... EXPENSIVE TASTES INDEED!
PERHAPS IT'S TRUE THAT CLOTHES MAKE THE PERSON, AS THE SAYING GOES...
CERTAINLY, BOBBY WOULD AGREE TO THE IMPORTANCE OF THE RIGHT APPAREL FOR EVERY OCCASION...
EXAMPLE: FOR A SPIKED WALL...
...A BOOT!
STRANGE... ONLY ONE WATCHGUARD!...
SCHWUMP!
<WHAT IS THAT NOISE?>
ALTO! <SHOW YOURSELF!>

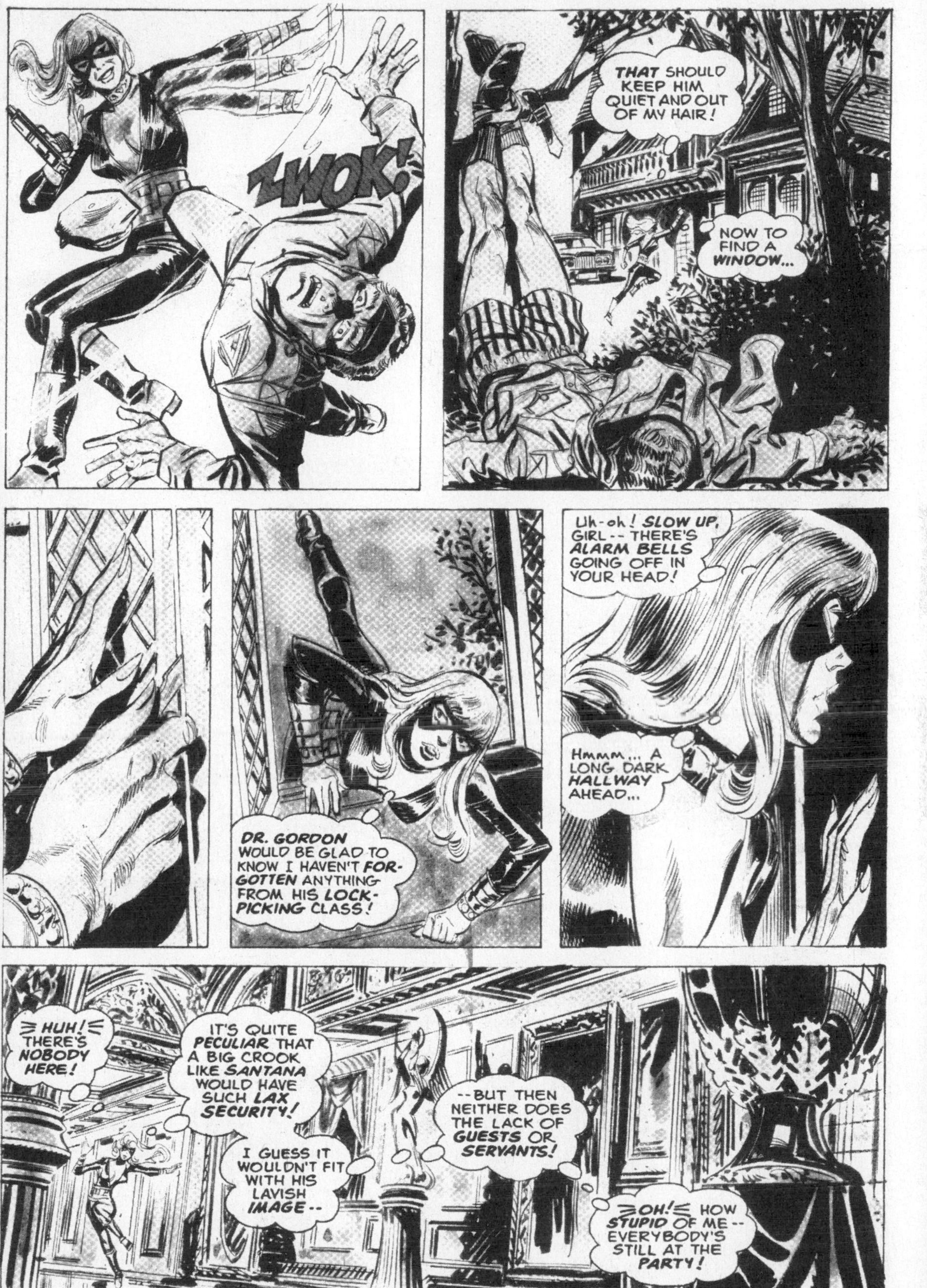
ZWOK!
THAT SHOULD KEEP HIM QUIET AND OUT OF MY HAIR!
NOW TO FIND A WINDOW...
DR. GORDON WOULD BE GLAD TO KNOW I HAVEN'T FORGOTTEN ANYTHING FROM HIS LOCK-PICKING CLASS!
Uh-oh! SLOW UP, GIRL -- THERE'S ALARM BELLS GOING OFF IN YOUR HEAD!
Hmmm... A LONG DARK HALLWAY AHEAD...
HUH! THERE'S NOBODY HERE!
IT'S QUITE PECULIAR THAT A BIG CROOK LIKE SANTANA WOULD HAVE SUCH LAX SECURITY!
I GUESS IT WOULDN'T FIT WITH HIS LAVISH IMAGE --
-- BUT THEN NEITHER DOES THE LACK OF GUESTS OR SERVANTS!
OH! HOW STUPID OF ME -- EVERYBODY'S STILL AT THE PARTY!

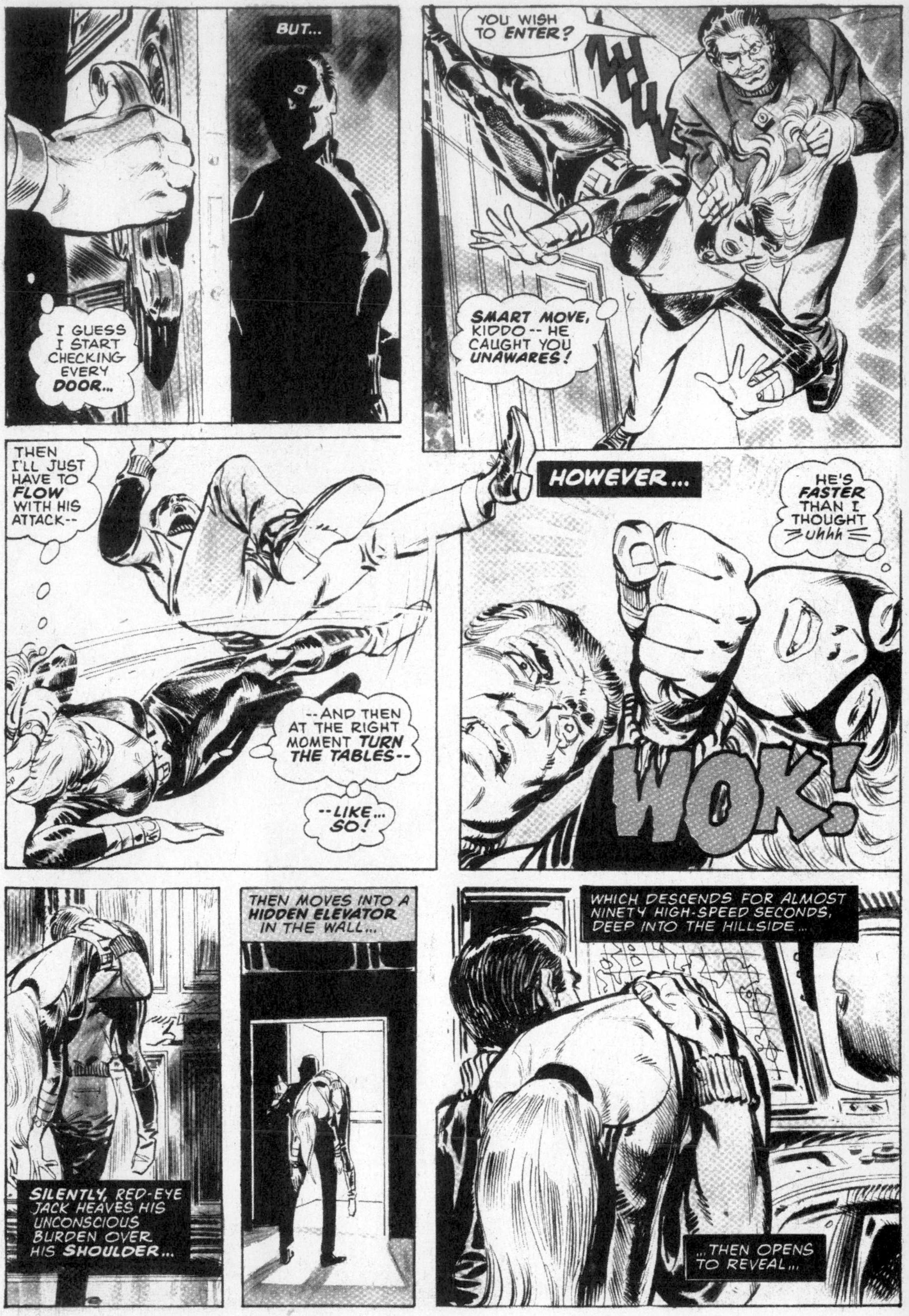
BUT...
I GUESS I START CHECKING EVERY DOOR...
YOU WISH TO ENTER?
THWUK
SMART MOVE, KIDDO-- HE CAUGHT YOU UNAWARES!
THEN I'LL JUST HAVE TO FLOW WITH HIS ATTACK--
--AND THEN AT THE RIGHT MOMENT TURN THE TABLES--
--LIKE... SO!
HOWEVER...
HE'S FASTER THAN I THOUGHT uhhh
WOK!
SILENTLY, RED-EYE JACK HEAVES HIS UNCONSCIOUS BURDEN OVER HIS SHOULDER...
THEN MOVES INTO A HIDDEN ELEVATOR IN THE WALL...
WHICH DESCENDS FOR ALMOST NINETY HIGH-SPEED SECONDS, DEEP INTO THE HILLSIDE...
...THEN OPENS TO REVEAL...

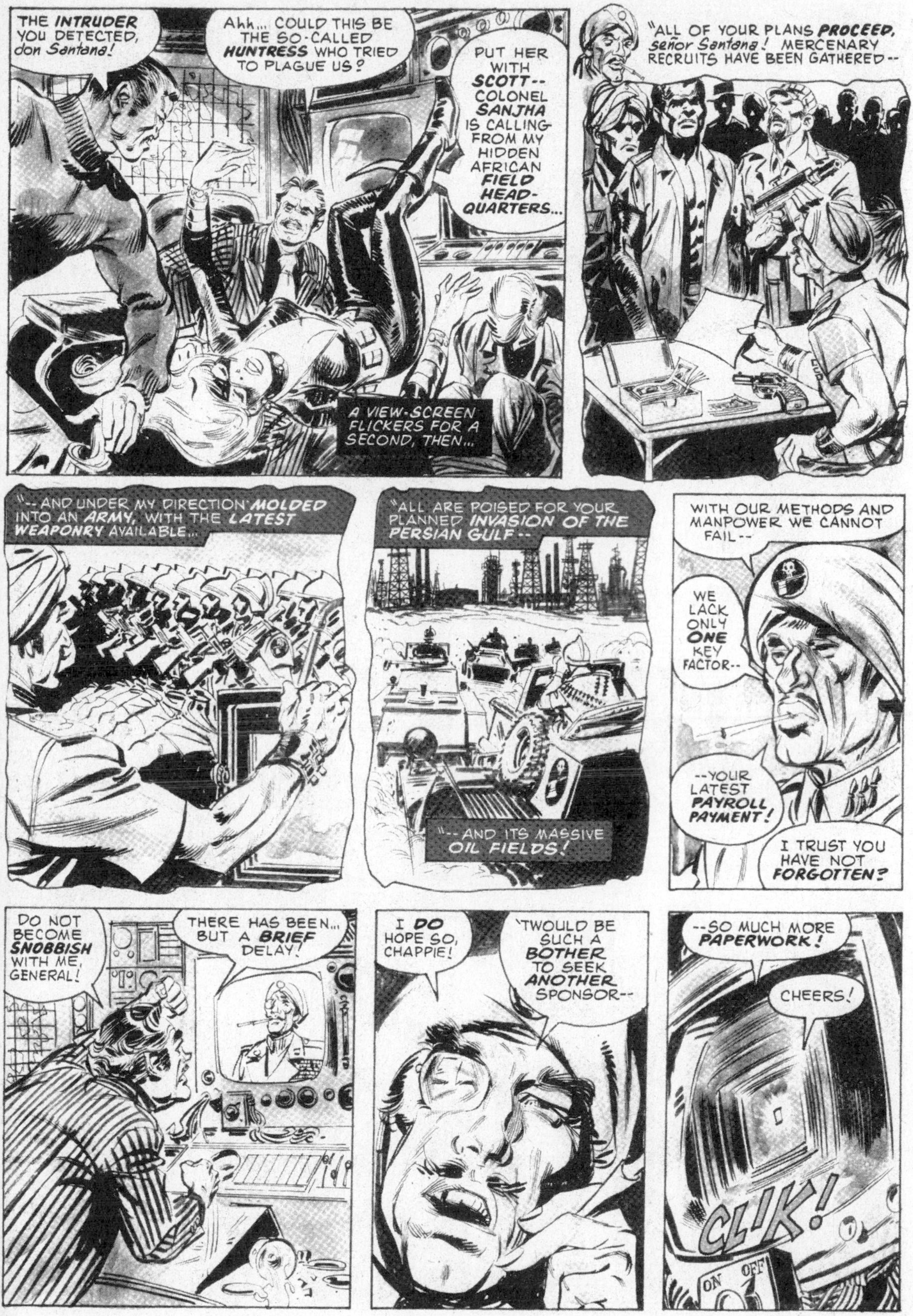
THE INTRUDER YOU DETECTED, don Santana!
Ahh... COULD THIS BE THE SO-CALLED HUNTRESS WHO TRIED TO PLAGUE US?
PUT HER WITH SCOTT-- COLONEL SANJHA IS CALLING FROM MY HIDDEN AFRICAN FIELD HEAD-QUARTERS...
A VIEW-SCREEN FLICKERS FOR A SECOND, THEN...
"ALL OF YOUR PLANS PROCEED, señor Santana! MERCENARY RECRUITS HAVE BEEN GATHERED--
"--AND UNDER MY DIRECTION MOLDED INTO AN ARMY, WITH THE LATEST WEAPONRY AVAILABLE...
"ALL ARE POISED FOR YOUR PLANNED INVASION OF THE PERSIAN GULF--
"--AND ITS MASSIVE OIL FIELDS!
WITH OUR METHODS AND MANPOWER WE CANNOT FAIL--
WE LACK ONLY ONE KEY FACTOR--
--YOUR LATEST PAYROLL PAYMENT!
I TRUST YOU HAVE NOT FORGOTTEN?
DO NOT BECOME SNOBBISH WITH ME, GENERAL!
THERE HAS BEEN... BUT A BRIEF DELAY!
I DO HOPE SO, CHAPPIE!
'TWOULD BE SUCH A BOTHER TO SEEK ANOTHER SPONSOR--
--SO MUCH MORE PAPERWORK!
CHEERS!
CLIK!
ON
OFF

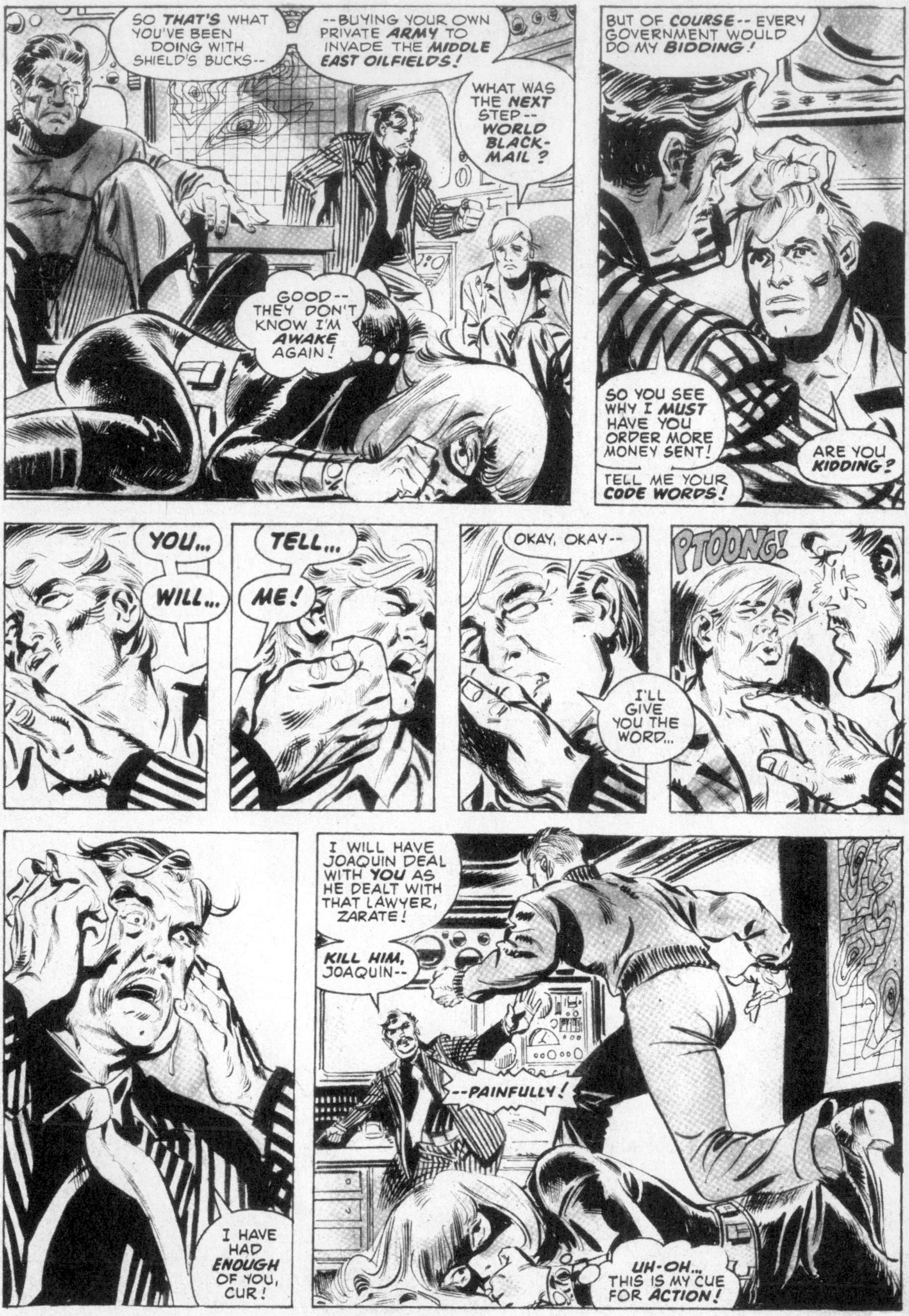
SO THAT'S WHAT YOU'VE BEEN DOING WITH SHIELD'S BUCKS--
--BUYING YOUR OWN PRIVATE ARMY TO INVADE THE MIDDLE EAST OILFIELDS!
WHAT WAS THE NEXT STEP-- WORLD BLACK-MAIL?
GOOD-- THEY DON'T KNOW I'M AWAKE AGAIN!
BUT OF COURSE-- EVERY GOVERNMENT WOULD DO MY BIDDING!
SO YOU SEE WHY I MUST HAVE YOU ORDER MORE MONEY SENT!
TELL ME YOUR CODE WORDS!
ARE YOU KIDDING?
YOU...
WILL...
TELL...
ME!
OKAY, OKAY--
I'LL GIVE YOU THE WORD...
PTOONG!
I HAVE HAD ENOUGH OF YOU, CUR!
I WILL HAVE JOAQUIN DEAL WITH YOU AS HE DEALT WITH THAT LAWYER, ZARATE!
KILL HIM, JOAQUIN--
--PAINFULLY!
UH-OH... THIS IS MY CUE FOR ACTION!

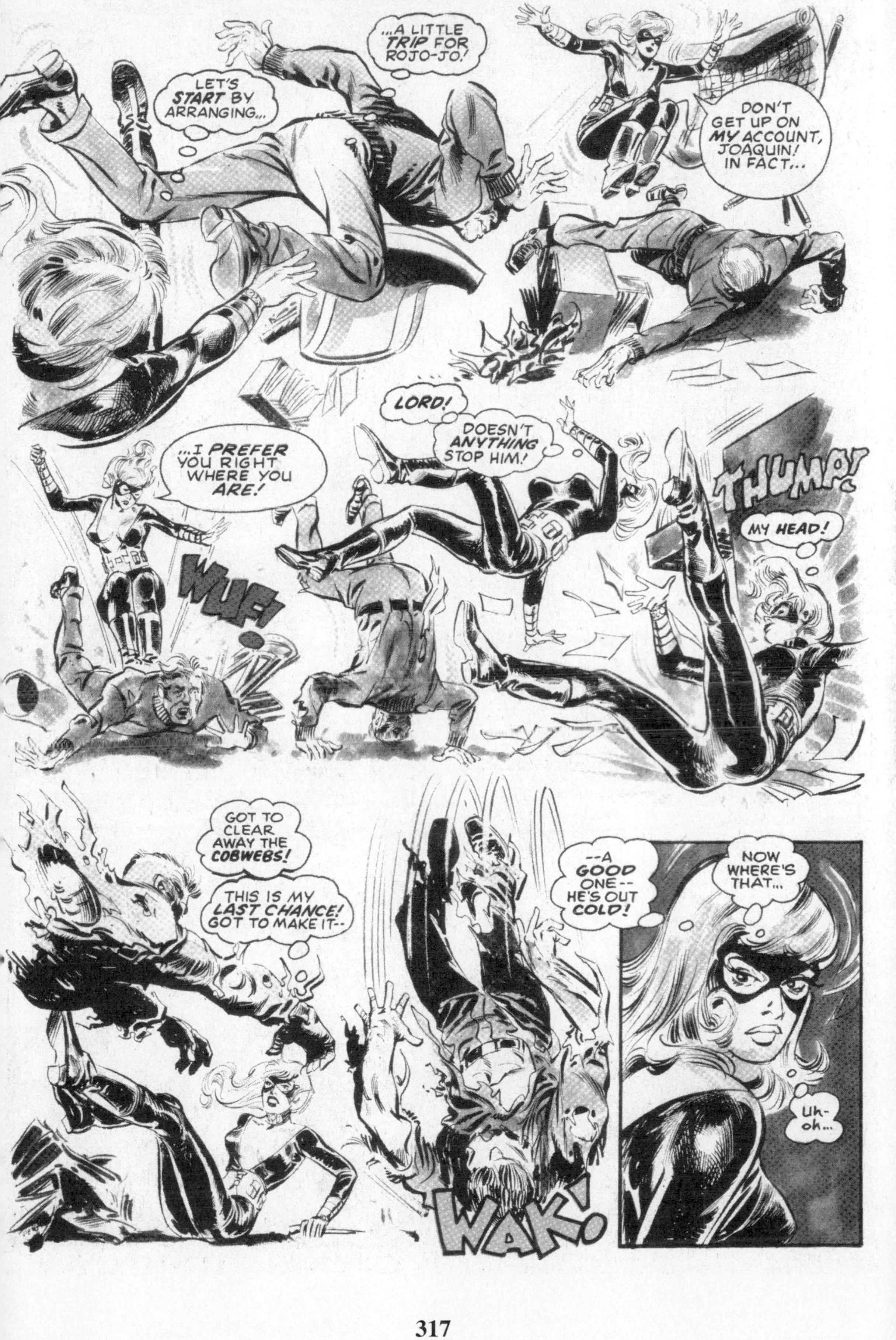
LET'S START BY ARRANGING...
...A LITTLE TRIP FOR ROJO-JO!
DON'T GET UP ON MY ACCOUNT, JOAQUIN! IN FACT...
...I PREFER YOU RIGHT WHERE YOU ARE!
WUF!
LORD!
DOESN'T ANYTHING STOP HIM!
THUMP!
MY HEAD!
GOT TO CLEAR AWAY THE COBWEBS!
THIS IS MY LAST CHANCE! GOT TO MAKE IT--
--A GOOD ONE-- HE'S OUT COLD!
WAK!
NOW WHERE'S THAT...
Uh-oh...

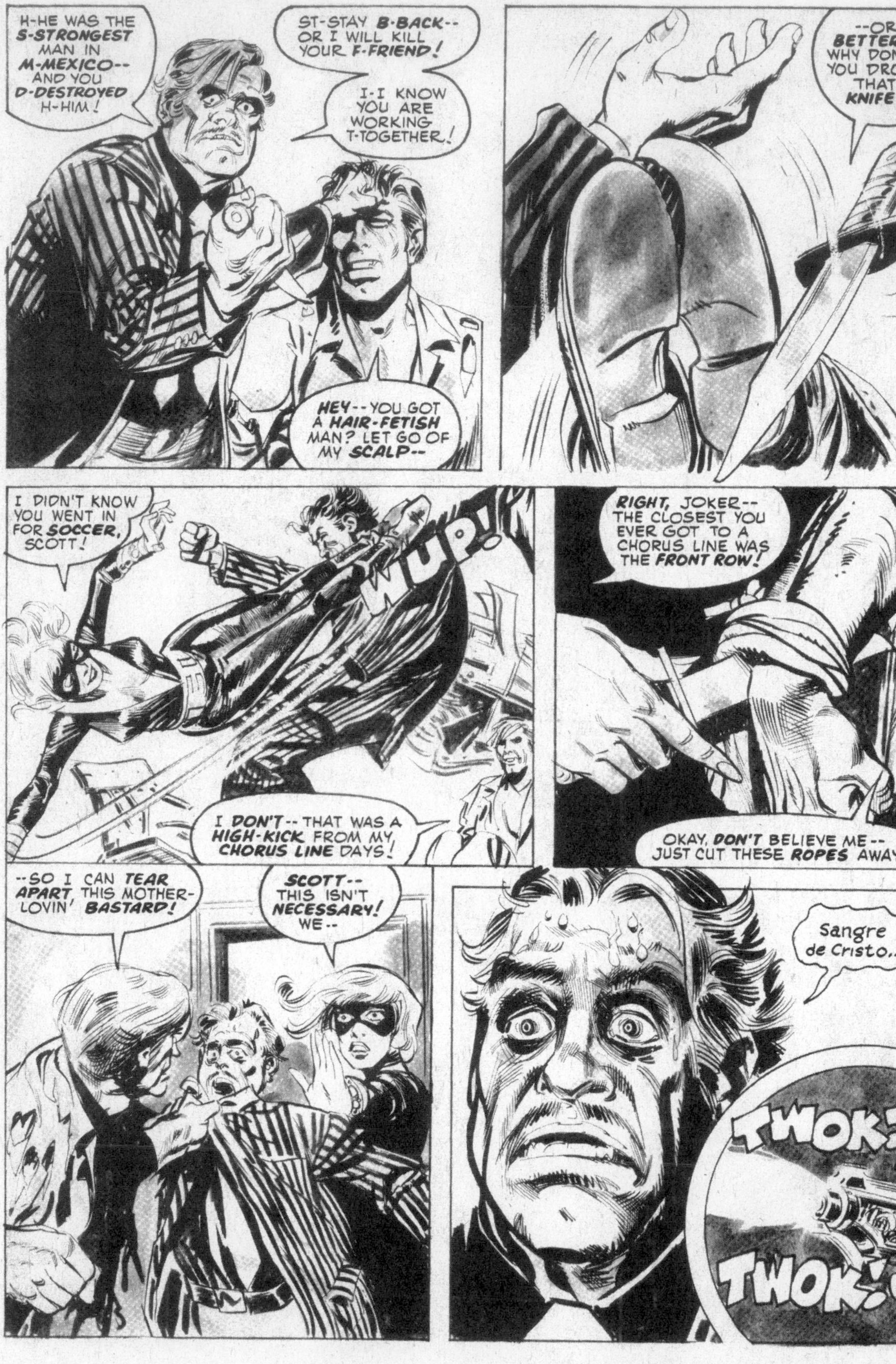
H-HE WAS THE S-STRONGEST MAN IN M-MEXICO-- AND YOU D-DESTROYED H-HIM!
ST-STAY B-BACK-- OR I WILL KILL YOUR F-FRIEND!
I-I KNOW YOU ARE WORKING T-TOGETHER!
HEY--YOU GOT A HAIR-FETISH MAN? LET GO OF MY SCALP--
--OR BETTER, WHY DON'T YOU DROP THAT KNIFE?!
I DIDN'T KNOW YOU WENT IN FOR SOCCER, SCOTT!
WUP!
I DON'T--THAT WAS A HIGH-KICK FROM MY CHORUS LINE DAYS!
RIGHT, JOKER-- THE CLOSEST YOU EVER GOT TO A CHORUS LINE WAS THE FRONT ROW!
OKAY, DON'T BELIEVE ME -- JUST CUT THESE ROPES AWAY--
--SO I CAN TEAR APART THIS MOTHER-LOVIN' BASTARD!
SCOTT-- THIS ISN'T NECESSARY! WE --
Sangre de Cristo...!
TWOK!
TWOK!

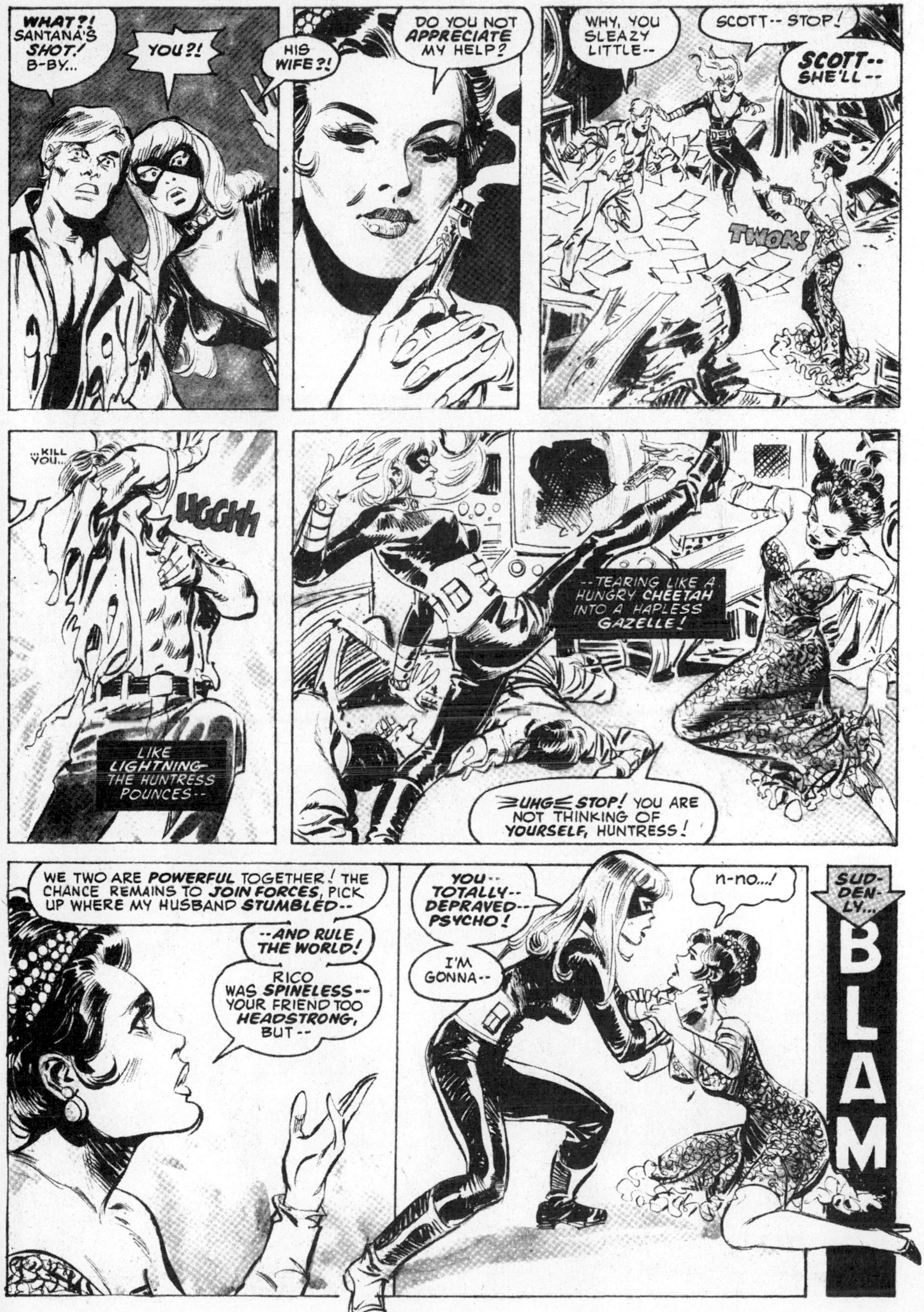
WHAT?! SANTANA'S SHOT! B-BY...
YOU?!
HIS WIFE?!
DO YOU NOT APPRECIATE MY HELP?
WHY, YOU SLEAZY LITTLE--
SCOTT-- STOP!
SCOTT-- SHE'LL--
TWOK!
...KILL YOU...
UGGHH
LIKE LIGHTNING THE HUNTRESS POUNCES--
--TEARING LIKE A HUNGRY CHEETAH INTO A HAPLESS GAZELLE!
UHG STOP! YOU ARE NOT THINKING OF YOURSELF, HUNTRESS!
WE TWO ARE POWERFUL TOGETHER! THE CHANCE REMAINS TO JOIN FORCES, PICK UP WHERE MY HUSBAND STUMBLED--
--AND RULE THE WORLD!
RICO WAS SPINELESS-- YOUR FRIEND TOO HEADSTRONG, BUT--
YOU-- TOTALLY-- DEPRAVED-- PSYCHO!
I'M GONNA--
n-no...!
SUD-DEN-LY...
BLAM

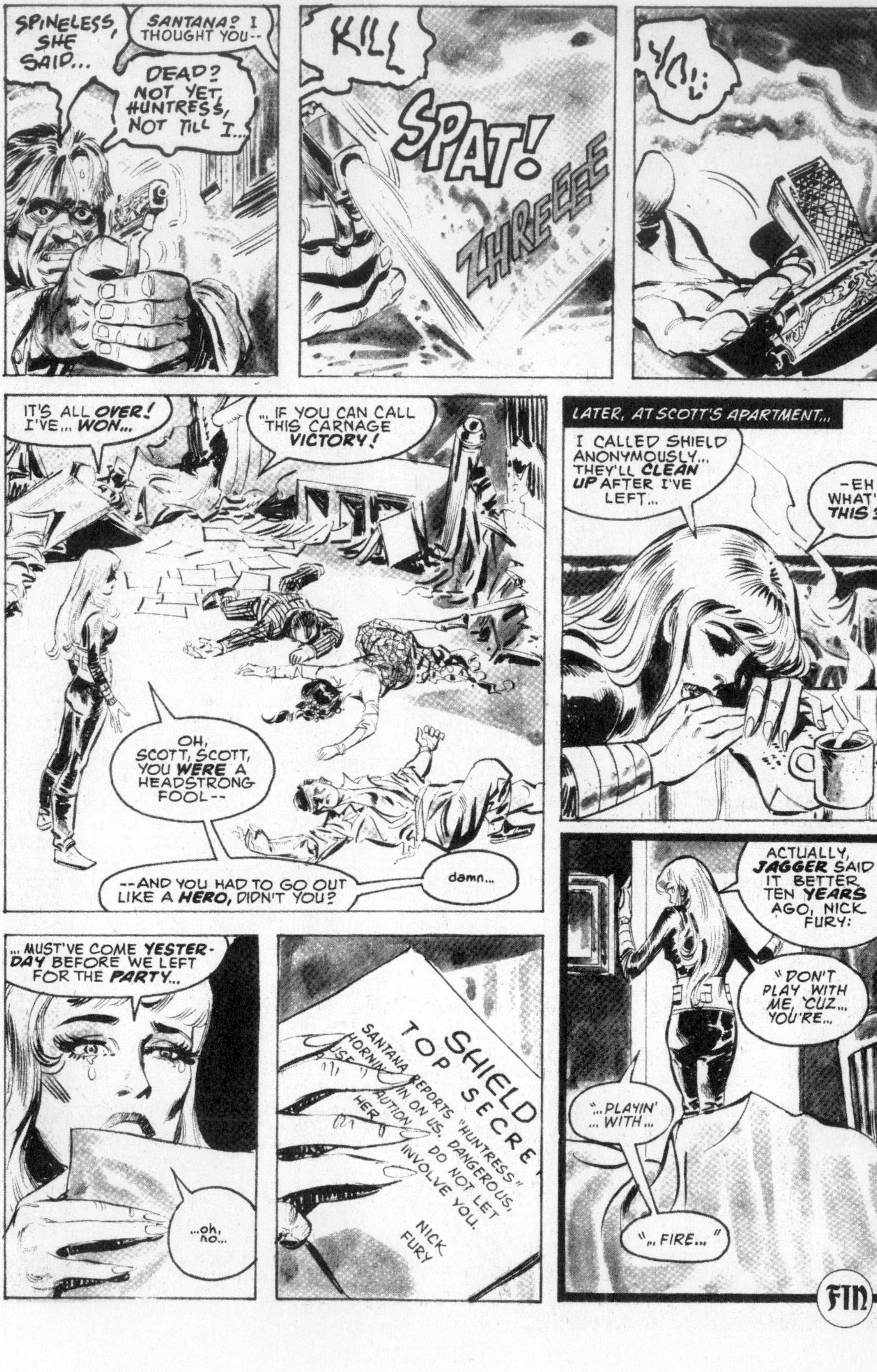
SPINELESS, SHE SAID...
SANTANA? I THOUGHT YOU--
DEAD? NOT YET, HUNTRESS, NOT TILL I...
KILL
SPAT!
ZHREEEEE
YOU!!
IT'S ALL OVER! I'VE... WON...
...IF YOU CAN CALL THIS CARNAGE VICTORY!
OH, SCOTT, SCOTT, YOU WERE A HEADSTRONG FOOL--
--AND YOU HAD TO GO OUT LIKE A HERO, DIDN'T YOU?
damn...
LATER, AT SCOTT'S APARTMENT...
I CALLED SHIELD ANONYMOUSLY... THEY'LL CLEAN UP AFTER I'VE LEFT...
-EH? WHAT'S THIS?
...MUST'VE COME YESTERDAY BEFORE WE LEFT FOR THE PARTY...
...oh, no...
SHIELD
TOP SECRE
SANTANA REPORTS "HUNTRESS" HORNIN IN ON US. DANGEROUS.
USE AUTION DO NOT LET HER INVOLVE YOU.
NICK FURY
ACTUALLY, JAGGER SAID IT BETTER TEN YEARS AGO, NICK FURY:
"DON'T PLAY WITH ME, 'CUZ... YOU'RE...
"...PLAYIN' ...WITH...
"...FIRE..."
FIN

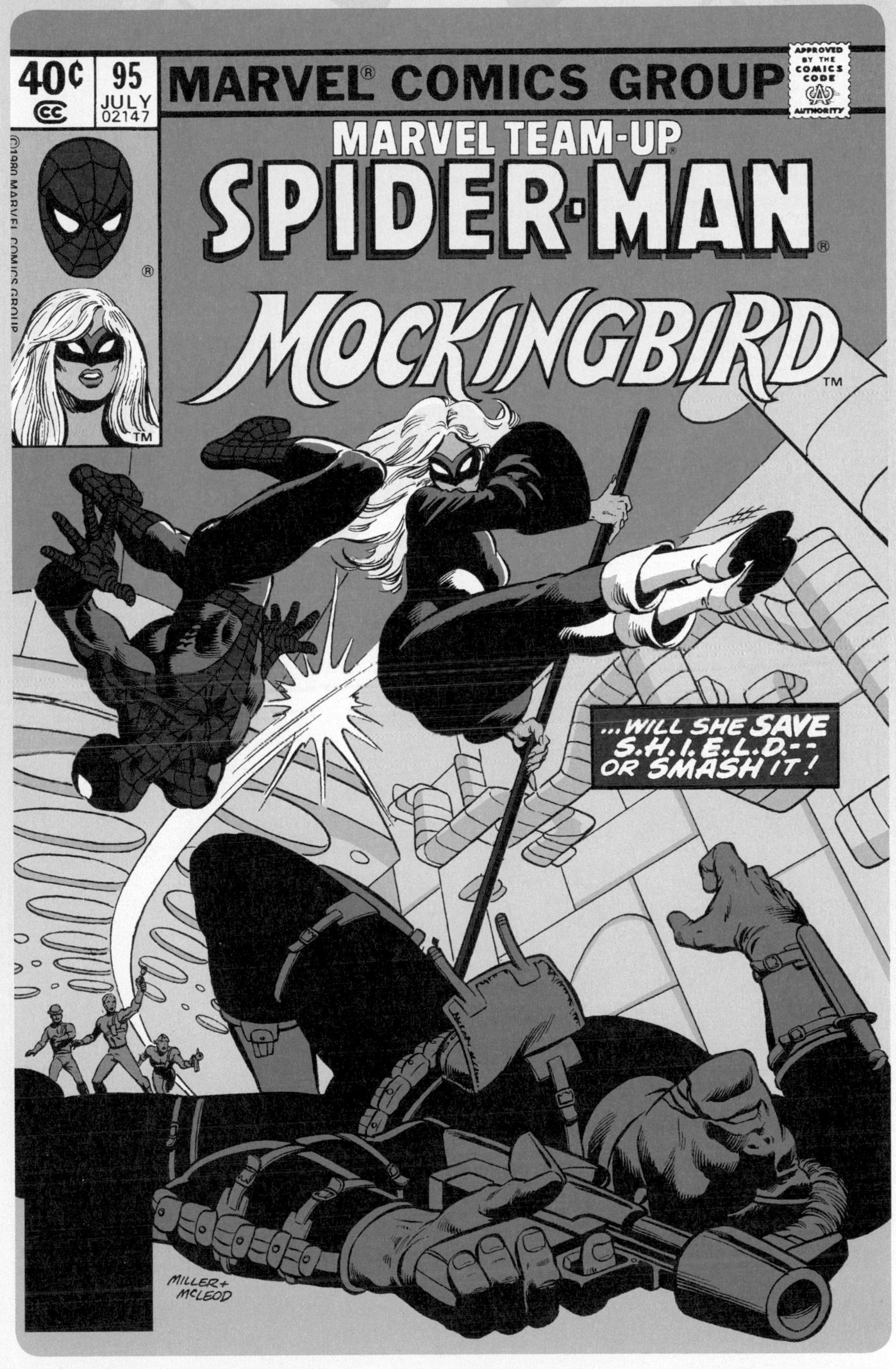
40¢
95
JULY
02147
MARVEL® COMICS GROUP
APPROVED BY THE COMICS CODE AUTHORITY
MARVEL TEAM-UP
SPIDER-MAN
MOCKINGBIRD
©1980 MARVEL COMICS GROUP
...WILL SHE SAVE S.H.I.E.L.D.-- OR SMASH IT!
MILLER+ McLEOD

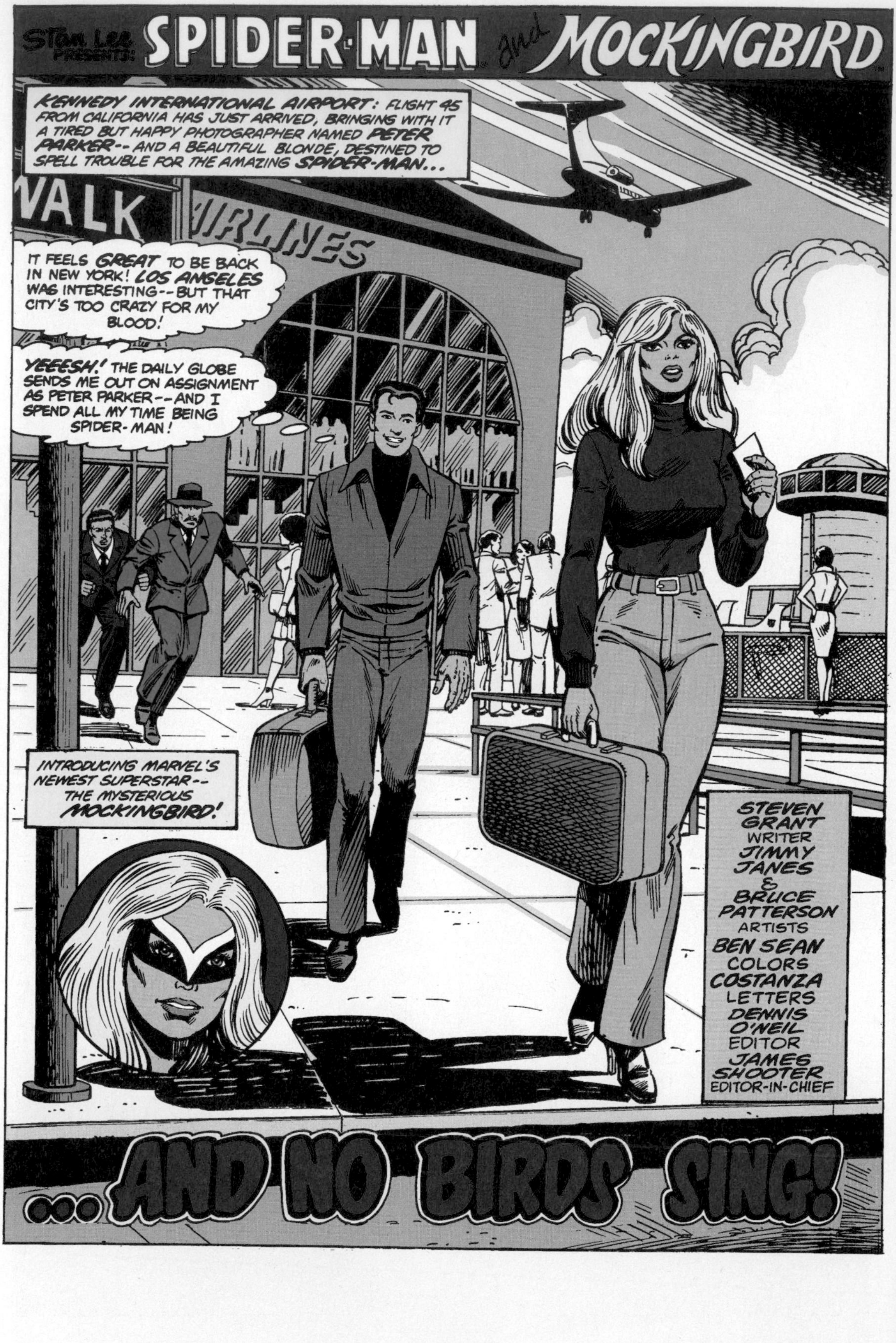
Stan Lee PRESENTS: SPIDER-MAN and MOCKINGBIRD
KENNEDY INTERNATIONAL AIRPORT: FLIGHT 45 FROM CALIFORNIA HAS JUST ARRIVED, BRINGING WITH IT A TIRED BUT HAPPY PHOTOGRAPHER NAMED PETER PARKER-- AND A BEAUTIFUL BLONDE, DESTINED TO SPELL TROUBLE FOR THE AMAZING SPIDER-MAN...
WALK
IRLINES
IT FEELS GREAT TO BE BACK IN NEW YORK! LOS ANGELES WAS INTERESTING-- BUT THAT CITY'S TOO CRAZY FOR MY BLOOD!
YEEESH! THE DAILY GLOBE SENDS ME OUT ON ASSIGNMENT AS PETER PARKER-- AND I SPEND ALL MY TIME BEING SPIDER-MAN!
INTRODUCING MARVEL'S NEWEST SUPERSTAR-- THE MYSTERIOUS MOCKINGBIRD!
STEVEN GRANT WRITER JIMMY JANES & BRUCE PATTERSON ARTISTS BEN SEAN COLORS COSTANZA LETTERS DENNIS O'NEIL EDITOR JAMES SHOOTER EDITOR-IN-CHIEF
...AND NO BIRDS SING!

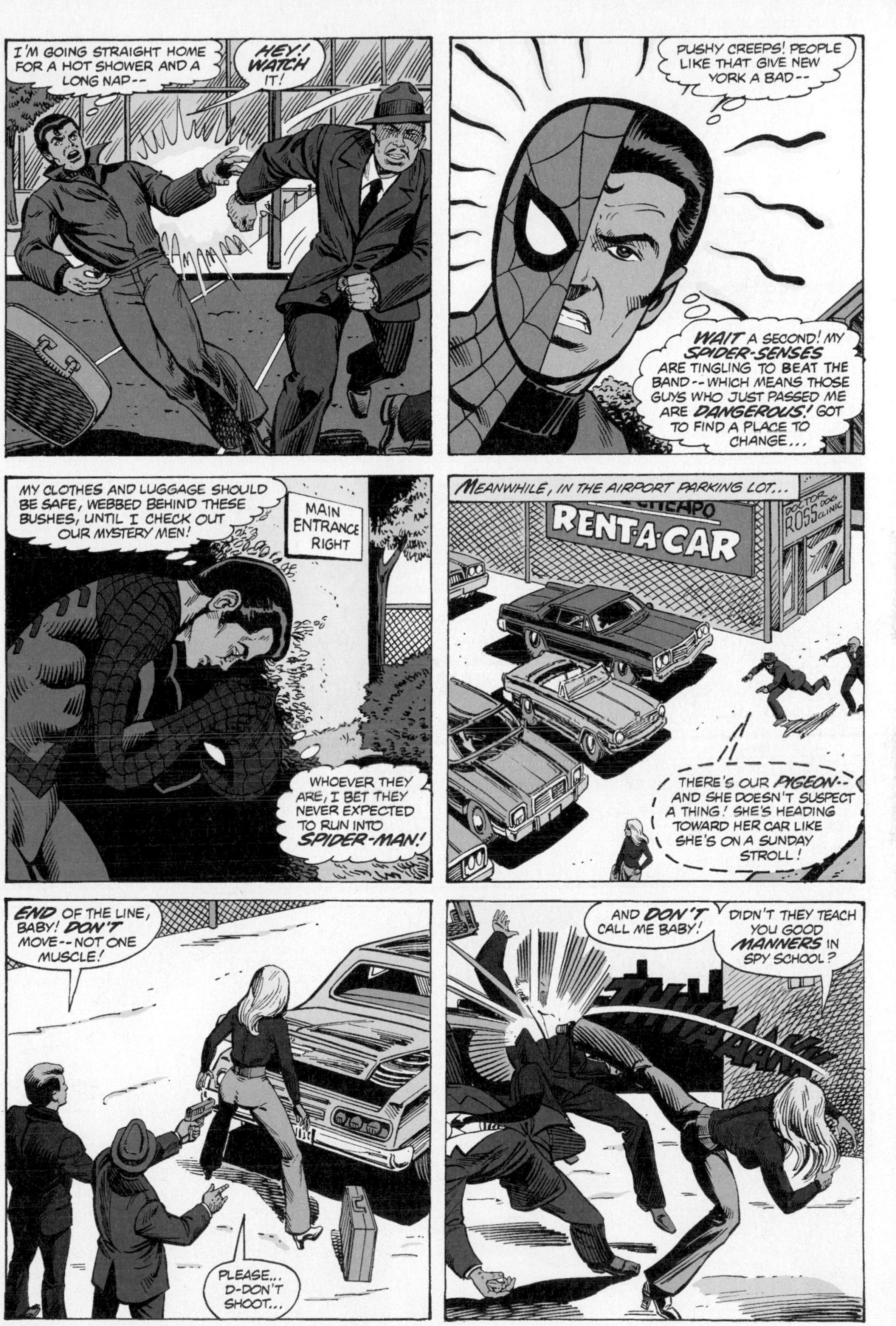
I'M GOING STRAIGHT HOME FOR A HOT SHOWER AND A LONG NAP--
HEY! WATCH IT!
PUSHY CREEPS! PEOPLE LIKE THAT GIVE NEW YORK A BAD--
WAIT A SECOND! MY SPIDER-SENSES ARE TINGLING TO BEAT THE BAND--WHICH MEANS THOSE GUYS WHO JUST PASSED ME ARE DANGEROUS! GOT TO FIND A PLACE TO CHANGE...
MY CLOTHES AND LUGGAGE SHOULD BE SAFE, WEBBED BEHIND THESE BUSHES, UNTIL I CHECK OUT OUR MYSTERY MEN!
MAIN ENTRANCE RIGHT
WHOEVER THEY ARE, I BET THEY NEVER EXPECTED TO RUN INTO SPIDER-MAN!
MEANWHILE, IN THE AIRPORT PARKING LOT...
RENT-A-CAR
DOCTOR ROSS DOG CLINIC
THERE'S OUR PIGEON--AND SHE DOESN'T SUSPECT A THING! SHE'S HEADING TOWARD HER CAR LIKE SHE'S ON A SUNDAY STROLL!
END OF THE LINE, BABY! DON'T MOVE--NOT ONE MUSCLE!
PLEASE... D-DON'T SHOOT...
AND DON'T CALL ME BABY!
DIDN'T THEY TEACH YOU GOOD MANNERS IN SPY SCHOOL?
THWAAANK

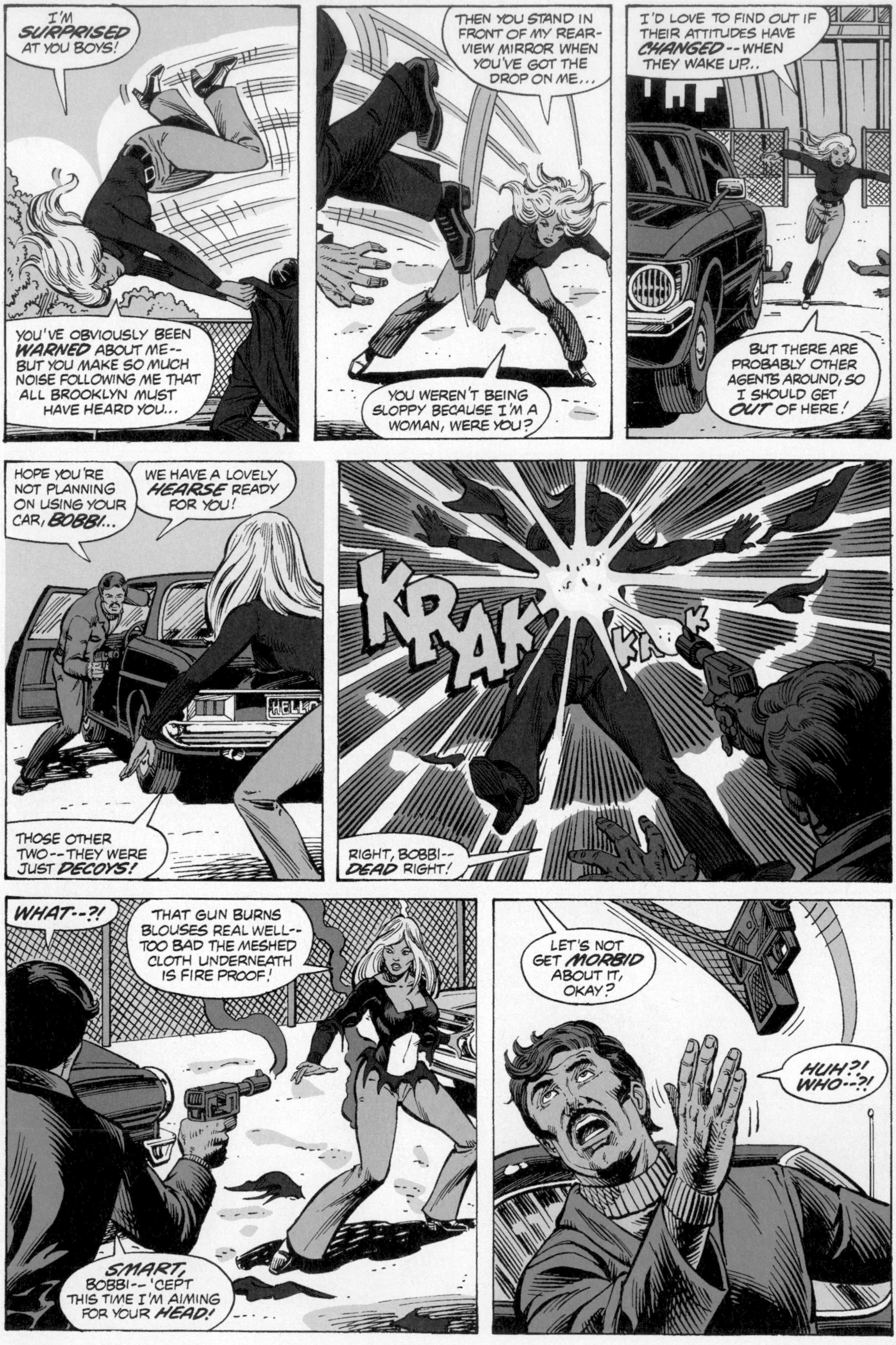

I'M SURPRISED AT YOU BOYS!
YOU'VE OBVIOUSLY BEEN WARNED ABOUT ME-- BUT YOU MAKE SO MUCH NOISE FOLLOWING ME THAT ALL BROOKLYN MUST HAVE HEARD YOU...
THEN YOU STAND IN FRONT OF MY REAR-VIEW MIRROR WHEN YOU'VE GOT THE DROP ON ME...
YOU WEREN'T BEING SLOPPY BECAUSE I'M A WOMAN, WERE YOU?
I'D LOVE TO FIND OUT IF THEIR ATTITUDES HAVE CHANGED--WHEN THEY WAKE UP...
BUT THERE ARE PROBABLY OTHER AGENTS AROUND, SO I SHOULD GET OUT OF HERE!
HOPE YOU'RE NOT PLANNING ON USING YOUR CAR, BOBBI...
WE HAVE A LOVELY HEARSE READY FOR YOU!
HELLO
THOSE OTHER TWO--THEY WERE JUST DECOYS!
KRAK
KRAK
RIGHT, BOBBI-- DEAD RIGHT!
WHAT--?!
THAT GUN BURNS BLOUSES REAL WELL-- TOO BAD THE MESHED CLOTH UNDERNEATH IS FIRE PROOF!
SMART, BOBBI-- 'CEPT THIS TIME I'M AIMING FOR YOUR HEAD!
LET'S NOT GET MORBID ABOUT IT, OKAY?
HUH?! WHO--?!

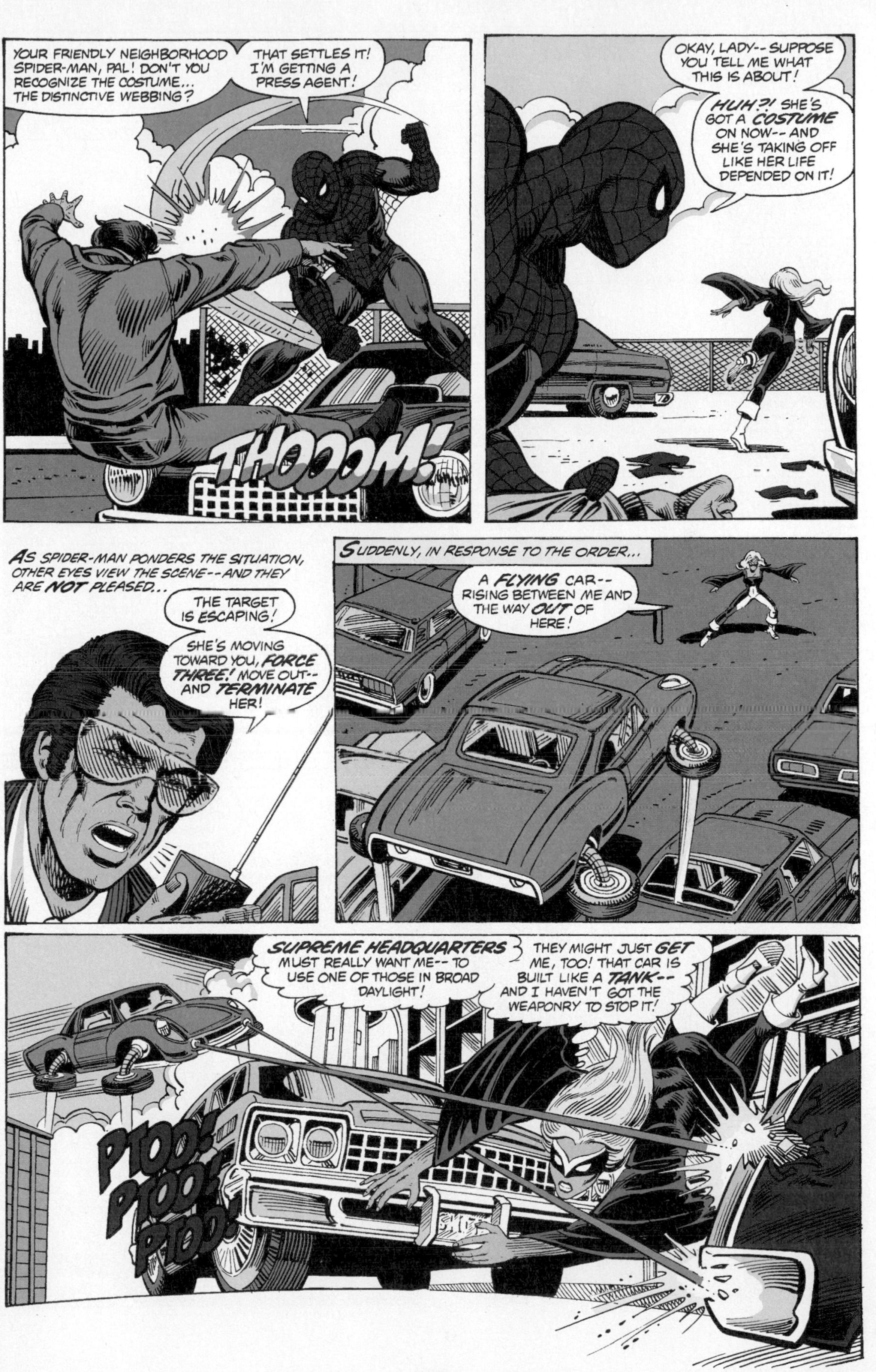

YOUR FRIENDLY NEIGHBORHOOD SPIDER-MAN, PAL! DON'T YOU RECOGNIZE THE COSTUME... THE DISTINCTIVE WEBBING?
THAT SETTLES IT! I'M GETTING A PRESS AGENT!
THOOOM!
OKAY, LADY-- SUPPOSE YOU TELL ME WHAT THIS IS ABOUT!
HUH?! SHE'S GOT A COSTUME ON NOW-- AND SHE'S TAKING OFF LIKE HER LIFE DEPENDED ON IT!
AS SPIDER-MAN PONDERS THE SITUATION, OTHER EYES VIEW THE SCENE--AND THEY ARE NOT PLEASED...
THE TARGET IS ESCAPING!
SHE'S MOVING TOWARD YOU, FORCE THREE! MOVE OUT-- AND TERMINATE HER!
SUDDENLY, IN RESPONSE TO THE ORDER...
A FLYING CAR-- RISING BETWEEN ME AND THE WAY OUT OF HERE!
SUPREME HEADQUARTERS MUST REALLY WANT ME-- TO USE ONE OF THOSE IN BROAD DAYLIGHT!
THEY MIGHT JUST GET ME, TOO! THAT CAR IS BUILT LIKE A TANK-- AND I HAVEN'T GOT THE WEAPONRY TO STOP IT!
PTOO! PTOO! PTOO!

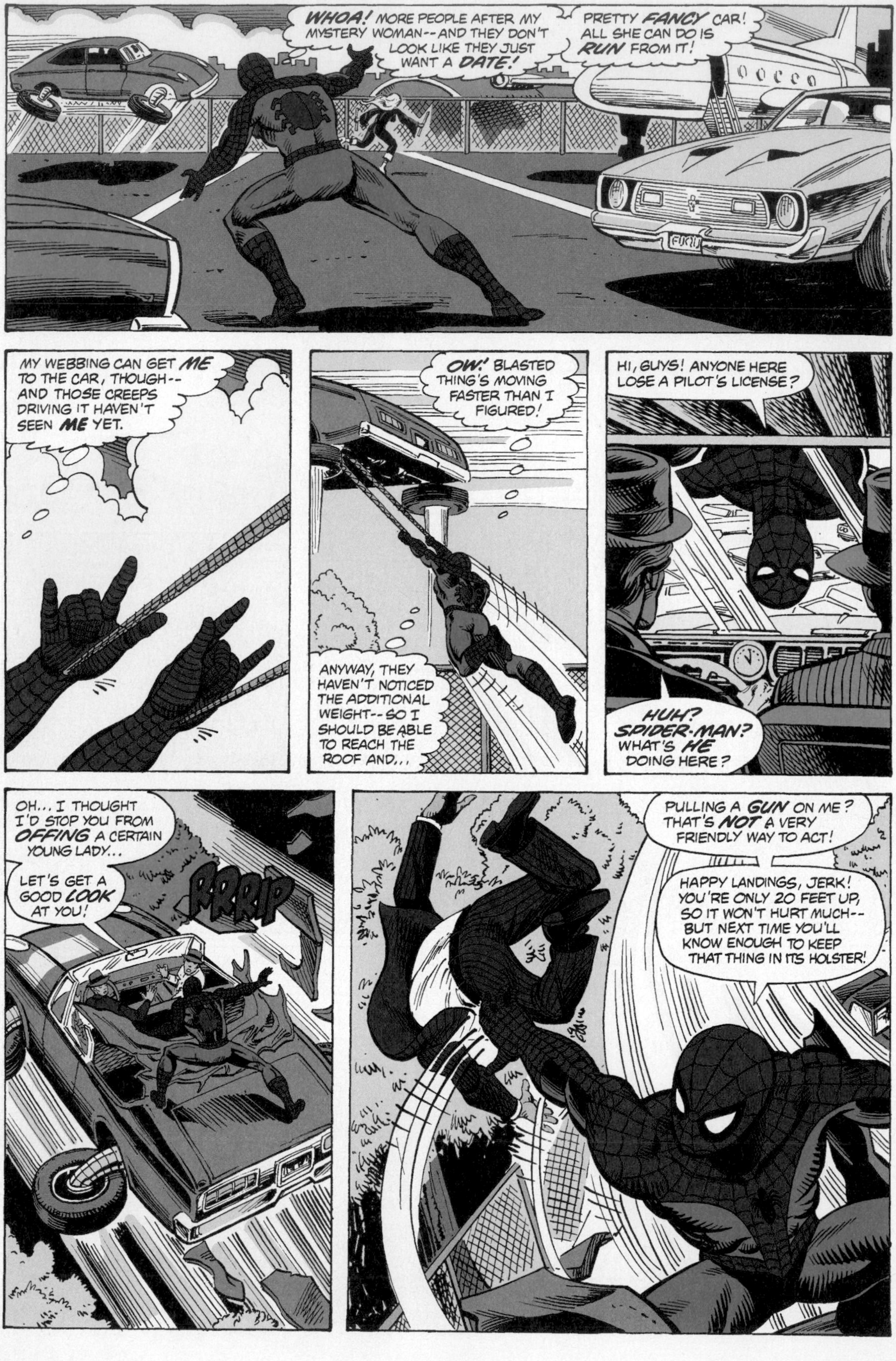
WHOA! MORE PEOPLE AFTER MY MYSTERY WOMAN--AND THEY DON'T LOOK LIKE THEY JUST WANT A DATE!
PRETTY FANCY CAR! ALL SHE CAN DO IS RUN FROM IT!
MY WEBBING CAN GET ME TO THE CAR, THOUGH--AND THOSE CREEPS DRIVING IT HAVEN'T SEEN ME YET.
OW! BLASTED THING'S MOVING FASTER THAN I FIGURED!
ANYWAY, THEY HAVEN'T NOTICED THE ADDITIONAL WEIGHT--SO I SHOULD BE ABLE TO REACH THE ROOF AND...
HI, GUYS! ANYONE HERE LOSE A PILOT'S LICENSE?
HUH? SPIDER-MAN? WHAT'S HE DOING HERE?
OH... I THOUGHT I'D STOP YOU FROM OFFING A CERTAIN YOUNG LADY...
LET'S GET A GOOD LOOK AT YOU!
RRRIP
PULLING A GUN ON ME? THAT'S NOT A VERY FRIENDLY WAY TO ACT!
HAPPY LANDINGS, JERK! YOU'RE ONLY 20 FEET UP, SO IT WON'T HURT MUCH--BUT NEXT TIME YOU'LL KNOW ENOUGH TO KEEP THAT THING IN ITS HOLSTER!

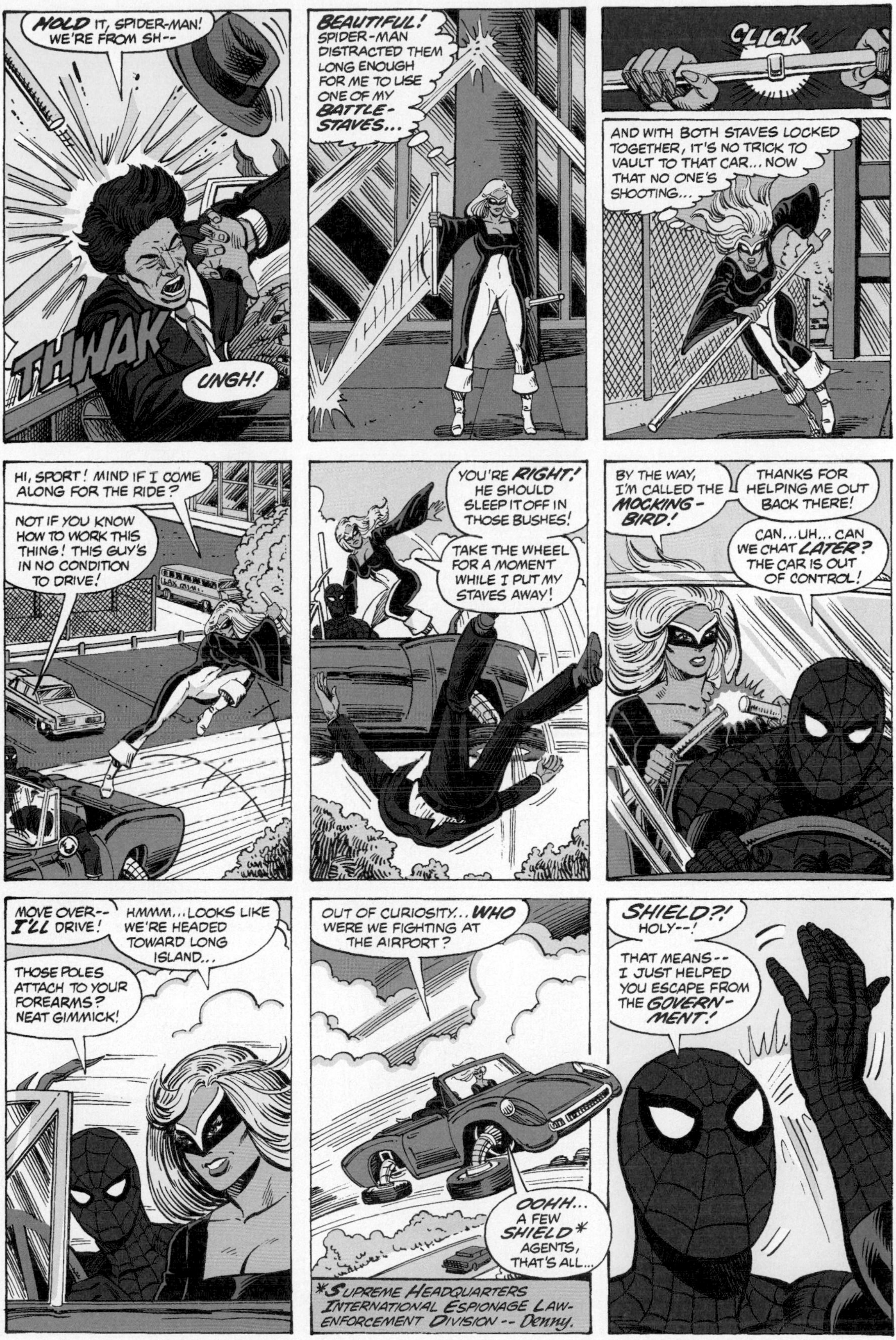
HOLD IT, SPIDER-MAN! WE'RE FROM SH--
THWAK
UNGH!
BEAUTIFUL! SPIDER-MAN DISTRACTED THEM LONG ENOUGH FOR ME TO USE ONE OF MY BATTLE-STAVES...
CLICK
AND WITH BOTH STAVES LOCKED TOGETHER, IT'S NO TRICK TO VAULT TO THAT CAR... NOW THAT NO ONE'S SHOOTING...
HI, SPORT! MIND IF I COME ALONG FOR THE RIDE?
NOT IF YOU KNOW HOW TO WORK THIS THING! THIS GUY'S IN NO CONDITION TO DRIVE!
YOU'RE RIGHT! HE SHOULD SLEEP IT OFF IN THOSE BUSHES!
TAKE THE WHEEL FOR A MOMENT WHILE I PUT MY STAVES AWAY!
BY THE WAY, I'M CALLED THE MOCKING-BIRD!
THANKS FOR HELPING ME OUT BACK THERE!
CAN...UH... CAN WE CHAT LATER? THE CAR IS OUT OF CONTROL!
MOVE OVER-- I'LL DRIVE!
HMMM... LOOKS LIKE WE'RE HEADED TOWARD LONG ISLAND...
THOSE POLES ATTACH TO YOUR FOREARMS? NEAT GIMMICK!
OUT OF CURIOSITY... WHO WERE WE FIGHTING AT THE AIRPORT?
OOHH... A FEW SHIELD* AGENTS, THAT'S ALL...
*SUPREME HEADQUARTERS INTERNATIONAL ESPIONAGE LAW-ENFORCEMENT DIVISION -- Denny.
SHIELD?! HOLY--!
THAT MEANS-- I JUST HELPED YOU ESCAPE FROM THE GOVERN-MENT!

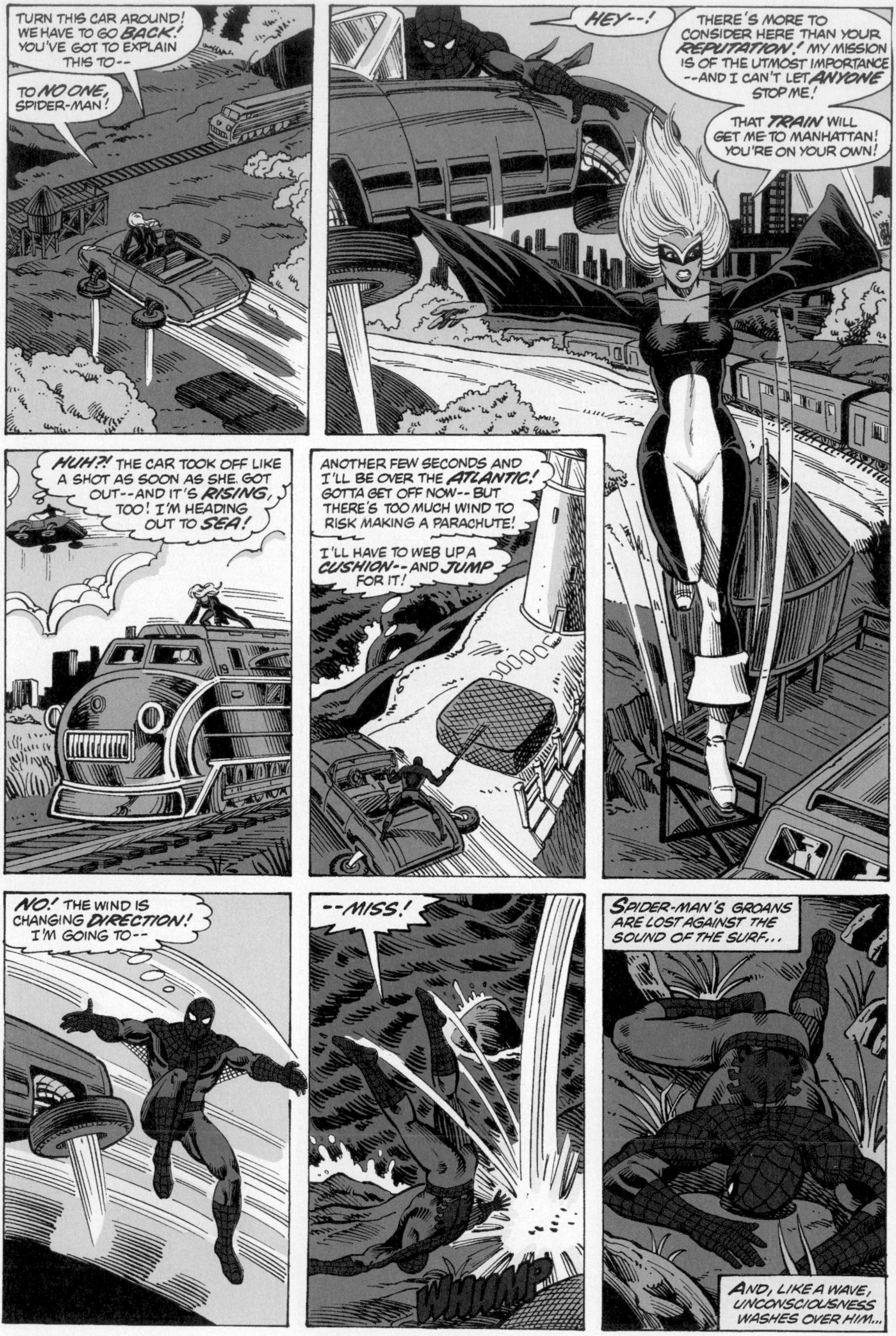
TURN THIS CAR AROUND! WE HAVE TO GO BACK! YOU'VE GOT TO EXPLAIN THIS TO--
TO NO ONE, SPIDER-MAN!
HEY--!
THERE'S MORE TO CONSIDER HERE THAN YOUR REPUTATION! MY MISSION IS OF THE UTMOST IMPORTANCE --AND I CAN'T LET ANYONE STOP ME!
THAT TRAIN WILL GET ME TO MANHATTAN! YOU'RE ON YOUR OWN!
HUH?! THE CAR TOOK OFF LIKE A SHOT AS SOON AS SHE GOT OUT--AND IT'S RISING, TOO! I'M HEADING OUT TO SEA!
ANOTHER FEW SECONDS AND I'LL BE OVER THE ATLANTIC! GOTTA GET OFF NOW--BUT THERE'S TOO MUCH WIND TO RISK MAKING A PARACHUTE!
I'LL HAVE TO WEB UP A CUSHION--AND JUMP FOR IT!
NO! THE WIND IS CHANGING DIRECTION! I'M GOING TO--
--MISS!
WHUMP
SPIDER-MAN'S GROANS ARE LOST AGAINST THE SOUND OF THE SURF...
AND, LIKE A WAVE, UNCONSCIOUSNESS WASHES OVER HIM...

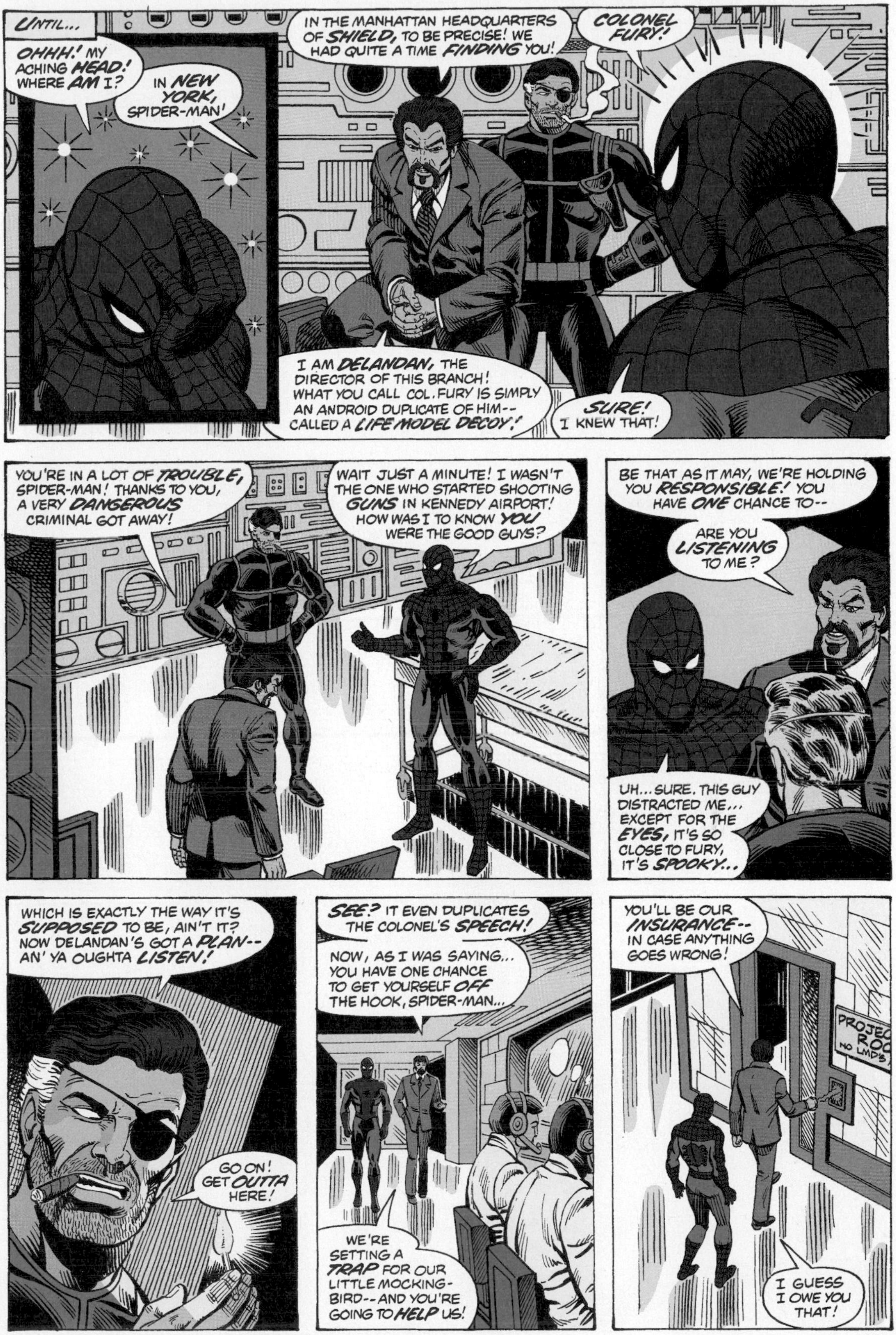
UNTIL...
OHHH! MY ACHING HEAD! WHERE AM I?
IN NEW YORK, SPIDER-MAN!
IN THE MANHATTAN HEADQUARTERS OF SHIELD, TO BE PRECISE! WE HAD QUITE A TIME FINDING YOU!
COLONEL FURY!
I AM DELANDAN, THE DIRECTOR OF THIS BRANCH! WHAT YOU CALL COL. FURY IS SIMPLY AN ANDROID DUPLICATE OF HIM-- CALLED A LIFE MODEL DECOY!
SURE! I KNEW THAT!
YOU'RE IN A LOT OF TROUBLE, SPIDER-MAN! THANKS TO YOU, A VERY DANGEROUS CRIMINAL GOT AWAY!
WAIT JUST A MINUTE! I WASN'T THE ONE WHO STARTED SHOOTING GUNS IN KENNEDY AIRPORT! HOW WAS I TO KNOW YOU WERE THE GOOD GUYS?
BE THAT AS IT MAY, WE'RE HOLDING YOU RESPONSIBLE! YOU HAVE ONE CHANCE TO--
ARE YOU LISTENING TO ME?
UH... SURE. THIS GUY DISTRACTED ME... EXCEPT FOR THE EYES, IT'S SO CLOSE TO FURY, IT'S SPOOKY...
WHICH IS EXACTLY THE WAY IT'S SUPPOSED TO BE, AIN'T IT? NOW DELANDAN'S GOT A PLAN-- AN' YA OUGHTA LISTEN!
GO ON! GET OUTTA HERE!
SEE? IT EVEN DUPLICATES THE COLONEL'S SPEECH!
NOW, AS I WAS SAYING... YOU HAVE ONE CHANCE TO GET YOURSELF OFF THE HOOK, SPIDER-MAN...
WE'RE SETTING A TRAP FOR OUR LITTLE MOCKING-BIRD--AND YOU'RE GOING TO HELP US!
YOU'LL BE OUR INSURANCE-- IN CASE ANYTHING GOES WRONG!
I GUESS I OWE YOU THAT!

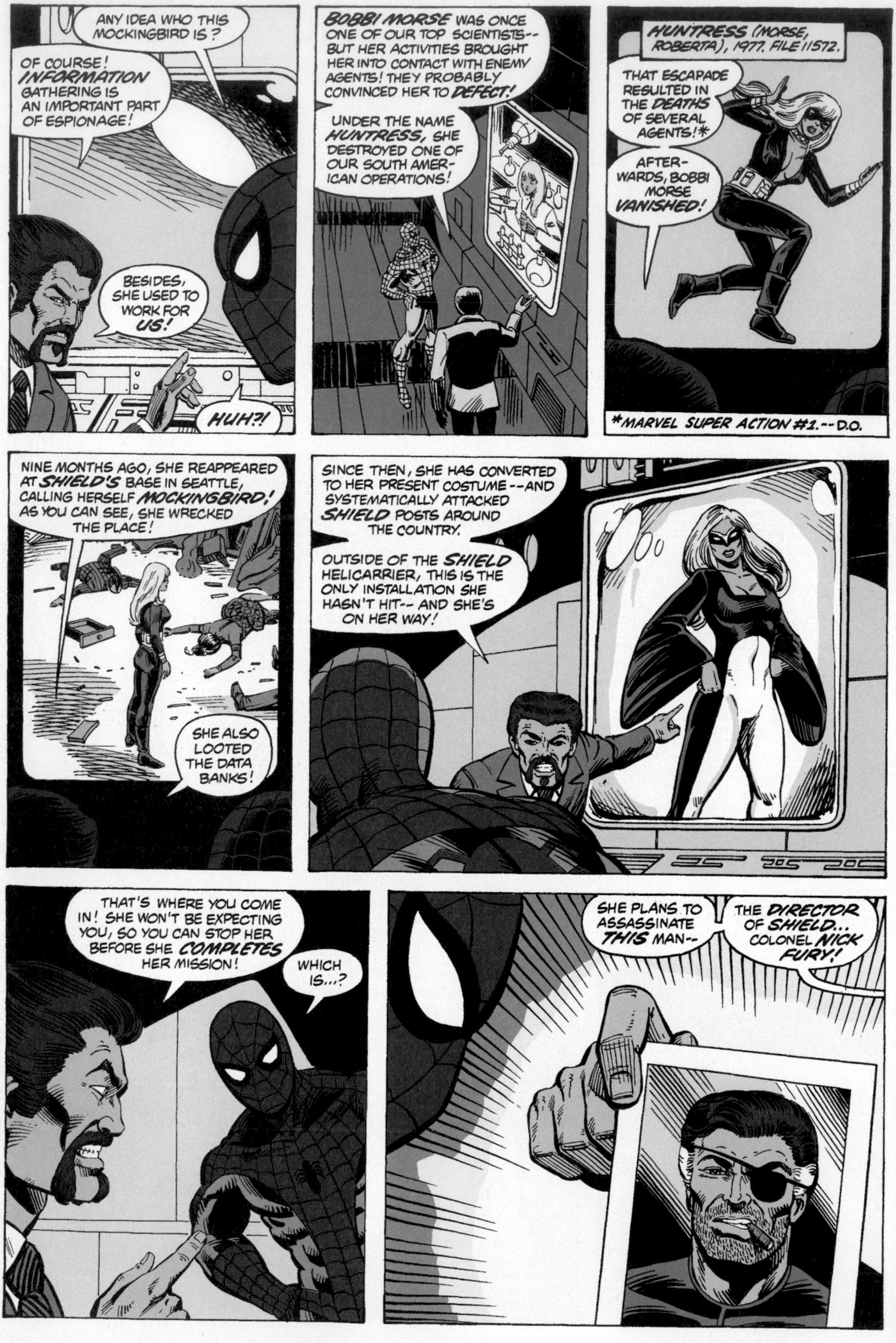
ANY IDEA WHO THIS MOCKINGBIRD IS?
OF COURSE! INFORMATION GATHERING IS AN IMPORTANT PART OF ESPIONAGE!
BESIDES, SHE USED TO WORK FOR US!
HUH?!
BOBBI MORSE WAS ONCE ONE OF OUR TOP SCIENTISTS-- BUT HER ACTIVITIES BROUGHT HER INTO CONTACT WITH ENEMY AGENTS! THEY PROBABLY CONVINCED HER TO DEFECT!
UNDER THE NAME HUNTRESS, SHE DESTROYED ONE OF OUR SOUTH AMERICAN OPERATIONS!
HUNTRESS (MORSE, ROBERTA), 1977. FILE 11572.
THAT ESCAPADE RESULTED IN THE DEATHS OF SEVERAL AGENTS!*
AFTERWARDS, BOBBI MORSE VANISHED!
*MARVEL SUPER ACTION #1.--D.O.
NINE MONTHS AGO, SHE REAPPEARED AT SHIELD'S BASE IN SEATTLE, CALLING HERSELF MOCKINGBIRD! AS YOU CAN SEE, SHE WRECKED THE PLACE!
SHE ALSO LOOTED THE DATA BANKS!
SINCE THEN, SHE HAS CONVERTED TO HER PRESENT COSTUME--AND SYSTEMATICALLY ATTACKED SHIELD POSTS AROUND THE COUNTRY.
OUTSIDE OF THE SHIELD HELICARRIER, THIS IS THE ONLY INSTALLATION SHE HASN'T HIT-- AND SHE'S ON HER WAY!
THAT'S WHERE YOU COME IN! SHE WON'T BE EXPECTING YOU, SO YOU CAN STOP HER BEFORE SHE COMPLETES HER MISSION!
WHICH IS...?
SHE PLANS TO ASSASSINATE THIS MAN--
THE DIRECTOR OF SHIELD... COLONEL NICK FURY!

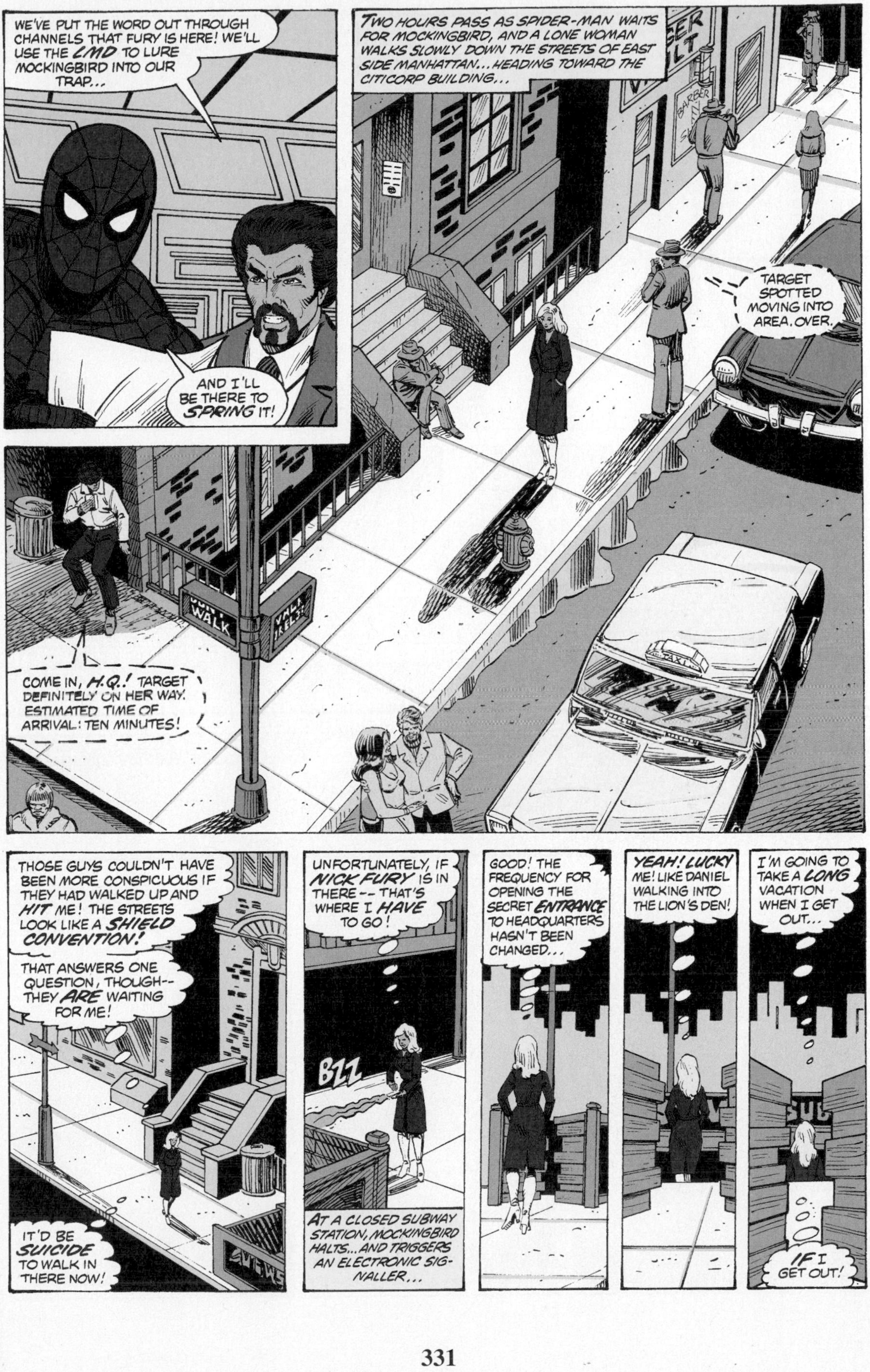
WE'VE PUT THE WORD OUT THROUGH CHANNELS THAT FURY IS HERE! WE'LL USE THE LMD TO LURE MOCKINGBIRD INTO OUR TRAP...
AND I'LL BE THERE TO SPRING IT!
TWO HOURS PASS AS SPIDER-MAN WAITS FOR MOCKINGBIRD, AND A LONE WOMAN WALKS SLOWLY DOWN THE STREETS OF EAST SIDE MANHATTAN... HEADING TOWARD THE CITICORP BUILDING...
TARGET SPOTTED MOVING INTO AREA. OVER.
COME IN, H.Q.! TARGET DEFINITELY ON HER WAY. ESTIMATED TIME OF ARRIVAL: TEN MINUTES!
WALK
TAXI
THOSE GUYS COULDN'T HAVE BEEN MORE CONSPICUOUS IF THEY HAD WALKED UP AND HIT ME! THE STREETS LOOK LIKE A SHIELD CONVENTION!
THAT ANSWERS ONE QUESTION, THOUGH-- THEY ARE WAITING FOR ME!
IT'D BE SUICIDE TO WALK IN THERE NOW!
UNFORTUNATELY, IF NICK FURY IS IN THERE -- THAT'S WHERE I HAVE TO GO!
BZZ
AT A CLOSED SUBWAY STATION, MOCKINGBIRD HALTS... AND TRIGGERS AN ELECTRONIC SIGNALLER...
GOOD! THE FREQUENCY FOR OPENING THE SECRET ENTRANCE TO HEADQUARTERS HASN'T BEEN CHANGED...
YEAH! LUCKY ME! LIKE DANIEL WALKING INTO THE LION'S DEN!
I'M GOING TO TAKE A LONG VACATION WHEN I GET OUT...
IF I GET OUT!

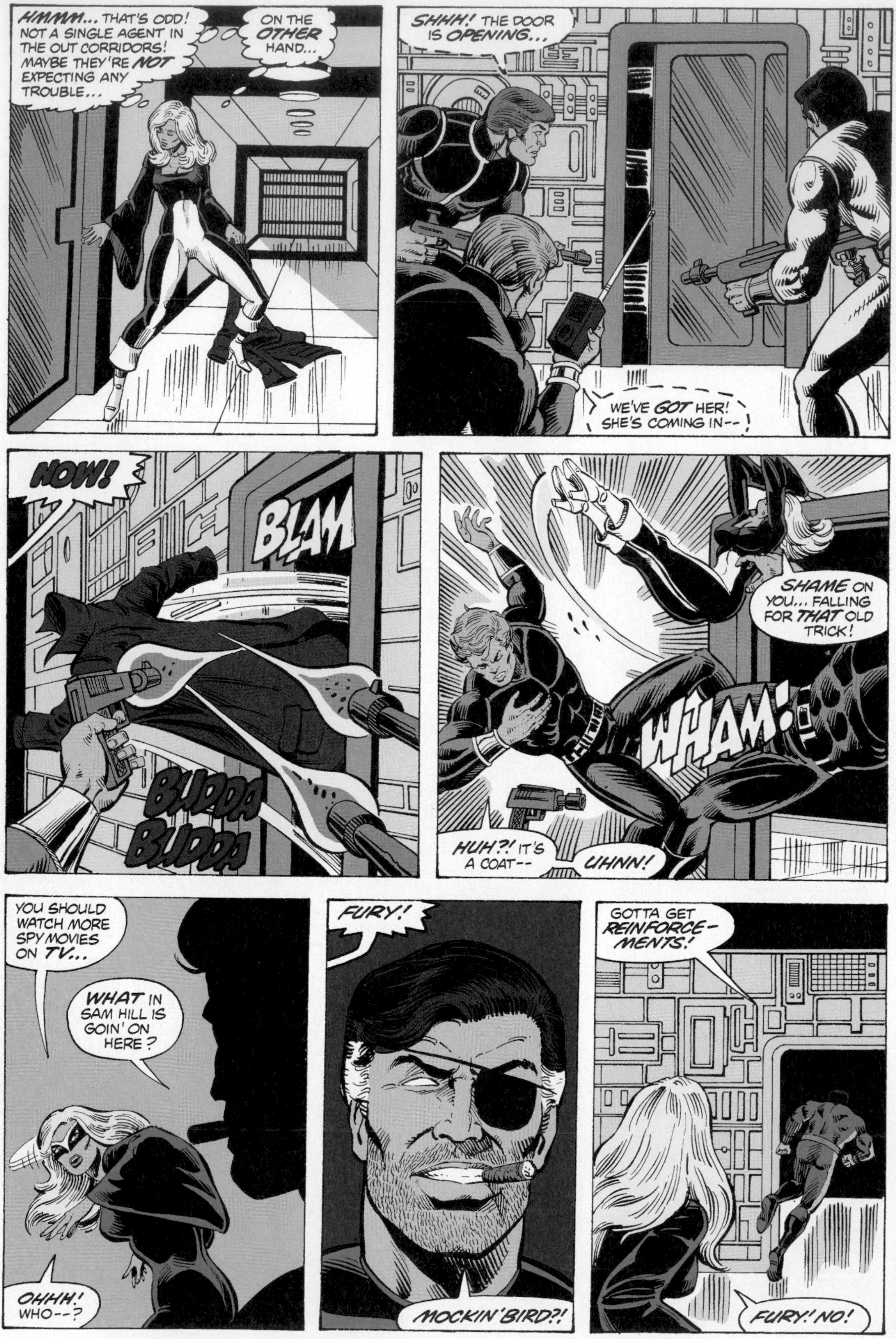
HMMM... THAT'S ODD! NOT A SINGLE AGENT IN THE OUT CORRIDORS! MAYBE THEY'RE NOT EXPECTING ANY TROUBLE...
ON THE OTHER HAND...
SHHH! THE DOOR IS OPENING...
WE'VE GOT HER! SHE'S COMING IN--
NOW!
BLAM
BUDDA BUDDA
SHAME ON YOU... FALLING FOR THAT OLD TRICK!
WHAM!
HUH?! IT'S A COAT--
UHNN!
YOU SHOULD WATCH MORE SPY MOVIES ON TV...
WHAT IN SAM HILL IS GOIN' ON HERE?
OHHH! WHO--?
FURY!
MOCKIN'BIRD?!
GOTTA GET REINFORCE-MENTS!
FURY! NO!

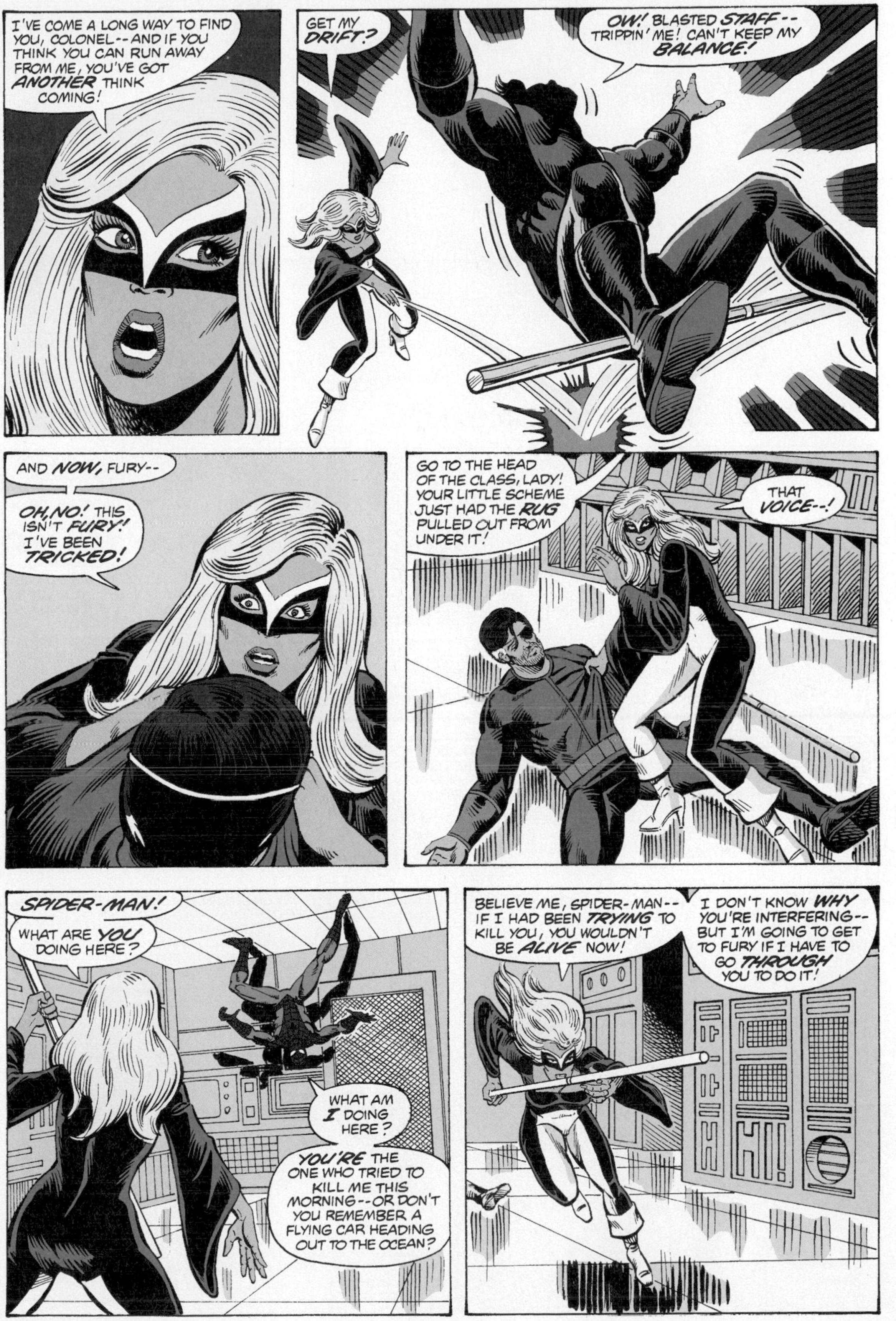
I'VE COME A LONG WAY TO FIND YOU, COLONEL--AND IF YOU THINK YOU CAN RUN AWAY FROM ME, YOU'VE GOT ANOTHER THINK COMING!
GET MY DRIFT?
OW! BLASTED STAFF-- TRIPPIN' ME! CAN'T KEEP MY BALANCE!
AND NOW, FURY--
OH, NO! THIS ISN'T FURY! I'VE BEEN TRICKED!
GO TO THE HEAD OF THE CLASS, LADY! YOUR LITTLE SCHEME JUST HAD THE RUG PULLED OUT FROM UNDER IT!
THAT VOICE--!
SPIDER-MAN!
WHAT ARE YOU DOING HERE?
WHAT AM I DOING HERE?
YOU'RE THE ONE WHO TRIED TO KILL ME THIS MORNING--OR DON'T YOU REMEMBER A FLYING CAR HEADING OUT TO THE OCEAN?
BELIEVE ME, SPIDER-MAN-- IF I HAD BEEN TRYING TO KILL YOU, YOU WOULDN'T BE ALIVE NOW!
I DON'T KNOW WHY YOU'RE INTERFERING-- BUT I'M GOING TO GET TO FURY IF I HAVE TO GO THROUGH YOU TO DO IT!

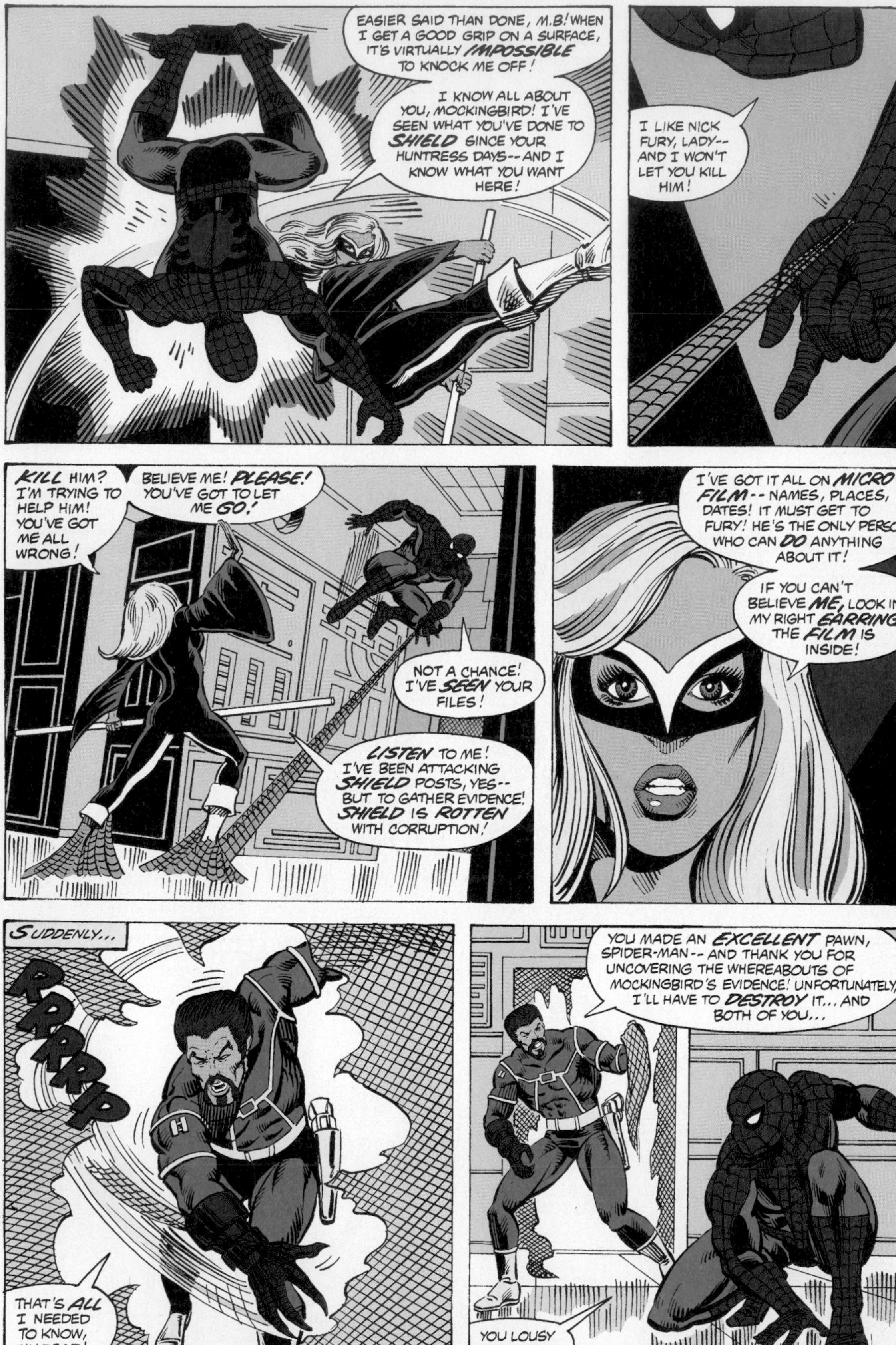
EASIER SAID THAN DONE, M.B.! WHEN I GET A GOOD GRIP ON A SURFACE, IT'S VIRTUALLY IMPOSSIBLE TO KNOCK ME OFF!
I KNOW ALL ABOUT YOU, MOCKINGBIRD! I'VE SEEN WHAT YOU'VE DONE TO SHIELD SINCE YOUR HUNTRESS DAYS--AND I KNOW WHAT YOU WANT HERE!
I LIKE NICK FURY, LADY--AND I WON'T LET YOU KILL HIM!
KILL HIM? I'M TRYING TO HELP HIM! YOU'VE GOT ME ALL WRONG!
BELIEVE ME! PLEASE! YOU'VE GOT TO LET ME GO!
NOT A CHANCE! I'VE SEEN YOUR FILES!
LISTEN TO ME! I'VE BEEN ATTACKING SHIELD POSTS, YES--BUT TO GATHER EVIDENCE! SHIELD IS ROTTEN WITH CORRUPTION!
I'VE GOT IT ALL ON MICRO-FILM--NAMES, PLACES, DATES! IT MUST GET TO FURY! HE'S THE ONLY PERSON WHO CAN DO ANYTHING ABOUT IT!
IF YOU CAN'T BELIEVE ME, LOOK IN MY RIGHT EARRING! THE FILM IS INSIDE!
SUDDENLY...
RRRRIP
THAT'S ALL I NEEDED TO KNOW, MY DEAR!
YOU MADE AN EXCELLENT PAWN, SPIDER-MAN--AND THANK YOU FOR UNCOVERING THE WHEREABOUTS OF MOCKINGBIRD'S EVIDENCE! UNFORTUNATELY, I'LL HAVE TO DESTROY IT... AND BOTH OF YOU...
YOU LOUSY CRUMB...

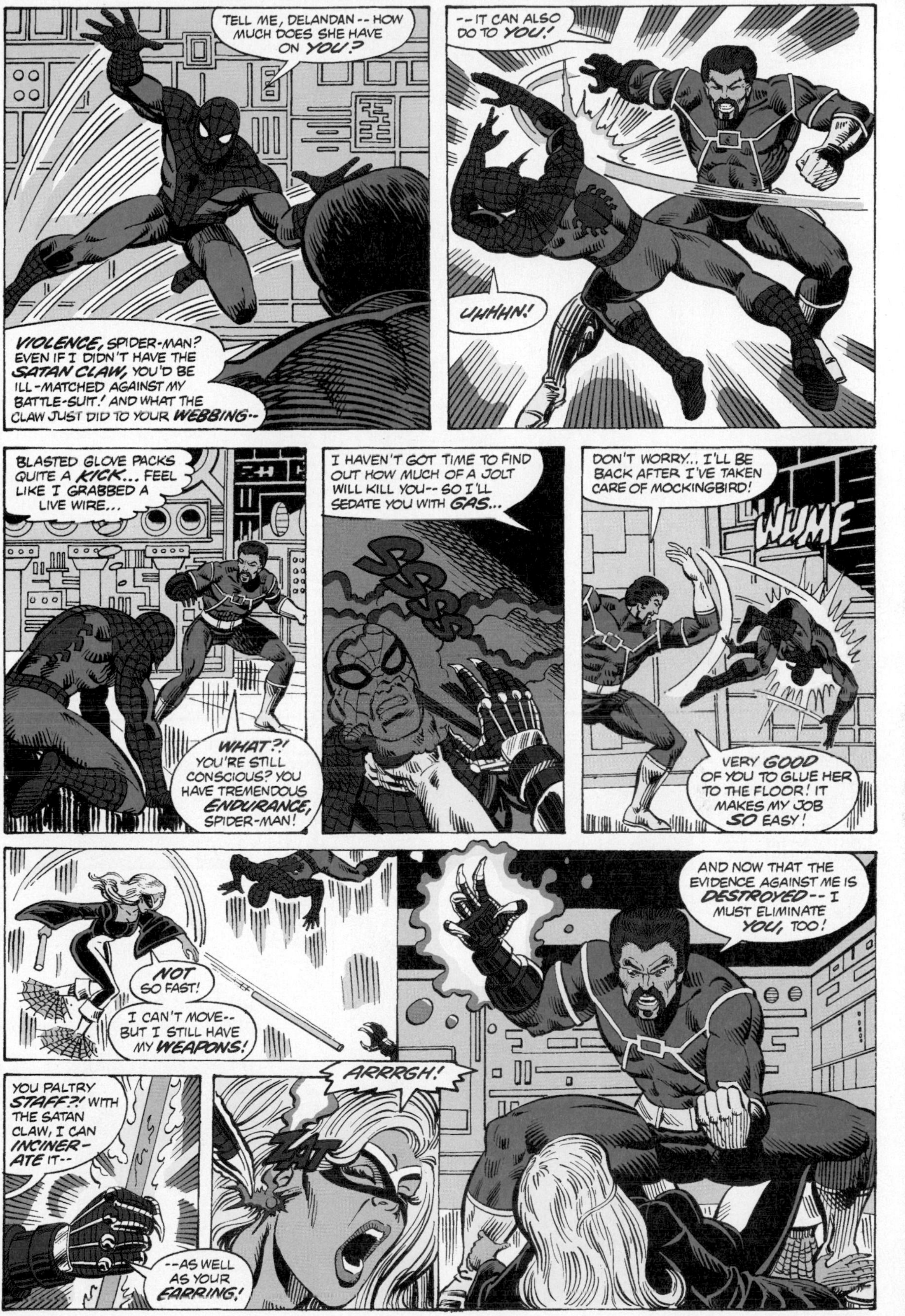
TELL ME, DELANDAN -- HOW MUCH DOES SHE HAVE ON YOU?
VIOLENCE, SPIDER-MAN? EVEN IF I DIDN'T HAVE THE SATAN CLAW, YOU'D BE ILL-MATCHED AGAINST MY BATTLE-SUIT! AND WHAT THE CLAW JUST DID TO YOUR WEBBING--
--IT CAN ALSO DO TO YOU!
UHHHN!
BLASTED GLOVE PACKS QUITE A KICK... FEEL LIKE I GRABBED A LIVE WIRE...
WHAT?! YOU'RE STILL CONSCIOUS? YOU HAVE TREMENDOUS ENDURANCE, SPIDER-MAN!
I HAVEN'T GOT TIME TO FIND OUT HOW MUCH OF A JOLT WILL KILL YOU-- SO I'LL SEDATE YOU WITH GAS...
SSSS
DON'T WORRY... I'LL BE BACK AFTER I'VE TAKEN CARE OF MOCKINGBIRD!
WUMF
VERY GOOD OF YOU TO GLUE HER TO THE FLOOR! IT MAKES MY JOB SO EASY!
NOT SO FAST!
I CAN'T MOVE-- BUT I STILL HAVE MY WEAPONS!
AND NOW THAT THE EVIDENCE AGAINST ME IS DESTROYED-- I MUST ELIMINATE YOU, TOO!
YOU PALTRY STAFF?! WITH THE SATAN CLAW, I CAN INCINER-ATE IT--
ARRRGH!
ZAT
--AS WELL AS YOUR EARRING!

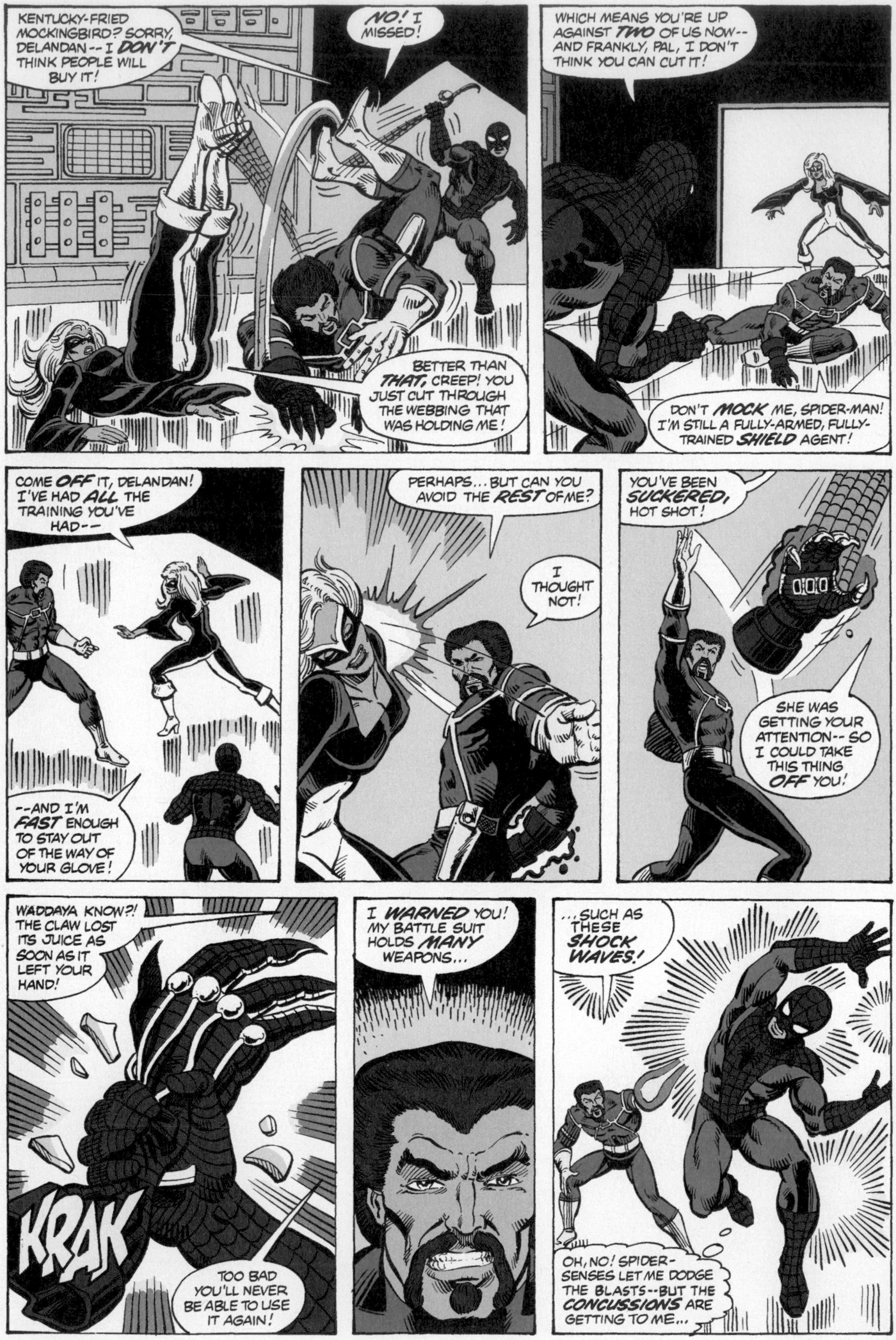
KENTUCKY-FRIED MOCKINGBIRD? SORRY, DELANDAN-- I DON'T THINK PEOPLE WILL BUY IT!
NO! I MISSED!
BETTER THAN THAT, CREEP! YOU JUST CUT THROUGH THE WEBBING THAT WAS HOLDING ME!
WHICH MEANS YOU'RE UP AGAINST TWO OF US NOW-- AND FRANKLY, PAL, I DON'T THINK YOU CAN CUT IT!
DON'T MOCK ME, SPIDER-MAN! I'M STILL A FULLY-ARMED, FULLY-TRAINED SHIELD AGENT!
COME OFF IT, DELANDAN! I'VE HAD ALL THE TRAINING YOU'VE HAD--
--AND I'M FAST ENOUGH TO STAY OUT OF THE WAY OF YOUR GLOVE!
PERHAPS... BUT CAN YOU AVOID THE REST OF ME?
I THOUGHT NOT!
YOU'VE BEEN SUCKERED, HOT SHOT!
SHE WAS GETTING YOUR ATTENTION-- SO I COULD TAKE THIS THING OFF YOU!
WADDAYA KNOW?! THE CLAW LOST ITS JUICE AS SOON AS IT LEFT YOUR HAND!
KRAK
TOO BAD YOU'LL NEVER BE ABLE TO USE IT AGAIN!
I WARNED YOU! MY BATTLE SUIT HOLDS MANY WEAPONS...
...SUCH AS THESE SHOCK WAVES!
OH, NO! SPIDER-SENSES LET ME DODGE THE BLASTS--BUT THE CONCUSSIONS ARE GETTING TO ME...

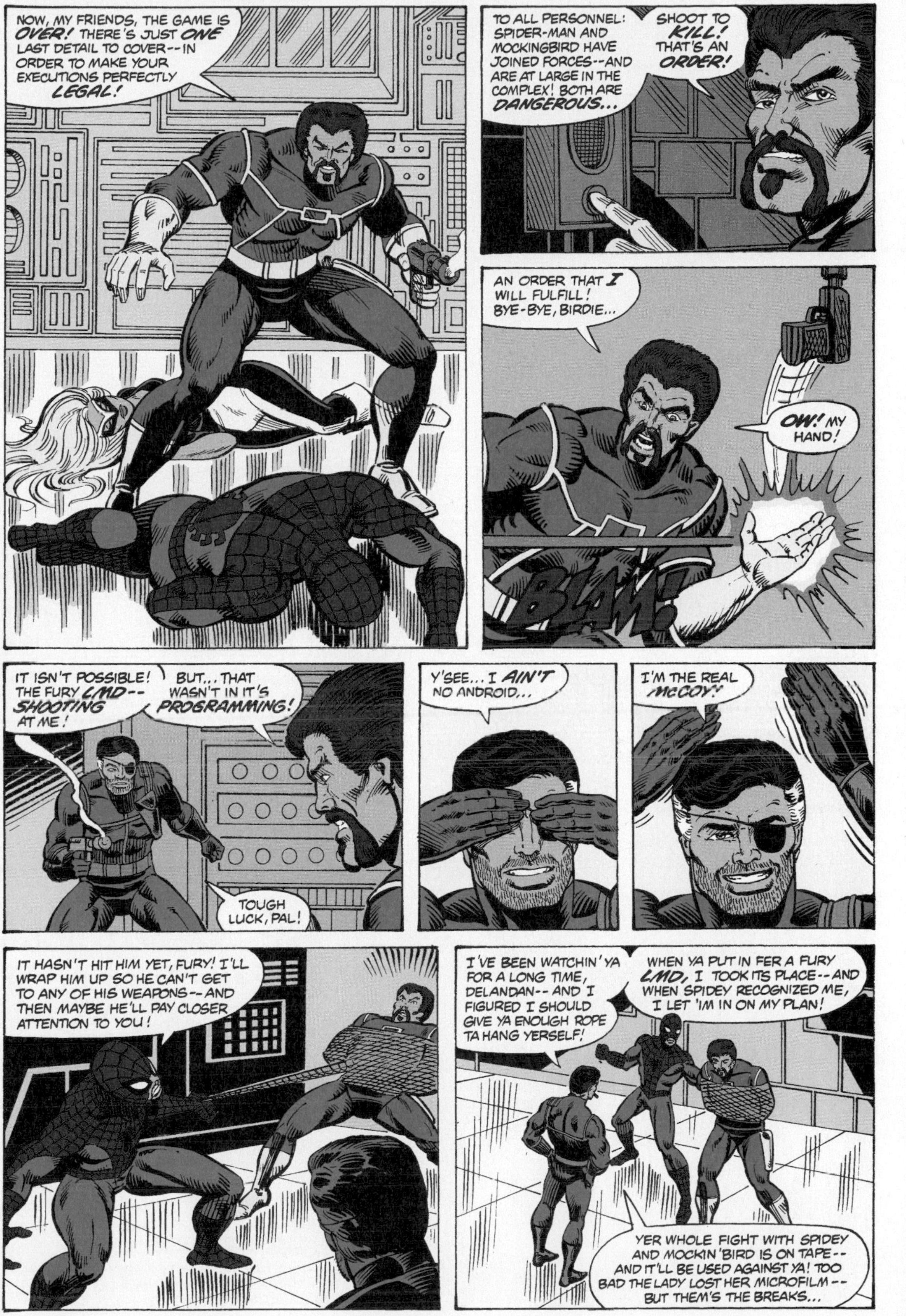

NOW, MY FRIENDS, THE GAME IS OVER! THERE'S JUST ONE LAST DETAIL TO COVER--IN ORDER TO MAKE YOUR EXECUTIONS PERFECTLY LEGAL!
TO ALL PERSONNEL: SPIDER-MAN AND MOCKINGBIRD HAVE JOINED FORCES--AND ARE AT LARGE IN THE COMPLEX! BOTH ARE DANGEROUS...
SHOOT TO KILL! THAT'S AN ORDER!
AN ORDER THAT I WILL FULFILL! BYE-BYE, BIRDIE...
OW! MY HAND!
BLAM!
IT ISN'T POSSIBLE! THE FURY LMD--SHOOTING AT ME!
BUT... THAT WASN'T IN IT'S PROGRAMMING!
TOUGH LUCK, PAL!
Y'SEE... I AIN'T NO ANDROID...
I'M THE REAL McCOY!
IT HASN'T HIT HIM YET, FURY! I'LL WRAP HIM UP SO HE CAN'T GET TO ANY OF HIS WEAPONS--AND THEN MAYBE HE'LL PAY CLOSER ATTENTION TO YOU!
I'VE BEEN WATCHIN' YA FOR A LONG TIME, DELANDAN--AND I FIGURED I SHOULD GIVE YA ENOUGH ROPE TA HANG YERSELF!
WHEN YA PUT IN FER A FURY LMD, I TOOK ITS PLACE--AND WHEN SPIDEY RECOGNIZED ME, I LET 'IM IN ON MY PLAN!
YER WHOLE FIGHT WITH SPIDEY AND MOCKIN'BIRD IS ON TAPE--AND IT'LL BE USED AGAINST YA! TOO BAD THE LADY LOST HER MICROFILM--BUT THEM'S THE BREAKS...

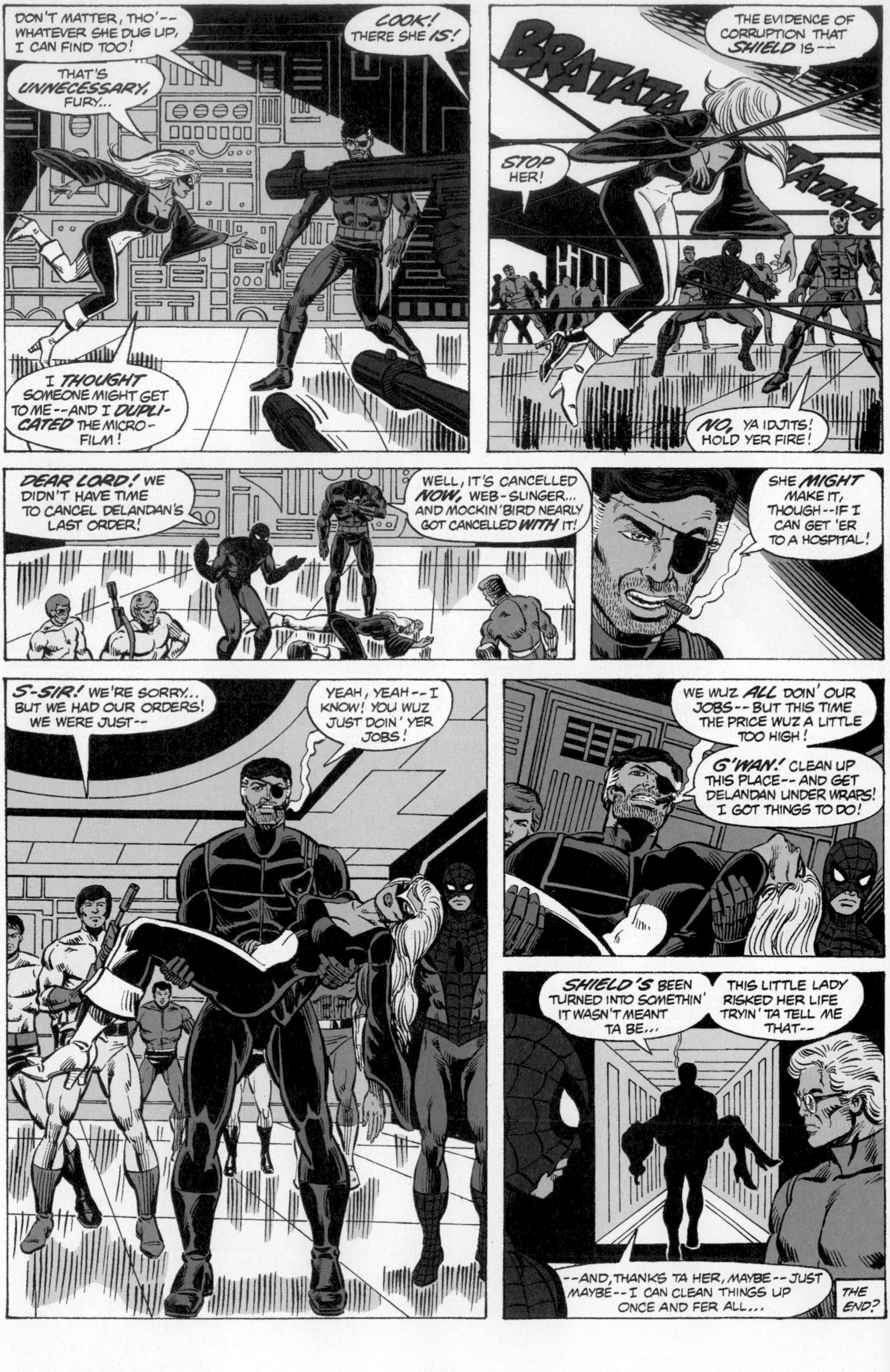
DON'T MATTER, THO'-- WHATEVER SHE DUG UP, I CAN FIND TOO!
THAT'S UNNECESSARY, FURY...
LOOK! THERE SHE IS!
I THOUGHT SOMEONE MIGHT GET TO ME--AND I DUPLICATED THE MICRO-FILM!
BRATATA TATATA
THE EVIDENCE OF CORRUPTION THAT SHIELD IS--
STOP HER!
NO, YA IDJITS! HOLD YER FIRE!
DEAR LORD! WE DIDN'T HAVE TIME TO CANCEL DELANDAN'S LAST ORDER!
WELL, IT'S CANCELLED NOW, WEB-SLINGER... AND MOCKIN'BIRD NEARLY GOT CANCELLED WITH IT!
SHE MIGHT MAKE IT, THOUGH--IF I CAN GET 'ER TO A HOSPITAL!
S-SIR! WE'RE SORRY... BUT WE HAD OUR ORDERS! WE WERE JUST--
YEAH, YEAH--I KNOW! YOU WUZ JUST DOIN' YER JOBS!
WE WUZ ALL DOIN' OUR JOBS--BUT THIS TIME THE PRICE WUZ A LITTLE TOO HIGH!
G'WAN! CLEAN UP THIS PLACE--AND GET DELANDAN UNDER WRAPS! I GOT THINGS TO DO!
SHIELD'S BEEN TURNED INTO SOMETHIN' IT WASN'T MEANT TA BE...
THIS LITTLE LADY RISKED HER LIFE TRYIN' TA TELL ME THAT--
--AND, THANKS TA HER, MAYBE--JUST MAYBE--I CAN CLEAN THINGS UP ONCE AND FER ALL...
THE END?

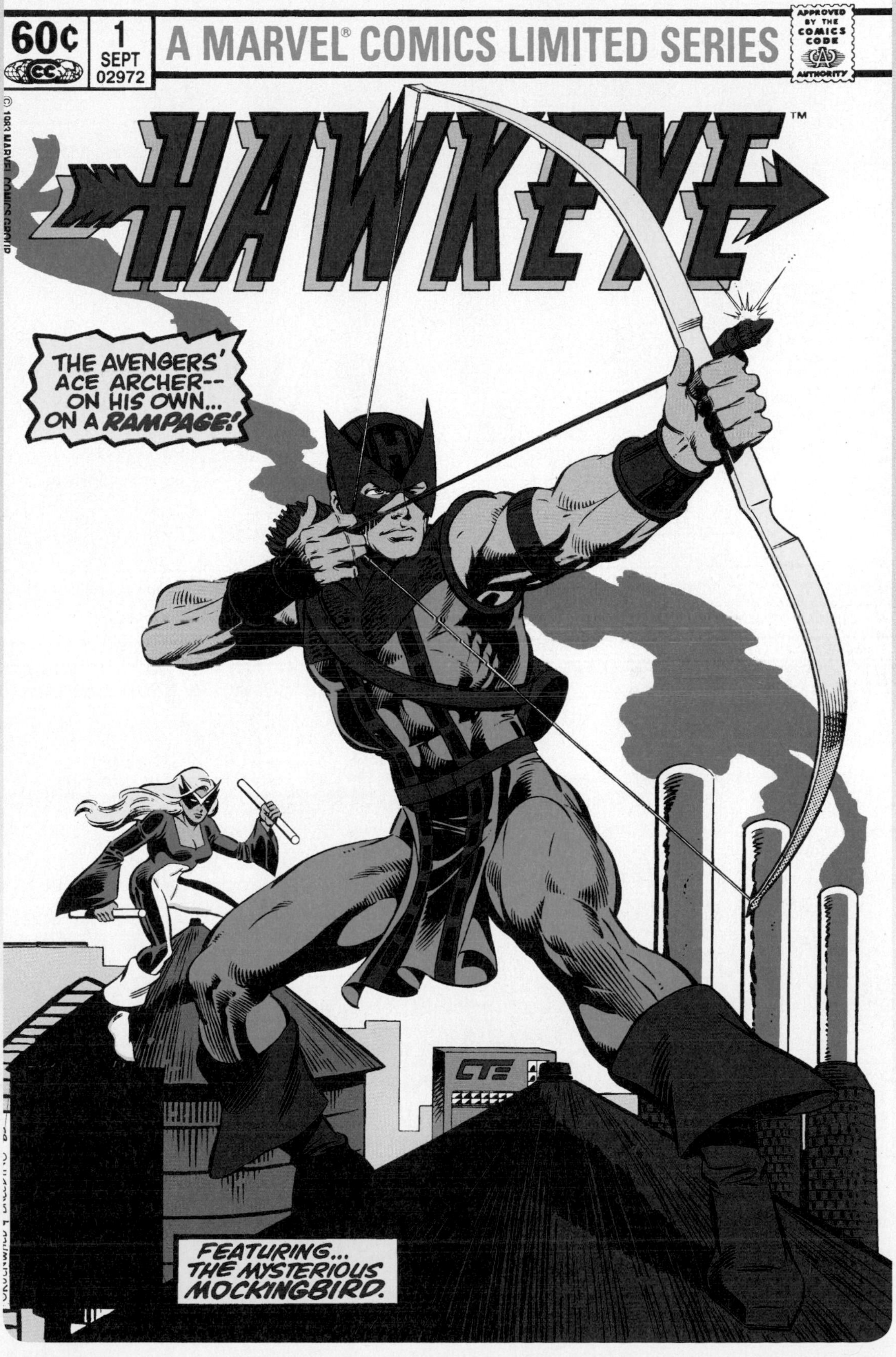
60¢
1
SEPT
02972
A MARVEL® COMICS LIMITED SERIES
APPROVED BY THE COMICS CODE AUTHORITY
© 1983 MARVEL COMICS GROUP
HAWKEYE™
THE AVENGERS' ACE ARCHER-- ON HIS OWN... ON A RAMPAGE!
FEATURING... THE MYSTERIOUS MOCKINGBIRD.

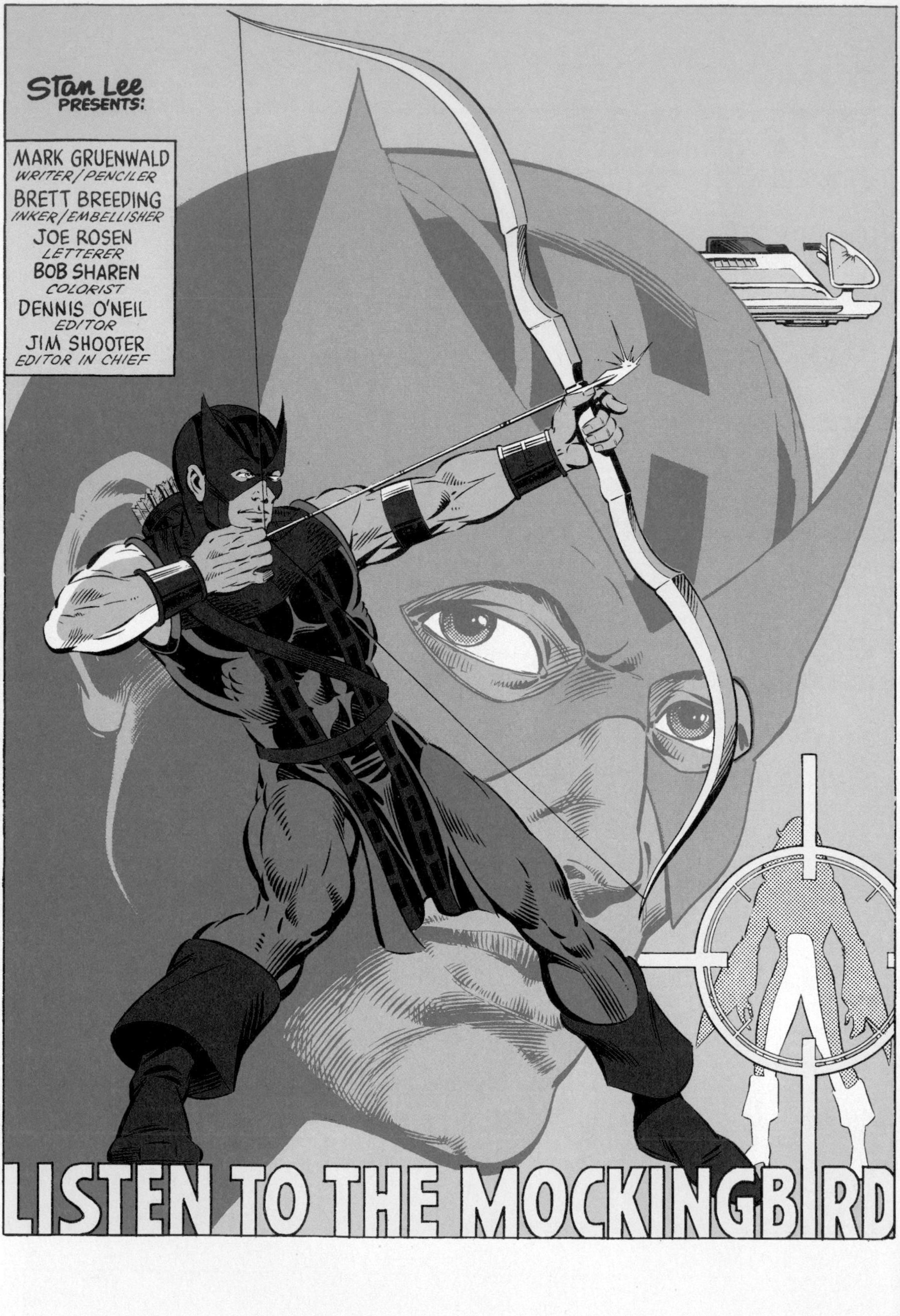
Stan Lee PRESENTS:
MARK GRUENWALD WRITER/PENCILER
BRETT BREEDING INKER/EMBELLISHER
JOE ROSEN LETTERER
BOB SHAREN COLORIST
DENNIS O'NEIL EDITOR
JIM SHOOTER EDITOR IN CHIEF
LISTEN TO THE MOCKINGBIRD

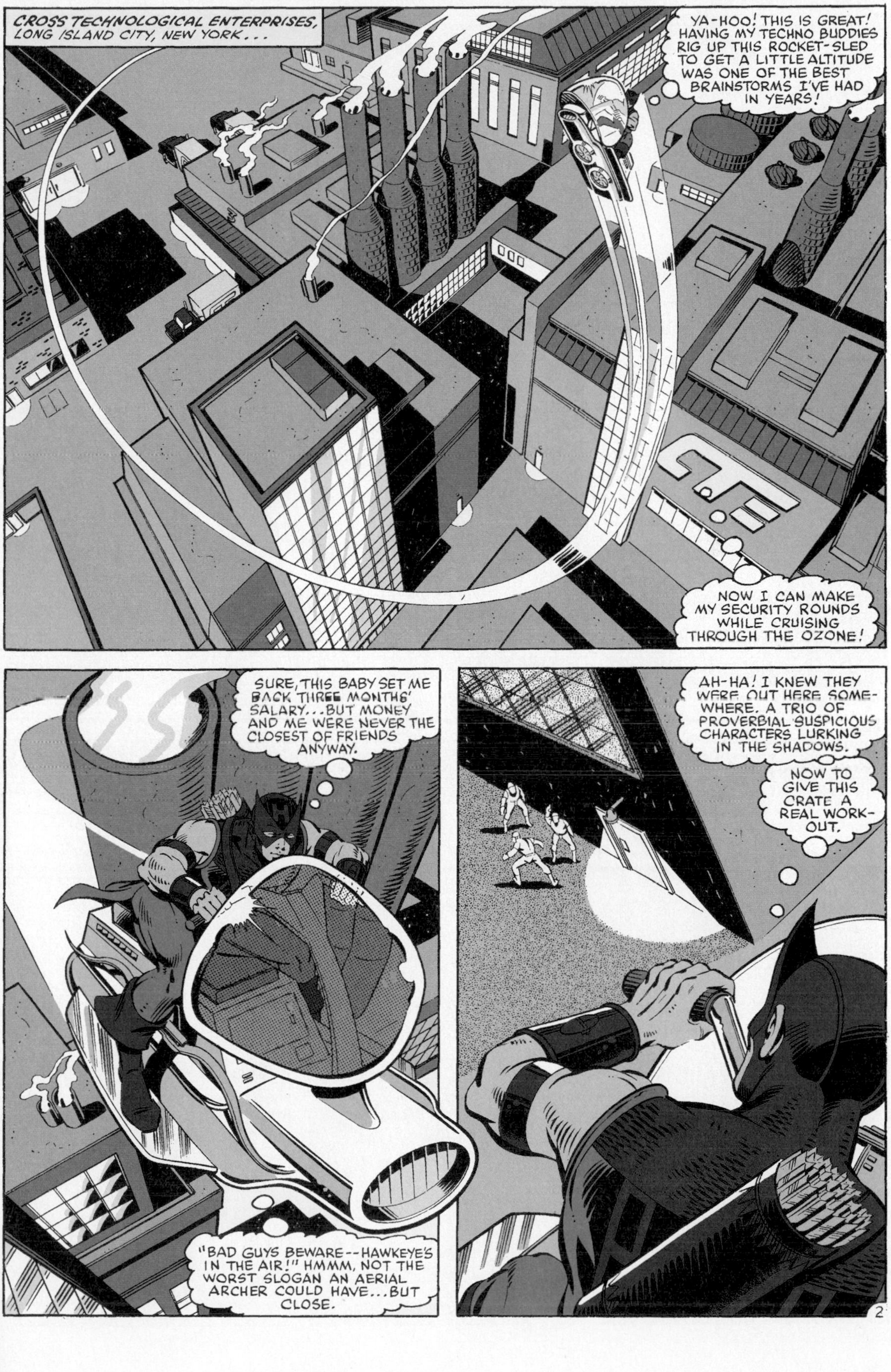
CROSS TECHNOLOGICAL ENTERPRISES, LONG ISLAND CITY, NEW YORK...
YA-HOO! THIS IS GREAT! HAVING MY TECHNO BUDDIES RIG UP THIS ROCKET-SLED TO GET A LITTLE ALTITUDE WAS ONE OF THE BEST BRAINSTORMS I'VE HAD IN YEARS!
NOW I CAN MAKE MY SECURITY ROUNDS WHILE CRUISING THROUGH THE OZONE!
SURE, THIS BABY SET ME BACK THREE MONTHS' SALARY...BUT MONEY AND ME WERE NEVER THE CLOSEST OF FRIENDS ANYWAY.
"BAD GUYS BEWARE--HAWKEYE'S IN THE AIR!" HMMM, NOT THE WORST SLOGAN AN AERIAL ARCHER COULD HAVE...BUT CLOSE.
AH-HA! I KNEW THEY WERE OUT HERE SOMEWHERE. A TRIO OF PROVERBIAL SUSPICIOUS CHARACTERS LURKING IN THE SHADOWS.
NOW TO GIVE THIS CRATE A REAL WORK-OUT.
2

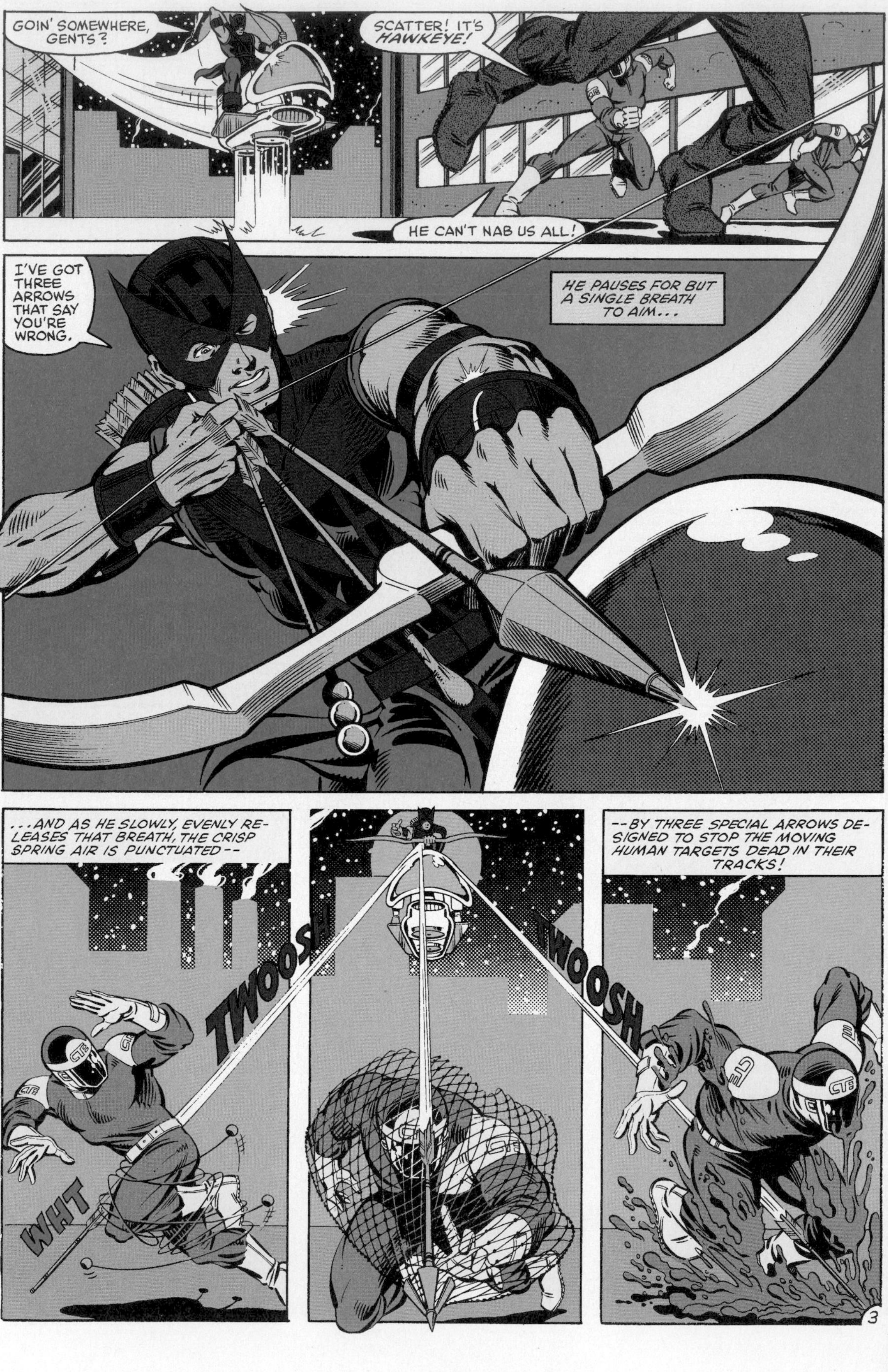

GOIN' SOMEWHERE, GENTS?
SCATTER! IT'S HAWKEYE!
HE CAN'T NAB US ALL!
I'VE GOT THREE ARROWS THAT SAY YOU'RE WRONG.
HE PAUSES FOR BUT A SINGLE BREATH TO AIM...
...AND AS HE SLOWLY, EVENLY RELEASES THAT BREATH, THE CRISP SPRING AIR IS PUNCTUATED--
TWOOSH
WHT
TWOOSH
TWOOSH
--BY THREE SPECIAL ARROWS DESIGNED TO STOP THE MOVING HUMAN TARGETS DEAD IN THEIR TRACKS!
3

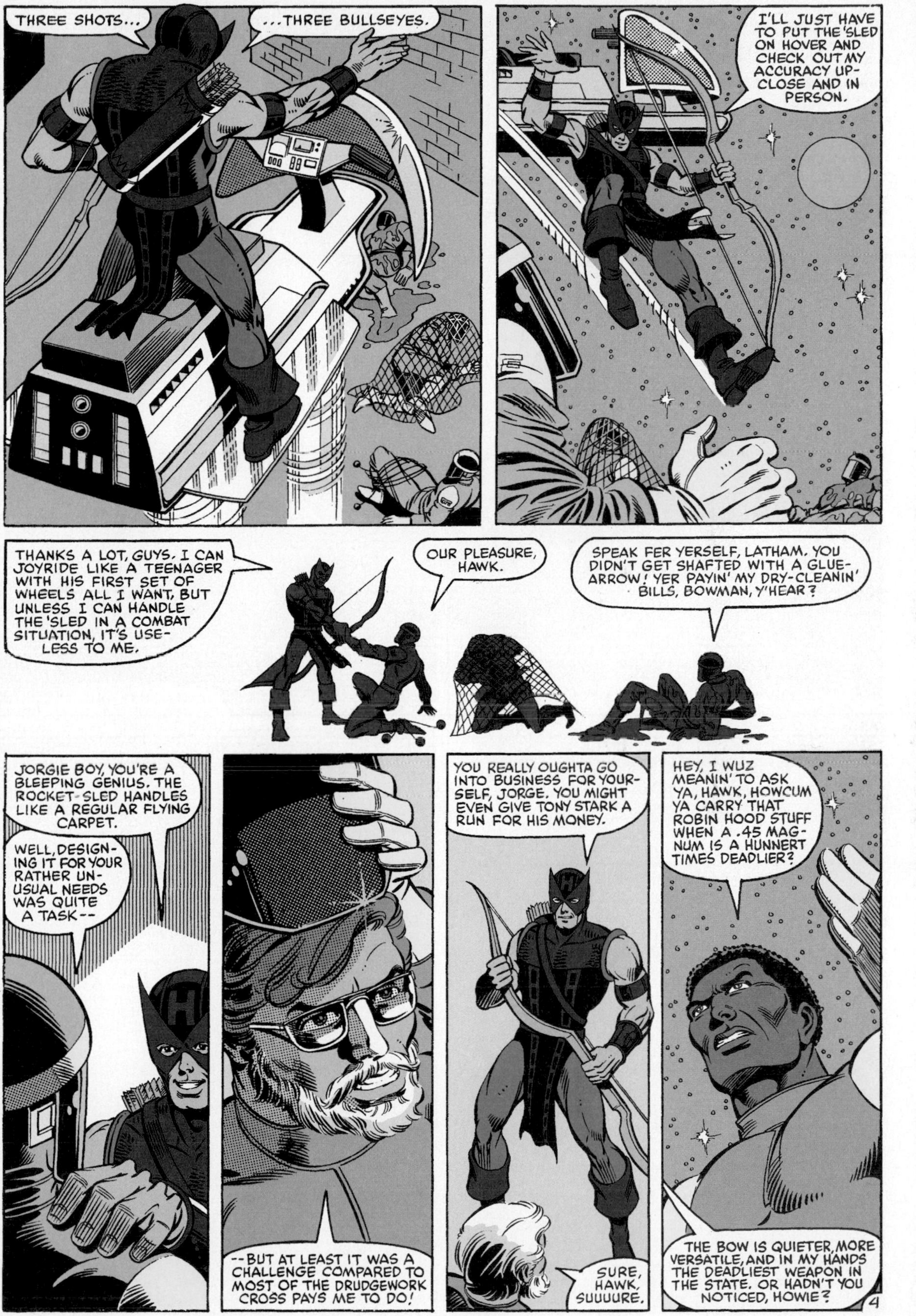
THREE SHOTS...
...THREE BULLSEYES.
I'LL JUST HAVE TO PUT THE 'SLED ON HOVER AND CHECK OUT MY ACCURACY UP-CLOSE AND IN PERSON.
THANKS A LOT, GUYS. I CAN JOYRIDE LIKE A TEENAGER WITH HIS FIRST SET OF WHEELS ALL I WANT, BUT UNLESS I CAN HANDLE THE 'SLED IN A COMBAT SITUATION, IT'S USE-LESS TO ME.
OUR PLEASURE, HAWK.
SPEAK FER YERSELF, LATHAM. YOU DIDN'T GET SHAFTED WITH A GLUE-ARROW! YER PAYIN' MY DRY-CLEANIN' BILLS, BOWMAN, Y'HEAR?
JORGIE BOY, YOU'RE A BLEEPING GENIUS. THE ROCKET-SLED HANDLES LIKE A REGULAR FLYING CARPET.
WELL, DESIGNING IT FOR YOUR RATHER UN-USUAL NEEDS WAS QUITE A TASK--
--BUT AT LEAST IT WAS A CHALLENGE COMPARED TO MOST OF THE DRUDGEWORK CROSS PAYS ME TO DO!
YOU REALLY OUGHTA GO INTO BUSINESS FOR YOUR-SELF, JORGE. YOU MIGHT EVEN GIVE TONY STARK A RUN FOR HIS MONEY.
SURE, HAWK, SUUUURE.
HEY, I WUZ MEANIN' TO ASK YA, HAWK, HOWCUM YA CARRY THAT ROBIN HOOD STUFF WHEN A .45 MAG-NUM IS A HUNNERT TIMES DEADLIER?
THE BOW IS QUIETER, MORE VERSATILE, AND IN MY HANDS THE DEADLIEST WEAPON IN THE STATE. OR HADN'T YOU NOTICED, HOWIE?
4

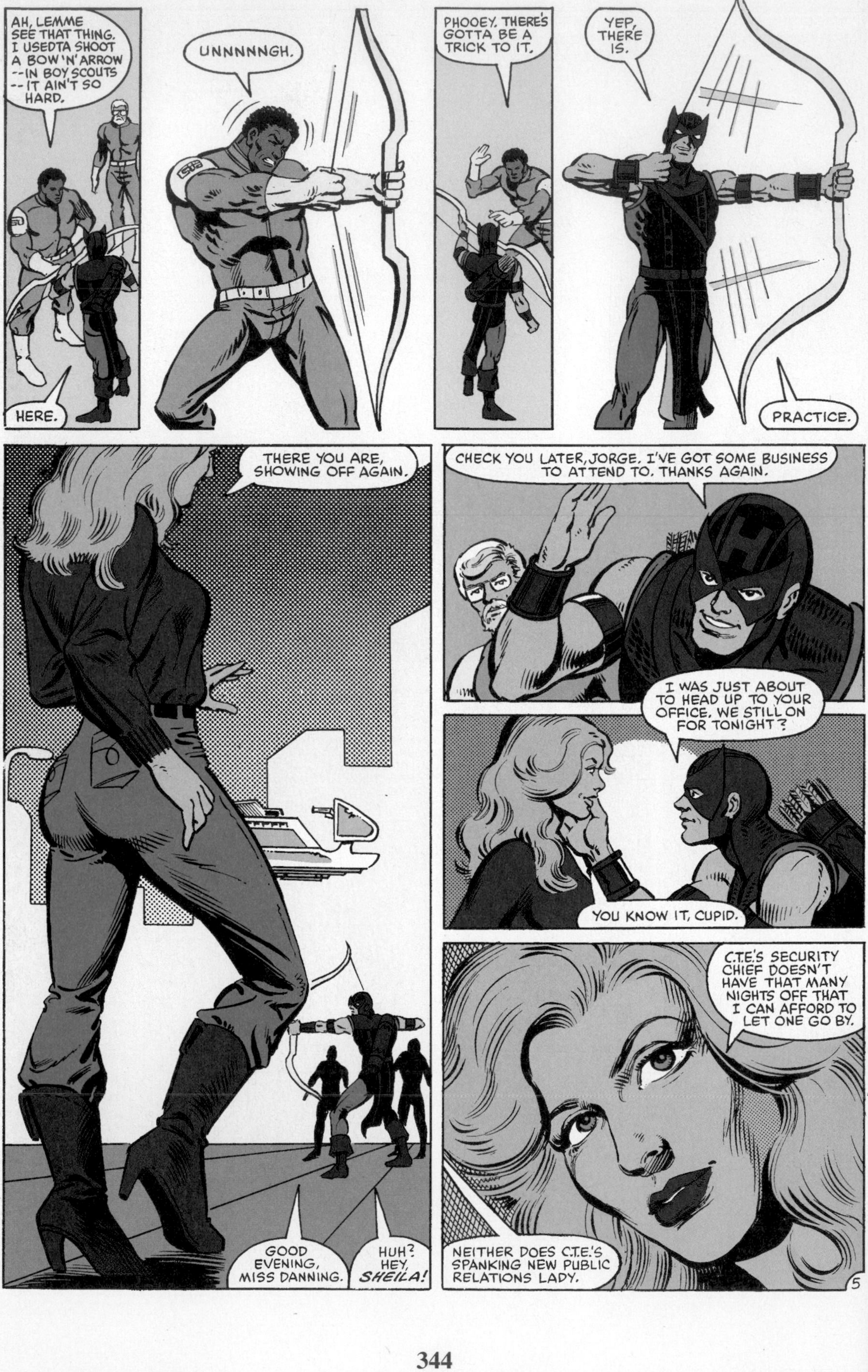
AH, LEMME SEE THAT THING. I USEDTA SHOOT A BOW 'N' ARROW --IN BOY SCOUTS --IT AIN'T SO HARD.
HERE.
UNNNNNGH.
PHOOEY. THERE'S GOTTA BE A TRICK TO IT.
YEP, THERE IS.
PRACTICE.
THERE YOU ARE, SHOWING OFF AGAIN.
GOOD EVENING, MISS DANNING.
HUH? HEY, SHEILA!
CHECK YOU LATER, JORGE. I'VE GOT SOME BUSINESS TO ATTEND TO. THANKS AGAIN.
I WAS JUST ABOUT TO HEAD UP TO YOUR OFFICE. WE STILL ON FOR TONIGHT?
YOU KNOW IT, CUPID.
C.T.E.'S SECURITY CHIEF DOESN'T HAVE THAT MANY NIGHTS OFF THAT I CAN AFFORD TO LET ONE GO BY.
NEITHER DOES C.T.E.'S SPANKING NEW PUBLIC RELATIONS LADY.
5

SO LET'S GET TO IT.

MILADY, YOUR CARRIAGE AWAITS.

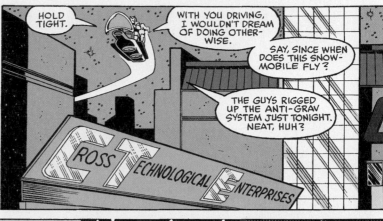

HOLD TIGHT.

WITH YOU DRIVING, I WOULDN'T DREAM OF DOING OTHERWISE.

SAY, SINCE WHEN DOES THIS SNOWMOBILE FLY?

THE GUYS RIGGED UP THE ANTI-GRAV SYSTEM JUST TONIGHT. NEAT, HUH?

CROSS TECHNOLOGICAL ENTERPRISES

SOON, CROSSING THE EAST RIVER INTO MANHATTAN...

MAN, THIS IS THE LIFE! A RIDICULOUSLY HIGH-PAYING JOB, A FAST MACHINE BETWEEN MY LEGS, AND A FOXY LADY WHO'S NUTS ABOUT ME. WHAT MORE COULD A GUY WANT?

UNTIL SHEILA CAME ALONG, I THOUGHT I WAS PUT ON THIS WORLD FOR WOMEN TO DUMP ON.

WOMEN... LIKE THE BLACK WIDOW AND SCARLET WITCH. NO MATTER WHAT I DID, I JUST COULDN'T GET THEM TO CARE FOR ME LIKE I DID FOR THEM.

SHEILA'S DIFFERENT.

EVEN THOUGH WE'VE BEEN SEEING EACH OTHER FOR ONLY A MONTH, WHAT WE HAVE IS SPECIAL, REAL, LIKE NOTHING I'VE EVER KNOWN.

ATTENTION, PASSENGERS, THANK YOU FOR FLYING HAWK AIR. WE'LL BE ARRIVING AT CLINT BARTON'S BACHELOR PAD IN FIVE SECONDS.

6

GREAT MACHINE, ISN'T IT?

I MAY GET USED TO IT.

AFTER YOU, MADEMOISELLE...

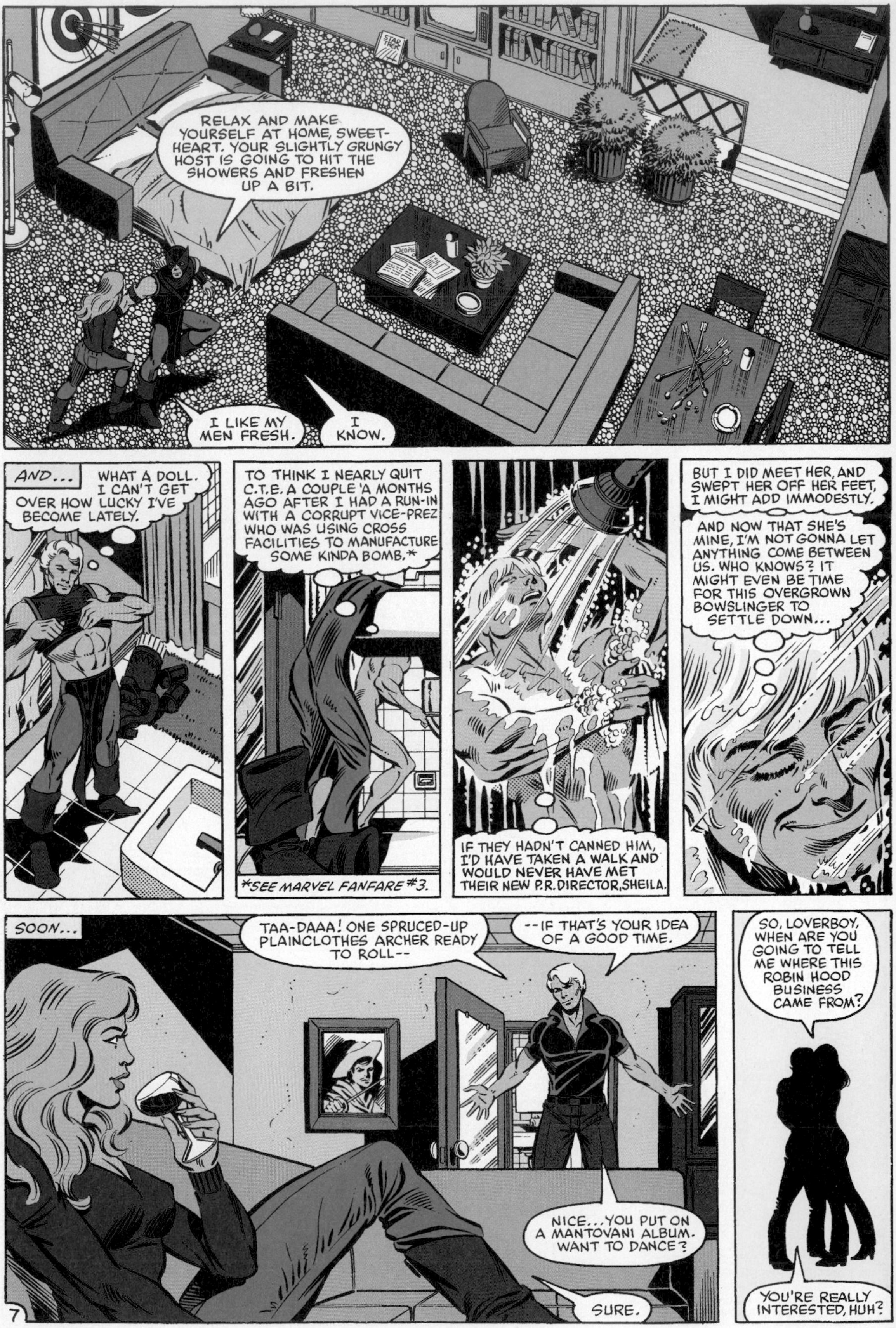
RELAX AND MAKE YOURSELF AT HOME, SWEETHEART. YOUR SLIGHTLY GRUNGY HOST IS GOING TO HIT THE SHOWERS AND FRESHEN UP A BIT.
I LIKE MY MEN FRESH.
I KNOW.
AND...
WHAT A DOLL. I CAN'T GET OVER HOW LUCKY I'VE BECOME LATELY.
TO THINK I NEARLY QUIT C.T.E. A COUPLE 'A MONTHS AGO AFTER I HAD A RUN-IN WITH A CORRUPT VICE-PREZ WHO WAS USING CROSS FACILITIES TO MANUFACTURE SOME KINDA BOMB.*
*SEE MARVEL FANFARE #3.
IF THEY HADN'T CANNED HIM, I'D HAVE TAKEN A WALK AND WOULD NEVER HAVE MET THEIR NEW P.R. DIRECTOR, SHEILA.
BUT I DID MEET HER, AND SWEPT HER OFF HER FEET, I MIGHT ADD IMMODESTLY.
AND NOW THAT SHE'S MINE, I'M NOT GONNA LET ANYTHING COME BETWEEN US. WHO KNOWS? IT MIGHT EVEN BE TIME FOR THIS OVERGROWN BOWSLINGER TO SETTLE DOWN...
SOON...
TAA-DAAA! ONE SPRUCED-UP PLAINCLOTHES ARCHER READY TO ROLL--
--IF THAT'S YOUR IDEA OF A GOOD TIME.
NICE... YOU PUT ON A MANTOVANI ALBUM. WANT TO DANCE?
SURE.
7
SO, LOVERBOY, WHEN ARE YOU GOING TO TELL ME WHERE THIS ROBIN HOOD BUSINESS CAME FROM?
YOU'RE REALLY INTERESTED, HUH?

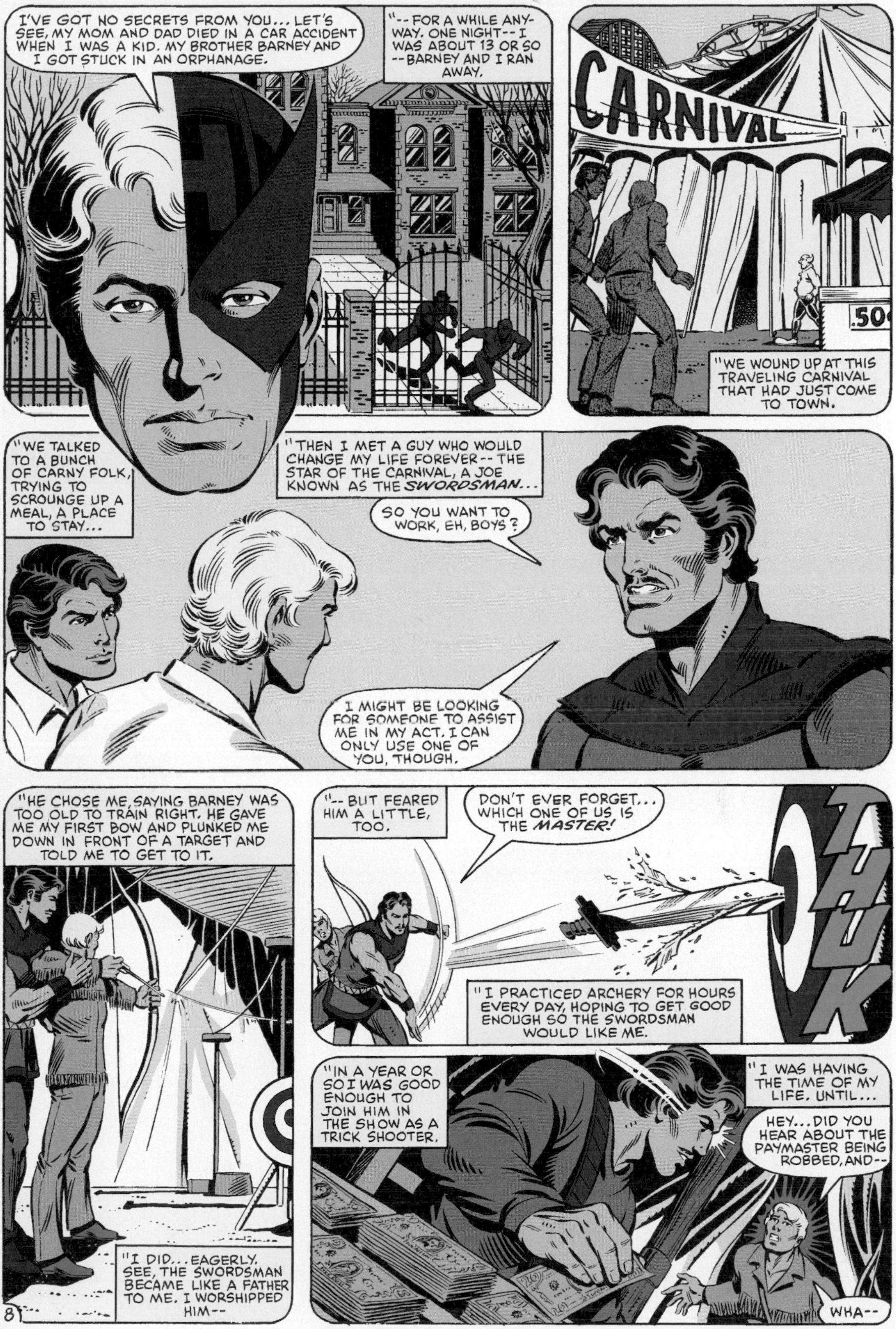
I'VE GOT NO SECRETS FROM YOU... LET'S SEE, MY MOM AND DAD DIED IN A CAR ACCIDENT WHEN I WAS A KID. MY BROTHER BARNEY AND I GOT STUCK IN AN ORPHANAGE.
"--FOR A WHILE ANYWAY. ONE NIGHT--I WAS ABOUT 13 OR SO --BARNEY AND I RAN AWAY.
CARNIVAL
.50
"WE WOUND UP AT THIS TRAVELING CARNIVAL THAT HAD JUST COME TO TOWN.
"WE TALKED TO A BUNCH OF CARNY FOLK, TRYING TO SCROUNGE UP A MEAL, A PLACE TO STAY...
"THEN I MET A GUY WHO WOULD CHANGE MY LIFE FOREVER--THE STAR OF THE CARNIVAL, A JOE KNOWN AS THE SWORDSMAN...
SO YOU WANT TO WORK, EH, BOYS?
I MIGHT BE LOOKING FOR SOMEONE TO ASSIST ME IN MY ACT. I CAN ONLY USE ONE OF YOU, THOUGH.
"HE CHOSE ME, SAYING BARNEY WAS TOO OLD TO TRAIN RIGHT. HE GAVE ME MY FIRST BOW AND PLUNKED ME DOWN IN FRONT OF A TARGET AND TOLD ME TO GET TO IT.
"I DID... EAGERLY. SEE, THE SWORDSMAN BECAME LIKE A FATHER TO ME. I WORSHIPPED HIM--
8
"--BUT FEARED HIM A LITTLE, TOO.
DON'T EVER FORGET... WHICH ONE OF US IS THE MASTER!
THUK
"I PRACTICED ARCHERY FOR HOURS EVERY DAY, HOPING TO GET GOOD ENOUGH SO THE SWORDSMAN WOULD LIKE ME.
"IN A YEAR OR SO I WAS GOOD ENOUGH TO JOIN HIM IN THE SHOW AS A TRICK SHOOTER.
"I WAS HAVING THE TIME OF MY LIFE. UNTIL...
HEY... DID YOU HEAR ABOUT THE PAYMASTER BEING ROBBED, AND--
WHA--

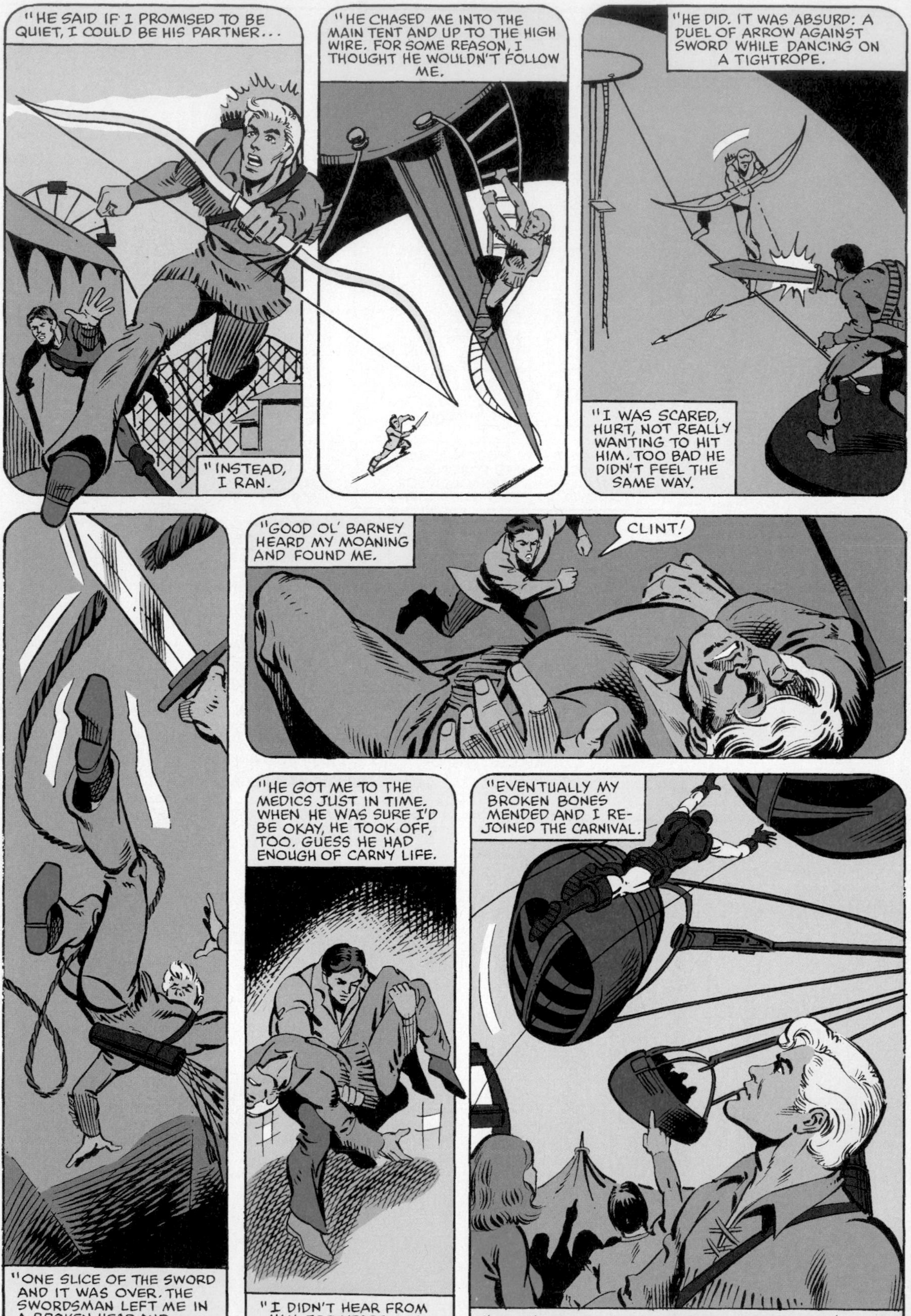
"HE SAID IF I PROMISED TO BE QUIET, I COULD BE HIS PARTNER...
"INSTEAD, I RAN.
"HE CHASED ME INTO THE MAIN TENT AND UP TO THE HIGH WIRE. FOR SOME REASON, I THOUGHT HE WOULDN'T FOLLOW ME.
"HE DID. IT WAS ABSURD: A DUEL OF ARROW AGAINST SWORD WHILE DANCING ON A TIGHTROPE.
"I WAS SCARED, HURT, NOT REALLY WANTING TO HIT HIM. TOO BAD HE DIDN'T FEEL THE SAME WAY.
"ONE SLICE OF THE SWORD AND IT WAS OVER. THE SWORDSMAN LEFT ME IN A BROKEN HEAP AND SKIPPED TOWN.
"GOOD OL' BARNEY HEARD MY MOANING AND FOUND ME.
CLINT!
"HE GOT ME TO THE MEDICS JUST IN TIME. WHEN HE WAS SURE I'D BE OKAY, HE TOOK OFF, TOO. GUESS HE HAD ENOUGH OF CARNY LIFE.
"I DIDN'T HEAR FROM HIM FOR YEARS. HE'S DEAD NOW.
"EVENTUALLY MY BROKEN BONES MENDED AND I RE-JOINED THE CARNIVAL.
"THAT'S WHERE I MET THE NEXT PERSON WHO'D TURN MY LIFE AROUND... IRON MAN!
9

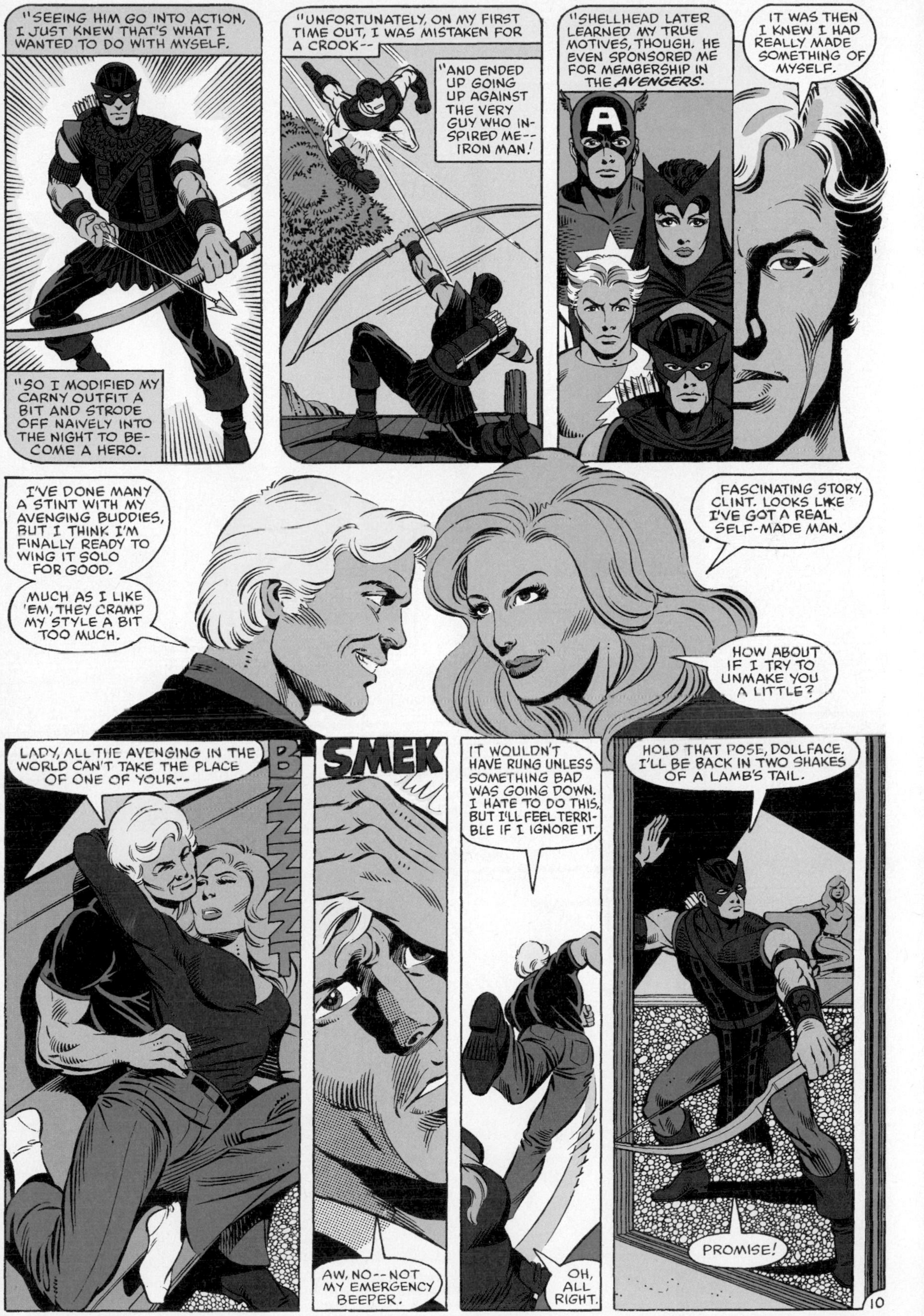
"SEEING HIM GO INTO ACTION, I JUST KNEW THAT'S WHAT I WANTED TO DO WITH MYSELF.
"SO I MODIFIED MY CARNY OUTFIT A BIT AND STRODE OFF NAIVELY INTO THE NIGHT TO BECOME A HERO.
"UNFORTUNATELY, ON MY FIRST TIME OUT, I WAS MISTAKEN FOR A CROOK--
"AND ENDED UP GOING UP AGAINST THE VERY GUY WHO INSPIRED ME-- IRON MAN!
"SHELLHEAD LATER LEARNED MY TRUE MOTIVES, THOUGH. HE EVEN SPONSORED ME FOR MEMBERSHIP IN THE AVENGERS.
IT WAS THEN I KNEW I HAD REALLY MADE SOMETHING OF MYSELF.
I'VE DONE MANY A STINT WITH MY AVENGING BUDDIES, BUT I THINK I'M FINALLY READY TO WING IT SOLO FOR GOOD.
MUCH AS I LIKE 'EM, THEY CRAMP MY STYLE A BIT TOO MUCH.
FASCINATING STORY, CLINT. LOOKS LIKE I'VE GOT A REAL SELF-MADE MAN.
HOW ABOUT IF I TRY TO UNMAKE YOU A LITTLE?
LADY, ALL THE AVENGING IN THE WORLD CAN'T TAKE THE PLACE OF ONE OF YOUR--
BZNNNNT
SMEK
AW, NO--NOT MY EMERGENCY BEEPER.
IT WOULDN'T HAVE RUNG UNLESS SOMETHING BAD WAS GOING DOWN. I HATE TO DO THIS, BUT I'LL FEEL TERRIBLE IF I IGNORE IT.
OH, ALL RIGHT.
HOLD THAT POSE, DOLLFACE. I'LL BE BACK IN TWO SHAKES OF A LAMB'S TAIL.
PROMISE!
10

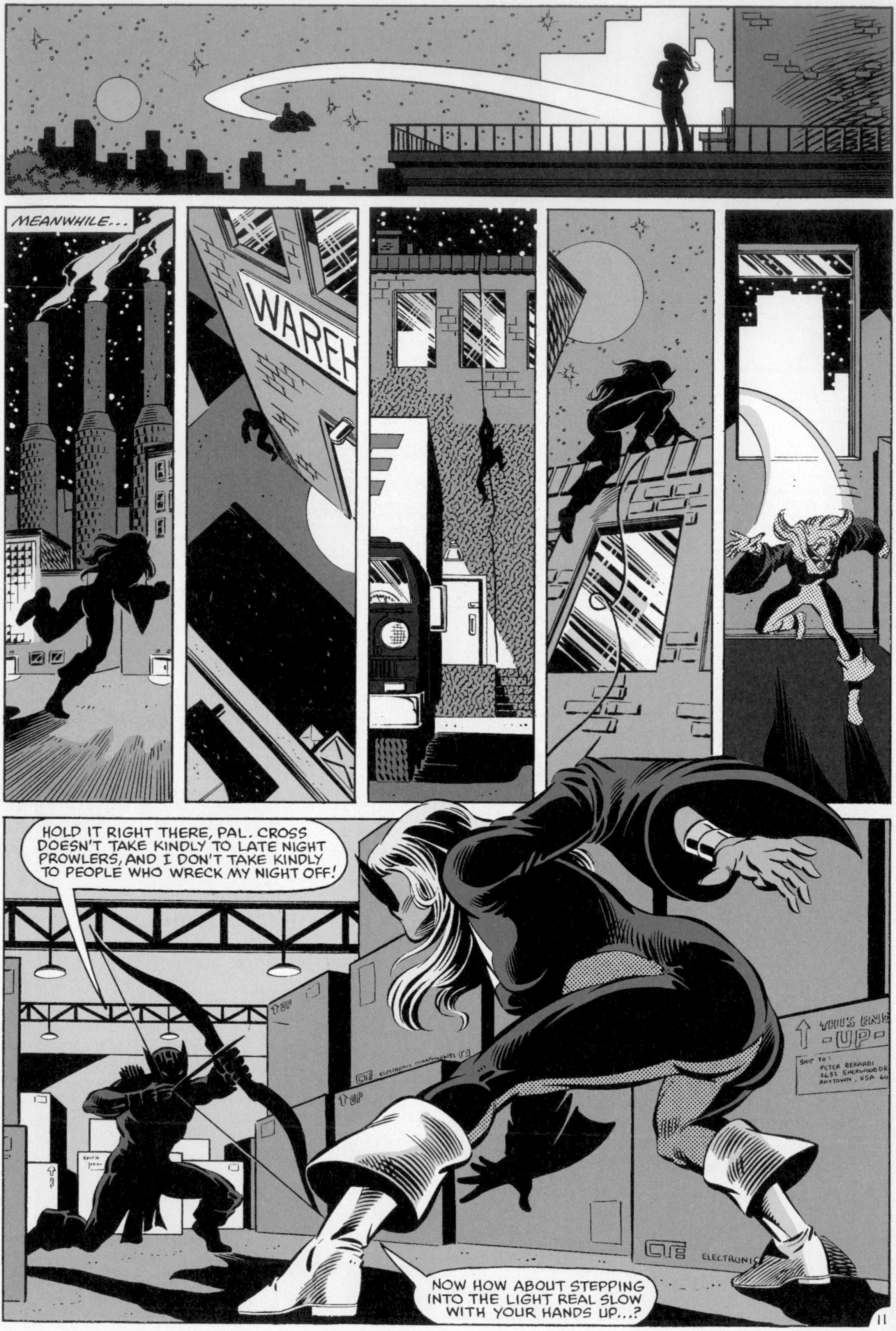
MEANWHILE...
WAREH
HOLD IT RIGHT THERE, PAL. CROSS DOESN'T TAKE KINDLY TO LATE NIGHT PROWLERS, AND I DON'T TAKE KINDLY TO PEOPLE WHO WRECK MY NIGHT OFF!
ELECTRONIC
NOW HOW ABOUT STEPPING INTO THE LIGHT REAL SLOW WITH YOUR HANDS UP...?
11

LISTEN, JERK. THIS ISN'T WHAT YOU THINK. I'M NOT SOME TWO-BIT PROWLER OR INDUSTRIAL SPY.

OH, YEAH?

YEAH.

WHST

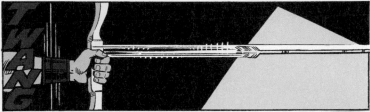

TWANG

THUK

WSSS

DNNK

GNNNG!

OKAY, BUSTER. JUST RELAX AND YOU WON'T GET HURT.

YOU'RE HAWKEYE, THE AVENGER, RIGHT?

YEAH, AND WHO MIGHT YOU BE?

12

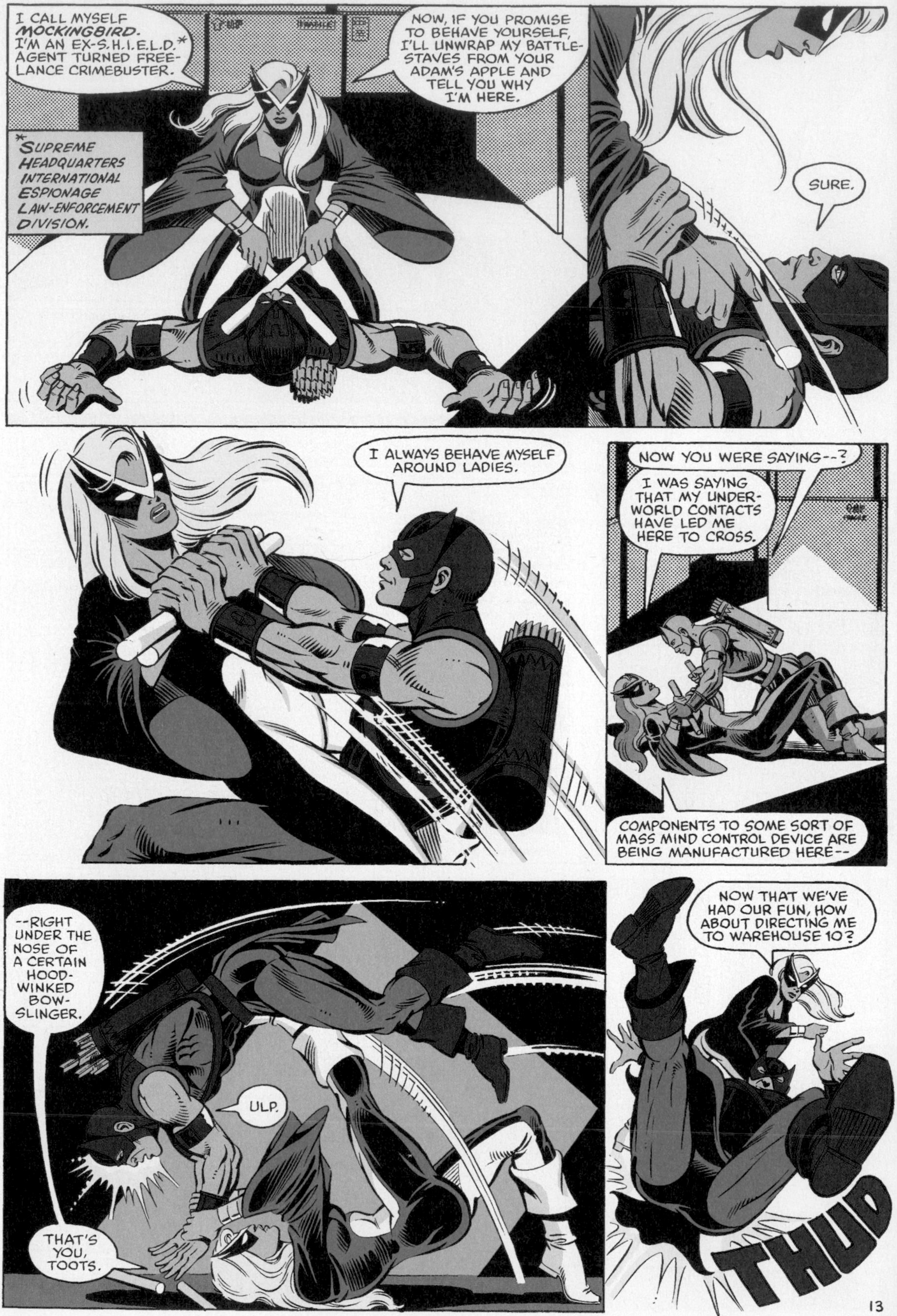

I CALL MYSELF MOCKINGBIRD. I'M AN EX-S.H.I.E.L.D.* AGENT TURNED FREE-LANCE CRIMEBUSTER.
*SUPREME HEADQUARTERS INTERNATIONAL ESPIONAGE LAW-ENFORCEMENT DIVISION.
NOW, IF YOU PROMISE TO BEHAVE YOURSELF, I'LL UNWRAP MY BATTLE-STAVES FROM YOUR ADAM'S APPLE AND TELL YOU WHY I'M HERE.
SURE.
I ALWAYS BEHAVE MYSELF AROUND LADIES.
NOW YOU WERE SAYING--?
I WAS SAYING THAT MY UNDER-WORLD CONTACTS HAVE LED ME HERE TO CROSS.
COMPONENTS TO SOME SORT OF MASS MIND CONTROL DEVICE ARE BEING MANUFACTURED HERE--
--RIGHT UNDER THE NOSE OF A CERTAIN HOOD-WINKED BOW-SLINGER.
ULP.
THAT'S YOU, TOOTS.
NOW THAT WE'VE HAD OUR FUN, HOW ABOUT DIRECTING ME TO WAREHOUSE 10?
THUD
13

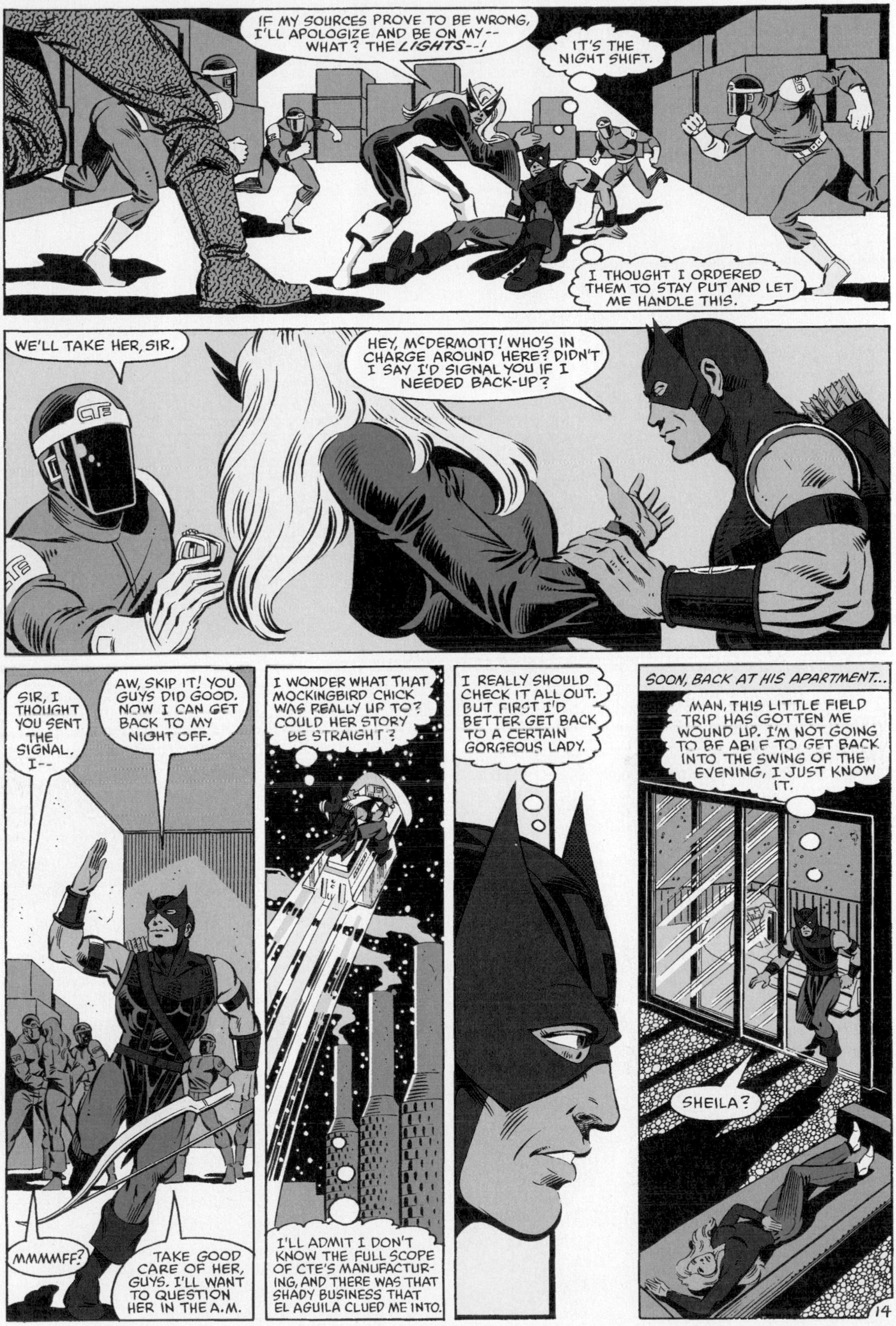
IF MY SOURCES PROVE TO BE WRONG, I'LL APOLOGIZE AND BE ON MY-- WHAT? THE LIGHTS--!
IT'S THE NIGHT SHIFT.
I THOUGHT I ORDERED THEM TO STAY PUT AND LET ME HANDLE THIS.
WE'LL TAKE HER, SIR.
HEY, McDERMOTT! WHO'S IN CHARGE AROUND HERE? DIDN'T I SAY I'D SIGNAL YOU IF I NEEDED BACK-UP?
SIR, I THOUGHT YOU SENT THE SIGNAL. I--
AW, SKIP IT! YOU GUYS DID GOOD. NOW I CAN GET BACK TO MY NIGHT OFF.
MMMMFF?
TAKE GOOD CARE OF HER, GUYS. I'LL WANT TO QUESTION HER IN THE A.M.
I WONDER WHAT THAT MOCKINGBIRD CHICK WAS REALLY UP TO? COULD HER STORY BE STRAIGHT?
I'LL ADMIT I DON'T KNOW THE FULL SCOPE OF CTE'S MANUFACTURING, AND THERE WAS THAT SHADY BUSINESS THAT EL AGUILA CLUED ME INTO.
I REALLY SHOULD CHECK IT ALL OUT. BUT FIRST I'D BETTER GET BACK TO A CERTAIN GORGEOUS LADY.
SOON, BACK AT HIS APARTMENT...
MAN, THIS LITTLE FIELD TRIP HAS GOTTEN ME WOUND UP. I'M NOT GOING TO BE ABLE TO GET BACK INTO THE SWING OF THE EVENING, I JUST KNOW IT.
SHEILA?
14

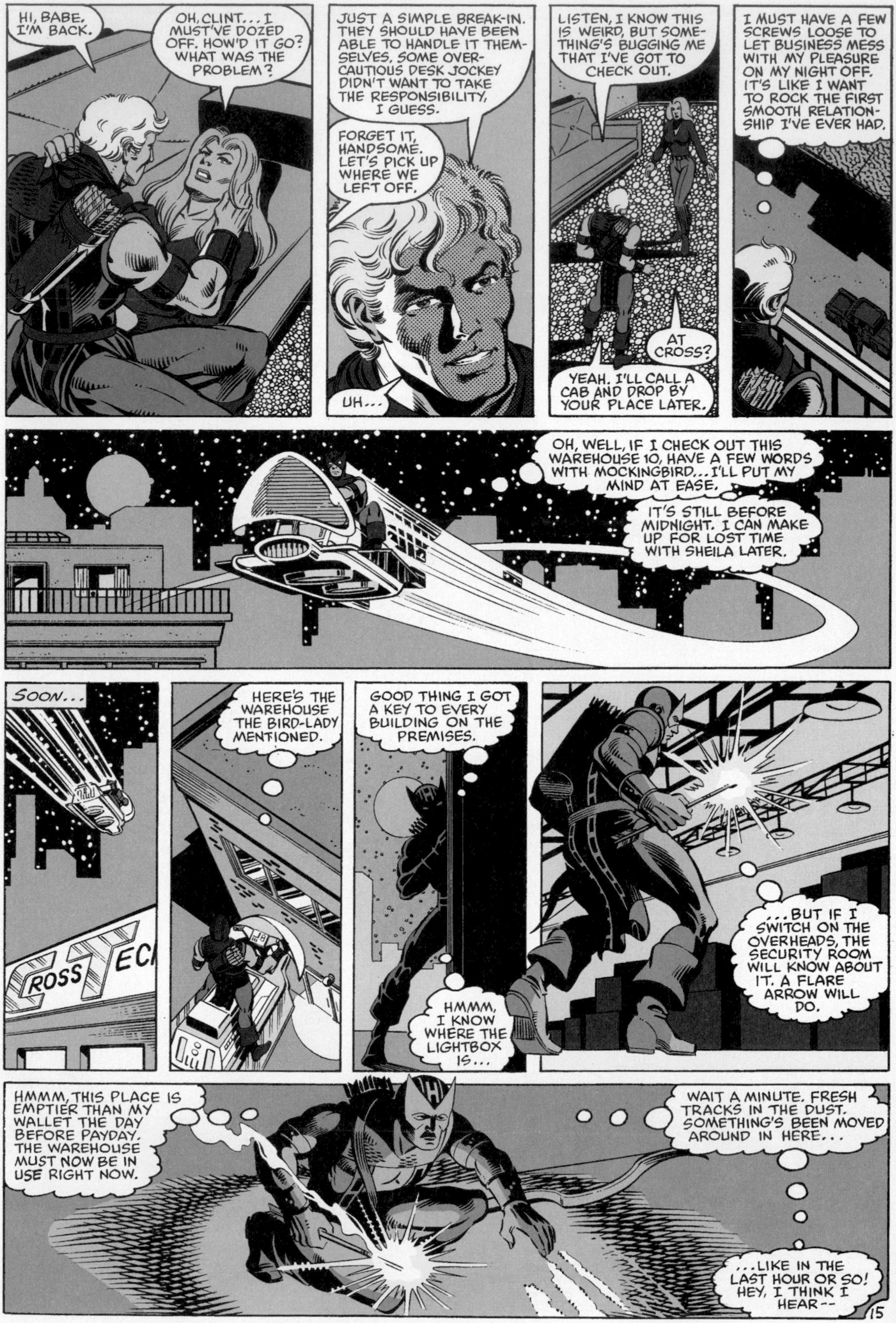
HI, BABE. I'M BACK.
OH, CLINT... I MUST'VE DOZED OFF. HOW'D IT GO? WHAT WAS THE PROBLEM?
JUST A SIMPLE BREAK-IN. THEY SHOULD HAVE BEEN ABLE TO HANDLE IT THEMSELVES. SOME OVER-CAUTIOUS DESK JOCKEY DIDN'T WANT TO TAKE THE RESPONSIBILITY, I GUESS.
FORGET IT, HANDSOME. LET'S PICK UP WHERE WE LEFT OFF.
UH...
LISTEN, I KNOW THIS IS WEIRD, BUT SOMETHING'S BUGGING ME THAT I'VE GOT TO CHECK OUT.
AT CROSS?
YEAH. I'LL CALL A CAB AND DROP BY YOUR PLACE LATER.
I MUST HAVE A FEW SCREWS LOOSE TO LET BUSINESS MESS WITH MY PLEASURE ON MY NIGHT OFF. IT'S LIKE I WANT TO ROCK THE FIRST SMOOTH RELATIONSHIP I'VE EVER HAD.
OH, WELL, IF I CHECK OUT THIS WAREHOUSE 10, HAVE A FEW WORDS WITH MOCKINGBIRD... I'LL PUT MY MIND AT EASE.
IT'S STILL BEFORE MIDNIGHT. I CAN MAKE UP FOR LOST TIME WITH SHEILA LATER.
SOON...
CROSS TECH
HERE'S THE WAREHOUSE THE BIRD-LADY MENTIONED.
GOOD THING I GOT A KEY TO EVERY BUILDING ON THE PREMISES.
HMMM, I KNOW WHERE THE LIGHTBOX IS...
...BUT IF I SWITCH ON THE OVERHEADS, THE SECURITY ROOM WILL KNOW ABOUT IT. A FLARE ARROW WILL DO.
HMMM, THIS PLACE IS EMPTIER THAN MY WALLET THE DAY BEFORE PAYDAY. THE WAREHOUSE MUST NOW BE IN USE RIGHT NOW.
WAIT A MINUTE. FRESH TRACKS IN THE DUST. SOMETHING'S BEEN MOVED AROUND IN HERE...
...LIKE IN THE LAST HOUR OR SO! HEY, I THINK I HEAR--
15

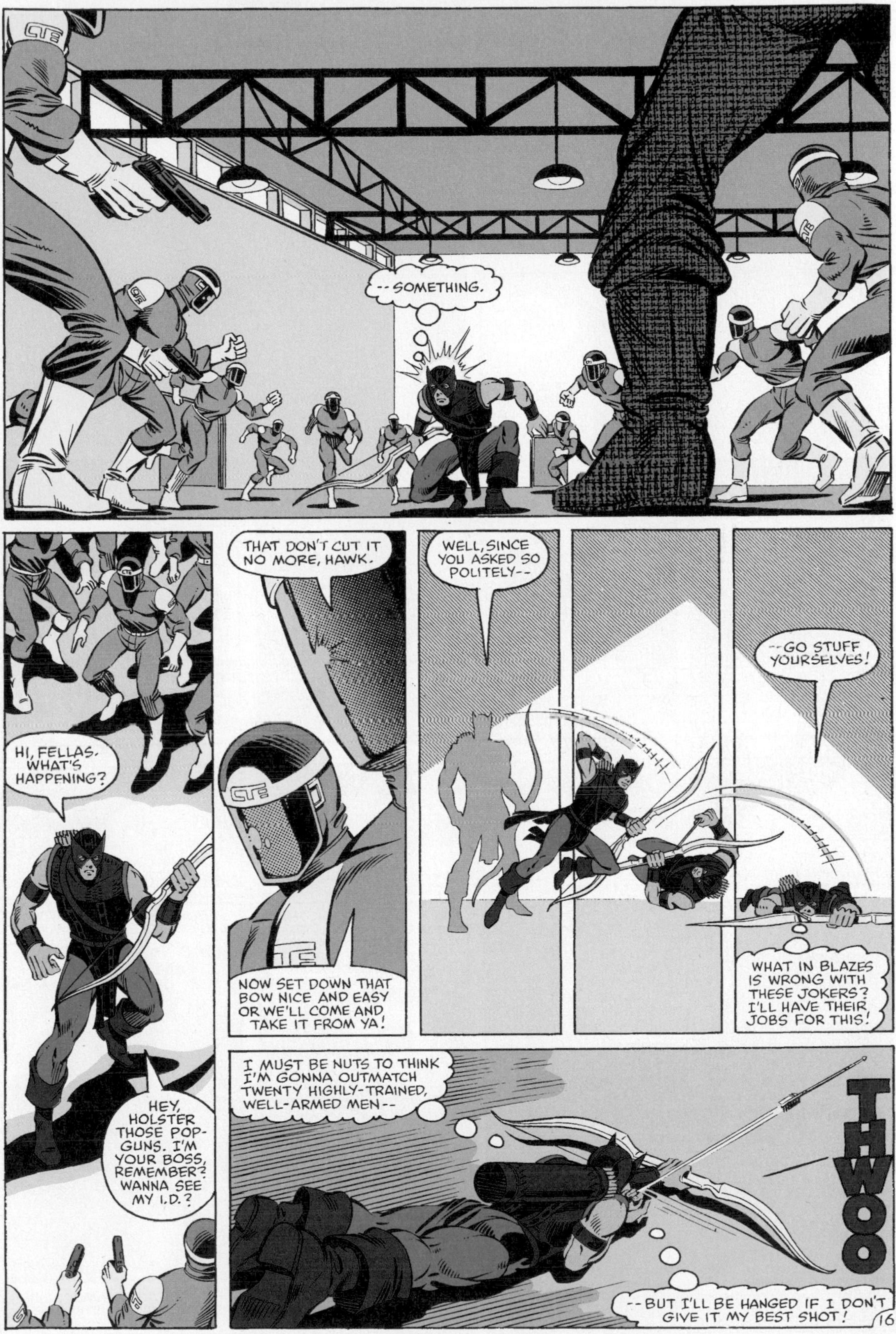
--SOMETHING.
HI, FELLAS. WHAT'S HAPPENING?
THAT DON'T CUT IT NO MORE, HAWK.
NOW SET DOWN THAT BOW NICE AND EASY OR WE'LL COME AND TAKE IT FROM YA!
HEY, HOLSTER THOSE POP-GUNS. I'M YOUR BOSS, REMEMBER? WANNA SEE MY I.D.?
WELL, SINCE YOU ASKED SO POLITELY--
--GO STUFF YOURSELVES!
WHAT IN BLAZES IS WRONG WITH THESE JOKERS? I'LL HAVE THEIR JOBS FOR THIS!
I MUST BE NUTS TO THINK I'M GONNA OUTMATCH TWENTY HIGHLY-TRAINED, WELL-ARMED MEN--
THWOO
--BUT I'LL BE HANGED IF I DON'T GIVE IT MY BEST SHOT!
16

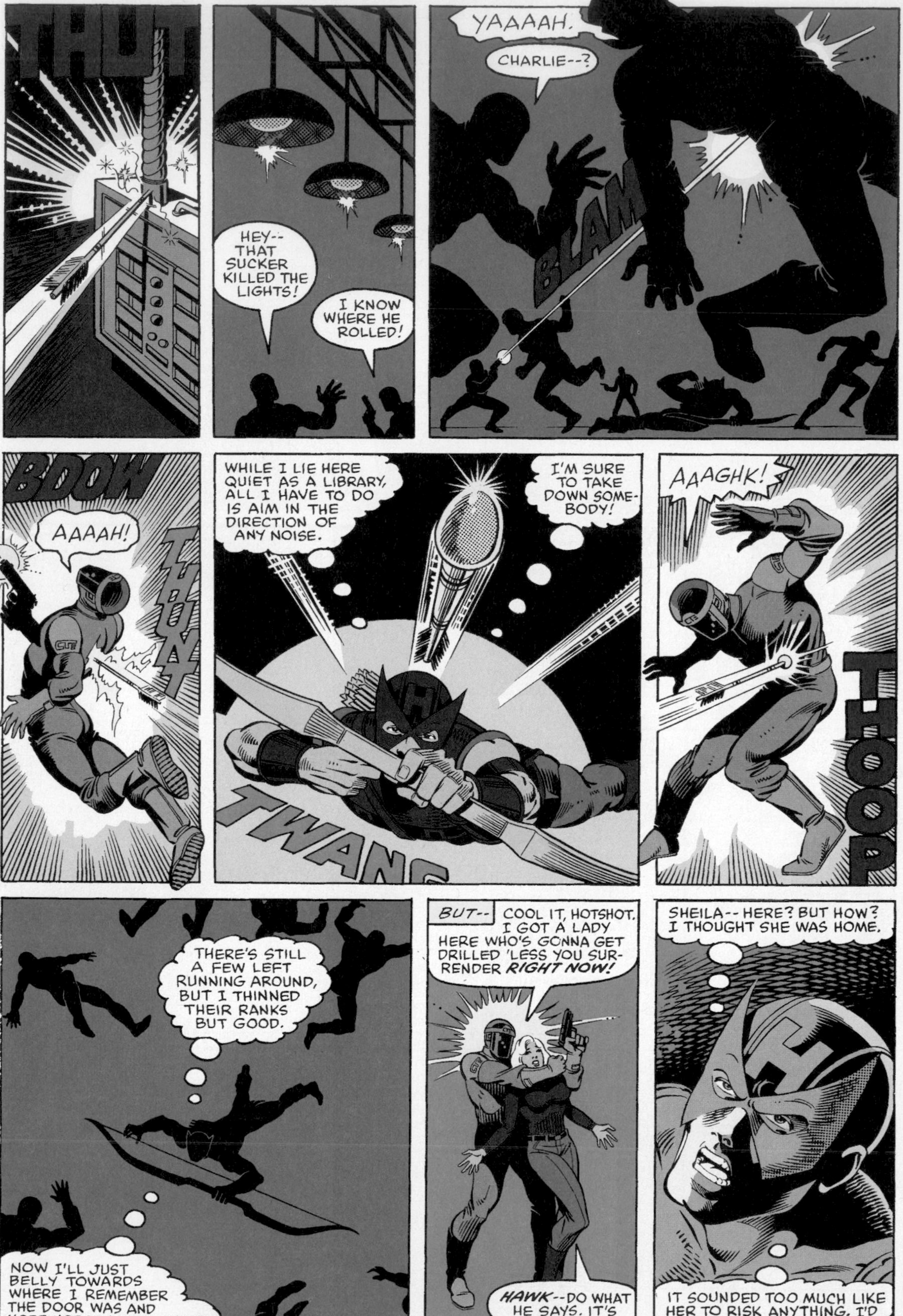
THUT
HEY-- THAT SUCKER KILLED THE LIGHTS!
I KNOW WHERE HE ROLLED!
YAAAAH.
CHARLIE--?
BLAM
BDOW
AAAAH!
THUNK
WHILE I LIE HERE QUIET AS A LIBRARY, ALL I HAVE TO DO IS AIM IN THE DIRECTION OF ANY NOISE.
I'M SURE TO TAKE DOWN SOMEBODY!
TWANG
AAAGHK!
THOOP
THERE'S STILL A FEW LEFT RUNNING AROUND, BUT I THINNED THEIR RANKS BUT GOOD.
NOW I'LL JUST BELLY TOWARDS WHERE I REMEMBER THE DOOR WAS AND HOPE NOBODY STEPS ON ME.
BUT--
COOL IT, HOTSHOT. I GOT A LADY HERE WHO'S GONNA GET DRILLED 'LESS YOU SURRENDER RIGHT NOW!
HAWK--DO WHAT HE SAYS. IT'S SHEILA!
SHEILA-- HERE? BUT HOW? I THOUGHT SHE WAS HOME.
IT SOUNDED TOO MUCH LIKE HER TO RISK ANYTHING. I'D BETTER GIVE UP.
17

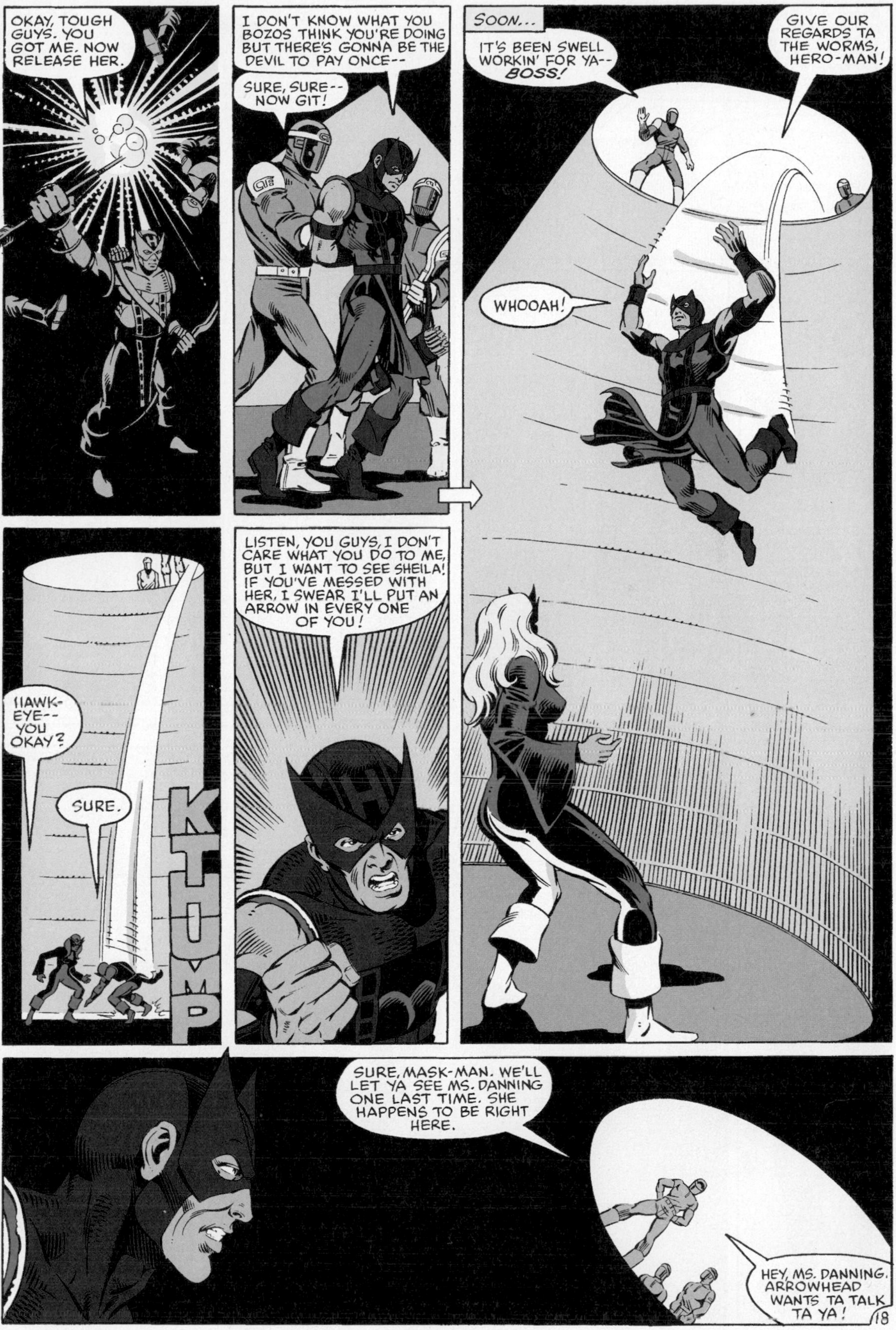
OKAY, TOUGH GUYS. YOU GOT ME. NOW RELEASE HER.
I DON'T KNOW WHAT YOU BOZOS THINK YOU'RE DOING BUT THERE'S GONNA BE THE DEVIL TO PAY ONCE--
SURE, SURE-- NOW GIT!
SOON...
IT'S BEEN SWELL WORKIN' FOR YA-- BOSS!
GIVE OUR REGARDS TA THE WORMS, HERO-MAN!
WHOOAH!
HAWK-EYE-- YOU OKAY?
SURE.
KTUMP
LISTEN, YOU GUYS, I DON'T CARE WHAT YOU DO TO ME, BUT I WANT TO SEE SHEILA! IF YOU'VE MESSED WITH HER, I SWEAR I'LL PUT AN ARROW IN EVERY ONE OF YOU!
SURE, MASK-MAN. WE'LL LET YA SEE MS. DANNING ONE LAST TIME. SHE HAPPENS TO BE RIGHT HERE.
HEY, MS. DANNING. ARROWHEAD WANTS TA TALK TA YA!
18

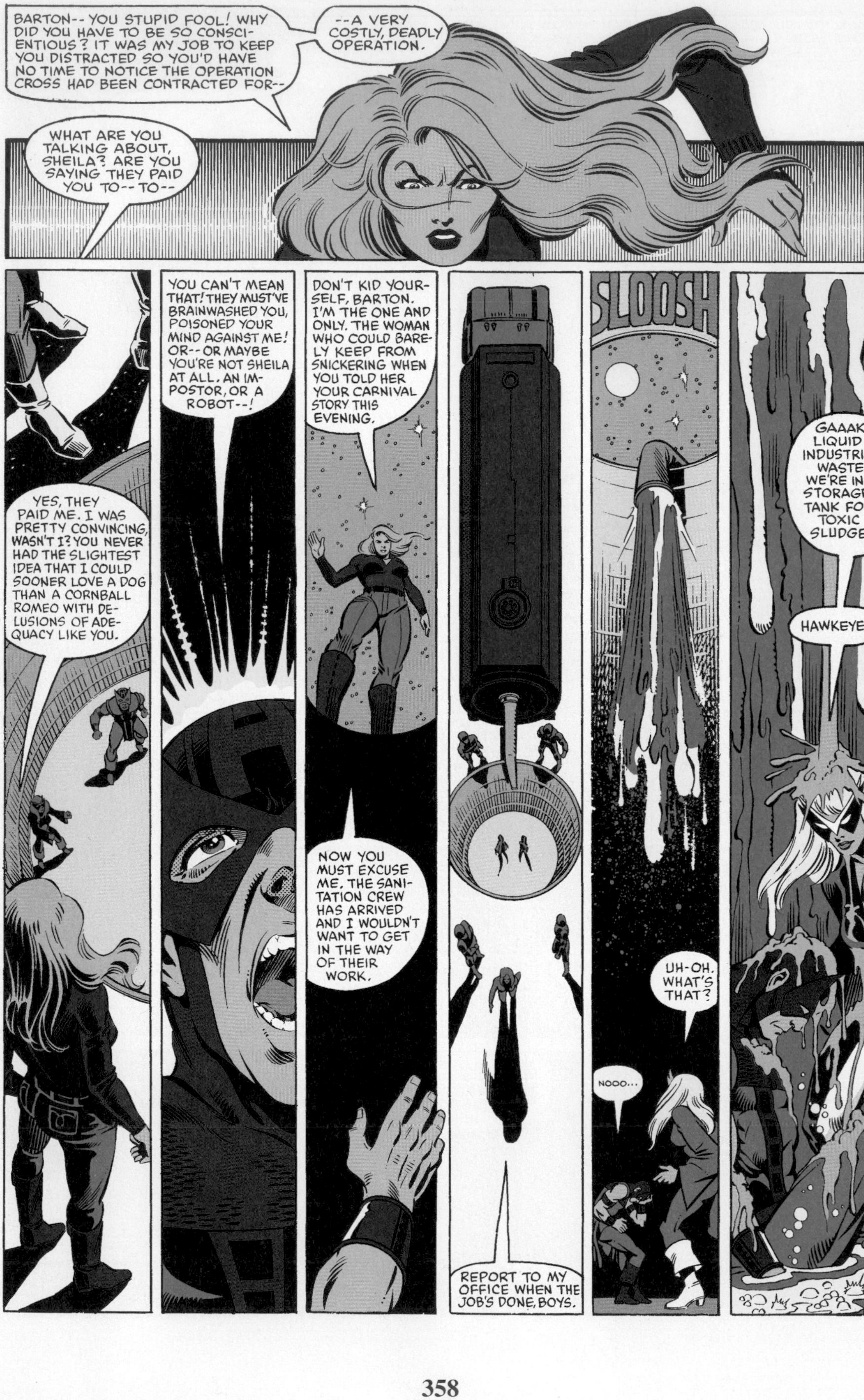
BARTON-- YOU STUPID FOOL! WHY DID YOU HAVE TO BE SO CONSCIENTIOUS? IT WAS MY JOB TO KEEP YOU DISTRACTED SO YOU'D HAVE NO TIME TO NOTICE THE OPERATION CROSS HAD BEEN CONTRACTED FOR--
--A VERY COSTLY, DEADLY OPERATION.
WHAT ARE YOU TALKING ABOUT, SHEILA? ARE YOU SAYING THEY PAID YOU TO-- TO--
YES, THEY PAID ME. I WAS PRETTY CONVINCING, WASN'T I? YOU NEVER HAD THE SLIGHTEST IDEA THAT I COULD SOONER LOVE A DOG THAN A CORNBALL ROMEO WITH DELUSIONS OF ADEQUACY LIKE YOU.
YOU CAN'T MEAN THAT! THEY MUST'VE BRAINWASHED YOU, POISONED YOUR MIND AGAINST ME! OR-- OR MAYBE YOU'RE NOT SHEILA AT ALL. AN IMPOSTOR, OR A ROBOT--!
DON'T KID YOURSELF, BARTON. I'M THE ONE AND ONLY. THE WOMAN WHO COULD BARELY KEEP FROM SNICKERING WHEN YOU TOLD HER YOUR CARNIVAL STORY THIS EVENING.
NOW YOU MUST EXCUSE ME. THE SANITATION CREW HAS ARRIVED AND I WOULDN'T WANT TO GET IN THE WAY OF THEIR WORK.
REPORT TO MY OFFICE WHEN THE JOB'S DONE, BOYS.
SLOOSH
UH-OH. WHAT'S THAT?
NOOO...
GAAAK. LIQUID INDUSTRIAL WASTE. WE'RE IN A STORAGE TANK FOR TOXIC SLUDGE!
HAWKEYE--?
19

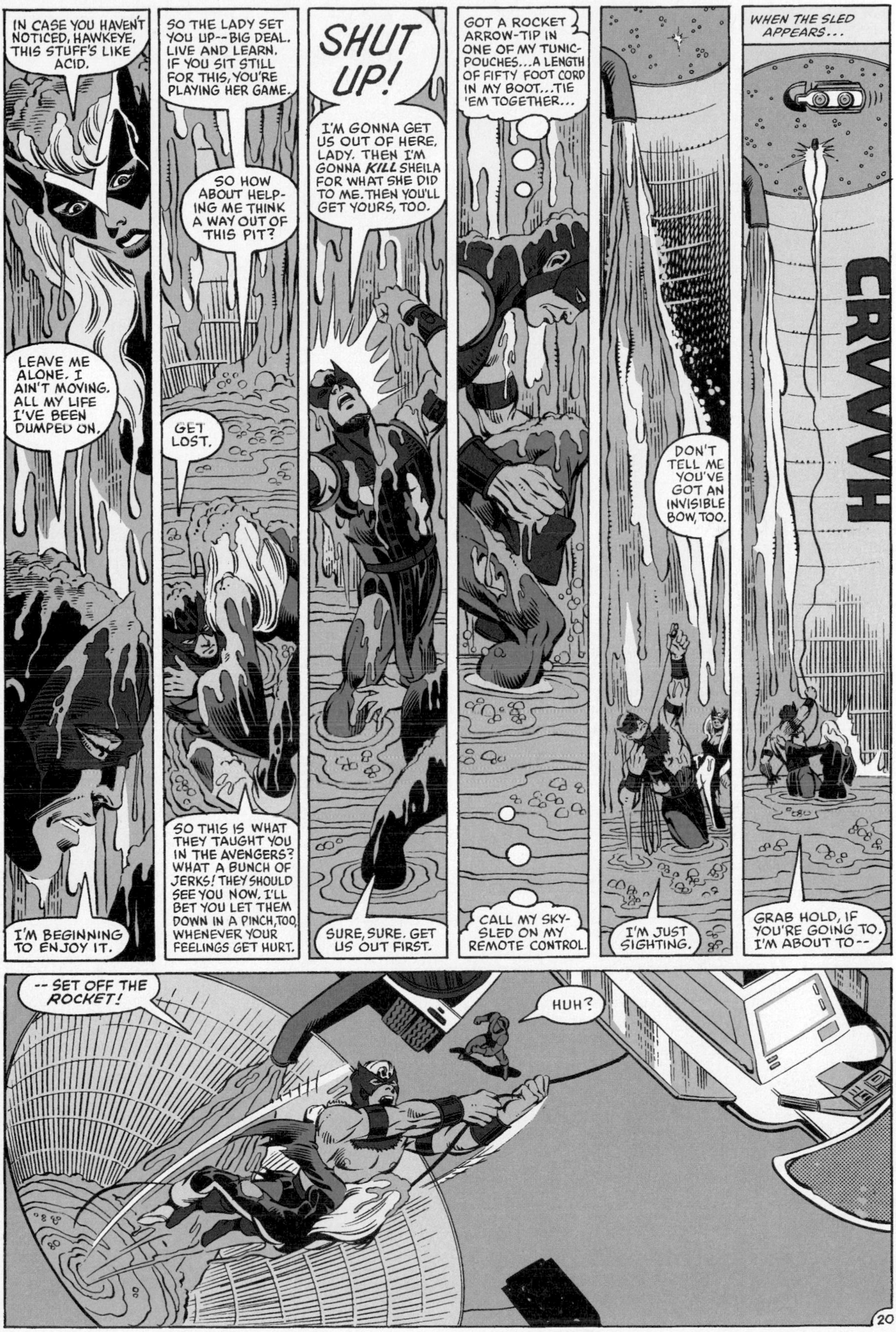
IN CASE YOU HAVEN'T NOTICED, HAWKEYE, THIS STUFF'S LIKE ACID.
LEAVE ME ALONE. I AIN'T MOVING. ALL MY LIFE I'VE BEEN DUMPED ON.
I'M BEGINNING TO ENJOY IT.
SO THE LADY SET YOU UP--BIG DEAL. LIVE AND LEARN. IF YOU SIT STILL FOR THIS, YOU'RE PLAYING HER GAME.
SO HOW ABOUT HELPING ME THINK A WAY OUT OF THIS PIT?
GET LOST.
SO THIS IS WHAT THEY TAUGHT YOU IN THE AVENGERS? WHAT A BUNCH OF JERKS! THEY SHOULD SEE YOU NOW. I'LL BET YOU LET THEM DOWN IN A PINCH, TOO, WHENEVER YOUR FEELINGS GET HURT.
SHUT UP!
I'M GONNA GET US OUT OF HERE, LADY. THEN I'M GONNA KILL SHEILA FOR WHAT SHE DID TO ME. THEN YOU'LL GET YOURS, TOO.
SURE, SURE. GET US OUT FIRST.
GOT A ROCKET ARROW-TIP IN ONE OF MY TUNIC-POUCHES...A LENGTH OF FIFTY FOOT CORD IN MY BOOT...TIE 'EM TOGETHER...
CALL MY SKY-SLED ON MY REMOTE CONTROL.
DON'T TELL ME YOU'VE GOT AN INVISIBLE BOW, TOO.
I'M JUST SIGHTING.
WHEN THE SLED APPEARS...
CRVVVH
GRAB HOLD, IF YOU'RE GOING TO. I'M ABOUT TO--
--SET OFF THE ROCKET!
HUH?
20

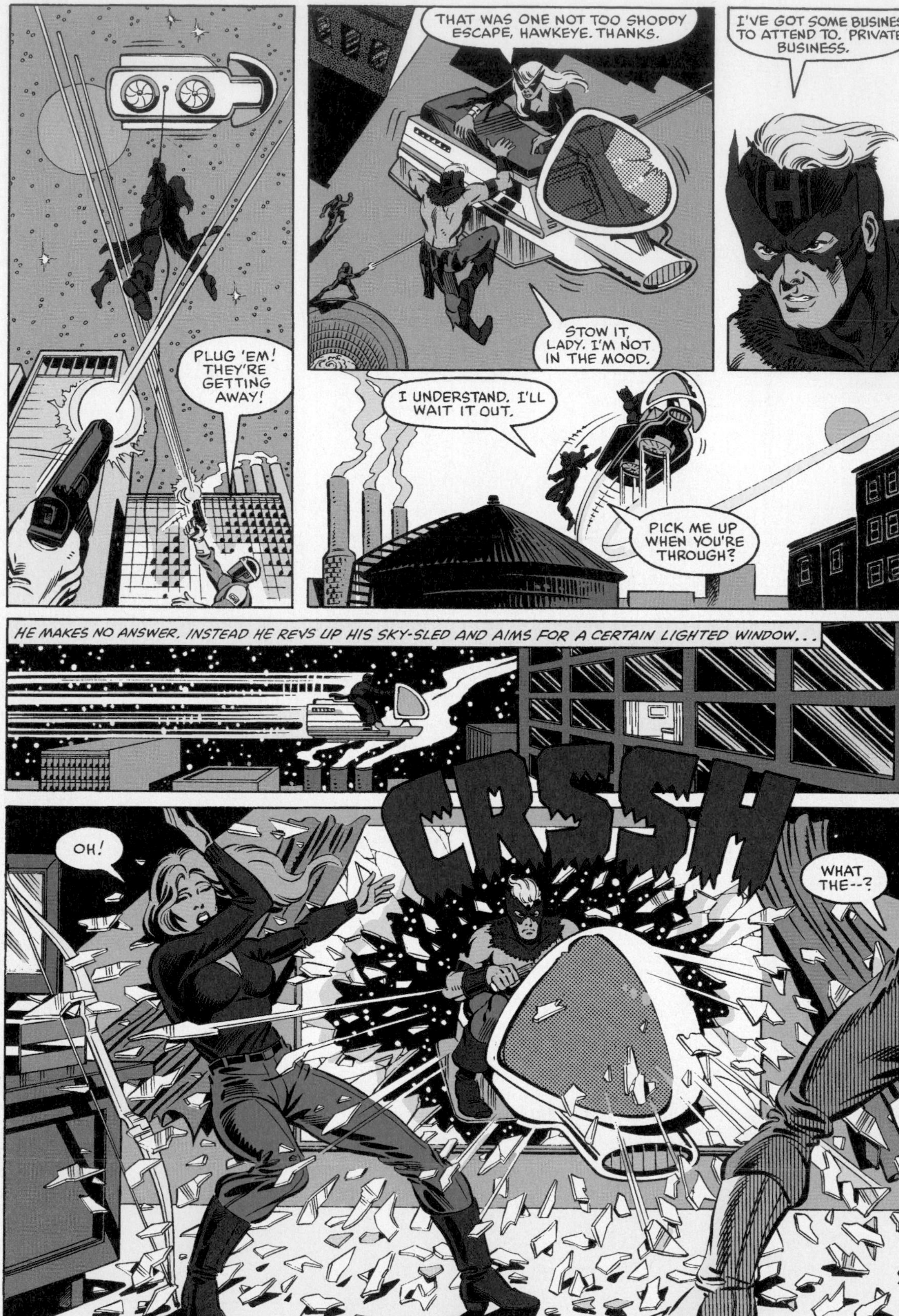
PLUG 'EM! THEY'RE GETTING AWAY!
THAT WAS ONE NOT TOO SHODDY ESCAPE, HAWKEYE. THANKS.
STOW IT, LADY. I'M NOT IN THE MOOD.
I'VE GOT SOME BUSINESS TO ATTEND TO. PRIVATE BUSINESS.
I UNDERSTAND. I'LL WAIT IT OUT.
PICK ME UP WHEN YOU'RE THROUGH?
HE MAKES NO ANSWER. INSTEAD HE REVS UP HIS SKY-SLED AND AIMS FOR A CERTAIN LIGHTED WINDOW...
CRSSH
OH!
WHAT THE--?
21

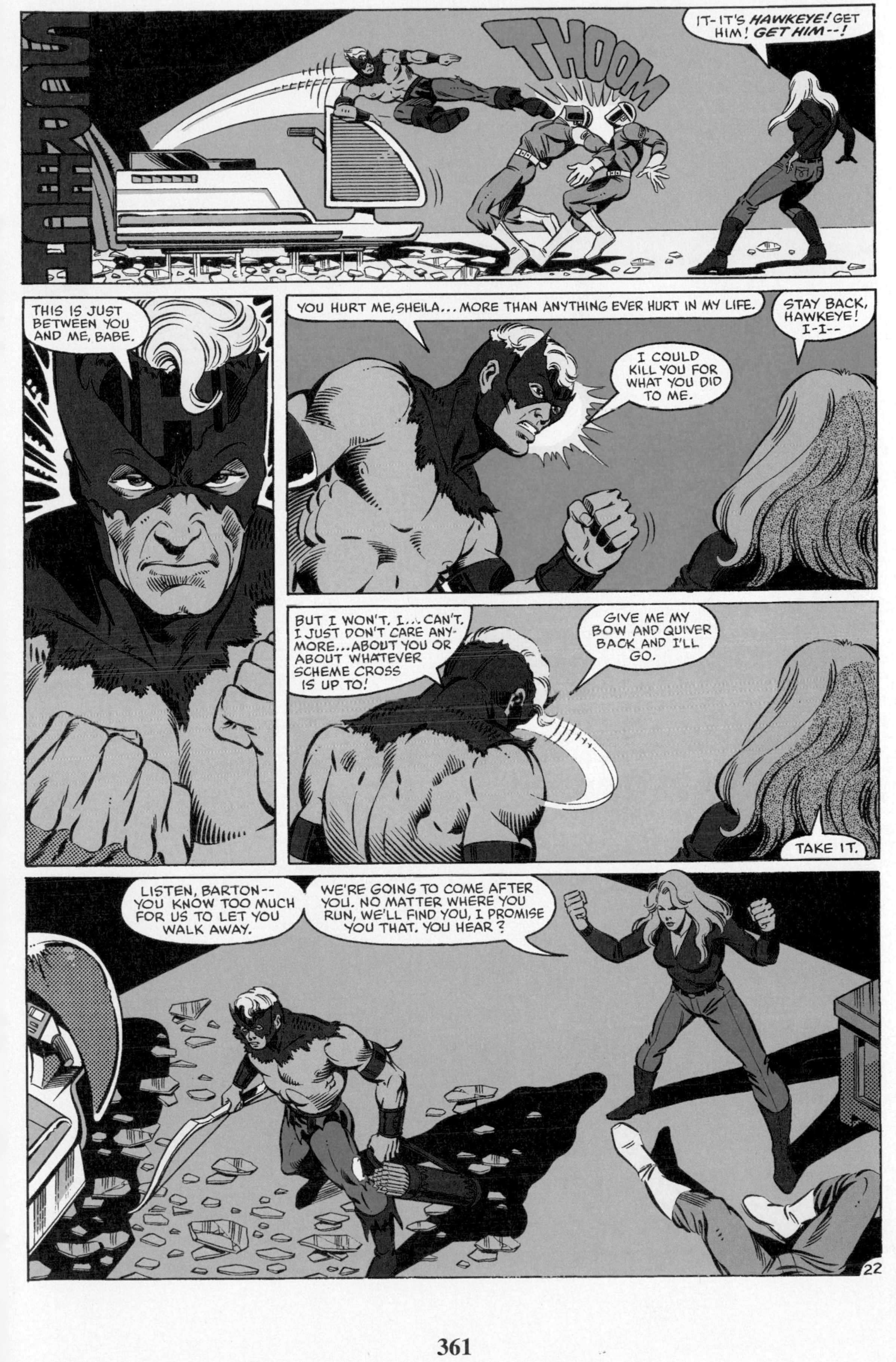

SCREECH
THOOM
IT-IT'S HAWKEYE! GET HIM! GET HIM--!
THIS IS JUST BETWEEN YOU AND ME, BABE.
YOU HURT ME, SHEILA... MORE THAN ANYTHING EVER HURT IN MY LIFE.
I COULD KILL YOU FOR WHAT YOU DID TO ME.
STAY BACK, HAWKEYE! I-I--
BUT I WON'T. I... CAN'T. I JUST DON'T CARE ANY-MORE... ABOUT YOU OR ABOUT WHATEVER SCHEME CROSS IS UP TO!
GIVE ME MY BOW AND QUIVER BACK AND I'LL GO.
TAKE IT.
LISTEN, BARTON-- YOU KNOW TOO MUCH FOR US TO LET YOU WALK AWAY.
WE'RE GOING TO COME AFTER YOU. NO MATTER WHERE YOU RUN, WE'LL FIND YOU, I PROMISE YOU THAT. YOU HEAR?
22

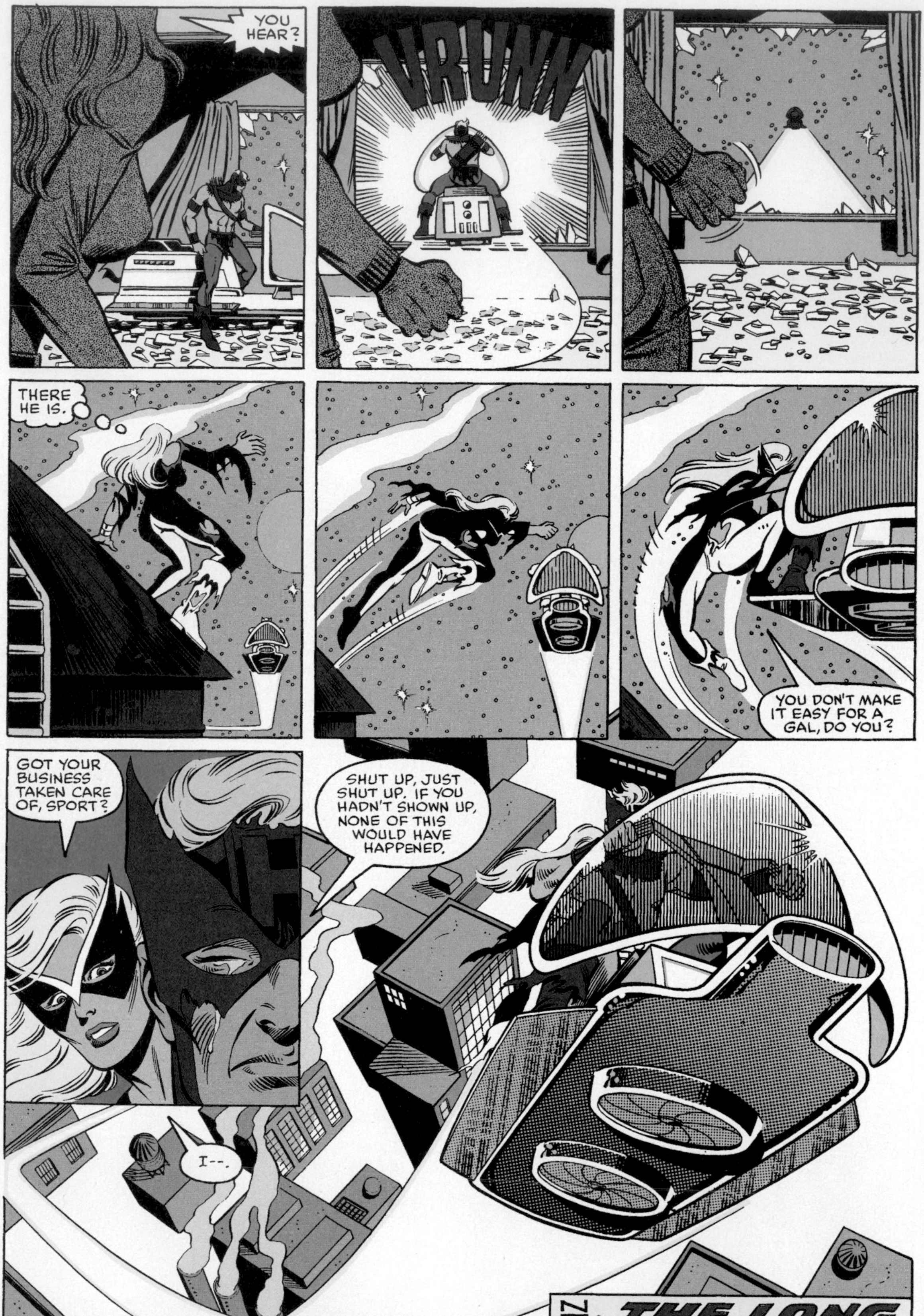
YOU HEAR?
VRUNN
THERE HE IS.
YOU DON'T MAKE IT EASY FOR A GAL, DO YOU?
GOT YOUR BUSINESS TAKEN CARE OF, SPORT?
SHUT UP, JUST SHUT UP. IF YOU HADN'T SHOWN UP, NONE OF THIS WOULD HAVE HAPPENED.
I--.
THE RIDE BACK TO MANHATTAN PASSES WITHOUT ANOTHER WORD.
NEXT: THE LONG SILENCE!

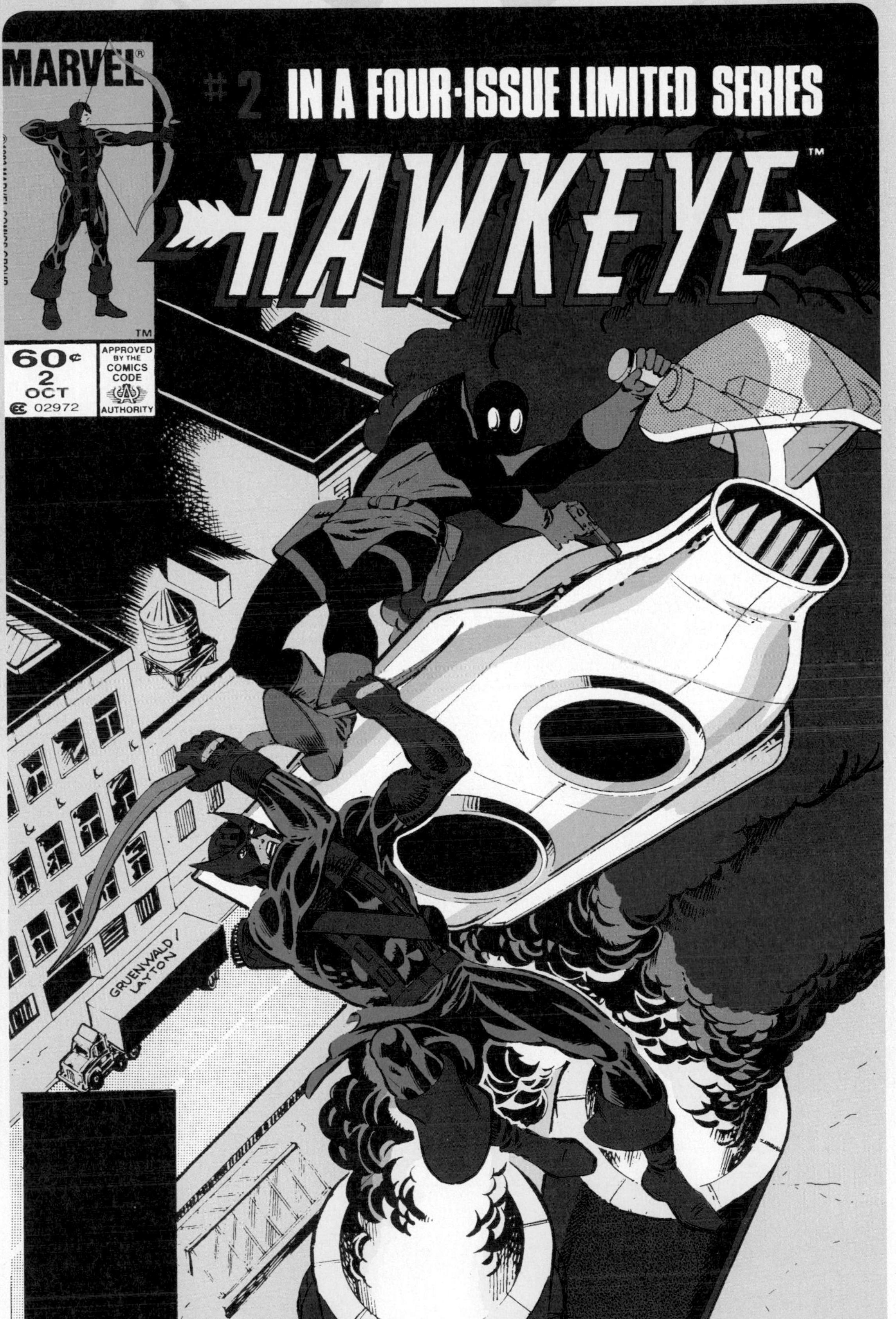
MARVEL®
TM
60¢
2
OCT
02972
APPROVED BY THE COMICS CODE AUTHORITY
#2 IN A FOUR-ISSUE LIMITED SERIES
HAWKEYE™
GRUENWALD / LAYTON

BENEATH THE WEST SIDE HIGHWAY IN MANHATTAN ARE SEVERAL MILES OF ABANDONED RAILROAD TUNNELS. IT IS THE FAMILIAR HAUNTS OF RATS, PIGEONS, DERELICTS, AND, FOR THE PAST 42 HOURS, THE BOWMAN CALLED...

HAWKEYE

STAN LEE presents

POINT BLANK!

MARK GRUENWALD	BRETT BREEDING	JOE ROSEN	BOB SHAREN	DENNIS O'NEIL	JIM SHOOTER
WRITER / PENCILER	EMBELLISHER	LETTERER	COLORIST	EDITOR	EDITOR-IN-CHIEF

REACH, NOTCH, DRAW, AIM...

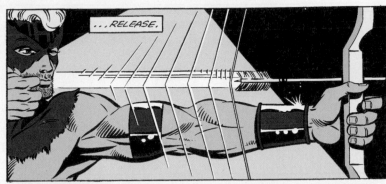

...RELEASE.

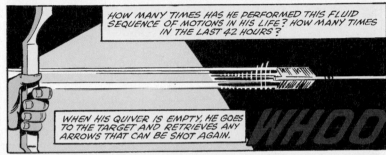

HOW MANY TIMES HAS HE PERFORMED THIS FLUID SEQUENCE OF MOTIONS IN HIS LIFE? HOW MANY TIMES IN THE LAST 42 HOURS?

WHEN HIS QUIVER IS EMPTY, HE GOES TO THE TARGET AND RETRIEVES ANY ARROWS THAT CAN BE SHOT AGAIN.

WHOO

THERE ARE NOW ONLY SEVEN.

KTUNK

SIX.

KRNP

TA

HE HAS SHOT AT HIS MAKESHIFT CEMENT TARGET CONSTANTLY SINCE HE CAME HERE.

HE HAS YET TO HIT A BULLSEYE.

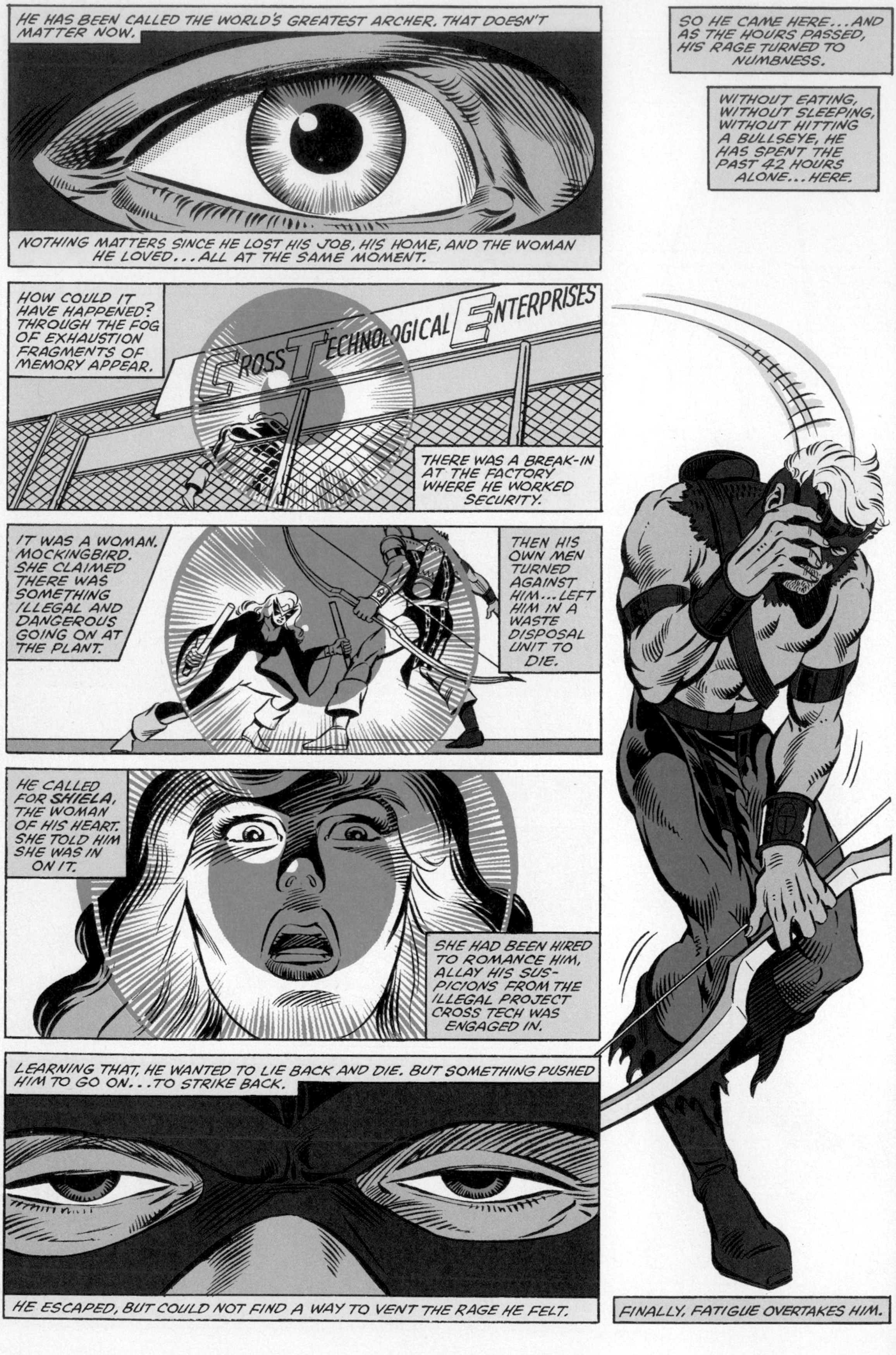
HE HAS BEEN CALLED THE WORLD'S GREATEST ARCHER. THAT DOESN'T MATTER NOW.
NOTHING MATTERS SINCE HE LOST HIS JOB, HIS HOME, AND THE WOMAN HE LOVED...ALL AT THE SAME MOMENT.
HOW COULD IT HAVE HAPPENED? THROUGH THE FOG OF EXHAUSTION FRAGMENTS OF MEMORY APPEAR.
CROSS TECHNOLOGICAL ENTERPRISES
THERE WAS A BREAK-IN AT THE FACTORY WHERE HE WORKED SECURITY.
IT WAS A WOMAN. MOCKINGBIRD. SHE CLAIMED THERE WAS SOMETHING ILLEGAL AND DANGEROUS GOING ON AT THE PLANT.
THEN HIS OWN MEN TURNED AGAINST HIM...LEFT HIM IN A WASTE DISPOSAL UNIT TO DIE.
HE CALLED FOR SHIELA, THE WOMAN OF HIS HEART. SHE TOLD HIM SHE WAS IN ON IT.
SHE HAD BEEN HIRED TO ROMANCE HIM, ALLAY HIS SUSPICIONS FROM THE ILLEGAL PROJECT CROSS TECH WAS ENGAGED IN.
LEARNING THAT, HE WANTED TO LIE BACK AND DIE. BUT SOMETHING PUSHED HIM TO GO ON...TO STRIKE BACK.
HE ESCAPED, BUT COULD NOT FIND A WAY TO VENT THE RAGE HE FELT.
SO HE CAME HERE...AND AS THE HOURS PASSED, HIS RAGE TURNED TO NUMBNESS.
WITHOUT EATING, WITHOUT SLEEPING, WITHOUT HITTING A BULLSEYE, HE HAS SPENT THE PAST 42 HOURS ALONE...HERE.
FINALLY, FATIGUE OVERTAKES HIM.

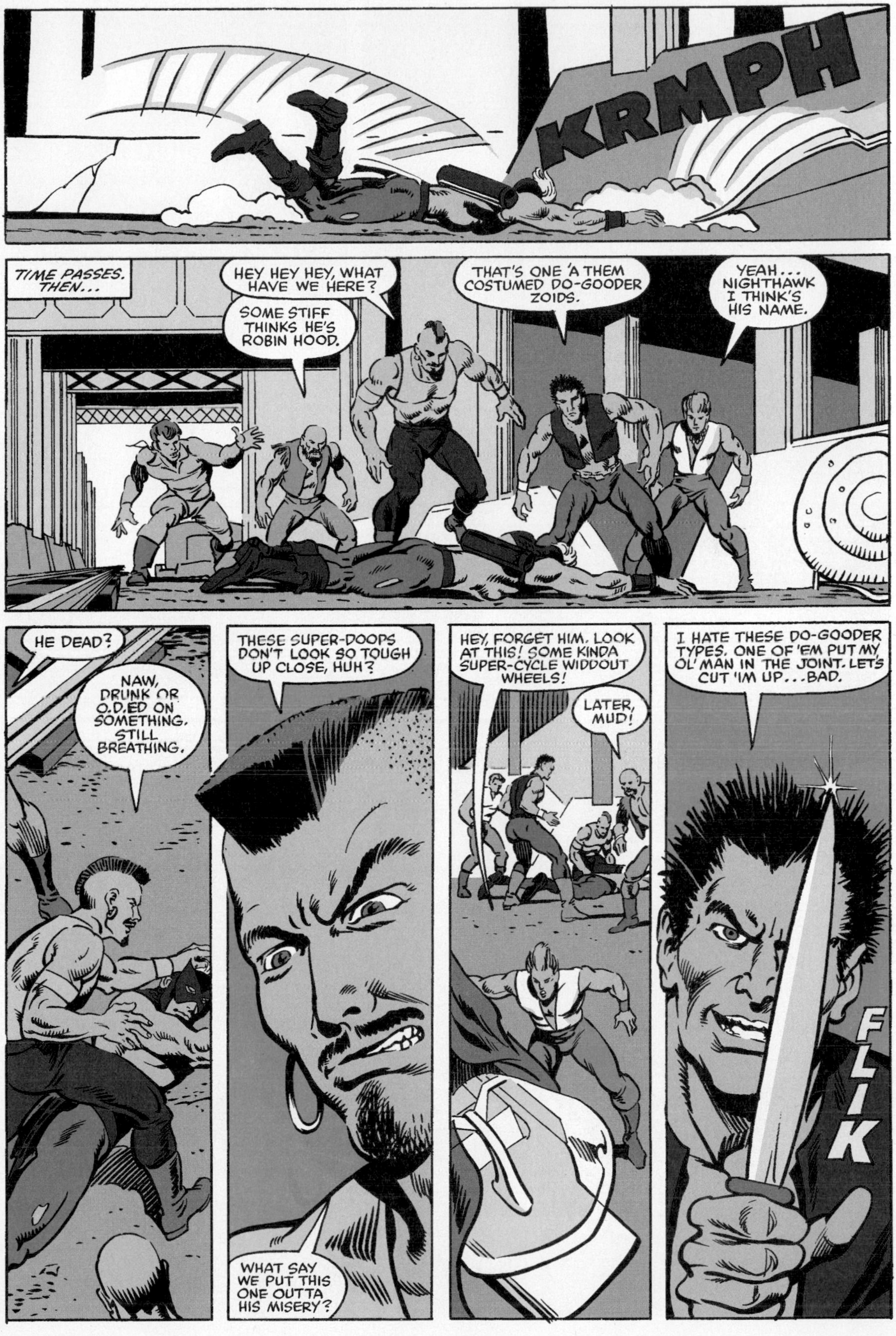
KRMPH
TIME PASSES. THEN...
HEY HEY HEY, WHAT HAVE WE HERE?
SOME STIFF THINKS HE'S ROBIN HOOD.
THAT'S ONE 'A THEM COSTUMED DO-GOODER ZOIDS.
YEAH... NIGHTHAWK I THINK'S HIS NAME.
HE DEAD?
NAW, DRUNK OR O.D.ED ON SOMETHING. STILL BREATHING.
THESE SUPER-DOOPS DON'T LOOK SO TOUGH UP CLOSE, HUH?
WHAT SAY WE PUT THIS ONE OUTTA HIS MISERY?
HEY, FORGET HIM. LOOK AT THIS! SOME KINDA SUPER-CYCLE WIDDOUT WHEELS!
LATER, MUD!
I HATE THESE DO-GOODER TYPES. ONE OF 'EM PUT MY OL' MAN IN THE JOINT. LET'S CUT 'IM UP...BAD.
FLIK

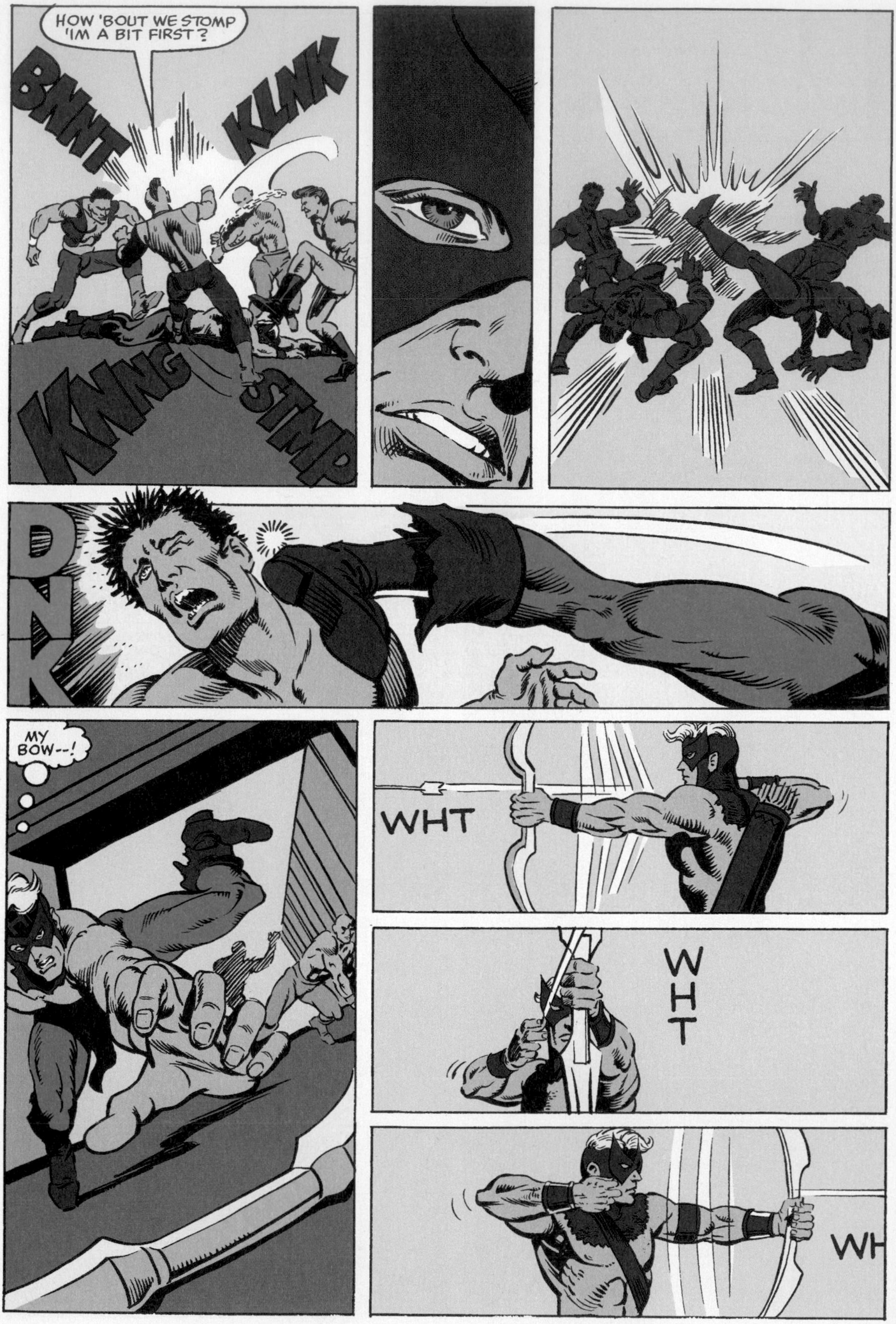
HOW 'BOUT WE STOMP 'IM A BIT FIRST?
BNNT
KLNK
KNNG
STMP
DNK
MY BOW--!
WHT
WHT
WH

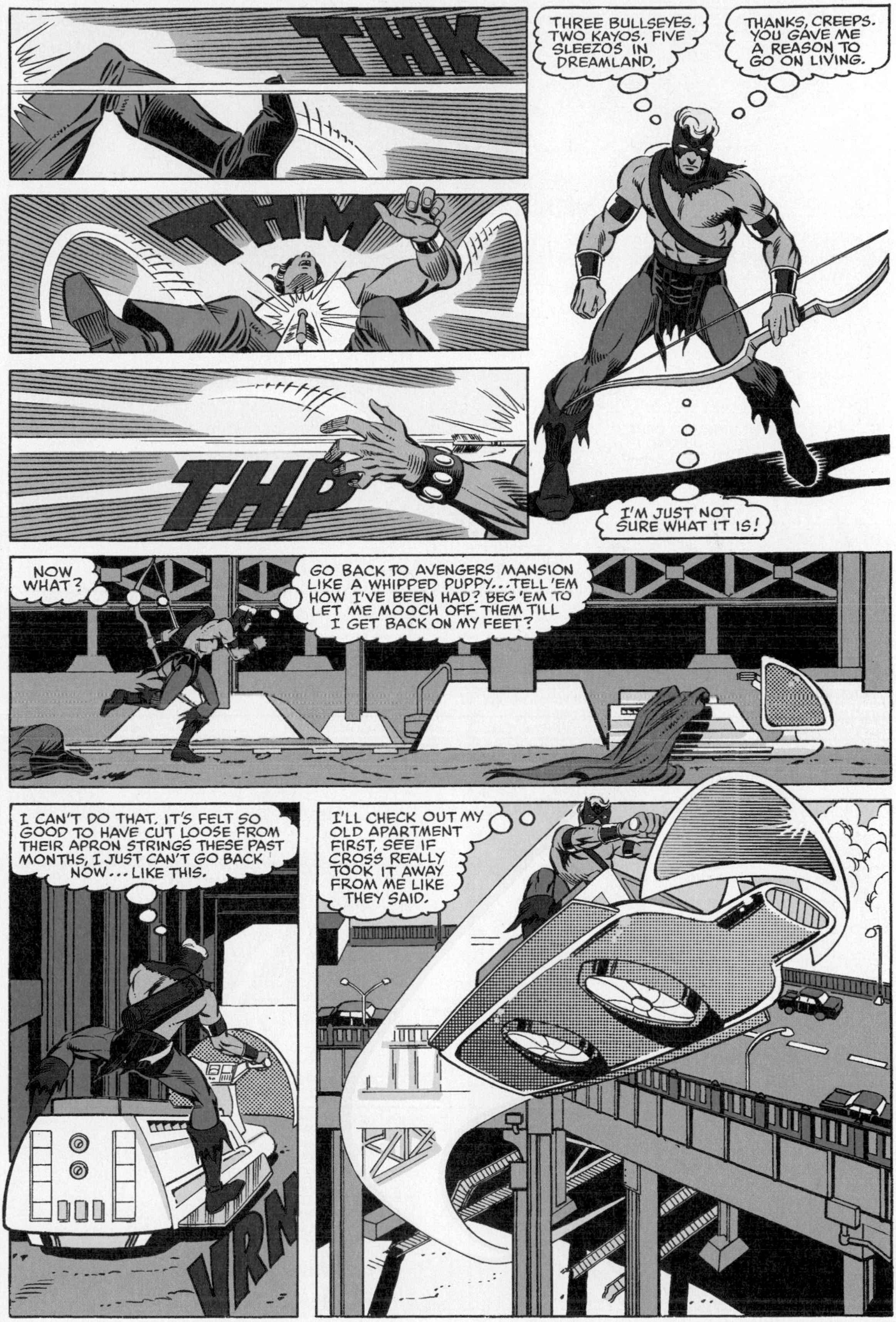
THK
THREE BULLSEYES. TWO KAYOS. FIVE SLEEZOS IN DREAMLAND.
THANKS, CREEPS. YOU GAVE ME A REASON TO GO ON LIVING.
THM
THP
I'M JUST NOT SURE WHAT IT IS!
NOW WHAT?
GO BACK TO AVENGERS MANSION LIKE A WHIPPED PUPPY... TELL 'EM HOW I'VE BEEN HAD? BEG 'EM TO LET ME MOOCH OFF THEM TILL I GET BACK ON MY FEET?
I CAN'T DO THAT. IT'S FELT SO GOOD TO HAVE CUT LOOSE FROM THEIR APRON STRINGS THESE PAST MONTHS, I JUST CAN'T GO BACK NOW... LIKE THIS.
VRM
I'LL CHECK OUT MY OLD APARTMENT FIRST, SEE IF CROSS REALLY TOOK IT AWAY FROM ME LIKE THEY SAID.

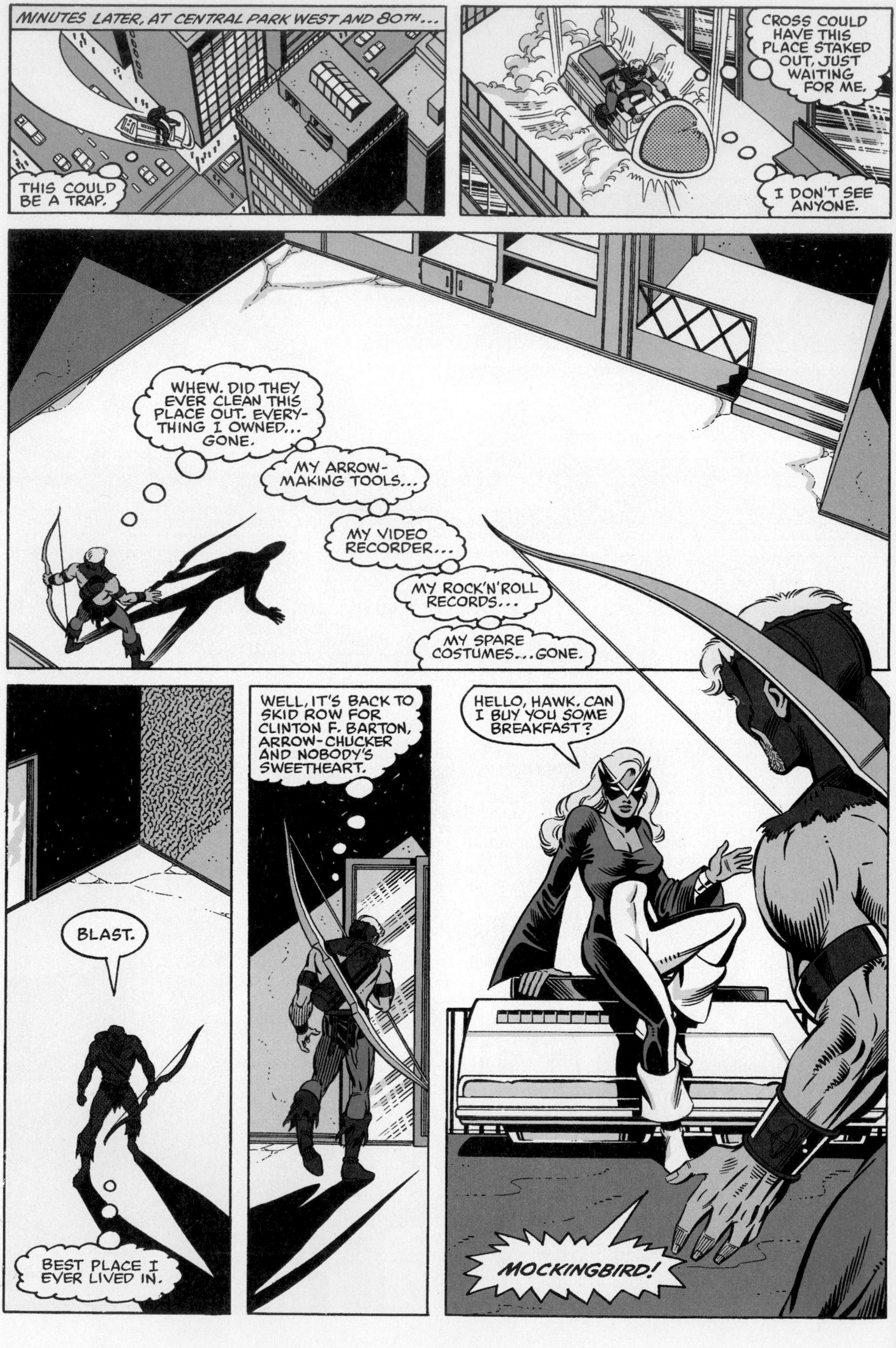
MINUTES LATER, AT CENTRAL PARK WEST AND 80TH...
THIS COULD BE A TRAP.
CROSS COULD HAVE THIS PLACE STAKED OUT, JUST WAITING FOR ME.
I DON'T SEE ANYONE.
WHEW. DID THEY EVER CLEAN THIS PLACE OUT. EVERYTHING I OWNED... GONE.
MY ARROW-MAKING TOOLS...
MY VIDEO RECORDER...
MY ROCK'N'ROLL RECORDS...
MY SPARE COSTUMES...GONE.
BLAST.
BEST PLACE I EVER LIVED IN.
WELL, IT'S BACK TO SKID ROW FOR CLINTON F. BARTON, ARROW-CHUCKER AND NOBODY'S SWEETHEART.
HELLO, HAWK. CAN I BUY YOU SOME BREAKFAST?
MOCKINGBIRD!

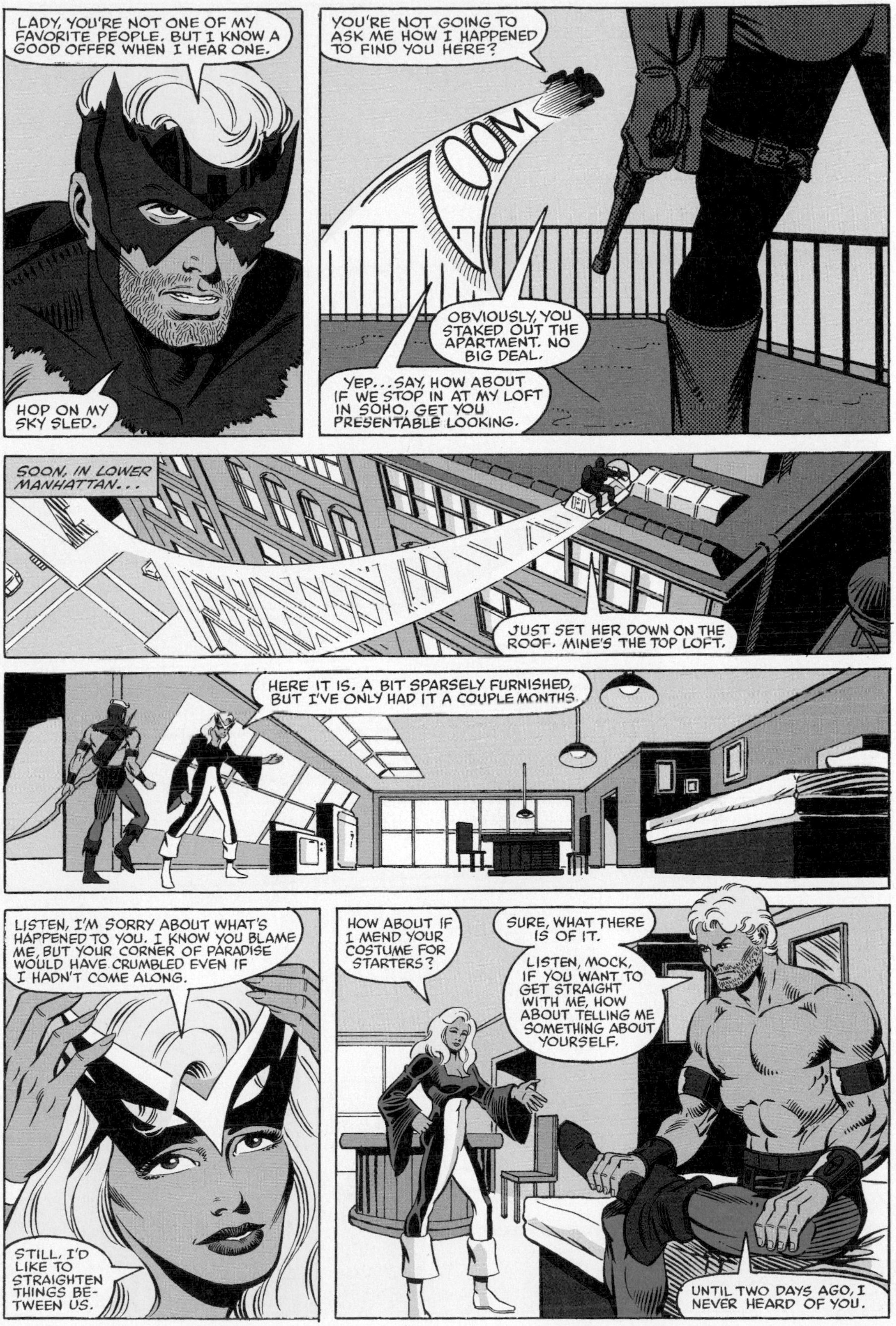
LADY, YOU'RE NOT ONE OF MY FAVORITE PEOPLE. BUT I KNOW A GOOD OFFER WHEN I HEAR ONE.
HOP ON MY SKY SLED.
YOU'RE NOT GOING TO ASK ME HOW I HAPPENED TO FIND YOU HERE?
ZOOM
OBVIOUSLY, YOU STAKED OUT THE APARTMENT. NO BIG DEAL.
YEP... SAY, HOW ABOUT IF WE STOP IN AT MY LOFT IN SOHO, GET YOU PRESENTABLE LOOKING.
SOON, IN LOWER MANHATTAN...
JUST SET HER DOWN ON THE ROOF. MINE'S THE TOP LOFT.
HERE IT IS. A BIT SPARSELY FURNISHED, BUT I'VE ONLY HAD IT A COUPLE MONTHS.
LISTEN, I'M SORRY ABOUT WHAT'S HAPPENED TO YOU. I KNOW YOU BLAME ME, BUT YOUR CORNER OF PARADISE WOULD HAVE CRUMBLED EVEN IF I HADN'T COME ALONG.
STILL, I'D LIKE TO STRAIGHTEN THINGS BETWEEN US.
HOW ABOUT IF I MEND YOUR COSTUME FOR STARTERS?
SURE, WHAT THERE IS OF IT.
LISTEN, MOCK, IF YOU WANT TO GET STRAIGHT WITH ME, HOW ABOUT TELLING ME SOMETHING ABOUT YOURSELF.
UNTIL TWO DAYS AGO, I NEVER HEARD OF YOU.

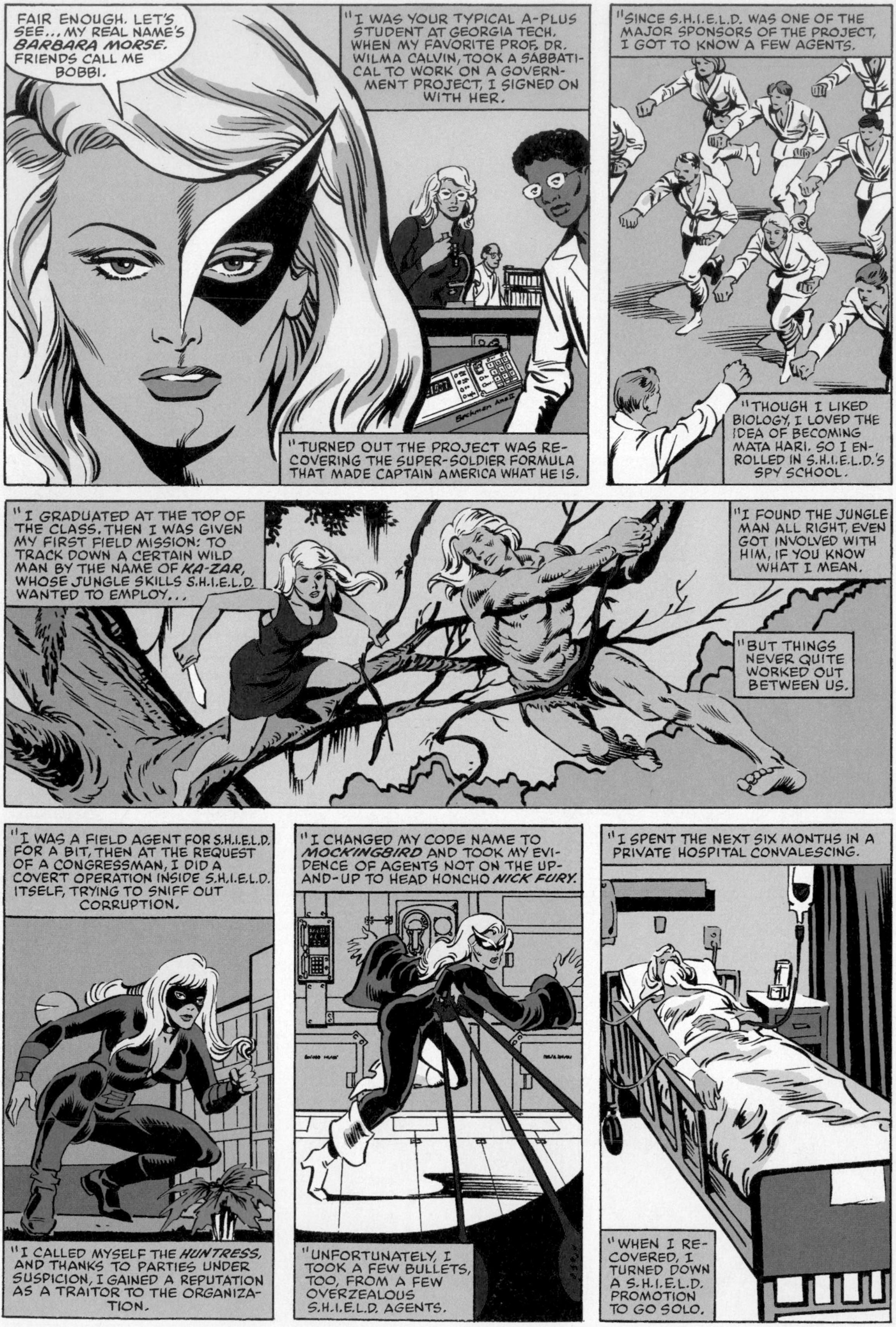
FAIR ENOUGH. LET'S SEE... MY REAL NAME'S BARBARA MORSE. FRIENDS CALL ME BOBBI.
"I WAS YOUR TYPICAL A-PLUS STUDENT AT GEORGIA TECH. WHEN MY FAVORITE PROF, DR. WILMA CALVIN, TOOK A SABBATICAL TO WORK ON A GOVERNMENT PROJECT, I SIGNED ON WITH HER.
"TURNED OUT THE PROJECT WAS RECOVERING THE SUPER-SOLDIER FORMULA THAT MADE CAPTAIN AMERICA WHAT HE IS.
"SINCE S.H.I.E.L.D. WAS ONE OF THE MAJOR SPONSORS OF THE PROJECT, I GOT TO KNOW A FEW AGENTS.
"THOUGH I LIKED BIOLOGY, I LOVED THE IDEA OF BECOMING MATA HARI. SO I ENROLLED IN S.H.I.E.L.D.'S SPY SCHOOL.
"I GRADUATED AT THE TOP OF THE CLASS. THEN I WAS GIVEN MY FIRST FIELD MISSION: TO TRACK DOWN A CERTAIN WILD MAN BY THE NAME OF KA-ZAR, WHOSE JUNGLE SKILLS S.H.I.E.L.D. WANTED TO EMPLOY...
"I FOUND THE JUNGLE MAN ALL RIGHT, EVEN GOT INVOLVED WITH HIM, IF YOU KNOW WHAT I MEAN.
"BUT THINGS NEVER QUITE WORKED OUT BETWEEN US.
"I WAS A FIELD AGENT FOR S.H.I.E.L.D. FOR A BIT, THEN AT THE REQUEST OF A CONGRESSMAN, I DID A COVERT OPERATION INSIDE S.H.I.E.L.D. ITSELF, TRYING TO SNIFF OUT CORRUPTION.
"I CALLED MYSELF THE HUNTRESS, AND THANKS TO PARTIES UNDER SUSPICION, I GAINED A REPUTATION AS A TRAITOR TO THE ORGANIZATION.
"I CHANGED MY CODE NAME TO MOCKINGBIRD AND TOOK MY EVIDENCE OF AGENTS NOT ON THE UP-AND-UP TO HEAD HONCHO NICK FURY.
"UNFORTUNATELY, I TOOK A FEW BULLETS, TOO, FROM A FEW OVERZEALOUS S.H.I.E.L.D. AGENTS.
"I SPENT THE NEXT SIX MONTHS IN A PRIVATE HOSPITAL CONVALESCING.
"WHEN I RECOVERED, I TURNED DOWN A S.H.I.E.L.D. PROMOTION TO GO SOLO.

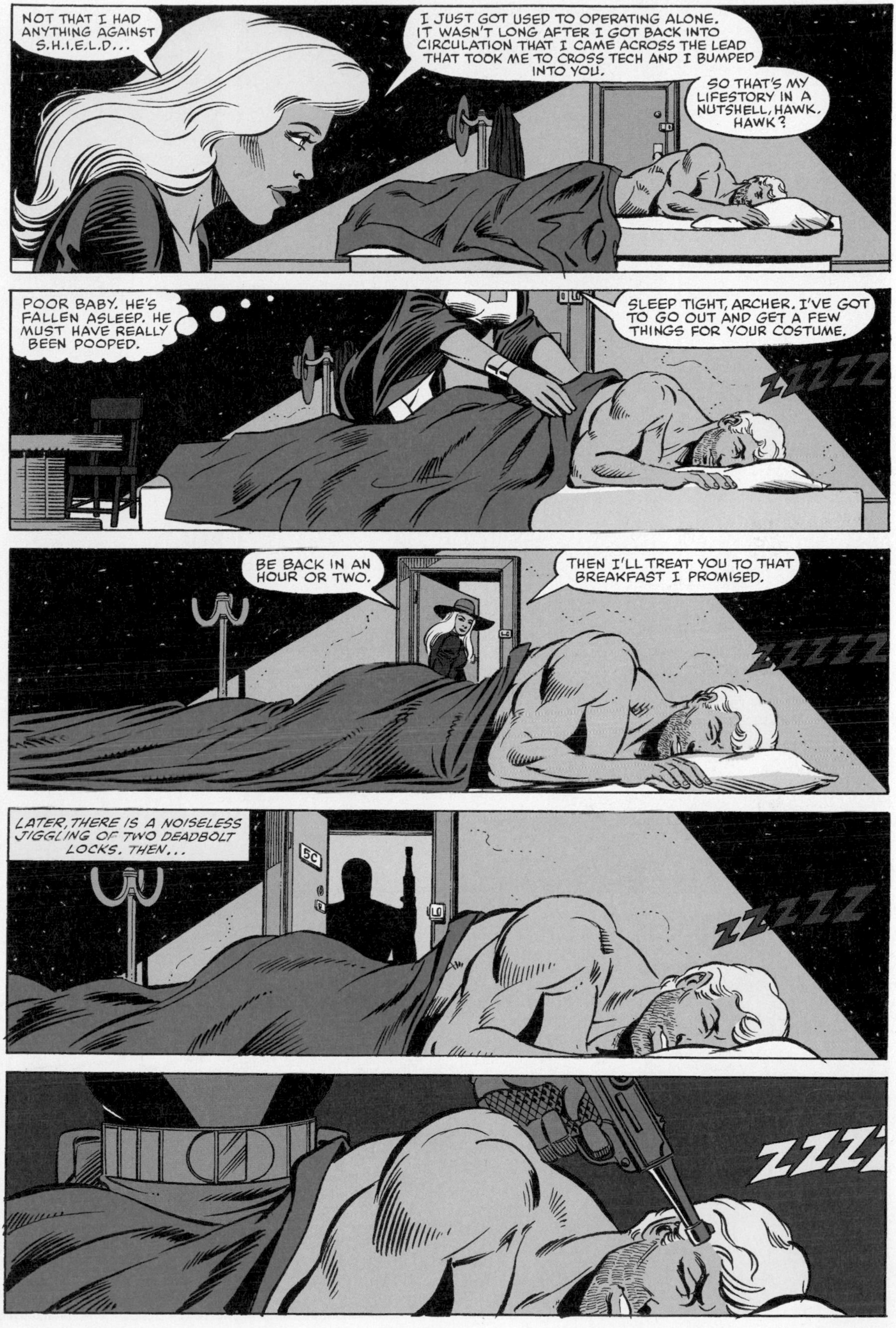
NOT THAT I HAD ANYTHING AGAINST S.H.I.E.L.D...
I JUST GOT USED TO OPERATING ALONE. IT WASN'T LONG AFTER I GOT BACK INTO CIRCULATION THAT I CAME ACROSS THE LEAD THAT TOOK ME TO CROSS TECH AND I BUMPED INTO YOU.
SO THAT'S MY LIFESTORY IN A NUTSHELL, HAWK. HAWK?
POOR BABY. HE'S FALLEN ASLEEP. HE MUST HAVE REALLY BEEN POOPED.
SLEEP TIGHT, ARCHER. I'VE GOT TO GO OUT AND GET A FEW THINGS FOR YOUR COSTUME.
ZZZZZ
BE BACK IN AN HOUR OR TWO.
THEN I'LL TREAT YOU TO THAT BREAKFAST I PROMISED.
ZZZZZ
LATER, THERE IS A NOISELESS JIGGLING OF TWO DEADBOLT LOCKS. THEN...
5C
ZZZZZ
ZZZZ

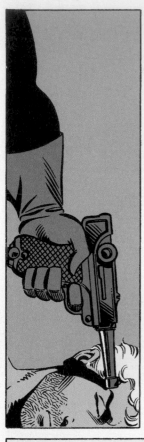

PERHAPS IT IS INSTINCT-- A SURVIVAL SENSE HONED IN HUNDREDS OF LIFE-AND-DEATH STRUGGLES...

BUT SOMEHOW CLINT BARTON FEELS THE COOL GUN METAL AT HIS TEMPLE, INSTANTLY RECOGNIZES IT FOR WHAT IT IS--

--AND REACTS.

374

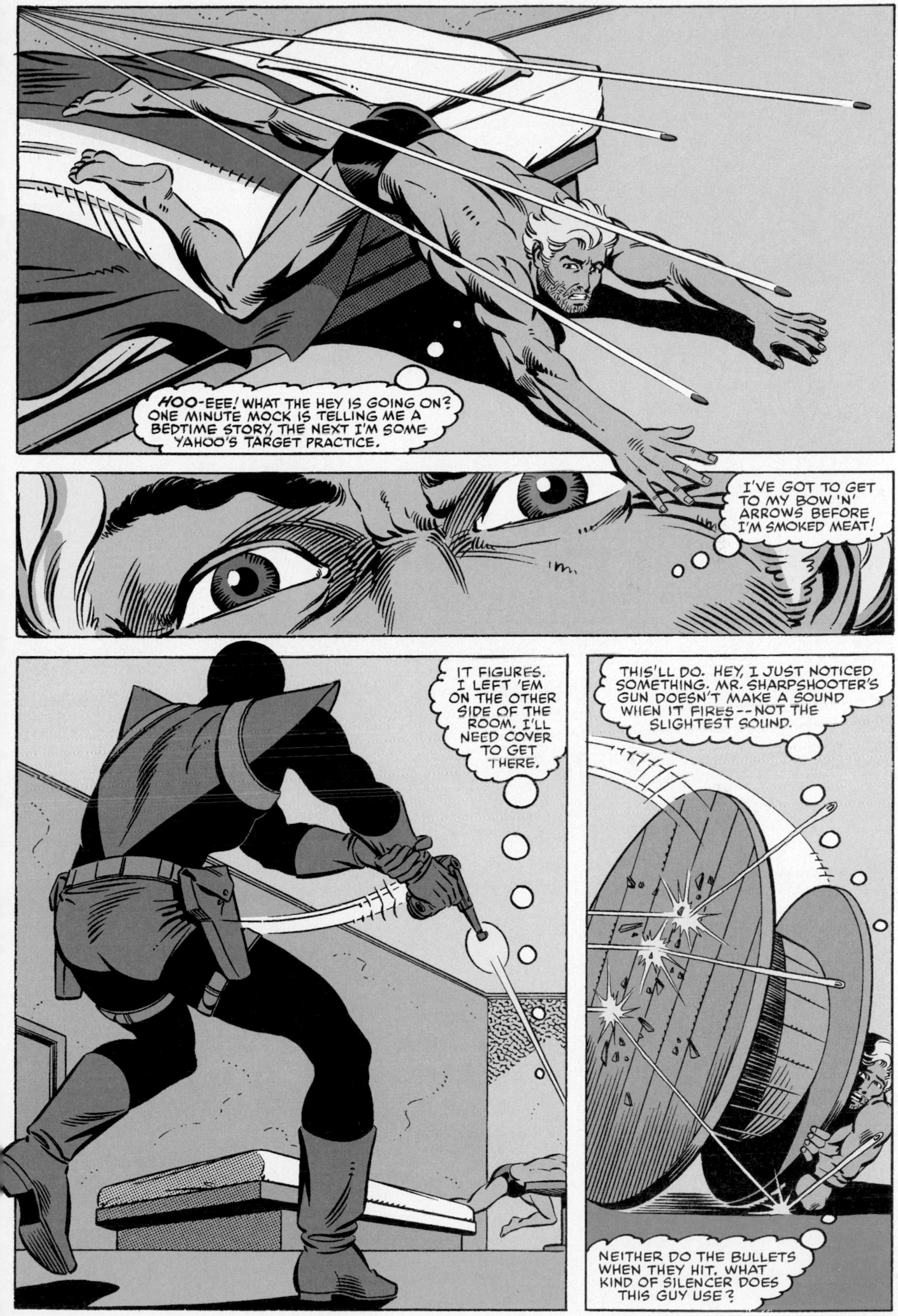
HOO-EEE! WHAT THE HEY IS GOING ON? ONE MINUTE MOCK IS TELLING ME A BEDTIME STORY, THE NEXT I'M SOME YAHOO'S TARGET PRACTICE.
I'VE GOT TO GET TO MY BOW 'N' ARROWS BEFORE I'M SMOKED MEAT!
IT FIGURES. I LEFT 'EM ON THE OTHER SIDE OF THE ROOM. I'LL NEED COVER TO GET THERE.
THIS'LL DO. HEY, I JUST NOTICED SOMETHING. MR. SHARPSHOOTER'S GUN DOESN'T MAKE A SOUND WHEN IT FIRES--NOT THE SLIGHTEST SOUND.
NEITHER DO THE BULLETS WHEN THEY HIT. WHAT KIND OF SILENCER DOES THIS GUY USE?

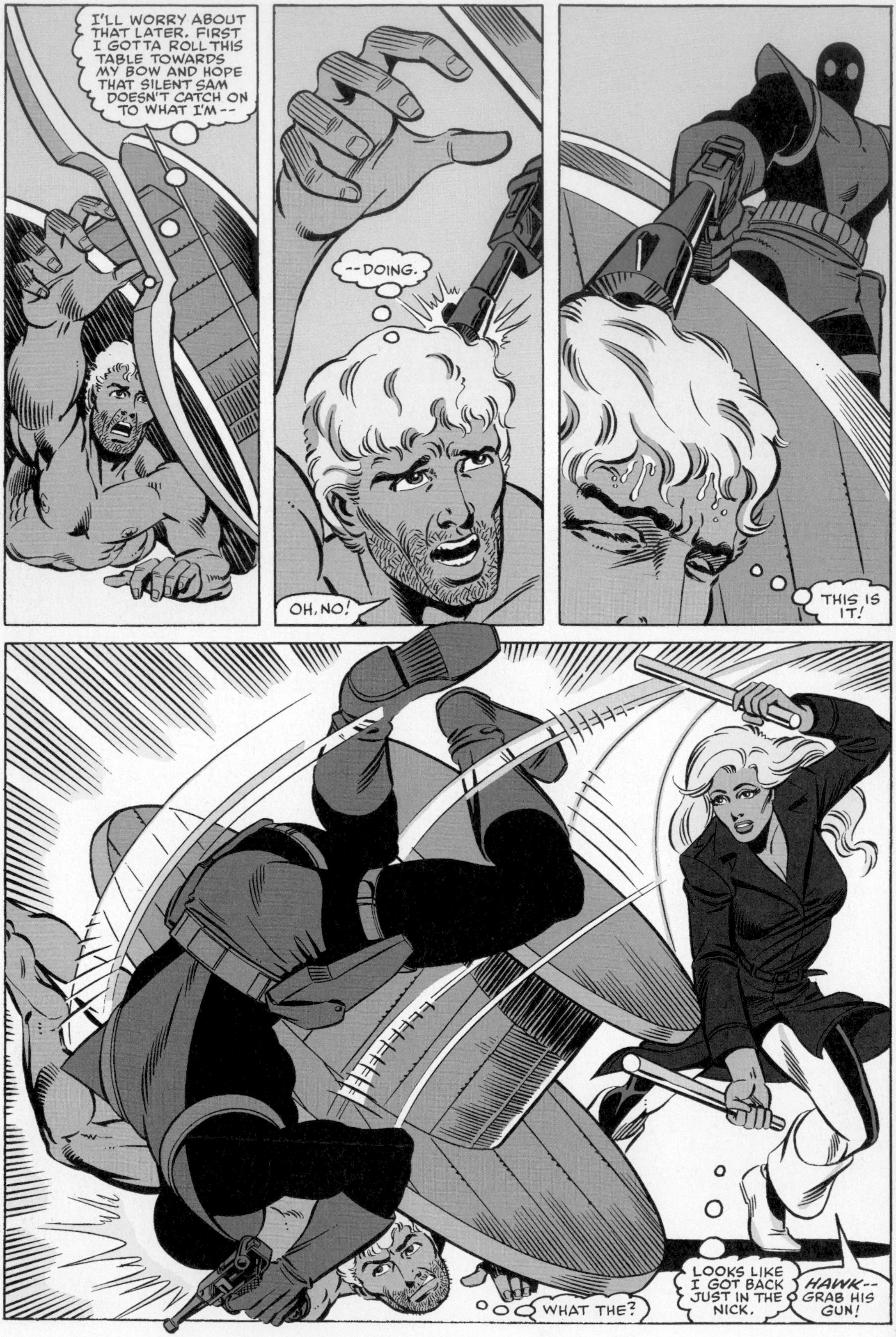

I'LL WORRY ABOUT THAT LATER. FIRST I GOTTA ROLL THIS TABLE TOWARDS MY BOW AND HOPE THAT SILENT SAM DOESN'T CATCH ON TO WHAT I'M--
--DOING.
OH, NO!
THIS IS IT!
WHAT THE?
LOOKS LIKE I GOT BACK JUST IN THE NICK.
HAWK-- GRAB HIS GUN!

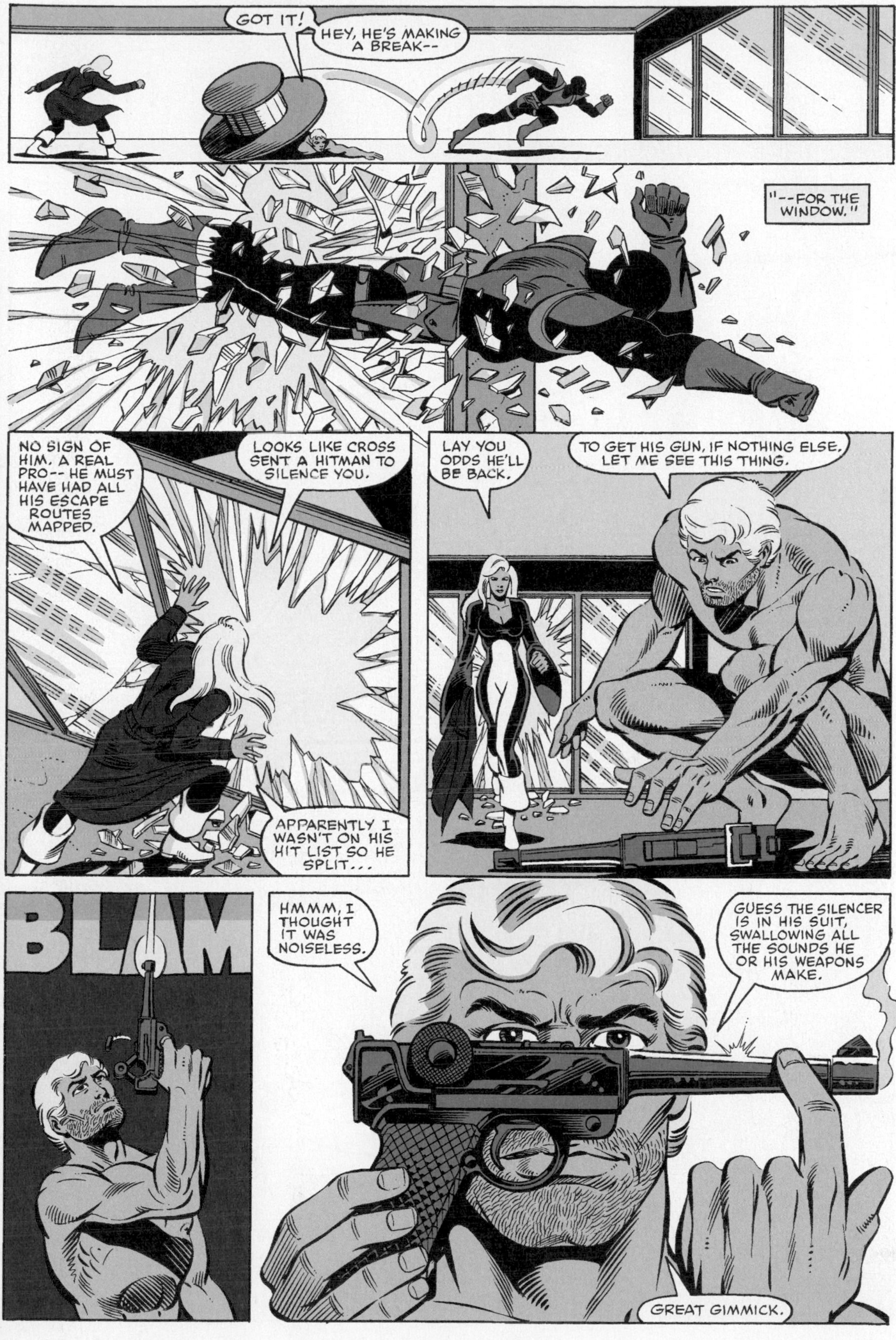
GOT IT!
HEY, HE'S MAKING A BREAK--
"--FOR THE WINDOW."
NO SIGN OF HIM. A REAL PRO-- HE MUST HAVE HAD ALL HIS ESCAPE ROUTES MAPPED.
LOOKS LIKE CROSS SENT A HITMAN TO SILENCE YOU.
APPARENTLY I WASN'T ON HIS HIT LIST SO HE SPLIT...
LAY YOU ODDS HE'LL BE BACK.
TO GET HIS GUN, IF NOTHING ELSE. LET ME SEE THIS THING.
BLAM
HMMM, I THOUGHT IT WAS NOISELESS.
GUESS THE SILENCER IS IN HIS SUIT, SWALLOWING ALL THE SOUNDS HE OR HIS WEAPONS MAKE.
GREAT GIMMICK.

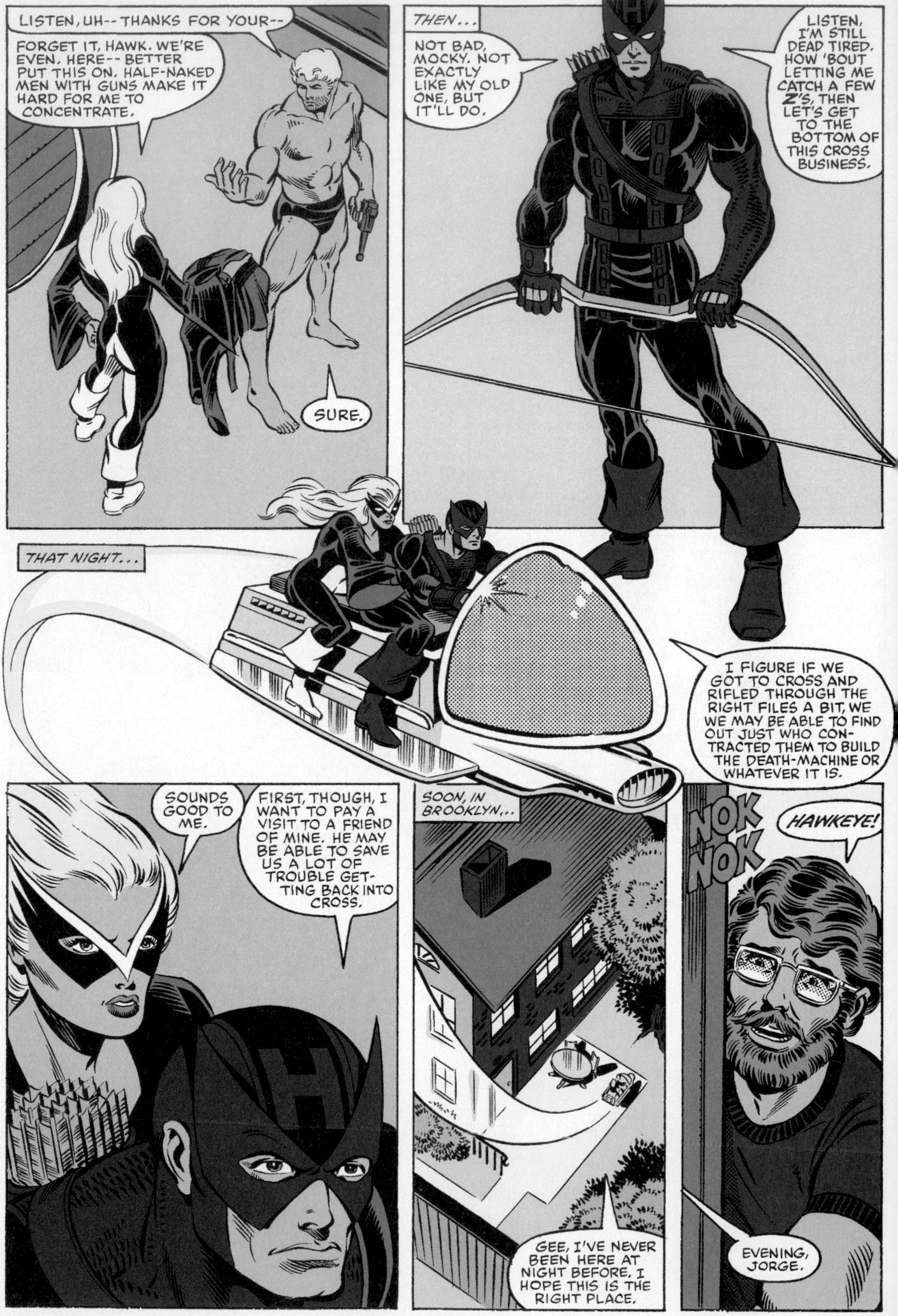
LISTEN, UH-- THANKS FOR YOUR--
FORGET IT, HAWK. WE'RE EVEN. HERE-- BETTER PUT THIS ON. HALF-NAKED MEN WITH GUNS MAKE IT HARD FOR ME TO CONCENTRATE.
SURE.
THEN...
NOT BAD, MOCKY. NOT EXACTLY LIKE MY OLD ONE, BUT IT'LL DO.
LISTEN, I'M STILL DEAD TIRED. HOW 'BOUT LETTING ME CATCH A FEW Z'S, THEN LET'S GET TO THE BOTTOM OF THIS CROSS BUSINESS.
THAT NIGHT...
I FIGURE IF WE GOT TO CROSS AND RIFLED THROUGH THE RIGHT FILES A BIT, WE WE MAY BE ABLE TO FIND OUT JUST WHO CONTRACTED THEM TO BUILD THE DEATH-MACHINE OR WHATEVER IT IS.
SOUNDS GOOD TO ME.
FIRST, THOUGH, I WANT TO PAY A VISIT TO A FRIEND OF MINE. HE MAY BE ABLE TO SAVE US A LOT OF TROUBLE GETTING BACK INTO CROSS.
SOON, IN BROOKLYN...
GEE, I'VE NEVER BEEN HERE AT NIGHT BEFORE. I HOPE THIS IS THE RIGHT PLACE.
NOK NOK
HAWKEYE!
EVENING, JORGE.

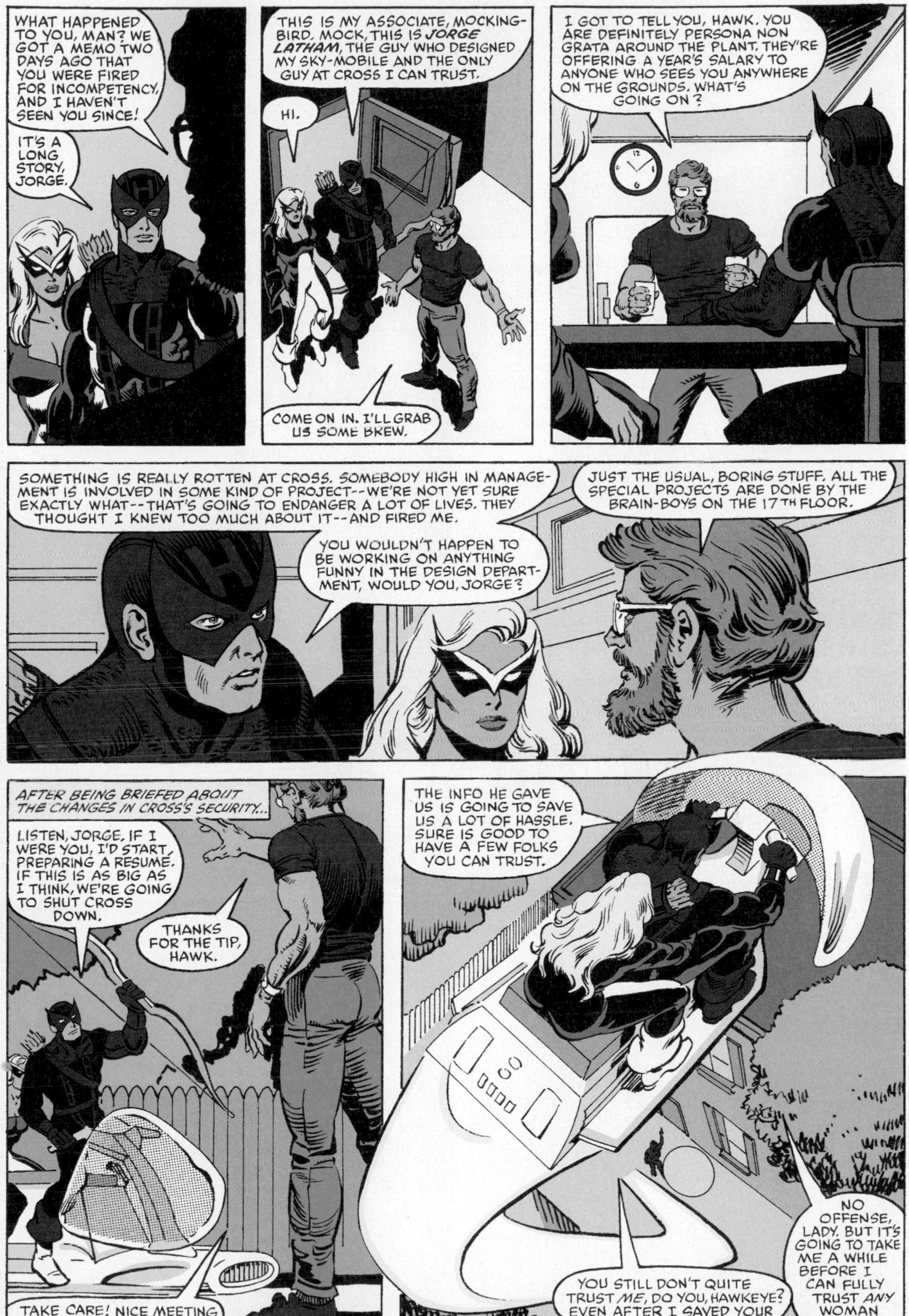
WHAT HAPPENED TO YOU, MAN? WE GOT A MEMO TWO DAYS AGO THAT YOU WERE FIRED FOR INCOMPETENCY, AND I HAVEN'T SEEN YOU SINCE!
IT'S A LONG STORY, JORGE.
THIS IS MY ASSOCIATE, MOCKINGBIRD. MOCK, THIS IS JORGE LATHAM, THE GUY WHO DESIGNED MY SKY-MOBILE AND THE ONLY GUY AT CROSS I CAN TRUST.
HI.
COME ON IN. I'LL GRAB US SOME BREW.
I GOT TO TELL YOU, HAWK. YOU ARE DEFINITELY PERSONA NON GRATA AROUND THE PLANT. THEY'RE OFFERING A YEAR'S SALARY TO ANYONE WHO SEES YOU ANYWHERE ON THE GROUNDS. WHAT'S GOING ON?
SOMETHING IS REALLY ROTTEN AT CROSS. SOMEBODY HIGH IN MANAGEMENT IS INVOLVED IN SOME KIND OF PROJECT--WE'RE NOT YET SURE EXACTLY WHAT--THAT'S GOING TO ENDANGER A LOT OF LIVES. THEY THOUGHT I KNEW TOO MUCH ABOUT IT--AND FIRED ME.
YOU WOULDN'T HAPPEN TO BE WORKING ON ANYTHING FUNNY IN THE DESIGN DEPARTMENT, WOULD YOU, JORGE?
JUST THE USUAL, BORING STUFF. ALL THE SPECIAL PROJECTS ARE DONE BY THE BRAIN-BOYS ON THE 17TH FLOOR.
AFTER BEING BRIEFED ABOUT THE CHANGES IN CROSS'S SECURITY...
LISTEN, JORGE. IF I WERE YOU, I'D START PREPARING A RESUME. IF THIS IS AS BIG AS I THINK, WE'RE GOING TO SHUT CROSS DOWN.
THANKS FOR THE TIP, HAWK.
TAKE CARE! NICE MEETING YOU, MOCKINGBIRD!
THE INFO HE GAVE US IS GOING TO SAVE US A LOT OF HASSLE. SURE IS GOOD TO HAVE A FEW FOLKS YOU CAN TRUST.
YOU STILL DON'T QUITE TRUST ME, DO YOU, HAWKEYE? EVEN AFTER I SAVED YOUR LIFE.
NO OFFENSE, LADY. BUT IT'S GOING TO TAKE ME A WHILE BEFORE I CAN FULLY TRUST ANY WOMAN AGAIN.

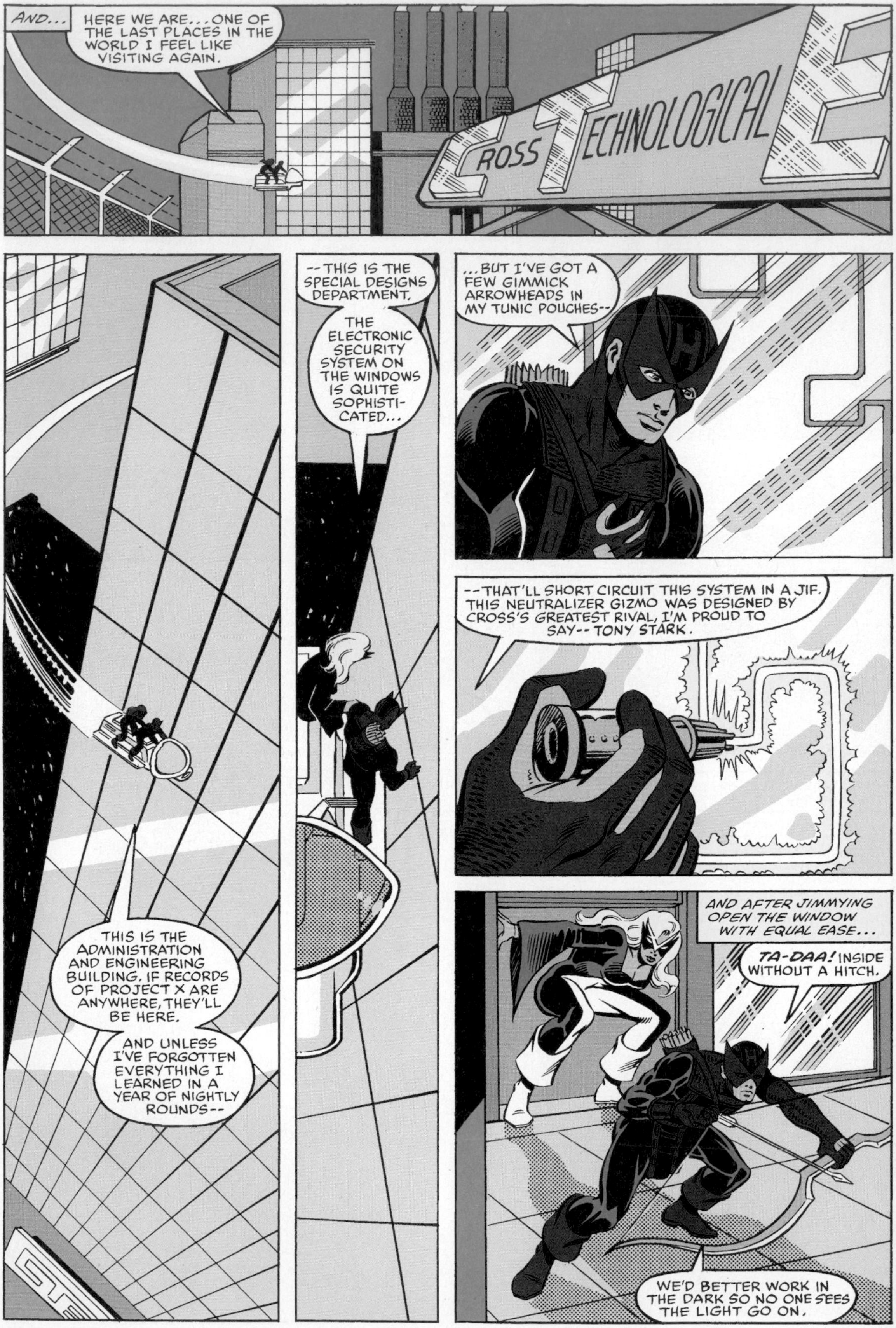
AND...
HERE WE ARE... ONE OF THE LAST PLACES IN THE WORLD I FEEL LIKE VISITING AGAIN.
CROSS TECHNOLOGICAL
THIS IS THE ADMINISTRATION AND ENGINEERING BUILDING. IF RECORDS OF PROJECT X ARE ANYWHERE, THEY'LL BE HERE.
AND UNLESS I'VE FORGOTTEN EVERYTHING I LEARNED IN A YEAR OF NIGHTLY ROUNDS--
--THIS IS THE SPECIAL DESIGNS DEPARTMENT.
THE ELECTRONIC SECURITY SYSTEM ON THE WINDOWS IS QUITE SOPHISTI-CATED...
...BUT I'VE GOT A FEW GIMMICK ARROWHEADS IN MY TUNIC POUCHES--
--THAT'LL SHORT CIRCUIT THIS SYSTEM IN A JIF. THIS NEUTRALIZER GIZMO WAS DESIGNED BY CROSS'S GREATEST RIVAL, I'M PROUD TO SAY-- TONY STARK.
AND AFTER JIMMYING OPEN THE WINDOW WITH EQUAL EASE...
TA-DAA! INSIDE WITHOUT A HITCH.
WE'D BETTER WORK IN THE DARK SO NO ONE SEES THE LIGHT GO ON.

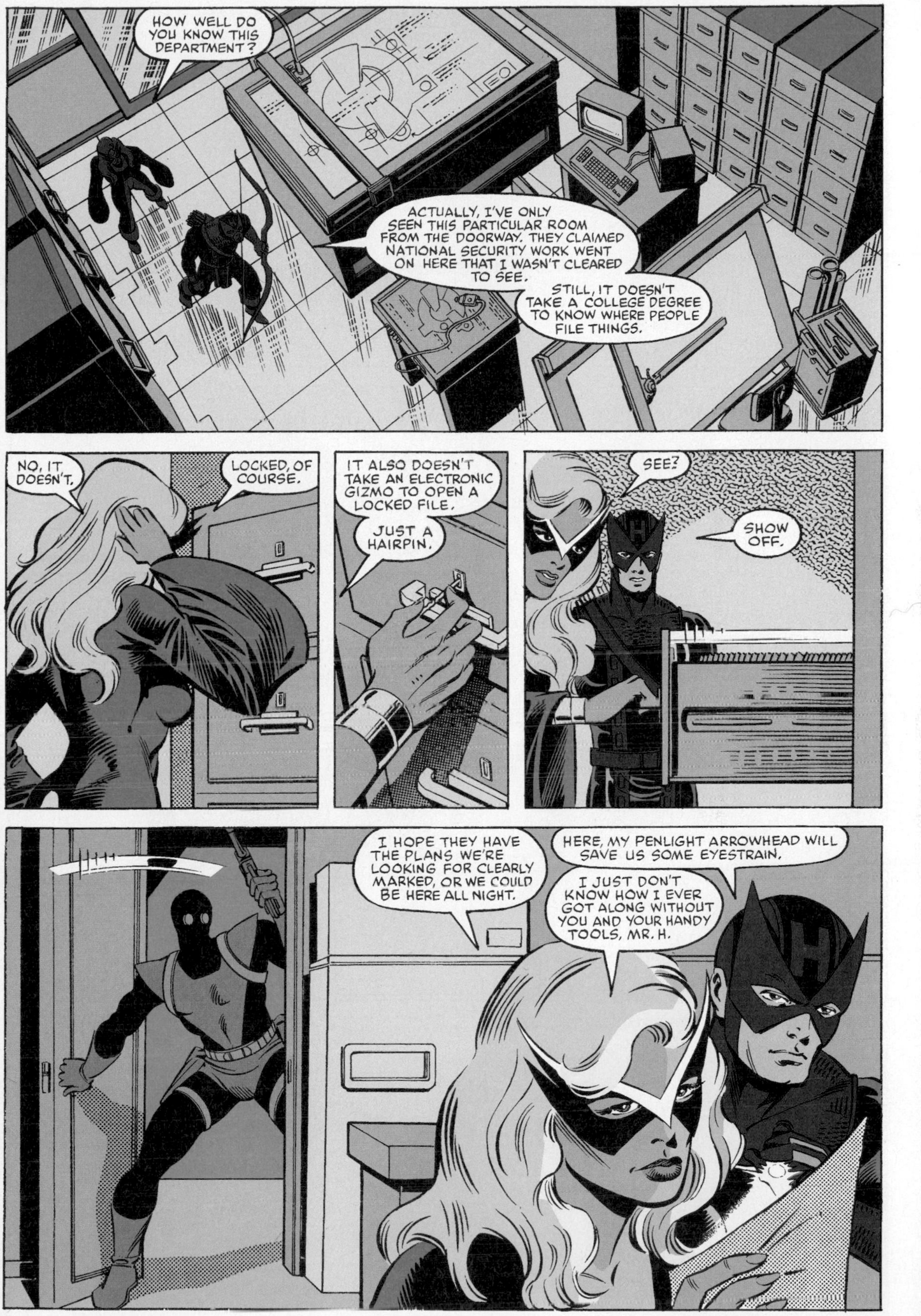

HOW WELL DO YOU KNOW THIS DEPARTMENT?
ACTUALLY, I'VE ONLY SEEN THIS PARTICULAR ROOM FROM THE DOORWAY. THEY CLAIMED NATIONAL SECURITY WORK WENT ON HERE THAT I WASN'T CLEARED TO SEE.
STILL, IT DOESN'T TAKE A COLLEGE DEGREE TO KNOW WHERE PEOPLE FILE THINGS.
NO, IT DOESN'T.
LOCKED, OF COURSE.
IT ALSO DOESN'T TAKE AN ELECTRONIC GIZMO TO OPEN A LOCKED FILE.
JUST A HAIRPIN.
SEE?
SHOW OFF.
I HOPE THEY HAVE THE PLANS WE'RE LOOKING FOR CLEARLY MARKED, OR WE COULD BE HERE ALL NIGHT.
HERE, MY PENLIGHT ARROWHEAD WILL SAVE US SOME EYESTRAIN.
I JUST DON'T KNOW HOW I EVER GOT ALONG WITHOUT YOU AND YOUR HANDY TOOLS, MR. H.

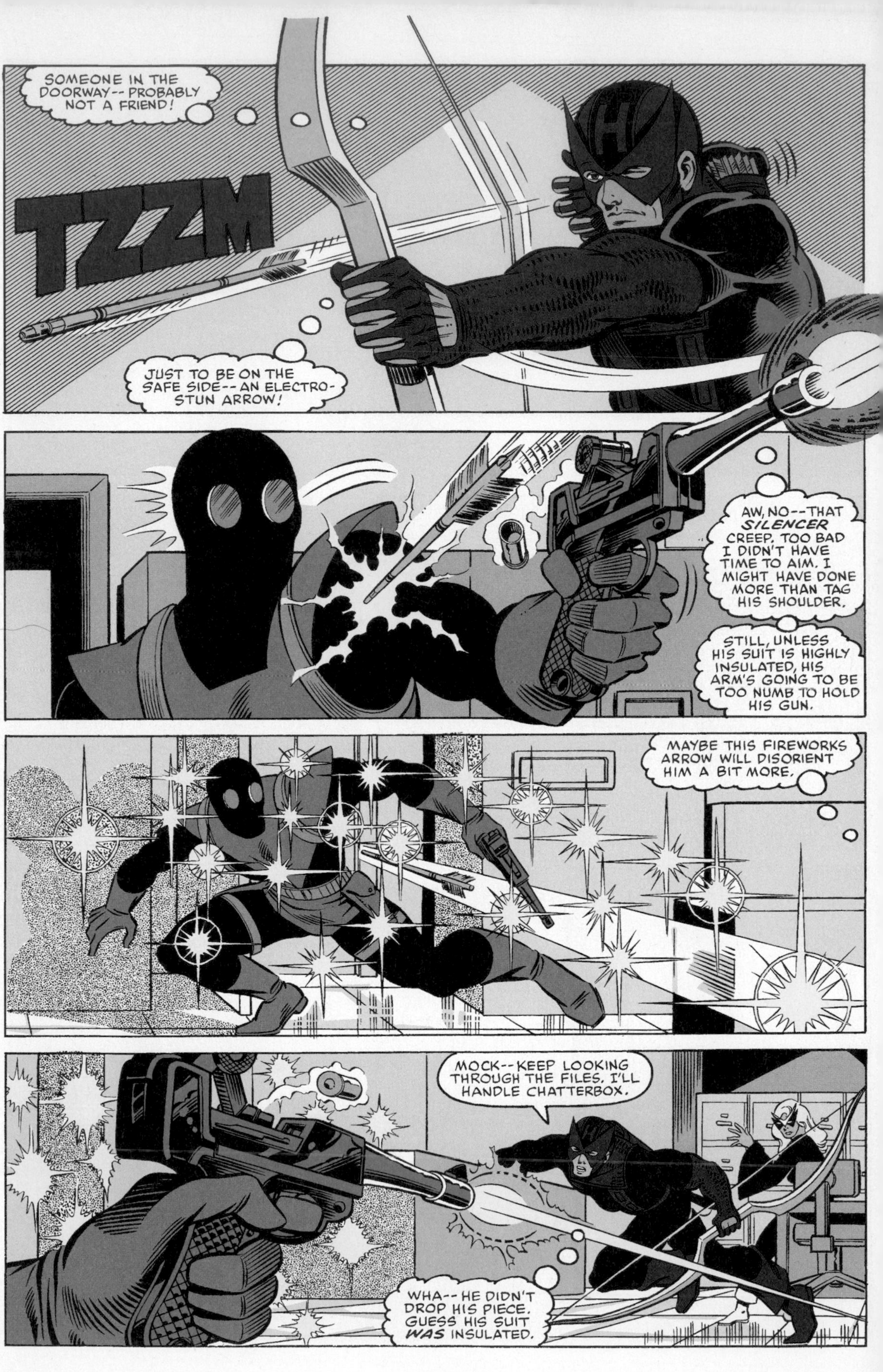
SOMEONE IN THE DOORWAY-- PROBABLY NOT A FRIEND!
TZZM
JUST TO BE ON THE SAFE SIDE-- AN ELECTRO-STUN ARROW!
AW, NO--THAT SILENCER CREEP. TOO BAD I DIDN'T HAVE TIME TO AIM. I MIGHT HAVE DONE MORE THAN TAG HIS SHOULDER.
STILL, UNLESS HIS SUIT IS HIGHLY INSULATED, HIS ARM'S GOING TO BE TOO NUMB TO HOLD HIS GUN.
MAYBE THIS FIREWORKS ARROW WILL DISORIENT HIM A BIT MORE.
MOCK--KEEP LOOKING THROUGH THE FILES. I'LL HANDLE CHATTERBOX.
WHA-- HE DIDN'T DROP HIS PIECE. GUESS HIS SUIT WAS INSULATED.

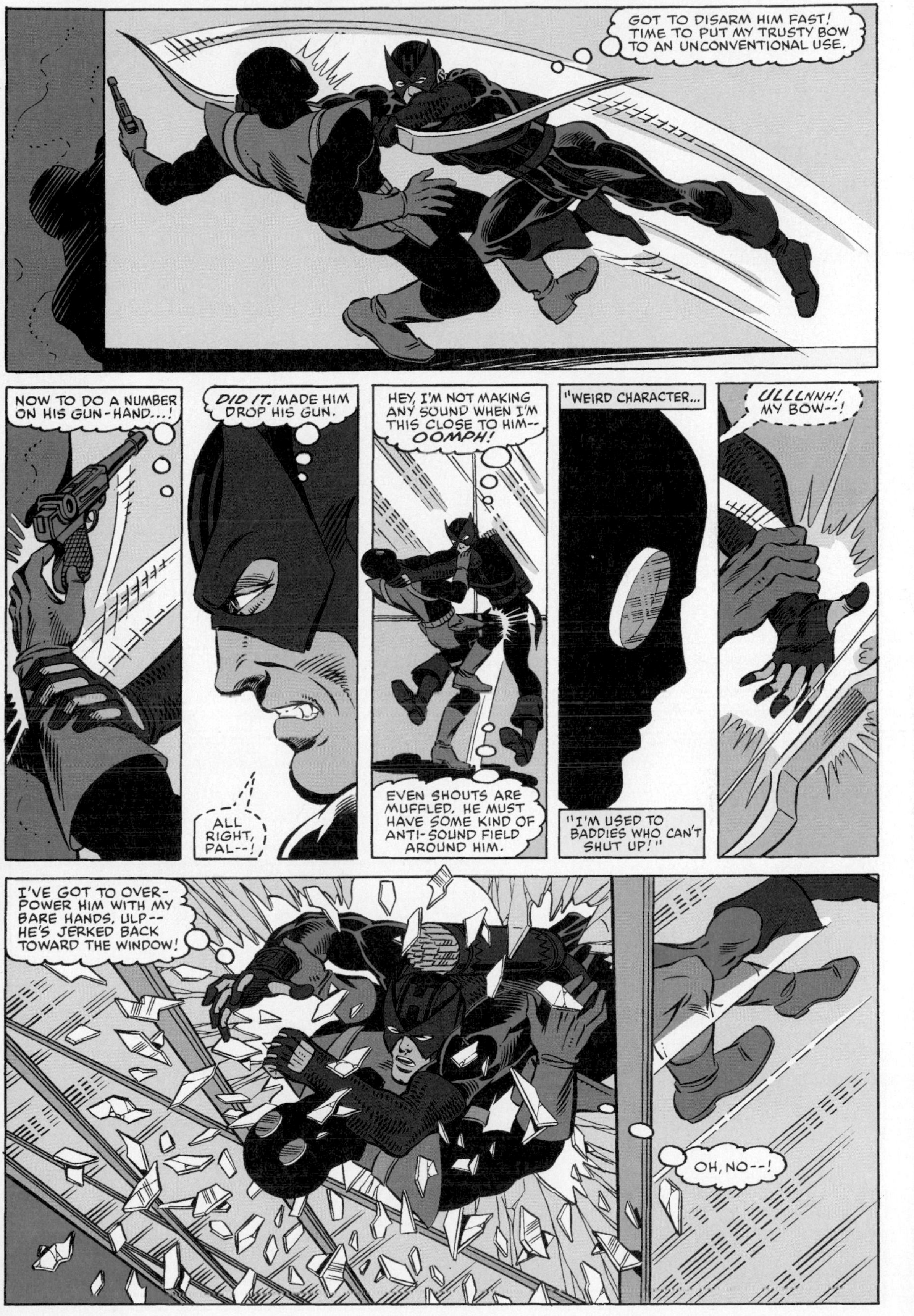
GOT TO DISARM HIM FAST! TIME TO PUT MY TRUSTY BOW TO AN UNCONVENTIONAL USE.
NOW TO DO A NUMBER ON HIS GUN-HAND...!
DID IT. MADE HIM DROP HIS GUN.
ALL RIGHT, PAL--!
HEY, I'M NOT MAKING ANY SOUND WHEN I'M THIS CLOSE TO HIM-- OOMPH!
EVEN SHOUTS ARE MUFFLED. HE MUST HAVE SOME KIND OF ANTI-SOUND FIELD AROUND HIM.
"WEIRD CHARACTER...
"I'M USED TO BADDIES WHO CAN'T SHUT UP!"
ULLLNNH! MY BOW--!
I'VE GOT TO OVER-POWER HIM WITH MY BARE HANDS. ULP-- HE'S JERKED BACK TOWARD THE WINDOW!
OH, NO--!

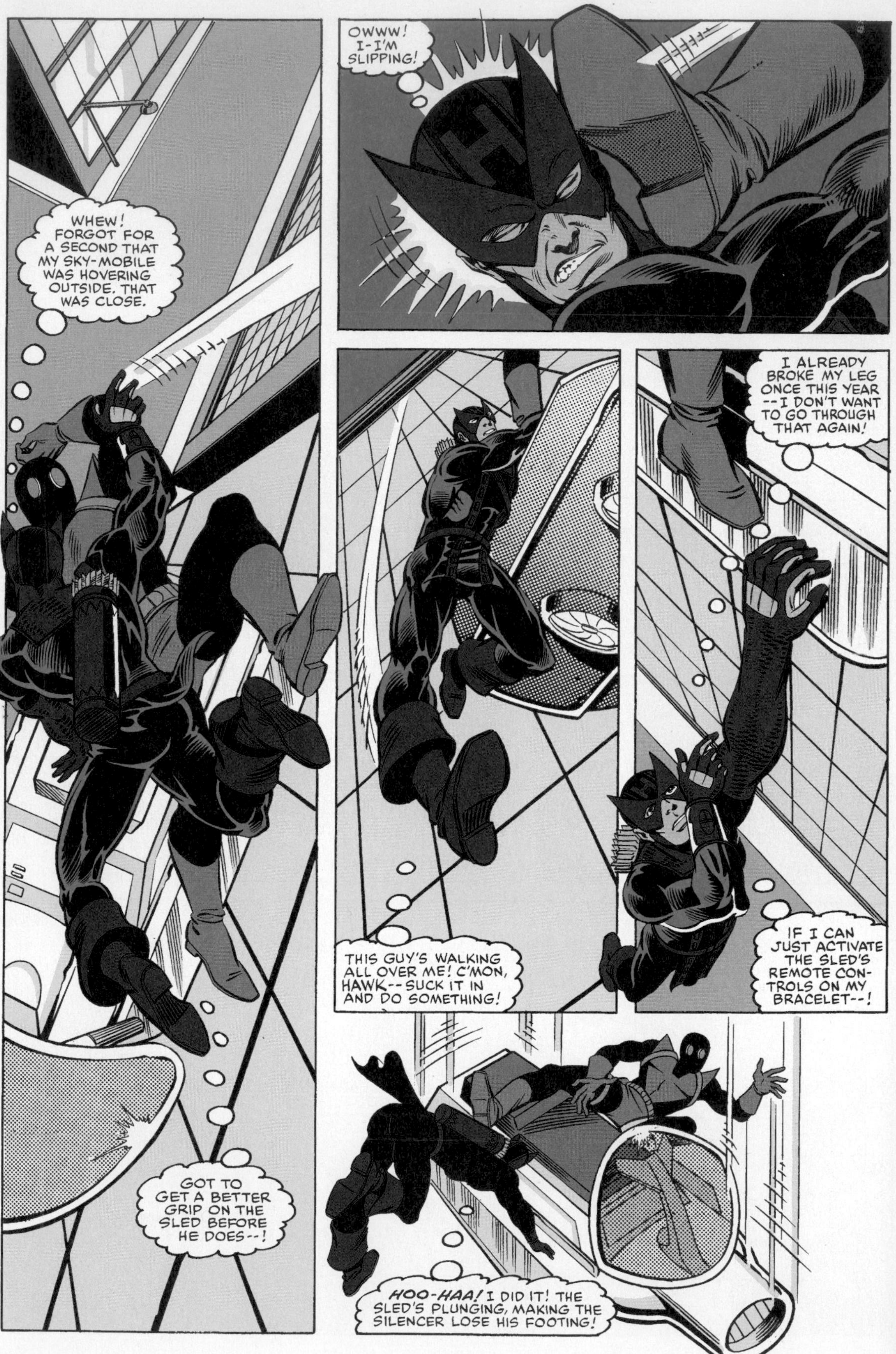

WHEW! FORGOT FOR A SECOND THAT MY SKY-MOBILE WAS HOVERING OUTSIDE. THAT WAS CLOSE.
GOT TO GET A BETTER GRIP ON THE SLED BEFORE HE DOES--!
OWWW! I-I'M SLIPPING!
THIS GUY'S WALKING ALL OVER ME! C'MON, HAWK--SUCK IT IN AND DO SOMETHING!
I ALREADY BROKE MY LEG ONCE THIS YEAR--I DON'T WANT TO GO THROUGH THAT AGAIN!
IF I CAN JUST ACTIVATE THE SLED'S REMOTE CON-TROLS ON MY BRACELET--!
HOO-HAA! I DID IT! THE SLED'S PLUNGING, MAKING THE SILENCER LOSE HIS FOOTING!

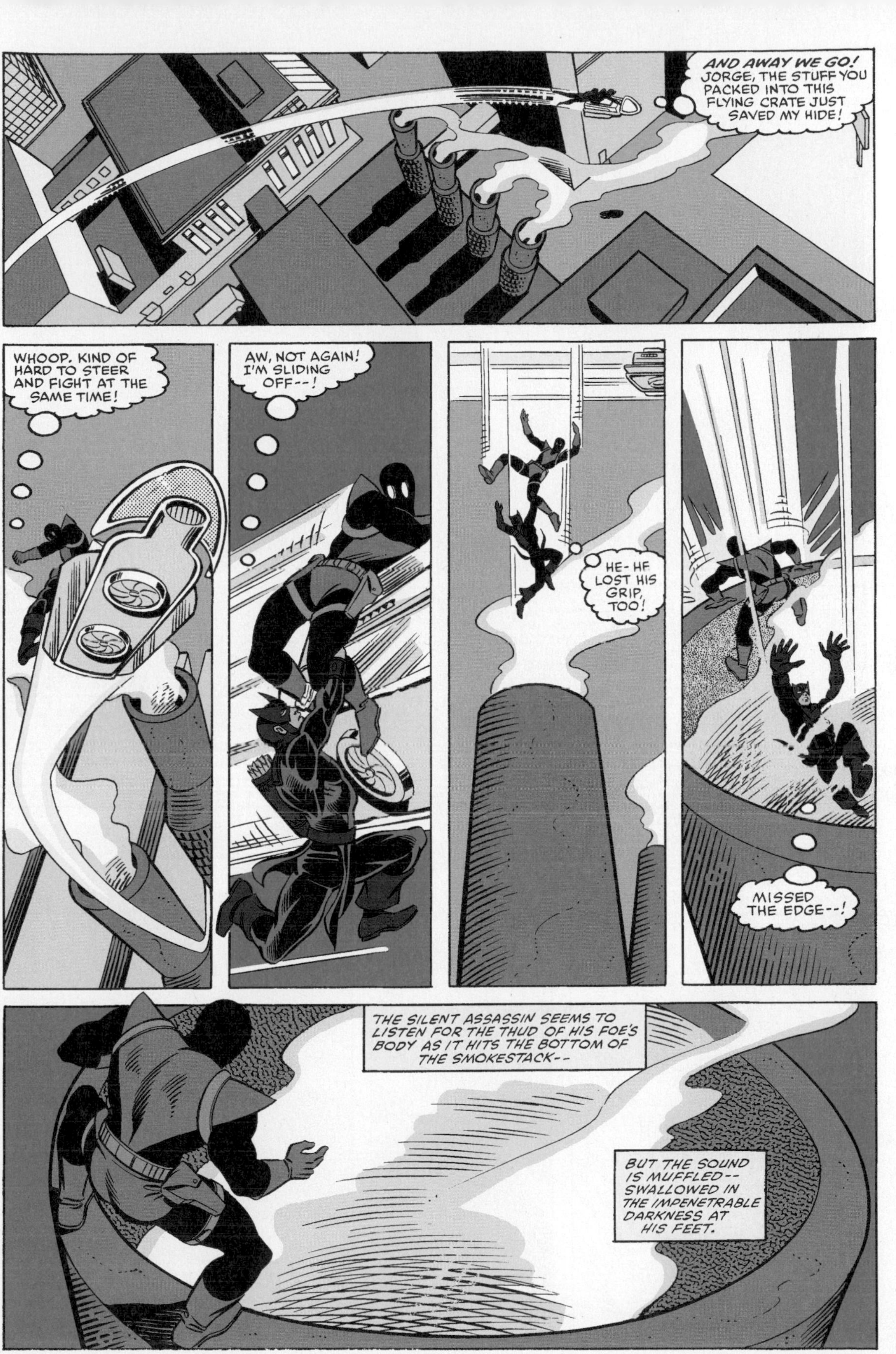
AND AWAY WE GO! JORGE, THE STUFF YOU PACKED INTO THIS FLYING CRATE JUST SAVED MY HIDE!
WHOOP. KIND OF HARD TO STEER AND FIGHT AT THE SAME TIME!
AW, NOT AGAIN! I'M SLIDING OFF--!
HE- HF LOST HIS GRIP, TOO!
MISSED THE EDGE--!
THE SILENT ASSASSIN SEEMS TO LISTEN FOR THE THUD OF HIS FOE'S BODY AS IT HITS THE BOTTOM OF THE SMOKESTACK--
BUT THE SOUND IS MUFFLED-- SWALLOWED IN THE IMPENETRABLE DARKNESS AT HIS FEET.

THE SILENCER TURNS, LOOKING FOR THE EASIEST WAY DOWN FROM HIS 200-FOOT HIGH PERCH.

HE SOON FINDS IT.

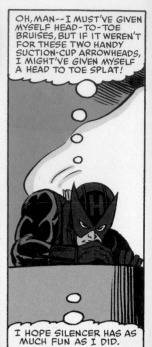

OH, MAN-- I MUST'VE GIVEN MYSELF HEAD-TO-TOE BRUISES, BUT IF IT WEREN'T FOR THESE TWO HANDY SUCTION-CUP ARROWHEADS, I MIGHT'VE GIVEN MYSELF A HEAD TO TOE SPLAT!

I HOPE SILENCER HAS AS MUCH FUN AS I DID.

AFTER SUMMONING HIS SKY-SLED...

WONDER HOW MOCKINGBIRD IS DOING. WE MUST HAVE TRIPPED SOME KIND OF ALARM IF SILENCER KNEW WHERE TO FIND US.

NO TELLING WHO ELSE MIGHT HAVE BEEN SENT.

HAWK! THERE YOU ARE. I WAS BEGINNING TO WORRY.

NO NEED. I'M A BIG BOY.

DID YOU GET THE INFORMATION?

YOU BETCHA. THE BLUEPRINTS, THE CLIENT'S NAME AND ADDRESS ...EVERYTHING.

RUN INTO ANY TROUBLE?

"NOT REALLY."

NEXT ▷ BEHIND THE ⑧-BALL!

MARVEL®
#3 IN A FOUR-ISSUE LIMITED SERIES
HAWKEYE™
©1983 MARVEL COMICS GROUP
TM
60¢
3
NOV
02972
APPROVED BY THE COMICS CODE AUTHORITY
GRUENWALD LAYTON

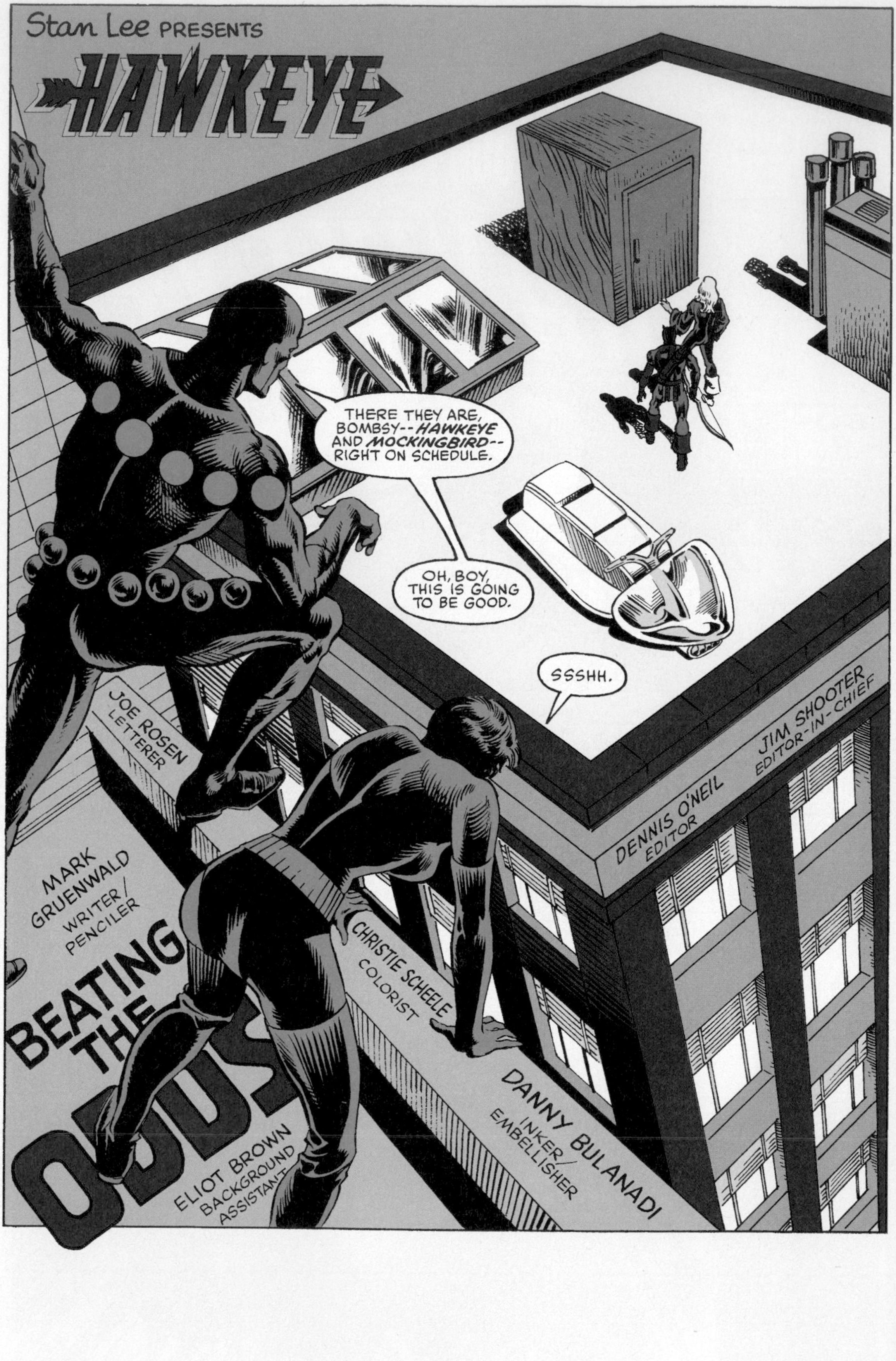
Stan Lee PRESENTS
HAWKEYE
THERE THEY ARE, BOMBSY--HAWKEYE AND MOCKINGBIRD--RIGHT ON SCHEDULE.
OH, BOY, THIS IS GOING TO BE GOOD.
SSSHH.
JOE ROSEN LETTERER
JIM SHOOTER EDITOR-IN-CHIEF
DENNIS O'NEIL EDITOR
MARK GRUENWALD WRITER/PENCILER
CHRISTIE SCHEELE COLORIST
BEATING THE ODDS
DANNY BULANADI INKER/EMBELLISHER
ELIOT BROWN BACKGROUND ASSISTANT

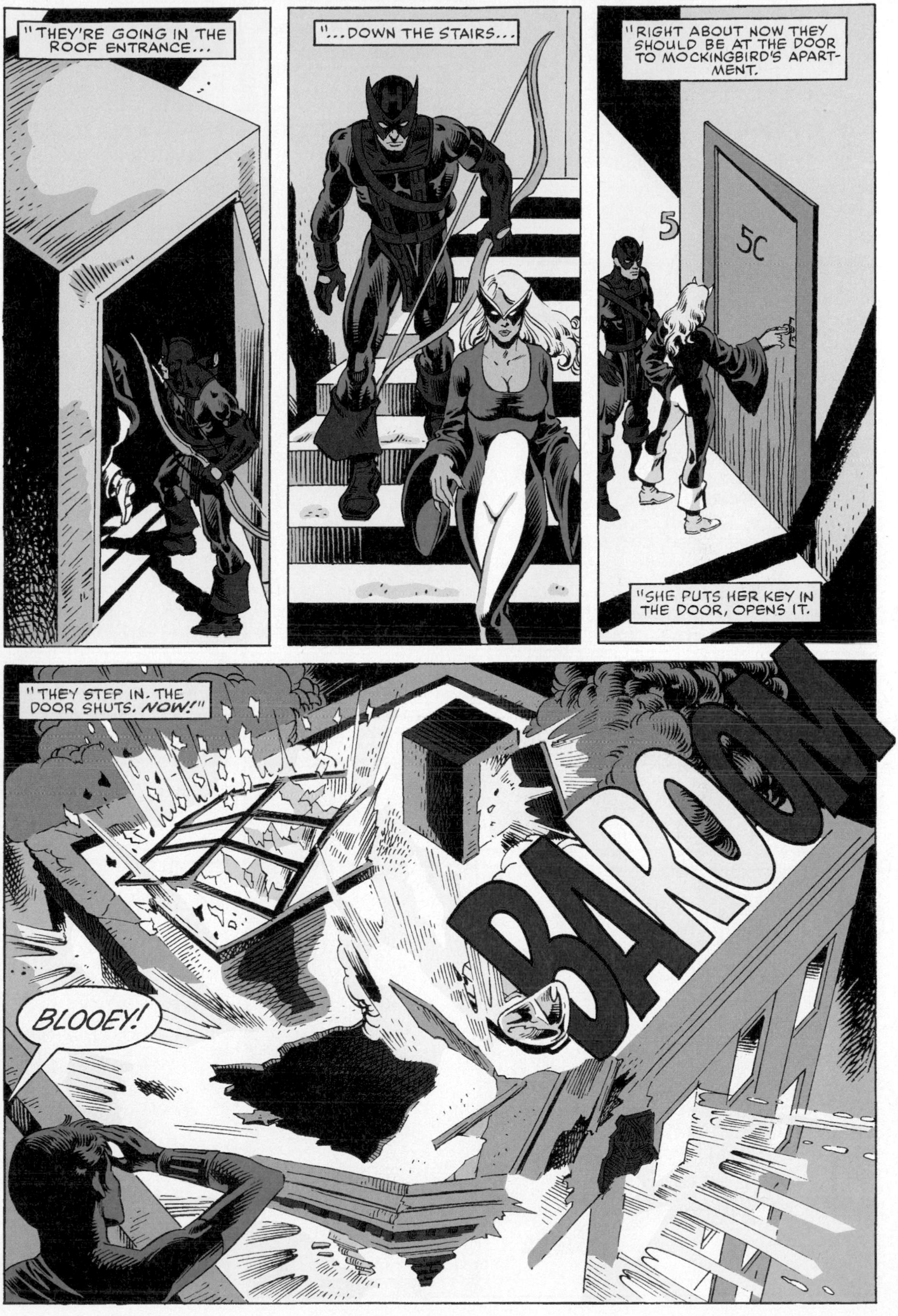

"THEY'RE GOING IN THE ROOF ENTRANCE...
"...DOWN THE STAIRS...
"RIGHT ABOUT NOW THEY SHOULD BE AT THE DOOR TO MOCKINGBIRD'S APARTMENT.
5
5C
"SHE PUTS HER KEY IN THE DOOR, OPENS IT.
"THEY STEP IN. THE DOOR SHUTS. NOW!"
BAROOM
BLOOEY!

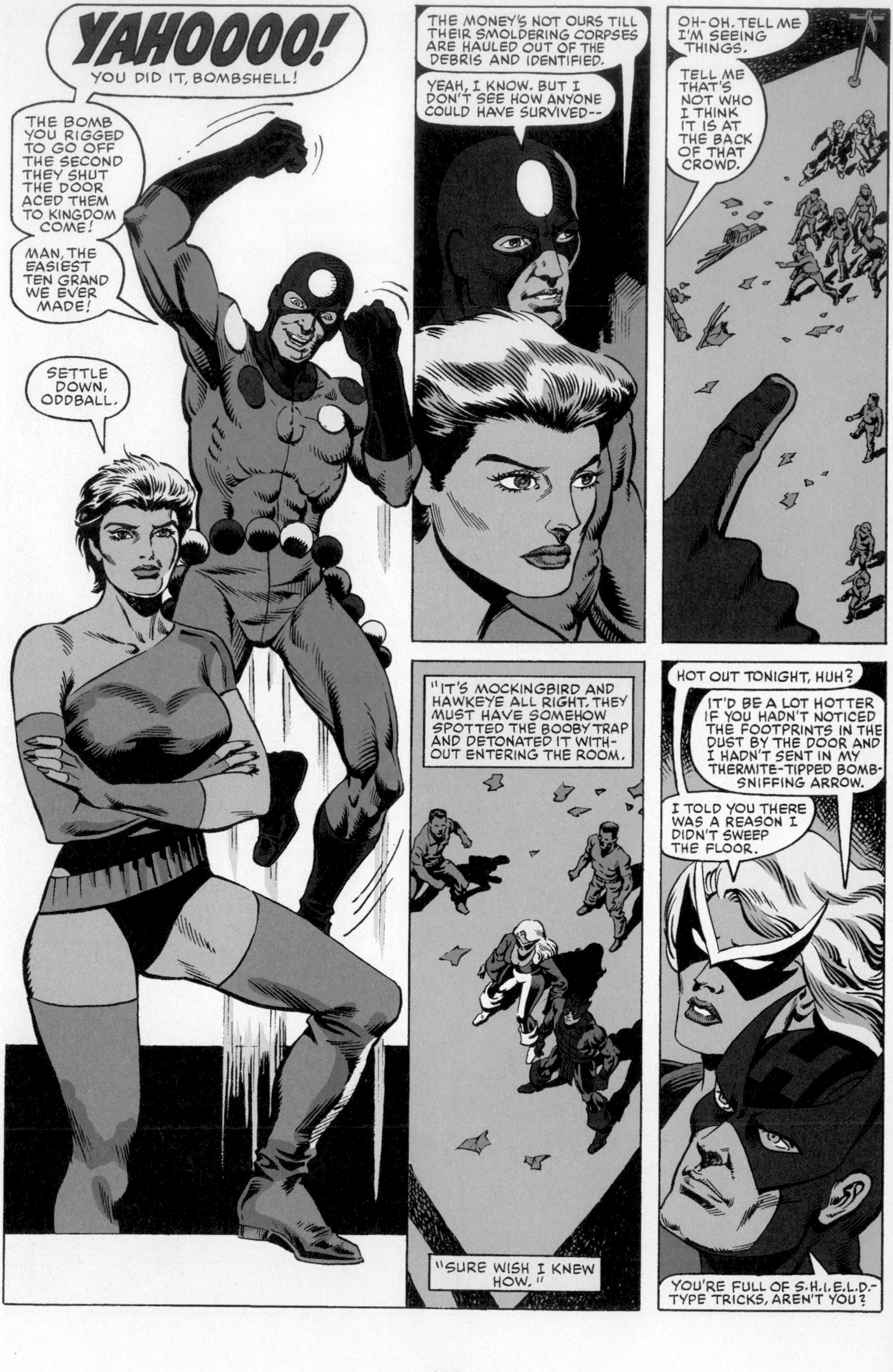
YAHOOOO! YOU DID IT, BOMBSHELL!
THE BOMB YOU RIGGED TO GO OFF THE SECOND THEY SHUT THE DOOR ACED THEM TO KINGDOM COME!
MAN, THE EASIEST TEN GRAND WE EVER MADE!
SETTLE DOWN, ODDBALL.
THE MONEY'S NOT OURS TILL THEIR SMOLDERING CORPSES ARE HAULED OUT OF THE DEBRIS AND IDENTIFIED.
YEAH, I KNOW. BUT I DON'T SEE HOW ANYONE COULD HAVE SURVIVED--
OH-OH. TELL ME I'M SEEING THINGS.
TELL ME THAT'S NOT WHO I THINK IT IS AT THE BACK OF THAT CROWD.
"IT'S MOCKINGBIRD AND HAWKEYE ALL RIGHT. THEY MUST HAVE SOMEHOW SPOTTED THE BOOBY TRAP AND DETONATED IT WITHOUT ENTERING THE ROOM.
"SURE WISH I KNEW HOW."
HOT OUT TONIGHT, HUH?
IT'D BE A LOT HOTTER IF YOU HADN'T NOTICED THE FOOTPRINTS IN THE DUST BY THE DOOR AND I HADN'T SENT IN MY THERMITE-TIPPED BOMB-SNIFFING ARROW.
I TOLD YOU THERE WAS A REASON I DIDN'T SWEEP THE FLOOR.
YOU'RE FULL OF S.H.I.E.L.D.-TYPE TRICKS, AREN'T YOU?

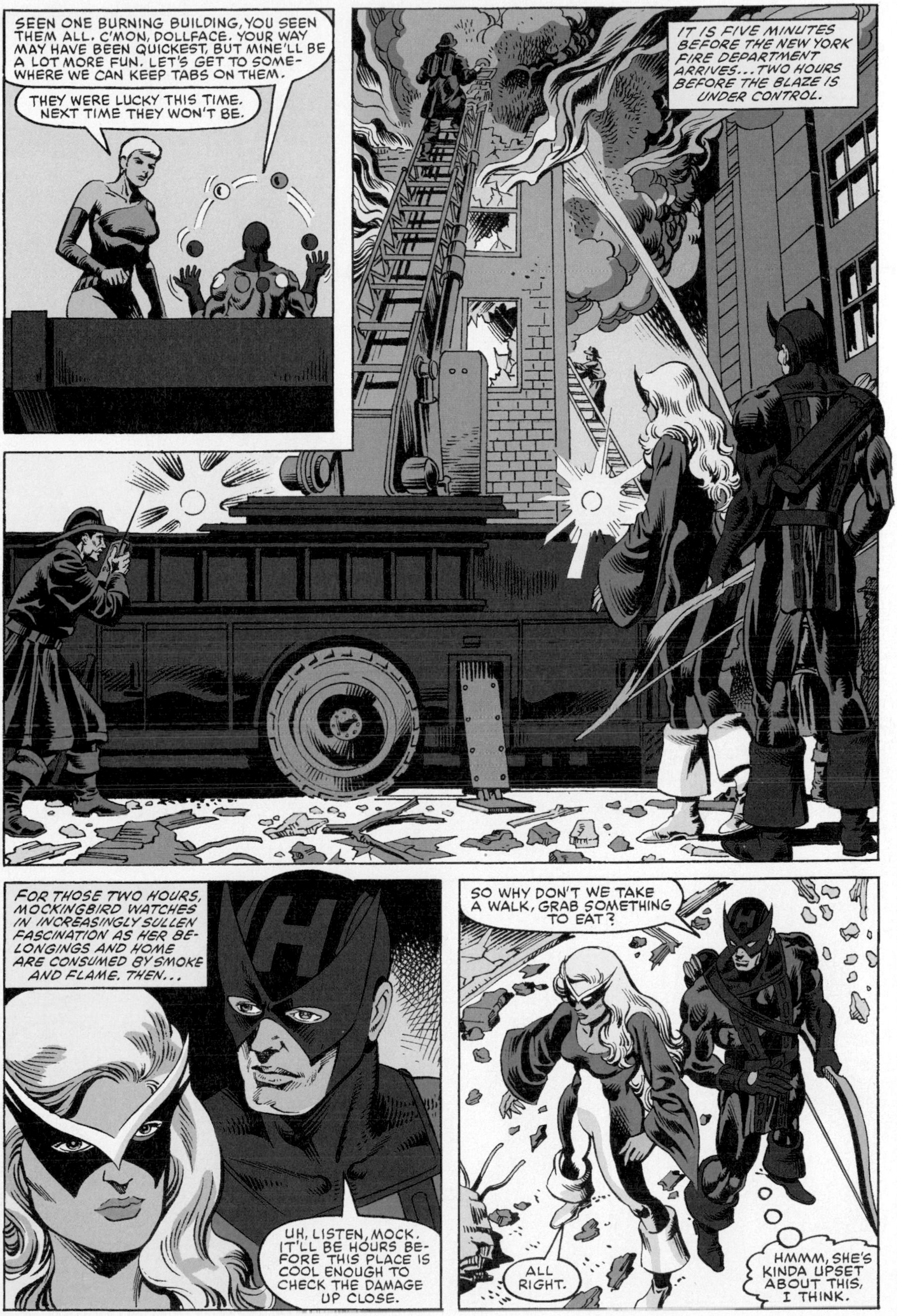

SEEN ONE BURNING BUILDING, YOU SEEN THEM ALL. C'MON, DOLLFACE. YOUR WAY MAY HAVE BEEN QUICKEST, BUT MINE'LL BE A LOT MORE FUN. LET'S GET TO SOMEWHERE WE CAN KEEP TABS ON THEM.
THEY WERE LUCKY THIS TIME. NEXT TIME THEY WON'T BE.
IT IS FIVE MINUTES BEFORE THE NEW YORK FIRE DEPARTMENT ARRIVES... TWO HOURS BEFORE THE BLAZE IS UNDER CONTROL.
FOR THOSE TWO HOURS, MOCKINGBIRD WATCHES IN INCREASINGLY SULLEN FASCINATION AS HER BELONGINGS AND HOME ARE CONSUMED BY SMOKE AND FLAME. THEN...
UH, LISTEN, MOCK. IT'LL BE HOURS BEFORE THIS PLACE IS COOL ENOUGH TO CHECK THE DAMAGE UP CLOSE.
SO WHY DON'T WE TAKE A WALK, GRAB SOMETHING TO EAT?
ALL RIGHT.
HMMM, SHE'S KINDA UPSET ABOUT THIS, I THINK.

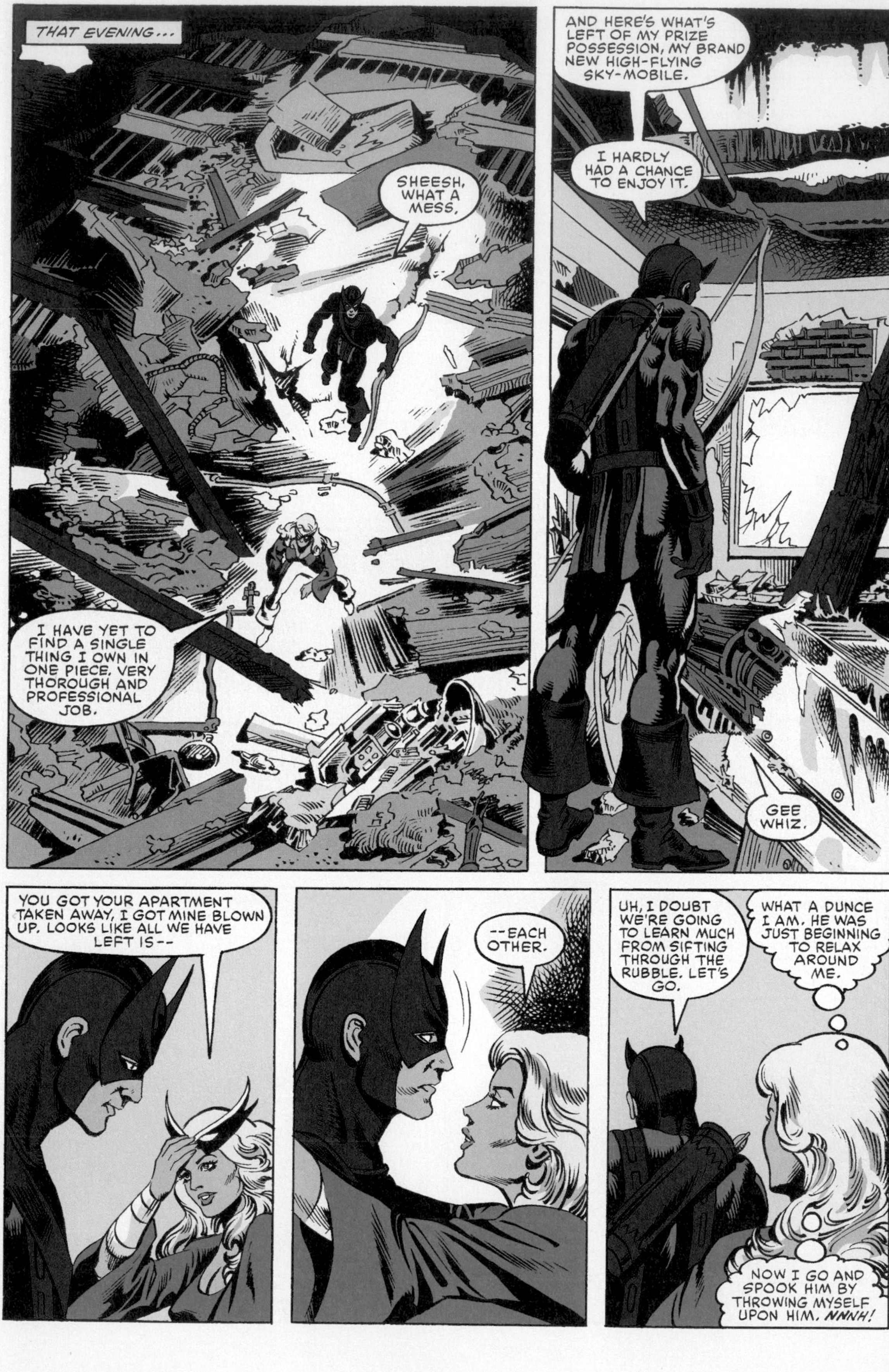
THAT EVENING...
SHEESH, WHAT A MESS.
I HAVE YET TO FIND A SINGLE THING I OWN IN ONE PIECE. VERY THOROUGH AND PROFESSIONAL JOB.
AND HERE'S WHAT'S LEFT OF MY PRIZE POSSESSION, MY BRAND NEW HIGH-FLYING SKY-MOBILE.
I HARDLY HAD A CHANCE TO ENJOY IT.
GEE WHIZ.
YOU GOT YOUR APARTMENT TAKEN AWAY, I GOT MINE BLOWN UP. LOOKS LIKE ALL WE HAVE LEFT IS--
--EACH OTHER.
UH, I DOUBT WE'RE GOING TO LEARN MUCH FROM SIFTING THROUGH THE RUBBLE. LET'S GO.
WHAT A DUNCE I AM. HE WAS JUST BEGINNING TO RELAX AROUND ME.
NOW I GO AND SPOOK HIM BY THROWING MYSELF UPON HIM. NNNH!

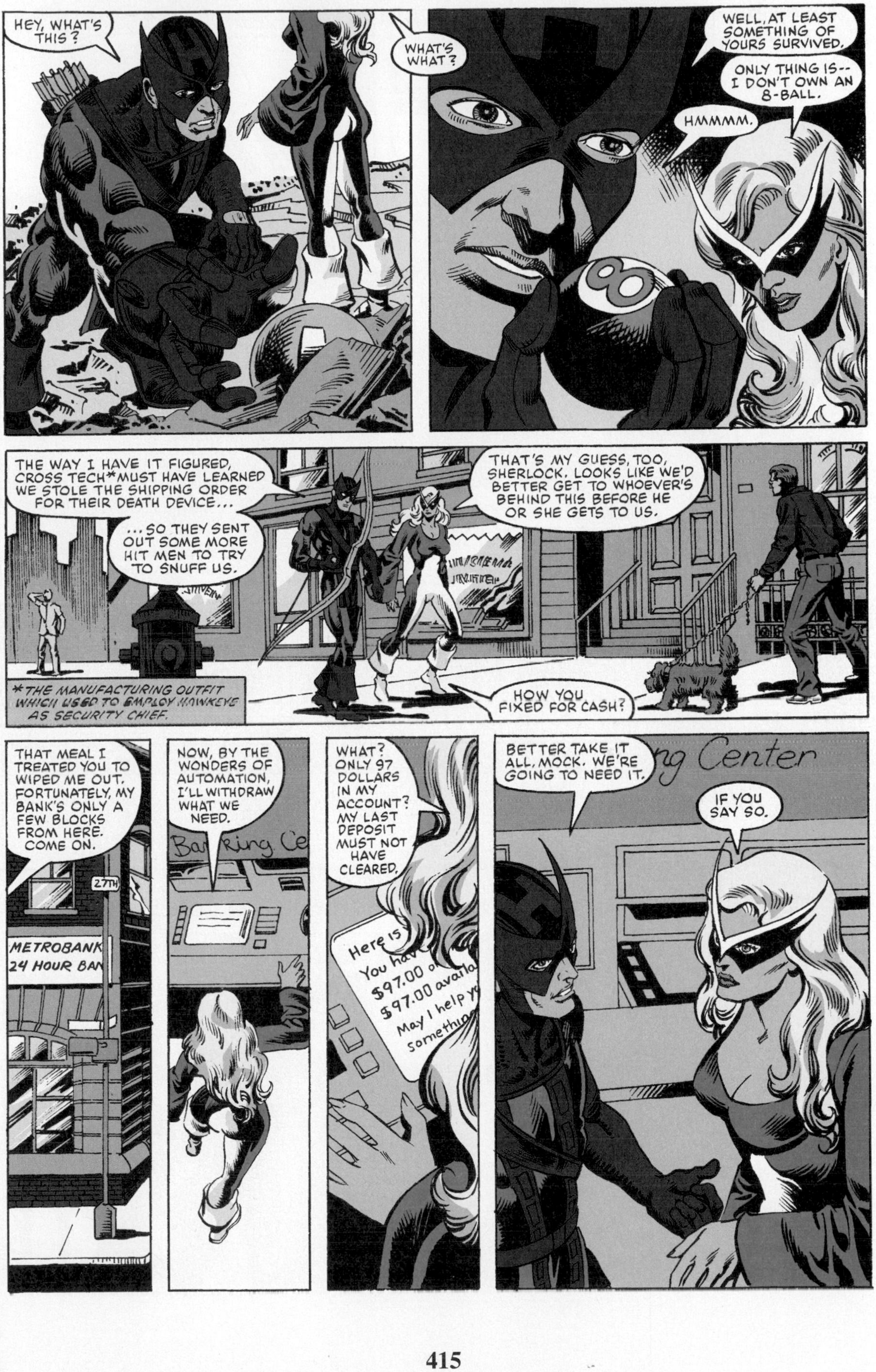
HEY, WHAT'S THIS?
WHAT'S WHAT?
WELL, AT LEAST SOMETHING OF YOURS SURVIVED.
ONLY THING IS-- I DON'T OWN AN 8-BALL.
HMMMM.
THE WAY I HAVE IT FIGURED, CROSS TECH* MUST HAVE LEARNED WE STOLE THE SHIPPING ORDER FOR THEIR DEATH DEVICE...
...SO THEY SENT OUT SOME MORE HIT MEN TO TRY TO SNUFF US.
THAT'S MY GUESS, TOO, SHERLOCK. LOOKS LIKE WE'D BETTER GET TO WHOEVER'S BEHIND THIS BEFORE HE OR SHE GETS TO US.
*THE MANUFACTURING OUTFIT WHICH USED TO EMPLOY HAWKEYE AS SECURITY CHIEF.
HOW YOU FIXED FOR CASH?
THAT MEAL I TREATED YOU TO WIPED ME OUT. FORTUNATELY, MY BANK'S ONLY A FEW BLOCKS FROM HERE. COME ON.
27TH
METROBANK
24 HOUR BAN
NOW, BY THE WONDERS OF AUTOMATION, I'LL WITHDRAW WHAT WE NEED.
WHAT? ONLY 97 DOLLARS IN MY ACCOUNT? MY LAST DEPOSIT MUST NOT HAVE CLEARED.
BETTER TAKE IT ALL, MOCK. WE'RE GOING TO NEED IT.
IF YOU SAY SO.

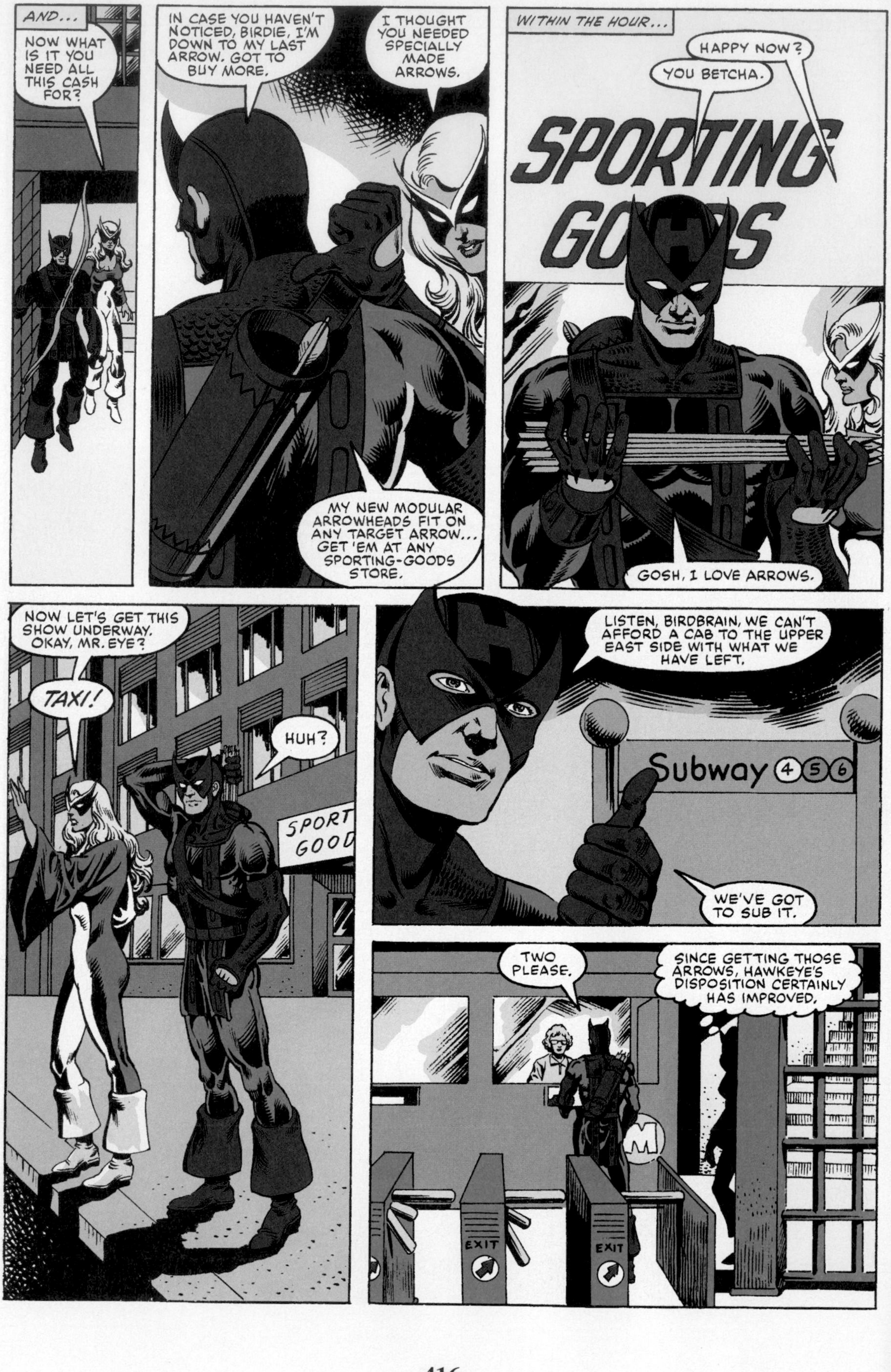
AND...
NOW WHAT IS IT YOU NEED ALL THIS CASH FOR?
IN CASE YOU HAVEN'T NOTICED, BIRDIE, I'M DOWN TO MY LAST ARROW. GOT TO BUY MORE.
I THOUGHT YOU NEEDED SPECIALLY MADE ARROWS.
MY NEW MODULAR ARROWHEADS FIT ON ANY TARGET ARROW... GET 'EM AT ANY SPORTING-GOODS STORE.
WITHIN THE HOUR...
HAPPY NOW?
YOU BETCHA.
SPORTING GO DS
GOSH, I LOVE ARROWS.
NOW LET'S GET THIS SHOW UNDERWAY. OKAY, MR. EYE?
TAXI!
HUH?
SPORT GOOD
LISTEN, BIRDBRAIN, WE CAN'T AFFORD A CAB TO THE UPPER EAST SIDE WITH WHAT WE HAVE LEFT.
Subway 4 5 6
WE'VE GOT TO SUB IT.
TWO PLEASE.
SINCE GETTING THOSE ARROWS, HAWKEYE'S DISPOSITION CERTAINLY HAS IMPROVED.
EXIT
EXIT

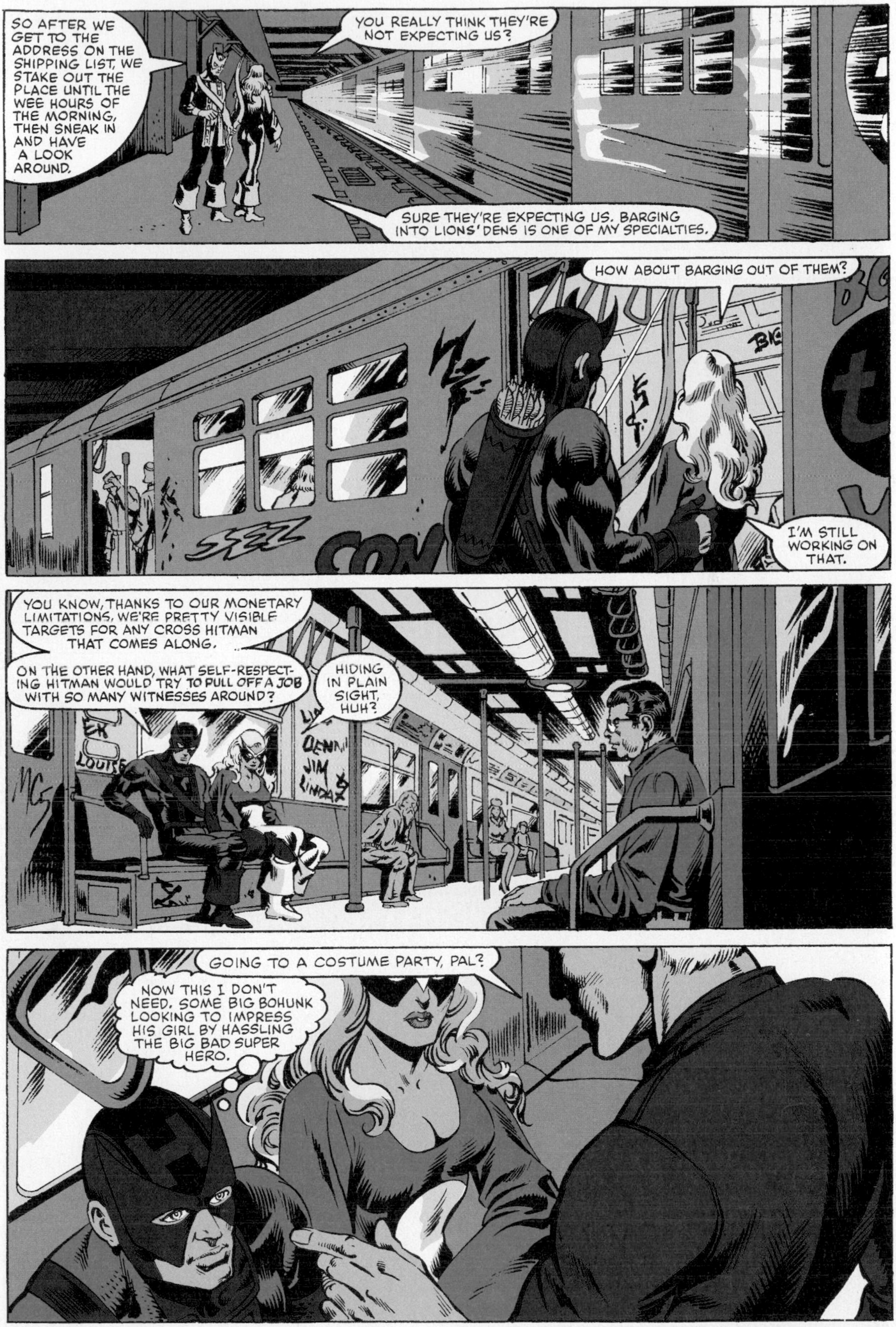
SO AFTER WE GET TO THE ADDRESS ON THE SHIPPING LIST, WE STAKE OUT THE PLACE UNTIL THE WEE HOURS OF THE MORNING, THEN SNEAK IN AND HAVE A LOOK AROUND.
YOU REALLY THINK THEY'RE NOT EXPECTING US?
SURE THEY'RE EXPECTING US. BARGING INTO LIONS' DENS IS ONE OF MY SPECIALTIES.
HOW ABOUT BARGING OUT OF THEM?
I'M STILL WORKING ON THAT.
YOU KNOW, THANKS TO OUR MONETARY LIMITATIONS, WE'RE PRETTY VISIBLE TARGETS FOR ANY CROSS HITMAN THAT COMES ALONG.
ON THE OTHER HAND, WHAT SELF-RESPECTING HITMAN WOULD TRY TO PULL OFF A JOB WITH SO MANY WITNESSES AROUND?
HIDING IN PLAIN SIGHT, HUH?
GOING TO A COSTUME PARTY, PAL?
NOW THIS I DON'T NEED. SOME BIG BOHUNK LOOKING TO IMPRESS HIS GIRL BY HASSLING THE BIG BAD SUPER HERO.

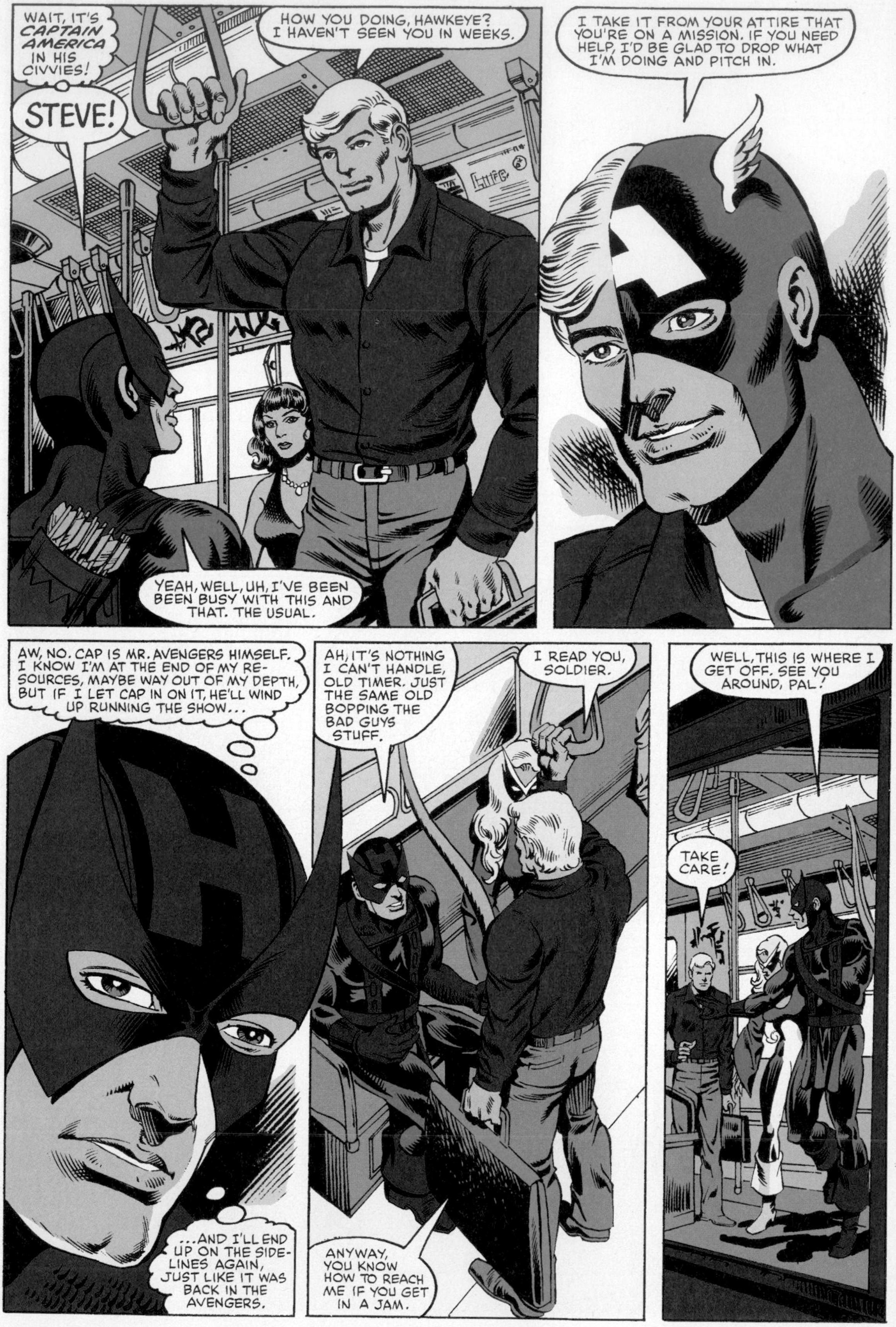
WAIT, IT'S CAPTAIN AMERICA IN HIS CIVVIES!
STEVE!
HOW YOU DOING, HAWKEYE? I HAVEN'T SEEN YOU IN WEEKS.
YEAH, WELL, UH, I'VE BEEN BEEN BUSY WITH THIS AND THAT. THE USUAL.
I TAKE IT FROM YOUR ATTIRE THAT YOU'RE ON A MISSION. IF YOU NEED HELP, I'D BE GLAD TO DROP WHAT I'M DOING AND PITCH IN.
AW, NO. CAP IS MR. AVENGERS HIMSELF. I KNOW I'M AT THE END OF MY RESOURCES, MAYBE WAY OUT OF MY DEPTH, BUT IF I LET CAP IN ON IT, HE'LL WIND UP RUNNING THE SHOW...
...AND I'LL END UP ON THE SIDELINES AGAIN, JUST LIKE IT WAS BACK IN THE AVENGERS.
AH, IT'S NOTHING I CAN'T HANDLE, OLD TIMER. JUST THE SAME OLD BOPPING THE BAD GUYS STUFF.
I READ YOU, SOLDIER.
ANYWAY, YOU KNOW HOW TO REACH ME IF YOU GET IN A JAM.
WELL, THIS IS WHERE I GET OFF. SEE YOU AROUND, PAL!
TAKE CARE!

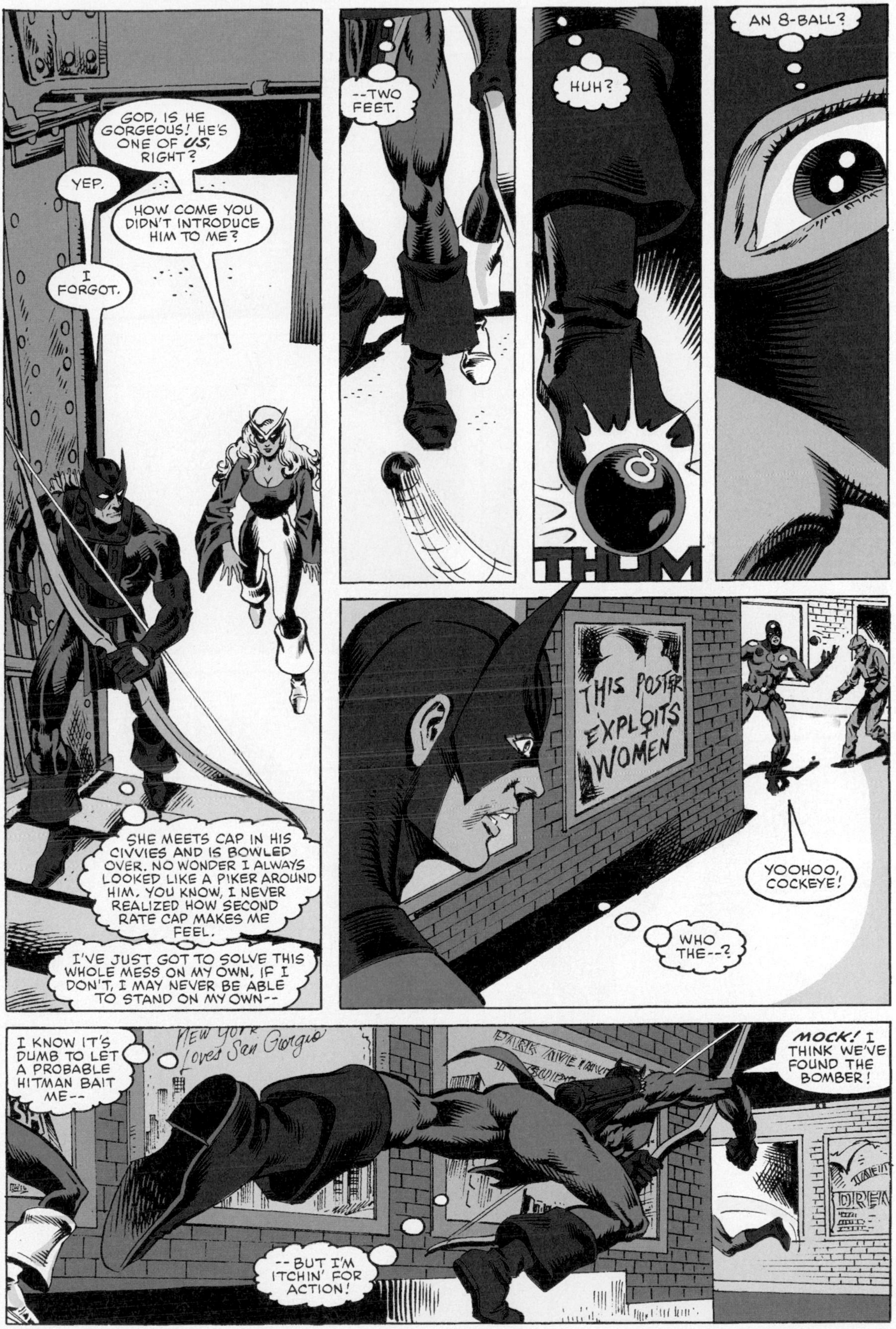
GOD, IS HE GORGEOUS! HE'S ONE OF US, RIGHT?
YEP.
HOW COME YOU DIDN'T INTRODUCE HIM TO ME?
I FORGOT.
SHE MEETS CAP IN HIS CIVVIES AND IS BOWLED OVER. NO WONDER I ALWAYS LOOKED LIKE A PIKER AROUND HIM. YOU KNOW, I NEVER REALIZED HOW SECOND RATE CAP MAKES ME FEEL.
I'VE JUST GOT TO SOLVE THIS WHOLE MESS ON MY OWN. IF I DON'T, I MAY NEVER BE ABLE TO STAND ON MY OWN--
--TWO FEET.
HUH?
THUM
AN 8-BALL?
THIS POSTER EXPLOITS WOMEN
YOOHOO, COCKEYE!
WHO THE--?
I KNOW IT'S DUMB TO LET A PROBABLE HITMAN BAIT ME--
New York Loves San Giorgio
MOCK! I THINK WE'VE FOUND THE BOMBER!
--BUT I'M ITCHIN' FOR ACTION!

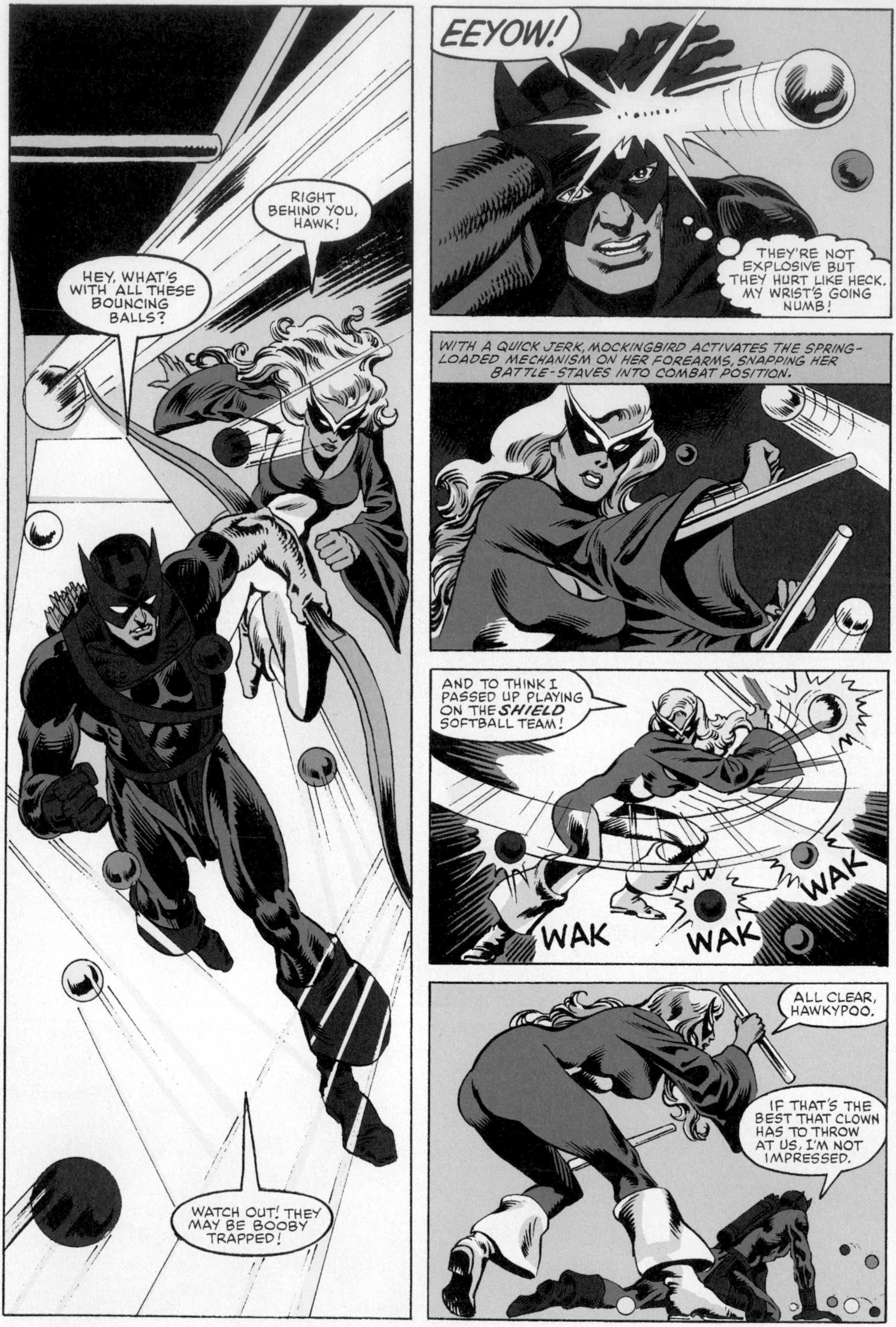
RIGHT BEHIND YOU, HAWK!
HEY, WHAT'S WITH ALL THESE BOUNCING BALLS?
WATCH OUT! THEY MAY BE BOOBY TRAPPED!
EEYOW!
THEY'RE NOT EXPLOSIVE BUT THEY HURT LIKE HECK. MY WRIST'S GOING NUMB!
WITH A QUICK JERK, MOCKINGBIRD ACTIVATES THE SPRING-LOADED MECHANISM ON HER FOREARMS, SNAPPING HER BATTLE-STAVES INTO COMBAT POSITION.
AND TO THINK I PASSED UP PLAYING ON THE SHIELD SOFTBALL TEAM!
WAK
WAK
WAK
ALL CLEAR, HAWKYPOO.
IF THAT'S THE BEST THAT CLOWN HAS TO THROW AT US, I'M NOT IMPRESSED.

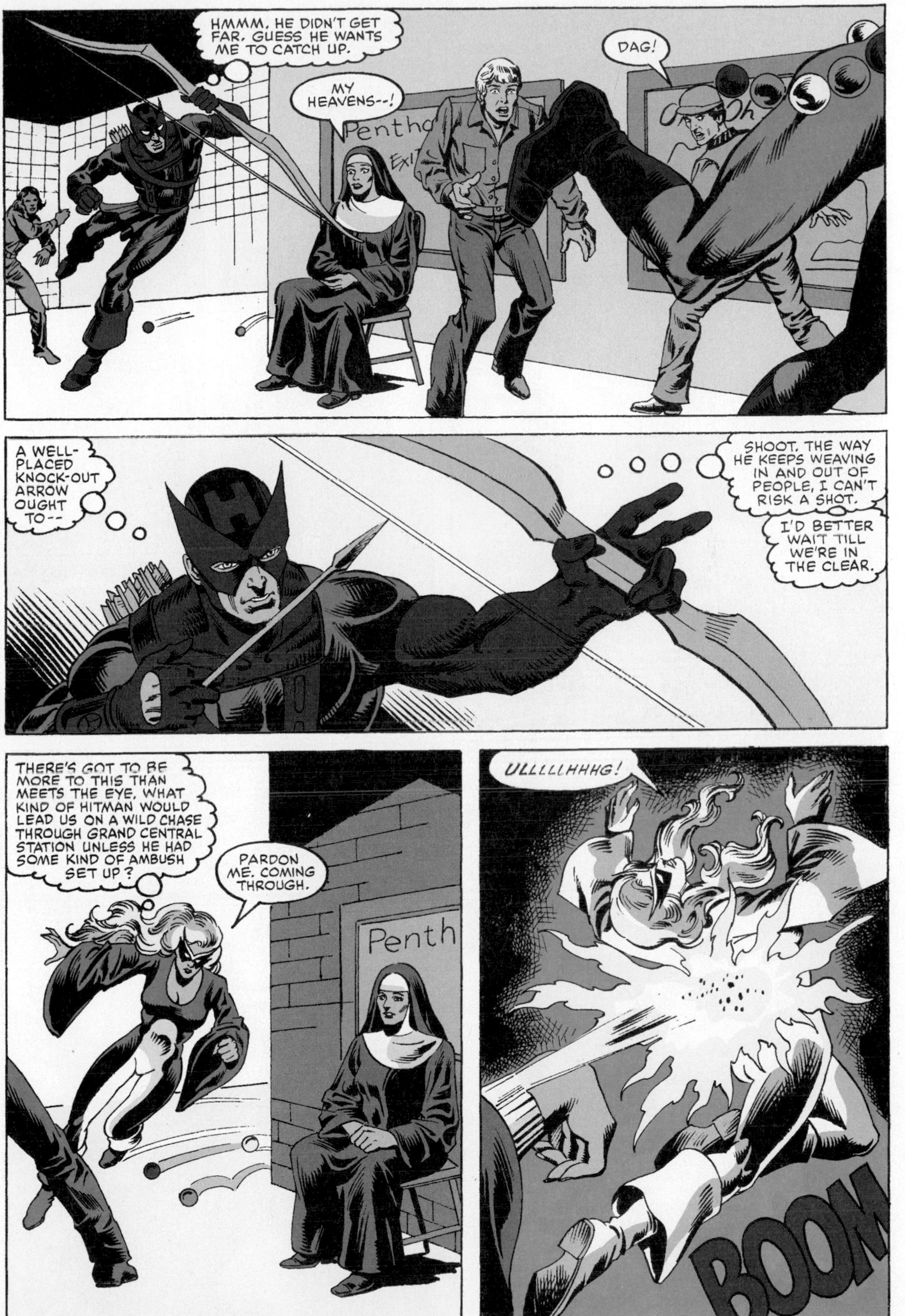
HMMM. HE DIDN'T GET FAR. GUESS HE WANTS ME TO CATCH UP.
MY HEAVENS--!
DAG!
Pentho
A WELL-PLACED KNOCK-OUT ARROW OUGHT TO--
SHOOT. THE WAY HE KEEPS WEAVING IN AND OUT OF PEOPLE, I CAN'T RISK A SHOT.
I'D BETTER WAIT TILL WE'RE IN THE CLEAR.
THERE'S GOT TO BE MORE TO THIS THAN MEETS THE EYE. WHAT KIND OF HITMAN WOULD LEAD US ON A WILD CHASE THROUGH GRAND CENTRAL STATION UNLESS HE HAD SOME KIND OF AMBUSH SET UP?
PARDON ME. COMING THROUGH.
Penth
ULLLLLHHHG!
BOOM

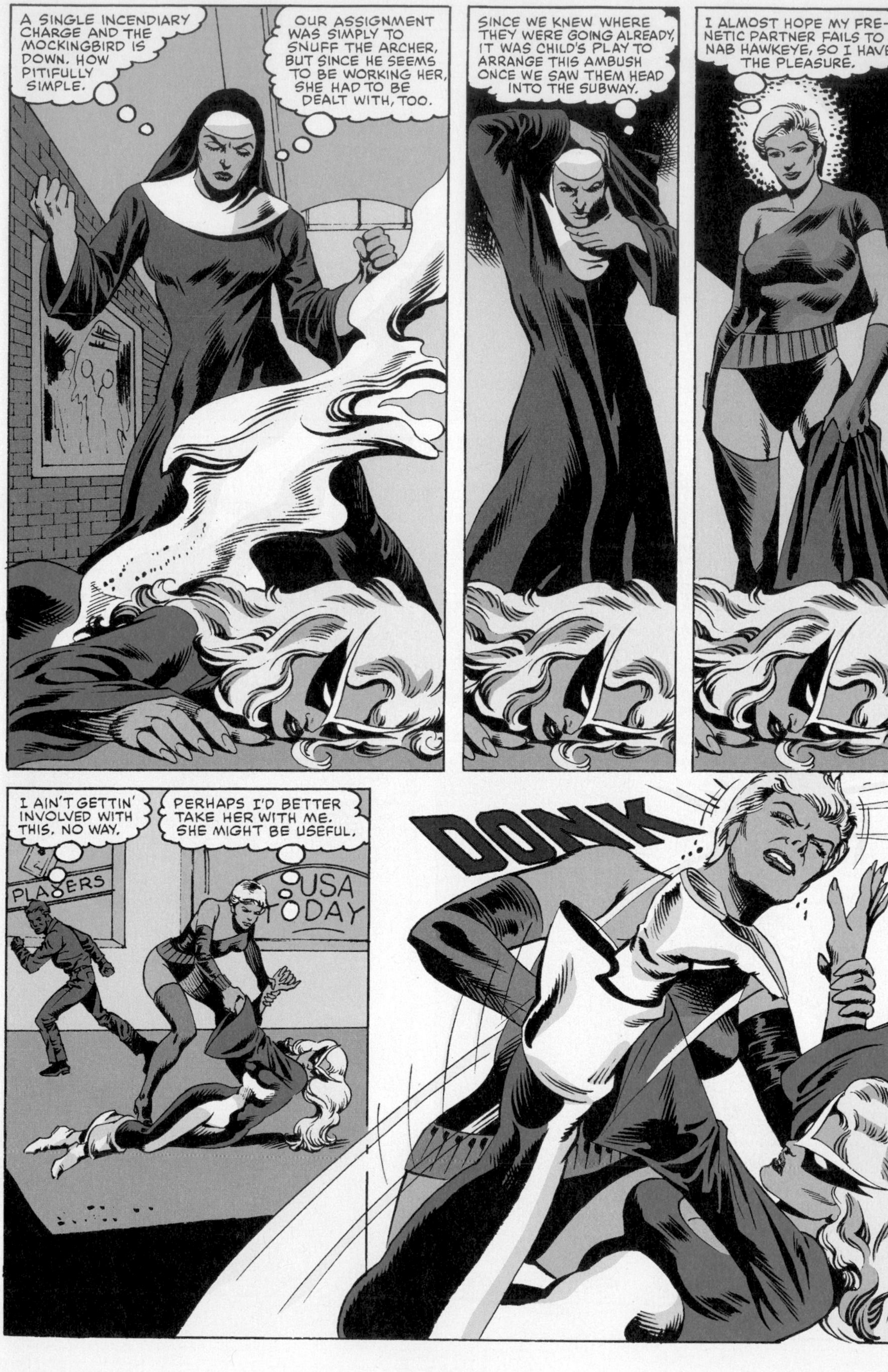
A SINGLE INCENDIARY CHARGE AND THE MOCKINGBIRD IS DOWN. HOW PITIFULLY SIMPLE.
OUR ASSIGNMENT WAS SIMPLY TO SNUFF THE ARCHER, BUT SINCE HE SEEMS TO BE WORKING HER, SHE HAD TO BE DEALT WITH, TOO.
SINCE WE KNEW WHERE THEY WERE GOING ALREADY, IT WAS CHILD'S PLAY TO ARRANGE THIS AMBUSH ONCE WE SAW THEM HEAD INTO THE SUBWAY.
I ALMOST HOPE MY FRENETIC PARTNER FAILS TO NAB HAWKEYE, SO I HAVE THE PLEASURE.
I AIN'T GETTIN' INVOLVED WITH THIS. NO WAY.
PERHAPS I'D BETTER TAKE HER WITH ME. SHE MIGHT BE USEFUL.
PLAYERS
USA TODAY
DONK

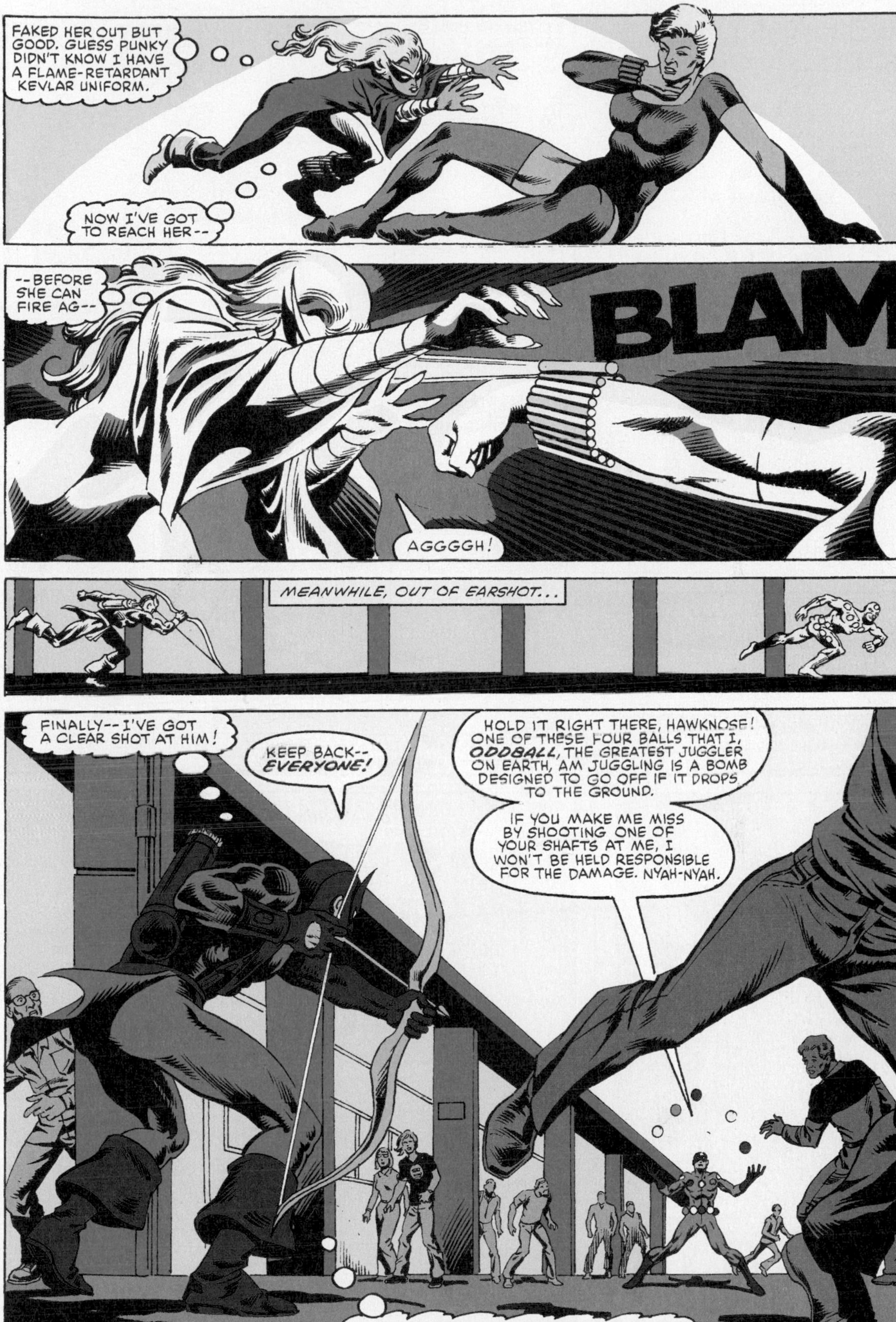
FAKED HER OUT BUT GOOD. GUESS PUNKY DIDN'T KNOW I HAVE A FLAME-RETARDANT KEVLAR UNIFORM.
NOW I'VE GOT TO REACH HER--
--BEFORE SHE CAN FIRE AG--
BLAM
AGGGGH!
MEANWHILE, OUT OF EARSHOT...
FINALLY--I'VE GOT A CLEAR SHOT AT HIM!
KEEP BACK-- EVERYONE!
HOLD IT RIGHT THERE, HAWKNOSE! ONE OF THESE FOUR BALLS THAT I, ODDBALL, THE GREATEST JUGGLER ON EARTH, AM JUGGLING IS A BOMB DESIGNED TO GO OFF IF IT DROPS TO THE GROUND.
IF YOU MAKE ME MISS BY SHOOTING ONE OF YOUR SHAFTS AT ME, I WON'T BE HELD RESPONSIBLE FOR THE DAMAGE. NYAH-NYAH.
IS HE BLUFFING? I'D HATE TO SEE A REPEAT OF MOCKINGBIRD'S APARTMENT MESS.

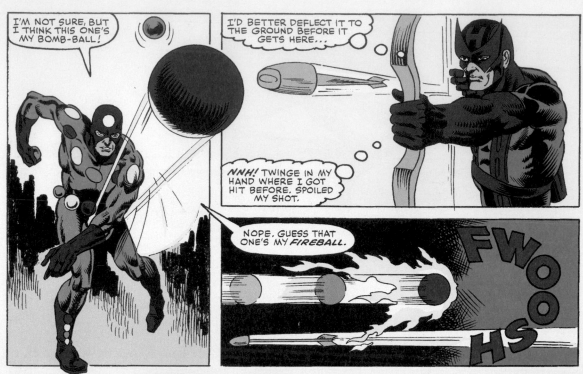

I'M NOT SURE, BUT I THINK THIS ONE'S MY BOMB-BALL!

I'D BETTER DEFLECT IT TO THE GROUND BEFORE IT GETS HERE...

NNH! TWINGE IN MY HAND WHERE I GOT HIT BEFORE. SPOILED MY SHOT.

NOPE. GUESS THAT ONE'S MY FIREBALL.

FWOO HSS

YOW. SIDESTEPPED BY JUST A HAIR.

GREAT SHOT, BOW-LEGS. IF YOU WERE AIMING AT THIS POST, THAT IS.

WE'RE HAVING FUN NOW, ALL RIGHTEE!

KANK

CARE FOR ANOTHER SHOT, SPORT? I'LL MATCH MY SPEED TO YOURS ANYDAY AND TWICE ON SUNDAY.

STAND CLEAR OF THE CLOSING DOORS!

TIME'S UP. GOTTA GO. TA-TA!

424

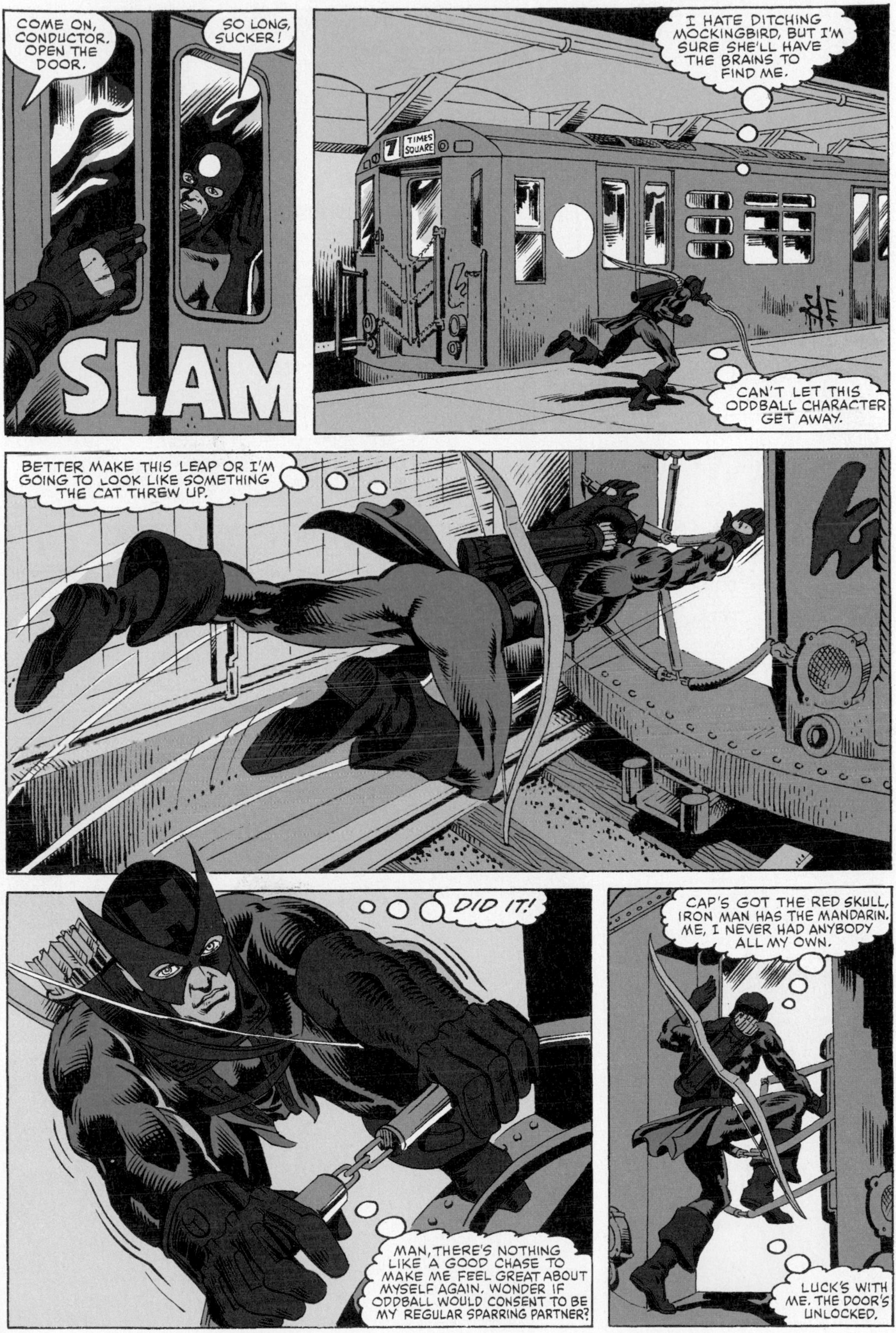
COME ON, CONDUCTOR. OPEN THE DOOR.
SO LONG, SUCKER!
SLAM
I HATE DITCHING MOCKINGBIRD, BUT I'M SURE SHE'LL HAVE THE BRAINS TO FIND ME.
7 TIMES SQUARE
CAN'T LET THIS ODDBALL CHARACTER GET AWAY.
BETTER MAKE THIS LEAP OR I'M GOING TO LOOK LIKE SOMETHING THE CAT THREW UP.
DID IT!
MAN, THERE'S NOTHING LIKE A GOOD CHASE TO MAKE ME FEEL GREAT ABOUT MYSELF AGAIN. WONDER IF ODDBALL WOULD CONSENT TO BE MY REGULAR SPARRING PARTNER?
CAP'S GOT THE RED SKULL, IRON MAN HAS THE MANDARIN. ME, I NEVER HAD ANYBODY ALL MY OWN.
LUCK'S WITH ME. THE DOOR'S UNLOCKED.

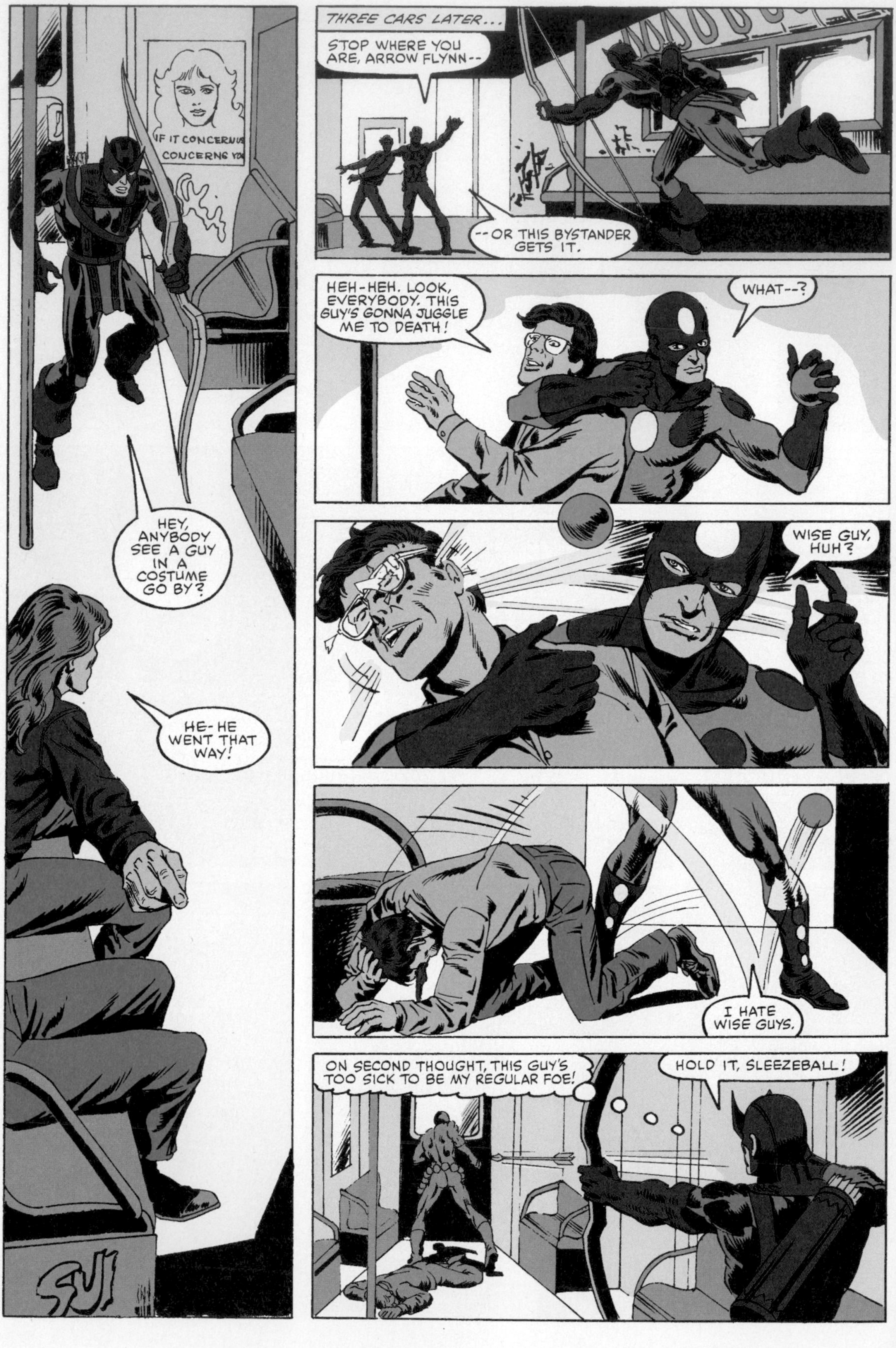
IF IT CONCERNS US
CONCERNS YOU
HEY, ANYBODY SEE A GUY IN A COSTUME GO BY?
HE-HE WENT THAT WAY!
THREE CARS LATER...
STOP WHERE YOU ARE, ARROW FLYNN--
--OR THIS BYSTANDER GETS IT.
HEH-HEH. LOOK, EVERYBODY. THIS GUY'S GONNA JUGGLE ME TO DEATH!
WHAT--?
WISE GUY, HUH?
I HATE WISE GUYS.
ON SECOND THOUGHT, THIS GUY'S TOO SICK TO BE MY REGULAR FOE!
HOLD IT, SLEEZEBALL!

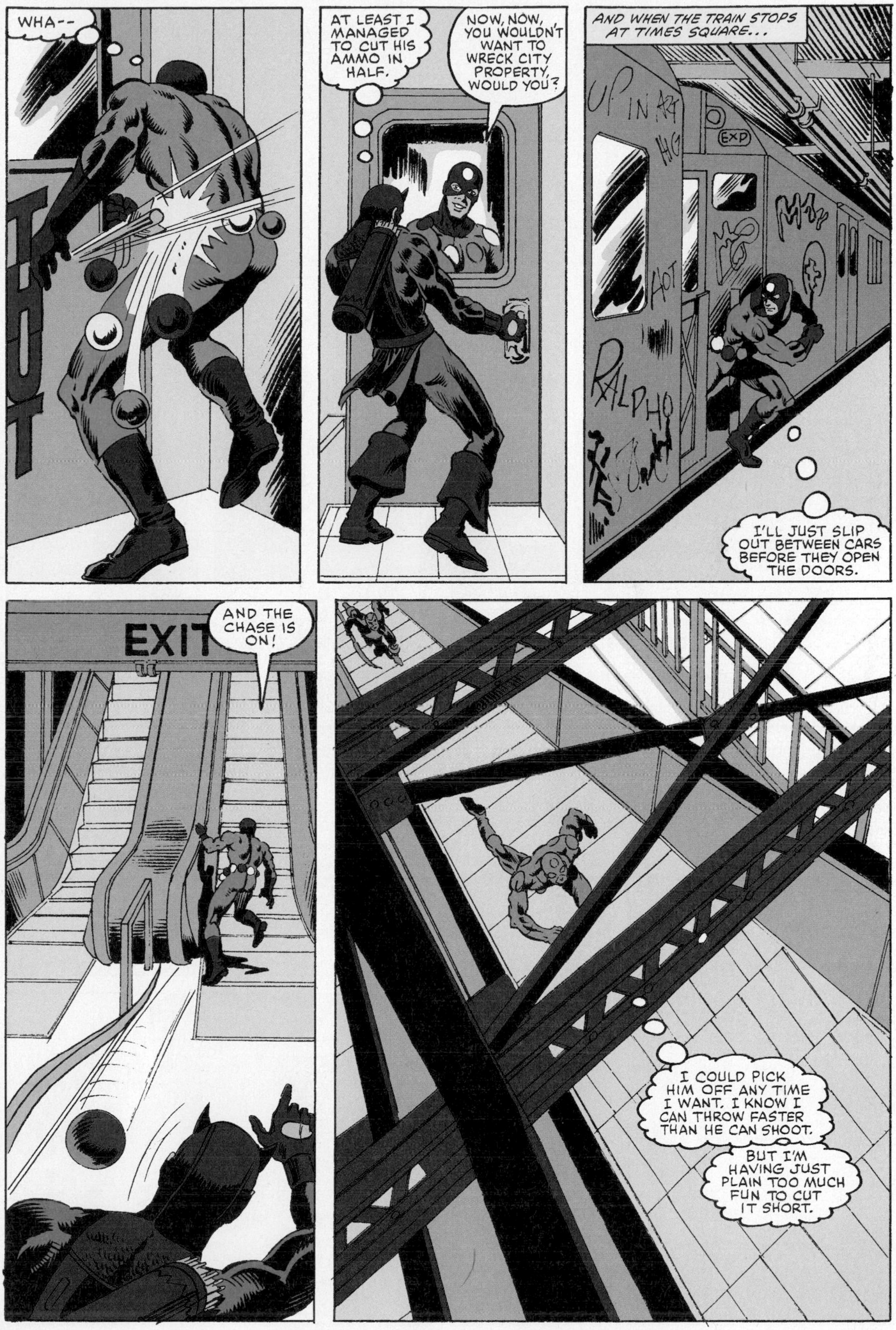
WHA--
AT LEAST I MANAGED TO CUT HIS AMMO IN HALF.
NOW, NOW, YOU WOULDN'T WANT TO WRECK CITY PROPERTY, WOULD YOU?
AND WHEN THE TRAIN STOPS AT TIMES SQUARE...
I'LL JUST SLIP OUT BETWEEN CARS BEFORE THEY OPEN THE DOORS.
EXIT
AND THE CHASE IS ON!
I COULD PICK HIM OFF ANY TIME I WANT. I KNOW I CAN THROW FASTER THAN HE CAN SHOOT.
BUT I'M HAVING JUST PLAIN TOO MUCH FUN TO CUT IT SHORT.

--I GOT LOTS.

I WANT TO TAKE YOU HIGHER, BOOMLACKA LACKA LACKA!

THIS GUY'S A LOON.

CAN'T GET A CLEAR SHOT FROM DOWN HERE.

OH, HE FLEW THROUGH THE AIR WITH THE GREATEST FINESSE--

--THAT DARING YOUNG MAN ON HIS FLYING BUTTRESS!

WHEN IT COMES TO TRICKS, BABY--

THIS IS A BIT BETTER. REMINDS ME OF THE HIGHWIRE BACK IN MY CARNY DAYS.

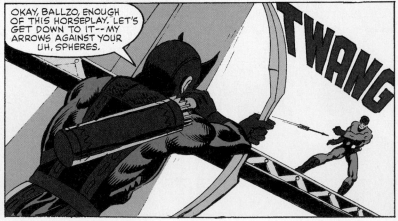

OKAY, BALLZO, ENOUGH OF THIS HORSEPLAY. LET'S GET DOWN TO IT-- MY ARROWS AGAINST YOUR UH, SPHERES.

TWANG

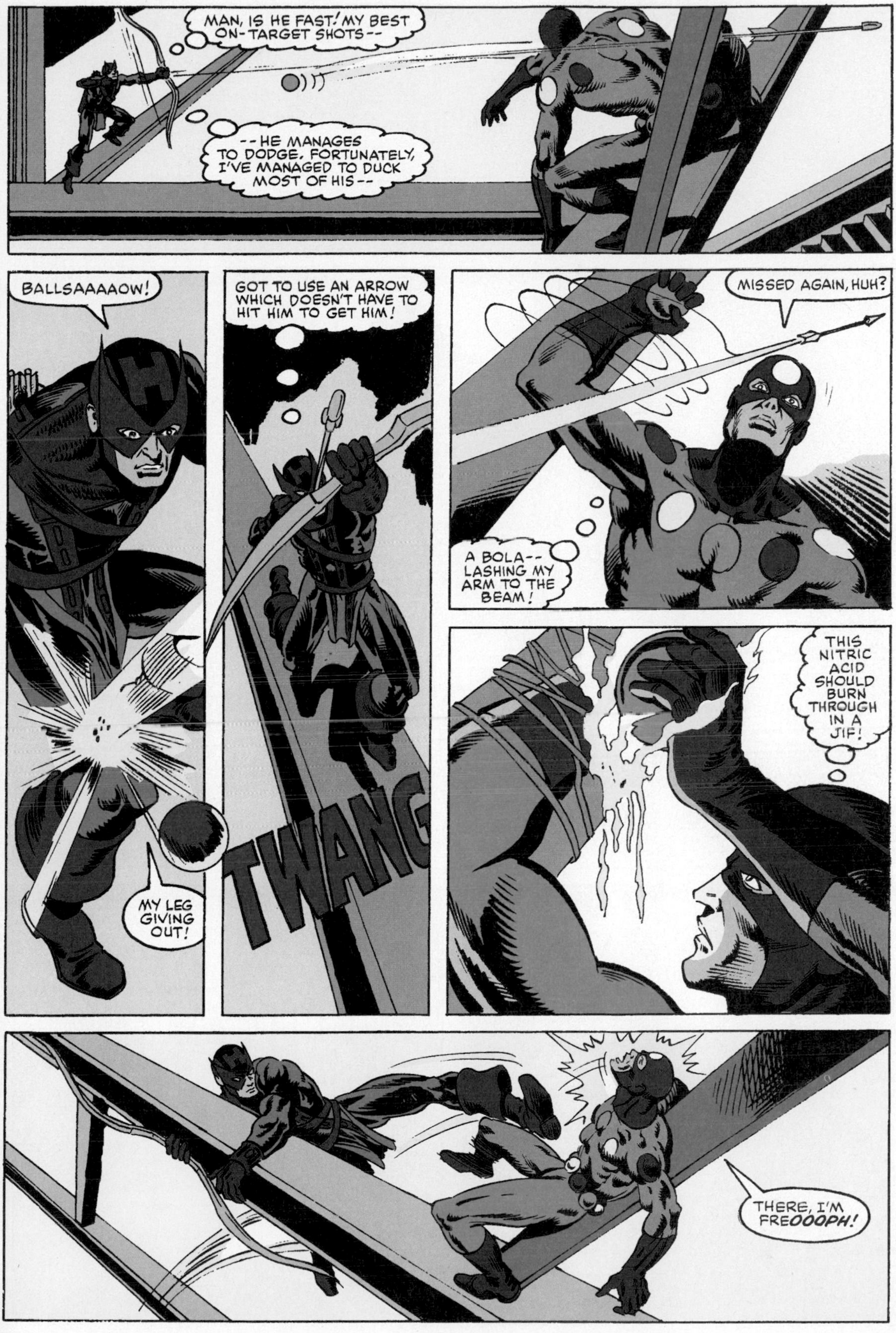
MAN, IS HE FAST! MY BEST ON-TARGET SHOTS--
--HE MANAGES TO DODGE. FORTUNATELY, I'VE MANAGED TO DUCK MOST OF HIS--
BALLSAAAAAOW!
MY LEG GIVING OUT!
GOT TO USE AN ARROW WHICH DOESN'T HAVE TO HIT HIM TO GET HIM!
TWANG
MISSED AGAIN, HUH?
A BOLA--LASHING MY ARM TO THE BEAM!
THIS NITRIC ACID SHOULD BURN THROUGH IN A JIF!
THERE, I'M FREOOOPH!

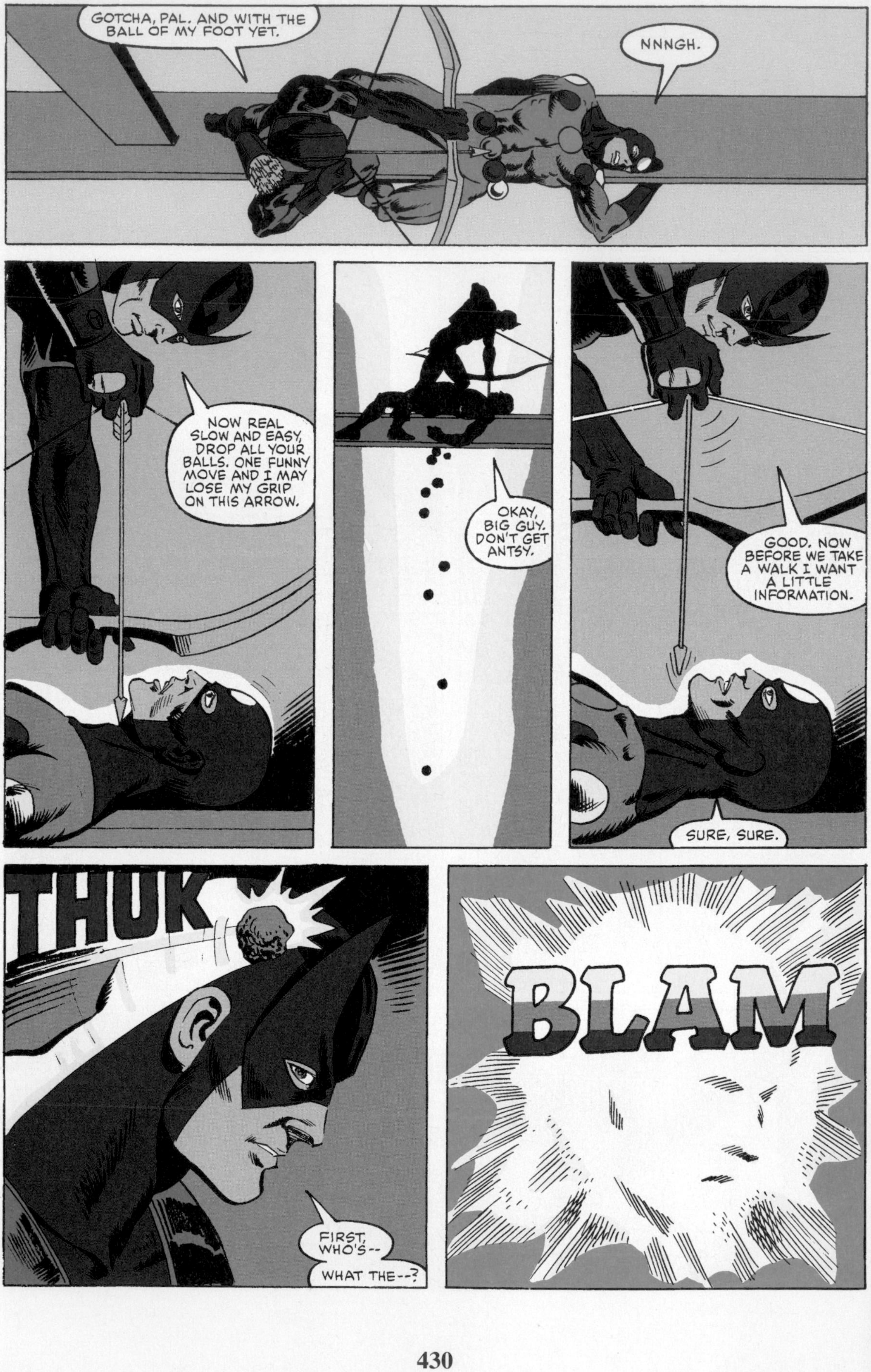
GOTCHA, PAL. AND WITH THE BALL OF MY FOOT YET.
NNNGH.
NOW REAL SLOW AND EASY, DROP ALL YOUR BALLS. ONE FUNNY MOVE AND I MAY LOSE MY GRIP ON THIS ARROW.
OKAY, BIG GUY. DON'T GET ANTSY.
GOOD. NOW BEFORE WE TAKE A WALK I WANT A LITTLE INFORMATION.
SURE, SURE.
THUK
FIRST, WHO'S--
WHAT THE--?
BLAM

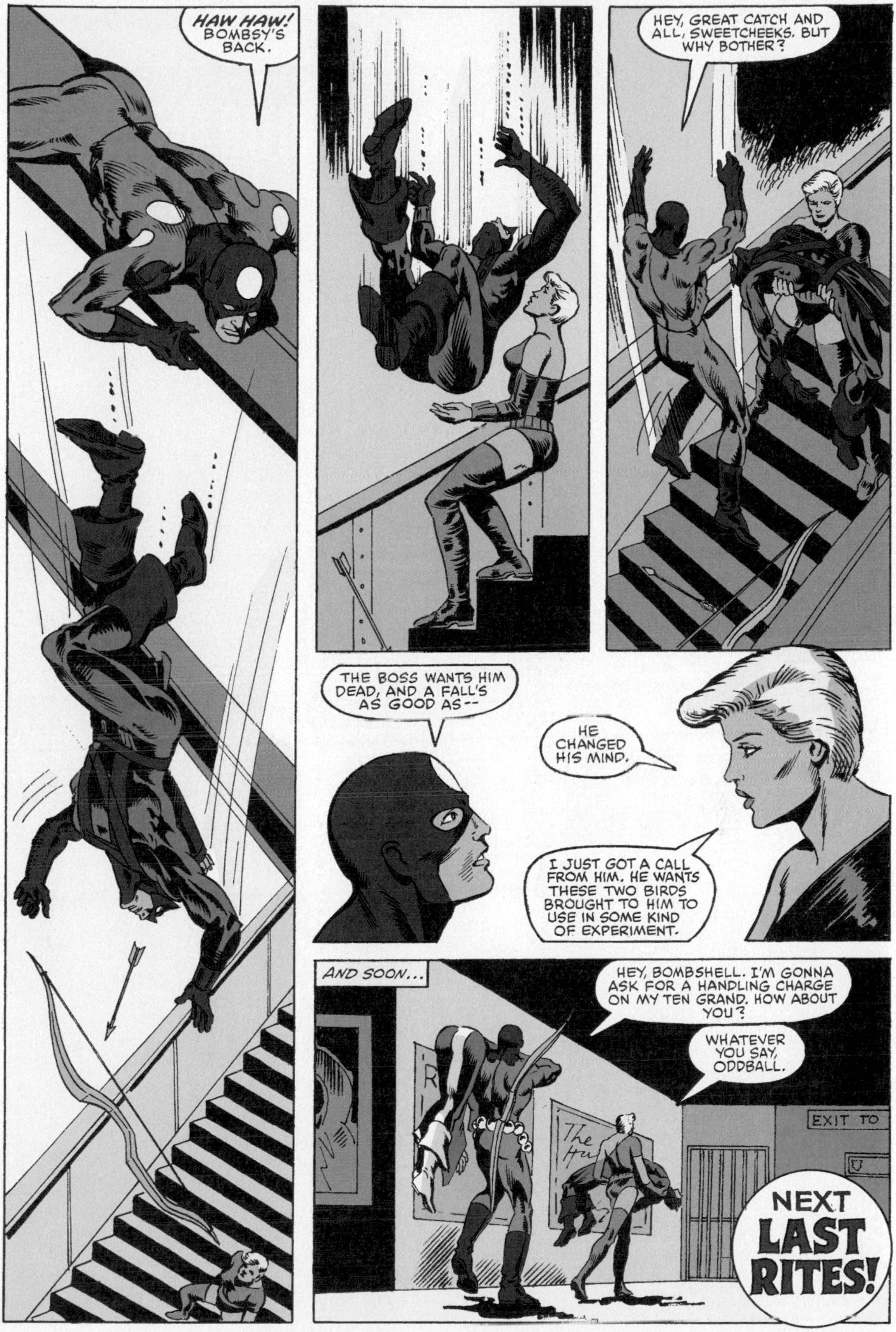
HAW HAW! BOMBSY'S BACK.
HEY, GREAT CATCH AND ALL, SWEETCHEEKS. BUT WHY BOTHER?
THE BOSS WANTS HIM DEAD, AND A FALL'S AS GOOD AS--
HE CHANGED HIS MIND.
I JUST GOT A CALL FROM HIM. HE WANTS THESE TWO BIRDS BROUGHT TO HIM TO USE IN SOME KIND OF EXPERIMENT.
AND SOON...
HEY, BOMBSHELL. I'M GONNA ASK FOR A HANDLING CHARGE ON MY TEN GRAND. HOW ABOUT YOU?
WHATEVER YOU SAY, ODDBALL.
EXIT TO
NEXT LAST RITES!

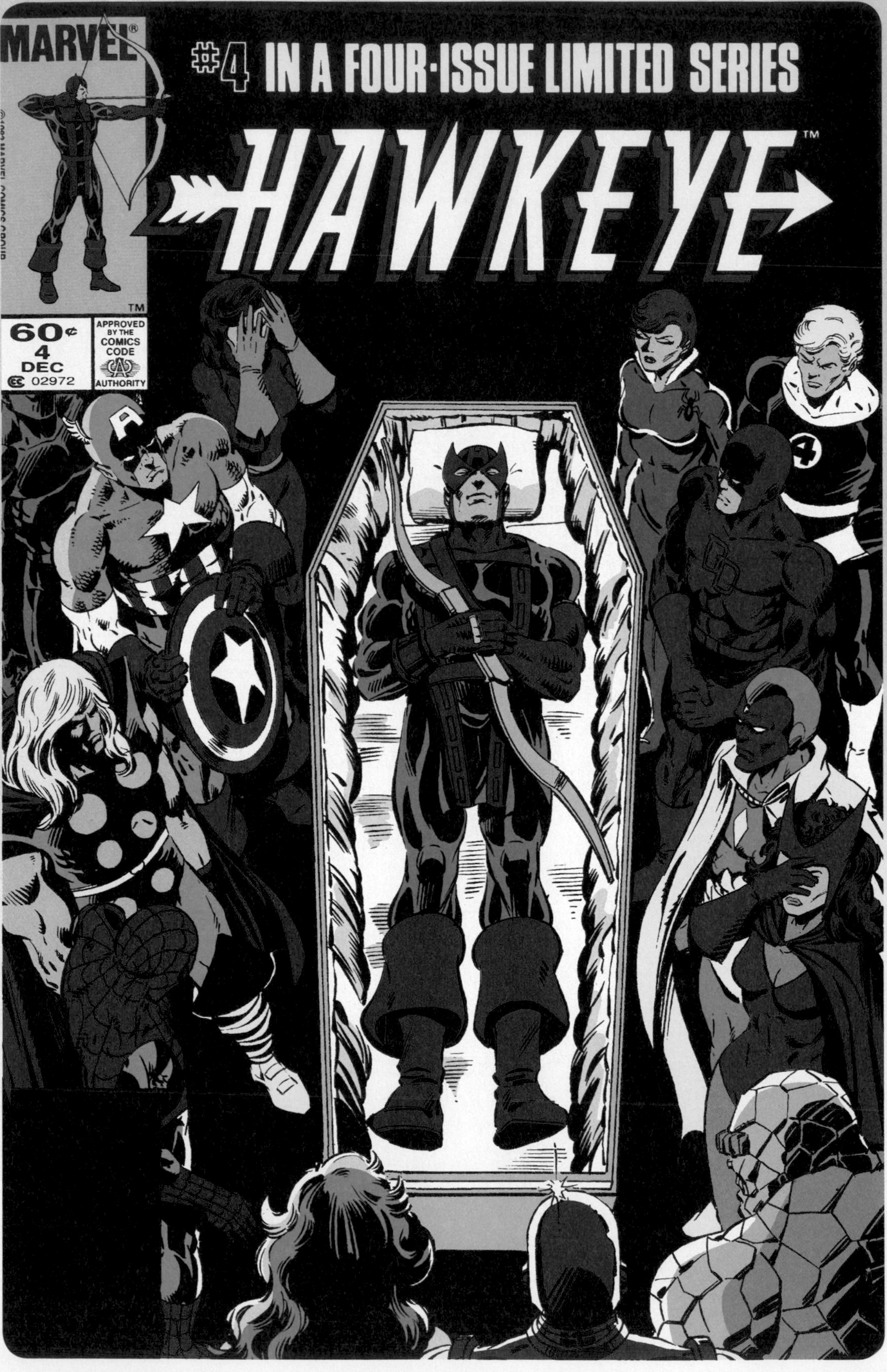
MARVEL®
#4 IN A FOUR-ISSUE LIMITED SERIES
HAWKEYE™
60¢
4
DEC
02972
APPROVED BY THE COMICS CODE AUTHORITY

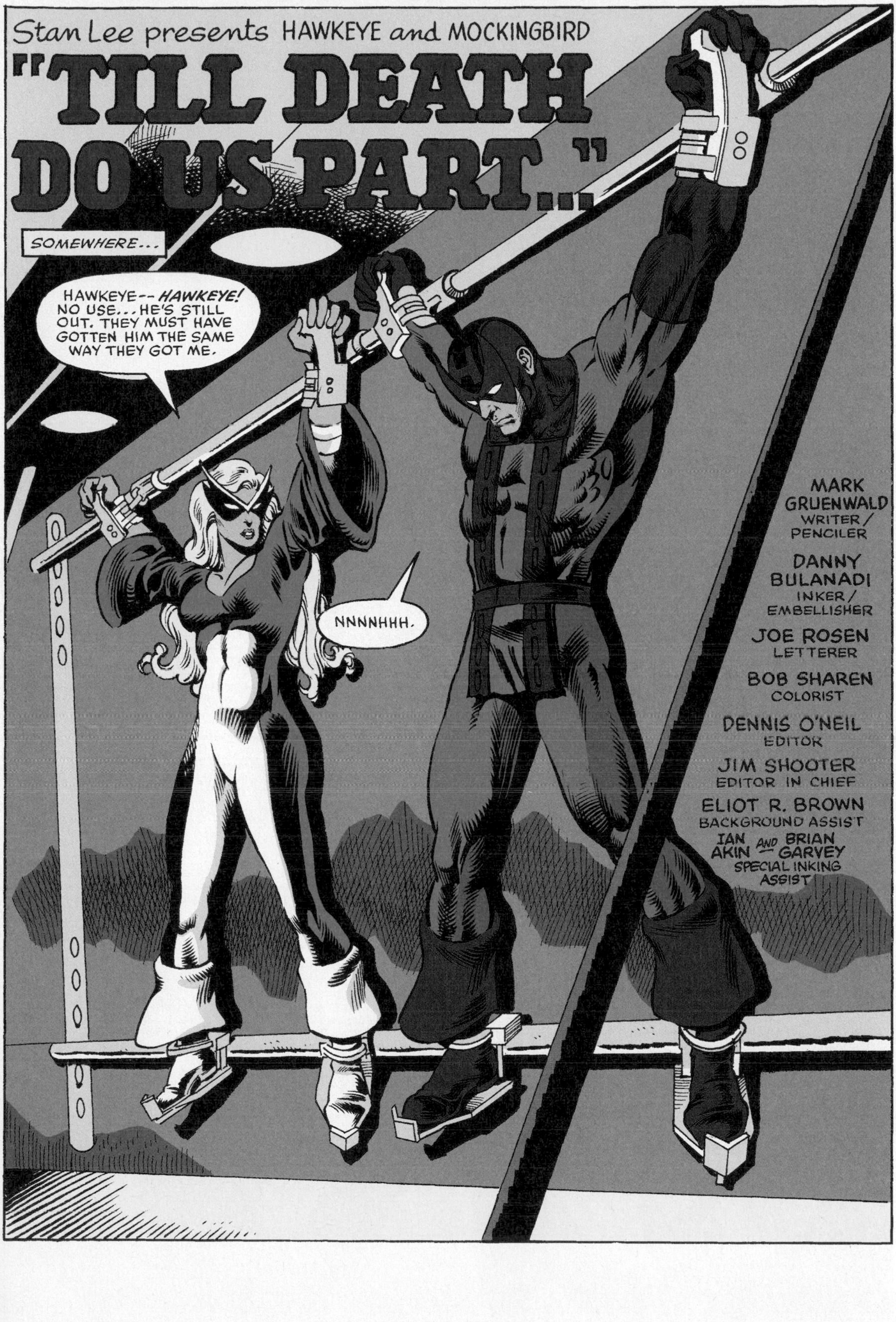
Stan Lee presents HAWKEYE and MOCKINGBIRD
"TILL DEATH DO US PART..."
SOMEWHERE...
HAWKEYE-- HAWKEYE! NO USE... HE'S STILL OUT. THEY MUST HAVE GOTTEN HIM THE SAME WAY THEY GOT ME.
NNNNHHH.
MARK GRUENWALD WRITER/PENCILER
DANNY BULANADI INKER/EMBELLISHER
JOE ROSEN LETTERER
BOB SHAREN COLORIST
DENNIS O'NEIL EDITOR
JIM SHOOTER EDITOR IN CHIEF
ELIOT R. BROWN BACKGROUND ASSIST
IAN AKIN AND BRIAN GARVEY SPECIAL INKING ASSIST

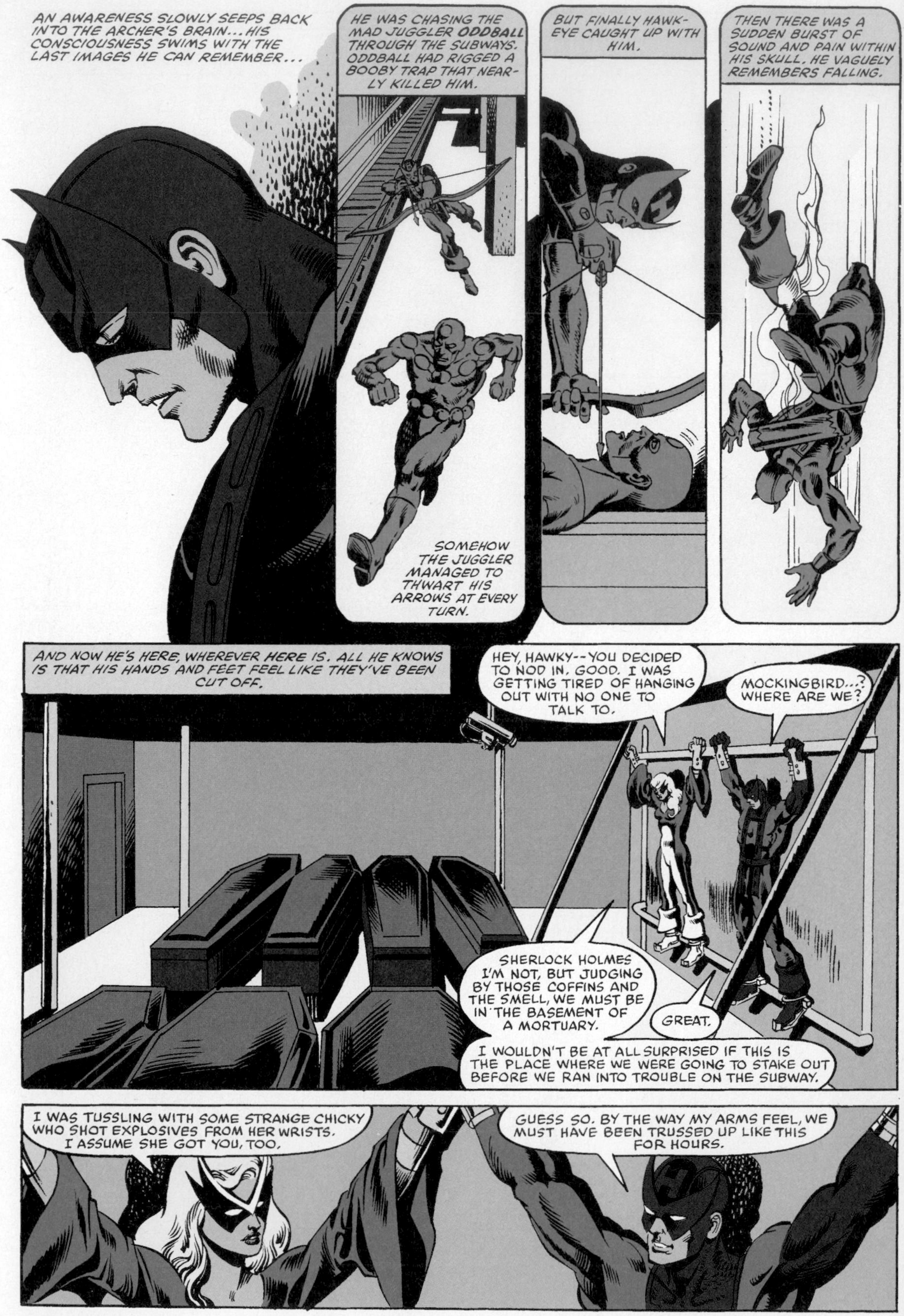
AN AWARENESS SLOWLY SEEPS BACK INTO THE ARCHER'S BRAIN... HIS CONSCIOUSNESS SWIMS WITH THE LAST IMAGES HE CAN REMEMBER...
HE WAS CHASING THE MAD JUGGLER ODDBALL THROUGH THE SUBWAYS. ODDBALL HAD RIGGED A BOOBY TRAP THAT NEARLY KILLED HIM.
SOMEHOW THE JUGGLER MANAGED TO THWART HIS ARROWS AT EVERY TURN.
BUT FINALLY HAWK-EYE CAUGHT UP WITH HIM.
THEN THERE WAS A SUDDEN BURST OF SOUND AND PAIN WITHIN HIS SKULL. HE VAGUELY REMEMBERS FALLING.
AND NOW HE'S HERE, WHEREVER HERE IS. ALL HE KNOWS IS THAT HIS HANDS AND FEET FEEL LIKE THEY'VE BEEN CUT OFF.
HEY, HAWKY--YOU DECIDED TO NOD IN. GOOD. I WAS GETTING TIRED OF HANGING OUT WITH NO ONE TO TALK TO.
MOCKINGBIRD..? WHERE ARE WE?
SHERLOCK HOLMES I'M NOT, BUT JUDGING BY THOSE COFFINS AND THE SMELL, WE MUST BE IN THE BASEMENT OF A MORTUARY.
GREAT.
I WOULDN'T BE AT ALL SURPRISED IF THIS IS THE PLACE WHERE WE WERE GOING TO STAKE OUT BEFORE WE RAN INTO TROUBLE ON THE SUBWAY.
I WAS TUSSLING WITH SOME STRANGE CHICKY WHO SHOT EXPLOSIVES FROM HER WRISTS. I ASSUME SHE GOT YOU, TOO.
GUESS SO. BY THE WAY MY ARMS FEEL, WE MUST HAVE BEEN TRUSSED UP LIKE THIS FOR HOURS.

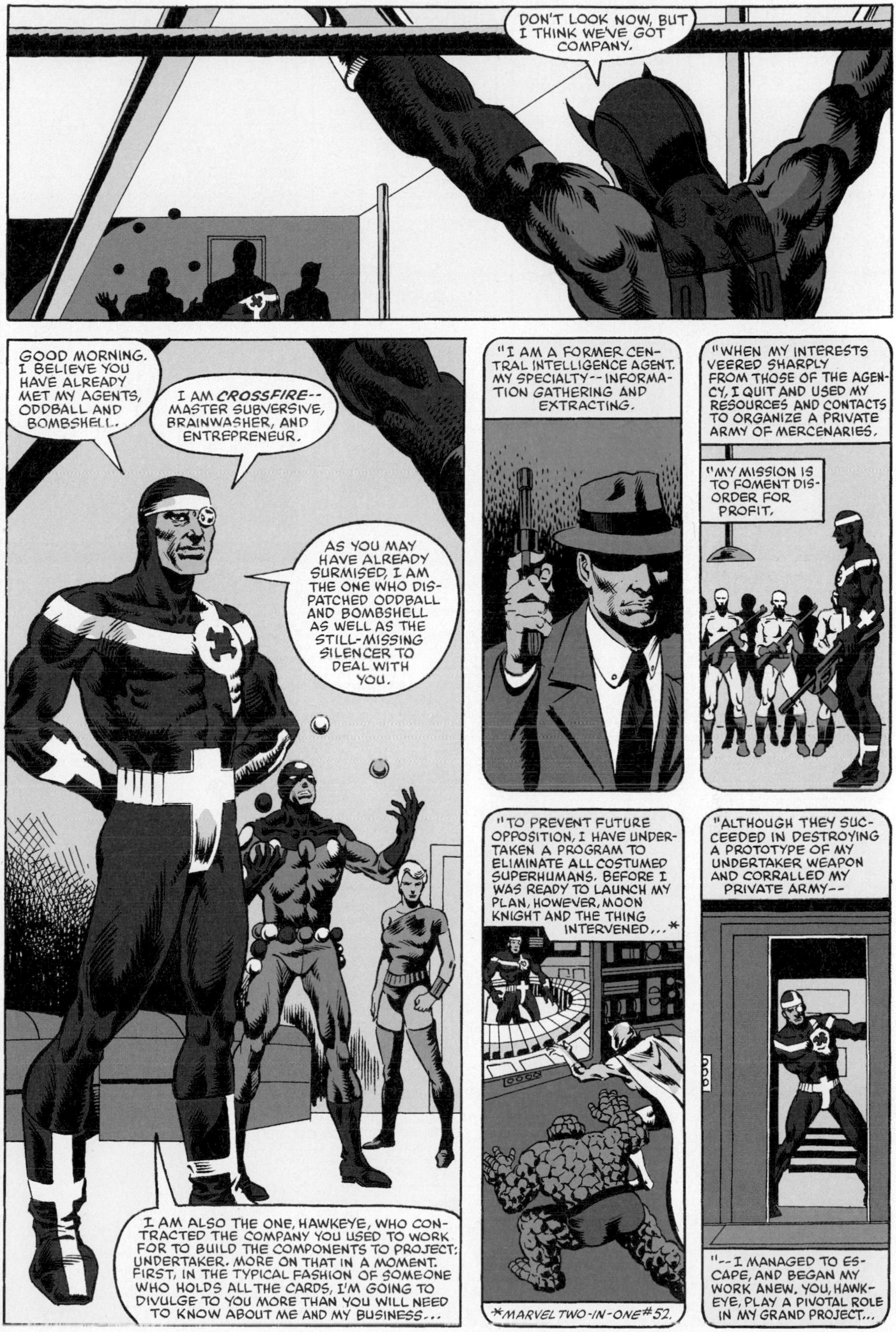
DON'T LOOK NOW, BUT I THINK WE'VE GOT COMPANY.
GOOD MORNING. I BELIEVE YOU HAVE ALREADY MET MY AGENTS, ODDBALL AND BOMBSHELL.
I AM CROSSFIRE-- MASTER SUBVERSIVE, BRAINWASHER, AND ENTREPRENEUR.
AS YOU MAY HAVE ALREADY SURMISED, I AM THE ONE WHO DISPATCHED ODDBALL AND BOMBSHELL AS WELL AS THE STILL-MISSING SILENCER TO DEAL WITH YOU.
I AM ALSO THE ONE, HAWKEYE, WHO CONTRACTED THE COMPANY YOU USED TO WORK FOR TO BUILD THE COMPONENTS TO PROJECT: UNDERTAKER. MORE ON THAT IN A MOMENT. FIRST, IN THE TYPICAL FASHION OF SOMEONE WHO HOLDS ALL THE CARDS, I'M GOING TO DIVULGE TO YOU MORE THAN YOU WILL NEED TO KNOW ABOUT ME AND MY BUSINESS...
"I AM A FORMER CENTRAL INTELLIGENCE AGENT. MY SPECIALTY-- INFORMATION GATHERING AND EXTRACTING.
"WHEN MY INTERESTS VEERED SHARPLY FROM THOSE OF THE AGENCY, I QUIT AND USED MY RESOURCES AND CONTACTS TO ORGANIZE A PRIVATE ARMY OF MERCENARIES.
"MY MISSION IS TO FOMENT DISORDER FOR PROFIT.
"TO PREVENT FUTURE OPPOSITION, I HAVE UNDERTAKEN A PROGRAM TO ELIMINATE ALL COSTUMED SUPERHUMANS. BEFORE I WAS READY TO LAUNCH MY PLAN, HOWEVER, MOON KNIGHT AND THE THING INTERVENED...*
*MARVEL TWO-IN-ONE #52.
"ALTHOUGH THEY SUCCEEDED IN DESTROYING A PROTOTYPE OF MY UNDERTAKER WEAPON AND CORRALLED MY PRIVATE ARMY--
"--I MANAGED TO ESCAPE, AND BEGAN MY WORK ANEW. YOU, HAWKEYE, PLAY A PIVOTAL ROLE IN MY GRAND PROJECT...

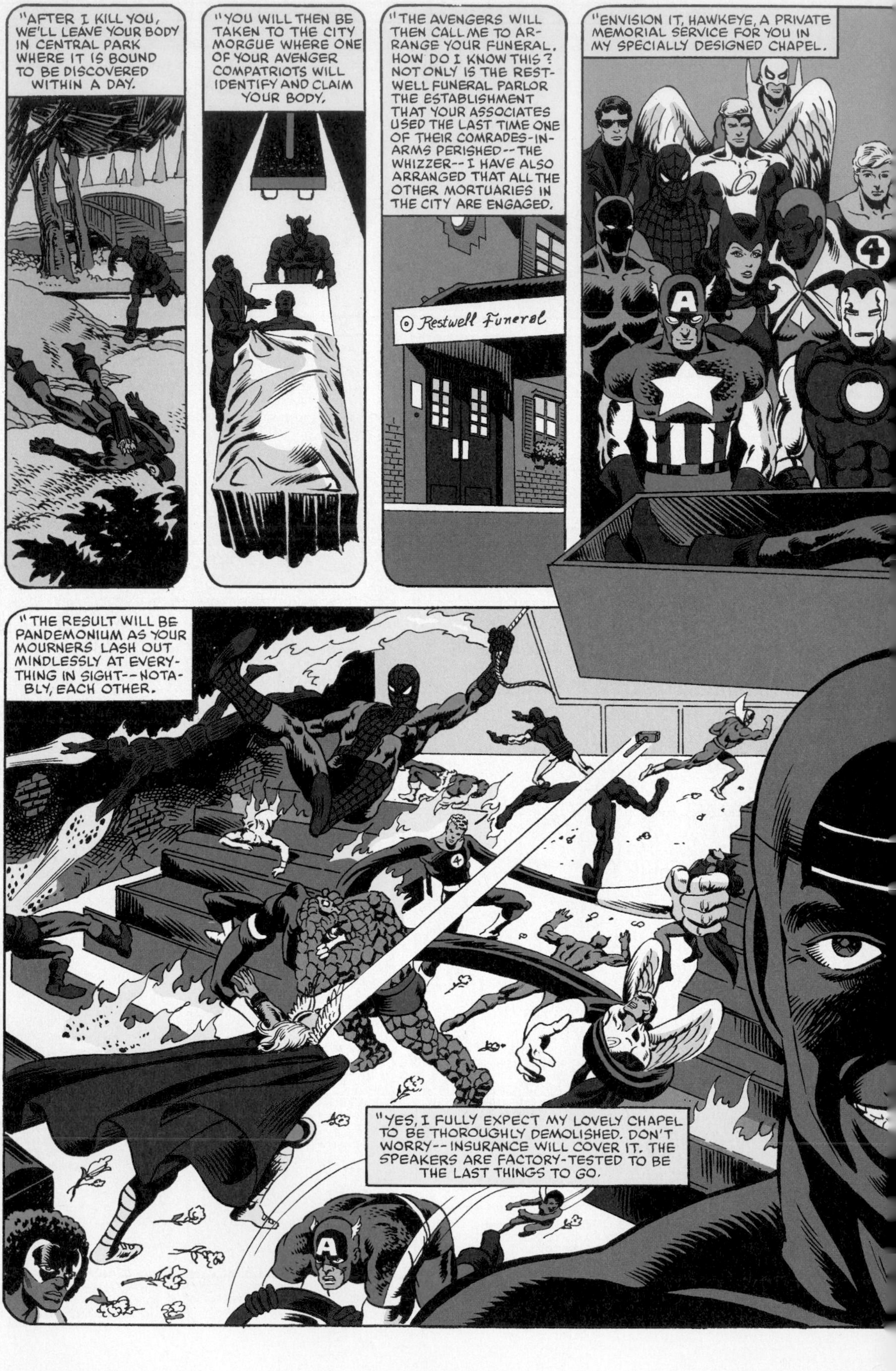
"AFTER I KILL YOU, WE'LL LEAVE YOUR BODY IN CENTRAL PARK WHERE IT IS BOUND TO BE DISCOVERED WITHIN A DAY.
"YOU WILL THEN BE TAKEN TO THE CITY MORGUE WHERE ONE OF YOUR AVENGER COMPATRIOTS WILL IDENTIFY AND CLAIM YOUR BODY.
"THE AVENGERS WILL THEN CALL ME TO ARRANGE YOUR FUNERAL. HOW DO I KNOW THIS? NOT ONLY IS THE RESTWELL FUNERAL PARLOR THE ESTABLISHMENT THAT YOUR ASSOCIATES USED THE LAST TIME ONE OF THEIR COMRADES-IN-ARMS PERISHED--THE WHIZZER--I HAVE ALSO ARRANGED THAT ALL THE OTHER MORTUARIES IN THE CITY ARE ENGAGED.
Restwell Funeral
"ENVISION IT, HAWKEYE, A PRIVATE MEMORIAL SERVICE FOR YOU IN MY SPECIALLY DESIGNED CHAPEL.
"THE RESULT WILL BE PANDEMONIUM AS YOUR MOURNERS LASH OUT MINDLESSLY AT EVERYTHING IN SIGHT--NOTABLY, EACH OTHER.
"YES, I FULLY EXPECT MY LOVELY CHAPEL TO BE THOROUGHLY DEMOLISHED. DON'T WORRY--INSURANCE WILL COVER IT. THE SPEAKERS ARE FACTORY-TESTED TO BE THE LAST THINGS TO GO.

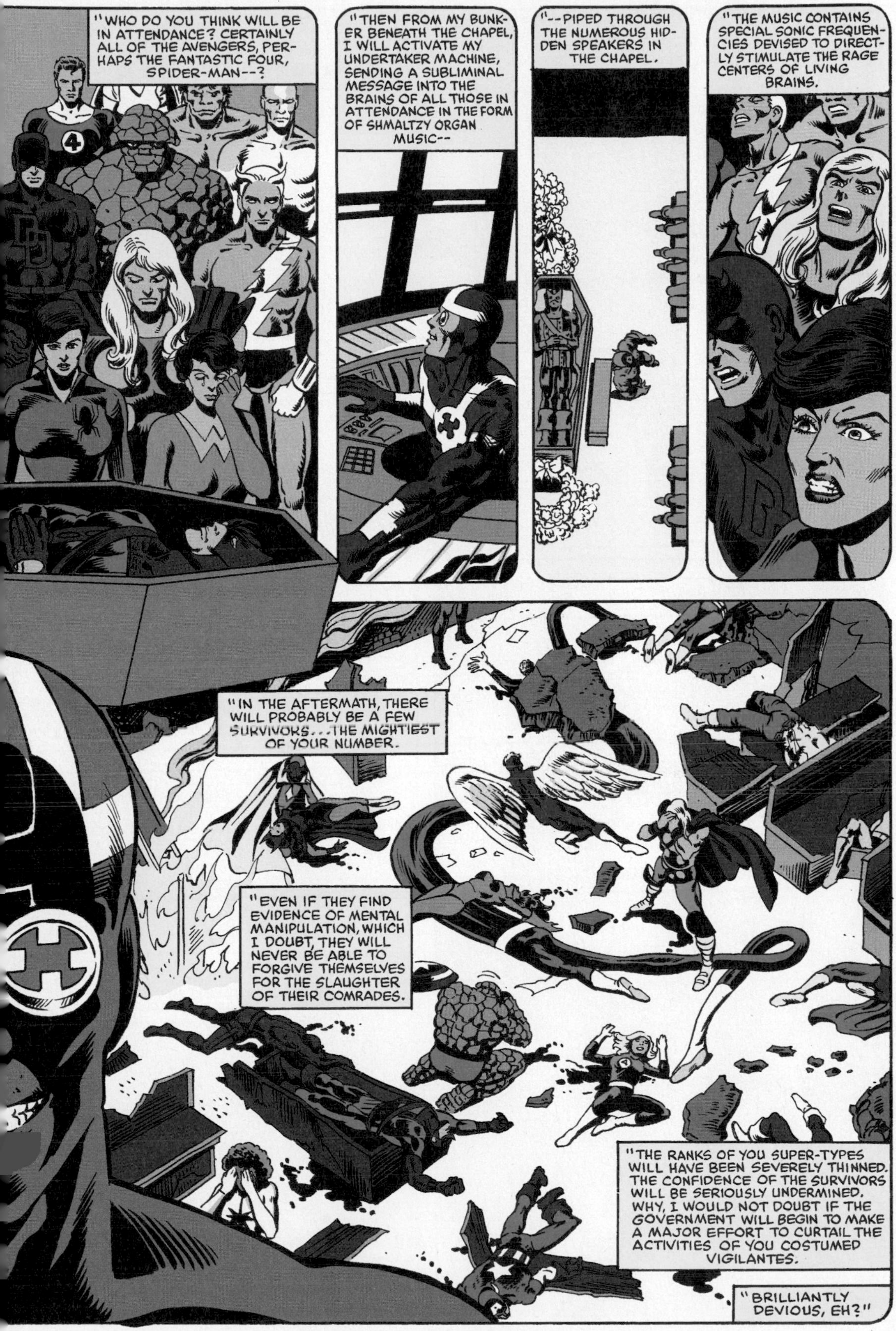
"WHO DO YOU THINK WILL BE IN ATTENDANCE? CERTAINLY ALL OF THE AVENGERS, PERHAPS THE FANTASTIC FOUR, SPIDER-MAN--?
"THEN FROM MY BUNKER BENEATH THE CHAPEL, I WILL ACTIVATE MY UNDERTAKER MACHINE, SENDING A SUBLIMINAL MESSAGE INTO THE BRAINS OF ALL THOSE IN ATTENDANCE IN THE FORM OF SHMALTZY ORGAN MUSIC--
"--PIPED THROUGH THE NUMEROUS HIDDEN SPEAKERS IN THE CHAPEL.
"THE MUSIC CONTAINS SPECIAL SONIC FREQUENCIES DEVISED TO DIRECTLY STIMULATE THE RAGE CENTERS OF LIVING BRAINS.
"IN THE AFTERMATH, THERE WILL PROBABLY BE A FEW SURVIVORS... THE MIGHTIEST OF YOUR NUMBER.
"EVEN IF THEY FIND EVIDENCE OF MENTAL MANIPULATION, WHICH I DOUBT, THEY WILL NEVER BE ABLE TO FORGIVE THEMSELVES FOR THE SLAUGHTER OF THEIR COMRADES.
"THE RANKS OF YOU SUPER-TYPES WILL HAVE BEEN SEVERELY THINNED. THE CONFIDENCE OF THE SURVIVORS WILL BE SERIOUSLY UNDERMINED. WHY, I WOULD NOT DOUBT IF THE GOVERNMENT WILL BEGIN TO MAKE A MAJOR EFFORT TO CURTAIL THE ACTIVITIES OF YOU COSTUMED VIGILANTES.
"BRILLIANTLY DEVIOUS, EH?"

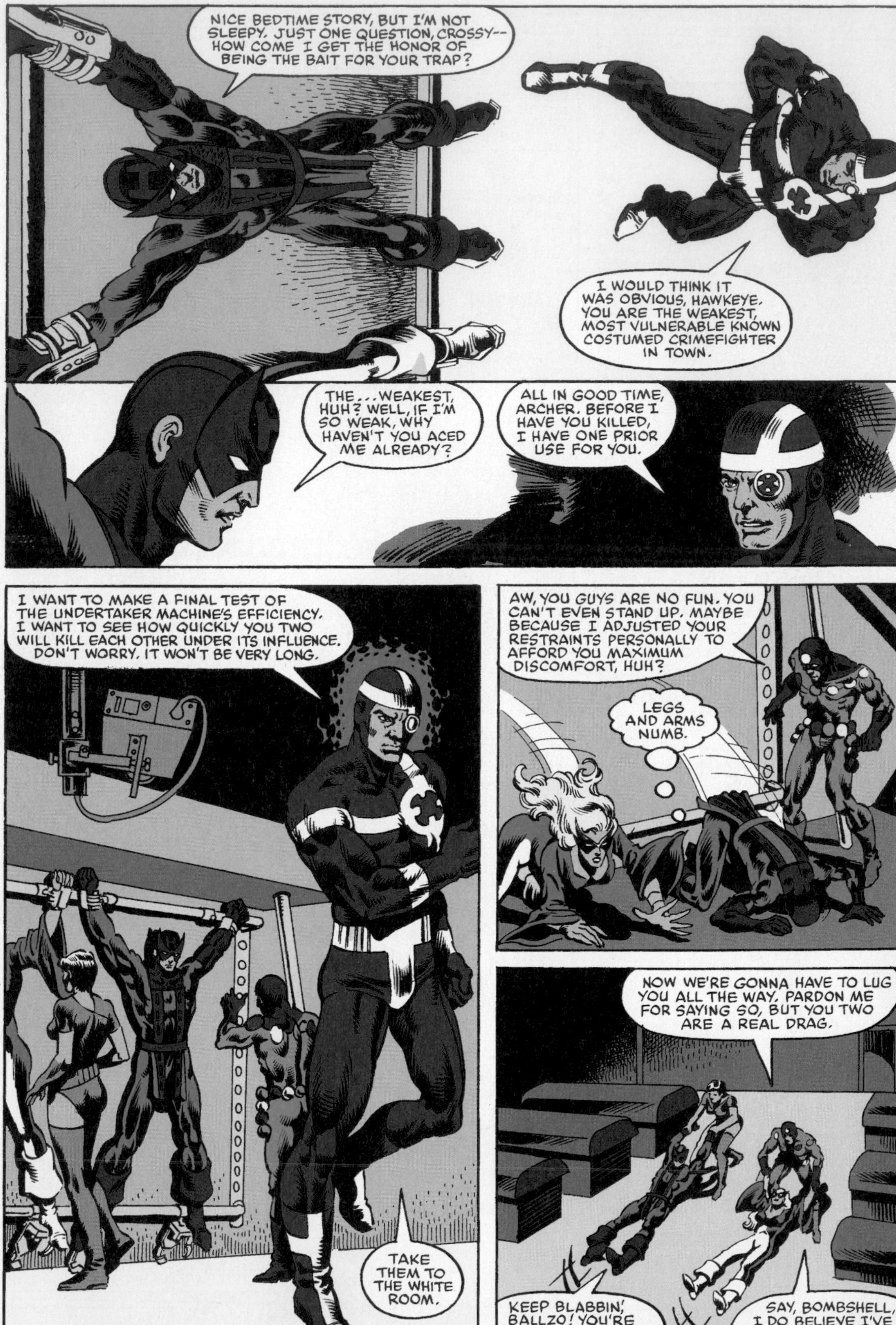
NICE BEDTIME STORY, BUT I'M NOT SLEEPY. JUST ONE QUESTION, CROSSY-- HOW COME I GET THE HONOR OF BEING THE BAIT FOR YOUR TRAP?
I WOULD THINK IT WAS OBVIOUS, HAWKEYE. YOU ARE THE WEAKEST, MOST VULNERABLE KNOWN COSTUMED CRIMEFIGHTER IN TOWN.
THE...WEAKEST, HUH? WELL, IF I'M SO WEAK, WHY HAVEN'T YOU ACED ME ALREADY?
ALL IN GOOD TIME, ARCHER. BEFORE I HAVE YOU KILLED, I HAVE ONE PRIOR USE FOR YOU.
I WANT TO MAKE A FINAL TEST OF THE UNDERTAKER MACHINE'S EFFICIENCY. I WANT TO SEE HOW QUICKLY YOU TWO WILL KILL EACH OTHER UNDER ITS INFLUENCE. DON'T WORRY. IT WON'T BE VERY LONG.
TAKE THEM TO THE WHITE ROOM.
AW, YOU GUYS ARE NO FUN. YOU CAN'T EVEN STAND UP. MAYBE BECAUSE I ADJUSTED YOUR RESTRAINTS PERSONALLY TO AFFORD YOU MAXIMUM DISCOMFORT, HUH?
LEGS AND ARMS NUMB.
NOW WE'RE GONNA HAVE TO LUG YOU ALL THE WAY. PARDON ME FOR SAYING SO, BUT YOU TWO ARE A REAL DRAG.
KEEP BLABBIN', BALLZO! YOU'RE GONNA GET YOURS.
SAY, BOMBSHELL, I DO BELIEVE I'VE BEEN THREATENED.

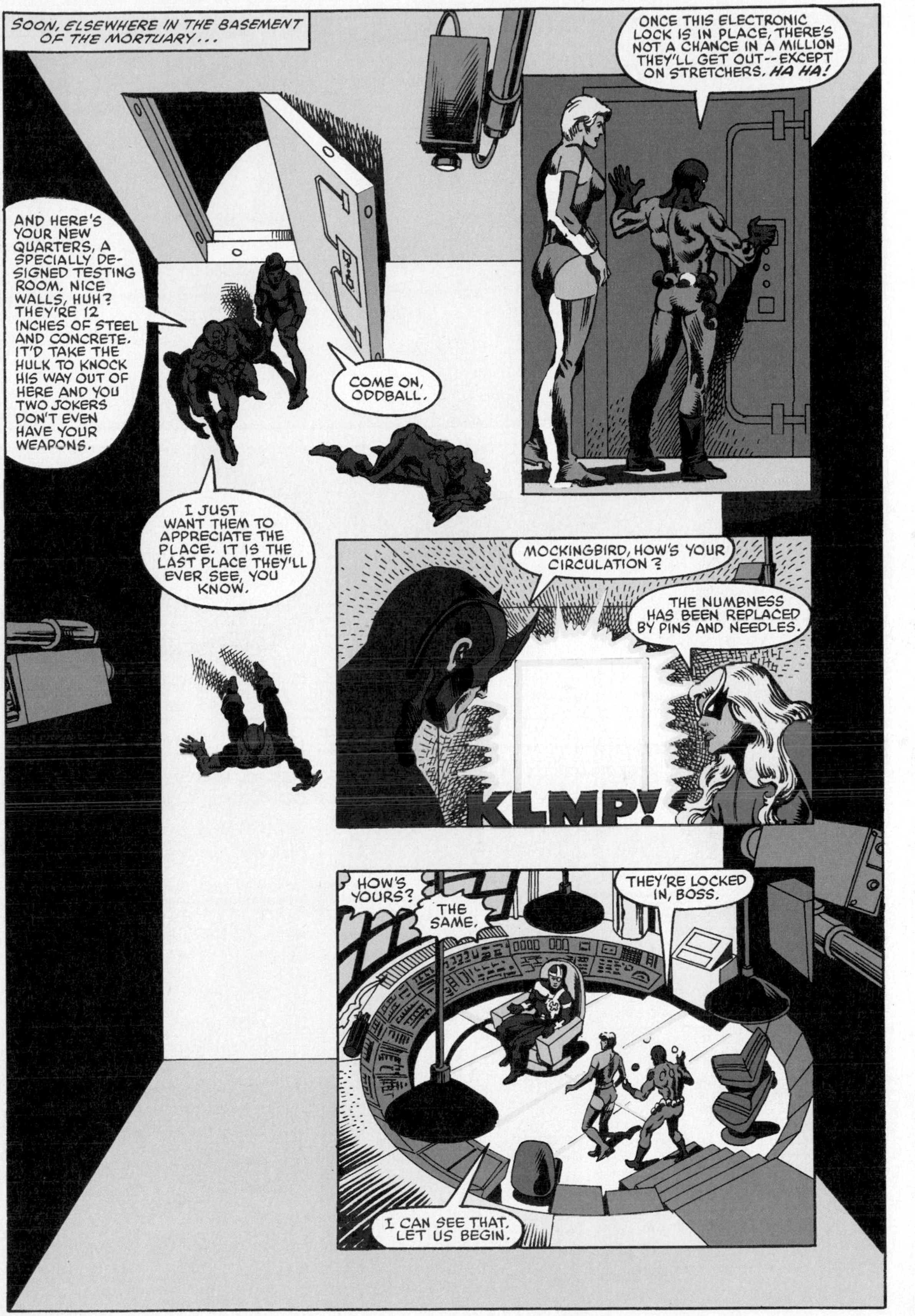
SOON, ELSEWHERE IN THE BASEMENT OF THE MORTUARY...
ONCE THIS ELECTRONIC LOCK IS IN PLACE, THERE'S NOT A CHANCE IN A MILLION THEY'LL GET OUT--EXCEPT ON STRETCHERS. HA HA!
AND HERE'S YOUR NEW QUARTERS, A SPECIALLY DESIGNED TESTING ROOM. NICE WALLS, HUH? THEY'RE 12 INCHES OF STEEL AND CONCRETE. IT'D TAKE THE HULK TO KNOCK HIS WAY OUT OF HERE AND YOU TWO JOKERS DON'T EVEN HAVE YOUR WEAPONS.
COME ON, ODDBALL.
I JUST WANT THEM TO APPRECIATE THE PLACE. IT IS THE LAST PLACE THEY'LL EVER SEE, YOU KNOW.
MOCKINGBIRD, HOW'S YOUR CIRCULATION?
THE NUMBNESS HAS BEEN REPLACED BY PINS AND NEEDLES.
KLMP!
HOW'S YOURS?
THE SAME.
THEY'RE LOCKED IN, BOSS.
I CAN SEE THAT. LET US BEGIN.

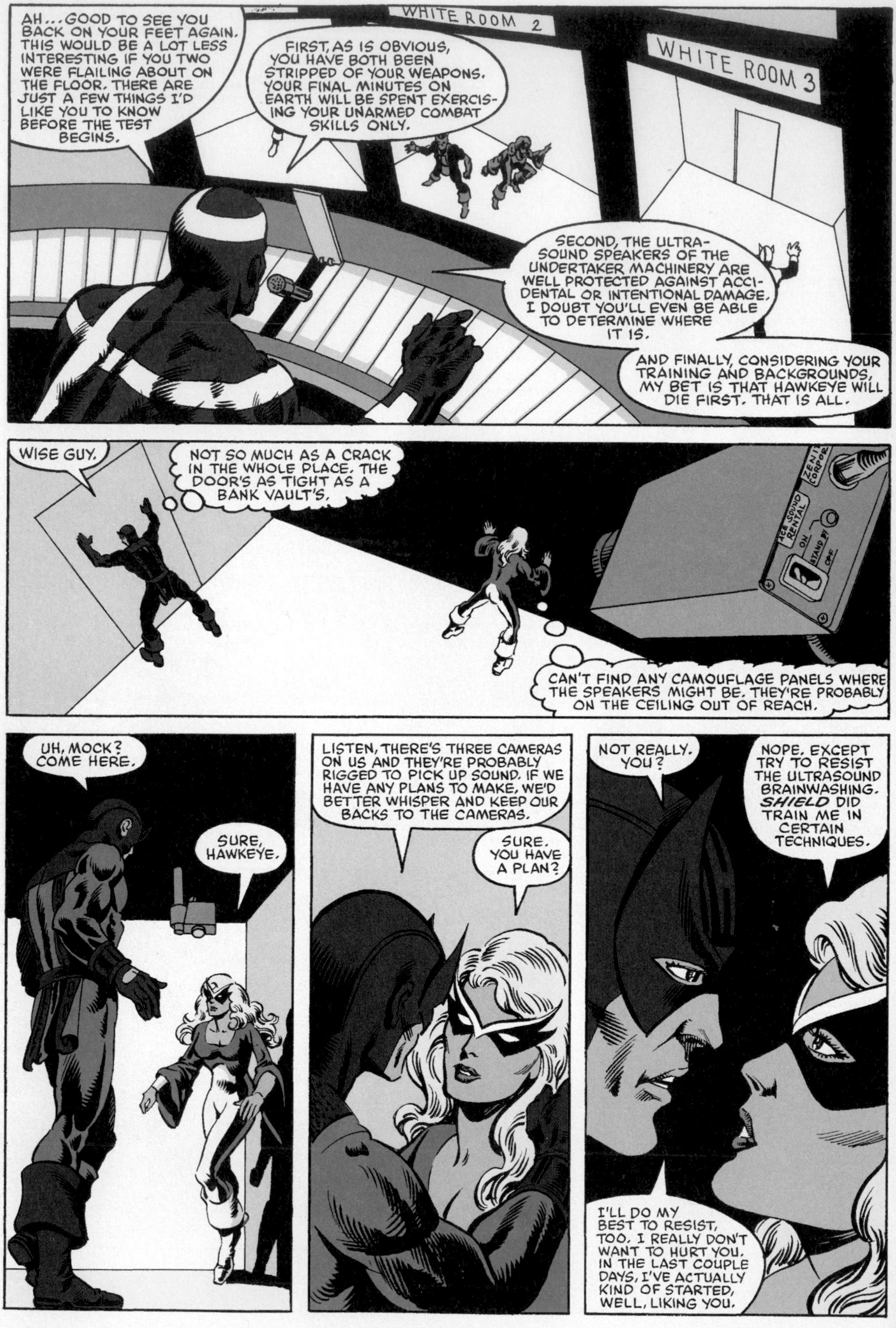
WHITE ROOM 2
WHITE ROOM 3
AH... GOOD TO SEE YOU BACK ON YOUR FEET AGAIN. THIS WOULD BE A LOT LESS INTERESTING IF YOU TWO WERE FLAILING ABOUT ON THE FLOOR. THERE ARE JUST A FEW THINGS I'D LIKE YOU TO KNOW BEFORE THE TEST BEGINS.
FIRST, AS IS OBVIOUS, YOU HAVE BOTH BEEN STRIPPED OF YOUR WEAPONS. YOUR FINAL MINUTES ON EARTH WILL BE SPENT EXERCISING YOUR UNARMED COMBAT SKILLS ONLY.
SECOND, THE ULTRA-SOUND SPEAKERS OF THE UNDERTAKER MACHINERY ARE WELL PROTECTED AGAINST ACCIDENTAL OR INTENTIONAL DAMAGE. I DOUBT YOU'LL EVEN BE ABLE TO DETERMINE WHERE IT IS.
AND FINALLY, CONSIDERING YOUR TRAINING AND BACKGROUNDS, MY BET IS THAT HAWKEYE WILL DIE FIRST. THAT IS ALL.
WISE GUY.
NOT SO MUCH AS A CRACK IN THE WHOLE PLACE. THE DOOR'S AS TIGHT AS A BANK VAULT'S.
CAN'T FIND ANY CAMOUFLAGE PANELS WHERE THE SPEAKERS MIGHT BE. THEY'RE PROBABLY ON THE CEILING OUT OF REACH.
UH, MOCK? COME HERE.
SURE, HAWKEYE.
LISTEN, THERE'S THREE CAMERAS ON US AND THEY'RE PROBABLY RIGGED TO PICK UP SOUND. IF WE HAVE ANY PLANS TO MAKE, WE'D BETTER WHISPER AND KEEP OUR BACKS TO THE CAMERAS.
SURE. YOU HAVE A PLAN?
NOT REALLY. YOU?
NOPE. EXCEPT TRY TO RESIST THE ULTRASOUND BRAINWASHING. SHIELD DID TRAIN ME IN CERTAIN TECHNIQUES.
I'LL DO MY BEST TO RESIST, TOO. I REALLY DON'T WANT TO HURT YOU. IN THE LAST COUPLE DAYS, I'VE ACTUALLY KIND OF STARTED, WELL, LIKING YOU.

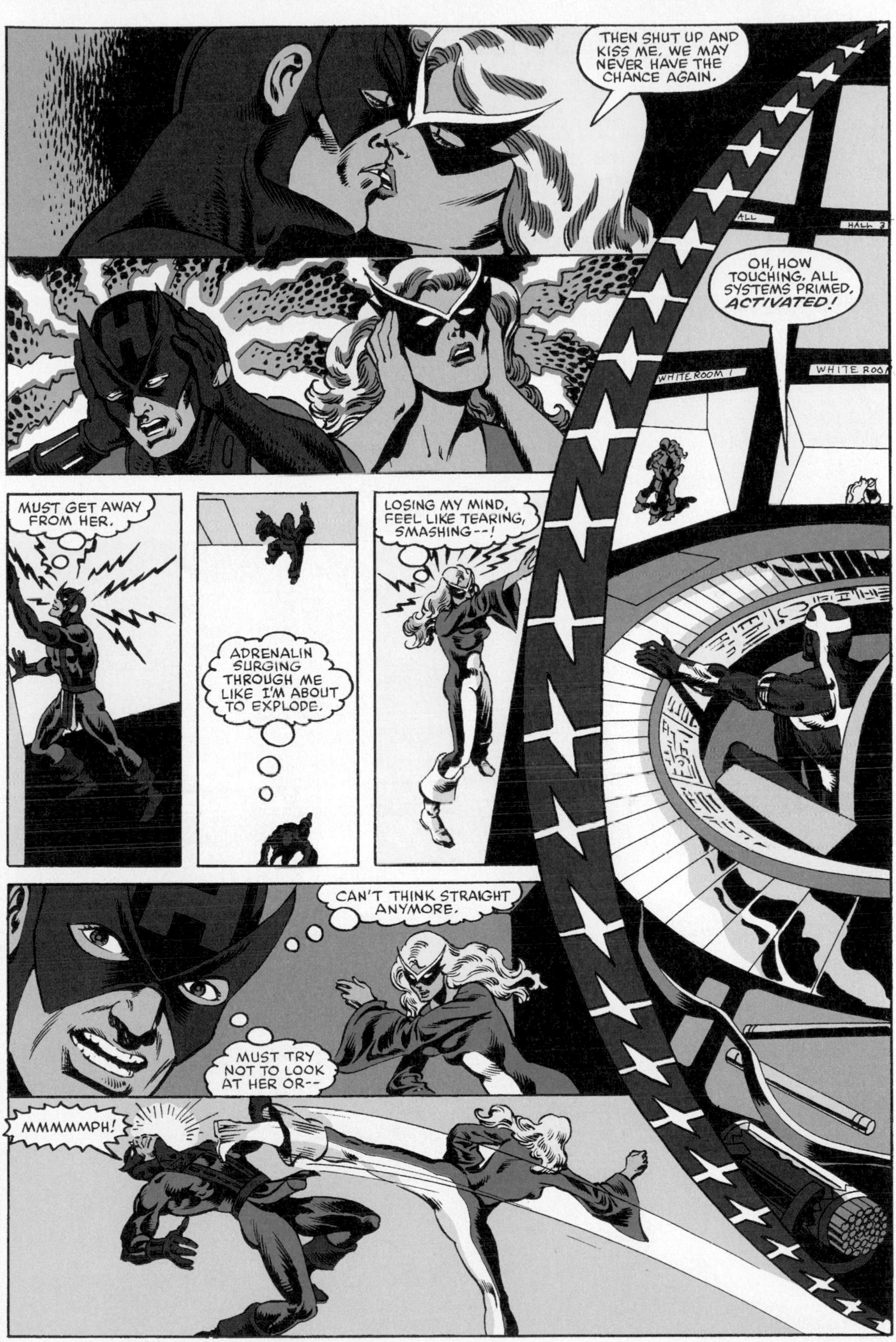
THEN SHUT UP AND KISS ME. WE MAY NEVER HAVE THE CHANCE AGAIN.
HALL
HALL 3
OH, HOW TOUCHING. ALL SYSTEMS PRIMED. ACTIVATED!
WHITE ROOM 1
WHITE ROO
MUST GET AWAY FROM HER.
ADRENALIN SURGING THROUGH ME LIKE I'M ABOUT TO EXPLODE.
LOSING MY MIND, FEEL LIKE TEARING, SMASHING--!
CAN'T THINK STRAIGHT ANYMORE.
MUST TRY NOT TO LOOK AT HER OR--
MMMMMPH!

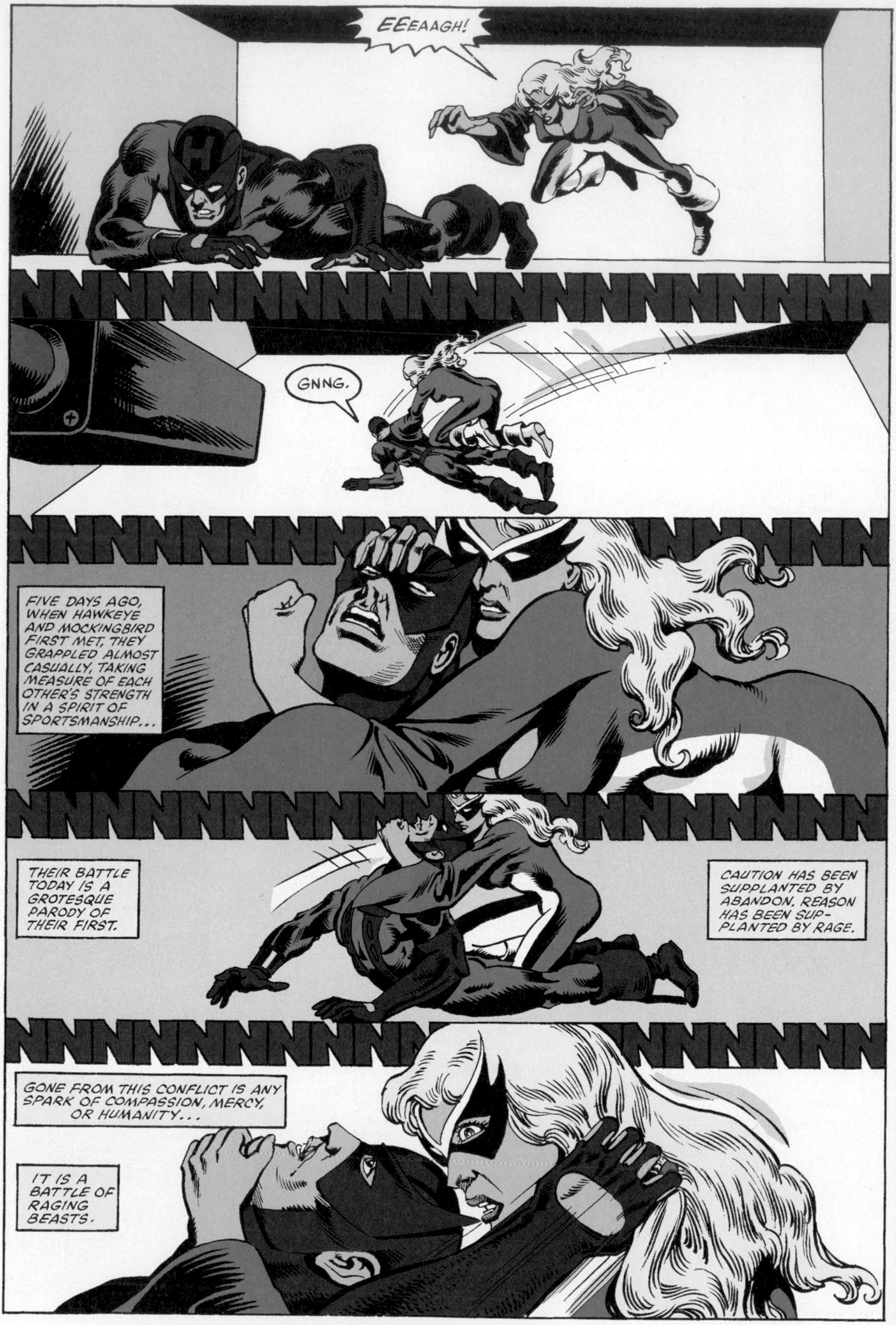
EEEAAGH!
NNNNNNNNNNNNNNNNNNNNNNNNN
GNNG.
NNNNNNNNNNNNNNNNNNN
FIVE DAYS AGO, WHEN HAWKEYE AND MOCKINGBIRD FIRST MET, THEY GRAPPLED ALMOST CASUALLY, TAKING MEASURE OF EACH OTHER'S STRENGTH IN A SPIRIT OF SPORTSMANSHIP...
NNNNNNNNNNNNNNNNNNN
THEIR BATTLE TODAY IS A GROTESQUE PARODY OF THEIR FIRST.
CAUTION HAS BEEN SUPPLANTED BY ABANDON. REASON HAS BEEN SUP-PLANTED BY RAGE.
NNNNNNNNNNNNNNNNNNN
GONE FROM THIS CONFLICT IS ANY SPARK OF COMPASSION, MERCY, OR HUMANITY...
IT IS A BATTLE OF RAGING BEASTS.

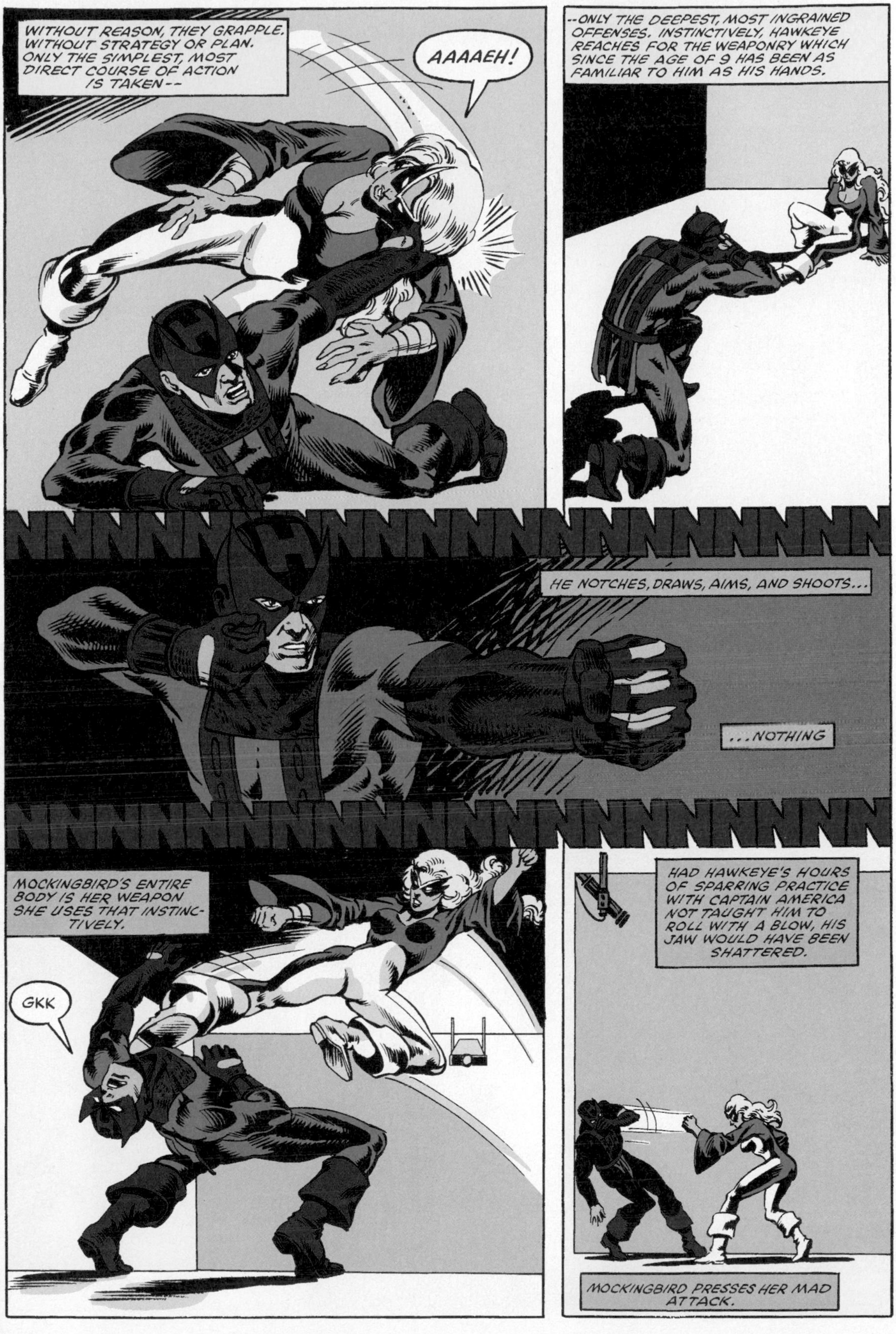

WITHOUT REASON, THEY GRAPPLE. WITHOUT STRATEGY OR PLAN. ONLY THE SIMPLEST, MOST DIRECT COURSE OF ACTION IS TAKEN--
AAAAEH!
--ONLY THE DEEPEST, MOST INGRAINED OFFENSES. INSTINCTIVELY, HAWKEYE REACHES FOR THE WEAPONRY WHICH SINCE THE AGE OF 9 HAS BEEN AS FAMILIAR TO HIM AS HIS HANDS.
NNNNNNNNNNNNNNNNNNNNNNNNNN
HE NOTCHES, DRAWS, AIMS, AND SHOOTS...
...NOTHING
NNNNNNNNNNNNNNNNNNNNNNNNNNN
MOCKINGBIRD'S ENTIRE BODY IS HER WEAPON SHE USES THAT INSTINCTIVELY.
GKK
HAD HAWKEYE'S HOURS OF SPARRING PRACTICE WITH CAPTAIN AMERICA NOT TAUGHT HIM TO ROLL WITH A BLOW, HIS JAW WOULD HAVE BEEN SHATTERED.
MOCKINGBIRD PRESSES HER MAD ATTACK.

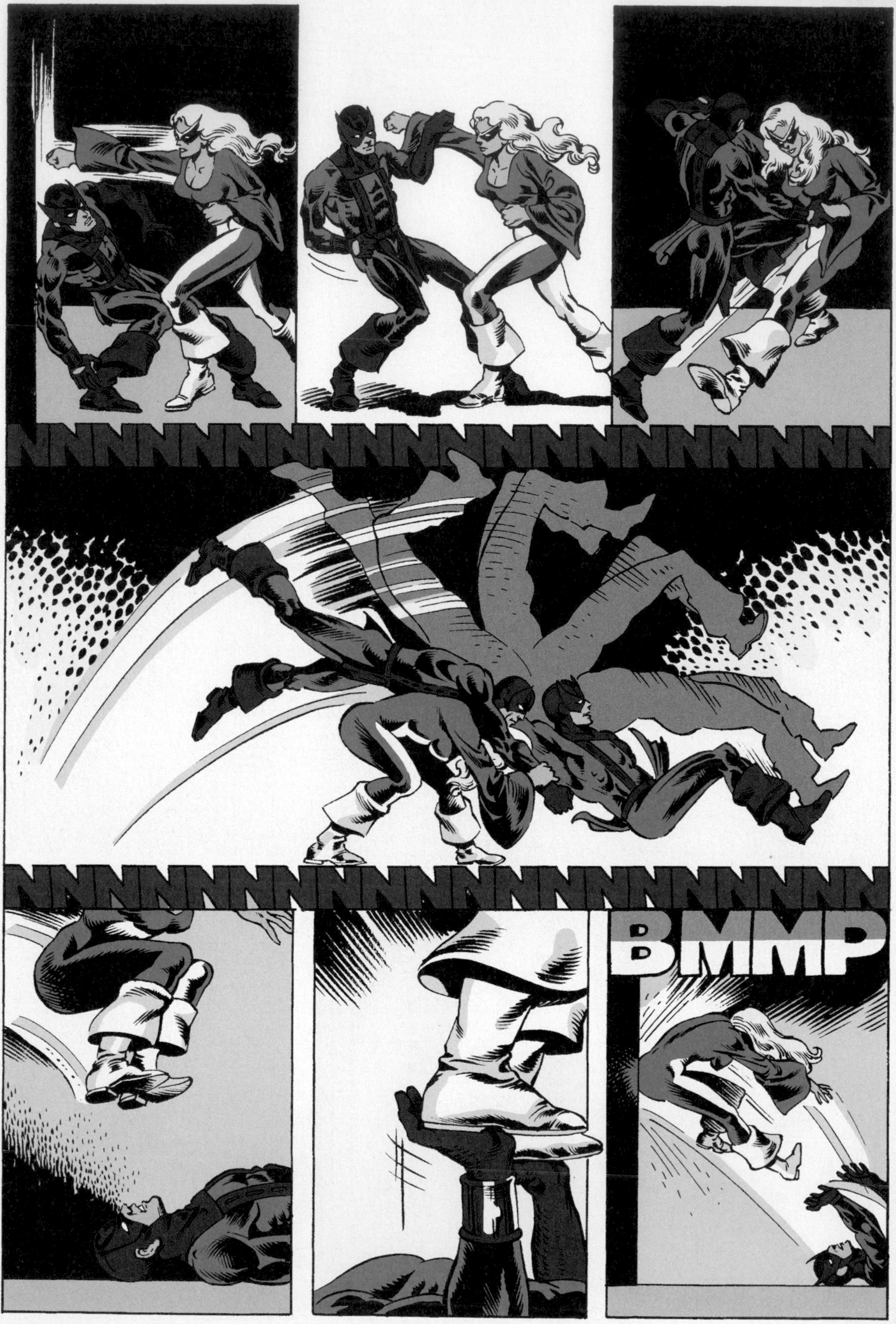
NNNNNNNNNNNNNNNNNNNNNN
NNNNNNNNNNNNNNNNNNNNNN
BMMP

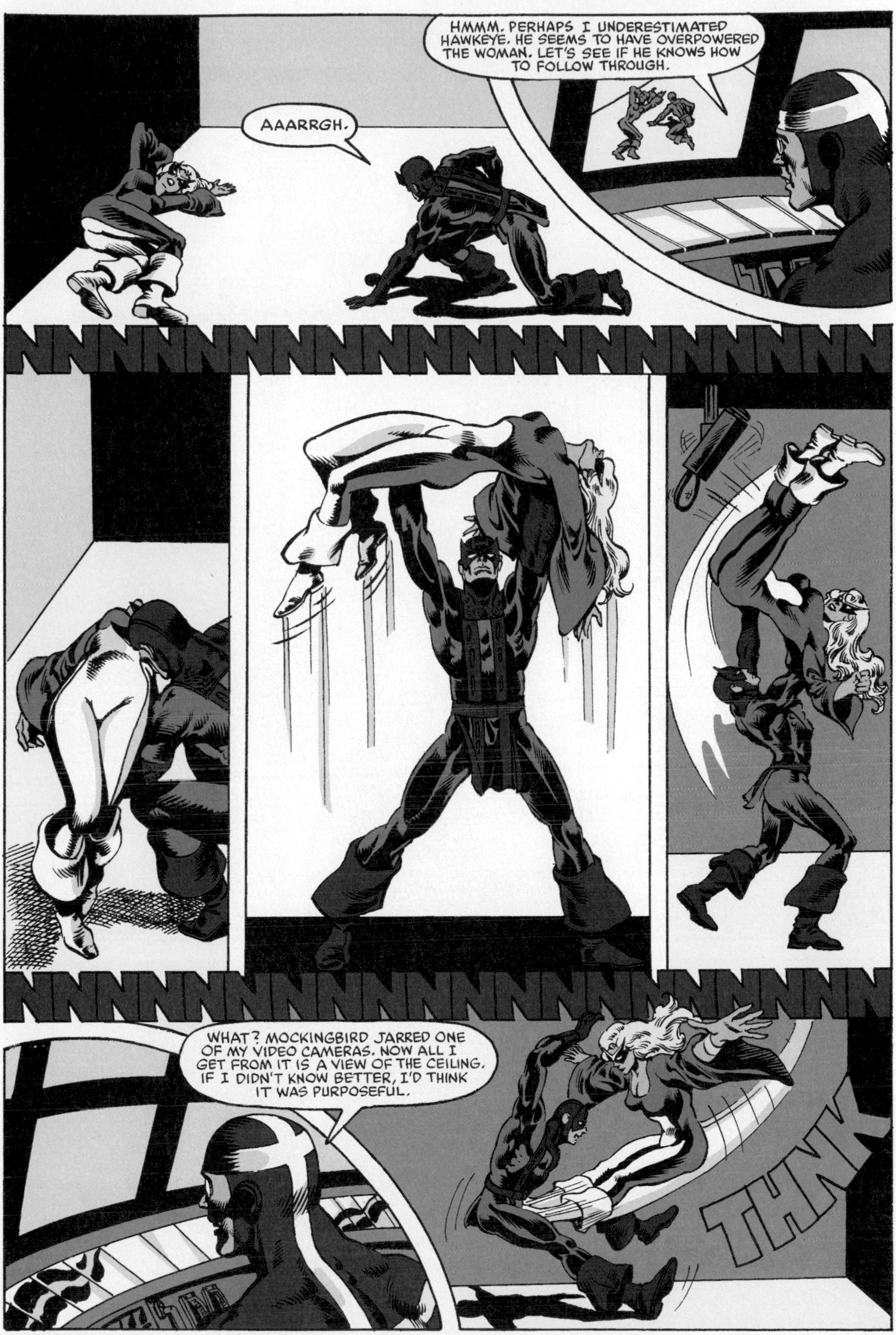
HMMM. PERHAPS I UNDERESTIMATED HAWKEYE. HE SEEMS TO HAVE OVERPOWERED THE WOMAN. LET'S SEE IF HE KNOWS HOW TO FOLLOW THROUGH.
AAARRGH.
NNNNNNNNNNNNNNNNNNNNNNNN
NNNNNNNNNNNNNNNNNNNNNNNN
WHAT? MOCKINGBIRD JARRED ONE OF MY VIDEO CAMERAS. NOW ALL I GET FROM IT IS A VIEW OF THE CEILING. IF I DIDN'T KNOW BETTER, I'D THINK IT WAS PURPOSEFUL.
THNK

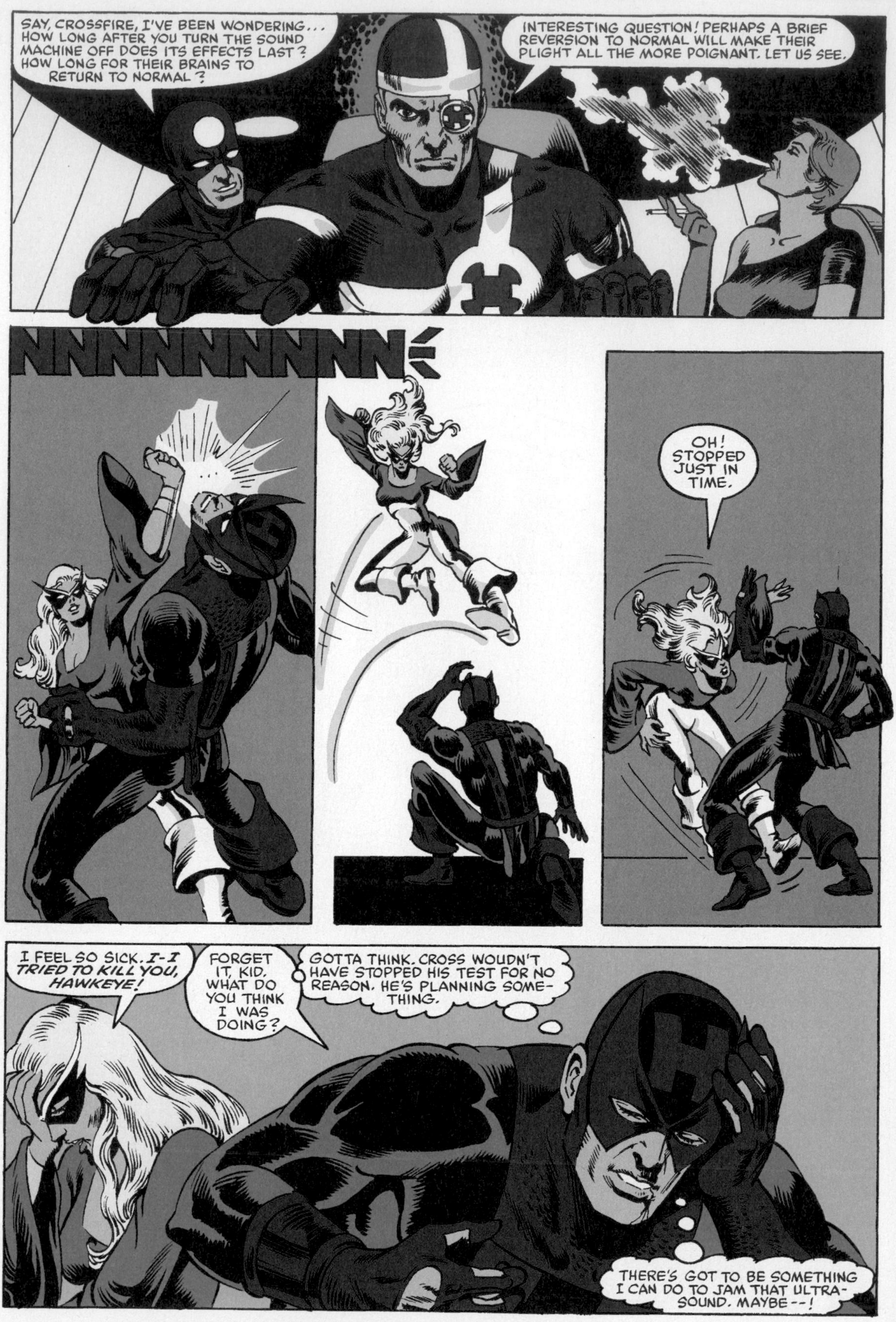
SAY, CROSSFIRE, I'VE BEEN WONDERING... HOW LONG AFTER YOU TURN THE SOUND MACHINE OFF DOES ITS EFFECTS LAST? HOW LONG FOR THEIR BRAINS TO RETURN TO NORMAL?
INTERESTING QUESTION! PERHAPS A BRIEF REVERSION TO NORMAL WILL MAKE THEIR PLIGHT ALL THE MORE POIGNANT. LET US SEE.
NNNNNNNNNN
OH! STOPPED JUST IN TIME.
I FEEL SO SICK. I-I TRIED TO KILL YOU, HAWKEYE!
FORGET IT, KID. WHAT DO YOU THINK I WAS DOING?
GOTTA THINK. CROSS WOUDN'T HAVE STOPPED HIS TEST FOR NO REASON. HE'S PLANNING SOME-THING.
THERE'S GOT TO BE SOMETHING I CAN DO TO JAM THAT ULTRA-SOUND. MAYBE--!

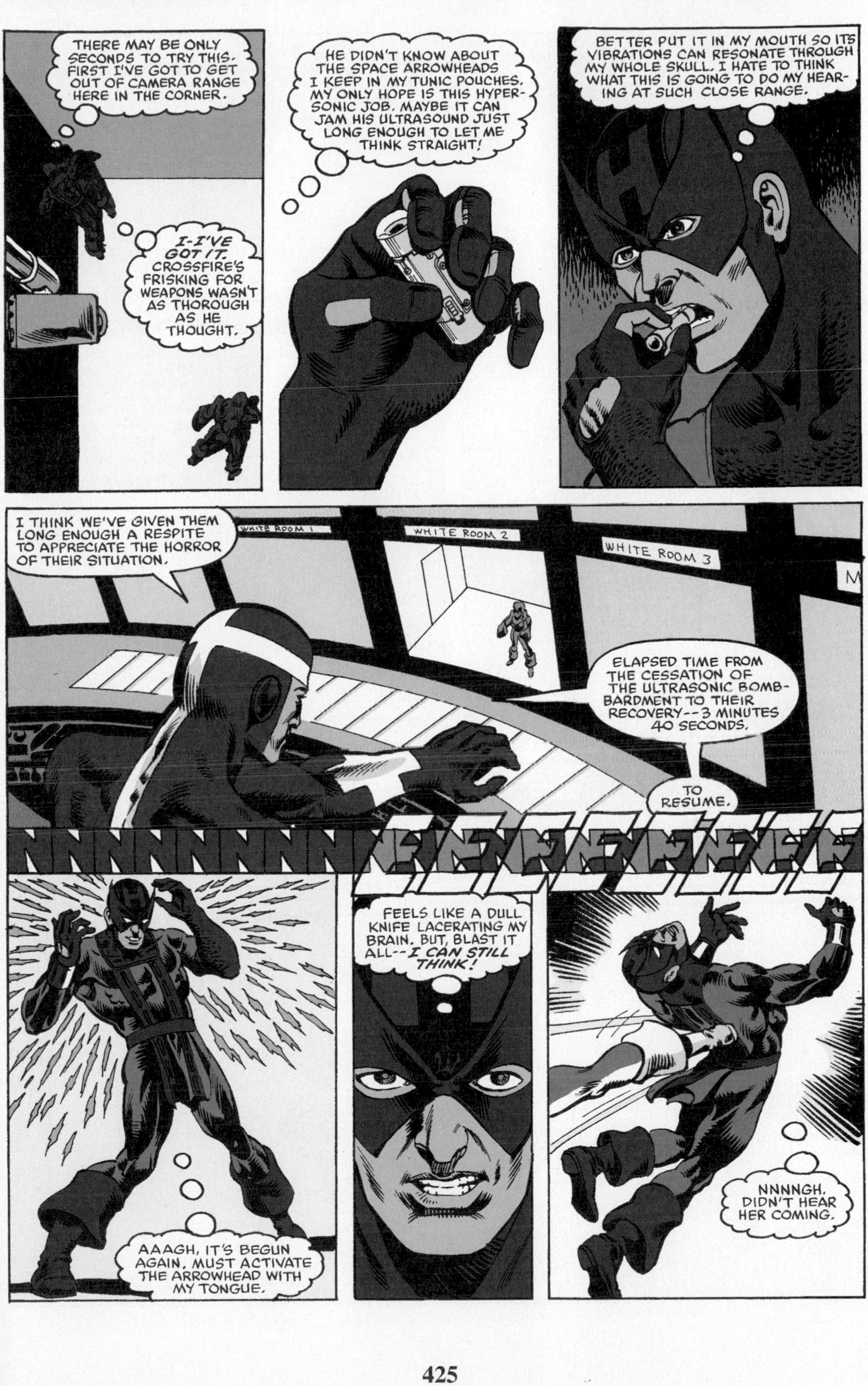
THERE MAY BE ONLY SECONDS TO TRY THIS. FIRST I'VE GOT TO GET OUT OF CAMERA RANGE HERE IN THE CORNER.
I-I'VE GOT IT. CROSSFIRE'S FRISKING FOR WEAPONS WASN'T AS THOROUGH AS HE THOUGHT.
HE DIDN'T KNOW ABOUT THE SPACE ARROWHEADS I KEEP IN MY TUNIC POUCHES. MY ONLY HOPE IS THIS HYPERSONIC JOB. MAYBE IT CAN JAM HIS ULTRASOUND JUST LONG ENOUGH TO LET ME THINK STRAIGHT!
BETTER PUT IT IN MY MOUTH SO ITS VIBRATIONS CAN RESONATE THROUGH MY WHOLE SKULL. I HATE TO THINK WHAT THIS IS GOING TO DO MY HEARING AT SUCH CLOSE RANGE.
I THINK WE'VE GIVEN THEM LONG ENOUGH A RESPITE TO APPRECIATE THE HORROR OF THEIR SITUATION.
WHITE ROOM 1
WHITE ROOM 2
WHITE ROOM 3
ELAPSED TIME FROM THE CESSATION OF THE ULTRASONIC BOMBBARDMENT TO THEIR RECOVERY--3 MINUTES 40 SECONDS.
TO RESUME.
NNNNNNNNNEEEEEEEEEEEEE
AAAGH, IT'S BEGUN AGAIN. MUST ACTIVATE THE ARROWHEAD WITH MY TONGUE.
FEELS LIKE A DULL KNIFE LACERATING MY BRAIN. BUT, BLAST IT ALL--I CAN STILL THINK!
NNNNGH. DIDN'T HEAR HER COMING.

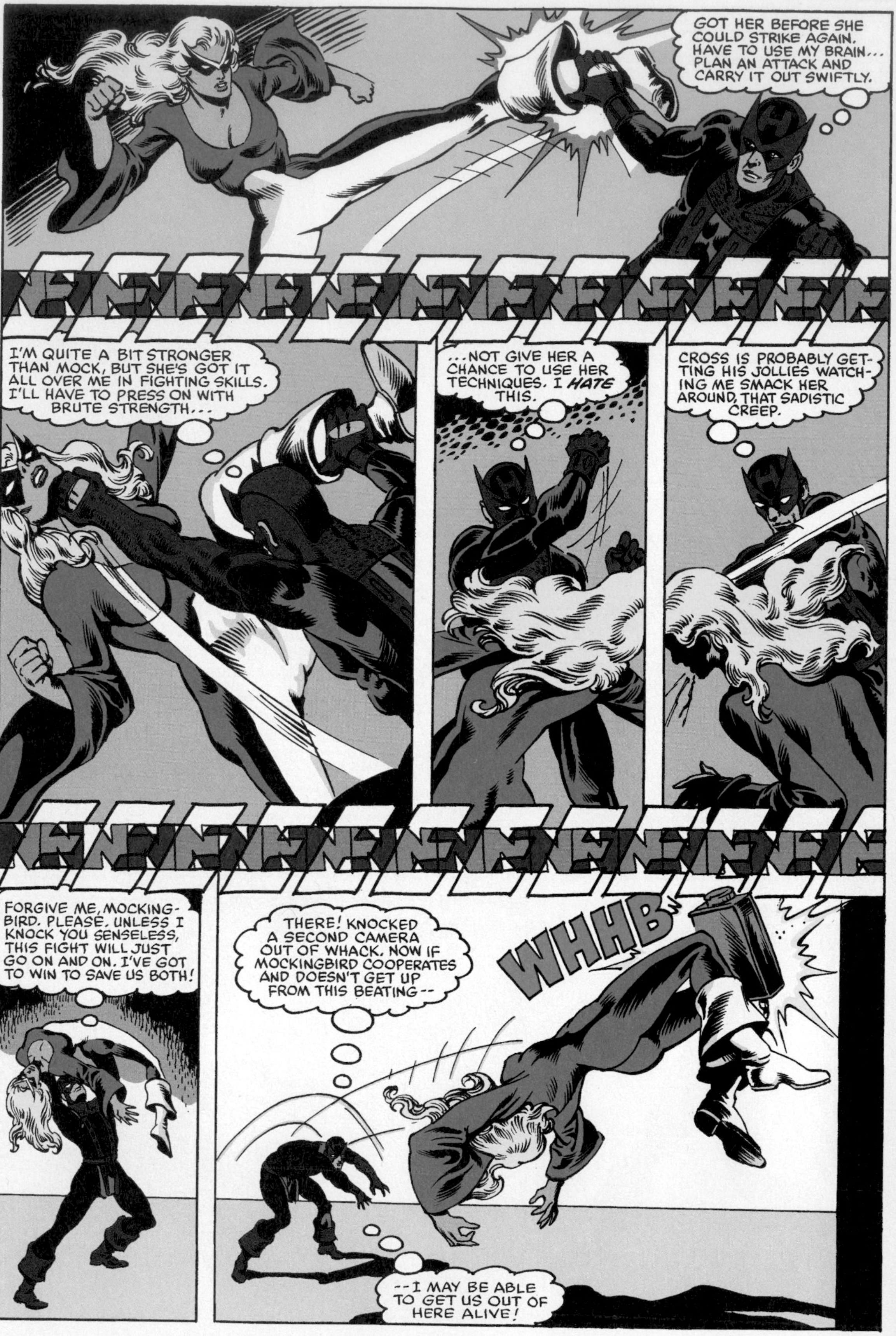
GOT HER BEFORE SHE COULD STRIKE AGAIN. HAVE TO USE MY BRAIN... PLAN AN ATTACK AND CARRY IT OUT SWIFTLY.
I'M QUITE A BIT STRONGER THAN MOCK, BUT SHE'S GOT IT ALL OVER ME IN FIGHTING SKILLS. I'LL HAVE TO PRESS ON WITH BRUTE STRENGTH...
...NOT GIVE HER A CHANCE TO USE HER TECHNIQUES. I *HATE* THIS.
CROSS IS PROBABLY GETTING HIS JOLLIES WATCHING ME SMACK HER AROUND, THAT SADISTIC CREEP.
FORGIVE ME, MOCKINGBIRD. PLEASE. UNLESS I KNOCK YOU SENSELESS, THIS FIGHT WILL JUST GO ON AND ON. I'VE GOT TO WIN TO SAVE US BOTH!
THERE! KNOCKED A SECOND CAMERA OUT OF WHACK. NOW IF MOCKINGBIRD COOPERATES AND DOESN'T GET UP FROM THIS BEATING--
WHHB
--I MAY BE ABLE TO GET US OUT OF HERE ALIVE!

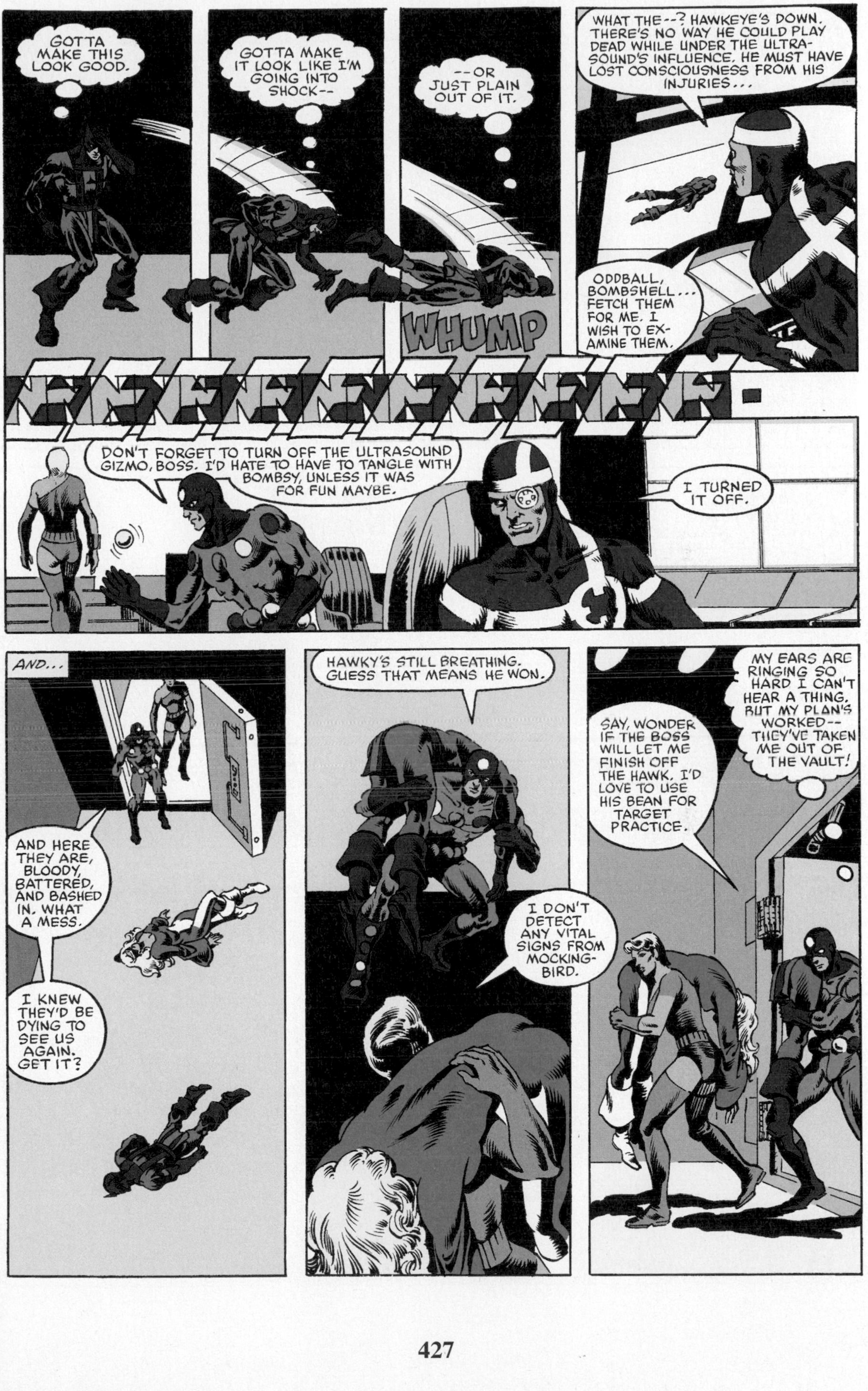

GOTTA MAKE THIS LOOK GOOD.
GOTTA MAKE IT LOOK LIKE I'M GOING INTO SHOCK--
--OR JUST PLAIN OUT OF IT.
WHUMP
WHAT THE--? HAWKEYE'S DOWN. THERE'S NO WAY HE COULD PLAY DEAD WHILE UNDER THE ULTRASOUND'S INFLUENCE. HE MUST HAVE LOST CONSCIOUSNESS FROM HIS INJURIES...
ODDBALL, BOMBSHELL... FETCH THEM FOR ME. I WISH TO EXAMINE THEM.
DON'T FORGET TO TURN OFF THE ULTRASOUND GIZMO, BOSS. I'D HATE TO HAVE TO TANGLE WITH BOMBSY, UNLESS IT WAS FOR FUN MAYBE.
I TURNED IT OFF.
AND...
AND HERE THEY ARE, BLOODY, BATTERED, AND BASHED IN. WHAT A MESS.
I KNEW THEY'D BE DYING TO SEE US AGAIN. GET IT?
HAWKY'S STILL BREATHING. GUESS THAT MEANS HE WON.
I DON'T DETECT ANY VITAL SIGNS FROM MOCKING-BIRD.
SAY, WONDER IF THE BOSS WILL LET ME FINISH OFF THE HAWK. I'D LOVE TO USE HIS BEAN FOR TARGET PRACTICE.
MY EARS ARE RINGING SO HARD I CAN'T HEAR A THING, BUT MY PLAN'S WORKED-- THEY'VE TAKEN ME OUT OF THE VAULT!

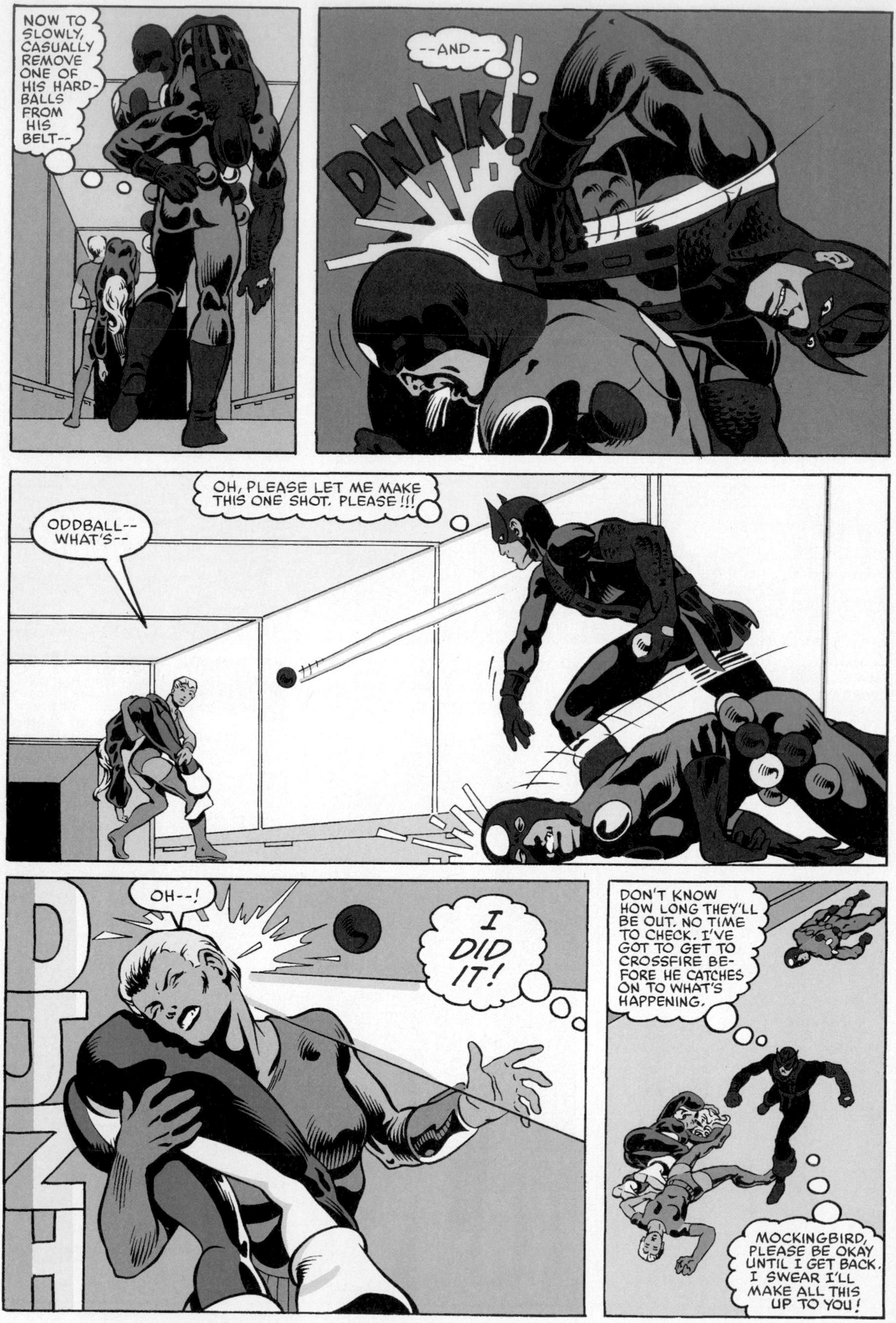
NOW TO SLOWLY, CASUALLY REMOVE ONE OF HIS HARD-BALLS FROM HIS BELT--
--AND--
DNNK!
OH, PLEASE LET ME MAKE THIS ONE SHOT. PLEASE!!!
ODDBALL-- WHAT'S--
OH--!
I DID IT!
DON'T KNOW HOW LONG THEY'LL BE OUT. NO TIME TO CHECK. I'VE GOT TO GET TO CROSSFIRE BE-FORE HE CATCHES ON TO WHAT'S HAPPENING.
MOCKINGBIRD, PLEASE BE OKAY UNTIL I GET BACK. I SWEAR I'LL MAKE ALL THIS UP TO YOU!

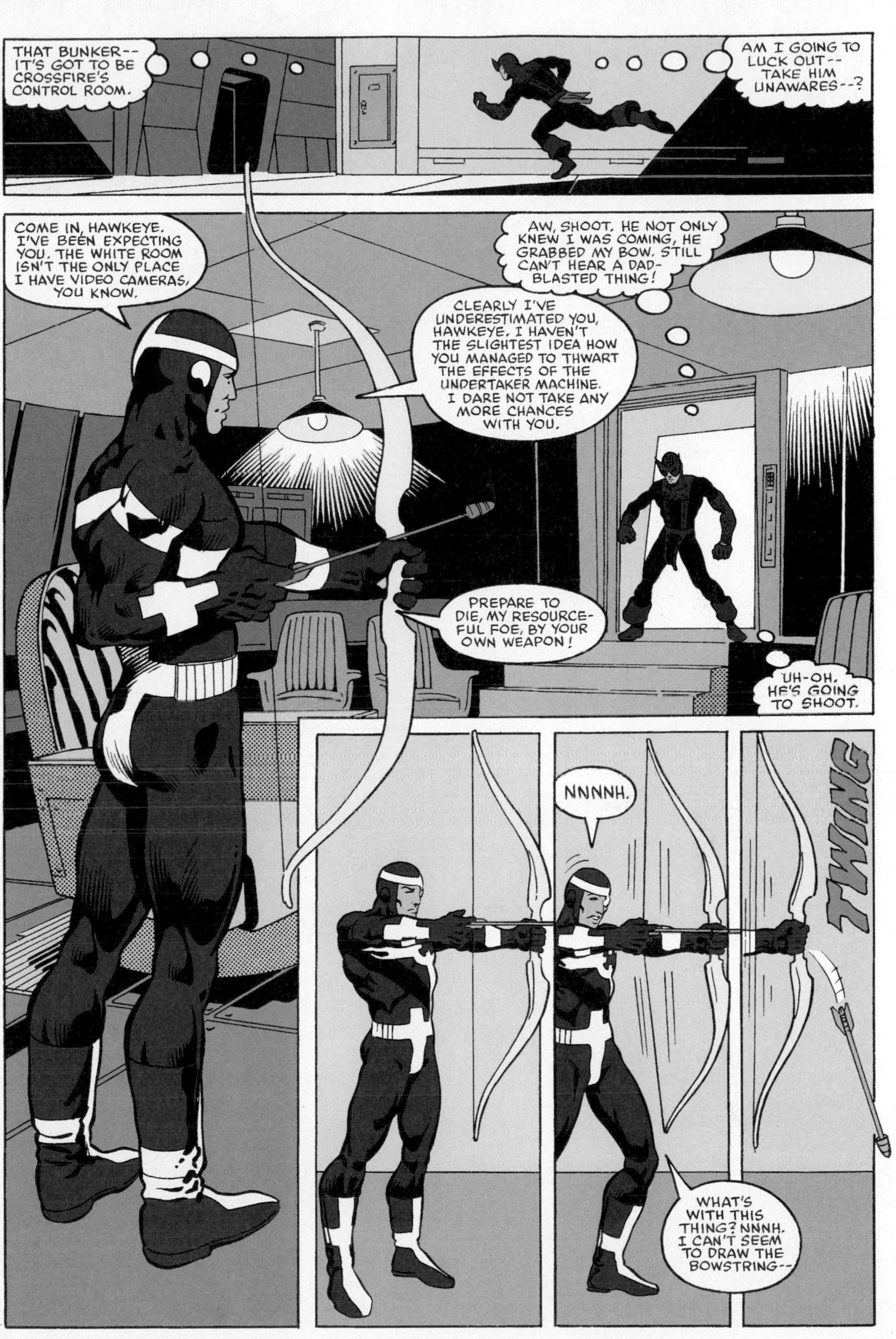
THAT BUNKER-- IT'S GOT TO BE CROSSFIRE'S CONTROL ROOM.
AM I GOING TO LUCK OUT-- TAKE HIM UNAWARES--?
COME IN, HAWKEYE. I'VE BEEN EXPECTING YOU. THE WHITE ROOM ISN'T THE ONLY PLACE I HAVE VIDEO CAMERAS, YOU KNOW.
AW, SHOOT. HE NOT ONLY KNEW I WAS COMING, HE GRABBED MY BOW. STILL CAN'T HEAR A DAD-BLASTED THING!
CLEARLY I'VE UNDERESTIMATED YOU, HAWKEYE. I HAVEN'T THE SLIGHTEST IDEA HOW YOU MANAGED TO THWART THE EFFECTS OF THE UNDERTAKER MACHINE. I DARE NOT TAKE ANY MORE CHANCES WITH YOU.
PREPARE TO DIE, MY RESOURCEFUL FOE, BY YOUR OWN WEAPON!
UH-OH. HE'S GOING TO SHOOT.
NNNNH.
TWING
WHAT'S WITH THIS THING? NNNH. I CAN'T SEEM TO DRAW THE BOWSTRING--

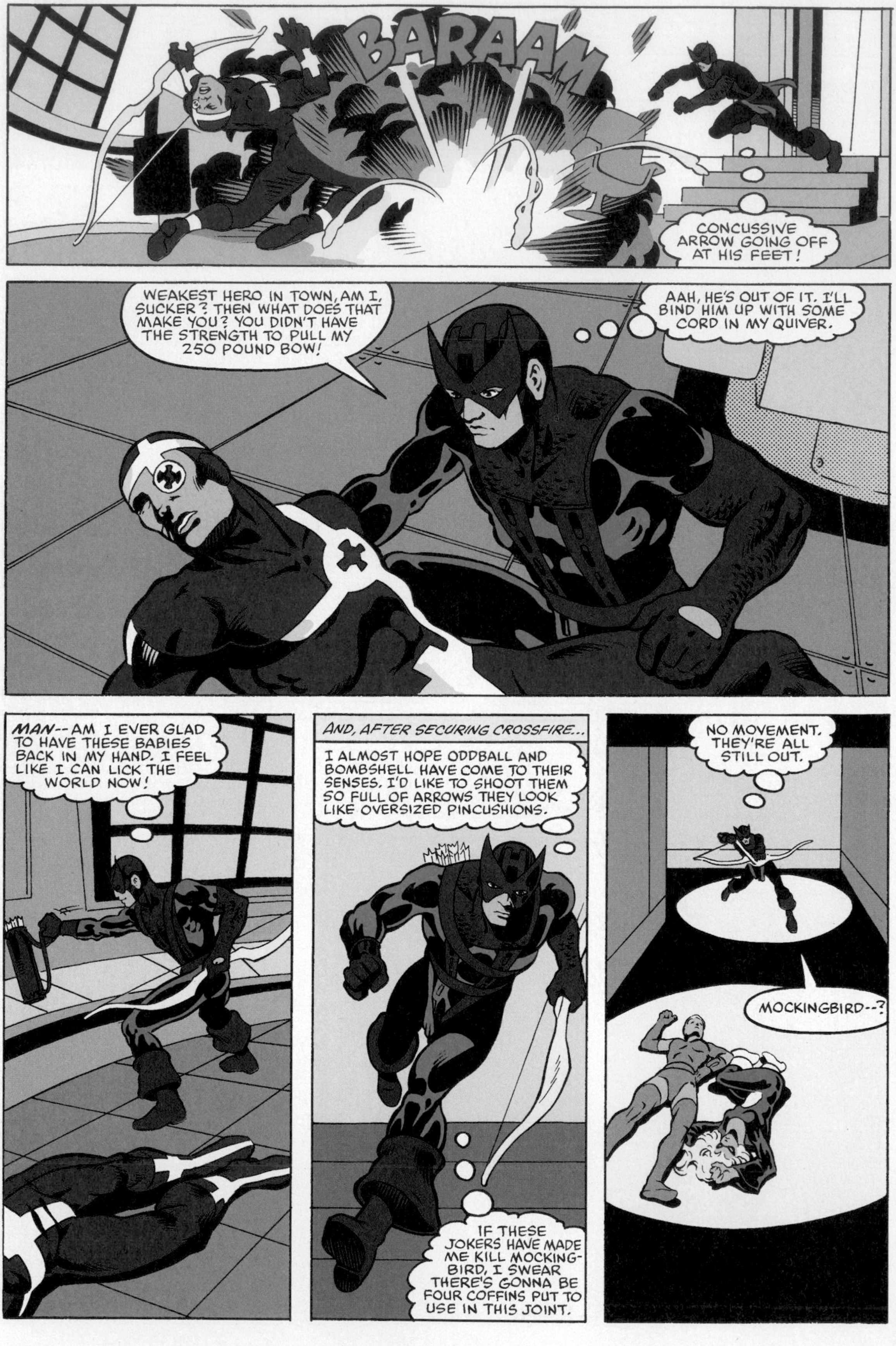
BARAAM
CONCUSSIVE ARROW GOING OFF AT HIS FEET!
WEAKEST HERO IN TOWN, AM I, SUCKER? THEN WHAT DOES THAT MAKE YOU? YOU DIDN'T HAVE THE STRENGTH TO PULL MY 250 POUND BOW!
AAH, HE'S OUT OF IT. I'LL BIND HIM UP WITH SOME CORD IN MY QUIVER.
MAN--AM I EVER GLAD TO HAVE THESE BABIES BACK IN MY HAND. I FEEL LIKE I CAN LICK THE WORLD NOW!
AND, AFTER SECURING CROSSFIRE...
I ALMOST HOPE ODDBALL AND BOMBSHELL HAVE COME TO THEIR SENSES. I'D LIKE TO SHOOT THEM SO FULL OF ARROWS THEY LOOK LIKE OVERSIZED PINCUSHIONS.
IF THESE JOKERS HAVE MADE ME KILL MOCKING-BIRD, I SWEAR THERE'S GONNA BE FOUR COFFINS PUT TO USE IN THIS JOINT.
NO MOVEMENT. THEY'RE ALL STILL OUT.
MOCKINGBIRD--?

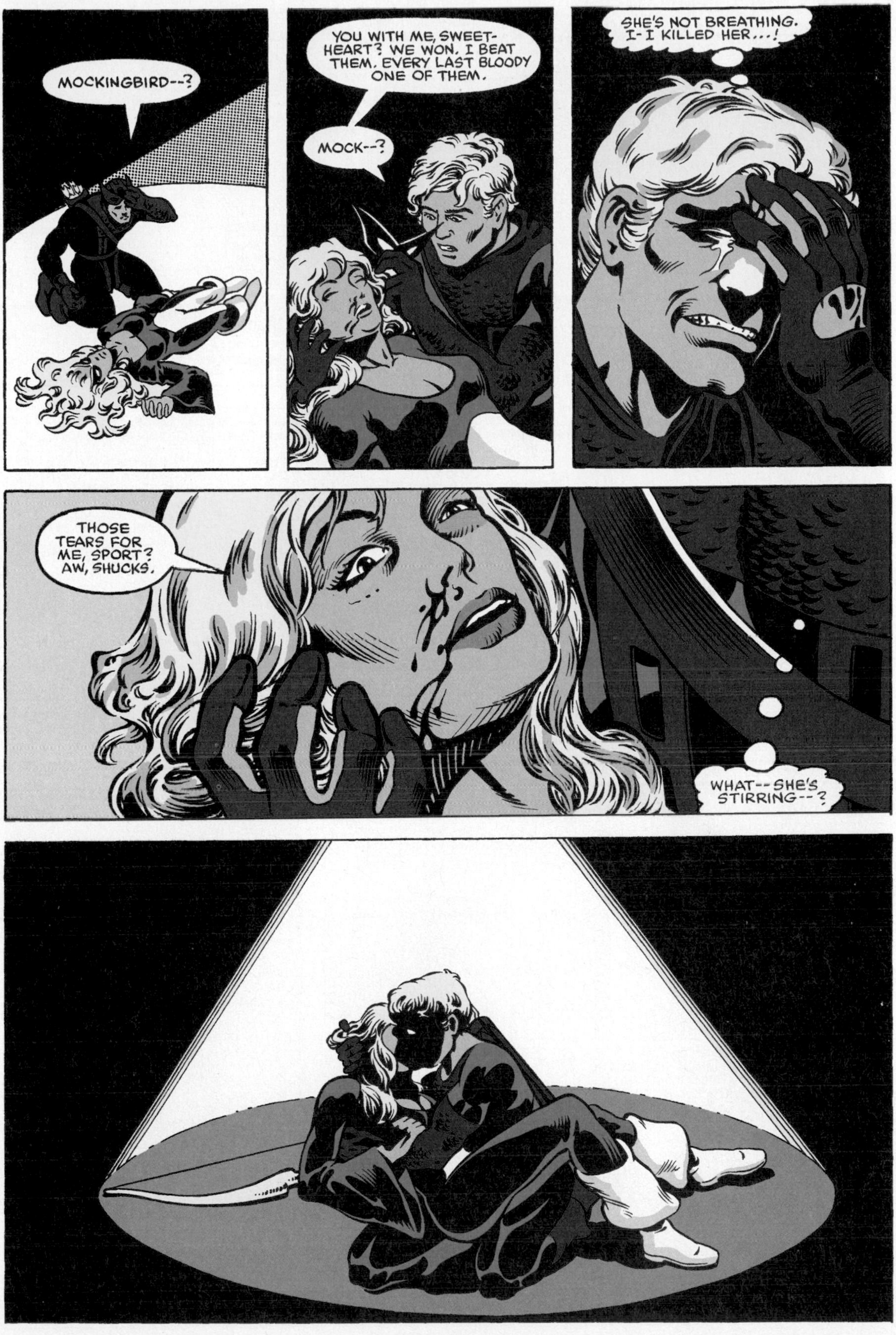
MOCKINGBIRD--?
YOU WITH ME, SWEET-HEART? WE WON. I BEAT THEM. EVERY LAST BLOODY ONE OF THEM.
MOCK--?
SHE'S NOT BREATHING. I- I KILLED HER...!
THOSE TEARS FOR ME, SPORT? AW, SHUCKS.
WHAT--SHE'S STIRRING--?

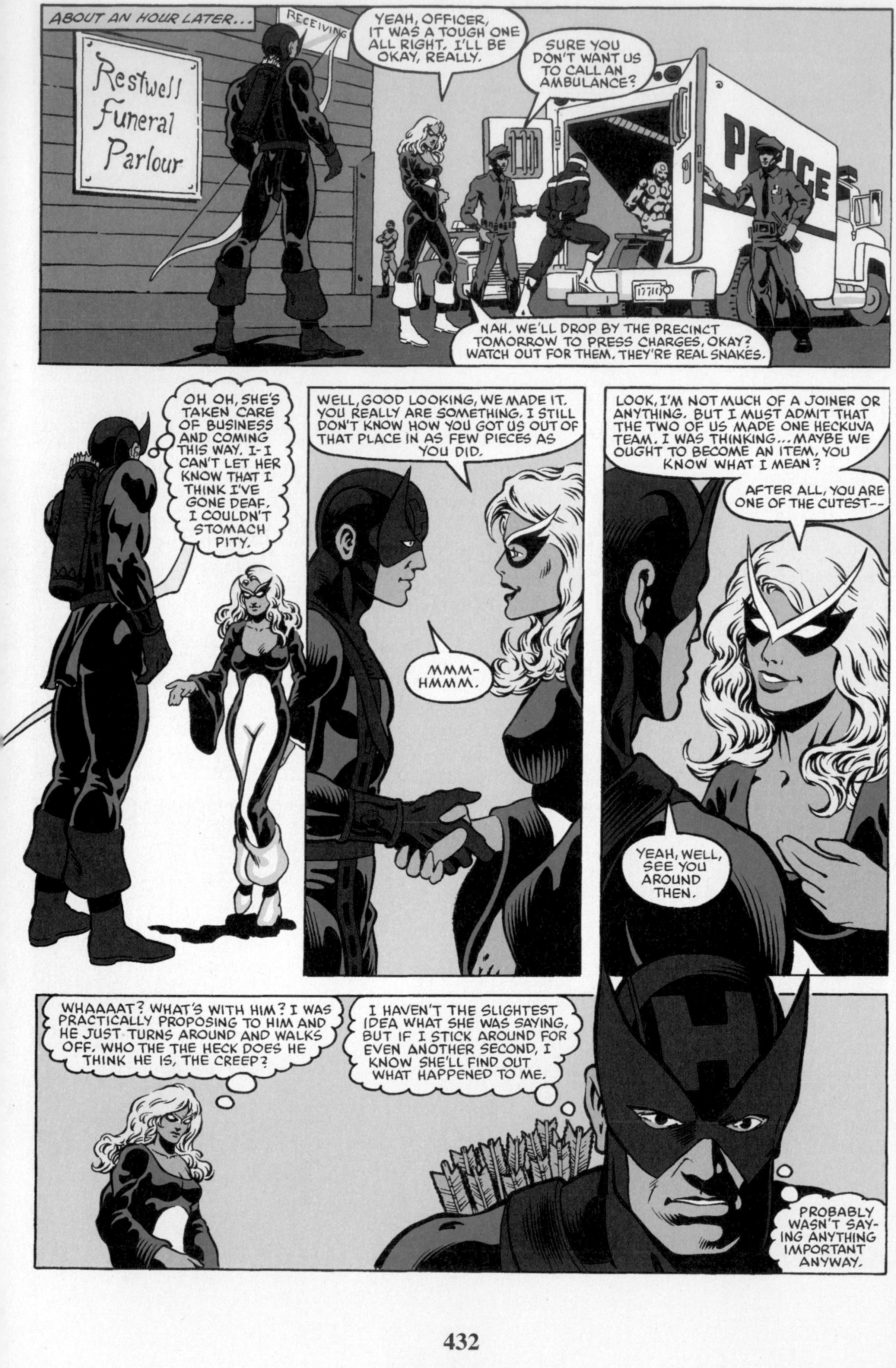
ABOUT AN HOUR LATER...
RECEIVING
Restwell Funeral Parlour
YEAH, OFFICER, IT WAS A TOUGH ONE ALL RIGHT. I'LL BE OKAY, REALLY.
SURE YOU DON'T WANT US TO CALL AN AMBULANCE?
NAH. WE'LL DROP BY THE PRECINCT TOMORROW TO PRESS CHARGES, OKAY? WATCH OUT FOR THEM. THEY'RE REAL SNAKES.
OH OH, SHE'S TAKEN CARE OF BUSINESS AND COMING THIS WAY. I- I CAN'T LET HER KNOW THAT I THINK I'VE GONE DEAF. I COULDN'T STOMACH PITY.
WELL, GOOD LOOKING, WE MADE IT. YOU REALLY ARE SOMETHING. I STILL DON'T KNOW HOW YOU GOT US OUT OF THAT PLACE IN AS FEW PIECES AS YOU DID.
MMM-HMMM.
LOOK, I'M NOT MUCH OF A JOINER OR ANYTHING. BUT I MUST ADMIT THAT THE TWO OF US MADE ONE HECKUVA TEAM. I WAS THINKING... MAYBE WE OUGHT TO BECOME AN ITEM, YOU KNOW WHAT I MEAN?
AFTER ALL, YOU ARE ONE OF THE CUTEST--
YEAH, WELL, SEE YOU AROUND THEN.
WHAAAAT? WHAT'S WITH HIM? I WAS PRACTICALLY PROPOSING TO HIM AND HE JUST TURNS AROUND AND WALKS OFF. WHO THE THE HECK DOES HE THINK HE IS, THE CREEP?
I HAVEN'T THE SLIGHTEST IDEA WHAT SHE WAS SAYING, BUT IF I STICK AROUND FOR EVEN ANOTHER SECOND, I KNOW SHE'LL FIND OUT WHAT HAPPENED TO ME.
PROBABLY WASN'T SAYING ANYTHING IMPORTANT ANYWAY.

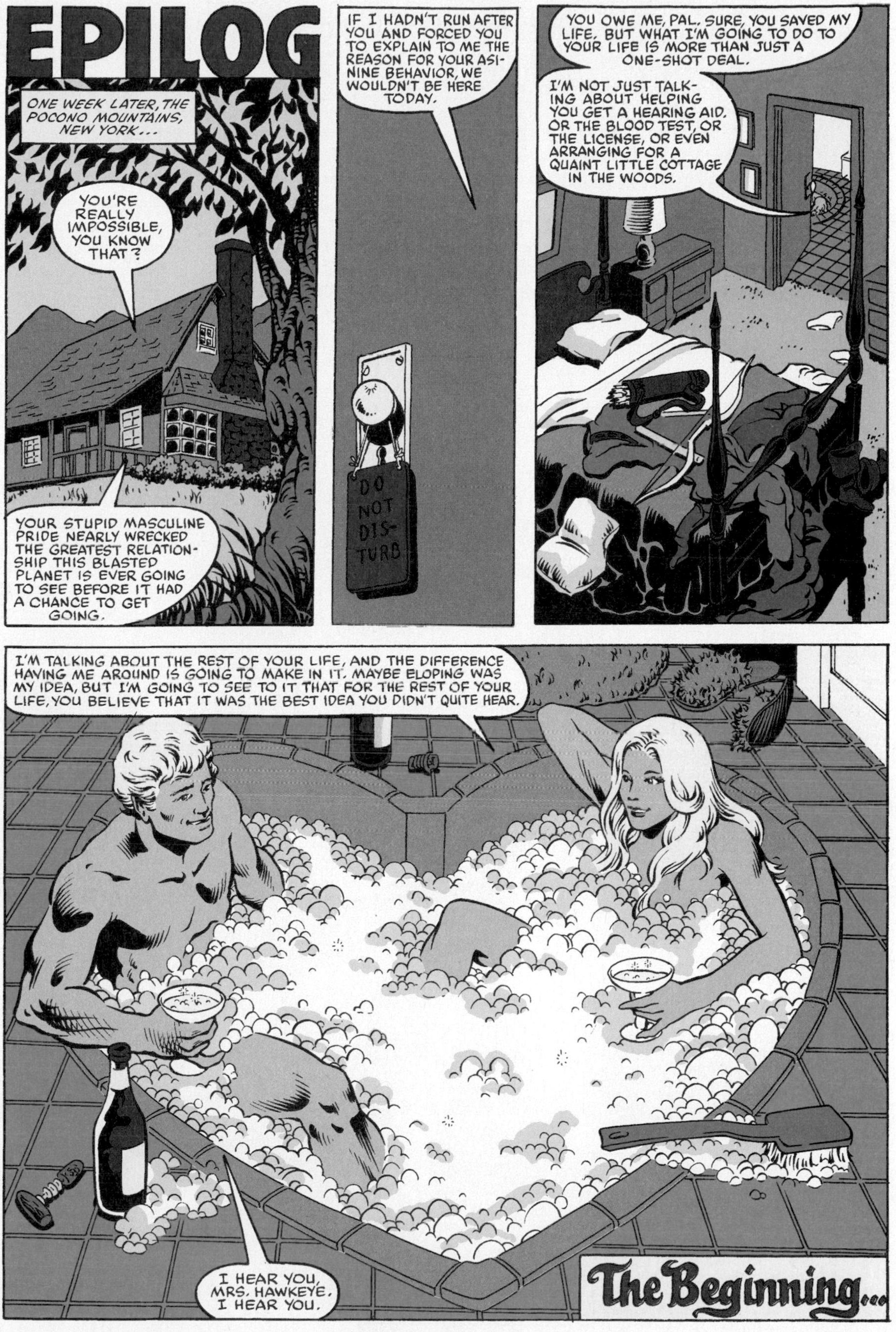

EPILOG
ONE WEEK LATER, THE POCONO MOUNTAINS, NEW YORK...
YOU'RE REALLY IMPOSSIBLE, YOU KNOW THAT?
YOUR STUPID MASCULINE PRIDE NEARLY WRECKED THE GREATEST RELATIONSHIP THIS BLASTED PLANET IS EVER GOING TO SEE BEFORE IT HAD A CHANCE TO GET GOING.
IF I HADN'T RUN AFTER YOU AND FORCED YOU TO EXPLAIN TO ME THE REASON FOR YOUR ASININE BEHAVIOR, WE WOULDN'T BE HERE TODAY.
DO NOT DISTURB
YOU OWE ME, PAL. SURE, YOU SAVED MY LIFE. BUT WHAT I'M GOING TO DO TO YOUR LIFE IS MORE THAN JUST A ONE-SHOT DEAL.
I'M NOT JUST TALKING ABOUT HELPING YOU GET A HEARING AID, OR THE BLOOD TEST, OR THE LICENSE, OR EVEN ARRANGING FOR A QUAINT LITTLE COTTAGE IN THE WOODS.
I'M TALKING ABOUT THE REST OF YOUR LIFE, AND THE DIFFERENCE HAVING ME AROUND IS GOING TO MAKE IN IT. MAYBE ELOPING WAS MY IDEA, BUT I'M GOING TO SEE TO IT THAT FOR THE REST OF YOUR LIFE, YOU BELIEVE THAT IT WAS THE BEST IDEA YOU DIDN'T QUITE HEAR.
I HEAR YOU, MRS. HAWKEYE. I HEAR YOU.
The Beginning...

Marvel Super Action #1 introduction excerpt
by **Archie Goodwin**

Being Marvel, we like to give you a little something extra or unexpected whenever we can. Hence, The *Huntress*. If revenge moves The *Punisher* and the need to fund his gambling drives *Dominic Fortune*, it seemed we could perhaps use someone operating out of a sense of commitment. I suggested the title and the notion of using S.H.I.E.L.D. to writer Mike Friedrich. He decided to draw upon a character he'd helped develop while scripting the color KA-ZAR comic, and wound up revamping her totally. With a bit of kibitzing from Mike and myself, artist George Evans designed the lady's costume and we were in business.

Well, almost.

SUPER ACTION was on the printing schedule as a bi-monthly book when a little something called the *recession* caught up with us. Or, more accurately, caught up with *everyone*. Rather than place an untried bi-monthly on already burgeoning newsstands, we decided to go with the one-shot you're looking at and see if your reaction to it is as great as the enthusiasm we feel.

This necessitated a small amount of revamping, mostly on the *Huntress* story. Mike's original synopsis called for it to be a two-part tale, completed in the second issue. By restructuring the story and adding some pages, he and George were able to turn it into an effective, complete-in-one-issue adventure yarn. And we were in business again.

Marvel Team-Up #95 letters page afterword
by **Mark Gruenwald**

"Where did this Mockingbird come from?" some of you may be asking. After all, it isn't every day that a brand new super heroine is premiered in MARVEL TEAM-UP. Well, the story behind her creation is this: when I had been writing the SPIDER-WOMAN book, one of my chief objectives was to build up a rogues' gallery that S-W could call her own. One of the several characters I conceived and designed was Mockingbird. Showing the sketch to Steven Grant, writer-about-town, he helped me work out her powers and weaponry. Well, I never got around to doing a Mockingbird story before I left SPIDER-WOMAN, so I put the idea on the back burner.

Time passed, and Steven was searching for something new and different to do in TEAM-UP. He was toying with the idea some of us have had to revamp the Bobbi Morse character (of KA-ZAR and SUPER-ACTION fame). Somehow we got the notion to amalgamate the two concepts and make Bobbi Morse the Mockingbird. (Anyone venture a guess why we abandoned the "Huntress" moniker?) All that was necessary was to change her hair and skin color since the original M.B. was going to be black. So that's the story behind the story. As for when and where Mockingbird will next appear, that's partially up to you readers. Let us know what you think of her, okay?

Hawkeye #1, page 13 panel 5 pencils by **Mark Gruenwald**

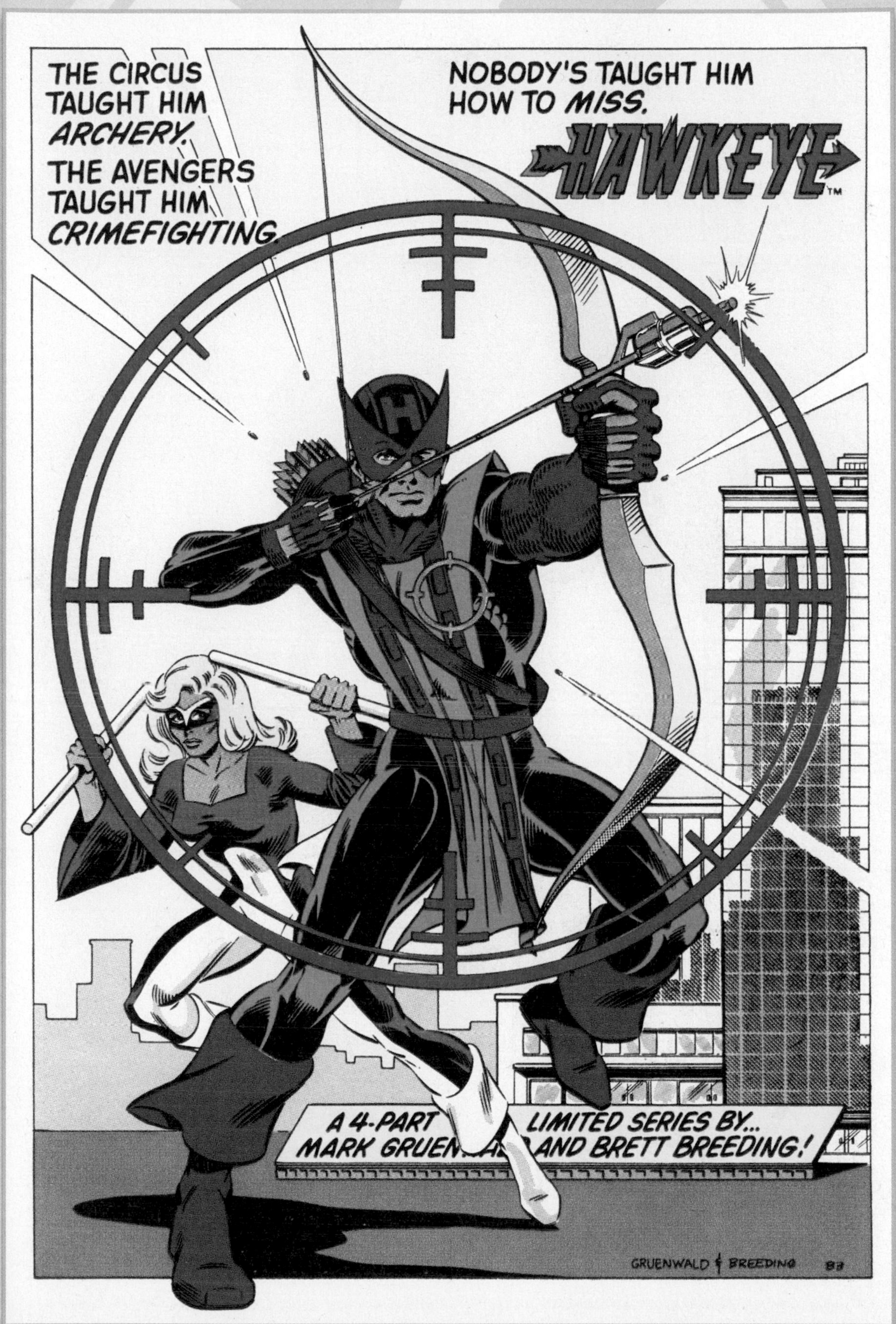

THE CIRCUS TAUGHT HIM *ARCHERY.*
THE AVENGERS TAUGHT HIM *CRIMEFIGHTING.*
NOBODY'S TAUGHT HIM HOW TO *MISS.*
HAWKEYE™
A 4-PART LIMITED SERIES BY... MARK GRUENWALD AND BRETT BREEDING!
GRUENWALD & BREEDING 83

Hawkeye house ad by **Mark Gruenwald** & **Brett Breeding**

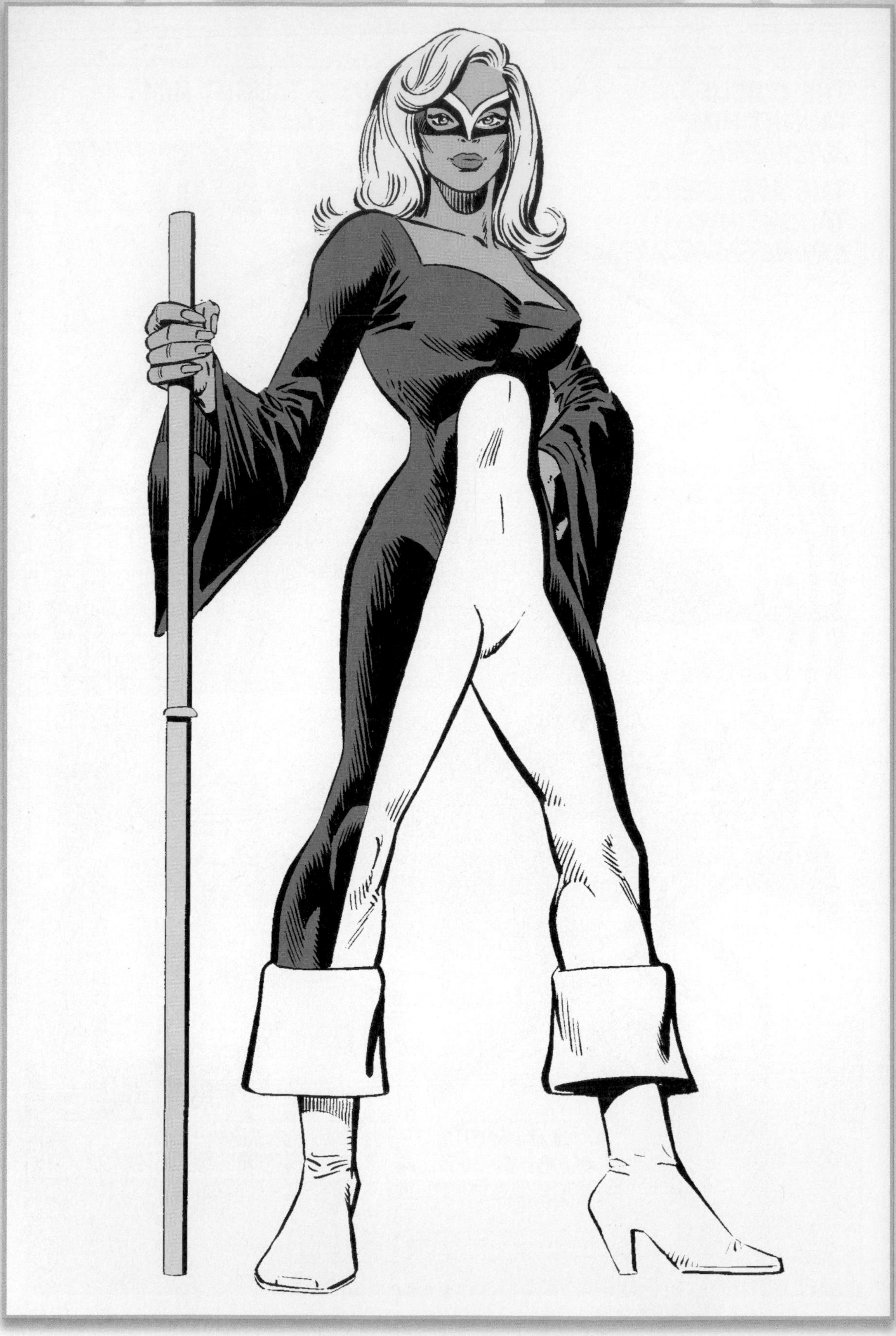

Official Handbook of the Marvel Universe #7 profile art by
Mark Richards, **Josef Rubinstein** & **Andy Yanchus**

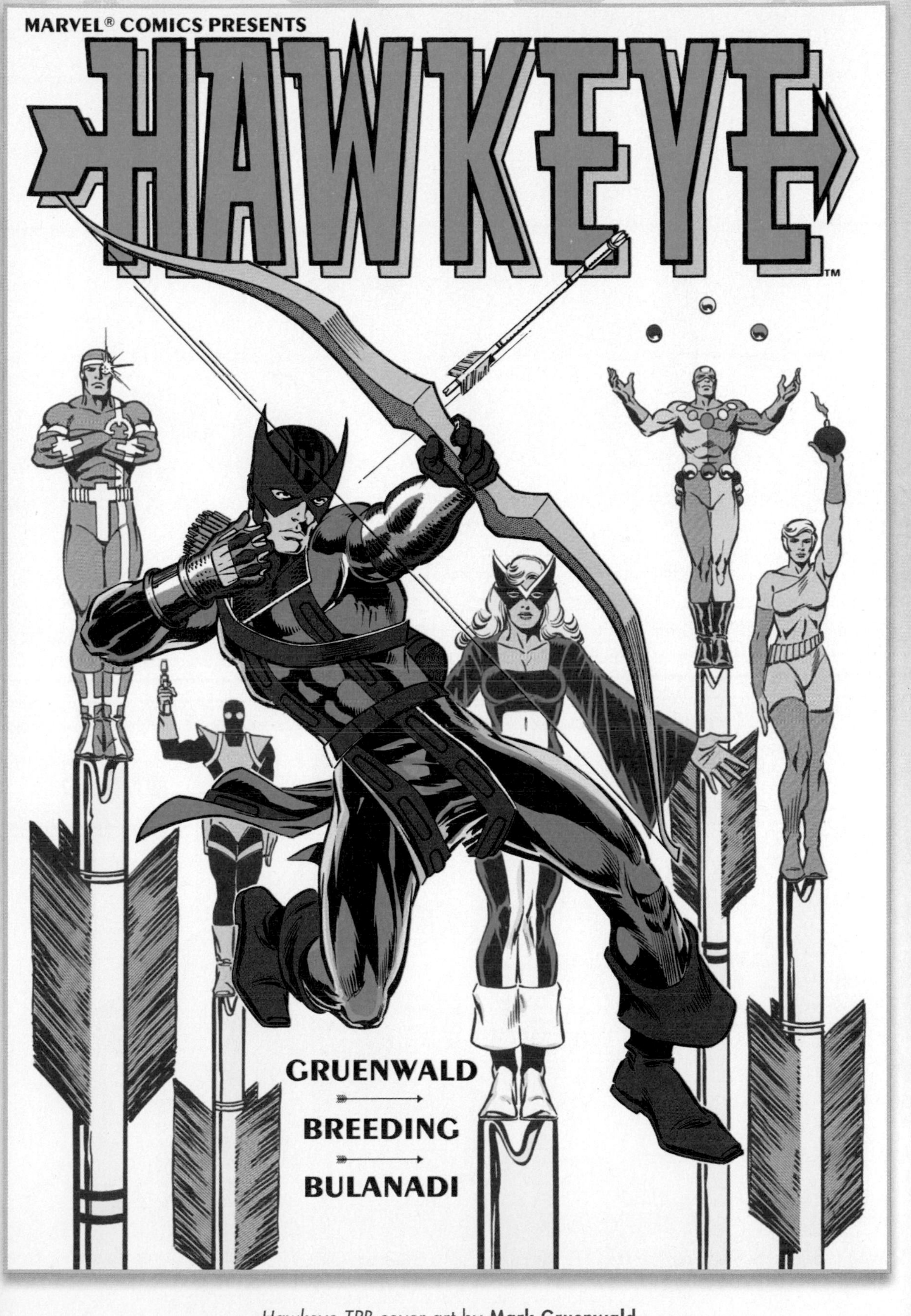
MARVEL® COMICS PRESENTS
HAWKEYE™
GRUENWALD
BREEDING
BULANADI

Hawkeye TPB cover art by **Mark Gruenwald**

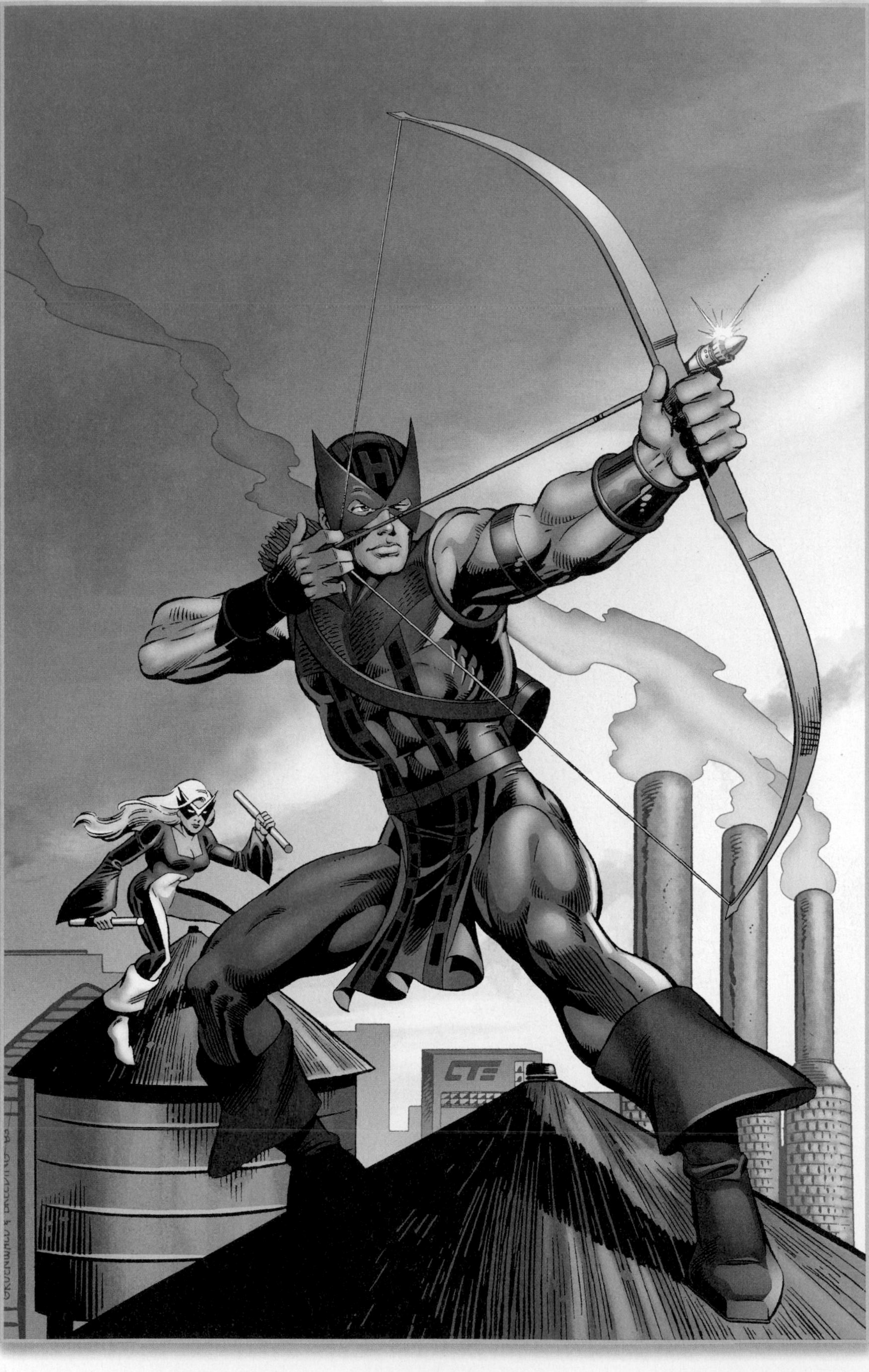

Avengers: Hawkeye Premiere HC cover art by **Mark Gruenwald**, **Brett Breeding** & **John Kalisz**

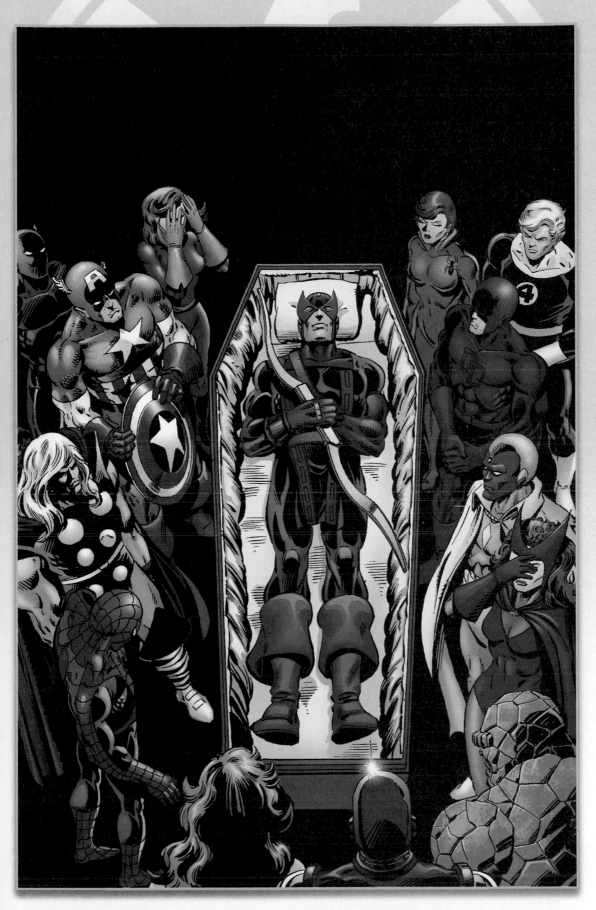

Avengers: Hawkeye Premiere HC back-cover art by **Mark Gruenwald** & **John Kalisz**

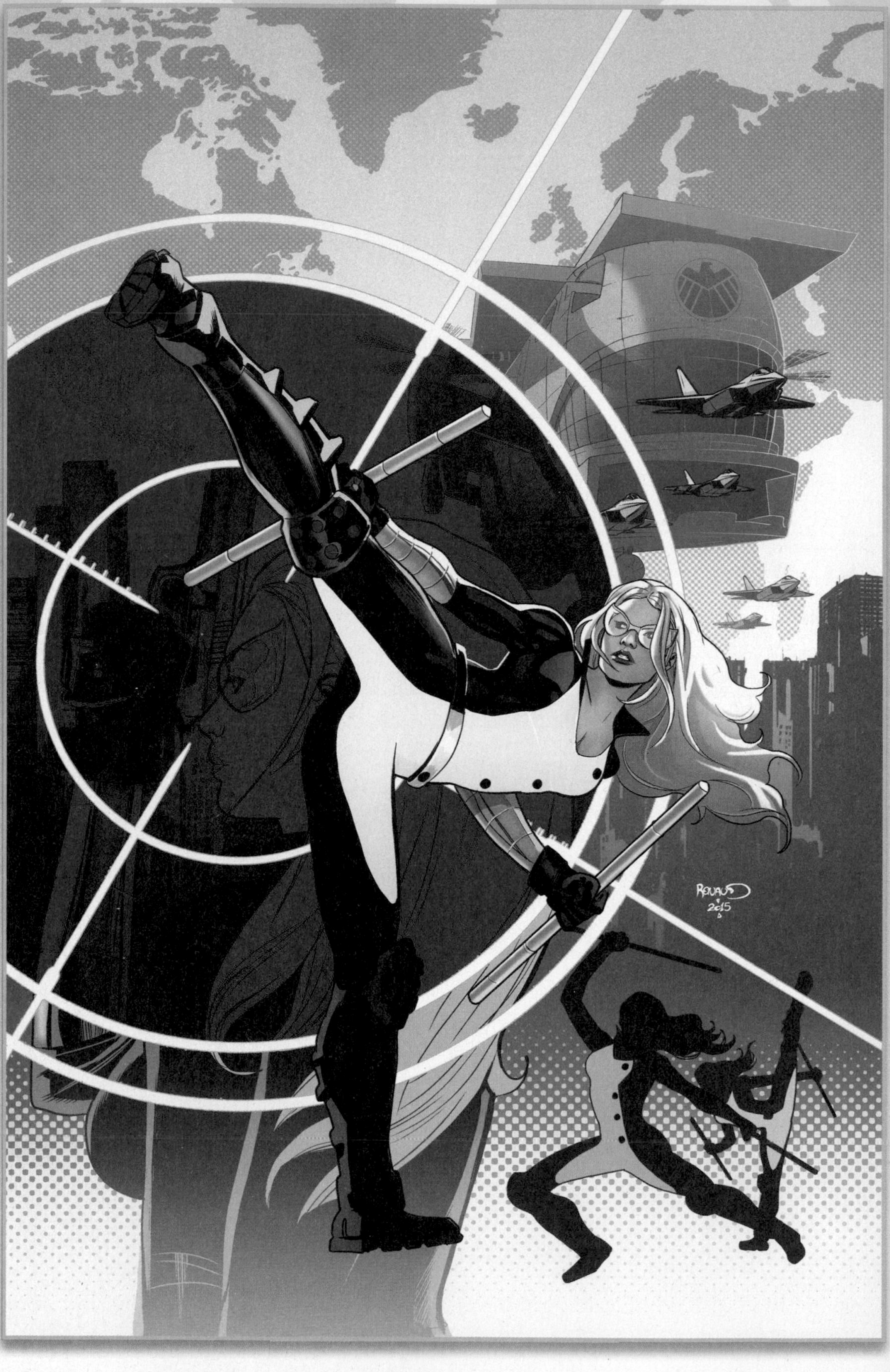

Mockingbird: S.H.I.E.L.D. 50th Anniversary #1 cover art by **Paul Renaud**